**CONTENTS :**
**1 v.**
**Computer optical disc (1)**

D0146382

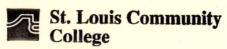

# Australia and the Pacific Islands

# THE GARLAND ENCYCLOPEDIA OF WORLD MUSIC

Advisory Editors
*Bruno Nettl and Ruth M. Stone*

Founding Editors
*James Porter and Timothy Rice*

The Garland Encyclopedia of World Music
*Volume 9*

# Australia and the Pacific Islands

Adrienne L. Kaeppler and J. W. Love
*Editors*

GARLAND PUBLISHING, INC.
A member of the Taylor and Francis Group
*New York and London*
*1998*

The initial planning of The Garland Encyclopedia of World Music was assisted by a grant from the National Endowment for the Humanities.

**Library of Congress Cataloging-in-Publication Data**

The Garland encyclopedia of world music / [advisory editors, Bruno Nettl and Ruth M. Stone ; founding editors, James Porter and Timothy Rice].
      p.    cm.
    Includes bibliographical references, discographies, and indexes.
    Contents: v. 9. Australia and the Pacific Islands / Adrienne L. Kaeppler and J. W. Love, editors.
    ISBN 0-8240-6038-5 (alk. paper)
    1. Music—Encyclopedias.    2. Folk music—Encyclopedias.
3. Popular music—Encyclopedias.    4. Dance—Encyclopedias.    I. Nettl, Bruno, 1930–    .
II. Stone, Ruth M.   III. Porter, James, 1937–   .  IV. Rice, Timothy, 1945–   .
ML100.G16   1998
780′.9—dc21                                           97-9671
                                                       CIP
                                                       MN

**For Garland Publishing:**

Vice-President and Editorial Director: Leo Balk
Managing Editor: Richard Wallis
Director of Production: Anne Vinnicombe
Project Editor: Eleanor Castellano
Copy Editor: J. Wainwright Love
Desktop publishing: Betty Probert (Special Projects Group)
Glossary and index: Marilyn Bliss
Music typesetting: Hyunjung Choi
Maps: Indiana University Graphic Services
Cover design: Lawrence Wolfson Design, New York

Cover illustration: At E Hula Mau, a Hawaiian *hula* competition at the University of California, Irvine, a seated female dancer performs a *hula kuolo*. She plays a gourd idiophone (*ipu*) by striking it on the floor and with her hand while moving her torso and arms to convey her vocalized poetry visually. Photo by Terry Lee Photography, 1996.

Printed on acid-free, 250-year-life paper
Manufactured in the United States of America

# Contents

## Part 3
## Peoples of Oceania and Their Music   405

# Audio Examples

The following examples are included on the audio compact disc packaged with this volume. For easy reference to text discussions, track numbers are indicated on the pages listed below. Complete descriptions of each example may be found on pages 1035–1040.

# About *The Garland Encyclopedia of World Music*

Scholars have created many kinds of encyclopedias devoted to preserving and transmitting knowledge about the world. The study of music has itself been the subject of numerous encyclopedias in many languages. Yet until now the term *music encyclopedia* has been synonymous with surveys of the history, theory, and performance practice of European-based traditions.

In July 1988, the editors of *The Garland Encyclopedia of World Music* gathered for a meeting to determine the nature and scope of a massive new undertaking. For this, the first encyclopedia devoted to the music of all the world's peoples, the editors decided against the traditional alphabetic approach to compartmentalizing knowledge from A to Z. Instead, they chose a geographic approach, with each volume devoted to a single region and coverage assigned to the world's experts on specific music cultures.

For several decades, researchers (following the practice of previous generations of comparative musicologists) have been documenting the music of the world through fieldwork, recording, and analysis. Now, for the first time, they have created an encyclopedia that summarizes in one place the major findings that have resulted from the explosion in such documentation since the 1960s. The volumes in this series comprise contributions from all those specialists who have from the start defined the field of ethnomusicology: anthropologists, linguists, dance ethnologists, cultural historians, folklorists, literary scholars, and—of course—musicologists, composers, and performers. This multidisciplinary approach continues to enrich the field, and future generations of students and scholars will find *The Garland Encyclopedia of World Music* to be an invaluable resource that contributes to knowledge in all its varieties.

Each volume has a similar design and organization: three large sections that cover the major topics of a region from broad general issues to specific music practices. Each section consists of articles written by leading researchers, and extensive glossaries and indexes give the reader easy access to terms, names, and places of interest.

Part 1: an introduction to the field, its culture, and its music

Part 2: major issues and processes that link the musics of the field

Part 3: detailed accounts of individual music cultures

The editors of each volume have determined how this three-part structure is to be constructed and applied depending on the nature of their regions of interest. The concepts covered in Part 2 will therefore differ from volume to volume; likewise, the articles in Part 3 might be about the music of nations, ethnic groups, islands, or subregions. The picture of music presented in each volume is thus comprehensive yet remains focused on critical ideas and issues.

Complementing the texts of the encyclopedia's articles are numerous illustrations: photographs, drawings, maps, charts, song texts, and music examples. At the end of each volume is a useful set of study and research tools, including a glossary of terms, lists of audio and visual resources, and an extensive bibliography. An audio compact disc will be found inside the back cover of each volume, with sound examples that are linked (with ⊙ᵀᴿᴬᶜᴷ in the margin) to discussions in the text.

*The Garland Encyclopedia of World Music* represents the work of hundreds of specialists guided by a team of distinguished editors. With a sense of pride, Garland Publishing offers this new series to readers everywhere.

# Preface

This volume introduces Oceanic musical traditions in a broad spectrum—from ancient traditions and their modern developments to musics introduced from near and far. The entries illustrate musical diversity, ranging from the famous, like Hawaiian *hula,* to the unfamiliar, like water-plunged idiophones of New Guinea, and reaching from the widespread novelty of the Macarena to the local Kaluli tradition of torching dancers' skin. The entries set contemporary developments into historical backgrounds. As insiders and outsiders continue to compose and perform, the music and dance of Oceania continue to change.

Letting people speak for themselves can be instructive, so even where no insiders contributed entries, outsiders frame their subjects in local terms, respecting culturally important categories and stylistic distinctions. Because the illustrative strength of data drawn from expressive behavior is partly a function of language, the volume has lyrics in more than eighty languages, with English texts translated from those and at least fifteen other languages. Most of the volume's authors speak the languages of the cultures they study, and many are indigenous to the traditions they expound. Others have interacted with Oceanic musical traditions for decades.

## HOW THIS VOLUME IS ORGANIZED

This volume embraces the performing arts of Australia and the Pacific Islands, grouped as New Guinea, Melanesia (often called Island Melanesia), Micronesia, and Polynesia. For some lands, the text uses indigenous names, including *Aotearoa* (New Zealand) and *Rapa Nui* (Easter Island). Other geographic names are outsiders' terms, local terms, or local pronunciations of outsiders' terms, such as *Kiribati* (Gilberts). The coverage is primarily that of indigenous and popular music, old and new.

After a short overview, Part 1 of the volume focuses on the people who have encountered Oceanic music by observing it or participating in it. ENCOUNTERS WITH "THE OTHER" presents descriptions and responses by early explorers, military personnel, writers, and filmmakers. ENCOUNTERS AMONG "OURSELVES" examines the music of festivals. It asks how indigenous peoples present themselves to themselves—and to outsiders, such as tourists. MUSICAL MIGRATIONS explores the movements of peoples and their musics.

Articles illustrate principles through short case-studies, which usually progress from west to east, south to north—starting with Australia and moving through New Guinea, Melanesia, Micronesia, and Polynesia. Cultural bonds modify this progression. For example, Aotearoa lies longitudinally west of most of West Polynesia, but texts about its performing arts appear among East Polynesian studies because it is culturally East Polynesian. Chronology too plays a part: because most cultural traits of the Polynesian outliers came from West Polynesia, the outliers are presented after the presentations on West Polynesia, though they lie west of that region. Discussions of musical instruments usually follow the standard organological order: idiophones, membranophones, chordophones, aerophones.

## Concepts in Oceanic music and dance

The articles in the first section of Part 2 explore concepts common to the musical cultures of Oceania. This section reviews how music works in society and how society works through music. Starting with local adaptations of imported musical sounds and how people in selected areas appreciate the sonic results, the texts move to music associated with commonly ingested substances—kava, betel, and alcohol. This section goes on to examine how music is embedded in religion, politics, theater, gender, and education—local interpretations of global issues.

An important topic of this section is popular music. Each tradition uniquely incorporates "the modern" into its musical system. As musicians have added and subtracted stylistic elements to enhance the local appeal of their music, sources of modernity have moved from nineteenth-century sailors' songs and Protestant hymns to gospel, country, rock, reggae, and worldbeat. Because stylistic preferences have generational implications, popular music often serves modernizing political strategies. It proves effective in dissent, protest, resistance, and other dynamics of political expression.

The articles in the second section of Part 2 present ideas and technical analyses in chapters focusing on music, dance, and language. This section explores the musical use of costumes, implements, and instruments, and examines the composing and teaching of music. The nature of knowledge—analysis itself—is an important element of the discussion.

No precontact Oceanic society had categories identical with European musical ones, and conceptualizations of musical contexts and sounds differed and continue to differ among Oceanic societies. Translations are often problematic, even between Australian and American English. Researchers may use a term like *flute* in a technical sense, referring to an aerophone whose sound is produced by a column of air vibrating within a solid object. To many readers, this term may conjure up images of a Boehm flute, a silvery, side-blown instrument having mechanical actions worked with metal rings, levers, and pads. But in Oceania, a flute is likelier to be a holed bamboo tube, blown on its side or an end, by mouth or nose.

Some instruments have an unsettled English terminology. Organologically precise names—like *percussion lamella, struck plaque,* and *idiochord bow*—may be new to casual readers, but fossilized literary terms can mislead. In the world at large, misnomers abound. Some foster obscurantism (a *bullroarer* is not a bull that roars). Some reflect eccentric exegesis (a *slit-drum* is not a drum with a slit). Some perpetuate antique prejudice (a *Jew's harp* is neither Jewish nor a harp, and a well-meaning substitute, *jaw's harp,* is etymologically inept). Instead of *bullroarer,* this volume uses the term *swung slat,* paralleling the standard term *swung vessel,* which denotes a holed nut or fruitshell whirled through the air on a string. For hollowed pieces of timber hit with an implement, the term *hollowed log idiophone,* rather than *slit-drum* or *slit-gong,* is accurate and neutral enough to be serviceable. For the instrument often misnamed Jew's harp and called *susap* in Bislama and Tok Pisin and *siusafo* and *suusafo* in Pijin, this volume uses the term *lamellaphone.*

## Selected local studies

Part 3 of the volume discusses individual cultures and societies, sorted geographically. Its sections—on Australia, New Guinea, Melanesia, Micronesia, and Polynesia—elucidate the contexts and events in which musical performances occur, and show how introduced sounds and movements have been adapted to indigenous artistic systems and incorporated into important contexts. Each section begins with an overview and continues with articles that sample an array of cultures.

These entries focus on peoples and places. They discuss musical systems holistically, sometimes from differing points of view. Their presentations are mainly empirical. Some summarize material assembled years ago. Some are the first publication of recent research. Some combine old and new observations. Some are first-person accounts of musical realities perceivable by cultural insiders. Some juxtapose outsiders' and insiders' perspectives. The ethnographic notion of a timeless present inevitably arises, but the texts try to avoid its biases.

Some cultures—indigenous and introduced—elude investigation. Of the music of Pitcairn Island, settled in 1789 by mutineers from H.M.S. *Bounty* and Tahitian men and women, little is known apart from the local festival celebrating the initial settlement. One morning each year, residents don eighteenth-century clothing, reenact the landing, sing "God Save the Queen," and lay wreaths on their ancestors' graves. At night, the Bounty Ball features old-time singing, barn dancing, and competitive waltzing. In 1856, some Pitcairn Islanders resettled on Norfolk Island, far to the west, carrying their musical traditions with them.

## Research tools

Part 4 of the volume summarizes information available about important musical archives, recordings, films, and books. Because the world has a vast number of these resources, the lists are selective. Different readers will inevitably have wished for different selections. In the rest of the volume, articles end with a list of references specifying cited publications. Cross-references to related texts appear in small capitals within brackets.

Visual imagery is an important part of the volume. More than 440 figures illustrate historical and contemporary music and dance, including formal presentations to knowledgeable audiences and informal incidents of daily life. These depictions range in time from 1771 to the present, and in type from drawings made by ships' artists to photos of modern-day festivals. Illustrations include one hundred musical examples, in notation that aims to be clear without being fussy, avoiding overfine precision of duration and pitch. Maps, in the Platte Carré projection, help locate places and peoples mentioned in the text. In maps 3, 5–8, and 10, international boundaries are 200-mile economic zones, set by the United Nations.

### Bibliography

The volumewide bibliography mainly includes late-twentieth-century publications that afford new perspectives on the performing arts in cultural contexts and are devoted primarily to music and dance. It lists only major monographs. It excludes useful older works, such as the reports of the Hamburg Südsee Expedition of 1908–1910, in which discussion of music and dance is usually a small part of the content. Such works, with other publications, are listed at the ends of articles that cite them. Most references are to publications in English.

### Discography

The discography provides references to commercially produced recordings. For many cultures, it lists at least one important early recording, though the recording may no longer be available for sale and may be heard only in archives and other institutions. Where hundreds of LP disks, cassettes, and CDs have appeared, the discography lists a small fraction of the known recordings. Where just a few commercial recordings have appeared, the list is more comprehensive.

### Glossary and Index

The glossary features terms undefined in the text or used frequently apart from passages that define them, and cites pages on which they are found. (Most of these terms do not appear as main entries in the index.) The given definitions apply to the special senses of the material in the volume. Selected terms are glossed at the tops of some pages throughout the volume. An analytical index singles out passages whose locations might not be apparent in the table of contents.

### Compact disc

A compact disc accompanying the volume samples the musics of Oceania. It has fifty-four items spanning the recorded history of Oceanic music—from 1893 to 1997—and illustrating distinctive instruments, genres, and styles. Some of these recordings were made under near-studio conditions with the latest technology. Others, full of ambient sounds, reflect vagaries of equipment and accidents of context. In the textual margins, the icon ⟨TRACK⟩ identifies the tracks of recorded examples illustrating particular discussions. Notes on the recordings, packaged with the disc, are duplicated on pages 1035–1040.

## The spellings of non-English terms

Most languages of Oceania use fewer distinct sounds than English. In careful pronunciation, many Oceanic vowels and consonants have approximately the sounds of their unmodified letters in the International Phonetic Alphabet.

Many languages of Oceania use a glottal stop, usually represented by an inverted comma, as in the word *Hawai‘i,* which, as pronounced in the islands, has a catch in the voice between the last two vowels. A notable instance of this convention is the word spelled *‘ukulele* in texts on Hawai‘i, but *ukulele* elsewhere. Some writers keyboard the glottal stop as an apostrophe, and French orthographic tradition adds French accents—so the spellings *‘Are‘are,* *’Are’are,* *’Are’are,* and *’Aré’aré* name the same people.

A macron lengthens its vowel and may change the meaning of a word. Lengthening has many functions, as in pluralizing (Sāmoan *fafine* ‘woman’, *fāfine* ‘women’). Some orthographies show extra length by doubling the written vowel, but others may use a macron or no sign at all. Because of certain word processors' limitations, some authors print macrons as umlauts—so *ö* in one text might represent *ō* in another. Some authors mark lengthening with a colon.

In some orthographies, *g* specifies the phoneme /ŋ/, usually spelled *ng* in English, as in "singer." For the same sound, other languages use *ng.* This inconsistency makes cognates less apparent—as with the word pronounced /toŋa/ and spelled *toga* in Sāmoan but *tonga* in Tongan. In languages that use prenasalized consonants, *b* may stand for /mb/, *d* for /nd/, and *q* for /ŋg/. These conventions cause confusion with languages like those of Malaita, where *g* is /ŋg/ (like Fijian *q,* unlike Sāmoan *g*), but *ng* is /ŋ/ (like Tongan *ng*). A standard orthography of the Solomon Islands uses *ḡ* to represent plain /g/.

## ACKNOWLEDGMENTS

The editors and authors especially acknowledge their Oceanic mentors who taught them the importance of music, dance, and poetry in daily life. Though this volume can only sample these mentors' knowledge and present mere tokens of their musical traditions, we hope it will reach, guide, and inspire a wider public that values their experience and creativity.

In the absence of clerical assistance, coordinating the efforts of 166 authors scattered among thirty countries and all continents would have been impossible without an access of goodwill. Bringing diverse authors' contributions into stylistic harmony while conserving their conceptual integrity proved a formidable task, and we are grateful for the trust that promoted whatever textual consistency the volume shows.

We thank the authors for checking and rechecking their edited words and happily tolerating the interweaving of their contributions into an ideally seamless texture, sometimes involving translation into U.S. English.

We are grateful to Ruth Stone and the editors of the other volumes in the series, who have given us pertinent counsel and taught us valuable lessons. At Garland Publishing, we thank Leo Balk, Richard Wallis, Eleanor Castellano, and others who helped see the volume through the press. We appreciate the early support and advice provided by Gary Kuris.

In reviewing manuscripts, experts offered inestimable aid: for Australia, Linda Barwick, Allan Marett, and Stephen A. Wild; for Papua New Guinea, Don Niles; for Micronesia, Barbara B. Smith; for the whole volume, Amy Kuʻuleialoha Stillman. Practical advice came from David Akin, Vida Chenoweth, Peter Russell Crowe, Catherine J. Ellis, Neville H. Fletcher, Helen Reeves Lawrence, Lamont Lindstrom, Jane Freeman Moulin, Steven R. Nachman, Jill Palmer, Anthony Seeger, Barbara B. Smith, Geoffrey M. White, Stephen A. Wild, and others. For the loan of illustrative material, we thank a host of contributors, who receive particular credit in the captions pertaining to their contributions. Jane Freeman Moulin, Don Niles, Mark Puryear, Amy Kuʻuleialoha Stillman, Stephen A. Wild, and especially Barbara B. Smith augmented the lists of recordings and films.

For the compact disc, individuals and archives lent important recordings, as listed in the Notes on the Audio Examples. At the Institute for Papua New Guinea Studies, Don Niles gave invaluable advice and assistance. At the Library of Congress, Joseph C. Hickerson and Judith A. Gray eased the search for materials. Technicians who prepared DAT copies of analog tapes included John Burke (examples 16, 42–47); Michael Grafton-Green (Canberra School of Music, Australian National University, examples 4, 21); Luise Hegedus (American Folklife Center, examples 2, 9, 32, 40); J. W. Love (examples 1, 5–7, 10–15, 17–19, 30–31, 34–39, 48–49, 52–54); Peter Medeiros (Department of Music, University of Hawaiʻi, examples 3, 41, 50, 51); Gerald Florian Messner (SBS Radio News, Artarmon, New South Wales, examples 8, 22–26, 29, 38); Robert Reigle (Department of Ethnomusicology, University of California at Los Angeles, example 33); and Pete Reiniger (Smithsonian Folkways, examples 20, 27, 28, 53). At Smithsonian Productions, mastering engineers Todd Hulslander and John Tyler oversaw the audio restoration and mastering of the compact disc.

—Adrienne L. Kaeppler and J. W. Love

# Contributing Authors

Te Ahukaramū Charles Royal
Otaki, New Zealand

David Akin
Ann Arbor, Michigan

Raymond Ammann
Agence de Développement de la Culture Kanak, Nouméa, New Caledonia

Ronne Arnold
National Aboriginal and Islander Skills Development Association, Woollahra, New South Wales

Kim Bailey
Extension Division, University of Guam, Saipan, Northern Mariana Islands (deceased)

Luke Balane
Creative Arts Faculty, University of Papua New Guinea

Linda Barwick
Music Department, University of Sydney, Sydney, New South Wales

Jean-Michel Beaudet
Département d'Ethnomusicologie, Musée de l'Homme, Paris, France

Niko Besnier
Department of Anthropology, Victoria University of Wellington, Wellington, New Zealand

Rokucho Billy
Saipan, Northern Mariana Islands

Peter Black
Sociology Department, George Mason University, Fairfax, Virginia

Jan Bolwell
Wellington, New Zealand

Paul Brennan
East-West Center, Honolulu, Hawai'i (emeritus)

Donald Brenneis
Department of Anthropology, University of California at Santa Cruz, Santa Cruz, California

Mary E. Lawson Burke
Department of Art and Music, Framingham State College, Framingham,
Massachusetts

Ka'ala Carmack
San Francisco, California

Vida Chenoweth
Wheaton Conservatory of Music, Wheaton College, Wheaton, Illinois (emerita)

Dieter Christensen
Department of Music, Columbia University, New York

Jennie Coleman
Research Center for New Zealand Studies, University of Otago, Dunedin,
New Zealand

Kathryn Creely
Melanesian Archive, University of California at San Diego, La Jolla, California

Peter Russell Crowe
Toulouse, France

William Davenport
Department of Anthropology, University of Pennsylvania (emeritus)

Tamsin Donaldson
Australian Institute of Aboriginal and Torres Strait Islander Studies, Canberra,
Australia

Bill Donner
Anthropology Department, Kutztown University, Kutztown, Pennsylvania

Peter Dunbar-Hall
Sydney Conservatorium of Music, Sydney, New South Wales

Reshela DuPuis
University of Michigan, Ann Arbor, Michigan

Catherine J. Ellis
Music Department, University of New England, Armidale, New South Wales
(deceased)

Catherine Falk
Faculty of Music, University of Melbourne, Parkville, Victoria

Richard Feinberg
Department of Anthropology, Kent State University, Kent, Ohio

Sir Raymond Firth
Department of Anthropology, London School of Economics, London, England
(emeritus)

Neville H. Fletcher
Department of Physical Sciences, Australian National University, Canberra, Australia

Juliana Flinn
Department of Sociology and Anthropology, University of Arkansas, Little Rock,
Arkansas

Judy Flores
Guam Council on the Arts & Humanities Agency, Agaña, Guam

Lawrence Foanaota
National Museum, Honiara, Solomon Islands

Randie K. Fong
Kamehameha Schools, Honolulu, Hawai'i

Larry Gabriel
Truman College, Chicago, Illinois

Maria Gaiyabu
Nauru Extension Center, University of the South Pacific, Nauru

Anne M. Gee
Hassocks, Sussex, England

Edward Gende
Keravat National High School, Rabaul, East New Britain, Papua New Guina

Clement Gima
Institute of Papua New Guinea Studies, Boroko, Papua New Guinea

David Goldsworthy
Music Department, University of New England, Armidale, New South Wales

Juan Pablo González
Instituto de Música, Universidad Católica, Santiago, Chile

Jane C. Goodale
Anthropology Department, Bryn Mawr College, Bryn Mawr, Pennsylvania (emerita)

Andrée Grau
Department of Dance, Roehampton Institute, London, England

Judith A. Gray
American Folklife Center, Library of Congress, Washington, D.C.

Margaret Gummow
Department of Music, University of Sydney, New South Wales

Michael Gunn
Metropolitan Museum of Art, New York

Hazel Hall
Canberra School of Music, Australian National University, Canberra, Australia

Lawrence Hammar
Department of Sociology and Anthropology, Willamette University, Salem, Oregon

Philip Hayward
Department of Media, Communication and Music Studies, Macquarie University, Sydney

Vilsoni Hereniko
Center for Pacific Islands Studies, University of Hawai'i, Honolulu, Hawai'i

Joseph C. Hickerson
American Folklife Center, Library of Congress, Washington, D.C.

Alan Howard
Department of Anthropology, University of Hawai'i, Honolulu, Hawai'i

Kirk Huffman
Ibiza, Balearic Islands, Spain

Rolf Husmann
Institut für den Wissenschaftlichen Film, Göttingen, Germany

Takiora Ingram
Ministry of Maori Development, Te Puni Kōkiri, Wellington, New Zealand

Allison Jablonko
Perugia, Italy

Hon. Jon Tikivanotau Jonassen
Cook Islands High Commission to Australia, Fiji, New Zealand, and Papua New Guinea and Ambassador to China

Jay W. Junker
Department of Music, University of Hawai'i, Honolulu, Hawai'i

Keri Kaa
Department of Māori Studies, Wellington College of Education, Te Whānau O Ako Pai Ki Te Upoko O Te Ika, Wellington, New Zealand

Adrienne L. Kaeppler
Department of Anthropology, Smithsonian Institution, Washington, D.C.

Betty Kam
Bernice Pauahi Bishop Museum, Honolulu, Hawai'i

Margaret Kartomi
Department of Music, Monash University, Melbourne, Victoria

Te Puoho Katene
School of Music, Victoria University of Wellington, Wellington, New Zealand

Kauraka Kauraka
Ministry of Cultural Development, Rarotonga, Cook Islands (deceased)

Jared Tao Keil
Department of Sociology and Anthropology, Carleton University, Ottawa

John Kelsey
World Music Archive, Olin Library, Wesleyan University, Middletown, Connecticut

Steven Knopoff
Department of Music Studies, The University of Adelaide, Adelaide, South Australia

Grace Koch
Australian Institute for Aboriginal and Torres Strait Islander Studies, Canberra, Australia

Junko Konishi
Faculty of Letters, Osaka University, Osaka, Japan

Rolf Kuschel
Psykologsk Laboratorium, University of Copenhagen, Copenhagen, Denmark

Wolfgang Laade
Music of Man Archive, Wädenswil, Switzerland

Helen Reeves Lawrence
Canberra School of Music, Australian National University, Canberra, Australia

Hervé Lecren
Agence de Développement de la Culture Kanak, Nouméa, New Caledonia

Rev. Dorothy Sara Lee
St. Paul's Episcopal Church, Indianapolis, Indiana

Michael D. Lieber
Department of Anthropology, University of Illinois at Chicago, Chicago, Illinois

Lamont Lindstrom
Department of Anthropology, University of Tulsa, Tulsa, Oklahoma

J. W. Love
Department of Anthropology, George Washington University, Washington, D.C.

Nancy Lutkehaus
Anthropology Department, University of Southern California, Los Angeles, California

Judith Macdonald
Department of Sociology and Social Anthropology, University of Waikato, Hamilton, New Zealand

Elizabeth Mackinlay
Aboriginal and Torres Strait Islander Studies Unit, University of Queensland, St. Lucia, Queensland

Vereara Teariki Monga Maeva
Rarotonga, Cook Islands

Fiona Magowan
Department of Anthropology, University of Adelaide, Adelaide, South Australia

Allan Marett
Music Department, University of Sydney, New South Wales

Martin M. Marks
Department of Music, Massachusetts Institute of Technology, Cambridge, Massachusetts

Mac Marshall
Department of Anthropology, University of Iowa, Iowa City, Iowa

Deirdre Marshall-Dean
Music Department, University of New England, Armidale, New South Wales

Lynn Martin
State Foundation on Culture and the Arts, Honolulu, Hawai'i

Raymond Mayer
Department of History, University Omar Bongo, Libreville, Gabon

Gerald Florian Messner
SBS Radio News, Artarmon, New South Wales

Barbara G. Moir
Faculty of Arts and Sciences, Northern Marianas College, Saipan, Marianas Islands

Megan Jones Morais
Salinas, California

Jane Freeman Moulin
Department of Music, University of Hawai'i, Honolulu, Hawai'i

Suzanne Mudge
Archives of Traditional Music, Indiana University, Bloomington, Indiana

Steven R. Nachman
Department of Sociology and Anthropology and Social Work, Edinboro University of Pennsylvania, Edinboro, Pennsylvania

Véronique Nagiel
Nouméa, New Caledonia

Jill Nash
Department of Anthropology, State University College, Buffalo, New York

Karen Nero
Department of Anthropology, University of Auckland, Auckland, New Zealand

Karl William Neuenfeldt
Central Queensland University, North Rockhampton, Queensland

Don Niles
Institute of Papua New Guinea Studies, Boroko, Papua New Guinea

Dorothy O'Donnell
Department of Music Studies, University of Adelaide, South Australia

Kathleen Oien
Jabiru, Northern Territory, Australia

Douglas L. Oliver
Department of Anthropology, University of Hawai'i, Honolulu, Hawai'i (emeritus)

JoAnne Page
Department of Linguistics, University of Sydney, Sydney, New South Wales

Anthony J. Palmer
Department of Music, University of Hawai'i, Honolulu, Hawai'i

Herbert Patten
Glen Iris, Victoria

Helen Payne
Department of Music Studies, The University of Adelaide, Adelaide, South Australia

Karen Peacock
Hamilton Library, University of Hawai'i, Honolulu, Hawai'i

Joakim Manniwel Peter
College of Micronesia, Weno, Chuuk, Federated States of Micronesia

Glenn Petersen
Department of Sociology and Anthropology, Baruch College, City University of New York, New York

Eve Pinsker
University of Illinois at Chicago, Chicago, Illinois

Alice Pomponio
Anthropology Department, St. Lawrence University, Canton, New York

Kim Poole
Waverley, New South Wales

Paul Vaiinupō Pouesi
Department of Education, Pago Pago, American Sāmoa

Ioannis Psathas
School of Music, Victoria University of Wellington, Wellington, New Zealand

Jacqueline Pugh-Kitingan
Ministry of Culture, Youth and Sports, Sabah, East Malaysia

Mark Puryear
National Council for the Traditional Arts, Silver Spring, Maryland

Boris N. Putilov
Pushkin's House, Russian Academy of Sciences, St. Petersburg, Russia (deceased)

Wendy M. Ratawa
Deakin University, Geelong, Victoria

Faustina K. Rehuher
Belau National Museum, Koror, Palau

Robert Reigle
Department of Ethnomusicology, University of California at Los Angeles, Los
Angeles, California

Dale B. Robertson
Brigham Young University, Lāʻie, Hawaiʻi

Jane Mink Rossen
Bagsvaerd, Denmark

Daisy Russell
Human Studies Film Archives, Smithsonian Institution, Washington, D.C.

Michael Ryan
Randwicke, New South Wales

Robin Ryan
Glen Iris, Victoria

Kevin Salisbury
Pukapuka Language Project, Auckland, New Zealand

Richard Scaglion
Department of Anthropology, University of Pittsburgh, Pittsburgh, Pennsylvania

Deborah J. Scratch
Department of Anthropology, University of Hawaiʻi, Honolulu, Hawaiʻi

Anthony Seeger
Center for Folklife Programs and Cultural Studies, Smithsonian Institution,
Washington, D.C.

Jennifer Shennan
Wellington, New Zealand

Artur Simon
Abteilung Musikethnologie, Museum für Völkerkunde, Berlin, Germany

Caroline Sinavaiana
Department of English, University of Hawaiʻi, Honolulu, Hawaiʻi

Barbara B. Smith
Department of Music, University of Hawaiʻi, Honolulu, Hawaiʻi (emerita)

Theodore Solís
School of Music, Arizona State University, Tempe, Arizona

Gordon Donald Spearritt
University of Queensland, North Maleny, Queensland (emeritus)

Regis Stella
Department of Language and Literature, University of Papua New Guinea, Port
Moresby, Papua New Guinea

Karen Stevenson
Department of Fine Arts, University of Canterbury, Christchurch, New Zealand

Lynn Stewart
Department of Anthropology, McMaster University, Hamilton, Ontario

Amy Ku'uleialoha Stillman
School of Music, University of Michigan, Ann Arbor, Michigan

Andrew Strathern
Department of Anthropology, University of Pittsburgh, Pittsburgh, Pennsylvania

Tialuga Sunia Seloti
American Sāmoa Community College, Pago Pago, American Sāmoa

C. Kati Szego
School of Music, Memorial University, St. John's, Newfoundland

Ryūichi Tai
Faculty of Music, Kurashiki Sakuyo University, Kurashiki, Japan

Helen Taliai
Melbourne, Victoria

Rev. Siupeli Taliai
Uniting Church in Australia, Melbourne, Victoria

Helga Thiel
Phonogrammarchiv, Vienna, Austria

Allan Thomas
School of Music, Victoria University of Wellington, Wellington, New Zealand

William R. Thurston
Department of Anthropology, Okanagan College, Kelowna, British Columbia

Ricardo D. Trimillos
School of Hawaiian, Asian, and Pacific Studies, University of Hawai'i, Honolulu, Hawai'i

Demeter Tsounis
Department of Music Studies, University of Adelaide, Adelaide, South Australia

Kenichi Tsukada
Faculty of International Studies, Hiroshima City University, Hiroshima, Japan

Kathleen O. Van Arsdale
Choral Department, Denver Christian High School, Denver, Colorado

Judy Van Zile, Department of Theatre and Dance, University of Hawai'i, Honolulu, Hawai'i

Hon. John D. Waiko
Vice Minister of Education, Science & Culture, National Capital District, Papua New Guinea

Jürg Wassman
Institut für Ethnologie, Heidelberg University, Heidelberg, Germany

Michael Webb
St. Paul's College, Thornleigh, New South Wales

James F. Weiner
Department of Anthropology, University of Adelaide, Adelaide, South Australia

Geoffrey M. White
Program for Cultural Studies, East-West Center, Honolulu, Hawai'i

Harvey Whitehouse
Department of Social Anthropology, Queen's University of Belfast, Belfast, Northern Ireland

Virginia Whitney
Waxhaw, North Carolina

Stephen A. Wild
Australian Institute of Aboriginal and Torres Strait Islander Studies, Canberra, Australia

Udo Will
Versonnex, France

Drid Williams
Dance Program, University of Minnesota, Hopkins, Minnesota

Pamela Wintle
Human Studies Film Archives, Smithsonian Institution, Washington, D.C.

Yoichi Yamada
Faculty of School Education, Hiroshima University, Hiroshima, Japan

Hugo Zemp
Department of Ethnomusicology, Musée de l'Homme, Paris, France

Susanne Ziegler
Phonogramm-Archiv, Berlin, Germany

## *Part 1*
# Introduction to Oceania and Its Music

In Oceania, music is not just for listening, but for seeing and feeling. Music is sung, played, danced, and acted as part of social, religious, and political events. In the world at large, fantasies and stereotypes about Oceanic peoples and their musics outweigh knowledge and understanding, even though thousands of individuals have traveled to the Pacific—as tourists, missionaries, scientists, or warriors, or for medical, economic, or political reasons.

Today, Oceanic music is performed in sacred spaces, on festival stages, in urban clubs, and at family gatherings. But above all, musical performances are markers of cultural and ethnic identity. The music of Oceania engages insiders and outsiders alike with its meaningful complexities and simplicities, its purposeful elegance and abandon.

The quadrennial Pacific Festivals of Arts are the premier venues for the performing, visual, and literary arts. Here, at the seventh festival, performers from Tikopia, wearing traditional costumes and striking their fans, appear for the first time. Photo by Adrienne L. Kaeppler, 1996.

# Profile of Oceania
*Adrienne L. Kaeppler*

**Prehistory and History**
**Oceania in the Larger World**
**Cultural Identity**
**Yesterday and Today**

The Pacific Ocean covers one-third of the earth's surface (map), and its lands are inhabited by hundreds of cultural groups. Oceania includes some twenty-five thousand islands, ranging in size from tiny specks of coral to the Australian continent. About fifteen hundred of the islands are inhabited by diverse peoples, many of whom have mixed and intermixed over millennia. Environments range from snowy mountains to raging volcanos, from steaming forests to searing deserts, from sparkling beaches to sheer cliffs (figure 1).

Some thirty million people inhabit Oceania. Many once lived in small, separate groups of only a few hundred people, while others were part of islandwide chiefdoms. Today, traditional living arrangements coexist with large ports and cosmopolitan cities. The people speak hundreds of dialects and languages—some mutually intelligible over wide expanses of ocean, others unintelligible to the residents of adjoining villages.

## PREHISTORY AND HISTORY

People probably began traveling eastward from southeast Asia about fifty thousand years ago. Exactly when they began to do so, why, in what numbers, where they came from, and how they traveled are matters for conjecture and research. It is certain that the physical conditions of lands they found differed from those of the same locations today. During the last Ice Age, sea levels throughout the world were lower than they are now; the sizes and shapes of islands were larger and more varied, and the distances between them were shorter.

At the eastern end of the Indonesian chain of islands, a continent lay athwart the passage to the Pacific Ocean: Sahul Land, as it is called, spanned what are now New Guinea, Australia, and Tasmania. Migrants and accidental voyagers from the west reached its coasts to become its earliest inhabitants. Succeeding millennia saw other contacts and other arrivals, who brought such treasures as pigs (possibly ten thousand years ago), dogs, fowl, and probably Asian bananas, breadfruit, taro, and yams. These they disseminated by trade and migration.

Much later, peoples with an archaeologically defined cultural tradition, now known as the Lapita cultural complex, spread from the Bismarck Archipelago

Oceania

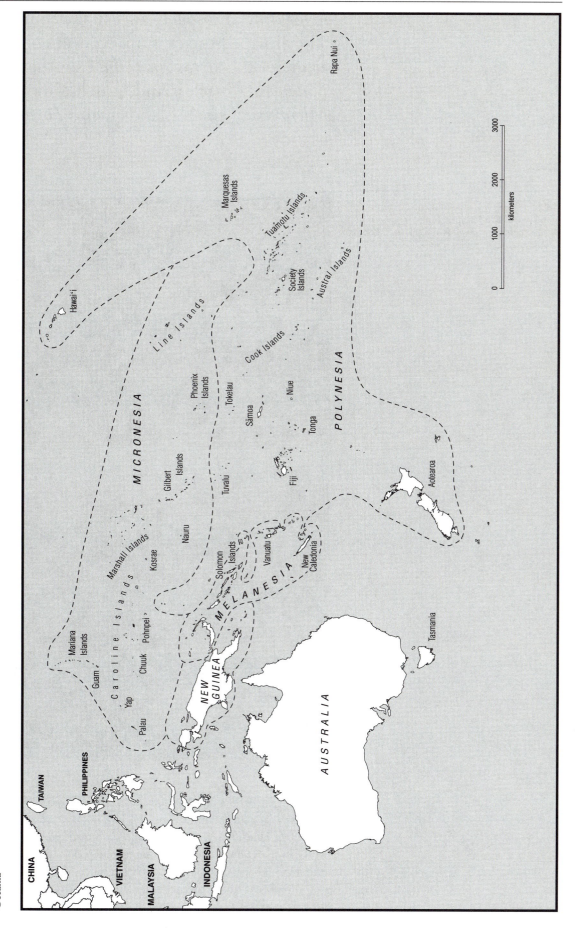

Over time and space, ancestral cultures diversified. They formed the cultural complexes grouped together under the terms *Australia* ('southern land'), *Melanesia* ('black islands', including New Guinea), *Micronesia* ('small islands'), and *Polynesia* ('many islands').

FIGURE 1    Oceanic environments: *a*, tropical island paradise in Ha'apai, Tonga; *b*, view from Kalalau Lookout, Kaua'i Island, Hawai'i. Photos by Adrienne L. Kaeppler, 1967.

(*a*)

(*b*)

(mainly New Britain and New Ireland), along the coast of New Guinea, throughout Melanesia, and finally into Polynesia. The Lapita complex, named after the site where it was first identified (in New Caledonia), is distinguished by earthenware ceramics with distinctive decorations. The Lapita complex is the most important cultural tradition for understanding the prehistory of much of Oceania.

Over time and space, ancestral cultures diversified. They eventually formed the historic cultural complexes usually grouped together under the terms *Australia* ('southern land'), *Melanesia* ('black islands', including New Guinea), *Micronesia* ('small islands'), and *Polynesia* ('many islands').

## OCEANIA IN THE LARGER WORLD

In addition to indigenous differences that existed in precontact times, colonial encroachments in Oceania included Britain, Chile, France, Germany, Indonesia, Japan, the Netherlands, Russia, Spain, and the United States of America, unilaterally and in various combinations.

Outsiders' influence on Oceanic societies has been uneven, ranging from areas of New Guinea where the primary contact has been with patrol officers, missionaries, anthropologists, and film crews, to lands that serve as overseas provinces of major outside powers, such as the Society Islands with France and Irian Jaya with Indonesia, to Hawai'i, now the fiftieth state of the United States. Between these extremes are Tonga, an independent kingdom (which, though extensively influenced by Britain, was never completely a colony, but only a protected state); newly independent states such as the Solomon Islands, Vanuatu (formerly the New Hebrides); Fiji, Kiribati (formerly the Gilbert Islands); Tuvalu (formerly the Ellice Islands); islands related to a larger political power, such as the Cook Islands (in association with New Zealand); and Guam (a territory of the United States).

## CULTURAL IDENTITY

Oceanic societies were extremely varied. The social systems within each part of Oceania—Australia, New Guinea, Melanesia, Micronesia, Polynesia—share core traits, but some societies do not easily fit into one of the major groups. New Caledonia has many elements in common with other Melanesian societies but has hereditary chiefs (more typical of Polynesia), and Fiji is in some ways a transitional area between Melanesia and Polynesia. Many Oceanic cultures are as different from each other as they are from other cultures in the world.

In the last decades of the twentieth century, separate peoples of Oceania have come to feel that they have more in common with each other than with outsiders. These feelings are not trivial or artificial, but derive from real concerns. What these societies have in common is the colonial experience, as varied as it may have been, and the love-hate relationship that has emerged with the colonizing power in the wake of efforts toward, and in some instances the achievement of, independence.

An important dilemma in independence is the necessity of interacting with other societies in international arenas, such as meetings of the United Nations and UNESCO, and the maintenance of embassies and other consular activities in foreign metropolitan areas, while maintaining cultural individuality and forging a national identity. Though politicians are usually not artists, performers, or sociologists, they legislate cultural policy. Throughout Oceania, cultural identity expressed through the performing arts has political and social value.

## YESTERDAY AND TODAY

Descriptions of music, dance, and performative contexts were written about by Europeans during the late 1700s, and especially the 1800s, when Christianity was introduced into most areas of Oceania and became part of the fashionable literature of exploration. Ethnographic collections of Oceanic objects, including musical instruments and costumes, were collected, and some of these treasures are now in Pacific metropolitan centers, including Auckland, Honolulu, Nouméa, Pape'ete, Vila, Suva, and Sydney; many books, manuscripts, and objects survive in collections in libraries and museums overseas, especially in Britain, France, Germany, and the United States.

The peoples of Oceania have continued many of their musical traditions, passing them orally from generation to generation. Modern Oceanic music has borrowed from abroad, but ongoing musical systems incorporate these intercultural borrowings to shape musical products into locally meaningful forms. New works depend on knowledge of traditional aesthetic systems in which musicians have immersed themselves. Modern composers and performers do not slavishly copy old products or processes: instead, they create forms based on their own backgrounds and experiences, often generating works that make old Oceanic themes understandable anew.

# Encounters with "The Other"

Adrienne L. Kaeppler        J. W. Love

Boris N. Putilov           Martin M. Marks

Lamont Lindstrom           Stephen A. Wild

Geoffrey M. White          Deborah J. Scratch

**Explorers and Expeditions**
**Warriors: World War II and Music**
**Writers**
**Filmmakers**

Millennia ago, peoples from Asia and Southeast Asia began moving into Oceania, bringing concepts of music, poetry, dance, and artistic performance. These cultural features evolved into traditions. Over time, owing to restyling from within and the influences of intercultural contact and renewed migrations, the traditions changed.

Encounters between peoples of Oceania and outsiders began in the 1500s and continue. Encounters among the people of Oceania began long before, but today intensify during festivals and competitions. The following discussions focus on encounters with "the other," here meaning people not indigenous to a perceiver's own tradition.

## EXPLORERS AND EXPEDITIONS

Beginning in the 1500s, Europeans began to travel the Pacific and to write about and illustrate what they experienced. These encounters recorded examples of music, movement, and costume as seen from the outside. Though sketchy, early eyewitness accounts are invaluable sources when used alongside reports from missionaries, traders, whalers, tourists, beachcombers, anthropologists, and indigenous peoples (figure 1). Numerous historic accounts made by outsiders are revealing about the outsiders themselves and their perspectives; but when used with contemporary research, they furnish insights into the nature of Oceanic music and data for studies of continuity and change.

### The 1700s

Eighteenth-century voyages of exploration were organized primarily by England, France, Holland, and Spain. The most reliable early descriptions of music and dance were from individuals who accompanied Captain James Cook on his Pacific voyages, focusing primarily on Polynesia. Other useful information appears in the accounts of Marion du Fresne's visit to Aotearoa in 1772 (Ling Roth 1891), Malaspina's visit to Tonga in 1793 (1885), Wilson's shipwreck on Palau [see PALAU], and others.

### *Dance*

Captain Cook's first Pacific expedition (1768–1771) employed scientists and artists to collect, illustrate, and describe important biological specimens, people, and events.

"They began to dance—putting their bodies into strange motions, writhing their mouths, and shaking their tails, which made the numerous plaits that hung about them flutter like a peacock's train." (1784)

FIGURE 1   Aborigines as "ourselves" and "the other": *a,* a corroboree in New South Wales, illustrated by Mickey of Ulladulla (photo Australian Institute of Aboriginal and Torres Strait Islander Studies); *b,* Aborigines dancing in Brighton, Tasmania, painted by J. Glover (Mitchell Library, State Library of New South Wales).

(*a*)

(*b*)

One of the artists, James Parkinson, made several sketches of Ra'iatea dancers. He successfully depicted their clothing, but did not have the skill to depict their movements. He died during the voyage, and Giovanni Battista Cipriani used his sketches

FIGURE 2    *A View of the Inside of a House in the Island of Ulietea, with the Representation of a Dance to the Music of the Country.* Engraving after a drawing by Giovanni Battista Cipriani, after sketches by James Parkinson, from Cook's first voyage, 1768–1771. Photo by Smithsonian Institution.

for a finished work (figure 2). This rendering bears little resemblance to any subsequent illustrations on later voyages, or to the dancing described by Parkinson in his journal (1784:74):

> A large mat was laid upon the ground, and they began to dance upon it, putting their bodies into strange motions, writhing their mouths, and shaking their tails, which made the numerous plaits that hung about them flutter like a peacock's train. Sometimes they stood in a row one behind the other, and then they fell down with their faces to the ground, leaning on their arms, and shaking only their tails, the drums beating all the while, with which they kept exact time. An old man stood by as a prompter, and roared out as loud as he could at every change. These motions they continued till they were all in a sweat; they repeated them three times alternately, and, after they had done, the girls began. In the interval, between the several parts of the drama, some men came forward, who seemed to act the part of drolls; and, by what I could distinguish, they attempted to represent the Conquest of Yoolee-etea, by the men of Bolabola; in which they exhibited the various stratagems used in the conquest, and were very vociferous, performing all in time to the drum. In the last scene, the actions of the men were very lascivious.

Rather than following this description, Cipriani placed Parkinson's dancers into a classical scene, to resemble an image with which he and presumably his audience were familiar—Botticelli's *Primavera*. An examination of the illustrations suggests that Cipriani simply turned the dancers of *Primavera* into Tahitians, setting them into a Tahitian scene. He did not develop the important elements of Tahitian dance (movements of the hips and hands), which Parkinson had failed to convey. Instead, Cipriani transferred the Europeans' mythological ancestors to Tahiti, illustrating Rousseau's ideas of the noble savage, rather than what the explorers actually saw.

Aotearoa was also visited during Cook's first voyage. No illustrations resulted, but Jonathan Monkhouse described dancing:

> They first prepared themselves by passing some Cloth, which they borrowed for the occasion, round their loins, till now totally without any covering: then placing themselves back to back a little asunder the foremost begins, the others following his motions minutely, with lifting up his right leg, at the same instant raising his arms to a

horizontal Position, and bending his forearm a little, he trembles his fingers with great quickness—begins a kind of song, and the right leg being raised as above, off they go, beating time singing & trembling the fingers in the most exact uniformity—the body is now and then inclined to one side or the other—sometimes they bend forwards exceedingly low and then suddenly raise themselves, extending their arms, and staring most hideously—at one time, they make a half turn and face one way, and in two or three seconds to their former position, in doing of which they bend forwards make a large sweep downwards with both Arms, extended, and as they turn upon the left foot, elevate their arms in the curve, stare wildly, & pronounce a part of the song with a savage hoarse expiration—this part of the ceremony generally closes the dance. (Beaglehole 1967:569)

Monkhouse mentioned a dance by three men "striking the thighs almost the whole time of the dance instead of trembling the fingers" (Beaglehole 1967:574)—apparently a *haka*. Joseph Banks described a performance in a canoe (Beaglehole 1962:2:29):

The War Song and dance consists of Various contortions of the limbs during which the tongue is frequently thrust out incredibly far and the orbits of the eyes enlargd so much that a circle of white is distinctly seen round the Iris: in short nothing is omittd which can render a human shape frightful and deformed, which I suppose they think terrible. During this time they brandish their spears, hack the air with their patoo patoos [weapons] and shake their darts as if they meant every moment to begin the attack, singing all the time in a wild but not disagreable manner and ending every strain with a loud and deep fetchd sigh in which they all join in concert. The whole is accompanied by strokes struck against the sides of the Boats &c with their feet, Paddles and arms, the whole in such excellent time that tho the crews of several Canoes join in concert you rarely or never hear a single stroke wrongly placd.

The Parkinson-Cipriani illustrations were refigured for some time, especially in France, where in 1805 a wallpaper entitled *Les Sauvages de la Mer Pacifique,* designed by J. B. Charvet and manufactured by J. Dufour, used the Ra'iatea scene, showing "a kind of dramatic dance, whose time is marked by an orchestra composed of flutes, drums, and a chorus of young girls, who sing sometimes of the sad events of life, but more often of its pleasures, marking time by clapping their hands" (McClelland 1924:407). Instead of wearing cumbersome cloth as depicted by Parkinson, the dancers wear flowing lightweight garments, more Roman than Polynesian. Instead of standing in a nearly static front-facing position, they are twirling—an un-Polynesian movement.

From Cook's third voyage (1776–1780) came more accurate views of Tahitian dancing: drawings by John Webber. Either Webber did not subscribe to the view of the noble savage, or he was more willing to take his time to study how the dancers were moving. Though most of his Polynesian figures are elongated and have slightly European features, his illustrations are quite accurate. Indeed, he became so familiar with what he was seeing that he was able to distill the essence from several performances and illustrate it. His illustration *A Dance in Otaheite* (figure 3) exquisitely refines his observations. It shows two female dancers performing the same movement while two men move differently from them and each other. The women wear long skirts, hairpieces, and flowers, while the men wear simple wraparound skirts—all of which survive in collections of Cook-voyage artifacts. Webber captures the two important movements of Tahitian dance—side-to-side movements of the hips and graceful flexions and extensions of the wrists. The movements of the hands were

harder to depict, but Webber conveys an accurate idea of what they actually were, just as he does in his illustrations of the hands playing the drums (figure 4).

In Tonga, Webber drew two elaborate dances and reworked the drawings into finished pieces: *A Night Dance by Men in Hapaee* (p. 766) and *A Night Dance by Women in Hapaee* (figure 5). A description of the event became part of the officially published journal of the voyage (Cook and King 1784:1:250–251):

> The concert having continued about a quarter of an hour, twenty women entered the circle. Most of them had, upon their heads, garlands of crimson flowers of the China rose, or others; and many of them had ornamented their persons with leaves of trees, cut with a great deal of nicety about the edges. They made a circle round the chorus, turning their faces toward it, and began singing a soft air, to which responses were made by the chorus in the same tone; and these were repeated alternately. All this while, the women accompanied their song with several very graceful motions of their hands toward their faces, and in other directions at the same time, making constantly a step forward, and then back again, with one foot, while the other was fixed. They then turned their faces to the assembly, sung some time, and retreated slowly in a body, to that part of the circle which was opposite the hut where the principal spectators sat. After this, one of them advanced from each side, meeting and passing each other in the front, and continuing their progress round till they came to the rest. On which two advanced from each side, two of whom also passed each other, and returned as the former; but the other two remained, and to these came one from each side, by intervals, till the whole number had again formed a circle about the chorus.
>
> Their manner of dancing was now changed to a quicker measure, in which they made a kind of half turn by leaping, and clapping their hands, and snapping their fingers, repeating some words in conjunction with the chorus. Toward the end, as the quickness of the music increased, their gestures and attitudes were varied with wonderful vigour and dexterity; and some of their motions, perhaps, would, with us, be reckoned rather indecent; though this part of the performance, most probably, was meant not to convey any wanton ideas, but merely to display the astonishing variety of their movements.

Webber's depiction of this shows two groups of women, one on each side of the musicians. The arms of each group's leaders are not in the same position. The leader

Tongan performers' "gestures were so expressive it might be said they spoke the language that accompanied them—if we allow that there is any connection between motion and sound." (1784)

FIGURE 4   *Drummers of the Society Islands.* Detail of an engraving after a drawing by John Webber, from Cook's third voyage, 1776–1780. Photo by Smithsonian Institution.

on the right has her right arm raised from the elbow and her left arm bent; her palms face backward, toward the body, and up. The leader of the group on the left has her slightly bent arms forward and palms facing away from her.

In Tongan dance today, these positions are two stages in a single movement, which begins in the position of the woman on the right. From this position, the lower arms rotate or turn outward while the fingers bend or curl. The curling starts with the little finger; the index finger is last to bend, and does not bend as far. Webber's illustration shows this curling in several stages, and often the index finger is curled less than the other fingers. The lower-arm rotation turns the palms outward and the fingers unbend, ending in the position of the leader of the group on the left. Webber's drawing, showing the women in various positions, is similar to modern photographs, for at any one moment the several dancers are in slightly different stages of the motif. Reconstructing the movement from the positions in the drawing suggests that Webber distilled the essence of the most important motif for women in the genre known as *me'elaufola*.

FIGURE 5   *A Night Dance by Women in Hapaee.*
Engraving after a drawing by John Webber, from
Cook's third voyage, 1776–1780. Photo by
Smithsonian Institution.

Webber's drawing of the men's dance is minutely described (Cook and King 1784:1:251–252), and it reveals a similar understanding of the movements of the arms. In the two illustrations, Webber conveys differences between men's and women's movements. Women seldom extend their arms, which they usually keep close to the body, gracefully bent at the elbows; men typically use extended arm positions and stronger movements at the wrists, and project more virile motions of the hands. Webber's illustrations correspond to the journal description that "some of the gestures were so expressive, that it might be said they spoke the language that accompanied them, if we allow that there is any connection between motion and sound" (Cook and King 1784:1:254–255). Cook's journal includes an excellent description of the *me'etu'upaki,* a dance in which standing men manipulate paddles.

When illustrating an important event, Webber placed his people into the elevated European artistic category of historical painting, activating his understanding of the appropriate conventions of that category: neomannerist bodies wear Polynesian clothing in unusual events, such as group dances, chiefly funerals, and human sacrifices. It is necessary to rethink these works, the purposes for which they were intended, their appropriations by others for other purposes, and the continuing processes of illustrating, portraying, constructing, and deconstructing to advance theoretical, philosophical, and revisionist views about art and the world.

From Bruni D'Entrecasteaux's expedition in search of the lost ship of La Pérouse comes another eighteenth-century example: a drawing and a description of a dance in Tonga from 1793. On this occasion, one of the prettiest girls rose to dance (Labillardière 1802:127–128). She sang only one phrase,

which she repeated for a least half an hour; but she displayed so much grace in the motions with which she accompanied this air that we were sorry she left off so soon. Her arms were brought forward, one after the other, and followed the time, while she raised her feet, standing, however, always in the same place: each division of the time was marked with the forefinger; this she struck on the middle-finger, which she kept extended by the thumb; and sometimes the thumb was carried against the middle-finger and the fore-finger. The charms of these motions were particularly owing to the beautiful shape of the hands and arms, so common among these people, and of which this young girl afforded a very striking example. Two other young girls then repeated the same tune, which they sang in parts, the one constantly a fifth under the other, and several men rose up to dance to the sound of their melodious voices: they beat time, by motions analogous to those of the young girls, first with their feet, and often by putting one of their hands on the opposite arm.

FIGURE 6 *A Dance at the Friendly Islands in Presence of Queen Tineh.* Engraving from Bruni D'Entrecasteaux's voyage, 1791–1793 (Labillardière 1802, following p. 157). Photo by Smithsonian Institution.

The illustration (figure 6) is remarkable for the delicate rendering of the hands and arms. One woman snaps her fingers, and another moves her hands gracefully while seated. Most remarkable are the five female dancers, who wear romantic versions of wraparound skirts, showing the grace of their upper limbs. The artist has depicted stages of the most important movement motif of the *ula.*

### Music

The fullest descriptions of eighteenth-century Oceanic music are from Cook's second voyage (1772–1775). They prove that vocal and instrumental polyphony was indigenous to Tonga, ensembles of stamped tubes and struck plaques accompanied danced poetry, struck log idiophones produced different tones, and Tongans sang in parts:

> two or 3 women began a Song which had something very cadenceful & musical in it and certainly ran through a greater variety of notes than at *Otahaite* and the Isles where all their Tunes are a variation of 3 notes only & at N. Zeeland of 5. To the song they beat time, with snapping the second finger & thumb, holding the other 3 fingers erect. Their voices were far from disagreable & what is still more remarkable they were accompanying one another harmonically. When these had done[,] an opposite set of singers took them up, & at last they all chorused. (J. R. Forster in Hoare 1982:3:378)

These remarks reflect the observations of Lieutenant James Burney (1750–1821), eldest son of the English composer and music historian Charles Burney (1726–1814). James Burney in his own journal noted that Tongan music used a flatted third:

> they sing in parts, keeping the Same time and varying the 4 notes without ever going beyond them. so many singers & so few notes you always hear the whole together. the difference of Words & Voices make some variety. the Singers (that I heard) were all women. one confined herself entirely to the Lower Note which acted as Drone. (Burney 1975:84)

He added that the final chord was a minor triad.

On Cook's third voyage, Surgeon William Anderson stated, "Where there is a great number they divide into several partys each of whom sings on a different key which makes a very agreeable music. . . . In the Same manner they vary the music of their flutes by playing on those of a different size" (Beaglehole 1967:2:944). On another occasion, J. J. Labillardière noted:

> We had, on our right, towards the north-east, thirteen musicians, who, seated in the shade of a bread-fruit tree loaded with a prodigious quantity of fruit, sang together in parts. Four of them held in their hand a bamboo, from a meter to a meter and a half in length, with which they struck the ground in order to beat time; the longest of these bamboos sometimes serving to mark all the divisions. These instruments gave sounds somewhat similar to those of the tambourine; and there was the following proportion between them: the two middle-sized bamboos were in unison; the longest was a note and a half lower; and the shortest, two notes and a half higher. The musician who sang the counter-tenor, made himself heard much above the others, although his voice was rather hoarse; he accompanied himself, at the same time, by striking, with two little *casuarina* sticks, on a bamboo six meters long, and split longitudinally. Three musicians, placed before the others, strove also to explain the subject of their song by gestures, which they had no doubt perfectly studied, for they repeated them together, and in the same manner. From time to time they turned towards the King, making with their arms motions which were not altogether devoid of grace; at other times they inclined their head suddenly against their breast, and shook it repeatedly. (1802:127)

Even the queen participated (1802:133):

> She was there giving a vocal concert, in which Futtafaihe [Fatafehi] sang and beat time, which all the musicians followed with the greatest exactness. Some performed their part in it, by accompanying with different modulations, the simple melody of the others. We now and then remarked some discordant notes, with which, however, the ear of these people seemed very much gratified.

But Europeans "eminently skilled in music" doubted Tongans sang in parts because they felt

> a great improbability that any uncivilized people should, by accident, arrive at this degree of perfection in the art of music, which we imagine can only be attained by dint of study, and knowledge of the system and theory upon which musical composition is founded. . . . It is, therefore, scarcely credible, that people semi-barbarous should naturally arrive at any perfection in that art which it is much doubted whether the Greeks and Romans, with all their refinements in music, ever attained, and which the Chinese, who have been longer civilized than any other people on the globe, have not yet found out. (Cook and King 1784:3:143–144)

Despite what armchair musicologists believed, these earliest visitors from the outside documented Polynesian polyphonic singing.

### Contexts

The English explorer George Vancouver's 1794 descriptions of music and movement illuminate the interaction of participants and observers, highlighting the importance of rank and taboo in Hawai'i:

> The heroine of the piece, which consisted of four parts or acts, had once shared the affections and embraces of Tamaahmaah [Kamehameha], but was now married to an inferior chief, whose occupation in the household was that of the charge of the king's apparel. This lady was distinguished by a green wreath round the crown of the head;

Each of the five Hawaiian performers
"pronounced, at the same time, the same note,
the same word, made the same gesture—and
moved his calabash in perfect time, either to
the right or to the left." (1850)

next to her was the captive daughter of Titeeree [Kahekili]; the third a younger sister to
the queen, the wife of Crymamahoo, who being of the most exalted rank stood in the
middle. On each side of these were two of inferior quality, making in all seven actresses. They drew themselves up in a line fronting that side of the square that was occupied by the ladies of quality and the chiefs. These were completely detached from the
populace, not by any partition, but, as it were, by the respectful consent of the lower
orders of the assembly; not one of which tresspassed or produced the least inaccommo-
dation.

This representation, like that before attempted to be described, was a compound of
speaking and singing; the subject of which was enforced by appropriate gestures and
actions. The piece was in honor of a captive princess, whose name was
Crycowculleneaow; and on her name being pronounced, every one present, men as
well as women, who wore any ornaments above their waist, were obliged to take them
off, though the captive lady was at least sixty miles distant. This mark of respect was
unobserved by the actresses whilst engaged in the performance; but the instant any
one sat down, or at the close of the act, they were also obliged to comply with this
mysterious ceremony. (1798:3:43–44)

Though we cannot be sure of the significance of the ceremonies described, early visitors offer tantalizing glimpses, still waiting to be interpreted.

**The 1800s**

British and French exploration of Oceania continued into the 1800s. Descriptions of
Polynesian performances made by British expeditions include those from *Port au
Prince* (Martin 1818) and *Blonde* (Bloxam 1925; Byron 1826). On the French ship
*Bonite*, Adolphe Barrot gave the following account of Hawai'i:

What was admirable in this song, which however had a compass of only two or three
notes, was the perfect accordance with which the five singers spoke and gesticulated.
They must have rehearsed many times to attain to this degree of perfection. Each one
of the five pronounced, at the same time, the same note, the same word, made the
same gesture, and moved his calabash in the most perfect time, either to the right or to
the left, or striking it against the ground he caused it to give forth sounds somewhat
similar to those of a bass drum. It might be said that they were all moved by the same
impulse of thought and will. Sometimes the gestures varied and became inconceivably
rapid, yet I was never able to discover a mistake. The voice, the hands, the fingers, the
calabashes, the bodies of the five singers were always extended, moved, regulated by a
spontaneous movement. (1850:33)

Barrot was less enthusiastic about the dancers:

Only one thing appeared remarkable in this dance; and that is, that the dancer regulated the measure, and, from time to time, gave the musician the subject of his song. The

FIGURE 7    *Young Woman from the Sandwich Isles Dancing.* Lithograph after drawing by Jacques Arago, from Louis de Freycinet's voyage, 1817–1820. State Archives of Hawai'i.

musician endeavored to make his time accord with the movements of her feet, and he succeeded with remarkable precision. Yet, at the end of half an hour, the dance began to seem long. . . . The dancing, so mean and monotonous, was far from realizing the idea we had formed of it. Only the singing and singers appeared to have preserved all the originality of ancient times. (1850:34)

Illustrations from nineteenth-century French expeditions are especially useful for studies of costumes and bodily ornaments and their changes over time. A drawing by Jacques Arago, artist with Captain Louis de Freycinet in 1819, illustrates a female dancer's clothing and tattoo (figure 7), and the drawing Barthelme Lauvergne made during the visit of *Bonite* in 1836 (figure 8) illustrates the incorporation of Western clothing by performers and their audiences. French descriptions of the Society Islands and the Marquesas made by Dumont d'Urville and J. A. Moerenhout are also important for understanding indigenous performance.

### Russians and Americans

During the 1800s, Russian and American explorers entered the scene. Some offered excellent descriptions and illustrations of performances. The second major Russian expedition into the Pacific (1815–1818), on the brig *Rurik,* commanded by Otto von Kotzebue, son of the German writer August von Kotzebue, sailed westward through the Tuamotu Islands to the Marshall Islands, and visited western North America, Hawai'i, and Guam before heading for the Philippines and back to Europe. It gleaned musical information mainly from Hawai'i:

Poetry, music, and dancing, which, in the South Sea islands, appear hand in hand, in their orignal [sic] union, to adorn human life, deserve to be particularly attended to. The spectacle of the Hurra [*hula*], the festive dances of the Owhyeeans [Hawaiians] filled us with admiration.

The words mostly celebrate, like the Pindaric Odes, the fame of some prince. Our knowledge of the language was not sufficient to judge of their poetry. The song is in

FIGURE 8   Detail from a drawing by Barthelme Lauvergne, during the voyage of the *Bonite,* 1836. Photo Bishop Museum.

itself monotonous. With the accompanying beats of the drum, it measures the turns of the dance, bearing, as it were, upon its waves a superior harmony. In the varying dance, the human form develops itself to this measure, in the most admirable manner, representing itself in a constant flow of easy unconstrained motion, in every natural and graceful position. We fancy that we see the antique starting into life, the feet only bear the dancer. He moves forward with composure. His body, his arms, all his muscles, are expressive; his countenance is animated. We fix our eyes upon him as upon the Mime when his art transports us. The drummers sit in the back ground, the dancers stand before them in one or more rows; all join their voices in the chorus. The song is at first slow and piano, and is gradually and regularly quickened and strengthened, as the dancers advance, and their action becomes animated. All execute the same motions. It is as if the same dancer stood several times repeated before us. These festal games of Owhyee remind us of the chorus of the Greeks, of tragedy before the dialogue was introduced; and, if we cast a look upon ourselves, we perceive into what a wrong path we have absurdly strayed, by reducing the dance to a motion of mere pleasure. These games intoxicate the Owhyeeans with joy. Their usual songs are danced in the same spirit, standing or sitting; they are of very different characters, but always accompanied by graceful motions of the body and the arms. What a school is here opened to the artist! What an enjoyment is here offered to the amateur! (Kotzebue 1821:3:253–255)

Useful information stems from the U.S. Exploring Expedition of 1838–1842, commanded by Commodore Charles Wilkes. In Fiji, the expedition witnessed an entertainment that included a men's dance with clubs (*meke i wau*), consisting of an entrance (figure 9), the dance proper (including a masked clown's antics), and the presentation of the clubs:

We were shown the way to the mbure [house], the platform or terrace of which, overlooking the whole scene, was assigned to us. The street, if so I may call it, widened and formed a square at the mbure, both sides being enclosed by stone walls; in front, at

FIGURE 9 *Club Dance, Feejee.* Engraving after a drawing by Joseph Drayton, from the U.S. Exploring Expedition (Wilkes 1845:3:191). Photo by Smithsonian Institution.

about thirty paces distance, were seated about one hundred men and boys: these we afterwards ascertained were the musicians. The stone walls in the vicinity were crowded by numbers of natives of both sexes, while beyond them an open space was apparently reserved, and surrounded by numbers of spectators.

We stood in expectation of the opening of the entertainment, and were amused to observe the anxiety manifested by the natives, both old and young. Suddenly we heard shouts of loud laughter in the open space beyond, and saw moving towards its centre a clown. His body was entirely covered with green and dried leaves, and vines bound round in every way; on his head he wore a mask somewhat resembling a bear's head, painted black on one side and orange on the other; in one hand he carried a large club, and in the other, one of the short ones, to which our men had given the name of "Handy Billy", his movements were very much like those of our clowns, and drew down immense applause from the spectators. The musicians now began a monotonous song on one note, the bass alternating with the air; they then sound one of the common chords in the bass clef, without the alternation. Some of the performers clapped their hands to make a sharp sound; others beat sticks together; while a few had joints of large bamboo, two or three feet long, open at one end, which they struck on the open end, producing a sound similar to that of a weak-toned drum. Although it could not be called music, they kept good time. . . .

To this air they use words applicable to the occasion. The dancers now advanced two by two, from behind a large rock which had served to screen them from view; they were all dressed in their gala dresses, with white salas and new masi on; the chiefs had around their turbans, wreaths of natural veins and flowers, which had a pretty effect; their faces were painted in various patterns, black and vermilion. In entering, their progress was slow, taking no more than three measured steps between each halt; as they drew nearer they changed their order to three and four abreast, using their clubs in a variety of attitudes, which are well represented in the admirable drawing Mr. Drayton has made of this scene. The whole number of dancers in the procession was upwards of a hundred. At the end of each strain of music they advanced three steps at a time, bowing gracefully to us, and changing the position of their clubs. When all had entered the square[,] they became more violent in their actions, jumping, or rather treading the ground violently, at the same time joining in the song. Each dance was finished with a kind of war-whoop at the top of their voices. (Wilkes 1845:3:188–190)

"Girls stand up, throwing their arms, feet, and hands in strange attitudes. Others sing amusing words in two or three parts. A third or fourth part is a coarse grunt or guttural sound." (1845)

In Sāmoa, the expedition found

> their dances and other amusements are in a great degree abolished, but they are still practised in the heathen villages, and even the Christian women may still be induced to exhibit the former, which they call *siva*. The mode of performing it differs from that of the Tahitians, but is like it lascivious, and neither of them would be called dances in our sense of the term. The dance is usually performed by young girls, who stand up before the audience, throwing their arms, legs, feet, and hands, in numerous strange attitudes, which are any thing but graceful. The others who are present sing amusing words, in two or three parts, while a third or fourth part is kept up in a coarse grunt or guttural sound, in the bass clef. The words are comprised in short sentences, each of which finishes suddenly with a staccato note, and a violent gesture. (1845:2:133–134)

A. T. Agate, an artist on the expedition, depicted the men dancing at night in a house (figure 10). Of this dancing, Wilkes said, "Clapping their hands, swinging them to and fro, or clasping them over their heads, they follow each other in a circle, leaping up and down, and turning suddenly around, keeping time to the music. The dances continue a considerable time, and end with a sudden clap of the hands and a simultaneous shout" (1845:2:134).

The 1890s brought a famous pair of Americans to Sāmoa, Fiji, and Tahiti: the historian Henry Adams, who used his visit to write about Tahiti, and John LaFarge, who painted Sāmoan and Fijian dancers.

FIGURE 10    *Samoan Dance.* Engraving after a drawing by A. T. Agate, from the U.S. Exploring Expedition (Wilkes 1845:2:135). Photo by Smithsonian Institution.

### Christian missionaries

Christian missionaries' writings added an evaluative slant to descriptions of music and dance. Some missionaries—E. E. V. Collocott in Tonga, William Ellis in Hawai'i, William Wyatt Gill in the Cook Islands, John Orsmond in Tahiti, Thomas Powell and George Pratt in Sāmoa, and others—collected texts and described performances. The Methodist missionary George Brown, using the medium of photography, documented performances in New Britain, Sāmoa, and elsewhere. In 1823, Ellis described a performance in Hawai'i:

> In the afternoon, a party of strolling musicians and dancers arrived at Kairua. About four o'clock they came, followed by crowds of people, and arranged themselves on a fine sandy beach, in front of one of the governor's houses, where they exhibited a native dance, called hura araapapa [*hula 'ala'apapa*].
>
> The five musicians first seated themselves in a line on the ground, and spread a piece of folded cloth on the sand before them. Their instrument was a large calabash, or rather two, one of an oval shape about three feet high, the other perfectly round, very neatly fastened to it, having also an aperture about three inches in diameter at the top.
>
> Each musician held his instrument before him with both hands, and produced his music by striking it on the ground, where he had laid the piece of cloth, and beating it with his fingers, or the palms of his hands. As soon as they began to sound their calabashes, the dancer, a young man, about the middle stature, advanced through the opening crowd. His jet-black hair hung in loose and flowing ringlets down his naked shoulders; his necklace was made of a vast number of strings of nicely braided human hair, tied together behind, while a paraoa (an ornament made of a whale's tooth) hung pendent from it on his breast; his wrists were ornamented with bracelets, formed of polished tusks of the hog, and his ankles with loose buskins, thickly set with dog's teeth, the rattle of which, during the dance, kept time with the music of the calabash drum. A beautiful yellow tapa was tastefully fastened round his loins, reaching to his knees. He began his dance in front of the musicians, and moved forwards and backwards, across the area, occasionally chanting the achievements of former kings of Hawaii. The governor sat at the end of the ring, opposite to the musicians, and appeared gratified with the performance, which continued until the evening. (1963 [1827]:58–59)

Despite the reportorial neutrality of the foregoing account and others, most missionaries condemned Oceanic music and dance as heathen rituals that led to licentiousness. In August 1859, an anonymous writer in *The Friend,* a Hawaiian missionary periodical, noted:

> For many years she [goddess of the *hula*] was forbidden to exhibit her licentious practices upon Hawaiian shores; but within a few years past she has returned and coquetted with persons of the "baser sort." According to the New Code, it appears that by paying $10.00, at the discretion of the Minister of the Interior, she may give a performance, or make an exhibition of her indecent and corrupting dances. In the names of decency, purity, virtue, morality, and Christianity, we hope the Minister will preserve the dignity and respectability of his high position, by making it tabu loa [really taboo] for a hula dance within the dominions of His Majesty Kamehameha IV.

And in an article signed "Truth" in the newspaper *Ku'oko'a* (27 May 1871), the author condemns Hawaiian dancing:

When the *meles* [songs] and instruments were used together it is as though a huge microscope is held and the little secret adulteries are magnified to adults and children. It then becomes a current, a whirlpool, drawing the spectators into the devils wringing machine that wrings out all the good in man, leaving him to swell like dry moss with lust and sinful desires. He feels that he must kiss a dancer and think of adultery to commit during the night. . . . See how well rounded is this nest of sin and lust where prostitution is hatched out. See how readily the *hula* leads to adultery. It is a great earthquake that shakes the graves open to swallow this glorious race of people, the foremost in the Pacific. See the heartlessness of those that are reviving this shameful and foolish thing of by-gone days. God will mete out to them their just rewards: For their stench in this world, there will be weeping in the next.

—ADRIENNE L. KAEPPLER

## Miklouho-Maclay

The Russian traveler Nikolai Nikolayevich Miklouho-Maclay (1846–1888) explored western Oceania from 1871 to 1883. He made important findings in natural history, geography, and the physical anthropology and ethnology of aborigines of the western Pacific and the Malay Peninsula. Observations on music and folklore were an organic part of his ethnological researches.

### Original findings

In 1871–1872 and 1876–1877, Miklouho-Maclay spent more than thirty months as the first European resident on the northeast coast of New Guinea. His diaries and scientific papers give many-sided descriptions of that area. He was the first to study indigenous musical instruments holistically: he noted their local names, described their appearance and structure, illustrated them, and told how to play them.

He bought specimens now displayed in Peter the Great Museum of Anthropology and Ethnography, St. Petersburg (Miklouho-Maclay 1992–1993). The idiophones include *orlan-ai,* a rattle made of a bunch of dried nuts, and *barum,* garamuts for long-distance signaling. The membranophones include the *okam,* a hand-held drum for dancing—a thin, hollowed-out trunk, whose upper part has a lizard-skin cover. The aerophones include *ai-kabrai,* a bamboo voice-modifying tube; *hol-ai,* a voice-modifying gourd; *munki-ai,* a two-holed coconut shell for modifying the timbre of whistling and vocalizing; *tyumbin,* a bamboo flute; and conchs of genus *Triton.*

On hearing these instruments, Miklouho-Maclay wrote of wild, ear-rending sounds, at night reaching his hut from the forest. Exploring the ritual functions of the instruments, he discerned among them one class, *ai,* reserved for use in men's rituals and feasts, and he described dances that *ai* accompanied. He reported a taboo: only men could use *ai.* Custom forbade women and children from looking at them, and even from hearing them up close; at the sound of *ai,* women and children had to hide.

Miklouho-Maclay analyzed local beliefs about the magical power of music. He left valuable reports on *mun,* local songs and dances. Giving sample texts, he described funerals, in which a person ritually wept over a dead spouse. He noted the words of a sago-preparing song. In some contexts (the arrival of guests, small events), he believed singing was improvisatory. He described festivals and dances. He singled out certain types of dancing (*mun-koror, mun-sel*) and made note of masks, ornaments, ritual costumes, and performers' placement and movements. Some festivals lasted three days and nights without interruption, and he was present all the time.

Miklouho-Maclay's observations on music elsewhere in Oceania were passing and casual. In the Admiralty Islands, he described a funeral rite, noting the performance of women's laments and dances to the accompaniment of a garamut (*mral*). In New Caledonia, he described women's laments, and the *pila-pila,* a dance now known as *pilupilu.* In some Micronesian islands, he observed the use of panpipes.

Miklouho-Maclay worked where European colonization had not yet reached, or where the outside world exercised little influence on culture. Later ethnologists collected, systematized, and published materials on the music of other areas of Papua New Guinea; though confirming the carefulness of Miklouho-Maclay's methods, they corrected and supplemented his observations.

### Ethnographic reprise

In 1971, a century after Miklouho-Maclay first landed in New Guinea, an ethnographical expedition of the Academy of Sciences of the Soviet Union studied music and folklore in Bongu Village. The expedition discovered in current use all the instruments Miklouho-Maclay had described, and got their names more exact (*aighabrai, ilol-ai, mongi-ai, schyumbin*). It discovered bamboo instruments in two variants, including a long voice-modifying tube, *ai-damangu.* It discovered three other instruments: *bembu,* a thick, hollow, closed-ended, bamboo tube, stamped by men only; *kongon,* a split piece of bamboo, held by the end, and struck with a stick; and *loblob-ai,* a slat tied to a bamboo pole and swung through the air. Amid a crowd of people in the village square, the expedition recorded its hum. The old taboo on women and children's participation had dissipated.

The expedition recorded the sounds of all the instruments. It collected more than fifty songs, performed by various groups and individuals: ritual songs (of male initiation, weddings, funerals), agricultural songs, and lyrics about love and war. The texts revealed a considerable stratum of mythological beliefs.

The expedition found that in character, melodies, rhythm, and costume, performances of men's dances matched Miklouho-Maclay's descriptions. The expedition filmed the dances and included excerpts in a documentary. On three audio discs (Putilov 1978), the expedition published its recordings of the music, with examples from other Oceanic sites. Alla Gomon notated and analyzed specimens of the music (Putilov 1974:35–35, 1975:252–257). The expedition did not confirm Miklouho-Maclay's assertion that local songs were improvisatory (Putilov 1974, 1975, 1979).

—BORIS N. PUTILOV

## The 1900s

As with the reprise of Miklouho-Maclay's studies, the 1900s saw the rise of more focused expeditions, especially those that included anthropologists. Scientific expeditions of the early twentieth century, especially in the Western Pacific, saw the introduction of German and Japanese descriptions of music and the widespread use of photography.

### German expeditions

The Hamburg Südsee Expedition collected artifacts and systematically presented information from Melanesia and Micronesia. Musical instruments were collected, wax-cylinder recordings were made, moving pictures were filmed, still photographs were taken, and written descriptions were printed. In the Mortlock Islands, the expedition collected examples of rare masks (now in the Hamburg Museum für Völkerkunde), filmed motion pictures (now in Göttingen), took photographs (now in Hamburg), and wrote down what they learned from the Mortlockese. Augustin Krämer (1935:118) noted that the masks were called *tapuanu,* gave an account of

The Pacific War (1941–1945) began a new era in Oceania. Its battles, bombings, and migrations disrupted and transformed many societies. Remote islands began to enter global networks.

FIGURE 11    Dance using *tapuanu* masks, staged for the Hamburg Südsee Expedition. Hamburgisches Museum für Völkerkunde.

their origin, and said they were worn for the performance of songs and dances to combat the wind. In a mock battle using staves, the men faced east, where Fangileng, the god of winds, lived. The masks were said to help breadfruit ripen. Because the rituals were seldom performed, the men of Satoan staged a performance for the expedition (figure 11).

### American expeditions

Scientific expeditions from North America before World War II were often made in collaboration with the Bernice P. Bishop Museum in Honolulu. These expeditions made collections of musical instruments, musical sounds, motion pictures, still photographs, and written documents. The most notable, the Bayard-Dominick Expedition (1920–1922), explored Tonga, the Marquesas, the Austral Islands, the Tuamotus, Mangareva, and Tahiti, generating numerous Bishop Museum Press publications by scientists including Robert T. Aitken, E. W. Gifford, E. S. C. Handy, Willowdean Handy, Ralph Linton, W. C. McKern, and John F. G. Stokes.

Other Bishop Museum expeditions included the Kaimiloa Expedition (1925) to Polynesia and Micronesia, by Kenneth P. Emory and others; the Tuamotu Expedition (1929) to the Tuamotus, the Society Islands, the Marquesas, Mangareva, and the Cook Islands, by Emory, Charles Nordhoff, Olaf Oswald, and others; the Zaca Expedition (1932–1933) to Fiji, Rotuma, and the Solomon Islands, by Gordon MacGregor and George T. Barker; the Mangareva Expedition, with the American Museum of Natural History (1934), to southeast Polynesia, by Emory, Peter H.

Buck, and others; the Franco-Belgian Easter Island Expedition (1935), by Alfred Métraux and others; the Itasca Expedition (1935) to Sāmoa, by E. H. Bryan and others; and the Micronesia Expedition (1936) to the Caroline Islands, by Yoshio Kondo and others. Other Bishop Museum staffers and associates collected throughout Oceania.

### Japanese expeditions

As part of the Bishop Museum's Micronesia Expedition (1936), a Japanese researcher, Iwakichi Muranushi, recorded Micronesian music and stories in Palau, Yap, and Pohnpei (Tatar 1985). Other Japanese researchers before World War II include Hisakatsu Hijikata and Hisao Tanabe, who researched music and dance in Palau, the Caroline Islands, and the Marshall Islands.

—ADRIENNE L. KAEPPLER

## WARRIORS: WORLD WAR II AND MUSIC

The Pacific War (1941–1945) began a new era in Oceania. Its battles, bombings, and migrations disrupted and transformed many societies. Remote islands began to enter global economic, communicative, and transportation networks. Social disruptions were variable: local effects depended on distance from major battles, sea-lanes, and bases. The results of the war included advances in the mobility of populations and in technologies of transportation and communication.

Wartime migrations included American and Japanese extensions into Oceania, by invasion and counterinvasion. These movements touched thousands of islanders—fleeing battles, seeking economic opportunities, or conscripted to work as native defenders and laborers. The intrusion of outside forces, islanders' increased mobility, and introduced technologies of communication affected the genres, instruments, performances, and themes of Oceanic music.

### Genres

Allied and Japanese military personnel moving into Oceania brought popular music of the 1930s and 1940s. On the Allied side, this included jazz, boogie-woogie, swing, jitterbug, big-band music, Tin Pan Alley music, blues, marches, national anthems, and children's music. In Bougainville, which the Japanese occupied in 1942, a Roman Catholic missionary lamented that children learned Japanese songs faster than they did his hymns (Lincoln 1979:6). Islanders working alongside Japanese and Allied troops picked up songs, many of which survived locally for decades. The melodies survived longer and more intact than the lyrics, whether English or Japanese.

Michael Somare, the first prime minister of Papua New Guinea, includes in his autobiography a version of the Japanese national anthem that he learned, with other songs, from a Japanese officer in the early 1940s (1975:4). On the Allied side, the most popular song may have been "You Are My Sunshine"; in the 1990s, people in Oceania continued to sing it, with local inflections of melody and meter (Thomas 1981:185 prints a Banaban version). Other locally popular songs were "Show Me The Way To Go Home," "Down Mexico Way," and "God Be with You 'Til We Meet Again." In 1944, a Marine officer in Vanuatu reported:

> I shall never forget one morning's sight of a native gang tramping to work to the harmonized chant of "God Bless America." The strains echoed feelingly through the jungle long after they had passed. Another favorite was "The Marine's Hymn." (Heinl 1944:240)

In the 1990s, older Vanuatuans could still sing "God Bless America."

Islanders in labor corps and local militias, and those who enjoyed more casual contacts with Japanese and Allied servicemen, learned songs from military supervisors, friends, and acquaintances. They had access to Western and Japanese music, transmitted by electronic media and systems of communication set up by soldiers. The combatants imported electric phonographs and recordings, and regularly screened films for the troops. The U.S. base on Espiritu Santo boasted forty-three mostly outdoor cinemas that islanders attended. On the U.S. side, touring shows of the United Services Organization (USO) featured performers such as Irving Berlin, Bing Crosby, and Bob Hope, who entertained troops and islanders. For morale and information, U.S. technicians set up radio stations on most larger bases. For the first time, some islanders listened to music transmitted by radio; others performed on live broadcasts. Over military radio, even Chamorro children sang American songs (figure 12). Sunday afternoons on the U.S. military's Radio Munda, a chorus from the Solomon Islands Defense Force performed regularly (figure 13).

As with songs, so with dances. The war offered opportunities for people to see Western patterns of dancing in mixed couples. This stimulated development of new, locally risqué styles of dancing, such as one in Vanuatu still called Texas. In 1944, people of Guadalcanal were practicing the jitterbug. Alongside borrowed Western and Japanese songs and dances, islanders absorbed musical styles from each other. People of northeast Ambae who during the war worked on Paama Island brought home a new style of singing in parallel thirds, which they incorporated into a dance (Peter Crowe, personal communication).

### Instrumentation and performance

Before the war, some Pacific Islanders used Western musical instruments, notably guitars, but the influx of Allied troops gave them greater access to Western instruments. Interviews with island veterans (Lindstrom and White 1990; White and Lindstrom 1989) have documented that men of the Solomon Islands and Vanuatu

FIGURE 12    Pedro, Ricardo, and José Cruz entertain U.S. Marines with their version of "Pistol Packin' Mama." Guam, 1945. National Archives, U.S. Marine Corps.

FIGURE 13    Bill Gina, David Hoto (guitar), and other members of the Solomon Islands Defense Force perform on the U.S. military's Radio Munda. New Georgia, Solomon Islands, 1944. Photo National Archives, U.S. Army Signal Corps.

learned to play guitar and harmonica from U.S. servicemen. During the war, four-stringed ukuleles, harmonicas, banjos, saxophones, and gutbuckets increased in popularity. Islanders sometimes got instruments as gifts from servicemen; some became skilled at making their own guitars, ukuleles, and gutbuckets.

In the 1990s, these instruments are the core of string bands, which provide accompaniment for Western dances promoted by the war. Three sets of fingerings and open position yield the commonly used chords. Musical styles differ from place to place, reflecting colonial histories and indigenous musical traditions. They share traits of Western popular music: 2/4 time; opening guitar and ukulele riffs; singing in falsetto; and basses often moving by fourths and fifths, on chordal roots.

For local performers, the war offered new opportunities and audiences. Military ceremonies often demanded musical accompaniment, and islanders joined bands that provided it. In Papua New Guinea, the Royal Papuan Constabulary Band gained an increased public role in supplying such music. Japanese and Allied military personnel attended dances organized as part of life-cycle feasts and the like. More commonly, islanders sang and danced to entertain military guests touring their villages. In July 1942, residents of St. Louis Village, New Caledonia, entertained members of the Americal Division, including U.S. Army nurses, who joined in a local dance. Similarly, on Bougainville in May 1944, members of Fiji's third battalion presented to Allied officers the music of a Fijian kava ceremony.

On the Japanese side, Michael Somare's people, in the Murik Lakes area of East Sepik Province, danced for occupying Japanese forces, who answered by dancing with swords (1970:32). In late 1945, children from Ngatpang, Palau, danced to entertain Japanese prisoners of war. Many labor-corps veterans from Vanuatu recall that while they worked, servicemen shouted out to them, "Dance, dance!"—and they obliged with impromptu performances.

String bands and Christian choirs entertained troops. Military radio stations broadcast some of these ensembles regularly. On 25 December 1943, U.S. Marines taped a Christmas program that included hymns sung by a choir from Miravari, Vella Lavella. To make the service available for local broadcasting and rebroadcasting in America, technicians laid eight kilometers of telephone wire. At bases where the lines of battle had pushed by, string bands provided music for military dances and other

Commenting on wartime experiences, Pacific Islanders composed thousands of songs. On Kolombangara in the mid-1990s, people still sang about "Captain Kennedy and the PT-109."

entertainments. On Guadalcanal, the so-called Jungle Rhythm Boys regaled the U.S. Marines. Clement Felo of Santa Isabel sang country songs he had learned from U.S. troops during a USO Christmas show in the Russell Islands. Western Sāmoan bands played for dances held by the crew of the U.S. Naval Hospital. A poster for a dance in 1942 advertised:

> DANCE Give by 'Fai Fai-Lemu Club' Admission 50 cents . . . Jazz Music, Mapusaga Orchestra . . . Come, don't miss the best dancers wonderful time Hawaiian hula and Polynesian dances and performances, will be taken place and also a knife dance. (Parsons 1945:155)

As the war disrupted traditional performances, islanders discontinued or postponed customary feasts. In Papua New Guinea, the Japanese banned the playing of log idiophones, fearing that drumming could send messages about troops' locations and movements. In the Buna area, for the same reason, they smashed the kundus they found. In late 1942, military administrators of Western Sāmoa banned all dances but those held in public buildings and sponsored by a military unit.

### Themes

Commenting on wartime experiences, Pacific Islanders composed thousands of songs. On Kolombangara in the mid-1990s, people still sang about "Captain Kennedy and the PT-109." Set in a variety of local and string-band styles (and in local languages, Pidgin English, or colonial languages), some of these songs are remembered and performed.

#### *Songs as archives*

In most Oceanic societies, songs serve as historical archives (Hezel 1988:103; Lindstrom and White 1993). Stylistic rules, established within local musical genres, give structure to the lyrics, patterning the informational content. Alongside aesthetic values, songs comment on notable events. Repeated in public, they highlight socially valued historical information, including the names of people and places. By revealing islanders' interpretations of the war, archives of locally composed war-era songs provide opportunities to investigate how indigenous peoples selected, arranged, and remembered historical events. These archives include songs about occupation and resistance, combat, working for military forces, "cargo" (novel goods and technologies), destruction, death, liberation, romance, farewell, and remembrance.

Many war-era songs record islanders' encounters with new people and objects and validate social associations and proprietary claims. These songs center on the nature of islanders' relations with military personnel, who suddenly began arriving in incomprehensible numbers. They focus on arrivals, departures, and the expectations and disappointments that surrounded these activities. Extending genres that expressed indigenous social relations, war-era songs tried to manage new relations, symbolically and practically, according to local frames of meaning.

### Songs of arrival

Songs of arrival often note feelings of wonder at the spectacle of unimagined kinds and quantities of vehicles, equipment, food, and material. A song from Tanna lists first contact with novelties (presented here, as with other texts, in English translation):

> Happiness, astonishment here!
> We saw many things:
> Airplanes, submarines, tractors, autos.
> The land was too small.
> They were like the sand, and the stars in the sky—
> Impossible for me to count.

A stanza from Lamotrek similarly chronicles people's first experiences: "The interpreters call the people together and show / The people Japanese movies. / The people feel happy they've seen the movies, / And that they've seen different kinds of modern things in the movies." Such songs resemble Oceanic myths about the origins of important objects and practices.

### Songs of naming

As usual in many Oceanic musical genres, war-era songs frequently name people and places. Verses from Santa Isabel record where people took refuge: "One runs away, / Another carries a child, / Another packs belongings. / Where will we all go? / Cross over to Gorogofa, / Kokodou, Pirikakau. / Where will we all go? / Kuboro, Tafrakhana, / Grurukupi, Sopasare." Though centered on wartime events, songs like this vaunt islanders' claims over their lands and celebrate their relations with neighbors.

### Dysfunctional relationships

Other songs comment on social relationships gone awry. Evident in many island wartime songs are disappointment and bitterness toward military units that did not share their wealth, or arbitrarily appropriated local food and labor, or mistreated local property and people.

In much of Oceania, a typical way to call public attention to social transgressions or exchange imbalances is to compose and perform a song. A song of Pohnpei laments the conditions of women conscripted to work on Japanese military farms:

> Our temporary quarters make us really lonesome.
> It's worse than being in jail,
> Because we've assumed the appearance of frogs,
> Creeping on all fours, gathering,
> Tearing up, looking straight ahead.

A song of Tuvalu deplores the destruction of gardens: "Tears are shed, when one thinks / Of the way Funāfuti used to look, / And of today's scarred land. / We are worse off for America's deeds. / America, America, the rich nation— / Loads of money. / But there's one problem: / They buried the taro pit."

*Emotion in songs*

Many songs did more than lament. As acts of resistance, they expressed anger, hurling curses at occupying forces. When, to clear land for an emergency airstrip, Americans cut down palms and other trees on Bellona, the landowner, Tekiuniu, lamented the loss of his property in retaliatory verse (recorded by Samuel Elbert):

> The heavens of the gods,
> I looked at sea for a ship
> As this was the place it fell.
>
> The treachery has not a single path;
> A path in the heavens, a path at sea.
> Lay waste my land for nothing.
>
> Dig up my coconuts, remove my house,
> Kill my forest trees
> As the *gemeji* of harvest-songs.
>
> Would there were a path to tread upon,
> As I would retaliate my thought;
> As I ravage America, I lay waste.

On Santa Isabel, where Americans recruited men to work on a base in the Russell Islands, women struggled to keep their families and communities intact. Americans asked them to supply the base with thatch for warehouses and barracks. As they sewed up the thatch, they musically cursed the British officer, Jack, who arrived periodically in a landing craft ("open-mouthed boat") to recruit labor and load thatch: "My husband, my husband! / Taking him out to sea / In that open-mouthed boat. / Jack, Ja-ra-ra-ke!" In local practice, slurring someone's name ("Ja-ra-ra-ke") causes illness, particularly diarrhea.

In other songs, Solomon Islanders taunted the Japanese, whose power deflated after the Americans invaded Guadalcanal. A song from Santa Isabel shows how villagers sided with the Allied counterinvasion of Japanese-held territory:

> The Japanese enemy
> Has reached Tulagi,
> With their strength,
> With their guns.
>
> Lunga and Tenaru,
> Kukum and Point Cruz,
> Maravovo and Hautabu:
> The Japanese went first.
>
> Capital Tokyo,
> From where they came.
> Seat of the war
> Has arrived here.
>
> Air force, weapons,
> Warships, submarines:
> These things, my friend,
> Surround the Solomons.

Come here to die.
Stay alive until
The Honolulu air force arrives.
*Ko hiʻe.*

Airplanes above,
Submarines below.
Come to take back
The headquarters at Tulagi.

You watch out, my friend.
America is facing you.
They want to drink you.
They want to consume you.

Solomon Islanders, working with American and British forces, composed a taunt that became one of the war's most widely known songs. An Australian officer in the Russell Islands collected it, and *Pacific Islands Monthly* printed it in November 1944. Two of its famous stanzas, in our edition of Solomon Islands Pidgin and our translation, are:

Mi flae olobaot long ist long west.
Mi sedere oloraon kipim Solomon;
Mi waka lukluk long lan long si.
Ha-ha, ha-ha, Japani, ha-ha!

Japani wandem simasem evri aelan Pasifiki.
Merika simasem Kapitan Tokio.
Iu lukaot, mae fren; oloman i kik bak.
Mi laf long yu, Japani, ha-ha!

I fly around the east and west.
I watch and keep an eye on you, O Solomons;
My work is to spy on land and sea.
Ha-ha, ha-ha, Japan, ha-ha!

Japan wants to smash every Pacific island.
America smashes Captain Tokyo.
You look out my friend, the men kick back.
I laugh at you, Japan, ha-ha!

In the 1990s, people of Oceania continued to sing versions of this song.

## Opportunities

As the war disrupted local life, it offered opportunities for new social relationships among islanders and servicemen—relations that exchanges of gifts created and deepened. Songs of celebration and praise countered the war's laments and taunts. An example from Kosrae rejoiced: "The American ship came, / Bringing freedom. / They carried a lot of food. / Everyone was given some / Cans of eggs, / Cans of hash. / There was also cheese and candy. / Eat and remember."

## Farewells

With the withdrawal of Allied and Japanese forces, songs of farewell commemorated relationships with outsiders. A Sikaiana song lamented the departure of U.S. pilots

Whether Marco Polo's Cathay, Columbus's Indies, Stoker's Transylvania, Lawrence's Arabia, or Dorothy's Oz, the land of "the other" has contrasted with habitual reality. Oceania easily fell into this role.

who had crashed on the atoll: "America, your plane circles the island. / When it turns to go, my heart swoons. / When [they] walk to climb [into the plane] I cry. / We have not yet said goodbye." On the other side, a Kiribati couplet dignified the Japanese withdrawal: "Japanese people, remember us and think of us, / As we are staying among you, filled with sadness."

On Palau, the administrative center of Japanese Micronesia, ambivalence marked the Japanese defeat and departure. Palauans deplored in songs the end of a long relationship. In August 1945, Shiro Bedul, of Ollei Village, Ngerchelong, composed a lament:

> Our departure was sudden.
> For us islanders and our mother country,
> We're sad for such a sudden goodbye.
> Japan, our mother country,
> Was destined to be defeated.
>
> We won't forget you, good people,
> Who were our teachers for thirty years.
> My favorite *sakura* [sentimental song].
> Our relationship with you has ended.
> We don't know which direction to go next.
>
> Goodbye, everyone; to home you go.
> With perseverance, do whatever you can.
> Perhaps someday we'll meet again.
> Please take care,
> And let us pray every day.

In the early 1990s, similar songs farewelling troops and evoking memories of shared experiences were known throughout Oceania.

*Commemorations*

Songs continue to rehearse and develop the memory of wartime events. Annually during a celebration for surviving the U.S. assault on Enewetak in 1945, local people sing songs about the war. On Kosrae, similar celebrations occur. On Tanna, war-era songs have entered the liturgy of the John Frum movement, whose members perform them publicly to string-band accompaniment every Friday night during ritual dances. In the Trobriand Islands, where cricket has become a sport, one village team, the Airplanes, enters the field dancing to music that evokes wartime strafing and bombing.

Postwar composers have drawn upon wartime events. The Vanuatu band Noisy

Boys, in a commercially released cassette (1986), included a song about the war: "*1000 Pipol i Kam long Port-Vila*" ('One Thousand People Came to Port-Vila'). In the 1990s, a new generation of islanders composed songs that, by celebrating the fiftieth anniversaries of wartime events, emphasized their identities as citizens of independent nations. In the Solomon Islands, to commemorate the fiftieth anniversary of the U.S. invasion of Guadalcanal (7 August 1992), Manuel Iyabora's composition "The Fiftieth Anniversary Song, WWII" received wide play on radio.

—LAMONT LINDSTROM, GEOFFREY M. WHITE

## WRITERS

In Western literature, notions of "the other" have long served as foils of the familiar. Whether Marco Polo's Cathay, Columbus's Indies, Stoker's Transylvania, Lawrence's Arabia, or Dorothy's Oz, the land of "the other" has contrasted with habitual reality. When Oceania came into European consciousness, it easily fell into this role. The French explorer Louis de Bougainville named Tahiti *La Nouvelle Cythère* (The New Cythera), identifying it with a Mediterranean island classically associated with Venus, goddess of beauty and love.

Visitors and nonvisitors to the Pacific have recorded in writing their representations of Oceania and its people. Many have tried to depict its reality realistically, and others have made it serve artistic invention. The boundaries between realism and artistry are imprecise. Some texts pose as factual records of "the other" mainly to reveal issues native to the society doing the viewing. Satire and utopian writing have made much of this process. *Travels into Several Remote Nations of the World* (Swift 1726) places in Oceania several societies visited by Gulliver: Brobdingnag, north of Irian Jaya; the flying island of Laputa, northwest of Hawai'i; and Lilliput, apparently in South Australia.

Satire seeks a sobersided style to construct an imaginary world, but ethnographic texts sometimes do the reverse, using an evocative style to construct a real one, in this manner of reporting:

> Many of those who have retired to sleep, drawn by the merry music, will wrap their sheets about them and set out to find the dancing. A white-clad, ghostly throng will gather in a circle about the gaily lit house, a circle from which every now and then a few will detach themselves and wander away among the trees. Sometimes sleep will not descend upon the village until long past midnight; then at last there is only the mellow thunder of the reef and the whisper of lovers, as the village rests until dawn. (Mead 1928)

Careful readers puzzle over such a representation. It recorded a writer's encounter with "the other," but how much was reality? And how much was imagination? What does it mean to say that thunder is mellow or that sleep descends? The images are obvious romanticisms, but are they mere tinges of innocuous decoration, or do they echo an attitudinal drone? These questions have no ready answers, but they deserve to be asked, and they underlie any worthwhile review of writers' encounters with the music and dance of Oceania.

—J. W. LOVE

### The 1700s

#### *Views from Britain*

Captain Cook's voyages contributed most to the content and philosophy of serious and satirical British literature of the late 1700s. Samuel Taylor Coleridge's *The Rime of the Ancient Mariner* owed its inspiration to Cook's second voyage (Smith 1956). To decry Europeans' effects on indigenous peoples, satire was often aimed at Sir Joseph Banks, a botanist on Cook's first voyage. An anonymous, 172-line poem—"An Epistle From Oberea, Queen of Otaheite, to Joseph Banks, Esq. Translated by T.Q.Z., Esq., Professor of the Otaheite Language in Dublin, and of All the Languages of the Undiscovered Islands in the South Seas; and Enriched With Historical and Explanatory Notes"—was published in 1774, purporting to reveal amorous incidents between Oberea and Banks. Another poem, "The Injured Islanders; Or the Influence of Art Upon the Happiness of Nature," also attributed to Queen Oberea, dwells on disastrous results of Europeans' visits to Tahiti (Kaeppler 1978:25–28).

Omai, a Tahitian taken to England on Cook's second voyage, became the hero and theme of many literary works. One of the most ambitious dramatic events of the 1780s in England was the production of the pantomime *Omai, or a Trip Round the World,* based on Cook's voyages and staged at Covent Garden in 1785–1787. Philippe Jacques de Loutherbourg (1740–1812) designed the spectacle; the Irish actor and playwright John O'Keeffe (1747–1833) wrote the libretto; John Webber, an artist on Cook's third voyage, was a consultant on clothing, properties, and scenery; and William Shield (1748–1829) composed the music. The piece was sung and mimed, to music said to be "beautifully wild" and therefore appropriate to the subject. Oberea again figured prominently, but this time as an enchantress. The final scene featured a procession of forty-six men and women dressed in authentic Polynesian clothing and a group of "Tahitian" dancers (Joppien 1979:122–127), whose male dancer (figure 14) was based on Webber's drawing of dancers from Tonga (p. 766).

*La Mort du Capitaine Cook* (1788), a French ballet based on Captain Cook's murder, was received in Paris with "uncommon applause." Its restaging in London the next year, as the pantomime *The Death of Cook,* generated "tears and hysterics at Cook's fatal stabbing" (Dening 1992:295). Only seven weeks after Captain William Bligh's return from the mutiny on the *Bounty* (1790), the pantomime *The Pirates, or, The Calamities of Capt. Bligh* was presented at the Royalty Theatre, London (Dening 1992:286–293). It included "an Otaheitian Dance." Who performed this dance, we do not know; but William Bourke, who played the mutineer Fletcher Christian, was known for dancing a double hornpipe, a dance that features rocking at the hips and ankles.

Said to be "fact told in action," such pantomimes were a series of historically connected scenes (*Omai* was said to resemble a travelogue) that tried to persuade the audience that "the other" was being presented realistically by the incorporation of authentic clothing, scenery, music, singing, and dancing.

—ADRIENNE L. KAEPPLER

### Views from the continent

Accounts of Captain Cook's voyages were joined by that of Bougainville (1771), which inspired Denis Diderot's philosophical *Supplement to the Voyage of Bougainville* (1796). The poet Friedrich Wilhelm Zachariä (1726–1777) composed an idyll, "Tayti oder die glückliche Insel" ('Tahiti or the Happy Islands', 1778), whose maidens dance:

> *Die Musik*
> *Ward schmelzender, und lockender, als sonst,*
> *Der nackten Nymphen Tanz. Sie fingen an*

FIGURE 14    *Tahitian Dancer.* Drawing by Philippe Jacques de Loutherbourg, about 1785. National Library of Australia.

*Im lichten Reigen fortzuschweben, nach dem Takt*
*Der Flöten, und nach der Castagnetten Schall*
*Aus Perlenmuscheln.*


                                    The music
        Was melting, and more enticing than usual
        Was the naked nymphs' dance. They began
        To float away in the light dance, to the beat
        Of flutes and the sound of castanets
        Made of pearl shells.


Flutes were authentic Tahitian instruments, as concussed pebbles or shells may have been, but their accompaniment to a "naked nymphs' dance" owed more to German imagination than to Polynesian reality.

On the continent, some knowledge of Oceania in the late 1700s stemmed from Johann Reinhold Forster and his son Georg, who served as naturalists on Cook's second voyage. Georg's *A Voyage Round the World* (1777) enjoyed editions in Dutch, French, and German. August Friedrich Ferdinand von Kotzebue (1761–1819) produced three Oceania-based plays. *Ich, eine Geschichte in Fragmenten* (I, a Story in Fragments, 1781), proposed an exchange of German and Polynesian girls, to benefit both peoples. His comedy *Bruder Moritz, der Sonderling, oder: die Colonie für die Pelew-Inseln* (Brother Moritz, the Strange One, or: the Colony for the Palau Islands, 1791) proposed that Europeans would benefit from living in an egalitarian society. *La Peyrouse* imagined that the famous explorer survived the wreck of his ship and took a local wife. Johann Wolfgang von Goethe (1749–1832) summed up the European use of the Oceanic other in his "wish to have been born on one of the South Sea islands as a so-called savage, in order only once to enjoy a human existence without false flavor and with perfect purity" (Schweizer 1982).

## The 1800s and after

### Fiction

Fiction set in nineteenth-century Oceania often incorporates authors' experiences, real or imagined. Feigning a degree of ethnographic verisimilitude, plots have a touristic sameness: told in the first person, they follow the acts and thoughts of a European or American man living among natives or other expatriates. Music, dance, and poetry enter narratives as bits of cultural authenticity. Reflecting European and American colonial realities, most fictional accounts of Oceania are in English, French, or German.

### In English

Widely read and financially successful nineteenth-century works of fiction set in Oceania included Herman Melville's *Typee* (1846) and *Omoo* (1847), novels drawn from experience in Polynesia. Melville's most profound novel, *Moby-Dick* (1851), though set mostly in Oceania, takes little notice of islanders. In *Typee*, Melville describes (chapter 20) girls' moonlit dances:

        They all consist of active, romping, mischievous evolutions, in which every limb is
        brought into requisition. Indeed, the Marquesan girls dance all over, as it were; not
        only do their feet dance, but their arms, hands, fingers, ay, their very eyes, seem to
        dance in their heads. In good sooth, they . . . sway their floating forms, arch their
        necks, toss aloft their naked arms, and glide, and swim, and whirl.

As a handy label for Oceanic song, the word *chant* appears in all forms of literature, in all periods, usually meaning that the described music did not have the tonal variety of European music.

As a generalized description of Polynesian women's dancing, this passage rings true, but it does not specify what makes the dance uniquely Marquesan. Also in *Typee*, Melville describes Marquesan singing, "a low, dismal, and monotonous chant. . . . The sounds produced by the natives . . . were of a most singular description; and had I not actually been present, I never would have believed that such curious noises could have been produced by human beings" (chapter 31). The terms *curious, low, dismal,* and *monotonous* effectively set this music aside from the musical styles of the writer's world. As a handy label for Oceanic song, the word *chant* appears in all forms of literature, in all periods, usually meaning that the described music did not have the tonal variety of European music. Melville also describes a common Polynesian instrument:

> It is somewhat longer than an ordinary fife; is made of a beautiful scarlet-coloured reed; and has four or five stops, with a large hole near one end, which latter is held just beneath the left nostril. The other nostril being closed by a peculiar movement of the muscles about the nose, the breath is forced into the tube, and produces a soft dulcet sound, which is varied by the fingers running at random over the stops.

Polynesian melodies do not move randomly, but this is probably otherwise an accurate representation.

In *South-Sea Idyls* (1873), sixteen stories set in Hawai'i and French Polynesia, Charles Warren Stoddard turns a simple idiophone into a fantastic instrument. He hears a "performance upon a rude sort of harp, that gave out weird and eccentric music. The mouth being applied to the instrument, words were pronounced in a guttural voice, while the fingers twanged the strings in measure. It was a flow of monotones, shaped into legends and lyrics" (1873:40). Describing "musical diversions," Stoddard says a song begins with "a few words, chanted on a low note, . . . when the voice would suddenly soar upward with a single syllable of exceeding sweetness, and there hang trembling in bird-like melody till it died away with the breath of the singer" (1873:53). In these passages, the terms *weird, eccentric,* and *monotonous* mark "the other." Stoddard even puts music into the scenery, against which the visitor's emotions play: "The night-wind was laden with music, and sweet with the odors of ginger and cassia; the spume of the reef was pale as the milk of the cocoanuts, and the blazing embers on shore glowed like old sacrificial fires" (1873:78).

More ethnographically honest are the Oceania-based stories of Louis Becke and Robert Louis Stevenson. Set in various islands, Becke's plots show an appreciation of social structures, revealing comprehension of the local purposes of public events, including feasts and dances. They sometimes take indigenous characters' points of view. Becke's attention to linguistic detail was keen: he spelled non-English terms with more phonetic accuracy than other writers of his day; he frequently used words and phrases from indigenous languages. Stevenson's collection *Island Nights'*

*Entertainments* (1893) contains three stories, which vividly capture encounters of indigenous people and outsiders, putting in sharp and sometimes violent contrast notions of "the other" that then prevailed.

Fiction in the early twentieth century—by Jack London, Frank T. Bullen, and others—maintained the tradition. One of London's stories, as Fijians are about to club a missionary, cites the "death song, . . . the song of the oven" (1909:77), but readers get no help in imagining how the music sounded. Somerset Maugham's short story "Rain," set in Pago Pago, American Sāmoa, possibly updates an actual event of the mid-1800s, a missionary's suicide; music points the dénouement, but the sounds are Western, played on a phonograph.

By the 1950s, literary exoticism had faded, reflecting the military encounters of the Pacific War. The most notable Oceanic work of this period, James Michener's *Tales of the South Pacific* (1947), uses the war as a framework. Most of its musical references are to Western pieces, heard live, or on a radio or a phonograph. A musical version of it, *South Pacific* (1949), with lyrics by Oscar Hammerstein and music by Richard Rodgers, adds stereotypical dancing, even of U.S. servicemen in drag, wearing "grass skirts" and coconut brassieres. The second half of the twentieth century gained new perspectives from indigenous writers, including Alan Duff, Patricia Grace (figure 15), Epeli Hauʻofa, Vilsoni Hereniko, Albert Wendt, and others [see MUSIC AND THEATER].

## In French

The novel *Le mariage de Loti,* by a French naval officer, Julien Viaud (calling himself Pierre Loti), tells the tale of the impossible love of a Tahitian maiden, Rarahu, and a British naval officer, Harry Grant (calling himself Loti). Its publication, in 1880, kindled a literary sensation in France, earning Loti election to the Académie Française. The story develops within Loti's diary, explicated by Plumkett, Loti's friend. Accounts of music and dance contribute exoticism:

> As in all the Tahitian districts, there was a choir called *himene,* which performed regularly under the direction of a chief and was heard at all the native festivals. Rarahu was one of the outstanding members of the choir and altogether dominated it with her pure voice. The voices of the choir that accompanied her were hoarse and somber— the men especially brought in low and metallic tones, a kind of roaring that . . . seemed more like the sounds of some savage instrument than those of the choristers of the Conservatory. (Loti 1976:53)

FIGURE 15   The cover of Patricia Grace's book *Watercress Tuna and the Children of Champion Street* (1984) features multicultural dancers.

This description may be true to life; but the plot is not, for the romantic love between Rarahu and Grant is an outsider's fantasy, as is the ending, in which Rarahu, consumptively pining for Grant, having dosed herself with whiskey, dies.

The themes of *Le mariage de Loti* found their way into European operas. On similar exoticism, romance, and social conflict, Edmond Gondinet and Philippe Gille based the plot of *Lakmé* (1883), a three-act opera, with music by Léo Delibes. The action occurs in India. Loti becomes Gerald, a British colonial officer, and Rarahu becomes Lakmé, a Brahmin's daughter. At the end, Lakmé, having poisoned herself, dies in front of Gerald. A similar cultural clash underlies John Luther Long's story "Madam Butterfly," the basis of David Belasco's play *Madam Butterfly* and Giacomo Puccini's opera *Madama Butterfly* (1904). The action occurs in Japan. Loti becomes Lieutenant Pinkerton, a U.S. naval officer, and Rarahu becomes Cio-Cio San, a geisha. At the end, Cio-Cio San, having stabbed herself, dies in front of Pinkerton.

Other French writers set tales in French Polynesia (Margueron 1989). They used music and dance, especially *hīmene,* to authenticate the setting. After being stationed in Tahiti, the naval doctor Victor Ségalen (1878–1919) published several books, of which *Les Immémoriaux* (1966) is well known. Between 1926 and 1938, Jean Dorsenne published twelve Tahiti-based novels and sketches, in which imagistic diction conveys exoticism. A typical passage describes a lead singer's phrases as "veritable vocal thrusts of a dagger, sublime arabesques of a bird that is about to die" (1931:84–85).

### In German

The French-German writer and poet Adelbert von Chamisso (1781–1838), after publishing the novel *Peter Schlemihl* (the man who sold his shadow, 1814), served as a naturalist on Otto von Kotzebue's first expedition to the Pacific. He took an interest in the Hawaiian language, of which he wrote the first grammar. He extolled the beauties of the *hula,* which he and others witnessed as Kamehameha's guests (figure 16).

Chamisso published three Oceania-themed poems. "Ein Gerichtstag auf Huahine" ('A Day in Court on Huahine') shows how missionaries' laws conflicted with Polynesian laws. "Idylle" translates a Tongan song. "Salas y Gomez" takes up the

FIGURE 16    Hawaiian women perform a *hula* in honor of Russian visitors. Drawing by Louis Choris, artist on Kotzebue's first voyage, 1815–1818. Photo by Smithsonian Institution.

motif of castaways on a desert island. "Frauen Liebe und Leben" ('Woman's Love and Life', 1830), lyrical poems later set to music by Robert Schumann, may have owed to the experience of Hawai'i some of its understanding of "the other"—in this case, feminine sentiments and perspectives.

The first written fiction set in Hawai'i in any language was possibly the story "Haimatochare" (1819) by the German composer E. T. A. Hoffmann (1776–1822). It misleads readers through a plot in which a European scientist visits Hawai'i and falls in love with a local beauty, only to reveal that the object of his affection is an insect. Its ethnographic details include information Hoffmann learned from Chamisso.

### Poetry

John Keats made "stout Cortez" stare at the Pacific, "silent, upon a peak in Darien," but few major British or American poets have set poems in Oceania. Alfred, Lord Tennyson, in "Kapiolani," praised a Hawaiian princess for embracing Christianity and freeing Hawaiians from the goddess Pele (1898:864):

> A people believing that Peelè the Goddess would wallow in fiery riot and revel
> On Kilauëä,
> Dance in a fountain of flame with her devils, or shake with her thunders and shatter
>     her island,
> Rolling her anger
> Thro' blasted valley and flaring forest in blood-red cataracts down to the sea!

As in the Oceania-based fiction of Tennyson's time, dancing is incidental, part of the natural—hence pagan and evil—process of life. It marks the old religion, doomed to fall.

In 1913–1914, the English poet Rupert Brooke (1887–1915) toured Polynesia. For him, as for other sightseers, the islands had relevance in comparison with home and the intended audience there. At Waikīkī, Brooke composed a sonnet whose beginning gains an edge from the sounds of an *ukulele*:

> Warm perfumes like a breath from vine and tree
>     Drift down the darkness. Plangent, hidden from eyes,
>     Somewhere an *eukaleli* [sic] thrills and cries
> And stabs with pain the night's brown savagery;
> And dark scents whisper; and dim waves creep to me,
>     Gleam like a woman's hair, stretch out, and rise;
>     And new stars burn into the ancient skies,
> Over the murmurous soft Hawaiian sea.

In "Fafaïa," composed in Sāmoa, Brooke emphasized the experiential distance between himself and "the other" as lover: "Heart from heart is all as far, / Fafaïa, as star from star." Inevitably, the traveler's encounters with beauty spurred thoughts of paradise. There, as Brooke wrote in Tahiti, is "Dance, but not the limbs that move; / Songs in Song shall disappear; / Instead of lovers, Love shall be; / For hearts, Immutability." The sequence of dance, song, and love nicely captures an important Polynesian aesthetic focus.

### Travelogues

Tourists who encountered Oceania, returned home, and wrote purportedly nonfictional accounts of their experiences are legion. One of the most widely read nine-

Women danced to accordion-provided music, repeatedly singing *Tu fra to potta mi,* which turned out to be "Shoo, fly, don't bother me"—a song that a Chinese immigrant to the Marquesas had learned in California.

teenth-century accounts is *Two Years Before the Mast* (1840), by a Harvard student, Richard Henry Dana (1815–1882). It recounts his life as a seaman, mostly in the Pacific. Music enters the narrative mainly in the form of sailors' calls and chanteys. One passage links Hispanic music in California with the Hawaiian sailors who heard it, reminding readers that in the 1830s, Polynesians were working aboard European and American ships, gaining musical knowledge they would eventually take back home.

Other travelers posted accounts directly from the Pacific. In the 1800s, the most adept of these was Robert Louis Stevenson (1850–1894), who spent the last six years of his life in Oceania. His book *In the South Seas* chronicles experiences of the Marquesas, the Paumotus (Tuamotu Islands), and the Gilberts (now Kiribati), and his study *A Footnote to History: Eight Years of Trouble in Samoa* (1892) enlivens its political accounts with observations on sounds and movements. A flutist, Stevenson had some technical knowledge of music; nevertheless, like everyone encountering "the other" and knowing little of the alternate culture, he judged local artistic values by his own. In Butaritari, he rated the dancing

> easily the first. The *hula,* as it may be viewed by the speedy globe-trotter in Honolulu, is surely the most dull of man's inventions, and the spectator yawns under its length as at a college lecture or a parliamentary debate. But the Gilbert Island dance leads on the mind; it thrills, rouses, subjugates; it has the essence of all art, an unexplored imminent significance. (1971 [1900]:253–254)

For Stevenson, dancing had no ties to language. He did not understand Hawaiian, so the *hula* did not entertain him as did dancing in Butaritari:

> A sudden change would be introduced (I think of key) with no break of the measure, but emphasized by a sudden dramatic heightening of the voice and a swinging, general gesticulation. The voices of the soloists would begin far apart in a rude discord, and gradually draw together to a unison; which, when they had reached, they were joined and drowned by the full chorus. The ordinary, hurried, barking, unmelodious movement of the voices would at times be broken and glorified by a psalm-like strain of melody, often well constructed, or seeming so by contrast. . . . The songs that followed were highly dramatic; though I had none to give me any explanation, I would at times make out some shadowy but decisive outline of a plot; and I was continually reminded of certain quarrelsome concerted scenes in grand operas at home; just so the single voices issue from and fall again into the general volume; just so do the performers separate and crowd together, brandish the raised hand, and roll the eye to heaven—or the gallery. Already this is beyond the Thespian model; the art of this people is already past the embryo; song, dance, drums, quartette and solo—it is the drama full developed although still in miniature.

This account highlights a difficulty with appreciating the aesthetic systems of "the other." Stevenson thought he understood the performance because its traits resembled those that had meaning for him—tonal harmony, the singing of psalms, drama, grand opera. In fact, the dancers' movements were evoking the activities of birds, allusively referring to the mythical origins of Butaritari society (Kaeppler 1996). Stevenson judged what was unfamiliar to him by using familiar canons of art for an aesthetic touchstone. His declaration that Butaritari performance was "the drama full developed" takes an evolutionary view of history—an interpretation that judged the achievement of an artist, a work of art, or a performance by the apparent rung achieved on an assumed ladder of progress.

With similar attitudes, another traveler, Jack London, described Polynesians' singing and dancing near Bora Bora:

> Tehei and Bihaura danced, accompanied by songs and choruses or by rhythmic hand-clappings. At other times a musical knocking of the paddles against the sides of the canoes marked the accent. A young girl dropped her paddle, leaped to the platform, and danced a hula, in the midst of which, still dancing, she swayed and bent, and imprinted on our cheeks the kiss of welcome. Some of the songs, or *himines* [sic], were religious, and they were especially beautiful, the deep basses of the men mingling with the altos and thin sopranos of the women and forming a combination of sound that irresistibly reminded one of an organ. (1908:195–196)

Most likely, the young girl's *hula* was the outsider's fictitious hula, not the authentic *hula* of Hawai'i; and as with Stevenson, the performance reminded London of a familiar musical instrument.

Another kind of travelog keeps the writer in the first person, but puts dialogue into the mouths of persons locally visited or seen. Hundreds—possibly thousands—of travelers have tried their hand at this genre. Among them were Frederick O'Brien (1919, 1921), Charles Nordhoff, and James Norman Hall, specialists in French Polynesia. On the Tuamotu atoll Rutiaro, Hall saw a dozen men dancing to sounds from an ensemble of idiophones. One was

> an empty gasoline tin, upon which the drummer kept up a steady roll while the dance was in progress. The rhythm for the movements was indicated by three others, two of them beating hollowed cylinders of wood, while a third was provided with an old French army drum. . . . The syncopation was extraordinary. . . . The music was a kaleidoscope in sound, made up of unique and startling variations in tempo, as the dance moved from one figure to the next. (Hall and Nordhoff 1921:156)

Women then danced to accordion-provided music, repeatedly singing *Tu fra to potta mi,* which turned out to be "Shoo, fly, don't bother me," a song that a Chinese immigrant to the Marquesas had learned in California in the 1870s (O'Brien 1919:175).

Another genre puts the writer's experiences in the form of letters or a diary, private in form, but intended for, or amenable to, publication. Stevenson's letters (1895) recount incidental musical performances in Sāmoa. Letters by the French writer Marcel Schwob (1930) recorded musical details of a voyage to Polynesia. Though highlighting music and dance, they often serve as opportunities for the indulgence of fine writing, as in his description of an onboard performance:

> The evening passes with improvised songs, in polyphony. . . . The voices harmonize in solemn chords; the song is sad and slow in the partial gloom, sometimes lifted by the fire of a Sāmoan cigarette rolled in a banana leaf; and the veiled moon marks a vast silver cutlass floating on the sea. (30 December 1901)

Writing about encounters with "the other" in Oceania continued through the twentieth century, as prominent outsiders, including Thor Heyerdahl (1950, 1958) and Paul Theroux (1992), unself-consciously recorded their understandings and misunderstandings of behavior. Typically, they said little about Oceanic poetry, music, and dance.

—J. W. LOVE

## FILMMAKERS

Filmmakers have recorded their encounters with the peoples of Oceania since 1898, when academic researchers first documented human behavior in the new medium. Some of these filmmakers were amateurs, but their films have become treasures of information. Of special importance are early films, many now available in archives. Films using old and new footage serve regularly for teaching in academic settings. Possibly the ultimate teaching film is the eight-hour study *Towards Baruya Manhood* series, filmed in New Guinea by Ian Dunlop and Maurice Godelier (1972), documenting an initiatory ritual. Some documentary films hold particular importance for the study of music and dance in the Pacific. Three films made by Chris Owen in Papua New Guinea—*The Red Bowmen* (1977), *Tighten the Drums: Self-Decoration Among the Enga* (1983), and *Gogodala: A Cultural Revival?* (1979)—show long sequences of music and dance. An instructional manual (Volkman 1986) helps introduce the films. Hugo Zemp's films on 'Are'are panpipe music (1993) are important for their emphasis on local music theory.

Films are not culturally transparent; they take viewpoints, distort, and even lie. Thus, the outtakes from professionally shot documentaries can become important documents. These outtakes are often difficult to find, and even the staff of reputable television stations, often responsible for filming the documentaries, forget what they have done with them. The effects of documentation on living traditions can be problematic (Moyle 1992).

Semidocumentary films, such as Robert Flaherty's *Moana of the South Seas* (1926), include dance sequences. Originally silent, this film has been updated to include ambient and spoken sound and music (Frassetto 1995:408–413). Commercial films with Oceanic subjects use performances only in passing but are important sources of historical representation and reflect societal changes in defining "the other." Often commercial films, and sometimes documentaries, tell more about their makers than about their subjects.

The introduction of video has expanded the possibilities of documenting and disseminating visual and aural images of Oceanic music and dance. Video has become especially important to indigenous filmmakers. Eddie Kamae's films, *Lia* (1988) and *The Hawaiian Way: The Art and Tradition of Slack Key Music* (1995), focus on Hawaiian music and its history. *Papakōlea: A Story of Hawaiian Land*, by Edgy Lee and Haskell Wexler (1993), records Hawaiians' frustrations about acquiring Hawaiian homestead lands in Honolulu. The 1995 video *And Then There Were None*, by Elizabeth Kapu'uwailani Lindsey, makes political statements about Hawaiian sovereignty and the dwindling population of full-blooded Hawaiians. All such films use music and dance in compelling ways to strengthen the impact of their message.

—ADRIENNE L. KAEPPLER

### Commercial films

The lands and peoples of Oceania have figured prominently in commercial films, going back to the first fiction and documentary features between 1910 and 1920; but these have not been indexed or systematically studied for their musical content. Many of the earliest films do not survive, or are inaccessible. This article charts attributes that worldwide audiences have seen and heard, and that thus have influenced popular understanding of Oceania and its arts.

Apart from Australia and to a lesser extent Aotearoa, no country in Oceania has developed a local cinematic industry. Instead, Oceania has been shown to the world by outsiders, principally within movies that originated in Hollywood. Consequently, authentic music of Oceania is a rare cinematic commodity, though in some films it makes a fleeting appearance. The scores are mostly hybrids, dominated by Western styles, sometimes with bizarre results; but distinctions can be made according to period and genre.

### Outsiders in paradise

Early on, the Pacific Islands offered exotic locales for stories focused on Americans or Europeans. Contrasting examples are *Male and Female* (silent, 1919), Cecil B. DeMille's seriocomic adaptation of the play *The Admirable Crichton,* partly set on an uninhabited island in the South Seas; and *Waikiki Wedding* (1937, songs mostly by Ralph Rainger and Leo Robin, arrangements by Victor Young), the pleasant vehicle in which Bing Crosby introduced the songs "Sweet Leilani" and "Blue Hawaii." In such pictures, music in quasi-indigenous styles functions as part of the scenery, a token of the setting. Even so, whether vocal or instrumental, whether foregrounded or backgrounded, it can be crucial to the effect of the film. As one commentator noted (Maltin 1997), it is obvious in *Waikiki Wedding* that none of the featured cast has actually set foot in Hawai'i; yet the songs help take us there.

A more opulent example is Elvis Presley's tropical vehicle, *Blue Hawaii* (1961, directed by Norman Taurog, musical score by Joseph L. Lilley). During the opening credits, Presley sings the title song—a sign of its continued potency. In contrast to the earlier version, this one combines colorful Panavision backdrops with flashy segments featuring Polynesian singers and dancers. *Blue Hawaii* is a late example of an important subcategory of exotic moviemaking: an American or European man romances an islander woman. (Presley's cinematic girlfriend is "Maile Duvall," whose grandmother is Hawaiian.) Such stories have long been favorites, with songs part of their appeal. One of the first examples was *Aloha Oe* (silent, 1915), in which, according to a synopsis, a brilliant San Francisco lawyer is shipwrecked on a Polynesian island, becomes a derelict, falls in love with the chief's daughter, and can save her and enjoy a happy life only after he hears the title song while suffering in a saloon! Two later examples were *Where the Pavement Ends* (silent, 1923) and *The Pagan* (sound, 1929), Metro films starring Ramón Navarro; though more tragic than *Aloha Oe,* each received an alohaesque theme song: "Neath the Passion Vine: South Seas Serenade," by Walter Hauenschild and Bert Herbert, and "Pagan Love Song," by Nacio Herb Brown and Arthur Freed.

*Aloha Oe* and *Where the Pavement Ends,* though silent, each had a complete score, prepared by Wedgwood Nowell and Ernst Luz, respectively. This procedure was unusual: for most silent films set in the South Seas, movie-house musicians had to improvise their own accompaniments; and if they sought help from anthologies, they usually found only one piece, Queen Lili'uokalani's "*Aloha 'Oe,*" which, with various incidental pieces like J. S. Zamecnik's "Tropic Isle" (1923) and Maurice Baron's "Prelude to 'Romances of the Seven Seas'" (1924), had to cover all of Oceania—unless they strayed into "Oriental" numbers.

Thus, musicians in silent cinemas relied on a handful of musical clichés, of which the most common seem to have been rippling arpeggios and diatonic

The stage version of *South Pacific* probably surpasses all films as an Oceanic landmark in the popular imagination. Its song "Bali Ha'i"—lush in harmony and orchestration—stands as a quintessential expression of longing for one's own "special island."

melodies, sweetened by chromatic ornaments. These clichés carried over into sound films, as did the idea of matching native backdrops to music in Western styles. A fascinating example is offered by *Tabu*, the Flaherty-Murnau film of 1931, shot silent and then given a synchronized score by Hugo Riesenfeld (figure 17). Gorgeous photography, rich visual storytelling, and a mostly nonprofessional Polynesian cast put the film on a high plane, but the compilation score, by making the film seem just another Europeanized tale of doomed romantic passion, pulls it down. One of the most jarring moments comes during a sequence when natives paddle toward an incoming ship—to the accompaniment of a sped-up version of *The Moldau*. When Max Steiner composed an elaborate landmark score for another romance, *Bird of Paradise* (1932), he dispensed with such borrowed material; all the same, he merged exotic instruments and melodies into a thoroughly symphonic, leitmotif-laden score. This sort of mixture became the norm of Hollywood practice for years.

### Outsiders and insiders interact

*Tabu* and *Bird of Paradise* fall into a second category of films, in which Westerners and natives interact with more subtle and serious consequences. Favorite sources for such stories were at first the popular sea-oriented fictions of Joseph Conrad, Jack London, Herman Melville, and a host of successful lesser writers, like Charles

FIGURE 17  A lobby card advertises the 1949 rerelease of *Tabu,* a film by Robert Flaherty and F. W. Murnau (1931). DeSoto Brown Collection.

Nordhoff and James Norman Hall. After World War II, new material came from American experiences in the South Pacific, as in James Michener's tales and the resultant Rodgers and Hammerstein musical. Indeed, though not of much critical value as a film, the stage version of *South Pacific* probably surpasses all films as an Oceanic landmark in the popular imagination; and its song "Bali Ha'i," lush in harmony and orchestration, stands as a quintessential expression of longing for one's own "special island."

Whatever the source, in such films the islands and their surrounding seas often become sites of romance and destruction. Influential examples from before the war include *Rain* (1931), an adaptation of Somerset Maugham's story of the same name; *Mutiny on the Bounty* (1935), an adaptation of Hall and Nordhoff's story of the famous insurrection; and *The Hurricane* (1937). All three have been remade (*Bounty* twice), and all show Western colonial, capitalist, and moral values colliding with indigenously innocent or barbaric behavior, usually with tragic results. In *Rain,* a scriptwriter expressed one of the tenets of such films when he gave the trader Horn the following to say about life in Pago Pago:

> Now take these islanders, Doctor; they're naturally the happiest, most contented people on earth. They ask nothing of life except to be allowed to eat, and sing, and dance and sleep. . . . They're satisfied with their gods of wind and wave, and along comes Mr. Davidson who tells 'em they're lost souls—they've got to be saved, whether they want to be or not.

Similarly though more grandly, in *Mutiny on the Bounty,* when Byam's mother proposes a toast to send *Bounty* off, the son, naive and idealistic, repeats her words and toasts "still waters and the great golden sea; flying fish like streaks of silver, and mermaids that sing in the night; the Southern Cross, and all the stars on the other side of the world."

*Rain* is an excellent example of an early sound film in which indigenous music is a minor, yet telling, component. The emphasis falls principally on jazz and blues to suggest Sadie Thompson's sexual allure, and on nonmusical sounds—especially those of rain—to convey a sense of monotony, covering incessant camera movement and suggestive montage. Key points in the film feature snippets of indigenous performance, once while men cast a net along the shore, and again after the net has fetched up Davidson's body. The buildup to the climax makes effective offscreen use of Sāmoan drumming, which, in ways reminiscent of *The Emperor Jones,* helps unleash a savage and finally irrepressible force, the missionary's lust.

As for *Bounty* and *The Hurricane,* each contains an elaborate symphonic score in a style that became typical during the mid-1930s (*Bird of Paradise* being a forerunner) and endured into the 1950s. *The Hurricane,* one of Alfred Newman's richest, benefits from a song later known as "Moon of Manukoora," Dorothy Lamour's signature piece. Its chromatics recall those of "*Aloha 'Oe*" (heard in passing), but it is one of an array of themes both Western and indigenous, the former Impressionist, the latter mostly Hawaiian. Stothart's score for *Bounty,* with its use of English naval songs and reliance on men's chorus, seems less compelling today; but in one respect, it offered a model for the remakes, as for other films to come: symphonic music is heard at the outset; but once the ship has reached Tahiti, local music takes over, making the cultural conflict audible. Bronislau Kaper's score for the 1962 remake follows much the same approach. More exciting than Stothart's, this version is ethnologically more accurate, even if the film overall is dramatically inferior—and still more so Vangelis's score for the 1984 remake, on both counts.

Study of such remakes suggests that the craft of cinematic storytelling has been

*Hawaii* could be described as the first revisionist epic. In it, outsiders—particularly missionaries and traders—are the source of all evil.

in decline, as has Hollywood's ability to mix music in radically different idioms within a late Romantic framework. Greater artistic success follows composers who work in films more modern in sensibility, better able to accommodate a new kind of fusion, in which modernist and indigenous styles join more equally. One of the first examples is *Hawaii* (1966), with a remarkably diverse score by Elmer Bernstein, rich in the sounds of Hawaiian instruments.

### Outsiders as problems

In some respects, *Hawaii* could be described as the first revisionist epic: in it, outsiders—particularly missionaries and traders—are the source of all evil, and in trying to accommodate them, Hawaiians suffer terribly. From Australia and Aotearoa in the late twentieth century came several pictures, including *The Last Wave* (1977, music by Charles Wain) and *The Piano* (1993, music by Michael Nyman), which presented similar conflicts and biases. In these films, a new trend emerges: natives themselves take center stage, suffering their own moral and cultural crises. Films like *Moana* and *Tabu* can be seen as ancestors, but the tone of recent films is altogether different.

The most disturbing examples of this type are *The Chant of Jimmie Blacksmith* (1978, music by Bruce Smeaton), *Utu* (1983, music by John Charles), and *Rapa-Nui* (1994, music by Stewart Copeland). With sympathy and irony, the first two depict natives on the rampage; the last presents an overwrought account of tribal strife and ecological disaster on Easter Island before European sailors encountered it.

None of the revisionist films offers anything like a traditional score. Only one aural point ties them together: recordings of indigenous music are not used as mere background, matched to scenes of natives or local life; on the contrary, the sinister Aboriginal drones heard in *The Last Wave,* the remarkable mixtures of orchestral styles and Māori flute in *Utu,* the Polynesian drumming and singing supported by symphonic instruments in *Rapa-Nui*—these are the central components of each film's score. Film music has always been a subordinate art; but these scores show that in films of Oceania there now exists as much freedom and as rich a potential for combining music, image, and narrative, as in films made about any other part of the globe.

—MARTIN M. MARKS

### Documentary films: Australia

Documentary films of Australian indigenous cultures enjoyed a vogue from about 1960 to 1985. Sound-synchronized filming outside studios became technically feasible from about 1960, and political and technical developments took documentary filmmaking in new directions after 1985. Most documentary films of that period were made by or for the Australian Institute of Aboriginal Studies, AIAS (Wild 1986a).

In films on music and dance, certain filmmakers stand out: Ian Dunlop, Roger

Sandall, Curtis Levy, and David MacDougall. Dunlop, employed by the Australian Commonwealth Film Unit (later Film Australia), shot *Dances at Aurukun* (1964) in Cape York, Queensland, and edited a shorter version in *Five Aboriginal Dances from Cape York* (1966). In northeast Arnhem Land, Northern Territory, he made *Madarrpa Funeral at Gurka'wuy* (1979), a more substantial film, with an accompanying monograph by Howard Morphy (1984), who, with Nancy Williams, was anthropological adviser for *Madarrpa*. Twenty more films by Dunlop on northeast Arnhem Land, mostly shot in the 1970s, were released between 1981 and 1996.

Sandall filmed in northern and central Australia. Like Dunlop, he specialized in religious rituals, and many of his films are for restricted viewing only. His films still available for unrestricted viewing include *Mourning for Mangatopi* (1975), which documents a Tiwi bereavement ceremony on Melville Island, and *A Walbiri Fire Ceremony: Ngatjakula* (1977), shot in Central Australia. Anthropological advisers were Maria Brandl for the former and Nicolas Peterson for the latter.

Like Dunlop and Sandall, Levy and MacDougall filmed Aboriginal ceremonies. Levy's film *Lockhart Festival,* shot in Cape York, was less a departure than the title implies, despite the presence of participants from Arnhem Land; *Lurugu* (1974b) documents the revival of an initiation ceremony on Mornington Island in the Gulf of Carpentaria, Queensland. MacDougall's *Goodbye Old Man* (1977) was another film of a Tiwi bereavement ceremony, and *The House Opening* (1980), directed by Judith MacDougall and filmed by David MacDougall, documented an amalgam of Aboriginal, Torres Strait Islander, and Western bereavement ceremonies in Cape York.

The films collectively titled *Groote Eylandt Field Project* (Moyle and Snell 1969a, 1969b, 1969c) represent a different approach to documenting Aboriginal music and dance. Instead of filming a ceremony, researchers had songs and dances performed specifically for filming, with no ceremonial context. The main purpose of the films was to aid the notation and analysis of music and dance. For this reason, the performers were simultaneously filmed from three angles (front, back, side), and the edited films retain these perspectives. Though the finished product is useful for notation, any cultural analysis it supports is limited in scope.

Perhaps the most remarkable documentary film made of Aboriginal music and dance is the award-winning *Waiting for Harry* (1980), by AIAS filmmaker Kim McKenzie. Shot in north-central Arnhem Land, it documents the politics of a ceremony of bereavement. Its success stimulated research on music and dance of the same people by Clunies Ross and Wild (1984), and was partly responsible for performances of a related ceremony, Rom, in Canberra in 1982 (Wild 1986b) and 1995 [see MUSIC AND THEATER: Australia].

—STEPHEN A. WILD

## Documentary films: Pacific Islands

Documentary films of the Pacific Islands range from low-budget productions that record events for posterity to high-budget productions made for television. *Tahiti Fête* (Polynesian Cultural Association 1992), *JVC Video Anthology of Music and Dance,* volumes 29 and 30 (Kunihiko and Yuji 1990), and *Beldeklel a Ngloik = Palauan Dance: The Process* (Babcock 1993) exemplify the former; *Nomads of the Wind* (Crawford 1994) and *Dancing in One World* (Bakal 1993) exemplify the latter.

*Tahiti Fête* records solo and collective performances in a two-day Tahitian-dance competition held in San Jose, California. It highlights one style of dancing done by performers of different ages and abilities, with Tahitian drumming. Apart from the competition, performances include other Polynesian music and dance. Sequences

Cricket matches are intervillage competitions. Each team has a theme—like "airplanes"—celebrated with mimetic entrances and exits. They dance when a player from the opposite team is bowled out.

unfold intact, giving a feel for the pace of the competition. Editing uses combinations of near and far shots. Since the film was meant for sale as a souvenir to contestants, friends, and families, the producers use neither narration nor captions. Similar commercial products show competitions in Hawai'i, Tahiti, California, and elsewhere, and archival copies of TV broadcasts of popular events—Merrie Monarch, Kamehameha Schools Song Contest, and others—are available.

Volume 29 of the *JVC Video Anthology of Music and Dance* shows dance and music from Australia, New Guinea (Iatmul, Sawos, Eipo), the Solomon Islands, New Caledonia, and Micronesia (Northern Marianas). Volume 30 covers Polynesia: Fiji, Sāmoa, Tonga, Tokelau, Tuvalu, Tahiti, the Marquesas, and Aotearoa. Meant as a sample of music and dance, it provides a montage of performances, captured in settings ranging from formal stages to backyards. Published guides provide additional information. Volumes 2 and 3 of the 1995 JVC/Smithsonian Video Anthology of Music and Dance of the Americas includes two Hawaiian examples.

The collaborative project *Beldeklel a Ngloik* documents Palauan dances. The film begins with shots of girls in hibiscus-bark skirts and woven pandanus tops, dancing and singing in front of a house. Clips of girls learning to dance provide background to this performance. The film shows Palauan men and women making the girls' costumes: they cut and process hibiscus for the skirts and prepare yellow-tinted turmeric oil for the dancers' skin. Also shown, with an explanation of how this form evolved, are clips of newer dances, performed to musical accompaniment.

Three aspects of filmmaking may inform the evaluation of a film: the filmmaker's intent, the intended audience, and the effect of a film on an audience (Banks 1992:117). Because *Tahiti Fête* is meant for an audience already familiar with Polynesian music and dance, the filmmakers did not explain the event beyond introducing the performers. The *JVC Video Anthology of Music and Dance* relies on supplementary published texts to provide additional explanation of the films' subject. In contrast, *Beldeklel a Ngloik* is meant as a visual record, combining detailed explanation of music and dance with visual documentation.

High-budget documentaries like *Nomads of the Wind* and *Dancing in One World* are made for mass audiences. *Nomads of the Wind* is a five-part series. Narrated by a male voice, it focuses on the transformation of natural habitats as a result of Polynesian—and later, European—activities. Scenes recreating Polynesians' arriving at islands, the culture they brought, and their activities often incorporate music and dance.

The closing scene of the first episode shows a tropic-bird-inspired dance, performed on a beach by Marquesans in white costumes ornamented with feathers and shells. The drumming, the singing, and the setting suggest how natural beauty inspired Marquesans to artistic expression. In another scene, a Marquesan man plays a nose-blown flute on a mountain while we watch a man being tattooed. The end of the last episode incorporates footage from the 1992 Pacific Festival of Arts. Drums play faintly in the background as we watch people arrive in Polynesian voyaging canoes, airplanes, and boats. Theme music weaves its way into sounds and images; the drums fade away until the music envelops surreal, slow-motion images of dancers.

*Dancing in One World* is the final part of the eight-hour series *Dancing*. Filmed at the 1990 arts festival in Los Angeles, it relies on narration, interviews, and subtitles to provide information about dance in multicultural contexts. It features dances by performers from Australia, Hawai'i, and 'Uvea, and shows performances by non-Oceanic troupes and modern-dance companies. Participants' discussions offer insiders' commentaries. In the same series, *Sex and Social Dance* (part 3) has a section on music and dance in the Cook Islands, focusing on how collective orientation is an organizing principle of local society.

The use of music in the two high-budget documentaries differs by audience and intent. For the most part, *Nomads of the Wind* uses theme music (composed by Brian Bennett), which rarely incorporates Polynesian elements. In contrast, *Dancing in One World* focuses on exotic and familiar forms of music and dance. Theme music, when used, features music from each of the film's subjects, blended into a single composition.

### Anthropological and ethnographic films

Anthropological films focus on comparing and explaining cultural differences; ethnographic films, a related genre, lack the explanatory power of anthropological films (Freudenthal 1988:124). Both genres often rely on music and dance to portray essential cultural traits. *Cannibal Tours* (O'Rourke 1987) and *Trobriand Cricket: An Ingenious Response to Colonialism* (Leach and Kildea 1973) exemplify anthropological films; *Turnim Hed: Courtship and Music in Papua New Guinea* (Bates and Agland 1992) is an example of an ethnographic film.

*Cannibal Tours* examines tourism along the Sepik River, Papua New Guinea. It opens with a caption: "There is nothing so strange in a strange land as the stranger who comes to visit it." As the film progresses, the truth of this proposition becomes apparent. The film records interactions between indigenous residents and European tourists who have come to experience the exotic "other." Interactions are stiff. The villagers perform dances for the tourists. They allow themselves to be photographed, sometimes with amused embarrassment, but sometimes with discomfort or barely disguised toleration. Personal statements show that neither side understands the other. The film uses music and natural sounds to contrast New Guineans and tourists. Classical music—Mozart!—accompanies clips that show the tourists doing touristic things: buying souvenirs, taking photographs, riding in speedboats. Indigenous music accompanies clips that show photographs from the days of early contact and when the local people talk of past customs, including cannibalism.

*Trobriand Cricket* opens with Trobriand Islanders adorned with feathers and paint, playing cricket. We then see footage of a British cricket match in a stadium, the players dressed in white. The film examines the history of cricket in the Trobriand Islands: how British colonialists introduced it, and how the islanders transformed it. Cricket matches are intervillage competitions. Each team has a theme, like "airplanes," celebrated with mimetic entrances and exits. They dance when a player from the opposite team is bowled out. *Trobriand Cricket* centers on these dances, which blend old and new cultural elements.

*Turnim Hed* focuses on the music of courtship in Chimbu Province, Papua New Guinea. A narrator's voice tells us that people of the highlands judge a man, not on his looks or personality, but on the quality of his singing. We see men practicing songs for courtship-related rituals and talking of an especially skilled yodeler (yodeling still serves for long-distance communication). The same men go to a young woman's house, where they entertain her family. We see women singing for rain and nourishment for their sweet potatoes.

*Trobriand Cricket* and *Turnim Hed* feature music generated by the subjects of the film. Because anthropological and ethnographic filmmakers know that music can influence an audience's interpretations, most want to minimize their impact on the audience, so they do not use background music (Freudenthal 1988:127). Anthropological and ethnographic films usually record music and dance in everyday contexts, in contrast to documentary films, which emphasize music performed for an audience or special event.

Other useful films that focus on New Guinea are *Tighten the Drums: Self-Decoration Among the Enga* (Owen 1976), which follows the stages of the manufacture of kundus, and *Maring in Motion* (Jablonko 1968), which describes movement and daily life among the Maring of Western Highlands Province. Several films by New Guinea filmmaker Chris Owen—*The Red Bowmen* (1977), *Gogodala: A Cultural Revival?* (1979), *Malangan Labadama: A Tribute to Buk-Buk* (1989)—have documentary importance for music, as does Les McLaren's film *Kama Wosi: Music in the Trobriand Islands* (1979). With consummate cinematographic artistry, Robert Gardner's *Dead Birds* (1961) portrays the Dani of Irian Jaya; it includes several clips of singing and dancing occasioned by warfare: a funeral and celebrations of victory.

—DEBORAH J. SCRATCH

## REFERENCES

*American Film Institute Catalog of Motion Pictures Produced in the United States.* 1971–. A: *Film Beginnings, 1893–1910.* F1: *Feature Films, 1911–1920.* F2: *Feature Films, 1921–1930.* Series in progress. Editor and publisher vary per volume.

Babcock, Lynn Kremer. 1993. *Beldeklel a Ngloik = Palauan Dance: The Process.* 16mm, 47 min. Worcester, Mass.: Lynn Kremer Babcock, Holy Cross College.

Bakal, Stephanie, and Mark Obenhaus. 1993. *Dancing in One World.* 16mm, 58 min. New York: RM Arts, BBC-TV, and Thirteen/WNET.

Banks, Marcus. 1992. "Which Films are the Ethnographic Films?" In *Film As Ethnography,* ed. Peter Ian Crawford and David Turton, 116–129. Manchester and New York: Manchester University Press.

Baron, Maurice. 1924. *Prelude to "Romances of the Seven Seas."* Baron Preludes, 8. New York: Belwin.

Barrot, Adolphe. 1850. "Visit of the French Sloop of War Bonite, to the Sandwich Islands, in 1836." Translation from the French, in *The Friend,* vol. 8.

Bates, James, and Phil Agland. 1992. *Turnim Hed: Courtship and Music in Papua New Guinea.* Princeton, New Jersey: Films for the Humanities and Sciences.

Beaglehole, J. C., ed. 1962. *The Endeavour Journal of Joseph Banks 1768–1771.* Sydney: Angus and Robertson.

———, ed. 1967. *The Journals of Captain James Cook on His Voyages of Discovery: The Voyage of the Resolution and Discovery 1776–1780.* Cambridge: Cambridge University Press.

Bloxam, Andrew. 1925. *Diary . . . of the 'Blonde' . . . 1824–25.* Special Publication 10. Honolulu: Bishop Museum.

Bougainville, Louis Antoine de. 1771. *Voyage autour du monde, par le frégate du roi "La Boudeuse," et sa flûte "L'Etoile."* Paris: Saillant et Vyon.

Bullen, Frank T. 1899. *The Cruise of the Cachalot.* New York: Appleton.

Burney, James. 1975. *With Captain James Cook in the Antarctic and Pacific.* Canberra: National Library of Australia.

Byron, George Anson. 1826. *Voyage of H. M. S. "Blonde" to the Sandwich Islands in the Years 1824–1825.* London: John Murray.

Chamisso, Adelbert von. 1814. *Peter Schlemihl.*

Clunies Ross, Margaret, and Stephen A. Wild. 1984. "Formal Performance: The Relations of Music, Text and Dance in Arnhem Land Clan Songs." *Ethnomusicology* 28(2):209–235.

Cook, James, and James King. 1784. A *Voyage to the Pacific Ocean.* London: Strahan.

Crawford, Peter. 1994. *Nomads of the Wind.* 16mm in 5 parts, 60 min. each. New York and London: Thirteen/WNET and BBC-TV.

Dana, Richard Henry. 1840. *Two Years Before the Mast: A Personal Narrative of Life at Sea.* New York: Harper.

Dening, Greg. 1992. *Mr Bligh's Bad Language.* Cambridge: University Press.

Diderot, Denis. 1796. *Supplement to the Voyage of Bougainville.* Paris.

Dorsenne, Jean. 1931. *Le baiser sous les palmes.* Paris: Librairie Alphonse Lemerre.

Dunlop, Ian, director. 1964. *Dances at Aurukun.* 16mm, 28 min. Sydney: Australian Commonwealth Film Unit, for Australian Institute of Aboriginal Studies.

———, director. 1966. *Five Aboriginal Dances from Cape York.* 16mm, 8 min. Sydney: Australian Commonwealth Film Unit.

———, director. 1979. *Madarrpa Funeral at Gurka'wuy.* 16mm, 88 min. Sydney: Film Australia.

Dunlop, Ian, and Maurice Godelier, directors. 1972. *Towards Baruya Manhood Series.* 16mm, 465 min.

Ellis, William. 1963 [1827]. *Narrative of a Tour of Hawaii, or Owhyhee; with Remarks on the History, Traditions, Manners, Customs and Language of the Inhabitants of the Sandwich Islands.* Honolulu: Advertiser Publishing.

Flaherty, Robert. 1926. *Moana: A Romance of the Golden Age.* Film, silent. Paramount.

Forster, George. 1777. A *Voyage Round the World, in His Britannic Majesty's Sloop, Resolution, Commanded by Capt. James Cook, during the Years 1772, 3, 4, and 5.* 2 vols. London: B. White.

Frassetto, Monica Flaherty. 1995. "New Birth for Moana (1995)." *Wide Angle* 17:408–413.

Freudenthal, Solveig. 1988. "What To Tell and How To Show It: Issues in Anthropological Filmmaking." In *Anthropological Filmmaking,* ed. Jack R. Rollwagen, 123–134. Chur, Switzerland: Harwood Academic Publishers.

Freycinet, L. C. Desaulses de. 1827–39. *Voyage autour du monde . . . pendant les années 1817–1820.* 2 vols. in 3. Paris: Pillet Aîné.

Gardner, Robert. 1961. *Dead Birds.* 16mm. Cambridge: Harvard University.

Grace, Patricia. 1984. *Watercress Tuna and the Children of Champion Street.* Auckland: Longman Paul.

Hall, James Norman, and Charles Bernard Nordhoff. 1921. *Faery Lands of the South Seas.* Garden City, New York: Garden City Publishing.

Heinl, R. D. 1944. "Palms and Planes in the New Hebrides." *National Geographic* 86:229–256.

Heyerdahl, Thor. 1950. *Kon-Tiki: Across the Pacific by Raft.* Translated by F. H. Lyon. Chicago: Rand McNally.

————. 1958. *Aku-Aku: The Secret of Easter Island.* Chicago: Rand McNally.

Hezel, Francis X. 1988. "New Directions in Pacific History: A Practitioner's Critical View." *Pacific Studies* 11:101–110.

Hoare, Michael E., ed. 1982. *The Resolution Journal of Johann Reinhold Forster 1772–1775.* 3 vols. London: Hakluyt Society.

Jablonko, Allison. 1968. *Maring in Motion.* 16 mm. College Park: Pennsylvania State University.

Joppien, Rüdiger. 1979. "Philippe Jacques de Loutherbourg's Pantomime 'Omai, Or a Trip Round the World' and the Artists of Captain Cook's Voyages." In *Captain Cook and the South Pacific,* ed. T. C. Mitchell, 81–136. London: British Museum.

Kaeppler, Adrienne L. 1967. "Preservation and Evolution of Form and Function in Two Types of Tongan Dance." In *Polynesian Culture History: Essays in Honor of Kenneth P. Emory,* ed. Genevieve A. Highland et al., 503–536. Honolulu: Bishop Museum Press.

————. 1978. *"Artificial Curiosities": An Exposition of Native Manufactures Collected on the Three Pacific Voyages of Captain James Cook, R. N.* Honolulu: Bishop Museum Press.

————. 1996. "The Look of Music, the Sound of Dance: Music as a Visual Art." *Visual Anthropology* 8:133–153.

Kamae, Eddie. 1995. *The Hawaiian Way: The Art and Tradition of Slack Key Music.* Honolulu: Hawaii Sons. Video.

————. 1988. *Lia.* 60 min. Honolulu: Hawaii Sons. Video.

Kotzebue, Otto von. 1821. *A Voyage of Discovery, into the South Sea and Beering's Straits, for the Purpose of Exploring a North-East Passage, Undertaken in the Years 1815–1818.* 3 vols. London: Longman, Hurst, Rees, Orme, and Brown.

Krämer, Augustin. 1935. *Inseln um Truk.* Hamburg: Friederichsen, de Gruyter.

Kunihiko, Nakagawa, and Ichihashi Yuji. 1990. *JVC Video Anthology of Music and Dance.* Vols. 29

and 30. 92 minutes each. Distributed by Rounder Records, Cambridge, Mass. 2 videos.

Labillardière, J. J. 1802. *An account of a voyage in search of La Perouse . . . under the command of Rear-Admiral Bruni D'Entrecasteaux.* London: Uphill.

Leach, Jerry W., and Garry Kildea. 1973. *Trobriand Cricket: An Ingenious Response to Colonialism.* 16mm, 54 min. University of California Extension Media Center, California.

Lee, Edgy, and Haskell Wexler. 1993. *Papakōlea: A Story of Hawaiian Land.* 57 min. Video.

Levy, Curtis, director. 1974a. *Lockhart Dance Festival.* 16mm, 30 min. Canberra: Australian Institute of Aboriginal Studies.

————, director. 1974b. *Lurugu.* 16mm, 59 min. Canberra: Australian Institute of Aboriginal Studies.

Lincoln, Satoko. 1979. "Japanese Schools in Bougainville, Papua New Guinea During the Pacific War, 1942–1945." Manuscript. Honolulu: Hamilton Library, University of Hawai'i.

Lindsey, Elizabeth Kapu'uwailani. 1995. *And Then There Were None.* 21 min. Honolulu: Pacific Islanders in Communication. Video.

Lindstrom, Lamont, and Geoffrey M. White. 1990. *Island Encounters: Black and White Memories of the Pacific War.* Washington, London: Smithsonian Institution Press.

Lindstrom, Lamont, and Geoffrey M. White. 1993. "Singing History: Island Songs from the Pacific War." In *Artistic Heritage of a Changing Pacific,* ed. Philip J. C. Dark and Roger G. Rose, 185–196. Bathurst, N.S.W.: Crawford House Press.

Ling Roth, Henry. 1891. *Crozet's Voyage to Tasmania, New Zealand, and the Ladrone Islands, and the Philippines in the Years 1771–1772.* London: Truslove and Shirley.

London, Jack. 1908. *The Cruise of the Snark.* New York: Harper.

————. 1909. *South Sea Tales.* New York: McClure.

Loti, Pierre [Julien Viaud]. 1976 [1880]. *The Marriage of Loti.* Translated by Wright Frierson and Eleanor Frierson. Honolulu: University Press of Hawai'i.

McClelland, Mancy. 1924. *Historic Wall-Papers.* Philadelphia: J. B. Lippincott.

MacDougall, David, director. 1977. *Goodbye Old Man.* 16mm, 70 min. Canberra: Australian Institute for Aboriginal Studies.

MacDougall, Judith, director. 1980. *The House Opening.* 16mm, 45 min. Canberra: Australian Institute for Aboriginal Studies.

McKenzie, Kim, director. 1980. *Waiting for Harry.* 16mm, 57 min. Canberra: Australian Institute of Aboriginal Studies.

McLaren, Les. 1979. *Kama Wosi: Music in the Trobriand Islands.* 49 min. Focal Communications. Film, video.

Malaspina, D. Alejandro. 1885. *La Vuelta al Mundo . . . desde 1789 a 1794.* 2nd ed. Madrid.

Maltin, Leonard, ed. 1997. *Leonard Maltin's 1998 Movie and Video Guide.* New York: Penguin.

Margueron, Daniel. 1989. *Tahiti dans toute sa littérature.* Paris: Editions L'Harmattan.

Martin, John. 1818. *An Account of the Natives of the Tonga Islands, in the South Pacific Ocean . . . Compiled and Arranged from the Extensive Communications of Mr. William Mariner, Several Years Resident in Those Islands.* 2nd ed. 2 vols. London: John Murray.

Mead, Margaret. 1928. *Coming of Age in Samoa.* New York: Morrow.

Melville, Herman. 1846. *Typee or a Peep at Polynesian Life.* London: John Murray.

————. 1847. *Omoo: A Narrative of Adventures in the South Seas.* London:

————. 1851. *Moby-Dick or, The Whale.*

Michener, James. 1947. *Tales of the South Pacific.* New York: Macmillan.

Miklouho-Maclay, Nikolai Nikolayevich. 1992–93 [1950–53]. *Sobranie sochinenii v shesti tomah.* New edition. Vols. 1–3 (1st part). Moscow and Leningrad: Institute of Ethnography, Academy of Sciences.

Morphy, Howard. 1984. *Journey to the Crocodile's Nest.* Canberra: Australian Institute of Aboriginal Studies.

Moyle, Alice, ed. 1992. *Music and Dance of Aboriginal Australia and the South Pacific: The Effects of Documentation on the Living Tradition.* Canberra: Oceania Monographs.

Moyle, Alice, and E. C. Snell, directors. 1969a. *Groote Eylandt Field Project: Aboriginal Dances (8.3).* 16mm, 30 min. Canberra: Australian Institute of Aboriginal Studies.

————, directors. 1969b. *Groote Eylandt Field Project: Eight Aboriginal Songs with Didjeridu Accompaniment (8.6).* 16mm, 20 min. Canberra: Australian Institute of Aboriginal Studies.

————, directors. 1969c. *Groote Eylandt Field Project: Five Brolga Dances, (8.4).* 16mm, 15 min. Canberra: Australian Institute of Aboriginal Studies.

Noisy Boys. 1986. *1986 Tanna Inta Distrik Gems.* Vila: Vanuata [sic] Productions.

O'Brien, Frederick. 1919. *White Shadows in the South Seas.* Garden City, New York: Garden City Publishing.

————. 1921. *Mystic Isles of the South Seas.* Garden City, New York: Garden City Publishing.

O'Rourke, D. 1987. *Cannibal Tours.* 16mm, 77 min. Direct Cinema, Los Angeles.

Owen, Chris. 1977. *The Red Bowmen.* 16mm, 58 min. Institute of Papua New Guinea Studies.

————. 1979. *Gogodala: A Cultural Revival?* 16mm, 58 min. Institute of Papua New Guinea Studies.

————. 1983. *Tighten the Drums: Self-Decoration Among the Enga.* 16mm, 58 min. Institute of Papua New Guinea Studies.

————. 1989. *Malangan Labadama: A Tribute to Buk-Buk.* 16mm, 58 min. Institute of Papua New Guinea Studies.

Parkinson, Sydney. 1784. *A Journal of a Voyage to the South Seas, in his Majesty's Ship, the Endeavour.* London: Charles Dilly and James Phillips.

Parsons, Robert Percival. 1945. *MOB 3: A Naval Hospital in a South Sea Jungle.* Indianapolis, New York: Bobbs-Merrill.

Polynesian Cultural Association. 1992. *Tahiti Fête of San Jose: A Polynesian Dance Extravaganza.* 16mm in 4 parts, about 135 min. each. Playback Memories, San Jose, California.

Putilov, Boris N. 1974. "Pesenno-muzykal'nie kollektsii MAE s ostrovov Okeanii" (Song and musical MAE collections from Oceanic Islands). *Sbornik MAE: Kultura narodov Avstralii i Okeanii* (MAE collected articles: the culture of Australia and Oceania) 30:27–35.

————. 1975. "Pesenno-muzykal'ni folklor bonguantsev" (Song-musical folklore of Bongu villagers). In *Na Beregu Maklaya: Etnograficheskie ocherki* (On the Maclay Coast: ethnographical essays), ed. A. S. Tokarev, 227–252. Moscow: Nauka.

————. 1978. *Rhythms and Music of Oceanic Islands, Following N. N. Miklouho-Maclay.* Leningrad: Melodiya M80-39597–39602. 3 LP disks.

————. 1979. "Contemporary Music of the Maclay Coast." In *The Performing Arts: Music and Dance,* ed. John Blacking and Joanne Wheeler Kealiinohomoku, 159–165. The Hague: Mouton.

————. 1987. "Musical Instruments." In *Matka Oseaniaan: Journey to Oceania,* 62–64. Helsinki: Museum of Applied Arts.

Sandall, Roger. 1975. *Mourning for Mangatopi.* 16mm, 56 min. Canberra: Australian Institute of Aboriginal Studies.

————, director. 1977. *A Walbiri Fire Ceremony: Ngatjakula.* 16mm, 21 min. Canberra: Australian Institute of Aboriginal Studies.

Schweizer, Niklaus R. 1982. *Hawai'i and the German Speaking Peoples.* Honolulu: Topgallant.

Schwob, Marcel. 1930. *Derniers écrits: Lettres à sa famille: Voyage à Samoa.* Edited by Pierre Champion. Complete works, 10. Paris.

Ségalen, Victor. 1966. *Les Immémoriaux.* Paris: Union Générale d'Éditions.

Smith, Bernard. 1956. "Coleridge's *Ancient Mariner* and Cook's Second Voyage." *Journal of the Warburg and Courtauld Institutes* 19(1–2): 117–154.

————. 1992. *Imagining the Pacific: In the Wake of the Cook Voyages.* New Haven: Yale University Press.

Somare, Michael. 1975. *Sana.* Port Moresby, Papua New Guinea: Niugini Press.

Stevenson, Robert Louis. 1892. *A Footnote to History: Eight Years of Trouble in Samoa.* London: Cassell.

————. 1893. *Island Nights' Entertainments.* London: Cassell.

————. 1895. *Vailima Letters,* ed. Sidney Colvin. London: Methuen.

————. 1971 [1900]. *In the South Seas.* Honolulu: University of Hawai'i Press.

Stoddard, Charles Warren. 1873. *South-Sea Idyls.* Boston: James R. Osgood.

Swift, Jonathan. 1726. *Travels into Several Remote Nations of the World.* London: B. Motte.

Tatar, Elizabeth, ed. 1985. *Call of the Morning Bird: Chants and Songs of Palau, Yap, and Ponape, Collected by Iwakichi Muranushi, 1936.* Honolulu: Bishop Museum, ARCS 2. Cassette.

Tennyson, Alfred. 1898. *The Works of Alfred Lord Tennyson.* New York: Macmillan.

Theroux, Paul. 1992. *The Happy Isles of Oceania: Paddling the Pacific.* New York: G. P. Putnam's Sons.

Thomas, Allan. 1981. "The Study of Acculturated Music in Oceania: 'Cheap and Tawdry Borrowed Tunes'?" *Journal of the Polynesian Society* 90: 183–191.

Vancouver, George. 1798. *Voyage of Discovery to the North Pacific Ocean and Round the World.* London: G. G. and J. Robinson.

Volkman, Toby Alice. 1986. *Expressive Culture in Papua New Guinea: A Guide to Three Films.* Boroko, Papua New Guinea: Institute of Papua New Guinea Studies.

White, Geoffrey M., and Lamont Lindstrom, eds. 1989. *The Pacific Theater: Island Representations of World War II.* Pacific Islands Monographs, 8. Honolulu: University of Hawai'i Press.

Wild, Stephen A. 1986a. "Australian Aboriginal Theatrical Movement." In *Theatrical Movement: A Bibliographical Anthology,* ed. B. Fleshman, 601–624. Metuchen, New Jersey, and London: Scarecrow Press.

————, ed. 1986b. *Rom: An Aboriginal Ritual of Diplomacy.* Canberra: Australian Institute of Aboriginal Studies.

Wilkes, Charles. 1845. *Narrative of the United States Exploring Expedition During the Years 1838, 1839, 1840, 1841, 1842.* 5 vols. Philadelphia: Lea and Blanchard.

Zachariä, Friedrich Wilhelm. 1778. *Poetische Schriften.* Amsterdam.

Zamecnik, J. S. 1923. "Tropic Isle." In *Sam Fox Moving Picture Music for the Piano,* 4:12. Cleveland: Sam Fox.

Zemp, Hugo. 1993. *'Are'are Music* and *Shaping Bamboo.* Audiovisual Series, 1. Society for Ethnomusicology. Video.

# Encounters among "Ourselves"

*Adrienne L. Kaeppler*
*Karen Stevenson*
*Stephen A. Wild*
*Don Niles*
*Vida Chenoweth*

**Festivals and Identity**
**Pacific Festivals of Arts**
**Australian Festivals**
**Papua New Guinean Festivals**
**Tannese Festivals**
**Heiva, a Festival of French Polynesia**
**Hawaiian Festivals**

The visits of Pacific Islanders from one island to another have always been important occasions. Though their purposes varied from island to island, they were often celebrated with performances of music and dance and presentations of gifts to hosts and guests. Whether given as necessities (as to the overlords of the "Tongan Empire" to keep peace, or to inhabitants of the high islands of the "Yap Empire" to ensure help to outlying atolls after devastating storms), as an adjunct to trading expeditions (as the *kula* ring of southeast New Guinea), or simply to visit (as the *malaga* of Sāmoan villagers), exchanges of music, dance, and objects were important cultural events. Clothing and performance spaces were important for the presentation of music, dance, and oratory. These visits were occasions for islanders to learn from each other. From these encounters, music, dance, costumes, and other artistic motifs were disseminated among cultures.

Today, musical encounters in Oceania still occur regularly—within traditional rituals, on days of importance for national or cultural identity, for regional festivals, or in the Festival of Pacific Arts, held every four years (figure 1). In the explosive world of the 1990s, where cultural identity has become ever more important, these encounters offer Oceanic answers to regionalism, unity within diversity, and national identity within multicultural nations (Kaeppler 1988).

Intended to promote cultural identity and regionalism, festivals in Oceania are aimed primarily at insiders, rather than outsiders. They bring visitors, as participants or audiences, to where they do not reside, and their organizers expect that the visitors will use local facilities (hotels, restaurants, shops), bringing financial benefit. The hope may be an influx of foreign currency, a temporary stimulation of local entrepreneurship, or the use of the national airline. Whatever the sponsors' expectation, festivals seem destined to be tourist attractions, and they have become part of the fabric of social life in Oceania.

Indigenous people themselves bring outside perspectives to their neighbors' music and dance. Though they sometimes bring understanding, they may also reinforce stereotypes and leave with false understandings or misconceptions. They come with various ideas about their neighbors, which they explore through festival performances and interpersonal relationships. They leave with new ideas, which, on their

Oceania is on its way to becoming one of the most important meeting places of the world. The lessons learned at festivals will influence the future of Pacific identity, politics, and tourism.

FIGURE 1   Final performances of the Sāmoan hosts at the seventh Pacific Festival of Arts. For individuals and groups throughout Oceania, these festivals are the premier venues for the performing, visual, and literary arts. Here, old and new coincide to honor the past while looking toward the future: *a*, in front of a skyscraper in downtown Apia, women perform a joyful farewell; *b*, audience and dancers behold each other in a colorful spectacle of Oceanic identity. Photos by Adrienne L. Kaeppler, 1996.

(*a*)

(*b*)

next meeting or the next festival, may have become reinforced, changed, or stereotyped. As with all productive touristic encounters, residents and visitors engage in a cultural dialogue that can challenge ideas about themselves and about Oceanic societies in the larger world.

The goal of attracting tourists has influenced some islanders to present their dances as entertainment in Polynesian floor shows. Even international venues, like the Brisbane Expo of 1988, included touristic Polynesian dance as an important part of the presentations. More audience-oriented, hence more familiar and accessible to outsiders, Polynesian dancing occurs during touristic entertainment in non-Polynesian Oceanic sites, where hotel entertainment often features less-than-high-quality examples. Even a Tongan-American rock band, The Jets, plays Polynesian numbers.

The festivals examined here are only a few of many similar events that occur each year in Oceania. Some, better known but hard to get to, are the Mt. Hagen Festival, held in the Highlands of New Guinea every second year, at an irregular date. Some festivals marking independence, as on outer islands of Vanuatu, are not only hard to get to, but difficult to learn about. Others, such as independence celebrations in Sāmoa, occur each year at a specific time and are easy to attend, though public accommodations may be in short supply.

Attendance at festivals is not only rewarding for the spectator as an aesthetic experience, but a chance to see cultural identity in action. For participants, the experience is more profound, for it is here that friendships are formed and understandings among neighbors and nations are forged. The preservation of diverse identities within a multicultural world promoted by festivals and enjoyed by tourists is especially relevant. According to all economic predictions, Oceania is on its way to becoming one of the most important meeting places of the world, and the lessons learned at festivals will influence the future of Pacific identity, politics, and tourism.

—ADRIENNE L. KAEPPLER

## FESTIVALS AND IDENTITY

Firmly rooted in the past, festival activity in Oceania has become a vehicle for ensuring and promoting Oceanic identities. Since the 1960s, when colonial governments began giving way to new nations, the importance of forging cultural identities has grown. Drawing upon indigenous traditions, political and artistic leaders have created national and local symbols of identity, to serve as rallying points for presentations by diverse performers.

Locally, nationally, and internationally, festivals promote cultural values of competition and cooperation, fostering and demonstrating subtleties of cultural variation, within fledgling nations and throughout Oceania. Contemporary festivals serve many of the functions as those of the past. They create venues for performing and competing in dance and athletics, occur in specially built arenas, honor guests and dignitaries, and bestow status and prestige upon winners. Stressing community values, historical continuities, and social identities, they serve symbolic roles. But they also serve political ends.

The creation of cultural policy tempts politicians and bureaucrats to decide which cultural values, events, and arts to spotlight, but implementing these policies can be difficult, especially in countries containing multiple cultures. One answer is the creation of composite symbols of identity. French Polynesians created a flag showing five stylized tiki, suggesting the separate, yet similar, cultural entities within the country. More problematic is Papua New Guinea: having to deal with more than seven hundred languages representing hundreds of cultures, the government had to look beyond local traits, so it created a flag incorporating a bird of paradise and the Southern Cross, a constellation seen as a Christian symbol. At festivals, such symbols accompany performers as visual representations of their national identities.

National festivals tend to promote cultural variation. Within Papua New Guinea are several national festivals, nineteen provincial ones, and many local ones. Within French Polynesia, in addition to the Heiva (see below), festivals in the Marquesas and the Austral Islands present unique local identities. The tourism-oriented Aloha Week

FIGURE 2 In Honolulu, the Aloha Week Court performs at the Kodak Hula Show. Photo by Adrienne L. Kaeppler, 1990.

in Hawai'i, while showcasing indigenous Hawaiian traditions (figure 2), celebrates the spectrum of cultures represented in Hawai'i.

### Identity and politics

National symbols help create national identities, the promotion of culture can attract tourist dollars, and focusing on cultural activity enhances knowledge of the past while offering a foundation for the future. These attempts at cultural affirmation counter colonial practice and missionary dogma, which often resulted in negative self-images. Pacific peoples now take pride in what remains (or what they have recreated) of their cultural heritage, which they sustain, advertise, and market in festivals.

Politics can also be seen in producers' and politicians' mixed messages and hidden agendas. A seemingly contradictory message is that of cultural growth and tourism. Some outsiders decry festivals as unauthentic because they attract tourists. Most Pacific governments do not deny their interest in tourists' dollars, but many festivals do not cater to tourists' whims. The promoted events, though superficially attractive to tourists, are for Oceanic peoples themselves. In Hawai'i, the Merrie Monarch Festival is primarily for the participants and their families and friends. In the Highlands of Papua New Guinea, tourists encounter festival singsings almost by chance.

Festivals embody a political present by defining and celebrating a cultural past. As traditions become objectified, commoditized, and institutionalized, they reflect political and economic realities. In 1996, as delegations prepared for the Pacific Festival of Arts, French Polynesian officials played down their financial role, waiting for the nuclear-testing uproar to subside. Their status as a colonial entity was awkward, but as in the past, they met European aggression with strong artistic statements of self-definition.

### The Tahitian Heiva

In Tahiti, culture is politically charged. Politicians and governmental officials decide which cultural values, events, and arts to spotlight. Though festivals have remained valuable assertions of Tahitian culture, their position within the social order has changed. At first contact with European explorers, they reinforced chiefs' prerogatives, status, and power; by the mid-1800s, they implemented the goals of a new French colonial government; today, they offer insight into how history is used to promote a sense of identity.

Dancing, singing, and racing canoes have been staples of the Heiva from its inception. In the mid-1950s, Marco Tevane, Minister of Culture, thought Tahitians needed education in their mythology, history, and culture, so he added cultural reenactments to the spectacle. Implementation of this ideal met politically tinged responses. The Roman Catholic Church protested that reenactments of pagan activities on indigenous religious enclosures (*marae*) were attempts to revive inappropriate forms of worship. Tahitians sympathetic to indigenous cosmologies protested that the reenactments were being exploited for tourists. Activists for independence saw the reenactments as pro-Tahitian and therefore anti-French—and immediately associated themselves with them. By the 1990s, these actions had come into line with widespread indigenous political and cultural ideologies. The Heiva promotes a cultural and political identity in distinction to a colonial presence (Stevenson 1992). Its reenactments are one event within the spectacle. The complete phenomenon—the competition, the atmosphere, the community—is what creates an indigenous (*māʻohi*) identity and generates feelings of cultural pride. Racing canoes and dancing are year-round activities, but in the spring, as participants train for the upcoming Heiva, such activities intensify. Competition was a fundamental element of precontact Tahitian life, and it is one reason the ancient activities and games translate easily to competitive athletics and dancing. For festival participants, competition remains a factor in achieving and preserving status. Monetary prizes and travel opportunities are also incentives.

### Festivals in the Marquesas and Austral Islands

By about 1950, the leeward islands of French Polynesia had organized small-scale versions of the Heiva, enabling people to witness competitions from within their own islands without traveling to Tahiti. The Marquesas Arts Festival, first produced in 1987 and intended to be restaged every other year, featured dancing and exhibitions of artistic and cultural activities. Its impetus came from Motu Haka, an association of carvers, dancers, makers of tapa, and tattooists. Charged with demonstrating the uniqueness of Marquesan culture, the festival distinguishes Marquesans from their French Polynesian neighbors, illustrating the banality of imposed political boundaries.

The Austral Islands Festival of Art, first produced in 1989 and intended to be restaged every other year, offers a contrast: it demonstrates the implementation of policy, rather than the assertion of identity. The idea for it came from artisans in the Austral Islands, but its events were organized by governmental agencies in Papeʻete—Office Territoriale d'Action Culturelle, Office de Promotion et d'Animation Touristiques de Tahiti et ses Îles, and the Ministry of Development in the Archipelagoes. Official events included dancing, sports (canoeing, fishing, carrying stones), material arts (plaiting, carving, making tapa), historical reenactments, walking on fire, and an agricultural fair. Unlike the Marquesan Arts Festival, it allowed Tahitians to participate.

—KAREN STEVENSON

## PACIFIC FESTIVALS OF ARTS

Since 1972, Pacific Islanders have had an international venue for their performances: the Pacific Festivals of Arts, planned to be held every four years in a different nation. Seven festivals have been held: Suva, Fiji, 1972; Rotorua, Aotearoa, 1976; Papua New Guinea, 1980; Tahiti, French Polynesia, 1985 (rescheduled from 1984); Townsville, Australia, 1988; Rarotonga, Cook Islands, 1992; and Apia, Western Sāmoa, 1996. Though these events have become increasingly political, they emphasize preservation and development in the performing arts. Troupes borrow from each other—and festival borrowings have appeared at later festivals.

"Too many academics today claim to know much about our cultures, yet do not even try to scrape the surface of our knowledge. It is now our responsibility to educate the outsider."

The third festival was billed as the Celebration of Pacific Awareness. The Honourable Stephen Ogaji Tago, M.P., Minister for Culture, Science, and Tourism, noted it would

> once again emphasise our cultural diversities and similarities. Our young genera-
> tion must be both directed and allowed the opportunity to know of their roots
> and practice their traditional culture. They should also learn to appreciate their
> neighbors' cultural practices as well as their own. . . . Too many academics today
> claim to know much about our cultures, yet do not even try to scrape the surface
> of our knowledge and the wisdom of our way of life. It is now our responsibility
> to educate the outsider and show him our true cultural ways. The South Pacific
> Festival of Arts is one way of doing this. (*Souvenir Programme* 1980:4–5)

Despite this objective, few outsiders attended, and they had not been encouraged to. Many participants were in some ways outsiders themselves. Their performances could not really be understood as "true cultural ways," partly because most were performed in local languages. Indigenous people of Oceania usually communicate across cultural boundaries in English or Melanesian pidgins (or French in French Polynesia and Wallis-Futuna), but at this festival, performers seldom tried to introduce or explain a performance so it could be understood as culture. Audiences did not understand if a performed item was old or new, what part it played in traditional culture, or how onlookers were supposed to react. The troupes that received the most acclaim (from large, mostly local audiences) were from Tahiti, the Cook Islands, and Hawai'i. The meaning or use or function of their dances was not communicated, but the use of the hips and legs in ways theretofore unseen—and even taboo for New Guinea performers—was a source of fascination. Troupes more experienced in performing for audiences could alter their performances on the spot, to capitalize on audience reaction. Mutual understanding of each other's cultures through each other's arts was not really accomplished; but getting to know one another on a personal basis and establishing new friendships were.

The fourth festival occurred in Tahiti, replacing the festival scheduled for 1984 in New Caledonia (aborted because of political unrest). Ensembles from twenty-two islands and nations took part in venues ranging from Vai'ete Square in downtown Pape'ete to stadiums on Tahiti and other islands of the Society Islands. In contrast to the previous festivals, more delegations made their presentations in a narrative theatrical manner. Indigenous performances would usually consist of a succession of dances not linked by a plot. This new, more narrative emphasis tended to transform the productions into more Western notions of theater. The dilemma of the artistic director of each cultural troupe can be appreciated: should the presentation take a more indigenous form, or should it be designed to appeal to understanding across cultural boundaries? A satisfactory solution has not been found—and exemplifies a problem that limits cross-cultural understanding.

FIGURE 3    A performance by dancers from
Papua New Guinea. Pacific Festival of Arts,
Townsville, Australia. Photo by Adrienne L.
Kaeppler, 1988.

The fifth festival, according to the festival publication, had two objectives: "to
maximize cultural exchange between the Australian and Pacific participants and to
increase the general public's awareness and understanding of these indigenous cultures." Though such an understanding may not have been fully achieved, the festival
was a feast for the eye, and observers could appreciate the programs as performance
(figure 3). Understanding must be accompanied by explanation of how socially constructed systems of music and movement are embedded in cultural forms. Cultural
borrowings appeared as a trend toward tahitianization and hawaiianization. Hawaiian
movements appeared in Tahitian dances; Hawaiians did a Tahitian-Hawaiian dance
in honor of *Hōkūleʻa*, the traditionally built ship that had voyaged between Hawaiʻi
and Tahiti. Wallis-Futuna tahitianized some of their drumming and singing,
Rotumans performed one Fijian-sounding song with thrusting hips that seemed to
caricature Tahitian movements, the Northern Marianas closed their program with a
hulalike item, and even Pari Village, from Central Province, Papua New Guinea, performed a hawaiianesque dance.

The sixth festival emphasized cultural identity through a focus on oceangoing
voyages. A large, new theater encouraged troupes to produce even more theatrical
and dramatic pieces, in addition to fashion shows and other more Western-oriented
productions. Nevertheless, these were presented alongside many performances similar
to those presented at earlier festivals. At the seventh festival, in addition to the usual
performances of music and dance, the focus was on tattooing and the literary arts.
Cultures not previously presented, including the Polynesian outlier Tikopia (see photo facing page 1), made memorable appearances.

—ADRIENNE L. KAEPPLER

## AUSTRALIAN FESTIVALS

The late twentieth century has seen a burgeoning of festivals in Australia, featuring
folk-derived arts, chamber music, country music, early music, choirs, jazz, theater,
and in 1995 the first National Australian Gamelan Festival. Also in 1995, associated
with the World Conference of the International Council for Traditional Music in
Canberra, was the Festival of Traditional Music—a title that can cover almost anything!

Australian festivals fall into three classes: those organized by nonindigenous people with nonindigenous performers; those organized by indigenous people with
mostly indigenous performers, but aimed at a nonindigenous audience; and those
largely indigenous in their organization, performers, and audience.

## Nonindigenously organized festivals

The major urban festivals in Australia—the Sydney Festival, the Melbourne Festival, the Adelaide Festival, the Perth Festival—are intended to appeal to a wide but fairly sophisticated audience. They regularly include indigenous elements from troupes such as Aboriginal and Islander Dance Theatre and Bangarra Dance Company (both based in Sydney), or dramatic productions from indigenous theatrical troupes or indigenous popular musicians or bands (Neuenfeldt 1995).

At the other end of sophistication are festivals of folk-derived and country music, also organized mainly by nonindigenous people and aimed at particular nonindigenous segments of the population. Aboriginal people have played a major role in the Australian pastoral industry, and country is this industry's preferred musical genre. Aboriginal musicians have always been prominent in the country scene and at country festivals. In the 1980s and 1990s, folk-derived festivals in Australia developed beyond their Anglo-Irish origins and became multicultural events. Their organizers try to include indigenous musicians and dancers. They emphasize ballads, protest songs, vocal ensembles, and what might be termed reconstructed traditional dances—traditional dances packaged for presentation to nonindigenous audiences.

The organizers of major urban festivals and festivals of country and folk-derived music highly value including indigenous performers. Indigenous arts, widely admired in Australia, constitute an important element in the national artistic identity. This is one reason for their inclusion in major festivals. But what is the motivation for indigenous performers? Irrespective of where on a continuum between traditional and contemporary an indigenous performance stands, a festival provides an opportunity to convey a message by presenting a point of view and to remind other Australians of an indigenous presence in their midst.

## Indigenously organized festivals

Some festivals organized by indigenous people have mostly indigenous performers but are aimed at indigenous and nonindigenous audiences. An example of this is the Kyana Corroboree, in Perth, Western Australia. This corroboree lasts several days in a major public outdoor area near downtown Perth. It includes outdoor performances of music and dance, and provides stalls selling indigenous arts, crafts, and "bush food." In 1993, it attracted an estimated audience of fifty thousand people. The focus is on Aboriginal culture of southwestern Australia, an area of intensive nonindigenous settlement and cultivation for more than one hundred fifty years.

Another example of an indigenously organized festival aimed at indigenous and nonindigenous audiences is the Kimberley Arts and Culture Festival, in Broome, a small coastal town in northwestern Australia, with a multicultural population, including a large proportion of indigenous people. It has been a fertile ground for contemporary indigenous music, and it is where the first Aboriginal musical (*Bran Nue Day*) was created.

In 1992, the Australian Broadcasting Corporation broadcast the entire main concert of this festival, which lasted from dusk till dawn, marketed under the title *Stompem Ground*. The music, almost entirely contemporary, featured local and nationally prominent bands and individual musicians. Interspersed between performed items were interviews with prominent musicians and footage depicting local traditions and important sites. Performers included Mixed Relations, a nationally prominent Aboriginal band from Sydney, playing urban rock; Johnny Albert Band, a local ensemble, and Warumpi Band, a nationally prominent ensemble from central Australia, playing a mixture of styles, including country and rock, and sometimes "singing in language" (with Aboriginal lyrics) and playing clapsticks; and Yothu Yindi, playing a mixture of rock and indigenous music of Arnhem Land, with accompaniment from clapsticks and a didjeridu and traditional decoration of performers' bodies.

The musical styles at these festivals are predominantly contemporary and popular, competing successfully with nonindigenous popular music. The music often includes indigenous stylistic elements and instruments. Singing is often in indigenous languages, with lyrics that have a strongly indigenous perspective, sometimes critical of other perspectives. During Stompem Ground 1992, the performers frequently exhorted indigenous attendees to be proud of their shared identity.

### Festivals for indigenous audiences

In the *Daily Advertiser* of the provincial city of Wagga Wagga on 24 August 1993 appeared an article headed "Aboriginal festival scheduled for city":

> Aborigines from throughout the Murrumbidgee [River] and Lachlan [River] regions are expected in the city for the three-day festival as part of International Year of Indigenous People celebrations. . . . Activities will include sporting events such as touch football, softball and netball, a talent quest featuring Aboriginal artists, Aboriginal dances and cultural events, and various displays.

Later, the text made clear that the main purpose of the article was to alert people that the park where the festival was to be held would be unavailable for other uses during the period reserved for the festival.

This kind of festival has a history, at least since the 1960s. Since then, Aboriginal people from a wide area of central Australia in the Northern Territory have congregated annually at the Aboriginal township of Yuendumu, about 200 kilometers northwest of Alice Springs. The event is called the Yuendumu Sports Weekend, though it involves more than sport. Activities include the competitive throwing of spears, a competition in the performance of popular music, and traditional singing and dancing. Aside from nonindigenous local staff, the organizers, the participants, and the audience are overwhelmingly indigenous.

Another example occurred on 29 and 30 May 1992 on Thursday Island, the administrative center of the Torres Strait Islands. (Fourteen of the islands are inhabited by Torres Strait Islanders, people who have tried to establish a separate identity in the national consciousness.) The Torres Strait Islander Festival is an annual event, when indigenous people from each of the inhabited islands gather for two days of interaction. Troupes from each island present singing and dancing, and set up stalls selling food, arts, and crafts. In a parade, troupes display themselves in their costumes. Each day, they perform their own songs and dances, one after another, announced over a public-address system. The festival of 1992 attracted nonindigenous onlookers, many of whom videotaped the dances, but Thursday Island is so remote and expensive to reach that the probability of attracting crowds is low. One presentation at the Torres Strait Festival of 1992, a story-dance by Boigu Islanders, was a lengthy tale, narrated over the public-address system while performers acted and danced the plot, accompanied by seated singers and drummers. Another presentation, a dance by Saibai Islanders, included an effigy of the sun, represented by decorated hoops carried by dancers, again accompanied by seated singers and drummers.

### Regionalism and politics

The festivals described above have in common a limited geographical scope—suggesting that their underlying purpose is the forging of a local identity. This is clear in the case of the Torres Strait Festival, through which indigenous people are trying to persuade the national government to grant them local autonomy. The heyday of the

Shows popularize certain types of dancing. Celebrated performers—Asaro mudmen wearing masks and moving silently, masked Angan performers with heads covered by cloth, Mekeo dancers wearing huge headdresses—have become staples.

Yuendumu Sports Weekend was the period leading up to passage of the Aboriginal Land Rights (Northern Territory) Act of 1976, which established procedures for claiming land in the Northern Territory on the basis of Aboriginal ownership. This festival contributed to building a sense of solidarity in central Australia. In the legislation, central Australia was to be represented by a Central Land Council, which has since mounted successful Aboriginal land claims.

Were festivals a part of indigenous culture? Large-scale ceremonial gatherings were held for religious and social reasons, but they brought together people of different clans, rather than different tribes or linguistic communities. The resources to sustain larger gatherings than this were probably unavailable, even if people had considered such gatherings desirable. It was not necessary to assert an indigenous presence when all inhabitants were indigenous and Aboriginal Australians had no apparent reason to imagine and create solidarity across linguistic boundaries. Festivals are an artifact of *multicultural* Australia, and indigenous participation in them seems to be motivated by a need to assert an indigenous identity and presence.

—STEPHEN A. WILD

## PAPUA NEW GUINEAN FESTIVALS

Shows or festivals in Papua New Guinea, in some areas known as singsings, provide occasions for the performance of music and dance outside of village environments, in competition with troupes from other parts of the country. Apparently the first such show was organized in 1952 at Kokopo, East New Britain Province. The next year, the first Port Moresby Show occurred, followed by the Goroka Show (1957), the Morobe Show (1959, in Lae), the Sepik Show (1960, in Wewak), and the Tolai Warwagira (1971). Today, most provincial centers have such shows every year or two.

All the early shows featured agricultural and industrial displays by appropriately named societies, as do many current shows. Some early shows were organized to enable enemies to gather peacefully, easing and hastening governmental operations. Visitors pay to enter and see the latest local work from governmental organizations and commercial companies. Stalls sell food, children's toys and hats, stenciled T-shirts, and so on. For many visitors, one of the main attractions is the competition in dancing.

At some shows, dancers are segregated from spectators; at others, visitors walk freely among performers during performances. Performers are often identified by a sign with a number (for the judges) and the name of the troupe or their village. Judges evaluate the "traditionality" of the performers' presentations: decorations, dances, and perseverance. Cash prizes are awarded to winners. Because troupes frequently come from disparate areas of the country and display unrelated traditions, judging one troupe's performance in comparison with another is difficult—and often the cause for complaints. To avoid such problems, since the mid-1980s, prizes have sometimes been divided among all the participants.

Such shows are excellent opportunities to see dances that would otherwise be performed in isolated locations, but the context is entirely different, and performances are sometimes modified to make them more appealing to spectators and judges. The importance of decorations in the judging means that sometimes this aspect is much more "traditional" than it would normally be back home.

Shows have done much to popularize certain types of dancing: celebrated performers—Asaro mudmen, wearing masks and moving silently; masked Angan performers, their heads covered with cloth; Mekeo dancers, wearing huge headdresses—have become staples. In addition to dancing, most shows schedule competitions for bands, providing opportunities for spectators to see live performances of bands they may know only from radio, cassettes, or television.

—DON NILES

## TANNESE FESTIVALS

In Tanna, southern Vanuatu, festivals are widespread, but they often draw no more than a few hundred people from an area of no more than 100 square kilometers. They mark long-standing systems of reciprocal exchange, without outsiders' participation. Festivals follow similar formats in different villages, though the names of their songs and dances vary by place and language.

### Feasts

The most elaborate and famous festivals of north-central Tanna are feasts (*nengaoiat*), often known as *toka,* an abbreviation of Enpitoka, on the eastern ridge of the volcano Yasur, where the dance called *toka* supposedly originated. To organize a feast, one village invites others: invitations go to four distinct *nakamal,* local sites of authority and governance, idealized as being under a banyan tree, a long-standing site of celebrations (Turner 1884:315–316). Three invitations go to men; one goes to women. The host village sets a date far enough in advance that the guests have ample time to rehearse. During the festival, dances are performed in a set order.

### *The first night*

Starting at nightfall, women begin singing and dancing, through two series of items. The first series, *naneluan,* begins with six songs, after which three songs are performed with actions. The actions of song seven mimic the making of the waistband from which strings or leaves are suspended to form a skirt: the actions portray soaking bark in water, washing the sap away and rolling the string on one's thigh. Song eight enacts digging a garden and piling the soil in a mound for planting yams; a stick of wild cane represents a spade. In song nine, the troupe divides into two columns, between which dance two women, one of whom symbolizes a fish being caught and landed by the other.

The second series, *napinapin,* is performed by women on the night the festival begins, and by men the next morning. It has three parts: singing two introductory songs, performed without a pause between them; singing the *napinapin*; and clapping the *napinapin,* so called in reference to the small rectangular pouch (*katum raha napinapin* 'basket for the *napinapin*') that each woman carries. This pouch, made of woven pandanus strips and stuffed with *nuo* leaves and ferns, is held in one hand and struck rhythmically with the other. For clapping the *napinapin,* the women separate into two groups.

### The second day

Men's songs and dances begin the second day with a *toka*. Men enter the arena carrying 1.5-meter-long, hooked sticks (*kenamin*), which they manipulate while dancing and singing. For each festival, the song for the *toka* is newly composed; as it is sung, two men break away to enact its words. Also essential is a hawk-feather-covered black-palm pole (*kweria* 'hawk'), borne on one person's shoulders and braced with guys steadied by four men following alongside. Chief Noanime relayed the story of the feathers (translated by Jill Gilbert, a Tannese woman):

> A man being chased by his enemies fell halfway down a cliff. He survived because a hawk supplied him with wood and a live coal, and then gave him a yam to cook. The hawk said if he clapped his hands, the hawk would come and lift him out by his hair. He did so, was rescued, and returned to his family, whom he asked for a pig and kava to give to the one who had helped him. The hawk said he would take only the intestines, and to put them, with the kava leaves, atop a tree. Today, if one finds a hawk's nest, a leaf of kava will be on either side of the chicks in the nest, placed there by the mother. When the chicks are ready to fly, the leaves— one long, one short—are switched in the nest.

Chief Noanime claims he has seen three such nests.

After the *toka,* men in two facing lines dance the *nau.* Each man carries a bundle of wild cane (*nau*), which he stamps on the ground or shakes as a rattle. Male and sometimes female dancers wear ankle-tied rattles (*noanipiripa*), made of the fruit of the *nipiripa* vine. The third dance, *kasasio,* is named for wooden implements, shaped like a wide-bladed scythe. Each man carries one, with his own design painted on it. The men face one another so each has a choreographic partner. The fourth dance (*nasil*) uses sticks. Every man carries in each hand a short club, with which he strikes the clubs of dancers behind, beside, and in front of him. The number of columns is variable, but each column is five men deep.

After the fourth dance, people of each *nakamal* bring in pigs and whole kava plants. Each dancer provides one live pig or more. These are tied up and placed on a platform, which six to eight men lift up and carry around. They tip it forward, and a man clubs the pig to death. The dead pigs are then lined up. Holding a kava plant, two dancers then step back and forth over them. People are then free to collect their pigs and kava, for later feasting at home.

## Boys' circumcision festivals and other celebrations

At Lamakaun Village, in the north-central area of Tanna (inland from Enpek Lapen), a typical boys' circumcision festival (*kaut*) occurred in 1995. (This village consisted of about 114 people, speakers of Nin-naka, an Austronesian language.) Tended by men, the boys stayed in a secluded house, built for the occasion. For meals, a woman would bring food to the gate, where she would strike a bamboo idiophone; a man would then take the food to the boys. Lest the boys be seen, initiated men sounded conchs (*tawi,* of genus *Triton*) while they led the boys to the river for bathing. Walking in single file, the trumpeters repeated a hocket pattern over and over (figure 4*a*). As the performance continued, a rhythmic variation occurred (figure 4*b*). To signal an end, player 1 omitted his second F♯, and player 3 omitted his note; all three conchs then sounded a chord (figure 4*c*). Women and girls were not allowed to see the boys until the initiation was over—a period of one to two months, depending on the time needed to organize the celebratory festival. Preparations involved making percussive pouches, bark-string skirts, and pandanus mats; gathering firewood; and building houses for guests on the *nakamal.* For the festival, the boys painted their faces and wore colorful cloth wraparounds.

FIGURE 4 Tannese conch-shell hocketing: *a*, the basic pattern, with the players designated by number; *b*, a variation as the performance continues; *c*, the final chord. Transcription by Vida Chenoweth.

At Lamakaun, the *mauyin,* once danced by men at yam-planting celebrations, can be performed at any festival, as can the men's *nalea,* once danced to celebrate the harvest of yams. For the mixed dance *rarikin* (also *larikin,* possibly from French *l'ouragan* 'the hurricane'), imported in the mid-twentieth century and often ending a festival, men perform in the center and women on the periphery; everyone shakes wildly and hilariously.

—VIDA CHENOWETH

## HEIVA, A FESTIVAL OF FRENCH POLYNESIA

Pacific Festivals of Art noncompetitively promote regionalism, national identity, and international cooperation, in contrast to the high-spirited competitive atmosphere of *heiva,* a Tahitian word for celebrations. The festival called Heiva promotes Polynesian identity as distinct from the European culture that impinges on French Polynesians' lives.

The distant roots of this celebration lie in Polynesian harvest festivals. These were transformed into the birthday celebration of the French Emperor Napoleon I, annually on 15 August; since 1881, the celebration of the storming of the Bastille (14 July 1789) was held annually in Tahiti (figure 5). But unlike France (which celebrates the Fête on 14 July), French Polynesia celebrates the Fête for weeks, hence its Tahitian name, Tiurai, the Tahitian word for July. Since 1985, the celebration, renamed Heiva, has begun at the end of June.

An important part of Heiva begins each evening at 9:00, a *spectacle folklorique.* A competition of music and dance, it draws participants from throughout French Polynesia, plus the Cook Islands, and occasionally Easter Island and even Hawai'i. Performers sing in vernacular languages, but these languages (and cultures) are closely related, and the intent of a performance is immediately understood. Widespread cultural borrowing of myths, legends, and movements is a feature of the celebration.

FIGURE 5 During the Bastille Day Fête in the late 1880s, a Tahitian group performs to the accompaniment of snare drums. Photo by Charles Spitz. Album of Rear Admiral Lewis Ashfield Kimberly, U.S. Navy. Bishop Museum Archives.

Festivals have roots in Hawaiian culture. The *makahiki* was a festival of harvesting and offering of tribute. Competitive games and sports were played under the eye of Lono, god of peace and agriculture.

Prizes are given, and participants perform with competitive spirit, emphasizing a Polynesian identity distinct from that of outsiders.

## HAWAIIAN FESTIVALS

Festivals are a major focus of Hawaiian identity, and the prospect of competing and performing in one or more of them is the glue that holds many *hula* schools together. Performances at these festivals do not necessarily reproduce old choreographies, but take old poetic, musical, and movement motifs and render them in a contemporary form. A thread that ties some performances to the past is the use of historic texts for recitational singing.

### The Merrie Monarch Festival

Festivals have roots in Hawaiian culture. The *makahiki* was a three-month festival of harvesting and offering of tribute, during which competitive games and sports were played under the eye of Lono, god of peace and agriculture. After 1819, with the overthrow of the state gods, such festivals became attenuated and eventually disappeared.

The most prestigious Hawaiian festival, a modern descendant of the *makahiki*, is the Merrie Monarch Festival, held annually in Hilo, Hawai'i, since 1964. Decades of continuity have made it a tradition in its own right. Named after King Kalākaua (1836–1891), the merry monarch, who in 1883 brought the *hula* back to public life, it exemplifies the renaissance of traditional Hawaiian music and dance. It includes a parade featuring brass bands and *pa'u* riders, women in wraparound clothing (*pa'u*) riding decorated horses; exhibitions of Hawaiian arts, crafts, music, and dance; and sometimes conferences, like "Future Directions of the *Hula*," a symposium held in 1979.

The most important part of the Merrie Monarch Festival is the *hula* competition, held on three consecutive evenings. On the first, that of the Miss Aloha Hula competition, solo dancers perform a traditional (figure 6) and a more recent *hula*; awards are presented that night. In a charged, competitive atmosphere on the next two evenings (from 6:00 P.M. until about midnight), troupes from all the inhabited Hawaiian islands, California, and sometimes other states, exhibit their dances. Each troupe performs twice—the first evening in *hula kahiko* 'ancient style', and the second evening in a more modern style, *hula 'auana*.

In *hula kahiko*, dancing accompanies older styles of singing and playing musical instruments, and costumes are modern versions of indigenous clothing. *'Auana* performances use *'ukulele*, guitar, string bass, piano, or other Western instruments, and their costumes are based on late-nineteenth-century clothing, made of *ti* leaves or dresses made of velvet, satin, or other lush fabrics. Each troupe demonstrates its leader's learned and new choreography. Each performs an old dance of the teacher's choice and sometimes a preselected song, choreographed traditionally. The teacher

FIGURE 6   Miss Aloha Hula Competition at the Merrie Monarch Festival. Photo by Adrienne L. Kaeppler, 1992.

choreographs the modern selection, with danced entrances and exits for both evenings.

Troupes seldom try to relate the whole performance to an overall theme; rather, they perform a dance or sequence of dances without context. Occasionally, a teacher relates the dances to a theme, such as stories about Kamapua'a, the pig god, or about Pele, the goddess of volcanoes. Besides being separated into *kahiko* and *'auana,* the competitions are separated by sex. In each of these categories, there are three or more awards for male troupes, three or more for female troupes, three overall awards for male troupes, and three overall awards for female troupes.

## Other Hawaiian festivals and trends

Other Hawaiian festivals include the King Kamehameha Traditional Chant and Hula Competition, held annually in conjunction with King Kamehameha Day, on or near 11 June. The original emphasis was on indigenous forms—no *ti*-leaf skirts or elegant dresses, no *'ukulele* or guitars, and little emphasis on showmanship; but by the 1990s, this festival, too, had added a second night, focusing on modern forms. Prizes are awarded for dancing and chanting. Other annual Hawaiian festivals are the Prince Lot Hula Festival (noncompetitive), the Queen Lili'uokalani Keiki Hula Festival for children, and the International Fair (figure 7).

FIGURE 7   Sāmoans perform at the International Fair, a regular event at the East-West Center, University of Hawai'i. Photo by J. W. Love, 1985.

### *Rockette-like presentations*

Another trend is what might be called the Rockette style of *hula.* This style is essentially a reinvention of shows of the 1930s and 1940s—the Kodak Hula Show, the dancing done to welcome Matson Liners into port, and USO performances for U.S. servicemen. An example of a Rockette-like hula was seen in the Hawaiian program of the fifth Pacific Festival of Arts, when a series of dances were performed by a single line of girls, all of whom were of the same height, build, and coloring. It seemed a moment frozen in time, as nine identical *hula*-Rockettes recreated "Sing Me a Song of the Islands" in a romantically sterile version harking back to the days and movies of Dorothy Lamour.

A similar focus on technique, performed with precise collective accuracy, is widespread in Hawaiian festivals. The emphasis given to maintaining straight lines and synchronizing movements has carried this trend beyond festivals and competitions to become part of most *hula* performances.

—ADRIENNE L. KAEPPLER

## REFERENCES

Kaeppler, Adrienne L. 1988. "Pacific Festivals and the Promotion of Identity, Politics, and Tourism." *Come Mek Me Hol' Yu Han': The Impact of Tourism on Traditional Music,* ed. Adrienne L. Kaeppler, 121–138. Kingston, Jamaica: Jamaica Memory Bank.

Neuenfeldt, Karl. 1995. "The Kyama Corroboree: Cultural Production of Indigenous Ethnogenesis." *Sociological Inquiry* 65(1):21–46.

*Souvenir Programme.* 1980. [Third Pacific Festival of Arts]. Port Moresby: published by the festival.

Stevenson, Karen. 1992. "Politicization of *la Culture Ma'ohi:* The Creation of a Tahitian Cultural Identity." *Pacific Studies* 15(4):117–136.

Turner, George. 1884. *Samoa a Hundred Years Ago and Long Before.* London: Macmillan.

# Musical Migrations

Adrienne L. Kaeppler

Amy Kuʻuleialoha Stillman

Demeter Tsounis

Catherine Falk

Dorothy O'Donnell

Linda Barwick

Michael Ryan

Helen R. Lawrence

Don Niles

Rokucho Billy

Kim Bailey

Donald Brenneis

Ricardo D. Trimillos

Ted Solís

Lynn J. Martin

Judy Van Zile

Allan Thomas

Jennie Coleman

**Chinese in Oceania**

**Australia**

**Papua New Guinea**

**The Mortlockese _Tokia_ in Saipan, Northern Marianas**

**Indians in Fiji**

**Hawaiʻi**

**Aotearoa**

**The U.S. Mainland**

Modern-day migration into Oceania has been uneven. Some islands and countries have received only a few immigrant settlers; others have received wave after wave, overwhelming the indigenous populations. Today, some areas—including Aotearoa, Australia, Fiji, New Caledonia, and Hawaiʻi—have many more immigrants (and their descendants) than indigenous peoples. Aside from sailors who jumped ship, the earliest immigration began in the late 1700s, with the resettling of British convicts into Australia.

This entry introduces the musics of immigrant groups in various islands and musics of Pacific Islanders in the United States. The discussion could extend in many directions—Filipino music in Guam (figure 1), Wallis-Futuna music in New Caledonia, Polynesian outlier music in Honiara, Indonesian music in Irian Jaya, Banaban music in Fiji (figure 2), or the music of one Micronesian island transplanted to a neighboring island. Immigrants have brought into Oceania many kinds of music and dance, often preserving traditions as they were when they left their homelands. Much of this music and dance is associated with the migrant groups' ethnic identity in the multicultural societies within which the migrants live.

—Adrienne L. Kaeppler

## CHINESE IN OCEANIA

Migratory waves from China into Oceania in the mid-to-late 1800s were fueled by two coinciding factors: in China, poor economic conditions; and in the islands, a developing need for cheap, unskilled labor on plantations and in mines. Historical sources, including photographs, demonstrate that Chinese migrants transplanted their music, dance, and theater. Configurations of these traditions, and their maintenance in the late twentieth century, vary with historical patterns of migration, interactions with islanders, and assimilative levels in local cultures.

From about 1850 to about 1900, migrants originated largely in the southeastern coastal areas of Guangdong and Fujian provinces. Most Chinese migrants into Oceania appear to have been Cantonese-speakers, but sizable numbers of Hakka peoples also migrated. In New Guinea, Chinese entered initially from Singapore, and lat-

Religious practices among Chinese communities vary. Buddhist and Daoist activities occur throughout Australia. A Chinese temple in Pape'ete, Tahiti, is notable for the absence of a surrounding Chinatown. Many Chinese have embraced Christianity.

FIGURE 1   Filipino influence is evident as dancers from Guam perform at the Pacific Festival of Arts. Photo by Adrienne L. Kaeppler, 1985.

er from other areas. Chinese laborers who fulfilled their contracts and opted to remain (rather than be repatriated back to China) often moved into urban areas, establishing Chinatowns, areas where Chinese businesses, religions, and cultural activities flourished. In the receiving countries during the early twentieth century, governmental policies limited immigration, but later, especially during and after the 1970s, renewed migration infused vitality into the Chinese presence throughout Oceania.

## Various activities

In the 1990s, Chinese performances throughout Oceania are diverse. In Honolulu and the state capitals of Australia, amateur instrumental and operatic clubs serve as conduits for contact with musicians and actors in China. With business and cultural associations, they sponsor community-based performances by their own members and touring artists.

Chinese opera by professional and amateur actors and musicians, especially that sung in the Cantonese dialect, flourishes in Honolulu and in Australia's Chinatowns. Professional Chinese-opera troupes reside in Australia; in 1991, a guild of profession-

FIGURE 2    Banabans who live in Fiji perform a
segment of the Fijian program at the Pacific
Festival of Arts, Townsville, Australia. Photo by
Adrienne L. Kaeppler, 1988.

FIGURE 2    Banabans who live in Fiji perform a segment of the Fijian program at the Pacific Festival of Arts, Townsville, Australia. Photo by Adrienne L. Kaeppler, 1988.

al and semiprofessional Chinese performers worked in Honolulu. Since the 1980s, increasing numbers of musicians, dancers, and actors professionally trained in China have moved to Australia and the United States, providing cultural expertise to Chinese communities there and aspiring non-Chinese students of Chinese music and dance.

Clubs that promote the study of martial arts maintain the performance of the Chinese lion dance. Martial arts are the primary attraction for participants, many of whom are neither first-generation immigrants nor native speakers of a Chinese language. The lion dance is an important marker of Chinese identity on occasions such as weddings, openings of restaurants and businesses, and gatherings of family associations (Kwok 1992:24). It is frequently included in public festivals and celebrations of holidays, including the Lunar New Year, the Mid-Autumn Festival, and Ching Ming, the sweeping of ancestral graves.

Religious practices among Chinese communities vary. Buddhist and Daoist activities occur in large urban areas and throughout Australia, where some temples may still be in active use (Lawrence 1992:37). A Chinese temple in Pape'ete, Tahiti, is notable for the absence of a surrounding Chinatown. Elsewhere, in multigenerational Chinese communities, many Chinese have embraced Christianity. Where Chinese immigrants have assimilated into local populations, they attend services in English or French; an increase in Cantonese and Mandarin services in the 1980s and 1990s served recent migrants, largely from Hong Kong and Taiwan.

Setting up schools to teach and promote Chinese cultural activities among children and adults has had varying results. An attempt on Guam in the 1970s disintegrated for the parents' lack of interest in Chinese culture and the children's preferences for contemporary Anglo-American popular culture (Sajnovsky 1992). Chinese schools in Tahiti, begun in the early 1900s, played an important role in maintaining a Chinese language, but they closed in 1964; the curriculum covered music, but whether it included Chinese music is unclear.

In the late 1990s, Chinese performative traditions are negligible in areas where early Chinese settlers intermarried and assimilated into surrounding communities. In the southern Cook Islands, residents of Chinese ancestry eschewed Chinese cultural traditions, as do long-term residents of Chinese ancestry in Aotearoa.

## Revivals

Chinese communities of long-standing residence in Tahiti and Fiji appear to be experiencing a reawakening of Chinese cultural identity. In Tahiti, photographs from the 1880s show musicians posing with Chinese instruments; a century later, their descendants were learning Chinese dances only for cultural festivals, by using taped music. Chinese people in Tahiti have consciously projected a pan-Chinese culture,

FIGURE 3    Chinese who live in Fiji perform a segment of the Fijian program at the Pacific Festival of Arts, Townsville, Australia. Photo by Adrienne L. Kaeppler, 1988.

adopting common components, as in the fan dance, and glossing over affinities with geographically based practices (Stillman 1992; Tung 1993). Likewise in Fiji, after decades of Fijian policies of discouraging multiculturalism, a Chinese school now presents pan-Chinese performing arts (figure 3).

Interactions between Chinese and indigenous traditions seem to have been negligible, but an illuminating case is Papua New Guinea, where Chinese residents are leaders in performing and promoting popular music. Two studios dominate the scene, and both are owned and managed by businesspeople of Chinese descent (Niles 1992:33–34).

—AMY KUʻULEIALOHA STILLMAN

## AUSTRALIA

### Greeks

About three hundred thousand Greek-Australians, nearly 2 percent of the national population, are the third-largest immigrant group in the country, after Anglo-Celts and Italians. Their migration began early, and they concentrated in cities (Tsounis 1988:17, 1993:25–26). A triad of traits are held to be integral to Greek diasporal culture: the Greek language, the Greek Orthodox religion, and extended families. Greek-Australians perform classical, rock, blues, jazz, and other musical genres. At services of the Greek Orthodox Church, they hear the chanting of Byzantine ecclesiastical hymns; and in various secular contexts (life-cycle celebrations, communal and mainstream events), they perform old and new musical genres.

Greek musical performance occurs at receptions for engagements and weddings (Tsounis 1986), civic and fraternity-sponsored dances, and commemorations of religious and public holidays, and in restaurants and pubs. Since the 1980s, Greek organizations, including the Hellenic Musicians Association of South Australia, have promoted concerts featuring particular genres and composers, including Manos Chatzidakis, Manos Loizos, and Vasilis Tsitsanis.

The Greek community also supports choirs that perform traditional, contemporary, and local Greek music—notably the Byzantine Chanters (Sydney), the Australian Greek Choir (Melbourne), and the Hellenic Symphonia and Sirens (Adelaide). For Greek and mixed audiences, annual festivals showcase Greek-Australian and international musicians and dancers. These festivals include Glendi (Adelaide), Dimitria (Adelaide), and Antipodes (Melbourne).

#### Musicians

Most Greek-Australian musicians work as semiprofessional musicians, rehearsing in evenings and performing on weekends. A few work full-time as professional musicians; others perform only for family and friends. A typical Greek band consists only of men: a vocalist and players of bouzouki (a long-necked lute), electric guitar, electric bass guitar, and drums. Greek-language vocals supported by bouzouki have become Australian icons of Greekness, but this instrumentation is changing to include female vocalists and other instruments, especially keyboard and violin.

Some first-generation immigrants play traditional instruments: the Pontian or Cretan upright fiddle (*lyra*), the violin, the clarinet, the hammer dulcimer (*santouri*), the long-necked lute (*lagouto*). They perform music associated with their places of origin (Chatzinikolaou and Gauntlett 1993:203). Younger, Australian-born musicians are learning to play urban popular instruments, including two kinds of bouzouki (*tzouras* and *baglamas*), the short-necked lute (*outi*), and a single-headed goblet drum (*toumberleki*).

To learn basic techniques, Greek-Australian musicians take lessons, but they also gain from studying recordings on records, cassettes, CDs, and videos, listening to Greek-community programs on radio, participating in Greek dancing, and above all, observing performances.

### Genres

Greek-Australian musicians mostly play genres that accompany spontaneous collective dancing: regional songs and dances (*dimotika*), songs and dances of the Greek islands (*nisiotika*), and urban popular songs and dances (*rebetika*). Peculiar to Australian contexts is the performance of at least nine Greek dances: *chasapikos* 'butcher's dance', a slow, duple-metered Anatolian line dance; *chasaposervikos* 'Serbian butcher's dance', a fast, duple-metered Anatolian line dance; *kalamatianos,* a dance in a circle, from the Greek mainland and islands, in seven-beat meter; *kotsari,* a duple-metered line dance from Pontus; *syrtos,* a dance in a circle; *tik,* the dance of Pontus, danced in duple meter in Australia; *tsamikos,* a triple-metered dance in a circle; *tsifteteli,* a solo Anatolian belly dance, in duple or quadruple meter; and *zeibekikos,* a solo dance in nine-beat meter, of the Zeibek people of western Anatolia. In the 1990s, patrons of Greek music request the *ballos,* a duple-metered couple dance from the Aegean Islands; the *ikariotiko,* a duple-metered Ikarian dance in a circle; the *karsilamas,* an Anatolian and Cypriot couple dance, in nine-beat meter; and the *pentozalis,* a duple-metered Cretan line dance.

The activities of troupes such as the Aristotelian Academy of Greek Traditional Dances (Sydney) and the Hellenic Youth Dancers (Adelaide) have intensified interest in regional dances. These troupes specialize in researching, performing, and teaching. Local musicians gain inspiration from the concerts and recordings of musicians who visit from Greece, including Chronis Aidonidis, Charis Alexiou, Kostas Boras, Giorgios Dalaras, and Domna Samiou.

Greek-Australian performances of traditional music retain much aural detail, including rhythmic complexity, modality, ornamentation, and improvisation. Local musicians harmonize melodies with triadic chords derived from the modal series, rather than from functional tonality. Since the mid-1980s, *rebetika* has enjoyed popularity in Australia, and ensembles such as Apodimi Kompania (Melbourne) and the Rockin' Rembets (Adelaide) have devoted themselves to it, performing songs and instrumental pieces in various styles: the earlier, *café-aman* and Piraeus styles, using modes (*dromous* 'roads') and asymmetrical rhythms; and the later, *laiko* style, using major and minor tonalities. Greek-Australian ensembles perform *rebetika* on acoustic instruments. Their instrumentation has included accordion, banjo, bouzouki (and related instruments), castanets, finger-held cymbals (*zilia*), guitar, *outi,* double bass, *toumberleki,* and violin. At festivals and multicultural carnivals, art exhibitions, and concerts celebrating Australian cultural diversity, *rebetika* attracts audiences of Greek and non-Greek enthusiasts (*merkalides*).

The *chasaposervikos*—the dance musicians often choose to encourage non-Greek patrons to participate in Greek dancing—is introduced as "the *zorba,* an easy dance to learn."

Greek bands mostly play modern styles of urban popular music: *laika* 'popular', *entechna* 'art-popular', and *elafro-laika* 'light-popular'. The musical components of these styles include traditional modalities, subjects, and dances, and Western and Arabian styles of pop. Greek-Australians prefer *elafro-laika* commercial hits associated with star singers associated with Greek nightclubs. Another common feature of this music is the use of *ousak,* the Phrygian minor mode, which emphasizes the flat second—a quality said to express yearning and heartache. Romantic texts contribute to the colloquial categorization of *ousak*-mode pieces as crying songs (*klapsourika*).

### Adaptations

The most striking adaptation to Australian contexts reflects the need to cater to the musical tastes of Greek people of diverse backgrounds. This need has resulted in unique programs, organized into standard brackets of music: floor show, Greek dance, and ballroom dance. In another example of adaptation, Greek bands perform at non-Greek-organized events, play rock and other pop music, sing in English and other languages, and provide English translations and introductions to Greek songs. The *chasaposervikos,* the dance musicians often choose to encourage non-Greek patrons to participate in Greek dancing, is introduced as "the *zorba,* an easy dance to learn."

### Greek-Australian composition

Greek-Australian composers draw from a heterogeneous set of raw materials: some compose within a traditional genre, setting new couplets to precomposed melodies (Chatzinikolaou and Gauntlett 1993:204); some use the rhythms and modes of *rebetika*; some compose symphonic music in an *entechna* style, orchestrating for theater and film; some compose in an *elafro-laika* style, employing the feel of rock.

The texts of some local compositions reflect experiences of bicultural identity and the need for cross-cultural understanding, as in the lyrics of "*Otan Anoichta Milo*" ('When I Speak Openly', Tsounis 1990):

> When I speak openly, you do not hear my voice.
> You hear only what you want to.
> You do not understand.
> Don't make me feel like a stranger,
> An orphan with a shattered life,
> An outcast on this earth.
> I've told you once, I'll tell you again:
> My memory runs deep.
> From the waters of the Aegean, it unfolds far to the south.
> Like the boundless ocean, which does not distinguish between lands,
> How will it be if we open up our hearts?

I composed this song for the project Shoulder To Shoulder, in which Greek people collaborated with Aboriginal Australians and Torres Strait Islanders to explore experiences of racism. The music, in the *chitzaz* mode (E♭–F♭–G–A♭–B♭–C♭–D♭–E♭), is for soprano, flute, viola, guitar, double bass, and piano. After a slow vocal section in triple meter, it moves into a moderate rumba (*syrtos*) with a repeated ascending vocal melody; it has a flamenco feel.

Greek-Australian composers who by performing and recording their own compositions have left their mark on Australian musical performance include Nick Arabatsis, John Kourbelis, Steve Papadopoulos, and Arthur Giannopoulos (Adelaide); Constantine Koukias (Hobart); Savvas Christodoulou, Christos and Tassos Ioannides, Costas Tsikaderis, and Stelios Tsiolas (Melbourne); and Themos Mexis (Sydney). Their activities owe much to annual competitions of the Greek Song Festival, held in Adelaide and Melbourne during the 1980s.

—DEMETER TSOUNIS

## Hmong

About thirteen hundred Hmong live in Australia. The vanguard arrived from Laos in 1968, when seven educated Hmong men undertook study in accounting, anthropology, economics, medicine, pathology, and theology. In and after 1975, they sponsored some of their relatives' immigration. Though small in numbers, the Hmong in Australia have a high local profile. Newspapers print photos of them in traditional dress. Markets exhibit and retail their handicrafts, with proceeds going to relatives in camps in Thailand.

The Hmong in Australia face many of the problems the Hmong in the United States face (Downing and Olney 1982; Hendricks et al. 1986), but unlike U.S. Hmong, most Australian Hmong have neither depended on churches for resettlement, nor felt pressure to convert to Christianity. They have maintained shamanic healing and divinatory rituals, funeral rituals, marriage negotiations, and New Year's celebrations. They accept marriage with non-Hmong, most frequently Laotian Australians. Because their ritual practitioners are few, their funerals and betrothals cannot always observe clan-specific requirements.

In 1978, individuals formed the Hmong-Australia Support Society, which for mutual assistance aimed to transcend clan boundaries. One of its most successful activities was lobbying the federal government, which in 1986, for a special intake of Hmong, accepted new criteria, including the knowledge of funeral texts, the power to call souls, and the ability to serve as a cultural leader. As a result, most Hmong communities in Australia have at least one cultural leader, one traditional musician, one marriage celebrant, and several shamans.

### The funeral ritual (kev pam tuag)

For the Hmong, death elicits the most important rituals, which instruct the soul of the deceased about its journey to the ancestors' world. The instructions require an elaborate, three-day ceremony (Symonds 1991; Tapp 1989), beginning with the *Qhuab Kev* 'Showing the Way', a recitation performed as soon as possible after a death. Later, a sectionalized piece, the *Qeej Tu Siav* 'Song of Expiring Life', is played on the *qeej* (Lao *khaen*), a multiple free-reed pipe. Recitations of the *Qhuab Kev* as recorded by two Hmong in Australia use a four-tone scale (related to lexical tones) and word-governed rhythms with one note per syllable. The Hmong do not regard these items as music (*kwv txiaj*).

The *qeej* symbolizes the Hmong, to themselves and other Australians. Multicultural events staged in Australia often feature a traditionally dressed *qeej* player. A Hmong anecdote tells how a boy who had recently arrived in Australia reacted to the country: against a background of the Sydney Harbour Bridge, he drew a picture of a kangaroo playing a *qeej*.

The demands of schooling and employment, with a lack of motivation and interest among younger Hmong, preempt traditional training in recitations. Youths can no longer learn the *qeej* and its texts while walking between fields. Because the texts are powerful, the Hmong believe they must not be performed inside dwellings, lest living souls inadvertently be sent to the ancestors' realm; in Australia, the Hmong discuss and learn this ritual in public parks and buildings.

Australian laws and customs have changed the text and conduct of the ceremony. Federal law permits the unrefrigerated storage of a corpse for not more than eight hours; accordingly, the Hmong have telescoped the ceremony. They may still sacrifice chickens, but do not slaughter an ox or a buffalo at the end of the ceremony, while the corpse is being taken to the grave. They have little choice of where to bury the body—a decision traditionally determined by divination. For accidental deaths, Australian law requires an autopsy. Since most Hmong believe *Qhuab Kev* should be recited to the soul of the deceased as soon as possible after death, the delay distresses them; they fear that doctors may sew foreign materials into the corpse, impeding the soul's rebirth (Falk 1994:19–24). Because the ancestors' realm lies in southern China, settlement in Australia has led to a problem of mortuary geography. A leader of the community, Dr. Pao Saykao, suggests altering the text to include instructions guiding a soul onto a Qantas plane bound for the southeast Asian mainland, where it can begin an overland journey to the ancestors' realm.

Most *qeej* players live in Melbourne. When a death occurs elsewhere, they and others travel overnight by bus to the home of the deceased. Because of their commitments to jobs, they conduct most funerals between Friday and Sunday evenings.

### Music of courtship

Traditionally used by lovers to talk in coded text, lamellaphones (*nja*) and free-reed pipes (*cha mblay*) have no place in the lives of Australian Hmong youth—who communicate by telephone. Young Hmong avidly consume cassettes of Laotian popular music, from Laos and Hmong and Laotian bands in the United States and France. The songs on these cassettes are usually songs of love (*nkauj*), such as "A Piece of My Heart" and "Do Not Disappoint Her."

There are two Hmong bands in Melbourne. Self-taught on drums, keyboard, and guitar, the musicians cover American Hmong, Laotian, Thai, and Chinese songs. In 1991, the band Déjà Vu (formerly The Boomerang Band) toured abroad, performing for Hmong communities in Canada and France. It and Neej Tshiab Band (New Life Band) perform at receptions after Hmong weddings, fund-raising events, and New Year's celebrations. In Melbourne, they engage in competition with the Laotian bands Mekong Band, Saythara, 7-Up, and Wodonga-Albury Band.

New Year's celebrations, a time of intense courtship, often result in marriages. Competing to invent witty rhymes, adolescent boys and girls face one another in a row, extemporizing songs in couplets. This custom occurs alongside bands, parades in traditional costumes, speeches, and Laotian-Hmong dances. In 1990, to preserve and promote Hmong culture, young Hmong in Victoria established the Hmong Youth Club. On Friday nights, members offer classes in English and mathematics.

### Extemporized solo singing (kwv txiaj)

This genre belongs mainly to the elderly, who rarely speak English, and neither read nor write Hmong. The texts express loneliness and estrangement from the traditional environment. Recorded on cassettes, performances are sent to relatives in Laos, in refugee camps, and in France and the United States. In these songs, people use poetic language as a vehicle to sing emotions they would be too shy to speak or write. Especially between 1975 and 1980, such songs helped Australian Hmong bypass Laotian censorship. Traditionally prohibited from singing while married, women often use this genre after they become widows. The words of these songs have changed to reflect their contexts: texts metaphorically cite yellow hair (people with fair hair), crows (airplanes), and "night-stars" (electricity).

—CATHERINE FALK

## Irish

The music of Irish immigrants in Australia encompasses songs, ballads, airs, marches, and dances, including jigs, reels, hornpipes, and polkas. Though many Irish immigrants have participated in their Australian contemporaries' social occasions and musical performances, some have maintained Irish musical traditions. From 1788, successive waves of Irish immigrants brought songs, some specific to Ireland, and others common to areas of Britain and Ireland. These immigrants included free settlers and involuntary immigrants, about one-third of the convicts transported to penal colonies in Australia. British- and Irish-created transportation ballads and broadside ballads gained wide currency in Australia.

The most prolific balladeer of the period of transportation (1788–1868) was Frank "the Poet" MacNamara, transported from Cork in 1832. "Moreton Bay," which chronicles the brutalities of convict life, is a famous Irish ballad attributed to him (figure 4); also known as "The Convict's Lament on the Death of Captain Logan," it is most commonly sung to "Boolavogue," a melody that derives from "Youghal Harbour."

Musical performance in nineteenth-century Australia was distinguished by social class. Genteel home entertainment favored the piano: sentimental, patriotic and music-hall songs, drawing-room ballads, Irish, Scottish, and Welsh airs, operatic overtures, and works by classical composers were performed in solo, duo, trio, or two-piano arrangements. The elegant drawing-room ballads of Thomas Moore (1779–1852), a Dubliner, were popular in Australia. By contrast, Australians hired traditional Irish musicians for horse-racing carnivals and life-cycle celebrations, which served as occasions for singing, dancing, and telling stories. Pubs, many owned

FIGURE 4 The first stanza of "Moreton Bay," a ballad attributed to Frank MacNamara, an Irish convict transported to Australia in 1832.

One Sun—day morn—ing as I went walk—ing, by Bris—bane wa—ters I chanced to stray; I heard a pris'—ner his fate be—wail—ing, as on the sun—ny ri—ver bank he lay. "I am a na—tive of Er—in's is—land, and ban—ish'd now from my na—tive shore; They tore me from my a—ged par—ents and from the maid—en whom I do a—dore."

The most common form of Irish immigrant social activity is the *céilí*, an evening of music and dancing. Dances popular in Australia include the Walls of Limerick, the Siege of Ennis, and the Waves of Tory.

and patronized by Irish immigrants, were often places of musical conviviality. As social centers, hotels provided venues for meetings, concerts, and balls. From the 1850s to the 1890s, Irish pubs, shebeens, and music pervaded Australian areas where Irish-born miners joined others seeking gold.

### Saint Patrick's Day

Since 1795 or before, this Roman Catholic feast (17 March) has been celebrated in Australia, where "patterns" (festivities associated with Irish saints' days) were marked by drinking and revelry. Official celebrations often took the form of a dinner-concert, featuring English and Australian songs, with occasional Anglo-Irish or sentimental American-Irish items. From 1897, many such concerts featured only Irish music—an innovation promoted by Cardinal Patrick Francis Moran (1830–1911), who arrived in Sydney in 1884.

At the St. Patrick's Day concert in Adelaide in 1905, fiddler Patrick O'Leary performed the reel "Kiss the Maid behind the Barrel," accompanied by his son on piano and four male dancers. Born in County Cavan in 1851, he spent a few years in North America, and arrived in South Australia in 1876. Corresponding with Francis O'Neill of Chicago, he wrote lyrically about Irish music. Passages from his letters appear in O'Neill's 1907 and 1913 publications. O'Neill's 1903 and 1907 collections remain sources of Irish music in many countries.

### The céilí

The most common form of Irish immigrant social activity in twentieth-century Australia is the *céilí*. In Ireland, a *céilí* was a neighborly social gathering that featured talk and gossip, but not necessarily singing and dancing. The first expatriate *céilí* occurred in London in 1897. Patterned on the Scottish *ceilidh,* it featured music, dancing, and refreshments. Since then, in immigrant Irish communities (and even in Ireland), a *céilí* has been an evening of music and dancing, usually held monthly. It may involve social dances (including the waltz), solo or group displays, and vocal solos. To replace dances considered foreign, teachers in Ireland developed specific dances for *céilí*; examples popular in Australia include the Walls of Limerick, the Siege of Ennis, and the Waves of Tory.

In the 1930s, the *céilí* band developed. It consisted of up to ten instruments, including fiddle, flute, accordion, piano, and drums. The Merry Moonshiners, formed in the 1960s, were the first Melbourne *céilí* band. Irish immigrants of forty or more years of Australian residence maintain the *céilí,* though its popularity with younger people has declined.

### Irish associations and musicians

In the 1800s and early 1900s, a solo fiddler or piper, or sometimes a duo or trio, accompanied the dancing of jigs, reels, and hornpipes. Irish dancing remains a popular social activity, supported in Australia by schools and competitions. Since the 1960s, Irish traditional musicians' recordings have usually provided music for classes and competitions in Irish dancing.

Though most Irish associations in Australia have promoted Irish culture in some form, systematic teaching of Irish music was introduced by branches of the Association of Irish Musicians (Comhaltas Ceoltóirí Éireann), established in Ireland in 1951. In Perth, a branch was founded by Seán Doherty, fiddler and performer on many other instruments, who arrived from County Mayo by way of England in 1968. In Melbourne in 1970, Irish singer Eileen Begley, from County Kerry, and her husband, Victor Loughnane, initiated another branch.

Some Irish immigrants influenced musicians in Australia, Irish and non-Irish. One such immigrant was Tim Whelan (1914–1989). In 1938, he left County Tipperary for Dublin, where he performed in halls and on radio. In 1967, after a period in England, he and his family arrived in Adelaide. He usually played an adapted piccolo, or his cherished Oliver Goldsmith walking-stick flute. By drilling an extra hole in the back of a tin whistle in D, he enabled himself to produce a C without cross-fingering; this adaptation became common in southern Australia. A charismatic musician, he exerted influence by performing at festivals that brought together musicians from across Australia. Other Irish immigrant musicians have attained high status within the Australian folk-oriented scene, where Australians of varied heritages readily adopt and adapt their music.

—Dorothy O'Donnell

## Italians

Since 1890, about 430,000 Italians have moved to Australia (Cresciani 1986:4). The Italian-born and their descendants in Australia, numbering more than half a million, about 3 percent of the national population, are the largest immigrant group of non-English-speaking origin. Nevertheless, no organized Italian community exists in Australia. The loyalties of the first generation are to particular geographical areas; the second and third generations have tended to lose the language, and with it their affiliation with other cultural forms.

During Australia's years as a penal colony, British authorities transported to New South Wales some Italians, usually sailors involved in brawls in British ports. In the 1850s and 1860s, gold attracted to Australia the first notable numbers of free Italian settlers, though the cost of passage was prohibitive to most, who preferred the Americas. Only in the 1920s, with the restriction of immigration into the United States, did substantial numbers of Italians, mainly of peasant or working-class backgrounds, enter Australia. Many settled in rural areas, where they carried on such occupations as gardening, cutting cane, fishing, manufacturing, and running small businesses. During World War II, the Australian government imprisoned many Italian-born men with known political connections, fascist and antifascist.

After the 1940s, mainly from 1955 to 1965, the Australian government promoted and assisted the passage of many Italians, especially those from poor, southern areas, especially Campania and Calabria. By the early 1990s, immigration from Italy had slowed to a trickle, and returnees to Italy had begun to outnumber new arrivals. The Italian-born population is thus aging and decreasing as a proportion of the national population. The profile of the Italian-born population varies from state to state; few Italians settled in Tasmania (0.5 percent in 1981); Victoria has the largest proportion of Australia's Italian-born (43 percent in 1981, mostly in Melbourne); and in Queensland, the Italian-born population is older and more concentrated in rural areas.

### Early immigrants' music

Most Italian immigrants have come from peasant and working-class backgrounds, and their culture has always included diverse musical styles, extensively documented in Italy only after 1945 (Leydi 1973). Almost no documentation of Italian musical activity in Australia before the 1970s exists, partly because the tradition was oral, and partly because social and official pressure to conform to the cultural norms of the English-speaking majority forced alternate musical expressions underground. Furthermore, Italians' patterns of settlement and hours of work afforded little incentive or support for maintaining musical activities, especially in the context of the second and subsequent generations' low retention of the language (Bettoni 1984).

History posts some tantalizing signs of Italian musical life in Australia. In 1868, the Victorian Register of Nationals listed five itinerant Italian musicians, and cited "musician" as the fifth most common occupation declared by Italians—after "miner," "sailor," "woodman," and "peasant" (Cresciani 1986:5). Melodies recorded from descendants of early Italian settlers in gold-producing areas of Victoria and cane-cutting areas of Queensland and New South Wales show that itinerant musicians probably earned their living playing in halls and other public spaces.

### The late twentieth century

In the 1970s, the Australian government shifted from a policy of assimilation toward a policy of multiculturalism, which encouraged the formation of Italian music-and-dance groups, often within the existing structures of regional clubs, such as the Fogolar Furlan (Friuli Club), the Associazione Puglia (Puglia Association), and the Associazione Toscana (Tuscany Association). Many such groups—Alpine choral societies, brass bands, dance groups, mandolin orchestras—modeled themselves on equivalent musical organizations and genres in Italy. The brass bands usually played popular arrangements, especially of operatic music (which in Italy, by degrees, has entered into oral tradition), and the choral societies performed a mix of standard choral pieces, such as Verdi's *Requiem*, and nontraditionally harmonized four-part arrangements of songs once circulating in oral tradition, such as "*Quel mazzolin di fiori*" ('That little bunch of flowers'). Folk-oriented groups usually dance to recorded music while wearing invented costumes. Especially in the context of festivals designed to celebrate the heritage of Australia's multiculturalism, the public demands spectacular symbols of Italian or regional identity.

The 1970s saw the formation of groups dedicated to reviving traditional Italian music. One of these, Adelaide's Italian Folk Ensemble (IFE, figure 5), developed out of theatrical performances and courses presented by the Italian Discipline at Flinders University, and its membership has sometimes included Italian-speaking Australians not of Italian descent. It sees the use of material from the popular traditions as more relevant to many Italians in Australia than highbrow culture, promoted by such Italian-Australian organizations as the Dante Alighieri Society; and it believes it presents to non-Italian Australians a truer expression of Italian popular culture than that of folk-oriented dancers. Most of the songs it performs are in dialect, not standard Italian.

Little recorded material on Italian-Australian traditional music is commercially available. Organizations such as the Federazione Italiana Lavoratori Emigrati e Famiglie (Federation of Italian Migrant Workers and Their Families) have sponsored the documenting of songs, though the result usually focuses on lyrics, ignoring music and other details of performance (figure 6).

In Adelaide in 1990, the IFE presented a *Ballata grande per Francesco Fantin* to mark a photographic exhibition on the life of the anarchist Francesco Fantin. Mixing

FIGURE 5    The Italian Folk Ensemble performs Italian traditional songs in English translation for the Adelaide Theatre Guild's production of Dario Fo's *The Fool's Mystery Play.* Photo by David Wilson, 1987.

spoken dialogue with songs in the forms and techniques of traditional itinerant singers of stories (*cantastorie*), the IFE retold his story: persecuted by Italian and Australian officialdom, he was killed by fascists in Loveday Internment Camp in 1942 (Barwick 1991). One text, set as a six-verse stanza (*sestina*) by the Sicilian *cantastorie* Cicciu Busacca, begins:

> Vogliu cuntarvi a la siciliana
> la storia di nu tristi avvinimentu
> successu qua in terra sud-australiana,
> menz' a lu campu di lu internamentu:
> è Loveday lu locu numinatu;
> puru Fantin Francescu ci è internatu.
>
> I want to tell you in the Sicilian style
> the story of a sad event
> that happened here on South Australian soil,
> inside the internment camp:
> Loveday is the name of the place;
> Francesco Fantin is interned there.

FIGURE 6    Ugo Bartolomei plays a piano accordion in Perth, Western Australia. Photo by Linda Barwick, 1995.

The melody begins high, repeatedly descends in one-verse phrases, and resolves on its lowest note, the tonic (figure 7). The singer adopts the improvisational flexibility of Southern Italian soloists. Maintaining melodic shaping and cadencing, he introduces tonal and rhythmic variations. He begins the first, second, and fourth verses a third lower than Busacca; in the third verse, he adds two eighths to make a 5/4 bar, incorporating two extra syllables. Unlike Busacca, he plays no accompaniment; exigencies of coordination with the guitarist force the standardization of tempo and phrasing.

Traditional Italian music has served other South Australian groups, most of them associated at some time with the IFE; these include Due Voci, Compagnia Folk, La Lega, Terra Mia, Local Import, and Doppio Teatro. Some productions have included traditional or new music drawing on standard idioms, like the suite of songs composed by Claudio Pompili for Doppio Teatro's production *La Madonna emigrante* (1986).

—LINDA BARWICK

Batuka is Australia's longest-established salsa band. Its members have been immigrants from Canada, Colombia, Cuba, El Salvador, France, Greece, Haiti, Jamaica, Lebanon, Peru, Poland, Puerto Rico, Russia, Spain, Uruguay, and Yugoslavia.

FIGURE 7   The first stanza of the fifth song in the Italian Folk Ensemble's *Ballata grande per Francesco Fantin,* performed in Adelaide, Australia, in March 1990, by Dino Porcaro, accompanied on guitar (not shown) by Lou Poiana. Text and English translation by G. A. A. Comin (after Comin and Barwick 1991:80).

## Latin Americans and Caribbeans

Between 1971 and 1984, Latin Americans and Caribbeans, fleeing political instability and fiscal inflation, became a new wave of immigrants to Australia. Most came from five countries: Chile (43.6 percent), Argentina (21 percent), Uruguay (15.6 percent), Peru (4.5 percent), and Brazil (3.7 percent). The remainder came from Colombia, Venezuela, Ecuador, Bolivia, and (in lower numbers) El Salvador, Cuba, Puerto Rico, Haiti, Jamaica, and Mexico. They settled mainly in urban parts of New South Wales and Victoria. In 1991, they totaled about 49,700, or 0.2 percent of the national population.

### Consensus and diversity

The immigrants' communal activities feature traditional dance-music styles. Genres that cross cultural boundaries in Latin America and the Caribbean do so in Australia. These include *huayno,* Peruvian and Bolivian dance-music; *cueca,* Chilean dance-music, also popular in Bolivia; and salsa, an African-Cuban urban contemporary music popular throughout the Americas. Immigrants from those countries enjoy participating in performances that feature those genres.

Also performed in Australia for communal and multicultural audiences are popular styles: from Argentina, *chacarera, milonga, resbalosa, tango, zamba*; from Bolivia, *bailecito*; from Brazil, bossa nova, *capoeira, choro, frevo, forro,* lambada, *maculele, marcha, samba batucada, samba enredo, samba canção*; from Chile, *refalosa*; from Colombia, *cumbia*; from Peru, *marinera*; from Uruguay, *candombe* and *murga*; from the Caribbean, calypso, cha-cha, mambo, merengue, reggae, soca (modern calypso), *son montuno*; and from Mexico, *mariachi.* Cross-cultural experimentation between immigrant and native Australian musicians has led to an array of original and innovative compositions, which blend elements of these styles with elements of jazz, pop, and rock.

### Performers

Few professional immigrant musicians from Latin America and the Caribbean live in Australia. Techniques and genres result mainly from the imitation of commercial recordings; performance changes the music further. The shortage of experienced immigrant musicians promotes multicultural artistic collaboration. Consequently, presentations vary much from indigenous models; often transformed and reinterpreted, such displays are more representative of a multicultural society than of homogeneous groups.

Batuka is Australia's longest-established salsa-playing band. Assuming its musicians share common cultural and musical backgrounds, promoters classify and hire it as a "South American band," though its members have been immigrants from Canada, Colombia, Cuba, El Salvador, France, Greece, Haiti, Jamaica, Lebanon, Peru, Poland, Puerto Rico, Russia, Spain, Uruguay, and Yugoslavia. Membership has included Australian-born musicians, who, like most other members, got their knowledge and experience of salsa only in Australia.

### Contexts

Performative contexts include community-based ventures, restaurants, clubs, festivals, and mass media. Annual festivals, such as The Sydney Festival del Sol (started in 1978), and the Bondi Festival of South American Music and Dance (started in 1979, governmentally sponsored), have permanent dates in the Australian calendar. Organizers promote those events to maintain their traditions and identities.

Through mass appeal, promotion, and sponsorship, certain Latin American styles have reached widespread audiences. Brazilian samba is one such style. In the 1950s and 1960s, American ballroom interpretations of Brazilian samba were popular in Australian social-dance circles. Since the early 1970s, Brazilian immigrants have introduced more spontaneous Brazilian samba variants and Brazilian-styled innovations. Carnival in Rio de Janeiro and Brazilian samba schools (*escolas de samba*) provided the models for the formation of two schools in Sydney: Sambação, in 1978–1982, and The Brazilian Samba Social Centre, in 1979–1984; a similar organization operates in Melbourne. At carnival, samba-school members (*sambistas*) organize the dancing; for a competitive parade (*Carnaval desfile*), each school composes its own narrative samba (*samba enredo*).

School membership has ranged from a majority of Brazilians to a majority of non-Brazilians; but "Brazilian" presentations in Sydney have involved cooperation between Brazilian-born and non-Brazilian organizers, musicians, singers, and dancers, whose efforts emphasize change and renovation, rather than stasis and preservation.

### Musical change

Many stylistic changes have occurred in the Australian context. Commercial recordings often substitute for live performances, and nontraditional musical instruments sometimes substitute for traditional ones. Virtuosic rhythms associated with certain instruments and styles—particularly the Brazilian friction membranophone (*cuíca*) and tambourine (*pandeiro*), the syncopations of salsa, and the sounds and rhythms of *capoeira,* produced by the musical bow (*berimbau*)—usually become simplified.

Other changes include reportorial standardization, partly because of dramatic changes of cultural environment and accompanying departures from old constraints and regulations, and partly because of the lack of composers. Realignment through conflict over vertical alignment of rhythm and melody is common in groups that mix musicians from disparate cultures. It is particularly clear in the basic beat of Brazilian samba, which comes from the *surdo,* a double-headed cylindrical bass drum, whose heads are attached by a metal hoop with regulating rods. Suspended at the waist, this drum serves in percussion sections (*baterías*) for *samba enredo* and related forms, *samba batucada* and *samba de partido alto.* Unusually by Australian standards, bass guitars provide a pulse that accents the fourth quarter in a 4/4 bar (Ryan 1989).

—MICHAEL RYAN

## Pacific Islanders

From about 1863 to 1904, the indentured-labor trade brought people from the southwest Pacific to work in eastern Australia. They mainly worked on cotton or sugarcane plantations in coastal Queensland. Known as kanakas (from Hawaiian *kanaka* 'person'), these laborers were Solomon Islanders and Ni-Vanuatu; some were Loyalty Islanders, and a few were from more distant groups, including Kiribati and Tuvalu.

In 1901, when Australia became a nation of federated states, the new parliament, supporting a racist doctrine that became known as the White Australia Policy, passed legislation to restrict non-European immigration. The government repatriated indentured laborers, but permitted those who had married local people, or could prove long-term residence, to stay. Their descendants are part of Australian multicultural communities living in the northeast. No research has been undertaken on their contemporary musical activities, nor is information readily available on the music and dance of the former indentured laborers in Australia.

### In Torres Strait

In the 1860s, Pacific Islanders worked in the strait as divers and crewmen, in pearling and collecting *bêche de mer.* Some of them were from Sāmoa, Niue, Rotuma, and the Loyalty Islands; others were Ni-Vanuatu and Solomon Islanders (Beckett 1987:36). From 1871, pastors from the London Missionary Society (LMS) converted the Torres Strait Islanders to Christianity. These missionaries—from the Loyalty Islands (mainly Lifu and Mare) and the Cook Islands (Aitutaki, Rarotonga, Manihiki)—were followed by missionaries from Niue and Sāmoa.

By 1900, the transformation of Erub (Darnley Island) and Ugar (Stephens Island) into Pacific Islander settlements was well under way. In 1908, an Anglican mission was established at Moa island, especially for Pacific Islanders permitted to stay in Australia after 1904. In 1915, the LMS ceded its churches in Torres Strait to the Anglican Church. By the 1990s, most Torres Strait Islanders could claim Pacific Islander descent. Thus, over a period of at least 130 years, Pacific Islanders' influence in Australia was strongest in the strait.

#### Musical influences in Torres Strait

The Pacific Islanders who visited or settled in Torres Strait brought musical traditions, influences of which remain in late-twentieth-century secular music and dance, such as *taibobo* and sit-down dances, the former an adaptation of songs and dances from Rotuma, and the latter based on Sāmoan dances. Pacific Islander missionaries introduced hymnsinging to the peoples of the strait. These hymns, with texts in the vernacular, are structurally comparable to the *hīmene* of the Society Islands and Cook Islands, "though simpler and less exuberant" (Beckett 1981:2):

> Its basic features are a two-part harmony, with the two parts moving independently, sometimes in antiphon, sometimes overlapping. . . . This style is in regular use in the Anglican churches of Torres Strait, usually accompanied by a drum.

In the 1800s, missionaries discouraged the performance of indigenous dances associated with former religious practices, and encouraged people to replace them with dances from the Pacific Islands (Haddon 1912:290). Many songs accompanying such dances retain texts in Pacific Islander languages, yet Torres Strait Islanders do not usually know the meanings of these texts.

In the early 1900s, Torres Strait Islanders developed a performative genre termed, in Eastern and Western language respectively, *segur kab wed* 'play-dance-song' and *kasa girer* 'gammon-dance' (Beckett 1981:3; Mabo 1984:34). This genre, known as island dance, incorporated music and movements introduced from the Pacific Islands. It is the most popular genre danced by Torres Strait Islanders throughout the strait (Beckett 1987:56). It spread north to Papua and south to Cape York Peninsula, where Torres Strait Islanders introduced it to Australian Aborigines. It has since spread to other parts of north Australia, such as the Roper River, Northern Territory (Black and Koch 1983:159), and to mainland areas where Torres Strait Islanders reside.

Some festivals and ceremonies in the strait show influence from Pacific Islanders. At least two—the tombstone-opening ceremony and the Mei—probably originated in Polynesia. The former marks the end of mourning a relative's death: while people sing Christian hymns, the headstone of the grave is unveiled; then the people feast and dance. The latter ceremony, incorporating public performances of music and dance, has roots in the LMS mission, which introduced the Mei as a competitive gift-giving activity, for giving gifts, with the church being the main beneficiary (Beckett 1987:42).

To meet local needs, Torres Strait Islanders have transformed or adapted such events. The instrumental accompaniment for some dances—provided by a length of bamboo, a rolled mat, or a kerosene tin (each beaten with two sticks), and later by guitars and ukuleles—derives from Pacific Islander usage, as does men's wearing cotton kilts while performing island dances.

### Migrants, mid-1970s to 1990s

In the mid-1970s, the Australian government adopted a nondiscriminatory immigration policy, removing all reference to racial restrictions. From that time, the greatest numbers of Pacific Islanders migrated to Australia. Some twenty-seven thousand Aotearoa Māori reside in Australia; about seven thousand are Australian-born (Lowe 1993:62–63). Many Papua New Guineans and Fijians live in Australia, as do some Solomon Islanders, Ni-Vanuatu, and New Caledonians. Almost one-fifth of immigrant Pacific Islanders are island-born Polynesians (mainly from Tonga, Sāmoa, the Cook Islands, Tuvalu, Niue, Tokelau, and the Society Islands); a minority are Micronesian (mainly from Nauru and Kiribati). Most reside in eastern Australia (in New South Wales, Queensland, and Victoria), with fewer numbers in other territories and states.

For Constitution Day, Cook Islanders hold competitions of music and dance. Groups compete as representatives of their cities of residence in Australia, rather than as representatives of any specific island or village.

*Alliances and associations*

Some Pacific Islanders have set up specialized centers of the arts, like the Samoan Centre for Arts and Culture, in Queensland. In larger cities, they attend their own church services, where they sing hymns in their native languages. Church groups are foci for social gatherings where people sing and dance.

In Sydney, most Pacific Islander groups have representatives on the Pacific Island Council, an umbrella organization, established to identify and represent Pacific Islanders' developing needs. Immigrants in the larger cities organize themselves into formal associations, according to their cultural background and birthplace. Some examples in the Sydney metropolitan area are the Tubati Association (formed by people from Tuvalu, Kiribati, and Nauru), a Tokelau Association, a Samoan Advisory Council, a Fijian Association, and a Tongan Association. Cook Islanders do not usually form associations in the cities, but belong to their own clubs and churches. In Sydney, these clubs are separate and independent of each other (Aloisio 1986:5). Because of long colonial, social, and economic ties with Papua New Guinea, numerous Papua New Guinean associations exist in northern and eastern Australia.

Where Pacific Islanders are more scattered or their populations are small, people of different archipelagoes sometimes form alliances. In this way, specific cultures may be subsumed under a generic Polynesian category to form a Polynesian performing-arts group. Such groups usually give public presentations for payment at international hotels, tourist resorts, and private venues. They present songs and dances of various Polynesian cultures. An example of this kind of group is the Polynesian Dance Theatre Group, of north Queensland; within a single presentation, it may perform items from Sāmoa, the Cook Islands, Hawai'i, and Tahiti.

*National days and festivals*

National-day celebrations are important to all Pacific Islander communities. Cook Islanders celebrate Constitution Day (commemorating self-government for the Cook Islands, in August 1965). In eastern Australia, they celebrate it during the Easter vacation, allowing time for people to travel between cities. They hold competitions of music and dance, using formats similar to those in the home islands, but groups compete with each other as representatives of their cities of residence in Australia, rather than as representatives of any specific island or village (figure 8). Favoring a generic culture, they ignore differences among the Cook Islands. For accompanying dances, they import musical instruments, such as drums, but they usually make costumes from substitute materials.

In Sydney, the Tubati Association celebrates Kiribati independence in July and Tuvalu independence in October (Aloisio 1986:3). Groups from Papua New Guinea celebrate the anniversary of their independence with performances of music and dance. In Townsville, which supports a high proportion of people (expatriate and indigenous) with a keen interest in Papua New Guinea, the performance occurs in

FIGURE 8 A mixed Cook Islander group in Australia competes in the celebration of Constitution Day, Springvale Community Hall. Melbourne. Photo by Helen Reeves Lawrence, 1988.

public, usually in the downtown mall. Other groups, such as Cook Islanders living in larger cities, hold celebrations indoors; musical performances are more specifically for the islanders themselves, plus invited guests. Family-based gatherings and other celebrations, such as nuptial receptions, provide appropriate occasions for singing and dancing. Pacific Islanders sometimes videotape such events for distribution to kinfolk abroad. For Australian national holidays, dances, and multicultural festivals, the organizers may invite Pacific Islanders to perform. These events usually encourage displays of handicrafts and the maintenance of food-selling stalls.

In Australian educational institutions that enroll overseas students, international organizations of students often arrange concerts and other events in which islander students sing and dance. In larger cities, community radio stations broadcast islander music; mainstream networks may broadcast larger public festivals, and national television may show selected performances.

*Funding for the performing arts*

Through clubs and formal associations, immigrant Pacific Islanders are eligible to apply as groups for funding from governmental organizations. The Ethnic Affairs Commission of New South Wales (1993:50) reported that between 1990 and 1993, it had granted A$6,050 to such groups in New South Wales, in amounts ranging from A$200 to A$1,000. These funds supported the purchase of costumes and musical instruments. These amounts were a small proportion of the total awarded to musicians and dancers in New South Wales.

Many Pacific Islanders, unaware that grants are available to them through governmental agencies, are not placing applications with these agencies. But support for artists of non-English-speaking backgrounds is "often refused on the basis that their art is supposedly traditional (that is[,] bound to the customs of a specific ethnic group) rather than of universal validity (that is[,] relevant for the whole of our culture and society)" (Castles and Kalantzis 1994:34). The question of access and equity in funding the arts is part of an ongoing debate in Australia, but Pacific Islanders seem particularly disadvantaged. The federal government's national policy on the arts, announced in October 1994, focused on multimedia technology, national-arts institutions, and individual fellowships for established artists; it also promoted arts-industry exports. Its implementation was likely further to marginalize minority Pacific Islanders, for whom such technologies, fellowships, and exports have little relevance.

—HELEN REEVES LAWRENCE

## PAPUA NEW GUINEA

Probably as long as human beings have lived in New Guinea, people have traded and learned music and dance from their neighbors. Such trading and learning continues in many areas of the country, and groups on border areas have long-standing relations with peoples of Indonesia, Australia, and the Solomon Islands. Music brought into Papua New Guinea from outside has resulted from extended contact with outsiders, initially in the form of missionaries and governmental officers. During earlier contacts (with explorers, whalers, sailors), exchanges of songs and instruments occurred; but such associations were usually brief, and had only short-term effects on local music (Webb and Niles 1987).

### Christian music

From about 1870 to about 1900, European powers subdivided the area politically, and Christian missions culturally invaded it. By 1900, the London Missionary Society (beginning work in 1871), Methodists (1875), Roman Catholics (1881), Lutherans (1886), and Anglicans (1891) had set up extensive networks, and in 1908 Seventh-Day Adventists began their work. Most missionaries entering the area were European or Australian, but some missions employed teachers and other workers from other parts of the Pacific, especially Polynesia, where the new religion was secure.

Different missions dealt with indigenous music and dance in different ways. Some banned it, fighting it by exposing secret paraphernalia; others added Christian texts to indigenous melodies. Hymnals in local languages began appearing in 1877, with texts usually sung to Western melodies. Roman Catholic missionaries taught Gregorian chant until the Second Vatican Council (1963–1965) permitted other styles.

Missionaries who banned indigenous music or dance recognized that replacements were necessary. Around Port Moresby, probably in the first decades of the twentieth century, Cook Islanders and other Polynesians associated with the London Missionary Society introduced a style of singing now known as *peroveta anedia* 'prophet songs'. The melodic lines, rhythms, harmonies, textures, and originally even the language derived from Polynesia. Quickly, *peroveta* spread up and down the coast, reaching other areas influenced by the London Missionary Society.

Lutherans became particularly interested in using indigenous melodies for hymns; after 1910, their hymnals in Morobe and Madang began to reflect their interest. After the mid-1960s, Anglicans in Northern Province and Roman Catholics in the Mamose and Island regions began using indigenous melodies for hymns. In contrast to the Lutherans and in common with the United Church (formerly, the London Missionary Society and Methodists), their hymns remain exogenously based. Workers of the Summer Institute of Linguistics, following the lead of Vida Chenoweth in her work among the Usarufa (Eastern Highlands Province, first outlined in Chenoweth 1972), composed hymns in indigenous styles.

In schools by 1901, children were learning Western songs in English, and occasionally in sol-fa and numeral notation. In the first few decades of the twentieth century, visitors sometimes brought phonographs to play recordings of Western popular and classical music; sometimes they recorded local music. In Port Moresby, the first cinema opened in 1914, with piano accompaniment to films; the first talking movies reached the country in 1933 (Stuart 1973).

Missions often formed choirs. In the Rabaul area, choral performance became an essential part of worship. In the 1930s, the London Missionary Society formed the Poreporena Choir, which still performs. Originally, most of its performances were of hymns in English, with only a couple in Motu; but probably by the 1940s, they were singing most of their hymns in Motu, often written by Motu composers. Later, in the 1950s, school choirs became common.

## Bands

Other ensembles began around the same time, or a bit later. From 1925 to 1927, the Lutheran missionary Heinrich Zahn formed a conch band (Gee 1991:135–179); since each shell produced one tone, as many shells were needed as tones in a melody. Zahn arranged Jabêm (a language of Morobe Province), English, and German hymns in four parts, published numeral notation for them (Zahn 1959), and made cylinder recordings of his band. He acquired brass instruments in 1927 and experimented with combining the two ensembles. In 1932, he returned to Neuendettelsau (Germany), where a conch band for girls was established.

About 1937, in Rabaul, Inspector David Crawley set up the Papua New Guinea Constabulary Band. In 1943, the band moved to Port Moresby, where it remains. Now known as the Royal Papua New Guinea Constabulary Band, it has received awards, and has repeatedly toured abroad.

The Kila Police Youth Band was formed in 1989–1990. Initially under the direction of the director of music of the police band, it consists mostly of unemployed youths in the Kilakila area of the capital; they know basic techniques of drumming and formations for marching. In early 1993, youths of Kerowagi (Chimbu Province) started a band in their home area.

In 1952, the Pacific Islands Regiment Pipes and Drums Band came into existence. It later split in two: one band in Port Moresby, one in Wewak. In the late 1960s, another pipe-and-drum band was formed, as part of the Corrective Institutions Services (later the Department of Correctional Services), responsible for prisons and prisoners. All three bands perform on the official occasions of their sponsoring force: during passing-out ceremonies, funerals, parades, and at other official functions.

## Popular performance

An important musical development occurred when songs began to be accompanied by guitar-based ensembles, often with the addition of ukuleles. These instruments were available before the 1940s, but only after 1945 did they became widespread. By the 1990s, some bands were using portable loudspeakers (figure 9).

FIGURE 9   Surrounded by onlookers, a Porgera string band (of Enga Province, Papua New Guinea) performs; a portable loudspeaker amplifies the sounds of the guitar on the left. Photo by Don Niles, 1991.

The bamboo band consists of a string band with the addition of tuned lengths of bamboo, whose open ends players strike with a rubber thong in patterns evoking a boogie-woogie bass.

In Central Province, singing reflected the influence of *peroveta*. Local styles began to develop, and styles such as Central, Tolai, Manus, New Ireland, Buka, Sepik, Highlands, Gulf, and Oro, are obvious to many listeners, whose criteria for differentiating them include guitar-playing methods, vocal harmonization, melodic contour, lead-guitar line, instrumentation, form, linguistic details, and so on. In addition to such distinctive features, much popular music uses only tonic, dominant, and subdominant chords. Formerly, the tuning of guitars and ukuleles varied from standard Western norms; tunings had such names as *Sunset, Five-Key, Sāmoan, D-Key,* and so on. By the 1990s, the use of nonstandard tunings had become less frequent.

A variant is the bamboo band, most often identified with Madang. It consists of a string band with the addition of tuned lengths of bamboo, whose open ends players strike with a rubber thong in patterns evoking a boogie-woogie bass. A further variant of the bamboo band occurs in North Solomons Province, where panpipes join the ensemble, and guitars disappear or play a smaller role.

In language, instrumentation, and locale, acoustic string bands contrast with electrically amplified bands, variously called electric bands, power bands (*pawa ben*) and live bands (*laiv ben*). String bands often sing original compositions in local languages and are associated with villages. In contrast, power bands often sing in English, add bass guitars and drums, and are associated with towns. Their rise began in 1962, when drinking was legalized for nationals, and mixed-race bands began playing in hotels and taverns. By the 1980s, with the greater availability of electric instruments, such contrasts were less valid. In some villages close to towns, power bands have usurped the position of string bands, and sing in local languages.

String bands and power bands remain popular. A thriving, highly competitive, local cassette-recording industry supports them. Since most bands sing in local languages, few can become popular outside the areas where their language is spoken. Successful exceptions are bands like Helgas and Paramana Strangers (both of Central Province), and Barike and Painim Wok (both of East New Britain). Some bands have tried to overcome linguistic barriers by including songs in Tok Pisin, Hiri Motu, and English. Shortly after Papua New Guinea gained independence, the focus for popular music was Central Province, which supported many bands and studios; but the mid-1980s saw a shift to Rabaul, because the studios there competitively promoted bands. In September 1994, volcanic eruptions in the Rabaul area devastated studios there.

Several bands have tried to incorporate into popular music some elements of indigenous music. Most of these bands, especially Sanguma, Tumbuna, and Tambaran Culture, have resulted from experimental work done at the National Arts School, now the Faculty of Creative Arts of the University of Papua New Guinea. Other bands have explored these lines in subtler ways, and the music of many bands reveals indirect influences from indigenous music. In the 1980s, gospel bands became important; these ensembles are a string band or a power band, but their songs, usually in English, are often covers of overseas religious songs, associated with fundamentalist or charismatic Christian movements.

In towns, hotels sometimes sponsor discos, in which young men and women, having paid an entry fee, dance to recorded rock, mostly from abroad. Some villages, borrowing the idea, fence off an area, where they sponsor dancing to the playing of cassettes or the music of a live band. Such parties are frequently called six-to-six parties, since they supposedly last from 6:00 P.M. to 6:00 A.M.

### Electronic media

Radio is an important carrier of exogenous music. Local broadcasting occurred sporadically in the 1930s and 1940s, and has continued regularly with the establishment of Papua New Guinea Services of the Australian Broadcasting Commission after 1945 (Mackay 1976). The National Broadcasting Commission, founded in 1973, maintains three services: Kundu (national, on medium- and shortwave frequencies), Karai (provincial, shortwave), and Kalang (national, FM, commercial). In addition to playing exogenous music, these services feature local indigenous and popular music; from station to station, the airtime percentage of each varies widely. Radio continues to be the main disseminator of information and all kinds of music.

In 1987, two commercial stations of broadcast television appeared. In 1989, the program "Mekim Musik" debuted on EMTV, the sole surviving station. This program played music videos continually. In 1990, it showed the first locally made Papua New Guinean music video, "Kame," by Pius Wasi and Jefferson Chalson. Since then, it—and in 1993, another program, "Fizz," devoted entirely to local music videos—promoted such videos, and in towns helped increase their sales.

—Don Niles

## THE MORTLOCKESE *TOKIA* IN SAIPAN, NORTHERN MARIANAS

Population movements in Micronesia have included Mortlockese of Chuuk State, Federated States of Micronesia, who have moved to Saipan, Northern Marianas. They took with them a series of stick dances (*tokia*), which in their new home they have maintained, though modified to suit the circumstances of a changed social environment.

In the Mortlockese homeland, *tokia* was a martial art, in which men used staffs for exercises to sharpen their alertness and agility. They needed this training for fitness in fighting with clubs in interinsular battles. *Tokia* had texts that refer to spirits, who in seers' dream-trances inspired the dances, and whom performances honor. The texts also contain terms for positions and movements. *Tokia* originated in several islands in Chuuk: Kuttu, Etal, and Nama (in the Lower and Upper Mortlocks), and Feffan and Udot (in Chuuk Lagoon). Through marriage, emigration, and public school activities, these dances spread.

German ethnologists (Bollig 1927; Girschner 1913; Krämer 1932; Kubary 1889–1895) described performances and their movement motifs. Named motifs included striking the ground with the staffs and making a shout, crossing paired staffs low, and then crossing paired staffs high.

### Performance

A series of dances or sections of dances progresses from easy to difficult, slow to fast, and sitting to squatting to standing. In this, it takes performers from a kind of warm-up into increasingly vigorous sessions of aerobic movements. A group consists of an odd number of performers: a caller and two lines of men, of any number divisible by four. Each man carries a carved and decorated hardwood staff. Typically, two lines of men walk into the dancing area. If a chief is present, both lines face him; if not, the lines face each other. The dancers sit cross-legged on the ground. The caller chooses one dancer to come to the front, engaging him in a mock demonstration of martial arts, calling out the movements as they proceed. The demonstration is supposedly to show both performers in their best light, but the leader can use this moment as a chance to shame his opponent by not calling out the attacking movements; the opponent cannot then anticipate the correct defense, and may be knocked down. After the demonstration, the chosen dancer, with torso and head bowed, respectfully walks back to his place.

The company then performs the first dance (*binemot* 'strike while seated'), sitting cross-legged. Performers strike each others' staffs and the ground. The second dance is performed squatting. The featured movement is *sorab* 'twisting'. The performers hold the staff with both hands, about 4 decimeters apart, right over left. By bringing the right arm downward toward the body and the left hand up and then reversing, the performers make the staff appear to twist. A series of dances, the number depending on how many dances can be performed in the time allotted, follows. The performers stand in squares of four, each man striking adjacent and opposite dancers' staffs. At the end of the series, the performers simply walk away from the dance space.

### *Tokia* in the present

Since fighting with clubs and spears belongs to a distant past, these dances are now performed as entertainment for feasts and nontraditional social events. The concept of *tokia* was introduced into Saipan in 1961 by Rokucho Billy, originally from Kuttu. He formed a troupe of young men, aged twelve to twenty-one, who called themselves the Agharubw Dancers, honoring a great navigator, who, about 1810, had led the first voyage of permanent residents from Satawal, Yap, to Saipan.

The dancers perform *tokia* for social occasions sponsored by or associated with the Roman Catholic Church, including feasts honoring patron saints, governmental entertainments for official visitors, local fairs and celebrations, and hotel dinnertime shows for tourists. The troupe represented the Northern Marianas at the 1980 Pacific Festival of Arts.

At each occasion, the dancers perform about fifteen *tokia,* their number depending on the time allotted, the facilities available, the audience, and the tone of the occasion. Often they perform only the standing dances. Since the 1970s, girls have participated in the troupe. Though the performance gains glamour and youthful exuberance from presence of teenage girls and boys, it loses the robustness and virility of older men. But Rokucho Billy formed the Agharubw Dancers because he wanted to connect young people with their cultural heritage, instill a sense of pride in it, provide young people with a positive way to use their free time, and create opportunities for them to make money by dancing in touristic venues. In Chuuk and Saipan, noncommercial performances occur several times a year under the evaluating eyes of Chuukese and Carolinian elders. These performances validate a revived sense of cultural pride, inspiring a new interest in the people's past.

—ADRIENNE L. KAEPPLER, based on a 1981 manuscript
by ROKUCHO BILLY and KIM BAILEY

## INDIANS IN FIJI

In Fiji live about 350,000 descendants of indentured immigrants who arrived from India mostly between 1879 and 1919. About two-thirds of the immigrants left through Calcutta, coming primarily from the Gangetic plain; others, mostly Tamil- and Telugu-speakers, departed from Madras; a few were Gujerati merchants and Sikhs. About 11 percent of the present-day community are Muslims, and some are Christians, but most are Hindus. Fiji Hindi, a cluster of linguistic varieties most closely related to Bhojpuri (of eastern Uttar Pradesh), is the most widely spoken and sung language in the community.

Exceptionally complex, the Fiji Indian musical world, though based on genres and instruments brought from India, includes new styles and genres from South Asia, introduced by visiting pandits and Muslim teachers, through printed song-books, Hindi films, and recordings; Western popular musics; and distinctively Fiji Indian kinds of performance, representing local transformations of these sources.

Some old genres, especially those associated with local subcastes (*jati*), have disappeared or are known by only a few singers, but music—live and, since the rise of a national cassette industry and increased local programming on Radio Fiji, on recordings—has consistently been a focus of entertainment, devotion, social life, and identity. Fiji Indian musical styles have distinctive forms and flavors, influenced by their South Asian antecedents but shaped by local interests, resources, and aesthetics (Brenneis 1983, 1985, 1987, 1991; Brenneis and Padarath 1975).

## Musical contexts and genres

The most common ensemble is a trio: harmonium; *dhol,* midsize double-headed drum; and *bottil,* a pair of upright, empty, one-liter Fiji Bitter bottles, struck rhythmically on the neck with a pair of heavy nails, or *majira,* finger-held cymbals. Singers usually play harmonium. Performing secular music and devotional pieces, these ensembles figure centrally at Hindu and Muslim gatherings, weddings, and informal social evenings at home.

Most rural Fijian Indian music is song (*git*). The most commonly performed genre is *bhajan kavvali,* a style of Hindu devotional singing associated with *kavvali* (or *qawwali*), a Muslim style. *Bhajan kavvali* consist of couplets, repeated whole or in part, with alternating slow and fast passages. Slow passages are usually sung solo; faster passages, often multiple repetitions of the same couplet, add drum and bottles, and often a harmonium, doubling the melody.

The melodic form of slow passages is usually a descending terrace, the lowest pitches being sung in the middle of the line. The slower lines often invert the terrace: the singer's voice rises to the highest tone, and then descends. Since melodies stay toward the top of singers' ranges, this pattern combines slow speed with considerable vocal tension, giving such passages what villagers interpret as a sense of stress and intensity. In contrast to the usually antiphonal and choral form of South Asian *qawwali,* and of antecedent Hindu forms (like *harikirtan*), *bhajan kavvali* is a solo style, as are related secular genres, including *Fiji kavvali,* narrative songs about historic or current events.

A second common genre, in this instance linked with the ritual calendar, is *cautal* or *faag,* named for the Hindu month when it is performed. A critical part of the Hindu festival of Holi, pieces in this genre stimulate in Fiji a sense of fun and hilarity. The songs are performed by a group of ten to twelve musicians, usually village men and boys, who go from household to household singing and being fed tea and sweets. Villagers call *cautal* an archaic form. Two lines of four to six men, each line facing the other, sing responsorially. Several men on either side play *jhajh,* 10-centimeter-diameter brass cymbals. A *dhol* player sits at one end of the lines; at the other end, one person shakes a sistrum (*jhika*).

One singer begins a couplet, joined briefly by a drummed flourish at the end of

Fiji Indian women's most frequent public performances occur at Hindu weddings. Songs for the various stages in the ceremony—anointing with oil and insulting the groom's party—are still common.

the first line, and by the drum and the other singers on his own side at the couplet's end. The initial side may repeat the same couplet several times, at increasing speed. The opposing side then joins in, overlapping with the end of the first singers' couplets. Instrumentalists play throughout, initially striking the same duple pulses as the singers, but shifting to a triple rhythm against the singers' continuing duple as the repetition of each particular couplet comes to an end. A new couplet is then declaimed, and the pattern repeats.

*Cautal* heard between 1970 and 1984 ranged from four to sixteen couplets in length. The melodic range is restricted when compared to that of *bhajan kavvali*; it usually stays within a fifth. The melody for each line of a couplet descends, though with frequent short midline rises. In contrast to *bhajan kavvali, cautal* are loud, multivoiced, and heard by their audiences as exceptionally exciting and festive. The moral didacticism of texts central to *bhajan* is unimportant for these songs, even when the texts are borrowed from *bhajan*.

The basic harmonium ensemble is often supplemented by Western instruments (especially a clarinet), and by other Indian percussive instruments, especially the *danda tal,* an iron bar, struck rhythmically with an iron rod. Other instruments are used with particular genres of devotional singing. Tambourines (*kajali*) are played with *dhol* in an antiphonal style associated with readings of the *Ramayana,* a sacred text.

For one variety of song, a soloist sings a *tambura bhajan* while accompanying himself on a two-stringed drone (*tambura*), plucked with the left hand, and small paired sistrums, shaken with the right. The *hudka,* an hourglass drum whose pitch is controlled by pulling or releasing the lacings around the head, is now primarily a curiosity, but was historically associated with specific lower castes in India. Similarly, the *mridang,* a large, double-headed drum brought to Fiji by members of the low-status Chamar subcaste, was initially used in caste-specific devotional and ritual settings, and now is occasionally played for secular performances, but not for religious music.

Some women have become known for singing *bhajan kavvali,* but women's most frequent public performances occur at Hindu weddings, whose events last several days. Songs for nuptial stages—anointing with oil (*telwan*), insulting the groom's party on its arrival at the bride's homestead (*galiya*) and on the day of the wedding—are still common, though women known to be specialists are often invited to help out. *Galiya* also figure in male singing at weddings and challenge-song sessions, in which two solo singers, each accompanied by harmonium, *dhol,* and bottles, question, challenge, and abuse each other. Such insults should be borne with good grace, though fights occasionally break out. In addition to older genres, film songs (*filmi git*) are exceptionally popular. As with earlier imports, they have provided a range of stylistic resources and inspiration for Fiji Indian singers.

—DONALD BRENNEIS

## HAWAI'I

In addition to music of the Hawaiian people, the State of Hawai'i conserves a wide range of music from abroad. Reflecting the local cultural mix, music serves as a major cultural marker. This discussion provides a synchronic overview, first of the setting, and then of selected cultures. It follows the Hawaiian practice of referencing people by their or their ancestors' homeland, thus *Chinese* rather than *Chinese-American* or *American-born Chinese* or *Asian-American*. It provisionally accepts the Western separation of music from dance—a concept antithetical to most indigenous perspectives from Asia and Oceania.

In Hawai'i, traditional musics reflect different relationships to their diasporic setting. Their diversity attests to the dynamism of cultural pluralism. Some traditions are public and accessible to all. The Japanese O-Bon (honoring departed souls) is a major outdoor event, accompanied by song and percussion. The O-Bon season lasts all summer; each weekend, a different Buddhist temple hosts the observance. Many non-Japanese attend and participate. Other music is more in-group: Santa Lucia Day (13 December) is observed primarily by the Scandinavian community, replete with Swedish songs and a crown of candles. Most non-Scandinavians are unaware of it.

A tradition may appropriate elements from the host culture or from another immigrant one. Filipino string bands often include a Hawaiian *'ukulele* or an American banjo. Other traditions are maintained by interested individuals. The Celtic Pipes and Drums of Hawai'i is a multicultural group active on O'ahu. It performs as part of every Kamehameha Day parade, honoring the monarch who first united the islands. Many of its members come from outside the Scottish community. A local ensemble for performing Japanese court music (*gagaku*) is a similar case: half its members are non-Japanese, and it is supported by the University of Hawai'i (figure 10). At official events, including the consular celebration of the emperor's birthday, it performs as a representative of Japanese culture.

In Hawai'i, music chosen as a cultural icon contrasts with music iconic on the mainland U.S., or even in the present homeland. The resident Puerto Rican community prefers the *jíbaro*, a genre of the Puerto Rican uplands, despite the prominence of salsa among Puerto Ricans on the mainland. Asian and European musical traditions in Hawai'i benefit from frequent contact with, and revitalization from, the homeland. Geographical distances from the mainland U.S. and homeland cultures do not isolate Hawai'i; rather, they provide a buffer that partially insulates the islands from the cultural pressures of dominant mainstream American, Asian, and European

FIGURE 10   In Japan, the Honolulu-based ensemble Hawai'i Gagaku Kenkyukai rehearses for a performance, 1972. Courtesy of the Rev. Masatoshi Shamoto.

FIGURE 11    In Honolulu, Yoshinae Majikina and Yoshino Majikina perform *Temizu No Yen,* an Okinawan dance, 1959. Courtesy of Yoshino Majikina.

homelands. Chinese music clubs are invigorated by visiting or emigrating artists or teachers from mainland China, Taiwan, or Hong Kong, and local Okinawan musicians and dancers travel to Okinawa for study or competition.

### Foregrounded traditions

The rhetoric of cultural pluralism and local identity foregrounds certain Asian and European cultures and their music. All of them are part of the multinational labor force recruited during the plantation era, 150 years of economic domination by sugar and pineapple agribusiness, now drawing to a close. The significant years of migration extend from 1852 until 1930, though actual immigration of these and other groups began earlier and continues.

In rough chronological order, the foregrounded cultures include Chinese, Japanese, Portuguese, Okinawan (figure 11), Puerto Rican, Korean, and Filipino. Each of these is recognized as a major stream and has contributed to the construction of local culture. A brief description of each illuminates the diversity of experience. European cultures not foregrounded in the island mix—including Germans, Norwegians, and Swiss—were management, rather than labor, within the plantation hierarchy.

#### *Chinese*

Chinese merchants were present in Hawai'i before the influx of laborers in 1852; musical customs, especially from southern China, are of long standing. The lion dance is the most widely recognized and practiced cultural icon. Its accompaniment includes a large barrel drum (usually mounted on a platform with wheels), a tam-tam, and cymbals. Performers are adolescent and young adult members of Chinese physical-culture or martial-arts organizations. The percussion, the din of exploding firecrackers, and noise of observers' conversation produce an exciting ambience. Leaders emphasize that the dance is a ritual, an aspect of training that includes music, martial arts, and ethics, though in nontraditional settings, including shopping centers and multicultural festivals, it functions as entertainment.

Amateur music clubs are by nature less public and more insular. Part of a benevolent or family-based society, they use Chinese language, either Cantonese or

Mandarin. A club specializes in a specific musical genre, such as Cantonese or Peking opera, or traditional music. Instruments, including *pipa, hu chin, di, yangchin,* and *sanhsien,* are brought from China, Hong Kong, or San Francisco. The clubs play principally for their own enjoyment. Sometimes a club or an individual musician appears in a multicultural festival or program.

Religious music includes Buddhist, Daoist, and Protestant Christian traditions. Only heard within the community, the ceremonial and ritual musics are predominately vocal, accompanied by percussion for the first two and piano or organ for the third. Christian congregations are subdivided according to Cantonese or Mandarin language and further by their origins (Hong Kong, mainland China, Taiwan), with concomitant contrasts in musical pieces and practices.

### Japanese

This group represents the largest Asian presence in Hawai'i. Musical activity has a high, professional profile, and is in regular contact with the homeland. O-Bon exemplifies this activity. Though five prefectural styles once existed, only two are locally extant: that from Fukushima and the Iwakuni style (from Yamaguchi Prefecture). The Fukushima style features a group of singers, a caller, and percussionists in the *yagura,* a tower 4.5 meters high. The music is sprightly, with texts sung to the accompaniment of a barrel drum, several small lashed drums, a bamboo flute, and a bell. In the Iwakuni style, a single singer in the *yagura* delivers an elaborate melody in a deliberate tempo, holding an umbrella, the signature of this style. The caller provides shouts of encouragement. A large barrel drum is located at the base of the tower, the drummers forming a circle before it. Each drummer approaches the drum with dancelike movements, plays a single phrase, and continues around the circle. The two ensembles alternate with each other and with recorded music.

Younger Japanese have begun participating in O-Bon, reversing a feared decline. Their interest parallels the popularity of *taiko* drumming, a genre popular in the homeland and the American diaspora. Drumming ensembles are on different islands, and Kenny Endo, a world-class performer, currently teaches in Hawai'i.

Professional teachers and performers of *koto, shakuhachi, shamisen* (with song), *shigin,* and *minyo* have been in Hawai'i a long time. Several local artists have binational careers, appearing regularly in concert or at major theaters in Japan. Non-Japanese musicians, too, are trained in Japanese music at the University of Hawai'i, and privately in Hawai'i or in Japan. The most active *shakuhachi* teacher and performer is a Caucasian of German heritage, trained in Hawai'i by a master of Chinese-Irish background.

Contact with the homeland includes regular visits by leading artists from Japan, who often combine a concert with vacation in Hawai'i. One tour company annually transports an entire O-Bon festival from Japan to Waikīkī. It includes hundreds of dancers, famous *minyo* singers and outstanding *taiko*-drumming ensembles. The local community is exposed to some of the finest artists of Japan, who in turn take pleasure in performing for a knowledgeable foreign audience.

### Portuguese

Immigration began in the 1800s, principally from Madeira and the Azores. Thus, Portuguese music in Hawai'i has few connections with continental Portugal. It is more remembered than practiced. The principal activity is concerted preservation and revival.

The most public Portuguese event in Hawai'i is religious, the Feast of the Holy Ghost, brought from the Azores. It is associated with the Roman Catholic observance of Pentecost, though not always on that Sunday. The religious procession is accompa-

Karaoke is making inroads into live Okinawan music in Hawai'i. Another popular tradition is *eisa*. Performers dance while playing hand-held drums and executing drills.

nied by Portuguese hymns. Subsequent festivities include songs and dances that connect the present English-speaking generation to its past. The procession is a popular event for the general Hawai'i population.

The remembered past frequently invokes nineteenth-century contributions to Hawaiian music—the *braguinha,* which developed into the *'ukulele,* and the Portuguese who crafted fine instruments. Old people remember a more recent past. The years just after World War II saw folk-styled, string band–accompanied dancing and concerts of emotional songs (*fados*) in public parks. Music was a vibrant part of the community. Every party or celebration included a session of sung debates (*desafio*). The lyrics had to be clever, improvised, and laced with double entendres. In a community with declining competence in Portuguese, the challenge of developing audiences and new performers among younger people is almost impossible.

A major ensemble is the Camoes Players of Maui, modeled after a plucked-string and accordion band of Madeira. It uses *'ukulele,* guitars, a string bass, and an electric keyboard. It accompanies singing and dancing throughout the state, often in collaboration with folkloric dancers. It collects and documents pieces brought during the early migration, and includes them in cultural presentations made to public schools and the general community. Its contacts with the homeland have been sporadic. In the 1980s and 1990s, it has focused on continental Portugal, rather than the islands of origin. No Portuguese music or dance is taught at the University of Hawai'i.

### Okinawan

The first workers from the Ryukyus came in 1900, some eighteen years after Japanese migration began. Though historically and presently ruled by Japan, Okinawans describe themselves as culturally distinctive. In the homeland, they constitute a minority culture; in Hawai'i, they are a foregrounded group of the island mix. Musicians in Hawai'i provide leadership for homeland and overseas populations.

Classical Okinawan music (*koten*) references the Shuri court of the 1400s–1500s, a golden age of local sovereignty. The primary performer is a singer self-accompanied on *sanshin,* a three-stringed lute. The vocal and instrumental lines are related. Highly elaborate, in a steady tempo, the vocal melody requires a specific timbre. The expanded ensemble for formal performance includes a zither, a side-blown flute, and drums. Regular musical gatherings become social occasions.

Public concerts of music and dance attract the general community. Seisho "Harry" Nakasone, a leading master and overall head (*iemoto*) of one of the schools, resides in Hawai'i; he travels frequently to Okinawa and to the mainland U.S. for teaching and consulting. He received a National Heritage Fellowship in 1991. Many young people are active in the tradition; they often win the music competitions in Okinawa. The zither (*kutu*) has developed solo pieces and grown in popularity.

Folk songs (*minyo*) are another major tradition of *sanshin*-accompanied song. The vocal line is less elaborate, the vocal production less demanding, and the tempo livelier. The texture includes whistles, calls, and rhythms of a bamboo castanet (*sanba*). *Minyo* often appear on programs of music and dance, but are equally at home in Okinawan bars, where song, *shamisen, sanba,* and *sake* combine to create an ambience distinct from that of concert stages.

Karaoke is making inroads into live Okinawan music. Another popular tradition is *eisa,* a massed music-and-dance genre. Performers dance while playing hand-held drums and executing drills. All the arts benefit from the Hawai'i Okinawa Center, which has encouraged and enhanced musical and cultural conservation.

### Puerto Rican

This group, which arrived around 1900, constitutes one of the smaller communities, but the popularity of its dance-music has pervaded general social life. Resident Puerto Ricans retain an older style with historic values; that choice distances them from the other Puerto Ricans, who are primarily military transients.

*Jíbaro* is simultaneously integral to local Puerto Rican social life and iconic for its cultural image. It comes from the uplands of Puerto Rico, more Spanish than African. The ensemble is a trio: guitar, plucked lute with five double courses of strings (*cuatro*), and gourd scraper (*güiro*); sometimes a button accordion joins in. The music includes older genres, mainly bolero, merengue, and waltz. All texts are in Spanish, though many of the younger musicians do not speak Spanish fluently.

Dancing to *jíbaro* was an important part of life on plantations. It still enjoys popularity in rural areas. At packed Saturday-night dances on Kaua'i, Puerto Ricans are joined by their Filipino, Japanese, and Portuguese neighbors. Music is part of almost every gathering. Saturday-afternoon baseball games include a jam session with *conjunto* or drumming during and following the game.

### Korean

The first group arrived in 1902 and became the foundation of the local Korean community. A second wave of immigration, after 1965, shaped present musical activity. Korean dance-music possesses the longest continuity, about fifty years. Music and dance are unified: dancers play hourglass drums (*changgo*) or racks of frame drums (*puk*) as part of the choreography. Dance accompaniment can include hourglass drums, gongs, zithers, and bamboo flutes.

Korean dance and its attendant music in Hawai'i are primarily the accomplishments of one individual, Halla Pai Huhm (figure 12). Her studio remains the only acknowledged representative of Korean performance in the state. Individual dancer-musicians, scattered throughout the islands, sometimes perform for local programs. The University of Hawai'i occasionally teaches farmer's-band music. Neither music nor dance is strongly supported or maintained within the community.

Other musical resources have been transient. An outstanding performer on the zither (*kayageum*) and her family of musicians settled in Hawai'i during the 1970s; after twenty years, the last member of the family left the islands. An accomplished *p'ansori* (storytelling) singer was in residence for ten years while studying at the University of Hawai'i; she finished her study and accepted a position at a mainland university. The status of religious music is similar to the Chinese case. Korean Buddhism and Korean Protestant Christianity maintain their own music, but each is little known outside its congregation.

Visiting artists from Korea concertize frequently for the local community. Government cultural troupes, drum ensembles on international tour, artists from the National Classical Institute, and Korean choral groups supplement the limited local resources.

FIGURE 12    In Honolulu, Halla Pai Huhm performs her signature "old man's dance" (*noin ch'um*), a piece in traditional Korean style. Photo by Cory Lum, 1993.

### Filipino

Beginning in 1906, Filipino migration reflected the final major recruitment by the sugar industry. Most Hawaiian Filipinos are Ilokanos, from northern Luzon; their language and culture contrast with the Tagalog-centric national culture of the Philippines. The fastest-growing population in Hawai'i, Filipinos have begun to establish leadership in its political and social life. They have maintained Filipino music while acquiring other genres.

String bands (*rondallas*) are iconic for the Filipino plantation experience. They formerly played for parties and dances. Today, they accompany lowland Philippine dances and songs in public and private settings. The ensemble consists of mandolin-like melodic instruments (*bandurria* and *laud*), guitars, and a bass, The musical style draws upon choral and brass-band idioms set to nineteenth-century European dances and marches. The ensemble can shrink to one *bandurria* and one guitar, or expand to a thirty-piece orchestra. Multigenerational family-based string bands can still be found in rural Hawai'i; amateur and senior-citizen groups are more common in urban areas.

Choirs performing arrangements of Filipino-language songs exist on each island. They participate in cultural celebrations like Rizal Day and for international festivals and communal events. The music encompasses major lowland languages—Tagalog, Ilokano, and Cebuano. The choral style is Western. It usually includes the choreography and theatricality of U.S. swing choirs. Hawaiian choirs are in touch with choirs in the homeland, and receive the latest compositions and arrangements.

*Kundiman* are Filipino songs composed as vehicles for a piano-accompanied soloist. They require a trained voice; some are virtuosic, with florid passages and a wide range. *Kundiman* are included in cultural programs as an artistic highlight.

An ensemble of Filipinos coming from upland tribes of Luzon was organized in 1990 to present upland Filipino music and dance authentically. Its formation is a response to the interpretation and reconstruction of upland traditions by lowland troupes.

### Other cultures and the public sector

Many groups, though present and recognized, are rarely acknowledged in the local rhetoric of cultural pluralism. From the European side, they include Ashkenazic Jewish, German, Greek, Norwegian or Scandinavian, Polish, Russian, and Spanish populations. From Asia, they include Indians—small, but long established—and the more recent Southeast Asians: Cambodians, Laotians, and Vietnamese.

Some immigrant communities—Greeks, Laotians, Vietnamese—already address the larger community through festivals and public celebrations. A small, but active, African-American gospel tradition brings Hawai'i into a broader American conversation on multiculturalism.

Though most cultural communities support their musical traditions in Hawai'i, the public schools, the state university, and the arts-and-culture agency provide external encouragement, validation, and assistance for these traditions. Every public school has a May Day program, featuring music from at least one of the foregrounded cultures. The University of Hawai'i, through its music, dance, and Asian-theater curricula, has provided training for students and performances of high artistic value to the community. Sometimes it has supported a tradition when the community has not. The State Foundation on Culture and the Arts provides financial and technical assistance for community organizations that conserve and preserve their musical traditions.

As a working multicultural society, Hawai'i inspires public and official rhetoric, invoked by the government, commodified by the tourist industry, validated by locally hybridized lifestyles, acknowledged by public education, and celebrated through cultural presentation, including music. Cultural diversity is constantly in dialogue with agendas of assimilation. Traditional music in Hawaiian settings particularizes cultural identity, provides a connectedness to homeland, establishes a platform for cross-cultural contact, and contributes to a rich and diverse aesthetic life.

—RICARDO D. TRIMILLOS

### Puerto Ricans

Like most culturally distinct peoples in Hawai'i, Puerto Ricans came as contracted sugar-plantation laborers. Beginning with about five thousand immigrants in 1901, their numbers increased in small increments. Most of their community, now numbering about twelve thousand, descend from the first group and live mainly on Hawai'i, Kaua'i, Maui, and O'ahu (Carr 1989; Souza and Souza 1985).

Local Puerto Rican musical traditions extend back to those of *jíbaros,* rural whites or mestizos in Puerto Rico, whose musical roots were essentially Hispanic (Solís 1994, 1995, 1996). During the twentieth century, Puerto Rico became urbanized, and cultural polarities between highland whites and coastal blacks blurred (Duany 1984). Puerto Ricans in the Caribbean and the eastern U.S. adopted more African-Latin musical traits than did those in Hawai'i. Partly because of isolation, Puerto Rican music in Hawai'i is archaic: genres current in Puerto Rico around 1900 but now obsolete there persist in Hawai'i, where Puerto Ricans preserve genres and practices found elsewhere only in self-consciously folkloric contexts.

Musical traditions associated with early migrants' descendants differ sharply from those of Caribbean and New York Puerto Ricans temporarily in Hawai'i. These transients form salsa bands (winds, full percussion sections, keyboard, electric bass, written arrangements), which, for Latinos on U.S. military bases, play salsas, merengues, boleros, *sones montunos,* and other popular genres. Local Puerto Ricans dance less flamboyantly than transient ones, with simpler footwork, fewer fancy turns and movements of the arms, and less rotation of the hips. The groups remain separate, musically and socially.

Though first-generation immigrants sang, composed, and improvised *décimas* (especially the *décima espinela*), their descendants seldom speak Spanish; even oldsters are more fluent in English than Spanish. Performers do not always understand the words they sing; they imitate and write down texts phonetically.

Some bands active in and after the 1970s include Silva's Rhumba Kings; Boy and His Family Troubadours (figure 13); and bands led by accordionist-vocalist Charlie Figueroa, *cuatro*-player-vocalists Julio Rodrígues, Jr., Joseph "Boy" Sedeño, Eva Rodrígues, Solomon Vegas, George Ayala, Bobby Castillo, Stanley Robley, and Angel Santiago. Mostly blue collar workers and skilled artisans, such performers have always been part-time musicians who learned by ear.

#### Contexts and genres

Puerto Rican music is most commonly heard at birthdays, weddings, softball games, luaus, clubs, and dances. Two civic organizations try to preserve traditional culture: the United Puerto Rican Association of Hawai'i sponsors monthly dances featuring local performers; the Puerto Rican Heritage Society archives music and sponsors cultural exhibitions.

Old-time Saturday-night dances, usually held in homes, were immigrant Puerto Ricans' principal recreation. Genres they brought from Puerto Rico included the waltz (*vals*), the *guaracha,* the *seis,* the *danza,* the polka (*polca*), the mazurka (*mazurca*), and the Christmas song (*aguinaldo*). All but the last are dances, some of which *cuatro*   Puerto Rican creole lead guitar with five steel-stringed double courses, originally four gut single strings

*danza*   Couple dance, usually without sung text, in duple meter and sectional form, often involving an initial promenade (*paseo*)

*guaracha*   Medium-fast strophic song-dance of Cuban origin, in duple meter and stanza-refrain form

*güiro*   Gourd (sometimes in Hawai'i, metal) scraper, of Amerindian origin, providing

usually stressed downbeats and rhythms varied according to the dance accompanied

*kachi-kachi*   Japanese-Hawaiian plantation term for the scratching of a *güiro*; in Hawai'i, a generic term for Puerto Rican dance-music

*plena*   Fast song-dance genre, of African–Puerto Rican origin, in duple meter and sometimes improvised stanza-refrain form

*seis*   Medium-fast duple strophic song-dance, set to the poetic form of a *décima*

FIGURE 13   The Puerto Rican ensemble Boy and His Family Troubadours, Honolulu, about 1947. *Left to right:* Sebastian Fernández, *marímbula*; Luciano Perez, Spanish guitar; Arthur Fernández, maracas; Joseph "Boy" Sedeño, Rickenbacker Electric tenor guitar; Raymond Fernández, güiro; Tito Fernández, guitar, Carmelo Fernández, claves; Tony Fernández, bongos. Courtesy of Joseph and María Sedeño.

are also sung. This nucleus attracted other genres, notably the coastal Puerto Rican *plena* in the 1920s, the Cuban bolero in the 1930s, and the Dominican merengue in the 1950s.

Waltzes, *guarachas, seises,* boleros, and merengues remain the core of any local Puerto Rican dance; *danzas* and *plenas* frequently occur, albeit in altered form. Older musicians, though remembering polkas, seldom play them; and of mazurkas, they recall only fragments.

Through the 1930s, Puerto Rican musical genres and styles were distinct from those preferred by other people in Hawai'i, but many local Puerto Ricans became proficient in the musics of Polynesian Hawaiians, playing 'ukulele and slack-key guitars, singing Hawaiian songs, and dancing *hula.* They now sing and play Filipino and Japanese songs (Solís 1989, 1994). To denote Puerto Rican dance-music, the people of Hawai'i frequently use the term *kachi-kachi,* a Japanese onomatopoeic term for the scratching of the *güiro.*

### Musical instruments

The nucleus of Puerto Rican musical instrumentation in Hawai'i since the early 1900s has been a trio: six-stringed Spanish guitar, *güiro* (or *guicharo,* a gourd or metal scraper), and creole guitar (*cuatro*)—instruments considered *jíbaro* in Puerto Rico. As lead instrument, a button accordion (*sinfonía*) sometimes replaces the *cuatro*. In the early 1900s, the *cuatro* was the keyhole-shaped *cuatro antiguo* 'old cuatro', with four single or double courses, tuned in fourths and a fifth. In the 1930s, those *cuatros* yielded to U.S.-made tenor guitars tuned like them.

Subsequent additions to the nucleus matched musical developments in mainstream U.S. popular music, and among Hispanics in the Caribbean and the U.S. mainland. They include maracas and claves in the 1930s, and bongos and congas after the mid-1940s. The *marímbula* (locally called box bass), a metal-tongued idiophone, often served as a bass instrument between about 1945 and 1955. Electronic amplification began in the 1930s. In the late 1960s, the modern *cuatro* arrived from Puerto Rico, where it had been developing for decades; a curved, violinlike instrument, it has five double courses, tuned in fourths.

Most bands (*conjuntos*) have had an electric bass guitar since the 1970s. A few have included drums (*timbales*) with attached cowbell. More traditional musicians reject congas and *timbales,* not perceiving them as authentically *jíbaro.* The last expert performer of the button accordion died in 1994, and this tradition seems headed for extinction.

In the 1980s and 1990s, the standard ensemble (*conjunto*) consisted of electric bass guitar, Spanish guitar, and modern *cuatro* (both having electronic pickups), *güiro*, and bongos, with optional double congas. The *cuatro* plucks the melody, and the guitar strums chords in syncopated rhythms. The bass guitar supports the chordal structure, usually in Cuban-derived anticipated-bass style. The *güiro* maintains a steady rhythmic background, and bongos and congas provide rhythmic variations based on Cuban rhythmic-timbral formulas, *martillo* and *tumbao* respectively. Anyone in the band may sing lead vocals. While someone sings, the *cuatro* adds countermelodies, improvised or (as with *seis* and *aguinaldos*) using stereotypical formulas; the ensemble serves as chorus.

—TED SOLÍS

## Pacific Islanders

Apart from the Polynesians who migrated to Hawai'i and became the Hawaiians, most Pacific Islander immigrants to Hawai'i arrived in the second half of the twentieth century. By the late 1990s, their largest numbers were from West Polynesia, mainly Sāmoa and Tonga. Lesser numbers had immigrated from East Polynesia. Others had come from Micronesia.

Mixtures of genders and generations provide contexts for continuing some customs that support social structures at home. Some Pacific Islanders come to attend the University of Hawai'i on campuses in Honolulu and Hilo, Hawaiian Pacific University, or a state community college. Most are unmarried; often residing in dormitories, they seek to connect with their home culture by forming student clubs, which, like extended families, provide security and companionship. An activity of many student clubs is to sing and dance for common enjoyment, at weekly meetings and special collegiate or universitywide functions.

One of the largest populations of Pacific Islanders in Hawai'i attends Brigham Young University at Lā'ie. To pay for their education, some of these students work at the Polynesian Cultural Center, adjacent to the university. Daily and nightly, for commercial audiences of tourists, they perform theatricalized versions of Oceanic music and dance, interspersed with recorded orchestrations of Western music.

### Sāmoans

In various denominations, Sāmoan churches support the singing of Christian religious music. Each church has a choir, which sings sometimes unaccompanied and sometimes accompanied by an organ. Sāmoan churches sponsor performances of secular music, but other groups form to entertain at Hawaiian hotels. Senior citizens, housed in government-subsidized, low-cost projects, sometimes form clubs and sing together weekly and on special occasions.

An occasion that brings the Sāmoan community together is Sāmoan Flag Day, commemorating the raising of the U.S. flag on Tutuila in 1900. In Hawai'i, the Council of Sāmoan Chiefs and Orators sponsors the observance of this celebration, featuring presentations of music and dance, demonstrations of cuisine, and athletic competitions. Groups rehearse in Sāmoan neighborhoods and projects. During the event, they may compete for prizes. Dances performed include the *sāsā,* in which seated performers synchronously execute rhythmic patterns by striking their hands against their arms, torsos, and legs. Excitement and fun increase with the tempo. The performers sometimes conclude by standing, yelling, and whistling. *Fa'ataupati* (a dance with slapping, performed only by seated men, though in Sāmoa performers may stand) and *mā'ulu'ulu* (interpretive songs and dances, done by women or mixed groups) may also be performed. As in the home islands, presentations of Sāmoan music and dance often end with a finale (*taualuga*), featuring a distinguished woman (*tāupou*), who dances with composure as antic men try to break her concentration; observers reward her by tucking dollars into her costume or dropping them at her feet.

### Tongans

In Hawai'i, Tongans perform Tongan music and dance in several contexts: religious services and annual celebrations, such as Christmas and Easter; communal picnics; and family celebrations, including weddings, birthdays, and funerals. Tongan Christian churches have choirs that sing hymns (*hiva himi*), anthems (*anitema*), and hymns based on indigenous songs (*hiva usu*). These are sung unaccompanied, or are accompanied by organ (figure 14). Since the 1980s, some have been accompanied by brasses. Churches also sponsor secular choirs, which usually rehearse weekly and perform at picnics and other church-sponsored events (figure 22).

The most frequently heard form of Tongan secular music in Hawai'i is *hiva kakala,* usually sung only by men, distinguished by rich harmonies and lilting melodies and sung unaccompanied or accompanied by guitars or ukuleles. Groups also perform *hiva kakala* without religious sponsorship. To drink kava and sing, the groups may meet weekly, or even nightly; they do not usually dance.

FIGURE 14   The Tongan choir of the First United Methodist Church of Honolulu. Photo by Phil Spalding, 1996. Courtesy of the State Foundation for Culture and the Arts.

FIGURE 15    The Kiribati Student Culture Club of Brigham Young University, Lāʻie. Photo by Tibor Franyo, 1996. Courtesy of the State Foundation for Culture and the Arts.

### Tahitians

Since the 1950s, Tahitian performing arts have been a featured part of the Kodak Hula Show and Polynesian revues mounted at hotels in Waikīkī and other commercialized zones in Hawaiʻi. What is presented as Tahitian has often included dances from other islands in French Polynesia and the Cook Islands. The costumes and music associated with Tahitian dance have often been misrepresented as Hawaiian. Tahitian dance is taught in many studios, some devoted exclusively to that tradition, others devoted primarily to Hawaiian *hula.*

The first Hawaiʻi-Tahiti Fête was held in Waikīkī in 1962. Later festivals were held on Kauaʻi and in Hilo. Most performers were local young people who had learned the dances from teachers who had studied with Tahitians. The festival on Kauaʻi thrives; for it, Tahitians visit regularly to work with the students and judge the competitions.

After 1976, when the Polynesian Voyaging Society's seagoing canoe, *Hōkūleʻa,* recreated a legendary voyage between Hawaiʻi and Tahiti, interest in Hawaiian-Tahitian relationships increased, and some Tahitians not active in commercial entertainment immigrated. In the 1990s, Tahitians in Hawaiʻi began to offer local presentations of Tahitian music. The annual Children's Competition (Keiki Fête), sponsored by the Kalihi-Palama Culture and Arts Society, gained popularity in support of traditional performances.

### Micronesians

Micronesians in Hawaiʻi came principally from Guam and the Trust Territory of the Pacific. Some Gilbert Islanders came as agricultural workers in the 1800s; their costumes as adapted by Hawaiians became known as grass skirts. Many Micronesians are short-term residents, living in Hawaiʻi to further their education. Most who have settled permanently have come for economic advancement, and usually remit some of their earnings to their families back home. The people of each Micronesian culture gather regularly—some at a church, some elsewhere—and sing religious or secular songs in their own language (figure 15). Such groups sometimes sing and dance for multicultural audiences in programs at academic institutions and civic events.

—Lynn J. Martin

Accompanied by Chinese drums and gongs, the lion darts back and forth. It wends its way to shops, where it cavorts until the owners, to bring luck in the year ahead, feed it money.

### Dance: American, Asian, European

Cultural diversity in Hawai'i fosters events that feature dancing. Besides dances of Hawaiians and people from elsewhere in Oceania, immigrants have brought dances from Asia, Europe, and the Americas. The first immigrants made dances from these areas an important part of local life, particularly on O'ahu.

Imported dances are perpetuated in old and new contexts. Young artists sometimes mix genres or develop new ones, and festivities often include traditional genres. Some people pursue activities related solely to their cultural heritage; others participate in various genres (Van Zile 1996).

#### Contexts

Some groups project a specific cultural identity through dance. At Buddhist temples in the summer months, people of Japanese ancestry celebrate O-Bon, the Japanese Buddhist commemoration of deceased friends and relatives. O-Bon festivities—large-scale, informal, outdoor events—occur throughout the islands, and some Japanese claim performances in Hawai'i resemble those of old Japan more closely than do performances in late-twentieth-century Japan. Bon dancing occasionally occurs on U.S. federal holidays and holidays unique to the state (like Statehood Day, 21 August).

For the Chinese lion dance, teenage members of Chinese martial-arts clubs are the usual performers. Taking turns being the lion's head or tail, they parade through streets, accompanied by drums and gongs. With movements rooted in martial-arts exercises, often including acrobatic tumbling and balancing, the lion darts back and forth. It wends its way to shops, where it cavorts until the owners, to bring luck in the year ahead, feed it money. It brings luck at weddings, birthdays, and other occasions, whether the celebrants are Chinese or not. Where and how people perform this dance typify the tradition in some areas of China, but the cultural origins of the individuals who perform may differ.

The European heritage of Hawai'i is evident in ballroom dancing, which has been in the islands since the early 1800s. In 1947, the opening of an Arthur Murray studio in Honolulu provided a setting for learning the latest couple dances. In the mid-1990s, the studio continued to flourish, and in Ala Wai Park, the City and County of Honolulu built a fine hall for ballroom dancing. Many older people participate avidly in this style. At clubhouses and recreation centers, dancers gather weekly to pursue what has often become more than a hobby. Some of them enter formal competitions; winners of local competitions seek prizes at national and international levels. Ladies may pay gentlemen to accompany them to "tea dances," held in the late afternoons at hotels.

The Scottish roots of some residents have been visible in presentational contexts. The Hawai'i Scottish Highland Games—including fighting with pillows astride wooden horses, tossing the caber, and competitive Highland dancing—were first held on Hawai'i Island in 1973. Participants included dancers from Canada and the

U.S. mainland, plus dancers trained in Hawai'i. Several years later, the games became simply gatherings based on the Scottish *ceilidh,* and they did not necessarily include dancing. Scottish dancing, originally recreational and social in purpose, maintains its original context. Participants gather weekly, to dance in circles and parallel lines ("longways sets"). Similar gatherings occur where people do the dances of Sweden or Israel, or dances from Europe and the Middle and Near East. In 1973, Hawaiian Scots formalized their tradition by setting up a branch of the Royal Scottish Country Dance Society.

Local members of the U.S. military, who in the mid-1990s numbered more than two hundred thousand (mainly on O'ahu), support country-western dancing in traditional social contexts. At the Pecos River Cafe (Honolulu), bluejean-clad men wearing boots and broad-brimmed hats join similarly attired women. To such songs as "Country State of Mind" and "Mamas, Don't Let Your Babies Grow Up to Be Cowboys," they do triple two-steps, polkas, and swing. On weekends, to prerecorded music that includes a caller, or that serves as background for moves prescribed by a live caller, some of them also participate in square dancing. National square-dance groups have held conventions in Hawai'i.

More than fifteen hundred American Indians from the mainland live in Hawai'i, mostly on O'ahu. Their powwows include fancy dancing and social dancing. Competitions occasionally provide an opportunity to recognize outstanding performers.

Beauty competitions provide a context that often includes dance; in contests for the title of Miss Filipiniana and Miss Koreana, traditional village and court dances serve as vehicles for earning points. Few conventions too, regardless of their focus, are complete without a banquet that includes performances of songs and dances of several cultures.

In recitals or concerts, studios often present dances. Students participate in informal programs in small halls or community centers, or more regularly (every year or two), on a larger and more formal scale, in theaters. These performances may be simple affairs, for which participants stitch makeshift costumes. They sometimes become lavish extravaganzas: studios rent costumes from the country where the dances began, import musicians to accompany the dancers, and host performances by the instructors who have taught their teachers. Among the most prominent dances presented in recitals or concerts are Japanese, Korean (figure 16), and Okinawan (figure 17), and Western ballet and modern dance.

FIGURE 16   In Honolulu, the Halla Pai Huhm Korean Dance Studio gives a recital. Photo by Cory Lum, 1993.

Hawaiians have transformed May Day into "lei day." School celebrations frequently include a program of songs and dances of cultures represented among the students.

FIGURE 17    In Honolulu, Yoshino Majikina dances "*Takadera Manzai,*" an Okinawan court dance, 1974. Photo courtesy of Yoshino Majikina.

Dance is a means of entertaining tourists. Entertainers sometimes try to evoke the original context of dances, but more often perform isolated items in programs designed as a series of cultural snapshots. Such programs most often restrict their depictions to Asia and the Pacific. Pat (b. 1923) and Orlando (b. 1921) Valentin, dancers of Philippine origins, put Asian dance in this context. In 1961, to introduce tourists to the dances of their area, they created the show "A Night in the Philippines," which their troupe performed regularly until 1971, when, elaborating on their original concept, they created the "Golden People's Show," which featured dances from China, Japan, Korea, Okinawa, Polynesia, Spain, and the Philippines. In the late 1970s, the two shows merged. By 1993, the Valentins were presenting their program only on request, and several members of their original company had founded separate troupes.

### Transmission

Dance is taught in Hawai'i in various contexts: some formally simulate educational environments in the country of origin; others are less formal, or adapt traditional settings to local circumstances. Some studios have rooms with polished wooden floors, mirrored walls, and elaborate audio equipment; others are the living rooms of private houses, whose owners, the teachers, after returning home from work, push the furniture aside. Formal classes occur at scheduled times, for fixed fees; less formal settings may provide free instruction, sometimes at sporadic intervals. Some who begin their studies at an early age and choose to continue beyond a temporary after-school diversion become the next generation of performers and teachers.

Practitioners of Western social dances—folk, ballroom, square, country—primarily nurture clubs for individuals who enjoy dancing as a hobby; they gather wherever they find a suitable space. Bon- and lion-dance clubs, though founded to assist in O-Bon temple celebrations and Chinese events respectively, also provide hobby groups for enthusiasts.

People learn some dances casually. Throughout the islands, old people gather in state and county facilities. Days are set aside for traditional activities of Japan, Korea, Okinawa, the Philippines, and newer immigrant groups, mainly from Laos and Vietnam. Instructors may be teachers who give instruction in studios by request, or old-timers, inspired to share their knowledge.

In elementary and secondary schools, some dances are taught in classes on physical education, social studies, or language. Hawaiians have transformed May Day—in Europe, a day to welcome the burgeoning of spring, or to celebrate human labor—into "lei day." School celebrations frequently include a public program of songs and dances of cultures represented among the students. Regular classroom teachers, who have learned the dances at the University of Hawai'i, or know them from participation in a studio or club, often teach the dances. Students who have learned in a local studio, parents who have learned in a studio in Hawai'i or the country of their origin, or invited specialists sometimes do the teaching.

The University of Hawai'i at Mānoa, the central campus of the state's leading university, offers instruction in Asian dance. In the 1950s, Barbara B. Smith (b. 1920), Professor of Music, and Earle Ernst (1911–1994), Professor of Drama and Theatre, laid the groundwork for the university's dance-ethnology program, which regularly offers courses on Hawaiian, Japanese, Korean, Okinawan, and Philippine dance. The program in drama offers courses in Japanese and Chinese theatrical forms, including dance. Advanced classes often present public performances.

The university's campus at Mānoa also supports ballet and modern dance. Students can earn undergraduate and graduate degrees in performance and choreography, participate in an annual concert, and benefit from the residencies of guest instructors. The university's campus at Hilo, several community colleges, and several studios offer classes in ballet and modern dance.

Several ballet companies exist on O'ahu, and small modern-dance companies occasionally arise on each island. The modern-dance companies have a harder time making a livelihood; the oldest, Dances We Dance Company, founded in New York in 1964 by Betty Jones (b. 1926) and Fritz Ludin, reopened in Hawai'i in 1979.

### Support

Governmental, public, and private organizations have funded the conservation of dance in Hawai'i, whose constitution says, "The State shall have the power to preserve and develop the cultural, creative and traditional arts of its various ethnic groups" (Hawai'i Revised Statutes, IX, 9). The legislature sometimes makes direct appropriations to the arts, but the State Foundation on Culture and the Arts is the primary distributor of funds. Through funding from the legislature and the National Endowment for the Arts, this foundation gives grants for performances, workshops, and instructors. According to annual reports, foundation funding for dance increased from $53,000 in 1984–1985 to more than $240,000 in 1990–1991. In the late 1990s, the federal and state governments decreased their funding for the arts.

The Hawai'i State Dance Council awards small grants for similar activities, and sponsors an annual choreographic competition. Most competitors have been exponents of modern dance and ballet, but the Council encourages participation by dancers who perform dances of other traditions. The university's Department of Theatre and Dance, sometimes independently and sometimes with other on-campus offices or the East-West Center, sponsors performances by groups visiting from Asia.

Dancing in Hawai'i has two opposite tendencies. Some dancers try to perform their dances as they learned them, or as they believe the dances were in their homelands. Other dancers try to produce blended forms.

It periodically coordinates special programs involving the residency of visiting Asian performers or teachers.

### Participants

Local dancers may have the same cultural background as the dances they perform, or they may have different ones. Most students at formal studios are girls whose ancestors came from the country of the dance they are studying. They frequently want to connect with their ancestral roots. Less often, people past middle age enroll in studio classes as a way to maintain ties with their homelands, or as a hobby.

The frequent participation of individuals of one culture in the dances of another is well exemplified in Mary Jo Freshley (b. 1934). An Ohioan of German-Swiss ancestry, she taught physical education at the elementary school level until 1995. After 1961, when she arrived in Hawai'i, she began participating in classes and dances of various cultures, including Europe, Hawai'i, Japan, Java, Korea, Okinawa, and the Philippines. Besides performing in diverse contexts, she adapted dances to her students' capabilities, and regularly included them in her syllabus. Perhaps more unusual, but also indicative of cultural crossovers in Hawai'i, is her involvement with Korean dance. The driving force behind this dance in the islands was Halla Pai Huhm (1928–1994), who immigrated in 1949, after studying dance in Korea and Japan. She set up a studio in 1950, and she and her students performed regularly. Most students at her studio were second-, third-, and fourth-generation Koreans, but Freshley began to study with her in 1962. Freshley studied the language, visited Korea to study dance, and became a major assistant at Huhm's studio (figure 18). With Huhm's death, Freshley assumed responsibility for maintaining the studio.

### Persistence and change

Dancing in Hawai'i has two opposite tendencies: conservation and innovation. Some dancers try to perform and transmit their dances as they learned them, or as they believe the dances were in their homelands; other dancers try to produce blended forms.

At the conservative end of the spectrum stands classical Japanese dance (*nihon buyo*), the most entrenched Asian dance in Hawai'i. Instructors teach it formally, according to Japanese practice. When students have achieved a sufficiently high level of skill, they go through formal name-taking ceremonies, as in Japan, where exact replication of dances is the ideal.

At the innovative end of the spectrum is the fusion choreography of "Mixed Plate," a theatrical concert-dance performed in the early 1980s. By incorporating movements from the dances of China, Hawai'i, and Japan, plus those of modern dance, it comically dealt with ethnic foods. Akiko Masuda, a third-generation Japanese choreographer, created the piece; she had studied ballet and modern dance, and had seen or casually participated in the dances of several cultures in Hawai'i.

FIGURE 18 In Honolulu, Mary Jo Freshley, a European-American from Ohio, performs a Korean crane dance (*hak ch'um*) choreographed by Halla Pai Huhm. Photo by Cory Lum, 1993.

Fusion choreography is less common in Hawai'i than in mainland U.S. communities with large immigrant populations.

Some fads that begin elsewhere make their way to Hawai'i. Though the lambada and break dancing never became as popular as they did in New York and Los Angeles, young people danced them in Hawai'i in the mid and late 1980s.

—JUDY VAN ZILE

## AOTEAROA

### Pacific Islanders

Aotearoa has long-standing connections with five Pacific areas: the Cook Islands, Sāmoa, Tonga, Tokelau, and Niue. These connections eased the islanders' immigration and promoted the formation of communities within the country. These communities continue their music and dance, though performances are largely not innovative, and they mostly occur within community gatherings, rather than for a wider, multicultural audience. The wider population notices islanders' traditions only at major festivals, or on one national occasion, the annual commemoration of the signing of the Treaty of Waitangi (6 February).

In metropolitan areas with Pacific Island pupils, many schools and colleges sponsor a "Poly club," which performs Polynesian dances. The foremost of these clubs has had a helpful effect on the public's perceptions of Pacific traditions, and has developed the self-esteem of participant pupils, who may speak English as a second language. In music and dance, secondary schools sponsor competitions. For younger generations, often those born in Aotearoa, "talent quests" give a chance to develop newer forms of older arts. Students mix styles of dancing and singing with popular genres, including rap. Within each tradition, in performances by some troupes, distinctive features of music and dance may blur. Few professional troupes exist. The only island-born tradition that nonislanders can hire for a performance is typically in Cook Island style: a few dancers and percussionists can create a show for use at parliamentary receptions, during municipal family-day festivals, or in nightclubs.

For adult communities, Christian churches are a traditional focus. Some churches hold services in a Pacific Island language; some larger Protestant congregations have their own building and minister. In addition to members' performances for their congregation (as entertainment, or in receptions for visitors), churches hold

In Aotearoa, Pacific Islanders' churches hold choral
competitions, cricket matches, and national assemblies. In these contexts, the community enforces
artistic standards that may be stricter than those in
the home islands.

national or regional gatherings, including Sāmoan choral competitions, cricket
matches between sections of an island population, and national assemblies. In these
contexts, the community enforces artistic standards that may be stricter than those in
the home islands.

### Sāmoans

Aotearoa had strong links with Western Sāmoa: in 1914, its soldiers ousted German
rulers there; until 1962, it kept political control. The colonial administration was
sometimes inept (as with the uprising known as the Mau) and negligent (as with the
1918 influenza epidemic), but many Sāmoans migrated to Aotearoa anyway. By the
late 1990s, immigrant numbers had swelled to nearly a hundred thousand, the largest
and most vocal Pacific Island body in the country. They became famous for vigorous
and spirited performances of Sāmoan music and dance. They succeeded in having
Sāmoan used at all educational levels, on radio, and in some publications. On 1 June
each year, by hosting receptions and shows of dancing, they celebrate the Sāmoan
Independence Day.

More than other islanders, Sāmoans boast prominent artists: novelist Albert
Wendt, painter Fatu Feu'u, television and theater actors, and popular musicians.
Many Sāmoan musicians formed bands that embraced other residents of Aotearoa.
Early in 1992, raising funds to repair damage from cyclone Ofa, a telethon brought
Sāmoan performers into national prominence.

### Cook Islanders

From 1891 to 1965, the Cook Islands were under the control of New Zealand. After
achieving independence, Cook Islanders retained rights of citizenship in New
Zealand. In the late 1990s, about forty thousand of them lived in Aotearoa. The similarity of their language to Māori sets up intercultural interests and rivalries.
Contrasts between these musical traditions are a source of continuing debate.

In gatherings of Cook Islanders in Aotearoa, the diversity of cultural traditions
in the homeland sparks lively exchanges. Single-island performances occur: the Atiu
Young Ones is a troupe in Porirua. Auckland annually hosts the Pukapuka Festival. A
festival in Wellington requires each island's troupe to display its heritage: in 1989,
each had to present traditional welcomes; in 1990, "songs of the sea." Competitive
dancing also occurs. Each October, with music and dance in the main centers, Cook
Islanders celebrate Gospel Day. Touring "*tere*" parties" from the islands often visit
Aotearoa. They stay among fellow islanders, from whom they raise funds for capital
works, church buildings, and other activities back home.

By the 1980s, expert drummers, dancers, composers, and singers from the Cook
Islands had become established in Aotearoa, where Turepu Turepu (d. 1990), tapping
a wealth of knowledge, strongly influenced performances. The composer Karitua
Makuare, in a choral piece (*īmene tuki*) premiered in Auckland on 1 January 1981

FIGURE 19    Excerpt from a New Year's choral piece (*īmene tuki*), composed by Karitua Makuare, a Cook Islander living in Aotearoa; a descant (*pele*) is not shown. Transcription by Kevin Salisbury.

(figure 19), combined English and Rarotongan; the piece instantly became popular for Cook Islanders' dancing.

### Tongans

In 1997, about twenty-five thousand Tongans were living in Aotearoa. In 1952, to promote the education and welfare of Tongan people, the Tongan royal family established a house in Auckland. Effectively the first diplomatic post from a Pacific Island nation, it served as a focus for cultural affairs.

Some of the main bearers of the Tongan musical tradition—'Ana Loumoli, Peni Tutuila, Pāluki Langi, Kioa Ve'ehala, Futa Helu, Tupou Posesi Fanua—became frequent visitors or residents in Aotearoa. In the 1980s and 1990s, immigrant Tongan composers, performers, and scholars included 'Okusitino Māhina, Taniela Vao, Sione Saafi, and the young Malukava.

### Tokelauans

Since 1925, the government of New Zealand has controlled the affairs of the Tokelau Islands. After about 1960, while maintaining economic links with New Zealand, Tokelauans progressively took on more self-administration. In 1997, about five thousand of them were living in Aotearoa, mostly in five centers: Auckland, Hutt Valley (Wellington), Porirua, Rotorua, and Taupo.

Every other Easter, in even-numbered years, Tokelauans organize a sports and cultural tournament, for which composers create or adapt songs with actions (*fātele*). In 1992, an immigrant Tokelau troupe issued a cassette of songs in new settings. The debut of Tokelau music in popular idioms, it combined acculturated singing with innovative guitar, drums, and vocals. It featured a new funeral lament (*haumate*), the first composed in more than ninety years.

### Other islanders

Under control of the government of New Zealand from 1901, Niue gained self-government in 1974, but its people maintained citizenship and a constitutional relationship with New Zealand. After the 1940s, Niue had trouble keeping its people at home; depopulation became a critical issue. In 1997, about fifteen thousand Niueans were living in Aotearoa (figure 20), far outnumbering those at home. They did not have a high national or community profile in the arts. Every year in October, they celebrated Niuean Constitution Day.

FIGURE 20    Niueans living in Aotearoa perform at the Pacific Drum Festival, Wellington, 1989.

Other Pacific islands with a resident presence in Aotearoa are Fiji and Tuvalu. In 1997, immigrants from each of these archipelagoes numbered about a thousand or fewer. In addition to the resources of diplomatic enclaves and visiting parties, their communities included several troupes in the Auckland or Wellington areas.

### Academic studies

Interest in islanders' music and dance can follow several educational leads: university Pacific studies centers (Canterbury, Auckland), undergraduate courses (Wellington, Auckland), colleges of education (Auckland, Canterbury, Otago, Wellington), and education resource centers (Auckland, Wellington). Theses on islanders' music include study within local populations, on music of Tokelau and the Cook Islands.

In 1988, to convene Tongan and international students of the music and dance of Polynesian immigrants to Aotearoa, Edgar Tuinukuafe organized the Tongan History Conference, one in a series of indigenous-oriented scholars' gatherings. Also in 1988, the Maori and South Pacific Arts Council of Wellington funded the Pacific Drum Festival, which involved people from six areas: Cook Islands, Fiji, Niue, Sāmoa, Tokelau, and Tonga. Representatives displayed their percussive heritage: rhythmic signals, structured movements, and drum-coordinated labor and sports. In preparing these displays, elders helped youths revive skills and knowledge.

—ALLAN THOMAS

## Scots

Scottish immigration to Aotearoa began in earnest about 1840. The largest concentration of Scots was in Otago, in the southern part of the South Island. There, in 1848, the Scottish Free Church founded a settlement combining strict religious principles with a vision of a highly stratified preindustrial social order, as articulated by the English colonial reformer Edward Gibbon Wakefield (1796–1862).

The settlement derived its religious choral music from the Scottish psalter and Calvinist hymns. Initially, congregations sang these items unaccompanied, led by a precentor, who for accuracy of pitch relied on a specially devised precentor's pipe. Only in the 1880s, when antagonisms toward organ accompaniment of singing hymns and psalms weakened, did the "kist o' whistles" find acceptance within religious puritanism. The Church of Scotland's *Scottish Psalter and Church Hymnary* remains central to Presbyterian choral music in Aotearoa.

During the first decade of the Otago settlement, about 80 percent of the migrants came from Lowland Scotland; the remainder were largely English. Highlanders, who arrived in small groups during successive decades, never made up more than 20 percent of Scottish immigration to Aotearoa (Brooking 1985). Though Highlanders and Lowlanders ostensibly shared the same nationality, the cultural differences between them found expression in language and music.

The Highlanders maintained their Gaelic singing only so long as they continued speaking Gaelic—usually no longer than a generation. Their musical contexts were usually domestic settings and rural enclaves. Institutionalized support for maintaining their vocal traditions affected a few sparsely scattered Gaelic or Highland or Celtic societies, only one of which remains functional.

### Bagpipes

The musical traditions introduced by migrant Scots are apparent in surviving shipboard diaries, held in the archive of the Otago Settlers Museum (Dunedin). These writings report an abundance of accordions, concertinas, fiddles, flutes, harmoniums, and pianos—instruments that typify Lowland traditions. The diarists, all of whom wrote in English, seldom mentioned the most idiosyncratic and symbolic of Scottish musical instruments, the Highland bagpipe. Yet the bagpipe became the most pervasive Scottish musical instrument introduced into Aotearoa, where it assumed a role in the expression of a homogenized national culture (Brooking and Coleman 1995).

The infrastructures of Scottish culture-based organizations were vital to this process. Caledonian societies provided an essential and literal platform by organizing competitions among their members. In rural and urban locations, they encouraged and sustained piping within the context of a Highland-style gathering, where the inseparability of bagpipes from the accompaniment of Highland dances continued.

In 1908, the formation of the Pipers and Dancers Association of New Zealand (later the Piping and Dancing Association of New Zealand) heralded increased uniformity in standards of performance, dress, and adjudication. Pipers' clubs and piping societies, most of which were formed after the Great War, have supported competition. Their principal roles have been to encourage performance and to further knowledge of bagpipe music. All official competitions of piping follow the regulations of the Piping and Dancing Association.

### Pipe bands

The most important contribution to the popularity of the Highland bagpipe in Aotearoa was the formation of bands. Modeled on the pipe-and-drum ensembles of the Highland regiments of the British Army, the first of these was formed in the southernmost city, Invercargill, in 1896. As a community-music functionary for ceremony and entertainment, such an ensemble spread rapidly up the eastern coast of the South Island's main urban centers, and throughout rural areas.

These bands were particularly demonstrative of the national population's militaristic consciousness and fervor, especially between the wars. Their existence clarifies a demarcation between solo piping and the more popular, twentieth-century phenomenon of piping in ensemble. Both styles of performing maintain the old pieces.

Strong patterns of inheritance occurred, of both the instrument and its performance (Coleman 1996). Though piping is an iconically male tradition, matrilineal transmission is an important element in its history. The most compelling reason for the local success of bagpipes may have been the determination of an immigrant minority to retain a unique and emblematic element of their cultural identity.

### Celebrations and social events

Unlike the festivals of other immigrant groups, few Scottish feasts and saints' days are locally celebrated. The main survival is Hogmanay, New Year's Eve (31 December), whose occurrence in the southern hemisphere's midsummer permits and encourages outdoor revelry. Midnight peals from churches and the piping of bands and soloists herald the new year, signaling an often prolonged round of "first-footing." This custom originates in the belief that the year's first visitor to a dwelling should bring

In Aotearoa, the neo-Celtic revival has a following. Accordions, concertinas, fiddles, flutes, Lowland or Border pipes, and the Scottish harp are its main instruments. The vocal tradition continues in English.

warmth and prosperity, symbolized by the gift of a piece of coal for the fire. Hospitality in the form of food and drink (normally alcoholic) is expected in return, regardless of the hour. Such well-wishing may continue throughout the remainder of New Year's Day, observed as a public holiday in Aotearoa, but emanating from the tradition of the Scottish national holiday.

In regular, usually monthly, concert meetings and occasional community dances, various communal organizations—such as the St. Andrew's societies (named after Scotland's patron saint), the Burns societies (named after Scotland's most famous poet), and the more generally named local Scottish societies—give expression to the popular, national, vocal tradition of Scotland. In these organizations, the Highland bagpipe maintains a ceremonial role, usually heralding the arrival and departure of officeholders and distinguished guests. Until the 1950s, a piper would have been expected to accompany the reel, the schottische, the gay Gordons, the Alberts, the lancers, the dashing white sergeant, and other popular dances; but knowledge of this music is declining.

The neo-Celtic revival, a modern expression of certain elements of Scottish music, has a local following. Accordions, concertinas, fiddles, flutes, Lowland or Border pipes, and the Scottish harp (*clarsach*) are its main instruments; the vocal tradition continues in English.

—Jennie Coleman

## THE U.S. MAINLAND

In the 1990 census, major Pacific Islander groups in the United States numbered 211,014 Hawaiians, 62,964 Sāmoans, 49,345 Chamorros, 17,606 Tongans, and 7,036 Fijians (apparently including Fijian Indians, who identify as Asian Indian). These numbers account for about 0.1 percent of the U.S. population.

Pacific Islander migration to the United States reflects factors that include access and motivation. Pacific Islander groups that enjoy direct access include Hawaiians (U.S. citizens through statehood), Chamorros (U.S. citizens through the Organic Act of 1950), and American Sāmoans (U.S. nationals, but not citizens). Sāmoans, Tongans, and Fijians frequently enter the United States via American Sāmoa. Guam and The Federated States of Micronesia serve as conduits for migration from other areas in Micronesia. Because emigration usually relates to former or ongoing colonial powers, migration from other Pacific Islands nations is negligible, and is usually due to marriage to U.S. citizens or nationals.

Sizable numbers of Hawaiians have migrated to the U.S. mainland, especially after 1945. In 1990, those in California numbered 34,447. Outside Hawai'i, Hawaiian communities face the same challenges in maintaining cultural traditions that other Pacific Islander migrants do. Enhanced employment opportunities draw islanders from all areas. Enhanced educational opportunities, especially in higher education, are particularly important for Micronesians, as is service in the U.S. military; those who migrate for these reasons often do so as individuals, rather than as families. Some Sāmoan and Tongan migration is related to Mormon Church activities in Utah and California.

In North America, the largest Pacific Islander communities are situated in Hawai'i and California. The greater Los Angeles and San Francisco areas in California house more than half the Sāmoan, Fijian, and Chamorro populations. Smaller communities have settled in Utah and Washington states.

## Music and identity

Strength in maintaining and transmitting the homeland's music and dance varies among islanders and locations. Environmental similarities between Hawai'i and other islands contribute to keeping more traditions intact there than on the U.S. mainland. In Hawai'i and on the mainland, the persistence of the extended-family system, prominent especially among Sāmoans and Tongans, supports performative traditions, which serve to bring communities together. Additionally, traditional music and dance are a focus of cultural association for second- and third-generation youth, born and raised in the U.S.

Pacific Islander groups vary in the extent to which performative events and participation extend beyond community enclaves. Sāmoan and Tongan special events occur largely within the respective communities and usually go unpublicized. American Sāmoans in major cities hold Flag Day celebrations, including the performance of prepared dances. Activities are often situated within churches: among Sāmoans, Congregational and Mormon denominations predominate; among Tongans, Methodist, Mormon, and Roman Catholic denominations do.

Singing hymns is a fundamental component of worship. Church-sponsored groups provide opportunities for learning and singing secular popular songs, like Sāmoan *pese* and Tongan *hiva kakala.* In Tongan communities, young women learn *tau'olunga* to perform at family, church, and community functions. An exceptional event was the visit of the King of Tonga to Hawai'i in 1993, for the thirtieth anniversary of the founding of the Polynesian Cultural Center. Parish-affiliated units in the Mormon Tongan community at Lā'ie performed specially composed *lakalaka,* elaborately sung poems, danced by entire villages in Tonga.

Events that attract attention and even participation from beyond the community showcase Hawaiian and Tahitian music and dance. Transmission of these traditions normally occurs within institutionalized settings, in schools and troupes. In hotels and places of entertainment in the 1960s and 1970s, pan-Pacific or pan-Polynesian troupes presented revues that usually included Hawaiian, Māori, Sāmoan, and Tahitian songs and dances. The variety of cultures represented depended on access to appropriate teachers and instruction in specific choreographies.

In the wake of the Hawaiian cultural resurgence begun in the late 1970s in Hawai'i, *hālau* (schools of *hula*) have multiplied. Two *hula* competitions are held yearly in California, and one is held in Washington state; in the mid-1980s, annual events were staged in Las Vegas, Nevada. In greater Los Angeles, at least three annual noncompetitive events draw Hawaiians together for cultural sharing and celebrating. A visible stylistic generational divide separates Hawaiian *hula* troupes. Teachers who migrated to the mainland before the cultural resurgence maintain older styles. In contrast, teachers who migrated later carry the innovative styles that emerged in the 1970s and 1980s in Hawai'i.

Ease of travel facilitates communication between migrant communities and their homelands. Cassettes from the islands are available in communal groceries, and larger chains are expanding their offerings of current Hawaiian compact discs. Interactions

Tahitian dance is flourishing, especially in California. Two competitions are staged annually, attracting more than twenty troupes. Most participants have not been to Tahiti.

FIGURE 21 At the Festival of American Folklife, celebrated on the Mall in Washington, D.C., members of the Sāmoan contingent from Hawai'i perform. Photo by J. W. Love, 1989.

are especially pursued in the Hawaiian community: teachers go to Hawai'i to attend and participate in major events and workshops; experts come from Hawai'i to conduct workshops on the mainland and judge competitions. Usually, migrant communities follow trends set in the homeland. As with Pacific Islanders in Hawai'i (figure 22), innovation in contemporary performance on the U.S. mainland flows largely in one direction.

Tahitian dance is flourishing, especially in California, in the absence of a sizable indigenous Tahitian community. Two competitions of Tahitian dance are staged annually in California, attracting more than twenty troupes. Participants of Tahitian and Hawaiian troupes overlap greatly, but most Tahitian dancers have not been to

FIGURE 22 In Honolulu, Tongan dancers perform at the second annual Liahona High School reunion. Photo by Adrienne L. Kaeppler, 1979.

Tahiti and have minimal access to reliable Tahitian-language consultation. In metropolitan areas, Pacific Islander communities are increasingly being requested to participate in larger multicultural events, such as the Smithsonian Institution's Festival of American Folklife in 1989 (figure 21), the Los Angeles Festival in 1990, Seattle's Northwest Folklife Festival in 1993, and San Francisco's Ethnic Dance Festival in 1995.

—AMY KUʻULEIALOHA STILLMAN

## REFERENCES

Aloisio, Pesamino Taualai. 1986 [?]. *Report on Pacific Islanders Minority Groups in the Sydney Metropolitan Area (August 13th–December 5th, 1986)*. Redfern: South Sydney Community Aid Cooperative.

Barwick, Linda. 1991. "Same Tunes, Different Voices: Contemporary Use of Traditional Models in the Italian Folk Ensemble's *Ballata grande per Francesco Fantin* (Adelaide, 1990)." *Musicology Australia* 14:47–67.

Beckett, Jeremy. 1981. *Modern Music of Torres Strait*. Canberra: Australian Institute of Aboriginal Studies AIAS 15. Notes to cassette.

———. 1987. *Torres Strait Islanders: Custom and Colonialism*. Cambridge: Cambridge University Press.

Bettoni, Camilla. 1984. "L'italiano in Australia: trasformazioni di una lingua o trasferimenti linguistici?" In *L'Australia, gli Australiani e la migrazione italiana,* ed. Gianfranco Cresciani, 118–126. Milan: Franco Angeli Editore.

Black, Paul, and Grace Koch. 1983. "Koko-Bera Island Style Music." *Aboriginal History* 7(2):157–172.

Bollig, Laurentius. 1927. *Die Bowohner de Truk-Inseln*. Münster: A. Schendorff.

Brenneis, Donald. 1983. "The Emerging Soloist: *Kavvali* in Bhatgaon." *Asian Folklore Studies* 42:67–80.

———. 1985. "Passion and Performances in Fiji Indian Vernacular Song." *Ethnomusicology* 29:397–408.

———. 1987. "Performing Passions: Aesthetics and Politics in an Occasionally Egalitarian Community." *American Ethnologist* 14:236–250.

———. 1991. "Aesthetics, Performance and the Enactment of Tradition in a Fiji Indian Community." In *Gender, Genre, and Power in South Asian Expressive Traditions,* ed. Arjun Appadurai, Margaret Mills, and Frank Korom, 362–378. Philadelphia: University of Pennsylvania Press.

Brenneis, Donald, and Ram Padarath. 1975. "'About Those Scoundrels I'll Let Everyone Know': Challenge Singing in a Fiji Indian Community." *Journal of American Folklore* 88:283–291.

Brooking, Tom. 1985. "Tam McCanny and Kitty Clydeside—The Scots in New Zealand." In *The Scots Abroad: Labour, Capital, Enterprise 1750–1914,* ed. R. A. Cage, 156–190. London: Croom Helm.

Brooking, Tom, and Jennie Coleman. 1998. "Piping in a Rough Equality: The Scots Contribution to the Making of New Zealand Culture." In *Scots in the Empire,* ed. John McKenzie. Lancaster: Lancaster University Press.

Carr, Norma. 1989. "The Puerto Ricans in Hawaii: 1900–1958." Ph.D dissertation, University of Hawaiʻi.

Castles, Stephen, and Mary Kalantzis. 1994. *Overview Report: Access to Excellence: A Review of Issues Affecting Artists and Arts from Non-English Speaking Backgrounds*. Vol. 1. Canberra: Australian Government Publishing Service.

Chatzinikolaou, Anna, and Stathis Gauntlett. 1993. "Greek-Australian Folk Song." In *The Oxford Companion to Australian Folklore,* ed. Gwenda Beed Davey and Graham Seal, 202–205. Melbourne: Oxford University Press.

Chenoweth, Vida. 1972. *Melodic Perception and Analysis: A Manual on Ethnic Melody*. Ukarumpa: Summer Institute of Linguistics.

Coleman, Jennie. 1996. "Transmigration of the *Piob Mhor:* The Scottish Highland Piping Tradition in New Zealand, with Particular Reference to Southland, Otago, and South Canterbury, to 1940." Ph.D. dissertation, University of Otago.

Comin, Antonio, with Linda Barwick. 1991. "*Ballata grande per Francesco Fantin*: Ballad for Francesco Fantin, as performed by the Italian Folk Ensemble, Adelaide 1990." *Musicology Australia* 14:68–85.

Cresciani, Gianfranco. 1986. "Italians in Australia: Past, Present and Future." Paper presented at the Third Australian Conference on Italian Culture and Italy Today, organized by the Frederick May Foundation for Italian Studies. Sydney: University of Sydney, 29 August–2 September 1986.

Downing, Bruce T., and Douglas P. Olney, eds. 1982. *The Hmong in the West*. Minneapolis: Southeast Asian Refugee Studies Project, University of Minnesota.

Duany, Jorge. 1984. "Toward an Anthropology of Salsa." *Latin American Music Review* 5(2):186–216.

Ethnic Affairs Commission of New South Wales. 1993. "The Ethnic Affairs Commission of New

South Wales and South Pacific Islanders: A Position Paper." In *A World Perspective on Pacific Islander Migration: Australia, New Zealand and the USA,* ed. Grant McCall and John Connell, 45–51. Kensington, New South Wales: Centre for South Pacific Studies, University of New South Wales.

Falk, Catherine. 1994. "Roots and Crowns: The Funeral Ritual of the Hmong in Australia." *Tirra Lirra* 4(4):9–13.

Faulkner, Andrea. 1988. "The Italian Contribution to South Australian Music-Making." In *From Colonel Light into the Footlights: The Performing Arts in South Australia, 1836 to the Present,* ed. Andrew McCredie, 356–369. Adelaide: Pagel Books.

Gee, Anne. 1991. "Contact, Change and the Church: Some Aspects of Papua New Guinea Church Music." M.A. thesis, University of New England, Armidale, Australia.

Girschner, Max. 1913. "Die Karolinen Inseln, Nomoluk und ihrer Bewohner." *Bässler-Archiv* 2:123, 3:165–190.

Haddon, A. C. 1912. "Dances and Dance Paraphernalia." In *Arts and Crafts,* ed. A. C. Haddon, 289–305. Reports of the Cambridge Anthropological Expedition to Torres Straits, 4. Cambridge: Cambridge University Press.

Hendricks, Glenn I., Bruce T. Downing, and Amos Deinard, eds. 1986. *The Hmong in Transition.* New York and Minneapolis: Center for Migration Studies of New York and Southeast Asian Refugee Studies Project of the University of Minnesota.

Krämer, Augustin. 1932. *Truk.* Ergebnisse der Südsee-Expedition 1908–1910, II.B.5. Edited by Georg Thilenius. Hamburg: Friederichsen, de Gruyter.

Kubary, Jan Stanislaw. 1889–1895. *Ethnographische Beiträge zur Kenntniss des Karolinen Archipels.* 3 vols. Leiden: P. W. M. Trap.

Kwok, Theodore J. 1992. "A View of Chinese Music in Hawaii." *Association for Chinese Music Research Newsletter* 5(2):20–26.

Lawrence, Helen Reeves. 1992. "The Chinese and their Musics in Eastern and Northern Australia." *Association for Chinese Music Research Newsletter* 5(2):35–38.

Leydi, Roberto. 1973. *I canti popolari italiani.* Milan: Mondadori.

Lowe, Jeremy. 1993. "Maori in Australia: A Statistical Summary." In *A World Perspective on Pacific Islander Migration: Australia, New Zealand and the USA,* ed. Grant McCall and John Connell, 61–66. Kensington, New South Wales: Centre for South Pacific Studies, University of New South Wales.

Mabo, Koiki. 1984. "Music of the Torres Strait." *Black Voices* 1(1):33–36.

Mackay, Ian K. 1976. *Broadcasting in Papua New Guinea.* Melbourne: Melbourne University Press.

Niles, Don. 1992. "The Chinese and Music in Papua New Guinea." *Association for Chinese Music Research Newsletter* 5(2):31–35.

O'Neill, Francis. 1979 [1903]. *The Music of Ireland: 1850 Melodies.* Ho-Ho-Kus, New Jersey: Rock Chapel Press.

———. 1986 [1907]. *The Dance Music of Ireland: 1001 Gems.* Dublin: Walton's Musical Instrument Galleries.

———. 1987 [1913]. *Irish Minstrels and Musicians with Numerous Dissertations on Related Subjects.* Cork: Dublin.

Ryan, Michael. 1989. "Brazilian Music in Sydney 1971–1984." Ph.D. dissertation, University of Sydney.

Sajnovsky, Cynthia B. 1992. "The Music of the Chinese in Contemporary Guam." *Association for Chinese Music Research Newsletter* 5(2):30–31.

Smith, Barbara B., ed. 1992. "The Chinese and Their Musics in the Pacific: Five Exploratory Reports from a Panel." *Association for Chinese Music Research Newsletter* 5(2):17–38.

Solís, Theodore. 1989. *Puerto Rican Music in Hawaii: Kachi-Kachi.* Smithsonian Folkways CD SF 40014. Cassette and compact disc.

———. 1994. *Puerto Rico in Polynesia: Jíbaro Traditional Music on Hawaiian Plantations.* Original Music OMCD 020. Compact disc.

———. 1995. "*Jíbaro* Image and the Ecology of Hawai'i Puerto Rican Musical Instruments." *Latin American Music Review* 16(2):123–153.

———. 1996. *"Kachi-Kachi Borinque": The Puerto Rican Musical Diaspora in Hawai'i.* Honolulu: University of Hawai'i Press.

Souza, Blase Camacho, and Alfred P. Souza. 1985. *De Borinquen a Hawaii: Nuestra Historia.* Honolulu: Puerto Rican Heritage Society of Hawai'i.

Stillman, Amy Ku'uleialoha. 1992. "Chinese Music in Tahiti." *Association for Chinese Music Research Newsletter* 5(2):27–29.

Stuart, Ian. 1973. *Port Moresby Yesterday and Today.* Revised edition. Sydney: Pacific Publications.

Symonds, Patricia V. 1991. "Cosmology and the Cycle of Life: Hmong Views of Birth, Death, and Gender in a Mountain Village in Northern Thailand." Ph.D. dissertation, Brown University.

Tapp, Nicholas. 1989. "Hmong Religion." *Asian Folklore Studies* 48:59–94.

Tsounis, Demeter. 1986. "Multicultural Music-Making and Dancing at Wedding Receptions: A Study of the Music-Making and Dancing Activities of Greek People in Adelaide." B.Mus. thesis, University of Adelaide.

———. 1990. *Shoulder to Shoulder.* Cassette. Adelaide: Multicultural Artworkers Committee of South Australia.

Tsounis, Michael P. 1988. "The History of Australia's Greeks: Some Signposts and Issues." In *Greeks in Australia,* ed. A. Kapardis and A. Tamis, 13–24. Melbourne: River Seine Press.

———. 1993. "Greek Community 'Paroikia' Formations in Australia, 1880s–1980s." In *Greeks in English Speaking Countries: Proceedings of the First International Seminar of the Hellenic Studies Forum: 27–30 March, 1992,* ed. Speros Vryonis et al., 25–40. Melbourne: Hellenic Studies Forum.

Tung, Yuan-Chao. 1993. "The Changing Chinese Ethnicity in French Polynesia." Ph.D. dissertation, Southern Methodist University.

Van Zile, Judy. 1996. "Non-Polynesian Dance in Hawai'i: Issues of Identity in a Multicultural Community." *Dance Research Journal* 28(1): 28–50.

Webb, Michael, and Don Niles. 1987. "Periods in Papua New Guinea Music History." *Bikmaus* 7(1):50–62.

Zahn, Heinrich. 1959 [1934]. *The Conchshell-Hymnal.* Edited by H. Wolfrum. Madang: Lutheran Mission Press.

# Part 2
# Concepts in Oceanic Music

What issues are important today in the musics of Oceania? How do these issues differ from those of times past? What concepts crosscut societies and pay no attention to cultural and national borders? Do insiders and outsiders view musical products and processes in the same way or different ways? What about the politics of music and the music of politics? How do cultural groups influence each other by borrowing, migrating, and participating in festivals? How has the wider scope of indigenous and gendered gazes affected views of musics and their social contexts? How do we probe the products of musical sound, movement, and language to understand the artistic processes that underlie them? What methods do we use to record, preserve, and analyze the elements of music at the end of the twentieth century?

These questions confront practitioners, scholars, and beholders of the myriad musics that find their homes in Oceania. They are worth asking. Some are answered here; some are refined, and their implications explored; others await the promise of new views and technologies.

One of the most potent issues in which music plays a part is the control of land. Here, Uncle Harry Kunihi Mitchell sings to encourage Hawaiians to reclaim Kahoʻolawe Island. Photo by Franco Salmoiraghi, 1979.

# Music and Society

The performing arts have always been important elements of culture and society. In Oceania, these arts look both back and ahead, promoting tradition while initiating change. The variety of music overwhelms—from bamboo tubes struck with rubber sandals to opera-house renditions of *The Mikado*; from singing, drumming, and moving on the grounds of outdoor temples to wailing at wakes in crowded huts; from nose-blown flutes to electric-wired ukuleles and beyond.

Now, at the end of the twentieth century, we look back at the music of Oceania—what it was when first encountered by outsiders and known from oral tradition, and what it is today. Sometimes obvious and sometimes subtle, as a means of sanctifying, politicizing, validating, and instructing, this music continues to serve social ends, even as it entertains.

Social structure is visually laid out in a Tongan dance by the village of Kanokupolu in honor of the coronation of King Tupou IV. The central positions are taken by Princess Pilolevu (the king's daughter) and Baron Vaea (now prime minister of Tonga). Two ladies standing behind the princess serve as "protectors" of her rank. Standing next to the princess in the first row is Latu, daughter of one of the chiefs of the village. Standing third (not shown) is Mafi, daughter of the ceremonial attendant Vakalahi. Next to Baron Vaea is Vili Fa'oa, son of one of the chiefs of the village. In the third position (not shown) is Halatoa Siale, the best male dancer of the village. Photo by Adrienne L. Kaeppler, 1967.

# Popular Music

*Adrienne L. Kaeppler*   *Peter Russell Crowe*   *David Goldsworthy*
*Don Niles*   *Kim Poole*   *Jay W. Junker*
*Robin Ryan*   *Kathleen R. Oien*   *Ioannis Psathas*
*Herbert Patten*   *Ryūichi Tai*
*Michael Webb*   *Mark Puryear*

**Musical Ensembles**
**Music in Place**

The concept of popular music changes over time and place, waxing and waning with the winds of time as they meet in the Pacific. A given style of popular music and dance may simply be one that has many adherents at a specific time or place. But often mixed into this definition is the sense of a musical style being created and performed by the nonelite, who have little or no political power, or are responding to economic and political colonialism.

On more specific levels, what is popular on Saturday may not be popular on Sunday, what is popular with indigenous people may differ from what is popular with migrants to the same area, and what is popular with one generation may differ from what is popular with another. The notion of popular music, though serviceable for analytical convenience, is not easily generalizable.

In the 1800s, Europeans transplanted their music to many areas of Oceania; by the late 1800s, brass bands and string bands had become popular. In the 1900s, American music became widespread (figure 1), and Japanese music became popular in Micronesia. American rock transformed traditional sounds in the 1950s, but in the 1980s, reggae again transformed what many want to see and hear. The people of each area, influenced by phonographs, radios, televisions, tape recorders, compact discs, and videos, determine for themselves what is popular for them.

Since the 1960s, the tide seems to have turned, and many Pacific peoples have begun to look inward and backward to their earlier traditions, indigenous and evolved. Though outside influences have continued and can be seen in Hawaiian jazz or the mellow sounds of entertainers such as Kui Lee, the exciting new wave can be characterized as contemporary traditional—traditional music and dance rendered in contemporary forms. Concerns over ethnic identity, festivals, and tourism spur a reemphasis on tradition.

But while these concerns pull Oceanic peoples toward older values, new waves of music from beyond the Pacific broaden the musical horizon. Reggae and other kinds of imported popular music have made inroads, especially where questions of independence and rights over lands are timely. Musical trends formerly entered the western Pacific from Polynesia, but newer concepts, such as the goal of a nuclear-free Pacific, the struggle to reclaim customary lands, and the assertion of indigenous

FIGURE 1    On Guadalcanal in 1943, two
Solomon Islanders spin records with an
American soldier. Photo U.S. National Archives,
U.S. Army Signal Corps.

rights, find expression in musical ideas that flow from the more politically active islands to islands throughout Oceania.

Much popular music is associated with entertainment, but some of the most popularly appreciated music in Oceania has been associated with religion. In the twentieth century, the musical display of political power has become more urgent, and the concept of gender and engendering music has gained popular interest. The processes by which children learn the music of their culture, absorbing relevant criteria of popularity along the way, invite research.

## MUSICAL ENSEMBLES

Outside influences on Polynesian music began in the 1700s with European explorers' bands. But it was not until Christian missionaries introduced hymns that profound changes began to occur. Other, more secular, music brought changes throughout the 1800s and 1900s, especially rock and country from the United States and cabaret music from France. During this time, interisland influences occurred, especially from Hawai'i to other parts of Oceania. Much of this music, using guitars, ukuleles, and similar Western stringed instruments, evolved into a style known as pan-Pacific pop.

Western musical instruments that Pacific Islanders adopted and adapted were primarily brass aerophones, membranophones struck with sticks, and strummed chordophones [see MUSICAL INSTRUMENTS]. Though sometimes played individually, they were usually combined into bands, specifically brass bands and string bands. Different instruments and combinations of instruments were favored in various places and have continued to change.

Brass instruments were usually accepted unchanged, but chordophones were adapted variously. In Hawai'i during King Kalākaua's time, strummed guitars (figure 2) and 'ukulele were common, usually as accompaniment for hula in the style known as hula ku'i. About the same time, experiments with using pocket knives and other objects to stop the strings led to the invention of the steel guitar.

Today in Hawai'i, a style known as chalangalang and changalang is popular. It is characterized by the manner of playing 'ukulele and guitar, sometimes called twangy: harmonic and rhythmic strumming (without picking out a melodic line), with

FIGURE 2    "The houlah-houlah, or native dance, in the presence of the king," detail of the color engraving *Entertainment given to British and American naval officers at Honolulu (Sandwich Islands).* Guitarists, singers, and dancers perform for King Kalākaua while a brass band waits (*upper right*). Bishop Museum Archives. Photo Bishop Museum.

uneven divisions of the beat. The singing, often in falsetto (*leo kiʻekiʻe*), includes vocal breaks that probably developed in relation to indigenous Hawaiian vocalization.

## Brasses

One of the most widespread popular musical traditions to enter Oceania was the brass band. Early voyages of exploration, such as those of Captain Cook, included marines trained in playing fifes and drums (and sometimes French horns and bagpipes) and parading. Though Pacific Islanders were not always impressed with these sounds, they understood that Europeans made rhythmic noises that could be found agreeable.

Military and civilian brass bands, at the height of their popularity in Britain and parts of Europe during the mid-1800s, were taken by migrants to their new homes in Oceania. During the colonial wars in Aotearoa, which involved ten thousand British troops, eleven of the fourteen British imperial regiments had military bands. Not long after, some Māori communities had their own brass bands.

In French Polynesia, brass bands are not popular; the sole brass band (RIMAP) plays primarily for military occasions. Membership is beginning to include French Polynesian males, who fulfill their military-service obligation while studying and experiencing Western music (Jane Freeman Moulin, personal communication).

The introduction of four-part tonal harmony, mainly by missionaries to enhance their work, set the stage for the local appreciation of brass bands. The association of these bands with military power may have played a part, but the combination of brass and percussion may have appealed to ordinary people, who, rather than music specialists, could without long training take part in collective displays.

—ADRIENNE L. KAEPPLER

### Papua New Guinea

In Papua New Guinea, brass bands are primarily associated with the national police force. Since the late 1800s, they were probably heard in local ports, in the form of British and German naval bands. Their continuing indigenous use began in 1928–1929, when the Lutheran missionary Heinrich Zahn (1880–1944) received a donation of eleven instruments—flügelhorns, tenor flügelhorns, trombones, and a tuba—for use by his students at Hocpoi, a training school for Lutheran evangelists in Bukawac Village, Morobe. In 1925, he had begun an experiment to improve local singing by using tuned conchs to play hymns based on German chorales; eventually,

FIGURE 3   The Papua New Guinea Police Band performs. Photo courtesy of Word Publishing, Papua New Guinea.

these arrangements were published (Zahn 1934, 1959). When the brass instruments arrived, his students were playing in four-part harmony, with one conch per note.

Though conchs and brasses are played with vibrating lips, brasses demanded the learning of new techniques and Western notation; nevertheless, Zahn's students quickly gained proficiency on their new instruments. The conch and brass bands performed separately and together, alternating with singing. After Zahn's return to Germany (in 1932), the brass band continued at Hocpoi, and conch bands spread to other parts of the province. The Pacific War interrupted such activities, but after 1945 conch bands were revived; they continue in three villages. Zahn's brass band did not continue, and attempts to revive it have not succeeded (Niles 1995).

In 1937, Inspector David Crawley began what is today known as the Papua New Guinea Royal Constabulary Band or, simply, the Police Band (figure 3). Impressed with a bugle band begun at a Methodist school in Rabaul, Crawley chose musicians from Nordup Village. He taught them to play instruments he provided. At the first public performance, the colonial administrator was so impressed that he urged Crawley to work solely on establishing a police band. A full set of instruments then arrived from Australia. In January 1942, Japanese troops captured Rabaul, and the bandsmen buried their instruments at Toliap Village. The band reformed in Port Moresby, and with new instruments toured Australia in 1945, playing arrangements of "Colonel Bogey on Parade," "Waltzing Matilda," and "God Save the King." Australians favorably received the performances, and more overseas trips followed (Kreeck 1991:136–142).

After Crawley's departure (in 1963), one of the original Nordup bandsmen, Sergeant-Major Tolek, directed the band until Thomas Shacklady arrived, in 1964. Experienced with military music, Shacklady added arrangements of local songs, like "*Raisi, raisi*" and "*Papua, oi natumu,*" and made recordings with Viking and the National Broadcasting Commission (Guzman-Alaluku 1981). Between 1965 and 1972, police divisional bands were formed in Mount Hagen, Madang, Lae, and Rabaul; they achieved local renown.

In 1974–1975, a competition was held to seek contributions for a national anthem for the independence of Papua New Guinea, on 16 September 1975. Controversy swirled around the five finalists, but just a few days before independence, the national cabinet decided that "O Arise All You Sons," composed by

Shacklady, would be the national song, and deferred a decision about a national anthem. Shacklady continued as conductor until 1981, when he was replaced by Chief Inspector Bill Harrison, who led the band until his replacement in 1994 by the current conductor, Superintendent Keith Terrett.

The Police Band, with about sixty-five members, participates in major official functions, including visits by dignitaries, the opening of important sporting events, and national holidays. When marching, they prove to be particularly entertaining because of the cymbalist's antics.                                    —DON NILES

### Tonga

The brass bands of Oceania have probably reached a cultural peak in Tonga, where they number in the hundreds. In addition to community bands, nearly every church and school has at least one brass band (*ifi palasa* 'to blow brass'). The most prestigious bands are the Royal Corps of Musicians (directed by the Honourable Ve'ehala, noble of the village of Fahefa); the Tongan Police Band, directed by Viliami Taufa; the Maopa Band, associated with the Maopa Choir of the Centenary Church in Nuku'alofa, directed by Viliami Esei; and the Tupou College Band, directed by Feke Kamitoni.

Every year, at least one large-scale competition for brass bands captivates the country (Linkels and Linkels 1994), with prizes given in several categories. The first prize might include a foreign tour for the members, or a new set of instruments. The music ranges from Bach, Handel, and Tchaikovsky, to John Philip Sousa, to local compositions of the *hiva kakala* genre. King Tāufa'āhau Tupou IV is especially fond of brass-band music. His arrival on ceremonial occasions is announced by a brass-band rendering of the national anthem. For his birthday and other holidays, school and community bands visit the palace to serenade him.

The origin of brass bands in Tonga may reflect British and German influences. In the mid-1800s, military and civilian bands were highly popular in Britain. If not imported into Tonga directly, they may have come by way of Aotearoa, where brass-band competitions have been held since the 1880s, more associated with expatriates than with Māori. It is said that Tongans were impressed by the band that traveled on the German warship *Nautilus,* which brought the body of the heir apparent, Tevita 'Unga, from Aotearoa, where he had died in 1879.

In 1882, the curriculum of Government College included singing, harmony, and "*ako tameaifi,* instrumental music" taught by a European, Mr. Wilson, whose brass band "would have done credit to any provincial town in Europe or Australia"; one of the "bandsmen became the conductor of an European brass band in Fiji" (Roberts 1924:113). Prince Wellington Ngū (grandson of King Tupou I), a graduate of the college, a "fine musician, who could play on almost any instrument" (Roberts 1924:121), was the patron of an ensemble whose thirteen members were depicted with him in the earliest known photograph of an all-Tongan brass band (figure 4).

Under a Tongan leader named Lulu, the Government College band was the subject of an account by Deputy Prime Minister Basil Thomson, who wrote that the band, with a lantern-slide lecture, toured Ha'apai and Vava'u, where it received popular acclaim, but its tour was cut short when the government, which owned the instruments, recalled it. The same bandleader was humiliated by his wife, who locked him out of the house so he could not get his cornet and conduct a rehearsal of the grand march from *Tannhäuser* (1894:144–148).

Tongan churches do not have organs: their choirs are accompanied by brass bands, performing European music often transcribed in Tongan numeral notation. In September 1994, the Maopa choir and brass band performed Handel's anthem "Zadok the Priest"; the seven-piece band included cornets, baritones, a euphonium,

FIGURE 4    Prince Wellington Ngū's band,
1884. National Library of Australia, Canberra.

and a sousaphone (called a bass). But the piece of European music the Tongans love most is the Hallelujah Chorus from Handel's *Messiah,* sung and played as loudly as possible. Every choir and band sings and plays this piece. Often choirs sing it en masse—a tradition that goes back at least to 1936, when a thousand singers from Tupou College, Kolisi Fefine, and graduates of these schools, accompanied by a brass band from Kolofoʻou, performed it, directed by the Rev. A. H. Wood.

The other brass-band favorites are *hiva kakala,* based in poetry and meant to be sung. Brass-band performance maintains the poetic emphasis: the band plays the first stanza and refrain, and while a few musicians continue to play, most of the bandsmen sing for several stanzas and refrains, eventually rejoining the others for a final instrumental section.

The usual instrumentation includes cornets (including one E♭ soprano cornet), E♭ horns, baritone, euphonium, trombones, either tubas or sousaphones, and percussion. To attain the mellowness of big-band music of the 1940s, the Tonga Royal Corps of Musicians and the Police Band add saxophones for concerts and ballroom dancing. In addition to playing in church and for concerts and competitions, most bands are marching bands. Some perform drills at agriculture shows and other events; some feature trombones in side-to-side and up-down choreographies. Their music at dances and balls often includes a grand march: at the ball honoring the twenty-fifth anniversary of women in the Tongan police force (in September 1995), the Police Band, following the tradition of the 1890s, played the grand march from *Tannhäuser.*

Why brass bands have become so popular in Tonga is a hard question, but the answer may relate to the Tongan love of complex harmony and group display. As in indigenous Tongan performing arts, individual parts are not elaborated; instead, multiple parts combine to make an intricate whole. Each instrument is considered to have a voice, and, as a metaphor of Tongan polyphony, the solo cornet carries the *fasi,* the melodic line; second and third cornet and E♭ horn carry alto or *kanokano;* baritone, E♭ horn, and trombones carry the tenor; tuba and sousaphone carry the *laulalo,* the lower, less melodic part; the euphonium adds decorative elements, which, like the *lalau* (the vocal part that it mimics), improvises around the *fasi*; other instruments, if available, add to the polyphonic texture, while drums keep the rhythm (as does a *nafa* in a *me'etu'upaki*). These polyphonic parts are elegantly displayed (as in a *lakalaka*) in precise timing to reach the aesthetic goal of aural and visual polyphony—a goal that Tongans liken to "one great machine."

### Hawai'i

In Hawai'i by 1836, The King's Band (later, The King's Musicians) was formed. In 1837, it played for the funeral of Nahi'ena'ena, Kamehameha's daughter, under a leader known as Oliver. The band's second director (1845–1848) was a former slave from Virginia, George Washington Hyatt. The third (1848–1870), William Merseburgh of Weimar, Germany, led an ensemble of at least ten members, who played flute, clarinet, bassoon, French horn, drums, and other brass instruments. This ensemble began with Hawaiian and non-Hawaiian players, but by 1860 all its personnel were Hawaiians. William Northcott, from Aotearoa, was the leader in 1870–1871, and for a few months in 1871, the leader was Frank Medina, from Portugal.

Finally, King Kamehameha V sent a request to the German kaiser to send a bandmaster to teach and conduct His Majesty's Band, and in 1872, Henry Berger arrived from Prussia; he remained in the islands until 1915 (figure 5). In Queen Emma Square, the band played concerts that concluded with a march around the square. The band played for incoming and outgoing vessels, and gave subscription concerts at the Hawaiian Hotel and Kapi'olani Park. In 1881, a full set of new instruments came from the maker, C. W. Mority of Berlin: seventeen brasses, ten woodwinds, two drums, and cymbals. In 1883, thirty bandsmen went with Berger to San Francisco; in 1887, Hawai'i won a competition over twenty-six other bands. Berger then added strings to the ensemble, so they could play symphonic music.

FIGURE 5     Henry Berger with his band on the steps of 'Iolani Palace. Photo Hawai'i State Archives.

*Bands and politics*

In 1891, a group of Berger's bandsmen toured the U.S. to try to gain support for Queen Lili'uokalani's cause. After the overthrow of the Hawaiian government, the band was classified as part of the military of the provisional government, and the bandsmen were required to sign an oath. Having refused, the Hawaiians were relieved of their duties, and two bands emerged: the Government Band, under the direction of Berger, and the Hawaiian National Band, under former bandsman José Libornio.

An important day in the history of struggles for sovereignty was 15 October 1894, a day of defiance that occurred at the dedication of Uluhaimalama Park in Pauoa. It began when the Hawaiian National Band played the national song, "*Hawai'i Pono'ī*," composed a few years earlier with King Kalākaua's words and Berger's music, derived from a Prussian anthem ("*Heil dir im Siegerkranz*"). The bandsmen then dramatically planted a stone, singing the now-acclaimed song "*Kaulana nā Pua*" ('Famous Are the Flowers'), composed by Kekoakalani Prendergast. Noting the members' refusal to sign the oath, this song asserts that Hawaiians would rather eat stones than support a government dominated by foreigners (after Elbert and Mahoe 1970:63):

| | |
|---|---|
| Kaulana nā pua a'o Hawai'i, | Famous are the children of Hawai'i, |
| Kūpa'a mahope o ka 'āina | Ever loyal to the land |
| Hiki mai ka 'elele o ka loko 'ino | When the evil-hearted messenger comes |
| Palapala 'ānunu me ka pākaha. | With his greedy document of extortion. |
| | |
| Pane mai Hawai'i, moku o Keawe. | Hawai'i, land of Keawe, answers. |
| Kōkua nā Hono a'o Pi'ilani. | Pi'ilani's bays help. |
| Kāko'o mai Kaua'i o Mano, | Mano's Kaua'i lends support, |
| Pa'apū me ke one Kakuhihewa. | And so do the sands of Kakuhihewa. |
| | |
| 'A'ole 'a'e kau i ka pūlima | No one will fix a signature |
| Maluna o ka pepa o ka 'enemi, | To the enemy's paper, |
| Ho'ohui 'āina kū'ai hewa | With its sin of annexation |
| I ka pono sivila o'o ke kanaka. | And sale of civil rights. |
| | |
| 'A'ole mākou a'e minamina | We do not value |
| I ka pu'ukālā a ke aupuni. | The government's sums of money. |
| Ua lawa mākou i ka pōhaku, | We are satisfied with the stones, |
| I ka 'ai kamaha'o o ka 'āina. | Astonishing food of the land. |
| | |
| Mahope mākou o Lili'u-lani, | We back Lili'u-lani, |
| A loa'a 'ē ka pono a ka 'āina. | Who has won the rights of the land. |
| (A kau hou 'ia e ke kalanu.) | (She will be crowned again.) |
| Ha'ina 'ia mai ana ka puana | Tell the story |
| Ka po'e i aloha i ka 'āina. | Of the people who love their land. |

For a while, Berger's band played non-Hawaiian music, and the Hawaiian National Band played Hawaiian music, but soon, in keeping with the Hawaiian spirit of compromise, the wounds were healed. By 1906, a newly named ensemble, the Royal Hawaiian Band, under Berger's direction as founder and leader, was performing in the U.S. and Canada, advertised as "Sixty Musicians and Singers, a Military Band, a Stringed Orchestra, a Choir, Mandolin, Guitar and Banjo Clubs and Solo Singers, Rendering Classical and Operatic Music and the Superb Native Music and 'Hula' Songs of Hawaii."

The Royal Hawaiian Band thrives, now under the direction of Aaron David

Aboriginal vaudeville troupes incorporated into their acts the sounds of jazz and the movements of clowning, corroboree-style stepping, and the *hula*. Virtuosos played gumleaves "no hands"—while playing an accordion with their hands or a harmonica with their nose.

Mahi, a Hawaiian. It plays at important local events and occasionally tours; in 1988, it played in Carnegie Hall. David Wayne Bandy compiled the history of the band in a master's thesis (1989), from which this entry draws.    —ADRIENNE L. KAEPPLER

### Gumleaves

Some Aboriginal peoples once played single-reed aerophones made from the leaves of local gums, trees or shrubs of genus *Eucalyptus*. Circumstantial evidence suggests that gumleaves served as hunting and bird-calling devices, signaling instruments, and musical toys (Ryan and Patten 1995:208). Responding to forced Christian evangelization in the late 1800s, detribalized Aboriginal peoples of southeastern Australia developed these aerophones into bands, which, depending on denominational influence, played European hymns, American gospel songs, popular music, and classical music.

The earliest documented gumleaf band appeared in 1892, when Salvation Army officers recruited tribesmen to play gumleaves in their street procession through Bordertown, South Australia (Temora 1892:7). This band may have had precedents, since the missionization of Aboriginal people began in the early 1850s, when conventional instruments were unavailable on the frontier. Gumleaf bands became nationally popular in the 1920s. No women belonged to major gumleaf bands, but women played gumleaves in church, and sometimes the whole congregation played.

#### Early twentieth-century bands

The Wallaga Lake Gumleaf Band from the south coast of New South Wales used a large kangaroo-skin drum to mark time. From the 1920s through the 1950s, apart from hymns, this band played popular and patriotic songs and dances. Bandsmen were known to play gumleaves in counterpoint while dancing (Breen 1989:22). In the late 1920s, the fourteen members spent months walking around the coast to perform at a ball in Melbourne; along the way, they did casual work, fished for food, and slept under bushes. Some members marched at the opening of the Sydney Harbour Bridge in March 1932, and during the same decade collaborated with the Cummeragunga Concert Party on the Murray River to tour the Goulburn Valley and Riverina District (Jackomos 1971:33). The Lake Tyers Gumleaf Band of Victoria performed for tourists. During World War II, leaders of army-recruiting drives employed its members in publicity stunts (Jackomos and Fowell 1993:25).

Gumleaves joined other instruments, variously including bones, spoons, ukuleles, fiddles, harmonicas, and accordions (figure 6). In the 1920s and 1930s, several Aboriginal vaudeville troupes toured the eastern seaboard. For paying audiences, they played in theaters, incorporating into their acts the sounds of jazz and the movements of clowning, corroboree-style stepping, and the *hula* (Ryan 1997). Virtuosos played gumleaves "no hands"—while playing an accordion with their hands or a harmonica with their nose (Sullivan 1988:65–66).

FIGURE 6     The gumleaf band of Darlington Point, New South Wales, Australia, 1932. *Left to right: back row,* Len "Busch" Kirby, Clancy Kelly, Edgar Howe, Freddy Christian (gumleaves); *center,* Billy Swindle; *front,* Roy Kennedy, Bon Hall (accordion), Stuart Clayton. Len Kirby Collection. Courtesy of the Australian Institute for Aboriginal and Torres Strait Islander Studies.

### From ensemble to solo tradition

By the 1960s, gumleaf quartets, trios, and duos came into vogue, overshadowing larger ensembles. The causes of this change included the Aboriginal urban drift, the rising popularity of guitars, the effect of rock, and the spread of television. Since 1977, informal and localized traditions have yielded to a national solo competition, open to Australians of any descent.

The leading Aboriginal exponent of the instrument is Herbert Patten (b. 1943), who as a child near Orbost, Victoria, observed the techniques of his great-uncle Lindsey Thomas. Like Thomas, Patten produces the deep, strong gumleaf tone of the open-air tradition, sometimes ornamented by wobbles (trills), vibrato, and wawa effects. He played at an exposition in Hong Kong in 1994. Recordings of his performances, ranging from Aboriginal and European songs to jazz items like "Birth of the Blues," are held at Monash University, Victoria. Dedicated female performer Roseina Boston (b. 1935) plays frequently on radio in Australia; she is descended from Possum Davis, former conductor of the Burnt Bridge Gumleaf Band of New South Wales.

Recordings of gumleaf performances are held in the Australian Institute of Aboriginal Studies, the National Library of Australia, and the archives of the Department of Music, Monash University. Two archival films are held in the National Film and Sound Archives.          —ROBIN RYAN, HERBERT PATTEN

### Bagpipes

Bands of bagpipes and drums are used in Aotearoa, Australia, and Hawai'i by members of immigrant Scottish communities. In Papua New Guinea, they are mainly associated with the national army and correctional staff. In December 1952, Pipe-Major L. MacLennan of Perth, Australia, formed the Pipes and Drums of the Pacific Islands Regiment in Port Moresby (figure 7). The band carries the tartan of Clan Cameron because of a visit at that time by Lord Rowallan, a member of that clan. Only six months after training began, the band joined the regiment on parade. In 1956, the band recorded two long-playing discs for the South Pacific Commission.

FIGURE 7    Pipers of the Papua New Guinea
Pacific Islands Regiment drill on parade, 1981.
Photo courtesy of Word Publishing, Papua New
Guinea.

In 1965, with the establishment of a second battalion (at Wewak), a second
band of bagpipes and drums emerged there. To perform jointly, both bands learn the
same pieces. The Pipes and Drums of the Pacific Islands Regiment have often toured
Australia, and commonly perform at Defence Force functions (Glanville 1984). They
have performed arrangements of local popular songs, including "*Papua, oi natumu*"
and "*Tripela de moa long Sohano.*"

The pipe band of the Correctional Institutional Services began in 1967, when
thirty custodial staff were trained by pipers and drummers of the Pacific Islands
Regiment. The band bought instruments from Pakistan, but now buys instruments
from Australia and Scotland. Since 1984, it has had female members, has played at
Port Moresby Show and Independence Day celebrations, and has won prizes at competitions in Australia.

—Don Niles

## Strings

European musical instruments transformed many Oceanic musical traditions by
being incorporated into indigenous musical systems. A useful example of this process
is the introduction of the guitar and its transformation into steel guitar and slack-key
guitar. Some of the earliest music on stringed instruments in the Pacific probably
occurred in Hawai'i, where the Portuguese *braguinha* was transformed into the
*'ukulele,* and Spanish guitars were transformed into Hawaiian guitars. The idiom that
derived from the combination of stringed instruments and the sung poetry with
which they were associated became known as Hawaiian music—developed in
Hawai'i by Hawaiians from musical ideas available during the second half of the
1800s. By the time of King Kalākaua in the 1880s, *'ukulele* and guitars were played
together. From Hawai'i, the concept traveled throughout Polynesia and to other areas
of Oceania—at least that is one story.

The proliferation of string bands has been phenomenal. Each island group has
its own preferred combination of instruments and styles of playing, with named
bands and famed individuals as composers, players, and singers. In Tonga, the band
of Tu'imala Kaho, Lou 'Ilima Koula 'o 'Amusia e 'A (The Golden 'Ilima Flower of
'Amusia e 'A) has ten singers, four of whom play stringed instruments: lead guitar,
rhythm guitar, and two *'ukulele.* The vocal parts include soprano (*fasi,* sung by
Tu'imala), two altos (one female, one male), one tenor, and six basses. Much of their
music is composed or arranged by Tu'imala Kaho and published in a booklet (1988b)

FIGURE 8    A Tongan amplified string band, with three guitars and a banjo. Photo by Adrienne L. Kaeppler, 1989.

and on cassette (1988a). At another point in the spectrum is the Tongan group The Old-Timers, who sing and play stringed instruments, including a violin. They play Tongan songs and American old-time songs, like "Home on the Range."

In each island area, band music is transformed by the indigenous music system into which it is incorporated. A colloquial term for the result is *pan-Pacific pop*. In many areas, string-band music is associated with local, cultural, ethnic, and national identity. In the late twentieth century, string bands have introduced amplifiers (figure 8) and electronic instruments, and are in the process of transforming themselves into power bands—bands that use power, in more ways than one.

—ADRIENNE L. KAEPPLER

### Papua New Guinea

Papua New Guinean string-band music, produced by ensembles variously including guitars, ukuleles, male singers, percussive instruments, and a one-string bass, is a subset of a pan-Pacific style-complex (Clark 1981, 1986; Donner 1987; Larcom 1982:337; Lindstrom 1990:108; Lindstrom and White 1990:159). Voices blend "in interlocked and overlapped polyphonies, in-sync and out-of-phase with strongly metric guitar or ukulele strums" (Feld 1988:96). Where geographically proximate indigenous music systems were mutually unintelligible, this musical practice became common.

The local genesis of these bands is unclear. They may have originated in Milne Bay Province (Dellman 1977:24), but more likely developed in several areas at once. In East Sepik Province, as many as twenty guitarists sometimes played together (Métraux 1990:525). In 1960, in Matupit, nontraditional performances by "teams of guitarists" occurred (Epstein 1969:310). The earliest string bands in Rabaul and Kavieng consisted of men returning from the Wau and Bulolo goldfields, where they had acquired rudimentary skills in playing guitars. The formation of string bands, and the birth and growth of distinct styles, may reflect a shift in the languages of musical texts. As more Tolai musicians formed bands, their language, Kuanua, came to replace Tok Pisin and other languages (Stella 1990; Waiko 1986).

Parallel to the rural development of string bands was, in the 1960s, the urban development of electric-guitar bands, which became locally known as power bands (*pawa ben*) or live bands (*laiv ben*). The first such bands, formed in Lae, Port Moresby, and Rabaul, consisted of mixed-race and Chinese musicians (Webb 1995:502–516), who performed the songs of the Everly Brothers, the Beatles, Chuck

Berry, and Elvis Presley ("Golden Opportunities" 1979). On a visit from Nouméa, New Caledonia, to Papua New Guinea, the band Freebeats introduced broadly Anglo-American music; its example encouraged more bands to form. Among Papua New Guinea's early power bands were the Kon Tikis, the Kopi Kats, the Porehoods, the Embers, and the Stalemates.

In 1975, the local commercial-recording industry began disseminating string-band recordings. By the late 1970s, regional substyles had developed. The most widely identifiable of these were Central, Tolai, Manus, New Ireland, and Madang (Susu 1983:16). Public recognition of regional styles masks the occurrence of stylistic variation within provinces and regions. This variation relies on precontact musical traits, particularly melodic, textual, rhythmic, and vocal timbre, and unique recombinations of features from Western and Pacific musics (Webb 1992).

*Musical styles*

Most string-band music uses tonic, dominant, and subdominant chords, and many bands play only in one key (Dellman 1977:25; Niles 1980:197). Some admired string bands come from Central Province, where bands emphasize intricate lead-guitar solos and accompaniments, exemplified in the recordings of groups such as Amazil Local (figure 9) and Bamogu Union Band. On the southeast coast of the province, bands use more complex chord progressions and modulations. While retaining the aesthetic sensibilities of string bands, many ensembles, including Paramana Strangers and Memehusa Company, changed over to electric instruments in the early 1980s. Paramana Strangers and Gaba Kaluks derived elements of their sound, including vocal style and guitar-fingering patterns, from Sakiusa and other Fijian musicians.

From other provinces, in various local substyles, came classic string-band songs or radio hits: "*Meri i Gat Namba*" ('The Girl Is Fabulous'), by Marawi Band, of East

FIGURE 9 Melodic outline and chordal accompaniment of an excerpt from the lead-guitar introduction to "*Garu Habare*," by Amazil Local (1981). After the introduction, as the vocalists enter, the key modulates to B♭, and then to A♭. Transcription by Michael Webb.

Sepik Province; "*Wanpela Liklik Meri*" ('A Young Girl'), by Kalibobo Bamboo Band, of Madang Province; and "*Poroman*" ('Friend'), by Yellow Top Band, a Tolai group (Webb and Niles 1986).

### String bands since 1975

When Papua New Guinea became independent, a proliferation of songs, most in Tok Pisin, exhorted communities to cooperate. String bands fostered a national consensus (Webb 1992). Catalyzing solidarity among youths, they exacerbated intergenerational conflict (Gewertz and Errington 1991:128–129; Stella 1990; Strathern 1984:64; Waiko 1986:36–38). Most were all-male, but East New Britain Province produced renowned female bands, including Lonely M. L. Daughters. Informally, women sometimes sing with men.

In educational institutions throughout the country, particularly schools not situated in or near the students' village homes, string bands provided an unequaled social and cultural context for reinforcing cultural solidarity in the face of temporary displacement (Dellman 1977). In the early 1970s, at annual festivals like the Tolai Warwagira, in Rabaul, a new tradition of string-band competitions (*stringben resis*) arose (Johnson 1983:39); it continued at multiple levels, including schools and colleges. Choirs too, and power bands, began to compete.

By the 1980s in many rural regions (particularly in the highlands), "six-to-six" electric-guitar bands were performing at all-night dances, from 6 P.M. to 6 A.M. Some bands traveled a lot; poorly paid, they consoled themselves with adventure and prestige. Attendees were usually unmarried men and women, who danced with each other in disco styles. By the mid-1980s, these events were supplanting the "dancing ceremonies and stringband parties . . . common in the past" (Matbob 1985). To supplement late 1950s and 1960s rock-and-roll classics, six-to-six bands performed medleys of string-band hits from the 1970s.

When string bands were new, they symbolized modernity. After the birth of power bands, residents of urban centers considered string-band music old-fashioned and outmoded; by the mid-1990s, however, some musicians were asserting that string-band style was the musical standard of national authenticity.

—MICHAEL WEBB

### Vanuatu

Pan-Pacific pop, supposedly based on pop-Hawaiian *hula*-music heard on 78-RPM disks, may have had currency in the 1920s and 1930s, via expatriates, but information on string bands in Vanuatu begins during the Pacific war, in 1942, with the arrival of U.S. forces at Luganville (Espiritu Santo) and Vila (Efate). In person and on the radio, local musicians heard and imitated U.S. servicemen's country and popular hits, and to their accompaniment young couples learned to dance Texas (*danis texas*), holding on to each other—a startling practice, since Vanuatu traditions had no mixed-sex dancing.

Michael Allen around Duindui district (West Ambae) presents boogie-woogie artists singing to guitars and ukuleles, with tea-chest one-string plucked basses, where the standard twelve-bar chorus may vary from nine to eighteen bars (with every odd length possible, say, sequences of thirteen, five, eleven, sixteen, and twelve bars), according to the texts. Guitarlike instruments use tunings to suit players' individual ways of finding basic I, IV, and V chords. Players strum, and are expected to sing choruses. String bands have such an appeal that the election of the Vanuaaku Pati to political power at independence in 1980 was aided by its string-band anthem.

High amplification is now rife, because players adopt Hendrix-style distortion and portable equipment has become efficacious and inexpensive, though responding to hotel guests' wishes, groups like Fatuana play cool and soft for middle-aged tourists, and use tuned soda bottles to add piano-like percussion. Annual string-band competitions are broadcast nationwide. From 1970 to 1990, Paul Gardissat of Vila played a major role in establishing and maintaining string bands on the radio.

Vanuatu string-band music includes striking examples of social commentary on local life. It is distinctive; any similarity to Hawaiian or Tahitian songs is accidental. Its rise parallels the rise of pidgins and creoles—from a mixture of adventitious vocabularies subjected to vernacular syntax.    —PETER RUSSELL CROWE

## MUSIC IN PLACE

### Australia

In Australia, popular music functions within contexts of leisure, most commonly in a prerecorded state, though live performances—at concerts, clubs, festivals—elicit support. Distinct styles of popular music attract definable social groups; many Australians remain loyal to a narrow range of musical styles.

### *Folk*

Australian folk includes old and new genres, descending from European and Asian states. Cross-cultural musical developments occur; but in immigrant communities, much of the music remains insular, actively recreated in reminder of an acknowledged homeland. Between 1788 and 1851, settlers from England, Ireland, and Scotland brought to Australia the first examples of the style (Watson 1987:50). In the 1990s, most Australians are of English and Irish extraction, but the proportion of non-British persons continues to increase.

Performances of Anglo-Irish folk, and of newly composed folk-styled music, occur within the context of musical sessions, clubs, and festivals. In each state, a central organizational committee oversees and aids organizers of clubs and festivals. The level of participation by audiences is highest in sessions and lowest at festivals. The historical accent of these gatherings shows in the participants' dress.

Most sessions occur weekly in public bars. The organizers encourage people to perform individually or join in choral singing. Clubs meet monthly in community centers or halls, where they present one or two headlining performers, and offer opportunities for floor singers (unbilled performers). The associated federations publish monthly newsletters.

Festivals occur annually. Smaller ones occur throughout the year, mostly between October and March; on Easter weekend, a national festival is held in Canberra. Large festivals celebrate non-Anglo-Irish musical traditions. To stress links with bygone days, smaller festivals occur in historically important rural towns, where they feature workshops. An annual Celtic festival occurs in Kapunda, South Australia. Other small festivals include Jamberoo and Wollombi in New South Wales, and Toodyay in Western Australia. At Kapunda, the restriction to Celtic traditions is unusual. Most Australian festivals encompass a range of musical styles.

At these events, particularly at sessions, the most widely enjoyed refreshment is alcohol, mainly in the form of beer. Festivals provide food, which, by representing various internationally derived cuisines, emphasizes multiculturalism. Smoking cigarettes is common at sessions, uncommon at clubs, and moderate at festivals.

In clubs and at festivals, perhaps 60 percent of performers and listeners are men. Audiences vary in age from preschoolers to nonagenarians, with a marked increase between the ages of thirty and fifty; performers are mainly between the ages of twenty-five and fifty. Only at major multicultural events, such as Carnivalé, a Sydney-based weekend-long display of the music and dance of various nations, do many different ethnic groups attend together.

*Music systems*

Organizers of clubs and festivals encourage the composition of new music, but composers must work within restrictive parameters, including melodic and harmonic simplicity and avoiding textual sentimentality. Composers usually introduce their own works to the public; later performances vary little.

In Anglo-Irish music, songs usually have stanzas and a refrain—a pattern composers of the 1990s still follow. Songs are ordinarily diatonic, in the major mode, in 3/4 or 4/4 time. Forms follow English, Irish, and continental European models: hornpipe, jig, mazurka, polka, reel, schottische, varsoviana. Few newly composed songs copy these styles; for collectors, older musicians continue to perform them.

New instrumental compositions draw equally from folk and jazz, plus ambient or New Age musical styles. Tempi are often free, and the music is tonal and repetitive. New compositions often reflect a wide range of temporal and tonal structures. Musicians prefer acoustic instruments, but they also play electric guitars and synthesizers. Textures range from the unaccompanied voice to bands made up of percussion (rarely drums), guitars (or other chordophones, such as mandolin, banjo, fiddle), bagpipes (or other aerophones), free-reed instruments (including concertina and button accordion), and vocals.

*Transmission and education*

Performers receive little or no formal training. They learn orally and aurally from other musicians, recordings, and notation. No Australian schools or institutions train people wanting to perform or compose folk. High schools include folk in the syllabus, but only students who have elected music as a course of study may enroll; teachers, who receive no training in the style, have meager knowledge of it.

The government fiscally supports the continuation of folk: to successful applicants, the Australian Folk Trust dispenses funds, in amounts that reflect political exigencies. Copyrights protect contemporary composers' work, but most pieces are in the public domain.

Folk receives little exposure on radio and television. The Australian Broadcasting Commission offers airplay on radio, as do several student- and community-supported stations. Journalists seldom comment on it, and most critical reviews stem from within clubs and committees. Most recordings depend on private funding: small, independent companies produce the exceptions, with limited distribution; performers themselves garner the most sales, in clubs and at festivals.

## Country

Australian country derives from North America, which continues to influence it. It presents distinctive subjects in recognizable musical forms for characteristic audiences (Watson 1987:48). Performances occur in diverse contexts, including clubs, concerts, and festivals. Amateur and peripheral musicians find opportunities to perform mainly in clubs, and musicians of higher public profile appear mainly at concerts and festivals. Clubs, festivals, and recording companies hold competitions. Festivals occur over weekends or annual public holidays, in rural towns. Performers and attendees dress in rural styles: hats, waistcoats, boots. By far the biggest festival occurs each January in Tamworth, New South Wales. Begun in 1973 and now a ten-day event, it attracts Australia's leading performers, national and regional broadcasts on television, and tens of thousands of fans (Smith 1984:126).

The textual and musical preoccupations of Australian country are conservative and restrictive; frequently sentimental, they explore the rural concerns of occupation and leisure. Common images in the poetry are "the homestead," "mother," "the old man," "cattle in the pasture," and "horses on the fields."

North American jazz reached Australia in 1917. Its initial performances provoked excitement and misinterpretation. The music appears to have emphasized comedy and abandonment. Critics condemned it as improper.

Following North American developments, Australian country in the 1990s adopted musical elements of rock. It also incorporated features of "bush music," the musical culture of rural Australians, as recorded and collected since the 1950s by folklorists, including Ron Edwards, John Manifold, and John Meredith. The songs mostly originated from 1850 to 1900. The conservatism of country provides sharp boundaries within which composers work; improvisations outside these boundaries risk alienating audiences.

Pieces in country-based styles are stanzaic in structure, often with a refrain. The most frequently employed tonality is the diatonic major scale, and music is usually in 3/4 or 4/4 time. Instrumental forms follow North American bluegrass models. Apart from human voices, steel-stringed acoustic guitars are the most frequently employed instruments. Australian musicians favor pedal steel guitars, fiddles, and (lately) electric guitars, electric bass guitars, and drums. The adoption of instruments and musical styles more commonly associated with rock has resulted in an increase in the sales of country. Some musicians have successfully crossed over into Australian popular music. Despite the success and increase in recognition the country-rock coalition has brought, change in the musical aesthetic of country has provoked censure (Watson 1987:48–77).

Country-music clubs provide some grounding for interested performers, but most performers and composers learn their craft at home, or by imitating other musicians. Australian schools and institutions provide little or no formal training in the subject. Lesser-known performers sometimes make their reputations by reinterpreting others' songs, but Australian country encourages the introduction of new songs. Many performers compose their own material.

Australian country receives its strongest media support from radio stations. In major cities, television and printed media present a low level of coverage, but the level increases in rural areas. Recordings provide a forum for musicians to reach audiences. Independent companies produce most marketed recordings. In 1990, at the Australasian Country Music Awards, forty-one of forty-six Australian-produced entries in the album-of-the-year category were on independent labels (Erby 1991:23). Publishers and copyrights protect composers' and performers' financial rights.

Country is most popular among rural Australians, including Aboriginals. Most performances occur in rural towns. Performers and audiences, predominantly of white European background, range from small children to old adults.

### Jazz

North American jazz inspired the beginnings of a jazz industry in Australia, but the history of jazz in Australia stands apart from that of its black-and-white models. It reached Australia in 1917 and grew in popularity throughout the 1920s. Its initial performances provoked excitement and misinterpretation. The music appears to have emphasized comedy and abandonment. Critics condemned it as improper. It has continued to rise and fall in public favor; it suffered neglect in the early 1930s, but enjoyed a boom in the early 1960s.

Performance of Australian jazz occurs in clubs, festivals, and concerts. All major Australian cities have nightclubs for jazz. These, plus supper clubs and bars, provide musicians with venues appropriate for short periods of residency, or for visiting interstate and international musicians. Musical scholarships and competitions, held annually, foster new talent. The level of interaction between audience and performer is fairly low, but audiences often express enjoyment and encouragement by applauding, during and after each piece. At jazz-oriented venues, the consumption of alcohol is common.

The strands of jazz usually performed in Australia are traditional (jazz in its early forms) and contemporary (bebop, cool, jazz-rock, avant-garde). Traditional performances offer reinterpretations of well-known pieces, but contemporary styles promote the composition of new ones. In both styles, improvisation is essential. The expectations of an audience and the limits of allowable innovation depend on the style: innovation, considered desirable in most contemporary forms, is less appropriate in traditional performance.

Song-based forms predominate. Instrumental pieces based on other structures have a "head arrangement": the head and improvised sections share a harmonic structure and sometimes melodic and rhythmic fragments. The temporal and tonal vocabularies are large; most jazz musicians have a thorough grounding in harmony and counterpoint. They perform solo, or in groups of any size. Bands support front-line instruments with a rhythm section of double bass, or of electric bass guitar and drums. Favored instruments include voice, saxophone, trumpet, electric or semiacoustic guitar, and piano.

Jazz is in the curriculum of most Australian conservatories. Secondary-school teachers of music have a rudimentary knowledge of it, and high-school students have contact with it as part of their schooling. Jazz musicians and composers learn their craft through a combination of theoretical study and aural experience. In the jazz-coordination program overseen by the Music Board of the Australia Council, the government provides administrative and financial support to jazz musicians.

The media aid in disseminating jazz: radio and television networks broadcast concerts and festivals, and printed journals specialize in the music. Independent companies produce most recordings, but established artists benefit from distribution by major companies. Some stores specialize in selling recorded jazz, but most retailers of cassettes and CDs give jazz recordings a small percentage of their displays. In 1990, jazz accounted for 2 percent of the recordings sold in Australia.

Almost uniquely to jazz, nightclubs reflect the socioeconomic status of contemporary audiences. Australian jazz is "predominantly a music for middle-to-upper-class audiences, with particular appeal to liberal intellectuals with a general interest in the arts" (B. Johnson 1987:61). Audiences of the jazz boom of the 1960s matured with the music: by the late 1990s, they were middle-aged, though some artists reported increasing attendance by younger patrons.

In contrast with jazz, the performance of early blues—Delta styles, on acoustic instruments—usually occurs in clubs, or at festivals. Urban blues, like those of Chicago in the 1940s and 1950s, occur mostly within rock-music contexts: in pubs, before an audience whose interests are more closely aligned with rock than with jazz.

## *Pop*

The rise of the recorded-music industry throughout the world echoed in Australia, from the earliest recordings of music-hall performers, through the jazz boom of the

1920s and the swing bands and light entertainment of the 1930s and 1940s, to the beginnings of rock and roll in the mid-1950s. Live presentations of pop in Australia occur in bars, clubs, large theaters, and outdoors. In dance-music clubs and at parties for dancing, prerecorded music is played. Performers and owners promote smaller events jointly; they sell tickets at the door, or consign them for sale in stores. Local promoters organize large concerts, featuring established musicians; they sell tickets in a single chain of outlets. Audiences and performers wear clothes reflecting current fashion. Audiences display pleasure with performances by dancing and applauding. They are more likely to voice displeasure in small settings, where the sale of alcohol accompanies performances.

The compositional processes of pop rely partly on the technology available to composers. Computer Musical Instruments (CMIs), widely used, emphasize a layering of instrumental textures. Alternatively, composers work with the aid of a guitar or a piano, or improvise with other musicians. Pop encourages a high level of stylistic conformity: excessively innovative composers reach narrow audiences.

Australian pop consists mainly of songs, with instrumental music mainly for dancing. Forms follow standard international conventions: stanza, refrain, and a third section (the "middle eight"). Chromaticism is rare; most compositions are diatonic, in 4/4 time. The most commonly used instruments are drums and other percussion, electric guitar, electric bass guitar, MIDI keyboards, sequencers, and vocals. (MIDI, or Musical Instrument Digital Interface, electronically links digital musical instruments; a sequencer stores encoded musical information, much like a multitrack tape recorder.) Less frequently used are acoustic instruments: accordion, fiddle, guitar, saxophone, trumpet.

The syllabus of secondary schools includes pop, but until the 1990s, music teachers in training received little instruction on how to present the subject. In 1990, Ausmusic, an organizational collective sponsored by the government and the music industry, started programs to train teachers. Technical and Further Education Colleges offer courses dedicated to the production of pop, but most musicians learn their craft from private teachers or other musicians. The government has introduced laws to ensure that Australian broadcasters air Australian productions. Artistically and financially, import-export laws aid local musicians. Music-video programs, and most AM and FM stations, broadcast pop. The print media offer a range of journals and magazines: in major cities, free weekly newspapers detail current musical events.

Bowing to market demands, major and (to a lesser extent) independent recording companies highlight pop in their releases. In 1990, it accounted for 87.5 percent of recordings sold in Australia. Pop has a wide appeal. Different musical styles emphasize specific social groups. An increase in the percentage of attendees under eighteen years of age has led to an increase in alcohol-free performances.

—KIM POOLE

### Aboriginal rock

Isolating rock from other forms of contemporary Aboriginal music is problematic, given the merging of genres, styles, and audiences, and individual musicians' versatility. Aboriginal rock reflects various tastes, "with country music, either ballad or country and western, not far in the background" (Chester Schultz, quoted in Breen 1989:130). It absorbs new styles and distantly created genres, including blues, hiphop, rap, and reggae [see TRADITIONAL AUSTRALIAN MUSIC: Contemporary Trends in Aboriginal Music]. Factors that have contributed to making it popular in Aboriginal music include the increased mobility of Aboriginal people, new funding for music, more political autonomy of Aboriginal communities, access (of consumers and producers) to the media, and formal Western musical training.

The late 1970s and early 1980s saw the emergence of Aboriginal organizations that funded the creation and dissemination of Aboriginal rock. These organizations included the Centre for Aboriginal Studies in Music (CASM), in Adelaide, where bands such as No Fixed Address, Us Mob, and Coloured Stone formed. Another seminal organization was the Central Australian Aboriginal Media Association (CAAMA), in Alice Springs. As a radio station serving remote communities, CAAMA realized that to broadcast what its constituency demanded, it needed to record more Aboriginal music, so it started the studio that has produced the largest number of Aboriginal contemporary recordings in Australia.

The 1980s saw the movement of Aboriginal lyrics from the narrative balladry or nostalgic storytelling of Aboriginal country styles to more confrontational, rhetorical, and overtly political texts of protest. The lyrics cover a range of topics, but most Aboriginal bands have composed or recorded political songs or songs of protest. Such songs represent an important aspect of the contemporary definition and expression of Aboriginal identity. A basic trope in current historiography is recognition of European colonizers' dispossession of Aboriginal people's land, livelihood, and culture; hence, lyrics addressing non-Aboriginal people often express anger and hostility.

Protest lyrics are often set as rock or reggae. Socially and historically, the development of Aboriginal rock parallels that of Afro-American blues and reggae (Davies 1993:83). The adoption of reggae by several Aboriginal bands after Bob Marley's concert tour of Australia (1979) provided an aesthetic and political medium for expressing frustration and anger.

*Conceptual traits of Aboriginal rock*
Aboriginal rock displays three main conceptual traits.

1. *Regional identification or affiliation authenticates Aboriginality.*—The grounding of a song, and therefore the producer of that song, to a particular physical and cultural area is often established linguistically. Examples include performing whole songs in Aboriginal languages ("*Ngura Panyatja Titjikalanya*" ['A Place Called Titjikala'], Desert Oaks Band 1989), using Aboriginal words in predominantly English-language songs ("Yil Lull," Geia 1988), referring to important places ("Yolngu Boy," Yothu Yindi 1994), and using Aboriginal English or Kriol ("Come-n-Dance," Blekbala Mujik 1995; "*Kapi Pulka*" ['Big Rain'], Coloured Stone 1987).

2. *Social issues are themes of Aboriginal life and culture.*—Examples include racism and discrimination ("Genocide," Us Mob 1981; "We Have Survived," No Fixed Address 1981), civil and land rights ("Australia for Sale," Casso and the Axons 1987), alcoholism ("*Woma Wanti*" ['Leave the Grog'], Areyonga Desert Tigers 1988), homeland movements ("*Kintore Lakutu*" ['Toward Kintore'], Warumpi Band 1987), jailhouse episodes, abuses by police, Aboriginal deaths in custody ("Jailbreak," Yothu Yindi 1995; "Justice Will Be Done," Shillingsworth 1988), and desires for returning to indigenous culture ("Take Me Back to the Dreamtime," Coloured Stone 1987).

3. *Rock spearheads other issues and agendas.*—To promote the use and maintenance of Aboriginal languages, CAAMA has produced a compilation CD, *In Aboriginal* (1994). CAAMA has also produced compilation albums on the subjects of Aboriginal community health (*UPK: Uwankara Palyanka Kanyinijaku* [A Strategy for Well-Being] 1989) and AIDS (*AIDS! How Could I Know* 1989).

*Regionalization*
The rock-related styles of Aboriginal bands vary by region. In the early 1980s, young, often urban Aborigines started bands at the Centre for Aboriginal Studies in Music,

in Adelaide. These bands' stance within Aboriginality is evidenced by their lyrics: texts set to reggae or hard rock are often political, dealing with issues of land or civil rights from pan-Aboriginal perspectives. Two of these bands, No Fixed Address and Us Mob, were featured in *Wrong Side of the Road* (1981), a film dealing with discrimination and hardships faced by young Aboriginal musicians.

Stylistic crossovers and borrowings occur throughout Australia, but bands often reflect the music prevalent in their area. Many Central Australian bands (like Warumpi Band and Desert Oaks Band) are heavily influenced by country and gospel music, and often utilize country-rock or gospel fusion styles. Yothu Yindi, from northeast Arnhem Land, and Blekbala Mujik, from central Arnhem Land, incorporate into their performances tribal singing, instruments, and dances. Joe Geia, from northeast Queensland, and Christine Anu, from the Torres Strait Islands, utilize island-style melodic and rhythmic elements.

In the mid-1990s, Yothu Yindi recorded two albums on a major label, garnered prestigious awards, and received international acclaim. Their main goal, that of most Aboriginal bands, is not money or fame. Aboriginal musicians see commercial profits as means to an end: they want to reseed into their communities what they have gained by interacting with the non-Aboriginal, market-run world. They view their work as a commentary on, and a reflection of, regional Aboriginal life. They feel they and their music should serve as a bridge between Aboriginal and non-Aboriginal Australia.                                                          —KATHLEEN R. OIEN

## Papua New Guinea

Music is a socially layered art (figure 10). Applied to music, the terms *traditional* and *introduced,* or *local* and *foreign,* are shifting and unstable notions. New Guineans experienced European musical instruments and forms in their earliest encounters with Europeans. In 1792, when Bruni d'Entrecasteaux's ships lay off Buka Island, a crewman played on the violin a melody that so pleased the islanders, they offered to trade clubs and bows for the instrument (Oliver 1991:72).

### Postcontact musical life

In the 1800s, fleeting musical encounters yielded to the sustained colonial influence of sacred music, military bands, and patriotic songs. In 1875, wanting to found a church, the Wesleyan missionary George Brown targeted Matupit Island, in Blanche

FIGURE 10     For the third Pacific Festival of Arts, a modern musical group of Papua New Guinea greets arrivals at the airport, playing garamuts, a kundu, panpipes, and a conch. Photo by Adrienne L. Kaeppler, 1980.

Bay: he and his Fijian "teachers stood offshore in their boats and began singing" (Mika 1976:24); attracted, residents welcomed them. So local peoples could grasp "a great truth through its repetition in song" (King 1909:194–195), missionaries taught them hymns, whose texts were among the first written items translated into indigenous languages (Webb and Niles 1987:51).

In the late 1800s, at missions in New Britain and New Ireland, and along the Papuan coast, Polynesian teachers taught their own musics, which they considered suitable substitutes for what they saw as accompaniments to licentious practices (Williams 1964:108). Consequently, some local musics and instruments fell out of use. On Kiwai Island by the early 1900s, empty kerosene tins frequently substituted for drums in dances "copied or adopted from Samoan mission teachers," or from men of various islands (Beaver 1920:179). Inland, European missionaries taught liturgical musics. In the 1920s, the artist Ellis Silas learned of a choir of local people in the mountainous region of Mafulu, Central Province, "whose rendering of the psalmody has been declared to be equal to that of any choir in Europe" (1926:33).

Patriotic songs, cheers, and salutes symbolized changes instigated by outsiders. In 1884, when British troops hoisted the Union Jack at Port Moresby, setting up a protectorate, a military band played "God Save the Queen," and a twenty-one-gun salute followed (King 1909:222). In the early 1900s, Sir William McGregor, a territorial administrator, registered surprise that Dobuans could sing the national anthem, "and all so decent like" (Burton 1949:96). By the 1920s, a bugle band was in training in the government school at Nodup, Gazelle Peninsula. By 1942, a parade band of Tolai policemen had formed in Rabaul (Clune 1951:234); after the war, it reorganized and traveled to Sydney, where it led a patriotic march (Neumann 1992a:58; "Tolala" 1950:53).

*European settlement and interisland travel*

After European settlement, music was a sign of colonial wealth. In 1896, Tolai dancers performed in Berlin, at the Colonial Exhibition (Nelson 1972:212; Neumann 1985:16, 1992b:312). Near the end of the 1800s, as crewmen and laborers, New Guineans from the mainland and various islands came into mutual contact, and music circulated as a commodity of exchange. Dances and songs were "the most easily and frequently diffused" of cultural traits (Powdermaker 1933:106). In the Trobriand Islands in the 1920s, workers from East Cape and Papua toured villages: for yams, breadfruit, and tobacco, they sold songs and dances (Silas 1926:175).

In early colonial times, ships helped transmit musics. In the northern Solomons in the 1880s, men of the survey ship *Lark* played a "pretty air . . . with the concertina in waltz time," music from the Duke of York Islands (Guppy 1887:141). In the 1920s, the Burns Philp schooner *Nuloa*, plying the waters off northern New Guinea, had crewmen drawn from across the Pacific, including a Buka quartermaster, a Solomon Islands cabin boy, and a Fijian steward; they sang "singsings of the sea and big-fella-s'ips" (Matches 1931:171). European passengers traveled with phonographs; on reaching their destinations, they held shipboard dances. Around 1960, on a trawler between Takuu and Nukumanu, a group of Takuu copra workers sang "romantic songs; 'pop' songs about topical events such as leaving their work and going home; other people's songs they had learnt while working in other places such as Rabaul; and their own old songs" (Spencer 1967:158).

Musical farewells migrated with commerce. In the Duke of York Islands in the early 1960s, young people played guitars, singing "songs that travel from island to island" (LeBrun-Holmes 1962). "*Yako Rah Oomanah,*" a guitar-accompanied song from the Solomon Islands, has this gloss: "Goodbye, my friend, my Solomon Islands, / Goodbye, I'm leaving. / Sad the wind, sad my heart, / Wait for my return."

*Folklorization and other innovations*

From the late 1800s, music and dance reinforced newly current ethnic-category terms. At competitive singsings sponsored by European planters or colonial officials, indentured laborers from the New Guinea mainland and various islands, and sometimes local villagers, simultaneously performed inside roped-off areas (Webb 1995:173–230). Intertribal rivalries often led to fighting; in the 1920s, at a singsing in Rabaul on the arrival of H.M.A.S. *Melbourne,* a clash resulted in a man's death (Overell 1923:98–99; Webb 1995:185, 189, 199–202).

In administrative centers, colonial officials merged multicultural displays of dancing with agricultural shows, where indigenous performers competed for prizes. The first Mount Hagen show (in the 1950s), the biggest such event, attracted forty thousand people from across the highlands. Many officials, including the governor general, attended. The show culminated in a parade, led by the constabulary brass band. A group from Mendi won £50 in the tribal-dancing contest, which lasted all "day and late into the night" (Williams 1964:344–350).

Singsing competitions still occur at regional shows in Goroka, Port Moresby, and Rabaul. Competitions and festivals continue at schools and colleges and in towns, incorporating the more recently developed styles of choirs, string bands, and other bands (Spencer 1967:47). The Warwargira Festival, founded by the Tolai in 1970, strongly contributed to the development of new musical forms and the rise of Rabaul as a commercial recording center (Johnson 1983:39; Neumann 1992a:223).

Before guitars were widely available, the Tolai pioneered triadically harmonized choral arrangements of indigenous songs (Australian Broadcasting Commission n.d.). Anticipating political independence, the colonial government held a competition to select a national song; it commercially released a recording of the finalists' entries (*Papua / New Guinea Independence Celebrations: Song Contest Finalists* 1975).

In some areas, indigenous songs became Christian liturgical music. In the 1920s, in a church on Sio (a small island in Morobe Province), an entire village met each morning to perform music that had mostly been "war chants and airs . . . connected with . . . ceremonial life," to which the people "had fitted appropriate Christian words" (Groves 1977 [1936]:97). Early plans for formal education included instruction in European music (Webb 1986), but at least one government school—set up at Kokopo in 1922—used "native songs with English words." In 1947, the territorial director of education, wanting "scientific surveys of certain aspects of native culture with a view to their inclusion in the educational programme of the future," appointed Ray Sheridan Native Music Officer (Groves 1977 [1936]:144–146).

Local contexts also changed, paralleling broader social trends. In the Okapa District, Eastern Highlands Province, redistribution of pigs became the new custom of commercialized festivals (*singsing bisnis*). Sponsors charged fees for admission, food, and drink; but to accumulate prestige, they put prominent guests in their debt by giving them gifts of pork, beer, and money (Foster 1992:291).

*New technology*

From the early 1900s, the gramophone became the "entertainer of the lonely outposts in the days before the space-annihilating wireless" (Booth 1929:18). As servants, indigenous peoples operated gramophones for outsiders (Mackellar 1912:131; Spencer 1967:187). At Rabaul in 1922, traveling Americans "danced to the music of a gramophone supervised" by islanders, who, for a fox-trot, "were liable to put on an opera selection" (Collins 1923:103). In the 1930s, at an Empire Day ball in Samarai, an islander played on a wind-up gramophone one record, "In a Little Spanish Town": "he made native music on it, playing one side of the record over and over again" (Mytinger 1946:40). The Tolai of Matupit were the first to own such devices (A. L.

Epstein 1992:237). In 1961, among the possessions of a domestic worker, departing Rabaul for Milne Bay, were "new suitcases and sewing-machine and gramophone" (Spencer 1967:191).

In 1935, from a hundred-watt radio transmitter in Port Moresby, experimental broadcasting began (Stuart 1970:114). The operation, the first in Oceania, took the name *4PM,* and broadcast news and music. Beginning in 1946, the Australian administration produced a "Native Peoples Session"; its audience was apparently an educated minority who had access to radios at missions, patrol posts, and council houses ("P-NG On Threshold of Dramatic Radio Development" 1963). At Port Moresby in the late 1940s and early 1950s, sixteen programmers and announcers ran Radio 9PA's "native broadcast section" ("Problems of Film Censorship and Radio Broadcasting"). Local peoples liked to listen to broadcasts of "their own singing—people singing and beating garamut, kundus, and things like that" (Australian Broadcasting Commission 1953). It was not until 1961 that the Australian Broadcasting Commission set up its first station, in Rabaul (L. W. Johnson 1983:86). Tolai audiences welcomed the "Rabaul Hit Parade," which covered Western popular music. In one month in 1963, the station received eleven thousand requests for songs ("Radio Rabaul Gives Them What They Want" 1963).

## Music during and after the Pacific War

During the war (1939–1945), entertainment for military personnel made a lasting impression on local populations; it included gramophones, a jukebox, motion pictures, and live performances. The latter included visits to a U.S. base in Torokina, Bougainville, by Bob Hope (with dancers and singers), and by Jack Benny with singer Martha Tilton and harmonica player Larry Adler (Jackson 1989:80–84, 87). At a base in Kiriwina, Gary Cooper (with singers Phyllis Brooks and Una Merkel) and John Wayne (with "two or three [singing] starlets") entertained troops and islanders (Powell 1945:116–126). In Port Moresby, the Australian musical-comedy star Gladys Moncrieff performed for Australian soldiers. The United Services Organization sponsored many shows. For an hour and a half, a show featuring American Jeannie Darrell, who sang in the Admiralty Islands, used three performers, but an Australian show displayed twenty performers in forty songs (Dawes 1943:120–121). Australian and U.S. styles of wartime entertainment contrasted further: the former offered "concert parties" headlining the "straight type of [vocal] solo"; the latter, "swing, or boogie-woogie" (Emanuel 1945; Powell 1945:125). Lighthearted comedy routines, ballet dancers known as the Tivoli Rockettes, Australian singers (including Victor Moore, known for his renditions of religious songs), swing bands—all contributed to musical entertainment (Powell 1945:116–126).

Servicemen and islanders also enjoyed movies. Early in the war, to screen old movies, Australia equipped trucks with projectors. Later, "American 16-mm units began making their appearance in large numbers, eventually showing the latest Hollywood releases" (Boyce 1945:6–7). Torokina base once had more than twenty "picture shows" (Medcalf 1986:35).

Other Pacific Islanders performed on New Guinean soil. In a show staged for officers, the Fiji Battalion, wearing "native garb," manipulated warclubs (Jackson 1989:87). Its song *"Bu Bu"* ("Drinking Coconut") shows how residents and troops shared their experiences. Composed in English, in a tight, four-part hymnodic style, its text refers to a Bougainvillean who profited from selling to Allied troops the coconuts enemy shelling had knocked from the trees (*'Isa Lei': Traditional Music of Fiji* n.d.). For themselves, Fijian soldiers held entertainments that included *taralala*—guitar-accompanied, informal, song-and-dance sessions (Ravuvu 1974:23).

> After 1945, guitars and ukuleles strongly affected the development of music in New Guinea. In the early 1960s, as soon as indigenous residents could legally drink alcohol, local string bands provided entertainment in hotels in urban centers.

Occupying forces encouraged the singing of hymns (Lindstrom and White 1990:165, 168). At one wartime service in Milne Bay, groups representing "many tribes" and "not a few islands" sang competitively: as Kiriwina Islanders walked home that night, they indulged "full-throated singing of hymns such as 'Yes, Jesus Loves Me'" (Powell 1945:52). In the Owen Stanley Range, indigenous carriers' singing inspired servicemen and carriers from other areas (Price n.d.:9).

Papua New Guineans recall Japanese marches and Shinto songs the Japanese taught them. In 1942–1943, they learned some of these songs formally, in schools on the Gazelle Peninsula and in the Sepik region; they learned other Japanese songs informally, around campfires. Japanese and Tolai sang, in their respective languages, versions of at least one song, about a submarine that accidentally sank. Christian Japanese servicemen learned Tolai hymns from the Methodist *Buk na Kakailai* (Leadley 1976:245, 247). With Tolai Christians, some sang Christmas carols and "Onward, Christian Soldiers" (Leadley 1975). On Los Negros Island, 150 marching Japanese soldiers sang "Deep in the Heart of Texas" as a decoy for U.S. Marines (Powell 1945:167).

### Guitar songs

After 1945, guitars and ukuleles strongly affected the development of music in New Guinea. In Rabaul before 1920, a Malay string band (Lyng 1919:131) and string orchestra (Lyng 1925:61) likely played Kroncong music, popular in Indonesia. As early as the 1920s, indigenous residents in urban centers probably heard Europeans' guitar-accompanied singing (Bassett 1969:51). Before 1939, stringed instruments— violin, banjo, banjo-mandolin, mandolin, guitar, ukulele—were popular in Rabaul, Port Moresby, and other urban centers. In the postwar years, from contacts with other Pacific islanders and American servicemen (Lindstrom 1990:154–161), music began to reflect a "marked guitar influence" (Sheridan 1972:819).

Guitars spread inland from seaports and other urban settlements, largely through the agency of indigenous and Pacific-Island evangelists, returning servicemen, schoolboys, and laborers. In the 1940s, guitar- and piano-accompanied duets, trios, and quartets by indigenous men occurred on missions in Milne Bay Province. Elsewhere during the Pacific War, a Solomon Islands missionary to Emirau, a small island in the St. Matthias group, sang to the accompaniment of his guitar the evangelical chorus "Fishers of Men" (Van Dusen 1945:16–17).

In the late 1950s in Rabaul, introduced musical forms went from town to village; older forms, from village to town (Spencer 1967:102). In the early 1960s, as soon as indigenous residents could legally drink alcohol, local string bands provided entertainment in hotels in urban centers. In the late 1950s and early 1960s, guitars reached rural regions (Stella 1990:58–59; Waiko 1986:36–37); by 1967, it had reached the present-day provinces of North Solomons, Eastern Highlands, East Sepik, Milne Bay, Morobe, Northern, Western Highlands, and West Sepik

(Chenoweth (1976:i, 76–79). Only in the late 1970s did ukuleles and guitars reach certain highland areas (Dellman 1976:25; Feld 1988:96).

For portability, cost, ease of construction, and rapid acquisition of skill, ukuleles were popular before the guitar. Most early string bands included at least one. Some bands used ukuleles exclusively (Dellman 1977:5; Niles 1980:190). In the late 1960s, in the Tambanum area of East Sepik Province, a status hierarchy that vaunted ownership and technical competency favored guitars over ukuleles (Métraux 1990:534).

*Early examples of guitar songs*
Guitar songs were initially minstrel, western, and hillbilly songs. In 1940, in the context of a music revue held in or near Port Moresby, Harry Mahuta provided a dance accompaniment on the steel guitar, with Siaka Heni on the banjo. Also featured were the unaccompanied Poreporena Choir.

In 1955, several ukulele- and guitar-accompanied songs were recorded in Manumanu, a Motu village in Central Province. One, with an original melody and an American text ("Carry Me Back to Old Virginny"), features yodeling like hillbilly or Hawaiian singing (British Broadcasting Commission 1958). Male string bands practiced on the beach. At least one song described wartime encounters among Papuans, Americans, and Japanese (Williams 1964:107).

Indigenous people soon began composing guitar songs. In the 1940s, Morea Hila of Hanuabada gained a reputation through his song "*Raisi Mo,*" and then through "*Poreporena Taumui*" and "*Base Veredia*" (Mackay 1975:59). A singer-composer who accompanied himself on guitar, he became the first Papuan broadcaster: in 1944, at Port Moresby, he joined Armed Forces broadcasting station 4PM.

Common traits of early guitar-accompanied songs include phrase-length variability, nonconsensual melodic beginnings among a band's singers, and irregular spacing between repetitions of stanzas. The song "*Meri Manam*" (figure 11), a parody of Sepik musicians by Rabaul's Kambiu String Band, illustrates the genre. The text, in Tok Pisin, recalls a woman from Manam Island, Madang Province.

> O a meri Manam, meri Manam!
> Sore peles, sore peles bilonga mia.
> O a meri Manam, meri Manam!
> Oo pat chit!
> Sore peles, ples bilong mi, meri Manam!
> O a meri Manam, meri Manam!
> O Yanini, O Yanini!
> Meri Manam, sitap long Aitape!
> Oo pat chit chit chit!

FIGURE 11  Excerpt from "*Meri Manam,*" with text as sung by Henry Lewerissa; recorded in Rabaul by Ray Sheridan for the Australian Broadcasting Commission in 1953. Guitar (which plays a G-major triad on every beat) and one-stringed bass not shown; original a semitone higher. Transcription by Michael Webb.

Oh Manam woman, oh Manam woman!
Homesick, pining for my home.
Manam woman, oh Manam woman!
*Oo pat chit!*
Homesick, pining for my home, Manam woman!
Oh Manam woman, Manam woman!
Oh Yanini, oh Yanini!
Manam woman, staying in Aitape!
*Oo pat chit chit chit!*

The song feels improvisatory. Stringed instruments provide a G-major setting for a repetitive, three-tone melody. A guitar strums a steady pulse. A string bass emphasizes every other pulse: after a few opening bars, it reiterates the chordal root. A ukulele improvises chordal embellishments, particularly at the end of sung phrases; it adds a sixth, and occasionally a major ninth. An open-throated, resonant voice, tempered by a light vibrato, recalls the vocal style of early-twentieth-century Hawaiian popular songs.

Blasius ToUna, a Tolai singer-composer, was among the first guitarists to become widely known in the country. In contrast with later practice, he performed without backup vocalists. On his recordings, his sons play ukulele and a second guitar. His recordings from the 1970s show familiarity with country-and-western ballads, hymns, European folksongs, and popular songs of the 1960s (Duvelle 1977). His song "*Bai Mi Maritim Gita Bilong Yu*" ('I'll Marry Your Guitar') comments on performances and their reception, as the translation of an excerpt shows:

Today, we come to the end of our performance.
We wish to go and leave you all.
Goodbye to all of you, and a very good night.
Perhaps you'll all have to come again.

When you [inclusive] began picking the guitar,
And we were seated, watching you play,
Your performance was really lovely,
And the sound of the guitars was like that of the breakers.

You must strum this guitar one more time;
I want to hear it once more, or I'll cry.
The sound of the guitar is really lovely:
It moves me, and I wish to marry it.

The song may refer to performances of the 1950s or early 1960s; ToUna had begun playing guitar in 1949. The reference to more than one player suggests an ensemble, the sound of which induced a profound emotional response from listeners. It suggests the achievement of musical competency by performers and listeners. The text refers to strumming, picking, and separation of performers and audience.

*Layers of practice*
In the late 1950s in Central Province, musical performances marked official openings of churches, cooperative stores, and other buildings of local significance. Villagers sorted themselves by age, in groups that had idiosyncratic dress, music, dance, and sex-based roles. In precontact costume, to the accompaniment of kundus, old people performed ancestral songs and dances. Attired in clean dresses and skirts, decked in

frangipani and hibiscus, middle-aged women danced bowdlerized versions of Polynesian dances, to the accompaniment of ukuleles strummed by men; they all sang hymns and *peroveta*. Led by officeworkers from Port Moresby, younger men formed a "jazz band of guitars and homemade percussion instruments, with a double-bass built from a tea-chest"; in nasal voices, they sang cowboy songs and "pseudo-Hawaiian love laments"; wearing "western frocks," girls danced fox-trots in pairs; separately, boys did the same (Williams 1964:75–76).

In the early 1990s, without the accompanying social stratification, the Tolai maintained a three-part division of musical styles (Neumann 1992b:307). In Tolai villages, neither "traditional dances," nor hymns, nor popular songs are the domain of a particular generation.

### Europeans' responses

Local peoples have been eager to learn European music, but most Europeans have paid little attention to local music. In 1912, with young people on Fergusson Island, Diamond Jenness learned courting songs with young people (Jenness and Ballantyne 1920:7–8). In the Trobriand Islands in the 1920s, an artist, Ellis Silas, tried to learn the movements of a dance (1926:174). While conducting fieldwork, Hortense Powdermaker (1966:112) in the 1930s, and Scarlett Epstein (1968:xi) in the 1960s, participated in dancing. Vida Chenoweth (1979) and Stephen Feld (1990) composed songs in the Usarufa and the Kaluli musical systems respectively. Christian missionaries discouraged and replaced local musical practices, but at least one advocated local musics as a medium for new religious expression (Chenoweth 1979:xv; 1980, 1984).

### Commercial recordings

On gaining national independence, the people of Papua New Guinea became preoccupied with the creation of public culture. Music figured in this process, helped by commercial recordings, which developed into an industry, complete with annually awarded "gold cassettes" (Niles 1984, 1985, 1986, 1987). In 1988, Port Moresby had three studios, and Rabaul had four (Niles 1988:3). Because of this concentration, ensembles from these areas issue more recordings, and are more musically influential, than those from elsewhere in the country (figure 12). Some songs became nationally popular. From Rabaul, Shutdown Band's "*Solwara Katim*" ('Separated by the Sea') became a radio hit in 1989; the national airline, Air Niugini, included it in its international in-flight entertainment. Largely as a result of Chinese involvement in recording and promotion, Port Moresby and Rabaul heavily influenced commercially recorded music (Niles 1992:34).

After 1975, commercially distributed recordings began tapping alternate styles. Acoustic string bands sang texts in indigenous languages. Gospel choirs were small and large; male, female, and mixed; unaccompanied or accompanied by acoustic guitars. Power bands were male-dominated groups that played on electric guitars. Generic, transnational, pop, and rock imitations sometimes featured texts translated into a highly anglicized Tok Pisin. Commercial studios released few traditional songs (*singsing tumbuna*), which in contrast with the practice of the 1950s and 1960s, broadcasts seldom featured (Simons 1988:68). Heavy doses of foreign top-forty hits on national radio (the AM *Karai Service* and the FM *Kalang Service*), available in pirated cassette copies imported from Singapore and Indonesia, exerted strong musical and cultural influences. The result was greater musical homogeneity.

From several perspectives, the growth of a recording industry fostered a national or generic culture. Rivalry among the leading recording studios inclined each to develop different strategies in the pursuit of a bigger audience. Beginning in the 1980s, Pacific Gold Studios (of Rabaul, East New Britain) released *Brukim Bus*

Technicians of the National Broadcasting Commission invited local bands to travel to studios to record. This practice permitted an unusual degree of grass-roots control over the formation and application of musics as symbols of identity.

FIGURE 12    Cassettes recorded and distributed from Rabaul and Port Moresby: *a, Junior Devils Stringband* (1986); *b, Nokondi Nama* (1988).

(*a*)                            (*b*)

'Shortcut', a series of cassettes, in which, to competently imitated versions of the songs of a famous revisionist band of the 1970s, Creedence Clearwater Revival, local musicians sang newly composed, topical texts in Tok Pisin. The use of commonly understood languages and musical styles helped recording firms expand.

Pacific Gold Studios also recorded the Tolai string-band-turned-power-band Molachs, which pioneered Tolai rock, an electric-guitar-based genre, which blended indigenous styles and standard rock. In 1982, the band's album *Painim Wok* proved string-band music had become a marker of local cultural identity ("Rely on Local Talent for Our Jingles" 1987; "Painim Wok Goes Back to Its Roots" 1990). Having renamed itself after the album, the band popularized a heavy-metal-like style. By the late 1980s, it had sold more than a hundred thousand cassettes (personal communication Greg Seeto). Early Tolai-rock songs—especially Barike's "*Bing Bing Lur*" and George Telek's "*Aumana Talaigu*" and "*Vunalaslas*"—inspired the formation of other Tolai bands: Droxy, Gravediggers, Junior Unbelievers, and Shutdown Band.

Later, Pacific Gold released a cassette album of versions of the song of the national television station, *Lukim Em-TV* 'Watch Em-TV'. The versions exemplified reggae, rock, and country-rock, plus several stylized string-band versions—in highland style (sung in Tok Pisin), Papuan-string-band style (sung in Motu), and bamboo-band style (also sung in Tok Pisin). An earlier version released by the same studio had featured an arrangement in semiacoustic Tolai-string-band style. The performance stressed a rhythm common in indigenous Tolai music (Anonymous 1987). Probably for the first time, a studio band had deliberately imitated regional string-band and bamboo-band substyles.

### Strategies for marketing

Broadcasting and recording-studio activity helped shape the representation of New Guineans to themselves. Peripatetic technicians of the National Broadcasting Commission, moving among urban provincial radio headquarters, invited local bands to travel to the studios to record. Though this practice resulted in the dissemination of musics of particular regions, it permitted an unusual degree of grass-roots control over the formation and application of musics as symbols of identity, since studio or technological intervention in the process remained minimal. In contrast, Pacific Gold invited musicians from other regions to record in Rabaul. Through multitrack-recording techniques, studio-employed musicians provided the accompanying band. In this way, Noan Wale, of Southern Highlands Province, produced *Hailanda*, a commercially successful cassette. From the mid-1980s, Pacific Gold, Chin H. Meen, and the National Broadcasting Commission emphasized studio production in shaping an ensemble's recorded output.

Chin H. Meen's main studio was in Port Moresby. In the late 1970s, it promoted the music of the Black Brothers, a reggae-oriented expatriate Indonesian band living in Papua New Guinea. The studio sponsored a commercially successful band, Deejays, known for a "free-flowing" style ("Getting to Grips with Gospel" 1984), clearly indebted to Fijian and other Polynesian guitar-based styles. Chin H. Meen issued this band's cassettes in the Australian Torres Strait Islands, the Solomon Islands, and Vanuatu. In the mid-1980s, to expand the market, the company broadcast in the Solomon Islands a taped weekly radio program, "Chin H. Meen Supersounds." In 1989, the company set up a second studio, in Rabaul.

In 1979, the neotraditional band Sanguma, formed at the National Arts School in Port Moresby, deliberately began hybridizing older New Guinean songs with rock and reggae. Sanguma represented Papua New Guinea at international events. In the 1980s, it recorded an album in Aotearoa, and made a video while touring in the United States. It disbanded in the late 1980s, but reformed in 1994 and played at a benefit for Rabaul-volcano victims. In 1995, another art-school ensemble, Tambaran Culture (since disbanded), released on Pacific Gold an album of neotraditional music.

In 1990, performers from Rabaul, working with performers from Melbourne, made the recording *Tabaran* (Not Drowning, Waving 1990). In 1993, George Telek, Pius Wasi, and Ben Hakalits performed with Not Drowning, Waving at world-music impresario Peter Gabriel's WOMAD festival in Adelaide, Australia. The song "Rowena," by the Rabaul band Barike was featured on the world-music compilation CD *Tribal Heart* (1994). In 1991, Rykodisc released an experimentally composed and recorded compact disc of a highland soundscape (Feld 1991). CD players are not yet widely owned in Papua New Guinea, but in 1995 several studios began releasing compilations, principally targeting tourists.                                  —MICHAEL WEBB

## Solomon Islands

Contact with the West, beginning in the mid-1800s, has resulted in extensive social and cultural change in the Solomon Islands. Hymns and other Christian-related music play an important role in people's lives. Western harmonies and scales, particu-

FIGURE 13    A bamboo band in Maleai Village, Shortland Islands, 1991. Courtesy of the MABO Project.

larly the diatonic scale, underlie musical performances. Interisland migrations and influences from Polynesia spur further changes.

In the New Georgia Islands in the early 1920s, Solomon Islanders lined up wide bamboo tubes of different lengths, which they tuned to Western scales and bound like a raft. They played these instruments by hitting individual tubes with coconut husks or rubber sandals (figure 13). With the addition of guitars, ukuleles, and voice, a new style of music appeared—an accompaniment for songs and dances that even assimilated sounds as nonindigenous as boogie-woogie. Bamboo bands and their associated dances remain popular in Western Province.

In 1950, an islander from Choiseul brought knowledge of this ensemble home to Sirovanga Village, where he founded the band Baliku, named after a yam-eating bird. The bandsmen made their own raft panpipes; for the strings of the guitars and ukuleles, they got wires from Allied forces. They created a new musical genre, *kela boru,* a term borrowing the New Georgia word *boru* 'something'; it has simple harmonies, a slow tempo, and a strong beat. To accompany it, Choiseul Islanders invented the *venga boru,* a women's dance, in which performers waved handkerchiefs in both hands, or put their hands on their waists and formed two concentric circles: one circle rotated clockwise; the other, counterclockwise. At the end, they clapped.

### Panpipe music

In Honiara, musicians developed a style based on panpipe ensembles of Malaita, especially 'Are'are ensembles. Increasingly important for special events and ceremonies, it is favored by the employees of private companies; children's ensembles from Christian secondary schools in Tenaru, a suburb of Honiara, are famous.

Musicians have altered old instruments and introduced new ones, arranging the music in a hybrid style built on Western harmonies. They use raft panpipes, of up to seventeen tubes each; to cover different scales and keys, these instruments come in pairs. Musicians pad one end of bamboo tubes so stamping the tubes produces a soft sound. Other new instruments for popular music include thick bamboo tubes arranged in a raft and hit by a stick, and seed rattles.

### Guitar music

Styles incorporating musical elements from Europe, the Americas, and elsewhere in Oceania, have appeared in the Solomons. Guitar songs (in Choiseul, *kela gitagita*) are hymnlike, countrylike songs, sung in local languages. Particularly popular with young people, they are accompanied by plucked or strummed stringed instruments,

FIGURE 14   Accompanied by guitars, people of Maleai Village, Shortland Islands, perform an island dance, 1991. Courtesy of the MABO Project.

mainly guitars and ukuleles, including homemade models using local materials (such as pandanus wood and leaves) and formerly having as few as three strings. Their style originates in musics introduced by Polynesian missionaries, heard by people who as migrant workers lived on Fijian plantations, and introduced during the Pacific war by U.S. military forces. Typically in strophic forms, guitar songs are sung by young men in high registers, sometimes in falsetto. They use simple chords, with rapidly strummed guitars and texts mostly about love.

Guitars paved the way for Polynesian music, from which Solomon Islanders developed songs and instrumentally accompanied dances. They developed the *hula,* locally a face-to-face line dance, from a dance brought to Western Solomons by Methodist missionaries from Tonga, and the *gongala,* a couple dance in a circle, from the *toralae,* possibly a local adaptation of the Fijian dance *taralala.* Invented in Choiseul in the 1970s and named for Gongala Village, the latter is a dance for a duet or a trio, who stand side by side, put their hands on each other's waists, shake their hips, and move their feet in tandem. At the end of each stanza, they stop; with torsos touching, they again shake their hips. In 1978 appeared a variation in which the dancers touch faces instead of torsos. *Gongala* music was fast, with light guitar ornaments. Later, a gutbucket—a string stretched across a board inserted into an empty petroleum can, struck with a stick—gave each ensemble a deeper, heavier sound.

The *gongala* became popular for several reasons. It maintained two important traits of indigenous dance: placing the feet neatly with every step, and a repeated up-and-down bodily movement. Young people enjoyed the novelty of cross-sex touching in public, the sensation of shaking their hips, and the happiness they felt in the sound of the guitars. In 1974, attendees at a Roman Catholic conference in southern Choiseul tried to ban it. By the 1980s, schoolchildren all over the Solomons were performing it, but village elders in Choiseul, defending the tradition that required physical avoidance between men and women, finally banned it.

Island dance, accompanied by string bands in a rapid tempo with lively rhythms, replaced it (figure 14). The texts of the accompanying songs are in local languages, or in Solomon Pidgin. The choreography (featuring intricate gesturing), costumes, and music are in effect a new Polynesian style, popular among the young. To perform these dances and songs, troupes are forming throughout the Solomons.

### Urban music

Performed by amateur bands, mainly in Honiara, and influenced by calypso, reggae, rock, and worldbeat, urban popular music is spreading in the Solomons. The means of its dissemination include radio (SIBC, including advertising jingles), cassettes produced by the radio station in villages, and live performances in hotels and discos. Typical urban groups are Fire and Ice (which by 1995 had disbanded), Okinawa Band, RYO (Rural Youth Orchestra), Sisirikiti, and Unisound. Each has five to eight members. Bandsmen live in Honiara, though most of the bands have origins elsewhere. Members tend to be speakers of the same language (*wantok* 'one-talks'). RYO are from Malaita Island, and Sisirikiti are from Santa Isabel.

Amateur bands use electric guitars, keyboards, and drums. In sound and beat, their songs are not wholly original, but they vividly express indigenous values and feelings, especially of those who, by living in towns, confront urban problems: unemployment, alcoholism, interethnic conflict, and women's hardships.

From the late 1980s to the mid-1990s, urban hits were "*Wakabaot long Saenataon Ia*" ('Walk Around Chinatown'), "*Master Liu*" ('An Unemployed Person'), "*Hibiscus Garu*" ('Prostitutes of Hibiscus [Hotel]'), and "*Mama Karae*" ('Mother Is Crying'). These songs show influences from calypso, reggae, and country, but their tempo is slower, their themes are more local, and their language is Pijin.

—Ryūichi Tai

## Micronesia

Long before Magellan's landing on Guam (1521), some peoples of Micronesia had occasional contacts with each other. Their encounters led to the sharing of cultural information, including music. Each culture modified and incorporated into its own musical system what it had learned from abroad. In now unknowable ways, the music of each culture reflected, and continues to reflect, the nature and intensity of these encounters.

Encounters with Westerners brought new kinds of popular music. The Mariana Islands and Guam have the longest histories of Western contact, but all Micronesian cultures have developed popular music in response to worldwide trends. Since the introduction of Western music and instruments, they have transformed old genres, producing dynamic composites, each popular in the judgment of particular audiences.

Micronesian peoples long maintained their genres of music and performance. Many genres remain in use, some in something like their original contexts, others in recontextualized settings, but popular music has joined them as a means of defining and perpetuating cultural identity and tactfully communicating about controversial subjects (Nero 1992).

### Earliest documented influences

The earliest documented influences on popular music in Micronesia were the Spanish sailors, soldiers, and missionaries who in 1668 began working toward Spanish colonial rule of Guam and the Marianas. These influences are evident in the vocal styles of contemporary Chamorro songs, including *kantan chamorrita,* solo and group songs distinguished by metaphors and other allusive verbal devices.

In the 1800s, North American Protestant missionaries' introduction of hymns immensely influenced singing in many parts of Micronesia. Three- and four-part tonal harmony, the musical grammar of those hymns, became an integral texture in religious and some secular singing. Also in the 1800s, Micronesia hosted whalers, merchant ships, and copra traders, who brought harmonicas, guitars, ukuleles, mandolins, accordions, and banjos. Kosrae and Pohnpei were whalers' frequent ports.

From 1899 to 1914, Germany administered all of the area but Guam, under U.S. control. Micronesians gained increased access to harmonicas and button accordions because these instruments were then popular in Germany. Another result was the *matmatong,* an unaccompanied Palauan song-dance, invented around 1900 by Chuukese laborers hired by Germans to work the phosphate mines. Later, German and Japanese words were intermixed into its text.

Beginning in 1914, Japanese administration of Micronesia led to increased Micronesian familiarity with Japanese people and their music. In 1934, Tanabe Hisao did fieldwork on several Micronesian islands, recording music. On Kosrae, he observed islanders singing Christian hymns; in the Marshalls, he documented performance on tin cans as percussion instruments. Cracker and biscuit tins still serve as percussion instruments in some areas, and even join the electronic instruments of contemporary ensembles. In 1936, Iwakichi Muranushi, a Japanese anthropologist, made recordings in Micronesia. In Palau, he recorded youths' songs (*derebechsul*), showing influence from Japanese popular music. In Pohnpei, many songs of that period showed influences of Western popular music (Tatar 1985). By then, Micronesians were performing Hawaiian songs like "*Aloha 'Oe.*"

### The Pacific War onward

Popular music in Micronesia underwent great changes after 1945 (figure 15). Micronesia was first administered by the U.S. military, later by the United Nations,

FIGURE 15    In Guam, a schoolboy plays a guitar during the lunch break. Photo by George M. Bain, 1945. Photographic Library, Bureau of Aeronautics.

and finally by the U.S. Department of the Interior. Military radio stations, USO-sponsored shows, and touring military bands began influencing local music. They were especially influential on Guam, Saipan, and other military and civilian administrative centers, where enterprising islanders set up bands to entertain troops.

The use of woodwinds, brasses, and other symphonic instruments increased in developed areas. In undeveloped areas, guitars, ukuleles, harmonicas, and other introduced instruments transformed indigenous songs, melodically and structurally. In the late 1940s, pop and country broadcasts on military stations—WLXI, "The Voice of Guam"; WXLD in Saipan; WVTY in Ulithi—increased the exposure of American music. The intermingling of elements of these styles, plus the use of fiddles, string basses, saxophones, and trumpets, became more widespread. Some islanders developed contemporary ensembles to perform at village functions.

By the 1950s, the Charfauros Brothers on Guam, David Sablan in Saipan, and others had gained recognition, locally and in expatriate communities abroad. Economic development occurred more slowly in other areas of Micronesia, especially Chuuk, Palau, Pohnpei, and Yap; in each area, at least one radio station, operated by the military or civilians, broadcast recorded music from the United States. The styles of popular music developing locally were distinguished by island-specific instrumentations, languages or dialects, and lyrical sentiments. In the Caroline Islands, slack-key guitar tunings became a feature of popular songs, as they remain.

By the mid-1960s, popular music on Guam and Saipan had become more attuned with worldwide trends than popular music elsewhere in Micronesia. During the 1960s, Candido (Candi) Tamen on Saipan, Johnny Sablan on Guam, and others released commercial recordings of popular music. From island to island, the style, form, and frequency of performance of popular music stretched over a continuum, depending on variable access to resources and technology. This pattern continues. Islands that host tourists have clubs and hotels, whose performances range from Micronesian and Polynesian variety shows to jazz, rock, and reggae. Some popular Micronesian groups are family-based (the Kaipat family on Saipan are a locally recognized example). Some soloists, like Johnny "B" Bekebekmad of Palau, accompanied themselves on guitar and, later, on electronic keyboard.

Since the 1970s, tourism has increased, primarily from Japan, and popular-music bands have sprung up in response. On Guam, vocalist Jesse Bias and the Taotao Tano Dancers, Jimmy Dee and the Chamorritas, the Sunshine Kids, and Mike Di Amore Jazz Quartet perform regularly, as do, on Saipan, Alex Falig and Max Pangelinan. Also on Saipan, the I Don't Know Band, a Sāmoan ensemble, performs their own reggae, sometimes called Jamoan music (combining the words *Jamaican* and *Sāmoan*). These bands' instruments, mirroring bands on the U.S. mainland, include electric guitars, keyboards, and synthesizers. These performers play for tourists and locals, adapting their style to suit the audience. Most bands record in the Philippines or Hawai'i, and market cassettes locally through retail sales.

In contrast, the development of international pop-musical styles has not been so thorough in Palau, the Federated States of Micronesia, and the Marshall Islands, where people live near transportational and governmental hubs, with residual populations on outlying islands and atolls. Since the 1970s, the dissemination of cassettes and electronic keyboards has enabled musicians, even there, to record on location. Since each island group has its own language or dialect and social structure, most lyrics are locally specific. Favored styles include those influenced by country, pop, and reggae. Since 1992, a unique style of rap has developed on the outer islands of Yap. Rap recordings from Chuuk are increasing in popularity among young people.

Popular music is performed in public social contexts, and for casual gatherings of friends in homes, clubs, and hotels. Portable keyboards are becoming the instrument of choice, joining acoustic and electric guitars. Keyboards preprogrammed with rhythmic sequences often replace drums. In the administrative centers of most islands, established bands and vocal soloists entertain at social affairs.

The production quality of recorded popular Micronesian music varies. Guam has nearly state-of-the-art recording studios, but their use is impractical for artists from less developed areas. Palauans have strong appetites for popular music by local artists, but most Palauan recordings are produced in the Philippines. In undeveloped areas, performers record on stereo cassettes or in local radio stations. Listeners then dub the cassettes for friends, losing acoustic fidelity with each successive duplication.

—MARK PURYEAR

## Fiji

Fijian popular music (*sere ni cumu* 'bumping songs') developed since the mid-1920s under the influence of European and American popular music. It relates to styles that developed elsewhere in Oceania under similar influences, most of which retain elements of their pre-European musical traditions.

At first, Fijians borrowed Western melodies and fitted them with Fijian words. They still do, but a more important development was the indigenous composition of Fijian popular music. Though words and melody are Fijian-composed, these songs take inspiration from Western or Westernized music, including music from other Pacific Islands and the Caribbean.

The history of *sere ni cumu* is obscure. The name probably refers to the context for singing such songs in their early days—parties where men clinked or bumped their glasses together. Several prominent Fijian musicians and scholars associate the rise of this style with the first legally allowed sales of beer to indigenous Fijians, who, for the first time in the 1920s, could buy and publicly drink beer; several bars opened to serve them. This development was centered in Suva, the capital. According to Eremasi Tamanisau, a Fijian composer, goldfields on Vanua Levu and Viti Levu were important locations where *sere ni cumu* were composed and sung at all-night parties. Many *sere ni cumu* still popular in Fijian villages were composed during the Pacific War (1939–1945), an intense period of creativity for this genre.

The residents of many Fijian villages associate *sere ni cumu* with informal kava-drinking sessions [see MUSIC AND INGESTED SUBSTANCES]. Usually served and drunk on ceremonial occasions, kava (*yaqona*) is associated with the singing of a special *meke* in indigenous style. After a day's work, people consume kava informally during sessions that may last until dawn. Villagers who have gathered to share a bowl may spontaneously perform *sere ni cumu*. Such singing, as it passes the evening hours, reinforces feelings of collective solidarity.

Fijians distinguish between village-style *sere ni cumu* and more sophisticated, commercial brands of Fijian popular music, found in towns. In Naselesele (Taveuni Island) and elsewhere in Fiji, singers call the village style *sere ni verada* 'veranda songs', in reference to their typical context. Informal and laid back, this style is said to be the oldest popular music current in Fiji. Village-style *sere ni cumu* are traditionally sung by men only, mainly because only men ordinarily participate in extended kava-drinking sessions. (Occasionally, these sessions include women.) Many lyrics of *sere ni cumu* concern love, human relationships, and the beauties of nature and homeland. "Never Say Die," an example from Baidamudamu (Kadavu Island), has a macaronic text about soccer.

### *Musical style*

Songs may be sung unaccompanied, or accompanied by slow and steady strumming on guitars and ukuleles. Village-based groups are renowned for distinctively tuning

In Fiji, the *taralala* enlivens festive occasions. People dance it in a line, taking slow steps forward and then backward. Missionaries introduced it as an entertainment for kindergartens.

their instruments. As with Hawaiian slack-key guitars, individuals and ensembles tune their guitars and ukuleles in special ways, developed to suit their styles of playing.

Ensembles sing in three- or four-part harmony, using progressions that usually follow Western models, mainly on tonic, subdominant, and dominant triads. Typically, the vocal lines are closely spaced, but the bass tends to be spatially separate and dynamically prominent. Its importance possibly relates to that of the bass drone, which harmonically anchors the singing of *meke.*

Though set in Western melodies and harmonies, many village-style *sere ni cumu* exhibit elements that link them to pre-European musical traditions. Some have narrative texts that contain the poetic imagery and symbolism typical of old *meke* and pre-European lyrics elsewhere in Oceania. Other features reminiscent of old *meke* include a triple subdivision of the basic beat and men's falsetto singing. Most examples are sung by performers sitting in a tightly bunched circle, with the leaders in the middle; this format is typical also of *meke.*

Most cultures of Oceania value collective performance more highly than solo performance. Similarly in Fiji, polyphony, albeit in Western tonality, is the prevailing texture for collective singing. Most *sere ni cumu* are merely songs (with or without instrumental accompaniment), not ordinarily associated or performed with dance. The *taralala* is an exception. A social dance, it enlivens festive occasions. Its music resembles that of other *sere ni cumu,* but with livelier rhythms. People usually dance it in a line, taking several slow steps forward and then backward. Methodist missionaries introduced it as an entertainment for kindergartens.

In urban centers, professional bands produce more up-to-date *sere ni cumu,* featuring electric instruments, upbeat rhythms, and varied harmonies. Modernized songs also accompany Western-style dancing. Village-based bands copy these styles, including Fijian adaptations of the major international varieties of rock of the 1980s and 1990s. Reggae, in particular, has had a big impact on Fijian music.

—David Goldsworthy

## Hawai'i

In popular music, Hawai'i is commercially marginal. Long distances from Japan and the U.S. mainland and high costs of travel keep all but the most daring off-island performers from risking the trip. But multiculturalism and prominence as a tourist destination make Hawai'i home to a varied mix.

### The club scene

Discussion of the clubs of Hawai'i benefits from distinguishing not only between tourist-oriented and local-oriented venues, but also between specifically ethnic and more generally inclusive venues. Many clubs act as bridges connecting disparate styles or peoples; others serve as buffers, sequestering and celebrating nonmainstream tastes, languages, and identities.

Clubs in Hawai'i developed with the cash economy of the early 1800s. Before then, music and dance centered on intoned poems (*mele*), tied to religious ritual and popular entertainment; dancing (*hula*) visually embellished sounded words. In the new contexts of the early 1800s, *mele* and *hula* probably supplied entertainment for paying customers. Through contacts with foreigners, musicians acquired and developed Western musical concepts, including the use of the fiddle (*pila*) and the guitar (*kīkā*). Older songs and dances coexisted with later forms, but are seldom performed in clubs, where most Hawaiian music is a blend of indigenous and Western styles.

Hawaiian music has long dominated the local club scene, not only in tourist areas of Honolulu (especially Waikīkī and the harbor district known as Hotel Street), but also in local communities. Many non-Hawaiians enjoy the music, and some perform it. Small bars off the tourist track feature Hawaiian music, live or recorded. Famed Hawaiian performers work a circuit that extends throughout the state. Music provides full-time employment for a few.

### The 1920s through the 1980s

In the 1920s and 1930s, at the height of Hawaiian musical popularity abroad, the major Hawaiian hotels and most theaters, many dance halls, cabarets, bars, cruise ships, community centers, and even bowling alleys, offered entertainment with local themes. The most famous site for live music was possibly the Moana Hotel, home of the first large orchestra, the first regular national broadcast from the islands ("Hawai'i Calls"), and a jam session that attracted legendary performers. The Moana Hotel Orchestra, under the direction of Johnny Noble (1892–1944), included piano, drums, saxophone and violin, with locally typical instruments: guitar, 'ukulele, double bass, and steel guitar. Arranging Hawaiian melodies as fox-trots and other dances, Noble drew heavily on mainland jazz and popular styles. Billed as the Hawaiian Jazz King, he set the standard for prewar commercial Hawaiian ensembles.

Since the 1920s, incorporating into Hawaiian music the stylistic elements of jazz has led Hawai'i closer to the international musical mainstream. These elements include hot solos, riffs, improvisation, augmented chords, swing, syncopation, call-response patterns, and plasticity. African-American, Chinese, Japanese, Filipino, European, Hawaiian, and Korean participants visit Hawaiian clubs together.

More segregated ethnic music venues have preserved the pluralism of Hawai'i's heritage. In the mid-1800s, agriculturists began establishing large plantations and importing labor from Asia and Europe. Throughout the rest of the century and into the early 1900s, immigrants came from China, Japan, Korea, the Philippines, Portugal, and Puerto Rico. Each group performed its music and dance on the plantations, sharing its arts with interested outsiders and reinforcing continuity with its homeland. As each group left the plantations, clubs and bars sprang up to serve them, providing environments where people still enjoyed the old language, food, and music. Newer communities—Hong Kong Chinese, Laotians, Sāmoans, Tongans, Vietnamese—have also founded clubs, which seldom attract outside attention. In keeping with Hawai'i's spirit of inclusion, these clubs tolerate outsiders, and sizable gatherings attract people of different races.

The most segregated clubs in Hawai'i are operated by the U.S. military. Most personnel and their families live on military reservations but frequent local clubs. Many military-oriented facilities, though they ban outsiders, feature mainland and local music, performed by mainland and local performers.

In the late 1950s in Hawai'i, as elsewhere, big bands yielded to smaller groups, as cooler forms of music attracted customers and young players. During this period, the exotic sounds of Martin Denny (replete with birdcalls) and Arthur Lyman held sway in Waikīkī, and young Don Ho, Kui Lee, and others experimented with a laid-back English-language balladic style, harmonically and rhythmically complex. The biggest young stars, Alfred Apaka and Don Ho, attracted tourists and local listeners. The differences between tourist and local tastes are complex; few major performers play exclusively for either audience.

Even in the 1970s, at the height of the revival of Hawaiian music and identity, most leading revivalist performers, including Sunday Manoa, Hui Ohana, and Olomana, worked regularly in Waikīkī. Political activist George Helm played the Gold Coin, a Chinese restaurant. The first major Hawaiian revivalist band, The Sons of Hawaii (with Eddie Kamae, Gabby Pahinui, and others), started by working bars outside Waikīkī, including the Sand Box on Sand Island Road, but later found regular employment, in and beyond Waikīkī.

As Hawaiian music experienced an upsurge among young people, concerts began to cut into club dates. With the Waikīkī Shell filling for local favorites like the Makaha Sons, hotels downsized their clubs. Several took their performers off the stage and made them stroll. Some groups, such as the Kahauanu Lake Trio, quit, but other performers, including the legendary Andy Cummings and Genoa Keawe, said they actually enjoyed strolling.

By the late 1970s and early 1980s, many nightclubs in Hawai'i, as elsewhere, had begun turning to more mediated music, using disco systems, commercial recordings, and karaoke. Because the Asian resident and tourist populations are large, Hawai'i picked up on karaoke earlier than other areas outside Japan. This innovation remains important to the local scene, mainly in clubs catering to Chinese, Japanese, Korean, Vietnamese, and other Asian participants.

The 1980s saw a sharp decline in the number of local clubs offering live music as a staple. Many bars that had featured music closed down or switched to satellite television. Even the strip joints, locally called Korean bars, switched to tapes. Factors local observers most commonly cite for this downsizing include the flexibility and inexpensiveness of mediated music systems, increased package tourism, a decline in the popularity of Hawaiian music abroad, new drunk-driving laws (which restricted "happy hours" and increased club liability), and young musicians' reluctance to pursue music as a full-time career. Additions to this list are skyrocketing land values (which forced small clubs to reduce operating expenses) and multinational hotel chains' standardizing their operations (which caused the local flavor of hotels to fade).

*The 1990s*
Spurred by the Jawaiian craze (see below), a revitalization of club activity began in the early 1990s. It started on the grass-roots level in small clubs, like Sparky's Lounge. Soon, Hawaiian reggae bands were playing regularly throughout the state, even on Moloka'i and Lāna'i.

Few clubs that feature mainstream rock have lasted long in Honolulu. Alternative rock at The Wave, opened in the 1980s in Waikīkī (figure 16a), and locally created world music at Anna Bannanas (located since the late 1960s in the university area), have survived much longer than any mainstream-rock establishment. In the 1990s, punk found a small, dedicated audience, willing to support local appearances by nationally known bands, including Fishbone, Fugazi, Invalids, Primus, and the Queers. Like ethnic and gay club scenes, punk is invisible to the mainstream, its advertising limited to radio, handbills, and word of mouth.

The most highly esteemed post-Jawaiian club music is an unplugged sound, blending Hawaiian music and pop. O'ahu favorites Ka'au Crater Boys, featuring

FIGURE 16    Performing spaces: *a,* The Wave, a Waikīkī home of alternative rock. *b,* Otto's Reef, a site for popular music on Beach Road, Apia, Western Sāmoa. Photos by Adrienne L. Kaeppler, 1996.

(*a*)

(*b*)

*ʻukulele* virtuoso Troy Fernandez, have sparked a revival of interest in the *ʻukulele.* Their Hawaiian standards, rock oldies, and English-language originals set the trend. The Maui performers Hapa and Kaliʻi Reichel have also had success. On Maui, a small world-music scene has evolved around the Casanova Restaurant, whose owner has flown in Buddy Guy (a nationally known bluesman) and afropop groups from New York, exclusively for weekends.

Hip-hop and rap, with their combination of prerecorded and live music, have not had a major impact on the local club scene. Both are popular on imported recordings, but only a few young local performers, most prominently the band Fiji, have fashioned original versions of the concept. The Hawaiian love of relaxing (*nahenahe*) sounds may be working against the jarring electronic effects of the pop mainstream. In clubs, even Fiji tends to tone it down.

### Hawaiian reggae (Jawaiian)

In the early 1990s, a localized blend of reggae and Rastafarian iconography dominated the indigenous popular music of Hawai'i. The term *Jawaiian* names this blend, which conforms to a wider Polynesian phenomenon: local reggae in Aotearoa, Sāmoa (figure 16*b*), Tahiti, Tonga, and elsewhere predates Jawaiian, which maintains the Hawaiian strategy of adapting foreign musics for recreational dancing.

Recorded by independent labels for local consumption, Jawaiian owes much of its inspiration to Jamaican superstar Bob Marley, promoted by globalized media. Disparaged by cultural conservatives for being insufficiently Hawaiian, it appeals largely to a youthful subculture, tied to land, beach, and local identity. Though it illustrates the power of transculturation, it retains or reinforces much from the past. Like ancient Hawaiian singing, it is word-based and metrically duple. Like much Hawaiian music since 1820, it uses major modality and triadic harmony. Its melodies and structures follow patterns familiar from hymnody and country, musical imports that previous generations absorbed.

Most Jawaiian bands perform with ukuleles and acoustic guitars—a combination that has dominated local popular music since the late 1800s. In the mid-1990s, groups increasingly used drums and electronic keyboards, but most solos continued to be played on guitars, with basic rhythms played on ukuleles. Jawaiian tempos tended to range between eighty and 150 beats per minute, faster than most Hawaiian music, but slower than hip-hop and other locally available mainstream dance-music. Like reggae of the late 1970s, Jawaiian of the 1990s featured motivic repetition; with short phrases presented in a responsorial pattern, or as a refrain, it encouraged listeners' participation.

Most Jawaiian texts are in English, sometimes with pseudo-Jamaican accents, but lyrics espouse Hawaiian values. A frequent theme is love of the land (*aloha 'āina*), expressed poignantly in Ho'aikane's "Kailua Kona." In a typically Hawaiian consensus-building manner, texts address social concerns, especially land and sovereignty. As in most pop musics, romance abounds, culturally encouraged in the context of celebratory and honorific attitudes. Other common topics include surfing (as in Butch Helemano's "Wave Rider"), and the music itself (as in Marty Dread's "Reggae Rock Maui Style" and Na Waiho'olu'u O Ke Ānuenue's "Jawaiian Slide"). With several reggaelike treatments of hymns, Del Beazley illustrated the compatibility between Jawaiian and *hīmeni*. For contemporary audiences, Israel Kamakawiwo'ole's "Hawaiian Superman" recontextualized legends of Maui the trickster.

### Evolution

Intensified communications and improved electronics helped Jawaiian evolve. In the 1970s, imported recordings, then live appearances (by Toots and The Maytals, Jimmy Cliff, and Bob Marley), attracted small but enthusiastic audiences. In 1979, Daniel Keiji Warner's program "Reggae from The Lion's Den" debuted on KTUH, the radio station at the University of Hawai'i. In 1980, Warner created Lion's Den Hi-Fi, a Jamaican-style sound system, which helped acquaint local musicians, such as Butch Helemano and Lydia Sur, with the music of expatriate Jamaicans, such as Harold "Rankin Scroo" Johnson and Maacho, an influential but enigmatic figure.

Playing by ear and learning from records, amateur bands formed on each island. Several small, commercial radio stations, most importantly KAOI (on Maui), began to integrate reggae into their playlists. Dubbing spread the music further, especially among high-school students.

Peter Moon ("Island Love"), Billy Kaui ("Mr. Reggae"), and Loyal Garner ("Koke'e") recorded reggae-styled songs in the 1970s, but Jawaiian coalesced in the early 1980s, when The Pagan Babies, Brother Noland Conjugacion, and others forged a distinctly Hawaiian style. In 1985, the Kahanu label released "Sweet Lady of Waiahole," the first Jawaiian standard. A medium-tempo *mele pana* 'landmark song' by Three Scoops of Aloha, with a marleyesque melody and a singable chorus, it quickly passed into popular circulation.

On the same label, three men fresh out of high school became the first Jawaiian stars, collectively known as Kapena. Their first hit, covering UB 40's cover of "Red-Red Wine," briefly quotes "Rapper's Delight." But Jawaiian does not emphasize toasting, the performance of rhymed narrative poems. The main exception, the group Ho'aikane, performs an electric style closer to current reggae than most Jawaiian. Jamin Wong, a member since age fourteen, models his raps on Jamaican and U.K. stars, especially Pato Banton and Terror Fabulous.

Throughout the 1980s, support for performers increased. Rastafarian symbols, usually blended with Hawaiian imagery, appeared with increasing frequency on clothing, stickers, and surfboards. Jamaican expressions, such as "*irie*" entered local slang, often free from the confines of their original meanings. In Hawai'i, *irie* covers senses from relaxed to excited; it can take on some of the meanings of the Hawaiian word *aloha*.

In 1990, KCCN, O'ahu's premier Hawaiian radio station, started an FM outlet targeting Jawaiian fans. Locally televised programs and advertisements featured the music. Between 1990 and 1993, many Hawaiian recordings and concerts incorporated Jawaiian elements. Some groups, including Bruddah Waltah and Island Afternoon, played only reggae, but most—including Kapena, Ka'au Crater Boys, Willie K, Hawaiian Style Band, Na Leo Pilimahana, Israel Kamakawiwo'ole, Henry Kapono, and Simplisity [sic]—adopted it into their style.

In the mid-1990s, local musicians were changing the name *Jawaiian* to *island music*. This change bespoke an ongoing process of localization. As off-island musicians accelerated tempos and roughened textures, Jawaiian performers maintained the gentleness (*nahenahe*) of Hawaiian music. As off-island producers turned to synthesizers and sampling, Jawaiian instrumentalists maintained their Hawaiian predecessors' relationship with ukuleles and guitars. As Kingston, New York, and London dance-hall stars fashioned personas as gangstas and ragamuffins, Jawaiian singers extolled the virtues of *aloha*.
                                                                —JAY W. JUNKER

## Aotearoa

New Zealand followed the pattern of other Western countries in appropriating American and British musical trends, but its isolation and biculturalism, blending Māori and European traits, resulted in unique eclecticism. Its position as a former British colony, with the American cultural influences that permeated the English-speaking postwar world, produced an unusually balanced ratio of British-American popular music.

Not all trends reached Aotearoa. Listeners virtually ignored skiffle and the surf-music craze. Similarly, although some groups—La De Das, The Underdogs, The Pleazers—enjoyed commercial success with rhythm-and-blues styles, no major rhythm-and-blues movement developed.

The major local genre of popular music in the late 1950s and early 1960s was country. Apart from the music of Scottish immigrants, little British rural music reached Aotearoa. Trends locally called folk reflected American models, in the form of country or the commercial style of such performers as Peter, Paul, and Mary.

In the late 1960s, the progressive popular music of Britain and America was largely unheard in Aotearoa, where the dominant format for bands remained lead guitar, rhythm guitar, bass guitar, and drums. Longer-lasting bands of that period changed repeatedly, adopting different models—psychedelia, British beat, middle-of-the-road ballads. These bands included Larry's Rebels and the La De Das. Overseas performers remained more popular in Aotearoa than local bands. Though some bands, such as the Underdogs, achieved prominence, none enjoyed the acclaim of the Beatles and the Rolling Stones.

By the early 1970s, local musicians had found their voices, leaving mannerly restrictions behind. Aotearoa rock developed a countercultural role, disdaining chart-oriented styles of music. Some musicians reassembled stylistic fragments from imported musical practices. During the postpunk boom of 1979 to 1982, garage bands like Proud Scum, Pop Mechanix, and the Screaming Mee Mees came to the fore.

### Māori and Pacific Island popular music

On the cabaret circuit in the 1950s and 1960s, Māori singers and bands mainly performed British-American music. The most popular of these artists was Sir Howard Morrison. Some artists tried combining Māori and British-American dances in songs such as "Haka Boogie" and "Poi Poi Twist." In the 1970s, Māori guitarists combined pyrotechnic blues and acid rock, imitating U.S. guitarists Jimi Hendrix and Carlos Santana, with *waiata* and Polynesian guitar rhythms.

After Bob Marley's visit (1979), reggae bands proliferated. These bands—including Aotearoa, and Dread Beat and Blood (later simply Dread Beat)—combined smooth indigenous harmonies with rough Jamaican rhythms and militant lyrics. Dread Beat's music included titles like "Colonial War," "No More War," and "One People." The Twelve Tribes of Israel, an Auckland-based Māori reggae band, carried these themes into the late 1990s. The longest-surviving Māori reggae band is Herbs, formed in 1980. Reggae, dancehall, and ragga have been important in hybridizing Māori popular music, demonstrating how reggae and its associated ideas and images can acquire new meanings when taken into a different social system.

The most distinctive entertainer in Māori popular music of the 1980s, Dalvanius Prime, produced "E Ipo" for the middle-of-the-road singer Prince Tui Teka. Its success led to "Poi E," first a hit single and video, and then a musical. "Poi E" combined Māori vocals, show bands, and concert-party forms with funk and break dancing. In Auckland, the 1980s saw the emergence of Māori soul, of which the most widely known exponent was the band Ardijah.

Hip-hop and rap inevitably served as a medium for Māori militancy. The most successful Māori rappers are Upper Hutt Posse, who found acceptance in Aotearoa and Australia. Their first releases (1988) put U.S. underclass rhetoric within a distinctly Māori frame of reference.

Māori and Pacific Island female singers in the 1990s operate mainly in dance-disco, a medium that has little room for non-Western traditions. Their musical styles reflect a need for marketable imagery. In 1992, Moana and the Moahunters, a Māori female trio, played at the New Orleans Jazz and Heritage Festival. That was the first major international exposure Māori popular music received. Moana and the Moahunters combine pop, reggae, funk, soul, and *waiata*. They play indigenous instruments, like swung slats (*pūrerehua*), and wield indigenous implements, like *poi*.

Many Māori regard broadcasting as a means of cultural empowerment. Māori popular-music bands, especially those that sing in Māori, rarely get airplay on national radio; they are heard mostly on university- and tribe-sponsored stations.

### Global and regional idioms

Most popular genres available in the United States and Europe have homegrown equivalents in Aotearoa. Techno is provided by Trasch; the dance-music scene is represented by NRA (Not Really Anything); white rappers MC, OJ, and Rhythm Slave have grafted themselves onto a U.S. underclass idiom; and Push Push represents the commercial end of a hardcore thrash-metal scene.

In 1981, a unique national musical identity crystalized around Flying Nun, an independent label based in Dunedin. Many bands that recorded on Flying Nun echoed U.S. bands of the 1960s and 1970s, such as Velvet Underground. The music of The Bats, of Christchurch, recalls that of the Byrds, and the music of The Jean Paul Sartre Experience recalls that of British independent-label bands like Lush and Ride. A sense of alienation is a trait of these bands' lyrics, as is an almost complete absence of a culturally oppositional stance.

Since exporting is necessary for a label's survival, national success inspires efforts to break into international markets. The first local band to achieve international recognition began in 1972 as Split Ends. With a changing roster of members, it became Split Enz in 1975 and Crowded House in 1986, though by then, none of the original members of Split Ends remained in the band.

Flying Nun is Aotearoa's most successful independent label. Founded to create an outlet for South Island bands, it became synonymous with the Dunedin sound. In the late 1980s, it added bands that had ambitions of reaching international markets; several of these—The Clean, The Chills, The Jean Paul Sartre Experience, The Verlaines—also appear on U.S. labels. Other producers, including Ode Records, Wingside, Tall Poppies, Rattle Records, and Tangata, have released recordings that have affected the local music industry, covering the stylistic spectrum.

While record companies are prominent in establishing local artists, other media and resources generate an infrastructure of support. The Arts Council of New Zealand Toi Aotearoa, NZ On Air, and Export Music New Zealand work with local musicians to fund debut albums and increase novices' airplay.

—IOANNIS PSATHAS

## REFERENCES

*AIDS! How Could I Know.* 1989. CAAMA Music 203. Cassette.

Amazil Local. 1981. *Amazil Local.* Walter Bay Trading Company. Vista NGK 6028. Cassette.

Anu, Christine. 1995. *Stylin Up.* Mushroom Records D 24325. Compact disc.

Areyonga Desert Tigers. 1988. *Light On.* Imparja Recordings 21. Cassette.

Australian Broadcasting Commission. N.d. *Songs of the Tolais.* T4LM-1482. 45-RPM disk.

———. 1953. "Ray Sheridan's Collection of Native Music of Papua and New Guinea Recorded July/August 1953." Interview with Ismael ToWolaka.

Bandy, David Wayne. 1989. "The History of the Royal Hawaiian Band 1836–1980." M.A. thesis, University of Hawai'i.

Bassett, Marnie. 1969. *Letters from New Guinea 1921.* Melbourne: Hawthorn Press.

Beaver, Wilfred N. 1920. *Unexplored New Guinea.* London: Seeley, Service.

Blekbala Mujik. 1995. *Blekbala Mujik.* CAAMA Music 244. Cassette.

Booth, Doris R. 1929. *Mountains, Gold and Cannibals.* Sydney: Cornstalk Publishing.

Boyce, Ralph L. 1945. "Introduction." In *Southwest Pacific Sketchbook,* by Cedric Emmanuel. New York: Prentice-Hall.

Breen, Marcus, ed. 1989. *Our Place Our Music: Aboriginal Music.* Australian Popular Music in Perspective, 2. Canberra: Aboriginal Studies Press.

British Broadcasting Commission. 1958. *Folk and National Music Recordings, Volume 1: Foreign Countries.* Recorded Programmes Permanent Library, 239–243, record 23176. LP disk.

Burton, John Wear. 1949. *Modern Missions in the South Pacific.* London: Livingstone Press.

Casso and the Axons. 1987. *Australia for Sale.* Mantree Industries. Cassette.

Chenoweth, Vida, ed. 1976. *Musical Instruments of Papua New Guinea.* Ukarumpa: Summer Institute of Linguistics.

———. 1979. *The Usarufas and Their Music.* Dallas: Summer Institute of Linguistics Museum of Anthropology.

———. 1980. *Music for the Eastern Highlands.* Ukarumpa: Summer Institute of Linguistics.

———. 1984. *A Music Primer for the North Solomons Province.* Ukarumpa: Summer Institute of Linguistics.

Clark, Ross. 1981. "Stringed Instruments and Stringbands." In *A New Song from the Islands,* Ross Clark and Allan Thomas, presenters. Broadcasts by Radio New Zealand.

———. 1986. "Some Notes on Neo-Melanesian Music." In *Asia Pacific Voices: Selected Papers from the Asia Pacific Festival and Composers' Conference,* ed. Allan Thomas and Ross Clark, 68–70. Wellington: Department of Music, Victoria University, and The Composers' Association of New Zealand.

Clune, Frank. 1951. *Somewhere in New Guinea.* Sydney: Angus and Robertson.

Collins, Dale. 1923. *Sea-Tracks of the Speejacks: Round the World.* Garden City and New York: Doubleday, Page.

Coloured Stone. 1987. *Black Rock from the Red Centre.* Rounder Records 5022. LP disk.

Darius, Walter. 1988. "Rock in Rabaul." *The Times of Papua New Guinea* (31 March–6 April): 27.

Davies, Chris Lawe. 1993. "Looking for Signs of Style in Contemporary Popular Aboriginal Music." *Australian Journal of Communication* 16:74–86.

Dawes, Allan. 1943. *'Soldier Superb': The Australian Fights in New Guinea.* Sydney: F. H. Johnston.

Dellman, Richard. 1977. *Aiyura String Bands.* Cassette tape and booklet. Aiyura: Expressive Arts Department, Aiyura National High School.

Donner, William W. 1987. "'Don't Shoot the Guitar Player': Tradition, Assimilation and Change in Sikaiana Song Performances." *Journal of the Polynesian Society* 96:201–221.

Desert Oaks Band. 1989. *Titjikala.* CAAMA Music. Cassette.

Donner, William W. 1987. "'Don't Shoot the Guitar Player': Tradition, Assimilation and Change in Sikaiana Song Performances." *Journal of the Polynesian Society* 96:201–221.

Duvelle, Frédéric. 1977. *Blasius ToUna: Guitar Songs of Papua New Guinea.* LRF 030. LP disk.

Elbert, Samuel, and Noelani Mahoe. 1970. *Nā Mele o Hawai'i Nei: 101 Hawaiian Songs.* Honolulu: University of Hawai'i Press.

Emanuel, Cedric. 1945. *South Pacific Sketchbook.* New York: Prentice-Hall.

Epstein, A. L. 1963. "The Economy of Modern Matupit: Continuity and Change on the Gazelle Peninsula, New Britain." *Oceania* 33(3):182–215.

———. 1969. *Matupit: Land, Politics, and Change among the Tolai of New Britain.* Berkeley: University of California Press.

Epstein, T. S. 1968. *Capitalism, Primitive and Modern: Some Aspects of Tolai Economic Growth.* Canberra: Australian University Press.

Erby, Nick. 1991. "Country Music." In *ARIA Yearbook,* ed. Paul Turner, 23–24. Sydney: ARIA Publications.

Feld, Steven. 1988. "Aesthetics as Iconicity of Style, or 'Lift-Up-Over-Sounding': Getting into the Kaluli Groove." *Yearbook for Traditional Music* 20(1):74–113.

———. 1990. *Sound and Sentiment: Birds, Weeping, Poetics, and Song in Kaluli Expression.* 2nd ed. Philadelphia: University of Pennsylvania Press.

———. 1991. *Voices of the Rainforest.* Rykodisc RCD 10173. Compact disc.

Foster, Robert J. 1992. "Commoditization and the Emergence of *Kastam* as a Cultural Category: A New Ireland Case in Comparative Perspective." *Oceania* 62(4):284–294.

Geia, Joe. 1988. *Yil Lull.* Gammin Records D3129. LP disk.

"Getting to Grips with Gospel." 1984. *The Times of Papua New Guinea,* 11 November, 20.

Gewertz, Deborah B., and Frederick K. Errington. 1991. *Twisted Histories, Altered Contexts: Representing the Chambri in a World System.* New York: Cambridge University Press.

Glanville, Ian. 1984. "Get the Tag Right." *Post-Courier* (5 September):5.

"Golden Opportunities." 1979. *New Nation* 3(10):31.

Groves, William C. 1977 [1936]. *Native Education and Culture-Contact in New Guinea: A Scientific Approach.* New York: AMS Press.

Guppy, H. B. 1887. *The Solomon Islands and Their Natives.* London: Swan Sonnenschein.

Guzman-Alaluku, Zende. 1981. "Old Tom Lays Down His Baton." *The Times of Papua New Guinea* (17 September):16, 19, 23.

*In Aboriginal.* 1994. CAAMA Music 241. Compact disc.

*'Isa Lei': Traditional Music of Fiji.* N.d. Columbia 330SX 7604. Notes to LP disk.

Jackomos, Alick. 1971. "Gumleaf Bands." *Identity* 1(1):33–34.

Jackomos, Alick, and Derek Fowell. 1993. *Forgotten Heroes: Aborigines at War from the Somme to Vietnam.* Melbourne: Victoria Press.

Jackson, Donald. 1989. *Torokina: A Wartime Memoir: 1941–1945.* Ames: Iowa State University Press.

Jenness, Diamond, and Andrew Ballantyne. 1920. *The Northern D'Entrecasteaux.* London: Oxford University Press.

Johnson, Bruce. 1987. *The Oxford Companion to Australian Jazz.* Melbourne: Oxford University Press.

Johnson, L. W. 1983. *Colonial Sunset: Australia and Papua New Guinea 1970–1974.* St. Lucia: University of Queensland Press.

Kaho, Tu'imala. 1988a. *Songs of Love.* Warrior Records Pacific Division WARC 2011. Cassette.

———. 1988b. *Songs of Love by Tu'imala Kaho of the Kingdom of Tonga.* Nuku'alofa, Tonga: Vava'u Press.

King, Joseph. 1909. *W. G. Lawes of Savage Island and New Guinea.* London: Religious Tract Society.

Kreeck, Ian Stuart. 1991. "The Touch of Voyagers: Polynesian and Western Influences on the Music of Southern Papua, 1871–1958." M.A. thesis, Deakin University.

*Ku'u Home: Hawaiian Songs of Home.* 1991. KGMB Television (Hawai'i), channel 9. Video.

Larcom, Joan. 1982. "The Invention of Convention." *Mankind* 13(4):330–337.

Leadley, Alan J. 1975. "The Japanese on the Gazelle." *Oral History* 3(3):33–72.

———. 1976. "A History of the Japanese Occupation of the New Guinea Islands, and Its Effects, with Special Reference to the Tolai People of Gazelle Peninsula." M.A. thesis, University of Papua New Guinea.

LeBrun-Holmes. 1962. *Music and Sounds of Melanesia.* HMV OELP 198. Notes to LP disk.

Lindstrom, Lamont. 1990. *Knowledge and Power in a South Pacific Society.* Washington, D.C.: Smithsonian Institution Press.

Lindstrom, Lamont, and Geoffrey M. White. 1990. *Island Encounters: Black and White Memories of the Pacific War.* Washington, D.C.: Smithsonian Institution Press.

Linkels, Ad, and Lucia Linkels. 1994. *Ifi Palasa: Tongan Brass.* PAN Records, Ethnic Series, 2044. Compact disc.

Lyng, James. 1919. *Our New Possession (Late German New Guinea).* Melbourne: Melbourne Publishing Company.

———. 1925. *Island Films: Reminiscences of "German New Guinea".* Sydney: Cornstalk Publishing Company.

Mackay, Ian K. 1975. "He Was the First Papuan Announcer." *Pacific Islands Monthly* 46(10):59.

Mackellar, C. D. 1912. *Scented Islands and Coral Gardens: Torres Straits, German New Guinea, and the Dutch East Indies.* London: John Murray.

Matbob, Patrick. 1985. "A Sign of the Times." *The Times of Papua New Guinea* (9 September):25.

Matches, Margaret. 1931. *Savage Paradise.* New York: Century.

Medcalf, Peter. 1986. *War in the Shadows: Bougainville 1944–45.* Sydney: Australian War Memorial.

Métraux, Rhoda. 1990. "Music in Tambunam." In *Sepik Heritage: Tradition and Change in Papua New Guinea,* ed. Nancy Lutkehaus et al., 523–534. Durham, N.C.: Carolina Academic Press.

Mika, John. 1976. "Matupit Village, Rabaul Sub-Province, East New Britain Province." *Oral History* 4(6):22–25.

Mytinger, Caroline. 1946. *New Guinea Headhunt.* New York: Macmillan.

Nelson, Hank. 1972. *Papua New Guinea: Black Unity or Black Chaos?* New York: Penguin Books.

Nero, Karen L. 1992. "Introduction: Challenging Communications in the Contemporary Pacific." *Pacific Studies* 15(4):1–12.

Neumann, Klaus. 1985. "Who Was ToKinkin?" *The Times of Papua New Guinea* (23 November):16–17.

———. 1992a. *Not the Way It Really Was: Constructing the Tolai Past.* Honolulu: University of Hawai'i Press.

———. 1992b. "Tradition and Identity in Papua New Guinea: Some Observations Regarding Tami and Tolai." *Oceania* 62(4):295–316.

Niles, Don William. 1980. "The Traditional and Contemporary Music of the Admiralty Islands." M.A. thesis, University of California, Los Angeles.

———. 1984. *Commercial Recordings of Papua New Guinea Music 1949–1983.* Boroko: Institute of Papua New Guinea Studies.

———. 1985. *Commercial Recordings of Papua New Guinea Music 1984.* Boroko: Institute of Papua New Guinea Studies.

———. 1986. *Commercial Recordings of Papua New Guinea Music 1985.* Boroko: Institute of Papua New Guinea Studies.

———. 1987. *Commercial Recordings of Papua New Guinea Music 1986.* Boroko: Institute of Papua New Guinea Studies.

———. 1988. *Commercial Recordings of Papua New Guinea Music 1987.* Boroko: Institute of Papua New Guinea Studies.

———. 1992. "The Chinese and Music in Papua New Guinea." *Newsletter* of the Association for Chinese Music Research, 5(2).

———. 1995. "Editor's Introduction." In *Mission and Music by Heinrich Zahn,* ed. Don Niles, trans. Philip W. Holzknecht, xvii–xcii. Boroko: National Research Institute.

No Fixed Address and Us Mob. 1981. *Wrong Side of the Road.* Black Australia Records PRC 196. Cassette.

Not Drowning, Waving. 1990. *Tabaran.* WEA 903172999.2. Compact disc.

Oliver, Douglas L. 1991. *Black Islanders: A Personal Perspective of Bougainville 1937–1991.* Honolulu: University of Hawai'i Press.

Overell, Lilian. 1923. *A Woman's Impressions of German New Guinea.* London: John Lane.

"Painim Wok Goes Back to Its Roots." 1990. *The Times of Papua New Guinea* (9 June): 19.

*Papua / New Guinea Independence Celebrations: Song Contest Finalists.* 1975. Viking VPS 392. LP disk.

"P-NG on Threshold of Dramatic Radio Development." 1963. *PIM* 23(7):33–39.

Powdermaker, Hortense. 1933. *Life in Lesu: The Study of a Melanesian Society in New Ireland.* New York: Norton.

———. 1966. *Stranger and Friend: The Way of an Anthropologist.* New York: Norton.

Powell, Gordon. 1945. *Two Steps to Tokyo: A Story of the R.A.A.F. in the Trobriand and Admiralty Islands.* Melbourne: Oxford University Press.

Price, Rhys W. N.d. *Papua Victory: With the Papuans in Peace and War.* Adelaide: Unevangelized Fields Mission.

"Problems of Film Censorship and Radio Broadcasting." 1961. *PIM* 31(7):80.

"Radio Rabaul Gives Them What They Want." 1963. *PIM* 23(10):21–25.

Ravuvu, Asesela. 1974. *Fijians at War.* Suva: Institute of Pacific Studies.

"Rely on Local Talent for Our Jingles." 1987. *The Times of Papua New Guinea* (26 November–2 December):15.

Roberts, S. C. 1924. *Tamai: The Life Story of John Hartley Roberts of Tonga.* Sydney: Methodist Book Depot.

Ryan, Robin. 1997. "Ukuleles, Guitars or Gumleaves? Hula Dancing and Southeastern Australian Aboriginal Performers in the 1920s and 1930s." *Perfect Beat* 3(2): 106–109.

Ryan, Robin, and Herbert Patten. 1995. "Eukalyptusblattmusik." In *Die Musik in Geschichte und Gegenwart,* ed. Ludwig Finscher, 3:208–211. Kassel: Bärenreiter.

Sheridan, Ray J. 1972. "Music (2)." In *Encyclopedia of Papua and New Guinea,* ed. Peter Ryan, 817–821. Clayton: Melbourne University Press.

Shillingsworth, Les, et al. 1988. *Justice Will Be Done.* Privately published. Cassette.

Silas, Ellis. 1926. *A Primitive Arcadia: Being the Impressions of an Artist in Papua.* Boston: Little, Brown.

Simons, Susan Cochrane. 1988. "The Cochrane Papua New Guinea Archive: Papua New Guinea Perspectives, 1949–1966." *Photophile* 6(3):64–70.

Smith, Jazzer, ed. 1984. *The Book of Australian Country Music.* Sydney: BET Publishing Group.

Spencer, Margaret. 1967. *Doctor's Wife in Rabaul.* London: Robert Hale.

Stella, Regis N. 1990. *Forms and Styles of Traditional Banoni Music.* Boroko: National Research Institute.

Strathern, Andrew. 1984. *A Line of Power.* London: Tavistock Publications.

Stuart, Ian. 1970. "Port Moresby: Yesterday and Today." 3:208–211. Sydney: Pacific Publications.

Sullivan, Chris. 1988. "Non-Tribal Dance Music and Song: From First Contact to Citizen Rights." *Australian Aboriginal Studies,* 1:64–67.

Susu, Stretim. 1983. "Bamboos Beat Out the Melanesian Sound." *The Times of Papua New Guine* (4 March):16.

Tatar, Elizabeth, ed. 1985. *Call of the Morning Bird: Chants and Songs of Palau, Yap, and Ponape Collected by Iwakichi Muranushi, 1936.* Honolulu: Bishop Museum.1:64–67. LP disk.

Temora (pseudonym). 1892. "The Eucalyptus Band." *The War Cry* (30 July):7.

Thomson, Basil. 1894. *Diversions of a Prime Minister.* Edinburgh: Blackwood.

Tolala (pseudonym). 1950. "Territories Talk-Talk." *PIM* 20(10):53.

*Tribal Heart.* 1994. Larrikin Entertainment AIM 1042. Compact disk.

*UPK: Uwankara Palyanka Kanyinijaku* (A strategy for well-being). 1989. CAAMA Music 208. Cassette.

Van Dusen, Henry P. 1945. *They Found the Church There: The Armed Forces Discover Christian Missions in the Pacific.* London: S. C. M. Press.

Waiko, John D. 1986. "Oral Traditions among the Binandere: Problems of Method in a Melanesian Society." *Journal of Pacific History* 21(1):21–38.

Warumpi Band. 1987. *Go Bush!* Festival Records C38707. Cassette.

Watson, Eric. 1987. "Country Music: The Voice of Rural Australia." In *Missing in Action: Australian Popular Music in Perspective,* ed. Marcus Breen, 47–77. Kensington: Verbal Graphics.

Webb, Michael. 1986. "Bi-Cultural Music Education in Papua New Guinea: A Quest for Unity and Identity." *International Journal of Music Education.* May.

———. 1992. *Lokal Music: Lingua Franca Song and Identity in Papua New Guinea.* Boroko: National Research Institute.

———. 1995. "'Pipal bilong music tru' / 'A truly musical people': Musical Culture, Colonialism, and Identity in Northeastern New Britain, Papua New Guinea, after 1875." Ph.D. dissertation, Wesleyan University.

Webb, Michael, and Don Niles. 1986. *Riwain: Papua New Guinea Pop Songs.* Goroka and Boroko: Goroka Teachers College and Institute of Papua New Guinea Studies.

Webb, Michael, and Don Niles. 1987. "Periods in Papua New Guinea Music History." *Bikmaus* 7(1):50–62.

Williams, Maslyn. 1964. *Stone Age Island: Seven Years in New Guinea.* London: Collins.

Yothu Yindi. 1994. *Yothu Yindi: Freedom.* Hollywood Records HR– 61451-2. Compact disc.

Yothu Yindi. 1995. "Jailbreak." In *Fuse/Box: The Alternative Tribute.* BMG 74321 286814. Compact disc.

Zahn, Heinrich. 1934. *Wê daucnga.* Finschhafen: Lutheran Mission.

———. 1959. *The Conchshell-Hymnal.* 2nd ed. Revised by Helmut Wolfrum. Madang: Lutheran Mission Press.

# Music and Ingested Substances

*J. W. Love*
*Lamont Lindstrom*
*Glenn Petersen*
*Dorothy Sara Lee*
*Lawrence Hammar*
*Peter W. Black*

**Kava**

**Betel**

**Alcohol**

In Oceania, music enhances the presentation and consumption of food and other substances. In formal and informal settings, people ingest kava, betel, and other natural substances that induce altered physiological states, attested by socially valued expressions of feeling or belief (Lindstrom 1987; Marshall 1979, 1982). In the past several centuries, beer, distilled alcohol, tobacco, and marijuana have become available—as have, in some areas after the 1950s, synthetic chemicals.

The trade, presentation, and consumption of these substances invites the performance of words, music, and dance. Customary economic protocols may govern their gift or exchange; elaborate rules of etiquette may surround their use. Their availability or presence may create interpersonally marked contexts, affecting and revealing social relations and political processes. Alone or with other ingested substances and context-defining materials, they take on symbolic significance.          —J. W. LOVE

**KAVA**

In most of Polynesia, Vanuatu, scattered locales of south-central and northeastern New Guinea, and the Micronesian areas of Pohnpei and Kosrae, people traditionally prepared, served, and drank kava, an infusion of the basal stems, stump, and roots of *Piper methysticum*, a tropical pepper, which grows up to 3.5 meters high.

Researchers have not fully explored fully the psychoactivity of kava and its neurological effects, but they classify it as a soporific, a drug that enhances feelings of happiness and sociability. Kava is almost everywhere ceremonial and social. At culturally important times and places, people prepare and consume it. Adult men are the main consumers.

Kava is a valuable token of exchange. Hosts of feasts and ceremonies present its stems and roots to visiting dancers and singers. In Sāmoa, orators mark formal exchanges with ornate speeches; quoting poetry, they refer to pieces of kava by metaphor, as "white doves," and by circumlocution, as "conjunctions-with-pith" (Love 1991:10–12). In Vanuatu, people who come to dance at feasts and exchanges usually receive gifts of kava.

In Tonga, Sāmoa, Fiji, and Pohnpei, public consumption of kava makes a political display, validating chiefly status. In Melanesia, and during less ceremonious occasions in Polynesia and on Pohnpei and Kosrae, people drink with less formality, sometimes with intoxication in mind. The physiological effects of kava, and the range of its political and religious functions, shape in important ways its interface with music. On Tanna, a person who wants to commission a song presents a special variety of kava to a songsmith. The composer retires to where he knows spirits frequent, prepares and drinks the kava, and sleeps, expecting to dream of new music and lyrics.

### Music associated with kava

Rhythm and song are important aspects of the preparation and serving of kava. In the Strickland River area of Western Province, Papua New Guinea, the Gebusi empower its freshly dug roots with ritual shouting (*yi-kay*), and bring the roots into their longhouses with whooping and stamping (Knauft 1987:82). On Pohnpei, men  process kava by pounding it on named flat, basaltic, stone slabs. To produce ringing tones, they prop these slabs on coconut husks or automobile tires, and strike them with stones. Typically, four men pound kava at each slab, using rhythms that mark the progress of the preparation. A final rhythm (*kohdi*), signaling the readiness of the powder, has seven rapid beats, a pause, two rapid beats, a pause, two long beats, a pause, two more rapid beats, and a final beat (Riesenberg 1968:105–106).

*Formal settings*

In much of Polynesia, kava validates political relationships. Preparers, orators, apportioners, servers, and drinkers follow culturally prescribed strictures of etiquette, covering placement, posture, gesture, and sequence (figure 1). Protocol may require poetry or music (Kaeppler 1985; Love 1991), often performed at set junctures in the process, as in eighteenth-century Hawai'i, when Captain Cook noted singing during the preparation of the beverage (1784:161).

As men strain kava in Fiji, seated male choruses do a song-dance that recounts the origins of the beverage or chronicles local histories. A text from Taveuni begins: "Sleeping at night; the day dawns, / The sun is on the warpath in the sky. / They go and pull up the kava to bring it" (after Hocart 1929:64–65). Associated movements include synchronized clapping and gesturing (Kennedy 1931:60). Three claps mark the end of the preparations, and again when each drinker empties the cup. As preparers finish straining kava in Sāmoa, the apportioner declaims a *solo'ava*, a poem recounting the origins of the beverage, or alluding to other myths or legends. A short formula declares the readiness of the beverage. Those who will drink applaud. Intoning apt epithets in a stentorian voice, the apportioner calls each party who will drink. On hearing one's call, one may clap several times, formally expressing delight.

FIGURE 1    Tongans prepare kava with stylized gestures. Photo by Adrienne L. Kaeppler, 1975.

FIGURE 2    Members of Fiji's Second Battalion Labour Corps, Lautoka, Fiji, enjoy music and kava. Photo Fiji Ministry of Information, 1944.

As individuals drink kava, etiquette may require that others be silent, or dancing and singing may continue, depending on the society and whether such performance implies hopes of intoxication. In most of Melanesia and Pohnpei, people believe noise and movement impede intoxication. On Tanna, dancers may consume kava when they arrive at a village hosting an all-night song-dance (*nupu*); but before dancing, they wait for the intoxicating effects to wear off. Dancing ends at sunrise, and drinkers may share a last round of kava before going home.

### Informal settings

In Polynesia, informal drinkers often entertain themselves musically (figure 2). On East Futuna in the 1930s, during evening concerts around the bowl, participants divided into two choruses, which exchanged songs (Burrows 1936:207). In old Sāmoa, young drinkers challenged one another to intone poems; the penalty for misstatement was to dance (Mead 1969:110), sometimes naked (Love 1991:43). In Tonga, during young people's informal kava-drinking parties (*faikava*), drinkers sing to the accompaniment of guitars, and women may dance. Female dancers also perform in the kava-drinking circles that serve as rotating credit associations among Tongans living in Honolulu: drinkers contribute to an association's funds by decorating the dancer with dollars. Some cities have kava bars. Singing songs and playing guitars are more common in such bars in Fiji than in those of Vila (Vanuatu) and Kolonia (Pohnpei), where drinkers worry more about the effects of noise on intoxication. However, by the mid-1990s, competition encouraged several bar owners to offer musical entertainment.

### Kava as a lyric subject

Like betel, kava is a topic of poetry, even where people do not commonly consume it. A Tikopian dance-song recalls its origin: *Te fitianga o te kava / E tu ra mai Tonga / I te tano o Tuipania, / E tao i te umu* 'The springing up of the kava / That stands there from Tonga / On the grave of Tuipania, / Who was cooked in the oven' (after Firth 1970:216). In Tikopian religious rituals, abandoned after the mid-1950s, people seldom drank the kava, but solemnly poured it onto the ground.

In the Lau Islands of Fiji, lyrics detail the stages of preparation (Thompson 1940:71). In Sāmoa, some poems do the same:

| | |
|---|---|
| 'Ava-pu'a ia, 'ava-le'a ia, | This *pu'a*-kava, this *le'a*-kava, |
| 'Ā ni sāsā o se mānaia. | Will be the beau's tokens. |
| Lia'ina mai ni 'ava mai Niniva; | Uproot some kava from Niniva; |
| Lūlūina, pōpōina, fatifatia. | Shake it, pat it, break it up. |
| Lafo ia 'i fafo 'i fa'alāina; | Toss it outside to be sunned; |
| 'Aumai 'i fale 'i silafia: | Bring it inside to be admired: |
| Lafo ia 'i fafo 'i māia; | Toss it outside to be chewed; |
| 'Aumai 'i fale 'i poupou'ia. | Bring it inside to be posted. |
| 'Ā maia, maia 'ia pala; | When chewing, chew it thoroughly; |
| 'Ae togi se tufa ma se tua-a-'ava. | But make an offering of back-kava. |
| 'Ā usi lo tātou 'ava, | When our kava shall be infused, |
| 'Ia mua'i 'o se mata-a-'ava. | Let the fore-kava be first. |
| 'I 'ata matua, matua a'e lava! | O mature, quite mature, stems! |
| 'A 'inā tufa lo 'outou 'ava! | Do indeed share out your kava! |

This text names two varieties of the plant. Traditionally, unmarried men, led by a formally recognized *mānaia* 'beau', chewed the kava and spat it into a bowl, in which a virgin woman mixed it with water and strained out the fibers.

A Hawaiian prayer-song transfers to the heavens the effects of drinking kava: "The Pleiades are becoming drowsy with the effects of kava. / They are drunk, drowsy, dizzy" (after Titcomb 1948:125). When stars get drunk on kava, humans can enjoy it all the more.                          —LAMONT LINDSTROM

## Kava in Pohnpei

Among the forces that shape Pohnpeian social relations lie the activities and values that accompany the preparation and consumption of kava (Pohnpeian *sakau*), a beverage that for Pohnpeians possesses mana (*manaman*). Its cultivation takes a large portion of the time and energy most Pohnpeian households expend on farming. For many, kava is an important source of income.

Competitive feasting, which entails the presentation of kava plants (with large pigs and yams), is fundamental to individual political advancement and the ebb and flow of community life (Petersen 1995). In most Pohnpeian communities, large feasts occur every few weeks, but every evening in every Pohnpeian community, small-scale kava sessions occur. These convene at private homes and in local formal houses (*nahs*), irregularly rotating within neighborhoods, families, and political factions.

In late afternoon and early evening, people gather at a site where someone has harvested a kava plant. After the root has been cleaned and pounded, its pulp and a small amount of water are squeezed through hibiscus bast into a coconut-shell cup, which passes from participant to participant, starting with the highest-ranking and proceeding down the hierarchy. Men and women, young and old, join in. Though the work is done primarily by young men, all but children are welcome to drink. Conversation about local and domestic issues, and sometimes broader political topics, accompanies the preparation of the beverage and the consumption of the first few rounds. Depending on the number of people participating (ordinarily from five to twenty-five), several subsets of conversations may be occur simultaneously.

Gradually, as drinkers begin to mull over their private thoughts, the talk slows down. Someone, usually a younger man, begins to sing. He may persist for a few bars or a few minutes. He may sing alone, or others may join in. After a few starts and stops, moving from song to song, someone may hit upon a tune that draws accompaniment from several of the participants. (Suitable melodies are slow, soft, and romantic or mournful.) If enough singers join in, four-part harmony ensues. Reflecting the amount of kava available, the number of people present, and more ephemeral factors, the singing may take only a brief period, or it may last for hours, and sometimes all night. Ordinarily, shared singing slowly shifts into shared silence.

During the preparation and consumption of the drink, especially the shared singing and silence, the participants may reach a vague consensus about a communitywide decision of some sort. As a consequence of kava sessions, without specifying the terms of an agreement, Pohnpeian communities come to understand what their common outlooks are. In the moods and sentiments evoked during the shared singing and silence, members of the community gain a sense of what they are collectively ready to endorse, or at least accept.    —GLENN PETERSEN

### Kava in Fiji

In Fiji, presentations of kava (*yaqona*) formally enact and reinforce established political and social bonds, reaffirming ties between families and friends, elevating everyday exchanges into dramatizations of the principles of village social structure—principles realized in the organization of the participants, the content of the texts, and the performance. Less formal presentations of kava accompany many daily activities, from a decorous request for assistance in a major project, which might be accompanied by an entire kava plant, to the casual act of joining an evening's social gathering by contributing a small portion of powdered kava to the communal supply.

To prepare kava for consumption, the root or stem is pounded (in large towns, powdered kava can be purchased from merchants) and infused in water (figure 3*a*). Each step is detailed in the text of a *meke ni yaqona,* from the initial preparations to the final mixing and straining of the fibers. In Naloto Village, Vanua Levu, warriors' patrilineages arrange formal kava ceremonies, assume the principal roles, and sing *meke ni yaqona* at important events. The singing of the principal vocal parts at such an occasion might require the services of particularly proficient singers, who contribute the vocal embellishments that measure the solemnity of the event.

In a classic *meke ni yaqona,* the words reflect on and direct the actions of the preparers and servers. In the most famous and most commonly used one, associated with the Ratu Kadavulevu School in Tailevu, the first stanza describes the preliminary preparation of the kava for the ceremony, consisting of cleaning and pounding the root or stem; the second describes the root to be presented to the guests, and reviews the secondary preparation stage of chewing and rinsing by the leading woman of the lineage; the third tells of the gathering for the ceremony. The final stanza details the actions of mixing and serving the drink. The following example was recorded in 1976 in Ucunivanua, and in 1977 in Naivunimono.

FIGURE 3    An informal kava ceremony in Naloto, Fiji: *a,* a man mixes powdered kava with water; *b,* a man stands to present a cup of kava to a visitor. Photos by Adrienne L. Kaeppler, 1984.

(a)

(b)

| | |
|---|---|
| Male oti na yaqona u cobola. | Clap your hands when the kava is mixed. |
| Kena bilo u vini ki na loga. | The cup is on the shelf. |
| Era sa solote levu loka. | We are all waiting. |
| O cei dina me na tu yaqona? | Who will be the cupbearer? |
| Rau qai bole a marama sola. | The two ladies have agreed to serve. |
| Adi Qanu na tu yaqona, | Lady Qanu will serve the kava, |
| Senikuba ka lava wai droka. | Senikuba will pour the opaque water. |
| Dru cerea, dru cerea matua, | Lift it up, lift it up high |
| Dru lave i kuba madua, | And go toward the front of the gathering |
| Tiko kunia na sau ni vanua. | Where sits the chief of the land. |
| Maca oti ru loka malua, | When the bowl is emptied slowly, |
| Cobo laki na yaqona ni vanua. | Clap the kava of the land. |
| Kena i 'obo e malau sausa. | The sound of the clap will echo down. |
| Vakabui matanivanua. | The chief's spokesman gives orders. |

The poem describes the steps in serving kava to a guest. The server conveys this through movement: at the beginning, he kneels beside the bowl; after the beverage is poured into his cup, he turns and stretches his arms forward toward the guest, slowly rising and straightening his knees until he is upright (figure 3b). Skilled cupbearers dance with the cup, tilting it slightly from side to side without spilling its contents. Once the server is upright, he walks toward the guest and presents the cup, either giving the guest the cup to drink, or pouring the cup's contents into the guest's own cup, timed to coincide with the word *biu* 'present it'.  —DOROTHY SARA LEE

## BETEL

In western Melanesia and the western Micronesian high islands (Palau, Yap, Marianas), the fruits of the areca palm, *Areca catechu* (a slender tree, which grows to 30 meters), are a socially important masticatory stimulant. Fresh or cured, the kernel of the seed—an astringent, red-orange drupe (colloquially, "nut")—is chewed with the leaves, stems, or catkins of betel pepper (*Piper betle,* a shrubby vine), slaked lime, and flavorings.

The consumption of betel is unceremonial. Men, women, and children chew it informally, at any time. During rituals, which may last several days and nights, betel is an important stimulant for musicians, dancers, and singers. It is an important item of exchange: in central New Ireland, Mandak hosts of a ceremony or feast often give it to dancers and singers, whom they may shower with nuts (Clay 1986:234).

### Music associated with betel

Many Oceanic peoples believe inspiration is an important source of knowledge, including that of songs, and attribute new knowledge to ancestral or spiritual guidance, which they seek in dreams, trances, and drugged states of consciousness, even the stimulated state associated with the use of betel. Individuals may sing spells into a nut, which symbolically serves as a route to the supernatural realm of lyrical inspiration.

Gifts of betel can embody a request that a composer produce new music. In New Britain, where musical composition is a specialized profession, a Tolai novice gains access to a publicly recognized spiritual source of musical inspiration by apprenticing himself to an expert. After paying shell money, the novice receives special nuts from a betel tree growing near the expert's source. To symbolize his access to the supernatural, he plants them. An inspirational source of a Tolai song is a guardian spirit (*turangan*), or simply betel (*buai*); new songs often start with a line like "Choose the betel of Mr. Expert" (Salisbury 1970:158).

Some people store slaked lime in gourds; often finely decorated, these and other containers may serve as percussive instruments. To accompany songs on Sudest, in the Louisiade Archipelago, people tap gourds with carved, shell-inlaid sticks, and lyrics about betel definitively mark a musical genre, *gia eledi* 'give betel' (Lepowsky 1982:340).

Betel occurs as a symbolic element in songs. A musical text translated from Tikopian begins: "O your aroma, friend, / Came first to me; / Then I peered over / Into your basket." It then celebrates the friendship implied in sharing betel: "And for our division, friend, / Of the scrap of betel leaf: / Chewing the morsel equally, / We two" (after Firth 1967:112).  —LAMONT LINDSTROM

## ALCOHOL

The general use of alcohol in Oceania stemmed primarily from contact with outsiders. Around 1800, escaped Australian convicts taught Hawaiians to distill a liquor from tī roots. This knowledge spread to the Society Islands, where experiments in the next decades led to the manufacture of orange-juice wine, around whose festive consumption Tahitians organized choral singing and dancing. Festivities included the consumption of "distilled coconut toddy made for the occasion (possibly learned from Marquesans), which became a signal for the beginning of nude dancing and promiscuous sexual pairings" (Lemert 1979:196). In the Cook Islands, ritualized parties developed (Lemert 1976): summoned by the sound of a conch trumpet, drinkers said prayers, sang hymns, listened to speeches, and from a barrel took rounds of drinks, brightened by the recitation of genealogies and the singing of *ūtē.*

Alcohol may set up contexts where drinkers speak words or tell jokes felt unsuitable for sober company, or sing songs that a person must not sing in the presence of someone of the opposite sex, or in public generally, as with Pohnpeian and Chuukese songs about sexual affairs, whose danger, except when dulled by inebriation, lies in their implications of adultery (Fischer and Swartz 1960). In Etal, an atoll in southern Chuuk, risky singing permitted by insobriety once took the form of shouting Japanese songs in the presence of an American (Nason 1979:246). Contexts conditioned by alcohol often include the partaking of other substances, as at a party in the Admiralty Islands in 1964, when "some drank and danced to ukulele and guitar music until morning, while others drank, joked, chewed betel, smoked cigarettes" (Schwartz and Romanucci-Ross 1979:262–263).

In many Oceanic societies, old festival and ritual contexts have continued or evolved with the substitution of alcohol for indigenous substances. Such was the case with orange-wine parties, which paralleled informal gatherings for drinking kava. The Enga of Papua New Guinea no longer conduct the *sanggai,* a ritual that made bachelors attractive and taught them to copulate without becoming affected by women's pollution, but parties organized for drinking store-bought beer show parallels:

> Drinking often occurs in seclusion. Young women come and sing songs. After much suggestive singing and dancing, sexual liaisons normally occur. This aspect of drinking parties seems to have an analog in *sanggai* in the form of particularly bawdy and explicitly suggestive songs sung by young women to the bachelors. (Wormsley 1987: 205–206)

By contrast, the settings of bars, though they usually associate drinking with music, have few parallels in precontact Oceanic societies.                    —J. W. LOVE

## Music, drugs, and sex in Daru, Papua New Guinea

A complex culture of rock, drugs, and sex flourishes on Daru Island, capital of Western Province, Papua New Guinea (Hammar 1996). Home to an ethnic majority of Kiwai (Landtman 1927), Daru is rich in music and sex, reflecting the combined effects of colonialism, capitalism, and Christianity.

Just south of the mainland, just east of the Indonesian border, Daru is four kilometers across, home unofficially to about fifteen thousand, conspicuous for overcrowding, poverty, and intense human traffic. It has a high school and four community schools, two banks, a hotel, a radio station, a prison, a police station, a hospital, a public market and wharf, and stores. Through it, smugglers import guns and drugs, gangs perpetrate crimes, and a variegated sex industry thrives. The collection and sale of firewood, beer bottles, and sea cucumbers provide licit income, as does employment with the provincial government.

Kiwai musical instruments included clappers (*marabo*), rattles (*korare*), susaps (*begube*), end-blown flutes (*turu, ugege*), panpipes (*piago*), and conch trumpets (*tuture*), but guitars and cassettes have replaced them. Daruans made rattles from seed pods and rattan, but they now string beer-bottle caps on fishing line. Dancing segregated people by gender, age, and marital status, but now, partly reflecting missionaries' prohibitions on indigenous dancing, dance parties (*disko pati*) rule. The Kiwai sang during ceremonies and the telling of narratives, but cassettes now play virtually round the clock. Drums, drummings, and drummers from particular villages were laden with symbols, meanings, and implications, but cassettes now come from Port Moresby's and Rabaul's recording studios and Australia, Indonesia, and the United States. Painim Nabaut, New Kumaisa, and Hollie Maea are talented Papua New Guinean bands, but Madonna, Technotronic, Elton John, and Rod Stewart dominate the airwaves.

### Drugs

On Daru as elsewhere, the consumption of alcohol presents health and social hazards. Male drinkers spend 20 to 25 percent of workers' average pay to consume about thirteen beers a week, often binging on payday. Wine, wine coolers, gin, rum, vodka, whiskey, and black-market beer are widely available. Enterprising Daruans make toddy (*tuba*) by collecting coconut sap and letting it ferment into a heady brew, said to foment drunkenness, kung-fu mimicry, and severe hangovers. To diluted cordial, male drinkers add methylated spirits (and occasionally gasoline), sometimes blinding and killing those who consume it.

Daruans enjoy ingesting other substances, particularly betel (*gore, buai*), chewed with betel-pepper catkins (*apure, daka*) daubed in lime (*amea, kambang*). They no longer drink kava (*gamoda*), a mild soporific, legendarily originating nearby, in the navel, semen, and dung of kangaroos. Smoking tobacco, of local and foreign brands, is common; as with alcohol and formerly kava, most users are males. Smoking marijuana is increasingly common, but it is severely stigmatized, said to turn women into prostitutes (*stupids*) and men into gang members (*raskols*).

### Contextual comparisons

The Daruan sex industry is ubiquitous, but some of its forms of labor are tightly patterned, marked by contrasting styles of music. *Sagapari,* a small mangrove garden, is an outdoor toilet and rubbish dump, where sex, primarily vaginal intercourse, is available for U.S. $2. From 8 A.M. (when beer shops open) till dusk, seven days a week, weather permitting, Bamu men prostitute their wives to non-Bamu laborers, villagers, clerks, and fishermen. (Bamu have been migrating to Daru since the 1960s.) Inside and near *sagapari,* Bamu women solicit customers to "do sex"—on the ground, against trees, behind the hardware store, or underneath upturned boats. Consumption of "S.P." ("little brown girls," bottles of South Pacific Lager) promotes male camaraderie, drunkenness, and sexual violence, inflicted by customer and Bamu husband alike (figure 4). Outside *sagapari,* plaintive stringband music plays on cassettes, sung in Tok Pisin, Motu, and local languages.

Dance parties exhibit other traits. Sex is not so commoditized or anonymous, and it involves fewer married people and less alcohol. Parties are advertised on store walls, telephone poles, and houses. Sponsors rope off and festoon the grounds, and collect fees for entrance. Teenage males oversee stereo components, and females prepare and serve refreshments: food, iceblock (frozen cordial), and sometimes beer. The favorite musical artists are British and American. In the early 1990s, Elton John's "Sacrifice" played solidly, and a recording of Technotronic's "Pump Up the Jam" often blasted its "Owwwwaiii, a place to stay. Getcher booty on the floor tonight—make my day!" Another favorite then was Right Said Fred's "I'm Too Sexy," with its lyrics "I'm too sexy for your body, too sexy for your body—the way I'm disco-dancing. . . . I'm too sexy for my cat. Come on, pussy, oh pussycat."

FIGURE 4   Advertising South Pacific Lager, a beer-bottle label features a bird of paradise.

A boy may wait for a girl walking behind him to catch up, and then ask her, "Where are you going? Can I have some sex?"; or he might say, "I paid your fees; I want sex with you." Alcohol is not a social glue holding the cultural center together, as once betel and kava might have been. It is a volatile fuel, poured onto the flames of socioeconomic distress.

Spatial parameters also differ. *Sagapari* is 75 meters deep and 90 wide; roughly concentric rings demarcate, in order toward the center, zones of clustered male drinking, solitary male urinating and defecating, and heterosexual coupling. By contrast at dance parties, teenagers cluster outside the grounds until they pay and enter. Audience and dancers segregate themselves by gender and age, males sitting here, females there, males handling "dance-mixes" (the order of pieces played on speakers), females passing messages, pairs exchanging hand-and-eye "actions." After connecting through these "actions," pairs disappear among banana trees, into showers, or behind partitions. Some boys and many girls have as many sex partners as they request: a boy may wait for a girl walking behind him to catch up, and then ask her, "Where are you going? Can I have some sex?"; or he might say, "I paid your fees; I want sex with you."

Sexual networking is intense in both locales. At *sagapari,* female supply, male need, and local name (*tu-kina bus* 'two-dollar bush [sex]') keep prices low. At dance-parties, payments ease sexual and material transactions; 43 percent of respondents to a 1992 questionnaire had given or received (or both) T-shirts, money, cassettes, food, and tobacco after their most recent sexual contact. Dance parties, new cassettes, and video shows promote sexual behavior in formerly unimaginable ways. *Sagapari* embodies a declining economy, Bamu stigmatization, and women's lack of sexual parity.

Alcohol is not a social glue holding the cultural center together, as once betel and kava might have been. It is a volatile fuel, poured onto the flames of socioeconomic distress. Locally preferred styles of music and dance show cultural loss and dislocation, even as they suggest culturally creative potential. Locally indulged sex—simultaneously pleasure and punishment—now carries heavy social and medical implications.    —LAWRENCE HAMMAR

### Music and alcohol on Palau and Tobi

On Tobi Island, out of a canoehouse near the beach, its interior lit by the flame of a hurricane lantern, a rough chorus erupted into the night: *Okei, okei! / Hanei tafei!* 'OK, OK! / Give him medicine!' Men sang it and burst into laughter. Emerging into the moonlight, a figure staggered down a path toward his house. Those he had left behind roared the song after him.

At the same time about 650 kilometers north, on Koror Island, young men were likely sitting on a bamboo bench, looking toward the sea from a hillside perch above their village. From a coconut, they were drinking a mixture of coconut water and vodka. They passed the coconut around, and each man took a sip. As the evening wore on, they added more and more vodka, making the beverage stronger and stronger. Occasionally, the coconut paused in its circuit, as the man holding it became engrossed in conversation, argument, or song. Then the man next in the circle would sing out (after a text and translation by Tony Ngiralbong):

FIGURE 5    Celebrating New Year's Eve, women of Tobi dance. The bottle contains only water; the supply of imported liquor ran out weeks ago. Deploying the bottle in this fashion expresses an important social fact: music and alcohol often go together in Palau. Photo by Peter Black, 1972.

Sechelik, momdasue e morchedii a kob.
Lilekong melemei leng uoi meketketang ir tilechang.
Engak a kurusii.

My friend, think and hurry up the cup that went your way.
Pass it back, because it's been too long with you.
I am longing [for the drink].

As soon as he finished singing, his "friend" would pass him the coconut.

These incidents reveal the role of alcohol-related singing in expressing social insights and processes ordinarily left unsaid—a common cultural feature of drinking songs in these societies (figure 5). They also reveal a paradoxical difference between Palauan and Tobian social worlds. If we name the competitive dimension of social life stressed in Palauan life Palauan, and the cooperative-solidarity dimension prominent in ordinary Tobian life Tobian, the Palauan song seems Tobian, and the Tobian song Palauan. Each social system has as a cultural counterpoint the main theme of the other, and that counterpoint is what these drinking songs express.

### The larger context

The Palau Islands are a tightly grouped archipelago, home to about fifteen thousand people. Once an administrative district of the U.S. Trust Territory of the Pacific Islands, these islands became the Republic of Palau, whose capital is the town of Koror. Included within the nation (as in the old district) are the remote Southwest Islands: Sonsorol, Pulo Ana, Merir, Tobi. The three hundred people who call them home have more in common with one another and the peoples of small coral islands to the east, in Yap and Chuuk, than with the people of Palau proper, who form a single cultural and linguistic unit.

The social systems of Palau and Tobi differ sharply. Palauan life stresses hierarchy and bilateral competition at multiple levels. Southwest-Island life stresses egalitarian and cooperative relations between people affiliated in roughly equivalent units. The contrast is between vertically and horizontally structured social systems. These are not autonomous: since the early 1900s, the Southwest Islands have been part of a Koror-centered political system. Both peoples occupy a single social field; nevertheless, important differences between them remain. These differences, which appear in many situations and contexts, help explain contrasts in the ways men in drinking parties use music.

### Drinking on Tobi

Tobi (Hatohobei) is a low, coral island, where traditionally men fished and women gardened, and on special occasions men engaged in communal drinking, consuming all available alcohol. Since most of what they drank was toddy (*hajii mwen*), locally gathered and fermented, drinking parties required planning. Once men had produced enough toddy, they began drinking, and they did not stop until the island was again "dry"—whether this took days, or even a week.

A typical Tobian drinking party occurred in the canoehouse and involved most of the men on the island. It was organized loosely into a central group of committed participants and a peripheral group, who for a few hours joined in, but then went home to sleep, or even to try to carry on some piece of their ordinary activities. Meanwhile, the island's women and children tried to lurk about without being noticed—to listen to the talk and jokes, to react if physical violence occurred, and especially to hear "bad" songs, which, after becoming inebriated, one or more of the men would likely bellow out.

Few Tobians considered local songs fit for mixed company. Most of those that were suitable were sung while persons of one sex danced for those of the other. Their lyrics tended to express the dancers' pride in their sex-specific attributes and activities. Nor did music from other places fall under this restriction: as people went about the ordinary life of the village, they publicly and unself-consciously sang Japanese, American, and Palauan songs. In contrast, many songs that men sang in their canoes as they fished, or women sang in their gardens as they worked and gossiped—songs with scatological and sexual meanings, buried beneath layers of metaphor—were unfit for situations in which people of the opposite sex might hear them.

Rules of avoidance and respect governed relations between men and women, especially sisters and brothers. One of the most important rules prohibited people from engaging in talk or song with a sexual or scatological content in the presence of a person of the opposite sex. Thus, local songs were seldom heard legitimately within the confines of the village, except when people danced for one another. These rules only heightened the interest that people of one sex had in the music of people of the other.

Men's songs moved into the women's world more rapidly than women's songs moved into the men's. Women's songs entered the men's world only when men (mostly teenaged boys) sneaked into taro fields to listen to women as they gardened. Men's songs moved into the women's world every time men mounted a drinking party because women (and children) gathered to overhear what they could. Therefore, when a man staggered out of the canoehouse, his wife and sisters were likely hidden somewhere within earshot—and they, too, might have laughed to themselves as the men inside repeated the phrase "*Okei, Okei! / Hanei tafei!*"

This phrase was a taunt. It poked fun at a man who, unable to keep up with the others, was withdrawing. Intensely egalitarian and cooperative, the Tobian social system permitted only indirect expression of male competition, but the competition was no less real for that. Letting alcohol release customary checks on the competitive aspects of Tobian male identity, drinking parties were exciting events because disallowed aspects of social relations, especially confrontation (verbal or, on rare occasions, physical), might occur. Men who left these parties before the toddy was gone appeared to be running away from that possibility. And those left behind used the song to point this out, in a direct and insulting fashion, unavailable in other contexts. The "medicine" the song cites was not just a remedy for alcohol-related illness: it was also a cure for unmanliness.

### Drinking on Palau

The Palauan song points in the opposite direction. Ordinary social life in Palau was characterized by structured, overt competition between most classes of persons, and as they went about their ordinary activities, young men were no exception. However, for drinking, they occasionally formed fellowships that momentarily suspended the lines of cleavage and competition in Palauan society.

In Palau, drinking was organized in a much more complex fashion than on Tobi. A cash economy and regular shipping made store-bought alcohol, rather than home-brewed spirits, the main intoxicant. Instead of one setting for drinking, Palau offered several: crowded bars filled with jukebox music, six-pack-fueled cruises in cars and pickups with amplifiers blaring, large house-parties, political gatherings. In many of them, men and women drank together, contrasting with Tobi, where women seldom drank, and then only in semi-secret parties of two or three.

Young Palauan men sometimes drank apart from community life. The lines of social cleavage which, in daily routine and politics, set these men and their families against one another, were ignored for the occasion, so the young men could drink in peace. Thus, the important word in that musical fragment from Palau calling the neglectful participant back to his obligation to the group is *sechelik* '[my] friend'.

In everyday life, Palauan men address one another in terms that call attention to differences in rank, differences the term *sechelik* denies. Like the Tobi song, the Palauan one gives explicit expression to ordinarily unspoken social truth, for, much as Tobian social activity includes a good deal of unacknowledged competition, so Palauan life contains a strong component of unexpressed comradeship.

—PETER W. BLACK

## REFERENCES

Burrows, E. G. 1936. *Ethnology of Futuna.* Bulletin 138. Honolulu: Bernice P. Bishop Museum.

Clay, Brenda Johnson. 1986. *Mandak Realities: Person and Power in Central New Ireland.* New Brunswick: Rutgers University Press.

Cook, James. 1784. *A Voyage to the Pacific Ocean. Undertaken by the Command of His Majesty, for Making Discoveries in the Northern Hemisphere.* Vol. 3. London: W. and A. Strahan.

Firth, Raymond W. 1967. *Tikopia Ritual and Belief.* Boston: Beacon Press.

———. 1970. *Rank and Religion in Tikopia: A Study in Polynesian Paganism and Conversion to Christianity.* London: Allen & Unwin.

Fischer, John L., and Marc J. Swartz. 1960. "Socio-Psychological Aspects of Some Trukese and Ponapean Love Songs." *Journal of American Folklore* 73:218–224.

Hammar, Lawrence. 1996. "Sex and Political Economy in the South Fly: Daru Island, Western Province, Papua New Guinea." Ph.D. dissertation, City University of New York.

Hocart, A. M. 1929. *Lau Islands, Fiji.* Bulletin 62. Honolulu: Bernice P. Bishop Museum.

Kaeppler, Adrienne L. 1985. "Structured Movement Systems in Tonga." In *Society and the Dance: The Social Anthropology of Performance and Process,* ed. Paul Spencer, 92–118. Cambridge: Cambridge University Press.

Kennedy, Keith. 1931. "A Fijian Yaqona Ceremony." *Mankind* 1:59–61.

Knauft, Bruce M. 1987. "Managing Sex and Anger: Tobacco and Kava Use Among the Gebusi of Papua New Guinea." In *Drugs in Western Pacific Societies: Relations of Substance,* ed. Lamont Lindstrom, 73–98. Association for Social Anthropology in Oceania Monograph 11. Lanham, Md.: University Press of America.

Landtman, Gunnar. 1927. *Kiwai Papuans of British New Guinea.* London: Macmillan.

Lemert, Edwin M. 1976. "Koni, Kona, Kava: Orange-Beer Culture of the Cook Islands." *Journal of Studies on Alcohol* 37:565–585.

———. 1979. "Forms and Pathology of Drinking in Three Polynesian Societies." In *Beliefs, Behaviors, and Alcoholic Beverages: A Cross-Cultural Survey,* ed. Mac Marshall, 192–208. Ann Arbor: University of Michigan Press.

Lepowsky, Maria. 1982. "A Comparison of Alcohol and Betelnut Use on Vanatinai (Sudest Island)." In *Through a Glass Darkly: Beer and Modernization in Papua New Guinea,* ed. Mac Marshall, 325–342. Monograph 18. Boroko, Papua New Guinea: Institute of Applied Social and Economic Research.

Lindstrom, Lamont. 1987. *Drugs in Western Pacific Societies: Relations of Substance.* ASAO monograph 11. Lanham, Md.: University Press of America.

Love, Jacob Wainwright. 1991. *Sāmoan Variations: Essays on the Nature of Traditional Oral Arts.* New York, London: Garland.

Marshall, Mac, ed. 1979. *Beliefs, Behaviors, and Alcoholic Beverages: A Cross-Cultural Survey.* Ann Arbor: University of Michigan Press.

———, ed. 1982. *Through a Glass Darkly: Beer and Modernization in Papua New Guinea.* Monograph 18. Boroko: Institute of Applied Social and Economic Research.

Mead, Margaret. 1969. *Social Organization of Manua.* Bulletin 76. Honolulu: Bernice P. Bishop Museum.

Nason, James D. 1979. "Sardines and Other Fried Fish: The Consumption of Alcoholic Beverages on a Micronesian Island." In *Beliefs, Behaviors, and Alcoholic Beverages: A Cross-Cultural Survey,* ed. Mac Marshall, 237–251. Ann Arbor: University of Michigan Press.

Petersen, Glenn. 1995. "The Complexity of Power, the Subtlety of Kava." *Canberra Anthropologist* 18(1–2):34–60.

Riesenberg, Saul H. 1968. *The Native Polity of Ponape.* Smithsonian Contributions to Anthropology, 10. Washington, D.C.: Smithsonian Institution Press.

Right Said Fred. 1992. "I'm Too Sexy." Charisma Records. EP disk.

Salisbury, Richard F. 1970. *Vunamami: Economic Transformation in a Traditional Society.* Berkeley, Los Angles: University of California Press.

Schwartz, Theodore, and Lola Romanucci-Ross. 1979. "Drinking and Inebriate Behavior in the Admiralty Islands." In *Beliefs, Behaviors, and Alcoholic Beverages: A Cross-Cultural Survey,* ed. Mac Marshall, 252–267. Ann Arbor: University of Michigan Press.

Technotronic. 1990. "Pump Up the Jam." Capitol Records. EP disk.

Thompson, Laura M. 1940. *Southern Lau, Fiji: An Ethnography.* Bulletin 162. Honolulu: Bernice P. Bishop Museum.

Titcomb, Margaret. 1948. "Kava in Hawaii." *Journal of the Polynesian Society* 57:105–171.

Wormsley, William E. 1987. "Beer and Power in Enga." In *Drugs in Western Pacific Societies: Relations of Substance,* ed. Lamont Lindstrom, 197–218. ASAO monograph 11. Lanham, Maryland: University Press of America.

# Music and Religion

*Adrienne L. Kaeppler*          *Peter Russell Crowe*

*J. W. Love*                    *Deirdre Marshall-Dean*

*Catherine J. Ellis*           *Helen Taliai*

*Harvey Whitehouse*            *Siupeli Taliai*

*Margaret J. Kartomi*          *Paul Vaiinupō Pouesi*

*Anne M. Gee*                  *Amy Kuʻuleialoha Stillman*

**Australia**

**New Guinea and Its Islands**

**Melanesia: Vanuatu**

**Micronesia: Yap**

**Polynesia**

Religion, the worship of the supernatural, goes hand in hand with music in the societies of Oceania, whose peoples practice it by intoning texts, sounding musical instruments, and making bodily movements. In indigenous Oceanic societies, the supernatural ranged from spirits of land and sea, to personifications of nature, to gods of war and peace. Worship varied from appeasing spirits and asking supernatural help in warfare, to blessing or harming crops and people, to invoking charms for calming the sea (figure 1).

## The processes of ritual

Religion is often associated with what is called ritual (though ritual is not always religious), and outsiders often conflate these concepts. Nevertheless, important concepts identified with ritual are useful for analyzing music and religion. Roy A. Rappaport, an anthropologist working in New Guinea, defined ritual as "the performance of more or less invariant sequences of formal acts and utterances not encoded by the performers" (1979:175). These acts and utterances are learned or memorized (or read) from ancestors' teachings, and are not generated by performers. According to this view, a ritual is "a form or structure" having "features or characteristics in a more or less fixed relationship to one another," and can exist only in performance. "The medium [the performance] is part of the message; more precisely, it is a metamessage about whatever is encoded in the ritual."

Likewise, while worshiping, performers may not fully understand what they are doing; they may know only that doing it is necessary. Thus, the process of performing is primary, while the product and its aesthetic evaluation are secondary. Religion is often part of a total cultural system, in which participation in religious activity is a social necessity.

In another sense, religious performance can be viewed as a kind of theater—the enactment of myths received from ancient times, or the reenactment of events in the history of spirits or gods. Aboriginal Australians believe that by ritually combining words, music, movements, and designs to reenact the events of the Dreaming, they make old powers work anew.

Early anthropologists, like E. B. Tylor and James G. Frazer, interpreted some rit-

FIGURE 1    An Ifalik navigator sings and performs movements to ensure the safety of his voyage, 1975. Printed from a videocopy of a film made by Scott Williams for the Smithsonian Institution.

uals as magic. Evolutionary views of human social progress led them to link their concept of magic with "primitive" societies and their concept of religion to "advanced" societies. Many anthropologists have discarded social evolutionism, but some older publications, including those of Bronislaw Malinowski (1922, 1955), are useful for their information about indigenous religion and "magic,"

> a specific power, essentially human, autonomous and independent in its action. This power is an inherent property of certain words, uttered with the performance of certain actions by the man entitled to do it through his social traditions and through certain observances which he has to keep. The words and acts have this power in their own right, and their action is direct and not mediated by any other agency. . . . The belief in the power of words and rites as a fundamental and irreducible force is the ultimate, basic dogma of their magical creed. Hence we find established the ideas that one never can tamper with, change or improve spells; that tradition is the only source from which they can be derived; that it has brought them down from times lying beyond the speculation of man, that there can be no spontaneous generation of magic. (1922:427)

The use of charms and spells, usually involving musical recitation, remains important in Oceania. A typical example is magic in Manus, which includes words and sometimes music: "It is recited aloud. It cannot be stolen by another. Its power is dependent on its having been rightfully obtained in marriage exchanges, peace-making exchanges or by more outright payment. After it is handed over it cannot be used by its former owner" (Fortune 1935:121).

## The wake of Christianity

The introduction of Christianity brought new supernatural and musical concepts, which have been adopted and adapted in myriad ways (figure 2). Across Oceania, Christianity has become a religious veneer, covering—and in some places irretrievably obliterating—indigenous religious systems.

The introduction of Christian music helped gain the widespread acceptance of

FIGURE 2    In a church in Rarotonga, the congregation sings. Photo by Adrienne L. Kaeppler, 1992.

TRACK 4

Christian beliefs. New musical genres combined precontact and introduced musical concepts into popular forms, such as *hīmene* in East Polynesia and *peroveta* in Papua New Guinea. In other areas, including Hawai'i and Aotearoa, poetic compositions were added to hymns. Still popular is *"Hawai'i Aloha,"* an unofficial national anthem, composed by the Reverend Lorenzo Lyons and set to the melody of "I Left It All with Jesus." One of the most popular pieces of music in parts of Oceania is the Hallelujah Chorus, sung in local languages, not only at Christmas and Easter, but at any time of the year.

One trait carries over into the new orthodoxy: performers still worship because they feel they must, and they may harbor only the vaguest understanding of the theology that underlies their beliefs. In the apostolic sects (Anglicanism, Lutheranism, Roman Catholicism), the language of the liturgy is simple and direct, but until the late twentieth century, Anglicans usually heard it in a sixteenth-century English version, and Roman Catholics always heard it in a medieval Latin one.

A widespread result of the introduction of Christianity has been the development of syncretic religious forms, in which Christian and indigenous ideas have blended. As part of this process, introduced Christian music has undergone reinterpretation (Barker 1990; Boutilier, Hughes, and Tiffany 1978). In some Oceanic societies, mainly those of Polynesia, Christianity has been the standard public religion for so long—about two hundred years in Tahiti—that old and now-secularized religious forms have without controversy been reintroduced into modern-day worship.

—ADRIENNE L. KAEPPLER, J. W. LOVE

## AUSTRALIA

Aboriginal cultures show basic similarities in myths about the Dreaming, the era of the creation, when great ancestral beings walked a featureless world, experiencing life and procreating. Every event that occurred to each of them resulted in the creation of geographic features, and so they sculpted the Australian landscape, creating

the plants, animals, and peoples of the known world. They also founded the religious ceremonies, marriage rules, food taboos, and other laws of human society.

. . . The Dreaming is . . . the generative principle of the present, the logically pri-
or dimension of the now. (Sutton 1989:15)

The ancestral beings created songs of their journeys, commonly known by Central
Australian performers as history songs, embodying laws for the maintenance of society, land, and totems. Since the beginning of time, performers claim, these songs
have passed unchanged from generation to generation.

History songs often cross linguistic boundaries, mapping places in ancestors'
journeys. The ancestral beings, when they created features or landmarks, left embedded in the earth inseminating, supernatural powers, which, through the correct ritualized performance of the ancestors' songs, knowledgeable people can tap. The
Dreaming is understood as morally neutral, and the power of the songs can serve
positive or negative ends (Strehlow 1971:262; Wild 1975:139).

Religious resonance is an important aspect of Aboriginal singing. Many extraordinary sonic experiences occur within the heightened emotional state of profound
performances. These experiences are hard to describe. They are not measurable by
electronic equipment, which deals only with the physical aspects of sound. Some
Aboriginal sounds are totally disorienting. They seem to disconnect participants from
the everyday world. Aboriginal society has mechanisms for introducing new songs,
especially through dreamed ancestral gifts. These songs are less sacred than history
songs, and appear to be more susceptible to change over time.  —CATHERINE J. ELLIS

## NEW GUINEA AND ITS ISLANDS

In New Guinea, the drama of music inspired and received enhancement from sensation and emotion. Collective ritual and musical performances often had a climactic,
and even traumatic, character. Moments of intense social drama, especially of
bereavement or physical pain (typically in initiations), they stimulated senses and
feelings, often as part of the workings of revelation. Actions, rather than words, or at
least not freely articulating speech, triggered experiences and meanings.

Some of this past remains. Participants in religious rituals still reach an understanding of ritual events by decoding the symbolism of performances. Baktaman
novices learn to appreciate the mystical connection between dew (rubbed on the
skin) and physical growth, because dew forms on leaves as if from nowhere (Barth
1987:32–35). At Wahgi feasts, men build a sacred structure on posts representing
subclans. For periods between festivals, they inter these posts in swampy ground. The
tenet that the posts never decay and may serve in later festivals reconceptualizes the
clan's immortality (O'Hanlon 1989:78).

For intensely moving, revealing, and mainly nonverbal experiences, music often
provides an important stimulus. Its communicative aspects sometimes lie in the ana-
logic principle of codification, as with Sepik flutes, tuned to mimic sacred species of
birds, whose behavioral and physical peculiarities bring into focus various cosmological mysteries. The Kaluli believe fruitdove calls convey sadness: when Kaluli songs
mimic their cries, the singer "becomes the bird," passing from life to death (Feld
1990:218–219). The Yonggom believe the hum of a swung slat resembles the noise
of engines, providing a musical vehicle for religious ideas about the origins of
European goods (Kirsch 1992).

Where lyrics are the means of religious communication, they are often ungram-
matical, and the words themselves may be archaic or secret (Barth 1975:70). The language may be foreign, as in Karavar ritual songs (Errington 1974:177). In some cases,
ritual actions and materials suggest verbal meanings; in others, participants may
interpret the meanings of strange sounds on the basis of subtle connotations with real
or modern words (Lewis 1980:59–60).

Music thus bolsters the cultivation of mysterious and multivocal symbols, but it is also emotionally arousing and expressive. Chambri music achieves poignancy in its beauty (Allen 1967:68; Mead 1935:245). When a conch accompanies singing, it may be discordant and awe-full (Williams 1928:38). Music can even be defiant, like cargo cultists' nocturnal drumming, expressing opposition to Christian missionizing (Trompf 1990:76). Emotion abounds in the Kaluli *gisalo*: the sadness of music so moves guests, they singe the skin of their hosts, who stoically endure the pain.

### Indigenous music and ritual

The grandness of musical performance may stimulate "collective effervescence," by which a community of people "assemble and become conscious of their moral unity" (Durkheim 1964 [1915]:387). In societies dispersed in hamlets or nuclear families for much of the time, the experience of large ritual gatherings is impressive. The concerted efforts of dancers, singers, and instrumentalists reinforce a sense of largeness; synchronized movements, voices, and rhythms produce intense solidarity. Baining men unite their voices in large choirs, accompanied by the beating of many bamboos: the force of their playing makes the earth vibrate; struck by feelings of common identity and collective strength, participants sometimes weep. In small, boundary-conscious societies, religious experience often inheres in an appreciation of the solidarity and immortality of clans or communities. In keeping with a Durkheimian vision of the throng as god, religious music integrates, represents, and sacralizes society.

In New Guinea, music has important mnemonic value (Lewis 1980:64–65). Its use with other sensory and emotional stimulation and an emphasis on concrete metaphors relate to performative infrequency. Where societies perform rituals rarely, ideas and feelings evoked by rituals must impress on memory a character strong enough to survive long periods of abeyance (Whitehouse 1992). In the highly elaborate and systematized ideas of routinized religions, language—liturgies, scriptural readings, sermons—codifies revelation. Unlike these, many New Guinean religious matters must persist in people's minds for years without transmissive contexts. Under these conditions, musical performance binds simple symbolic processes and potent emotional states. How the metaphors of Kaluli songs compel guests to weep "dominates both the aftermath and the remembrance" (Feld 1990:215).

Infrequency of transmission also affects the material form of instruments. When elaborate instruments, whose manufacture requires skilled labor, are not in use, people keep them strictly separate from the social world. In many areas of New Guinea, garamuts and other instruments remain within ceremonial houses. The Chimbu carefully preserve flutes in leaf coverings within men's houses (P. Brown 1978:223). A safer method of ensuring that exposure to instruments occurs only on appropriate ritual occasions is to develop a disposable musical technology. When Sambia initiations end, the participants discard the sacred flutes (Herdt 1981:230). Within a few minutes, the Mali Baining can fashion and tune simple reed instruments (*kelarega*), which, immediately after use, they deliberately destroy.     —HARVEY WHITEHOUSE

## An indigenous context: Asmat

A legend of creation anchors Asmat religious beliefs and arts. According to the legend, the people's full name is *Asmat Ow Kaenak Anakat* (Asmat People Who Are Real Humans), that is, Asmat people who are not carvings. Real Asmat people descended long ago from their creator, Fumiripits, who one day landed unconscious on the shore. When he awoke, birds rescued him; henceforth, he saw birds as symbols of the ancestors. He gathered timber and rattan to build himself a longhouse, and spent his days carving wooden figures. Eventually, he filled his house with carved likenesses of humans and birds, yet he felt lonely.

One day, Fumiripits made a drum (*em*). He hollowed out a log, used his blood and some white lime to attach the skin of a lizard over one end, and secured the skin with a rattan band. He started to play, and the carvings began to move, jerkily at first. He beat the drum faster, and the figures moved less stiffly. They turned into living, dancing humans.

Fumiripits then moved to a succession of sites, where he similarly created the populations of villages. The people he created were called Asmat. People who inherited his skills at carving, *wowipits,* learned to carve ancestral figures, some of which were attached to drums, houses, boats, and so forth. Only Fumiripits can create human beings, but *wowipits* are important people, because ancestral souls (*bis*) can inhabit carved figures. Unlike other craftsmen, who create useful implements and other objects and services for consumption, *wowipits* create drums and other artworks for use in religious rites.

### Ceremonial performances

Some ceremonial Asmat dance-movements are based on avian movements, emphasizing the legendary link between human beings and ancestral symbols. Songs and stories say the soul of a newly deceased person travels in a boat along rivers, building a house at various places until it reaches the ancestors' land.

After a sago or coconut harvest or a successful wild-pig hunt, the Asmat hold ceremonies to invite ancestral spirits to meet the living and strengthen them. Whenever customary leaders decide to hold a ceremony—to honor the ancestors, to listen to their demands for revenge from wrongdoers, for initiations, to launch canoes, when an important decision needs to be reached—men gather in the communal longhouse for days and nights. Women periodically bring them meals. In the longhouse, men stand to sing and dance, or sit to rest or listen to speeches, each with a spear and a shield.

#### *A ceremony witnessed in a longhouse in Agats*

In a ceremony held to request ancestral advice about a division of land, all participants were males. They wore mainly red, white, and black clothes, with belts and monkey-fur headbands, shell necklaces, rattan armlets, white feathers, and bone nose ornaments. Ocher-red symbolized strength, shell-white signified human skin, and charcoal-black symbolized relief from pain. Participants clustered around fireplaces situated every few meters along the floor. Periodically they stood up, sang in chorus, and engaged in dancing (*bis pok mbui* 'ancestral spirit-dancing'). They stepped right and left, or simply swayed their bodies while standing or sitting. The floors rippled and swayed.

The tempo of the singing (whose melodies mainly used two or three tones) and drumming kept changing. After a vocalist began to sing, everyone stood to join in, each man dancing in place. Some of the men shouted out comments, whereupon the tempo of the music and dancing increased, only to stop altogether some time later. While resting, participants smoked or ate a snack of sago, and at mealtimes they ate fish or pork, with rice. They then resumed the next bout of music and dancing, repeating the process all day and all night for as long as they believed the ancestors required. The movements, based on those of birds, emphasized the mythological link between human beings and birds.

### Carving ritual drums

Asmat ritual art is largely men's business. Women are not allowed to be present while a *wowipits* is carving a ritual object or design, or to be in the longhouse on the most sacred occasions, while male musicians play and sing, though they are expected to bring meals. Some ceremonies, however, are for women only; men and women may participate in warfare-related ceremonies.

The main Asmat instrument is a single-headed hourglass drum with a wide waist and a handle attached to one side. Drums from the east and Brazza-northeastern areas are usually plain; drums from the coastal-central and northwestern areas are often decorated with carvings representing ancestral spirits. The handles of the latter drums have carvings of animal, bird, and geometric designs on their bodies; on their handles they bear elaborately carved ancestral figures facing two directions, often combining human and avian faces. In some cases, white and black feathers and beads hang from the body and the handle.

The drums vary in size, depending on their area of origin, with large ones being about 80 to 100 centimeters long, and small ones about 50 centimeters. The drumhead, about 14 to 18 centimeters in diameter, has lizardskin stretched across it, kept firmly in place by a plaited rattan band just below the rim. To keep drums dry and insect-free, the Asmat usually store them on a rack above a fireplace. Before playing, they tauten the skin by holding it over a fire. Normally, they play only one drum at once. The player holds it in his left hand, beating the head with his right hand.

For a carver-artist to make a ritual drum takes about a month. On its handle and body he may carve designs of spirits' hands and ears, fruitbats' feet, hornbills' heads, monkeys' tails, wriggling snakes, and human figures. For his labor, he and his family receive gifts of cooked meals.

### *Insiders and outsiders*

Partly as a result of Dutch military presence from 1904 to 1913, the world began to find artistic value in Asmat ancestral carvings (including musical instruments) and masks, and such items are found in the world's major museums. In 1953, after the Dutch had defeated local fighters, the Roman Catholic mission in Agats became influential. Its leverage increased after 1963, when the Indonesian government invaded and took control. This government tried to stop local warfare and cannibalism, yet ancestral rituals were still commonly held. The mission's museum in Agats has collected Asmat carvings, musical instruments, and other artifacts. In 1988, it became known as the Asmat Museum of Culture and Progress, and received financial assistance from by the government's Department of Education and Culture. The mission and the government encourage Asmat carvers and performers to resist being swamped by tourists' demands for cheap artifacts.

Promoting trade and enhancing Indonesia's image, the government has sent Asmat performers to the United States, Britain, and elsewhere. To some Asmat participants and foreign observers, the presentations—of rural sacred arts to urban secular audiences—have seemed incongruous. Such presentations bring to the fore the conflicting perceptions of "insider" Asmat performers and "outsider" foreign audiences.                                                           —MARGARET J. KARTOMI

## A syncretic context: Mali Baining

Among the Mali Baining in the early 1970s, a millenarian religious movement, Pomio Kivung, spread widely (Whitehouse 1995). Its main goal was to prepare for and expedite a miracle—in which ancestors would return to life, bringing material wealth. According to the movement's Christian-syncretic doctrines, those who invested this wealth wisely would merit salvation.

In 1987, mainly in two villages, a splinter party emerged and claimed it could work the miracle on its own. Renouncing its allegiance to the overall movement, it vowed loyalty to local leaders. These acts did more than assert a new and modified religious dogma: they confirmed the autonomy and unity of a small political unit,

The ancestor Aringawuk journeyed to the world of the dead. Returning home, he revealed a new morality, which he urged his people to accept. They did not, and in protest, he hanged himself.

upholding its leaders' authority. The splinter party relied heavily on new forms of collective ritual, in which music played a prominent role.

The model for leadership in the splinter party came from a myth relating the adventures of the ancestor Aringawuk, who experienced a mystical journey to the world of the dead. Returning home, he brought news of a new morality, similar to the Ten Commandments. He urged his people to accept this morality, but they did not, and in protest, he hanged himself.

The details of this story appeared in a song partly remembered by elders. As the splinter party coalesced, they pieced the song together, rehearsing in secret. They finally performed it in public, celebrating one man's dream—that the ancestors had chosen a new leader, Tanotka, to complete Aringawuk's task. Tanotka was a young man with little communal influence, but in the light of dreams and other sources of revelation, the community elected him to a position of authority and likened him to the central post of a house: as that post supported the rafters, people expected him to carry the community in its quest for the miracle. These ideas found expression in musical performance.

### Celebrating the dream

The climax of the celebration of the dream about Tanotka occurred in a meetinghouse. Men occupied about one-third of it, crammed together on a wooden platform. They handled lengths of bamboo, with which they beat rhythms on the planks beneath them. Contrasting with the complexity of their neighbors' rhythms, which the Mali often copy, "authentic" Mali rhythms are simple. In the song about Aringawuk, an even beat alternated with a polka-like rhythm, three beats followed by a rest.

The accompanying melody had the character of a dirge. It began on a low note (the pitch varying by verse), slid up to a rapid succession of high notes, and fell to the original one. The oscillation between a low register and a high one corresponded to changes of volume: the low note was quiet and somber; the high notes, loud and stirring. While the choir remained strong, melodies and lyrics repeated; but when several of the men's voices became weak or fell silent, somebody (usually an elder) would begin a new verse, cueing others to unite behind him and sing with gusto. The same technique introduced songs, often selected according to the mood of the man introducing them, or his perceptions of the mood of the assembly. Sometimes few in the choir knew the new song, and another person might introduce a change. The main criterion for a successful rendition was that it be moving or evocative, and this feeling rose and fell with the energy invested in performing.

Fervent singing inspired the women and girls to dance. When the choir sang the song of Aringawuk, men raised a post, symbolizing the leader Tanotka; women danced around it, in a tight, shuffling crowd. Every couple of hours, on average, all rested for up to fifteen minutes. The singing and dancing lasted until dawn:

### Syncretic music and ritual

The musical rendition of the story of Aringawuk inspired perceptions that ordinary speech, or even the most practiced and persuasive oratory, could not have animated. The story itself recounted the failure of the ancestors to unite behind an inspired leader, with tragic results. It recognized the arrival of a new leader and the opportunity for redemption; this time, it asserted, the community would, in the prevalent metaphor, "stand as one person."

Unified thought and action achieved its most dramatic display in synchronized drumming and singing, the result of careful and strenuous rehearsal. A solid relationship linked the synchrony of musical performance and the unity of the community. The women's dancing around the housepost affirmed communal allegiance to Tanotka, around whom everyone symbolically gathered. A series of individual declarations of solidarity, however impassioned, could not adequately have conveyed a similar impression.

The advantage of music was that it could communicate the idea of a body of people greater than the individuals of which it was composed—and within that collectivity, it could cultivate strong emotions. The juxtaposition of differing melodies, intensities, and rhythms created ever-shifting moods, from lamentation in grief to affirmation of allegiance. These moods were meanwhile enhanced by the participants' movements, heat, and odors.

—HARVEY WHITEHOUSE

## Christian contexts

In 1871, the London Missionary Society (LMS) ventured into New Guinea. At first, it represented all Protestant religious denominations; later, it became increasingly a society of independent or congregationalist churches. British missionaries saw themselves as leaders in spreading civilization. For many, imperial expansion was a providential means for making converts to Christianity. Some foreign critics concluded that British colonialists were extending their political control under the cloak of Bibles, prayers, sermons, and hymns.

Political events in 1868 and 1869 required the missionaries to withdraw from French territories in Oceania (Prendergast 1968:69). The French government allowed only islanders under its administration to work as religious teachers in French Polynesian territories. Polynesians played important roles as missionaries in New Guinea, where they first arrived in 1872.

The tools of conversion included hymns. The missionaries began with texts in English and German, but soon added local languages. Kâte, once spoken by about six hundred people in a handful of villages, spread through the peninsula into upland areas as far west as Mt. Hagen; by the 1950s, about seventy-five thousand persons understood it. In the same way in northeast New Guinea, the Lutheran mission used Gedaged and Jabêm. Between 1898 and 1984, it printed nearly forty hymnals containing texts of hymns, most of which were Western hymns with indigenous texts (Wagner and Reiner 1986:445). Other missions and their languages are Wesleyan (Dobu, Kuaua), Anglican (Binandere, Wedau), Kwati (Suau), LMS (Hiri Motu, Kiwai, Toaripi), and Unevangelized Fields Mission (Gogodala). After the late 1950s, when English became the national language of education, the religious importance of these languages declined.

### The 1880s and after

In 1886, Roman Catholic priests founded a mission on Yule Island. Rivalry with Protestants erupted, but with less dissension than in other areas of the Pacific. By 1887, five organizations were working in New Guinea: the LMS; the Order of the Sacred Heart (Roman Catholic); Wesleyan Methodists; and Lutherans from

Neuendettelsau, Bavaria, who in 1886 had established a mission at Simbang, near Finschhafen. These missions were on coastal strips or in the islands.

In 1890, the leaders of the Protestant missions divided British New Guinea (Papua) into spheres of influence. The Methodists took responsibility for the islands off the eastern coast. The LMS, the largest mission, took responsibility for the southern coast. The Church of England agreed to evangelize the northeastern coast, where its missionaries first arrived in 1891.

The missions recognized the importance of getting to know the people to whom they were preaching. Roman Catholics demanded obedience on questions of doctrine, but in other matters allowed converts to continue their old ways. Methodists emphasized an ethical, rather than a doctrinal, manner of life, which did not tolerate "heathen" customs. As late as 1925, one LMS missionary, Charles Abel (at Kwato), condemned indigenous drumming and dancing. Anglican missionaries never fully believed that without their intervention the peoples of the Pacific would die out. They seesawed between demanding the eradication of indigenous culture and tolerating some indigenous activities; but they always condemned dancing because they thought its sexual connotations sinful.

New Guineans learned hymns quickly. Communal singing in church paralleled their experience, since indigenous religious rites involved music. The Anglican Church offered pieces by Handel, Keble, Sankey, and Wesley. Nonconformist works, especially those in gospel-song hymnals, were popular at Dogura in 1894, but Anglican clergymen tried to replace them with plainsong. The gospel-song style gained and held popularity. Certain musical influences at Dogura came from the Kwato mission, where children learned sol-fa singing.

Wherever the music came from, each mission stamped it with unique intonation and rhythms. Wesleyan hymns were "bright rousing choruses, while Anglican singing was always slow and lugubrious" (Wetherall 1977:179). Hymns presented Papua New Guineans with particular problems: the music followed a diatonic scale, with a functionally tonal syntax, in Western structures. Indigenous peoples could not understand the words. Their own songs were repetitive, with only a few notes (often only three to five), sung from memory. Western hymns—in books, with many words and long stanzas—required literacy.

### The indigenization of hymns

For missionaries in New Guinea, the choice of music for Christian worship was never straightforward. New Guineans sang the Christian message in local languages before they could read. Is a German chorale sung in a vernacular language not wholly indigenous? If an indigenous Christian composes a hymn in imitation of Western examples, is the new composition indigenous? If a text is a translation of an English or German text, but the melody is indigenous, is the new piece indigenous? The permutations of these variables illustrate the complexity of service music in New Guinea. Identified and listed, they illuminate the word *indigenous* when applied to hymns.

These are the main kinds of MUSICAL indigenization in New Guinea:

A. Existing Western music, printed in hymnals
B. Music composed in a Western style by an indigenous person
C. Music using indigenous musical material, adapted by an indigenous person
D. As C, but adapted by a Westerner
E. Music composed by a Polynesian, as in *peroveta*
F. Music composed by an indigenous person in a traditional style
G. "Popular" Western style, as in gospel songs

H. Traditional percussion: kundus, garamuts, or kundus with garamuts
I. Conch trumpets
J. Rattles, or other traditional instruments
K. Western instruments, as an organ
L. Guitars, ukuleles

These are the main kinds of TEXTUAL indigenization in New Guinea:

M. Existing Western texts, printed in hymnals
N. Western texts (as M), but translated into an indigenous language
O. Composed by an indigenous person in English or German, based on Western theology
P. Composed by an indigenous person in an indigenous language, based on Western theology
Q. Composed by an indigenous person in an indigenous language, based on New Guinean theology
R. Western (as M), but translated into Tok Pisin
S. Composed in Tok Pisin by an indigenous person
T. Composed in Tok Pisin by a Polynesian

These are the main kinds of local indigenization in DANCE:

U. Movement and costume from indigenous traditions
V. Movement and costume from Polynesia

In some missionaries' minds, any permutation except A + M marked a hymn as indigenous, even if only one of the other variables were present. There could therefore be shades of indigenization: A + N, A + O, B + N, B + O, and so on. The most common pattern, in all religions throughout Papua New Guinea, is A + R, a Western hymn with words translated into Tok Pisin.

### Peroveta

In Central, Gulf, and Western provinces, one unique influence remains: *peroveta* 'prophet', Polynesian music brought by Polynesian LMS missionaries. The people of those provinces believe this influence came from Fiji, Tonga, Sāmoa, or Rarotonga. To learn to sing and dance *peroveta,* delegations from Western Province annually visit Rarotonga.

The singing of *peroveta* falls mainly to a mixed choir in two parts. The texts tell of biblical prophets. Dance, an essential element of the genre, illustrates the narratives (figure 3). The songs, often responsorial, frequently use percussive vocalizations typical of certain Polynesian male singing. Though some local people consider *peroveta* to be thoroughly indigenous, its phrases are longer than those of local songs, and many of its pieces are in a language unknown to the singers.

### Conch bands

From 1902 to 1932, the Rev. Dr. Heinrich Zahn served in New Guinea as a Lutheran missionary. To accompany singing in Christian contexts, he formed bands whose instruments were shells of gastropods of genera *Cassis, Fusus, Strombus,* and *Triton* (figure 4). Through holes drilled through the apex or the side, players buzzed their lips. Instruments were of graded sizes: the larger the shell, the lower the pitch.

In 1920, Zahn saw the chance of using these trumpets in four-part harmony—an effect that occurred in precontact music only as the result of accidental melodic overlapping. Zahn's first band, in 1925, consisted of nineteen conchs. Each shell produced one note, tuned to the diatonic scale. Zahn's bands gave intonational support

FIGURE 3    During the Hiri Moale Festival, a choir performs in a *peroveta* competition. Photo by Don Niles, 1991.

to New Guinean Christians who had difficulty singing in tune. Another solution might have been to import a harmonium, but the Lutherans took pride in using locally available materials. These bands were unique in Oceania. Their heyday lasted three years (1925–1927). One band played at Hocpoi, one in the middle school at Watsutieng-Logaweng, and one in the church at Malalo.

Before Zahn could form the band, he had to overcome two problems: to obtain conchs and devise a method by which the players could read music. He introduced a notation using the numerals 1 to 7, with 1 representing the tonic (figure 5). He marked lower and upper octaves with dots below or above the numerals respectively. Two (or more) dots below (or above) indicate two (or more) octaves down (or up). Zero denotes a rest. A dot after a figure doubles a duration. Lines above numerals show rhythm: one line marks an eighth; two lines, a sixteenth. An asterisk indicates a flat.

*The Conchshell-Hymnal* (Zahn 1959) contains eighty-three hymns, some with multiple titles in English, German, and Jabêm. Some hymns have up to five titles. The disposition of the languages hints at the popularity of a particular hymn or the suitability of a text to a language area. Having each person play one tone imposes restrictions on the music, since the coordination of fast notes would be difficult. Zahn responded to this concern by choosing hymns in block chords with simple harmonies, mostly triads in root position.

Around 1927, trumpets, tubas, a baritone, and a trombone—a gift from the Evangelical Trumpet Band Association of Bavaria—arrived at Hocpoi. Zahn taught young people to play these instruments. He then amalgamated his bands: for a few months, ten brasses and twenty-five conchs accompanied hymns in Hocpoi.

Several conch-band revivals have occurred. At Lae around 1955, an expatriate teacher formed a band at Bumayong High School, near the Lutheran headquarters. Revivals occurred briefly at Asaroka Lutheran High School in the 1960s; Bukawa in 1964 and 1983; Logaweng Seminary, Finschhafen, in 1982; and Germany in 1953 and 1972 (Muhlenhard 1983).

### Later trends

After Papua New Guinean independence, the missions formulated a policy of indigenizing the liturgy, music, language, and clergy. This policy changed the emphasis

FIGURE 4   The Rev. Dr. Heinrich Zahn and his band at Hocpoi, 1927. By permission of Neuendettelsau Seminary Archives, Germany.

from mainly Western-based music to what remained of indigenous music. Services began to feature indigenous musical instruments. In the Anglican Church, especially at feasts, kundu-playing choirs sang and danced their way to the sanctuary, often in a version of indigenous dress. In varying proportions, worship added hymns accompanied by kundus, rattles, and conchs; newly composed hymns in local languages; and most popularly, hymns with stanzas and refrains, accompanied by one or two guitars.

In rural performances of the 1990s, the distribution of musical styles might be 10 percent hymns (English and translated versions), 10 percent choruses (with guitar), and 80 percent indigenized music (with kundus). The proportions in urban parishes are possibly 45 percent, 45 percent, and 10 percent, respectively.

Papua New Guinean Anglicans have their own hymnal, with 280 hymns. Many of its texts come from standard British hymnals (*Hymns Ancient and Modern Revised* 1947; Vaughan Williams, Shaw, and Dearmer 1925), but churches use many modern hymns, often with a repeated chorus. *The Lutheran Hymnbook,* reflecting its origins, features German chorales. The United Reform Church uses Wesleyan hymns, whose texts expound the strict morality of nineteenth-century Nonconformism. Evangelical churches favor the musical simplicity of gospel songs, encouraging congregations to clap and dance as they sing.

—ANNE M. GEE

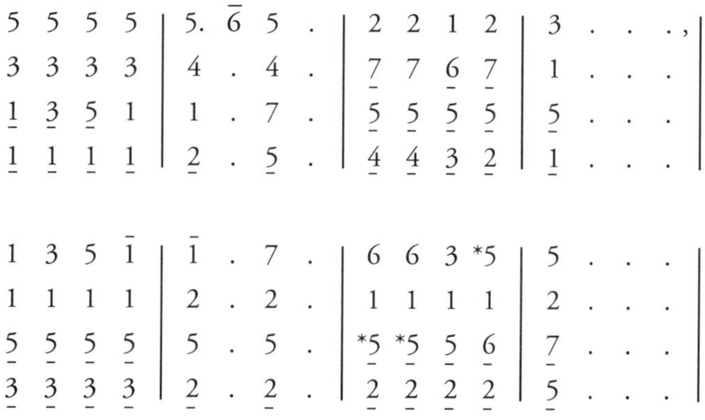

FIGURE 5   Conch-band notation: the beginning of "Onward Christian Soldiers" (Zahn 1959). The symbol *5 is a flat fifth, though the functional tonality of the note is a sharp fourth. By permission of Kristen Pres Incorporated, Madang, Papua New Guinea.

## MELANESIA: VANUATU

In Vanuatu, where notions of the secular are importations, all music bears the influence of religious experience. The ni-Vanuatu (indigenous peoples) distinguish between animistic practices and Christian sects, often nominal, in that elements of old beliefs permeate them. The national motto is We Stand With God (*Long God Yumi Stanup*), but savvy pagans—15 percent of the population, living mainly on Espiritu Santo, Pentecost, and Malakula—ask which god politicians and clerics have in mind. The resulting conflicts have overt musical implications.

On many northern islands, neighboring villages compete in *sawagoro*-like dance-songs. In numbers, vigor, volume, and choice of music, one side tries to surpass another. Historical interpretation is a field for combat, on which villagers define their local identities by mobilizing myths and metaphors. To show sophistication, performers select pieces illustrating heroic or even antiheroic stances. One side waits for the other to finish, and fills pauses between items with smartly apposite items. On Ambae in the early 1990s, an Adventist village might have sung popular "Christian choruses" from the European-American campfire ecumenical tradition, advocating puritan virtues. Other villages might have answered it with a *sawagoro* about a hero who achieved renown by apparent transgressions: lies, adulteries, murders, wars. Comprehensive and subtle, the irony may elude missionaries' ken. Villages that have renounced custom because of sectarian dictates (Seventh-Day Adventists, Apostolic Church, Church of Christ) often appreciate most sharply the importance of indigenous music. To keep up the interface between custom and importation, they maintain links with laxer Christian sects (Anglicans, Roman Catholics).

Despite rejuvenating events, musical variety often gives way to imported uniformity. By the 1990s, Vanuatu's 105 languages of the 1970s (each with music related to specific terrains) had dwindled. Conscious of loss, peoples looked inward to cultural specificities in their languages, and produced songs in a mixture of dialect and neo-Melanesian—in what outsiders sometimes thought to be innocuous string-band music, a pan-Pacific style, in which, typically, performers recount boy-meets-girl situations. Though some of the music builds false happiness, some is social commentary in disguise. Apt subjects are adultery, incest, rape, murder, treason. The pretty mask of innocence cozens missionaries and ni-Vanuatu politicians, struggling to homogenize their peoples. Once pierced, the surface of much pan-Pacific pop never looks the same. The ubiquitous string band, Vanuatu's vigorous, cutting-edge form, where "you have to know the words," has a deadly, religious-political side.

The content of string-band lyrics comes directly from indigenous song. The government bans some old forms, such as the East Ambae *tanumwe*, which musicians no longer compose because they deal with technical incest (intramoiety cohabitation), a matter religious people do not tolerate, though they know it persists. Whenever someone sings one of these songs, a crowd gathers and weeps.

Songs and dances join religious forms in marking notable public events. The completion of a building, a well, a windmill—all demand rituals of consecration. In 1977, the Nagriamel Party celebrated with a ceremony the opening of a new road. A suicide eased the question of who should inherit the land, resident colonial commissioners unknowingly ate forbidden pigeons (which they had put on a protected list), and people from the hinterland danced *na polo* counterclockwise and killed hermaphrodite pigs. At the other end of the road, performers did double-line dances to the accompaniment of an accordion, instead of double raft panpipes; they said the accordion played "much the same sounds." At any point in such ceremonies, people may break out into nineteenth-century evangelical hymns, such as "Shall We Gather by the River?"

In church-run schools, students typically learn music from a blackboard display of sol-fa notation, taken from hymnals published in England. They ignore end-line and mid-line pauses or prolongations, and the sung result is irregular tempo, often with novel rhythmic effects. Neither in hymns nor in string-band songs, their popular offspring, are phrases equal in duration. The aesthetically admired manner of singing requires volume as loud as possible, and no vibrato.

In 1977, a religious performance used inaudible music. For tribute at a bishop's consecration, all communities of the diocese presented dances. People from Mota, Motalava, and Maewo displayed elaborate headgear and dress. In perfect synchrony, they danced silently, to music heard only in their heads. Conclusively, punctiliously, they then destroyed their garb. None in the audience knew what religious sentiments they had been expressing.

In the 1970s, high-church Anglicans encouraged a fusion of indigenous and Christian cultures, and local composers set the text of the Anglican Mass to Mota melodies. Fundamentalist Christian sects have pushed ritual music to elementary levels, but more complex religious music might arise from inspiration by international contact on occasions such as the Pacific Festival of Arts.   —PETER RUSSELL CROWE

## MICRONESIA: YAP

To Yap in 1886 Spanish Capuchin missionaries brought Gregorian chants, the music of the Roman Catholic Church. Distributed among the sections of the Mass, and proper to the day and time, these pieces display various monophonic styles and structures.

In 1903, German missionaries brought another language and different customs. Hymns performed on Yap in the mid-1990s show that the linguistic legacy of German missionaries exceeded that of Spanish ones. German words have made their way into Yapese, most likely as a result of being in religious music. An example is the text of the Agnus Dei, "*Saaf ku Goot*" ('Lamb of God', figure 6). The Yapese word *saaf* comes from the German word *Schaf* 'sheep'; and *Got,* from the German *Gott* 'God' (Jensen 1977).

Most hymns performed on Yap have been adapted from conventional hymns or carols. "*Felfelan'dad*" ('Let's Be Joyful') is widely known beyond Yap as "Joy to the World," and "*Nep ni Zozup*" ('Holy Night') is based on "Silent Night." Not all such melodies, however, come from international classics; often, though, the texts are literal translations from English into Yapese.

Yapese hymns have been collected and printed in *Ngadatanggad ku Samol* (Songs of the Savior), which sorts them by their role in the Mass, their seasonal use, or their topic, such as songs of Mary (*tang ku Maria*), songs of the dead (*tang ko yam*), songs

FIGURE 6  The Agnus Dei as performed on Yap in the mid-1990s. Transcription by Deirdre Marshall-Dean.

The principles through which Polynesians interpreted their world included mana and taboo. Mana, 'supernatural power', was a generative force. It was protected by taboos, some of which were activated by the recitation of verbal formulas.

of the Mass (*tang ko Misa*). At the beginning of the book is a collection of general hymns, not all of which conform with the melodies of standard Roman Catholic hymns.

Taking melodies from international pop, local composers have created hymns. The most notable of these is the Christmas song "*Ke Yib Fare Raen*" ('The Light Has Come'), based on Simon and Garfunkel's melody "The Sound of Silence."

Yapese sing hymns outside religious services—at parties and village celebrations, usually unaccompanied and in unison. One such piece is the communion hymn "*Kammagar Samol*" ('Thank You, Lord'), based on the song "Kumbaya." A possible reason for using that music with Yapese words is the phonetic similarity between *kumbaya* and *kammagar*.                         —DEIRDRE MARSHALL-DEAN

## POLYNESIA

Important religious concepts of Polynesia included the origin of the universe and connections among gods, ancestors, and humans. These connections were ritually maintained through music and dance, systems of knowledge that hereditary experts held in memory. Gods and people formed a continuum of the sacred and the profane. As gods were sacred and people profane, so were chiefs sacred and commoners profane. This axiom underlay Polynesians' sociocultural organization, justifying ranked social and kinship structures. It still underlies many Polynesian interpersonal relationships.

The details of Polynesian cosmogony remain to be worked out, but the Proto-Polynesian universe probably began with a primary void. From it came heaven and earth, personified as a sky-father and an earth-mother, who clung in a warm embrace until they were pushed apart by one of the four great Polynesian gods—Tāne, Tangaroa, Tū, and Rongo—or sometimes by a lesser god (or demigod), Maui. In Hawai'i, rather than rending heaven and earth, the sky-father and earth-mother, with various partners, gave birth to the individual islands of the Hawaiian chain.

These gods took various forms throughout Polynesia. They concerned themselves with the creation of the universe, most elements of nature, the other gods, and human beings. They displayed human dispositions, and had to be honored, worshiped, and appeased. Each island or cluster of islands had a unique cast of lesser deities, emphasizing locally salient plants, animals, and natural phenomena. Special gods—like Pele, the goddess of volcanos in Hawai'i—met the requirements of special natural environments (figure 7).

The underlying set of principles through which Polynesians interpreted their world and organized their social lives included mana and taboo (*tapu*), concepts intertwined with ideas of rank based on divine descent. Mana, possibly best glossed 'supernatural power', was a generative force, often linked with genealogical rank, fertility, and protocol. It was protected by taboos, some of which had musical significance because they were charms, activated by the recitation of verbal formulas. As

FIGURE 7    Near the edge of Hale Maʻumaʻu Crater, Hawaiʻi, Hālau o Kekuhi perform a *hula* in honor of Pele, the volcano goddess. The teachers of this school, the Kanakaʻole sisters Nalani and Pualani, received a National Heritage Fellowship in 1993. Photo by Adrienne L. Kaeppler, 1982.

restrictions on behavior, some taboos were made visible by signs, like a bent branch, or a specially plaited frond attached to a tree to protect its wood, its leaves, or its fruit. Other taboos were conceptual, supported by myths and other intangible tokens of morality (Handy 1927).

## West Polynesia

In West Polynesia, Tangaloa (East Polynesian Tangaroa) and Maui were the important male god and demigod, respectively, and Hikuleʻo (Tonga) or Saveasiʻuleo (Sāmoa) governed Pulotu, the underworld. In Tonga, Maui pushed up the skies, ordered in ten layers. Tangaloa was the sole creator, whose universe was the ocean and a many-tiered sky. In Sāmoa, he threw a rock into the ocean, and it became the island of Manuʻa. (Alternate myths exist.) The Tongan islands were said to have been created when the gods threw down chips of wood from their workshops. Maui or Tangaloa used special fishhooks to fish up certain islands from the sea.

### *The origin of the universe*

The organization of the universe and important events in the lives of gods or chiefs were embodied in songs and dances that became chronicles of history and geography. The following excerpt, from Tonga, describes the role of Maui and the layers of the heavens (after Kaeppler 1976:202–203).

| | |
|---|---|
| Naʻe fakatupu hotau fonua, | Our land was created, |
| ʻO fakapulonga mei ʻolunga, | Shrouded from above, |
| Pea tau totolo hangē ha unga. | And we crawled like crabs. |
| Langi tuʻo taha, langi tuʻo ua, | The first and second skies |
| Tala ange kia Maui Motuʻa | Tell to Maui Motuʻa |
| Ke ne teketeke ke maʻolunga | To push them high |
| Ke havilivili he ʻoku pupuha, | So the breeze can come in, for it is hot, |
| Pea fakamaama e fanua. | And bring light to the land. |
| Pea tau tuʻu hake ki ʻolunga, | And then we stood up, |
| ʻO ʻeveʻeva fakamafutofuta. | And walked about proudly. |
| Langi tuʻo taha, langi tuʻo ua, | The first and second skies |
| Ko e langi pe ʻa Maui Motuʻa. | Are the skies of Maui Motuʻa. |
| Langi tuʻo tolu, langi tuʻo fā, | The third and fourth skies, |

| | |
|---|---|
| Nofo ai ‘a ‘Ūfia mo Latā: | Are the living places of ‘Ūfia and Latā: |
| Ko e langi kehe, langi ‘uha, | These are separate skies, the rainy sky, |
| Na ‘ufia e langi ma‘a, | That covers the cloudless sky, |
| Pea lilo ai Tapukitea. | Where Tapukitea is hidden. |

Tapukitea is Venus, the morning and evening star. Later verses mention the origin of the Milky Way and certain climatological features.

West Polynesian myths also recount the origin of chiefly titles and kava rituals, linking political structures with other beliefs, and making political and religious concepts suitable topics for the poetry performed at kava ceremonies. In Sāmoa, Tagaloa (Tangaloa) had kava brought from heaven to slake his thirst (Pratt 1891:164). In Futuna, a man obtained kava from spirits in a trance (Burrows 1945:59). A Tongan and Sāmoan myth says kava first grew from the buried body of a chief's leprous daughter.

### The maintenance of order

Taboo contrasted with permitted behavior. The contrast was sometimes explicit, as in Sāmoa, where notions of the bound (*sā*) and the free (*fua*) affected many aspects of life. In Sāmoa since missionization, the Christian day of restricted behavior has been Sunday (*aso Sā* 'bound day'), and the people's first day free of its restrictions has been Monday (*aso Gafua* 'free day'). Hence a song of Savai‘i, current around 1900:

| | |
|---|---|
| ‘O le tulī ma le ve‘a fiafia aso Gafua. | The tern and the rail enjoy Mondays. |
| Kilekuā aso Sā, kilekuā! | *Kilekuā* Sundays, *kilekuā!* |

As with many Polynesian lyrics, even in children's songs, this text is metaphorical: by saying a seabird (the tern) and a landbird (the rail) enjoy Mondays, it means that all birds—all *people*—do.

Belief in gods and spirits occasioned the performance of several kinds of music. Recitations of prayers were common, by heads of households on behalf of families, and village priests on behalf of communities. In old Sāmoa, annual offerings of food to gods were "associated with games, sham-fights, night-dances" (Turner 1884:20), and a conch served as the emblem of certain gods of war (Stair 1897:221). In the West Polynesian outlier Tikopia, a cycle of seasonal rituals, the Work of the Gods, occasioned the performance of kava, reciting, singing, and dancing (Firth 1967).

Religious beliefs also underlay funeral customs. Laments were a standard feature of indigenous music; some were performed with conventionally intoned sighing, wailing, and sobbing (Kaeppler 1993b; Mayer and Nau 1976), but others were not always somber, weepy, or lugubrious. In old Sāmoa, survivors let a dead chief's body decompose; they eventually severed the head and interred it, but did so with feasting and dancing (Brown 1972 [1910]:405). After the Western missionaries' arrival, funerals became Christian events, which followed Christian liturgies. In Sāmoa, Protestant funerals end with a performance of the hymn "‘*Ia Fa‘atasi Pea Iesū ma ‘Oe*," a version of the nineteenth-century evangelical hymn "God Be with You."

Today, most West Polynesians are Christians. Elaborate churches are familiar aspects of the landscape. In addition to furnishing music for worship, choirs compete in festivals, in their home countries and abroad.

—ADRIENNE L. KAEPPLER, J. W. LOVE

### Christian music in Tonga

In 1822, Wesleyan missionaries arrived in Tonga and immediately saw how important music was in Tongan life. On 2 December 1827, a simple hymn of two stanzas, composed by the missionary Nathaniel Turner, was sung at a religious service—the first time a Christian hymn was sung in the Tongan language. During the first thirty years of Christianity in Tonga, Methodist missionaries translated many hymns composed by Charles Wesley (1707–1788). The Te Deum was sung in Tongan as early as 1839, at the marriage of Sālote, daughter of Taufaʻāhau (later King Tupou I), to a high-ranking chief, the Tuʻi Pelehake. The first Tongan hymnal (1849) contained 189 hymns. Missionary Walter Lawry, in a visit in 1850, observed the worship in Nukuʻalofa: "The beautiful harmony with which they went through the responses in the Morning Service was very affecting, in tones like the sound of many waters" (Wood 1975:1:91).

### James Egan Moulton and his numerical notation

In 1865, the Rev. (later Dr.) James Egan Moulton (1841–1909) came from England as a missionary and teacher. In 1866, he founded Tupou College, now the biggest boys' secondary boarding school in the South Pacific. His brilliance as a theologian, linguist, and musician is still recognized. Words and phrases from his hymns have become proverbial in the Tongan language, quoted in public in various settings. Moulton retranslated hymns and the liturgy into stately Tongan, replacing what the early missionaries, with a less fluent knowledge of the language, had produced.

Though the Roman Catholic and Methodist churches shared the pioneering of Christianity in Tonga, it is Moulton's contribution that is musically outstanding. Composing hymns for the students of Tupou College, he began to introduce music written in sol-fa, but when he started to teach, he learned that certain combinations of syllables were indelicate words in Tongan. He then devised a numerical notation, which Tongan churches and schools still use, even for eight-part anthems and music for bands.

By introducing a system of notation, Moulton brought to Tonga the European oratorio tradition. Handel's *Messiah,* Haydn's *Creation,* and Mendelssohn's *Elijah* soon became familiar. Moulton's Tongan translations of favorites such as "Abide with Me," "Jesus, Lover of My Soul," "Nearer, My God, to Thee," and "When I Survey the Wondrous Cross" have become part of the cultural heritage of the Tongan people.

### Moulton's techniques of translating

Moulton used his linguistic and theological skills to weave meaningful illustrations into his interpretations of hymns. In the Tongan version of Joseph Scriven's text "What a Friend We Have in Jesus," especially the lines "Are we weak and heavy-laden, / Cumbered with a load of care," Moulton used the idea of a father and son going to the garden to get food for the family. The food was carried in a coconut-leaf basket hung on a long stick, the father resting one end of the stick on his shoulder, and the son taking the other end. When the father would draw the basket closer to his end, he would take more of the weight of the load, lightening it for his son. Reinterpreting the hymn, Moulton wrote:

> Ka ne ʻave ki he ʻEiki, siʻo ngaahi fuʻu moʻua,
> Te ne ala pe ʻo hiki, hilifaki hono uma:
> Te ne toho pe ke ofi ʻau pe hono maʻamaʻa.
> Tuʻu totonu ʻo malohi, faingofua ʻa e faingataʻa.

> If you take your burdens to the Lord,
> He will lift them on to his shoulder:
> He will pull the burden closer to make your load lighter.
> Stand tall and be strong, and the burden will be easy.

For Frances Havergal's hymn "Master, Speak! Thy Servant Heareth," Moulton began with the idea of a master-servant relationship. He added the story of the calling of Samuel, to produce what has become a favorite Tongan children's hymn, "'*Amusia 'a Samiuela hono ui 'e he 'Eiki*" ('Oh that I were Samuel to be called by the Lord').

Some favorite hymns are Moulton's own lyrics, set to widely known tunes. "'*E 'Eiki, ke ke mé a mai 'a e anga 'eku nofo*" ('See, Lord, the way I live') illustrates his skill in evoking culturally important imagery. His lyrics meditate on the temptations that surround our lives, trying to trap us:

> 'Omi ha konisenisi hange ha tama'imata,
> Ke u kalo 'oka lave si'i ha mé'i angahala.

> Give me a conscience as sensitive as the pupil of the eye,
> So that I will turn away if a speck of sin touches it.

In other texts, Moulton used illustrations from the sea, deeply familiar to an ocean-bound people. In Tongan minds, his hymns evoke important meanings and values associated with outriggers, sails, masts, harbors, storms, and anchors. Noted Tongan scholars have said that no Tongan has equaled his use of the Tongan language.

### Moulton's followers

Moulton imbued his students with his love of hymns. When they graduated and returned to their villages, they formed choirs and taught their congregations music they had learned at the college. In 1935, Dr. A. Harold Wood (1896–1989, another musician, also principal of the college) introduced choral competitions, which became so popular that choirs of a hundred or more voices now travel from all over the islands to participate.

Over the years, outstanding Tongan musicians have worked in Christian musical idioms. Tevita Tu'ipulotu Taumoefolau (1915–1981) and Feleti Sitoa Siale (1912–1996) of the Free Wesleyan Church, and Sofele Kakala (1916–1991) of the Roman Catholic Church, were exceptional Tongan choirmasters. Kakala composed Tongan-language masses that incorporated indigenous Tongan melodic contours, and the Vatican honored him for his music.            —HELEN TALIAI, SIUPELI TALIAI

### Christian music in Sāmoa

In 1830, LMS missionaries arrived in Sāpapāli'i, Savai'i, and King Mālietoa Vaiinupō accepted them. At first, Tahitian and Rarotongan teachers conducted hymns and services in their own languages (Faleto'ese 1961:85); later, missionaries composed Sāmoan texts, for which they borrowed simple melodies from various sources. After the 1840s, when the missionaries established seminaries (Mālua and Pīula), Sāmoans learned English hymns. Graduates from these institutions, as pastors throughout the islands, took these hymns to villages, where they can still be heard in churches and family prayers.

### Musical traits of hymns

In modern arrangements, the melody can occur in the soprano or the tenor, or be distributed among four parts; or its melodic line may be hidden and carried by one or two voices. Descants, mostly in the major mode, sometimes decorate hymns. The crossing of voices is uncommon.

Harmonic structure resembles that of English hymns. The diminished chord, a foreign trademark, is popular; it appeared early in Sāmoan hymnals, and later in songs by local composers. Parallel fourths rarely occur. Vocal duets and trios have become popular in late-twentieth-century sacred music. A feature of sacred music original to local composers is a parallel movement of inner voices (alto and tenor) in a final cadence or final chord that, in an amen gesture, restates the last line or words of a verse or refrain.

Harmonic modulation between stanzas came from abroad. In the 1980s, modulation a semitone upward became a favorite way to connect stanzas and hymns, and to end the last section of a song. As a result of repeated upward modulations, sopranos sometimes approach final cadences straining to reach the pitch. The singing of high notes results in straining and nasality, named by several Sāmoan terms: *fa'ataiō, fa'aumu,* and *pese i le isu* 'sing through the nose'.

Rhythms, whether fast or slow, usually derive from textual pronunciation. Short vowels tend to have notes of shorter duration than long vowels. Directors or organists usually start with the music before adding words. Using a text improperly in borrowed music may violate the relationship of vowel length and rhythm, making certain words sound awkward, and even changing their meaning.

In the treatment of tempos, pace reflects mood: texts about tragic events are slow, and texts about joyful events are fast. To specify tempo in written music, local composers write a Sāmoan word that describes the tempo they prefer; for example, the term *laulausiva* (in other contexts the name of an introductory item with gestures and claps) prescribes a lively, fast tempo.

Strophic form, a trait of many indigenous songs, occurs in Sāmoan hymns. Anthems based on biblical texts are through-composed, with or without repeated sections. Large works called psalms (*salamo*) have three movements—fast, slow, fast—with an introduction and interludes. Other religious compositions have a development and a coda. Strophic and through-composed hymns have a tendency to repeat each stanza, the refrain after the last stanza, and the last lines of the refrain.

Variations in dynamics are uncommon in Sāmoan religious performances. A piece is sung loudly until the last refrain, which the choir first sings softly and then loudly; the soft singing signals that the hymn will soon end.

The singing of hymns once had a nasal timbre, especially in soprano and tenor voices, which, by carrying the melody in alternation or doubling, stood out from other parts; but in the late 1990s, this nasality is diminishing. Most Sāmoan choral directors do not like it, and try to change it during warm-up exercises (figure 8). Directors also try to control vibrato, three kinds of which are becoming popular in sacred choirs: a fast tremolo, as if quivering (*tete pei e ma'alili* 'tremble as if shivering'); a yelling vibrato, with the mouth widely open (*tete fa'aumu,* or *tete fa'ataiō*); and a slow, hollow vibrato, resulting from lowering the jaw (*leo tete fa'a'ō'ō*).

The texts of Sāmoan religious music use the formal register, with the phoneme /t/ pronounced [t]; this register also serves for reciting religious verses, saying prayers, and giving sermons. A controversial textual practice in religious music of the 1980s and 1990s has been to use secular terms, like proverbs and legendary allusions—phrases typically spoken by orators and chiefs in settings outside the church.

### Typical plans of worship

Each denomination follows its own order of worship, with slight variations. In Protestant churches, this plan is typical:

1. Organ prelude, optional
2. Invocation (*tatalo 'āmata*), said by the pastor or catechist (*ta'ita'i*)
3. Hymn (*pese fa'afetai* or *Agāga Pa'ia*), sung by the choir and the congregation
4. Long prayer (*tatalo 'umi*), said by the pastor or the catechist

FIGURE 8    In Pago Pago, the choir of the
Congregational Church of Jesus in Sāmoa
rehearses. Photo by Leua Frost, 1995.

5. The Lord's Prayer, sung by everyone present in a musical version standard throughout Sāmoa. In the Mass, many Roman Catholic congregations also sing this version of the music
6. Hymn, sung by the choir and congregation
7. Skits, optionally inserted by Sunday-school students; especially in Methodist churches in Tutuila, the idea of skits was introduced by the late Rev. Fa'atauva'a Tapua'i, pastor of Susana Uesile Methodist Church in Tafuna and chairman of the National Council of Churches in American Sāmoa
8. Sermon (*lāuga*), by the pastor or the catechist
9. Hymn, sung by the choir and congregation; at special services, like the anniversary of the founding of the local parish, the choir may at this point present an anthem, or the congregation may sing a psalm to a European psalmodic formula
10. Organ postlude, optional

Solo singing is popular in weddings, funerals, and sections of some anthems and psalms.

Protestant congregational singing includes hymns from Britain and the United States, especially Sunday-school songs, some in versions maintained orally from the 1800s. Their texts are usually Sāmoan translations by LMS missionaries (whose churches now form the 'Ekālesia Fa'apotopotoga Kerisiano i Sāmoa) and Methodist missionaries. Protestant services may feature solo, duet, trio, or other small-ensemble performances of gospel or pop adaptations, accompanied by synthesizers or other musical instruments.

Roman Catholic churches follow the order of worship specified in standard liturgical books, but Sāmoan priests make minor adjustments for special services. Many congregations sing hymns—music and text—borrowed from Protestant hymnals. Musical traits particular to Roman Catholic services include responsorial singing between a cantor or a priest and the congregation; the singing of Latin texts, or of Sāmoan texts translated from Latin; and the adaptation of Sāmoan texts and music.

TRACK 6

Much music is felt equally appropriate for Roman Catholic and Protestant churches. The main reason is that Roman Catholic churches hire Protestant choir directors. The major forces behind this trend were two composers from the Congregational Church of Jesus in Sāmoa, Mata'utia Pene Solomona and Elder Mr.

Ioselani Pouesi, who taught many of today's choir directors, and composed music for Roman Catholic and Protestant hymnals.

*Musical philosophy*

Protestant pastors believe musicians play an important part in religious services. A common phrase they use when thanking musicians is *E mafai e le pese ona lāuga, 'ae lē mafai e le lāuga ona pese* 'A song can preach, but a sermon can't sing'. Pastors who graduated from theological colleges are said to have been the first choristers (*faipese*) in village choirs; in some areas, this tradition continues. Some congregations accept that pastors must control the choir; others reject this relationship. Disgruntled members of the church voice their disagreement to pastors by quoting a common phrase: "The job for which we brought you here to our village is your Bible, not music."

Before the mid-1900s, pastors allowed organists and choirs to select songs for Sundays because the organists could play only by ear (*tā fa'alogo*) or by fluke (*tā fuluka*): they needed time to learn to play new hymns and teach them to the choir. By the 1990s, however, most village choirs included one or more persons who could read musical notation, and pastors exercised more choice in selecting hymns.

Conservative pastors prefer to maintain older styles of performing: singing accompanied by an organ (pump or electric), or unaccompanied. They believe the use of keyboards with small log idiophones (*pātē*) distracts congregations; they disparage the use of pop tunes. But some choristers quote biblical phrases to support the idea that the use of drums and other instruments to praise the deity is theologically acceptable. Some pastors allow drumming, clapping, and dancing in Sunday school and during special services, like White Sunday (*Lotu a Tamaiti*), the second Sunday in October, when children regale the congregation with religious recitations, songs, and skits.

In the western islands, some Methodist churches put the organ aside and employ sets of *pātē*, each instrument with a unique pitch; some Roman Catholic churches also allow *pātē*. Other churches use brasses, woodwinds, and an electric organ. The Assembly of God has begun using electric guitars. Portable keyboards with built-in percussion are fashionable in several denominations. Innovation comes from musicians influenced by popular music, and from American popular or gospel artists, including Michael Jackson and Gloria and William J. Gaither.

—Paul Vaiinupō Pouesi

## East Polynesia

Religious experience in East Polynesia underwent dramatic transformations when, largely by the mid-1800s, Polynesians devalued indigenous religious practices to embrace Christianity. Within each society, the role of music has remained central, albeit in different ways. The continuity of certain structural concepts from indigenous spirituality suggests uniquely Polynesian configurations in religious experience, many of which manifest themselves in musical performances (Forman 1982; Garrett 1982) (figure 9), including those in secular contexts.

Several core concepts mark spirituality throughout East Polynesia. The central concept is mana, a dynamic force, regulated through interdictions (*tapu*, Hawaiian *kapu*), which keep the sacred separate from the secular. Regulating the flow of mana in and through people and objects was an objective of religious and spiritual practices on at least two levels. First, elaborate state rituals of invocation to major deities, performed on stone temple platforms, legitimized ruling chiefs and maintained stratified social orders, especially in Hawai'i (figure 10) and Tahiti; an elite class of priests closely guarded knowledge of these rituals (Kaeppler 1993a). Second, lesser rituals of supplication to minor deities and animistic spirits permeated daily life; these were

FIGURE 9   Pushing up the sky with the feet is a recurring theme in Polynesian religious texts, here featured in sculpture as part of the stand of a Hawaiian *pūniu*. Photo by Bishop Museum.

FIGURE 10    Religious architecture in East Polynesia: *center,* a reconstructed Hawaiian temple (*heiau*) at Kailua-Kona, Hawai'i; *right,* the spire of Mokuaikaua Church, on the site where, in 1820, missionaries from Boston established the first Christian church in the Hawaiian archipelago. Photo by Adrienne L. Kaeppler, 1996.

performed in front of altars whose purposes and locations varied from domestic to occupation-specific concerns.

Central to rituals on all levels were prayers. Uttered in various styles of declaimed speech, these were rendered conceptually distinct from speech by generic classifications, simultaneously in three domains: subject, rhetoric, and declamation. Prayers were believed to effect desired ends because of sanctity inherent in the formulaic statements, as is illustrated in the Hawaiian proverb *I ka ʻōlelo ke ola, i ka ʻōlelo ka make* 'In the word is life, in the word is death', and in a belief in dire consequences for prayers incorrectly uttered (Tatar 1982; Valeri 1985).

In the earliest postcontact decades, East Polynesians saw outsiders transgress *tapu* without retribution, and experienced the compromised effectiveness of *tapu* in the face of new technologies of production and warfare. They widely considered Christianity a means for obtaining prestige-associated foreign goods. On missionization, they had already renounced the *tapu* system, or were on the verge of doing so.

### Effects of Christianity

Locale-specific configurations of historical circumstances accounted for important differences in denomination and colonization, affecting musical practices. LMS missionaries began evangelical work in the Society Islands in 1797. Helped by Tahitian catechists, they expanded westward to the Austral and Cook islands in the 1820s. American Congregationalists of the American Board of Commissioners for Foreign Missions began a mission in the Hawaiian Islands in 1820.

Roman Catholic priests, regarded as a religious arm of French colonial aspirations, faced initial resistance in areas where substantial populations had converted to Protestantism and Protestant missions enjoyed ranking chiefs' support; the priests had their greatest successes in the Gambier, Marquesas, and Tuamotu archipelagoes, which have remained predominantly Roman Catholic. Among the Māori in Aotearoa, denominational diversity prevailed, as Anglican, Roman Catholic, and Wesleyan Methodist missionaries competed for converts, beginning in the 1820s and 1830s.

Musical ramifications of conversion to Christianity vary throughout East Polynesia. In Protestant areas, missionaries vigorously worked to suppress indigenous practices; those that survived decades of censure did so underground. In Roman Catholic areas, priests tolerated some indigenous activities as resources that could be developed for devotional purposes: hence the emergence of Mangarevan *'akamagareva,* devotional hymns in the format of *kapa,* and Marquesan *ru'u,* chants with devotional texts. American missionaries in Hawai'i taught musical literacy and the use of Western musical notation (Stillman 1993); in contrast, LMS missionaries in the Society, Austral, and Cook islands relied on oral instruction and transmission (Babadzan 1982).

Indigenous practices, resurfacing with vigor in the 1830s and 1840s, began to coexist with the singing of Christian hymns. Out of that coexistence emerged new musical styles, which fused aspects of Western melody and harmony with indigenous vocal styles and textures, chief among them the multipart choral tradition of central East Polynesia, known as *hīmene* in the Society and Austral islands, and *'īmene* in the Cook Islands. (These are vernacular forms of the English term *hymn.*) These styles emerged largely within Christian worship and devotional contexts, where they have strengthened and enhanced the expression of Christian faith. Many of them, taken into secular contexts and infused with secular subjects, coexist alongside their models (Stillman 1991).

### Survivals and revivals

Christianity in East Polynesia accommodates beliefs and practices stemming from indigenous spirituality. Notions of mana continue to inform Christian supplications, as do notions of rank, status, and prestige in the social organizations of village parishes; this is especially notable in village pastors' and priests' oratory. Such hierarchies are leveled, however, in congregational singing, which requires cooperative participation. Belief in, and respect for, ancestral spirits persists.

Though Christian hymns continue to play a major role in islanders' daily lives, indigenous spirituality has been reawakening in the 1980s and 1990s. This trend has especially characterized colonized areas, where political activism is aimed at restoring self-determination. Struggles to regain access to lands and redress environmental imbalances (formerly regulated by *tapu*) have focused on lands identified as having precontact religious significance.

Since the mid-1970s, a resurgence of voyaging, through the revival of Polynesian navigation, has stimulated a revival of corresponding rituals, ceremonies, oratory, invocations, and styles of performance required for their presentation. In 1995, the convergence of sailing canoes from various East Polynesian areas at the sacred site of Taputapuatea (Ra'iatea, leeward Society Islands) marked a formal reestablishing of ancestral relationships among Polynesian peoples.   —AMY KU'ULEIALOHA STILLMAN

## REFERENCES

Allen, Michael R. 1967. *Male Cults and Secret Initiations in Melanesia.* Cambridge: Cambridge University Press.

Babadzan, Alain. 1982. *Naissance d'une tradition: Changement culturel et syncrétisme religieux aux Iles Australes (Polynésie française).* Travaux et Documents de l'ORSTOM, 154. Paris: ORSTOM.

Barker, John, ed. 1990. *Christianity in Oceania: Ethnographic Perspectives.* ASAO monograph 12. Lanham, Md.: University Press of America.

Barth, Frederick. 1975. *Ritual and Knowledge among the Baktaman of Papua New Guinea.* New Haven, Conn.: Yale University Press.

———. 1987. *Cosmologies in the Making: A Generative Approach to Cultural Variation in Inner New Guinea.* Cambridge: Cambridge University Press.

Boutilier, James A., Daniel T. Hughes, and Sharon W. Tiffany, eds. 1978. *Mission, Church, and Sect in Oceania.* ASAO monograph 6. Ann Arbor: University of Michigan Press.

Brown, George. 1972 [1910]. *Melanesians and Polynesians.* London: Macmillan.

Brown, Paula. 1978. *Highland Peoples of New Guinea.* Cambridge: Cambridge University Press.

Burrows, Edwin G. 1945. *Songs of Uvea and Futuna.* Honolulu: Bishop Museum. Bulletin 183.

Durkheim, Émile. 1964 [1915]. *The Elementary Forms of the Religious Life.* Translated by Joseph Ward Swain. London: Allen & Unwin.

Errington, Frederick Karl. 1974. *Karavar: Masks and Power in a Melanesian Ritual.* Ithaca, N.Y., and London: Cornell University Press.

Faleto'ese, K. T. 1961. *A History of the Samoan Church (L.M.S.).* Malua: Malua Printing Press.

Feld, Steven. 1990. *Sound and Sentiment: Birds, Weeping, Poetics, and Song in Kaluli Expression.* 2nd ed. Publications of the American Folklore Society, New Series. Philadelphia: University of Pennsylvania Press.

Firth, Raymond. 1967. *The Work of the Gods in Tikopia.* 2nd ed. New York: Humanities Press.

Forman, Charles. 1982. *Island Churches of the*

*South Pacific: Emergence in the Twentieth Century.*
American Society of Missiology Series, 5.
Maryknoll, N.Y.: Orbis Books.

Fortune, Reo. 1935. *Manus Religion.* Memoir 3.
Philadelphia: American Philosophical Society.

Garrett, John. 1982. *To Live Among the Stars:
Christian Origins in Oceania.* Geneva and Suva:
World Council of Churches, with the Institute of
Pacific Studies, University of the South Pacific.

Handy, E. S. Craighill. 1927. *Polynesian Religion.*
Bulletin 34. Honolulu: Bishop Museum.

Herdt, Gilbert H. 1981. *Guardians of the Flutes:
Idioms of Masculinity.* New York: McGraw-Hill.

*Hymns Ancient and Modern Revised.* 1947.
London: William Clowes.

Jensen, John Thayer. 1977. *Yapese-English
Dictionary.* Honolulu: University Press of Hawai'i.

Kaeppler, Adrienne L. 1976. "Dance and the
Interpretation of Pacific Traditional Literature."
In *Directions in Pacific Traditional Literature,* ed.
Adrienne L. Kaeppler and H. Arlo Nimmo,
195–216. Special Publication 62. Honolulu:
Bishop Museum.

———. 1993a. *Hula Pahu: Hawaiian Drum
Dances: Volume 1: Ha'a and Hula Pahu: Sacred
Movements.* Bishop Museum Bulletin in
Anthropology 3. Honolulu: Bishop Museum
Press.

———. 1993b. "Poetics and Politics of Tongan
Laments and Eulogies." *American Ethnologist*
20(3):474–501.

Kirsch, Stuart. 1992. "Myth as History-in-the-
Making: Cult and Cargo along the New Guinea
Border." Paper presented at the annual meeting of
the Association for Social Anthropology in
Oceania, New Orleans, 8 February 1992.

Lewis, Gilbert. 1980. *Day of Shining Red: An
Essay on Understanding Ritual.* Cambridge:
Cambridge University Press.

Malinowski, Bronislaw. 1922. *Argonauts of the
Western Pacific.* New York: Dutton.

———. 1955 [1925]. *Magic, Science and
Religion.* Garden City, N.Y.: Doubleday.

Mayer, Raymond, and Malino Nau. 1976.
"Chants funèbres de l'île Wallis." *Journal de la
Société des Océanistes* 32(51–53):141–184,
271–279.

Mead, Margaret. 1935. *Sex and Temperament in
Three Primitive Societies.* London: George
Routledge and Sons.

Muhlenhard, E. 1983. "Local Music Should Be
Promoted." *Weekend Nius* (Port Moresby), 4
September.

O'Hanlon, Michael. 1989. *Reading the Skin:
Adornment, Display and Society Among the Wahgi.*
London: British Museum Publications.

Pratt, George, trans. 1891. "Some Folk-Songs and
Myths from Samoa," ed. John Fraser. *Journal of
the Royal Society of New South Wales* 25:70–86,
97–146, 241–286.

Prendergast, P. A. 1968. "The History of the
London Missionary Society in British New
Guinea 1971–1901." Ph.D. dissertation,
University of Hawai'i.

Rappaport, Roy A. 1979. "The Obvious Aspects
of Ritual." *Ecology, Meaning, and Religion,*
173–221. Richmond, Calif.: North Atlantic
Books.

Stair, John B. 1897. *Old Samoa: Or Flotsam and
Jetsam from the Pacific Ocean.* London: Religious
Tract Society.

Stillman, Amy Ku'uleialoha. 1991. "*Hīmene
Tahiti:* Ethnoscientific and Ethnohistorical
Perspectives on Protestant Hymnody and Choral
Singing in the Society Islands, French Polynesia."
Ph.D. dissertation, Harvard University.

———. 1993. "Prelude to a Comparative
Investigation of Protestant Hymnody in
Polynesia." *Yearbook for Traditional Music*
25:89–99.

Strehlow, T. G. H. 1971. *Songs of Central
Australia.* Sydney: Angus and Robertson.

Sutton, Peter, ed. 1989. *Dreamings: The Art of
Aboriginal Australia.* Ringwood, Australia, and
London: Viking Penguin.

Tatar, Elizabeth. 1982. *Nineteenth Century
Hawaiian Chant.* Pacific Anthropological
Records, 33. Honolulu: Department of
Anthropology, Bernice P. Bishop Museum.

Trompf, Gary W. 1990. "Keeping the Lo Under a
Melanesian Messiah: An Analysis of the Pomio
Kivung, East New Britain." In *Christianity in
Oceania: Ethnographic Perspectives,* ed. John

Barker, 59–80. ASAO Monograph 12. Lanham:
University Press of America.

Turner, George. 1884. *Samoa a Hundred Years Ago
and Long Before.* London: Macmillan.

Valeri, Valerio. 1985. *Kingship and Sacrifice:
Ritual and Society in Ancient Hawaii.* Translated
by Paula Wissing. Chicago and London:
University of Chicago Press.

Vaughan Williams, Ralph, Martin Shaw, and
Percy Dearmer. 1925. *Songs of Praise.* London:
Oxford University Press.

Wagner, Herwig, and Harmann Reiner, eds.
1986. *The Lutheran Church in Papua New
Guinea: The First Hundred Years 1886–1986.*
Adelaide: Lutheran Publishing House.

Wetherall, David. 1977. *The Reluctant Mission:
The Anglican Church in Papua New Guinea:
1891–1942.* St. Lucia, Queensland: University of
Queensland Press.

Whitehouse, Harvey. 1992. "Memorable
Religions: Transmission, Codification, and
Change in Divergent Melanesian Contexts." *Man*
27(4):777–797.

———. 1995. *Inside the Cult: Religious
Innovation and Transmission in Papua New
Guinea.* Oxford: Oxford University Press.

Wild, Stephen A. 1975. "Warlbiri Music and
Dance in Their Social and Cultural Nexus."
Ph.D. dissertation, Indiana University.

Williams, F. E. 1928. *Orokaiva Magic.* Oxford:
Oxford University Press.

Wood, A. Harold. 1975. *Overseas Missions of the
Australian Methodist Church.* 2 vols. Melbourne:
Aldersgate.

Yayii, Filip Lamasisi. 1983. "Some Aspects of
Traditional Dance within the *Malanggan* Culture
of Northern New Ireland." *Bikmaus* 4(3):33–48.

Zahn, Heinrich. 1959 [1934]. *The Conchshell-
Hymnal.* Edited by H. Wolfrum. Madang:
Lutheran Mission Press.

# Music and Politics
*Adrienne L. Kaeppler*
*Hervé Lecren*
*Lamont Lindstrom*
*J. W. Love*
*Reshela DuPuis*

**Kaneka: Political Music of Kanaky**
**John Frum Music of Vanuatu**
**Imagery in Sāmoan Political Songs**
**Hawaiian Land, Politics, and Music**
**Hawaiian Documentary Videos as Political Tools**

Using music to convey political messages is prevalent in Oceanic societies (figure 1). Politically charged songs are popular with young people and exhibit various musical styles. Ranging from innocuous "wry comment from the outback" in the Niua Islands of Tonga conveyed through traditional musical forms (Pond 1995), to full-blown political activism conveyed through the idioms of reggae and rap, songs of protest have had a phenomenal impact on politics.

In 1995, when the French government restarted nuclear testing on Mururoa Atoll, French Polynesia, peoples of Oceania protested vehemently. Pacific Islanders in Fiji used performance to protest in a so-called antinuclear *tāmūrē*. Singing songs about the natural beauty of the environment and wearing bikini bathing suits, the performers demanded "no more Bikinis"—recalling U.S.-controlled H-bomb testing on Bikini Atoll in the 1950s.

## The politics of ethnic identity
Possibly the most important reason for the reemphasis of tradition in Polynesian music and dance is ethnic identity and its visual manifestation—the preservation and development of indigenous arts as a way of distinguishing indigenous peoples from outsiders. Until the 1960s, many Pacific communities saw the continued erosion of their arts as young people, modernizing and internationalizing themselves, took little interest in their history. Concerned individuals began to take steps not only to preserve what they had learned from their own parents and grandparents, but to cast their nets wider and deeper to bring back into the living tradition forms of music and dance on the verge of extinction. Polynesian pride in their own culture and traditions has intensified, as younger people, finding themselves less and less distinctive just as the outside world has started becoming more interested in non-European culture and its distinctive musics, have become more political, valuing their traditions more highly.

In Hawai'i in the 1960s, a renaissance of the *hula* began, and Hawaiians and concerned outsiders established the State Council on Hawaiian Dance (now the State Council on Hawaiian Heritage), which brought together individuals knowledgeable about traditional *hula* and its music, and persuaded these individuals that they

FIGURE 1    The Royal Guard marches at the
closing of parliament in Nuku'alofa, Tonga.
Photo by Adrienne L. Kaeppler, 1965.

should share their knowledge more widely than they had formerly done. The process
generated by the council included workshops in which the most respected exponents
of *hula* taught a wide spectrum of students. These teachers also performed, and
Hawaiian politicians set up a statewide system of recognition of culturally knowledgeable artists: each year, the governor designates one or two individuals as intangible cultural treasures. Several such individuals have received the honor for their contributions to the preservation and study of music and dance.

## The politics of tradition

Related to the politics of ethnic identity is the more divisive matter of the "politics of
tradition," an issue that gained prominence in the Pacific during the late 1980s.
Debate centers on "the invention of tradition," a notion introduced by Hobsbawm
and Ranger (1983) to extend to nationalistic movements that did not have historic
dimensions the analysis of European traditions created for artificial communities,
such as nations and states. These concepts were transformed in Pacific research as
debates about *kastom,* led by Roger Keesing (1989) in the Solomon Islands, Allan
Hanson (1989) in Aotearoa, and Jocelyn Linnekin (Handler and Linnekin 1984) in
Hawai'i. As used in Oceania, the term referred to the continual (re)creation of culture by manipulating symbolic elements and reordering and refocusing cultural constructs to reflect present-day politics (figure 2). It was read by indigenous scholars,
however, as a case of genuine versus spurious, with Haunani K. Trask (1991) leading
the opposition. Indigenous scholars thought new creations and invented traditions
implied dishonest and unworthy fabrication. The debate then changed to what *tradition* means, who has authority to speak or write about it, and how postmodern
modes of analysis should apply (Linnekin 1992).

   The debate sometimes invoked music, dance, theater, and the visual arts, but
quickly changed to use more appropriate concepts. In "The Arts and Politics," a special issue of *Pacific Studies* (1992), these concepts included transformation, recontex-
tualization, recreation, retention, resurrection, revision, negotiation, and the inter-
mixture of indigenous and foreign. It appears that the bandwagon of the invention of
tradition, onto which many jumped, has now crashed.

   Some of the most politically potent songs in Oceania derive from so-called
fourth-world cultures, indigenous peoples who have become minorities in their
homelands: Aboriginal people of Australia, Kanaks in New Caledonia, Māori in
Aotearoa, and Hawaiians in the fiftieth state of the United States of America. In addition to the examples below, the association of music with political processes is a
recurring theme in the areal entries of Part 3 of this volume.

—ADRIENNE L. KAEPPLER

FIGURE 2    Combining old and new on 16 September 1996, the twenty-first anniversary of national independence, Papua New Guineans attending the seventh Pacific Festival of Arts parade their traditional costumes and national flag through the streets of Apia, Western Sāmoa. Photo by Adrienne L. Kaeppler.

## KANEKA: POLITICAL MUSIC OF KANAKY

Long treated as an insult, the term *Kanak* has been reclaimed by the indigenous people of New Caledonia in their political struggle: Kanak And Proud Of It (*Kanak et fier de l'être*) has become a slogan. From this word, which denotes the Melanesian population of New Caledonia, people seeking national independence have adopted the name *Kanaky* for their country.

Since 1985, Kanak musicians have used the term *kaneka* to denote their music. In it, they want to take inspiration from yesteryear's rhythms, melodies, and harmonies. It is at heart a quest, an affirmation of identity (Goldsworthy 1997). Elders' rhythms—the beat of the *pilu,* stamped bamboo tubes, percussion sticks—these resound again with the new generation, but accompanied with modern instruments: electric guitars, synthesizers, and drums.

In the 1970s, French and international stars of music—Claude François, Johnny Halliday, the Beatles—were also the stars of Caillou (Pebble), the nickname of New Caledonia because of its reserves of nickel. Soon after, the samba and a Tahitian version of the waltz became locally prominent. Among Kanak youth in the 1980s, Bob Marley's reggae ruled. Today, the Jamaican style competes with a new arrival, one that has previously been around. The beat of *kaneka* makes the youngest dance, as it does the oldest, because it does not come from abroad. It strongly attracts the Kanak population, but has not yet crossed over into the other populations who live in its territory.

Kanak musicians are self-taught, and nobody makes much of a living out of *kaneka.* Precarious material conditions are the lot of most Kanaks. Some areas do not have electricity. For musicians who have hardly any money, modern instruments of quality are beyond price.

### Musical style

What makes *kaneka* unique is the presence of percussion that takes its beat from indigenous dances, mostly *pilu* (Ammann 1997:54–79). Rhythmic motifs use paired percussive sounds. When the difference between them is marked in rhythmic values, one of the sounds is longer, and each pair is transcribable as a sixteenth and a dotted eighth. When the difference is marked by dynamics, one of the sounds is heavier, and each pair can be transcribed as two eighths, of which the second receives the stronger accent. Both patterns can be played together (Ammann 1994:31).

Local listeners distinguish two styles of *kaneka*: that of the Loyalty Islands and that of Grande Terre. Musicians of the 1990s blend these styles. In the Loyalty Islands, rhythms are played with sticks on bamboos brought from Grande Terre. For percussion, the people of Grande Terre use fig-bark beaters or, more rarely, the spathe of a cabbage palm.

In *kaneka,* the sounds of a bass drum or—functionally the same thing—a snare drum are preferred to those of stamped tubes, which performers may put aside because of on-site difficulties of voicing. The tubes sound most effectively when stamped against the ground. Stages have no soil, hence yield an inferior sound. A membranophone serves as a substitute, because its sound more closely approximates the ideal. To that instrument, performers add congas, bongos, and other imported instruments. Shouts, whistles, and whispers join the sounds of a rhythmically accompanying ensemble.

Tempo varies somewhat by locality. The strumming of guitars strengthens the beat; the melodic playing of guitars is rare. Brasses are nearly nonexistent. Keyboards function rhythmically. Harmonies are simple: most songs use no more than four chords, reflecting Christian hymnody most clearly in the Loyalty Islands. Reinforcing the Kanak tendency of *kaneka,* singers ordinarily use local languages, not French.

Musical texts often take their thematic content from current events, or those of 1984 to 1989, whose protests gave the first push to *kaneka*. The demand for independence is the nursemaid of *kaneka:* on account of it, Kanak politics have taken their first steps. The year 1995 began a new decade of *kaneka*. At that age, many popular musics have already died, or at least grown old; *kaneka* continues raising itself up. It knows where it is going, and it may someday march all through the societies of the Pacific.                    —Hervé Lecren, translated by J. W. Love

## JOHN FRUM MUSIC OF VANUATU

By asserting claims to land and other important resources, songs can establish and document a collective political identity. In southern Vanuatu in the 1800s, Christian missionaries saw that music had political functions, so they worked to secure their missions by replacing local songs with Christian hymns (Inglis 1887:136–153). In Southeast Tanna, Presbyterian missionary William Watt, with Christian converts, translated into the Kwamera language 145 hymns (Watt 1919), adapted from compilations of Sankey, McGranahan, and other evangelical standbys. Many of these hymns remain popular. After 1945, church-based hostility to indigenous music and dance abated, and Christian islanders, except members of fundamentalist sects, participated in traditional performances.

Into this milieu came the John Frum movement. Begun in Tanna in the late 1930s, it combined a protonationalistic drive, a cargo cult, and a political party (Lindstrom 1993). The distinct musical styles of Tanna distinguish John Frum events from those of Christian churches and traditions elsewhere. The remembered person of John Frum, now a spiritual middleman, links Tanna with the powers of the outside world, particularly the United States (figure 3). John Frum music reflects influence from string-band styles of 1942 to 1945. Its lyrics, like those of string-band music, usually incorporate words in Bislama, the local pidgin.

Each Friday, the movement's holy day, teams of John Frum supporters gather at Sulphur Bay, the religious headquarters. There, they dance until Saturday morning. Songsmiths, inspired by spiritual guides, present new songs at Friday services, after checking the lyrics with leaders of the movement. Annually on 15 February, thousands of John Frum supporters and guests gather to celebrate the founding of the movement. Drill teams and string bands perform.

John Frum lyrics, like those of indigenous songs, celebrate heroes, events, guardian spirits, and notable places. The following song records John Frum's appearance at Green Point and his promises to enrich Tanna—promises marked by a memorial of two stones he left behind.

FIGURE 3    John Frum people raise the U.S. flag during 15 February celebrations at Sulphur Bay, Tanna. Photo by Lamont Lindstrom, 1985.

> 1941 kamini kasik ira fwe ia Krin Poen.
> Rini riti, nakwa rini riti.
> Ripamimri *nimorial* kwipwier kiru:
> "Iakevin mo *stat* ruvehe mi mo *pus*
> Ia narimnari me pam ia *wol* ia *rum* rouihi."
> Karari kasik ira ia Krin Hil.
> *Nesin kan* rini nei tukwe.
> Kurira rariri pehe iesa mwi.
> Nirhi *pis* tukwe ti nermama pam.
> Iahisikir imwamiaha nermama pam.

> In 1941, someone [John Frum] told about it at Green Point.
> Join together, orders are to join together.
> He placed two memorial stones:
> "I am going to start coming and pushing
> Everything in the world into a small room [Tanna]."
> It spread [until] one calls for him at Green Hill.
> The machine-gun shoots up the tree because of him.
> After, he will enrich this place also.
> Send his peace to all people.
> We greet people of all lands.

Distinctive musical pieces differentiate local John Frum organizations and stress shared identity as supporters of the movement, against political opposition from Christians and traditionalists.                                        —LAMONT LINDSTROM

## IMAGERY IN SĀMOAN POLITICAL SONGS

After the early 1800s, the musical and verbal processes of Sāmoan political singing changed. The musical changes matched those affecting the rest of the music; the verbal ones were more ambiguous.

Sāmoan political songs of the mid-1800s were monophonic, based on a scale that can be transcribed as B–D–E–F–G, with B and G being auxiliary tones, D and F the principal melodic tones, and E often the final; textures were sometimes in two parts, with a lead voice (*usu*) and an answer (*tali*), and melodic rhythms fitted to those of the words. This system gave way to one based on diatonic scales and the four-part textures of European common-practice tonality, with melodic rhythms fitted to harmonic and metric requirements, independent of the words.

Lyrics underwent more subtle changes, which minimized metaphor (the technique of saying one thing and meaning another) and abandoned indigenous themes in favor of Christian and European imagery. Verbal indirection enhances much Sāmoan sung poetry, but Sāmoan political poetry often avoids it, preferring statements of plain facts and blunt opinions. Where political songs use figurative diction, the imagery may now be biblical.

### Indigenous political contexts and styles

Before European contact, intervillage warfare climaxed Sāmoan politics. Customary rules governed when, where, and how battles occurred, who was eligible to fight, and who was safe from harm. Battles began after an exchange of ceremonial courtesies, including the presentation of kava [see MUSIC AND INGESTED SUBSTANCES]. Hand-to-hand combat with clubs was the preferred technique. Each fighter's goal was to kill his opponent and cut off his head. Warfare of this kind lasted into the 1890s, and music was an important part of it. After a battle, a victors' camp boasted

> a pyramid of human heads. . . . Round this hideous trophy stood some women with baskets, waiting until the enemy should give them permission to take them away and bury them. . . . Every house was more or less full of armed men, begrimed with dust and paint and gunpowder. . . . Some of them had their brows bound, not with laurel, but with shells, while their bodies were only clad with a few scanty ivy-leaves. Others had dressed their long locks in elaborate style, and had painted their faces black or red or blue, as the taste of the owner had prompted. Muskets, rifles, battle-axes, spears, and shields were lying about in all directions, while amid all the confusion were . . . young girls busily and quietly engaged in chewing *kava*. With this native nectar the warriors pledged each other as they sung their paeans of victory. (Forbes 1875:430–431)

These included songs praising successful fighters and lamenting the loss of defeated ones. The laments (*fatu, lagisolo*) were often long and complex; the songs of praise (*vīʻi*) were usually short, like a song of the 1860s, praising ʻUaʻua Esekia of Manono: *ʻĀ fati le pua, / Vīʻi Tinilau ma ʻUaʻua* 'When plucking a gardenia, / Praise Tinilau and ʻUaʻua'. Tinilau was a Polynesian legendary hero, and plucking a flower meant a man's sexually conquering a woman.

A song composed about 1869 exemplifies the indigenous style of verbal imagery (Love 1991:184–204). It recalls two youths' deaths in battle, sad news made sadder by being associated with what should have been the happiness of their friends' courting party (*aumoega*), a time of sexual fun:

| | |
|---|---|
| ʻO fetai o le Papa Lauina: | Morning glories of the Papa Lauina: |
| Faʻi mai; e fua ma faʻamita. | Pluck them; they bloom and boast. |
| ʻAu mai, mātou sūʻia | Bring some here, for us to thread |
| ʻUla mā Le Filifiliga, | In garlands for Le Filifiliga, |
| ʻAe le miō e taʻalilina. | While the crowd makes noise there. |
|    Laʻu tāmaē, |    O my boy, |
|    ʻUa tātou pēnei ai! |    For whom we've done this! |
|    Oi! oi! le taūae! |    *Oi! oi!* O the war! |
|    Ta te lē fia manatūae! |    O I don't want to remember it! |
| | |
| ʻUlutūnue, le e tuʻu mai, | O ʻUlutunu, which appears before me, |
| Ta te lē fia vaʻai ʻi ai. | I don't want to look at it. |
| Sā mātou lau pae ai | We were strewn about there, |
| Ma teine o le Mosi ʻŪlae. | O with girls of the Crimson Prawn. |
|    + *Refrain.* |    + *Refrain.* |
| | |
| ʻĀtonu lava ni māsaloga, | Perhaps indeed some suspicions, |
| ʻIna neʻi faʻataga-a-fofola, | So as not to make false promises, |
| ʻAe tupu ai se aʻa ʻoʻona. | From which a bitter root would grow. |
|    + *Refrain.* |    + *Refrain.* |

Tinged with regret, this song keeps the war in the background, its details compressed and muffled. Scenes ensue ambiguously, telling a story in glimpses, not in a logical progression. The text cites the Papa Lauina (Leveled Rocks), a lava cliff overlooking the sea. It names ʻUlutunu, the ceremonial center of Gāuta-a-vai Village, where the singing, dancing, kava ceremonies, and other party-related events occurred. To specify the local women, it uses an honorific formula, "girls of the Crimson Prawn." Showing missionaries' influence, the third stanza uses biblical imagery, "from which a bitter root would grow" (Hebrews 12:15); this phrase recalls the ceremonial hostess's opinion of her suitor, though the leaders of her village made her marry him anyway.

In political songs, honorific epithets designated armies and their supporters. An excerpt from a song about a war of the 1860s includes such an epithet, though the text minimizes metaphor:

| | |
|---|---|
| Na'u fa'alogo 'i le tālae: | O I listened to the talk: |
| 'Olo'ua tofi le taūae. | O they've decided on war. |
| 'O Manono lava e sau i tai, | Manono itself comes by sea, |
| Fa'apea Sā Fotulāfai | Likewise Sā Fotulāfai, |
| Ma ali'i o le Lōmēae, | O and fellows of the Reddish *Lō,* |
| 'Ae te'a Tuamāsāgae. | O but Tuamāsaga is cast out. |

The text alludes to the people of Matāutu, Savai'i, by citing their emblem, the reddish *lō,* a fish. Otherwise, these lines run more like versified prose than many nonpolitical Sāmoan lyrics. The statements are straightforward, not full of hidden meanings.

## The politics of European influence

During the 1800s, as European powers scrambled to colonize Oceania, Britain had the local advantage. Most Protestant missionaries had come from there, as had respected traders. High Chief Mālietoa, in effect the political head of the Sāmoan Protestant church, sided with Britain. His rivals, Matā'afa and Tamasese, took parallel or alternate positions, often siding with Germany. In a war of 1889, Mālietoa's side sang a song saying Germans spoke with forked tongues (*gutulua*), telling lies (*talapelo*) because they wanted to turn Sāmoans into slaves (*pologa*). It ended with an appeal (after Krämer 1902:355–356): *Le 'aufaipule 'o i Peretānia, / Ma Tupu a Vitōria, / Fa'molemole se'i tou 'aumaia / 'O se tonu mātou te faia* 'The government that's in Britain, / And Queen Victoria, / Please do bring here / A plan for us to follow'. The style is merely versified prose, the import is clear, and figurative diction is absent.

### German rule, 1900–1914

The Treaty of Berlin (1900) awarded Western Sāmoa to Germany. On Savai'i Island arose anti-German complaints, fomented by the orator Lauati, whom the colonial government exiled with his retinue. In 1906, protests included a song containing this excerpt:

| | |
|---|---|
| La'u tupe na pa'ū i le vai, | My coin that fell into the water, |
| 'Ailoga 'ā toe a'e mai. | I probably won't get it back. |
| Lauati, po'ofea? | Lauati, where is he? |
| Tēvaga 'ua 'āvea; | Tēvaga has been taken; |
| Taupule 'ua opeopea. | Taupule has been exiled. |
| 'O le kōvana, ta'u mai 'ea: | Governor, do tell me: |
| 'O ali'i na 'āvea, | The chiefs that were taken, |
| Pe toe a'e 'āfea? | When will they come back? |

The coin stands for Lauati, but the text is minimally metaphorical.

'Let's all congratulate / George the Fifth with his praises. . . . / The eagle stands naked; / It won't shake hands again. / Britain and the lion / Have tossed the kaiser's pals out'.

### Rule from New Zealand, 1914–1962

In 1914, troops from New Zealand relieved Germany in Western Sāmoa. Authorized by the League of Nations, New Zealand administered the country as a mandated territory. Thinking of Britain, Sāmoans at first celebrated this change, as expressed in song by a choir of Neiafu, Savai'i: *Se'i tātou fa'apaleina / Siaosi Lima i ni vi'iga. . . . / Tū telefua 'o le 'āeto; / 'Ua lē toe lūlū lima. / Peletānia ma le leona / 'Ua lafoia 'au o le kaisa* 'Let's all congratulate / George the Fifth with his praises. . . . / The eagle stands naked; / It won't shake hands again. / Britain and the lion / Have tossed the kaiser's pals out'. The text cites a European king, a European point of etiquette (shaking hands), and European icons: the eagle, symbolizing Germany, and the lion, symbolizing Britain.

The situation worsened. The worldwide flu epidemic of 1918 embittered Western Sāmoans for the administrative incompetence that admitted the disease to their country, killing thousands. (By a contrast that did not go unnoticed, a U.S. naval quarantine protected American Sāmoa.) Official disrespect of Western Sāmoan rights sparked protests, which in 1926 coalesced into a political movement, the Mau (Opinion), headquartered in the bandstand of Vaimoso Village (figure 4), near the capital, Apia.

During a Mau-sponsored demonstration on 28 December 1929, policemen shot into the crowd, wounding sixteen and killing eleven. The most prominent victim was High Chief Tamasese, who said: "My blood has been spilt for Samoa. I am proud to give it. Do not dream of avenging it, as it was spilt in maintaining peace. If I die, peace must be maintained at any price" (Rowe 1930:278). His dignity in dying strengthened the Mau, whose adherents followed his advice and protested peacefully, often in song, as with these lyrics:

FIGURE 4    The bandstand of Vaimoso Village, rebuilt as an office, became the headquarters of the Sāmoan political movement known as the Mau. Photo by J. W. Love, 1973.

| | |
|---|---|
| Mea a Nu'u Sila 'ua fa'atupu sela, | Things of New Zealand make us gasp, |
| Pe'ī 'o se tagata e alu 'i se a'ega. . . . | Like a person going up an incline. . . . |
| 'O Mose lava 'oe, 'o le ta'ita'iala; | You're Moses himself, the pathfinder; |
| 'O Isalā'elu lēnei 'ua malaga. | This is Israel that's on a journey. |
| E ui ina leva ma tele tausaga, | Though it's been long and many years, |
| 'Ae fa'amoemoe pea lava i fōlafolaga: | We still hope in the promises: |
| 'O lo tātou tofi 'o le nu'u o Kanana. | Our goal is the land of Canaan. |
| Tamasese, 'ou te fa'afetai | Tamasese, I give thanks |
| 'Ua iloga, sē, lou tōmai. | That your encouragement, *sē*, is exemplary. |
| 'Ua 'avea 'oe 'o le tautai, | You've become the captain, |
| Ma si o'u loto e ma'ama'ai. | And my poor mind is fierce. |
| E ui lava 'i gutu o fana ma mata o pelu, | Despite the mouths of guns and the faces of swords, |
| 'O au malelega 'ole'ā tātou liu lefulefu, | Your words that we'll all turn to ashes, |
| 'O au afioga e leai se lauulu e mave'u! | Your words that not a hair be disarranged! |

FIGURE 5   The Southern Cross is a visual metaphor for Christianity. *Top to bottom:* national flags of Australia, New Zealand, Papua New Guinea, Sāmoa.

| | |
|---|---|
| 'O Tāvita 'oe, 'o le toa o Isalā'elu. | You're David, the warrior of Israel. |
| 'Ofea Kiliata, sā fa'atauemu? | Where's Gilead, who was mocking us? |
| 'O le lale 'ua sola: 'ua tutū lona selu. | He has run away: his comb is up. |

Here, aside from a proverb (the last line refers to the feathers on a cock's head, raised when he loses a fight), the text is thoroughly biblical. Tamasese tells his followers to maintain their march. He leads them toward the guns. In metaphorical terms, he must therefore be Moses, and his followers must be the people of Israel, en route to Canaan, the promised land. And for Tamasese's bravery against overwhelming force, he must be David, killer of the giant Goliath. The biblical name *Gilead* refers to the Mau's first opponent, Major-General Sir George Richardson, who left office as administrator in 1928. The conceptual process of this text is metaphorical, but the imagery does not come from indigenous culture. Gone are the lists of places and series of honorifics. Gone are the Polynesian heroes and gods. Triumphant is the Christian Bible, and with it a novel array of ideals and images.

### The Sāmoan national anthem

At schools in Sāmoa, each day begins with an affirmation of political allegiance, a performance of the national anthem. As the flag starts up the pole, schoolchildren in haydnesque harmonies sing the command: *Sāmoa, tūlaʻi ma sisi ia lau fuʻa, lou pale lea* 'Sāmoa, stand up and raise your flag, your crown'. That a flag is a crown has figurative potential, but by focusing on what will actually happen, this phrase is basically antimetaphorical.

Noting the flag's depiction of the Southern Cross (figure 5), the anthem takes an idea that could easily become a metaphor—that today's stars are yesterday's cross—and by explaining it, destroys it:

| | |
|---|---|
| Vaʻai 'i nā fetū | Look at those stars |
| 'O loʻua agiagia ai. | That are waving on it: |
| 'O le faʻailoga lea o Iesū, | This is the symbol of Jesus, |
| Na maliu ai mō Sāmoa. | Who died on it for Sāmoa. |

Explanation destroys figurative imagery in the sense that anatomical dissection destroys the tissue dissected. This text explains to instruct. Older texts may have instructed, but they did so by merely displaying images, not by deconstructing them. Similar distinctions characterize other Sāmoan public speaking: political orations display indigenous images, but Christian sermons deconstruct biblical ones.

With the flag at the top of the pole, the anthem concludes: *Sāmoa, tūlaʻi: 'ua agiagia lau fuʻa, lou pale lea* 'Sāmoa, stand up: your flag is waving, your crown'. Again, by stating the obvious, the lyrics evade the processes of figurative art.

—J. W. LOVE

## HAWAIIAN LAND, POLITICS, AND MUSIC

In Hawaiʻi, political songs have a long history. The most famous Hawaiian song of protest is "*Kaulana nā Pua,*" composed by Kekoakalani Prendergast [see POPULAR MUSIC: Musical Ensembles]. It asserts that Hawaiians would rather eat stones than support a government dominated by foreigners. In the wake of the overthrow of the monarchy (1893), several hundred proroyalist lyrics were published in Hawaiian-language newspapers (Stillman 1989). Songs for political campaigns date back to the 1920s or before. They range from attracting voters and soliciting votes, to implications that the candidate was God's choice (Williamson 1976).

The late 1970s and the 1980s saw the rise of protests demanding that the U.S. government return Kahoʻolawe Island to the Hawaiian people. For decades, the navy had been using the island as a practice-bombing site. After a string of small-scale protests, a grass-roots movement coalesced into Protect Kahoʻolawe ʻOhana. Uncle Harry Kunihi Mitchell (p. 122), one of its leaders, composed *Mele of Kahoʻolawe,* a song that became the unofficial anthem of the movement (after Edith Kanakaʻole Foundation 1993:72–73):

Aloha kuʻu moku ʻo Kahoʻolawe.
Mai kīnohi kou inoa ʻo Kanaloa.
Kohemā lamalama, lau kanakaʻole
Hiki mai nā pua, e hoʻomalu mai.

Alu like kākou, lāhui Hawaiʻi.
Mai ka lā hiki mai i ka lā kau aʻe,
Kūpaʻa a hahai, hoʻoikaika, nā kanaka.
Kauliʻi mākou, nui ke aloha no ka ʻāina.

Hanohano nā pua o Hawaiʻi nei
No ke kaua kauholo me ke ʻaupuni.
Paʻa pū ka manaʻo, no ka pono o ka ʻāina,
I mua, nā pua, lanakila Kahoʻolawe!
I mua, nā pua, lanakila Kahoʻolawe!

Love for my island, Kahoʻolawe.
From the beginning your name was Kanaloa.
You are the southern beacon, barren, without population
Until the rescue of nine people to grant you peace.

Let us band together, people of Hawaiʻi
From sunup to sundown,
Stand together and follow; be strong, young people.
We are few, but our love for the land is unlimited.

Glorious are the young people of Hawaiʻi
For the civil strife against the government.
Together in one thought, for the good of the land,
Go forward, young people, bring salvation to Kahoʻolawe!
Go forward, young people, bring salvation to Kahoʻolawe!

In 1976, nine people, in defiance of military regulations, visited Kahoʻolawe, initiating the movement to increase awareness of the island's devastation.

Since the 1980s, with the rise of the Hawaiian-sovereignty movement, songs of protest against outsiders have become more ardent. The musical styles of these songs are rock, reggae, and rap, usually rendered in a more laid-back manner than are their parallels in North America and the Caribbean. One of the most popular of these songs in the mid-1990s was "Hawaiian Lands" (Bruddah Waltah & Island Afternoon 1990):

Talk to me, my brother,
Love one another.
It's plain to see
This land is here for you and me.

Keep Hawaiian lands in Hawaiian hands, yeah.
Keep Hawaiian lands in Hawaiian hands, yeah, eah.
On the road we go; far from life we stroll.
It's an uphill climb, yeah; stays with you all the time.

This is our plea, our destiny-flight.
We got to be free to claim our rights.
Stand up, be heard, and declare our creed.
We got to preserve our dying breed.

This text emphasizes land, whose ownership and use—always meaningful concepts for Polynesians—have gained new political dimensions in the modern world.

—ADRIENNE L. KAEPPLER

## HAWAIIAN DOCUMENTARY VIDEOS AS POLITICAL TOOLS

"Instead of guns, we use a videocamera. That's my gun. That's my weapon." Blunt and uncompromising, this is the view of Hawaiian videographer Puhipau, who with Joan Landers has produced nearly eighty videos promoting Hawaiian national sovereignty. Their work is part of an indigenous-rights movement that has parallels across the Pacific. It often depicts the performance of indigenous culture, especially music and dance.

During the mid-1970s, when affordable video-making technologies became available, videos began serving as symbolic, public enactments of cultural and political values. Activists across a spectrum of political opinion—environmental professionals, single-issue lobbyists, elders concerned about the preservation of their indigenous cultures—have used them in campaigns for political action. In 1988, a leading Hawaiian-sovereignty organization recognized that its efforts to reassemble an independent Hawaiian nation must include the creation of a "tool to provide the social and cultural and political basis for nationhood" (Puhipau and Landers 1988).

Documentary videos produced by or for these activists display collective beliefs and goals. Their effectiveness can be measured by their influence on voting patterns and changes in public awareness about social problems. Produced on low budgets, with borrowed equipment under nonprofessional conditions, many have been faulted for displaying inferior artistry, following unimaginative narratives, reflecting low production values, and making a meager impact.

Politically oriented videos can be understood in the context of their production and distribution, processes often as important to the activists and local communities who make them as are the products themselves. Researching, writing, funding, filming, editing, and distributing local videos can be important mechanisms for social and personal transformation. Because documentaries are processes and products, they can function as sites of multivalent practices, including the preservation, transmission, and transformation of cultural and historical knowledge. As arenas of political struggle over the control and representation of that knowledge, they can be fields on which the boundaries of national, ethnic, communal, and personal identities are negotiated.

Using networks developed through video-production processes, activists have initiated changes in their communities' physical and cultural landscapes. Many activists' documentaries, fostering revisions in public historical memory, have encouraged politicized reassessments of historical sites, actors, and events. Noncommercial distribution networks, which promote screenings in community halls, schools, churches, and private homes, contribute to the local impact of these videos. Public screenings often lead to discussions, and sometimes to fund-raising and voter-registration drives, the introduction of issue-specific legislation, and other political tactics.

Activists' documentaries are distributed through public-access television channels, federal- or state-owned television networks, and commercial cable networks. An increase in homeowned VCRs has furthered their distribution. Few locally produced documentary videos have been distributed through commercial broadcast networks. Island-based videographers show their work mainly in their home countries. Regional film festivals provide international exposure, as do occasional showings at universities and other noncommercial venues, such as museums, art academies, and political rallies. Increasingly since the 1980s, these images have described and reaffirmed the links of shared histories across the Pacific.

Politically conceived videos are dynamic topics in debates over the representation of ethnic identity. Videographers share imagistic iconographies, narrative tactics, genres, and organizational strategies. Most of these schematics show the influence of U.S. mass-media culture, but many videographers use indigenous notions of history, storytelling, culture, and nature. Their shift toward the videotaped creation of islander-centered portrayals of social and historical issues is an important political strategy. Since the late 1970s, they have told their own histories, defined their communities' problems using indigenous values, and proposed nonmainstream solutions to local and regional problems. They continue to do so, though few make a living from their craft. A longtime video activist, Hawai'i-based Victoria Keith, has said, "If I didn't think we could make a difference, I would have stopped long ago. Of course I believe we can change the world."

## The politics of "The Stone-Eating Song"

In many indigenous Hawaiian songs, metaphors suggest double meanings (*kaona*), sometimes politically charged. In the late 1800s, Hawaiian lyrics set to Western-influenced tunes functioned similarly. After the overthrow of Queen Lili'uokalani's government (1893), Hawaiians composed songs of protest. One of these, now known as "*Kaulana Nā Pua*" ('Famous Are the Children'), was composed by Ellen Kekoaohiwaikalani Prendergast in 1893 [see POPULAR MUSIC: Musical Ensembles]. Responding to the new government's demands that employees sign oaths of allegiance or lose their jobs, members of the Royal Hawaiian Band told Prendergast they would not sign, but would "be satisfied with . . . the stones, the mystic food of our native land" (Nordyke and Noyes 1993). Prendergast transcribed bandsmen's sentiments in the lyrics: *Ua lawa mākou i ka pōhaku, / I ka 'ai kamaha'o o ka 'āina* 'We are satisfied with the stones, / With the wondrous food of the land' (Stillman 1989:24). The next year, at a tree-planting ceremony in the queen's honor at Uluhaimalama Gardens, bandsmen and royalist women sang the song under its original title, "*Mele 'Ai Pōhaku*" ('The Stone-Eating Song').

In a community-produced video about the 1894 planting ceremony (*The 'Āina Remains,* 1983), native Hawaiian elder (*kupuna*) and dance teacher (*kumuhula*) Auntie Ma'iki Aiu Lake refused to allow the song to be included. She was concerned that non-Hawaiians would misunderstand the spiritual and political *kaona* of the song. Over the next few years, however, the song became popular at rallies for sovereignty. By 1993, it had appeared in at least two pro-sovereignty videos produced by native Hawaiians: Heather Haunani Guigni used a sung version in *Ho'āla: Awakening* (1992), and Nā Maka o ka 'Āina featured it in *Act of War: The Overthrow of the Hawaiian Nation* (1993), sung by activist Didi Lee Kwai. In one of this video's most moving sequences, the lyrics, translated into English, appear at the bottom of the screen over photos from the monarchic era.                                    —RESHELA DUPUIS

## REFERENCES

Ammann, Raymond. 1994. *Les danses kanak, une introduction.* Nouméa: Agence de Développement de la Culture Kanak.

———. 1997. *Kanak Dance and Music: Ceremonial and Intimate Performance of the Melanesians of New Caledonia, Historical and Actual.* Nouméa: Agence de Développement de la Culture Kanak.

"The Arts and Politics." 1992. *Pacific Studies* 15(4). Special issue, edited by Karen L. Nero.

Bruddah Waltah & Island Afternoon. 1990. *Hawaiian Reggae.* Platinum Pacific Records PPR 1005CD. Compact disc.

Edith Kanaka'ole Foundation. 1993. *E Mau Ana o Kanaloa, Ho'i Hou: "The Perseverance of Kanaloa, Return!"* Honolulu: Kaho'olawe Island Conveyance Commission.

Forbes, Lytton. 1875. "The Navigator Islands." *Overland Monthly* 15:209–218, 422–433.

Goldsworthy, David. 1997. "Indigenisation and Socio-Political Identity in the Kaneka Music of New Caledonia." *Perfect Beat* 3(2):15–31.

Handler, Richard, and Jocelyn Linnekin. 1984. "Tradition, Genuine or Spurious." *Journal of American Folklore* 97(385):273–290.

Hanson, Allan. 1989. "The Making of the Maori: Culture Invention and Its Logic." *American Anthropologist* 91(4):890–902.

Hobsbawm, Eric, and Terence Ranger. 1983. *The Invention of Tradition.* Cambridge: Cambridge University Press.

Inglis, John. 1887. *In the New Hebrides: Reminiscences of Missionary Life and Work, Especially on the Island of Aneityum, from 1850 till 1877.* London: T. Nelson and Sons.

Keesing, Roger. 1989. "Creating the Past: Custom and Identity in the Contemporary Pacific." *Contemporary Pacific* 1:19–42.

Krämer, Augustin, 1902. *Die Samoa-Inseln: Entwurf einer Monographie mit besonderer Berücksichtigung Deutsch-Samoas.* Vol. 1. Stuttgart: Nägele.

Lindstrom, Lamont. 1993. *Cargo Cult: Strange Stories of Desire from Melanesia and Beyond.* Honolulu: University of Hawai'i Press and Center for Pacific Islands Studies, University of Hawai'i.

Linnekin, Jocelyn. 1992. "On the Theory and Politics of Cultural Construction in the Pacific." *Oceania* 62(4):249–263.

Love, Jacob Wainwright. 1991. *Sāmoan Variations: Essays on the Nature of Traditional Oral Arts.* New York and London: Garland Publishing.

Nordyke, Eleanor C., and Martha H. Noyes. 1993. "'Kaulana Nā Pua': A Voice for Sovereignty." *Hawaiian Journal of History* 27:27–42.

Pond, Wendy. 1995. "Wry Comment from the Outback: Songs of Protest from the Niua Islands, Tonga." *South Pacific Oral Traditions,* ed. Ruth Finnegan and Margaret Orbell, 49–63. Bloomington: Indiana University Press.

Puhipau and Joan Landers. 1988. *The Story of the Struggle of the Native Hawaiian People for Self-Determination.* 22 mins. Honolulu. Video.

Rowe, N. A. 1930. *Samoa Under the Sailing Gods.* London and New York: Putnam.

Stillman, Amy K. 1989. "History Reinterpreted in Song: The Case of the Hawaiian Counter-revolution." *Hawaiian Journal of History* 28:1–30.

Trask, Haunani K. 1991. "Natives and Anthropologists: The Colonial Struggle." *The Contemporary Pacific* 3(1):159–167.

Watt, William. 1919. *Naresien em Nupume ya Nafwakien ya Nagkirien Kwamera.* Melbourne: Brown, Prior.

Williamson, Eleanor. 1976. "Hawaiian Chants and Songs Used in Political Campaigns." *Directions in Pacific Traditional Literature,* ed. Adrienne L. Kaeppler and H. Arlo Nimmo, 135–156. Special publication 62. Honolulu: Bishop Museum Press.

# Music and Theater

*Adrienne L. Kaeppler*        *Caroline Sinavaiana*
*Stephen A. Wild*             *Allan Thomas*
*Ronne Arnold*               *Helen Reeves Lawrence*
*Vilsoni Hereniko*

**Australia**
**The Pacific Islands**

Theater is a performative category that requires the participation of performers and an audience. Theatrical actions usually occur in a specially defined space (figure 1). These actions are often regulated by rules that distinguish them from everyday conduct, sometimes to the point of inverting the norms of ordinary behavior.

Unlike the formal acts and utterances of ritual, which need not be encoded by performers, theatrical acts and utterances *are* encoded. The message in theater must be derived from the performance. In theater, it is the *product,* not the *process* of performance, that is the message. In ritual and theater, process and product are important: in ritual, the process is primary; in theater, the product usually is. A Tongan *lakalaka* is a cultural form in which poetry, music, movement, scent, and dress coalesce into theater. An aesthetic construction, it is a complex form of discourse, built on culturally understood symbols within sociopolitically marked contexts, conveying information and meaning as entertainment.

The grammar of a theatrical idiom, like the grammar of a language, involves structure, style, and meaning: to understand the event, one must learn its theatrical conventions, how they can vary, their syntax (rules about how they can and cannot be put together), and what meanings are ascribed to them. In the Cook Islands, theatrical dance-dramas incorporate old legends in contexts marked by Christian concepts. Combining hymns, biblical pageantry, and enacted legends with singing and dancing, these theatrical performances are the centerpieces for the *nuku,* an annual festival commemorating the arrival of Christianity, and for celebrations of the national constitution (McMath and Parima 1995). Such pieces are also performed at Pacific Festivals of Arts and on other occasions overseas. When performed for other Cook Islanders, the poetry and movements convey important cultural values; outsiders, however, may admire the performances primarily for collective display, fascinating sounds, and incredible hip movements.

Theatrical performances can be approached in least three ways: as ritual, as theater, and as spectacle. Among Pacific Islanders, most staged performances can be considered theater or religious ritual. For outsiders, the performance is spectacle. How a performance is decoded depends on what the beholder brings to the performance. It determines if he or she will be an engaged observer or simply a spectator.

FIGURE 1   At the Pacific Festival of Arts, a contingent from Papua New Guinea performs on a stage in front of a painted backdrop. Photo by Adrienne L. Kaeppler, 1996.

## National dance-and-theater companies

A further expression and extension of theater is the development of national companies. Two productive national troupes are the New Guinea National Theatre Company (formerly the National Dance and Drama Company) and the Cook Islands National Arts Theatre, both of which have performed on stages of the world for non-Pacific audiences. The New Guinea National Theatre Company and Raun Raun Theatre (see below) perform for local audiences throughout Papua New Guinea. They have traveled to international festivals and performed in many parts of the world, integrating dances and dramatic pieces from various parts of the country into theatrical events that they represent as being typical of Papua New Guinea and understandable to themselves and to outsiders.

The performance of the Cook Islands National Arts Theatre at the 1985 Pacific Festival of Arts was a new program, which the members hoped to develop and present on tour. In a narrative theatrical manner, they told the story of their religious heritage and the coming of Christianity. Interspersed with dancing were religious speeches culminating with the presentation of Bibles to selected members of the audience. Though mixing rapid-hip-movement dances with speeches about Christian salvation seemed incongruous to some outside observers, this juxtaposition was not incongruous to the performers.

Other touring troupes from Oceania include young people from the Torres Strait and the American Sāmoan Cultural Choir. The former simply presents a set of dances, but the latter has become a staged presentation of culture, which interweaves dances and songs with a drama of everyday and ceremonial life, including making kava, playing games, and parading and presenting bark cloth and mats. The troupe's staging of culture has developed the storyteller's art into the arts of acting and mime, playing down the traditional emphasis on language.

Touring troupes are not new in Oceania. A Māori troupe from Aotearoa performed in England in 1862, and singer-dancers from Hawai'i and West Polynesia performed at the World's Columbian Exposition in Chicago in 1893. Other Polynesian troupes performed at the world's fair in St. Louis in 1904, and troupes from German colonies in Oceania performed in Europe in the years immediately before 1914.

Modern national dance companies or touring troupes may function as tourist attractions, in the sense that such performances attract tourists to visit the performers' homelands. These presentations make it possible for nonresidents of Oceania to have a touristic experience without traveling. Some such viewers, intrigued by performances, may subsequently visit the Pacific. Once tourists have traveled to the homeland of the performances, however, comparable performances may not be so easy to find, unless their visit happens to coincide with a festival [see ENCOUNTERS AMONG "OURSELVES"]. Touring companies, at least those now springing up in Oceania, seem directly related to the same urge as the rise of festivals: the promotion of identity, politics, and tourism.

—ADRIENNE L. KAEPPLER

## AUSTRALIA

With reference to theatrical concepts in Aboriginal societies, the term *theater* requires particular examination. Stock notions of theater imply processes of enactment, evident in special uses of time and space, embodied by performers acting prescribed roles for collective purposes. Many Australian Aboriginal performances follow similar processes. On several levels and from several points of view, they involve enactment. In marked ways, they use time and space. They employ performers who sing, move, and use props and special decorations.

More generally in keeping with stock notions of theater, Aboriginal performances realize specific themes, sometimes evoking plotlike imagery. They are special occasions, set apart from everyday life, for which attendance may require an invitation. Over and above the duty of conveying the referential content of the communication, the performers have the duty of displaying communicative competence.

### Time

The use of time in Aboriginal performances often varies from its common theatrical use. A performance may consist of a series of shorter performances with periods of rest between them. It may last for months. Outsiders may have difficulty perceiving when a performance begins, but endings are usually obvious. A performance routinely consists of a long period of preparation, which passes, often almost imperceptibly, into the main part of the performance; the line between preparation and performance is often blurred. This is not to imply that, once under way, Aboriginal performances cannot be precisely coordinated. They can achieve a brilliant coordination, involving many performers and complex sets of roles (Clunies Ross and Wild 1981; Eyre 1964 [1845]).

Aboriginal performers may execute their roles spectacularly. They can do so partly because they make elaborate and careful preparations. Before a performance, they discuss their prospective roles and actions. By singing relevant songs and discussing myths, they remind themselves of the themes they will be enacting. Some ease into their roles by preparing props for use in their performance and getting their bodies decorated.

### Space

A stock notion of theater implies a presentation to an audience. Aboriginal theater challenges this idea, since in Aboriginal performances all the participants are usually also performers. Some participants may not even be permitted to see or hear the main part of the performance, but they are nonetheless participating in some other way, somewhere else.

Aboriginal performances commonly include participants often called managers, but the managers, though not always visible at the center of the apparent action, are not offstage: they are part of the performance, for which they often provide musical accompaniment. The owners of a performance enact theatrical movements and are the focus of attention.

The actions of many Aboriginal performances occur within a recognizably bounded area, but other aspects of what may be called staging can differ from widespread notions of theater. Performances may occur in several places, sometimes simultaneously. As a performance proceeds, performers may move from one place to another, sometimes performing important parts of the event in transit.

### Context

Most Aboriginal theater intimately connects with religious rituals. Secular performances are limited in scope, and even they often relate to religious themes or goals. Because of outsiders' ignorance or ethnocentric prejudice, many early reports of Aboriginal performances did not mention this aspect of the performers' intent (Berndt 1974:1).

Underlying and unifying ritual performances are myths of ancestral spirits, whose activities continue to shape the patterns of Aboriginal life. By framing the cultural coding of fetal conception and genetic descent, myths relate people to people, and people to land. Ethnographies abound with translated accounts of myths as narratives, but they contain little information about how the myths were presented and collected. Published Aboriginal narratives that take stories through coherent plots may merely approximate authentic genres of expression. Aboriginal myths are usually enacted, not told. Their realizations as stories may entail only imagistic explanations of their enactments (Berndt 1974; Stanner 1966).

### Content

Many features of Aboriginal theater are illustrated in Rom, a ceremony performed in Arnhem Land by one people as a mark of friendship toward another (figure 2). In 1995, Rom was performed in Canberra as a greeting to delegates at the World Conference of the International Council of Traditional Music, and as a gesture of friendship to the people of Canberra.

Twenty-one women and men, carefully selected for theatrical competence, performed. (Since Arnhem Land singers are specialists, who learn their craft as apprentices to older singers, the inclusion of a child in the performance added further authenticity.) Preparations, directed by a ritual manager, lasted several months in Arnhem Land; they consisted of elaborately decorating two ceremonial poles, selecting the performers, and selecting and rehearsing the items to be performed.

In Arnhem Land, songs and dances associated with the pole or poles to be presented are ordinarily performed each day for several weeks, gradually building up to

FIGURE 2   At Nagalarramba, central Arnhem Land, performers present the Rom pole (*left*). Photo by Axel Poignant, 1952.

the climactic day when all the relevant mythological subjects have been expressed in performance. In Canberra, under the direction of the ritual manager, the ceremony lasted three days, with the presentation of the poles on the last day, when dancers' bodies were elaborately decorated and several new dances were performed to symbolize particular meanings and intentions.

Symbolism projected in performance included a danced farewell, when the performers (and the ancestors whom they represented) mimetically paddled away from the audience. Each of the performed dances represented an ancestral spirit, of whom the central ones were Morning Star and Wild Honey. Morning Star shines brightly each morning before dying, and reappears at night as the Evening Star; Wild Honey, a symbol of fertility, is found in hollow logs, the receptacle of bones of the dead.

The symbolism of Rom comes from central Arnhem Land mortuary ceremonies. It expresses the eternal tragedy of human existence: "Life, with its delicious accompaniments, burgeons in an entanglement of pain under the shadow of death" (Hiatt 1994:6–7). In this ceremony, as in much Aboriginal theater, performance ritualizes bereavement.                                                    —STEPHEN A. WILD

## NAISDA

The National Aboriginal and Islander Skills Development Association (NAISDA) College has been described as one of the most exciting and innovative dance colleges in Australia. With its conceptual creativity embedded in Aboriginal and Torres Strait Islander (ATSI) cultures, it has initiated new directions in dance and the performing arts (figure 3).

In 1988, NAISDA evolved from the Aboriginal Islander Skills Development Scheme, established in early 1975, when the Arts Council of Australia (now the Australia Council) and the Aboriginal Arts Board sought to stimulate and initiate Aboriginal and Torres Strait Islanders' artistic activities. By June of 1975, the Urban Theatre Committee of the Aboriginal Arts Board of the Australia Council had initiated a six-week training course at the Black Theatre in Redfern, Sydney. Selected nationally to participate, twenty-eight students took the course, sponsored by the Aboriginal Arts Board in association with the Aboriginal Study Grant Section of the

FIGURE 3    A NAISDA student performs the "Buffalo Dance" from Christmas Creek, Western Australia. Photo by Elaine Pelot Kitchener, 1987.

Commonwealth Department of Education. The areas of study included dance, drama, playwriting, and the Pitjantjatjara language. In October 1975, "Careers in Dance" commenced as the first project under the scheme. It functioned as a three-year unaccredited course in dance and related fields, but it was recognized by the Commonwealth Department of Education.

Though focusing on the songs and dances of indigenous Australian cultures, NAISDA College has gone in new creative directions using contemporary arts, with cultural links to ATSI communities throughout Australia. Because these links inform the curriculum, the college encourages students to use indigenous dances and songs for their creative works. By fusing these movements and concepts with Western arts, a dynamic transformation has developed within contemporary ATSI dance and song. Since training at the college insists that traditional values associated with cultural dances and songs be maintained, preserved, and respected, young ATSI artists are continuing to create and develop ways of presenting dances and songs representative of contemporary ATSI society. The college offers three nationally accredited programs in Aboriginal and Torres Strait Islander artistic studies, a certificate in dance, an associate diploma in dance, and a diploma of dance.

A further development of the Aboriginal Islander Skills Development Scheme was the creation of the Aboriginal Islander Dance Theatre, which enabled ATSI dancers to present their creative efforts to the public (figure 4). This company has performed nationally and internationally.          —RONNE ARNOLD

## THE PACIFIC ISLANDS

Theater in the Pacific Islands may be divided into three classes: traditional, popular, Western. These classes partly overlap, though each has features that distinguish it from the others. In the late 1990s, the emergence of a genre that combines elements of these classes heralded a new phase in the development of Pacific theater.

### Traditional theater

In the 1500s, when Europeans first saw the Pacific, Oceania had its own theatrical forms. Three centuries later, Christian missionaries frowned on some of them. Interpreting outward expressions of joy as works of the Christian devil, missionaries banned certain forms of music, dance, and theater. Some of these forms are being revived, at the cost of concessions to Christian notions of decency and propriety.

Traditional theater was either sacred or secular. Sacred theater was linked with the supernatural world and ideas of fertility. Performances often coincided with planting and harvesting, marriages, funerals, and other important events. Expeditions to neighboring islands were opportunities for these displays. Sometimes the ʻarioi of Tahiti acted under the cover of houses built for public entertainment, though they also performed in the open air, or on canoes as they approached the shore. ʻArioi ranged from "a society of comedians" to "human harpies, . . . in whose character and habits all that is most loathsome—earthly, sensual, devilish—was combined" (Oliver 1974:913–914). According to some views, societies akin to the ʻarioi existed in Aotearoa, the Caroline Islands, the Cook Islands, Hawaiʻi, Mangareva, the Mariana Islands, the Marquesas, and the Tuamotu Islands (Angas 1866:296; Webster 1968 [1908]:164–170).

Touring Sāmoans performed theatrical sketches (*faleaitu*) in the villages where they stopped. Performances climaxed evenings of oratory, dancing, and singing. Sources of amusement and social commentary, they lampooned authority and foreign ideas. This institution continues in Sāmoa, Tokelau, and overseas urban centers where large numbers of Sāmoans live. *Faleaitu* sometimes serve as comic interludes between dances. At the University of the South Pacific in 1992, Sāmoan students

FIGURE 4    Original members of the Aboriginal Islander Dance Theatre. Photo by Lee Chittick, 1980.

performed about twenty different dances; midway through, they presented a sketch that satirized beauty pageants. It ended with cross-dressed male contestants performing in idiosyncratic styles: speaking in high-pitched voices, wearing skirts, lipstick, and high heels, the men careened around the stage. The audience, mainly of Pacific Islanders, roared with laughter.

In Fiji, clowns performed during harvesting embargoes and firstfruit festivals, where they mocked "earthly authority with a licence normally undreamt of" (Clunie and Ligairi 1983:57). During the months before these festivals, taboos were placed on certain crops, fish, and pigs. For exchanges between hosts and visitors, people rehearsed dances and manufactured various goods and stuffs. Clowning also occurred in the contexts of cannibalistic feasting (Britton 1884:144) and funerals.

In Hawai'i, byplay and buffoonery enlivened *hula ki'i,* a theatrical genre with puppets. About one-third human life-size, the puppets wore human clothing and enacted human situations. Standing behind a screen, a performer (or performers) manipulated the puppets while reciting the words the puppets were apparently uttering. Human dancers sometimes imitated the puppets (Luomala 1984:5).

At Rotuman weddings, a woman past childbearing, chosen by the bride's relatives, performs the role of *hàn mane'àk su* 'woman who plays the wedding'. Overturning the social hierarchy and assuming the role of supreme ruler, she prances around with a stick in her hand. Sometimes she performs alone; sometimes other women join her, forcing chiefs and other men to dance. This situation often leads to the development of a comic sketch in which the *hàn mane'àk su* threatens a man with her stick: he reacts verbally to the demand, she answers, and he obliges by doing what she wants. A demanding *hàn mane'àk su* is a customary catalyst, whose banter and antics entertain everyone.

### Dance as theater

In some cultures of Oceania, dancing had religious dimensions, though this link is no longer readily apparent in most dances. Often performed with singing and the playing of musical instruments, dance may be interpreted broadly as theater. Its movements may illustrate or decorate lyrics. Dancers may mimic the activities of creatures, such as sharks or iguanas. Hints of spiritual possession are sometimes evident, as when dancers from Nauru and Kiribati imitate the quivering movements of frigate birds.

Dances in Oceania often tell stories. Dancers not uncommonly break out of frame to take on the role of clown, who moves freely around the arena, as in the ancient Rotuman *tautoga,* shouting out comments and stirring things up (figure 5). Some Fijian dances with clubs or spears included a human representative of an elflike creature (*veli*), until it became marginalized because of the seeming frivolousness of the role. In some Kiribati dances, one or two dancers clown by emulating the flight of frigate birds.

The Sāmoan *taualuga* and its Tongan counterpart (*tau'olunga*) also support theatrics. Around a single female dancer, often distinguished by an elaborate costume, men frisk and frolic. Focusing their attention on her, they jump, whoop, and make faces. They shake the houseposts. They slap themselves. They throw themselves onto the ground—anything to highlight the female dancer's dignity by contrasting it with their antics. Reinforcing the contrast, men and women from the audience may join their abandon.

Secular performances were not linked with religion, and are therefore still practiced. The main function of this type of theater is to entertain or to tell a story. Performances may use a chorus and several actors to dramatize a myth or legend. Sometimes, as during feasts and competitions in the Cook Islands and Hawai'i, the story reveals itself as a dance-drama, into which clowns spontaneously insert hilarious displays.

### Other contexts as theater

Sports sometimes serves as a context for spontaneous performance. Cricket matches, particularly among Sāmoans and Trobriand Islanders, are often occasions for spectators to dance, sing, and clown. The entertainment offered by the clowning may be more engaging than the game; for days after, spectators may recount the entertainment and the verbal and sometimes physical exchanges. Unless fighting has broken out and disrupted the peace, this clowning often brings communities closer together.

The people of some parts of Oceania are reviving ancillary elements of traditional theater: tattooing or painting their bodies, reciting poems, and performing with

Popular theater primarily serves rural people, with actors performing in the open air. Using colorful costumes, singing, dancing, dialogue, and sometimes puppets, they present didactic sketches and try to communicate messages to a general audience.

FIGURE 5    At a presentation of taro to the district chief, a Rotuman man clowns. Photo by Alan Howard, 1960.

masks. At the Pacific Festival of Arts, observers are likely to witness these traits in various permutations.

Where missionization has been particularly thorough, theater may have disappeared altogether, or may have been coopted by the church for its own purposes. The clearest examples of the latter result are biblical pageants (*nuku*) of the Cook Islands and skits done by children throughout Oceania on Palm Sunday.

### Popular theater

Popular theater, usually called community theater, is a twentieth-century introduction to Oceania. It primarily serves rural people. Its focus is inward, specific to times and places. Local people and their needs mainly dictate the kinds of plays that popular theatrical companies produce. Another distinguishing trait is an educational focus on economic, environmental, medicinal, and political issues.

Popular-theater actors usually travel to villages and perform in the open air. Using colorful costumes, singing, dancing, dialogue, and sometimes puppets, they present didactic sketches. They seek simplicity in story, props, and other aspects of the production. They may employ theatrical techniques, but try to communicate messages clearly to a broad and general audience. Raun Raun Theatre of Papua New Guinea, Wan Smolbag of Vanuatu, and Sei! of the Solomon Islands are examples flourishing in the late 1990s.

Popular theater is likely to grow. From Community Aid Abroad, the World Health Organization, and the South Pacific Commission, Wan Smolbag received funding that enabled it to offer theatrical workshops in Aotearoa, Australia, the Cook Islands, Fiji, Papua New Guinea, the Solomon Islands, and Tonga. In Fiji, Women Action for Change uses popular theater to get its messages across. Sei! has traveled to the Philippines to learn new skills and share ideas with its counterparts.

### Western theater

A hallmark of Western theater is the scripted play. As written by playwrights of Oceania, plays are usually in the language of the colonizer or former colonizer, performed within the confines of a building and often on a proscenium stage, and intended primarily for an urban audience. They are often supported by urban theatrical companies whose mission is to produce local and/or European or American plays. The Fiji Arts Club, Kumu Kahua Theater of Honolulu, and Taki Rua of Aotearoa are such companies.

Plays written by Pacific islanders have graced stages in Auckland, Honolulu, Port Moresby, Suva, and other urban centers. Pacific playwrights who have written successful plays include John Kasaipwalova and Nora Brash of Papua New Guinea, Larry Thomas of Fiji, Hone Kokua and Riwia Brown of Aotearoa, and John Kneubuhl (1920–1994) and his niece Victoria Kneubuhl of Sāmoa. Modeled on Western notions of dramatic structure, works by Pacific playwrights are distinguished from their foreign counterparts primarily by their focus on Pacific issues or themes. The plays of John Kneubuhl best exemplify this type of theater. *Think of a Garden,* his last play, focuses on a half-caste boy's identity crisis; within two years of its composition, it had been produced in Auckland, Honolulu, Pago Pago, and Wellington.

A host of Papua New Guinean playwrights emerged in the 1960s. In Fiji in the 1970s, under the leadership of Albert Wendt and Marjorie Crocombe at the University of the South Pacific, a similar flowering occurred. In 1973, the founding of the South Pacific Creative Arts Society and its journal *Mana* fostered the writing of plays, poetry, and fiction, usually following Western ideas of characterization and structure.

### Crossing the millennium

In the 1990s, a theatrical genre that draws from oral forms but exploits techniques of Western and popular theater emerged. Its main practitioners, though familiar with Western forms and values, feel a need to assert their cultural heritage, fusing the old and the new. This development coincides with increased politicization of the arts and the revival of ancient dances, as in Aotearoa and Hawai'i.

Plays of this genre often have a sustained narrative and complex character development. They use singing, dancing, and clowning to assert their geographic origins. They are not easily pigeonholed: they may resemble a musical with a Pacific flavor, or a serious play with comic or satirical undertones. Raun Raun Theatre's production of John Kasaipwalova's poem *Sail the Midnight Sun* (1980), the New Guinea National Theatre Company's *Sana Sana* (1992), Victoria Kneubuhl's *Ola Na Iwi* 'May the Bones Live' (1994), and Vilsoni Hereniko's play *Last Virgin in Paradise* (coauthored with Teresia Teaiwa, 1991, 1994) exemplify this kind of theater.

The new plays reflect influences from old oral forms, but scripts continue to be vehicles for exploring local issues and concerns. New plays show a shift from presentations of social realism to works that confound neat classification. A full-length production that combines traditional elements with modern theatrical techniques is the most exciting challenge awaiting Pacific playwrights who want to reach audiences everywhere.                                        —VILSONI HERENIKO

## New Guinea

Theatrical companies in New Guinea have developed indigenous concepts in ways that establish an artistic commonality with concepts of theater in the outside world. Unlike traditional performers, who often reenact abstract, timeless encounters between spirits and their descendants, theatrical companies dramatize plots portraying realistic people whose lives interconnect, and sometimes interconnect with spirits.

Though movements derive from traditional ones, women participate almost equally with men. Here too is the kind of drama that unfolds through the workings of a plot, often featuring a hero or a star. Traditional antecedents, such as masks, become stage properties, which cast a brooding sense of history over the proceedings.

This new form of dance-drama is an appropriate medium for the perpetuation of old movements in new settings. It has universal appeal, appropriate not only for outsiders, but for the inhabitants of New Guinea. Viewers do not have to know tribal lore or village customs. They may simply immerse themselves in dramatized struggles common to life anywhere, but here these struggles are filtered anew through the local experience.

### *Raun Raun Theatre*

Begun in 1975 in Goroka, this is a grass-roots company dedicated to make theater available and understandable to all people of Papua New Guinea. It frequently performs in small villages, but has graced stages in Sydney, New York, and San Francisco. It focuses on modern life in Papua New Guinea, especially cultural history and traditions that seem to be slipping away. Educational plays on nutrition, health, and other subjects alternate with indigenous operas, in which dialogue, mime, and dance are amalgamated into a popular theater using traditional material.

*Sail the Midnight Sun,* the company's sixth production, stages a poem by John Kasaipwalova, a Trobriand Islander. The plot encapsulates the view "that balance is essential between the sea and the sky, sun and moon, male and female, night and day, expectation and achievement" (Murphy 1980). An individual representing what the script calls Everyman reveals the origins and history of Papua New Guinea as a political entity. Addition of a plot and emphasis on dramatic encounter have profoundly changed narrative structure while encapsulating a traditional emphasis on movement as a visual extension of rhythm.

### Other companies

The National Theatre Company consists of performers from many parts of Papua New Guinea. They too perform indigenous operas, dances learned from village elders, and modern-dance compositions. At provincial and smaller levels, regional theatrical companies have developed, emulating their national counterparts. Because they focus more on local communication, they may employ local languages. The national companies often use Tok Pisin.          —ADRIENNE L. KAEPPLER

## Sāmoa

Sāmoan theatrical performance occurs largely in two types of narrative show: comic sketches, and legendary or biblical plays. Its most common context is the concert (*koniseti*), a tropical vaudeville: "There are pantomimes and comic songs in it and a clown and a funny man and, of course, always dancing" (Flaherty 1925:796). Before the mid-1800s, Sāmoan theatrical expression required dancing. With Christian suppression of licentious contexts, entertainment began to include skits, as separate dramatic interludes between songs (Sinavaiana 1992). In legendary and biblical plays, a more Western mode of performing developed: props, costumes, and makeup became more elaborate; and to sing a narrative of the plot, a Greek-style chorus emerged.

### Contexts

To raise funds, village associations—churches, schools, men's or women's organizations—sponsor concerts. Other than a hired comedian or two, performers belong to the sponsoring organization. During each number, to show support, onlookers lay money at performers' feet, or tuck it into performers' costumes. If the sponsors seek an extraordinarily large sum, their troupe may travel to other villages, islands, or countries. Since conspicuous populations of Sāmoans live abroad (in Aotearoa, California, Hawai'i), such troupes make an important cultural link with the homeland. In addition to fund-raising events, major occasions for theatrical performance are national celebrations: Flag Day (in American Sāmoa), Independence Day (in Western Sāmoa), school-sponsored cultural days, and religious holidays.

### Comic sketches

Of several types of narrative show, *faleaitu* are probably the oldest surviving form of Sāmoan theater. Small troupes of amateurs orally script, rehearse, and perform them. The most accomplished comedian of the troupe trains and directs the others. By reversing normative status-roles, *faleaitu* satirize authority-figures and social conventions. The former may include officials (indigenous and foreign), parents, teachers, elders, and pastors. Conventional textual devices include hyperbole, punning, caricature, slapstick, and burlesque. Audiences rate acting by the variety and fluidity of characters.

In the twentieth century, several comedians became famous throughout the islands, and even toured overseas. In competitions honoring the British King George's birthday in the 1920s, the comic Reupena and his troupe, from Neiafu, Savai'i, regularly won prizes. The comic Sale is remembered for his bawdiness, and the comic Siaki for his impersonations and vocal modulations (Shore 1977:319). In the late twentieth century, Petelo dominated the field. Specializing in satire with the comic Ta'ai, he skillfully played with differences between the polite and the vernacular registers of the language. Two younger stars, Ioelu and Ioane, tend more toward burlesque, as of marital disagreements, and famously impersonate pop icons, including Elvis Presley and John Wayne (Sinavaiana 1992).

Comedians are traditionally males. A typical stage persona is that of a transvestite female impersonator (*fa'afāfine*). Women usually perform as comedians only in

An important religious holiday is White Sunday. Before the congregation, children recite poems and ensembles perform biblical plays. In a reversal of social norms, adults pamper children—showering them with gifts and treats.

the context of an all-female audience. Remarking on the skill of female clowns, commentators of both sexes agree that sexual joking makes women's *faleaitu* in mixed company inappropriate.

Most skits use few costumes or props and little makeup. Comedians wear ordinary attire, consisting of skirts and shirts. The only actor in costume is often the lead comedian, who may affect some form of female dress, either Sāmoan or European.

*Legendary and biblical plays*

Legendary and biblical plays commonly feature more elaborate stagecraft: costumes, props, makeup, and casting. The intent and tone of these shows are explicitly serious, but comic moments abound, encouraged by repartee between the comedians and the audience. Plots come from tales (*fāgono*), legends (*tala*), and biblical stories (*tala fa'alotu,* usually from the Old Testament). Dialogue may be sparse: while a chorus conveys the story in song, actors mime the action. The cast and chorus may total fifty or more, depending on the occasion, with men and women equally represented.

Fund-raising events occur in the evening; the usual venue is the village center (*malae*), unless rain drives the performance into a communal meetinghouse. Culture-day events occur in the daytime, often as competitions among student organizations within a school or schools within a district. Performances celebrating religious holidays also occur by day, though without competition.

An important religious holiday is White Sunday (Lotu a Tamaiti), the second Sunday in October. Before the congregation, children recite memorized poems, and ensembles perform biblical plays. Instituted by the Congregational Church, this event has become a major cultural occasion. In a reversal of social norms (which valorize seniority), adults pamper children, showering them with gifts and treats.

**Nineteenth-century forms**

The earliest written accounts locate theatrical performance primarily in the context of dances, when performers might mimic animals or present common scenes, like fishermen using nets and spears. In the mid-1800s, at "evening sports,"

> *theatricals* were in vogue. Illustrations would be given of selfish schemes to take things easy at the expense of others, clownish processions to create laughter, or marriage ceremonies in which, when it came to the point, the bride rebelled and would not have her husband. Ventriloquism also was attempted, in which, as they say, "voices spoke to them without bodies." (Turner 1884:132)

In the 1880s, one comic skit featured an actor playing the role of Death, whose designs on an infant were thwarted by a "medicine man" (Trotter 1888:774). Performers often lampooned outsiders. In the early 1890s, the Countess of Jersey saw a sketch acted with immense spirit, great contortion of face, and an enjoyment so keen that it could not fail to communicate itself to onlookers. One series of gesticulations was supposed to represent "German fashion"; the imitation of walk and countenance. (1893:257)

In Manu'a about 1940, a comedy spoofed a visiting American photographer: with songs and dances, villagers performed a skit with a clown who, in a white suit, strutted with his shoes on the wrong feet (Sloan 1940:67–69).

### Outside influences

In the early 1900s, as colonialism influenced Sāmoa, theatrical performance, like other indigenous cultural practices, took on Western features. Itinerant troupes would set up makeshift stages, lit by torches. Such plays were apparently fanciful enactments of European stories, usually with a king and queen, arrayed in splendor on glittering thrones. In the 1940s, this kind of performance was a "recent development" (Grattan 1985:123–124), popular at Christmas and New Year's.

If programs were extensive, troupes might spend the night with their audiences. These programs may have developed into concerts (*koniseti*), which included songs, dances, and plays, with elaborate costuming, effects, and instrumental accompaniment. Plots might come from sources like Shakespeare, but troupes localized the material. In the 1920s, Alice Fergusson cited the ingenuity of an adaptation of *The Winter's Tale*.

The production was excellent; there was never a hitch or a pause—nothing dragged. Another feature was the intense appreciation of the audience. The dialogue, always crisp and telling, was closely followed; every hit was appreciated. The people have a strong sense of humour, and roars of laughter greeted each touch of comedy. (Hereniko 1990:74–75)

On one occasion in the 1940s, costumed actors provided additional props.

A man who was to represent a house covered himself with thatch and squatted out in the middle of the square. A river was represented by another man covered with blue tapa cloth who continually shook and waved the cloth to represent flowing water. A forest was represented by half-a-dozen boys carrying palm fronds. Whenever a change of scenery was required these people got up and walked off and others took their places. (Sloan 1940:101–102)

The performance incorporated into the dramatic setting the natural one: malae, beach, lagoon.

Other major occasions for festive performance were village celebrations of important communal events. In the 1930s, when trade in copra for export flourished, one such occasion occurred at harvesttime. In Manu'a after a feast, the community assembled at the malae, lit by torches, fires, and the light of a full moon. Comic sketches mimicked Western copra-traders' attempts to seduce Sāmoan women. One legend portrayed certain introduced species (weeds, nettles, thornbushes) as the offspring of Fijian chiefs and gods' wives, whom they had raped (Sloan 1940:103–104). More than a hundred actors performed for more than an hour, mostly in mime, to songs sung by a chorus of fifty, seated to one side. The pageant also had a romance and "two orthodox plays wherein the actors spoke their own parts" (Sloan 1940:104).

### Technological change

After the 1940s, electronic technologies spurred important developments. Since the early 1970s, technicians have taped major performances; repeatedly throughout the year, local radio and television stations air the tapes. An increase in noninstitutional taping has helped preserve and disseminate performances to audiences far beyond local stages. Cultural and aesthetic implications of this technology remain academically unexplored. Within the boundaries of culturally Sāmoan territory (now effectively spanning the Pacific from Aotearoa to California), traditional theater persists as an important vehicle for the exchange of resources.    —CAROLINE SINAVAIANA

## Tokelau

Into the festivities of Tokelauan celebrations, performers may interpolate humorous skits (*faleaitu*), scenes staged to amuse onlookers. A skit may take as a comic theme any of a variety of incidents, like an argument, the capsizing of a canoe, an accident in a kitchen. It may mock boasters, brutes, and bunglers. It may parody outsiders, such as the crews of Korean and Japanese trawlers, or scientific investigators. Medical examinations with probing instruments are a favorite theme.

The performers may wear costumes appropriate to their roles in the skits. Older women, dressed in ill-fitting male attire, may act as clowns. Actors shout their lines to one another, sometimes drowned out by roars of laughter from the audience. The coarseness of the presentation—in costume, clowning, and language (which may veer into bawdry and indelicacy)—counterpoints the elegance of the rest of the celebration.    —ALLAN THOMAS

## Manihiki

In Manihiki, theatrical presentations (*nuku*) may have sacred or secular themes. The former are *nuku puka tapu* 'biblical plays' or *nuku tuatua tapu* 'sacred-story plays'. The latter are *nuku henua* 'land plays', centering on stories and legends concerning the land; predating Christian times, they are sometimes called *nuku hetene* 'heathen plays'.

The actors perform among the spectators, not on a stage. The location is often in the open, for secular plays, or in a Sunday-school building, for sacred plays. Dressed in appropriate costumes, actors represent a village or a congregation, and may enhance the drama with singing, dancing, and drumming (figure 6). Young people's presentations often include songs accompanied by guitars and ukuleles. Music and dance serve as devices for emphasizing ideas or actions, or for explaining parts of a story the actors cannot or choose not to act out. Theatrical performances also provide a vehicle for presenting newly composed songs and dances.

Theatrical presentations occur at national competitions, including the constitutional celebrations in Rarotonga, in the category *peu tupuna,* a Rarotongan term meaning 'in the ancestors' manner or custom'. (Rarotongans apply the term *nuku* to sacred plays only.) In national competitions, theatrical presentations occur on a stage in front of an audience and judges.    —HELEN REEVES LAWRENCE

## REFERENCES

Angas, F. L. S. 1866. *Polynesia: A Popular Description of the Islands of the Pacific.* London: Society for the Promotion of Christian Knowledge.

Berndt, R. M. 1974. "Australian Aboriginal Religion." In *Iconography of Religions,* ed. T. P. van Baaren, L. Leertouwer, and H. Bunting. Leiden: E. J. Brill.

Britton, Henry. 1884. *Loloma, or Two Years in Cannibal-Land: A Story of Old Fiji.* Melbourne: Mullen.

Clunie, Fergus, and Walesi Ligairi. 1983. "Traditional Fijian Spirit Masks and Spirit Masquers." *Fiji Museum Quarterly* 1:46–71.

Clunies Ross, Margaret, and Stephen A. Wild. 1981. "The Relations of Music, Text and Dance

FIGURE 6    Inside a Sunday-school building in Tukao Village, Manihiki, performers dramatize the story of Adam and Eve. Photo by Helen Reeves Lawrence, 1987.

in Arnhem Land Clan Songs." Paper presented at the Conference on Transmission in Oral and Written Traditions, Humanities Research Centre, Australian National University, Canberra, August.

Eyre, Edward J. 1964 [1845]. "Manners and Customs of the Aborigines of Australia." In *Journals of Expeditions of Discovery into Central Australia,* 2:145–507. Adelaide: Libraries Board of South Australia.

Fergusson, Alice. 1928. "Shakespeare Amongst the Samoans." *Blackwood's Magazine* 224:365–370.

Flaherty, Frances Hubbard. 1925. "Behind the Scenes with Our Samoan Stars." *Asia* 25:746–753, 795–796.

Grattan, F. J. R. 1985. *An Introduction to Samoan Custom.* Auckland: Macmillan.

Hereniko, Vilsoni. 1990. "Polynesian Clowns and Satirical Comedies." Ph.D. dissertation, University of the South Pacific.

Hiatt, Les. 1994. "Wild Honey and Morning Star." In *'It's About Friendship': Rom: A Ceremony From Arnhem Land,* 5–7. Canberra: Aboriginal Studies Press.

Jersey, M. E. 1893. "Three Weeks in Samoa." *The Nineteenth Century* 33:52–64, 249–260.

Krämer, Augustin. 1902. *Die Samoa-Inseln.* Vol. 1. Stuttgart: Nägele.

———. 1903. *Die Samoa-Inseln.* Vol. 2. Stuttgart: Nägele.

Luomala, Katherine. 1984. *Hula Kiʻi: Hawaiian Puppetry.* Honolulu: Institute of Polynesian Studies.

McMath, Marivee, and Teaea Parima. 1995. "Winged Tangiʻia: A Mangaian Dramatic Performance." In *South Pacific Oral Traditions,* ed. Ruth Finnegan and Margaret Orbell, 215–255. Bloomington and Indianapolis: Indiana University Press.

Murphy, Greg. 1980. Introduction to *Sail the Midnight Sun,* by John Kasaipwalova. Waigani, Port Moresby: National Arts School.

Oliver, Douglas L. 1974. *Ancient Tahitian Society.* 3 vols. Honolulu: University Press of Hawaiʻi.

Shore, Bradd. 1977. "A Samoan Theory of Action: Social Control and Social Order in a Polynesian Paradox." Ph.D. dissertation, University of Chicago.

Sinavaiana, Caroline. 1992. "Comic Theater in Samoa: A Holographic View." Ph.D. dissertation, University of Hawaiʻi.

Sloan, Donald. 1940. *The Shadow Catcher.* New York: Book League of America.

Stanner, W. E. H. 1966. *On Aboriginal Religion.* Oceania monograph 11. Sydney: University of Sydney.

Trotter, Coutts. 1888. "Among the Islands of the South Pacific: Tonga and Samoa." *Blackwood's Magazine* (June):759–776.

Turner, George. 1884. *Samoa a Hundred Years Ago and Long Before.* London: Macmillan.

Webster, Hutton. 1968 [1908]. *Primitive Secret Societies: A Study in Early Politics and Religion.* 2nd ed. New York: Octagon Books.

# Music and Gender

*Adrienne L. Kaeppler*
*Linda Barwick*
*Helen Payne*
*Nancy C. Lutkehaus*
*James F. Weiner*
*Judith Macdonald*

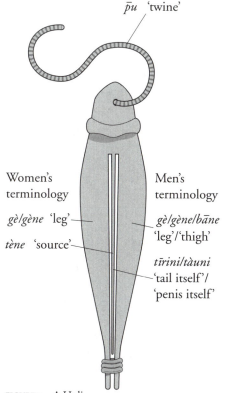

*p̄u* 'twine'

Women's
terminology

*gè/gène* 'leg'

*tène* 'source'

Men's
terminology

*gè/gène/bāne*
'leg'/'thigh'

*tīrini/tàuni*
'tail itself'/
'penis itself'

FIGURE 1  A Huli lamellaphone and its parts as named by men and women. Drawing by Jacqueline Pugh-Kitingan.

Sex is a physical attribute, but gender is a social construct. Worldwide, participation in musical performances often depends on gender. In Oceania, male and female sexuality may be supplemented by culturally constructed concepts, like *māhū* (Tahitian and Hawaiian term for effeminate men), *geligeli* (Tok Pisin for the same), *fakafefine* and *fakatangata* (Tongan terms for male and female homosexuals, respectively), and *fakaleiti* (a new Tongan term for gay men).

Though many societies usually separate human activities by gender, studies of music in Oceania have mostly been carried out by male researchers, who have had access mainly to male rituals and interpretations. Recent studies by female researchers have added missing pieces. For example, the indigenous terms for parts of a Huli instrument may differ according to the gender of the person describing it (figure 1).

In old Polynesia, access to rituals was not usually restricted by gender, though priests were usually male. Dances were often separated by gender. Tongan *me'elaufola* were performed by women or men, but today's *lakalaka* are performed by women and men, each conveying the poetry simultaneously with different choreographies (figure 2). Women's movements are soft and graceful; men's are strong and virile. In Hawai'i, however, men and women perform the same movement motifs, but the style varies by gender.

In Australia and New Guinea, relationships of gender as manifested in music are more complex and gender-specific (figure 3), and musical instruments may incorporate sexual attributes. The following entries focus on these areas. By contrast, the entry on Tikopia, a Polynesian outlier, emphasizes gender-based insults as a sexually provocative art.
—ADRIENNE L. KAEPPLER

## GENDER IN AUSTRALIAN MUSIC

In music and dance, as in other dimensions of Aboriginal life, differences of gender are centrally important and clearly visible. Most sources published before the 1970s, however, misrepresent or ignore women's roles (Bell 1983). Performances by mixed-sex gatherings and men only are well documented. In some areas, notably Central Australia and the northwest, women's-only ceremonies, like men's, reenact ancestors' actions in the Dreaming. Women and men receive songs from spirits in dreams, pass-

FIGURE 2    In the *lakalaka* of Kanokupolu Village performed at the centenary celebration of the Tongan constitution, women's soft and graceful movements contrast with men's virile movements. Photo by Adrienne L. Kaeppler, 1975.

ing on to a spouse or other close relative the ownership of songs properly performed by members of the opposite sex (Keogh 1989; Marett and Page 1995; R. Moyle 1986; Wild 1975). Because women's-only and men's-only ceremonies are culturally restricted, comment on their content is inappropriate.

In public ceremonies, participation is often differentiated by sex and other socially significant categories, including kinship moiety and land affiliation. Women usually keep apart from men. Depending on genre and location, further restrictions may affect their actions and musical behavior. Differential participation complementarily emphasizes the complexity of interdependence that characterizes gender relations and other social relationships in Aboriginal societies (Bell 1983; Magowan 1994; Rose 1992).

### Accompaniment and musical style

Sex-specific forms of percussive accompaniment to singing have been documented throughout Aboriginal Australia. People of either sex may clap. Exclusively male per-

FIGURE 3    At the Pacific Festival of Arts, Enga men (*left*) perform with kundus while Enga women perform separately on the periphery. Photo by Adrienne L. Kaeppler, 1980.

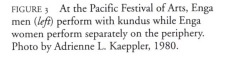

cussive instruments include clapsticks and other objects struck against each other or the ground. In the southeastern area and along the eastern seaboard as far north as Cairns, women place a possum-skin pillow in their lap and strike it with a hand (Dixon and Koch 1996). Elsewhere, women use similar movements for slapping: a kneeling woman strikes her lap or crotch with a cupped hand grasped at the wrist by the other hand (A. Moyle 1978). Women usually perform this percussion at half the rate of idiophonic accompaniment: two strokes of the men's clapsticks correspond to one beat of the women's slapping or clapping. The didjeridu, formerly used only in Northern Australia, is played in that area only by men, though women in the Daly River area are reported to play it occasionally.

In Central Australia, a single musical system with texts set to flexibly descending melodies is common to men's and women's songs, but women's songs differ in important ways (May and Wild 1967; R. Moyle 1979):

tempo: slower for women
duration of item: longer for women
proportion of unaccompanied songs: higher for women
number of accompanimental patterns: lower for women
variety of text-repetition patterns: lower for women
vocal and accompanimental rhythmic relationship: simpler for women
predominant meter of vocal rhythm: triple for women, duple for men
melodic notes: higher for women
melodic range: smaller for women
melodic movement: governed by absolute duration for women, by poetic meter
    for men

Melodic unison is standard in Central Australia, but in mixed performances, departures from unison occur (Barwick 1995). In Warlpiri *purlapa,* men and women may sing different melodies at once (Wild 1984).

### Dance

Public ceremonies throughout Aboriginal Australia frequently restrict performers' roles by sex. In many public genres across the continent, men dance while women sing or accompany (Gummow 1992; Keogh 1990; R. Moyle 1986; von Sturmer 1987). By contrast, in Northern Australian *wangga* and public segments of Central and Northern Australian initiations, women may dance but not sing (Ellis 1964; Keen 1978; Marett and Page 1995; R. Moyle 1986).

Styles of movement also differ by sex. In Central Australia, women frequently make a special shuffle-jump (Pitjantjatjara *nyaṉpinyi*), a step designed to leave tracks on the ground (Morais 1995); men make stamps (Pitjantjatjara *kantuṉi*) not used by women (Ellis et al. 1978). In Northern Australian *wangga* and clansong dancing, women's movements are frequently nontraveling (performed in place, or with minimal forward movement), and upper-body movements mark beats (figure 4). This style contrasts with men's, which marks beats by lower-body movements, including running and stamping, and deemphasizes upper-body movements (Anderson 1992; Keen 1978; Marett and Page 1995). To represent concepts in Yolngu dancing, movements and bodily positions may differ by sex.

A further distinction occurs in Warlpiri public ceremonies, where only men may dance mimetically, embodying ancestors' actions. Women's dancing, though nonmimetic, encodes information about ancestors' direction and mode of travel; men matrilineally related to the owners of the ceremony sometimes use this style.

—LINDA BARWICK

FIGURE 4   At Belyuen community, Northern Territory, during a *kapuk* ceremony for disposing of a deceased woman's belongings, women dance a *wangga.* Photo by Linda Barwick, 1995.

## WOMEN'S MUSIC IN CENTRAL AUSTRALIA

Central Australian Aborigines regard ceremonies featuring music as belonging either to males or to females. They permit public ceremonial performances by mixed-sex gatherings, but restrict private performances to members of one sex, acting in secret. For a women's public ceremony, women lead the singing, undertake the painting and dancing, and tell attendees how to behave; for a men's public ceremony, men play these roles. Sexual segregation and genderization are most apparent in the Central Australian desert, where men and women have private ceremonies apart, choosing place, time, and participants.

For women's ceremonial enactments, the female owner of the ceremony assigns the performative roles. Those who, through childbirth, have proved their fertility train those who have not. For a girl, instruction in women's ceremonial practices begins at menarche and continues until she herself may teach correct ceremonial procedures—a freedom she usually reaches after menopause. A girl who shows interest in women's ritual domains is expected to learn the multiplicity of structures being presented to her in performance. At first, she participates in the beating that accompanies singing; later, she joins in the singing itself. Until she has borne children, the designs painted on her body and the movements of her dancing will be restricted, but once she has gained the appellation of woman (following the birth of a child) she is expected to participate responsibly in all aspects of the ritual. Deep levels of meaning inherent in women's ceremonial life are revealed to her little by little.

In women's ceremonial enactments, licenses and privileges accrue to post-menopausal women, who have crossed the gender-distinctive boundary that separates men from women. Aboriginal society permits such women to have an understanding of men's ritual domain. It holds these women's wisdom sufficient to reveal to them when and under what circumstances they may disclose their knowledge of men's secrets (Kaberry 1939:229; White 1975:126). What matters socially is the public acknowledgment of knowledge, not its acquisition. Sharing across genderized private realms of knowledge authenticates the suggestion that the members of one sex duplicate material in the ceremonial property of the other (Strehlow 1971:653).

### Scholarly research

Research in the area of women's rites has been less extensive than in the area of men's rites. Since the 1970s, as female researchers, in increasing numbers and with increasing authority, began asserting a female-oriented view of reality, women's ceremonial contributions to society have been better communicated to outsiders (Bell 1983; Berndt 1978, 1983; Brock 1989; Ellis 1970; Gale 1978, 1983; Hamilton 1980; Payne 1984; White 1975). Conventional statements by male authors, like Richard Moyle (1983:92), implying that women's rites concern childbirth and love-controlling magic, show that more work is needed before the world will accept that Aboriginal women, like men, hold autonomous but complementary social responsibilities.

Some female keepers of knowledge and guardians of rites and sites are women who have proved their value in healing and have achieved special status as healers; other such women possess the much-coveted *illpintji* knowledge, often mentioned by male researchers, but rarely in terms that adequately portray the breadth of the maintenance of society and land that women's performance assures (Payne 1992:276).

Understanding women's places in Aboriginal society complements a "hearing" of the voices of contemporary urban Aboriginal performers like Tiddas and The Seven Sisters, and soloists like Ruby Hunter. Paralleling their sisters' songs, these songs carry messages about women's situations and concerns—violence, incest, rape, murder—so

no matter where Aboriginal women are living, they summon through music others'
awareness of their strength, their desires, their spirit.          —HELEN PAYNE

## GENDER IN NEW GUINEAN MUSIC

As distinctions of gender and the division of labor by sex are fundamental principles
of culture and social organization in New Guinea, so the performance of music is
structured by principles of gender. Only men carve and play garamuts, especially in
association with men's houses or clanhouses. Men also make and play kundus, water-
sounded drums, bamboo flutes (especially flutes called *tambaran* in Tok Pisin), rattles, clickers, trumpets, and swung slats. In performance with dance, men often stand
or move in a circle, with women on the outside, circling them or dancing in place,
alone or in clusters of a few individuals.

Singing is mainly associated with women. In Manam society, women's work at
mortuary ceremonies is to perform *tang rang* 'laments', mourning a person's death;
women also sing these songs at marriage ceremonies, and formerly for male and
female initiatory rites. Though Manam women are expected to sing *tang rang,* the
songs are not their exclusive property. Men sing them in the context of their own
gender-exclusive rituals performed in the men's house, and sometimes with women
after the initial round of ritual crying at a funeral.

### Gender, musical genres, and power

Some musical genres and instruments are useful simply for pleasure, but others are
imbued with supernatural power and meaning. Lullabies, songs associated with children's games, and other musical genres have no gendered dimension, but some genres
are associated with relations between the sexes, as when men court women, either in
ensemble (as in the highlands), or individually. A man may serenade his sweetheart
by playing a bamboo flute, or signal a midnight tryst by clicking a small instrument
carved from a canarium nut (Tok Pisin *galip*).

Singsings, important public contexts for mixed singing and dancing, are partly
secular and partly sacred. Clan or village ensembles seek the admiration and envy of
rivals by excelling at singing and dancing, showing off their physical beauty and
prowess. The competitiveness of these events—often performed in association with
competitive exchanges of pigs or other valuables—is implicit in the tension induced
among hosts and guests.

Genres of music and instruments most intimately associated with supernatural
power, thus most sacred, are performed exclusively by men. Formerly, the performance and the instruments were kept secret from women. Men threatened to kill
women who saw a performance or viewed the sacred instruments.

### *The gendered power of musical instruments*

The iconography of kundus may declare the sex of those who play them (figure 5),
but the beliefs and practices surrounding flutes and swung slats are possibly the stark-
est example of the relationship between gender and music in New Guinea, where
strict taboos keep women from performing, or even seeing men perform, certain
instruments.

In Sepik societies, gender and sexuality affect performance on flutes. The
Manam, living on a volcanic island off the mouth of the Sepik River, formerly had a
secret male practice in which initiated men learned to perform bamboo flutes 1.5 to
1.8 meters long. Though men no longer practice secret activities surrounding the
performance of the flutes, men still play flutes in pairs, one flute about a decimeter
longer than the other, producing a lower pitch. The longer flute is said to be male;
the shorter, female. Performance thus involves a couple, with the male flute taking

FIGURE 5    A drum with male sexual traits from
along the Fly River, New Guinea. The Field
Museum, Chicago.

the lead and the female flute (as men enjoy saying) following. Men make the metaphor explicit: describing the behavior of the performers, who stand facing one another, their bodies moving with the rhythm of heavy breathing, men say that a performance is like sexual intercourse (Lutkehaus 1995).

The creation of music with these flutes is a gendered physical activity, producing pleasure for the performers and the audience. It is also a product, the sensual and supernatural sounds of nonhuman beings. Women and children, including uninitiated males, were formerly told that the sound of the flutes came from a birdlike supernatural spirit (Manam *nanaranga*, Tok Pisin *masalai*).

### The mythical validation of gendered power

Many New Guinean societies that associate bamboo flutes with male initiations and secret societies use myths to validate this association. A Manam myth says women discovered the flutes, which only they could play. Their fascination with the flutes led them to neglect their familial duties. When the women's husbands discovered the cause of their wives' neglect, they stole the flutes. But the women, in revenge, told the men they would have to undergo rigorous and painful training to be able to play them. It is this training, and the taboos on food and sex that accompany it, that young male initiates must undergo.

Perhaps the most telling reason some New Guinean men give for restrictions on women and flutes stems from a gendered notion of the division of labor. Men of Wogeo, who share the same flute-origin myth as the Manam, have said "men play flutes, women make babies" (Hogbin 1970). Carrying the analogy of sexual intercourse with flute performance to its logical conclusion, we might say that for men, symbolic intercourse results in the creation of the superhuman voices of spirits, the production of powerfully sacred music; but for women, sexual intercourse results in the creation of a new human voice, the production of a baby.

## Gender and opportunity for musical performance

New Guinean men appear to have formerly had more options for performing music and playing musical instruments than did New Guinean women. With the introduction of new musical instruments and genres—ukuleles, guitars, and Western vocal music, especially church-oriented choral singing—men continue to dominate musical performances.

Village string bands and urban electrified bands, which record music cassettes and videos, are ordinarily all-male ensembles. Some church-based bands are of mixed sex, but few New Guinean bands feature female vocal singers, and fewer still are all-female bands. In many New Guinean societies, men and women sing, but instrumental music has long been predominantly the purview of men, and it remains so.

—NANCY C. LUTKEHAUS

## GENDER, EMBODIMENT, AND MOVEMENT IN FOI SONG

Though Foi men's and women's memorial songs (*sorohabora*) are considered by men and women to be identical, they have markedly different performative, metrical, melodic, and linguistic structures, which emphasize what Foi construe to be gender dichotomy in their world. The structure of men's performances is dominated by couplets, a function of the fact that the songs are sung by a pair of men (*soro ira* 'song tree').

The first line of a male-produced couplet describes an image: an animal trap in the bush, a habitually recited spell or myth, a canoe moving along the river. It identifies a condition of active vitality. The second line offers a contrasting assertion of what has happened to that condition: an abandoned bush track, a spell forgotten and not passed on, a fallen tree. It offers a view of life's finality.

Performing an actual *sorohabora,* three to six *soro ira* sing together. This is the second level of performance, called the song base (*soro ga*). The alternating structure of the *soro ira*'s recital of verses replicates at this level: each pair sings one verse at a time in turn, going from one end of the ensemble to the other and returning to the original pair. After each pair has sung its first verse, the first pair sings its second verse, and so on.

### Men's and women's performances contrasted

While men sing or stand waiting their turn, they bob up and down, bending their knees in time to the music. In one hand, each man holds a bundle of arrows and a bow, or a spear. These they strike against the floor on downbeats. Often, each man begins his line by stamping his heel on the floor to coincide with his first syllable. One or two men in each *soro ga* hold a seed-pod rattle, shaken in the same rhythm as the other percussive accompaniments.

Men's public postures are standing, with the opening up of the chest and upper torso area. In singing, as in oratorical encounters, men use their arms to emphasize their discourse: arms provide the percussive rhythm of the *sorohabora,* and they enact and underline men's speech.

Women's characteristic singing positions are sitting, with an emphasis on closing up the central body and assuming close-in crouches. Women's use of a full-length cape (concealing the entire body except for the face) and a chestcloth emphasizes the public closing-off of the torso. Women's singing and formal wailing occur in a sitting position, with legs bent upward toward the body, as when making sago, or folded underneath, as when sitting cross-legged next to a corpse in the longhouse. Women's positions emphasize stasis, compactness, motionlessness; men's postures emphasize a dynamically charged motion, an openness and potential for vigorous rhythmic expression.

—JAMES F. WEINER

## GENDERED MUSICAL INSULTS OF TIKOPIA

Tikopia dances may separate the sexes. In *mako,* entertaining daytime dances, men dance in front waving paddles, women to the rear with fans, but men and women of one village may dance together against those of another. In unmarried people's night-time activities, girls dance against boys, each party insulting the other by singing gendered musical insults (*tauāngutu* 'mouthwars'). These performances air personal rivalries and heartbreaks, and make general statements about intersexual relationships (Firth 1995).

*Tauāngutu* allow the young of either sex to titillate one another with songs about courtship or sexual behavior. They grant catharsis by allowing insult and challenge, especially from females to males. At their core, they establish stereotypes in the definition of gender-based roles. Such stereotypes in Western society may be developed through the simple crudity of the dirty joke—amazing performance and incongruous conjunction—counterpointed by accepted wisdom of the no-man-wants-a-slice-of-a-cut-cake variety. *Tauāngutu* embody the same dichotomy between desire and reality. Boys criticize girls for promiscuity and rapacious sexual appetite while praising themselves for strength and desirability. Girls celebrate their virginity in the face of boys' importunity and their discrimination in choosing partners. They characterize the boys as immature, sexually greedy, and boastful. Each party slanders the other and praises itself.

The war of words escalates. The boys sing that the girls are wantons who chase them shamelessly. The girls reply that the boys are like motorboats—buzzing around, trying to get into any bay.

The boys may start a dance with a general comment on female behavior:

Te likoliko i fofine fio touongutu.
Tu ki runga o sava moi, karanga
Pe ko ai tou manongi.
Kuou, kuou, kuou.

The circling of girls who like to *tauāngutu*.
Stand up to indicate, call out
Who your sweetheart might be.
Me, me, me.

On the last line, the boys point toward themselves.

The word *likoliko* means 'circle, weave', as eels do in the lake. That the girls move like eels, associated with male lust and rape, comments on the girls' sexual activities. The word *sava* can be glossed 'gesture' or 'indicate', but only men are supposed to *sava*. Therefore, when the boys tell the girls to *sava moi*, normally pronounced *sava mai* 'gesture to us' [see LANGUAGE IN MUSICAL SETTINGS: Sonics: Phonemic play in Oceanic verse], they are suggesting that the girls behave like men, taking the lead in indicating the object of their desire.

The girls may sing back at the boys:

Te viki pure faka-Ravenga
E loliloli ke avongo.
Ku se morumoru ke tou viki pure
Ku fokomorumoru ki ou foi rou.

The little senior men of Ravenga
Are hurrying to marry.
But growing up has not come to the little senior men
From coming to make a score.

The phrase *foi rou*, normally pronounced *fai rau*, can be glossed 'tally', as in counting fish; but it also has the sexual implications of the colloquial English 'score'.

From there, the war of words escalates. The boys sing that the girls are wantons who chase them shamelessly; they ask why the girls take such trouble to choose a white nasal shell, a sign of virginity, since none of them is entitled to wear it. (This is a time-honored insult, as virgins no longer wear such shells.) The girls reply that the boys are like motorboats, buzzing around, trying to get into any bay. Some of the songs are old ones, their composers forgotten; the authors of others are remembered, as are their objects. A rejected lover of either sex can compose a *tauāngutu* of scorn against the deserter and teach it to friends; the text does not name names, but many people may know the story behind it.

*Tauāngutu* are songs of the unmarried, but married people could formerly join in, mothers singing with their sons, fathers with their daughters. This is a nice inversion: the opposite-sex parent joins what is, in effect, the battle of the sexes; however, because some of the songs derogated an individual, rather than the sex generally, and because the individual's identity was usually known, the dance could degenerate into a brawl, as normally happened when a father was present and resented a slur on his daughter's reputation. In the 1960s, to prevent trouble arising from parentally protective feelings, the chiefs forbade adults to join the young at these dances.

Older people say that previously the singing of *tauāngutu* was a game, but that modern musical insults are more personal and bitter. This may well be true, because many of the girls felt badly treated by the boys. Males' migration to plantations elsewhere in the Solomon Islands, where they may marry local girls, has led to a shortage of potential husbands in Tikopia; only one of three girls there will find a husband and acquire the only respectable status possible for a Tikopia female, that of married woman. Young women cannot leave the island alone. If they go abroad with their families, they are discouraged from marrying non-Tikopia. Therefore, unmarried girls' competition for a husband has a ferocity that was probably not seen before labor migrations began.

Unmarried males are flattered by the attention, use the girls ruthlessly, and avoid marriage, at least until they have traveled. *Tauāngutu* often express tensions and stresses that arise from boys' and girls' incongruent desires. In 1980, the songs carried so much venom that the local Anglican priest considered banning them.

—JUDITH MACDONALD

## REFERENCES

Anderson, Gregory D. 1992. "Murlarra: A Clan Song Series of Central Arnhem Land." 3 vols. Ph.D. dissertation, University of Sydney.

Barwick, Linda. 1995. "Unison and 'Disagreement' in a Mixed Women's and Men's Performance (Ellis Collection, Oodnadatta 1966)." In *The Essence of Singing and the Substance of Song: Recent Responses to the Aboriginal Performing Arts and Other Essays in Honour of Catherine Ellis,* ed. Linda Barwick, Allan Marett, and Guy Tunstill, 95–105. Oceania monograph 46. Sydney: University of Sydney.

Bell, Diane. 1983. *Daughters of the Dreaming.* Melbourne, Sydney: McPhee Gribble and Allen & Unwin.

Berndt, Catherine. 1978. "Digging Sticks and Spears, or, the Two-Sex Model." In *We Are Bosses Ourselves: The Status and Role of Aboriginal Women Today,* ed. Fay Gale, 64–84. Canberra: Australian Institute of Aboriginal Studies.

———. 1983. "Mythical Women, Past and Present." In *We Are Bosses Ourselves: The Status and Role of Aboriginal Women Today,* ed. Fay Gale, 13–21. Canberra: Australian Institute of Aboriginal Studies.

Brock, Peggy, ed. 1989. *Women, Rites and Sites.* Sydney: Allen & Unwin.

Dixon, Robert M. W., and Grace Koch. 1996. *Dyirbal Song Poetry.* St. Lucia: University of Queensland Press.

Ellis, Catherine J. 1964. *Aboriginal Music Making: A Study of Central Australian Music.* Adelaide: Libraries Board of South Australia.

———. 1970. "The Role of the Ethnomusicologist in the Study of Andagarinja Women's Ceremonies." *Miscellanea Musicologica: Adelaide Studies in Musicology* 5:76–208.

Ellis, Catherine J., A. Max Ellis, Mona Tur, and Antony McCardell. 1978. "Classification of Sounds in Pitjantjatjara-Speaking Areas." In *Australian Aboriginal Concepts,* ed. Lester R. Hiatt, 68–80. Canberra: Australian Institute of Aboriginal Studies and Humanities Press.

Firth, Raymond. 1995. "Sex and Slander in Tikopia Song: Public Antagonism and Private Intrigue." In *South Pacific Oral Traditions,* ed. Ruth Finnegan and Margaret Orbell, 64–84. Bloomington and Indianapolis: Indiana University Press.

Gale, Fay, ed. 1978. *Woman's Role in Aboriginal Society,* 3rd edition. Canberra: Australian Institute of Aboriginal Studies.

———, ed. 1983. *We Are Bosses Ourselves: The Status and Role of Aboriginal Women Today.*

Canberra: Australian Institute of Aboriginal Studies.

Gummow, Margaret J. 1992. "Aboriginal Songs from the *Bundjalung* and *Gidabal* Areas of South-Eastern Australia." 2 vols. Ph.D. dissertation, University of Sydney.

Hamilton, Annette. 1980. "Dual Social Systems: Technology, Labour, and Women's Secret Rites in the Eastern Western Desert of Australia." *Oceania* 51:4–19.

Hogbin, Ian. 1970. *Island of Menstruating Men.* Scranton, Pennsylvania: Chandler Publishing.

Kaberry, Phyllis. 1939. *Aboriginal Woman: Sacred and Profane.* London: Routledge.

Keen, Ian. 1978. "One Ceremony, One Song: An Economy of Religious Knowledge among the Yolngu of Northeast Arnhem Land." Ph.D. dissertation, Australian National University.

Keogh, Raymond D. 1989. "*Nurlu* Songs from the West Kimberley: An Introduction." *Australian Aboriginal Studies* 1989(1):2–11.

———. 1990. "*Nurlu* Songs of the West Kimberleys." Ph.D. dissertation, University of Sydney.

Lutkehaus, Nancy C. 1995. *Zaria's Fire: Engendered Moments in Manam Ethnography.* Durham, N.C.: Carolina Academic Press.

Magowan, Fiona. 1994. "'The Land Is Our *Märr* (Essence), It Stays Forever': The *Yothu-Yindi* Relationship in Australian Aboriginal Traditional and Popular Musics." In *Ethnicity, Identity and Music: The Musical Construction of Place,* ed. Martin Stokes, 135–155. Oxford and Providence, Rhode Island: Berg.

Marett, Allan, and JoAnne Page. 1995. "Interrelationships between Music and Dance in a *Wangga* from Northwest Australia." In *The Essence of Singing and the Substance of Song: Recent Responses to the Aboriginal Performing Arts and Other Essays in Honour of Catherine Ellis,* ed. Linda Barwick, Allan Marett, and Guy Tunstill, 27–38. Oceania monograph 46. Sydney: University of Sydney.

May, Elizabeth, and Stephen A. Wild. 1967. "Aboriginal Music on the Laverton Reservation, Western Australia." *Ethnomusicology* 11:207–217.

Morais, Megan J. 1995. "Antikirinya Women's Ceremonial Dance Structures: Manifestations of the Dreaming." In *The Essence of Singing and the Substance of Song: Recent Responses to the Aboriginal Performing Arts and Other Essays in Honour of Catherine Ellis,* ed. Linda Barwick,

Allan Marett, and Guy Tunstill, 75–93. Oceania monograph 46. Sydney: University of Sydney.

Moyle, Alice M. 1978. *Aboriginal Sound Instruments.* Australian Institute of Aboriginal Studies AIAS 14. LP disk.

Moyle, Richard M. 1979. *Songs of the Pintupi: Musical Life in a Central Australian Society.* Canberra: Australian Institute of Aboriginal Studies.

———. 1983. "Songs, Ceremonies and Sites: The Agharringa Case." In *Aborigines, Land and Land Rights,* ed. Nicolas Peterson and Marcia Langton, 66–73. Canberra: Australian Institute of Aboriginal Studies.

Moyle, Richard M., with the help of Slippery Morton. 1986. *Alyawarra Music: Songs and Society in a Central Australian Community.* Canberra: Australian Institute of Aboriginal Studies.

Payne, Helen. 1984. "Residency and Ritual Rights." In *Problems and Solutions: Occasional Essays in Musicology Presented to Alice M. Moyle,* ed. Jamie C. Kassler and Jill Stubington, 264–278. Sydney: Hale & Iremonger.

———. 1992. "Matriarchs of Myth." In *The Feminist Companion to Mythology,* ed. C. Larrington, 268–287. London: Harper Collins.

Rose, Deborah B. 1992. *Dingo Makes Us Human: Life and Land in an Australian Aboriginal Culture.* Cambridge, New York, Melbourne: Cambridge University Press.

Strehlow, T. G. H. 1971. *Songs of Central Australia.* Sydney: Angus and Robertson.

von Sturmer, John. 1987. "Aboriginal Singing and Notions of Power." In *Songs of Aboriginal Australia,* ed. Margaret Clunies Ross, Tamsin Donaldson, and Stephen Wild, 63–76. Sydney: University of Sydney.

White, Isobel M. 1975. "Sexual Conquest and Submission in the Myths of Central Australia." In *Australian Aboriginal Mythology,* ed. Lester R. Hiatt, 123–142. Canberra: Australian Institute of Aboriginal Studies.

Wild, Stephen A. 1975. "Walbiri Music and Dance in their Social and Cultural Nexus." Ph.D. dissertation, Indiana University.

———. 1984. "Warlbiri Music and Culture: Meaning in a Central Australian Song Series." In *Problems and Solutions: Occasional Essays in Musicology Presented to Alice M. Moyle,* ed. Jamie C. Kassler and Jill Stubington, 186–203. Sydney: Hale & Iremonger.

# Music and Education

*J. W. Love*  
*Hazel S. Hall*  
*Kenichi Tsukada*  
*Gerald Florian Messner*  
*Peter Russell Crowe*  
*Maria Gaiyabu*  
*Dorothy Sara Lee*

*Paul Vaiinupō Pouesi*  
*Rolf Kuschel*  
*Jane Freeman Moulin*  
*Kauraka Kauraka*  
*Anthony J. Palmer*  
*Randie K. Fong*  
*Allan Thomas*

**Australia**  
**Iatmul**  
**Baluan**  
**Vanuatu**  
**Nauru**  
**Tahiti**  
**Fiji**

**American Sāmoa**  
**Bellona**  
**Tahiti**  
**Cook Islands**  
**Hawai'i**  
**Aotearoa**

Learning the music of one's culture is an important social process. It falls mostly to children, who imitate what they see and hear. Throughout Oceania, schools sponsor events in which children perform for adults' approval. Apart from formal schooling, some Oceanic societies expect children to perform music and dance (figure 1). A European visitor watched such a performance in Tuvalu:

> when all the visitors had arrived, one dusky damsel, with head thrown back, lids half closed, lips parted in a dreamy smile, but teeth tightly closed, began to clap slowly and sing a few words in a high-pitched, nasal, reedy voice; one after another the boys and girls joined in, swaying their bodies dreamily and gracefully, and clapping their hands to mark the time. The whole body of natives behind the stars chimed in lustily too, and several of them banged vigorously with sticks on the rolls of mats, which I now discovered were used as drums, to mark the time more sharply. . . .
>
> The singing was in several parts, making a full, rich, though barbarous harmony; the actions were varied and all graceful, and were changed with lightning rapidity at each change of phrase. It was an excellent drill in fact, perfectly done, and yet these children have no drill or musical instructor—they just watch, listen, and imitate.
>
> It was amusing to see the small children, some of them not more than a year old, with wide-open eyes watching the older ones, and lisping some of the words, while imitating the movements cleverly. Any Funafuti child of four could teach our best Kindergarten children both singing and drill. (David 1899:61–62)

Similarly in Sāmoa, children take over Protestant religious services one Sunday a year, when they stage skits, recite memorized texts, sing, and dance [see MUSIC AND THEATER: The Pacific Islands].

In Aboriginal Australia and parts of New Guinea and Melanesia, musical education includes cultural training and psychological development in initiatory schools, which primarily involve adolescent boys, whom older men remove from their villages and sequester in secluded locations. The boys learn important cultural information,

FIGURE 1    Kiribati children perform at the Pacific Festival of Arts, Port Moresby, Papua New Guinea. Photo by Adrienne L. Kaeppler, 1980.

including restricted musical knowledge, esoteric meanings of myths and lyrics, and how to make and play secret musical instruments. In the Sepik area of New Guinea, restricted knowledge covers the performance and significance of sacred flutes. In Australia, it covers swung slats, which

> symbolize the sky-heroes or totemic ancestors, are carefully looked after, and only shown to those who have been "prepared" to seem them. The sight of them stirs the deepest feelings of reverence. . . . They are usually kept in sacred storehouses, and only handled with the permission of the headmen. No uninitiated person may go near the storehouses. (Elkin 1964:185)

Other music geared to initiations occurs when the boys are brought back into public society, a time often celebrated in singing, dancing, and feasting. Female musical education is less formally organized or celebrated. Many informal songs, by recounting or alluding to people and events, instill in children a sense of their culture's collective past.

Children's forms of expression, including singing and dancing, reflect children's special places in society (Merriam 1964:247). As individuals grow up, they abandon their old songs and learn new ones. Adults may remember songs from their childhood. In response to overhearing performances, they may think of them, or even sing them, but Oceanic societies usually lock adults into styles deemed appropriate for their age. To the extent that children's lack of experience conditions their perception and creativity, their songs may simplify the typical traits of adults' music (Jones 1959; Koizumi 1957). Children's music, however, may have structural peculiarities of its own. Followed over time, a given children's song may show refinements that imply an increasingly simplicity (Love 1991).

### Play as school

Like children around the world, the children of Oceania enjoy games, pastimes, and spontaneous performances. Many of these activities require speaking, singing, and moving, as young minds and bodies learn their culture by playing with it. Many children's games use musically performed counting and other repetitive processes that help children form conceptions of quantity, volume, and space. Such games include juggling (figure 2), often accompanied by singing.

FIGURE 2    Three girls of Tungua, Tonga, perform *hiko,* a vocalized text accompanied by juggling. Photo by Adrienne L. Kaeppler, 1967.

### *Making string figures*

A widespread pastime in Oceania is the making of string figures, known to English-speakers as cat's cradles. The string figures of Oceania belong to a huge family of string-manipulating games that includes those of native Americans (Jayne 1906:xii). In the opening position of examples in this family, a loop of string lying across the dorsal side of each hand crosses the palm between the little finger and the thumb.

The making of many Oceanic figures requires singing, usually by the person or persons manipulating the string. Texts may refer to images suggested in the string. Repeatedly handling string-made images teaches socially important metaphors, reinforcing the cognitive mastery of metaphorical processes. Persons of all ages enjoy making string figures, but acquiring the cultural information encoded in them has a subtle urgency for the young.

Surveys of string figures in Oceania are incomplete, but some distributional patterns are clear. The string figures of related cultures, like the Society Islands and the Marquesas, share typical moves (Handy 1925:5–9). The name for the genre may bespeak an evolutionary relationship, as with cognate terms in Tahitian (*fai*), Hawaiian (*hei*), and Māori (*whai*). Names for identical figures, however, vary widely because the images take on the names of salient topographies, plants, animals, and legendary persons. String figures have been classified as stationary, progressive, sliding, two-party, and three-dimensional figures, each class with examples that require the player to sing (Handy 1925).

Comparative analysis of the educational significance of string-figure imagery remains to be done, and psychosocial implications need to be worked out, but some researchers, most notably Honor Maude, have profitably studied technical features of the game. Inspecting examples that Raymond Firth collected on Tikopia, Maude concluded that the first settlers of that island had brought

> basic Polynesian-type figures, many of which were, however, known throughout most of the Pacific region; that superimposed on those is found an interesting group of Micronesian figures, possibly derived from the Gilbert group (direct, or via the Ellice Islands, where a large percentage of Gilbertese figures are known); while yet a third group apparently came from Melanesia. (1970:7)

The geographical distribution of string figures reflects cultural histories. String figures travel among cultures with more accuracy of reproduction than the spoken and sung elements they may accompany. Their moves and images are interculturally more stable than their words and melodies. In turn, it appears that music, especially as singing incorporates verbal rhythms and meanings, may be more culturally specific than visual modes of perception and cognition.          —J. W. LOVE

## AUSTRALIA

### Children in school

In 1994, the Australian government implemented Creative Nation, a policy that made a commitment to promoting and supporting "cultural industry," tourism, and new technology in the arts, and to assisting emerging artists. Addressing national trends that had emerged in the 1980s, this policy began an era in Australian cultural development.

Before 1991, curricula in music and dance were disparate. Each Australian state had developed its own curriculum, enabling its schools to devise courses in dance and music. In 1991, the federal government, lobbied by the National Affiliation of Arts

Educators (representing the nation's arts associations), officially recognized five arts—music, dance, drama, media, and visual arts—as a Key Learning Area (KLA).

Development of the National Arts Statement and Profiles followed. Profiles are suggested outcomes for each of eight bands (levels of learning), ranging from kindergarten to tenth grade. Within every band, each recognized art has five strands (kinds of thinking): creating, making, presenting; exploring and developing ideas; using skills, techniques, and processes; presenting criticism and aesthetics; and understanding past and present artistic contexts. Allocation of curricular time is the responsibility of individual schools. As the states move toward responding to the statement and profiles, parity of curricular time among the five arts and the eight KLAs remains rare.

### New directions

Eighteen trends have affected education in music and dance.

1. Music and dance are now components of a discipline called the arts.

2. Most scholastic curricula are required to implement a series of cross-curricular frameworks, addressing issues of employment, social justice, national identity, education of Aborigines and Torres Strait Islanders, multiculturalism, and the environment. Curricula in music and dance have been extended and enriched through their inclusion (figure 3).

3. With the national curriculum already crowded, a major concern is adequate allocation of time for each of the recognized arts.

4. Specialist music or performing-arts schools exist in most states, often taking the role of junior conservatories. Some high schools, collaborating with outside institutions, have developed specialist programs in ballet.

5. Music and dance may combine with other arts to form "related" or "integrated" curricula in the arts. This combination is more likely to occur in schools where students have access to the recognized arts.

6. Primary schools often integrate music and dance with other subjects in a holistic curricular approach to learning.

7. Australia is moving toward outcome-based curricula. When the national profiles are fully implemented, educators will regularly map students' progress in music and dance to determine their levels of achievement.

FIGURE 3   NAISDA's Phillip Langley, of Mornington Island, dances in front of Normanton Primary School. Photo by Lee Chittick, 1980.

8. Curricula have a renewed focus on creativity, refined by performance and appraisal.

9. High schools and colleges usually employ at least one specialist teacher of music. More primary schools are seeking specialists in music. Specialists in dance are rare; they may have to teach also in other fields.

10. In many special fields, the therapeutic use of music has created a growing need for music therapists.

11. To attract new students in an atmosphere of school closures (demanded by economic rationalism), schools showcase the arts, possibly overemphasizing the presentational performance of music and dance.

12. Australian schools prefer instrumental music. They favor concert bands (featuring woodwinds, brasses, and percussion) over symphonic orchestras (featuring strings). Instruction in playing strings is less popular because of student preferences, fewer tutors, and budgetary constraints. Of concern is the lack of choral programs, more likely to be developed in elementary and private schools.

13. As a $15 billion-a-year industry, the arts are a powerful twenty-first-century megatrend. The "arts industry" is already shaping the curriculum. It runs the National Rock Eisteddfod, a competitive arena for creative dance, which profoundly affects students' stylistic preferences for education in dance and music. Already bodies such as Arts Training Australia and industry-based courses like those at Southern Cross University at Lismore, New South Wales, are producing a new wave of artists and teachers.

14. Educators in music and dance are liaising more and more with local artists, particularly for professional development and individual tutoring. Artists' organizations provide children's tuition in making music and dancing, as do some major institutions, notably the Canberra School of Music.

15. Many professional associations for music-and-dance education provide or sponsor advocacy, networking, newsletters, publications and resources, history and research, professional development, summer schools, and national conferences. They plan and organize projects and events.

16. Computers have become important tools in developing musical literacy. They serve for exploring, experimenting, and creating, self-paced learning, recording students' work (often replacing handwritten tests), and improving students' performance, as with interactive programs and playback devices.

17. A national drive toward implementation of safe dancing in schools is gathering momentum.

18. Professional artistic associations—notably Ausdance, the Australian Society for Music Education, the Kodaly Music Education Institute of Australia, and the Australian National Council of Orff Schulwerk—provide forums for research through conferences and archives. Major institutions, including the Frank Callaway Institute in Western Australia and the Curriculum Corporation in Melbourne, provide research and archival services.

As a multicultural nation with indigenous music and dance, Australia faces many aural and kinesthetic choices. The National Arts Profiles have provided consistency of outcomes in music-and-dance education, but schools may specialize further, diversifying to develop partnerships with institutions, industry, and everyday communities.

## Children at play

Children's music in Australia includes the musical rhymes, recitations, and songs that belong to the private world of children's play. These are intoned at varying levels between speech and song. The mode of intonation, number of participants, kind of text, and nature of activities are integral to the performance.

Children mimic adults. Young people borrow musical material and texts from adults, manipulating it, parodying it, and ultimately claiming ownership of it. They may borrow whole texts or melodies, or they may combine fragments to produce new creations. From playground rhymes and songs, they learn the basic elements of verbal, aural, and kinesthetic arts that characterize the culture from which they spring. Australian society of the late 1990s provides a rich and diverse source of cross-cultural material.

Interest in the musical traits of Australian children's play has been stimulated by social and linguistic studies (Davey and Factor 1980; Lowenstein 1960; Turner 1969). Researchers into Australian children's music have included M. Brunton (1976), Cheryl Romet (1980), and Hazel Hall (1984, 1988, 1993). Margaret Kartomi (1980) has explored Aboriginal children's lore. Kathryn Marsh (1995) has been working in multicultural lore.

### Traits of Australian children's lore

Beginning in the early 1980s, I have studied the playground music of primary-school children in Melbourne, Victoria. My study and others show that Australian children's lore has at least ten musical traits.

1. *Diverse modes of intonation.* Children use a continuum of intonational styles within two basic forms of spoken intonation (with unstable pitches) and one form of sung intonation (with stable pitches).

2. *Repeated tones.* Certain tones occur more frequently than others and often repeat consecutively. Repeated tones are likeliest to correspond with the first or fifth degree of the major scale. More than half the songs I recorded contain repeated tones in the first bar. The commonest form of tonal repetition was tonic hammering, reiteration of the tonic.

3. *Vocal and choral traits.* In choral recitations, pitches are more stable and intonation tends more toward singing than in solo recitations.

4. *Childlike rhythms.* In South Australia (Brunton 1976), children use six fundamental rhythmic patterns, all of which can be adapted, varied, syncopated, and made into composites.

5. *Childlike motifs and melodic formulas.* Researchers of Australian children's play have identified a specific melodic formula of three notes (*sol–la–mi*; or in C major, G–A–E). My study shows that this is most likely to emerge if the rhyme is used for skipping (and is therefore performed by girls), scanned in trochaic tetrameter (transcribable as four pairs of eighths, with stress on the first of each pair), and performed chorally, rather than soloistically.

6. *A narrow melodic range.* Children's melodies usually employ three to six tones of a major scale.

7. *A tendency to parody.* I identified four categories of parody: popular songs and advertising jingles, folk songs, songs for special occasions (like Christmas carols), and nursery rhymes. In youthful exploration, children discover that twisted language and music make humorous creations.

8. *Diverse thematic material.* More popular themes include make-believe and fantasy (especially heroes and heroines in stories, cartoons, and media), reinforcement of common gender roles, poking fun at images representing authority (schools, teachers, parents, police), indelicate lyrics (exploring children's curiosity about bodily and sexual functions), and nonsense rhymes.

9. *Diverse kinetic formulas.* Australian children from varied ethnic backgrounds

tend to transmit kinetic formulas more readily than textual formulas (Marsh 1995), as do their American counterparts.

10. *Various rhetorical devices.* Australian children use verbal patterns similar to those of adult rhetoric. These patterns are often emphasized by musical rhetoric, notes or phrases whose repetition underlines the text. Common rhetorical devices in children's lore are repetition of sounds (assonance, alliteration, onomatopoeia, rhyme) and structures (words, phrases, lines, stanzas). Concatenations consist of tags (verbal codas), series (lists of texts and numbers), and floating melodies and texts (items appended without relevance to the original melody or text). The following text illustrates some of these devices.

> Under the bamboo, [original rhyme]
> Under the tree, *cha-cha-chá.* [tag]
> True love for me, my darling,
> True love for me, *cha-cha-chá.* [tag]
> When we get married, we'll raise a family [rhyme]
> Of sixty thousand children in a [formula that links floating text]
> Row, row, row your boat [floating text]
> Gently down the stream. [floating text]
> Chuck your teacher overboard
> And listen to her scream: [rhyme]
> Aaaaaaaaah! [tag]

Through playground music, children develop skills and knowledge in important areas of sensory communication. Through the exploration of verbal, aural, visual, kinesthetic, and tactile ways of thinking and knowing, they approach an understanding of themselves, their schoolyard society, their culture, and the world at large.

—HAZEL S. HALL

## IATMUL

Iatmul people of all ages recognize three kinds of polyphonic children's songs. The most innovative are taught in school. Their texts are in English. Their harmonies evoke the tonic, dominant, and subdominant functions of standard tonality. Children learn songs of another kind from schoolteachers and other adults. Their texts are in Tok Pisin, and their tonal structures are diverse. Songs of the third kind have texts in the local language (*tok ples* 'place talk'). Their meters are triple. Their scales are transcribable as the triad C–E–G, with a D sounded only in passing. An example performed by one child in 1978 (figure 4) stresses the rhyming syllables *nya, kwa, da, ya, la,* and *wa.*

Iatmul songs of scarification (*kisim pukpuk* 'getting crocodiles') mark a transition from childhood to adulthood. Men sing these songs for initiatory procedures in which boys undergo scarification on their backs and chests, receiving marks that symbolize the skin of crocodiles (Bateson 1932:435–437, 1958:77). One such song reiterates the harmony of a major third, as do other initiatory songs. The tonalities of Iatmul children's local-language songs and songs of scarification resemble those of fanfare melodies of Irian Jaya and elsewhere (Kunst 1967:102–103), including melodies of the Bunun, aboriginal inhabitants of Taiwan (Kurosawa 1952).

FIGURE 4 A melody performed by a Iatmul child in 1978 shows the typical children's scale C–E–G, with a D sounded only in passing. Transcription by Kenichi Tsukada.

Kn din nya    n na kwa    la lin da    a me ya    lo ngo la    vo da na wa

From their earliest days, Baluan children hear musical performances. Relatives formally teach them the rules and techniques of singing and instrumental playing.

Iatmul adults traditionally sing monophonically. Their melodies, first recorded in 1912, move in small steps over a narrow range (Christensen 1963), usually defined by three tones in any of three sets, transcribable as E–F–G, D–E–F, and C–D–E. A melody of the song "tʃagi" exemplifies the second set (Tsukada 1983:90:1b); a melody transcribed by Richard Thurnwald exemplifies an elaboration of the third (Schneider 1969: example 60). The middle tone of each set tends to be the tonal center.

Iatmul children's triad-based songs and Iatmul adults' three-tone songs may echo melodies played on aerophones. At boys' initiations, men play sacred flutes (*wavi* 'birds'), whose sounds they regard as ancestral voices. Two flutists, facing each other, play in a fast tempo (Yamada 1982). The flutes are tuned to tones slightly less than a tempered major second apart—an interval rooted in local aesthetics (Spearritt 1974:107, 1976:400). By sounding partials four, five, and six, each flute provides tones approximating a major triad and combining in a scale transcribable as C–D–E–F♯–G–A.

Playing paired flutes tuned a second apart provides an opportunity to hear triad-based tonal structures and other three-tone scalar structures (Spearritt 1982). By a possibly analogous process in Africa, the same triadic scale may derive from two fundamentals and their partials, sounded by Faŋ performers on a musical bow (Kubik 1968). The derivation of vocal tonality from the acoustical properties of musical instruments has been an important analytical issue since Erich M. von Hornbostel addressed it (1912). An unanswered question is how Iatmul children could base their music on sounds heard mainly by adults and adolescent boys in the seclusion of initiatory schools.

—KENICHI TSUKADA

**BALUAN**

On Baluan, musical education occurs in two ways: first, from the earliest days, children hear musical performances; second, under strict guidance, relatives formally teach children the rules and techniques of singing and instrumental playing.

To a baby or a small child, relatives sing lullabies, rhymes whose stanzaic structures match the main patterns of local drumming on garamuts. Performing the poetry ensures the proper development of children's reproductive organs. While reciting, a singer may stretch a baby boy's penis to provide the adult man with a large one, or massage a baby girl's vagina to provide the adult woman with a relaxed posture and a strong, fetus-nourishing womb. A typical text makes the action clear:

| | |
|---|---|
| Nanat puyoi parun kanum: | A stone broke at the garden's *parun:* |
| Selpong parun kalalou, | It broke the *parun* of food, |
| Parun kalalou ran pul. | *Parun* of the food of the moon. |
| Pul palan mat pala kareu. | The moon's penis is bruised. |
| Yekyek tan kapuen tau. | Rub the penis for a big man. |

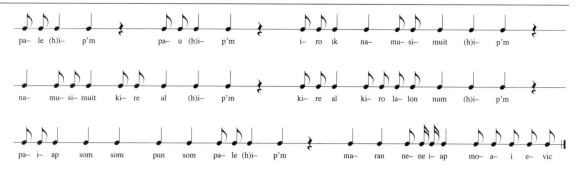

pa— le (h)i— p'm          pa— u (h)i— p'm          i— ro ik na— mu—si— muit (h)i— p'm

na— mu—si—muit ki— re al (h)i— p'm          ki— re al ki— ro la— lon num (h)i— p'm

pa— i— ap som som pun som pa— le (h)i— p'm          ma— ran ne— ne i— ap mo— a— i e— vic

Another text (figure 5) remains metaphorical: "This is a shell: / Pull it; / Play with it. / This is good play. / It stays in its house. / Paiap with his turtle takes a shell; / Its eye looks stronger at him." Adults recite such lullabies with a soft, smooth voice at a comfortable pitch, inflecting the ends of verses a fourth downward. The texts often encode metaphors and symbols whose sexual connotations embarrass Westernized adults. Children easily memorize the texts, which they perform happily. Stressing rhythms more than adults, they improvise, using one melodic pattern for old and new texts. They recite most texts on a single tone, preceded by a pickup of a major second or minor third.

Baluan children's games and tales show common archetypal features. The protagonists are native birds, fish, lizards, pigs, and crocodiles. Narrative songs have four tones and a single melodic model. By the 1970s, as government-sponsored schooling pigeonholed curricular subjects into classes and grades, games and tales had become relics of a holistic system of education.          —GERALD FLORIAN MESSNER

## VANUATU

Learning music and dance entails memories of things heard, seen, and felt; but in oral traditions, it has a particular character. Enculturation starts in the womb, and the motherliness of the familial world is impressed on newborn infants. As a child grows, its memory records experiences, but only according to subconsciously expanding codes, which include myriad sonorous and gestural details.

It is hard to record or memorize experiences that do not fit into patterns, so the acquisition of music, dance, and language may run analogously and in parallel, and the power of memory shown by many in Vanuatu may directly relate to oral and visual means of transmission, flowing with little impediment. School interferes with these processes, introducing reliance on mechanical means of recording information, via books, tapes, photos, and films.

This process has been illustrated among adults. At Vuingalato (North Central Ambae), I recorded local histories. For an hour, a committee of old men checked one story minutely, recalled the integrated songs, and added verses. The chosen reciter then retold the story and sang the songs, all to the committee's satisfaction. The telling took ten minutes in the vernacular, and again in Bislama, the local pidgin. On transcription, the telling and details of each repeated version proved equivalent. Local power of recall is often near-total, so that hearing a song and its text once may be enough to fix it. The same process can apply to a dance or a speech. The Vuingalato committee was happy to have good versions of their histories on tape, as school did not teach them and they doubted their children's ability to memorize.

Imitation is said to be the way of learning, but this begs questions as to what imitation in fact consists of—how to imitate a hidden code. On Maewo, children improvise in the morning in the *bolo Ambae* form while their parents sleep after having danced it all night. On Ambae, children conduct games of killing pigs, in which pieces of banana trunk serve as pigs, exposed roots of nearby shrubs are beaten as if log idiophones, and children venture inside the ring to make speeches, playing through whole rites and social grades. Raga and East Ambae boys learn log-idiophone rhythms by sitting beside an expert drummer and imitating him with sticks on the ground. When a boy is seen to be correct, he will be invited to try the real thing, but he should make small payments for the chance to acquire such skills.

At Saranabuga (West Ambae), a method of teaching log-idiophone rhythms was devised by the late Samuel Lengge, who with the fingers of both hands on a bamboo pillow or hand-held instrument tapped skeletal versions of the ensemble items, five idiophones in three parts: bass, tenor, and three trebles. Apprentice players learn the gestalts of the items like that, and in full rehearsals are expected to discern their parts within the whole. As codes, Vanuatu custom-oriented men hold savvy systems, comparable to expert systems in computerese.

Children learn dances in their totality. They do not usually find the movements hard, either to do or to memorize: their problem is more often in songs and texts, especially when their sequence lasts several hours. In rehearsal, participants may spend just as much time on selecting appropriate songs for dancing as in ensuring that everybody grasps them, because when sung chorally, the words may be unclear.

—PETER RUSSELL CROWE

## NAURU

In Nauru, music begins with lullabies for babies, like *Mimiy ko, mimiy ko, Lachalan, / Bwe ngam orre bita atsinogaga me kamiduw. / Mimiy ko* 'Go to sleep, go to sleep, Lachalan, / For the monster will come and bite you. / Go to sleep'. Adults sometimes change "the monster" to another animal, such as a cat.

Some chants (*iruwo*) for children are playful, and usually begin slowly and repeat, the tempo increasing. Children respond by laughing, clapping, and moving. One lullaby praises fat, a sign of beauty:

| | |
|---|---|
| Ouwak nanan, ouwak nanan, | Big legs, big legs, |
| Ouwak an deidi, ngea ean o, ean o. | Big bottom, the girl O, the girl O. |
| Enimon kabur, kabur, | She washes, washes, |
| Enimon kabur, kabur, kabur raid. | She washes, washes, washes rice. |
| Ouwak nanan, ouwak nanan, | Big legs, big legs, |
| Ouwak an deidi. | Big bottom. |

Another favorite is for gesturing: *Le, le, le; bum, bum, bum. / Le, le, le; bum, bum, bum. / Letsa bum, letsa bum. / Bum, bum, bum.* An adult moves a child's hands while others join in.

A chant used for teasing goes: *Edugiago, Edugiago, eken ngea, eken ngea. / Babaiya, babaiya, babat doromeren.* An adult sings this while twinkling the baby's fingers and swaying its body. Sometimes adults use it to tease older children about their carelessness, anger, silliness, or stubbornness; it annoys some, but makes others burst into laughter. Women formerly used it to provoke each other when competitively playing ball games: they made faces and cavorted with hands on hips, implying that their opponents were "as soft as watermelon."

First birthdays are big events, which require extensive preparations. Some parents start preparing as soon as their baby is born. More than a hundred people may attend. Often the party begins on the eve of the birthday, when relatives and friends shower the child with gifts and good wishes. Men and women, young and old, with guitars and ukuleles, sing songs. They pass the child around and dress it in expensive garments, decorated with money and beads. They place the child on a mat, piled with colorful textiles, towels, pillows, clothing, toys, and a cake. Specially composed songs express beauty, admiration, and goodwill. To giftgivers, the child's family gives baskets or dishes of food. Children dance hulas and disco, and everyone present eats and drinks. A famous song tells the child to wake up and "Listen to the beauty and goodness / Of songs that are sweet and melodious."

## Schoolchildren

Children come home from preschool (five years) singing songs such as "Humpty Dumpty," "Twinkle, Twinkle, Little Star," and "Baa, Baa, Black Sheep," or this song: *Ongadan Nauru; ongadan Nauru. / Kania ino; kania ino. / Aei, aei; aei, aei. / Duduat ebok; duduat ebok!* 'Nauru's burning; Nauru's burning. / Look yonder; look yonder. / Fire, fire; fire, fire. / Pour on water; pour on water!' Older sisters, brothers, and adults sometimes join in. The commotion may turn competitive, as each tries to impress the other with songs. When a child runs out of songs to sing, it usually gets upset.

Nauruan children ages five to eleven entertain themselves with song-games, performed seated. Each song has unique movements. Singing in English or Nauruan, children rhythmically clap and tap each other's hands, laps, shoulders, and other parts. Favorites include "A Rubber Dolly": "My mother told me / That she will buy me a rubber dolly. / If I was good, good, good. / But when I told her that I kissed a soldier, / She wouldn't buy me / A rubber D-O-L-L-Y." One song consists of nonsense: *Eamo, eamo ekeramwan. / Eamo, eamo ekeramwan. / Bwi yegen bwe te gugure. / Bwi yegen bwe te gugure. / Tsan ta rian tsan, tsan ta rian tsan. / Tsan ta rian; tsan, tsan, tsan. / Tsan ta rian; tsan, tsan, tsan.* Children teach each other this song and its actions, which require skill and coordination.

At school, Nauruan children learn songs about history, legends, love, and patriotism. A song that children like to act out is based on the legend of Arere:

| | |
|---|---|
| Tsimine engame ion Arere egen, | There was a man named Arere, |
| Tsimine bet aget Eworowin. | With wife named Eworowin. |
| Ar emeg epoa atai eoning | They lived with ten children |
| Ian ebeben Naeoro oque. | On the island of Nauru. |
| | |
| Nuwawen Arere bwe enim tuwon oka. | Arere went fishing. |
| Me eoning rerir akora, | The children dug up white crabs, |
| Ngaga eita inora oreita | While their parents looked |
| Kanani ara komoraro. | And gathered food for them. |
| | |
| Rodut Eomakwan adun apoe | Along came Eomakwan from inland |
| Bwe nim tuwin kongang eoning. | To ask for a child. |
| Ngaga eita inora eo oiya, | When their mother refused, |
| Egirowedut Eomakwan. | Eomakwan got angry. |
| | |
| Ngaga Eomakwan oren abi | As Eomakwan was about to kill |
| Eita Eworowin me eoning, | Eworowin and her children, |
| Arere tomidaten toborogu. | Arere threw his club at him. |
| Pudu Eomokwan me eman. | Eomakwan fell and died. |

Teachers accompany such songs by playing guitar, ukulele, or portable electric organ, but normally use recorded music to teach songs. Brass-band instruments are taught mostly in secondary school.

In the 1960s and 1970s, teenage girls and boys drove around the island at night, singing songs of fun and courtship. By the 1980s, teenagers were preferring to drive in all-terrain sports vehicles, with loudspeakers blaring the music of recorded songs.

Every Nauruan household has electrical stereo equipment, cassettes, and compact discs. For countless hours, some people, especially men, listen to popular music. On weekends, playing recorded music over loudspeakers draws crowds. People stop to listen and admire the beat. Children join in the fun: some watch passively; others sing and dance. Sometimes, in a battle-of-sound competition, people blast music from the loudspeakers.

### Holidays and major events

Families celebrate holidays together. Some attend several functions, indulging in food and fun. Children entertain adults by singing Christmas carols; older boys flaunt their new recordings on cassettes or compact discs. New Year's is another big celebration. After church at midnight, some families enjoy a feast, exchanges of gifts, and children's improvised dancing. Kiribati, Tuvalu, and Solomon organizations go from house to house, singing and wishing a happy new year. Some perform elegant cultural dances. A new-year song known to every adult and child is a Nauruanized version of "The Birthday Song": *Hapi Nu Ya to you. / Hapi Nu Ya to you. / Hapi Nu Ya, Hapi Nu Ya. / Hapi Nu Ya to you.* It is also sung in Kiribati: *Ekam te maure kamie. / Ekam te maure kamie. / Ekam te maure, ekam te maure. / Ekam te maure kamie.*

For concert performances, children learn songs and dances of local Asian Indians, Filipinos, Kiribati, Tuvaluans, and others, from whom teachers request aid. Schools stage nighttime concerts, which children open by singing the national anthem. A priest or pastor says a prayer. Then, dressed in colorful costumes, children perform music and dances from cultures overseas.

At the Pacific Festival of Arts in 1985 and 1988, sixth-graders at the Nauru Primary School presented the frigate bird (*iti*), a Nauruan dance. The students practiced daily for two months. The boys clapped and sang while the girls danced, portraying the birds' flying and perching:

> Ema reko, ngamie dangoma, bwam aiae iti ya ro aoeta
> Ma ye rawedu animat tea ni Baitsi.
> Ekania ko dabugura ya ro meiy adun ituga owesake.
> Kabeiy kabeiy kor dabugura me ya renim eow eat engora.
> Kwokwon ko me ibwa me wo eab gona.
> Keyeya, gonaen inga? Weden ngage koko pe!

> Come, our friends, and see the frigate birds flying
> And landing on the roosts in Baitsi.
> Look how beautiful as they scoop down from above.
> Just imagine how beautiful as they land onto their perch.
> You try and catch them, but you won't be able to.
> It's hard, so what will you do? Go and eat stone!

In 1994, at the Children's Convention in Fukuoka, Japan, ten eleven-year-old boys and girls from Nauru performed the *dogoropa,* a dance with sticks, which men and women from Nauru had performed at the Festival of Arts in 1980.

Independence Day (31 January), Constitution Day (17 May), Nauru Phosphate Corporation Hand-Over Day (1 July), and Angam Day (26 October) are festivals. On Constitution Day, district teams of children and teenagers participate in track meets. Each team has its own songs, encouraging itself and teasing opponents. Winners and their supporters circle the island celebrating their superiority. Adults in cars and on motorbikes, and children in buses, shout songs that humiliate the losers.

At school assemblies and other important events, children and adults sing the national anthem:

Nauru bwiema, ngabena ama auwe.

Ama detaro bwe dogum.

Ama otota bet egom.

Atsin ngago bwien akor ama bagadugu.

Epoa ngabuna re nan orre bet imur,

Ama memag ma nan epodan eredu wam engiden

Me iyan aema ngeyin ouge, "Nauru eko dogi."


We love Nauru, our homeland.

We'll pray for you.

We'll praise your name.

Long ago lived our ancestors and forefathers.

And for those who are yet to come,

We will all together respect your flag

In our saying, "Nauru forever."

—MARIA GAIYABU


## FIJI

*Vakawelegone* are songs, amusements, and diversions performed for Fijian children. They have two subclasses: *vakamocegone,* similar in intent to lullabies; and *vakawelegone* proper, including songs, rhymes, and nonsense verses associated with counting and juggling games (*meke ni moli*), the making of string figures (*meke ni ciuciu*), hand games, and games of elimination. Adults or older siblings perform *vakawelegone* to entertain their charges while babysitting at home, but spontaneous performances occur when relatives and friends must subdue rambunctious children at informal gatherings.

All *vakawelegone* involve rhythmic movements, which vary from a simple up-down rocking motion to the complex strategic interactions of formal games. Some games, including *karikari bilo* 'scrape the coconut' and *tukituki, Senimulomulo, Seniyatayata* 'pound it, Senimulomulo, Seniyatayata', mimic the activities of everyday life. Others involve random gestures likely to appeal to children. Adults sometimes abstract the basic rhythmic patterns from *vakawelegone* for play with small children, or add pitched vocables and simple hand-and-body movements to carry the rhythm along.

Texts have a basic structure. The first lines, setting up a basic rhythmic pattern, identify the text and main characters. Then follow one or more episodic lines, evoking images familiar to children: a dove calling nearby, the fire of a playful goddess, two brothers tending a great chief's garden soon destroyed by a hurricane, a grand octopus dance. Closing patterns range from formulaic expressions to the recitation of the first ten cardinal numbers. Texts last from two lines to more than forty, and often have several rhymes. Most *vakawelegone* are known by their first lines; some, by the game they accompany. Their lengths adjust to listeners' moods, player's skills, and singer's memories.

In most *vakawelegone,* the narrating voice is that of an adult, often a grandmother. Urban parents often send children to grandparents in a village to be raised and instructed in customary ways. Even when several generations reside in the village, grandmothers often babysit while parents farm and fish. In *vakawelegone* texts, core verses typically begin with the guardian's trying to comfort a distressed child by conjuring up the image of parents engaged in some familiar food-gathering activity so the child can have a treat. Any kind of subsistence activity can be substituted.

Many texts refer to a vaguely remembered past—obsolete counting systems, old political alliances, ancient roads, deities supplanted by Christianity. *Vakawelegone* are filled with supernatural beings, legendary human ancestors, and the animal lords of the kingdoms of ducks, fish, and land-dwelling mammals. They feature wordplay.

By example and ridicule, *vakawelegone* provide behavioral lessons for children. Grandmothers' voices mock sullen, uncooperative, crying children, comparing their behavior unfavorably with that of unruly animals. In the following *vakamocegone,* the petulant child Ququ, whose name connotes the image of a child being dragged along in the tight clasp (*ququ*) of its grandmother, parallels its mother's actions, dragging (*ququ*) the sand of the reef in search of food.

| | |
|---|---|
| Wawa, wawa, Bui kei Ququ. | Wait, wait, Granny and Ququ. |
| Tinamu a se lai a ququ. | Your mother has gone dredging. |
| Ia, ia cerea mati ruku. | The reef is exposed by low tide. |
| Tale vale va ruburubu, | Go home and be sullen, |
| Matana tu ki na vuniduru. | And turn your face to the corner. |
| Rubu tu, rubu tu, | Stand sullen, stand sullen, |
| Rubu tu, rubu tu. | Stand sullen, stand sullen. |

Since *vakawelegone* have no known or acknowledged composers, each has variant texts, sometimes imported through marriage, as wives bring new texts with them to pass on to their children. Most textual differences occur in sequence of episodes, or in the names of people and places. Differences in dialect may account for other variants.

## Vakawelegone proper

*Vakawelegone* proper are gently physical games and amusements, enacted to the accompaniment of sung or (more often) spoken humorous, rhythmic verses. They help babysitters keep babies and children occupied and quiet. They can be performed by individuals of all ages, but parents and grandparents usually perform the most.

The verses are usually in duple meter, performed with as much speed as memory and skill allow. The simplest are games of touch and tests of dexterity, involving tickling, stroking, pinching, tapping, or grabbing. In the following, the leader and the charges sit facing one another, with hands palms up on the mat in front of them. The performer counts off to eliminate one of the players. At the end of the verse, the losing player blows on or licks the eliminated hand and tucks it under one leg: *Karikari bilo, / Karikari bilo, / Se ni qomoqomo, / Tu mai, tacitaci Roma* 'Scrape the coconut cup, / Scrape the coconut cup, / Qomoqomo Flower, / Stand up, Roma's little brother'. Then the leader advances a hand toward the hand of one of the children, and pinching it sharply, says: *Meu la' ki mada, me'u la'ki mada, / Vaka rai qairi ki vei tiri* 'Just let me go, just let me go, / To look at the crab among the mangroves'. Still pinching the top part of the child's hand, the leader thumps it with the free hand, gesturing as if listening to the resulting sound, and says: *O! Sa dua na qari matua: / Me kedra na turaga* 'Oh! A mature (fleshy) crab: / That's the chief's food'. Folding the captive hand into a fist, the leader puts it back on the mat, picks up the other hand, and says: *O! Sa dua na qari lala: / Me kedra na marama* 'Oh! An empty crab: / That's the woman's food'. The leader places the second hand on top of the first, and repeats the sequence with the other players, piling the fists up, one on top of the other, until the winner emerges.

*Meke ni moli* are games of juggling citrus fruits. The juggler's skill is measured against the length and speed of the verse, whose sense may be silly or whimsical.

| | |
|---|---|
| Tutu na ivi teitei | Standing in the chestnut plantation, |
| Lololoma bale ki Vei | Send love to Vei |
| Baleta na sala ko Vugalei. | Along the road to Vugalei. |
| Da tu lia, da raicia. | Just stand up and look around. |
| Da raica ra, luve ni Gasau: | Look at them, the children of Gasau. |
| Da vakaseru, da vakasau. | They are combing their hair, behaving like chiefs. |
| Da mai tutu ko Viti Lau, | They are chiefs in eastern Fiji, |
| Tu na Viti Levu. | Standing in Viti Levu. |
| Gau na yatemu. | Your liver is mine to eat. |
| Tava na vonu, kau ni Bau. | Roast the turtle, take it to Bau. |
| Kau muri rau ko Suvalau. | Follow them to Suvalau. |
| Sucu mai na gone, gone damudamu. | A child is born here, a fair child. |
| Vakatokatoka e vei na yacana? | After whom will the child be named? |
| Lele Soqiri, lele Soqara. | Go to Soqiri, go to Soqara. |
| Tukituki toka na koro ni Waqa. | There is hammering in Waqa's village. |
| Waqa ki cei vaka votu laca? | Whose sail is so strongly worked on? |
| Laca ka Toro ni Salialevu. | Toro's sail for Selialevu. |
| Sesekoto cakau levu, | They missed the landing at the big reef, |
| Batinitabua ko na Viti Levu, | At Batinitabua in Viti Levu. |
| Tara se au, ua levu. | I reached there before high tide. |
| Ua levu kakaba na saro: | High tide at Kaba, the crabs start to climb: |
| I vei tiri, i vei dogo, | All over the mangroves, all over the fruit, |
| I vei vaka vutu lakolako. | All over the *vutu* trees they go. |
| Ka koto moli titeqe. | Walking on tiptoe, |
| Sucu a teqe, tara o teqe. | Hit a young one, catch another. |
| Dua, rua, talu, va, | One, two, three, four, |
| Lima, ono, vitu, walu, | Five, six, seven, eight, |
| Ciwa, tini! | Nine, ten! |

This looks like a random mixture of unrelated scenes, but the text strings together several episodes: the chestnut plantation, the children of Gasau, the turtle, the birth of the fair child, Toro's sail, the reef at high tide, the crabs, and the numbers from one to ten.

### Vakamocegone

*Vakamocegone* are the songs that ease children into sleep and the up-and-down rocking motion that characterizes it; merely on hearing the word, older women may begin to rock. *Vakamocegone* are also called *meke ni gone* 'choreographed verse for children' and *meke ni bui ni gone* 'granny songs'. Grandmother imagery is integral to the genre, for grandmothers do most of the performing. Many texts feature a grandmother, who comforts and distracts a child with images of food and fantasy. In performance, younger performers try to achieve the vocal quality of a genuine *bui ni gone* 'grandmother with small children in tow': distant, hollow, toothless, deep, scratchy, with the voice fading into a whisper at the ends of verses.

*Vakamocegone* are shorter than *vakawelegone* proper, but share some basic features. Longer ones episodically embrace many of the fabled creatures and events as juggling games and other diversions of the broader genre. Sung *vakamocegone* tend toward triple meter, but a single melody can be adapted to different texts and meters.

—Dorothy Sara Lee

## AMERICAN SĀMOA

Public schools in American Sāmoa are under the supervision of the Department of Education. Implementing the goals outlined by the U.S. National Standards for

Two to eight Bellonese children usually play together. Besides affording the excitement of social activity, the games foster three classical components of psychological development: forming cognitive awareness, improving motoric skills, and controlling fear.

Music Education, the department expects by 2001 to have hired qualified teachers from abroad and to have purchased band instruments for all schools. For teachers at all levels of schooling, the Division of Curriculum Instruction conducts summer workshops, which review curricular guidelines and ensure that teachers acquire the methods and skills necessary to teach theory, choir, and band. In public schools, principals and music teachers set aside time for students to practice for major public events, including Sāmoan Flag Day, whose activities feature competitions in singing and dancing, and performances sponsored by the drug-free program under the Department of Education and the Arts Council of American Sāmoa.

### Elementary schools (grades K–8)

American Sāmoa has nineteen elementary schools in Tutuila and three in Manu'a. Educational goals specified in the elementary curriculum are adapted from the National Music Education Guidelines. Elementary beginning band was introduced into the curriculum starting with Alofau Elementary School in December 1995, and it made its first public TV performance for the Christmas program organized by the Arts Council. In 1996, special two-week workshops were arranged for guidance from experts from the University of Southern California.

All public elementary schools in American Sāmoa have one or two teachers with no formal training who can play an instrument, usually guitar or ukulele. Some schools have teachers who work as church organists. The basic methods of teaching utilize singing and dancing Sāmoan and other music (accompanied on tape or cassette), listening, reading, creating, playing instruments, and practicing rhythms and movements.

### Secondary schools (grades 9–12) and other schools

American Sāmoa has six public high schools: five on Tutuila and one in Manu'a. Individual instruction is given in voice and band instruments, concert choir, jazz or swing choir for advanced singers, intermediate band, advanced band, and music theory, building on basic theory, introduced at the elementary level. In 1997, four high schools have Sāmoan teachers who hold bachelor's degrees in music. Through these teachers' efforts in the mid-1990s, school-based choirs underwent important improvements. Most schools lack band instruments and full-time band directors.

American Sāmoa has private elementary and secondary schools, sponsored by the Roman Catholic, Baptist, and Congregational churches. Lacking specialists in music, these schools have no written curriculum in music. The students participate in special events, performing in Flag Day activities and presenting Christmas programs. Sāmoan dances are taught by teachers who have that skill; choirs are directed by those who are organists in village churches.

American Sāmoa Community College offers the degree of associate in arts; students may major in music to pursue a bachelor's or master's degree abroad. From the

United States, the college hires graduate-degree-holding teachers, usually on short-term contracts. Courses offered in 1998 include music theory, music literature, concert and swing choir, jazz ensemble, and private instruction in piano and voice.

—Paul Vaiinupō Pouesi

## BELLONA

Two to eight Bellonese children usually play together, sometimes joined by an adult caretaker. Residential patterns and fear of enemies or malevolent supernaturals impede the interactions of children of different households. Only during periods of feasting do large groups of children meet.

Children's music is more vocally centered than adults' music, for children do not use struck plaques. Like adults, they have songs accompanied by clapping, with hands cupped or flat. Children usually imitate other children; but teenagers, mothers, and other females sometimes teach smaller children.

### The psychology of children's singing

Of twenty-eight recorded children's games, nine involve singing (Kuschel 1975). Besides affording the excitement of social activity, the games foster three classical components of psychological development: forming cognitive awareness, improving motoric skills, and controlling fear.

#### Forming cognitive awareness

Cognitive awareness includes a capacity for understanding numerical concepts. Bellonese children about three and four years old learned to count in a game where a child repeated the numbers after an adult, who at the end of the counting touched and tickled the child. This game (*te taunga babange a Sikingimoemoe* 'Sikingimoe-moe's counting game') was mostly a play with words, and the adult counted only to three before the tickling began. Afterward, children would run around repeating *tasi, ngua, tongu* 'one, two, three' and burst into laughter. This practice differs from other numerical rhymes of Polynesia, where a more realistic, matter-of-fact counting occurred.

The creating of new string figures (figure 6) was an appreciated cognitive challenge. Several Bellonese figures were three-dimensional. Some required players to get the whole figure, or parts of it, to move. To remember the structures of string figures demanded concentration and elaborate cognitive skills. Sometimes a child or several children tried to develop a new figure; those who succeeded became heroes of the day.

#### Improving motoric skills

Among games developing motoric skills were those known as *tanimalenge* 'bite the yam', *ha'uha'u kongoa* 'wind the loincloth', *hetau'aki o ngigho* 'encircle fish', *baa'aki* 'riding horseback (being carried on a person's back or shoulder)', *hai ngenge* 'swinging', *te ingi* 'climbing trees', *hakatau hana* 'archery', and *hai pake* 'making string figures'.

In "wind the loincloth," children concentrate on keeping their balance while walking forward and backward. They stand in a straight column, holding each other's hands. They then start walking, repeatedly singing "Wind the loincloth." After a few meters, the person in front stops walking. The other participants move around him or her in a spiral march until all the participants are standing close together, still holding hands. The participants then walk backward, until the "loincloth" has unfolded and everyone is again standing in a straight line. Stepping backward, small children, whose motoric skills have not fully developed, usually fall down, eliciting bigger children's laughter.

FIGURE 6    Sengeika Tepuke of Matahenua Village demonstrates the Bellonese string figure named *te hakatahinga* 'a party, a gathering'. Photo by Rolf Kuschel, 1991.

The game "encircle fish" enables children to develop and practice their abilities to anticipate others' movements and react quickly to them. All but two children hold hands, forming a circle. One child is inside, and one is outside. The outside child tries to sneak into the circle and catch the inside one. With arms and hands, the children in the circle try to block the way, but by stealth and speed, the outside child may manage to slip inside. Then others become the chaser and the chased. During the game, the outside children holding hands sing about the surgeonfish and the squirrelfish.

### Controlling fear

On pitch-dark nights, a special test of courage was the game *tuku mataku* 'forsake fear', in which the object was to go as far as possible along the main trail, passing taboo areas. Bellonese said this challenge was suited to older children—young teenagers, and even adults.

Play attacks (*tau'a babange*) resembled adult raids. While one party hid, another tried to sneak up on them. Starting the attack, the attackers let out a battle cry. They metaphorically killed their enemies with spears (papaya stalks). With clubs, axes, and machetes (the butt ends of coconut fronds), they chopped off their enemies' arms and legs, and sang songs of victory. Their play was realistic and violent. It often ended with some of the players crying. It taught children lessons necessary in adult situations: agility, alertness, cooperation, cunning, stealth, control of fear, and endurance of pain.

### Traits of game-playing songs

Bellonese game-playing songs were simple and repetitive. The melody of the ant-pinching game (*kubikubi ngoo'ata*) consisted of four tones. Sitting in a circle, players put their clenched fists on top of each other, so each new hand's thumb and index finger pinched the back of the hand below. The fist on the bottom did not pinch another. When the tower of fists was complete, the participants sang:

| Kubikubi ngoo'ata, | Pinching ant, |
| 'Aabake hia? | Pass up how many times? |
| 'Aabake tongu! | Pass up three times! |
| Hohonga, hohonga! | Spread out, spread out! |

At the word *hohonga* 'spread out', the bottommost hand was splayed out on the ground, palm down. The children repeated the song until all the hands were flat. After the ant-pinching, children would play "tap your feces." Two children sitting opposite each other touched each other's fingertips, one by one, singing *Kini ou ta'e* 'Tap your feces'. They sang this strophe ten times, once for each digit, until all the opposed fingertips were touching.

An ancient clapping-accompanied song enlivened the game "bite the yam." Children stood in a circle around one child. Hopping on one leg, with hands clasped in back, that child tried to snap a yam pierced on a stick. Clapping cupped hands, the others repeatedly sang:

| Taku ghaasigho, na bangai: | My *ghaasigho*, the *bangai:* |
| Ma hinatu kinai. | Let's go to them. |
| Kua toghi'ia te kala nei. | This *kala* has been picked. |
| E 'uingaa, hia e sii. | The picking of nuts, hia e sii. |
| Takoto, kau takoto, takoto. | Lie down, I lie down, lie down. |
| | |
| Kau ngongongohu, ai i ee! | I bite, *ai i ee!* |
| Kau tanimalenge, oo i ee! | I walk back and forth, *oo i ee!* |
| Ngoni, ngoengoe, sii. | *Ngoni, ngoengoe, sii.* |
| Takoto, kau takoto, takoto. | Lie down, I lie down, lie down. |
| Sii, sii, sii, sii! | *Sii, sii, sii, sii!* |

Like the lyrics of many Oceanic children's songs, these are often metaphorical and sometimes obscure. The *ghaasigho* (a vine), the *bangai* (a tree), and the *kala* (edible nuts) may represent the yam; the *ngoni* is a sea slug, and the *ngoengoe* is an edible beetle. The term *sii* denotes a hissing or spurting sound.

### Introduced games

Since the early 1970s, many ancient games have been replaced by Western ball games like rugby, soccer, and volleyball. Children now sing songs from hymnals and songs they have heard on radio or learned in school. Older children may accompany themselves on guitars or homemade ukuleles.

Two striking traits differentiate ancient Bellonese games and modern ones. Most ancient games were played by children in small numbers, but the new games demand the participation of large numbers. This change has been eased by residential shifts: people now live in villages instead of single homesteads. And though the ancient games had simple rules, releasing fun and laughter, the new games have complex rules, and are seriously competitive.

—ROLF KUSCHEL

## TAHITI

In the late twentieth century, Tahitian schools have modeled themselves on the French educational system, which provided national guidelines for curriculum and evaluation, but allowed for local design of primary- and secondary-school programs. Written statements regarding national goals for music education existed, and local teachers used primarily Tahitian music to achieve them. All teachers in training studied singing and learned Western musical notation; those who enjoyed music and dance included them in their elementary-school classes.

During the first cycle of secondary school (ages twelve to fifteen), students in public schools may receive musical instruction from teachers sent from France and local volunteers, respected for performing music and dance. Teachers increasingly view music and dance as excellent ways to strengthen skills in the Tahitian language, but music at this level competes with other goals, such as computer literacy. In the early 1990s, only two high schools (one Roman Catholic, one public) had choirs, and musical education in school depended primarily on initiatives from nonspecialists. Even in schools that do not offer regular instruction in music, music is an important part of school celebrations, for which students learn songs and dances.

The Conservatoire Artistique Territorial, Te Fare 'Upa Rau, opened in 1978 in Pape'ete as the government-sponsored school for instruction in Western voice and musical instruments. In 1981, offerings expanded to include Tahitian dance, instrumental music (ukulele, guitar, drumming), and singing (*pātā'uta'u, tārava*). In 1996, almost one thousand students enrolled in about twenty kinds of classes, and 350 applicants were turned away for lack of space. Classes in Tahitian music and dance attracted almost five hundred students (figure 7).

In the late 1980s, the conservatory example of formal classes and the subsequent popularity of these classes contributed to the appearance and growth of private dance schools. In 1995, four—run by noted female dancers Makau Foster, Jeannine Maru, Tumata Robinson, and Moeata—flourished on Tahiti; some had more than three hundred students.

Formalized, paid, class instruction is a departure from older ways of passing on knowledge. It contrasts with a model in which youths learn music and dance by joining an established troupe. Classes focus on abstractly acquiring technique and learning pieces, but troupes rehearse under the guidance of a director (*ra'atira*), whose duties encompass choreography, musical composition, costume design, and overall coordination, but not necessarily the demonstration of musical or movement patterns and their individualized correction. Many directors choose experienced performers to demonstrate new pieces, and students repeat complete compositions until the words and movements are secure. Dancers and musicians do not pay the director. Teachers are peers; the methodology is imitation. Troupes usually form to prepare for upcoming occasions or (as do professional troupes) a series of ongoing occasions.

André Tschan's studio of ballet and modern dance, an established and respected school, has since 1970 served a small, mostly European and Chinese segment of the population—75 percent and 15 percent, respectively, of the 250 students enrolled in 1993. In the mid-1990s, this was changing, as some Tahitian and part-Tahitian children began studying Western dance formally. Two new Pape'ete schools, Vital California (1982) and Andréa (1984), were popular among young people on Tahiti during the 1980s and 1990s. These schools offered instruction in aerobics, modern jazz, and Tahitian dance. They regularly presented shows highlighting specific themes: music of the 1930s, the 1950s, Broadway, and Michael Jackson. Such shows appealed to Tahiti's teenagers and young adults.    —JANE FREEMAN MOULIN

## COOK ISLANDS

In the Cook Islands, the major forms of singing and dancing are the *hupahupa* and the *kaparima*, which have gender-specific movements. Children begin learning to sing and dance it as soon as they can walk. Parents encourage them, especially to dance for the amusement of grandparents or visitors. Parents may even bribe them with lollies. At the age of three or four, some children become junior members of the village troupe; they and others may begin to play a musical instrument, sing, and join a band.

Schools in the Cook Islands do not teach music as a formal subject, but schoolchildren perform music at school during concerts for raising funds, as part of the Māori Culture Program, for entertaining important visitors, and so on (figure 8). The schools of Manihiki usually have a fund-raising event during Parents Day (Rā-no-te-au-Metua), on a date determined annually by the staff of the schools. The schoolchildren's *hupahupa* is the highlight of the occasion.

The day begins as parents visit their children in their classrooms. The students and teachers then assemble in the open, and each class from grades 1 to 4 sings and dances. In front of the performers is a bowl, into which members of the audience put donations of money while the performance goes on. Donors may join the children and dance before putting a few coins or notes into the bowl. Occasionally, a parent tucks money into parts of a child's clothing; that money remains the child's property unless the child decides to put it into the bowl.

FIGURE 8    Rarotongan boys practice their movements while a seated girl looks on. Photo by Aileen K. Wiglesworth, 1995.

An extremely talented dancer usually becomes the center of attention. Adults may express pleasure for the excellence of the performance by placing money on this dancer's person. After the performances, the money is counted and its amount is announced. Certificates of merit are awarded to students who excelled in their schoolwork. Everyone joins in a feast. The parents, as the guests of the day, eat first, while some children entertain them with singing and others act as waiters, serving coconuts for drinking and running other errands. If the weather is fine, the feasting occurs under trees in the playground; otherwise, it occurs in the classrooms. As with most communitywide events, it begins and ends with a Christian prayer, recited by an adult.

Most schoolteachers in the Cook Islands can play a musical instrument and sing, but they do not often teach music formally. Children learn how to play an instrument, how to sing, and how to compose music, almost all by themselves. Hearing the sounds of drums, guitars, ukuleles, adults' singing in church, and music on cassettes and radio, children form their own appreciation of what their music should be.

—KAURAKA KAURAKA

## HAWAI'I

For decades in Hawai'i, the Department of Education has promulgated a curriculum that embraces instruction in music. The present curriculum echoes goals set by the U.S. Music Educators National Conference, but it adds instruction in concepts particular to the state. Meeting its educational ideals remains a challenge.

The state's Foundation Program proposes that "students in grades K through 6 receive instruction in art, health, language arts, mathematics, music, physical education, science, and social studies" (*Music Curriculum Guide K–12* 1986:17). For these grades, it allots ninety minutes of musical study a week, but recommends that grades K through 3 spend 120 minutes on music. For students in grades 7 and 8, it institutes a one-year fine-arts requirement, for which art and music are alternatives; students who have completed the requirement may take music as an elective. The music courses offered are band, orchestra, chorus, and glee club; high schools add music appreciation. To graduate from high school (grades 9–12), students need twenty-two credits, which must include the following years of study: English, four; social studies, four; mathematics, three; science, three; physical education, one; health, one-half; guidance, one-half. The remaining credits are electives. The curriculum requires no course in any of the arts, but authorizes music as an elective at all levels.

The curriculum sorts musical concepts into those of tone, rhythm, harmony, tonality, texture, form, and melody. Kindergartners learn basic concepts of pitch, loudness, timbre, duration, tempo, tonic key, and accompaniment, and are expected to recognize the symbols *p, f, pp, ff* and the signs for crescendo and diminuendo. Further technical information comes in a graded order. The treble clef appears in third grade, the fermata in the fourth, and accidentals (sharps, flats, naturals) in the sixth, when students ideally learn about chordal roots, binary form, fugal processes, opera, twelve-bar blues, and other concepts. The curriculum emphasizes Hawaiian-related material in fourth and eighth grades. Students learn about the *'ukulele* in fourth grade and the guitar in seventh (figure 9). The curriculum introduces Polynesian musical instruments in second grade, and reinforces that instruction in all subsequent grades.

On an extracurricular basis, intermediate and high schools offer Hawaiian cultural activities, including singing and dancing. They hold an annual *hula* competition each May; the winning ensemble is invited to perform in the (noncompetitive) Prince Lot Hula Festival each July. In evening, weekend, and summer classes,

FIGURE 9  The curricular plan for introducing knowledge of musical instruments in Hawaiian schools (*Music Curriculum Guide K–12* 1986:32).

**Introduction of Musical instruments for Grades K-12**

| INSTRUMENTS | GRADE LEVELS | | | | | | | | | |
|---|---|---|---|---|---|---|---|---|---|---|
| | K | 1 | 2 | 3 | 4 | 5 | 6 | 7 | 8 | 9-12 |
| Resonator bells, autoharp, rhythm instruments | ● | ○ | ○ | ○ | ○ | ○ | ○ | ○ | | |
| Tonette | | | ● | ○ | ○ | | | | | |
| Ukulele | | | | ● | ○ | ○ | ○ | | | |
| Recorder | | | | | ● | ○ | ○ | | ○ | |
| Band and Orchestra | | | | | ● | ○ | ○ | ○ | ○ | |
| Guitar | | | | | | | ○ | ● | | |
| Polynesian | | | ● | ○ | ○ | ○ | ○ | ○ | ○ | ○ |

Introduced = ●     Reinforced = ○

Hawaiian dancing is taught in city and county playgrounds. On Oʻahu, these courses culminate in a festival at Kapiʻolani Park each August.          —J. W. LOVE

## Kūpuna in the curriculum

The Hawaiian Studies Program, operated in Hawaiian public schools by the State Department of Education, relies heavily on the participation of *kūpuna* (sing. *kupuna*), Hawaiian-speaking elders, living repositories of indigenous culture. Though many students in the schools are not of Hawaiian blood and some are recent immigrants, *kūpuna* lead them to understand indigenous culture and how they can play a role in it.

This educational development began in the late 1970s in the wake of a rise in support for Hawaiian music, dance, and language, leading to the creation of the Office of Hawaiian Affairs. By amendment in 1978, the state constitution included (as article X, section 4) a mandate that the state promote Hawaiian cultural, historical, and linguistic knowledge and involve Hawaiian experts, the *kūpuna*.

Hawaiian public schools had taught Hawaiian culture before 1980, but the Hawaiian-culture curriculum had not been systematic through all the grades. The new program promoted "elements of affective development," listed as "*aloha,* sharing, cooperation, consideration and caring for others, respect for self and others, responsibility, industriousness," and other cultural values (*Hawaiian Studies Program Guide* 1986:2:1).

The program relies on *kūpuna* to supplement the instruction given by regular classroom teachers, who "have direct responsibility for aiding the classroom teacher in planning and providing instruction that focuses on Hawaiian language development and the modeling of Hawaiian cultural values." When they discuss Hawaiian cultural elements like songs and places, students receive instruction in the Hawaiian language.

To implement the announced goals, the Hawaiian Studies Program established six programmatic objectives (*Hawaiian Studies Program Guide* 1986:2:5–10):

1. Awareness of the origin and culture of the native Hawaiian people
2. Appreciation of the students' own cultural backgrounds, and of other cultures and heritages
3. Knowledge of historical and cultural developments and influences in Hawaiʻi
4. Interest in and opportunities to pursue further in-depth study of the Hawaiian language and other aspects of culture
5. Understanding and appreciation of the concept of *alohaʻ āina,* the love, sense of harmony and proper use, respect and environmental awareness which the Hawaiians and other island people have for the land

Princess Bernice Pauahi Bishop, last direct
descendant of King Kamehameha I, determined to
help Hawaiian children. She bequeathed her estate,
consisting of about 9 percent of the land of Hawai'i,
to be held in trust for educating Hawaiians.

6. Awareness and demonstration of the essence of the so-called *aloha* spirit—a spirit of cooperation, hospitality, sharing, and reciprocated respect and interpersonal amiability

Each of these statements has objectives, which the program details.

### The curriculum for grades 1–6

The program has nine strands. The music-and-dance strand trains students in singing, performing *hula,* creating new songs, and using musical materials to further their understanding of Hawaiian culture, particularly its integration with nature. Students learn that music serves Hawaiian poetry because sounded words have power.

#### Singing

In the use of music, the curriculum asks kindergartners and first-graders to identify a melody as Hawaiian, "to imitate simple melodic and rhythmic phrases, and to sing simple Hawaiian melodies and lyrics." It asks second-graders to sing Hawaiian melodic phrases while performing appropriately choreographed movements, and "to compose and perform simple rhythmic patterns." It asks third-graders to sing "using correct Hawaiian pronunciation, to recognize rhythmic patterns in Hawaiian songs, and to use Hawaiian rhythm instruments."

The curriculum expects fourth-graders to memorize and sing a simple Hawaiian song, to compose lyrics "in English and Hawaiian expressing feelings about Hawaii, to compose melodies with a Hawaiian theme," to enlarge their Hawaiian vocabulary, to study immigrants' roles in the history of Hawaiian music, "to become aware that composers utilize environmental themes to inspire their music and lyrics," and "to discuss music as an aspect of culture."

The curriculum expects fifth- and sixth-graders to make music "an integral part of their skills and knowledge of Hawaii." It asks them "to compare music in previous times with that of today" and to discuss early Hawaiian songs and dances.

#### Movement and dance

The curriculum addresses the Hawaiian structured-movement system. It requires kindergartners and first-graders to make simple gestures with their hands. Second-graders perform a seated dance (*hula noho*) and learn to coordinate their hands and feet while performing a *hula.* Third-graders "create motions for songs based on personal interpretation." Fourth-graders "continue to develop their skills previously learned." Fifth-graders choreograph and perform more advanced or complicated movements. For the whole school, sixth-graders plan, organize, and present exhibitions of Hawaiian dancing. The basic approach of the program is holistic and integrative. Woven into the music-and-dance strand of the fourth-grade curriculum is the expectation that students will relate selected name songs (*mele inoa*) to the historical figures the songs honor.

### Resources

Each subject in the curriculum has its own resources (Mitchell 1992). The music-and-dance strand relies on *Nā Mele Ho'ona'auao,* a music-resource book (1985), divided into three sections. The first, *"Nā Mele,"* contains preexistent songs, for which permission has been granted for use. The second, *"Mele,"* consists of songs composed for the Hawaiian Studies Program, some based on familiar items. The third, *"Nā Mele Ho'onānea"* ('Songs to Enjoy'), are additional songs to enhance instruction as the occasion demands.

*Nā Mele Ho'ona'auao* has seven appendices, containing basic information about the songs, *'ukulele* chords for the songs, cross-references for lyrical content, a discography, a bibliography, an annotated list of videotapes available within the school district, and a list of Hawaiian instruments, with their descriptions, uses, and pictures. The book's contents range from old songs to hapa haole songs to contemporary Hawaiian songs.

The program has several qualities for multicultural music programs in public schools. What it brings to students is relevant and appropriate to the substance of Hawaiian culture. *Kūpuna* brought in to teach are highly qualified representatives of their culture. Classroom teachers at the schools collaborate with *kūpuna* to carry on additional instruction as they learn and become proficient in Hawaiian culture. This program has wide support from administrative staff and the Hawaiian community.

—ANTHONY J. PALMER

## Kamehameha Schools

On 19 December 1831, Princess Bernice Pauahi Bishop, great-granddaughter and last direct descendant of King Kamehameha I, was born. From a world of chaos and change, she emerged as a beacon of hope for her people. Moved by the social catastrophe around her, she determined to help Hawaiian children become contributing citizens of society. To this end, she bequeathed her estate, consisting of about 9 percent of the land of Hawai'i and other holdings, to be held in perpetual trust for educating Hawaiians. In 1887, four years after her death, the Kamehameha School for Boys opened; in 1894, the Kamehameha School for Girls followed.

Today, the campus of the Kamehameha Schools covers about 240 hectares on Kapalama Heights, overlooking downtown Honolulu. From kindergarten through twelfth grade, its programs educate some thirty-two hundred native Hawaiian children.

### The curriculum and educational goals

From its founding through World War II, Kamehameha Schools functioned like a military school, with vocational curricular goals. Classes were geared toward preparing Hawaiians for blue-collar jobs. The Boy's School provided training in areas such as carpentry, farming, and other practical trades; the Girl's School prepared young women for domestic life, with extra training in skills needed for officework. Only a few students were counseled onto a college track.

By the 1960s, the curriculum had begun to provide a wider range of courses. In 1966, the school became coeducational. Though essentially "college prep" through the 1970s, it was not officially called that until the 1980s. Today, about 95 percent of graduating seniors go on to experience some form of higher education. Kamehameha graduates now occupy a range of socioeconomic levels, locally and abroad.

*Nineteenth-century perspectives*

The early performing-arts curriculum featured choir, band, and piano, and offered opportunities in drama. Singing was thoroughly a part of Hawaiian culture, hence unaccompanied choral singing became a curricular hallmark. Early instructors introduced the glee-club concept, borrowed from East Coast Ivy League traditions.

During the first century, with the choral foundation firmly laid, the Kamehameha Schools nurtured their own dynamic Hawaiian choral tradition. Indigenous dance (*hula*) was considered inappropriate in the early days, and for much of the schools' history it was not encouraged. Ballroom dancing, however, remained a part of the program for many years. The Hawaiian language was the first language for most students through the 1920s, but it too was discouraged. Over time, local educational and social beliefs regarding culture and arts evolved.

*Culture and performing arts in the late 1990s*

Today, the philosophy of the Performing Arts Department is to provide students with various artistic experiences. It is the department's belief that performing arts can improve the quality of life, and that learning to recognize and create beauty is crucial to a complete and effective education. At the secondary level, the department features a seventy-five-voice concert glee club, a 210-piece marching band, a fifty-five-piece orchestra, a fifty-member drama program, a fifty-member contemporary dance troupe, and a *hula* program, which annually instructs some two hundred students in indigenous dancing.

The department offers a guitar program and private instruction in voice, slack-key guitar, violin, viola, cello, and bass. It has a computer lab, with instruction in music theory, listening skills, and composition using keyboards and a MIDI interface. The elementary school (grades K–6) and the middle school (grades 7 and 8) emphasize band, orchestra, choral programs, and a general music program at the lower levels. An elementary children's chorus performs at community events.

*Choral singing*

Choral singing is an important part of the Kamehameha experience. All secondary-school students are required to participate in the Song Contest, a legacy of the 1920s. It features male, female, and mixed unaccompanied choral singing by the freshman (mixed only), sophomore, junior, and senior classes. Each class enrolls nearly 450 students, who compete for trophies. Hawaiian songs are arranged and taught in required sectionals over a two-month period. Each class elects its own musical and organizational leaders. The Hoʻike, a multimedia production based on the *hula,* is presented while scores are tallied. Its themes and images often influence dance trends and cultural interpretations. The event is broadcast live over statewide television.

Every December, the entire student body assembles to celebrate the birthday of the school's founder (figure 10). Students perform name songs (*mele inoa*) in their original, late-nineteenth-century, choral arrangements. In May, at the end of the academic year, commencement exercises for graduating seniors feature choral singing.

**Late-twentieth-century trends**

Since the early 1970s, a resurgence of Hawaiian culture has affected the community, and the schools have begun to offer more culturally oriented courses. *Hula* has become extremely important in ceremonies and performances. Some eight hundred students are now studying the Hawaiian language, and many are fluent in it. For cultural exchange, performing-arts troupes from the schools have traveled throughout the United States, Europe, Asia, and Oceania. The Hawaiian performers at the Pacific Arts Festivals in 1988 and 1992 were Kamehameha students. Reestablishing

FIGURE 10    Students at Kamehameha Schools commemorate the birthday of the founder, Bernice Pauahi Bishop. Photo Kamehameha Schools.

connections with other Polynesians is now a prominent part of indigenous Hawaiian identity. These changes reflect the evolution of attitudes about the educational value of Hawaiian culture and arts. In the face of a new millennium, Kamehameha Schools strive to prepare native Hawaiian children for a globally connected future, based on the solid and secure foundation of their artistic and indigenous past.

—RANDIE K. FONG

## AOTEAROA

Popular Māori songs appeared in *The Dominion Song Book,* a fifteen-volume collection, whose publication and use in schools began in 1930. The Māori songs stood among shanties, songs of various countries, and items by Mozart, Schubert, and Schumann. In the 1940s, as New Zealand marked its first century of European settlement, a desire to use the curriculum to build a national identity spurred the inclusion of Māori material.

In the 1940s, indigenous cultural items were prominent features of independent Māori schools, including Queen Victoria Girls School, Auckland and Te Aute Boys College, Hawkes Bay. Run by religious denominations, these schools educated many leaders of the Māori community, incorporating traditional skills into their curricula. They became renowned for choral performances, called concert parties, whose programs included Māori pieces. Most secular schools lacked such training; but Sir Apirana Ngata, prominent Māori leader and member of parliament, led an initiative to appoint the composer Tuini Ngawai as a teacher of song and dance in schools in the rural east coast of the North Island.

As the Māori population moved from tribal areas into cities, the people set up new formal centers (*marae*). The first of these was Ngāti Pōneke (Wellington, in 1936), which concentrated on the performance of cultural items. At such *marae* today, traditional and acculturated musics are important features of preschool education (*kohanga reo*). These musics figure prominently in Māori-language schools (*kura kaupapa*), such as those established by Dr. Peter Sharples at the Hoanui Waititi *marae* in West Auckland, and in bilingual units at mainstream schools.

### The rise of multiculturalism

By the 1970s, immigrant Pacific Islanders' increasing enrollment in city schools was providing opportunities for multicultural curricular developments. Experts from

FIGURE 11    At New Camp Hamlet, Mapiri Village, Nissan, children join the adults' dance. Photo by Steven R. Nachman, 1971.

immigrant communities began to teach in public schools. In Porirua (in greater Wellington), a troupe from Brandon Intermediate School provided public performances at festivals, civic receptions, interschool meetings, and conferences. Its director was Teremoana Hodges, a Cook Islander. Teachers and parents agreed that curricularizing the music and dance of islanders' cultures helped boost pupils' self-esteem and scholastic achievement. The bonds forged between teachers and parents were important features of this movement. Similar developments occurred in Auckland and other centers. The music and dance of multicultural troupes featured Sāmoan *māʻuluʻulu,* Tokelauan *fātele,* and genres from the Cook Islands. In many schools, these troupes burgeoned, and students held annual festivals, attracting hundreds of performers. As elsewhere in Oceania (figure 11), performances of music and dance served to join the world of children with the world of adults.

Curricular changes enabled students in secondary schools to offer skills in Māori and Pacific music as an aspect of their academic assessment. By 1995, the syllabus drafted for the final three years of school had a different outlook from syllabi current in the 1940s. Māori and Pacific musics had become practical music studies, and students taking written examinations could choose to answer questions on Māori, Pacific, or Asian music. The syllabus encouraged study of local composers, popular music, and music of indigenous peoples and Pacific Islanders.    —ALLAN THOMAS

## REFERENCES

Bateson, Gregory. 1932. "Social Structure of the Iatmul People of the Sepik River (Part III)." *Oceania* 2:401–453.

———. 1958. *Naven.* 2nd ed. Stanford: Stanford University Press.

Brunton, M. 1976. "The Usage of Music Patterns by Primary School Children." M.A. thesis, University of Adelaide.

Christensen, Dieter. 1963. "Melodiestile am mittleren Sepik." *Bässler-Archiv* 10:9–44.

Davey, G., and Factor, J. 1980. "Cinderella and Friends: Folklore as Discourse." Paper presented at the ANZAAS Conference, Melbourne.

David, Mrs. Edgeworth [Lady Caroline David]. 1899. *Funafuti, or Three Months on a Coral Island: An Unscientific Account of a Scientific Expedition.* London: John Murray.

Elkin, A. P. 1964. *The Australian Aborigines.* Garden City, N.Y.: Doubleday.

Hall, Hazel. 1984. "A Study of the Relationship between Speech and Song in the Playground Rhymes of Primary School Children." Ph.D. dissertation, Monash University.

———. 1988. "From Playground to Schoolroom: the Joy of Rhyming." Proceedings of the eighteenth national conference of the Australian Early Childhood Association; Canberra, A.C.T.

———. 1993. "Musical and Poetic Characteristics of Children's Folklore." In *Oxford Companion to Australian Folklore,* ed. Gwenda Beed Davey and Graham Seal, 257–270. Melbourne and New York: Oxford University Press.

Handy, Willowdean Chatterson. 1925. *String Figures from the Marquesas and Society Islands.* Bulletin 18. Honolulu: Bishop Museum.

*Hawaiian Studies Program Guide.* 1986. Honolulu: Office of Instructional Services, General Education Branch, Department of Education, State of Hawaii.

Hornbostel, Erich M. von. 1912. "Die Musik auf den Nord-Westlichen Salomo-Inseln." In *Forschungen auf den Salomo-Inseln und dem Bismarck-Archipel,* vol. 1, ed. Richard Thurnwald, 461–504. Berlin: Dietrich Reimer.

Jayne, Caroline Furness. 1906. *String Figures.* New York: Scribner.

Jones, A. M. 1959. *Studies in African Music.* Oxford: Oxford University Press.

Kartomi, Margaret. 1980. "Childlikedness in Play Songs—A Case Study among the Pitjantjatjara at Yalata, South Australia." *Miscellanea Musicologica* 11:172–214.

Koizumi, Fumio. 1957. *The Study of the Japanese Traditional Music.* Tokyo: Ongaku no Tomo.

Kubik, Gerhard. 1968. *Mehrstimmigkeit und Tonsysteme in Zentral-und Ostafrika.* Vienna: Hermann Böhlaus.

Kunst, Jaap. 1967. *Music in New Guinea.* The Hague: Martinus Nijhoff.

Kurosawa, Takatomo. 1952. "The Musical Bow of the Bunun Tribe in Formosa and Suggestion as to the Origin of the Pentatonic Scale." *Toyo Ongaku Kenkyu* 10–11:18–32.

Kuschel, Rolf. 1975. "Games on a Polynesian Outlier Island." *Journal of the Polynesian Society* 84(1):25–66.

Love, Jacob Wainwright. 1991. *Sāmoan Variations: Essays on the Nature of Traditional Oral Arts.* New York and London: Garland.

Lowenstein, Wendy. 1960. Field recordings from Western Australia. Melbourne: State Library.

Marsh, Kathryn. 1995. "The Influence of the Media and Immigrant Groups in the Transmission and Performance of Australian Children's Playground Singing Games." Paper presented at the Conference of the International Council for Traditional Music; Australian National University, Canberra.

Maude, Honor. 1970. "The String Figures of Tikopia." In *Tikopia String Figures,* ed. Raymond Firth and Honor Maude, 7–11. London: Royal Anthropological Institute.

Merriam, Alan P. 1964. *The Anthropology of Music.* Evanston, Ill..: Northwestern University Press.

Mitchell, Donald D. Kilolani. 1992. *Resource Units in Hawaiian Culture.* Revised edition. Honolulu: Kamehameha Schools Press.

*Music Curriculum Guide K–12.* 1986. Honolulu: Office of Instructional Services/General Education Branch, Department of Education.

*Nā Mele Hoʻonaʻauao: Hawaiian Studies Music Resource Book.* 1985. Honolulu: State of Hawaiʻi, Office of Instructional Services, General Education Branch, Department of Education.

Romet, Cheryl. 1980. "The Play Rhymes of Children—A Cross Cultural Source of Natural Learning Materials for Music Education." *Australian Journal of Music Education* 27:27–31.

Schneider, Marius. 1969. *Geschichte der Mehrstimmigkeit.* Tutzing: Hans Schneider.

Spearritt, Gordon D. 1974. "Music of the Middle Sepik River." *Studies in Music* 8:101–109.

———. 1976. "The Musical Ingenuity of the Men of the Sepik River." In *Challenges in Music Education,* ed. Frank Callaway, 399–403. Perth: University of Western Australia Press.

———. 1982. "The Pairing of Musicians and Instruments in Iatmul Society." *Yearbook for Traditional Music* 14:106–125.

Turner, Ian. 1969. *Cinderella Dressed in Yella: Australian Children's Play-Rhymes.* Melbourne: Heinemann Educational.

Tsukada, Kenichi. 1983. "Bamboo Flutes and Iatmul Musical Heterogeneity." *Bikmaus* 4(4):85–92.

Yamada, Yōichi. 1982. "An Analysis of Wavijangut of the Iatmoi, Papua New Guinea: A Proposal of a Method of Ethnomusicology." *Jikenzan Ronso* 15:5–27.

# The Many Dimensions of Music

The study of the music of Oceania invites multidimensional methods of approach and analysis. Poetic text, melodic and rhythmic rendering, visual expression in movement, musical instruments, costumes, and performing spaces are examined with the social contexts of the activities and events of which music is a part. Symbolism and aesthetics contribute to the understanding of concepts associated with the recording, preservation, notation, and analysis of sound, movement, language, and musical instruments.

This carved wooden drum, acquired in 1929 in Ambunti (then part of British New Guinea), was donated to the Smithsonian Institution. It is now on exhibition in the Pacific Hall at the National Museum of Natural History, Washington, D.C. But what bird did it represent, and what did this symbolism mean to the people of Ambunti? What sounds came from this instrument, and how did they relate to local singing and dancing? Research on such questions and many others lies ahead. Photo Smithsonian Institution.

# Understanding Music

J. W. Love          Steven Knopoff

Dieter Christensen      Vida Chenoweth

Udo Will              Jürg Wassmann

Jacqueline Pugh-Kitingan   Junko Konishi

C. K. Szego         Amy Ku'uleialoha Stillman

**Music as a System of Knowledge**

**Transcription**

**Time**

**Pitch**

**Timbre**

**Structure**

What is music? Everyone seems to know, but not everyone agrees on a definition. The thing comes in packages of audible events, and these result from artful play, but the concept implies more: unity and continuity, performers and listeners, givers and receivers, makers and consumers. It includes, beyond what we see and hear, a *system* of aural knowledge, *processes* that produce the system, and *contexts* that guide performance and appreciation.

Since individual responses to music vary, no musical system is wholly perceptible. Each varies from place to place, from time to time, and from person to person. Even the sounds of a performance vary, depending on where, in relation to performers and other participants, an observer is taking them in. No single site has privilege of place, and no single person has privilege of time.

As with all knowledge, musical information is imperfectly imparted by teachers and imperfectly received by students. The pooling of knowledge, as among coordinated performers or researchers, may bring clarification, but the means and bounds of a musical system, because the system remains ideational, elude rational awareness. Nor are musical systems static: as events add experience to knowledge, their attributes change; each new piece or performance changes the whole.

## MUSIC AS A SYSTEM OF KNOWLEDGE

The term *music* specifies, not merely performances or pieces, but an aesthetic framework, the result of creative activities that formalize sounds. The analysis of Oceanic music reaches out to many contexts, including rituals, ceremonies, sports, games, courtship, and entertainment. Analysis that would separate music from nonmusic according to indigenous theories has seldom occurred. Researchers simply use the term *music* for certain kinds of structured sounds, but the term is Western. The sounds for which it stands are unique. Only by hearing them in context or knowing them in reference to their cultures can observers feel the social energies that give them currency. Playing with sounds, the musical segments of society show structured contents, betoken interpersonal relationships, realize aesthetic values, and bear messages that find meaning in cultural templates.

As systems of knowledge, systems of structured sound are the products of

FIGURE 1 A Solomon Islands panpipe ensemble combines singing, sounds from musical instruments (panpipes and stamped tubes), and structured movements into a complex system of knowledge. Photo by Ōtani Mayumi, 1993.

human activity and the processes through which that activity unfolds. In any society, they bind with other systems of knowledge into a larger system, socially and culturally formed (figure 1). These systems are mental processes—inaudible, intangible, and invisible. Except by inference and imagination, they are inaccessible.

Within the limits imposed by the nature of the subject, an ideal study of the music of a society might analyze the social situations that drive people to structure their sounds, the technical processes that produce the structures, and the human values that give meaning to the products. The sounds and their structures can be analyzed *etically*—on their own terms, as sets of acoustic events, cultureless vibrations, phonetic articles. But they can also be analyzed *emically*, according to the sense they make to participants in the cultures that generate or value them. Hence, musical analysis confronts an array of potentially productive tensions: between sound and meaning, science and art, musicology and anthropology, etic facts and emic percepts, outsiders' ears and insiders' minds.

### The process of performing

The people of Oceania make music to do many things. They perform to welcome and honor friends, menace and revile enemies, make political statements, enact rituals, and support other actions. They may make music for no apparent reason. They may want a given sequence of sounds to be decoded differently if performed for fun, in competition, for a human audience, or for spirits or deities. Human decoding may reflect personal backgrounds and abilities, grounded in the artistic protocols of a specific place and a specific time, and its evaluation may vary with prevailing criteria of beauty.

Analyses of musical meaning focus on cultural insiders' reasons for performing particular pieces and their perceptions of musical classes, variably called genres, types, and forms. To gain a foothold on insiders' perceptual terrains, researchers routinely seek information on these topics, so publications on Oceanic music often structure themselves by listing conspicuous social functions or musical classes and analyzing the messages communicated in them.

Like dance and language, music presents its messages in structured forms. It is thoroughly grammatical. Its syntax, the technical process of its coding, follows conventional patterns, analyzable etically as a set of rules and emically as the conveyance of meaning. An exhaustive set of etic rules may be impossible to chart, but basic sets, covering typical uses of time, pitch, timbre, structure, and texture, may describe and differentiate pieces, genres, and systems.

### The analysis of recordings

What can we learn by listening to recordings? How can we use recorded information? A recording is a product, an artifact created when a performance meets a recorder. How we use that product depends on our goals. At varying levels of fidelity, a recording tells how aural sequences occurred on a specific occasion, but our hearing cannot fully elucidate the musical system, because the system is inaudible and invisible (Kaeppler 1995). It partly depends on unrecorded and unrecordable perceptual responses and knowledge.

Increasingly, researchers are looking for systems. They use recorded music as a window to the processes that went into making it. They transcribe recordings and compare transcriptions to uncover, behind the veil of contingent variation, aesthetic stabilities that enable musical systems to cohere. They may experiment by asking musicians to perform repeatedly, the better to tell the potential range of variation among performances (see "Pitch: Normal scores," below). Or they may record rehearsals and compare the recordings with those of public performances, the better to learn how presentation changes the music.

Recordings of Oceanic music are geographically haphazard. Performances by people of several societies, including Sāmoa in 1893, the Torres Strait in 1898, and other locations in the next decade, were recorded early in the history of the phonograph. Some Oceanic societies have had their musical performances documented on successively more accomplished technologies: wax cylinders, vinyl disks, wires, tapes, cassettes, films, videos, and digitally mastered CDs. For some of these societies, the temporal depth of these recordings has exceeded, or will soon exceed, a century. The music of other Oceanic societies may never have been recorded.

## TRANSCRIPTION

Recordings are useful for many purposes, but they do not replace notation. Reduced to writing and disseminated by printing, sounds become interculturally useful commodities, no matter how culturally specific their origins. By making sounds visible, transcriptions ease analysis. For much analytical work, transcriptions are adequate, but they do not record the whole of performances, and it would be foolish to pretend that by understanding a set of transcriptions, we can fully understand the musical system behind them.

Most transcribers of Oceanic music have passed through curricular programs that train students in techniques of musical notation without regard for the notational theory of other arts, even of allied ones, like poetry and dance. Their transcriptions therefore do not always reflect awareness of, or interest in, the nonmusical artistry of musical performances. In certain genres or cultures, this artistry encompasses observers' reactions. Responding to impressive performances, the Kaluli, of Southern Highlands Province, Papua New Guinea, cry and jab torches against the singer-dancers' skin (Schieffelin 1976); but the crying and the burning are accompaniments

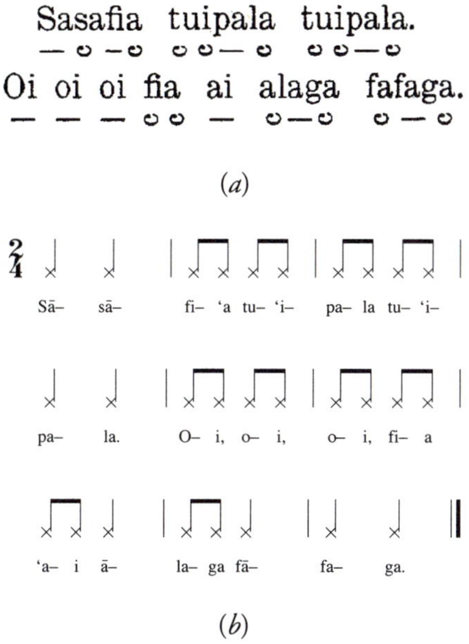

Sasafia tuipala tuipala.

Oi oi oi fia ai alaga fafaga.

(a)

(b)

FIGURE 2 Transcriptional uses of signs for scansion: *a,* marking the rhythms of a Sāmoan children's song (after Sierich 1905:188); *b,* the rhythms of the text of *a,* as performed in Sāmoa in 1973 (transcription by J. W. Love).

that would not ordinarily leave a transcriptive residue. Similarly, though with varying specifics, Oceanic observers shout, clap, and make other actions during musical performances. These responses can contribute to the social meaning of performances, and an ideal notation might accommodate them.

Transcriptions of Oceanic music often take the form of notation on five-line staffs, augmented with signs for special sounds. Researchers have also used tablature, graphic, numeral, symbolic, and electronic notations. A rarely used notational method borrows the signs developed centuries ago to mark the scansion of classical poetry: the macron (long mark) and the breve (short mark), traditionally used for long vowels and short vowels respectively. In 1825, to suggest stressed and unstressed rhythms of two Micronesian songs, Adelbert von Chamisso used these signs, as did Otto Sierich for a Sāmoan children's song (figure 2*a*), though unusually, with placement under the words; evidence obtained in the 1970s revealed that Sierich used the macrons not to mark scansion, but to mark downbeats (figure 2*b*).

A major decision in making a transcription is how much detail to notate. Obviously, too much detail impedes analytical progress: "It is possible . . . to carry the exactitude of a transcription to a point where one cannot see the wood for trees, so that the structure of the piece transcribed has got completely out of hand" (Kunst 1950:39). Researchers usually show only what suits their analytical goals.

## Notation on five-line staffs

Notation on five-line staffs, inherited from Western music and basically unchanged for centuries, serves as a standard. It is the form of notation in which musical performances of many Oceanic peoples were first transcribed, as on Captain Cook's second voyage, when James Burney used it to notate Tongan music. Conventionally, it shows time as running from left to right, so serial events occur on the horizontal dimension. Transcriptions of multiple performers show simultaneity on the vertical dimension, with higher-pitched sources ordinarily set above lower-pitched ones. (The vertical order of symphonic scores is usually inappropriate for indigenous Oceanic ensembles.) The conventions of reading this notation are widely known, so transcribers assume basic knowledge and explain only how their notations differ. Some transcribers use nonstandard key signatures, with each indicated accidental (sharp, flat, natural) governing all instances of notes occurring at its tonal level; other transcribers prefer to write an accidental before every such instance.

Because this notation is recognized worldwide, even nonstandard prints of it or its derivatives can usually be understood. A print of log-idiophone signals transcribed by an amateur musician in Vanuatu (Deacon 1934:505), eliminates staffs, puts the lowest-sounding instrument on top, and misaligns the notes, but it gives enough information for readers to tell that the instruments were jointly producing a pattern in which the smallest and highest-pitched log, shown at the bottom, sounded the most often.

Staff-notated tones usually imply an underlying tempered scale, so to accommodate systematic deviations from that scale, transcribers add special signs, typically lines and squiggles to depict sliding between tones, and pluses and minuses or arrows to depict notes whose pitches differ, in the direction implied or pointed, from those of tempered tuning. These signs have no universal meanings, and the meanings they do bear may be valid only in the transcription in which they appear. Their use can betray unwarranted theoretical assumptions. In 1855, James Davies published transcriptions of Māori music using altered signs for sharps and flats to show what he believed to be quarter-tone deviations from tempered intonations; in local contexts, the precision of these supposed deviations was worthless. Further signs accommodate other musical traits, or otherwise augment the staff-borne information. Transcribing

FIGURE 3 Icons representing an ‘Are‘are solo panpipe augment a transcription: the widened tubes are the ones producing the transcribed notes. After Zemp 1981:403.

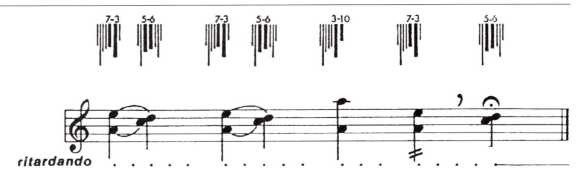

polyphony performed on an ‘Are‘are panpipe, Hugo Zemp (1981) set instrumental icons above the staff: for each chord, the pipes that produced the transcribed notes are widened; Arabic numerals identify the pipes (figure 3).

Adaptations of staffs have proved useful. Transcribing texts articulated on Huli lamellaphones and musical bows, Jacqueline Pugh-Kitingan (1975, 1977) adapted staffs to show the frequencies obtained through modifications of the shape of the player’s oral cavity and throat. Each line in such transcriptions [see HIGHLAND REGION OF PAPUA NEW GUINEA: figure 12] represents the main pitches in hertz, not scalar tones. The sizes of notes show relative intensities. Dotted vertical lines mark each pluck of the tongue of the instrument, and solid vertical lines mark phrasal boundaries. Notating performances on the Huli musical bow was more complex: the instrument produces three fundamental pitches, and the player’s oral cavity resonates selected partials. Pugh-Kitingan used two staffs: as in standard notation, the lower staff shows the notes of the fundamentals; the upper staff is a set of horizontal lines indicating the most prominent partials, specified in hertz.

A simplified staff-based notation has proved useful for melodies concentrated on one tone. For recitations associated with Hawaiian *pahu,* Elizabeth Tatar (1993) used one horizontal line for the main tone of the melody, with extra lines for auxiliary tones on either side of it.

## Tablature

For guitars and ukuleles, the dominant introduced chordophones of Oceania, musicians often write music in tablature, a notational device showing on which frets the performer presses (“stops”) strings against the fingerboard. Additional symbols may show other actions. Tablature usually depicts the fingerboard and the strings as if the viewer were looking at the instrument with the first fret at the top.

Ukulele tablature typical of the craze of the 1920s shows stopped strings as darkened circles and open strings as undarkened circles. Reading left to right as one looks at the tablature, the strings are tuned and named G–C–E–A (conventionally sung as “My dog has fleas”), but any appropriately transposed tones are possible, as in Will D. Moyer’s *National Self Teacher for Hawaiian Ukulele, Banjuke or Taro Patch Fiddle* (1922), which uses strings tuned A–D–F♯–B (figure 4). This kind of tablature has no symbols to convey temporal information. For showing rhythms and patterns of

FIGURE 4 In an early manual on how to play the ukulele, tablature below a five-line staff shows with darkened circles the strings the performer is to stop. After Moyer 1922:5.

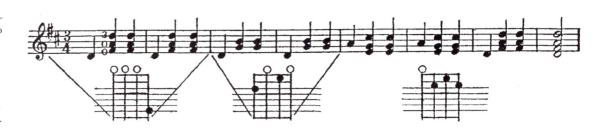

FIGURE 5   Oceanic examples of graphic notation: *a,* music of the Marquesas Islands, with exclamation points denoting claps (Handy and Winne 1925:38); *b,* levels of vocal performance and the phonetic structure of the music (after Tatar 1981:487).

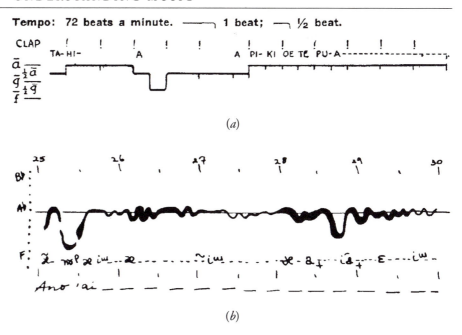

strumming, modern notation may use headless, conventionally flagged stems, with chords named by their tonic notes [see POPULAR MUSIC: figure 16].

In a pattern borrowed from piano notation, tablature may designate the fingers by the numerals from 1 to 5, with the thumb as 1. For teaching ukulele fingering using staff-based notation, it was once conventional to designate the thumb with an X over or under the note, the index finger with one dot, and the middle finger with two dots.

## Graphic notations

Graphic notations transcribe sounds in ways resembling charts and graphs. Time usually moves from left to right, and low tones print lower than high tones. A melody, instead of being shown as a series of rhythmicized notes, may be a line. This notation, which differs most from staff-based notation in the way it shows temporal values, was used in Russia so early as 1912 (Seeger 1958:188). An early-twentieth-century Oceanic example of it (figure 5*a*) appears in an analysis of music of the Marquesas Islands (Handy and Winne 1925).

Investigating the timbral qualities of precontact Hawaiian singing, Tatar used graphic notation "to show the most specific levels of the vocal performance and therefore the nature of the phonetic structure" of the music (1981:486). The thickness of the lines represents loudness, the thicker the louder (figure 5*b*). Below the wiggly line, representing the sung tones, is a phonetic transcription of the words, with an orthographic version of the same. Part of J. W. Love's construction of a normal score (see below) is a form of graphic notation, as are George List's transcriptions of a Māori *haka* (1963a:8) and what List called a Palauan intonational recitation (1963a:11).

## Numeral notations

Numeral musical shorthands, sometimes called cipher notation, derive from European voice-training practices. These notations took hold only in certain parts of Oceania. Introduced by Christian missionaries for teaching hymns, they survive strongly in Fiji, Tonga, and New Guinea.

Numeral notations represent the notes of the diatonic scale (*do, re, mi,* and so on) as numbers (1, 2, 3, and so on). A related notation uses letters derived from

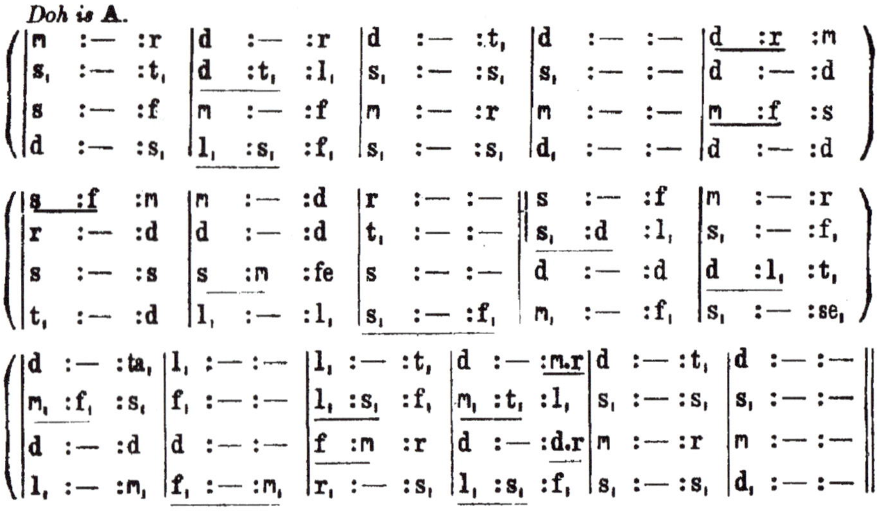

FIGURE 6   Beginning of a Rotuman hymn: the notes of the diatonic scale are represented by the first letters of their names (*do, re, mi,* and so on).

*Doh is* **A.**

```
( |n  :—  :r  |d  :—  :r  |d  :—  :t, |d  :—  :—  |d  :r  :m )
( |s, :—  :t, |d  :t, :l, |s, :—  :s, |s, :—  :—  |d  :—  :d )
( |s  :—  :f  |m  :—  :f  |m  :—  :r  |m  :—  :—  |m  :f  :s )
( |d  :—  :s, |l, :s, :f, |s, :—  :s, |d, :—  :—  |d  :—  :d )

( |s  :f  :m  |m  :—  :d  |r  :—  :—  ‖ s  :—  :f  |m  :—  :r )
( |r  :—  :d  |d  :—  :d  |t, :—  :—  | s, :d  :l, |s, :—  :f, )
( |s  :—  :s  |s  :m  :fe |s  :—  :—  | d  :—  :d  |d  :l, :t, )
( |t, :—  :d  |l, :—  :l, |s, :—  :f, | m, :—  :f, |s, :—  :se, )

( |d  :—  :ta, |l, :—  :—  |l, :—  :t, |d  :—  :m.r |d  :—  :t, |d  :—  :— ‖
( |m, :f, :s, |f, :—  :—  |l, :s, :f, |m, :t, :l, |s, :—  :s, |s, :—  :— ‖
( |d  :—  :d  |d  :—  :—  |f  :m  :r  |d  :—  :d.r |m  :—  :r  |m  :—  :— ‖
( |l, :—  :m, |f, :—  :m, |r, :—  :s, |l, :s, :f, |s, :—  :s, |d, :—  :— ‖
```

solmization syllables (figure 6). Various marks denote suspensions, rests, octaves, and chromatic alterations [see MUSIC AND RELIGION: figure 5]. Subscripts and superscripts mark tones in a lower or a higher octave. In Tonga, missionaries found that the local word for the number three could in some contexts bear an unseemly sense, so they numbered the tones of the scale uniquely.

In New Guinea, the first printed numeral notation appeared in a Roman Catholic hymnal in the Roro language (*Romano Katoliko Katekismo* 1898). Lutheran conch-playing ensembles have employed it, notated in one to four parts, most famously in *The Conchshell-Hymnal* (Zahn 1959 [1934]). It continues in use primarily for Western or Western-inspired music, but has served to notate indigenous melodies: Julian Quinlan (1974) used it to transcribe more than six hundred melodies of the North Solomons.

### Symbolic notations

The use of individual signs apart from a standard staff might be called symbolic notation. Jon Jonassen (1991) devised such a notation for percussive musical instruments. It describes and prescribes musical performance on *pātē* and other log idiophones, the most important percussive instruments of the Cook Islands. It takes either of two forms: a simple figuration of dots and dashes, and a combination of dots, dashes, letters, and virgules. In both forms, the most rudimentary sound, a hit to the side of the instrument (called *tī* in Rarotongan), is a dot, and one hit to the center (*tō*) is a dash. Double quick hits against the side (*tiri*) are two dots or the letter *n,* respectively. Double quick hits to the center (*toro*) are two dashes or the letter *u.* Triple hits are three dots or *m,* and three dashes are *w.* Virgules mark rests, and *o* marks the completion of a sequence. Jonassen shows the example

$$(-\,n\,n\,-\,-\,)^2$$

explained as "one hit at the center . . . , two double hits at the center, followed by two single hits at the center" (1991:38), and the superscript means the performer plays the pattern twice. For a related instrument, the *tōkere,* often played with the *pātē,* Jonassen adds the letters *R* and *L* to specify the hand, and uses other letters to stand for combinations of the simple actions.

For textual analysis, transcribers reserve another kind of symbolic notation, the abbreviation of intervals by obvious letters. In this use, for example, *P4* denotes a perfect fourth, *M3H* denotes a major third higher than a referential point (usually the tonal center), and *m6L* denotes a minor sixth lower.

### Electronic notations

Printouts of music registered etically by an electronic device are gaining increased use in musical transcription; several examples appear in this volume. Even to novice eyes, such printouts can dramatically depict important musical traits, as Tatar proves in four examples of Hawaiian singing (1981:488–489), showing contrasts among systematically critical techniques of vocal production specified as laryngealization, pharyngealization, velarization, and glottalization.

An advantage of electronic transcriptions is their handling of detail. The Melograph, a device invented by Charles Seeger (1951, 1958), produces a finely detailed graph of frequency, duration, amplitude, and harmonic spectrum, leaving to researchers the task of interpreting the printed patterns. But the advantage of detail can become a disadvantage, because musical meaning generated mechanically is not always clear, and "all details in any graph are not equally meaningful" (List 1963b: 195). Though the amount of emic information conveyable in electronic notations may approach zero, such notations can serve as springboards for reasoning about emic rules. To analyze rhythms that the Kwoma, of East Sepik Province, Papua New Guinea, use for signaling, Hugo Zemp fed recordings into a Bruel Kjoer level recorder; the precision of its continuous-line graph helped him study subtleties of the rhythms (Zemp and Kaufmann 1969).

### Multiple notational methods

Since each notational method has advantages and disadvantages, deploying an array of methods can be an effective strategy in examining complex issues of musical analysis. Many Oceanic performances include song, percussion or concussion, and dance (figure 7), but analysts may make separate transcriptions of language, music, and movement, depending on which element they want to foreground.

To ease the analysis of sounds played on garamuts by the Iatmul, Gordon Spearritt (1979) used two methods. An electronic transcription showed changes in intensity and time by using continuous lines. In the recorded performances, the predominant rhythm was triple, so on graph paper Spearritt marked off beats in multiples of three squares. Guided by the printouts, he put a dot in squares representing the points he heard each impact of a garamut. This procedure is not unlike that of time-unit box system notation (TUBS), devised for transcribing West African drumming (Koetting 1970). To guide transcriptions of rhythms played on Hawaiian *pahu,* Elizabeth Tatar similarly used graph paper (1993:317), and combined spectrograms with other forms of notation.

FIGURE 7 At the Pacific Festival of Arts, Enga performers sing, dance, and play kundus. Photo by Adrienne L. Kaeppler, 1996.

### TIME

Music takes myriad kinds of time. It uses short units, several to the second, as in Polynesian drumming. It uses the somewhat longer units often suitable for reciting syllables at their usual spoken pace and singing the notes of Christian hymns. It uses the phrasing of human breaths. It uses the spans that make up stanzas and songs, the stretches of suites, and the courses of whole days or nights of performing. It uses the seasons and the years. In Aboriginal Australia, it uses all of eternity.

Time is highly important in musical composition, performance, and perception. Regional metrical traits may distinguish stylistic areas. East Polynesian and Sāmoan music is mainly in duple meter, but Tongan and 'Uvean music often follows triple meters (as in 3/4 and 6/8 time), and some cultures of Melanesia favor quintuple

**inner tempo** The number of rhythmic impulses per minute, regardless of their periodicity or regularity of occurrence, the distribution of accents, and the presence of a meter

**meter** An underlying pattern of strong and weak stresses (beats), notationally indicated by a time signature and marked off in measures by bar lines

**note** A tone occurring as part of a musical piece; a transcriptive sign of such a tone or any other musically significant sound

**pitch** The perceived height or "location" of sound, measurable in mels; often used loosely in reference to frequency, measurable in hertz

**rhythm** A pattern of strong and weak elements in a flow of sound, sometimes recurring or grouping at multiple levels of organization

**tempo** The perceived speed of a musical performance

**tone** A sound of definite frequency; a pitch or range of pitches treated within a musical system as a sonic identity, often analyzable as a scalar unit

---

meters. Documentation is patchy, however, and interculturally comparative studies focusing on time in Oceanic music are lacking.

In some areas, distinctions of tempo—the number of perceived changes in musical sounds in relation to measured time—differentiate musical genres. Some West Polynesian songs for dancing get faster as they go along. In Tuvalu in the 1890s,

> The curious thing about the singing was that the longer the natives sang the more excited they got, and the faster ran both words and actions, and the louder were the voices; and just when the din became all but insupportable the whole choir and orchestra would suddenly stop dead, and one's ears crackled painfully in consequence. I never could find out how they knew when to stop, for there was no signal given that I could detect, but they always stopped clean, not one singer ever being the veriest shade behind the others. (David 1899:62)

Some areas distinguish between songs that keep a steady tempo and songs that change it. Data provided by Richard Feinberg show that Anutan laments maintain a steady tempo, but Anutan songs for dancing speed up. The increase can become drastic: in a sample of recordings of performances of the genre *mataavaka,* the first statement of the melody begins at sixty to seventy-two beats a minute, but the last ends at 240 to 306; correspondingly, the dancers' movements go from deliberate to frenzied.

—J. W. LOVE

## Tempo

As an analytical concept, tempo raises hard questions. Perceptions of what is significant in a performance are culturally determined. They may differ among individual participants, and among participants and outside observers. Researchers have found no universally apt measures for tempo in music, nor is there much intercultural agreement on the elements that enter into the perception of musical speed.

To gain analytical tools for describing and comparing musical sounds, I transcribed recordings of songs performed by the Kâte and the Sialum of Morobe Province, Papua New Guinea. From the transcriptions, I developed the concepts of "inner tempo," "melic (melodic) tempo," and "harmonic tempo," which I applied to the analysis of other Oceanic music, including that of Tuvalu (Christensen 1957, 1960; Christensen and Koch 1964).

Inner tempo counts the number of rhythmic impulses per minute, regardless of their periodicity or regularity of occurrence, the distribution of accents or emphases, and the presence of a meter. Any sudden change perceived by a careful observer in the music counts as an impulse. If a regular meter is present, such impulses would often occur within the meter, hence the term *inner tempo* to distinguish this concept from the one conventional in Western music. Alternatively describing the rate of these impulses, some researchers speak of *chronometric density.*

The formula for calculating inner tempo is analogous to that for metronomic tempo. Where $N$ is the number of rhythmic impulses and $D$ is duration in seconds,

inner tempo = $N \times 60\ /\ D$

Similarly, a formula for melic tempo counts the changes of tones per minute that an observer perceives in a melody. A rapid repetition of one tone would yield a high inner tempo, but a low melic tempo. An analogous formula for harmonic tempo relates the changes in multivoiced sounds to time.

A comparative analysis of recorded songs of the Kâte and the Sialum showed that the inner tempo of Sialum songs is significantly higher than that of Kâte songs (Christensen 1957:104). Similar studies of music on recordings from Tuvalu allowed me to assess not only differences among various genres of singing and dancing there, but also dramatic increases in intensity during the performances of individual dance-songs (Christensen and Koch 1964:165).        —DIETER CHRISTENSEN

## PITCH

Possibly because issues relating to pitch are highly important in Western music, Western-trained researchers have concentrated on those issues (List 1974). Some indigenous musical systems of Oceania, however, are indifferent to precision in pitch, though they may prescribe the broad outline of melodic contours. In repeated performances, the "absolute pitches" (frequencies) of tones having musically identical functions may differ drastically.

For musical analysis, it is convenient to distinguish among three concepts: a *pitch* is a sound that has a specific vibrational frequency, measurable in hertz; a *tone* is a culturally meaningful range of pitches treated as a musical identity and analyzable as a scalar unit; a *note* is a tone that has a duration in a specific musical performance or piece. An object vibrating 440 cycles a second, a rate describable as 440 hertz, is commonly said to have a pitch of 440. In 1939, the International Standards Association set that frequency as the standard of the tone A. (Each tone occurs at multiple octaves, but the nomenclature of these is not uniform; a widely followed system uses the designation a′ for the level of A defined by 440 hertz.) Other standards have prevailed: the Paris Academy in 1859 adopted a′= 435 as a standard; Handel's and Mozart's tuning forks gave a standard far below that. Today, many symphony orchestras "tune high," at a′= 441 to a′= 444. Musicians who tune their own instruments, including Oceanic guitarists and ukuleleists, pitch their standard at whatever level suits them; bands collectively decide on how high to tune their instruments.

In musical contexts, the *name* of a pitch—the tone by which it may be called—is not precisely determinant. Even in performances using a′= 440 as a standard (especially performances featuring wide vibrato), a note whose sound touches a pitch of 440 hertz may be perceived, not as a′, but as a tone as low as g♯′ or as high as b♭′. Thus, perceived tonalities can differ from measured frequencies.

### The analysis of pitch

Issues relating to pitch can be too fine for the human ear to manage, so researchers may use mechanical and electronic devices, mainly the Stroboconn, the Sonagraph, the Spectrograph, and the Melograph. Because musical style, and therefore musical analysis, mostly depend on the movement of tones in relation to each other, researchers have seldom investigated absolute pitches. When wax-cylinder recording was in vogue, researchers often sounded a tuning fork at the start of a recording, ensuring that the absolute pitch of the playback would match that of the performance.

Catherine Ellis (1964, 1967) studied pitch in Central Australian vocal music. In the 1990s, she and Udo Will devised methods for measuring and analyzing pitch. Studying unfiltered, complex sound waves, they analyzed songlines from Central Australia and songs from Northern Australia (see below). Hugo Zemp (1981), using a Stroboconn, investigated relationships of pitch in 'Are'are panpipe music. Elizabeth Tatar (1981) used a Spectrograph to study Hawaiian singing; in comments on disks of Hawaiian music, she analyzed the recorded pitches.

Melodies can be understood as sequences of intervals, the distances between tones. The artistically important aspect of these sequences is usually the relative relationship of the tones, not their absolute placement on a pitch-based continuum. Therefore, transcriptive work often ignores questions of pitch to focus on questions of tonality. Especially in the early days of the academic analysis of Oceanic music, this tendency led to preoccupation with tonal inventories, as in Mervyn McLean's discovery of 651 Māori scales (1969). But scales are raw materials. More complex and culturally revealing issues concern how musical tones go together—sequentially to make melodies and simultaneously to make harmonies.

Any musical system probably has theoretical concepts of what tones are, and of how tones can (and should) relate to one another. For music that regulates rhythms tightly but tones loosely, a reductive methodology has proved useful in finding melodic tendencies hidden in performative variation (see "Normal scores," below). For music that builds melodies around a single tone, the concept of a tonal center has proved useful (see "Tonal center," below). A lack in most musical scholarship of Oceania concerns how indigenous makers and receivers of music think about pitch and tonality. Probing into the nature and specifics of musical perception, mainly as that perception is coded in aesthetic terminology, has proved a fruitful line of inquiry. Because the number of indigenous scholars has been increasing, this aspect of musical analysis has begun yielding important results.　　　　　—J. W. LOVE

## Concepts of pitch in Central Australia

In 1965, Catherine Ellis found evidence that small intervals (multiples of 3 to 5 hertz) consistently occurred in Central Australian singing. She interpreted these intervals as building blocks for arithmetic (equidistant) scales. Will and Ellis (1994, 1996) confirmed that the complete tonal space of a songline consists of a set of consistently recurring frequencies, with intervals as small as 2 to 6 hertz; however, they found the arrangement of intervals to be nonequidistant. Even melodic elements like glides and inflections can be interpreted as well-defined, consistent movements. They contradict a widely held belief: that Aboriginal melodies move indeterminately and inconsistently among fuzzy pitches.

Nonequidistant arrangements of intervals were also found in a comparative study of six Pitjantjatjara songlines (Will 1995b). The tonal space of these songlines can be considered linearly structured because the size of the intervals, expressed in hertz, does not correlate with their frequency. In addition, intonational variation, in linear terms, appears constant throughout the range of vocal activity.

Though tonal-space structures—sets of distinct pitches within a song—do not indicate the organization of intervals in actual melodies, three lines of evidence show that indeed, "melodic" interval sequences and melodic gestalts are organized linearly. In melodies with a range greater than an octave, the frequency with the longest duration is often the octave of the final (the last note, the tonal center). The crest above this octave is a linear transposition of the crest above the final (crests in frequency-duration graphs correspond to the terraced-pitch areas in the generally descending melodic line of a song): the difference between the octave and the main peak of the crest above it is about the same as that between the final and the main peak of its

FIGURE 8    A frequency-of-occurrence graph: one verse of a Pitjantjatjara songline, whose linear intervals among the three lowest peaks (111, 118, 121 hertz) appear in several other songlines, with the "octave" range linearly replicating the subsequent series of eight peak intervals at 126–157 hertz. Graph by Udo Will.

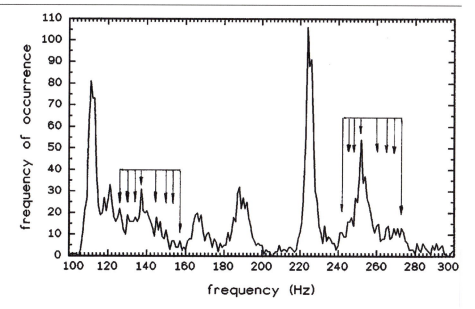

adjacent crest; and the differences between the peaks of the crest above the octave are the same as those of the crest above the final—that is, in this "octave" transposition, the linear intervals of the crest are maintained (figure 8). In 1965, Ellis observed such an "octave" shift for a sequence of two intervals above the final.

In transpositions within songlines, differences between peak frequencies of the crests tend to be maintained; however, because the tonal space is nonequidistant, some intervals must be readjusted, but they are not changed according to ratios (Will and Ellis 1996). This process may be compared to the change from one mode to another in modal music.

Three peaks with a constant frequency difference seem to be a common feature of the crests of the final of several songlines (as at extreme left of figure 8). In all analyzed examples, the differences between the final and the two upper-side peaks are about 6 and 9 hertz, though the frequency of the finals varies between 95 and 155 hertz; if based on a logarithmic system, the intervals would vary from about 6 to 9 hertz and from 9 to 16 hertz, respectively.

In the organization of melodies, ratios are an additional principle. Though the intervals of crests appear transposed according to a linear, nonequidistant system, the relation (distance) between at least the main crests appears regulated according to ratios; in songlines with different final-frequencies, the ratios between the main peaks and their adjacent upper or lower crests are the same. Whether ratios regulate the relation among all or only a few crests is unclear. In either case, the ratios do not seem to approximate small-integer ratios (harmonic ratios), and no link between these ratios and the spectral structure of the performer's voice is evident.

"Octave identity" appears to exist only for the final (Will 1997). With an average size of 1,225.23 cents in four songlines, the octave stretch is much larger than in Northern Australian songs accompanied by the didjeridu, or in Western music (Ward 1954). All intervals in the upper "octave" are linear shifts, not octave transpositions of their counterparts in the lower octave. However, musical practice suggests a more general concept of octave identity: under certain conditions, singers sing the same song or parts of it in octaves (Ellis 1965).

### Concepts of pitch in Northern Australia

Major differences exist between unaccompanied and didjeridu-accompanied songs. In Northern Australia, singers adjust their singing so the fundamental frequency of the voice lies in the range of the first and second octave of the didjeridu drone; hence, didjeridu-accompanied melodies have a higher pitch level than unaccompanied ones. In a sample of didjeridu-accompanied songs (Lauridsen 1983), the average frequency of the drone of the didjeridu was 74.5 hertz, and the average of the final was 224 hertz. Will (1995) found didjeridu drones between 68 and 102 hertz, and corresponding final-frequencies between 114 and 205 hertz.

Adjustment of vocal frequencies to the sound spectrum of the didjeridu leads to the systematic appearance of harmonic intervals: two or three pitches match the second, third, and fourth harmonic of the didjeridu, with a mean deviation of only 7.88 cents ($N = 10$) from the precise harmonic ratios, and the pitches adjusted to the octaves of the didjeridu drone are not necessarily those of the final and its octave.

Jan Lauridsen (1983:62) reported that didjeridu-accompanied songs have a pronounced "bias towards natural intervals," but apart from intervals formed by frequencies adjusted to harmonics of the didjeridu, I found (1995a, 1995b) no other simple-ratio intervals. Instead, the main peaks tend toward equidistant spacing, in terms of ratios (cents). These ratios are greater for songs with a lower final than for those with a higher one. The series of intervals between the main peaks—starting with about 20 hertz (the level of the final), ending with about 50 hertz (the octave)—is similar for all analyzed songs, irrespective of the pitch of the final. These and other traits show that in some Northern Australian songs, the organization of frequencies does not exclusively follow logarithmic principles. —UDO WILL

## Normal scores

Much of the effort of transcribing goes into notating what is aurally evident. But some of the work of analysis concerns how to discover a performer's musical tendencies. For each song, a performer has a concept of what constitutes the essential musical elements. A mental construct, it remains locked in mind. Outsiders cannot scrutinize it directly. Inferential techniques must come into play.

A preliminary task of analysis may be to predict which sound a singer is most likely to produce at any given point. Analysts can make such an inference only by following procedures that take into account the variation inherent in samples of the performer's musical behavior, reductive processes like those developed by Bertrand H. Bronson (1951) to construct an "ideal melodic contour." Of any melody found by quantitative inference, the music may be called a normal score, adapting Percy Grainger's concept of a "normal tune" (1908:154). By compassing the most invariant aspects of a variously realized artifact, it can serve as the best guess about a performer's concept of a piece.

The work of finding the central tendency in performances begins with performers. Multiple renditions by one person must be recorded and transcribed, for without them, no sense of the range and character of personal variation will be available. In only one performance of an otherwise unstudied piece, the typical blends with the idiosyncratic, and an analyst has no reliable basis for distinguishing permanent aesthetic features from contextually accidental ones.

Treatment of one song illustrates the successes and limitations of the concept. The Sāmoan song "*O fetai o le Papa Lauina*" (composed about 1867 by a man of Falealupo, Savai'i) consists of three stanzas, each followed by a refrain. In 1972–1973, it was sung for the record by Fa'animo, a learned lady, then in her nineties. For many years, she had been the last person to know the song. But in what form did she know it? During twelve sessions, quasi-randomly spaced over nearly two years, she performed its first stanza sixteen times; its second, fifteen; and its third, fourteen: she added forty-five performances of the refrain. Transcriptions of these performances became the raw material for analysis.

FIGURE 9    The Index of Tonal Consistency shows the percent by which every metrically salient unit in a normal score matches notes documented in multiple performances. Transcription by J. W. Love.

### Deriving the normal score

A mechanical process of tabulation to derive a normal score uses five basic steps: by matching the melodic contours, transpose all versions of the melody to the same scalar level; superimpose all melodies on a grid, and take the modal rhythmic unit for a standard, so columns represent units and rows represent tones as sung; for each column and row, tabulate the number of performances in which each musical event (symbolized by rests and tones) occurs; select the symbol of highest plurality in each unit to be represented in the normal score; edit the melody in the staff, adjusting the notation to account for phrasing, accentuation, and other persistent attributes.

The percent of correspondence of the normal score with the performances can be expressed as the Index of Tonal Consistency, $C$. Computed for an excerpt, a piece, or a set of pieces, it serves as a guide to the degree of variation within the sample (figure 9). Secondarily, it shows how much detail the derivation of the normal score has discarded. A value of $C$ of 75 shows that the normal score corresponds with 75 percent of the tones actually sung, and that 25 percent of the detail has been eliminated as being variation of little compositional significance.

### Ideal and actual

Construction of a normal score raises the issue of the relationship of the ideal and the actual. In a set of variously realized sounds, the central tendency, defined as the normal score, may be clear; but we do not necessarily know how closely it matches any ideal set of sounds intended by a performer or imagined by a listener.

In the broadest sense, the detail discarded in construction of the normal score is insignificant. A comparison of the distribution of tones in the normal score of "'*O fetai o le Papa Lauina*" and the performances that support its derivation (Love 1991:201) shows the tones D and F are slightly more favored in the normal score, but the tones E and G occur about 2 percent more often in the performances. Differences of these amounts are too small not to be negligible and ascribable to error—on the part of the recorder, the transcriber, or even the singer.

In the study of an art known only from performance, two kinds of witness cooperate in telling a single truth: a best guess of what in performance constitutes the artwork, and an indication of how reliable that guess is. Lack of the first would keep us from understanding systematic tendencies behind the performance; lack of the second would keep us from presenting evidence that might enable others to weigh our success in seeing the system. Without a normal score, a researcher cannot fully demonstrate how a melody constitutes an artistic system; without an index to measure that variation, other researchers cannot effectively evaluate the evidence. These witnesses find their function in analytical concepts: a normal score, objectively abstracted from raw information, is a reasonable guess about the essential tones and rhythms of a song, and the Index of Tonal Consistency qualifies that guess by specifying, at every temporally relevant point, the amount of correspondence between the normal score and the raw material.

—J. W. LOVE

### Tonal centers

Through an aural logic resembling verbal grammar, a society invents and maintains its music. This logic often involves the concept of tonal centers, whether verbalized as such or not. This concept has proved useful in analyzing the music of New Guinea and Melanesia. It corresponds to the Western concept of "key."

Musical grammar controls the aurally meaningful elements of a musical system. It gives coherence to their distribution, in relation to each other, and to the larger units of which they are components (Chenoweth 1972). It presupposes and underlies the meaningful progression of sounds.

Because tonal intervals relate to one another serially, the logic of musical grammar works through time. Like lexical terms, the tones of a musical composition function within short units of time, to articulate motifs and phrases. In some musical systems, they sound together to form harmonies. Like syntactical structures, these tones function in larger temporal units to bring into musical coherence the memories of serially disposed sonic events. During performance, they enhance the expectation and appreciation of musical form.

The grammar of music takes into account the interrelationship between serial progressions of significant units (musical syntax); it often has to address the underlying vocabulary of tonal possibilities (musical tonality). The potentialities of the latter give dynamic power to the former.

In the melodies of previously unanalyzed musical systems, the location of a tonal center is sometimes evasive. Several expectations aid in locating it: it occurs in rhythmically strong positions, its distribution within a melody has few restrictions (it may be approached and left by the greatest variety of tones), and it is often the final tone. When these conditions occur in a musical piece, frequency of occurrence may offer further confirmation of a tonal center, which may or may not occur more frequently than other tones. In language, the words most frequently used are not necessarily focal points: in English, the most frequently used word is the article *the,* but that word is seldom the focal point of a sentence; so also the tones of a melody. The concept of tonal center concerns the referential plane of a melody, the so-called gravitational tone (Chenoweth 1979:140). It activates other tones, acoustically coloring their motion.

Analyzing the structure of any unwritten music or language, one seldom finds solutions in a predictable order; only the final product bears descriptive elegance. Often, the analyst may remain undecided about the tonal center of a song until tabulations reveal the central tendencies of the tones.

Some melodies have dual tonal centers, both of which seem to have equal importance. If this is the case and the analyst wants to explore the possibilities of having just one tonal center, the tone on which the song ends would seem to break the tie, but only if in many melodies it is consistently the cadential tone.

## TIMBRE

The musical analysis of timbre, the quality given to tones by their harmonics, is a thorny issue. Timbre may affect listeners' appreciation of a performance, yet because it entails complex acoustical information, it has proven harder to study than rhythms and melodies. Terms listeners choose to describe it are usually imprecise. Academic studies of its aesthetic and social relevance to the peoples of Oceania are rare.

The perception of timbre depends on the presence and relative prominence of harmonics. A given tone produced on different instruments may have the same fundamental, but if the intensities of the harmonics differ, we attribute different qualities to the sounds and recognize that the instruments are of different kinds. The identifying harmonics of an instrument typically lie within fixed vibrational bands, called formants. In speaking and singing, the articulatory actions of the parts of the oral cavity and the throat invoke different formants. As a result, for each vowel, the human voice becomes a separate instrument; accordingly, the orchestration of vowels throughout musical texts is an important compositional task and an alluring analytical issue [see LANGUAGE IN MUSICAL SETTINGS: Sonics].

In Oceania, timbre may broadly mark registers of speech and song, and its details may code subtle plays of sense and intent. The ideal timbres of political oratory and Christian sermons may differ markedly from those of conversation. In cultures that use rhyme in poetry, the timbres of rhyming sounds may reveal underlying aesthetic principles. Sāmoan oral poetry has rhymes that by featuring the open vowel /a/ differ widely from vowel-produced timbres in samples of conversation and lexicons (Love 1991:97–100). Emphasizing a series of emotional transformations from worry to hope, one Sāmoan poem starts with the back-shifting pairs *ao* and *au,* reverses to *oa,* and ends with the front-shifting pairs *ae* and *ai.*

## Falsetto

Falsetto, a timbre resulting from limitations of the tone-making apparatus, has been reported from many areas of Oceania. Its use enables singers to reach pitches above their full-voice range. In some societies, men and women sing in falsetto; in others, falsetto is typical of one sex, usually males. Falsetto singing may be singers' improvisational choice, or it may help define specific genres, whose performance would seem wrong without it. In societies where it marks genres, it contrasts with other genres. It serves many social functions. In some areas, it empowers magic performed to produce desired outcomes. In the highlands of New Guinea, it is a standard style for songs sung and giggled by courting teenagers of both sexes. Along the Rai Coast of New Guinea, it marks singing into voice-modifying instruments for sacred purposes. In many parts of Oceania, narrators use it for voicing characters' dialogue.

Falsetto singing by males occurs throughout Oceania in solo and ensemble singing to chordophone accompaniment, reflecting either an indigenous aesthetic or twentieth-century influence from Hawai'i [see POPULAR MUSIC], or a blend of these foundations. Usually in polyphonic singing, the falsetto pitches are the highest of the vocal ensemble; even when they are not, their timbre may give the impression that they are. Falsetto may have a cadential function, marking the ends of stanzas, as in Sāmoa (figure 10), and laments, as on Anuta. It may be a marker of rehearsing, as on Bellona. In Hawaiian singing, it reached a high degree of elaboration, and retains important affective and evaluative implications (see below).

Falsetto singing may be unusually loud, as with the Buang, or tense, as with the Siasi; but it more typically occurs at subdued levels, as with the Irumu, the Managalasi, the Maring, the Sursurunga, and many other peoples. Yodeling, the rapid alternation of falsetto and full-voice singing, can be piercingly loud. It occurs famously among many peoples of Irian Jaya and Papua New Guinea (see below), and it marks certain musical genres of the Solomon Islands.                    —J. W. LOVE

TRACK 10

FIGURE 10   In an excerpt from a Sāmoan song, brackets mark where the singer uses falsetto to extend his melodic range; ukulele accompaniment not shown. Transcription by J. W. Love.

♩ = 120

Ma– li– e ma– ia 'i se 'u– pu 'u– a sa– la:    'i la– fo a– ne 'i– a    'i fo– gā– va– 'a.

'O ai lēi– lo– a le ta– ga– ta lē se– sē    'ai– lo– a mai e 'o– e?

Huli collective yodeling occurs when men work together. It synchronizes individual actions, informing listeners of the activity in progress. It has several genres, each based on patterns of interlocking calls.

FIGURE 11    Excerpts of Huli yodeling: *a, nògo ú; b, gèla; c, àliwa.* Transcriptions by Jacqueline Pugh-Kitingan.

## Huli yodeling

Yodeling is an important musical activity of the Huli, of Southern Highlands Province, Papua New Guinea [see HIGHLAND REGION OF PAPUA NEW GUINEA]. The Huli differentiate two main types of men's yodeling: solo yodeling (*ú*), and collective yodeling (*ìwa*). Solo yodeling helps people communicate across mountainous terrain. Men yodel whole statements; each ends with a high-called *ú*. Purely yodeled signals also occur, including *à–ú–à–ú* 'Where are you?' and *háko–háko* 'I'm here'.

Collective yodeling occurs when men work together. It synchronizes individual actions, informing listeners of the activity in progress. It has several genres, each based on patterns of interlocking calls: the high-falling *ú* begins all collective yodeling, is usually started by one man, and can spring from a low pitch on the vowel /a/, the same level to which it falls; *pēge, pēbe, hēbe, pēbo,* or *bēbo* is a level, lower-pitched call; the level *kē* is the highest falsetto call; *ī,* a medium-level call, follows *kē; gèla* is a rising call, yelled in a medium range; *púlu* or *úlu,* the lowest call, resembles a falling exclamation. The Huli have six main genres of collective yodeling.

1. *Nògo ú* 'pig yodel' (figure 11*a*) is performed by men carrying cuts of butchered pigs to the *hòmanogo,* a feast held after mourning a death. It is based on

the pattern *ú–gèla,* which pivots on the piercing call *ú.* It signals that the death has been compensated for, so mourning must cease.

2. *Gèla* (figure 11*b*) is the name of the *ìwa* yodeled in public processions of the fertility rituals *tēge* and *gáia tēge.* It also occurs in *tēge púlu* initiations, as the initiates run to the culthouses with their guardians and during rituals inside the house. It follows the *ú–gèla–púlu* pattern, where *púlu* often overlaps *gèla.* Boys sometimes cry the *kē* call above the men's *gèla* and *púlu.* The call *gèla,* with its syllables a major second apart, has a clearer melodic structure than that of the pig yodel; the syllable *kē* lies an octave above the syllable *là.* The *gèla* coordinates collective movements, summons spirits, and frightens younger initiates to toughen them.

3. As victorious warriors return after battle or men work jointly, they cry a fast yodel simply named *ìwa,* based on the pattern *ú–pège.* The high *ú* lies an octave above *pège,* with the vowel /a/ a major third (rarely a minor third) above *pège.* The *ú* sometimes falls a major third, its low point sounding an octave above *pège.* The *kē* then occurs on the high *ú* in time with *pège.*

*TRACK 11*

4. Male dancers yodel *màli ìwa* at nighttime rehearsals for daytime *màli*-dance celebrations. It has the same repeated pattern as the *ìwa.* The dancers form two facing rows. In time to the beating of their kundus, the yodeling synchronizes their sideways-jumping steps; it announces the *màli,* attracting spectators.

5. As rain approaches, boys walking together may yodel the *àliwa* or *àli ìwa* ('man's *ìwa*'). It follows the syllabic pattern *ú–pège–kē–ī,* where *kē* and *ī* coincide with *pège* (figure 11*c*). The *ú–pège* relationship resembles that of the men's *ìwa; ī* lies a major third above *pège* and an octave below *kē.* The *àliwa* expresses coldness, informs listeners of approaching rain, and trains the boys' voices for yodeling as adults. The word *àliwa* denotes a form of *ú,* boys' solo yodeling in wet weather.

6. Women have solo and collective calls. In rage or excitement, a woman shouts *hèagola!* Peaceful groups of women walking to their gardens in fine weather call out *hēao.* The Huli recognize that these calls have communicative functions, but do not classify them as yodeling because they do not use falsetto.

If not enough men for collective yodeling are available at a feast, one man imitates the relevant *ìwa* using a short bamboo tube (*pīlipè*), closed at one end by a node. Pressing this pipe against his lower lip, he blows while groaning in falsetto (Pugh-Kitingan 1986). The resultant textures—pipe fundamental, overblown partials, falsetto voice—resemble collective yodeling, with vocal melodies outlining characteristic tunes.

—JACQUELINE PUGH-KITINGAN

## Interpreting timbre in Hawai'i

For contemporary Hawaiians, listening to music is not just auditory pleasure, but social practice, informed by the knowledge of indigenous Hawaiian and Western musics. In 1991–1992, the Kamehameha Schools [see MUSIC AND EDUCATION: Hawai'i] served as a site for studying this process. Students in grades nine through twelve listened to music of Hawaiian and European-American origins, and monitored the thoughts, images, and sensations that came into their consciousness. Coded and analyzed, their responses revealed distinctive attitudes toward timbre.

The students preferred vocal timbres over purely instrumental timbres, whether Hawaiian or Western. This preference reflects indigenous aesthetics. The most important musical genre of the precontact period, *mele,* is no longer part of everyday life, but highlights significant social events. Young people study it in *hula* schools [see EAST POLYNESIA: Hawai'i: Dance] and courses on Hawaiian culture, where they learn that performances were prized for the delivery of poetry rich in descriptive imagery and euphonious devices, and subject to multiple interpretations of *kaona,* meanings hidden in allusions and metaphors (Roberts 1977 [1926]:57; Wong 1965:9).

Indigenous Hawaiian philosophy emphasized the agency of sounded words, whose power could deeply affect performers, listeners, and their environment. The students displayed their understanding of this principle by quoting the proverb *I ka ʻōlelo nō ke ola; i ka ʻōlelo nō ka make* 'In language is life; in language is death'. Most students, though skeptical of the extreme power of sounded words, maintained a language-centered view of music. They valued text-driven music for its capacity to tell stories.

### Social interpretations of vocal timbre

The student listeners also imputed personal attributes to singers on the basis of timbre. This interpretive strategy reveals a cultural focus on vocal nuance, reflecting contemporary Hawaiians' social concerns. Timbre was an important artistic feature in Hawaiʻi, which had more than forty terms describing *mele*-related vocal qualities (Tatar 1979, 1982). Singers drew from many vocal techniques to mark their individual styles and communicate affect (Trimillos 1989). The cultural focus on vocal quality, particularly for exploiting changes in vocal register, later facilitated singers' adoption of non-Hawaiian styles of falsetto singing, such as yodeling.

The students' social interpretation of vocal timbre reflects the centrality of harmonious and lasting interpersonal relations. Hawaiians' investment in affiliation requires them to develop strategies for determining others' trustworthiness. They "have discovered that . . . focusing on expressive cues is the surest path to reliable knowledge" (Howard 1974:31). Such cues include proxemic behavior, facial expression, and vocal timbre.

Implementing these sensitivities to expressive nuance, the students often treat musical performances as social encounters. On the basis of vocal quality, they impute personal attributes and intentions. A voice whose raspiness and creakiness remind them of aging people may inspire feelings of trust, invoking the affection they feel for their elders, but the same voice may receive criticism if it does not blend sufficiently in a choral setting. Because of the emphasis on interpersonal harmoniousness, listeners perceive equally blended voices to imply cohesive social relationships. Students at Kamehameha Schools acquire this interpretive strategy, in part, through their choral-singing tradition, which associates musical success with singers' attainment of psychological, rhythmic, intonational, and timbral unity.

—C. K. Szego

## STRUCTURE

Above the level of single pitches and tones, music has many kinds of structure. Notes may combine into phrases, phrases into sections, sections into pieces, and pieces into suites. Performances begin and end, and in between they undergo structure-implying processes. All sorts of performative events—Australian Aboriginal ceremonies, Christian liturgies, festival concerts, touristic floor shows, New Guinean singsings— may have complex structures entailing distinct segments, each of which has its own structure. Even the musical system of a whole society can be called a structure.

Much of the structuring of music involves the passage of time. Most notations, by graphing time on a left-right axis, reinforce the conceit that synchronic sounds are *vertical* structures (harmony), and diachronic sounds are *horizontal* structures (melody). For most practical purposes, melodies in which only one meaningful sound occurs at a time can be considered the simplest horizontal structures. As a succession of discrete acoustic events, they naturally have no shape, but because they may give culturally informed minds the illusion that they do, their analysis concerns the processes that give that impression.

The simplest melodic structures of Oceanic music are *formulaic*. A melodic formula may consist of a tone or a series of tones (some variously optional or alternative), whose rhythmic realization depends mostly on the words that give it breath. Such formulas serve throughout Oceania in monophonic recitational singing. Compositional processes can develop formulas into extended works of beauty and power. A formula may divide into segments, as in an opening phrase and a closing phrase. On the interplay of such segments, and of optional or alternative tones, much of the art of formulaic structure depends. Because formulaic singing can tire listeners unfamiliar with the language, it seldom attracts intercultural interest, especially in the absence of dancing. It often receives the name of "chant."

*Strophic* structures, which expand the idea of contrast to include the regular recurrence of larger or more numerous segments, can be viewed as complex formulas, but they usually have more tightly fixed rhythms, are metrically stricter, and depend less on words. They are the usual structures of Christian hymns, and of styles commonly called country, rock, and reggae. They are therefore the typical structures of current Oceanic popular music. Plenty of songs in indigenous musical systems, however, were strophic, and they remain so, whether preserved from the past or newly composed in older styles.

Vertical structures sounded in sequence may be regarded as *texture*. Voices that move in unison, with everyone singing or playing the same note at the same time, are said to be *monophonic*. Voices that move somewhat independently from each other are said to be *polyphonic*. Musical systems may develop unique textures: the interweaving human voices of Eipo *mot,* Fataleka *'aukwee,* and Tahitian *hīmene* make textures that differ unmistakably from each other. Variant textures within a musical system may interrelate: human voices, a didjeridu, and clapsticks combine to make a defining texture of certain Australian Aboriginal music; but even without the didjeridu, voices and clapsticks may sound against each other in similar ways. Rock, reggae, and other internationally popular styles stand apart. One or more human voices sing against guitars or keyboards and drums, weaving a texture that crosscuts the musical systems of Oceania.

—J. W. LOVE

### Yolngu clansong scalar structures

Yolngu clans assert collective identities by owning and maintaining unique sets of songs. They may claim ownership of series, ancestral spirits sung within a given series, musical words (*dharuk*) or dialect (*matha* 'tongue') used in singing, skeletal melodic structures (*dhambu* 'head'), "sound" (*rirrakay* 'noise'), concussive rhythms (*biḻma* 'clapsticks'), and dances accompanying sung performances.

*Dhambu* are important because they are regarded as inviolate ancestral creations. Unlike clapstick patterns, vocal and didjeridu rhythms, and certain textual aspects (all of which may be subject to reinterpretation in certain public contexts), the basic tonal structures of *dhambu* are said to be closed to innovation. *Dhambu* are the most consistently distinguishing acoustical traits of a clan's songs. Each clan is associated with a variety of clapstick patterns, didjeridu rhythms, and vocal rhythms, but it has only one—rarely two or three—*dhambu.*

Each *dhambu* consists of a scale (sometimes with two modal variants) and an idiomatic set of brief melodic formulas. The number of discrete scalar tones associated with various clans' *dhambu* range from two to six, including the octave, where applicable. In each performed verse, singers improvise one or more descending melodic lines based on the underlying scalar structure of a given *dhambu.* Within the constraints of this structure, melodic lines are built up through the use of associated motivic formulas, the choice of which may be determined by clapstick pattern(s) or other rhythmic features.

The scales of some clans' *dhambu* may be analyzed as having two modal variants. This possibility commonly arises where the range of the basic scale spans an octave.

FIGURE 12    Three Yolngu skeletal melodic structures: *a,* of the Guyula Djambarrpuyngu clan; *b,* of the "Top" Djapu clan; *c,* of the "Top" Ngaymil clan. The tones indicate averaged or possible intervals, and do not imply a standard tuning. For ease in comparison, the tonal levels of the given scales have been adjusted to have a final note of middle C. Brackets show the tones of modal variants. Transcriptions by Steven Knopoff.

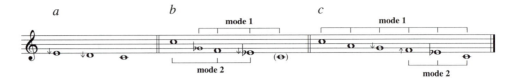

Singers typically sing in one mode for a long time before switching to the other. These modes may be thought of as *registral modes,* in that one of the main reasons for changing mode is to allow the singer(s) to shift from a lower to a higher vocal register, or vice versa. Switching modes is primarily how singers effect changes in register. Adjusting vocal range by transposition is rare.

Unlike Western tempered tuning, Yolngu tuning is variable: in a given *dhambu,* some intervals tend to remain fairly constant while others vary, sometimes by more than a semitone, depending on context. Yolngu singing allows for the insertion of microtonal passing notes and neighbor notes in certain contexts.

### Three examples of structures

The Guyula Djambarrpuyngu clan's *dhambu* has a scale of three tones (figure 12). The interval between the first and second tones is commonly about 200 cents, a major second. The interval between the second and third tones is usually somewhat smaller, often varying between 120 and 170 cents.

Melodies of the "Top" Djapu clan are based on two modal variants of a four-note scale (not counting the ornamental pitch given as G♭ in figure 12). Mode 1 of the Djapu *dhambu* may have two to four tones; it involves the alternation of F and flat-E♭, but often includes a prominent ornamentational pitch, G♭. The lowest tone of the scale rarely occurs, and then only during the final part of the verse. Mode 2 uses two of the same tones as mode 1, plus the lowest tone of mode 1 transposed up an octave, but does not use an ornamental tone.

The "Top" Ngaymil clan's *dhambu* also appears in two modal variants. Mode 1 involves descending melodic phrases using all six scalar tones, the first and sixth about an octave apart. The intervening tones are spaced at alternately large and small intervals, which sometimes roughly approximate distances of 300 cents (a minor third) and 150 cents (1½ semitones), respectively. Mode 2 uses a subset of the full scale. The three tones of mode 2 are often sung an octave higher, allowing a shift to singing in a higher vocal register.

—STEVEN KNOPOFF

## Melodic structures in Eastern Highlands Province, Papua New Guinea

Melodies typical of the province have three to eight tones; four-tone melodies are the most common. Because syntactic restraints curtail melodic movement in a single direction, vocal lines have wavy contours. After a maximum of four tones in one direction, the movement stops in repeated notes, or reverses. Tonal progressions show a tendency for movement to and from the tonal center.

All songs of the province have tones selected from the summary in figure 13. Regardless of the selection, each of them progresses commonly to and from the tonal center. When they occur, tones a perfect fourth and a minor third below the tonal center move freely from one to the other; when tones a major second and major third occur above the tonal center, the lower typically proceeds to the higher, but not the reverse.

Apart from women's octave doubling, harmonic intervals do not occur. Cadences are unprepared, but more than half the songs collected end on a tonal center. The duration of songs averages three to four minutes, but performances extend by linking the songs of one composer, one class (such as fight songs), or one ritual (such as male purification).

FIGURE 13    Melodic structures of Eastern Highlands Province, Papua New Guinea: the arrows show syntactically permitted movement among scalar tones; the tonal center is A. Transcription by Vida Chenoweth.

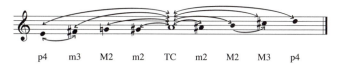

Compositional plans rely mostly on the presence of two contrastive phrases. Most songs follow this plan, but when texts are long and the ceremony is not in focus, more kinds of phrases are present, up to five in Usarufa. When a song consists of only two contrastive phrases, they may repeat in various combinations, but no examples show a combination longer than five phrases in sequence before some repetition of the pattern occurs. No restrictions govern the combinations of A-phrases and B-phrases, except that phrase B occurs consistently as the second phrase in all combinations. Melodies develop by variation within phrases. Devices for variation include the omission, the addition, and the substitution of tones. Melodic rhythm varies likewise, as changes in the text dictate (Chenoweth 1979:97–113).

Songs with multiple phrases are usually through-composed, with derived phrases: each new phrase grows from motifs of preceding phrases (Chenoweth 1979:158). The melody thus develops like a spiral. In content, examples of these are usually less serious than ceremonial songs. Multiple phrases are typical of songs within stories, girls' coming-of-age songs, and songs associated with preadolescence.

—VIDA CHENOWETH

## Yupno personal tunes

About six thousand Yupno inhabit a rugged, isolated region in the eastern Finisterre Range, at an altitude of about 2 kilometers, along the slopes of the Yupno Valley, Madang Province, Papua New Guinea. Several months a year, they occupy dispersed settlements at higher altitudes, collecting pandanus nuts, and hunting marsupials. Surrounded by high fences, their houses resemble haystacks—a style that occurs only in this area of New Guinea. Having no windows, the houses provide shelter from the cold. In the middle of each house, an elongated fire (as long as 10 meters), which provides the only light, burns continually.

The Yupno have a unique type of vocal music: the *konggap* 'ghost voice'. Each is a short tune, lasting just a few seconds (figure 14). Texts consist of vocables. Each Yupno person has a *konggap*, just like a name (Keck 1992:80–82). Shortly after a baby's birth, the mother invents a melody for the child. The melody is provisional, and the child may later replace it with another. Children find their tunes in several ways: some play with different melodies until one seems right; others dream their tune (a spirit communicates it to them in a dream). The *konggap* accompanies the person through life; after the person's death, relatives can sing it in mourning or remembrance: neither inheritable nor transferable, it is inseparably linked with its owner's personality.

*Konggap* most frequently identify persons over wide distances. When crossing a garden or stretch of bush, a Yupno sings the landowner's tune, showing knowledge

FIGURE 14    *Konggap* melodies of Gua Village, Madang Province (after Niles 1992:155).

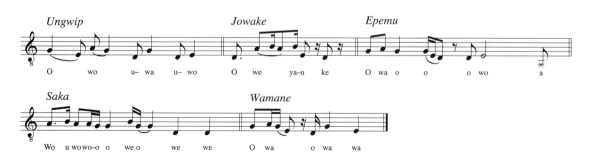

and revealing intent; only strangers—that is, enemies—would remain silent (Wassmann 1993:170). People use a *konggap* to summon a person: they sing the *konggap* of the individual they wish to call, followed by the word *wupwup* 'come'. A person may sing someone else's *konggap* simply because he or she is thinking of that individual at that moment, or just for private pleasure. From all directions during the day, an alert listener constantly hears *konggap,* sung by men, women, and children.

One does not normally sing one's own melody in the presence of others, or during the day. To do so would be considered hot (pretentious, arrogant, immodest), elevating oneself above the cool social midst of others. People, however, do sing their own melody, as when a groom, derided for incompetence ("coldness"), is unexpectedly able to contribute to the bride-price payment; or when someone manages to steal a piece of another's body-soul (clinging to some betel), to make that person ill ("heat up"); or, formerly after a battle, when someone returned victorious to his village. In these cases, the person concerned sings as a sign he has humiliated or defeated others: this is "letting out the hidden feelings by singing the *konggap.*"

### Simultaneous performance

One occasion requires every man to sing his tune: during the *njaguo konggap,* a dance accompanied by drumming in unison, each man sings his tune at the same time the other men are singing theirs. Consequently, the sound of a *njaguo konggap* is distinctive: a multipart mass of asynchronous vocalizations, unified by percussive rhythms and synchronous steps. Such dances occur only in the darkness of night; by incessantly repeating a tune, some singers attain a trancelike state.

Dancers move counterclockwise in a circle, bending alternate knees with each beat. Each male plays a kundu, closed with a skin at one end, open at the other, with a carved handle at the center. Decorations for such a performance are distinctive. A correct performance includes at least one man, but preferably as many as possible, wearing a large, umbrella-shaped decoration (*njaguo*). The wearer of this decoration fastens to his waist a piece of cloth painted with clan-specific designs; it covers his buttocks and hangs to the backs of his knees (figure 15).

The Yupno hold group performances to announce that a man can marry, celebrate the opening of a new house, honor a couple's first pregnancy, prepare for war, or close a successful battle. Women dance outside the men's circle, but do not sing.

Each Yupno adult knows the *konggap* of hundreds of people in his or her own and neighboring villages. With this number of individual tunes in circulation, it might be tempting to assume the tunes would feature certain common traits, say, among *konggap* of members of the same social group; however, this is not the case. Melodic and rhythmic patterns vary widely; they have no relationship to the spoken language, nor do they imitate the sounds of birds or other animals.

—JÜRG WASSMANN

## Wavy processes in Yapese music

Micronesian music often features melodies of three to seven notes, grouped in strophic forms or sequences of phrases. Popular Micronesian melodies based on Western styles are syllabic, with minor or (mainly) major scales, in 4/4 or 2/4 meter, though irregular time sometimes appears. The music of these pieces has abandoned many features of indigenous styles.

Distinctions between older and newer musical styles may have little consequence. The Yapese regard indigenous and Western-influenced songs as Yapese; what, if anything, matters to the Yapese is the difference between their music and that of other Micronesians. The Yapese say they can distinguish between their songs and those of other areas—not only by the words, but also by the melodic patterns.

FIGURE 15    Men decorated for the *konggap* dance of Gua Village, Madang Province. Photo by Don Niles, 1987.

### Foregrounding waves over scales

Yapese melodies tend to consist of successive upward and downward motions, locally said to resemble a wave. For this reason, the most important element in the Yapese conceptualization of their music is not the scale or the rhythm, but the waviness of the melodies. Yapese composers of popular music say they use wavy patterns to catch the Yapese spirit. They prefer to select notes from major scales, rather than to use the Yapese scale, which has five tones, transcribable as C–E–F–G–B. Yapese composers harmonize and rhythmicize melodies on Western instruments—electric guitars, keyboards, and drums.

To emphasize the waviness, composers sometimes use wide ranges between the highest and lowest notes. "*Fanam toorel*" (figure 16*a*), composed in the late 1960s (and still popular with young people thirty years later), shows this tendency. In the initial phrase, the range from the highest tone to the lowest is an octave and a perfect fifth. When upward motion reaches the highest tone, downward motion begins; when downward motion reaches the lowest tone, upward motion begins. Thus, the song consists of a continuous wavy movement.

A typical performance of an older Yapese topical song (*meleng*) also shows wavy patterns (figure 16*b*). This genre, popular until the mid-1940s, uses a melodic pattern that clarifies a wavy movement when repeated. Each phrase begins on the lowest tone and moves to the highest; the downward movement ends with the second-lowest tone. The next phrase begins with the lowest tone, the same as the first phrase.

Yapese singers, young and old, often use short scalar glides, with no effect on basic melodic waviness. During dances, each dancer may sing these ornaments idiosyncratically, varying a unison melody. Even in the mid-1990s, some Yapese singers used these ornaments while performing popular songs, though their listeners did not always know how indigenous the style was. Wavy ornaments sometimes occur when older Yapese perform Japanese songs for schoolchildren, though these singers are conscious of singing as their Japanese teachers taught them.

### Upward movement

A conspicuous feature of wavy patterns in Yapese music is that they usually begin with upward motion. When the leader recites at the start of a Yapese dance, the recitation is expected to start on a low pitch and slide up to a high pitch. Many Yapese popular songs also begin with upward motion, an element that may distinguish Yapese songs from other music in Micronesia.

Yapese say that beginning a melody with an upward movement is a good way for drawing participants into the performance. For this reason, when a group of men exchange love-related songs with a group of women, they sing in this manner. Further, when Yapese hail someone at a distance, they accent the name on the second syllable; they sound the response in a high range, not heard in ordinary conversation.

Though wavy patterns are a prominent feature of Yapese music, similar features appear in the music of other parts of Micronesia. As a result of frequent cultural exchanges among the islands, non-Yapese dances have reached Yap. People who live on small islands with similar physical resources naturally have common musical concepts, often differing from that outside their area. Some Yapese composers say that

FIGURE 16    Two Yapese melodies: *a,* the beginning of "*Fanam toorel,*" a song composed by Joel Fa'lady, performed by Nexsus, and dictated by John Gilmatam; *b,* "*Gobal,*" a song composed by twelve men of Anoz Village, performed by Tethin, and recorded by Osamu Yamaguti in 1965 (transcription by Junko Konishi).

Anutan music is monophonic. Melodies move in unison or octaves: while some singers skip from a unison down to a note, others skip upward to the octave of that note; later, the performers coalesce on a unison.

when they go to the shore, the surf gives them inspiration. Figuratively, they imply, they learn their music from the sounds of the waves.    —JUNKO KONISHI

### Musical structures of Anuta

Recordings and information provided by Richard Feinberg permit certain structural processes to be illustrated by the music of Anuta, a Polynesian outlier in the Solomon Islands. An Anutan choral song normally consists of two stanzas of text, each with its own melody (*aro reo*): but some songs have three stanzas, and a few have four; almost none have just one. The term *kopu* 'parcel, package' designates a stanza. A stanza normally consists of three phrases, which can be reduced to verses (lines of text); but many stanzas have four, and some extend to five or more; a few stop after two.

The formal progress of these songs is the same in all performances: each stanza repeats immediately, before the next begins; and after the repetition of the last stanza, the whole cycle may begin anew. Thus, a three-stanza piece might in performance take the structure AABBCC, or AABBCC + AABBCC, or AABBCC + AABBCC + AABBCC. To provide smooth tonal transitions, the melody of a stanza may have first and second endings; some melodies reserve a miniature coda to follow the last repetition of the last stanza. Almost any number of cycles may occur: public performance involves about ten to twenty cycles of a *mako,* or about five to ten cycles of a *puatanga.* Only rarely does one cycle suffice for a satisfactory performance.

Melodies of dance-songs flow continuously, with no rests: individual singers inhale at self-chosen times. They may continue to mouth the words during inhalation. Only rarely and by accident do they all pause at once. The cyclical sense of the formal progress of a melody receives reinforcement, and the end of the repetition of the last stanza leads without a break into the beginning of the first.

#### Scalar structures

Apart from stray harmonic intervals, Anutan music is monophonic. Melodies move in unison or octaves: while a few singers skip from a unison down to a given note, others skip upward to the octave of that note; later, and possibly even on the next note, the performers coalesce again on a unison. The effect is of monophonic motion in which harmonic octaves occasionally occur (figure 17*a*).

An individual singing alone may realize a given note first in one register, and then at the octave, as shown by the placement of C in figure 17*b,* from successive renditions of the same phrase. Anutans' indifference to octaves reinforces the point that they conceive music monophonically. Anutan melodies usually stay within a range defined by about a major sixth below middle C and a minor third above it; however, when soloists perform (as for a recording), their melodies wander beyond these limits.

#### Typologies

Scalar and metrical structures sort Anutan songs into two classes. Songs of the first

FIGURE 17  Harmonies in Anutan melodies (brackets): *a,* a unison melody breaks out into parallel octaves; *b,* excerpts from one person's successive renditions of the same phrase of a song show indifference to the octave in which the tone transcribed as C sounds. Transcriptions by J. W. Love.

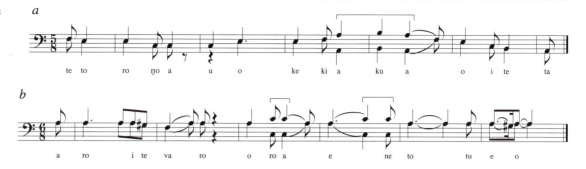

class are somewhat homogeneous in tonal resources, but heterogeneous in meter. They share a scale notatable as A–B–C–E–F. The most frequently heard tone, a kind of tonic, is C. A common melodic feature in the performance of songs of this type is the reiterated semitone E–F; the notes E and F follow C in frequency of use. The B, a tone of unremarkable duration, occurs exclusively in unstressed positions, either in passing, or as a quick lower auxiliary before a stressed C.

Metrically, the songs of the first class display groupings of 4, 5, and 6 temporal units, which can be transcribed as 4/8, 5/8, and 6/8 (or 3/4). These meters occur in about the same frequency in Feinberg's sample. Verbal information about local conceptions of the musical organization of time is lacking.

Songs of the second class are heterogeneous in tonal resources, but somewhat homogeneous in meter. Its melodies use a scale of six or seven tones. The steps of this scale may include a semitone, but melodies do not feature, by reiteration or frequency, the notes that define it. The meters almost exclusively involve groupings of four units; but in the recordings, examples that involve groupings of five occur.

Anutan scalar distinctions do not reflect Anutan classificatory criteria. The basic local division into genres corresponds to differences of meter, tempo, timbre, text, and context. *Mako* exploit triple, quadruple, and quintuple meters; *puatanga* are in quadruple meter. Compared with the pace of *mako,* the pace of *puatanga* seems extremely slow: each note lasts several seconds, giving the impression of nonmetrical music. Anutans sing dance-songs in an approximation of unison, but sing laments with multivoiced quivering; microtonal sighing and sobbing set up a timbral effect that Anutans call heavy (*mamapa*), contrasting with the sound of *mako,* which they call light (*maamaa*).

—J. W. LOVE

### Polynesian multipart singing

Polynesian music usually involves sounded words. Analysis of relationships among topics, linguistic traits of poetic diction, and melodic settings reveals how named categories may prescribe musical aspects of performance, though the names ostensibly refer to poetic aspects. Kevin Salisbury's analysis of Pukapukan singing (1983), J. W. Love's analysis of Sāmoan performative genres (1991), Elizabeth Tatar's analysis of Hawaiian singing (1993), and other studies demonstrate the interrelatedness of textual and melodic components.

Since many poetic categories provide a foundation for dancing, choreographic considerations are important. Because poetic expression is primary, poetic texts are composed first; choreography is often the final component of the creative process. Named categories of dance incorporate conventions of combining kinetic motifs and sequences within prescribed formations, as analyzed by Adrienne L. Kaeppler for Tongan dance (1972) and Jane Freeman Moulin for Tahitian dance (1979). Choreographic patterns and prescribed structures can serve analytically as visible manifestations of corresponding or noncorresponding structures in melodic and rhythmic organization.

TRACK 12

Conceived as multiple parts sounding together, musical polyphony is but one dimension of multipart relationships. Traces of indigenous polyphony survive in the central areas of Polynesia, including Tonga and the Society Islands, but are apparently absent on the periphery, in Aotearoa, Hawai'i, and Mangareva. In the Society Islands, configurations of multiple parts reported by voyagers before 1800 can be interpreted as polyphonic even if they combine a sung melody with rhythmic accompaniment by one or more drums.

Analysis of polyphony must account for historical circumstances and the presence or absence of frameworks for polyphonic organization. In the 1990s, Polynesian polyphonic configurations include multipart choral singing in two streams: conventional, Western, three- or four-part performances of Christian hymns, in styles taught by missionaries; and indigenous styles, many of which have incorporated Western chordal harmonies. In the domain of Christian hymns, analyzing chords by identifying tonal harmonies is relevant. Outside that domain, however, the analysis of tonal harmonies may be inappropriate, for polyphonic organization may proceed on bases other than functional tonality, despite the presence of seemingly Western harmonies.

### Tahitian hīmene tārava

In Tahitian *hīmene tārava,* an analysis in terms of tonal harmony could identify triads such as a supertonic (ii) in an opening measure resolving to a tonic (I) for the remainder of a stanza, or alternating measures of a dominant (V) and a tonic throughout a stanza. An analysis on Tahitian terms, however, reveals that the musical content of each vocal part is determined by its named function, and that tonal harmony results from the combination of the parts (Stillman 1991). The primary functions of the vocal parts are textual declamation, rhythmic punctuation, and melodic decoration. The primary declamatory part, performed by most of the women in a choir, centers at or near the tonic; the men's counterpart usually centers on the dominant below. Other texted parts performed by pairs of soloists, usually men, center on the third degree of a major scale. The rhythmic punctuation performed by the remainder of the men consists of a vocalized grunting pitched on the lower tonic.

The terms by which Tahitians articulate the procedures of singing reveal an emphasis on combining the parts—one woman awakens the *hīmene,* others catch on to her lead, the chorus joins in and secures the *hīmene,* and the *hīmene* is said to rise. An analysis that merely identifies the harmonies fails to account for indigenous conceptions underlying the production of those harmonies.

### Tongan lakalaka

Tongan *lakalaka* can have up to six vocal parts, each of which fulfills one of three functions: melody (or leading part), drone, and decoration: "The leading part consists of essential features, the drone defines or outlines the space in which the essential features operate, and the decoration is an elaboration of specific features which are not necessary for its existence or function" (Kaeppler 1978:262).

The harmonic analysis of the combined vocal parts is extended by Larry Shumway, who demonstrates how Western harmonizations, in particular the pattern I–vi($^6_4$)–I$^6_4$–(V$^7$)(vi)–I, though evidence of Western musical influence, are apparently a fleshing out of pre-Christian harmonic conventions (1981:470). The mere applicability of the vocabulary of Western tonal harmony does not indicate the absence of an indigenous conceptual framework, which may itself be an important clue to understanding relationships among performing parts.

### Coordinate polyphony

An unusual example of a multipart tradition is the *suahongi,* a ritual of Bellona. All sections, combining multiple vocal parts simultaneously, are polyphonic; several,

FIGURE 18    At the coronation of Tupou IV as King of Tonga, men of Lapaha, Tonga, divide into parts in the *meʻetuʻupaki*. Photo by Adrienne L. Kaeppler, 1967.

combining two distinct texts, are polytextual (Rossen 1978). The Tongan *meʻetuʻupaki* can be polytextual, polyphonic, and polykinetic (figure 18): three texts are simultaneously sung in three melodic contours and realized in three movement sequences. The lower part of this polyphony, a drone bass, is the prototype for the *lakalaka* drone (Kaeppler 1991, 1994). Unlike fixed instrumental drones of the Solomon Islands (figure 19), the *lakalaka* drone is movable: the drone-producing voices may shift among several tones.          —AMY KUʻULEIALOHA STILLMAN

TRACK 13

## REFERENCES

Bronson, Bertrand H. 1951. "Melodic Stability in Oral Transmission." *Journal of the International Folk Music Council* 3:50–55.

Chamisso, Adelbert von. 1825. *Entdeckungsreise in die Südsee.* Vienna: Kaulfuss & Krammer.

Chenoweth, Vida. 1972. *Melodic Perception and Analysis: A Manual on Ethnic Melody.* Ukarumpa,

Papua New Guinea: Summer Institute of Linguistics.

———. 1979. *The Usarufas and Their Music.* Dallas: SIL Museum of Anthropology.

Christensen, Dieter. 1957. *Die Musik der Kate und Sialum: Beiträge zur Ethnographie Neuguineas.* Berlin: Freie Universität.

———. 1960. "Inner Tempo and Melodic Tempo." *Ethnomusicology* 4:9–14.

Christensen, Dieter, and Gerd Koch. 1964. *Die Musik der Ellice-Inseln.* Veröffentlichungen des Museums, Neue Folge 5, Abteilung Südsee 2. Berlin: Museum für Völkerkunde.

David, Mrs. Edgeworth [Lady Caroline David].

FIGURE 19    Multiple structures are evident in music for a Blablanga men's dance. After a four-bar introduction, the music moves through time in an ABA structure. Over a trumpet drone, panpipes add block chords, creating a distinctive texture. Transcription by Vida Chenoweth.

1899. *Funafuti, or Three Months on a Coral Island: An Unscientific Account of a Scientific Expedition.* London: John Murray.

Davies, James A. 1855. "Appendix: On the Native Songs of New Zealand." In *Polynesian Mythology and Ancient Traditional History of the New Zealanders,* ed. George Grey. London: Willis.

Deacon, A. Bernard. 1934. *Malekula: A Vanishing People in the New Hebrides.* Edited by Camilla H. Wedgwood. London: George Routledge & Sons.

Ellis, Catherine J. 1964. *Aboriginal Music Making: A Study of Central Australian Music.* Adelaide: Libraries Board of South Australia.

———. 1965. "Pre-Instrumental Scales." *Ethnomusicology* 9(2):126–137.

———. 1967. "The Pitjantjatjara Kangaroo Song from Karlga." *Miscellanea Musicologica* 2:171–268.

Grainger, Percy. 1908. "Collecting with the Phonograph." *Journal of the Folk-Song Society* 3:147–162.

Handy, Edward S. Craighill, and L. Jane Winne. 1925. *Music in the Marquesas Islands.* Bulletin 17. Honolulu: Bishop Museum.

Howard, Alan. 1974. *Ain't No Big Thing: Coping Strategies in a Hawaiian-American Community.* Honolulu: University of Hawai'i Press.

Jonassen, John. 1991. *Cook Islands Drums.* Rarotonga: Ministry of Cultural Development, Cook Islands.

Kaeppler, Adrienne L. 1972. "Method and Theory in Analyzing Dance Structure With an Analysis of Tongan Dance." *Ethnomusicology* 16:173–217.

———. 1978. "Melody, Drone and Decoration: Underlying Structures and Surface Manifestations in Tongan Art and Society." In *Art in Society,* ed. Michael Greenhalgh and Vincent Megaw, 261–274. London: Duckworth.

———. 1991. "Me'etu'upaki and Tapaki: Paddle Dances of Tonga and Futuna, West Polynesia." *Studia Musicologica Academiae Scientarum Hungaricae* 33:347–357.

———. 1994. "Music, Metaphor, and Misunderstanding." *Ethnomusicology* 38(3):457–473.

Keck, Verena. 1992. *Falsch Gehandelt—Schwer Erkrankt: Kranksein bei den Yupno in Papua New Guinea aus Ethnologischer und Biomedizinischer Sicht.* Basel: Wepf.

Koetting, James. 1970. "Analysis and Notation of West African Drum Ensemble Music." *Selected Reports,* vol. 1, no. 3. Los Angeles: University of California.

Kunst, Jaap. 1950. *Musicologica.* Mededeling 90, Afdeling culturele en physische anthropologie 35. Amsterdam: Koninklijke Vereeniging Indisch Instituut.

Lauridsen, Jan. 1983. "Musical Scales in Australian Aboriginal Music: Structure and Social Implications." Ph.D. dissertation, University of Maryland.

List, George. 1963a. "The Boundaries of Speech and Song." *Ethnomusicology* 7(1):1–16.

———. 1963b. "The Musical Significance of Transcription." *Ethnomusicology* 7(3): 193–197.

———. 1974. "The Reliability of Transcription." *Ethnomusicology* 18(3):353–377.

Love, Jacob Wainwright. 1991. *Sāmoan Variations: Essays on the Nature of Traditional Arts.* New York: Garland.

McLean, Mervyn. 1969. "An Analysis of 651 Maori Scales." *Yearbook of the International Folk Music Council* 1:123–164.

Moulin, Jane Freeman. 1979. *The Dance of Tahiti.* Pape'ete: Christian Gleizal.

Moyer, Will D. 1922. *National Self Teacher for Hawaiian Ukulele, Banjuke or Taro Patch Fiddle.* Chicago: Chart Music.

Niles, Don. 1992. "*Konggap, Kap* and *Tambaran*: Music of the Yupno/Nankina Area in Relation to Neighbouring Groups." In *Abschied von der Vergangenheit: Ethnologische Berichte aus dem Finisterre-Gebirge in Papua New Guinea,* ed. Jürg Wassmann, 149–183. Berlin: Dietrich Reimer.

Pugh, Jacqueline. 1975. "Communication, Language and Huli Music: A Preliminary Survey." B.A. thesis, Monash University.

Pugh-Kitingan, Jacqueline. 1977. "Huli Language and Instrumental Performance." *Ethnomusicology* 21(2):205–232.

———. 1986. *The Huli of Papua Niugini.* Bärenreiter-Musicaphon BM 30 SL 2703. LP disk.

Quinlan, Julian. 1974. *Bougainville Sings.* Rigu: St. Joseph's High School.

Roberts, Helen. 1977 [1926]. *Ancient Hawaiian Music.* Gloucester, Mass.: Peter Smith.

*Romano Katoliko Katekismo.* 1898. Port-Leon (Yule Island): Roman Catholic Mission.

Rossen, Jane Mink. 1978. "The *Suahongi* of Bellona: Polynesian Ritual Music." *Ethnomusicology* 22:397–439.

Salisbury, Kevin. 1983. "Pukapukan People and Their Music." M.A. thesis, University of Auckland.

Schieffelin, Edward L. 1976. *The Sorrow of the Lonely and the Burning of the Dancers.* New York: St. Martin's Press.

Seeger, Charles. 1951. "An Instantaneous Music Notator." *Journal of the International Folk Music Council* 3:103–106.

———. 1958. "Prescriptive and Descriptive Music-Writing." *Musical Quarterly* 44:184–195.

Shumway, Larry V. 1981. "The Tongan *Lakalaka*: Music Composition and Style." *Ethnomusicology* 25:467–479.

Sierich, O. "Samoanische Märchen." *Internationales Archiv für Ethnographie* 17: 182–188.

Spearritt, Gordon D. 1979. "The Music of the Iatmul People of the Middle Sepik River (Papua New Guinea) with Special Reference to Instrumental Music at Kandangai and Aibom." 2 vols. Ph.D. dissertation, University of Queensland.

Stillman, Amy Ku'uleialoha. 1991. "*Himene Tahiti*: Ethnoscientific and Ethnohistorical Perspectives on Choral Singing and Protestant Hymnody in the Society Islands, French Polynesia." Ph.D. dissertation, Harvard University.

Tatar, Elizabeth. 1979. "Chant." In *Hawaiian Music and Musicians,* ed. George S. Kanahele, 53–68. Honolulu: University Press of Hawai'i.

———. 1981. "Toward a Description of Precontact Music in Hawai'i." *Ethnomusicology* 25(3):481–492.

———. 1982. *Nineteenth Century Hawaiian Chant.* Pacific Anthropological Records, 33. Honolulu: Department of Anthropology, Bishop Museum.

———. 1993. *Hula Pahu: Hawaiian Drum Dances: Volume II: The Pahu: Sounds of Power.* Bulletin in Anthropology, 4. Honolulu: Bishop Museum.

Trimillos, Ricardo D. 1989. "*Hālau, Hochschule, Maystro,* and *Ryū*: Cultural Approaches to Music Learning and Teaching." *International Journal of Music Education* 14:32–43.

Ward, W. D. 1954. "Subjective Musical Pitch." *Journal of the Acoustical Society of America* 26:369–380.

Wassmann, Jürg. 1993. *Das Ideal des leicht gebeugten Menschen: Eine Ethno-kognitive Analyse der Yupno in Papua New Guinea.* Berlin: Reimer.

Will, Udo. 1995a. "Frequency Performance in Australian Aboriginal Vocal Music, with and without 'Tone'-Producing Instruments." Paper presented at the thirty-third ICTM World Conference, Canberra.

———. 1995b. "Structures of Frequency Organization in Central Australian Aboriginal Music." In *Proceedings of the Xth European Seminar in Ethnomusicology, 1994.*

———. 1997. "Two Types of Octave Relationships in Central Australian Music." *Musicology Australia* 20:3–10.

Will, Udo, and Catherine Ellis. 1994. "Evidence for Linear Transposition in Australian Western Desert Vocal Music." *Musicology Australia* 17:1–11.

Will, Udo, and Catherine Ellis. 1996. "A Re-Analyzed Australian Western Desert Song: Frequency Performance and Interval Structure." *Ethnomusicology* 40(2):187–222.

Wong, Kaupena. 1965. "Ancient Hawaiian Music." In *Kamehameha Schools' 75th Anniversary Lectures,* 9–15. Honolulu: Kamehameha Schools Press.

Zahn, Heinrich. 1959 [1934]. *The Conchshell-Hymnal.* Edited by H. Wolfrum. Madang: Lutheran Mission Press.

Zemp, Hugo. 1981. "Melanesian Solo Polyphonic Panpipe Music." *Ethnomusicology* 25(3):383–418.

Zemp, Hugo, and Christian Kaufmann. 1969. "Pour une transcription automatique des 'langages tambourines' mélanésiens (un exemple kwoma, Nouvelle-Guinée)." *L'Homme* 9(2):38–88.

# Understanding Dance

*Adrienne L. Kaeppler*

Dance as a System of Knowledge
Preserving the Product through Film and Video
Preserving the Product through Notation

Cultural forms that result from the creative use of human bodies in time and space are often glossed as *dance,* but the word itself carries with it preconceptions that mask the importance and usefulness of analyzing the movement dimensions of human action and interaction. Dance is a multifaceted phenomenon. It includes, in addition to what we see and hear, the "invisible," underlying system, the processes that produce the system and the product, and the sociopolitical context.

Indigenous Pacific societies had no categories comparable to the Western concept of dance. Movement analysis has been enlarged to encompass all structured-movement systems, including, but not limited to, those associated with religious and secular rituals, ceremonies, entertainment, martial arts, sign languages, sports, and games. What these systems share is that they result from creative processes that manipulate human bodies in time and space. Some categories of structured movement may be further distinguished or elaborated by being integrally related to music (a specially marked or elaborated category of structured sound), and text.

## DANCE AS A SYSTEM OF KNOWLEDGE

Separating dance from nondance in cross-cultural contexts is problematic because to do so would require comparing cultural conceptions that separate a series of specialized movements from what is culturally conceived as ordinary, mundane, or nonformalized movements. Analyses that would make it possible to separate dance from nondance according to indigenous points of view (or even if there are such concepts) have not yet been carried out in many areas. Most researchers simply use the term *dance* for bodily movement associated with music, but this is a Western term (as is *music*). The cultural forms produced, though transient, have structured content, are visual manifestations of social relationships, are part of complex aesthetic systems, have meanings that refer to deep structures of the society and the nondance world, and may assist in understanding cultural values.

Structured-movement systems are systems of knowledge, the products of action and interaction, and processes through which action and interaction occur. They are usually part of a larger activity. They are socially and culturally constructed—created by, known, and agreed upon by people, and primarily preserved in memory.

An ideal study of movement of a society or social group would analyze all activities and cultural forms in which human bodies are manipulated in time and space, the social processes that produce them according to the aesthetic precepts of specific people at a specific point in time, and the components that group or separate the various dimensions of movements and activities they project into kinesthetic and visual form. Indigenous categories can best define which movement systems, if any, fit these, or other, characterizations, and how they should be classified. Is it the content, the context, or both that blur the classification boundaries? Discovering the structure and content of structured-movement systems, and the creative processes, movement theories, and philosophies from indigenous points of view is a difficult task, but it is necessary for understanding culture and society.

## The process of performing

Here, I use the term *dance* to denote specially marked or elaborated systems of movement (how movements are specially marked or elaborated is culturally specific) that result from creative processes that manipulate human bodies in time and space in such a way that movement is formalized and intensified in much the same manner as poetry intensifies and formalizes language. Often the process of performing is as important as the cultural form produced. These specially marked movement systems may be considered art, work, ritual, ceremony, entertainment, or any combination of these, depending on the society and context. A person may perform the same or a similar sequence of movements (consisting of grammatically structured motifs) as a ritual supplicant, as a political act, as an entertainer, or as a marker of identity. Thus, the same movement sequence may be meant to be decoded differently if performed for gods, if performed for a human audience, or if performed as a participant for fun; and it may be decoded differently depending on an individual's background and understanding of a particular performance and the individual's mental and emotional state at the time. Choreographers, performers, and viewers are socially and historically placed individuals, who operate according to sociocultural conventions and aesthetic systems.

Specially marked or elaborated, grammatically structured human movement may convey meaning by mime, dramatic realism, storytelling, or metaphor, or with abstract conventions. The movements may be signs, symbols, signifiers, in any combination. Essentially, movements are cultural artifacts that convey the idea that these movements belong to a specific culture or subculture, or that a specific type of movement is being activated for a particular purpose. Movement sequences may be audience-oriented to admire as art or work, they may be participatory to be enjoyed as entertainment, they may make political or social statements, they may bring religious ecstasy or trance, they may be performed as a social duty. Movements given by gods and ancestors may be perpetuated as cultural artifacts and aesthetic performances, even if their meanings have been changed or forgotten as points of reference for ethnic or cultural identity.

## The analysis of structure

Dance becomes visible as a product of human action and interaction in the context of a socially constructed movement system. The system itself is invisible, existing in the minds of people as movement motifs, specific choreographies, and meaningful imagery.

### *Kinemic and morphokinemic analysis*

The first type of analysis is kinemic and morphokinemic analysis. It is basically an analysis of movement using linguistic analogies to derive what would be comparable to phonology and syntax or grammar in spoken-language analysis. Starting with the assumption that only a small segment of all possible movement is significant in any single dance or movement tradition and that these significant units can be discovered, the first step is to isolate minimal units of movement. These units, termed kinemes, are derived through contrastive analysis. Kinemes are minimal units of movement recognized as contrastive by people of a given dance tradition. Though having no meaning in themselves, kinemes are the basic units from which the dance of a given tradition is built.

The next level of structural organization in this system is the morphokinemic level, and is analogous to the morphemic level of linguistic structure. A morphokine is the smallest unit that has meaning as movement in the structure of a movement system (meaning here does not refer to narrative or pictorial meaning). Only certain combinations are meaningful, and multiple kinemes often occur simultaneously to form a meaningful movement. The resulting grammar groups morphokines into classes in a way that is specific to a particular movement system. As the first aim of this method is to derive dance *structure,* and not dance *meaning,* further analogies with language (such as lexemes or sememes) are not used. Morphokines, which have meaning as movement, but do not have lexical or referential meaning, are organized into a small number of motifs, which, when ordered simultaneously and chronologically (that is, choreographed), form dances.

There are essentially two analytical processes involved here: the derivation of the emic units or kinemes by observing movement, and questioning which etic behaviors are cognitively grouped or separated into emes (that is, are they the same or different? do they contrast?) and the derivation of the movement system by observing and questioning how the emic units are structured or grouped into classes and what the relationships are between them.

### Motif and choreographic analyses

The next structural level is motif analysis. This is probably the most important step in analyzing dance structure. Motifs are culturally grammatical sequences of movement made up of kinemes and morphokines. They are movement pieces that combine certain morphokines in characteristic ways, and are verbalized and recognized as motifs by the people themselves. The ordering of motifs simultaneously and chronologically is the process of choreography, and a dance can be analytically broken down or built up from its component parts. This system of structural analysis was developed by Kaeppler (1967, 1972), and has been used by Raymond Mayer (1986–1987) for analyzing 'Uvean dance.

### Genre or local-category analysis

This kind of analysis examines the local taxonomy of culturally recognized dances within a specific culture and how the categories differ from each other. In Tonga, several types of sung speeches with choreographed movements are grouped together as *faiva,* but are separated from *tau'olunga* movements, which accompany *hiva kakala.*

## PRESERVING THE PRODUCT THROUGH FILM AND VIDEO

The medium of film records the visual and sometimes the acoustic dimensions of movement—that is, the product. What can we learn by looking at (and listening to) film? How do we put this visual imagery to use in studying movement? What we see and hear in a film is how kinetic and aural sequences were performed on a specific occasion, but it cannot elucidate the system, which is invisible (Kaeppler 1995b).

Repeated viewings as captured on film make possible the analysis of the importance of certain movement motifs, how motifs are varied in time and space, and how sequences of motifs are transferred from ritual to dance and today to rituals of identity. Film is important as a mnemonic aid, for repeated viewing of specific events, or to more closely examine minutiae.

An important study using film is the continuing work of Alison Jablonko on the movement dimensions of the Maring of Western Highlands Province, Papua New Guinea. Her early Laban-based microanalysis of movement used short filmed segments, ranging from five to fifteen seconds, and focused on an examination of synchrony, the use of specific traceforms, and the patterns of body-part use. Her more recent macroanalysis (Jablonko 1991) used ten-minute segments to examine flow and pulse as visible analogies between movement patterns and social patterns. Also using film, Megan Jones Morais (1995) applied Labananalysis to analyze Aboriginal dances to reveal deep structures of the society.

Studying the Umeda of West Sepik Province, Papua New Guinea, Alfred Gell used film to analyze gait by measuring angles between the upper and lower leg, and then plotting the angles on a graph:

> The advantage of this method of representation is that it permits instant visual comparisons between different versions of the step cycle seen as wholes, with the possibility of easy identification of the distinctive features wherein they differ. Moreover, it becomes possible in this way, to see the different styles of movement adopted by participants in *ida* [ritual] as a set of transformations of a single form. (1985:189)

Further work by Gell in analyzing *The Red Bowmen,* both the finished film (Owen 1977) and outtakes, demonstrates the usefulness of repeated viewings to draw out the movement dimensions of ritual transformations as conceived by the participants, and how through movement these people construct their ideas of nature, culture, and gender.

Alan Lomax and his study of choreometrics used film to describe distinctive patterns of movement and interaction so that dance styles might be compared and classified cross-culturally. Lomax's grand scheme for an evolutionary taxonomy of culture was based on coding dancing from viewing films. From this, he concluded "dance style varies in a regular way in terms of the level of complexity and the type of subsistence activity of the culture which supports it" (1968:xv). This work has been of little service in the study of Oceanic dance; it used only a few examples, and even these have been found unacceptable (Kealiinohomoku 1974).

## PRESERVING THE PRODUCT THROUGH NOTATION

Film is useful for many analytical purposes, but it is not a substitute for notation. The use of movement notation in Oceania includes pictorial representations and notation in the Laban and Benesh systems.

### Pictorial representations

At least five kinds of pictorial representations of dance movement have been used in Oceania. Beth Dean's representation shows poetic text and sticklike drawings (*Three Dances of Oceania* 1976). Alan Armstrong and Reupena Ngata (1960) devised a pictorial system for notating Māori dance. They describe and illustrate forty-seven important movements with full-figure drawings (figure 1*a*). These motifs are associated with stick figures that subsequently represent these actions in the dances that follow. Included are: the poetic text in Māori and English, musical notation with text, melodic contour, and rhythm, and an integrated score, consisting of the poetic text and the associated actions in stick figures (with their numbers from the previous-

FIGURE 1    Pictorial system used by Alan Armstrong and Reupena Ngata (1960) for analyzing Māori dance: *a*, full human figures and their rendering in stick-figure form; *b*, the stick-figure form related to the melodic contour and poetry it accompanies.

(a)

(b)

ly presented inventory), and sometimes a notated musical line to indicate the rhythmic rendering of the actions (figure 1*b*). Jane Mink Rossen's analysis of a *pati* from Bellona uses a similar presentation (1987:1:157–163). For a specific performance, she gives a verbal description, a musical score in staff notation, a diagram of musical rhythm and dance movement, and upper-body drawings of a dancer. Jane Freeman Moulin (1979) presents drawings and verbal descriptions of important Tahitian dance motifs.

Judy Van Zile presented a pictorial notation (1982), including full-figure drawings and verbal descriptions in addition to full scores in Labanotation, and musical notation for some dances. Dorothy K. Gillett presented her system in 1972. Her directions for a seated Hawaiian dance included the poetic text in Hawaiian and English, musical notation, full-figure drawings, and verbal directions (figure 2).

FIGURE 2    Pictorial notation used by Dorothy K. Gillett for analyzing a seated Hawaiian dance (1972:76).

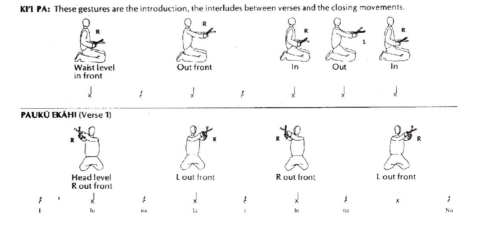

FIGURE 3    Pictorial notation used by Adrienne L. Kaeppler for analyzing a dance of the Cook Islands (1983:77).

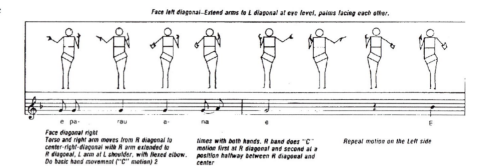

FIGURE 4    Pictorial notation used by Raymond Ammann for analyzing a New Caledonian dance (1992:40).

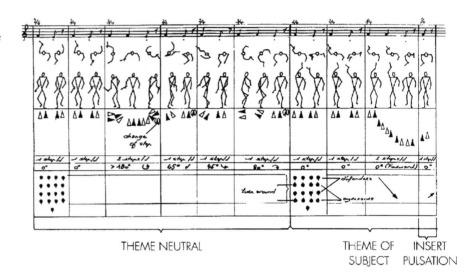

FIGURE 5    Drawing depicting movement from above: the gong-raising dance at Atchin, an island off the coast of Malakula, Vanuatu. After Layard (1942:326).

Adrienne L. Kaeppler presented a pictorial representation (1983). This included the poetic text in the Polynesian language and English; musical notation with text, melodic contour, and rhythm; remarks with basic movements used in the dance and choreographic notes; and an integrated score, which included text, music, verbal descriptions, and a modified stick-figure pictorial notation (figure 3). Raymond Ammann presented a pictorial representation of a New Caledonian dance (1992). This included an integrated score with musical notation with melodic contour and rhythm; stick-figure pictorial representations of movement from eye level and above; foot patterns; and relationships among the dancers as they move in the performance space (figure 4).

Drawings may depict movement from above to show the positioning of the performers on the ground, their alignment (as with symbols pointing the direction individuals are facing), and their movement from place to place, or with arrows pointing the direction of travel. Possibly the simplest form represents each performer with a letter of the alphabet, aligning letters in columns and rows. To illustrate dancers' movements in a Tongan *me'etu'upaki*, Kaeppler used a series of diagrams made up of X's (1991). For the *maginogo,* a "bamboo dance" of the Hohodai Koita of Papua, C. G. Seligmann (1910:156) represented each dancer as a black (male) or white (female) circle, with an attached arrow showing the direction faced and moved, and larger arrows showing the direction the columns of performers moved. John Layard (1942) used symbols for male and female to show the directions the individuals faced, with larger arrows showing the direction the rows of men moved (figure 5).

### Laban and Benesh movement notations

Today in dance and anthropological literature, movement is increasingly notated in two internationally recognized systems. Labanotation (known in Europe as

Kinetography Laban) is similar in concept to musical and phonetic notation. Benesh notation was originally devised for notating ballet, but is applicable to other forms of dancing. Laban and Benesh notations can notate in minute detail the movements of individual dancers and group choreography. Reading and writing these systems require specialized study, just as understanding and using musical notations do. The basic notational systems are not difficult to learn, and a notated score can tell us much more than graphic representations or films.

Labanotation has been used by Kaeppler (1967, 1993, 1995a) in her analyses of Tongan and Hawaiian dance, and by JoAnne Page in her analysis of *wangga* [see TRADITIONAL AUSTRALIAN DANCE, figure 3]. Judy Van Zile (1982) has used Labanotation to analyze Japanese *bon* dance in Hawai'i. Benesh notation has been used by Andrée Grau (1992) in her analyses of Tiwi dances in Australia. Megan Jones Morais (1992, 1995) has used Labanotation and Benesh to analyze Walpiri dances in Australia [see TRADITIONAL AUSTRALIAN DANCE, figure 6].

Notation can be considered the most important tool for preservation and analysis, but should ideally be augmented by film or video. Notation can capture an ideal version of movements and movement motifs and how the dancers wished them to be preserved, whereas film captures only how a dance was performed on a specific occasion. However, film preserves the style and feeling of the dance and how the choreography was performed on a particular occasion. Notation can be emic, in that the dancers can be questioned about what makes the movements the same or different—the same process a linguist uses for eliciting if spoken utterances are the same or different, the hallmark of the method of contrastive analysis.

Dance analysis is a complex composite of observing, learning, recording, and conveying the crucial visual dimension of music. A full analysis consists of learning the content and contexts, and their presentation by notation, film, and the written word. But the ultimate aim of analysis of human movement is not simply to understand dance in its cultural context, but to understand society through analyzing systems of movement. To attain these ends, we must study meaning, intention, and cultural evaluation, the activities that generate movement systems, how and by whom they are judged, and how the study of movement can assist in understanding society.

## REFERENCES

Ammann, Raymond. 1992. "Ty.Ga: Timidou Galilée." In *Who We Are: Delegation of New Caledonia: VI^Th Festival of Pacific Arts—Rarotonga—Cook Islands—1992*, 38–40. Nouméa: Comité du Festival/A.D.C.K.

Armstrong, Alan, and Reupena Ngata. 1960. *Maori Action Songs*. Wellington: Reed.

Dean, Beth. (1976). *Three Dances of Oceania*. Sydney: Opera House Trust.

Gell, Alfred. 1985. "Style and Meaning in Umeda Dance." In *Society and the Dance*, ed. Paul Spencer, 183–205. Cambridge: Cambridge University Press.

Gillett, Dorothy K. 1972. "Hawaiian Music for Hawaii's Children." *Music Educators Journal* Washington, D.C.: Music Educators National Conference, 57–63.

Grau, Andrée. 1992. "Danses Rituelles Tiwi." *Cahiers de musiques traditionnelles* 5:205–216.

Jablonko, Alison. 1991. "Patterns of Daily Life in the Dance of the Maring of New Guinea." *Visual Anthropology* 4:367–377.

Kaeppler, Adrienne L. 1967. "The Structure of Tongan Dance." Ph.D. dissertation, University of Hawai'i.

————. 1972. "Method and Theory in Analyzing Dance Structure with an Analysis of Tongan Dance." *Ethnomusicology* 16(2):173–217.

————. 1983. *Polynesian Dance, With a Selection for Contemporary Performances*. Honolulu: Alpha Delta Kappa.

————. 1991. "Me'etu'upaki and Tapaki: Paddle Dances of Tonga and Futuna, West Polynesia." *Studia Musicologica Academiae Scientiarum Hungaricae* 33:347–357.

————. 1993. *Hula Pahu: Hawaiian Drum Dances: Volume 1: Ha'a and Hula Pahu: Sacred Movements*. Honolulu: Bishop Museum Press.

————. 1995a. "The Paradise Theme in Modern Tongan Music." *The Essence of Singing and the Substance of Song: Recent Responses to the Aboriginal Performing Arts and Other Essays in Honour of Catherine Ellis*, ed. Linda Barwick, Allan Marett, and Guy Tunstill, 159–183.

Oceania monograph 46. Sydney: University of Sydney.

———. 1995b. "Visible and Invisible in Hawaiian Dance." In *Human Action Signs in Cultural Context,* ed. Brenda Farnell, 31–43. Metuchen, N.J.: Scarecrow Press.

Kealiinohomoku, Joann W. 1974. "Review Number One (Discussion of Choreometrics)." *CORD News* 6(2):20–24.

Layard, John. 1942. *Stone Men of Malekula: Vao.* London: Chatto & Windus.

Lomax, Alan. 1968. *Folk Song Style and Culture.* Washington, D.C.: American Association for the Advancement of Science.

Mayer, Raymond. 1986–1987. "Les Codes de la Danse à l'île Wallis (Uvea)." 2 vols. Ph.D. dissertation, University of Paris 5.

Morais, Megan Jones. 1992. "Documenting Dance: Benesh Movement Notation and the Walpiri of Central Australia." In *Music and Dance of Aboriginal Australia and the South Pacific,* ed. Alice Marshall Moyle, 130–144. Oceania monograph 41. Sydney: Oceania Publications.

———. 1995. "Antikirinya Women's Ceremonial Dance Structures: Manifestations of the Dreaming." In *The Essence of Singing and the Substance of Song: Recent Responses to the Aboriginal Performing Arts and Other Essays in Honour of Catherine Ellis,* ed. Linda Barwick, Allan Marett, and Guy Tunstill, 75–93. Oceania monograph 46. Sydney: University of Sydney.

Moulin, Jane Freeman. 1979. *La Danse à Tahiti.* Translated by Pierre Montillier. Pape'ete: Christian Gleizal.

Owen, Chris. 1977. *The Red Bowmen.* 16mm, 58 min. Institute of Papua New Guinea Studies.

Rossen, Jane Mink. 1987. *Songs of Bellona Island.* 2 vols. Language and Culture of Rennell and Bellona Islands, 6. Copenhagen: Forlaget Kragen.

Seligmann, C. G. (1910). *The Melanesians of British New Guinea.* Cambridge: Cambridge University Press.

Van Zile, Judy. 1982. *The Japanese Bon Dance in Hawaii.* Honolulu: Press Pacifica.

# Language in Musical Settings

*J. W. Love*
*Adrienne L. Kaeppler*
*Niko Besnier*
*Jane Mink Rossen*
*Michael D. Lieber*
*Allan Thomas*

*Don Niles*
*William Davenport*
*William Donner*
*James F. Weiner*
*Jürg Wassmann*

**Linguistic and Musical Systems of Oceania**
**The Analysis of Speech in Musical Contexts**
**Transcription**
**Metrics**
**Sonics**
**Strophics**
**Metaphor and Symbolism**

In Oceania, performance often packages music with language (figure 1), but sung words may escape analytic notice: musical researchers focus on rhythms and tones, often not underlaying transcriptions with the performed words, and linguists focus on spoken discourse, often disregarding musically equipped performances of speech. For words uttered in such performances, the terms *poems* and *poetry* are often serviceable, and terms like *lyrics* and *texts* can work in their place. But the stylistic gap between spoken words and sung words can be wide, and many Oceanic societies have performative genres that fall into it. Acts of speaking and singing are not absolutely distinct, though they can be viewed as separate dimensions (List 1963).

In addition to what we hear, sung speech involves unheard musical-linguistic systems, the creative processes that make the systems and their products, and the social contexts in which performances unfold. Linguistic analysis centers on "ordinary" discourse, in which it assumes performative competence; but it can examine other kinds of speech.

## LINGUISTIC AND MUSICAL SYSTEMS OF OCEANIA

Before the 1500s, at least three linguistic families had established themselves in Oceania: Australian languages in the Australian continent and Tasmania, Austronesian languages in Micronesia and Polynesia, and both Austronesian and non-Austronesian languages in New Guinea and Melanesia. Whether the non-Austronesian languages represent one (huge, diverse, ancient) family is a focus of scholarly debate.

Of these families, the Austronesian is the newcomer. Possibly more than five thousand years ago, Austronesian-speakers moved southward from the Chinese coast and Taiwan. They settled in the Indonesian islands and parts of coastal Southeast Asia. Their farthest known westward reach was Madagascar, off the coast of Africa. Others moved east, touching coastal New Guinea and extending into the Pacific, through Melanesia into Micronesia and Polynesia. Their farthest known eastward reach was Rapa Nui. After the peopling of the Pacific, long-distance voyages continued, leaving in Melanesian and Micronesian seas isolated pockets of Polynesians.

Since language and music are intertwining cultural systems, the basic picture of

FIGURE 1    Tuiasosopo gives metrical direction to the Sāmoan contingent at the Pacific Festival of Arts, Tahiti. Photo by Adrienne L. Kaeppler, 1985.

linguistic history in Oceania is relevant to the study of music. Musical pieces and genres can cross linguistic barriers, but many do not, and it is reasonable to believe that the musical history of Oceania parallels the linguistic history. Language moves with people, but people can learn second languages. The musical situation is similar. Probably for millennia, people of Oceania have learned songs from neighbors and strangers whose linguistic and musical systems they did not understand; and they continue to do so, highly valuing songs in foreign languages. The most elaborate ceremony of the Kaluli of Southern Highlands Province, Papua New Guinea, uses only songs in a non-Kaluli language (Schieffelin 1976:178). In many cultures, English supplies prestigious words. Terms borrowed from foreign languages sometimes have value simply because they sound different, and some cultures have developed genres using nonsense verse, supposed to be in some foreign language.

Proto-Polynesian, a hypothesized ancestor of the Polynesian languages, broke up between two thousand and three thousand years ago (Pawley and Green 1973), making its analysis less complex than that of the Australian languages, whose divergence, if they do diverge from a common ancestor, may have lasted five times as long. The Polynesian languages are fairly homogeneous, but other Oceanic languages are more diverse. Because researchers have not developed methods to quantify the degrees of similarity among musical systems, it is not known how closely the degrees of homogeneity in the musical systems of Oceania match those of the linguistic systems.

### The process of performing

Performing words in musical settings has deep social and aesthetic implications (Bauman and Briggs 1990; Feld and Fox 1994; Hanks 1989). With intonation and sometimes movement, sung speech may function as art, work, ritual, ceremony, entertainment, or a combination of these, depending on the social context. People may sing words as a ritual plea, a political statement, a private diversion, or a marker of identity. The meaning these words convey may vary according to the perceiver's background, mental state, and contextual understanding.

Like spoken language, sung speech may convey meaning by plain statements, but it often emphasizes metaphorically loaded diction and vocables, sounds that convey meaning without making lexical references. Singing may add nuances that speaking lacks. Sung words serve purposes particular to specific cultures or subcultures, and their effects may differ, or carry a different force, from the effects of the same or similar words if spoken.

## THE ANALYSIS OF SPEECH IN MUSICAL CONTEXTS

Language has multiple registers (kinds or levels of diction), governed by context and intent, and sometimes analytically categorized under terms like *formal, informal, colloquial,* and *polite.* All utterances have their music, but utterances that artfully formalize rhythm or intonation may be examples of performance in a special communicative channel, whose norms may differ from those of nonsung channels.

The people of many Oceanic societies rate the special intonation of poetry and oratory more highly than everyday spoken language, and they may value sung language even more. In Australia, singing is the medium of choice for communications from the ancestral beings who created the world, gave the land its features, and ordained principles for people to follow. Throughout Oceania, singing perfects the camaraderie of cordial inebriation in drinking songs, the perception of spiritual experience in Christian hymns, the exhibition of political allegiance in national anthems, the progress of sociable competition in children's games, and the assertion of cultural identity in festival performances.

Unlike most spoken language, singing may require many people simultaneously to articulate long strings of words. It may use precisely measured rhythms and paces, require instrumental accompaniment, and invite human movement and the participation of an audience that must behave in prescribed ways. But it may not be universally exceptional: in technical ways relating to time and pitch, it may be *less* complex than spoken language. Hence, singing and speaking should be treated as alternately normative kinds of performance.

Singing and speaking can be viewed as arbitrarily demarcated segments of a continuum or intersecting continua. Some Oceanic societies categorize vocalizations depending on melodic tones and rhythms and their relationship to how words are pronounced. Outside observers often distinguish less melodically varied and more rhythmically word-dependent renditions by a term like *chant,* which, for the more melodically varied and less word-dependent rendition, they contrast with a term like *song.* Some Oceanic cultures, such as Nauru and the Marquesas, terminologically distinguished between such classes. Since the introduction of the words *chant* and *song,* many cultures have used these terms to categorize the old and the new.

### Reconstruction as an analytical process

By comparing words known from living languages, researchers reconstruct words that must have existed in ancestral languages, of which no written or aural record exists. They can do this because over time, any language spoken in isolated communities breaks up into mutually unintelligible languages, which retain in their sounds and structures proof of their descent from a common parent. Because the changes that produce this differentiation follow regular principles, researchers can deduce from living languages the existence and traits of a dead and otherwise unknown ancestral language.

Methods of measuring the history of related languages are called lexicostatistics (Dyen 1965; Grace 1961) and glottochronology (Swadesh 1972). Using words likely to be in any complete vocabulary, researchers compute the degree by which languages share cognates, semantically similar words having phonetically similar sounds. The method assumes a constant rate of change, derived from documented cases of linguistic divergence. Estimating how long interrelated languages have been diverging, linguists relate their conclusions to other cultural evidence, particularly the results of archaeological investigation.

Reconstructive methods that work for language might work for music, but musical researchers have been slow to explore this possibility. Part of the reason may be that linguists, by acquiring competence in speaking a language, feel free to play at reconstructing. Musicians are likelier to stick to the sounds of actual performances, which do not raise questions of intercultural comparison. To reconstruct older musical forms, we must ask a series of questions. What are musical cognates? Do musical systems have discrete and minimally distinctive units of sound? If so, what are they? Would cognates at elementary levels emerge if sought by usual methods of transcription and analysis, or are they so subtle as to be measurable only by electronic machinery? What about rhythmic configurations and instrumental timbres? Does the use of similar tonal inventories prove related musical histories? Do the minor thirds reported from all over Polynesia represent cognate tonal structures? Is the cadential downglide of some Polynesian musical systems a reflex of a Proto-Polynesian melodic motif? Words like Tokelauan *pehe* 'song', Sāmoan and Sikaianan *pese* 'song', Tikopian *pese* 'song, hymn', Bellonese *pese* 'clapsong', and Anutan *pete* 'song' are cognates, but are the musical genres or styles they name also cognates? If so, what does this evidence prove about the history of these musical systems? If not, is it possible that musical and linguistic systems, though mutually reinforced in the nexus of sung speech, drift and evolve independently? Beyond that, what can we possibly know about musical systems thousands of years ago, analogous with reconstructed protolanguages?

## The elements of sung speech

Linguistic analysis uses elementary concepts relevant to the study of music. The minimal unit of distinctive linguistic sound is called a phoneme. From the adjective *phonemic,* researchers take the shortened form *emic* to denote distinctive elements and patterns conceived or conceivable by persons native to a tradition; in turn, they use *etic,* derived from *phonetic,* to denote elements and patterns taken as objectively observable. In other fields, including music and dance, researchers put the terms *emic* and *etic* to analogical use.

Since performed words and tones may independently reveal patterns, their juncture offers opportunities for exploring similarities and contrasts. Verbal structures may move in parallel to musical structures, as when a stanza whose lines rhyme ABAB goes with musical phrases also analyzable as ABAB. Or words may move in counterpoint to music, as when textual phrases patterned ABCABC come from alternate sides of a choir (see "Strophics and society in the Santa Cruz Islands," below). The possibilities of verbal and nonverbal interaction in musical contexts are myriad, and many remain unexplored.          —J. W. LOVE, ADRIENNE L. KAEPPLER

## TRANSCRIPTION

Transcribing linguistic utterances is a complex endeavor that raises many questions of analytic import. A small but significant body of works in discourse analysis and linguistic anthropology (including Edwards 1993; Ochs 1979; Tedlock 1983) addresses some of these questions, but little has been written about the special problems that the transcription of sung language raises, and most scholars of Oceanic music continue to treat the process of linguistic transcription unproblematically. The following overview presents problems of transcribing spoken language and identifies possible avenues of inquiry in the analysis of sung language. This discussion takes as its object of inquiry the performance of singing in a social context, rather than decontextualized music.

## Basic principles of transcription

The transcription of language in sociolinguistics and linguistic anthropology has traditionally been a contingent, project-specific process, for which no standardized procedures exist: researchers have devised their own systems, inspired in part by previous research, in part by their own analytic requirements.

Everything in language can potentially have semantic or pragmatic significance. Meaning, be it referential (literal), affective (emotive), or social, can potentially be conveyed by every aspect of linguistic behavior, including subtle shifts in pronunciation (particularly if they give rise to nonstandard pronunciations), intonation, vocal quality, loudness, and tempo, plus nonphonological features including choice of words, syntactic variation, false starts, hedges, and other "noise" in delivery. This observation leads to the first basic principle of linguistic transcription: everything in linguistic performance must be encoded in a transcript, including material that the researcher might initially consider extraneous.

Competing with this principle are several concerns. One, first discussed in print by Elinor Ochs (1979), is that a transcript too rich in detail is unanalyzable. Transcribers must therefore find a compromise between the inclusion of detail sufficient for a careful analysis of the transcript and enough clarity to enable analysis. How this compromise is achieved depends on the ultimate goals of the research, the nature of the linguistic material, and the method utilized in the analysis of the transcript. However, transcribers must take seriously Ochs' insistence that each transcriptive decision has theoretical import. The compromise itself will give subsequent analysis a particular theoretical slant, which would differ if an alternate compromise were made.

Ochs provides an example regarding the transcription of child-language data. Conversational turns between adults are commonly transcribed in a vertical arrangement: when one speaker yields the conversational floor to another, the transcriber, following the age-old practices of dramaturgical writing, usually begins transcribing the next turn on a fresh line. This arrangement provides a visual impression of equality between the conversationalists. Though it may be adequate for most conversations between adults, it is poorly suited to the transcription of asymmetrical interactions, as between children and adults.

Elaborating on Ochs' insights, Jane A. Edwards (1993) identifies several components in transcript design. First, transcribers must decide which categories to include, and once they have made this decision, the transcription of each category must be systematic; a transcriber who decides that pause length is of potential importance to the transcript and its analysis must indicate pause length for every instance of a pause. Second, the transcript must be readable: the notational system must be sufficiently transparent and conventional to be readily interpreted by other users. Third, related events, like turns of the same conversation, must be transcribed in close proximity to one another, while unrelated events must be separated visually. Fourth, the spacial arrangement of the transcript must be iconic of the temporal arrangement of events.

## Transcribing musical material

Discussions of the problems that transcription raises have mostly concerned conversational data, but most of the issues raised in this literature are directly relevant to the transcription of musical material. Sung performances in Oceania are often punctuated by audience responses, including applause, laughter, weeping, or verbal evaluation. In Tongan song-and-dance performances, observers express approval by shouting *mālie* 'well done'. In Sāmoan song-and-narrative performances, listeners show appreciation by saying '*aue,* or any of several other terms. Thus, sung performances

TRACK 14

are as potentially dialogic as informal conversation, and a performance-centered analysis of singing must treat this dialogism as an object of inquiry. As John M. Atkinson (1984) has demonstrated, skillful politicians carefully control the timing of their audience's applause in response to speeches, and use the applause in designing the course of their subsequent delivery. Formal spoken discourse can be as sensitive to nonverbal response cues from the audience as informal conversation, and while it remains an empirical question, the same could probably be said of many musical performances worldwide (witness the timing of applause in performances of jazz). The transcription of singing must thus provide information about the inception, completion, and quality of applause.

In short, the transcription of any verbal and nonverbal data is a theoretically fraught activity, and researchers must approach the task of transcribing as an integral part of the analytic process.　　　　　　　　　　　　　　　　—NIKO BESNIER

## METRICS

Metrics is a subset of rhythmics, the study of the relationship of language and time. The metrical organization of sung verse is more complex than that of spoken verse because it joins two systems, language and music, which play off each other by using similarity and contrast.

Oceanic musical phrases, especially those for dancing, realize meters that subdivide into beats grouped into twos, threes, fours, and so on; but their texts, if viewed apart from their music, rarely subdivide into linguistically analogous patterns, the regularly repeating configurations called iambs, trochees, anapests, dactyls, and the like. Oceanic verbal meter often realizes a different strategy: the accumulation of an ideal number of units per phrase, as in Chuuk, Kosrae, and Pohnpei, where most lines "contain five or seven syllables" (Fischer 1966:206). In Polynesia, poetic lines may ideally contain fixed numbers of moras (short vowels): twelve-mora lines are evident in poetic texts from Sāmoa, Tonga, and 'Uvea (Love 1991:288), and have been reported from Bellona and Pukapuka. The Māori of Aotearoa have poetry disposed in eight-mora lines, revealing a principle called the rule of eight (McLean 1981).

The Sāmoan metrical system exemplifies the variety possible in mora-focused verse. Documented nineteenth-century songs fall into three metrically based classes: some have fourteen-mora verses, some have twelve-mora verses, and some have paired verses of contrasting lengths. Of the last (figure 2), some combine eight- and twelve-mora verses, and some combine six- and fourteen-mora verses, formerly rendered in alternation by choruses, whose timbral contrasts, when matched with the meanings of the sung words, offered artful effects.　　　　　　　　—J. W. LOVE

### The metrics of Bellonese verse

The sung poetry of Bellona, a Polynesian outlier, uses marked diction, sometimes including archaic words and phrases and always avoiding non-Bellonese words. Because of a strong interest in ancestral history and the role of songs as carriers of historical information, the repertory retains ancient songs. The texts of some, in the language of the putative homeland ('Ubea) as the Bellonese remember it, have no intelligible gloss. Some ancient songs are introductory songs, *pese,* and the *suahongi* (Rossen 1987). Common themes are everyday subjects: fishing, building houses, doing domestic activities, praising gods, insulting enemies. Musical genres exemplify different poetic forms (*na noho o na hatu'anga* 'the kinds of poetic composition').

Some musical texts have lines of widely varying lengths, and some have lines of twelve moras each. The first four lines of a seventeen-line lament (*tangi*) illustrate the latter trait:

FIGURE 2　Distributions of Sāmoan verses in one *fatu* (solid line) and two other *fatu* (dashed line), measured in moras, with percents on the vertical axis (after Love 1991:126).

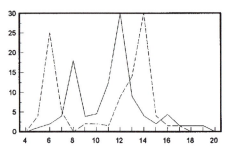

FIGURE 3   Beginning of the Bellonese "*Te Tangi Tu'ai*" ('The Ancient Lament'): the refrain, sung by a man; the first verse, sung by a woman; and the refrain, sung by ten men and three women (after Rossen 1987:2:50).

| Hakatahi ake ki te 'aso 'eha. | A crowd gathered for the big day. |
|---|---|
| Na ngaoi tau sa'enge i ngoto. | Good, your movements therein. |
| Maghiiti ma te huu hakaiho na. | Songs of praise and clapsongs. |
| Tangi ai tou nge'o i ngoto na. | Your smooth voice [heard] therein. |

After each of these lines, a chorus sings a refrain (figure 3). In length, seldom do the lines differ from the norm: line three is one mora longer. Another lament (*mako*) has twelve-mora lines. Rhymes and a one-word refrain reinforce the metrics of each line (Rossen 1987:2:53–55):

| Mangu poo u hesingi, aea. | In the night I asked, *aea.* |
|---|---|
| 'Atua hea ka sisi'i, aea. | Where the god was with us, *aea.* |
| 'Atua na ngoto tamaki, aea. | The god was big of mind, *aea.* |
| 'Abaki ki toku masaki, aea. | It helped my sickness, *aea.* |
| Longi oku ba'e kua piki, aea. | I hold my stiff legs, *aea.* |
| 'Oha oku niho kua siki, aea. | My teeth are gone, *aea.* |

The moras in these lines number 12, 12, 12, 12, 13, and 13. The lines cluster in couplets, rhyming (before the refrain) in *i–i, a–i,* and *i–i,* respectively. Unusually, the rhyme of the second and third couplets receives the consonantal reinforcement of /k/ in the combinations *-aki* and *-iki.*

—JANE MINK ROSSEN

## SONICS

Sonics is the study of the pure sound of utterances. It covers rhyme, alliteration, and other ways by which recurring sounds create pleasing effects. Rhyme, an attribute of twentieth-century popular music, was rare in precontact Oceanic musical texts. The only region that favored it was West Polynesia, where, stressed at the ends of lines, it took the form of two vowels, with or without an intervening consonant, so *mata* and *maa* were, and are, acceptable rhymes for *mana.* Because the people of East Polynesia and the Polynesian outliers do not readily use this kind of rhyme, it may have originated in West Polynesia after the primary settlers of East Polynesia and the Polynesian outliers had departed.

Hawaiian poets developed a technique called linked assonance, by which the first word of a phrase (conveniently written as a line) echoes the last word of the preceding phrase. Instances appear in a Hawaiian musical text (Beckwith 1951:205):

In some cultures of Oceania, phonemes shift between speaking and singing: spoken /a/ may become sung /o/; spoken /k/ may become sung /t/. Why this happens, and how it affects observers' apprehension of meaning, are consequential questions.

Hanau ka muki, muka, mukekeke
Muka, kukuku, kunenewa
Moku, monu, mumule ana
Mumule wale ana Kane i ka mule
I mule, i keʻeo, i ka maua
I ka wahine weweli wale.

There was whispering, lip-smacking and clucking
Smacking, tut-tutting, head-shaking
Sulking, sullenness, silence
Kane kept silence, refused to speak
Sullen, angry, resentful
With the woman for her progeny.

In addition to linked assonance, as between *mumule ana* and *Mumule wale,* this passage alliterates thoroughly—on /m/, /k/, and finally /w/—and has other salient recurrences, like the pattern of *-ale, -ule,* and *-eli.* Unlike West Polynesian rhyming, linked assonance occurs only intermittently in Hawaiian sung words. Farther west, it connects verses in Buin laments and stanzas in Kuman songs of courtship.

Alliterative play also marks Oceanic texts. Recurring word-initial /y/ and /s/ and word-final rhymes mark a line in a Kiwai song: *Yóromo sóromo óromo yáramawío sáramawío* 'Along outside, sea he breaks along canoe, spray he come' (Landtman 1927:434). In a forty-three-verse Kiwai song, forty of the verbs begin with /d/. Other kinds of sonic recurrence probably contribute to the art of musical poetry in Oceania, but await further research.

**Phonemic play in Oceanic verse**

In addition to formalizing rhythms and intonations, music permits words to change their structures. Typically, the process involves phonemic play, the substitution of sung phonemes for different phonemes normal in nonsung speech. In Western Australia, Pilbara singers "modify a vowel or avoid a consonant entirely if they think fit" (von Brandenstein and Thomas 1975:[13]). Similar activity modifies the phonemes of Asmat sung verse (Voorhoeve 1977). In Western Province, Papua New Guinea, the Kiwai "pronounce the words so hastily as to make them almost incomprehensible, and they modify them freely by abbreviating or by adding extra syllables" (Landtman 1927:422–423). In the Southern Highlands, "Kaluli vowels vary considerably from speech to song," particularly from spoken /e/ to sung /ɛ/, and similarly from /o/ to /ɔ/ (Feld 1990:19). In Morobe, some Jabêm sing vowels

quite differently as to how they sound in normal speech, for example, *losia* instead of *lasio, i lausi* instead of *i lasi,* or *ŋaô êjom o losico* instead of *ŋao êjam o lasicac.*

The singer wants to embellish his text somewhat, 'it sounds so much finer and more unusual' than in normal speech. (Zahn 1996:339)

In the North Solomons, similar substitutions highlight Buin verse (Laycock 1969). In the Trobriand Islands, "*valu* becomes *vanu* and *vanui, mokita* becomes *monita,*" and phonemic play effects a "well understood" register (Baldwin 1945: 202–203).

Most reported information on phonemic play concerns superficial performative attributes; but for at least one Oceanic society, Kapingamarangi, a deep-structural analysis is available (see below). In addition to, and possibly in replacement of, phonemic play, the ideational play of metaphor aids aesthetic strategies. In some Polynesian societies, an etiquette that encourages the public avoidance of prominent persons' names or titles leads to context-dependent lexical shifts, but it does not usually force the phonemic shifts discussed here.

### The substitution of one phoneme for another

In some cultures of Oceania, phonemes shift between speaking and singing: spoken /a/ may become sung /o/; spoken /k/ may become sung /t/. Why this happens, and how it affects observers' apprehension of meaning, should prove fruitful questions, but little research has been done on the musical side of the process. Probably the answer concerns the social functions of performance, as speaking and singing differentially set the frames within which communication occurs.

#### Play between vowels

Possibly because vowels do most of the work of sustaining intoned sounds, they bear the most documented phonological activity. Abundant data on one-to-one shifts between vowels come from the Polynesian outliers. Another documented phonemic shift is the assimilation of a vowel to the quality of the next vowel [see EAST POLYNESIA: Cook Islands: Northern Cook Islands: Pukapuka].

The most widely reported shift is between spoken /a/ and sung /o/. In a Kapingamarangi musical text (see below), this shift occurs in the word formally pronounced *hangahanga* but sung, with other changes, as *hangona.* Material collected in the early 1980s by William Donner shows that in Sikaiana, a change from spoken /a/ to sung /o/ is the commonest local shift, in stressed position (*hati* → *hoti*) and unstressed position (*manava* → *monavo*). In Bellona, "*a* is often sung as *o*," reflecting "an aesthetic preference for *o* as a sustained (sung) vowel" (Rossen 1987:1:312–313). In Tikopia, this shift occurs "either medially or terminally. So *tapu* becomes *topu* and *mua* becomes *muo*" (Firth 1990:40). Material collected by Richard Feinberg shows that in Anuta, this shift occurs in stressed and unstressed positions, especially in frequently used nouns: *moana* 'ocean' → *moono* and *tamaaroa* 'bachelor' → *tomooroo.*

A shift from spoken /a/ to sung /u/ has been reported from Sikaiana (*Alohi* → *Ulohi*). A shift from spoken /o/ to sung /u/ has been reported from Anuta (*moana* → *muono*). Environment may condition these variances: in Anutan musical texts, /a/ seems able to shift to /u/, but only after /e/, or after /o/ that remains /o/; it also can shift to /e/, but only before /u/; /o/ can also rise to /u/. Material collected by Michael Lieber shows that in Kapingamarangi sung speech, a shift from spoken /a/ to sung /i/ occurs (*whanaga* → *whanogi*), as does that from spoken /u/ to sung /i/ (*gulu* → *guli*).

#### Play between consonants

Apart from sung changes in /n/, /ŋ/, and /t/, Polynesian consonants are fairly stable. In Sāmoan singing, even in extremely informal contexts (as for singing about indelicate subjects), the formal /t/, reflecting Proto-Polynesian /*t/, is often pronounced /t/, not the informal /k/. Hawaiian singers trained in the mid-1800s and recorded in the 1920s pronounced the reflex of Proto-Polynesian /*t/ as /t/, not the orthographic /k/ (Roberts 1926:73); some Hawaiian singers now indulge the /t/, but inconsistently articulate /t/ and /k/ in the same performance. In Sāmoa, the formal /n/ usually remains /n/ in musical contexts, and is not informalized to /ŋ/. Elders sometimes add voicing to give /s/ the character of /z/, otherwise absent from the language.

### *The addition of phonemes*

Ordinarily in Oceanic cultures whose languages differentiate short and long vowels, sung short vowels receive short rhythmic values, and sung long vowels receive long rhythmic values. The absolute duration of these values, and their lengths relative to each other, depend on tempo, genre, and context. Exigencies of phrasing also affect these relationships. The usual alteration is lengthening, a process reported from all cultures of West Polynesia and some Polynesian outliers.

Scattered reports of the insertion of vowels for metrical necessity exist, as on Chuuk, Kosrae, and Pohnpei (Fischer 1966:206) and in Buang music (Hooley 1987). In Fiji, musical settings enable "syllables to change the stress in words. For instance, the word *cere* may become *ceyececeyere* to suit the rhythm" (Quain, in Rothenberg 1968:517). In Kapingamarangi, the tongue moves downward to add vowels after /i/ (*daahili* → *daahieeli*) but upward after /a/ (*nghaga* → *nghaiiki*). Some Sikaianan genres permit the optional insertion of vowels: the line *e ni naenae ko nau* becomes *ea nia naenaeia koa naeua*, and *te taaina nei e hahano mai* becomes *tea taaeianoa neaia e hahano a moaia*. In Bellona, only the vowels /a/ and /e/ may undergo this process, producing /aua/ and /eie/, and the resultant augmentation may itself receive lengthening: *e* → *eie* → *eeiee* (Rossen 1987:1:312–313).        —J. W. LOVE

### Concealing and revealing on Kapingamarangi

Doing research on Kapingamarangi Atoll, a Polynesian outlier in Micronesia with a population of five hundred, I had expected to find that personal names would mark some important event or feature surrounding a child's birth. I was disappointed. Personal names are nonsense syllables, I was told. They are chosen because they sound good. Further questioning revealed that precontact names for a newborn were not invented on the spot, but were taken mainly from musical texts about fishing expeditions, or eulogies for a relative of the newborn. But why choose words and phrases that are nonsense? And why create compositions with nonsense syllables in them?

Experts said that in a good song, it is the sound that counts. "Sound" (*lee*) refers to an aesthetic fit among four components: tempo, rhythm, content, and metaphor. (Pitch is irrelevant because singing is monotonic.) Of these, rhythm is compositionally the most demanding: it requires judicious use of consonants for accenting beats (nasals /h/ or /wh/ being more frequent than stops), and for combining accented and unaccented beats (using vowels, flaps, and nasals). In the following excerpt, acute accents (otherwise unorthographic) mark stressed syllables; the vowels of the words *whale, loi, niu, magi, binu, ala,* and *mai* have half the rhythmic value of the others.

> Mée nogó moe ló di whale lói niu e,
> Hángona dí agi dú magi de bínu ala mai.

> He slept in the coconut-leaf house,
> Was roused by the tern in the pandanus.

To maintain the rhythm, every syllable must fit, but the basis of the first word of the second line does not. The verb 'rouse' is *hangahanga,* whose four syllables could be shortened to three, but *aha* as two full beats is considered awkward. By substituting *o* for *a* and *na* for *ha,* the composer fits the word to the rhythm while varying vowel height (low-to-mid-to-low, with a nasal to make the unaccented beat), giving a smooth flow. The resulting form of the word, however, is unrecognizable: it is a nonsense word, but not the sort of nonsense that enhances a composer's reputation or serves as a name.

Substituting *hangona* for *hangahanga* is regarded as an example of craft and competence, not art and brilliance. This is so because the manipulation fits the rhythm with the pleasing sound expected of any competent composer. But it lacks brilliance because the meaning of *hangona* is transparent. The root, *hanga,* is apparent in form and semantic placement. Anyone could guess, given the context of a sleeping person and a word beginning *hang–,* that the word means 'to rouse', whatever the rest of the form (whose context is completed by the agent that awakened the sleeper). To be artful, phonemic manipulations have to be opaque to listeners, with the transformed word or phrase being sensible once explained by the composer.

The more phonemic transformations applied to a word or a phrase, the more opaque its meaning. A mere excess of transforming is too easy to be artful. The real coup for a composer is to make only one phonemic change sufficient to mask an entire phrase. But that requires the composer to set up a narrative so the next event in a sequence being depicted could be any number of different events; that is, the narrative reaches a point of near total ambiguity about what the next event is likely to be, followed by a phrase with one phonemic change that is equally ambiguous.

In a song about a fish-netting expedition, a fleet of canoes is heading toward the main channel through the reef. One man looks back. Then, as the song says, "the thing *gu ada mudi.*" What is the thing? And what does it do? It could be a fish, as if the transformation were from *gu ae di muu* '(then) surfaced the *muu* (sea bream)' with two changes, or *gu ada di muu* '(then) first (to appear) the *muu*' with two changes. Another possibility is *gu ada mai* '(then) first to appear', and another is *gu ada mua* '(it was) shadowy before (us)', or *gu adaada (matau) mua* '(it was) reflected light (as on the water) before (us).' The word *ada* has homophones meaning 'picture', 'reflection', 'shadow' and 'be first, be older'. But *ada* could also be a transform of *dada* 'pull, drag, start, grab', or of *daga* 'attach (as a leader on a fishhook, or ends of a net), or of *mada,* 'look', and so on.

At this point in a performance, any of these possibilities would fit. The authentic meaning is *gu ada muli* 'then the thing (another canoe) came late (was last to appear)'. Just one phoneme changes: /l/ becomes /d/. And the only way we can know that is to ask the composer, or someone who learned the authentic meaning of the line from the composer. And yes, Guadamudi is indeed a personal name.

### The aesthetics of naming

Why should these meaningless (and once learned, trivial) musical phrases be choice items for people's names? Because the process of their composition and exegesis— encoding and decoding, concealing and revealing, investing the meaningless with meaning—are precisely the processes by which infants become persons and persons become particular kinds of persons.

Like most Oceanic peoples, Kapinga people define the person as a relatum, part of a social relationship, a locus of shared biographies. People's expectations of one another reflect their knowledge of others' biographies, what they themselves have done, and their styles of doing what they do. But for a social order to operate on the basis of individual biographies, each person must act and interact *consistently.* People develop personal, distinctive consistency by cultivating personal styles—distinctive ways of interacting with their natural and social environments. Personal styles are the bases of personal reputations, those thumbnail sketches that summarize their personal biographies.

A person has a series of names. At the death of a loved one, a person abandons his or her first childhood name, signaling the end of the relationship (Lieber 1991). For the same reason, he or she will abandon in turn the next name and later names. Since no two people ever use the same name at the same time, names uniquely distinguish living people. But since most names are those of long-deceased relatives, names conjoin kin. It is the name an adult has at his or her death that historically identifies him or her. That identity, however, is uniquely invested in the name by the person's lifetime of doing particular things in a distinctive way. The name denotes a reputation, developed and cultivated: Kapinga people do, as they say, "make their names."

Kapinga people distinguish the *tangata,* the public persona (or 'person'), from the *lodo* 'inside(s)', one's inner, private self. Kapinga individuals carefully cultivate the public persona for, organize it around, and define it by, the particular relationships that contextualize their actions and utterances. The *lodo* is the domain of chaos. Will, desires, emotions, thoughts—processes that comprise a person's inner life—these develop at different times from infancy onward. Each acts independently of the others. Without surveillance and control, any of them may arise unbidden to dominate a person's actions, with disastrous results.

But the *lodo* is also the domain of creativity and decision. People keep it hidden. They never talk about their feelings and musings, for nobody wants to know what is going on inside anyone else. It is the refractions of the self to which people attend—outward manifestations of inner processes, edited and filtered for public presentation. Even knowledge is a feature to be hidden until a moment strategically calculated for its display and use. While the *tangata* is visible, even transparent, the *lodo* is opaque. People reveal it in fragments, at carefully timed moments of revelation, when people come to know one another. Afterward, they sometimes revise their mutual estimations.

Kapinga people choose personal names from nonsense phrases in songs because the patterns by which each is comprised, composed, disseminated, and knowable are identical. The process of dissembling, concealing, and revealing make these bits of nonsense appropriate metaphors for labeling persons. In a larger context, Kapinga conceptions of personhood are products or outcomes of applying cultural principles that we call axioms or premises. Kapinga conceptions of particular persons—living, interacting, named, knowable—-are products or outcomes of applying cultural principles that we call aesthetics.

—Michael D. Lieber

## STROPHICS

Strophics is the study of patterning at levels larger than lines. Many musical systems of Oceania structure songs at such levels. A performance in Tuvalu in the 1890s had "a constant repetition of words or phrases; the same phrases were repeated over and over again to the same tune with the same actions; at each change of phrase there was a change of tune and action, and a considerable increase of speed" (David 1899:61). Most Oceanic societies have not developed nomenclatures for the processes by which their musical systems achieve strophic structures, but the names of genres can indicate theoretical recognition of the artistic effects of these processes. In old Mangaia, in the Cook Islands, choral songs had an introduction (*tumu*), a foundation (*papa*), a first section (*unuunu tai* 'first offshoot'), a second section (*unuunu rua*), sometimes a third section (*unuunu toru*) and a fourth (*unuunu ā*), and always a finale (*akareinga*). The sections usually did not have parallel structures; they included solo and choral passages, specified by the composer (Gill 1876). Songs of Tikopia divide into sections (*kupu* 'word'). In a two-section piece, the first is the foundation (*tafito*) and the second is a *kupu*; in a piece having three sections or more, the last section is called *safe* (Firth 1990:15–16). Much popular Oceanic music of the twentieth century has forms using regularly repeating stanzas and refrains.                    —J. W. LOVE

### Epigrammatic songs of Oceania

Epigrammatic songs—with short texts, repeated many times in performance—occur throughout Oceania. Their words often make abbreviated, elliptical references, fully understood by only a few. Their semantic compression is extreme. Performances emphasize the excitement of singing (and often dancing), rather than the logic of narrative sequentiality. Many postcontact texts allude to biblical stories, but some use precontact motifs and cite current events.

Epigrammatic texts require composers to exercise skill in distilling the essence of a topic: a crucial incident, capturing a single moment, opens a story for contemplation. A Tokelauan example (after Thomas et al. 1990:30–31) shows the process:

| | |
|---|---|
| *Tuia ko te atu:* | The bonito is hooked: |
| *Te tiuvaka e!* | O the swordfish! |

This means that a fisherman hooked a bonito, but before he could land it, a swordfish had impaled it, illustrating the fickleness of fate. With similar compression, a song in the Ngarluma language of Western Australia recalls a predicament in a dinghy: *Jardiŋarraba, kudjardikudjardi; / Jardiŋarraba pirndura kalbana* 'Waves can come, one by one; / Waves can rise in a heavy swell' (after von Brandenstein and Thomas 1975:10, 61). This text does more than record an incident at sea: it advertises the composer's name—Jimmy Dougall-Kudjardikudjardi, Jimmy Dougall-One-By-One. As these examples show, the full meaning of epigrammatic songs may not be a textual attribute: it may be an activity of an informed listener's mind, where it develops from contextual knowledge and experience.

Because of the compression of epigrammatic texts, the story behind them can be opaque to outsiders, as in a song from Tuvalu: *'Ia 'outou ilia le sofao ikepea ma le pū / i totonu o le nu'u o Lama* 'Blow the shofar and the conch / Among the people of Ramah' (after David 1899:78). This text could originally have referred to any of the five cities the Bible names Ramah, but it might have named a local personage (*Lama* 'Torch' is a plausible Tuvaluan personal name). Only Tuvaluans of the 1890s may have understood why linking aerophones with the people of Ramah or Lama was apt for them.

The link between the lines of a couplet sometimes gains intensity from rhyme, as in many West Polynesian texts and in one from near Wagawaga, Milne Bay Province, Papua New Guinea: *Mai Del laulauua; / Mai Del gonugonua* 'People of De have been talking; / People of De have been grumbling' (after Seligmann 1910:588). In this text, only the rhyming words vary. Elsewhere, their place can be filled by identical words or vocables, as in a Tok Pisin song that Amanab-speakers of West Sepik Province, Papua New Guinea, sing while cutting grass: *Gras katim, e-e! / O-e-o, e-e!* 'Cutting grass, e-e! / O-e-o, e-e!' (after Webb and Niles 1990:113–114). Musically, this song follows the five-part vocal harmony of the *yaubug* genre, in which each part is named after one of the wooden trumpets (*fuf*) that play in five-part polyphony.

In another intensifying technique, different words fill the same slots in matching structures, as with the coordinate tripling of *O Kuki* 'Cook' and *Neborau e* 'O sailed' in a song from Kiribati (after Farrell 1921:312):

| | |
|---|---|
| O Kuki, O Kuki, O Kuki, te arikivaka, | Cook, Cook, Cook, the captain, |
| Neborau e, neborau e, neborau e, ki Sāmoa. | O sailed, O sailed, O sailed, to Sāmoa. |

This assertion, if it is about Captain Cook, is false, showing that the truth of epigrammatic songs can be in their forms and their contexts, not in the senses of their words.

Forms larger than couplets may show similar compression. (For special uses of triplets, see "Strophics and society in the Santa Cruz Islands," below, and COMPOSITIONAL PROCESSES: Binandere compositional processes.) Performance can turn couplets into quatrains. A taro-harvest song (*kasama*) as created by Hunjara-speakers of Oro Province, Papua New Guinea (after Webb and Niles 1990:94–96), goes: *Aha, maha, sova vuvija! / Ere Jenifo Aijau, Jenifo Aijau!* 'Mother, father, the spirit is coming! / Wake up, Jennifer Aijau, Jennifer Aijau!' Performers sing the first line twice, add the second, and sing the first again. Continuing the performance, they may repeat the formula, substituting other persons' names, while elaborately decorated dancers accompany drumming on kundus.

—ALLAN THOMAS, J. W. LOVE, DON NILES

## Strophics and society in the Santa Cruz Islands

Formal songfests of Santa Cruz merge poetry and costumery in performances that make ritual petitions to deities. Taken together, these elements paint a symbolic picture of Santa Cruz society (Davenport 1975). The ruling part of a songfest is the music, whose force depends on the strophics of the lyrics. Most songs are triplets, like these examples (Mamini is a haunted reef, and Tengaviti is a deity):

> The house of the unmarried men,
> Located at the village of Bumalu:
> Many unmarried girls come to sleep over.

> The baton draws them from Mamini;
> A conch trumpet announces their arrival:
> Tengaviti awaits them, the dancers, with money.

The most distinctive stylistic device of each strophe is the order of the lines. The meaning of the first line is usually ambiguous. The second line compounds the ambiguity. The last line supplies a missing element of meaning.

TRACK 15

Each strophe repeats over and over, making a circular structure. The dancing, too, is circular. It occurs in a ring built for the event, near a men's clubhouse, the focus of local rituals. Builders pay attention to the quality of the earth: with care, they prepare the ground so it will resonate with dancers' stamps, which, on a still night, are audible a kilometer away.

The main dancers are handsome young men, who perform in pairs (figure 4). Their beauty attracts female deities, so each man guards his partner lest a deity seduce him. Because these men wear feathers, they are called birds. The performance challenges their stamina: without resting, they dance from late afternoon until well into the next morning.

The men form a choir and a percussion section, which regulates the beat. Dancers stamp their feet mainly in unison on downbeats, while taking small steps forward. The choir leads. Behind follow elder men, also in special garb, trailed by women and children. Many participants hold freshly cut branches, signifying they have come overland from another village. Slowly, the crowd moves counterclockwise around the ring. The back merges with the front, just as the last line of each strophe returns to the first. Illuminated by a bonfire, the mass of participants resembles a slowly revolving grove of trees, leaves trembling to the beat of the stamping and singing.

FIGURE 4    Handsome Santa Cruz men perform in pairs, each guarding the other from female deities attracted by their beauty. Photo by William Davenport, 1959.

The choir divides in half. One half sings one line; the other half answers with the next. Since most songs have three lines, this process results in strophic counterpoint between the halves of the choir. With the first lines of the poetry designated by letters, the first section of the choir represented as a subscript 1, and the second section as a subscript 2, the full pattern can be symbolized as $A_1B_2C_1A_2B_1C_2$. The back-and-forth redistribution of the lines of a strophe gives the phrasing a large-scale two-against-three syncopation, a rhythmic propulsion that adds to the aesthetic effect.

As excitement mounts, the tempo accelerates. The choir introduces a lag between stamped downbeats and the meter of the poetry. Forward movement may stop while all participants bear down on their stamping. When the performance reaches a climax, some participants start stamping on offbeats. The tempo decelerates, and people leave off singing to shout, yell, and grunt in enthusiasm.

A single song lasts as long as enthusiasm for it does. If a song does not arouse much enthusiasm, it is abandoned after a few minutes. But appreciation of a song can keep it going through several climaxes, for as long as an hour. The objective is to keep spirits as high as possible for as long as possible. The members of the choir do not select the songs. After the performance of one strophe winds down, an elder man begins another, and the choir joins in.

Costumes consist of clothing, accessories, and cosmetics. The principal item is a delicately carved facial pendant, hung from the nose. Some accoutrements—earrings,

Santa Cruz dancers perform the round of social life. The lyrics extol the quest for wealth and prestige, the defense of life and property, occupations and hazards, loves and frustrations, mysteries and banalities.

breast ornament (and a smaller replica at the back of the neck), armbands, belt, breechcloth—are finely crafted versions of what, before World War II, men wore daily. Each dancer may wear a rattle tied to each knee. Each holds in his right hand a bamboo baton, which ordinarily serves as the storage case for his ceremonial breechcloth. Some accoutrements—plumes, coloring for the hair, upright nasal skewers, facial paint, shell necklaces, decorations tucked under armbands, wristlets, anklets—are worn only on this occasion. Every piece has deep symbolic significance. Many are heirlooms. All emanated from deities, who gave humans important knowledge, recorded in myths.

The lyrics of a songfest follow a theme, such as fighting. They may develop a subtheme, such as places where fights occurred. A common theme is the life of unmarried men, as in the following examples.

> Unmarried girls cry for their village;
> A young man in a canoe appears:
> They watch him fade into the distance.
>
> You are a handsome unmarried man,
> But I must cover my head and avoid your gaze:
> Soon I am to become your taboo relative.
>
> They say I am a handsome young man;
> But when I stand in the ring of Luli,
> *Eiaa!* one of my legs is gimpy.
>
> At night, your body looks beautiful,
> Unmarried man of Nonia Village:
> But studying it now—no!
>
> Stamping vigorously around the ring,
> You see my footprints there:
> I, the rooster of Tēmotū Noi, have come.

Lyrics are sung to three kinds of melodies. The most frequently chosen one, because its melodic line is fairly level, is called horizontal. In contrast is a melody termed vertical. The third, always sung fast, may be called lively. The horizontal form is used only at night, the vertical form is for singing by day, and the lively one serves as relief from the other two.

Like the triplets of the strophes, the participants divide into three groups: costumed impersonators of the deities, mature men, and the rest of the community. These groups merge into a single body, which in sung poetry performs the round of social life. The lyrics extol the values of human existence—the quest for wealth and prestige, the defense of life and property, occupations and hazards, loves and frustrations, mysteries and banalities.

—WILLIAM DAVENPORT

### The strophics of Sikaiana verse

The Sikaiana musical system has names for at least eight kinds of stanzas in several genres (*sau, siva, tuki, tani, tuuhoe*), but seldom in songs composed for guitar accompaniment. Not all named stanzas must appear in a song.

A refrain (*akoako*) guides the structure of many songs: it introduces the textual theme and recurs throughout the structure. Stanzas (*puku*) do not repeat: a song begins with a refrain, followed by the first stanza; the refrain then recurs, followed by the second stanza; and so on. A preface (*mua* 'front') can precede the initial refrain. Some songs have a *hhati* 'split' after the refrain and a *liaki* 'scatter' after the *hhati*. The *haopuku* is a repeated phrase that introduces each stanza (*puku*). Some songs have a second refrain (*tualua* 'twofold'). The first time a *tualua* is sung, it follows a *tutalua*, which does not recur when the *tualua* repeats. The link of the *tualua* and the *tutalua* parallels that of the refrain and its preface.

The textual resources of a *sau* composed for the *puina,* a local celebration, illustrate some of these principles; all but phrase B consist of one line each.

A    I te tulana o toku tanata e ku nonoho ma a nau
B    He mokoaa nau ku moe lolono ai nei.
      Te laakau e sina nei: e lavaka ki hakatuu ake? ii oo!
C    I te hiahia o toku tanata ku nonoho ma a nau.
$D_1$    Te hea na lautama mua, ku oti i te mamate?
E    A te mate laa o tatae mai taku otiana ma te henua.
$F_1$    Toku moe i he kaakena taku otiana ma te henua.
$D_2$    Te hea na lautama loto, ku oti i te mamate?
$F_2$    Toku moe i he tuuloto taku otiana ma te henua.
$D_3$    Te hea na lautama muli, ku oti i te mamate?
$F_3$    Toku moe i he mulivaka taku otiana ma te henua.

I think about my youth
Whenever I sleep soundly.
This tree that falls: can it be made to stand? *ii oo!*
The happiness of my youth remains with me.
Where are the prior generations, who departed in death?
At death, my departure from the island occurs.
My sleep on a bier is my departure from the island.
Where are the middle generations, who departed in death?
My sleep in state is my departure from the island.
Where are the latter generations, who departed in death?
My sleep at the stern is my departure from the island.

The names of these textual structures are *mua* (A), *akoako* (B), *tualua* (C), *haopuku* ($D_1$, $D_2$, $D_3$), *tualua o te haopuku* (E), *puku* ($F_1$, $F_2$, $F_3$). Respondents in 1983 said the correct sequence of stanzas is: A–B–C–B, $D_1$–E–B–$F_1$–E–B, $D_2$–E–B–$F_2$–E–B, $D_3$–E–B–$F_3$–E–B. In a recording made in 1983, an extra *akoako* occurred after the second *puku*. The cited mortuary customs include the funeral bier, lying in state in the center of a house, and committing the corpse to sea in a canoe.

—WILLIAM DONNER

## METAPHOR AND SYMBOLISM

Metaphor—saying one thing and meaning another, hearing one thing and understanding another—abounds in Oceanic lyrics. Explanations of metaphorical processes are legion (Lakoff and Johnson 1980; Sacks 1979), but conventional analysis accepts that each metaphor has a *stated* denotation, sometimes called the vehicle, which delivers an *unstated* message, sometimes called the tenor. The vehicle may stand as a symbol of the tenor. A poet may talk of birds but mean girls; a singer may lament storminess but mean death. Simile—the process of merely *likening* a tenor to a vehicle (saying girls are *like* birds, death is *like* a storm)—is rare in Oceanic poetry. A sharp distinction between these processes is that superficially, a metaphorical statement is false (girls are not really birds), but a simile may be true (girls may be *like* birds).

Examples of two metaphorical processes, the Tongan *heliaki* and the Hawaiian *kaona,* are famous, but analysis of most is lacking. Sikaianans [see POLYNESIAN OUTLIERS] understand musical texts to have two senses, an open meaning and a hidden one, whose metaphorical play (*hulihulisala*) expands or intensifies textual meaning. Complex or difficult metaphors they call *nnoto* 'deep', a term otherwise applied to the sea.

Metaphors flaunt as they mask, setting up artistic tensions that appeal to wordsmiths. They safely convey sung criticisms and references to illicit behavior because their meaning is inferential and therefore unprovable, protecting composers and performers from retaliation (Monberg 1974). Though metaphorical imagery may be so conventional as to be unfresh, its use in musical settings is purposeful (Berndt and Berndt 1971:676).

### Content

Unfolding semantic patterns and textual trends can give purpose to artistic discourse, but many lyrics are too brief to provide conclusive evidence about what composers and performers intend. Checking the meanings of individual words does not explain why performance can make an ostensibly humdrum passage—like Shakespeare's "Pray you, undo this button"—a stunning emotional moment. Taken alone, each word is ordinary. The power of words lies in their context; hence, the most implicative unit of analysis can be a song or a repertory.

Semantically focused analysis can be a profitable line of research. The lyric eminence of natural features—reefs, shores, mountains, plants, birds, fish—is obvious and expected, but the processes by which poets and societies select and manipulate the vehicles for their ideas is little understood; nor have researchers done much analytical work on how Oceanic poet-composers understand those processes.

A common metaphorical vehicle in Oceania is a bird. Famous examples include beautiful fruitdoves of Kaluli weeping, frigatebirds of Micronesian singing and dancing (figure 5), parrots whose feathers adorn costumes in New Guinea and Bougainville, the birds of the *Sia* of the Siassi Islands and elsewhere, and bird-men of Rapa Nui. Each of these vehicles carries a unique tenor, particular to the society that generated it.

Musical texts of Anuta, as collected by Richard Feinberg, exemplify the range possible within an impopulous society. In 1971, a dance-song called a member of an expedition to Anuta *ko te manu o te moana* 'a bird of the ocean'; a few years later, another called an American researcher *ko te manu mai Amerika* 'a bird from America'. An erotic song celebrated that *ka eva temanu o te moana* 'the bird of the ocean will venture forth'—a lover will go to his sweetheart, who serves as *te noponga o te manu-tai* 'the seabird's residence'. The phrase *te manu ku eva* 'the bird has ventured forth' recalled a youth's death.

FIGURE 5     Banabans dance a story about frigate birds. Photos by Adrienne L. Kaeppler, 1988.

*(a)*     *(b)*

## Tales as extended metaphors

On the surface, tales are imaginary sequences of events that concern imaginary characters; but their underlying subjects are the lives of the listeners they attract. Narrative themes resonate with the common experience of audiences. They spring from a culture the listeners call or make their own. Without such resonance, tales would fail to captivate an audience; and the evidence of centuries of investigation shows that every culture of Oceania has a repertory of life in fiction.

Tales hold their popularity to the extent their themes are familiar. They appeal mainly to persons who share in the cultural background behind the themes, but they can travel anywhere if they undergo the transformations necessary to bring their figurative plans into concordance with local expectations (Lévi-Strauss 1969; Thompson 1977 [1946]). Broad environmental similarities, particularly those relating to the interface of Oceanic land and sea, have ensured the persistence of themes across wide expanses. Accidental voyages ending in unanticipated landfalls may have furthered the transmission of tales over long distances. Many narrative themes are widespread in Oceania (Kirtley 1971).

In addition to language, the narration of tales may involve musical sounds and movements. For characterization and dialogue, the narrator may modulate vocal timbres, sprinkle the story with exclamations, make abrupt changes of pitch and intensity, and emphasize passages with inclinations of the torso, nods and shakes of the head, exaggerated facial expressions, and gestures.

Oceanic tales track the magical exploits of ancestral figures and mythical creatures. They tell of witches and ogres, enchanted fish and animals, wise and cruel elders, brave and foolish children. They explain the origins of familiar objects, landmarks, and practices. But their underlying and unstated subjects, their tenors, carried in the vehicle of metaphor, are the lives of the people who tell and listen to them.

### Narrative as a musical context

Throughout Oceania, tales furnish contexts in which a narrator sings to an audience. Their bulk is action, told in oral prose; their sung parts, often emotionally charged soliloquies, may occupy a small portion of the time taken in performance. Such songs may be high points of performances. They are usually solo and unaccompanied, in simple and formulaic diction, ending even in spoken words. Claps and other nonvocal sounds may enhance performances. Audiences may participate by clapping (figure 6), or by calling out formulaic phrases of appreciation, either at liberty or at set points, as after each stanza of a song. Listeners may respond to sung verses by calling out a refrain, or even by joining a narrator's singing. Rarely, a person other than the narrator undertakes the primary musical performance.

### Polynesian tales

Tales throughout Polynesian cultures share many motifs. In West Polynesia, the sung

FIGURE 6   On Rapa Nui, Kiko Pātē sings a story, adding movements of his arms, while listeners participate by clapping. Photo by Adrienne L. Kaeppler, 1984.

parts of tales bear names that generically distinguish them from most other kinds of singing: in Sāmoa, tales are *fāgono*, usually pronounced *fāgogo*; in 'Uvea, *fagono* (Bataillon 1932); in Tonga, *fananga*. In much of West Polynesia and the Polynesian outliers, the singing and the songs are specified by a term for the act of crying, reflecting Proto-Polynesian *\*taŋi*.

A sung text in a tale widely known in West Polynesia and the Polynesian outliers illustrates poetry typical of tales. In Sikaiana, the text of one tale (*ttani kkai*) concerns the boys Te Laupounini and Te Laupounana (data courtesy of William Donner), whom the mother calls:

> Te Laupounini a, Te Laupounana ei!
> Tuutuu mai i ki naa;
> Tuutuu mai i ki naa.
> Ka te nei alua uhi maa lua talo—*taloo?*
>
> Te Laupounini, Te Laupounana!
> Stand right there for me;
> Stand right there for me.
> What's with your yam and your taro, *taro?*

And the boys answer:

> Ahe i ki naa e ki tinana e;
> Ahe i ki naa e ki tinana e.
> Ki maaua ka hulo o sesepu i te ava haimano, *huloo!*
>
> Turn aside there, O mother;
> Turn aside there, O mother.
> We're running to dive into the sharky passage—*running!*

As in most sung poetry in tales, the phrases are short, the diction is clear, the syntax is simple. Metaphorical processes are working themselves out at levels higher than words and phrases.

—J. W. LOVE

## Foi memorial songs

Throughout interior Papua New Guinea, metaphorical processes are deployed in a variety of contexts. Particularly in magic, dream interpretation, and oratory, interior Papua New Guinea men use metaphor as a route to discursive efficacy and power. In song too, metaphor plays a decisive role. Among the Foi of the Southern Highlands Province, memorial songs (*sorohabora*) are composed by women and sung by men and women in different formats and settings (Weiner 1991). Chiefly, these songs commemorate deceased men.

The primary metaphoric link established in memorial songs is between a human life and a journey. A common format is to list the names of places the deceased inhabited:

| | |
|---|---|
| Ibu Barua ga iga— | The path to Barua Creek— |
| Iga ereʻe! | Look at the path! |
| Kumagi iga— | The path to Kumagi Creek |
| Iga ereyiyaʻabe? | Do you not see it? |
| | |
| Baʻa naʻa ibu Fayaʻa ga iga— | Boy, the head of the Fayaʻa River— |
| Iga ereʻe! | Look at it now! |
| Baʻa naʻa ibu Fayaʻa ga iga— | Boy, your Fayaʻa River source land— |
| Iga ereʻe! | Just see what it looks like now! |
| | |
| Kumagi tage iga— | The path leading to the mouth of the Kumagi Creek— |
| Iga kigibaʻae. | It is covered with bush. |
| Sese faiyu wabu iga— | The path along which the *faiyu* marsupial travels— |
| Iga aodibaʻae. | Has been covered over with bush. |
| | |
| Orodobo Meremo— | The Orodobo man Mere— |
| Baʻa Baruma. | His son Baruma. |
| Tirifadobo ka Gairame— | The Tirifadobo woman Gairame— |
| Kabe Memenemabo. | Her son Memenemabo. |
| | |
| Tirifadobo ka Gairame— | The Tirifadobo woman Gairame— |
| Kabe Daribu. | Her son Daribu. |
| Orodobo Mere— | The Orodobo man Mere— |
| Kabe Baruma. | His son Baruma. |

Actively used paths through the forest stay free and clear of vegetation, but a man's path soon becomes overgrown after his death. For the Foi and other interior Papua New Guinean forest-dwelling peoples, the disappearance of this geographical material trace is a poignant image of the erasure of life.

Metaphors commonly employed in other discursive domains find their way into song. A dream of a large tree falling down portends a leader's death. The following song uses that image to commemorate the death of the Hegeso leader Iraharabo, of the Tirifadobo clan.

| | |
|---|---|
| Ira furabu derare— | The tall *furabu* tree— |
| Forabibiʻae. | Fallen. |
| Ira furabu derare— | The tall *furabu* tree— |
| Forabibiʻae. | Long fallen. |
| | |
| Baʻa naʻa ao dumaroʻo— | Your tree-covered mountain— |
| Aodobobaʻae. | Covered with bush. |
| Baʻa naʻa kö tegeri maʻayaroʻo— | Your *tegeri* cordyline seeds— |
| Forabobaʻae. | Broken off. |

| | |
|---|---|
| Ba'a na'a ira furabu derare— | Your tall *furabu* tree— |
| Forabi'ae. | Fallen. |
| Ba'a na'a kegebe abu derare— | Your *abu* vine— |
| Forabo'owa'ae. | Long cut down. |
| | |
| wa'ari hubobi dobo kabe Degayomore— | He of the *hubobi* palm clan Degayo— |
| Kabe Harabi. | His son Harabi. |
| Wa'ari hubobi dobo kabe mege bamore— | That sole man of the *hubobi* palm clan— |
| Kabe Iraharabo. | The man Iraharabo. |
| | |
| Yo hua ka mege bamo— | That sole woman, his mother— |
| Kabe Iraharabo. | Her son Iraharabo. |
| Bi'a huba dobo ka mege ba ma'ame— | That only woman of the *huba* black-palm clan— |
| Ba'a Harabi. | Her son Harabi. |

The communal and dramatic properties of the public performance of songs ensure that metaphors of this sort achieve a great discursive effect on people's imagination and emotion. Their evocative powers are part of what make the songs effective for Foi audiences.

—JAMES F. WEINER

## Iatmul mythological suites

Iatmul stories of creation recount the founding of the clans. Before creation, water was everywhere. A crocodile appeared and split in two: its lower jaw became the earth; its upper jaw, the sky; hence, Iatmul society would divide into earth-based moieties and sky-based moieties. Then the first pair of human brothers came into existence. From them sprang other pairs, who founded the clans.

The locale of these events was an area north of the Middle Sepik, near Gaikorobi Village. In the beginning, all people were there. Then the clan-group founders and their relatives left, following the crocodiles' tracks. The most important ancient event was the migration into the areas of present settlement. During the journey, the founders took possession of tracts of land, bush, and watercourses. They founded villages. At each place, they left a few men and women behind. They assigned to them an animal, a plant, or some other object, into which they could transform themselves; thus, each place had its totem. This totem and all other salient objects and landmarks received names, paired in lists. The inhabitants of the villages also received names.

These creations and migrations have visual and aural representations. The visual representation is a *kirugu* 'knotted cord', which in performance serves as a mnemonic device. Each clan has a unique cord. Between 5.5 and 6.5 meters long, it has knots of different sizes at regular intervals. Each cord enacts an ancient migration. Each large knot represents a place along the route; each small knot represents the name of a totem associated with a place.

Aurally, the ancient events find their representation in the reciting of mythological suites (*sagi*). These start with a special rhythm, beaten on two garamuts: it is the voice of the crocodiles (figure 7). Every suite consists of a fixed sequence of songs, including three elements: localities, names, and tales.

### The mythological processes of suites

Each suite follows the course of a migration, that of the Yagun clan maps part of the Sepik River and certain tributaries, Chambri Lake, present-day villages, and abandoned villages. The migration started at Gaikorobi, moved through Marap, Silai,

FIGURE 7   The beginning of a Iatmul mythical cycle: as the main singer (*center*) awaits his turn, the voice of the crocodiles rings out from jolted garamuts. Photo by Jürg Wassmann, 1973.

Tugut, and so on, and ended at Mansipambangi. Each song marks a station where a founder halted: a settlement, a village, a swamp, a river.

Each Iatmul suite centers on a totem, which has hundreds of names. The etymology of these names involves the totem, or recalls past events associated with it. The first song of the Yagun cycle mentions twenty-two names for the primeval crocodile and twenty names for Gaikorobi, the first place in existence. In it, the crocodile emerges from the primal sea and turns in a circle, so the land comes into being. It goes on turning, so over parts of its body, the earth solidifies. At first, the earth shakes; it gradually firms up. The totem is the primeval crocodile, the newly risen land. The names recall events that coincided with the creation of the earth. The first two names of the primeval crocodile are synonyms: Andi-kabak-meli (*andi* 'earth', *kabak* 'primeval crocodile') and Kipma-kabak-meli (*kipma* 'earth'). The morpheme *meli* is a masculine suffix. Both names mean 'The crocodile is both primeval crocodile and earth'. The first two names of Gaikorobi are Lili-lipma (*lili* 'slip away'; *lipma* 'palmtree', a metaphor for "place") and Kwakwa-lipma (*kwakwa* 'stand up and fall down'). Both names mean 'The newly created place still rocks'.

### Songs and the tales behind them

Each song within a mythological suite relates a short tale, in which the totem of the place accomplishes a set action (Wassmann 1991). The texts the songs convey are simple, small, harmless extracts from secret myths, which describe ancient events in detail. An excerpt from the Yagun suite illustrates the process. After the crocodiles' voices resound from the garamuts, one singer stands and begins the first song. It relates to the creation of the earth and the formation of the first village.

> Father, your upper jaw,
> Father, your upper jaw,
> Ancestor, your lower jaw,
> Father, your jaw.
> Father, you Andikabakmeli,
> Andikabakmeli, Kipmakabakmeli,
> O you water spirit!

The primeval crocodile rises to the surface of the water, bringing a piece of earth. It later splits in two: its upper jaw becomes the sky; its lower jaw, the earth.

Father, in this place,
In the place Lililipma,
Near the palm Kwakwalipma,
You lay down,
And your upper jaw became the sky.

Only in the light of events is the pattern clear. The myth invokes the primeval crocodile: with a rotary motion, it rises to the surface of the water, bringing a piece of earth. It later splits in two: its upper jaw becomes the sky; its lower jaw, the earth.

After this song, nineteen more places follow. For each, men perform a song, recite tales, and mention totemic and ancestral names. The songs cite events that happened en route: the dog Koruimbangi ran across the land, enlarging it; the clan's founder, Wolindambwi, built the first men's house; a dove and a cockatoo showed women how to give birth; a crocodile floated a village on its back. But the main event was the ancestral women's murder of Kabiragwa, Wolindambwi's sister. In dudgeon, the men turned into bats and departed.

All clans migrated from Gaikorobi, but each clan's journey involved particular places, events, and totems. For each clan, the most important migratory role falls to a cardinal totem: sea and west wind, eel, borassus palm, sun and moon, crocodile.

—JÜRG WASSMANN

### Sāmoan nuptial cheers

Sāmoan nuptial cheers (*tini*) illustrate metaphors in multiple ways. On the simplest level, the bridegroom's success in getting a wife is equivalent to an athlete's victory. The ordinary sense of the name of the genre, *tini*, is 'goal'. At Sāmoan weddings, a cheer for the bridegroom, performed by his supporters, goes: *Mua! 'inā mua! mua ō* 'Shout! do shout! shout O'. During dart-throwing games (*tāga-a-ti'a*), participants and onlookers shouted *mua!* to celebrate a competitor's prowess, in effect that he had scored. Shouting it for the bridegroom carries the idea into a different context.

In a more complex sense, this cheer can become the refrain of a larger piece, a shout that links the names of the husband and wife. On a monotone, a soloist or a small number of persons recited the names, and the rest of the company sang the refrain.

Finally, the cheer can become allusive and elaborate, a series of stanzas, as in the text of a *tini* sung for the marriage of a chief of Falealupo, Savai'i, before 1918. One or two orators intoned the quatrains, and the bridegroom's party sang the refrains.

Paopao le galu i Fagafo'i,     The wave is restrained at Fagafo'i,
'A e sua le fetai 'i Māunu.     But the tide rises at Māunu.
Tili'ava ma le Fau-o-le-Tagaloa:     Tili'ava and the Fau-o-le-Tagaloa:
'O vāifanua ia o le tamāloa.     These are the man's homelands.
    *Mua! 'inā mua! mua ō!*     *Shout! do shout! shout O!*

Naumati, Falepipi na tua 'i le sīliga:      Parched, Falepipi waited for the quest:
'O 'aiga-a-nonu a le fūna'iga,              The *nonu*-eating of the feast,
Ma le malama e tonu ai Tapusita:           And the dawn Tapusita justifies:
'O lēnā le e seu māta'ina.                  That's what's snared in view.
    *Mua! 'inā mua! mua ō!*                      *Shout! do shout! shout O!*

Na 'ou sīlia 'i 'ā teu e ā?                 I asked, hey, why store it?
E tu'u e ā? e nā e ā?                       Why leave it? why hide it?
Tōle'afōae, lau lupe lēnā,                  O Tōle'afoa, that's your dove,
'E te seu ai 'i le fīsā.                     Which you snare in the crowd.
    *Mua! 'inā mua! mua ō!*                      *Shout! do shout! shout O!*

The text cites pieces of land, of less than a hectare each: Fagafo'i is the beach seaward of Māunu, a tract in Avātā (subvillage of Falealupo); Tili'ava and Falepipi are tracts nearby. All are the bride's habitats, now in the bridegroom's power. The bride is a bird (*lupe* 'dove'), for which the bridegroom and his party have been hunting. From the flock, Tōle'afoa has snared her. Some words bear archaic glosses: the singer thought *fetai* (here treated as *tai* 'tide') possibly an alternate form of the modern *fa'afetai* 'thanks'; a *fūna'iga* 'feast' was anciently a band of men assembled for a bonito-fishing expedition, but the singer said the phrase referred to the crowd present at the event; the archaic form *sīlia* 'ask' has yielded, even in formal speech, to *fesili*; the term *fīsā* 'crowd' could alternatively be a variant of *fīsaga* 'northwesterly breeze', though the singer explained it as a reference to the crowd. Many of these variations are between the vehicles of metaphors, not the tenors, but changes in one can lead to changes in the other. This text reveals the same technical processes—symbolic referral, semantic indirection—that endow with artistic interest the texts of many Oceanic oral productions.

—J. W. LOVE

## REFERENCES

Atkinson, John M. 1984. "Public Speaking and Audience Responses: Some Techniques for Inviting Applause." In *Structure of Social Action: Studies in Conversation Analysis,* ed, John M. Atkinson and John Heritage, 370–409. Cambridge: Cambridge University Press.

Baldwin, B. 1945. "Usituma! Song of Heaven." *Oceania* 15:201–238.

Bataillon, P[ierre]. 1932. *Langue d'Uvea (Wallis): Grammaire-Dictionnaire Uvea-Français-Uvea-Anglais.* Paris: Librairie Orientaliste Paul Geuthner.

Bauman, Richard, and Charles L. Briggs. 1990. "Poetics and Performance as Critical Perspectives on Language and Social Life." *Annual Review of Anthropology* 19:59–88.

Beckwith, Martha Warren. 1951. *The Kumulipo: A Hawaiian Creation Chant.* Chicago: University of Chicago Press.

Berndt, Catherine H., and Ronald M. Berndt. 1971. *The Barbarians: An Anthropological View.* London: C. A. Watts.

Davenport, William. 1975. "Lyric Verse and Ritual in the Santa Cruz Islands." *Expedition* 18(1):39–47.

David, Mrs. Edgeworth [Lady Caroline David]. 1899. *Funafuti, or Three Months on a Coral Island: An Unscientific Account of a Scientific Expedition.* London: John Murray.

Dyen, Isidore. 1965. *A Lexicostatistical Classification of the Austronesian Languages.* Anthropology and linguistics memoir 19. Bloomington, Ind.: International Journal of American Linguistics.

Edwards, Jane A. 1993. "Principles and Contrasting Systems of Discourse Transcription." In *Talking Data: Transcription and Coding in Discourse Research,* ed. Jane A. Edwards and Martin D. Lampert, 3–31. Hillsdale, N.J.: Lawrence Erlbaum.

Farrell, Andrew. 1921. "Micronesia Under the Moon." *Asia* 21(4):312.

Feld, Steven. 1990. *Sound and Sentiment: Birds, Weeping, Poetics, and Song in Kaluli Expression.* 2nd ed. Philadelphia: University of Pennsylvania Press.

Feld, Steven, and Aaron A. Fox. 1994. "Music and Language." *Annual Review of Anthropology* 23:25–53.

Firth, Raymond. 1990. *Tikopia Songs.* Cambridge Studies in Oral and Traditional Culture, 20. Cambridge: Cambridge University Press.

Fischer, John L. 1966. *The Eastern Carolines.* Revised edition. New Haven, Conn.: Human Relations Area Files Press.

Gill, William Wyatt. 1976. *Myths and Songs from the South Pacific.* London: H. S. King.

Grace, George W. 1961. "Lexicostatistical Comparison of Six Eastern Austronesian Languages." *Anthropological Linguistics* 3:1–22.

Hanks, W. F. 1989. "Text and Textuality." *Annual Review of Anthropology* 18:95–127.

Hooley, Bruce A. 1987. "Central Buang Poetry." In *Perspectives on Language and Text: Essays and Poems in Honour of Francis I. Andersen's Sixtieth Birthday,* ed. Edgar W. Conrad and Edward G. Newing, 71–88. Winona Lake, Ind.: Eisenbrauns.

Kirtley, Bacil F. 1971. *A Motif-Index of Traditional Polynesian Narratives.* Honolulu: University of Hawai'i Press.

Lakoff, George, and Mark Johnson. 1980. *Metaphors We Live By.* Chicago and London: University of Chicago Press.

Landtman, Gunnar. 1927. *Kiwai Papuans of British New Guinea.* London: Macmillan.

Laycock, Donald. 1969. "Sublanguages in Buin: Play, Poetry, and Preservation." Papers in New Guinea Linguistics, 10:1–23; Pacific Linguistics, A 22. Canberra: Australian National University.

Lévi-Strauss, Claude. 1969. *The Raw and the Cooked.* Translated by John Weightman and Doreen Weightman. New York and Evanston, Ill.: Harper & Row.

Lieber, Michael D. 1991. "Cutting Your Losses on Kapingamarangi: Death and Grieving on a Polynesian Atoll." In *Coping with the Final Tragedy: Cultural Variation in Dying and Grieving,* ed. Dorothy Counts and David Counts, 161–190. New York: Baywood Press.

List, George. 1963. "The Boundaries of Speech and Song." *Ethnomusicology* 7:1–16.

Love, Jacob Wainwright. 1991. *Sāmoan Variations: Essays on the Nature of Traditional Oral Arts.* New York and London: Garland.

McLean, Mervyn. 1981. "Text and Music in 'Rule of Eight' Waiata." In *Studies in Pacific Languages and Cultures,* ed. Jim Hollyman and Andrew Pawley, 53–63. Auckland: Linguistic Society of New Zealand.

Monberg, Torben. 1974. "Poetry as Coded Messages: The *Kananga* of Bellona Island." *Journal of the Polynesian Society* 83(4):427–442.

Ochs, Elinor. 1979. "Transcription as Theory." In *Developmental Pragmatics,* ed. Elinor Ochs and Bambi B. Schieffelin, 43–72. New York: Academic Press.

Pawley, Andrew, and Roger Green. 1973. "Dating the Dispersal of the Oceanic Languages." *Oceanic Linguistics* 12:1–67.

Roberts, Helen Heffron. 1926. *Ancient Hawaiian Music.* Bulletin 29. Honolulu: Bishop Museum.

Rossen, Jane Mink. 1987. *Songs of Bellona Island.* 2 vols. Language and Culture of Rennell and Bellona Islands, 6. Copenhagen: Forlaget Kragen.

Rothenberg, Jerome, ed. 1968. *Technicians of the Sacred: A Range of Poetries from Africa, America, Asia & Oceania.* New York: Doubleday.

Sacks, Sheldon, ed. 1979. *On Metaphor.* Chicago and London: University of Chicago Press.

Schieffelin, Edward L. 1976. *The Sorrow of the Lonely and the Burning of the Dancers.* New York: St. Martin's Press.

Seligmann, C. G. 1910. *The Melanesians of British New Guinea.* Cambridge: Cambridge University Press.

Swadesh, Morris. 1972. *The Origin and Diversification of Language,* ed. Joel Sherzer. London: Routledge & Kegan Paul.

Tedlock, Dennis. 1983. *The Spoken Word and the Work of Interpretation.* Philadelphia: University of Pennsylvania Press.

Thomas, Allan, Ineleo Tuia, and Judith Huntsman. 1990. *Songs and Stories of Tokelau: An Introduction to the Cultural Heritage.* Wellington, New Zealand: Victoria University Press.

Thompson, Stith. 1977 [1946]. *The Folktale.* Berkeley, Los Angeles, London: University of California Press.

von Brandenstein, C. G., and A. P. Thomas. 1975. *Taruru: Aboriginal Song Poetry from the Pilbara.* Honolulu: University Press of Hawai'i.

Voorhoeve, C. L. 1977. "Ta-Poman: Metaphorical Use of Word and Poetic Vocabulary in Asmat Songs." In *Language, Culture, Society and the Modern World,* ed. Stephen A. Wurm, 19–38. New Guinea Area Languages and Language Study, 3; Pacific Linguistics, C 40. Canberra: Australian National University.

Webb, Michael, and Don Niles. 1990. *Ol Singsing Bilong Ples.* Boroko: Institute of Papua New Guinea Studies. Institute of Papua New Guinea Studies IPNGS 010. Book with two cassettes.

Weiner, James F. 1991. *The Empty Place: Poetry, Space and Being among the Foi of Papua New Guinea.* Bloomington: Indiana University Press.

Zahn, Heinrich. 1996. *Mission and Music: Jabêm Traditional Music and the Development of Lutheran Hymnody.* Edited by Don Niles. Translated by Philip W. Holzknecht. Apwitihire, 4. Boroko: National Research Institute.

# The Accouterments of Musical Performance

*Adrienne L. Kaeppler*

**Dress and Undress**

**Masks and Rhythmic Clothing in Melanesia**

**Dress as Sociopolitical Discourse in Tonga**

Music and dance are performed in various spaces and settings, corresponding to the purpose of the performance. Settings may relate the performance to mythological or religious concepts, the universe, or the modern cultural landscape. A full understanding of music should include orienting the performance in the layout of space—how one moves in it, what one wears and carries while moving, how and which objects are placed in it, and how all these elements encode contexts and activities. People create their spatial and conceptual organization, and their actions are influenced by these creations. Creative processes and actions influence the forms that verbal and visual expressions take, and these forms embody and convey meaning.

Oceanic settings for the performance of music and dance vary from sandy deserts in Australia to tropical forests in New Guinea, from white beaches in Micronesia to village greens in Polynesia, or in modern theaters from Sydney to Rarotonga to Honolulu. Tracing a Dreaming tract or a songline by Australian Aboriginals involves a group of related people who sing many small songs while traveling the desert: wearing designs painted on their skin (figure 1), they perform patterned musical structures and associated movement motifs, leaving footprints in the sand. At the same time only a short distance away, at the Sydney Opera House, similar sounds and movements might be performed, but their setting and audience change a participatory ritual into spectacle.

Properties—implements such as sticks used to strike each other, and fans struck against the costume or a hand—add to the aural texture of a performance, creating patterns and motifs in their own right. Skirts add sounds as they swish against themselves, and add visual enhancements when performers spin or move their hips from side to side (figure 2). Wooden floors, or the platforms of structures built for dancing, resonate the stamping of performer's feet.

## DRESS AND UNDRESS

Like music and dance, dress is a grammatically structured part of the larger activity for which it is worn. Its grammar involves structure, style, and meaning—what its various pieces are, from what materials they are made, how they can be stylistically varied, what their syntax (rules about how they can and cannot be put together, and

FIGURE 1    Paint elaborates the bodies of performers of the Rom ceremony. Photo by Alana Harris, 1995. Courtesy Australian Institute of Aboriginal and Torres Strait Islander Studies Pictorial Collection.

for what occasions) is, who can wear them, what meanings are ascribed to them, and what effect they have on the production of sounds and movements (figure 3). Clothing is another part of the construction of performance, an aesthetic assemblage that places sound and movement into complex forms of discourse, built on culturally understood symbols within sociopolitical contexts to convey information and meaning.

Pieces of dress derived from gods, ancestors, or historic figures may have been retained and perpetuated as cultural and aesthetic artifacts. But dress can also be creative and innovative. It can convey messages of modernity, or even protest. The August 1995 antinuclear fashion show in Suva to protest French nuclear testing was

FIGURE 2    Wearing a thick grass skirt and flower-and-fiber adornments, with a conductor and a seated chorus in the background, a Kiribati woman performs in a temporary performing space at the Pacific Festival of Arts. Photo by Adrienne L. Kaeppler, 1980.

TRACK 16

FIGURE 3    A Melpa man wears various pieces of clothing structured in a specific way to form a costume. Photo by Andrew J. Strathern.

framed by an antinuclear Tahitian-inspired dance, "No More Bikinis," performed by Pacific Islanders as a reminder that the bikini bathing suit was named for nuclear testing on Bikini Atoll, in the Marshall Islands. Dress and its history are important, even if their meanings have been changed or forgotten as points of reference for cultural identity. Like all symbolic systems, dress creates new meanings by combining old forms in new ways, relying on shared understandings among designers, wearers, and viewers.

## Propriety, presentation, and aesthetics

Linked with aesthetics, propriety, personhood, and where one fits into the overall scheme of things, clothing was traditionally important during structured sound-and-movement ritual presentations, and for performances of music and dance in which poetry, music, movement, scent, and dress coalesced into sociopolitical theatrical events. The parts of the body that required coverings varied with gender, wealth, and sometimes rank. Women were usually covered from the waist to the knees, and men usually covered the genital area. People of status wore finer clothing, ornaments, and combs. Decoration of the setting—with cloth derived from the inner bark of the paper mulberry, mats plaited from dried pandanus leaves, paints, green leaves, and flowers—was also infused with meaning.

### The presentation of clothing

Clothing for Polynesian and Micronesian formal gifts and performances was traditionally made from bark cloth, woven textiles, plaited mats, and coconut fiber. Gifts of cloth valuables might be attached to a person of rank and presented in a dramatic flourish. In Fiji, a chief presented himself to a higher chief clothed in hundreds of meters of cloth—and then disrobed, either by spinning to unravel wrapped cloth, or by dropping a huge looped dress as an aesthetic gesture in honor of the receiving chief. In Tahiti, cloth was unwound from the giver and rewound onto the receiver. In Tonga, the missionary George Vason noted that the manner of presentation was as important as the gift itself (Orange 1840). The missionary John Williams described the context, clothing, movements, and sounds that characterized the nuptial ceremony of a woman of status in Sāmoa:

> Her dress was a fine mat, fastened round the waist, reaching nearly to her ankles; a wreath of leaves and flowers, ingeniously and tastefully entwined, decorated her brow. The upper part of her person was anointed with sweet-scented cocoa-nut oil, and tinged partially with a rouge prepared from the turmeric root, and round her neck were two rows of large blue beads. Her whole deportment was pleasingly modest. While listening to the chanters, and looking upon the novel scene before us, our attention was attracted by another company of women, who were following each other in single file, and chanting, as they came, the praises of their chief. Sitting down with the company who had preceded them, they united in one general chorus, which appeared to be a recital of the valorous deeds of Malietoa and his progenitors. This ended, a dance in honour of the marriage was commenced, which was considered one of their grandest exhibitions, and held in high estimation by the people. The performers were four young women, all daughters of chiefs of the highest rank, who took their stations at right angles, on the fine mats with which the dancing-house was spread for the occasion, and then interchanged positions with slow and graceful movements both of their hands and feet, while the bride recited some of the mighty doings of her forefathers. To the motions of the dancers, and to the recital of the bride, three or four elderly women were beating time upon the mat with short sticks, and occasionally joining in chorus with the recitative. (1837:324–325)

These arts of propriety and presentation were locally meaningful, and they activated the social and cultural landscape.

### The presentation of skin

The *absence* of costume can make a statement about propriety. In Sāmoan kava ceremonies, the (male) server ideally shows dignity by wearing no covering above the waist, no flower in his hair, no necklace, no armband, no wristwatch, no decoration of any kind. In precontact times, some Polynesian performances featured or ended with the removal of clothing. In Sāmoa into the 1890s, women dancers removed

FIGURE 4    Waiting to perform at the Pacific Festival of Arts, a Telefolmin musician holds the end of his kundu. Photo by Mary Jo Freshley, 1980.

their skirts by degrees, ending in a few seconds of complete nudity. Betrothal festivities in Luangiua were marked by a public parade of unclothed virgins.

Skin was, and still is, tattooed, painted, or scarified, in different parts and degrees for men and women, and scented with perfumed coconut oil. Among Aboriginal Australians, elaborate painted designs with the addition of feathers adorn the skin. In the Highlands of Papua New Guinea, paint on the face and body conveys messages about physical status and fertility (Strathern 1981). In the Marquesas, yellow and reddish paint enhanced the color of the skin; an herb commonly used for its yellow-orange pigment is turmeric (*Curcuma sp.*). For dancing in Rapa Nui, men adorned their skin with elaborate painting.

In Polynesia, tattoo visually proclaimed its owner's social status and its maker's artistic ability. The Polynesian term *tatau,* or some variation of it, is the source of the English word *tattoo.* The process was carried to high points in the Marquesas (where some men were completely tattooed, including the face) and Aotearoa, but large portions of the body were tattooed in Sāmoa, Tahiti, and elsewhere, men more elaborately than women. Sāmoan tattoo is displayed when a man lifts his skirt while dancing—an action that can have aesthetic significance, especially in accompaniment to a woman's *taualuga.*

## The materials of dress and ornament

Clothing and ornaments demonstrate the status, sanctity, rank, and wealth of people who wear them and the skill and patience of the specialists who make them. Decorated shells and shaped gourds serve as penis decorations (figure 4). Materials used for ornaments often have high value, either because of their sacred qualities, such as feathers or hair, or because of their rarity, such as jade, whale ivory, tortoiseshell, pearls, and seashell. Ephemeral ornaments were made of flowers (often sewn in elaborate, painstaking constructions), seeds, and other parts of plants. In Polynesia, human hair had a sacred quality because it came from the *tapu* part of the body, from ancestors or defeated enemies, thus capturing their mana. There and elsewhere, human hair was used in wigs, headdresses, necklaces, fans, and belts. Feathers, especially the tail feathers of tropicbirds or birds of paradise and red feathers of various kinds, were used in headdresses, waist girdles, and ornaments for fingers. Human and animal teeth (including those of sharks, dogs, and pigs) were used in rattles, necklaces, bracelets, and ornaments for the head and chest. Coconut fiber was used in combs and belts. Rare materials—jade, bones and teeth of whales—served as earrings, pendants, and combs. Tortoiseshell was used on headdresses and bracelets, pearls were used as earrings, and pearlshells were used in necklaces and headdresses, and to decorate costumes.

Today, in addition to traditional materials, people of Oceania use European cloth, plastic, and mirrors in old and new ways. Analyzing a Kiribati dance costume, Phillip Dark (1990) describes the introduction of glass beads and paper, and notes that shiny materials are valued in old and new forms. Helen Lawrence (1993) describes the combination of old and new materials as markers of Manihiki identity.

## MASKS AND RHYTHMIC CLOTHING IN MELANESIA

In many parts of Melanesia, the rhythmic emphasis of music is emphasized by clothing, and masks add mystery and drama. The rhythmic environment of drumming and singing is made visual by human bodies as they move vertically—in contrast to horizontal movements, more characteristic of Polynesia. Costumes—composed primarily of attachments, most of which move—emphasize this rhythm. Bird-of-paradise plumes and other feathers extend from headdresses, backs, bustles, or arms. Hanging rattles of seeds or shells are attached to legs or costumes, or are held in the hand. Cuscus skin ripples like vertical waves, and shredded leaves and fibers cascade and bounce. Penis coverings of gourd, shell, or bark are curved forward and upward to emphasize the up-down movement of this part of the body. It is difficult to discern if the costume is aimed at emphasizing rhythm or if the rhythm is a way of showing off the costume. All these elements conspire to make a mass rhythmic statement.

In Kaluli music and dance, up-and-down bouncing activates the sounds of streamers and rattles attached to the costumes. The sound of the streamers represents the sound of a waterfall (Feld 1988). In *ida,* a fertility ritual of the Waina-Sowanda (West Sepik Province, Papua New Guinea), costumes—or their absence—are intertwined with biological and social regeneration, which encapsulates the formalized opposition between the sexes and among men of different ages (Gell 1975). Some *ida* masks are constructions held on the shoulders. Others cover only the face and neck.

As purveyors of disguise and elaboration, masks and paint worn for musical events are an important artistic form in many Melanesian societies, intimately involved with gender and the social role of the individual. Performers often take the roles of mythical or ancestral beings celebrated in oral literature, and their dress consists of a mask and a full, otherworldly costume.

Among the Baining of New Britain, animals, plants, stones, water, rain, wind, earthquakes, sickness, and death relate to spirits that in performance become visible, embodied in huge bark-cloth-mask constructions. Fire dances placate spirits of the dead, who live in the underworld and at night interfere in human affairs. Moving in these costumes is difficult, and performance focuses on the legs and swaying bodies; arms are covered, and serve to steady the costume and the mask.

Masked performers become supernatural beings, and usually do not interpret poetry or speak; their voices—often conveyed by musical instruments, especially whirring disks—can be understood only by initiated men. Rhythm is elaborated by the mask and its attachments. Melanesian masks are often made and worn for a specific event, and are then discarded. Made of leaves, feathers, cloth, and other ephemeral materials, many are not found in museums.

In New Ireland, masks are worn for *malanggan,* dramatic rites of commemoration, in which hundreds of people assemble around an open area on a beach. When darkness begins to fall, the sound of shell rattles is heard from inside a cremation enclosure. Large masked figures, answering their mortal kin's call to appear, advance toward the crowd. They move with a slow, stately, heavy tread. After each step, accented by shell rattles, they pause and slowly turn their masked heads, looking uncertainly at this now unfamiliar world of the living. Recognizing the designs on the masks, people call the performers (who have become the dead ancestors) by name, and soon each figure is surrounded with wailing relatives.

Such dramatic moments are small parts of *malanggan,* a dominating feature of life in New Ireland. Essentially a postmourning ceremony occurring one to five years after a person's death, *malanggan* honors the dead in a large-scale community ceremony in which relatives and the whole society express sympathy and reverence. The most important masks, *murua,* represent the reincarnated dead; the designs and the way they combine reveal the lineage and the individual they represent. Helmetlike *tatanua* masks, worn during many performances, represent mourning-period hairstyles of a shaved head with a crestlike strip down the center (figure 5). The masked individual becomes a medium between the living and the dead, pays respect to his human ancestors, worships his totem, demonstrates his wealth, and strengthens his position in a society that highly regards the striving for prestige.

FIGURE 5   At the Pacific Festival of Arts, men of New Ireland give a *malanggan* performance with *tatanua* masks. Photo by Adrienne L. Kaeppler, 1980.

## DRESS AS SOCIOPOLITICAL DISCOURSE IN TONGA

Dress can be seen as sociopolitical discourse. In a *lakalaka* performance from Kanokupolu, Tonga, performers are enveloped in bark cloth. The costume for Kanokupolu (but not for any other village) and the name for their performance, no matter which one, is *fola'osi,* the term for a specific size of bark cloth. This name was given to Kanokupolu's *lakalaka* by Queen Sālote, who designed the costume as a metaphor that refers to the most highly valued Tongan movements, *fola* 'outstretched-arm movements' and *'osi* 'finished'. This refers to the work of the queen's choreographer, Vaisima, whose movements are embodied in the costume (Kaeppler 1994).

Dancers perform for their father's village, but Kanokupolu's costume shows the importance of the mother's line—in this case, Queen Sālote herself and her contribution to Kanokupolu. The making of cloth is women's work, and the cloth is considered part of the *koloa* or valuables of the society. In this *lakalaka,* the material valuable wraps or encircles the oratorical valuable presented to the sovereign and the nation.

The central performers (*vāhenga*) dress distinctively, showing their status by their clothing. In 1975, the central female performer was Princess Pilolevu, the king's daughter, who danced for Kanokupolu because it was her father's village (figure 6).

FIGURE 6   Men and women of Kanokupolu, Tonga, perform a *lakalaka* for the centennial Tongan constitution, November 5, 1975. Photo by Adrienne L. Kaeppler.

Pilolevu wore a *puleotu* attached to a black velvet ribbon. According to tradition, if the *puleotu* lies still and does not turn over, the wearer is a virgin. During the entire performance, Pilolevu's *puleotu* did not turn over.

The central male performer was Baron Vaea, noble of the village of Houma, who descends from the same line. Pilolevu and Vaea demonstrate their special individual statuses by their clothing. Pilolevu wore a costume made for the occasion. Scallops were cut from an old and finely plaited mat (*kie*) and sewn in rows to a backing that formed a sleeveless blouse and skirt that ended just above the knees. Each scallop was decorated with a valuable white cowrie shell (*puleotu*) in the middle and outlined with tiny white shell beads. The skirt was tied at the waist with a belt of darker curled fibers. Around her neck, Pilolevu wore a *puleotu* attached to a black velvet ribbon. According to tradition, if the *puleotu* lies still and does not turn over during a performance, the wearer is a virgin; during the entire *lakalaka*, Pilolevu's *puleotu* did not turn over.

Baron Vaea, as male *vāhenga*, wore a white shirt and a leaf girdle that matched those worn by the other male dancers; but showing his special status, he wore a plain black wraparound skirt (in contrast to the other male dancers' skirts) and a large fine mat, layered between the skirt and the girdle.

The political discourse, verbally and visually displayed by the clothing worn during Kanokupolu's *lakalaka,* is one of history and social relationships that make up the government. Each village *lakalaka,* including its costume, develops what is distinctive about the village and its performers.

Understanding what the *lakalaka* of Kanokupolu or other performances (Kaeppler 1995) are discussing with their audiences depends on knowledge of Tongan politics, culture, history, and shared values. Symbolic clothing informs the sociopolitical discourse, and musical dress is an integral part of the frame for painting historical and political metaphors.

## REFERENCES

Dark, Philip J. C. 1990. "Tomorrow's Heritage Is Today's Art, and Yesteryear's Identity." In *Art and Identity in Oceania,* ed. Allan Hanson and Louise Hanson, 244–268. Bathurst, Australia: Crawford House Press; Honolulu: University of Hawai'i Press.

Feld, Steven. 1988. "Aesthetics as Iconicity of Style, or 'Lift-up-over Sounding': Getting into the Kaluli Groove." *Yearbook for Traditional Music,* 74–113.

Gell, Antony Francis. 1975. *Metamorphosis of the Cassowaries: Umeda Society, Language and Ritual.* London: Athlone Press.

Kaeppler, Adrienne L. 1994. "Dance and Dress as Sociopolitical Discourse." *Proceedings of the Study Group on Ethnochoreology 17th Symposium,* 45–51. Nafplion, Greece: Peloponnesian Folklore Foundation.

———. 1995. "The Paradise Theme in Modern Tongan Music." In *The Essence of Singing and the Substance of Song: An Anthology for Catherine Ellis,* ed. Linda Barwick, Allan Marett, and Guy Tunstill, 159–183. Oceania monograph 46. Sydney: Oceania Publications.

Lawrence, Helen Milton Reeves. 1993. "The Material Culture of Contemporary Music Performance in Manihiki, Northern Cook Islands." Ph.D. dissertation, James Cook University.

Orange, James. 1840. *Life of the Late George Vason of Nottingham.* London: John Snow.

Strathern, Andrew. 1981. "Introduction." In *Man as Art: New Guinea,* by Malcolm Kirk, 15–36. New York: Viking.

Williams, John. 1837. *A Narrative of Missionary Enterprises in the South Sea Islands.* London: John Snow.

# Compositional Processes

*Allan Thomas*          *Peter Russell Crowe*
*Allan Marett*          *Lamont Lindstrom*
*Steven Knopoff*          *Mary E. Lawson Burke*
*Vida Chenoweth*          *Adrienne L. Kaeppler*
*John D. Waiko*          *Vereara Teariki Monga Maeva*

**Australia**

**New Guinea**

**Vanuatu**

**Kiribati**

**Polynesia**

In most Oceanic societies, composers are responsible for more than inventing musical sounds: they versify texts, choreograph movements, direct rehearsals, and lead performances. The English word *composer* is therefore inadequate to convey the range of activities managed by musically active individuals in Oceania.

Prominent political leaders of Oceania in the 1800s and 1900s composed music, or exerted influence on the development of their music. These leaders included Queen Sālote of Tonga, Sir Apirana Ngata in Aotearoa, and Queen Liliʻuokalani of Hawaiʻi, whose words for "*Aloha Oe*" became iconic of her country (figure 1). Some features of Oceanic music are inexplicable without reference to musical leaders or composers.

FIGURE 1    Sheet music of "*Aloha Oe*," composed by Queen Liliʻuokalani. DeSoto Brown Collection.

## Sources of inspiration

Many cultures of Oceania formerly considered composing a spirit-inspired activity, and composers served as musical intermediaries between spirits and human beings. In Kiribati, special rituals and incantations readied composers for contact with the spiritual world and increased their compositional ability (Teruruia n.d.). In Fiji, some songs had spiritual origins: elflike creatures inspired light, quick, and sometimes unpredictable compositions, and ancestral spirits inspired epic songs (Finnegan 1977:171). In the Trobriand Islands, individuals spiritually journeyed to paradise, where they learned songs (McLaren 1979).

Many cultures permitted or enforced seclusion for composers. For inspiration in Kiribati, composers utilized secluded locations and specific times, the most dramatic being the open sea in the early morning (Laxton 1953). In the Marquesas, until finishing a composition, a composer lived alone in a specially built house (Handy and Winne 1925:11). Compositional seclusion can occur in sleep, and the mental apartness of dreaming often figures in local interpretations of compositional processes.

Some composition involves recomposition: a composer changes the personal names and other references in a text so it is relevant to an event. Recomposition may not gain composers the prominence accorded to customary composition; as in the Tokelau Islands (Thomas and Tuia 1990), it may be an activity among the compositionally inexperienced.

## Payment and status

Composers may receive payment for their work. Many communities reward composition with status, which in Kiribati and Fiji may inhere in a special name or title. The title and its prestige may go to a senior practitioner who has garnered recognition through many compositions. Other societies, however, expect composition of any adult of high status, as occasion demands. In Sāmoa, chiefs who commission a song may give the composer mats, cloth, or other valuables. The books of poetry collected by Sir Apirana Ngata (1959) reveal that many songs respond to crises—deaths, wars, lovers' rejections, libels—and that many composers worked in response to a specific act. In Bellona, a man's musical prestige reflected his generosity in giving feasts and his artistic craftsmanship—a concept that included composing and dancing (Rossen 1987:87). Such prestige is also conferred in Tikopia (Firth 1990).

Some societies expect composerly skill of everyone. The Kaluli believe every adult is a competent performer, interpreter, and songsmith; they explain the differences between performances, and those between compositions, "by interest and desire, and not by special biological endowment or talent" (Feld 1984:390). Other societies restrict composition to individuals of recognized talent, of either or both genders. Ngata emphasizes that in classic Māori society, composers were predominantly women, for whom songs were forms of public retaliation for wrongs. The Bellonese consider women "superior to men in the composition and singing" of laments, but dance-songs "are almost exclusively the domain of men" (Rossen 1987:86).

## Ownership and authority

Compositions often belong to families. Bellonese singers tend to perform their ancestors' compositions (Rossen 1987), preserving songs within bloodlines. In Māori music, a composer's extended family and descendants have custody of the composer's songs, which they control in performing, teaching, recording, and publishing. The family of the Māori composer Tuini Ngawai has published an edition of her collected works (Pewhairangi 1985), with an account and photographic mementos of her life. In a study of Kiribati, personal accounts of twenty-two composers "bring their experiences to life" (Lawson 1989:273), illustrating variation in their training and practice. A study of Bellona (Rossen 1986) gives biographies of fourteen composers, with lists of their compositions.

FIGURE 2   Ihaia, composer and repository of Tokelauan musical knowledge. Photo by John Casey, 1990.

Biographical information contributes to an understanding of how a community receives songs. Allan Thomas and Ineleo Tuia (1990) studied a Tokelau composer, Ihaia (figure 2). They compared his works to those of other composers of his generation. He worked in the genre of short dance-songs (*fātele*), and was a repository of information about *mako*, personal songs sung solo by men. He enjoyed challenging and surprising his community. In compositions from the 1930s to the 1980s, he heavily influenced the aesthetics and forms of Tokelau music. Considering his compositions, Thomas and Tuia suggest that knowledge of a composer's personality and actions leads communities to appreciate the composer's works: the "resonances" of the music involve the composer's attitudes and personality, because the composer "has left his mark on the composition in a way that the community who know him will identify" (1990:163).

In complex hierarchic societies, major composers have bent their energies to eulogizing royal lines and supporting the status quo (Kaeppler 1990), but other composers have created critical works. Even Tonga has songs of dissent from outlying areas (Pond 1990). Surveying Aotearoa in the 1980s (a "decade of protest"), Tīmoti S. Kāretu accumulated examples of protests against governmental policies and Māori lawbreaking, physical abuse, and alcoholism, and concluded: "The venting of one's spleen and the vilifying of others has always been a source of inspiration for the Māori lyricist and composer" (1991:159).

For only a few cultures of Oceania have researchers carefully studied composers, composition, and musical leadership. Extant studies show that such information enhances scholarship in four respects: understanding the creation of new material, locating influences on change and development in the musical system, examining the effects of copyright and other restrictions, and seeing individuals' imprints on events and styles. Future work might examine whether the assertions that songs have "no known composer" (Burrows 1945:118) and that the composer and owner of every song is known (Bell 1935:108) reflect observers' prejudices, or are real cultural contrasts.

—ALLAN THOMAS

## AUSTRALIA

The most spiritually powerful songs are believed to have been created by ancestral spirits. Revealed at the beginning of time, in the period known as the Dreaming, the texts of such songs are inviolate, since they record the utterances of the ancestors themselves. Strong sanctions, including (formerly) the threat of death, have been invoked to prevent their alteration. In performance, these texts are rhythmically realized, mapped onto appropriate melodic contours, and interlocked with the execution of movements and designs. Correctly performed, such songs are believed to release ancestral power. Except as performance involves exploring the limited oral-compositional processes that will yield a correct "fit," such songs cannot be said to be composed (Barwick 1989, 1990).

Other kinds of song believed to have been created in the Dreaming, including the Central-Eastern Arnhem Land clansongs (*manikai* and *bunggurl*), involve freer processes of oral composition, ensuring that no two performances of a song, though similar, will be exactly the same. For any given subject, singers draw on a set of stock epithets, mapping them onto a melodic contour and adjusting their overall structure to fit that of danced structures. Performances involve complex negotiations between one or two singers, the player of a didjeridu, and (where present) dancers.

### Songs received in dreams

Certain categories of Australian Aboriginal song may be regarded as having been "composed," but even in these, the process whereby a song comes into being usually involves spiritual intervention. *Wangga* and *lirrga* of Northwest Arnhem Land are normally received by singers from spirits in dreams. Alan Maralung (1925–1990) received the *wangga* song "Minmin Light" from the spirit of the deceased songman Balandjirri:

> It came from the west, that Minmin Light. Yeah, it came up close. Like, you know, I saw it. I thought, oh, this might be a *debil-debil* coming up. I was asleep then. I was watching.
>
> Balandjirri said, "Boy, are you asleep? I'm coming into your camp. Bunggridj-Bunggridj and I are coming." Then both of them came to me. "Get up," said Balandjirri. "Come here. We're going to sing for you. We're going to show you a song."
>
> Well, Balandjirri and that didjeridu player [Balandjirri's son, Narolga] showed me that song. He looked at that light and then followed it. It was Balandjirri who made me know. When that light appeared, he followed it himself. It was dangerous because that other *debil-debil,* the Minmin Light, was then at the same place that he had gone to. He got that song then. He got it from there for sure.
>
> Then he came to me and said, "Boy, you listen. You might be frightened. Are you asleep?"

"Come here," I said; "I can see you."

"Well," he said, "we've got to show you this song, 'Minmin Light'."

"You show yourself now. Come here and sing to me," I said.

This is how he got those—what do you call them?—corroboree sticks. They were about two feet long. They just appeared there. He got them all of a sudden. He split that cloud. They were enormous, those corroboree sticks.

That didjeridu player, he sat down. There were two men. Balandjirri called the didjeridu player son. It wasn't a short didjeridu. It was enormous. Really long. And he played that didjeridu right there for me.

Well, he went back from there then. Yeah, he went back. "Don't lose this song," he said. "Well, boy," he said to the didjeridu player, "I'll take you back now."

"All right," I said.

"Bye-bye," he said. "Don't you lose it. You keep this one. I sang this *wangga* for you. It's yours." (after Marett and Barwick 1993)

For all this, it is clear that Maralung works new songs before singing them. On one occasion, he rehearsed fragments of a song given to him by Balandjirri, rearranging the melodic material in a whisper to himself before singing it (Marett and Barwick 1993).

Other song-giving spirits include animals and the small, dwarflike spirits known as *walakanda* in the Daly region of Northwest Arnhem Land. The receipt of songs from spirits also characterizes categories of song in Central Australia, where spirits can restore songs that have fallen out of use because their performance was tabooed (Wild 1987).

Singers from Northwest Arnhem Land occasionally say they have made some songs "with the brain"—without spiritual intervention. Such explanations appear to coexist easily with claims of spiritual intervention, even for the same song. In the Kimberleys, songs of the genre *lildjin* are also said to be made with the brain (Moyle 1977); they mainly treat topical events.                                    —ALLAN MARETT

## Yolngu newsong verse

As in many other Australian Aboriginal musics, the textual and musical content of Yolngu clansongs is regarded as ancient, created by ancestral spirits, handed down from the beginning of time and not subject to revision. Yolngu clansong performance, however, allows for the addition of contemporary thematic and musical elements (Knopoff 1992). One of the main ways these elements are introduced is through composing and performing newsong verse (*yuṯa manikay* 'new song').

Newsong verses are not entirely new. They involve the addition of new thematic, textual, and musical elements to extant ancestral songs. Unlike strictly ancestral creations, they are considered the creations of living singers, or of deceased singers whose identities are usually still known. Their creation is inspired by contemporary events, which, through perceived metaphoric or physical affinities, are associated with the subjects of ancestral songs. Many newsong verses are inspired by worrisome events, involving concern for someone's safety, anxiety for a recently deceased person's spirit, and sorrow for a relation's absence.

Newsong verses do not always incorporate newly added text. When they do, the added material is usually brief, and it supplements, rather than replaces, the ancestral text, frequently as part of a vocal or instrumental refrain. The use of refrains is itself an attribute of newsong verse. Newly added text often includes words someone spoke or felt, or references to living individuals by name or kinship term.

### Dolphins and dingoes

During a funeral held at Yirrkala, two grieving women asked a male relation to make a newsong verse for the occasion (Knopoff 1997). He chose the ancestral dolphin as his primary subject. He added some text, which included a refrain on the drawn-out sounds *yooo, yooo* (made by dolphins) and references to the women's names, sung in the context of dolphins jumping out of the water and falling on their side—an idiomatic action that metaphorically relates to an idiomatic Yolngu ritual act: at certain times during funerals, grieving women throw themselves to the ground. The verb *duryunmirr* specifies both these actions.

In another instance, a singer and his wife found themselves lost while driving en route from Yirrkala to their homeland center. They heard their children back at camp calling out for their mother. This experience inspired the singer to compose a newsong verse about *birrdji,* the ancestral dingo. Small amounts of new text include a refrain in which the children call for their mother (*ngän̲di-gay!* 'oh! mother'), and phrases in which the parents ponder the children's whereabouts (including *ngala dhika?* 'where is that place?', *nhaltjarr dhawal ngarrak?* 'where was that place of mine?'). No explicit references are made to *birrdji,* but a connection is implicit, since the ancestral dingo is a habitual wanderer, a lost dog in search of a road.

Distinctive musical features of newsong verses include newly composed clapstick patterns, unison vocal refrains (less common in purely ancestral verses), and contemporary styles of vocal and didjeridu rhythm and syncopation. Comparison of recordings of "the same" newsong verses performed in the 1950s and the 1990s shows that, at least in these cases, some of the musical contents (especially vocal and didjeridu rhythms) undergo revision, while other elements (especially the words of the vocal refrain and the basic clapstick patterns) remain constant.   —STEVEN KNOPOFF

## NEW GUINEA

### Investigating Usarufa composition

The who and why of communally based activities may pose problems to outsiders, and may puzzle insiders. A lengthy stay is necessary to discover how any culture's music came into being; particularly perplexing are cases involving monolingual cultures. Focused elicitation, even in the vernacular, does not always produce the information wanted, as the greater analytical problem concerns how people conceptualize their culture.

The first few years I lived with the Usarufa [see HIGHLANDS REGION OF PAPUA NEW GUINEA: Eastern Highlands Province], I asked about the meaning of each recorded text and who had made the song. When transcribing the music, I discovered that recordings of the same song had been attributed to different composers. Investigation revealed that these were textual variants, but who had made the music? Often people did not know. They emphasized the text more than the music. Making a song could be understood to mean fitting a new text to an old melody. Their language had no term to denote the concept of composing a melody.

Among the Usarufa and other highland cultures, I never found a verb meaning 'to compose a melody'. In the Eastern Highlands, instrumental music consisted of short melodic phrases alternated between players of paired flutes or unbound panpipes. Melodic instruments were said to talk. Often the use of these instruments was secret and ceremonial. For playing musically, such expressions as 'fighting a drum' and making flutes 'speak' were common. To discover the inventors of specific pieces of music required a different set of questions.

### Asking about music

When Linguist Darlene Bee and I asked the Usarufa basic questions about music, we resorted to the form "Out of whose mouth did this song at first come?" The Usarufa apparently understood this as "Who first sang the song?" or "Who first taught you the song?" and the reply did not necessarily disclose the composer. When we learned that the most highly valued local songs came in dreams, we knew to ask "Who dreamed the song?" But not all Usarufa songs are dreamed. Night after night, sitting around the fire and recording the singing, we listened as friends discussed songs and their import. Sometimes a composer's identity emerged in the telling, but, for this kind of conversing, a researcher needs fluency in the vernacular.

I once asked about the origin of a song, and was told that a child—about five or six years old—had made it. On further questioning, all present gave assurance of this. On another occasion, a song was attributed to Dr. Bee, who had never composed an Usarufa song. Through this experience, we learned that one aspect of making a song was to name the source of inspiration. Something said or done by the child and Dr. Bee had prompted the compositions, though neither had invented them.

A question researchers invariably ask is "Who makes songs?" The generic Usarufa reply was "Everyone." This might lead a novice to believe that all people compose songs—or that all are expected to, and are therefore capable of composing. The question is misinterpreted. No insider has to ask such a question, so when an outsider asks it, people hear it as "Who 'sings' songs?" A synonym for making a song is singing, and everyone in Usarufa society can participate. As soon as youngsters know the songs, they join the singing. To sing a song is to make a song. An Usarufa composer gains no special status. Some are not surprised that they are unable to create a melody memorable enough to transfer to another person, but they know men and women who can do so. The musical output of several generations, shows that certain families produce composers, and that talent for musical composition is often found in composers' offspring.                    —VIDA CHENOWETH

## Binandere compositional processes

The Binandere, of Oro Province, Papua New Guinea, have developed the art of turning private cries into public songs. Elsewhere (Waiko 1984, 1986, 1990), I have examined the skills involved and how they pass from one generation to another. Here, I concentrate on the terminology, structure, and analysis of one kind of oral tradition.

The primary form (*ji tari*) starts with a person's expression of emotion. A death summons relatives to mourn the loss of the loved one. While they cry over the corpse, other adults—especially gifted poets—listen attentively, to record mentally the individuals' exact words, their *ji tari*. Later, the poets recall these words, which they turn into two other artistic forms.

If a *ji tari* has meter and rhythm, poets adjust it to the form of a chorus (*guru*), whose structure reveals three features: images, meter, and repetition. Each has a unique role—for evocation, repeating syllabic patterns, and recurring themes. If the *ji tari* does not contain repeating patterns of syllables, poets adapt it into the form *yovero,* which an individual sings while performing a manual task, such as cutting down a tree to make a garden.

Converting *ji tari* into *guru,* a skillful poet and singer turns a momentarily felt emotion into an artistic product. In 1979, the poet-dancer-singer Warari explained that in his mind, this process "sorts out the different forms between the *ji tari* with the three characteristics and those without them. As you listen to the cry, the mental pitch does all the work, and the vocal cord just sings according to that abstract form: either *guru* or *yovero.*" The poet changes the form into a new structure, with stanzas and refrains. This structure is standardized in a fashion that on public occasions helps oral artists recite from memory.

*Ya jiwari* is the singing of *ji-tari*-derived songs, accompanied by drums. Because *guru* demand accuracy, strict social sanctions control the adaptation between *ji tari* and *guru,* and help clansmen remember the songs. *Ya jiwari* requires the control of meter, image, association, cue, and—most importantly—the repetition of a choral unison. Men sing *guru* in a standard sequence: the male lead is the first precentor (*kumbari*), often called the cue (*maemo*); he is immediately followed by the second precentor, often called the real (*be*), who takes his cue so the items in both precentors' lines match, or come from related categories of animals and plants. When the *jiwari* (the chorus, the rest of the men in the group) join in, they repeat the *be.*

*Guru* are often sung at public gatherings, such as feasts honoring the dead, when young men beat drums to the appropriate pitch of the *guru.* Synchronizing the drumming, a conch is blown. Verbal allusions make this oral art almost impenetrable to outsiders.

### Composing with metaphors

Binandere lyrics exemplify metaphorical integrity and complexity. The *guru* "*Waewo E'nano Teure*" (Waiko 1982) contains the following stanza.

| | |
|---|---|
| Kendere ano teure. | It might become yellowish. |
| Pugeo ano teure. | It might become gray-brownish. |
| Pugeo ano teure. | It might become gray-brownish. |

According to the standard sequential rules, when the first precentor sings the word *kendere* (a yellowish color, taken by a leaf just before it falls to the ground), the second precentor follows immediately with *pugeo* (the gray-brownish tint of a leaf after it has fallen, and just before it turns to compost), and the chorus then repeats the second precentor's line. This song has nearly twenty stanzas—all of which, to complete one formal *guru* (*ya be*), must follow in order.

Another artistic rule is that a *ya be* must be performed twice before another *guru* can start. The repeat leads into a buffer or break (*kewoia*), which affords an opportunity for people to recall more *guru.* The *kewoia* is also sung twice before another *ya be* begins, and this kind of singing goes on all night.

Another example, "*Yavita Mamo Erae*" ('Yavita's Motionless Father'), has this stanza:

| | |
|---|---|
| Raga da rare, erae. | Muddy silt, motionless. |
| Dude da rare, erae. | Sticky mud, motionless. |
| Dude da rare, erae. | Sticky mud, motionless. |

In this cry, my great-great-grandmother, Dauda, expressed how she saw her husband passing from life to death. She sat beside his bed, feeling his pulse falter. His passage to death was like a canoe going from clear water toward muddy silt (*raga*); then the canoe reached sticky mud (*dude*), and came to rest on the bank. The *jiwari* of this example is *erae* 'motionless'—death itself. Dauda's position is that of a person in a stranded canoe.

In another stanza, Dauda sees herself as the punter of the canoe:

| | |
|---|---|
| Bogo piena, erae. | Punting and pushing poles, motionless. |
| Demo piena, erae. | Steer and punt away, motionless. |
| Demo piena, erae. | Steer and punt away, motionless. |

As soon as she reaches the danger, she wants to change direction: she uses the poles to steer and punt away, but escape is impossible. In reality, when Dauda realized the

Vanuatu composers regularly say that thinking up melodies is secondary. Once the text is straight, melodies come by themselves. There are only so many ways a melody can turn.

time of her husband's death had come, she tried to persuade him to live a few moments more; but her plea was futile—the canoe was *erae,* motionless, still.

—JOHN D. WAIKO

### Musical composition in Irian Jaya

In the highlands of Irian Jaya, many songs have unknown or superhuman origins. The Yale say many of their songs came from a skull in the wall of a house: a man from Kosarek Village stole the skull, from which he learned songs. Beginning in 1981, songs with biblical texts developed among the Yali (not to be confused with the Yale), as with the Dani before them. These songs follow rules of the local musical system. An adult may improvise a text or compose a song, but groups usually compose hymns: in repeated trials, verses that "do not flow right are modified," and when participants "are happy with them," someone writes them down (Wilson 1988:93). Within six years, the Yali were singing more than 150 new compositions.

Along the north coast, the Isirawa believe one group of dance-songs (*fatiya*) came from a mythological woman whom people killed and butchered; as various sub-tribes carried off parts of her body, her head and each of her limbs sang songs, which now bear the highest prestige and serve for dancing (Oguri 1981:13). Of lesser status are *karame,* which, consciously or dreaming, individuals continue to invent. Most are composed by young unmarried girls. One *karame* derides a boy who could not dance: "They taught him and taught him, but it was no use." Other Isirawa songs (*kona*) came from a water-dwelling spirit. People believe songs learned in dreams come from supernatural sources, including spirits and ghosts.

Little is known of composition along the south coast of Irian Jaya, where the Asmat regard their music as an art equal to that of carving wood and telling stories. No ritual occurs without music, and collective participation assures homogeneity and solidarity (Van Arsdale 1982).

In Fakfak Regency, the Mairasi say they do not know how to compose melodies, but adults create new texts for existing melodies. They distinguish between songs sung by night and songs sung by day. Neither compositional nor performative features classify songs: long ago, ancestors determined which songs people would sing by day and which by night. Musical texts may contain clues about performance; for example, songs to the sun, as it rises or sets, are day-appropriate songs. Mairasi believe melodies are "part of the original universe that 'just happened' . . . 'they were born by themselves.' Therefore new tunes cannot be made." To existing melodies, people may still add new texts, with one exception, the *bajeni* class of day-appropriate songs, whose lyrics come "from dreams at the beginning of time" (Hughes 1989 2:1). The Mairasi believe religious specialists receive melodies only under spirits' control.

In Sorong Regency, the Abun divide songs into three classes. The first, dance-songs (*sukne*), mainly have vocables for texts, with no semantic meaning but the names of villages. Ancestors, inspired by natural objects, created the first lines, one of which imitates a bird at play. Keith Berry, a linguist analyzing the Abun language, reports (personal communication) that a leader sings hundreds of "first lines," and other singers continue melodically while arbitrarily inserting words or phrases that fit the rhythm. A second class (*sukba*) is more personal in expression. Topics range from songs about love to remarks on the immediate ("You have come to learn to speak Abun"). For a farewell, one old woman sang: "When the sun rises above the mountain, Duane [Clouse] and Vida will be going back to where they came from; now it is cloudy, overcast, and raining, preventing your going." The third class (*sukrot*) consists of two-step melodies sung in a little-known improvisatory style, considered the oldest Abun music.                                                                —VIDA CHENOWETH

## VANUATU

In Vanuatu, composition is in principle open to anyone, but some individuals achieve renown as songsmiths. Christopher Lui of Lowainasasa (Ambae Island) said he would dream the outline of a song, get up at about 4 A.M., write it down in a notebook, and later revise it. If it were a *sawagoro* (a popular genre, possibly derived from campfire sing-alongs), he would wait for a session, join the group, and introduce his new item. He would be attentive to its acceptance, hoping for a hit. He inserts foreign or obsolete words for reasons of assonance or symbolic suggestion, but knows no systematic song-dependent language, as Codrington (1885:308–310) postulated for the Banks Islands. He accepts commissions to compose, but frequently offers new songs simply for his own renown. To a European, he says his best composition is "The Godden Memorial Song," possibly because of its hymnodic elements.

Women compose with skill and subtlety. Eleanor Voi of Umlonggo (Maewo Island) made a song about academic researchers' attempts to make a windblown flute and what that recalled to her of "time before." George Boe of Ngota (Maewo) composed one about meeting researchers. Vanuatu composers regularly say that thinking up melodies is secondary: once the text is straight, melodies come by themselves, in a particular form: there are only so many ways a melody can turn.

A songsmith carefully designs the strategy of a typical narrative song. In the *sawagoro* form, events unfurl like leaves, one after another. Eventually a bud appears. In the penultimate stanza, it bursts open. Only in the last stanza does the composer name the subject, unveiling the floral metaphor. This process exploits an art of suspense, often paralleled by crescendo and (when danced) by quickening tempo. The most highly regarded composers create songs whose endings seem to erupt, spewing their signification in a torrent. The dreaming of new dances involves symphonic conception because a ritualized spectacle is involved, with many songs, much decoration, and perhaps instrumental accompaniment.

### Syncretic compositional processes

Today, Vanuatu people use many syncretic adaptations of customary elements, assembled to satisfy new performative occasions, such as festivals, where performers from various areas contribute items to a proposed medley. Results are usually attractive to local audiences, but claims of tradition can be specious, barring the principle that the overall formula, the way of working it, may be culturally basic.

The syncretic political movement Nagriamel has supported revivals of half-remembered, half-understood elements, mixed regardless of place of origin. A dance with paired couples in moving diagonal lines at Tanafo in 1977 followed the ostinatos of a harmonica, replacing panpipes, no longer manufactured. Log-idiophone rhythms for killing pigs on the same occasion (to give honorific rank to the then-colonial resident commissioners) made loud and erratic noises, with neither territori-

FIGURE 3     Ansen, composer and leader of women's dancing in Mariu and Lotawan villages, Mota Island. Photo by Dan Garst, 1995.

al validity nor accuracy. This mixture was acceptable as Nagriamel President Jimmy Stevens's new dance, which he had dreamed. The log idiophones of Espiritu Santo had long since disappeared. Imported instruments were given to Ambae and Malakula people to play—individuals who had no common musical system and were untrained drummers.

—PETER RUSSELL CROWE

## Dreaming music on Mota

In Lotawan Village, Mota [see VANUATU: Banks Islands], lives the middle-aged singer Veve (Mother) Ansen (figure 3). A prolific composer, she can sing a prodigious number of songs, some remembered from her childhood. She claims to know hundreds of songs, "more than can be recorded." As the leader of women's dancing in Mariu and Lotawan villages, she controls the rehearsals and performances of women's dances there.

Songs come to Ansen in dreams, complete as to events, images, words, and melodies. Though not many persons of the Banks Islands are currently composing new songs, she and her daughter Keit Florita have obtained songs in dreams, and she has composed songs when fully awake. Some of Ansen's songs are adaptations of other persons' songs. She says she knows songs suitable for healing the sick, but will not record them because of the risk of losing their power. She paid someone from another island for them and the power they hold. She does, however, appear willing to sell them.

In one dream, Keit Florita saw a deceased man, Father Lindsay, sitting in the shade of a tree, looking out at the beautiful island of Nawila, which has a white-sand beach and plentiful fish in its waters. He called for his little boy, Lotlot (nickname for Launcelot), who began crying. Father Lindsay awakened, and Keit Florita's dream ended. Three recorded versions of the song dreamed in this dream are extant. Figure 4 is the melody as dreamed by Keit Florita and sung by Ansen, to whom Keit taught it. In another performance, Ansen sang and accompanied female dancers by striking a bamboo idiophone. She used introductory beats to set the tempo, to which the dancers marched, single file, accenting each beat with one footfall. Ansen compressed the melody into one statement of phrases $A_1$ and $A_2$, followed by a high G♭ on the syllable *hē*, sustained for more than eight beats while the dancers ran in place in double time, kicking backward with each step. All ended with the shout *ai-yai-yo*. In a third performance, Keit Florita and her husband, Paul, sang the first phrase in unison. Their rhythms approximated those of Keit's solo rendition, but their tones sometimes differed. The beginning of phrases $A_2$ and $A_3$, A♭–B♭–D♭–E♭–D♭, they sang as A♭–B♭–E♭–F–E♭, and their melody ended on B♭, not A♭.

—VIDA CHENOWETH

## Commissioning music on Tanna

The Tannese believe inspiration by external authority generates artistic productions (Inglis 1887:151). Local authorities include spirits, ancestors, people, and written texts from beyond the community. Artists who produce new objects, designs, songs, or stories explain that they merely pass along a revealed message or idea. Songsmiths

FIGURE 4    Keit Florita's song about Father Lindsay's dream of Nawila as sung for the record by Ansen. Transcription by Vida Chenoweth.

get new compositions by overhearing ancestral or spiritual voices. To encourage ancestral revelation, some songsmiths retire to spiritually active glades, drink kava, sacrifice a fowl, and settle back to await inspiration.

People hosting festivals may commission songs by sending requests to song-smiths with good ancestral connections. A songsmith works into the lyrics the names of those who have requested the song; or he uses the name of the plant representing a participant within the token of the commission (*norirupwien*), or the name of a plot of land or kin associated with that individual. From ancestral sources, a songsmith may receive extra compositions (*takutai nupu* 'backside of song'). From the commissioners, he receives kava, fowl, and pigs.

To teach the new music, the composer visits the sponsor's kava-drinking ground. At one occasion in 1984, men practiced a new *nupu* melody and lyrics seated. They did not slow the tempo, nor did they break the lyrics into segments. They hummed the tune and sang the lyrics; later, they stood and added movements. Such movements may stem from the commissioned composer. In 1979, Sam Tukumha, a West Tanna leader, choreographed *kepui* so the men's circle split into halves, between which four women danced before the halves rejoined; this pattern, he said, symbolized islandwide unity, which he found a scarce virtue.

Lyrics commonly cite people, places, and events, and highlight reasons for an exchange. Longer songs may combine unrelated topics. Lyrics are elliptical, allusive, and metaphorical, as in a *nupu* that begins:

| | |
|---|---|
| Kariuak revi nuai reia. | Kariuak pulled out the tail feather. |
| Navahi pen Maririg. | He sent it to Maririg. |
| Iauha ramavahi raka, | Iauha is already taking it, |
| Muvsini pehe ti nupu Ikurupu. | And changing it into an Ikurupu song. |
| Iramanien ramisua apwiri iou. | The spiritual dream woke me. |

For the second turn of the dancing, the lyrics go: *Hianekwihi nimrig ia nitete sakimi-aha, Naraimene. / Kamata nimigi nep. / Nasipmene hata, minisua mata tafaga* 'You have destroyed the canoe's heritage that belongs to you, Naraimene. / One sees the handle of the club. / Nasipmene sees, understands that behavior'. For the third turn of the dancing, the lyrics continue: *Rikuarkuar; uvuta pukah. / Manasanas iatakurei nakogar, / Mosatuk menu ianueiuei. / Ravahi uta roas misansani* 'There is plenty; lift up the pigs. / Overflowing atop the *nakogar* tree, / The bird stretches in the wind. / It lifts the bark-cloth skirts and exposes [women]'. The feather was part of the bundle given the songsmith to commission the song. Naraimene is a local group.

Beyond metaphor and elision, many songs are semantically opaque. Some of these are antique, their meaning lost. Others purposefully contain exotic language. The East Tanna missionary William Gray noted, "A native . . . readily uses the prefor-matives [tense- or aspect-marking prefixes] of his own dialect with the stem root words of another dialect. I have found these corruptions and foreign words in all native songs I have examined" (1894:43). Even new songs have nonsensical words, whose babble symbolizes ancestral power (Lindstrom 1990). Festival songs, especially those without associated mime, contain vocables, as in this *nirup* stanza.

| | |
|---|---|
| Iaruaina iaruaina. | *Iaruaina iaruaina.* |
| Iaruaina iaruaina. | *Iaruaina iaruaina.* |
| Iaruaina iaruaina. | *Iaruaina iaruaina.* |
| Samo kurkurau | We circle |
| Ipinien, ia rukwanu rasori | At Ipinien, at the large village |
| Savai Namereisi. | Of Namereisi. |
| Takirui uta kamakwein a. | We will beat [our baskets] and sing out. |

As here, repeated vocables at the beginning cue recognition of songs, and let singers coordinate their voices before semantically explicit verses begin.

—LAMONT LINDSTROM

## KIRIBATI

In Kiribati, composing musical texts and related rituals involved ancestral spirits and deities, overseen by a *tia-kainikamaen,* a priest specializing in *kainikamaen,* skills of composing and performing, which paralleled other religious practices. Composition required skillfully executing *kario* 'bring-down' rituals, of which an excerpt goes: *Rio mai, ao nako mai, au manewe. / Uouona ma uangiana mai nano, ba I abokia rake* 'Come down to me, come to me, my inspired verse. / Come forth and be drawn forth from below, for I begin above' (after Laxton 1953:344). Assistants, called *tia-ototo, rurubene,* and *tauanikai,* memorized the words as the *tia-kainikamaen* transmitted them from spirits, and suggested suitable arrangements of words and phrases into completed texts.

The domain of the *tia-kainikamaen* included training other composers, enhancing a song's appeal and power, increasing performers' attractiveness, and conducting rituals necessary for competitive performance (figure 5). As the spiritual protector of the village, he was admired and feared. Compositional rituals occurred on the shore, at a composing shrine, or in the ocean; they required fires, coconuts, leaves, fishing rods, sticks, and other implements. Composers could compose less powerful songs alone, at home or on the shore.

Becoming a *tia-kainikamaen* took extensive training. At intervals from the age of two weeks to about twenty-five years, a trainee would learn about spirits, incantations, and ceremonies, and undergo ritual and psychological conditioning. Typically, he stood on a reef, rinsed his mouth with seawater, and addressed spirits with a recitation such as the following (after Teruruia 1970:38–39):

| | |
|---|---|
| Tebuna mai kanne. | I learn a song. |
| Tera mai kanne? | What do you teach me? |
| Te ang mai ikai. | I learn about the wind. |
| Tera mai kanne? | What do you teach me? |
| Au manewe ni kuna raraoi. | The poetic words of my song. |
| Ma i kanna, i kanna, i kanna. | For I learn and learn and learn. |

FIGURE 5    Taanea Buretiu, trustee of his family's *kainikamaen* knowledge, performs a *bino* for people of Tekaman Village, Tabiteuea North, Kiribati. Photo by Mary E. Lawson Burke, 1985.

Eventually, people considered the trainee a *tia-ototo* 'song-doer'. To be regarded as a *tia-kainikamaen,* he had to receive popular recognition that he possessed unsurpassed spiritual and practical knowledge pertaining to all other aspects of performance. A final step was the communal construction of his composing shrine.

Rarely today does someone call himself a *tia-kainikamaen;* knowledgeable persons insist that their role as descent-group protector is now irrelevant. Expertise varies among composers. Their selection is no longer so exclusive, and most have been trained by methods of varying rigor. Some specialize in choral songs (*kuaea*) or dance-songs (*maie*), but others compose in both genres. The most prevalent title for a composer is *tia-ototo,* though one known to use assistants or rituals may be called a *tia-kamaen* or *tia-kario.*

The impact of missionaries' work, differing degrees of training, and other influences have loosened the observance of ritual methods. Many knowledgeable composers prefer not to rely on traditional methods, believing their texts will be powerful and appealing simply because of their heritage. As rituals have shortened and moderated, composition has largely become a private matter.

Composers and their assistants teach songs by rote during rehearsals, dance-training sessions, and performances. They may write their texts down. Schools teach old and new songs and dances, and in some areas Western notation; hymnals are often in numeral notation. Radio has become a powerful means of disseminating newly composed songs.

—MARY E. LAWSON BURKE

## POLYNESIA

### Tonga: the music of Queen Sālote

Composers in Tonga are known as *pulotu* or *faʻu.* A person who composes poetry is known as *pulotu taʻanga* when the poetic composition is meant to be the basis for a *lakalaka,* or *faʻu maau* (or sometimes *fatu maau*) when the poetic composition will be the basis for a *hiva kakala* (*hiva* is the gloss for 'sing'). A person who composes the melodic and rhythmic setting for the poetic composition is known as *pulotu hiva* for a *lakalaka,* or *faʻu hiva* for a *hiva kakala.* A person who choreographs movements for a poetic composition is known as *pulotu haka* for a *lakalaka,* or *faʻu haka* for a *tauʻolunga* (*haka* is the gloss for 'arm movement'). A person who can compose poetry, music, and movement is known as *punake,* a distinguished and elevated term.

*Punake, pulotu,* and *faʻu* can be either male or female. Their compositions are judged by the same criteria, the most important of which is *heliaki* 'to say one thing but mean another'. *Heliaki* is realized through indirectness, metaphor, and allusion, never approaching a subject directly, but making reference to a subject by going around it and enhancing it with layers of meaning. The words of a song do not necessarily reveal the meaning of the song, and the movements of the accompanying dance can allude to either the words themselves or the hidden meaning.

Tongan compositions are based on motifs—culturally grammatical verses of poetry, culturally grammatical sequences of pitched and rhythmic sounds, and culturally grammatical sequences of movement. Motifs are held in memory by the composer, who can create images from them, making a social statement.

Genealogy and gender are important elements of Tongan poetry, song, and dance—which verbally and visually embody ideas and cultural values dealing with prestige and power. Sung poetry conveys allusions and metaphorical references, whose meaning is enhanced by gender-specific movements. Tongan composers are influential in producing and reproducing social values, deciding which subjects and symbols will be brought to public attention at a specific time, and what will be sung and danced about. They have the power to honor or be silent.

FIGURE 6    Queen Sālote (1900–1965), the most famous composer of twentieth-century Tonga. Courtesy of the Palace Office.

### Queen Sālote

Queen Sālote (1900–1965) was the most famous composer of twentieth-century Tonga (figure 6). Reigning as Tupou III from 1918 to 1965, she embodied Tongan values, which she conveyed through her compositions of allusive poetry, realized through melodic and rhythmic settings in two or more parts, and often projected kinetically in dance. Many of her compositions continue to be performed regularly; some are revived and restaged for special occasions.

Expert in cultural, social, and artistic forms, Queen Sālote gave each of her compositions an underlying theme. Drawing on her knowledge of social structure, genealogy, history, and culture, she applied to old Tongan cultural forms a new veneer, superficially Westernizing them. Her compositions, reproducing cultural values that combine the old with the new, offer a virtually untapped source for studying the production and reproduction of social and cultural values in Tonga (Kaeppler 1990).

### The queen's hiva kakala

*Hiva kakala* is a major Tongan musical genre of the 1900s. Its melodies are often borrowed from hymns, Western secular songs, and earlier *hiva kakala*. An example of transforming a Western tune into the musical setting of a Tongan text is "*Toli Fisi*" ('Pick Blossoms', figure 7), for which Queen Sālote's poetry received a musical setting from Lavaka Kefu. The poetry declares the queen's love for her consort, Prince Tungī, cited by the names of sweet-smelling flowers:

> Toli fisi pea 'aikona 'o 'omai;
> Huni, fahina, langakali.
> Talanoa hua 'o ka malu efiafi,
> Holo ai e 'eva 'oku fetaki.
>
> Tu'u kae 'ai hao sei,
> Alamea tekiteki.
> Toki luva ha'o maheni
> Oku fai feluteni.

Pick blossoms and bring them in your skirt;
*Huni, fahina,* and *langakali* [flowers].
Sociable talk in the shade of evening,
Happily strolling arm in arm.

Stand there while I place a flower decoration for your ear,
Your hair ornament made of *alamea* [flowers].
Only give it away
To one you dearly love.

More directly, the second stanza extols simple joys: "You appear to me in the middle of the night, / The smile that makes me happy. / Round and round flow the leaves of Mailemomo. / Hooray! when we are happily making love."

Tongan composers delight in fitting such poetry to radio-broadcasted melodies, which may be heard only once or twice, and the result often bears little resemblance to the original, especially when it reflects the Tongan view that one takes a tune that one likes and improves on it. In music, as in poetry, the obvious is hidden: a singer can add to a melody by singing in harmony with it, and the musical product, like the poetry, can illuminate, enhance, or hide.

Queen Sālote also composed *hiva kakala* for public occasions. Here, the poetry is carefully composed, given a melodic and rhythmic setting, and played and sung by a famous group or band. Movements are choreographed to emphasize the performer's beauty, to allude textually through *heliaki,* and, in the best compositions, to have an overall *heliaki.* One such composition is *"Manu 'o Palataisi"* ('Bird of Paradise'), in which Queen Sālote compares Tonga to paradise (Kaeppler 1995).

### The queen's lakalaka

Queen Sālote's *lakalaka* brought history and mythology to bear on contemporary events, and the values imparted dealt primarily with the overall societal structure and the people of rank through whom it operates. The poetry of a *lakalaka* is a series of concepts and references, rather than a complete story; it is usually composed for performance at a specific event.

One of the queen's most engaging *lakalaka* is the text about the supernatural turtle Sangone, composed about 1948 (Kaeppler 1993 [1967]). "'*Otu Langi*," her last

FIGURE 7 The first stanza and refrain of *"Toli Fisi."* Transcription by J. W. Love.

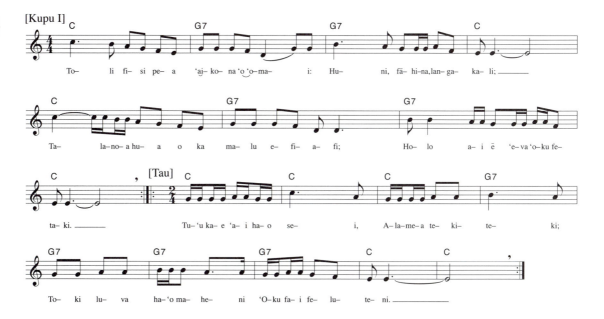

I compare music with the parts of a growing tree: roots, trunks, stems, branches, twigs, leaves, flowers, fruits. The parts of a musical composition work together. Its words and lines connect to form an organic whole.

composed for Lapaha Village, was performed in 1953 for the state celebration honoring the visit of Queen Elizabeth II. The text preserves information about the ancient stone tombs. Its social meaning lies in the values it conveys about the importance of history and the appropriateness of tradition.

Queen Sālote's compositions are important in the production and reproduction of social and cultural values, especially these relating to concepts of extended families, gender, and the hierarchical structure of Tongan society. Her compositions are also important because they embody the essence of the Tongan aesthetic of indirectness, which she was instrumental in evolving to its present form; but they can be understood only by a knowledgeable audience. That audience is decreasing because much of the younger generation does not understand the *heliaki* through which the queen tried to convey these values.

—ADRIENNE L. KAEPPLER

## A Cook Islands composer at work

Each musical composer in the Cook Islands has an individual style of composing songs. None of these composers could claim his or her way as the best or the right way. Many have produced beautiful pieces of music, which remain popular (Herrmann 1988).

Composers develop and produce their own pieces of music, taking pride in their talent and skill. If a composer is happy and satisfied with the result, he or she must be doing the right things, but to improve one's skills, it is helpful and advisable to listen to other's music and seek others' advice. This is how I have gained and improved on my experiences. Coming from a musical society and family, I became aware of the importance and usefulness of music in portraying personal feeling and identity, or marking a special event. I started to develop my compositional skills as a hobby, and through four decades have continued to do so in earnest. My first composition was "*Taku ei roti*" ('My Garland of Roses'), in 1958, when I was nineteen. During the years, my compositions have celebrated school-festival activities, community activities, sports, women's organizations, special national events, loved ones, and a host of other topics.

### *A method of composing*

Music is a living process, born and developing within us. I compare music with the parts of a growing plant or tree: roots, trunks, stems, branches, twigs, leaves, flowers, fruits. Like these parts, all the parts of a musical composition work together. Its words and lines connect to form an organic whole. To produce a meaningful, accessible piece of music, one must select or identify a theme or a title, collect relevant information, formulate appropriate lyrics or script, develop a suitable rhythm and tune, and choose an appropriate accompaniment.

*Theme.*—A theme is a set of thoughts, a composer's guideposts for describing a feeling or a situation. When I compose, I direct my imagination toward a theme. An appropriate theme could be "The South Pacific Mini Games," or the "Cook Islands Constitution Silver Anniversary," or feelings of love for a particular person. Some themes, as in my song "*Tiare,*" composed for the Secondary Schools Culture Festival (1977), are about natural objects, in this case a flower. Other themes come from tales, as in "*Ina i te Kumuitonga,*" about a maiden betrothed to the chief Tinirau. Others reflect biblical principles, as in "*Te Iti Vaine o te Kuki Airani,*" developing the passage "Cast thy bread upon the waters: for thou shalt find it after many days" (Eccles. 11:1). Once I identify a theme, I choose words or thoughts to suit it.

*Information.*—Focusing on a theme, I do not have to look far for relevant information so long as I have a clear picture or understand the identified theme or title of the song. The process of gathering information may entail answering a set of questions: What is the background of the situation? Who is involved? What actually happened? Where did it happen? When did it happen? Why or how did it happen? These are the questions I consider, but not all compositions need to answer all of them.

*Lyrics.*—Because composing a song is like growing a plant, with all its parts interconnected, I next compose the lyrics. Each line of poetry, and the links between the lines, must make sense! Careful selection of words to form a series of thoughts makes a piece of music more meaningful and beautiful.

*Rhythm and melody.*—This part of the composition is important because these attributes inspire the inner beauty of the song, expressing the true feeling or depth of the situation or event. The words must match the mood. If the song is about a happy occasion, the rhythm and melody must be cheery and lively. The process of inventing or adapting rhythms and melodies reflect the composer's feeling and understanding in relation to the theme of the song.

*Accompaniment.*—Composers have a choice of accompaniment, depending on how the song will be sung, by whom, and where. There are really no restrictions on accompaniment, unless the composer or the singers decide otherwise. I believe that any kind of accompaniment is suitable to any piece of music, so long as the composer is satisfied.

—VEREARA TEARIKI MONGA MAEVA

## REFERENCES

Barwick, Linda. 1989. "Creative (Ir)regularities: The Intermeshing of Text and Melody in Performance of Central Australian Song." *Australian Aboriginal Studies* 1:12–28.

———. 1990. "Central Australian Women's Ritual Music: Knowing Through Analysis Versus Knowing Through Performance." *Yearbook for Traditional Music* 22:60–79.

Bell, F. L. S. 1935. "The Social Significance of Amfat Among the Tanga of New Ireland." *Journal of the Polynesian Society* 44:97–111.

Burrows, Edwin G. 1945. *Songs of Uvea and Futuna.* Bulletin 183. Honolulu: Bishop Museum.

Codrington, R. H. 1885. *The Melanesian Languages.* Oxford: Oxford University Press.

Feld, Steven. 1984. "Sound Structure as Social Structure." *Ethnomusicology* 28(3):383–409.

Finnegan, Ruth. 1977. *Oral Poetry: Its Nature, Significance and Social Context.* Cambridge: Cambridge University Press.

Firth, Raymond. 1990. *Tikopia Songs.* Cambridge: Cambridge University Press.

Gray, William. 1894. "A Song of Aniwa." *Journal of the Polynesian Society* 3:41–45.

Handy, Edward S. Craighill, and L. Jane Winne. 1925. *Music in the Marquesas Islands.* Bulletin 17. Honolulu: Bishop Museum.

Herrmann, John J., ed. 1988. *E Au Imene Tamataora: Songs and Songwriters of the Cook Islands.* Suva, Fiji: Institute of Pacific Studies and Cook Islands Centre, University of the South Pacific.

Hughes, Valori E. 1989. "An Analysis of Mairasi Music." Senior document, Wheaton College.

Inglis, John. 1887. *In the New Hebrides: Reminiscences of Missionary Life and Work, Especially on the Island of Aneityum, from 1850 till 1877.* London: T. Nelson.

Kaeppler, Adrienne. 1993 [1967]. "Sangone, a *Lakalaka* from Lapaha: Folklore as Expressed in the Dance in Tonga." In *Poetry in Motion: Studies of Tongan Dance,* 40–47. Nuku'alofa, Tonga: Vava'u Press.

———. 1990. "The Production and Reproduction of Social and Cultural Values in the

Compositions of Queen Sālote of Tonga." In *Music, Gender and Culture,* ed. Marcia Herndon and Susanne Ziegler, 191–219. Berlin: International Institute for Comparative Music Studies and Documentation.

———. 1995. "The Paradise Theme in Modern Tongan Music." In *The Essence of Singing and the Substance of Song: Recent Responses to the Aboriginal Performing Arts and Other Essays in Honour of Catherine Ellis,* ed. Linda Barwick, Allan Marett, and Guy Tunstill, 159–183. Oceania monograph 46. Sydney: University of Sydney.

Kāretu, Tīmoti S. 1991. "Te Ngahurutanga: A Decade of Protest, 1980–1990." In *Dirty Silence,* ed. Bill Manhire, 159–175. Oxford: Oxford University Press.

Knopoff, Steven. 1992. "*Yuta Manikay:* Juxtaposition of Ancestral and Contemporary Elements in the Performance of Yolngu Clan Songs." *Yearbook for Traditional Music* 24:138–151.

———. 1997. "Accompanying the Dreaming: Determinants of Didjeridoo Style in Traditional and Popular Yolngu Song." In *The Didjeridu: From Arnhem Land to Internet,* ed. Karl Neuenfeldt, 39–67. Sydney: John Libbey and Perfect Beat Publications.

Lawson, Mary Elizabeth. 1989. "Tradition, Change, and Meaning in Kiribati Performance: An Ethnography of Music and Dance in a Micronesian Society." Ph.D. dissertation, Brown University.

Laxton, P. B. 1953. "A Gilbertese Song." *Journal of the Polynesian Society* 62:342–347.

Lindstrom, Lamont. 1990. *Knowledge and Power in a South Pacific Society.* Washington, D.C.: Smithsonian Institution Press.

Love, Jacob Wainwright. 1991. *Sāmoan Variations.* New York and London: Garland Publishing.

Marett, Allan, and Linda Barwick, ed. 1993. *Bunggridj-Bunggridj: Wangga Songs by Alan Maralung.* International Institute for Traditional Music: Traditional Music of the World, 4. Smithsonian Folkways CD 40430. Compact disc.

McLaren, Les. 1979. *Kama Wosi: Music in the Trobriand Islands.* 49 mins. Focal Communications. Film, video.

Moyle, Alice. 1977. *Songs of the Kimberleys.* Canberra: Australian Institute of Aboriginal Studies. Companion booklet for LP disk.

Ngata, Apirana T. 1959. *Nga Moteatea.* Wellington: Polynesian Society.

Oguri, Kiroko. 1981. "The Music of the Isirawa." *Irian* (Cenderawasih University) 9(3):1–33.

[Pewhairangi, Ngoi.] 1985. *Tuini: Her Life and Songs.* Gisborne: Te Rau Press.

Pond, Wendy. 1990. "Wry Comment from the Outback: Songs of Protest from the Niua Islands." *Oral Tradition* 5(2–3):205–218.

Rossen, Jane Mink. 1987. *Songs of Bellona Island.* 2 vols. Acta Ethnomusicologica Danica, 4. Copenhagen: Forlaget Kragen.

Teruruia, Ten. 1970. "A Study of Gilbertese Culture in Song and Dance." In *Gilbert and Ellice Islands,* ed. T. R. C. Coppack, 33–59. Tarawa: Tarawa Teachers College.

Thomas, Allan, and Ineleo Tuia. 1990. "Profile of a Composer: Ihaia Puka, a Pulotu of the Tokelau Islands." *Oral Tradition* 2(3):267–282.

Topolinski, Kaha'i. 1986. *Nou E, Kawena: For You, Kawena.* Pumehana Records PS 4926. LP disk.

Van Arsdale, Kathleen O. 1982. "Music and Culture of the Bismam Asmat of New Guinea: A Preliminary Investigation." *An Asmat Sketch Book,* 17–94. Publication 8. Asmat Museum of Culture and Progress.

Waiko, John Douglas Dademo. 1982. "*Be Jijimo:* A History According to the Tradition of the Binandere People of Papua New Guinea." 2 vols. Ph.D. dissertation, Australian National University.

———. 1984. "Binandere Songs." *Bikmaus* 5(3):87.

———. 1986. "Oral Tradition Among the Binandere: Problems of Method in Melanesian History." *Journal of Pacific History* 21:21–38.

———. 1990. "'Head' and 'Tail': The Shaping of Oral Traditions Among the Binandere in Papua New Guinea." *Oral Tradition* 5(2–3):334–353.

Wassmann, Jürg. 1991. *The Song to the Flying Fox: The Public and Esoteric Knowledge of the Important Men of Kandingei about Totemic Songs, Names and Knotted Cords (Middle Sepik, Papua New Guinea).* Translated by Dennis Q. Stephenson. Apwitihire, 2. Boroko: National Research Institute.

Wild, Stephen. 1987. "Recreating the *Jukurrpa:* Adaptation and Innovation of Songs and Ceremonies in Warlpiri Society.' In *Songs of Aboriginal Australia,* ed. Margaret Clunies Ross, Tamsin Donaldson, and Stephen A. Wild, 97–120. Oceania monograph 32. Sydney: Oceania Publications.

Wilson, John D. 1988. "Scripture in Oral Culture: The Yali of Irian Jaya." Master's thesis, University of Edinburgh.

# Musical Instruments

*J. W. Love*  
*Neville H. Fletcher*  
*Don Niles*  
*Douglas L. Oliver*  
*Allan Thomas*  
*Gerald Florian Messner*  
*Adrienne L. Kaeppler*  

*Michael Webb*  
*Amy Kuʻuleialoha Stillman*  
*Jay W. Junker*  
*Allan Marett*  
*Karl William Neuenfeldt*  
*Hugo Zemp*  
*Raymond Ammann*  

**Idiophones**  
**Membranophones**  
**Chordophones**  
**Aerophones**  

TRACK 17

All peoples of Oceania play musical instruments, whose contributions to musical performance vary widely. Solomon Islanders use combinations of precisely pitched flutes, from whose tunings they verbalize a musical theory. Indigenous Australians minimize their instruments to a few acoustic tools. Most peoples incorporate into musical performance the slaps, claps, tramps, and other nonvocal sounds of human bodies in motion.

The study of musical instruments relies on objective classification, but no proposed taxonomy has proved universal, and all taxonomies have difficulty with perplexing cases. The system codified by Erich M. von Hornbostel and Curt Sachs (1914, 1961) has gained international acceptance as a standard. Applied to Oceania by Hans Fischer (1986) and others, it informs the discussions of musical instruments in this volume.

Sounds are vibrations, so researchers sort musical instruments primarily by the nature of the object that vibrates (figure 1). Idiophones are instruments whose *own substance* vibrates without having previously been stretched. Membranophones yield sounds by the vibration of *stretched skins.* Chordophones yield sounds by the vibration of *stretched strings.* Aerophones make *air itself* the primary vibrating object. Researchers sort musical instruments secondarily on the basis of other physical traits or the action that gets the vibration going—striking, plucking, rubbing, blowing, and so on.

Every culture has a unique set of musical instruments, embodying a history of collective choices. Throughout Oceania, these choices favor idiophones, mainly for signaling, cueing, and marking musical meter. In cultures that combine multiple idiophones, ensembles have developed the musical potential of rhythmic and timbral contrasts.

The instrumentation of symphonic music, now heard in major urban centers, differs from indigenous Oceanic instrumentation. A typical example is Mozart's opera *The Magic Flute,* whose performance in 1973 inaugurated the Sydney Opera House. Its orchestra has a foundation of chordophones (of the violin family), enhanced with aerophones (including flutes, oboes, bassoons, and trumpets), but relegates an idiophone (glockenspiel) and a membranophone (kettledrum) to a special

FIGURE 1    Four kinds of Oceanic musical instruments: *a,* at the Pacific Festival of Arts, men of Papua New Guinea strike log idiophones (photo by Adrienne L. Kaeppler, 1992); *b,* Lani Correa plays the Hawaiian membranophones *pūniu* with her right hand and *pahu* with her left hand (photo by George Bacon, about 1950); *c,* Gagime plays the Huli chordophone *gáwa,* a two-stringed musical bow (photo by Jacqueline Pugh-Kitingan, 1977); *d,* in Nukuʻalofa, Tonga, at the steps of the palace, Veʻehala plays a nose-blown flute, an aerophone (photo by Adrienne L. Kaeppler, 1975).

(*a*)

(*b*)

TRACK 18

(*c*)

class, often called the percussion section. Similarly, the popular music of Oceania, mostly deriving from European-American sources, builds ensembles on chordophones (guitars and ukuleles), but these are usually plucked, whereas symphonic strings are usually bowed, and the use of percussion in Oceanic reggae and rock bands gives idiophones and membranophones greater musical emphasis. On such points, researchers can examine a culture's preferred combinations of instruments to explore what aesthetic values they imply and what social functions they serve.

The search for ethnological implications in the spread of individual instruments has attracted academic interest. For New Guinea, Jaap Kunst (1967) produced an interregional chart of the distribution of instruments, turning up leads later pursued by Kenneth A. Gourlay (1975), Don Niles (1983), and Mervyn McLean (1994). For Polynesia, Edwin G. Burrows (1937) studied material culture, including musical instruments. Some Oceanic musical instruments incorporate visual and acoustic symbolism, which may arise from deep social structures to embody mythical charters and religious beliefs.

Some researchers, using a narrow definition of music, do not extend to all sound-producing artifacts the status of musical instrument. This tendency points up

FIGURE 1 *(continued)*

TRACK 19

*(d)*

differences between insiders' and outsiders' outlooks, and suggests the importance of respecting the classificatory thinking of the people to whom instruments are cultural-ly meaningful.

—J. W. LOVE

## IDIOPHONES

Objects that by virtue of their shape and the materials from which they are construct-ed make musically useful sounds when mechanically excited are classified as idio-phones, meaning that they sound "of themselves." Mechanical excitation usually involves hitting the object with some sort of hammer (as with log idiophones, wood-en plaques, and xylophones), or hitting one part of the object against another (as with clapsticks, paired stones, and castanets). The first case is percussion; the second, concussion. In each case, the vibrating object radiates its sound directly, though some idiophones (hollowed log idiophones, castanets) have an air-cavity resonator. Other methods of excitation include hitting the object against the ground or water (figure 2), or against a person's hand or body (the Hawaiian stick rattle, *pū ili*).

A struck object vibrates in sonic patterns called normal modes, each of which has a characteristic form, determined by the shape of the object, and a characteristic frequency, determined by the size, shape, density, and elasticity of the material. The shapes of some idiophones make one mode acoustically dominant. Known as the fundamental, this mode is usually that of the lowest frequency. It gives a definite pitch. More precisely tuned idiophones, such as the slats of xylophones, bring the next higher mode (the first overtone) into harmonic relation with the fundamental, enhancing the sensation of pitch. Tuned idiophones may be played as sets, allowing the production of melodic motifs.

The sounds of Oceanic idiophones are transient. The time each sound persists depends on the material from which the instrument is made. A prolonged sound requires a large mass of heavy material, such as metal, with small internal losses of energy. Indigenous Oceanic societies did not forge metal, so their idiophones are typically of wood, whose sound dies away more quickly because its lower density stores less energy and has higher internal losses. Metal idiophones used in Irian Jaya are imported from Indonesian islands farther west.

### Log idiophones

Socially and musically, the most important indigenous Oceanic idiophone may be the log idiophone, a percussion instrument hewn and hollowed from a solid piece of wood. Log idiophones are played in part of northeastern New Guinea, much of Melanesia and West Polynesia, and parts of East Polynesia. Log idiophones take many sizes and shapes. Ensembles of differently sized instruments are notable in central East Polynesia (Cook Islands, Society Islands) and Melanesia. Most versions in western Oceania have a slit narrower than the width of the cavity; Polynesian versions usually have a slit about as wide as the cavity. Most Oceanic log idiophones lie horizontal, but peoples of central Vanuatu set them upright in the ground.

The enclosed air plays a large part in defining the sound and pitch of a log idiophone, since the cavity and slit together form a Helmholtz resonator, excited by vibration of its walls under the influence of a sharp knock. The larger the cavity and the narrower the slit, the lower the pitch. Stamped bamboo tubes, closed by a node below and open above, work similarly, but the air takes the form of a long cylinder.

Players obtain sounds from log idiophones by either of two actions: striking and jolting (see below). Striking gives a short time of contact because the stick rebounds, and the stroke is light because it is determined mostly by the weight of the stick. Jolting gives a heavy stroke and a long time of contact because the weight of the player's hand and arm is effectively attached to that of the stick, and must move with it.

### Other idiophones

Indirectly struck idiophones often fuse dance and music by turning human movements into sounds. Held, or tied to a human torso or limbs, they use a dancer's energy to excite the vibration of various objects: natural bells, made from snail shells, and especially in western Oceania the fruits of *Pangium edule;* chain rattles, in which resonating bodies fastened in series to a string hang from a belt circling the dancer's waist, arms, or legs (figure 3); and bundle rattles and frame rattles, in which resonating bodies fastened to a string cluster in bundles, inside a frame, or on a stick, usually held in a hand. Other Oceanic rattles include suspension rattles, like shark-catching rattles, in which coconut-shell halves are threaded onto rattan rings or sticks, and the *'ūlili,* a Hawaiian pulled rattle, with three empty gourds attached to a string; vessel rattles, usually a gourd containing pebbles, as in the Hawaiian *'ulī'ulī;* and stick rattles, in which the end of a stick is split so individual lengths vibrate against each other, as in the Hawaiian *pū'ili.*

Some idiophones are sounded by plucking. The lamellaphone has a flexible tongue, set or cut within a frame and twanged by a finger or knocked by an attached cord. A quiet instrument, it can produce multiple timbral effects, determined by the size and shape of the player's oral cavity and vocal tract, which act as a resonator. Lamellaphones can convey the illusion of speech, and they may have social value as means of communication among friends and lovers. Especially in Melanesia and New Guinea, they serve as agents of love-controlling magic. In keeping with this symbolism, several western Oceanic societies liken the rhythmic twanging of a lamellaphone to the sexual action of a penis.

Rarely, the vibrations of Oceanic idiophones—notably, an instrument of New Ireland (see below)—are excited by friction. Depending on the materials involved, an

FIGURE 2    An idiophone rhythmically plunged into water to produce sounds said to be the voice of an ancestral crocodile. East Sepik Province, Papua New Guinea. Photo by Museum der Kulturen Basel.

TRACK 20

appropriate degree of friction between the rubbing hand and the surface of the idiophone is achieved by the application of moisture or resin. The vibrations excited often have a high pitch because they are predominantly parallel to the surface rubbed, and the rubbing tends to excite a single mode, giving a definite pitch.

—J. W. Love, Neville H. Fletcher

FIGURE 3　A Hawaiian dancer wears chain rattles (*kūpe'e niho'īlio*) tied under his knees, and in his hand shakes a feather-decorated vessel rattle ('*ulī'ulī*). Drawing by John Webber during Cook's third voyage, 1778. Photo by Smithsonian Institution.

## Hollowed log idiophones of Papua New Guinea

The hollowed log idiophone (Tok Pisin *garamut*) is one of the largest instruments in Papua New Guinea. Garamuts are frequently made of *Vitex cofassus,* a tree also called garamut. The inside of the instrument is hollowed out through a 10-to-15-centimeter-wide slit, running its length. Carved representations of spirits or other images may adorn one or both ends of the log. Most garamuts are between two and three meters long, but some are more than four meters long.

On the New Guinean mainland, garamuts are used in an area that extends from just west of the border with Indonesia (near Jayapura), eastward along the coast and up major rivers, to the vicinity of Lae. It is used throughout the insular provinces, but is absent from Wuvulu-Aua (Manus) and the Baining area of East New Britain. This distribution and that of cognate terms for the instrument suggest that garamuts may have arrived with secondary settlers, long after initial settlements.

Garamuts are played with sticks, whose number and manner of use differ. Instruments are *jolted* if the garamut is hit with the end of a stick (figure 4); they are *struck* if hit with the side of a stick (figure 1a). Jolted garamuts are usually hit with a single stick; in the Middle Sepik area, they are hit with two short sticks, one in each hand. In Manus Province, most garamuts played in ensemble are struck with two sticks.

An isolated example of a garamut-like idiophone appears in the Yonggom area of Western Province, where the instrument is shaped like an oblong bowl with a wide mouth, and is struck on the inside with a stone. Another major deviation from the general form of the garamut occurs at the westernmost limit of its distribution: at Wutung, near the Indonesian border, players strike a suspended plank.

FIGURE 4　Men of Balil Village, Nissan Island, jolt hollowed log idiophones with bundled sticks. Photo by Steven R. Nachman, 1971.

Garamuts function to communicate messages and support singing and dancing. They may make public announcements, as for the arrival of visitors, a call to gather, a request for some item, a death, and so on. Rhythms and textures may specify individuals, clans, objects, numbers, and actions; in combination, such patterns can convey detailed information. For singing and dancing, garamuts may play in unison; but in Manus and parts of North Solomons provinces, differently sized instruments play different rhythms [see ISLAND REGION OF PAPUA NEW GUINEA, figure 4], and in the middle Sepik, paired instruments play interlocked rhythms.

Garamuts may be kept hidden in men's houses in the Middle Sepik and parts of the Rai Coast, but in most other areas they are played publicly by men (rarely by women). In North Solomons Province, people build special, open-sided houses for storing garamuts.

Distinct from large wooden garamuts are small, often hand-held, instruments, made of bamboo and used especially in New Ireland, New Britain, and North Solomons, and for Kiwai dances of Western Province. An internodal slit is cut out of the wall of the bamboo, and the instrument is struck with one stick or, more commonly, two sticks. In the absence of larger wooden instruments, such instruments can be used for signaling, but they most commonly accompany dancing.

—DON NILES

## A Siwai garamut ensemble

In Siwai villages in the late 1930s (Oliver 1955), each clubhouse had a set of *moikui*-wood garamuts, ranging from 1 meter long and 30 centimeters wide to 3 meters long and 1.5 meters wide. Ideally, these instruments stood in a rough circle, placed and labeled by size from largest to smallest: the big one (*ho kou*), his younger brother (*paramoŋ*), their younger brother (*perimoŋ*), *muvomiŋ* (unglossed), fifth one (*aŋumukaŋ*), sixth one (*no'oriki naraŋu*), seventh one (*ki'irike naraŋu*), and *tapivo* (unglossed). The leader's instrument, *ragoi* (a term in Buin, the language of the Siwai's eastern neighbors), was the smallest, placed in the center of the circle. The seven largest instruments were collectively called the body (*mumu*). Some instruments had proper names, like *The Thunderer* and *The Killer*. When clubhouses had more than nine instruments, intermediate ones sat near those of nearest size, from which they took their names.

The garamuts rested on small wooden sleepers (*kupekupe*). With the butt of a stick about 1.2 meters long, players jolted the center of the lip of the slit. The tones produced were not conceived as implying any fixed scalar structure. The garamuts sounded patterns that players linked to make rough narratives. Six signals were beaten on one instrument, usually their younger brother:

- *kuŋkuŋkuŋ*, a call to assemble, usually for work;
- *antara*, an announcement, usually made in the evening, alerting people that an assembly would occur the next morning;
- *akarumiŋimiŋno*, that a special pudding was being prepared;
- *kavoero*, that the pudding was ready;
- *kuroto*, that someone of consequence was approaching;
- *enopi*, that the owner of the clubhouse was angry, as when he discovered that a pig had broken through his garden fence, or learned that someone had slandered him or had tried to seduce his wife.

Four signals were beaten on the big one:

- *aokoto*, that a renowned leader or his wife had died, or that a large pig had been penned up for a feast;

- *eruoto,* that a man had been killed in fighting;
- *ekueku,* that a man who had died by falling from a tree was being cremated (on hearing this, adult males kept away from the funeral, to avoid similar fates);
- *takiruoto,* that warriors should gather to go on a raid.

For a large feast, garamuts announced preparatory stages. The night before, the host's supporters would assemble, one player for each log. The most expert player sounded *ragoi,* and the strongest man present sounded the big one. The host usually assigned these posts, but the other players picked their own; since more players than garamuts were always available, the playing was done in relays.

When everyone was ready, the leader sounded "Vitality-Getting," a warm-up signal. He played it twice through, on *ragoi.* As he began it for the third time, *tapivo* joined in. These instruments then played the signal once in unison, and as they started again, seventh one joined in—and so on, until all the garamuts were sounding in unison. After several repetitions of the signal by the whole ensemble, *ragoi* would sound a quick series of terminal beats and stop playing. *Tapivo* would then do likewise, and so on, around the circle until only the big one would be playing, and then the big one would stop.

After a minute or two, *ragoi* would begin another signal, any of a class called shell ornaments, signals sounded for pleasure. Expert leaders knew forty or fifty of these, and they took pride in their ability to lead for hours without repeating. Shell ornaments varied in length and complexity. Some were simple, like "One at a Time" (*no'no'-ori*), a series of ten moderately slow beats, evenly spaced without variation in accent. Others described real or imaginary events, such as a widely known lament for a *kouakoua* bird: "As I, the *kouakoua,* was warming my eggs on the bank of the stream, the water suddenly rose and washed me downstream; and now I search for my mate." When the player of *ragoi* reproduced the syllabic stresses of these words, Siwai hearers would recognize the poem. The text of a shorter shell ornament illustrates the technique:

| Morokiŋ pupu | The flying-fox sap-of-wild-banana |
| Neuitoŋ, neuitoŋ. | It-is-drinking, it-is-drinking. |

When spoken, the text carries these accents: *Mórokiŋ púpú néuitoŋ, néuitoŋ.* By rhythm and tempo, the garamuts reproduced this pattern.

Some shell ornaments evoked laughter. These included the plaint of the faithful wife who tells how her husband dreams of seeing her fornicating with strangers—and believing his dreams to be true, beats her every morning on awakening. Others were solemn, like the sorrow of the man driven out of his hamlet on the untrue accusation of sorcery. Some described little events of daily life: "The frog is caught in the fish-trap"; "The eel swims down the stream"; "Pigs have eaten my taro"; and so on. Many of them were borrowings from Buin music.

When the stock of shell ornaments ran out, the ensemble would be silent for a few minutes. The leader would then introduce the climactic "Pig-Counting" signal, with a few repetitions of "Man-Killing," the phrase formerly played to announce the killing of an enemy. When this phrase resounded, people would say: "Now it is coming; now they will make the host's renown"—whereupon the whole set of garamuts would beat out the value, in units of shell money, of each pig to be given at the feast. People three and four kilometers away would rouse one another to listen to these signals. To many Siwai, this tally was the high point of the feast.

—Douglas L. Oliver

Since the late 1800s, biscuit and kerosene tins have served as musical instruments in Polynesia. Each instrument is beaten by one person with two sticks. Several tins may be beaten at once.

### Struck plaques of Anuta

For musical accompaniment, many peoples of Oceania musically struck wooden plaques. Particularly in West Polynesia, struck pieces of lumber, whether flat boards or wooden bodies of other shapes, were a cultural icon. They have been reported from Fiji, Sāmoa, Tonga, and Tokelau, and from Polynesian outliers including Bellona, Luangiua, Nukumanu, and Tikopia. Data and recordings provided by Richard Feinberg extend to Anuta their known musical use.

The Anutan struck plaque (*napa*) is a wooden plank, beaten with polished hardwood sticks (*kautaa*) about 50 centimeters long. Musicians use it exclusively for sounding rhythms for dancing; they do not tune it to a specific pitch (in relation to any sung or imagined pitch), nor do they ordinarily use several instruments together. In performance, one percussionist takes control; others may participate. Certain genres invite or require multiple players, who augment or reinforce the leader's rhythms. Most players are males.

### *Musical style*

The Anutan struck plaque emphasizes downbeats. In that musical function, it is roughly analogous to the bass drum in Western marching bands. It does not provide offbeat rat-a-tat-tats typical of more famous Polynesian idiophones, like the *pātē* and the tin.

In the simplest pattern played on a struck plaque, beats sound at a regular pace (figure 5*a*); this pattern may persist from the beginning of the performance to the end. In all the recorded performances on a struck plaque, most downbeats receive emphasis with a hit of at least one stick on the board. In a more complicated pattern (figure 5*b*), an upbeat complements the downbeat, making a metrical contrast with the melody, a two-against-three pattern. The exactness of this metrical relationship does not begin at the beginning of the performance. There, as recorded (not shown),

FIGURE 5 Excerpts from recorded performances of Anutan music show the use of a struck plaque: *a,* stressing downbeats; *b,* stressing downbeats and offbeats that set up a two-against-three pattern; *c,* stressing a downbeat after a rest, in measures 4 and 5. Transcriptions by J. W. Love.

the struck plaque reinforces the melodic meter by strengthening the third beat of the measure; as the performance continues, the temporal position of the percussive upbeat slides to that shown in figure 5c. This change ensues gradually, as the tempo accelerates; but once the illustrated metrical relationship appears, no more shifting occurs, though the tempo may keep accelerating. In the performance from which figure 5c comes, one of the players made a slight variation: from time to time, he struck the offbeat early, or struck a grace note with one stick and the offbeat with the other. This variation did not persist or become regular.

A higher level of rhythmic patterning gives structure to recorded performances of one piece: in each of four stanzas, the percussionists consistently omitted a certain upbeat, and struck the next downbeat especially hard. Such a pattern begins in the fourth full measure of figure 5c. The recorded instances of this pattern mark no common element throughout the melody; nor do the sounds or the senses of the lyrics at those points share any apparent similarity. This pattern may merely emphasize the start of an extended rhythm.

—J. W. LOVE

### Struck tins of Polynesia

Since the late 1800s, light metal biscuit tins and kerosene tins have served as musical instruments, especially in Polynesia. Each instrument is ordinarily beaten by one person, who strikes it with two sticks. Since vigorous percussion deforms its shape, it is soon discarded, and another takes its place. Several tins may be beaten at once.

Though most researchers have ignored the tin, it has value in local music. It has been considered an intruder, but most islanders regard it with respect. In several archipelagoes, the tin takes its local name from English 'copper' via Tongan *kapa* 'sheet metal': Sāmoan *'apa,* Tokelauan *apa.* The Manihikian, Pukapukan, and Tongan name, *tini,* copies the English.

The tin serves prominently in activities that require synchronization: for collective labor, like cutting grass; for sports, like racing canoes and cheering in Sāmoan cricket; for dances with weapons, like the *kailao* of 'Uvea, Tonga, and elsewhere; and for dances that accelerate, like the *fātele* of Tokelau.

The sound of the tin, readily accepted in much Polynesian music and dance, must be understood as an extension of an indigenous aesthetic, traditionally involving percussive sounds gotten from small log idiophones. The tin extends and enhances the range of the highest such instrument, to whose musical role it adds a rattling brittleness. Sāmoans play one or more tins alongside one or more small log idiophones (*pātē*). In Sikaiana, under the name *pulotu,* the tin probably replaces a wooden instrument of the same name. In Takuu, five-gallon tins play with log idiophones. In percussive ensembles of the Cook Islands, a tin may replace the highest-pitched log idiophone.

Throughout the Society Islands since 1900 or earlier, percussionists accompanied dancers by beating on tins (Tahitian *punu*). Starting in 1948, the rules of competition have specifically banned this practice, as they have in competitions in the Cook Islands. For Tahitian dancing in Hawai'i in the 1960s and early 1970s, percussionists also used the tin.

Tins may serve alternately with other idiophones as a distinguishing element of a genre. In Mangareva, a tin accompanies indigenously conceived dramatic enactments (*pe'i*), but Tahitian dances are accompanied by small log idiophones (*tō'ere*).

In Tokelau, Protestant missionaries encouraged playing on tins. On Fakaofo in 1882, their followers played to drown out the log idiophone (*lali*) that Roman Catholics struck to signal the start of services (Thomas 1996). The instrumentation of *fātele,* century-old dances, may be a compromise between the sounds of wood and those of tin (perhaps earlier representing Roman Catholic and Protestant sonorities

FIGURE 6    While Tokelau dancers perform at the Festival of Pacific Arts, drummers hit a wooden box (*pōkihi*) with their hands. Photo by Adrienne L. Kaeppler, 1988.

respectively), either through the partnership of wooden box (*pōkihi*) and tin, or by the incorporation of tins as resonators within the wooden box (figure 6).

—ALLAN THOMAS

TRACK 22–26

### Friction blocks of New Ireland

Friction blocks (*lounuat,* figure 7), wooden idiophones unique to New Ireland, have three tongues (seldom four or five), which when rubbed make a piercing sound. Only in the late twentieth century, when the instrument lost its deeper spiritual significance, could its background be explored. Its production, use, and playing remain secret and concealed from noninitiates.

The instrument comes in three sizes. A small version (12–20 centimeters) produces a shrill, penetrating squeak. Some of its names are Nalik *karao* 'lizard', Kara *qatqat* 'small frog', Tabar-Mandar *kulekuleng* 'tiny night-active bird', Noatsi *ngutsikande* 'small noisy bird'. A medium version (25–35 centimeters) produces a smoother, high-pitched sound. Some of its names are Nalik *manibobos* 'night-active bird', Kara *paleseqau* 'smaller bird'), Tabar-Mandar *kinato* 'small night-active bird with a smooth cry'. A large version (40–65 centimeters) produces a medium-high-pitched sound. Some of its names are *launut, lounut, lounuat, leinuat, lunuat* (from Tabar *lunit,* probably the generic term for the instrument*)*; Noatsi *miluk* 'big night-active bird'; Tabar-Mandar *ma* 'bird'; Noatsi *ma(n) lounuat, ma(n) lavinuat* 'bird-*lounuat*'.

Other names, collected by researchers when the tradition was intact, do not indicate size: *gulwochnak* (a nonsense word); *lapka, lauka, livika, pika, vika* (birds of the Lelet Plateau, central New Ireland); Tigak *taparpar* 'bird' and *gulle bangenggeg* 'going into the forest to mourn'; Nalik *manu vezaq* 'the bird cries'; Noatsi *vutsikande,* a misinterpretation of *ngutsikande* 'small, noisy bird'.

Larger versions are said to sound like a bird; smaller ones, like geckoes, frogs, or squeaking birds. Bird-related names prevail. This fact and the legend of the origin of the *lounuat* suggest that latter-day cults have acquired the instrument from a preexisting cultural stratum. The legend says a woman discovered the instrument upside-down in a cave on the beach, where waves were pushing it to and fro, making it cry. Afraid, she ran home to tell her husband. He seized it and tried to make it work. In vain he knocked it, and then blew air onto it. Finally, by rubbing it, he made it cry. In *lounuat*-using societies, all important customary objects originated with women, who yielded them to men.

FIGURE 7    A friction block from New Ireland. Institut für Völkerkunde, Göttingen, Germany.

### Manufacture and learning

The *lounuat* is made from the wood of the tree *savaf,* which also serves for canoes, masks, and sculptures. Knowledge of its manufacture, restricted to the men of a few subclans, passes down through maternal moieties. This copyright is valuable cultural property.

Customs relating to the manufacture of *lounuat* vary locally. All require ritual payments at certain stages. While fasting and abstaining from sex, Noatsi men carve them in a cave near the beach. The freeing-of-the-tongue ritual requires a feast for initiated maternal clansmen. Having used stone knives to cut the wood, glowing coconut shells to hollow the tongues, and the skin of a shark or a ray for polishing, the carver saws into the wooden plates a delicate cut with a specific rope. Then the instrument can reproduce ancestral voices.

A *lounuat* master accepts only adepts displaying appropriate behavior and customary knowledge. He initiates apprentices into its secrets by making them reenact the legend. Starting with silent observation, they move stepwise through its plot. He expels students who fail his tests.

Players rank high. Their office, kept for life, requires them to behave perfectly. In return for playing, they receive prestigious gifts, including the most highly valued parts of butchered pigs, other high-prestige foods, and shell money. Formerly, when a performer died, his instruments would be cremated with him, or thrown with his body into the sea.

### Tuning and playing

The tongues are tuned relatively. Each instrument has a unique tuning, but all feature a sequence of low–medium–high. (One exception shows a medium–low–high pattern.) The intended sound is a piercing, beating cluster, with a frightening effect for noninitiates. *Lounuat* are played in different sizes simultaneously, in ensembles of twenty or more. At grand occasions, like funerals, they join an ensemble of reeds and swung slats.

Players hold small instruments in one hand. They address medium and large ones in either of two ways: sitting with the instrument between their thighs, and standing with the instrument between their legs. To get enough friction, they moisten their palms and fingers with the sap of rubber or breadfruit trees. Each player rubs the tongues in the direction of his body, from the farthest (with the lowest pitch) to the nearest. While hearing the sound of the instruments, noninitiates may not look at the players or the instruments.

Most of the music has been forgotten. It served for signaling (as did that of log idiophones), when it announced the deaths of important men or women. Only three ritual pieces survive. Their structure is intricate: a rhythmic series of low, medium, and high pitches, in slow and fast modes. In Nalik, these pieces are "*Di Vozi*" ('A Gasping Man Climbs the Hill'), "*Di Buak a Rangana Urima*" ('Pluck a Branch from the *Urima*'), and "*A Vel(e) Sikau Ina Gom i Varakaum*" ('Two Singing Birds Alternate').

### Acoustics

Played indoors, one instrument was measured at a sound-pressure level of 115 decibels, almost painfully loud. (The human threshold of pain is about 130 decibels.) Sonagrams of the sound show no overtones—probably because overtones more than 30 decibels below the level of a fundamental do not register on the equipment. Fourier analysis of the waveform shows that some overtones are insignificantly involved. The *lounuat* produces a quasi-sinewave tone, mixed with friction-produced noise. This pattern is unusual among idiophones. In culturally conditioned noninitiates, the sound of twenty or more of these instruments being played at once may indeed arouse fear.

—GERALD FLORIAN MESSNER

## MEMBRANOPHONES

Instruments of the drum family—membranophones—have as their vibrating element a thin membrane stretched elastically over a supporting rim. The membrane controls the vibrations and is responsible for efficiently radiating the sound. The frequencies of the vibrations are set primarily by the thickness of the membrane, the tension with which it is stretched, and its area. A thin membrane of small area under high tension produces a high fundamental pitch. The shape of the membrane has a less important effect on frequency.

The membranes of drums are usually supported on deep cylindrical rims, partly for convenience and mechanical strength, and partly to separate acoustically the two sides of the membrane, increasing the loudness of the radiated sound. The rim of some drums extends to form a nearly closed cavity or a long pipe, and the elastic properties of the air in this cavity can modify the vibrational frequencies of the membrane. The general effect of such a cavity is to act as a resonator, reinforcing the radiation from particular low modes of the membrane's vibration, giving the drum a distinct pitch.

Changing the tension of the membrane can vary its pitch over a moderate interval, typically about a major third up or down. The frequency can be lowered by the attachment of a heavy object or objects to the center of the membrane. This attachment has the effect of making the first few membrane-generated frequencies nearly harmonics of its fundamental, giving the drum a pronounced tonal character. Such a technique is common on kundus, hourglass-shaped drums of New Guinea, to whose membranes players often affix pellets of wax or resin. Vigorous strokes increase the tension of the membrane, so that its pitch, at first slightly high, falls as the sound decays; this effect may be more noticeable with a loaded membrane.

The indigenous drums of Oceania have only one membrane, typically the skin of a lizard in New Guinea and Melanesia, and of a shark in Micronesia and Polynesia. Western Oceanic drums are normally tubular or hourglass-shaped instruments held in the hand; most Polynesian drums are free-standing, footed kettledrums. Kundus and East Polynesian kettledrums often bear intricate carvings: kundus on the handle and the body; kettledrums on the feet and supporting stand, often depicting stylized human shapes holding up the rest of the instrument.

Oceanic drums are typically played with the fingers and the palms. The palm, which remains in contact with the membrane, gives a heavier sound, but strokes of fingers or sticks give lighter and more ringing tones. The Tahitian *pahu* and the Tongan *nafa,* huge double-headed drums played with a stick or sticks, derive from European bass drums (figure 8). The Hawaiian *pūniu,* a fishskin-headed coconut shell often tied to a dancer's knee, is played with a braided fiber thong [see MUSIC AND RELIGION, figure 9].

Snare drums, introduced for use in brass bands and pipers' bands, have two membranes, usually at opposite ends of a cylindrical shell. With sticks, the player strikes the upper membrane. The acoustic effect of the lower membrane can be varied by tuning it in unison with the first or to some other interval. The lower membrane has cords (snares) running just above its surface, so its vibration causes impact with the snares and generates a high-frequency rattle, emphasizing rapid rhythms.

The sound of a drum decays rapidly because the membrane, being light, cannot store much mechanical energy, and being large in relation to its thickness, loses its energy quickly by radiating its sound. Sounds produced by drums with snares decay

FIGURE 8    At the Methodist conference of
1967, Tongan men play three *nafa*. Photo by
Adrienne L. Kaeppler.

FIGURE 8    At the Methodist conference of 1967, Tongan men play three *nafa*. Photo by Adrienne L. Kaeppler.

rapidly, but sounds produced by drums with a large coupled-air volume have longer times of decay. These traits affect how various membranophones function: in Oceanic brass-band music, bass drums normally accent downbeats; snare drums, though they often reinforce downbeats, add decoration on offbeats.

The timbre of a drum can vary in two ways. First, striking the drumhead in different places can excite its vibration modes to different relative amplitudes. Because a fundamental excited by a central blow is rapidly damped, drummers usually strike the head near one edge, so as to make the next higher mode the prevailing one in the excitation. Second, changing the hardness of the beater can vary the timbre: a small, hard beater excites all modes of the membrane, giving a sound describable as hard and dry; a large, soft beater damps out higher-frequency modes, concentrating vibrations into modes of lower frequency and giving a deeper sound.

—J. W. LOVE, NEVILLE H. FLETCHER

## Kundus of Papua New Guinea

The drum known in Tok Pisin as kundu (Hiri Motu *gaba*) is one of the most widespread instruments of Papua New Guinea. It is so important that it adorns the national emblem [see THE MUSIC AND DANCE OF MELANESIA: figure 1]. It is found in every province of the country, but in parts of the Island Region it is absent, especially in much of Manus, the eastern part of New Ireland, the Baining area of East New Britain, and most of North Solomons.

Most commonly, the body of the kundu is shaped like an hourglass; cylindrical, conical, and goblet shapes also occur. A typical length is about 80 to 90 centimeters, but in some areas, instruments are small (about 27 centimeters) and long (about 280 centimeters). The wood used for kundus varies by local preference and availability. The most common species are *Pterocarpus indicus* (Tok Pisin *nar*), *Vitex cofassus* (*garamut*), *Intsia bijuga* (*kwila*), and trees of genus *Litsea*.

The wood is hollowed out by a combination of scraping, chiseling, and burning. The people of some areas carve a central handle from the wood. Designs may be carved into the body of the instrument and painted; the presence or absence of such decorations and their form are culturally specific. The open end of the instrument is usually left in its round shape, but in parts of Gulf and Western provinces it may be carved into jawlike forms. As a substitute for wood, bamboo sometimes serves. In the Adzera area of Morobe, the body of the *simpup gur* is made of clay—apparently the only such occurrence in the country.

Many kinds of skin serve for the drumhead. In lowlands, the skin of the monitor (*Varanus indicus*) is commonly used; in the highlands, where large lizards are absent, the skin of the ringtail (*Pseudocheirus forbesi*) is frequently used. Skins from other large lizards, crocodiles, sea snakes (especially *Acrochordus arafurae* in coastal areas of

Gulf and Western provinces), wallabies, tree kangaroos, cuscuses, bandicoots, fish, and pigs are occasionally used, as are skins of more recently introduced animals, including cats, cows, deer, dogs, and goats. The Hewa of Southern Highlands use the skin of a megapode, *Talegalla jobiensis*—the only known instance of birdskin serving as a drumhead in Papua New Guinea. The skins of cassowaries are used in parts of Irian Jaya.

Removed and dried, the skin is glued with sap to one end of the instrument. String may be wrapped around the skin; especially in the highlands, a rattan ring may be placed over it. Lacing through holes in the skin is apparently restricted to parts of the Sepik and Wuvulu and Aua Islands in Manus; this trait links the latter area to Micronesia. The use of wedges between the skin and a supporting ring—occurring only on instruments of some Sepik villages, and on the Gogodala *diwaka* in Western Province—is also uncommon in the country.

Each kundu is tuned to whatever pitch enables it to resonate well. For tuning, players increase the mass of the vibrating membrane, most often by adding blobs of beeswax (*Trigona sp.*) to the central area of the skin, which they further tune by adjusting the blobs and heating the skin over a fire. In the Nankina and Teptep area of Madang, they tune the membrane by smearing moist clay onto it, and they cannot use heat, which would dry the clay out.

Most kundus are held in one hand and struck on the head with the other. Seated players lay the instrument across their laps; the large Gogodala instrument lies on the floor. Scattered reports say certain kundus are hidden from females and uninitiated males, but only in Mountain Ok areas of West Sepik and Western provinces is playing restricted to men who have completed a certain initiatory stage. Elsewhere, women play special music on kundus.

Kundus often accompany singing, for which they provide a basic rhythmic pulse. Their rhythms can be complex, with players cueing changes of rhythm, and thus of movement. In much of the country, performers play the same rhythm at the same time. In Eastern Highlands, where kundus are a new concept, playing is asynchronous. In parts of Northern and Milne Bay provinces, differently sized kundus play different rhythms together. String bands occasionally use kundus. Bands that meld indigenous and Western musics, like Sanguma and Tambaran Culture, place kundus upright in stands for playing with both hands.    —DON NILES

## Drums of East Polynesia

Single-headed cylindrical membranophones standing vertically on a carved footed base that raises the septum above the ground are found in the Austral Islands, the Cook Islands, Hawai'i, Mangareva, the Marquesas, the Society Islands, and the Tuamotus. Usually designated *pahu* or *pa'u,* they likely developed within East Polynesia, and were not known elsewhere in Oceania.

Hawaiian *pahu,* ranging in height from 22 to 114 centimeters, are usually carved from coconut or breadfruit wood (Kaeppler 1980); Marquesan examples, carved of *Cordia subcordata* or other woods, range in height from 33 to 243 centimeters (Moulin 1997); examples from the Austral Islands are quite tall in relation to their diameter.

Covered with specially prepared skin of a shark or a ray, *pahu* are usually lashed with coconut fiber. The player strikes the head with various parts of the hand—the flat palm, the cupped palm, the fingers, the heel, and the sides. Striking the center of the membrane produces sounds different from those produced by striking at the edge—differences that players rhythmically exploit for musical effects (Tatar 1993).

The languages of most areas of East Polynesia differentiate these drums simply by size, but in Hawai'i, a secondary drum (*pūniu* or *kilu*), a fishskin-headed coconut

FIGURE 9    A Hawaiian *pahu* with human images, whose upstretched arms form crescents; collected during Cook's third voyage, 1778–1779. British Museum, London. Photo by British Museum.

TRACK 27

shell, provides an additional sound when a player strikes the skin with a braided fiber thong. A rich vocabulary—denoting the size and the shape of the drums, the musical parts various drums play, the sounds of the drums, the techniques used in drumming, and the social functions of the drumming—has cognate terms throughout East Polynesia.

### Performance using pahu

A performance can combine a text, the sounds through which it is articulated, a drum, the sound of the drum, the human movements through which the drum sounds, and associated ritual movements. *Pahu* may be played singly; or, for an array of different pitches and timbres, they can be played in pairs or sets of different sizes (Tatar 1993).

Early written references to *pahu* usually situate them in sacred ritual use in outdoor temples, played for the articulation of texts on one tone or a few tones usually described by outsiders as chanting, and often associated with ritual movements usually described by outsiders as dancing. The carving of the base often portrayed a series of upturned crescents (Hawaiian *hoaka*), which in the earliest surviving examples (from the late 1700s) appear to be abstracted symbolic representations of upstretched arms (figure 9). These crescents may have housed the drum's spiritual strength, its mana (Kaeppler 1993).

*Pahu* are sounded in rhythmic motifs that often bear names. In Hawai'i, typical motifs are played with *pahu* and *pūniu* in standard forms, though with varied stresses. As high-status ritual objects, *pahu* received personal names, and they were fabricated in association with rituals dealing with carving the body and lashing the membrane. The sound they produced was considered a voice, and they were inherited within chiefly or priestly lines. Besides being used in the service of gods, *pahu* announced important births, opened and closed wars, and marked funeral and memorial services. Today, they accompany dances and rituals of ethnic identity, especially in Hawai'i and Tahiti.

—ADRIENNE L. KAEPPLER

## CHORDOPHONES

Since the late 1800s, the inventory of chordophones in Oceania has probably undergone more drastic changes than have that of the other classes of instruments. As indigenous musical instruments, chordophones were rare; but in the form of guitars and ukuleles, they have become common, and their music has crossed cultural and national borders in ways other indigenous instruments have not.

The indigenous chordophones are quiet instruments. Their sound is usually audible only to their players and to listeners no more than a few meters away. Most cultures of Oceania highly value the noisiness of public display, correspondingly devaluing soloistic instrumental performance. Indigenous chordophones therefore do not enjoy public prestige. They are often instruments of private magic, lovers' communication, and children's amusement. Introduced chordophones—banjos, guitars, mandolins, ukuleles—are louder; when played in ensembles, and especially when amplified electrically, they accompany singing and dancing in public venues, and even furnish instrumental music without singing.

Stretched strings are musically important because their pitch can readily be changed. The fundamental frequency of a string varies directly as the square root of its tension and inversely with its length. To reach a given frequency, thick and heavy strings require greater tension than light strings. String tension is usually adjusted to fix the basic pitch of the full-length string, and stringed instruments can have strings of different lengths for different tones, as do multistringed idiochord tube zithers of

In the New Guinea islands, modern instrumental music and nomenclature show Polynesian influence. As a musical shorthand, this nomenclature enabled musicians to play together without rehearsal. Musical leaders could give verbal cues to guide performances.

FIGURE 10    Mabu plucks the string of a Huli musical bow. Photo by Jacqueline Pugh-Kitingan, 1978.

Irian Jaya (Van Hille 1907:621) and two-stringed musical bows of New Ireland and the Solomons (Kunst 1967:47). In New Britain and the Sepik area of New Guinea, a tuning noose enables one string to produce two tones (Fischer 1986:71).

Stopping, usually with a finger, can reduce the vibrating length of a string and raise its pitch. Halving the length of the string doubles the frequency, raising the pitch by an octave. Pitch may be varied in fixed steps (when a fingerboard has frets), or continuously (when a fingerboard is smooth). The former method is typical of introduced chordophones; the latter, of indigenous ones.

### Exciting vibrations

A player may excite vibrations simply by plucking or striking a string (figure 10). The position of the pluck or strike affects the relative amplitudes of the overtones: high overtones have greater relative amplitude when the excitation point is near one end of the string. The amplitude of the vibration is proportional to the force of the pluck or strike.

Typical methods of playing chordophones in Oceania are plucking with a finger or a plectrum, and striking with a light stick. Each of these methods is used for musical bows of New Guinea, the Solomons, Vanuatu, and East Polynesia. An important Polynesian musical bow is the ʻūkēkē, a half-meter-long multistringed Hawaiian bow, held crosswise in the mouth, with unstopped strings plucked by the fingers or a plectrum. Similar bows, with cognate names, are used in the Marquesas, the Tuamotus, and the Society Islands; a comparable bow with a different name is used in Aotearoa.

The amplitudes of high overtones are reduced if the string is made of soft material, which dissipates high-frequency energy. Such is sometimes the case with idiochord instruments, whose string may be a fiber separated and raised up from the body of the instrument.

Strings can also be excited by the friction of a transversely moving bow, made from hair stretched on a wooden frame and treated with material such as resin to increase the friction. That is the usual method of sounding violins and related instruments, but it was rare or unknown in precontact Oceania.

### Resonating vibrations

A simple vibrating string radiates almost no acoustic energy because its diameter is small relative to the wavelength of the sound. For this reason, at least one end of the string is usually connected to a larger structure, like a gourd or a wooden box, which the string sets into vibration, radiating the sound. The resonances of this structure selectively reinforce overtones of the string's vibration in particular frequency ranges, giving each instrument a characteristic timbre.

The musical quality of a stringed instrument depends on the acoustic properties of the resonant body. The connection between the string and this body is sometimes made by anchoring the end of the string to it, or (in the case of idiochord bows) raising fibers up from the bow. On instruments of the violin family, a light structure, called a bridge, is placed between the strings and the body. Plucked stringed instruments, like guitars and ukuleles, have one end of the strings usually attached to a light anchoring bridge mounted on a thin part of the body, the soundboard.

Musical quality can also depend on attachments to the resonator. The *belembaotuyan,* an introduced musical bow of the Marianas, exemplifies this use. A player cups the open side of the resonator against his belly. Its pressure against his skin, and the tautness of his abdominal muscles, affect the timbre of the resonated sound.

—J. W. LOVE, NEVILLE H. FLETCHER

## Guitars in the New Guinea islands

Between 1945 and 1965, chordophone-based ensembles known first as *pilai gita* 'play guitar' (or simply *pilai*) and now as string bands (Tok Pisin *stringben*) emerged in Melanesia. Guitars and ukuleles, largely because of their portability and affordability, were the foundation of these ensembles. Melanesians especially liked the guitar's potential for stylistic versatility, since it was equally adaptable to styles performed in Allied camps during the war—swing, boogie-woogie, cowboy—and gospel and Hawaiian songs. Guitar proficiency became a desirable social skill (Attenborough 1960:164).

### Tunings

In the New Guinea islands, modern instrumental music and its associated nomenclature show strong Polynesian influence. Fundamental to this music was the concept of tuning (Tok Pisin *ki* 'key'). The term *ki* originated with slack-key guitars (Kanahele 1979:353) in Hawai'i, where, as in the New Guinea islands, the word *ki* forms part of local names for specific slack-key tunings.

In the 1940s, New Guinea islanders learned a tuning known as *Fiji ki* 'Fijian tuning'. This may have been an alternative name for *faiv ki* 'five tuning' or *tri ki* 'three tuning', or for both terms, which, with *blu maunten* 'blue mountain' (also *blu ki*), New Guinea islanders favored in the 1950s. Tolai guitarists were familiar with tunings known as *Suva ki* 'Suva tuning', *Awai ki* 'Hawaiian tuning', *Taiti* 'Tahitian', and *Spenish* 'Spanish'; they believed, as did others (Lomax n.d.; Waterman 1990:46–47), that Spanish tuning had originated in Hawai'i. By the late 1950s, numerous guitar tunings were circulating in the New Guinea islands. Jack Tonga, an outstanding guitarist and songwriter from the Duke of York Islands, composed songs in at least ten tunings. Other performers, including the Tolai master John Wowono, specialized in only one or two tunings, developing idiosyncratic styles.

Around Rabaul, performers used the term *ki* in more general ways. *Rong ki* 'wrong tuning' designated the modification of a standard tuning, usually in the islands by lowering the pitch of one string. Most tunings had associated *rong ki*; some players used *rong ki bilong faiv ki* 'wrong tuning of five tuning'. The term *rap ki* 'rubbed tuning' distinguished tunings capable of being picked or strummed. Jack Tonga says the Hawaiian, Fijian, and Spanish tunings are all *rap ki*.

### Stylistic elements in the New Guinea islands

The existence of a standardized pidgin nomenclature bespeaks a process of social cooperation involving the pooling of knowledge about pieces and practices. As a musical shorthand, this nomenclature enabled musicians to play together without rehearsal. Strong musical leaders could give spontaneous verbal cues to guide ensembles through performances.

The harmonic vocabulary of most songs in most tunings was limited to the primary triads: chords I, IV, and V, known as *wan, tu, tri,* respectively. A major chord built on the second scalar degree (functioning as V of V) was known as *flat.* The use of this chord signaled a fleeting modulation to the dominant key. Bands of the 1940s and 1950s confined it mostly to instrumental sections framing vocal sections, but bands later incorporated it into the harmonic structure of songs. Vocal harmonization consisted of a simple improvisatory layering of thirds with much parallel movement—a practice learned from singing hymns.

The instrumental passage known as step was an important stylistic feature of guitar ensembles. It served as an introduction and conclusion to every song. The term *step* gained wide currency in Papua New Guinea, as its use in a remote area indicates (Kelsey 1993:215). By 1970, Tolai string bands had codified the harmonic sequence of the step as a bipartite phrase: I–IV–I–V, I–IV–V–I. Numerous string bands employed this pattern with little variation; others experimented with alternatives. The step became these bands' signature, wherein their most skilled guitarist would perform a planned but improvisatory-sounding sequence of jaunty, country-style melodic runs, interspersed with hammer-ons and strummed or plucked chords. In the step, a solo guitar would often play a brief, "harmonically deceptive" line, leading into an "engaging group strum" (Clark 1981). In steps, to catch listeners' attention, musicians playfully disrupted Western harmonic relationships.

Until the 1970s, most guitarists in the New Guinea islands tended to play the same step for every song. The leader signaled a return to the step (after all the stanzas of a given song had been sung) by calling out *step* or some other commonly understood cue, like *taxi*—a signal in imitation of hailing a taxi. Rarer signals include the Tolai term *marue* 'vomit', the borrowed term *hula* (used by a shipboard Nauruan string band), and the Tok Pisin term *holim* 'hold it'. In many recordings of the 1960s, the step sounds as if it has simply been tacked on to the beginning and ending of songs.

In the years before the chordophone ensemble became standardized as the string band, notions of musical foreground and background, or of melody and accompaniment, were absent. The instruments and voices built up a dense, mid-to-high-range texture, with minimal sound-source stratification. Musicians did little specializing in instrumental roles, but a guitarist often filled sung phrases with bass runs, connecting chordal roots. Guitarists often used picking patterns, but ukuleleists strummed. Guitarists preferred a jangle, achieved by plucking close to the bridge—a technique that probably developed to project the sound of the guitar, particularly when playing outdoors.

The guitars and ukuleles set up a metrical foundation, employing rhythms relevant to the dances they were accompanying. In the early 1960s, use of the alternating bass-strum cowboy pattern, with its four-beat metrical groupings, became common. In the 1970s, string bands' primary function, providing music for dancing, shifted with creative challenges newly posed by public competitions, held in urban centers. Giving indigenous musical elements the highest priority, musicians discarded the square patternings of beats—a musical change reflecting the climate of political determination, particularly in Rabaul.

By the mid-1980s, transnational popular music had established itself as the preferred music of urbanized youth in the New Guinea islands. Bands systematically replaced their techniques with techniques specific to the new idioms. Without consistent support from the recording industry, the older-style bands by the early 1990s had become marginal, but some of their stylistic elements carried over into the styles loosely called Pacific country and island reggae.          —MICHAEL WEBB

## Slack-key guitars

The term *slack-key guitar* denotes an orally transmitted, Hawaiian-developed method of playing acoustic guitar. The Hawaiian-language equivalent of the term, *kī hōʻalu,* means 'to slacken the key'. This refers to the practice of loosening the strings to alter the standard guitar tuning.

Many slack-key tunings produce diatonic chords when strummed. Specifically named tunings vary among players, who formerly guarded them and handed them down within families, or from teacher to student. Since the 1970s, instructional books specifying tunings have been published by famous players, including Keola Beamer, Raymond Kāne, Leonard Kwan, and Mike McClellan. Beamer and Kane have published instructional videos [see FILMS AND VIDEOS OF OCEANIC PERFORMING ARTS]. Among the most common tunings are taro patch (from low strings to high, D–G–D–G–B–D), *wahine* (D–G–D–F#–B–D), and Mauna Loa (D–G–D–D–G–D).

Slack-key playing involves picking a melody on the higher-pitched strings while playing an accompaniment on the lower-pitched strings. Slack-key guitarists use three techniques. To hammer on refers to stopping a string on the fretboard after plucking it, producing two successive sounds on one string. Pulling off refers to the opposite, of plucking a string stopped at a fret, then pulling the finger off the fretboard, leaving the open string to continue vibrating. Chimes are harmonics, produced by lightly stopping a string at simple fractions of its length.

In its basic form, slack-key playing consists of repetitive patterns that can serve as accompaniment. Though any song may be rendered in slack-key style, Hawaiians have most often applied the method to *hula kuʻi,* strophic songs, each strophe consisting of one or two couplets of poetry and offering the guitarist opportunities to embellish basic patterns.

The introduction of the guitar to Hawaiʻi is credited to Mexican cowboys, brought over in the 1830s to manage cattle. Among Hawaiians who eventually assumed the skills and responsibilities of ranching, the guitar remained popular in times of leisure. The slack-key method of playing developed largely in rural, and specifically ranching, contexts, and emerged in commercial recordings of Hawaiian music in the late 1940s.

One performer in particular, Gabby Pahinui (1921–1980), is widely revered for his virtuosity, heard on recordings on the Waikiki, Hula, and Panini labels, spanning three decades. In 1987, Raymond Kāne was awarded a National Heritage Fellowship from the National Endowment for the Arts. In the early 1990s, two documentary films about slack-key guitar (Friedman 1994; Kamae 1993) were released.

—AMY KUʻULEIALOHA STILLMAN

## Steel guitars

The steel guitar (Hawaiian *kikā kila*) is possibly the most influential and iconic musical instrument of Hawaiʻi. Its sweet, gliding sounds, made by sliding a metal bar across the strings of a guitar, is widely diffused through recordings, films, television, and live performances. Besides Hawaiian music, the steel guitar has crossed over into country, pop, blues, rock, and many world musics.

Most scholars credit eleven-year-old Joseph Kekuku of Lāʻie with discovering the steel guitar in 1885. Walking along a railroad track, he picked up a loose bolt, which he rubbed across the strings of the guitar he was carrying. The resulting slides inspired him. After seven years of experimenting with materials and shapes, he settled on a 10-centimeter-long, bullet-shaped steel bar, with which he crafted the microtonal slides, augmented chords, harmonics, and timbral variations that became basic to the steel-guitar tradition. Other important aspects of playing the steel guitar include metal picks for plucking or strumming, open tunings, and an unusually high bridge ("high action") to avoid bumping the frets.

After popularizing the steel guitar in Hawaiʻi, Kekuku left the islands in 1904 to tour America and Europe in shows that included the Broadway musical *Bird of Paradise.* Many other steel-guitar pioneers—Frank Ferera, Ben Hokea, Sol Hoʻopiʻi, Andy Iona, Joe Kaipo, Walter Kolomoku, Pale Lua, Dick McIntire, Tau Moe, Benny Nawahi, and July Paka, and others—also emigrated, enticed by an international demand for Hawaiian music. Many of them followed the vaudeville circuit and taught other musicians through private lessons and instruction books. Most recorded prolifically, performing a broad spectrum of material, Hawaiian and non-Hawaiian. The closest bonds developed with jazz and country. Sol Hoʻopiʻi and Benny Nawahi often played hot swing with Hawaiian melodies. Among Hoʻopiʻi's students was Roy Smeck, who achieved fame as a jazz virtuoso. Frank Ferera, who recorded more than a thousand titles under his own name, accompanied early cowboy star Vernon Dalhart. On several releases, Joe Kaipo backed up country legend Jimmie Rodgers. By the 1930s, a steel guitar was an integral part of country ensembles.

The popularity of the instrument led to mainland manufacture and important innovations in design. The metal-resonator guitars created by National and the Dopra brothers in the 1920s gave way in the 1930s to electric instruments, the first of which surfaced in western swing bands. By the 1940s, all the major steel guitarists in Hawaiʻi had gone electric. They used the features of electric amplification to perfect a soothing, relaxing (*nahenahe*) sweetness that complemented the crooning of Hawaiian melodies and helped set up an idyllic atmosphere in nightclubs.

In the 1940s and 1950s, Hawaiian electric steel guitars enjoyed international popularity, largely because of major-label recordings, Hollywood movies, and "Hawaiʻi Calls," a radio program that opened with a steel guitar beckoning softly above the waves of Waikīkī. Masters of the electric steel guitar in Hawaiʻi during this era included Pua Almeida, Barney Isaacs, David Keliʻi, Annie Kerr, Billy Hew Len, Benny Rogers, and Jules Ah See.

In the 1970s, the steel guitar began losing favor. The causes of its decline were its connection to tourism, the difficulty of mastering it, the popularity of standard guitars in contemporary pop music, and the ascendancy of slack-key guitar, a style that predated steel, but had never been associated with commercial music. The public still supported some steel-guitar performances like the work of David Feet Rogers with the Sons of Hawaiʻi, and of Gabby Pahinui with his own group and Ry Cooder. Younger players, like Alan Akaka and Eddie Palama, emerged, but the average age of players and fans began to rise.

In the early 1990s, the Hawaiian steel guitar enjoyed a revival. Several groups now perform with electric steel, and a few musicians are returning to acoustic steel, often named by the country term *dobro.* No important innovations in the mechanics of the instrument or the style of its music have occurred. Once Hawaiʻi's trendiest innovation, steel has become a voice of nostalgia.                —JAY W. JUNKER

## ʻUkulele

The roots of the *ʻukulele* (known in English as the ukulele) lie in the four-stringed *braguinha,* a Portuguese version of the guitar, brought to Hawaiʻi by agricultural workers immigrating from Madeira in 1879. Favored at the court of King Kalākaua in Honolulu, the instrument was incorporated into performances of the nascent Westernized *hula kuʻi* by the early 1880s. It has since functioned as an icon of Hawaiian music, especially in the wave of interest that swept the U.S. mainland from about 1910 to the 1920s.

The earliest makers of *ʻukulele* in Hawaiʻi were Portuguese. Augusto Diaz and Manuel Nunes, who had established shops in Honolulu by 1884, were joined by Jose do Espirito Santo in 1888 (Felix et al. 1980). Samuel Kamaka began a manufacturing business in 1916; other Hawaiian manufacturers in the 1920s and 1930s included the Kaai, Kahola, and Kumalae brands. During the instrument's mainland vogue, American guitar manufacturers Gibson, Martin, and Weissenborn began producing *'ukulele.* In the 1990s, Kamaka's grandsons still operate the sole mass-production factory in Hawai'i, though independent makers have established businesses.

*'Ukulele* come in several sizes. The smallest, called soprano or standard *'ukulele,* is about 46 to 53 centimeters long, with twelve to seventeen chromatic frets. The next size, called concert *'ukulele,* is about 61 centimeters long, with up to nineteen frets. Next larger is the tenor *'ukulele,* about 71 centimeters long, with eighteen to twenty-two frets. The largest, called baritone or bass *'ukulele,* is up to 81 centimeters long, and has up to twenty-two frets. Strings are most often nylon. Four-stringed instruments predominate. On tenor and baritone *'ukulele,* six-, eight-, ten-, and twelve-stringed models are produced by doubling or tripling the courses—a construction that enriches the sonority of the instrument (*Extraordinary Ukuleles: The Tsumura Collection from Japan* 1993).

The body of the *'ukulele* normally resembles that of the guitar. An oval-shaped body, affectionately nicknamed pineapple, has also been developed. The highest-quality instruments manufactured in Hawai'i use local woods, especially *koa* and *kou.*

### Tunings and strumming

In Hawai'i, the *'ukulele* uses one standard tuning. From top to bottom as a right-handed player holds the instrument, the strings are tuned G–C–E–A, all within the compass of the sixth C–A, and with arbitrary referential pitch. The *'ukulele* offers melodic leads and chordal accompaniments. Accounts from the 1880s reveal its virtuosic appeal. Players dazzled audiences with rapid picking, hence the instrument's Hawaiian name: *'uku* means 'flea', *lele* means 'to fly'; thus the term *'ukulele* is most often rendered as 'flying fleas' or 'jumping fleas', referring to the action of the fingers.

Since the 1950s, two patterns of strumming have emerged in the accompaniment of modern *hula 'auana* (figure 11); both relate to rhythmic patterns on the gourd idiophone (*ipu*) used to accompany ancient *hula kahiko* [see EAST POLYNESIA: Hawai'i]. The straight strum corresponds to the *kūkū* or *pā* pattern on the *ipu.* The double strum, also called *'ōlapa* strum, corresponds to the *kahela* pattern on the *ipu;* this strum is for songs in quick tempo. In the accompaniment of modern *hula,* an *'ukulele* is played in an ensemble that includes at least a guitar and a string bass; the ensemble may be augmented by a piano and an electric steel-stringed guitar. The *'ukulele* player and cowboy singer Clyde "Kindy" Sproat received a National Heritage Fellowship in 1988.

### Tahitian adaptations

During the early twentieth century, Tahitians adopted the Hawaiian *'ukulele* (which they pronounce *'uturere*), for which they devised alternate methods of construction. One method uses half of a coconut shell for the body; the top and the fingerboard are made from a piece of wood, typically with mother-of-pearl inlay. The other method uses one piece of wood for the top and the fingerboard, and another for the sides and the bottom, where a resonating hole is cut. The sound is amplified when the instrument is held against the musician's abdomen and the strings are strummed with a pick.

The four basic strings are tuned to the same tones as the Hawaiian *'ukulele;* but in Tahiti and throughout French Polynesia, the C is tuned a fourth above the G, in contrast to the Hawaiian use of C a fifth below the G. Additional strings, if present, duplicate the tones of the basic four. Tahitian strumming (*ta'iri pa'umotu* 'Pa'umotu [Tuamotu] beat'), differs from Hawaiian strumming (figure 11c). Quick strokes combine even divisions of the beat and syncopations.   —AMY KU'ULEIALOHA STILLMAN

FIGURE 11   Basic rhythms strummed on *'ukulele,* showing upstrum (U) and downstrum (D): *a,* the Hawaiian straight strum, corresponding to the *kūkū* or *pā* pattern on the gourd idiophone; *b,* the Hawaiian double strum (also called *'ōlapa* strum), corresponding to the *kū* or *kahela* pattern on the gourd idiophone; *c,* the Tahitian *ta'iri* strum. Transcriptions by Amy Stillman.

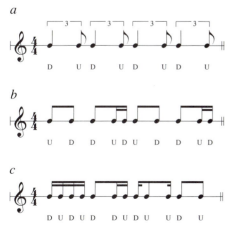

## AEROPHONES

Instruments in which air is excited into vibration are called aerophones. They include purely air-driven instruments (flutes, whistles) and those that have an air-driven valve, like a reed (oboes, clarinets, saxophones) or a player's lips (conchs, didjeridus, trumpets). The sound of most aerophones is largely controlled by the behavior of a column of enclosed air. This behavior is best understood in terms of the properties of ideally cylindrical or conical tubes, either open at the point of blowing, as with flutes, or effectively closed, as with reed-driven or lip-driven instruments. The deflecting jet, vibrating reed, or buzzing lips are controlled in part by the vibrations of the column of air, but the physical mechanism is different for each of these classes.

Any enclosed column of air has characteristic vibrational modes, in which pressure waves propagate from one end to the other. No sound escapes directly from a closed end, and surprisingly little escapes from an open end, most of the wave being reflected back inside the tube. For a flute open at or near both ends, the possible vibrations of the enclosed air are those for which the length of the tube is an exact number of half waves, leading to a complete harmonic series with frequencies $f$, $2f$, $3f$, and so on.

For a cylindrical flute closed at the remote end, or for a cylindrical reed-blown or lip-blown tube open at the remote end and effectively closed at the blowing end, the possible vibrations of the air are those with an odd number of quarter waves in the tube, giving only the odd harmonics $f$, $3f$, $5f$, and so on. Because the fundamental $f$ corresponds to a quarter wave in this case, it is an octave below the frequency of a doubly open pipe of the same length. A complete conical tube blown with reed or lips at the small end has the same resonance frequencies as a doubly open cylindrical tube of the same length. Lip-driven instruments with flaring tubes have resonance properties intermediate between those of cones and cylinders, usually producing a series about like $0.8f$, $2f$, $3f$, and so on.

On some aerophones, a skilled player can produce all the modes of the air column separately, giving bugle-call capabilities by varying the blowing pressure, the tension of the lips, and the volume of the mouth. Many aerophones have facilities for changing the effective length of the air column to fill in intermediate notes. The player may shorten the column by successively opening holes along its length (as with oboes, clarinets, and most Oceanic flutes) or inserting a stick into the open end (as with piston flutes), or may lengthen it by adding cylindrical tubing engaged by a slide (as with trombones) or a series of valves (as with trumpets, valved horns, and tubas).

TRACK 24  The swung slat, common in New Guinea, Melanesia, and Aboriginal Australia, occurs only sporadically elsewhere in Oceania. An extremely simple aerophone, it does not have any column of air or associated cavity. It is usually a thin, lens- or rhomboid-shaped wooden slat, attached to a string and swung through the air. Its fundamental pitch is determined by the aerodynamic forces of lift and drag on the rotating slat, and hence by the size and shape of the wood, the length of the string, and the speed of the player's swing. It often has a sacred significance, and how a player makes it hum is kept secret from uninitiated persons.

Oceanic end-blown flutes include piston flutes, water flutes (which work similarly, but consist of an open-ended tube set into water), and flutes with holes for fingering. Most are made of bamboo. The commonest in Vanuatu and the Island Region of Papua New Guinea is a notched flute; the player blows against a notch at one end. In side-blown flutes, the player blows into a hole near one end of the tube. Side-blown flutes with one end closed occur in several areas, but are typical of New Guinea. A few side-blown flutes have both ends closed.

In the flutes discussed above, the player sets the air column in motion by exhal-

(a)

(b)

FIGURE 12    Two kinds of panpipe: *a,* a man of the Shortland Islands plays a double raft pan-pipe (photo 1991, courtesy of the MABO Project); *b,* Ibidali plays a common Huli bundle panpipe, *gúlupòbe* (photo by Jacqueline Pugh-Kitingan, 1978).

ing through the mouth. A typical Polynesian flute is a nose-blown instrument [figure 1*d,* and see THE MUSIC AND DANCE OF POLYNESIA, figure 1]. Having closed one nostril with a finger or a thumb, the player exhales through the other nostril into the instrument. West Polynesian flutes include side-blown instruments closed at both ends. The hole for blowing is the same size as the holes for fingering, which often lie symmetrically and equidistantly from each other, so the flute can be blown from near either end.

An elaboration of flutes occurred in Aotearoa, which developed a three-holed end-blown flute open at both ends and having three holes with two close to each other (*kōauau*), a similar flute with three equidistant holes in the middle (also *kōauau*), a similar flute with three holes close to one end (*porutu, whio*), a side-blown flute with a hole for blowing near the closed end and three holes for fingering near the open one (*rehu*), a short nose-blown flute open at both ends (*nguru*), and a tapering tube usually open at both ends and with one hole in the middle (*pūtōrino*) (Fischer 1986:107).

Some Oceanic societies formerly used aeolian flutes, instruments whose sound is produced by the action of wind. These flutes were usually tall bamboo poles set up on the beach, where sea breezes made them give out variable sighs and moans, thought to represent the voices of ancestors or spirits.

Another important Oceanic instrument is the panpipe, a set of end-blown flutes (figure 12). *Raft panpipes* have tubes bound in a row; *bundle panpipes* have tubes bunched together. The former are more widely used, and often play in ensembles of instruments in several sizes, whose fundamental tones cover a range of several octaves. From observing the acoustical results of blowing into measured lengths of bamboo tubes, the 'Are'are of the Solomon Islands have verbalized a theory of musical tonality (Zemp 1979).

Other kinds of Oceanic flutes are vessel flutes, whose body is neither cylindrical nor conical, including the Hawaiian *ipu hōkiokio,* a nose-blown gourd with three holes for fingering. In these instruments, the body acts as a Helmholtz resonator, and only the sizes, not the positions, of the holes have acoustical importance. Other Oceanic vessel flutes are whirring nuts and other swung vessels, and humming tops.

End-blown wooden trumpets are especially common in New Guinea. A special case is the didjeridu of Aboriginal Australians (see below). Another important lip-driven aerophone, the most widely used indigenous Oceanic musical instrument, is the conch trumpet, made from shells of marine gastropod mollusks of genera *Triton* (less commonly the similar genera *Fusus* and *Strombus*) and *Cassis.* Internally, each shell is a short conical spiral. Penetrating the point of any of these shells results in an end-blown instrument; all but *Cassis* can be blown from a hole made in the side. Conchs usually serve as instruments of signaling. Each instrument produces just one tone, and overblowing to the difficult second mode is not employed. After the introduction of European four-part tonal harmony, the sound of these instruments led to the invention of unique ensembles, the conch bands of New Guinea [see POPULAR MUSIC: Bands].

—J. W. LOVE, NEVILLE H. FLETCHER

## Didjeridus of Australia

The didjeridu, a wooden trumpet about 1 to 1.5 meters long, is played by Aborigines of northern Australia (figure 13). The bore, usually slightly conical, is about 4 to 5 centimeters in diameter at the near end and up to 13 centimeters at the far end. The wall is 5 to 10 millimeters thick. Commonly encountered names of the instrument are *bambu* 'bamboo' (throughout northern Australia), *kulumbu* (Kimberleys), *kanbi* (Western Arnhem Land), *djalapu* (Central Arnhem Land), and *yidaki* (Eastern

Performers blow into the didjeridu with loose lips. The expulsion of air creates pulsations, tonal variations, and slight rises in pitch. In Eastern Arnhem Land, lightly spat overtones are produced in virtuosic displays.

FIGURE 13    In a gymnasium in Apia Park at the Pacific Festival of Arts, a man plays a didjeridu while others sing and dance. Photo by Adrienne L. Kaeppler, 1996.

Arnhem Land). Because of the popularity of Yothu Yindi, a rock band from Yirrkala, the last of these is gaining currency among English-speaking Australians. The didjeridu accompanies one or more singers and rarely serves as a solo instrument.

### Ethnography

Didjeridus are usually made from termite-hollowed branches of eucalyptus trees. The bark is stripped, and the internal bore is cleared of any obstruction. Both ends of the tube may be smoothed with a file. To give a better seal between lips and instrument, and to protect the lips, players may add beeswax or eucalyptus gum to the blowing end. Any cracks in the tube are sealed with wax. Instruments are sometimes soaked, sealing the tube further; for the same effect, water is blown through the tube during a performance. Didjeridus are often painted with elaborate totemic and other designs.

Trees commonly used in making didjeridus include stringybark (*Eucalyptus terodonta*), woollybutt (*Eucalyptus miniata*), red river-gum (*Eucalyptus tetrodonta*), bloodwood (*Eucalyptus polycarpa*), and ironwood (*Erythrophlaeum laboucherii*). In Western Arnhem Land, the trunks of pandanus trees are frequently used; because pandanus instruments are quite porous, they are thoroughly soaked before being played, or sealed with oil-based paints or plastic tape. Bamboo was formerly used, and plastic and metal piping have recently been used.

### Distribution

The didjeridu primarily accompanies public songs in northern Australia, most notably *wangga* and *lirrga* (or *gunborgg*) of Western Arnhem Land and the Kimberleys, and the clansongs *bunggurl* (or *manikai*) in Central and Eastern Arnhem Land, including Groote Eylandt. An exceptionally large didjeridu was used in *ubar* (or *ngulmark*), a ceremony not performed since the 1950s or earlier. A large wooden trumpet is used in *djungguwan,* a ceremony of Eastern Arnhem Land, where it has a representational, rather than a musical, function. Didjeridus were widely reported in northern Queensland around 1900 (Moyle 1974:37–38), but now are seldom heard there.

During the twentieth century, the instrument became established, with the genres *wangga* and *lirrga,* in the Kimberley region of Western Australia. By the 1970s or before, it was widely played throughout the continent (especially in the southeast and the southwest), where in the local revival of Aboriginal culture it became a symbol of Aboriginality. Its use in popular music of the 1990s has extended its performance overseas.

### Technique

Differences in didjeridu technique are important elements in defining the musical styles and substyles found in northern Australia. Most importantly, didjeridu-accompanied genres of Central and Eastern Arnhem Land, such as clansongs and *djatpangarri,* use an overblown hoot not found in genres of Western Arnhem Land.

Performers blow into the didjeridu with loose lips to sound the fundamental as a drone. In Central and Eastern Arnhem Land, by tightening the lips and increasing the air pressure, players sound an overblown note a tenth to an eleventh above the fundamental; the exact interval varies from instrument to instrument. Except in some metrically free styles in Central Arnhem Land, the drone on the fundamental articulates rhythmic and metric patterns through the mouthing of vocables into the instrument. Some of these vocables—*didjeridu-didjeru, didjemro-didjemro, didjeramo-rebo didjeramo-rebo*—suggest how the instrument may have acquired its English name (Moyle 1967:3–4).

Further patterning of the drone occurs as a result of circular breathing: the player snatches breaths through his nose while expelling air held in his cheeks. The expulsion of air creates pulsations, tonal variations, and slight rises in pitch, further patterning the drone. Perhaps the most spectacular patterning is found in Eastern Arnhem Land, where complex patterns involving lightly spat overtones are produced in virtuosic displays (Moyle 1967:2B, with mouth sounds recorded separately). To mark structural points (such as the beginning or end of sections of a song), or to produce variant patterns that mark off internal formal divisions, players produce sustained overtones. In unmeasured styles (such as *ngarkana,* used in the central Arnhem Land clansong series *Murlarra*), the didjeridu sustains unpatterned notes of irregular length, and introduces overblown hoots at important structural points.

Songs of Central-Eastern Arnhem Land use overtones in both ways described above, but *wangga* and *lirrga* make no use of overblowing. There, a major technical element is the humming of a tone near the pitch of the second harmonic to produce a complex chord, rich in harmonics. With this technique, performers articulate rhythmic patterns typical of Western Arnhem Land. Special patterns may cue metrical changes in *wangga* (Marett and Barwick 1993); in Western Arnhem Land, where the didjeridu stops before the voice, players use terminating formulas with their own mouth sounds (Marett 1991). In Western and Central Arnhem Land, the pitch of the drone normally coincides with the final of the singer's melody. Didjeridus used in *wangga* and *lirrga* are usually shorter and higher in pitch than those used in clansongs of Central Arnhem Land. Longer, deeper-pitched instruments are used in Eastern Arnhem land, where players apparently do not try to match the pitch of the didjeridu with that of the singer's voice.

Players may perform standing or sitting. For parts of ceremonies that involve procession, they often stand or walk. Postures while sitting vary between Western and Central-Eastern Arnhem Land: in the west, where the didjeridu is shorter, the player holds the far end of the instrument off the ground, or supports it on his foot, resting his right arm on his raised right knee, supporting the didjeridu on his wrist or holding from below; in Central-Eastern Arnhem Land, the player rests the far end on the ground, or places it in a resonator (such as a bucket or a large seashell), and in time with clapsticks may tap the tube with his fingernail or a stick.    —ALLAN MARETT

### Acoustics

The basic sound of a didjeridu is a drone, which a performer elicits by buzzing his lips into the tube. At the frequency of this drone, the instrument acts approximately as a quarter-wavelength resonator. (The flare of the tube sharpens its resonance slightly.) This frequency ranges from about 60 hertz (about $B_1$) for longer instruments, to about 90 hertz (about $F_2$) for shorter ones. The player can also produce the second mode of the tube. Its frequency, a little less than 1.5 times the fundamental (this figure depending on the flare), sounds a rather flat twelfth above the drone (Fletcher 1983, 1996).

Despite the inharmonicity of these resonances, the steady sound of the didjeridu

FIGURE 14 Frequency analysis of two versions of the steady drone of a didjeridu, showing the evenly spaced harmonics. In each graph there is a formant band near 500 hertz. There is a higher formant band near 2 kilohertz in the upper curve and 1.4 kilohertz in the lower. The player accomplishes this frequency shift by changing the effective volume of his mouth. Measurement by Neville H. Fletcher.

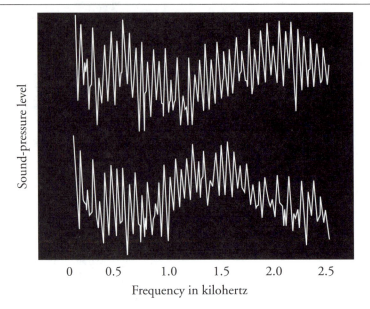

(figure 14) consists of a series of strictly harmonic overtones, as with all sustained-tone instruments unless they are playing multiphonics. Because of the form of the air pulsating past the player's lips, the acoustic spectrum of the drone is moderately rich in harmonics. The acoustic-power output of a didjeridu is comparable with that of other wind instruments, around a milliwatt. The player usually keeps the dynamic level constant, apart from rhythmic pulsations.

*Special effects*

Many of the acoustic effects of the sound of a didjeridu derive from the absence of a constriction, such as a mouthpiece. This absence causes the column of air to couple closely to the player's vocal tract. The player can markedly change the timbre of the sound by moving his tongue and cheeks to tune his oral cavity. Such actions emphasize harmonics of the frequency of the drone within a formant band determined by the volume of the oral cavity. This band typically lies in the range of 1,000 to 3,000 hertz (the range of human whistling), and bears a strong analogy to one of the formants that characterize the sounds of human vowels. Rapidly tuning the formant frequency produces impressive timbral effects. There is also a lower formant, with a frequency around 500 hertz, corresponding to the resonance of the lower vocal tract.

Playing a didjeridu uses a lot of air. To prolong the drone almost indefinitely, players use circular breathing: while storing air in distended cheeks, they suddenly inhale through the nose. This technique yields a marked pulsation, with a period between one and two seconds. Players usually decorate this pulsation by rhythmically articulating syllables such as *ri-to-ru* (with a rolled /r/ and a long /u/) or *did-je-ri-du*. In addition to these articulations, players often vocalize while playing.

Because vibrations of the lips and vocal folds affect the flow of air into the instrument in a multiplicative, rather than an additive, way (vocal folds and lips have to be open before any air will flow), the voiced sound does not simply add to the sound of the drone, but modulates it to produce sum and difference frequencies. If the frequency of the drone is $f_1$ and the player sings a frequency $f_2$, he produces frequencies $(nf_1 \pm mf_2)$, where $n$ and $m$ are whole numbers. Thus, if he sings a note a major tenth above the drone ($f_2 = 2.5 \times f_1$), he produces a strong difference-tone of frequency $0.5 \times f_1$, an octave below the drone. For a major third ($f_2 = 1.25 \times f_1$), the result is $0.25 \times f_1$, two octaves below the fundamental. These tones are unsubtle; because they have high harmonic content, they have a strident quality.

Players may use many additional vocal effects to mimic the sounds of wild animals. In such cases, the voiced sound usually has a much higher pitch than the drone. The difference frequencies are then unnoticeable, and the sound seems superimposed upon the drone.

Since the didjeridu is made from hardwood and is hollow, its mechanical resonances—basically deformations of the walls of the tube—are also musically useful. A player can excite these resonances by hitting the instrument with a stick, rhythmically embellishing the drone.                                —NEVILLE H. FLETCHER

### Studio technology

Once heard only in the music of Arnhem Land and eastern Kimberley, and now heard as a feature of Australian Aboriginal popular music, the didjeridu has become an ingredient of worldwide musical genres: rock, jazz, new age, and symphonic music. For internationally released recordings in these genres, commercial studios have attracted such Aboriginal performers as David Hudson, Richard Walley, and Makuma Yunupingu, and such non-Aboriginal performers as Stewart Dempster, Andrew Langford, and Charlie McMahon.

The didjeridu may look and sound simple, but is neither, as musical instrument or sociocultural artifact. The use of nontraditional materials, such as polyvinyl plastic pipe or resins, and the electrical manipulation of recorded acoustic impulses are affecting its dissemination into new musical and geographic domains. Throughout the twentieth century, technology has driven the evolution of the entertainment industry, of which nonsacred didjeridu music is a part. In the context of popular musical genres, studio handling of the didjeridu involves recording, remixing, and reshaping.

### Recording

The didjeridu produces a wide signal, involving a deep drone and one or more prominent overtones. A large-diaphragm microphone best captures these qualities, especially with large instruments. Also helpful are using a large area to add natural ambience, and using a medium level of compression to attenuate the width of the signal. Placing the microphone off the floor directly in front of the far end of the instrument results in a full sound, but often with noticeable attack in the form of the performer's breathing—an inherent part of the performance, which some listeners find intrusive. An alternative method is to position the microphone off to the side. Different microphone techniques suit different goals of production, such as where the didjeridu is to appear within the soundscape of the recording, and which other instruments complete the ensemble. In live applications, technicians commonly use various techniques of placing the microphone. One is to suspend the microphone over the far end of the instrument; this technique has the advantage of controlling feedback. Another technique is to set a microphone directly on the floor. Placements vary according to whether the performer sits or stands.

### Remixing

When vinyl was the principal means of recorded reproduction, the didjeridu was best located in the middle of an ensemble. If placed elsewhere, its signal overpowered others, creating difficulties in mastering. Formats using tape and CDs have eliminated this problem, so placement is more flexible—such as off to one side when responding to a centered vocal or instrument. In live applications, perspective is also important, especially since the didjeridu occupies the same tonal register as the string bass and the bass drum. Placing it off to one side can help keep these instruments from setting up competing sound waves. For onstage monitoring, large woofers are best.

FIGURE 15    Tanimae plays a four-tube 'Are'are bundle panpipe (*'au ware*). Photo by Hugo Zemp, 1969.

*Reshaping*

Aside from equalizing specific frequencies, technicians frequently add reverberation, of which a delay is useful in creating the illusion of space and reinforcing the drone. Another facet of the reshaping of sound is the matter of tuning: when overdubbing, technicians can in effect electronically tune other instruments to the didjeridu. Since the didjeridu produces a sound so complex an electronic tuner often fails to read it, one method is to tune a guitar string to the didjeridu's fundamental, and then make an electronic tuner read that note. The note is then recorded at normal speed on a machine that can be tuned up or down with a variable-speed adjustment. The didjeridu is then recorded in its own pitch against the backing tracks. When the machine is returned to normal speed, the didjeridu is in tune with the rest of the recording.

—KARL WILLIAM NEUENFELDT

## Bundle panpipes of the Solomon Islands

The Solomon Islands are famous for the sophistication of their panpipe music. Transcriptions and musical analyses of panpipe ensembles playing in two-, three-, and four-part polyphony among the 'Are'are, and in up to eight parts among the Kwaio, have been published (Zemp 1979, 1982, 1994a). Like many peoples of the Central Pacific, the 'Are'are and the Kwaio enjoy polyphony: the former make no less than nine variants of a type of solo panpipe with irregular distribution of tubes, allowing a soloist to perform two-part polyphony by blowing simultaneously into adjacent tubes (Zemp 1981).

Two types of bundle panpipes that the 'Are'are classify as *hoko ni 'au* 'bundles of bamboo' are solo instruments designed for polyphonic playing (Zemp 1978). The physical differences between them involve the number of tubes and the form of mouthpieces. The first type, *'au waa* 'open bamboo', has seven tubes open at both ends. Its range extends from Vanuatu to New Guinea (Fischer 1986:119–121), and it is known even farther west, among Austronesian-speaking montagnards of Vietnam (Dournes 1965:231–233). The second type has four tubes in Kwaio and northern 'Are'are, and three in southern 'Are'are. A small hole, pierced in the node of the bamboo at one end of each tube, forms a mouthpiece; hence the name of the instrument in northern 'Are'are: *'au ware* 'bamboo [with the] tiny [mouthpiece]'. The other end is open (figure 15).

Another difference between the types of bundle panpipes is in the technique of playing: some panpipes are held vertically, and some are held obliquely. The vertically held 'Are'are bundle panpipe (*'au waa*) is blown from a distance of one to three centimeters. In contrast to the usual means of playing flutes (in which the stream of breath breaks at the edge of the tube, oscillating the column of air), the tubes apparently serve as resonators. On observing the playing of an *'au waa* on film (Zemp 1994b), Gilles Leothaud, acoustician at the University of Paris IV, confirmed this hypothesis. A player directs his breath successively into different tubes, but part of the stream penetrates neighboring tubes (Zemp 1973a, track 8; 1995a, track 3).

The obliquely held bundle panpipe of the 'Are'are and Kwaio is put between the lips like the obliquely held end-blown flute of northern Malaita, which also has a small hole cut into the node as a mouthpiece (Zemp 1971:47). This placement enables musicians, by delicately adjusting the pressure of their breath with the technique of overblowing, to choose successive partials from the harmonic series. These partials become basic melodic notes. Musicians turn the instrument with a movement of their wrists; hence its names: Kwaio *'au bulobulo* 'turning bamboo, twisting bamboo' and southern 'Are'are *'au po'o* 'sideways bamboo, turning bamboo'. Musicians consciously direct air into one or two neighboring tubes, obtaining subtle chords (Zemp 1994b).

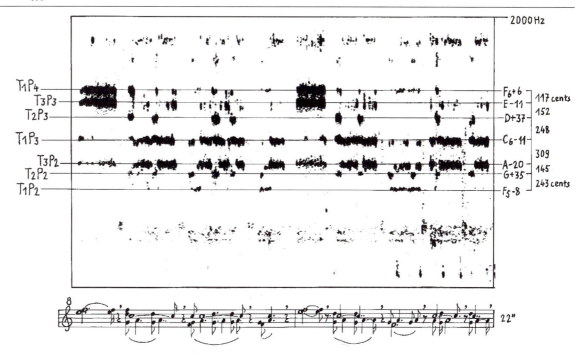

FIGURE 16 Sonagram of the first twenty-two seconds of "*Nanarata*" ('Weeping'), played on a three-tube bundle panpipe ('*au po'o*) by Kohea'eke in 1975. Transcription by Hugo Zemp (1995a: track 2a).

### Spectrograms and analysis

Since partials from one tube might be perceived as simultaneous pitches (rather than timbral components), a transcription on a five-line staff gives an imperfect picture of the playing of this instrument. The spectrogram, traces all the harmonics—those a listener perceives as the melody and those an analyst may define as components of the timbre. A combination of the assumed objectivity of the spectrogram and the assumed subjectivity of standard notation may give the most useful overall picture.

Using the Sona-Graph 5500 in the Ethnomusicology Department of the Musée de l'Homme (Paris), I made spectrograms of two performances (figures 16 and 17). Horizontal lines traced by hand upon the spectrograms mark melodically and polyphonically exploited partials. The legend at left gives the numbers of the tubes and partials; thus, $T_1P_2$ means "tube 1, partial 2." The legend at right identifies partials converted from frequencies. Differences in cents are relative to the degrees of the tempered scale (A=440); between two pitches, the intervals are in cents.

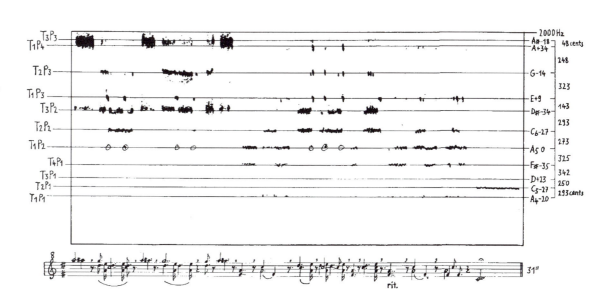

FIGURE 17 Sonagram of the last thirty-one seconds of "*Aamamata*" ('Formal Lament'), played on a four-tube bundle panpipe ('*au ware*) by Tanimae in 1969. Transcription by Hugo Zemp.

Cents give only a rough idea of pitches and intervals: because of fluctuations of pitch and limitations of sonographic analysis, measurements are approximate, plus or minus 10 cents. Despite this imprecision, the intervals clearly do not belong to the equally spaced seven-tone system of panpipe-ensemble music: 243 cents (figure 17) and 250 cents (figure 16) correspond to an interval between a major second and a minor third. Between higher partials, intervals narrow.

None of these intervals normatively appears elsewhere in 'Are'are music, though on film (Zemp 1994b), the musician 'Irisipau demonstrates a second (*rapi 'au*) and two thirds (*hoa ni 'au*) derived from a scale that divides the octave into seven equal parts: measurements of the second partials of the four tubes give figures of 157 cents (close to the 171.4 cents of this theoretical second) and 351 and 327 cents (close to the 343 cents of this theoretical third). As an expert theorist of 'Are'are music, 'Irisipau may have attached importance to the tuning of solo instruments according to the demands of panpipe ensembles, his favorite music.

The sonagrams clearly show the pulsation of breath, six beats a second, as in playing panpipes in ensemble. In the transcriptions on a five-line staff, a beat has the value of a sixteenth. A sonagram of a different piece (Zemp 1995a: figure 3, track 2b) shows an even stronger pulsation.

### The 'au po'o

Figure 16 reproduces the sonagram and standard notation of the first twenty-two seconds of a piece played on a three-tube *'au po'o* by Kohea'eke. Pitches melodically and polyphonically perceived by the ear have the range of an octave. Fundamentals are not sounded; the music uses partials 2 and 3 of all tubes and partial 4 of the longest. A main chord in length and strength, appearing at the beginning of each melodic segment, is made up of $T_3P_3$ and $T_1P_4$, producing the minor second (E–F) mentioned above. Another important chord in the structure of this piece is made up of $T_3P_2$ and $T_1P_3$, producing a minor third (A–C). Shorter chords, having the length of one to three beats at most, combine three pitches, or even four. They give the music of this instrument a special flavor, and give the spectrograms a characteristic design.

### The 'au ware

Figure 17 shows the second part of a piece played by Tanimae on a four-tube *'au ware* (Zemp 1973a: track 9a). Since the fundamental pitches are here used in the structure of the piece ($T_1P_1$ being weak), the range of this piece is two octaves. The smallest tube ($T_4$) produces only $P_1$. The beginning of the piece and of the second melodic segment has a strong dissonance in the treble, $T_1P_4$ and $T_3P_3$ producing two pitches about a quarter tone apart. A notable feature is a short chord consisting of $T_1P_2$ and $T_1P_3$, with or without a longer note of $T_2P_3$ or $T_2P_2$: the ear distinctly hears an A (corresponding to $P_2$), which the sonagrams mark only weakly or not at all (indicated by a hand-drawn circle). The ear may reconstitute that pitch from $P_3$ and the upper partials.

This is a magical instrument! The delicacy of its sound, enhanced by the recitation of sacred formulas and the application of secret substances, formerly helped boys court girls (Zemp 1995b). Nowadays, boys try to please girls with the sound of guitars (if possible, electrically amplified), but one can imagine that the whisper of the obliquely held bundle panpipes, hardly rising above the chirping of insects, should surprise a girl who, not being able to see the performer in the darkness, might wonder who her suitor was and try to find out.

According to a myth, a man invented the *'au ware* to aid his escape from a bounty hunter: the pursued man placed it under his nose, so that when he would be asleep, his breath would sound the pipes, making the bounty hunter believe he was awake (Coppet and Zemp 1978:24).

### Geographical distribution

A systematic survey of all eleven peoples of Malaita, with a brief sampling of Guadalcanal and Savo Islands, shows that the obliquely held bundle panpipe exists among only three neighboring peoples, all on Malaita: 'Are'are, Kwaio, and Kwarekwareo (Zemp 1971). The Kwarekwareo, adjoining the linguistic boundaries of 'Are'are and Kwaio, speak a dialect of the Kwaion language subgroup "heavily overlain with 'Are'are borrowings, linguistic and cultural" (Keesing 1975:viii). In New Britain, the Solomons, and Vanuatu, men play bundle panpipes with mouthpieces of small holes in the nodes (Fischer 1986:119–121, 208–209); but observers' accounts and organological features (six to eleven pipes) imply that those panpipes are blown from a distance, so each tube is probably used as a resonator, and cannot produce melodically and polyphonically exploited partials. No further evidence about the existence of the obliquely held bundle panpipes with overblowing technique has come to my knowledge, so I must tentatively conclude that this instrument is a local invention of the 'Are'are or the Kwaio or both—and thus is unique in Oceania.

—HUGO ZEMP

## Side-blown flutes of New Caledonia

Only a few elders of New Caledonia remember a side-blown flute that once played an important role in Kanak life (figure 18). Its particularity was its form: all known examples are curved—some a little, some a lot. Their length varied between 1 and 1.5 meters, and their diameters rarely exceeded 2 centimeters. The flute had only one hole for fingering, near the far end. Flutes of this form do not exist on other islands of the Pacific. No elders play this instrument today, and ancient specimens survive only in museums.

This flute formerly had high social value. Excluding percussive instruments, it was the *only* indigenous musical instrument (Brou 1987:243; de la Hautière 1980 [1869]:113). A traveler in 1911–1912 said it was the "most important" Kanak instrument (Sarasin 1929:229). Respondents in 1994 remembered that it had been widespread in the center and north of Grande Terre until the 1930s, when a sharp and fast decline began. They attributed this decline to the introduction of harmonicas. In the first decades of the twentieth century, Japanese people had come to New Caledonia to work in the nickel mines. Some opened stores and sold harmonicas, which soon replaced the flute in popularity.

Early writings contain confusing statements about this flute. Some writers (de la Hautière 1980 [1869]:113; Leenhardt 1980 [1930]: plate 11, no. 2; Rochas 1861:189) say the flute could have been played with the mouth or the nose. But Kanak elders questioned about that in the 1990s said the flute was played only with the mouth. Legends that mention the flute never say it was played with the nose.

Each flutist made his own instrument, using measurements of his body to determine its length and the positions of the holes. He cut a reed to its proper length, and with a hot iron rod burned the holes in. With a thin hardwood rod, he pierced the node walls inside the reed. This action made the reed lose strength; when bent, it could break, and at the places of the buds, small holes could develop. To prevent these results, the maker spread a sticky paste around each node on the outside of the reed; as the paste dried, it hardened. To curve the reed, the maker tied a rope to both its ends, and bent it like a bow. Keeping the rope tight, he hung the reed under a roof, where the heat and smoke of the household fire made the flute retain its curve.

As a symbol of social rank, the flute was reserved for elite men, such as chiefs or high chiefs. When posing for photographs more than a hundred years ago, some

FIGURE 18    A man holds a Kanak side-blown flute (after Garnier 1990:6).

The flute is a chiefly instrument. Strong taboos in relation to it must have existed. One legend says a whole family had to die because a disobedient child had touched his father's flute.

Kanak, to assert their social position, held their flutes beside their weapons. One of these pictures shows the high chief Mindia Neja of Houaïlou, holding his flute in front of himself. A legend from the Cèmuhî language-area says a person who emerged from a tree was accepted as a high chief because he possessed a flute (Guiart 1963:87); another legend confirms that the flute is a chiefly instrument (Rivierre 1994:43). Strong taboos in relation to the flute must have existed, but only one surviving legend tells of them. It says a whole family had to die because a disobedient child had touched his father's flute (Ronny Phadom, personal communication).

The only known authentic recording of the Kanak flute is a melody lasting forty-seven seconds, recorded by André-Georges Haudricourt in 1963. The melody was played by Kallen Bova of Tiouaé, in the north of Grande Terre. Kallen is long dead. In the 1960s, he was the last person who knew how to play this flute. When his daughter heard a recording of his performance, she remembered the melody, and confirmed that the music had been played on a slightly curved, one-holed, side-blown flute, in her language (Cèmuhî) called *a opwêê*.

Analysis of the recorded melody showed that this music used two overtone-derived scales: the scale with the hole for fingering closed consisted of overtones 3 to 6, and the scale with the hole open consisted of overtones 4 and 5. The interval between the two corresponding overtones from each scale is about a semitone. The resulting scale can be notated D–F♯–G♯–A–B–C, with the tones made when the hole for fingering is open (G♯ and B) sounding a little sharper than their counterparts in the tempered scale.

### A modern revival

Benoît Boulet, an elder Kanak of Weraap, a village in northern Grande Terre, has not learned to play the Kanak flute; but as a boy, he watched flutists of his family make their instruments. In his language (Fwâi), the reed used to build the flute is called *hago,* as is the flute. In 1994, his knowledge and the results of the analysis of the recording enabled the Agence de Développement de la Culture Kanak to organize a workshop to share this knowledge with young Kanak. Most of them had not even heard about the Kanak flute, but under Boulet's guidance, each participant built at least one instrument. A flutist myself, I helped the participants elicit their first notes from their new instruments. Today, young people build and play flutes in the old style. They are sharing their experience with friends, and the number of people who play the revived instrument is growing. —RAYMOND AMMANN

## REFERENCES

Attenborough, David. 1960. *Quest in Paradise.* London: Lutterworth Press.

Brou, Bernard. 1987. *Préhistoire et société tradi-* *tionelle de la Nouvelle-Calédonie.* Nouméa: Société d'Études Historiques de Nouvelle- Calédonie.

Burrows, Edwin G. 1937. "Western Polynesia: A Study in Cultural Differentiation." Ph.D. dissertation, Yale University.

Clark, Ross. 1981. "Stringed Instruments and

Stringbands." Part 4 of "A New Song from the Islands." Broadcasts presented by Ross Clark and Allan Thomas. Radio New Zealand.

Coppet, Daniel de, and Hugo Zemp. 1978. *'Aré'aré: un peuple mélanésien et sa musique*. Paris: Le Seuil.

Dournes, Jacques. 1965. "La musique chez les Jörai." *Objets et Mondes (La Revue du Musée de l'Homme)* 5(4):211–244.

*Extraordinary Ukuleles: The Tsumura Collection from Japan*. 1993. Catalog of an exhibit at Honolulu Academy of Arts, 8 September through 3 October 1993. Honolulu: Akira Tsumura.

Felix, John Henry, Leslie Nunes, and Peter F. Senecal. 1980. *The 'Ukulele: A Portuguese Gift to Hawaii*. Honolulu: Authors.

Fischer, Hans. 1986. *Sound-Producing Instruments in Oceania*. Edited by Don Niles. Translated by Philip W. Holzknecht. Boroko: Institute of Papua New Guinea Studies.

Fletcher, Neville H. 1983. "Acoustics of the Australian Didjeridu." *Australian Aboriginal Studies* 1:28–37.

———. 1996. "The Didjeridu (Didgeridoo)." *Acoustics Australia* 24:11–15. Reprinted in *Acoustics Bulletin* (United Kingdom) 21:5–9.

Fletcher, Neville H., and T. D. Rossing, 1991. *The Physics of Musical Instruments*. New York: Springer-Verlag, New York.

Friedman, Susan, director. 1994. *Kī Hoʻalu: That's Slack Key Guitar*. 57 mins. Half Moon Bay: Studio on the Mountain. Video.

Garnier, Jules. 1990 [1867–1868]. *Voyage à la Nouvelle-Calédonie*. Paris: Éditions du Cagou.

Gourlay, Kenneth A. 1975. *Sound-Producing Instruments in Traditional Society: A Study of Esoteric Instruments and Their Role in Male-Female Relations*. New Guinea Research Bulletin 60. Port Moresby and Canberra: Australian National University.

Guiart, Jean. 1963. *Structure de la chefferie en Mélanésie du sud*. Travaux et Mémoires, 66. Paris: Institut d'Ethnologie.

Hornbostel, Erich M. von, and Curt Sachs. 1914. "Systematik der Musikinstrumente." *Zeitschrift für Ethnologie* 46:553–590.

———. 1961. "Classification of Musical Instruments." Translation by A. Baines and Klaus P. Wachsmann. *Galpin Society Journal* 14:3–29.

Jones, Trevor A. 1967. "The Didjeridu." *Studies in Music* 1:23–55.

Kaeppler, Adrienne L. 1980. *Pahu and Pūniu: An Exhibition of Hawaiian Drums*. Honolulu: Bishop Museum.

———. 1993. *Hula Pahu: Hawaiian Drum Dances: Volume I: Haʻa and Hula Pahu*. Bishop Museum Bulletin in Anthropology, 3. Honolulu: Bishop Museum Press.

Kamae, Eddie, director. 1993. *The Hawaiian Way*. Produced by Myrna J. Kamae and Rodney A. Ohtani. 68 mins. Honolulu: Hawaii Sons. Video.

Kanahele, George S. ed. 1979. *Hawaiian Music and Musicians: An Illustrated History*. Honolulu:

University of Hawaiʻi Press.

Keesing, Roger M. 1975. *Kwaio Dictionary*. Pacific Linguistics, series C, 35. Canberra: Australian National University.

Kelsey, John Russell. 1993. "The Music of the Irumu People, Morobe Province, Papua New Guinea." Ph.D. dissertation, Wesleyan University.

Kunst, Jaap. 1967. *Music in New Guinea*. The Hague: Martinus Nijhoff.

La Hautière, Ulysse de. 1980 [1869]. *Souvenirs de la Nouvelle-Calédonie: 1869*. Nouméa: du Cagou.

Leenhardt, Maurice. 1980 [1930]. *Notes d'ethnologie Néo-Calédonienne*. Travaux et Mémoires, 8. Paris: Institut d'Ethnologie.

Lomax, Alan. N.d. "Interview #1" with Muddy Waters. Track 2 in *Muddy Waters: The Complete Plantation Recordings*. CHD-9344. Compact disc.

Marcuse, Sybil. 1975. *A Survey of Musical Instruments*. New York: Harper & Row.

Marett, Allan. 1991. "Variability and Stability in *Wangga* Songs of Northwest Australia." In *Music and Dance of Aboriginal Australia and the South Pacific*, ed. Alice Marshall Moyle, 194–213. Sydney: Oceania Publications.

Marett, Allan, and Linda Barwick. 1993. *Bunggridj-Bunggridj: Wangga Songs by Alan Maralung*. Smithsonian Folkways CD 40430. International Institute for Traditional Music: Traditional Music of the World, 4. Compact disc, with photos by Allan Marett and commentary by Allan Marett and Linda Barwick.

McLean, Mervyn. 1994. *Diffusion of Musical Instruments and Their Relation to Language Migrations in New Guinea*. Occasional Papers on Pacific Music and Dance, 1. Boroko: Cultural Studies Division, National Research Institute.

Messner, Gerald Florian. 1980. "Das Reibholz von New Ireland." *Studien zur Musikwissenschaft* 31:221–312.

———. 1983. "The Friction Block *Lounuat* of New Ireland: Its Use and Socio-Cultural Embodiment." *Bikmaus* 4(3):49–55.

Moulin, Jane Freeman. 1997. "Understanding Traditional Function and Usage in Marquesan Musical Instruments." *Journal of the Polynesian Society* 106(3):250–283.

Moyle, Alice M. 1967. *Songs from the Northern Territory*. Institute of Aboriginal Studies, M-001/5. 5 LP disks with booklet.

———. 1974. "North Australian Music. A Taxonomic Approach to the Study of Aboriginal Song Performances." Ph.D. dissertation, Monash University.

Niles, Don. 1983. "Why Are There No Garamuts in Papua?" *Bikmaus* 4(3):90–104.

Oliver, Douglas L. 1955. *A Solomon Island Society: Kinship and Leadership among the Siuai of Bougainville*. Cambridge: Harvard University Press.

Rivierre, Jean-Claude. 1994. *Dictionnaire Cemuhi*. Langues et Cultures du Pacifique, 9. Paris: SELAF.

Rochas, Victor de. 1861. "Voyage à la Nouvelle-Calédonie: 1859." *Le Tour du Monde* 1861(1):129–134.

Sarasin, Fritz. 1929. *Nova Caledonia: Forschungen in Neu-Caledonien und auf den Loyalty-Inseln*. Munich: C. W. Kreidel.

Tatar, Elizabeth. 1993. *Hula Pahu: Hawaiian Drum Dances: Volume II: The Pahu: Sounds of Power*. Bishop Museum Bulletin in Anthropology, 3. Honolulu: Bishop Museum Press.

Thomas, Allan. 1996. *New Song and Dance from the Central Pacific: Creating and Performing the Fātele of Tokelau in the Islands and in New Zealand*. Dance and Music, 9. Stuyvesant, New York: Pendragon Press.

Van Hille, J. W. 1907. "Reizen in West-Nieuw-Guinea." *Tijdschrift van het Koninklijk Nederlandisch Aardrijkskundig* 24.

Waterman, Christopher A. 1990. *Jùjú: A Social History and Ethnography of an African Popular Music*. Chicago: University of Chicago Press.

Webb, Michael. 1995. "'Pipal bilong music tru'/ 'A truly musical people': Musical Culture, Colonialism, and Identity in Northeastern New Britain, Papua New Guinea, after 1875." Ph.D. dissertation, Wesleyan University.

Zemp, Hugo. 1971. "Instruments de musique de Malaita." *Journal de la Société des Océanistes* 30:31–53.

———. 1973a. *Melanesian Music, 'Are'are, vol 3*. Vogue LDM 30106. Collection Musée de l'Homme. LP disk.

———, with J. Schwarz. 1973b. "Echelles équiheptaphoniques des flûtes de Pan chez les 'Aré'aré (Malaita, Îles Salomon)." *Yearbook of the International Folk Music Council* 5:85–121.

———. 1978. "'Are'are Classification of Musical Types and Instruments." *Ethnomusicology* 22(1):37–67.

———. 1979. "Aspects of 'Are'are Musical Theory." *Ethnomusicology* 23(1):5–48.

———. 1981. "Melanesian Solo Polyphonic Panpipe Music." *Ethnomusicology* 25(3):383–418.

———. 1982. "Deux à huit voix: polyphonies de flûtes de Pan chez les Kwaio (Îles Salomon)." *Revue de Musicologie* 68(1–2):275–309. Special number André Schaeffner, *Les Fantaisies du voyageur: XXXIII variations Schaeffner*.

———. 1994a. *Solomon Islands: 'Are'are Panpipe Ensembles*. Collection CNRS/Musée de l'Homme. Le Chant du Monde LDX 274961–62. 2 compact discs.

———. 1994b [1979]. *'Are'are Music and Shaping Bamboo*. Society for Ethnomusicology, Audiovisual Series, 1. 2 videos of 16-mm films.

———. 1995a. *Solomon Islands: 'Are'are Intimate and Ritual Music*. Collection CNRS/Musée de l'Homme. Le Chant du Monde CNR 274963. Compact disc.

———. 1995b. *Écoute le bambou qui pleure: récits de quatre musiciens mélanésiens*. Collection "L'aube des peuples." Paris: Éditions Gallimard.

# Part 3
# Peoples of Oceania and Their Music

Geography and nature influence people and their music, just as people and their music influence geography and nature. Aboriginal song lines created the geographic features of Australia, just as Christian hymns sung in Yapese confirm the ordering of the universe. Views differ about whether the gods are responsible for music, or whether music was created for the gods. Interactions between individuals, families, and communities are often carried out through music, while music helps construct and invigorate the interactions themselves.

Music can best be understood in its cultural context and geographical location. Though the emphasis of the following articles is on music, sketches of the environmental and social backgrounds of sounds and movements are presented to help the reader appreciate and understand the music. Some musics, having been exhaustively studied, are summarized; some are described in depth for the first time; others yet await their initial appearance in print.

Performing spaces influence music, as at the Pacific Festival of Arts, where dancers' steps have been transferred from a grassy surface to a stage in front of a concrete building. Photo by Adrienne L. Kaeppler, 1996.

# Australia

A cosmopolitan nation with musics of indigenous peoples coexisting and intermingling with musics of immigrants is the destiny of Australia in the twenty-first century. From didjeridus to beer-cap rattles, from clapsticks to symphony orchestras, from island songs to urban reggae, from wallaby mimes to the postmodern dancer Pina Bausch, Australian music encompasses the expected and the fantastic.

Secret rites of Aboriginal men and women are performed in songlines of the Dreaming. The Sydney Opera House hosts hometown operas and Russian ballets. Greek songs, Brazilian sambas, and Vietnamese instruments grace performing spaces inhabited by trompe-l'oeil Parthenon fragments and dot-painted murals. Australia mixes old and new, global and local, with music at the heart of a creative nation.

Traditional musical analysis focuses on sounds, but a multidimensional approach deepens our understanding by incorporating the study of structured movement, costume, and musical instruments, as in the seagull (*mirrijpu*), a dance of Goulburn Island, Arnhem Land. Photo by Axel Poignant, 1952.

# The Music and Dance of Australia

*Stephen A. Wild*
*Adrienne L. Kaeppler*

**Indigenous Music**
**Indigenous Musical Instruments**
**Popular Music**
**Institutionalizing Musical Maturity**
**Australian Dance in the 1990s**

Australia, containing 7,682,300 square kilometers, is home to a multicultural population of eighteen million (map). The first Australians migrated from the north more than forty thousand years ago. They spoke more than two hundred languages, and occupied ecological zones varying from a vast continental desert to small tropical islands. The modern history of Australia began in 1788, when representatives of the British government established a penal station at Port Jackson (now Sydney). The people of this settlement, mostly convicts and soldiers, were outnumbered by the indigenous population, and this imbalance probably continued for decades. Thus, even if Australia's history is counted only since 1788, the predominant music for a significant period was indigenous. Social interactions between the original inhabitants and the newcomers were inevitable, often with disastrous consequences for the former. These interactions included the hospitality some indigenous people extended to the newcomers in the form of invitations to entertainments of music and dance.

The earliest accounts of indigenous performance were recorded in settlers' and explorers' diaries and drawings (figure 1a). The latest performances, incorporating modern Western dance, take place on urban stages and are recorded by photography (figure 1b). In an indigenous language spoken around Port Jackson, the word for a performance of music and dance was documented as *carib-berie,* a term that in the form *corroboree* was widely adopted by immigrants and indigenous peoples who spoke other languages.

Little is known of indigenous performances in the 1700s and 1800s. By the 1900s, when serious musical research began, the music of southern Australia, the region of most intense European settlement, had changed substantially. In the northern half of Australia, as in the center, outsiders' values intruded less, enabling old practices to continue. Regional differences in indigenous musical styles and cultures of longer standing than the last two hundred years remain.

## Lurching toward multiculturalism

Though in the 1800s some composers tried to use indigenous material in Western styles of composition, most musical influence between indigenous and immigrant populations was from the latter to the former. The two concepts of music were not

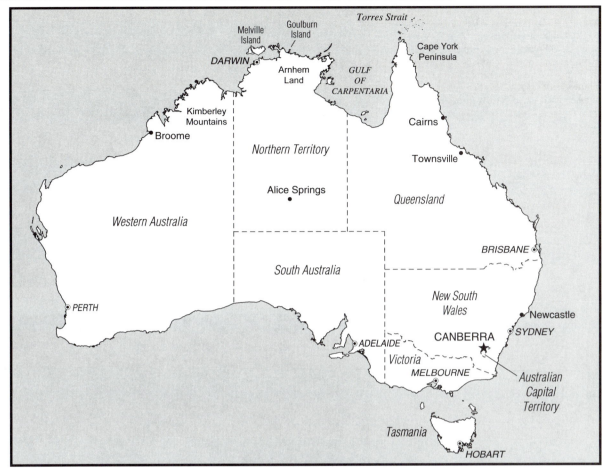

Australia

easily compatible, and indigenous music was gradually overwhelmed by introduced music, particularly in the south.

Because Port Jackson was a military settlement, the immigrants' organized musical life for about the first fifty years centered on regimental bands. A steady and increasing flow of free settlers, beginning about 1830, swelled after 1851, when rich deposits of gold were discovered. In the late 1800s, institutionalized classical music became more professional, with the establishment of symphony orchestras, professional choirs, and musical conservatories in universities.

English and Irish music, brought by lower-class immigrants, provided the musical experience of many Australians, particularly in rural areas. Music in the goldfields was dominated by professional entertainers, who sang current music-hall or popular-theater songs from Britain and North America. These traditions evolved into Australian folkloric music in the twentieth century (Covell 1967:49–54). A little-known aspect of music in nineteenth-century Australia was the music of non-European immigrants, particularly the Chinese. In 1901, with the federal government's adoption of an immigration policy that allowed entry only to Europeans, an Asian presence in Australia and Australian music virtually disappeared.

In the latter half of the twentieth century, an initially European-based Australian school of composition began turning toward Asia. Composers again tried to use indigenous musical elements in classical compositions. Jazz and country were also adopted, and a local popular-music industry developed and flourished. Other European traditions, particularly Greek and Italian, influenced the Australian musical landscape following large-scale immigration after World War II. In the 1960s, with the abandonment of selective immigration, Asian music began to contribute to Australian culture.

FIGURE 1   Australian dancing: *a*, in 1840, Aboriginals perform a corroborree (engraving by E. G. Dunnel after a drawing by A. T. Agate, from the U.S. Exploring Expedition, Wilkes 1844:2: facing p. 198, photo by Smithsonian Institution); *b*, in 1996, the Bangarra Dance Theatre performs *Ochres*, choreographed by Stephen Page, using modern-dance-inspired movements to evoke the Dreaming (photo by Adrienne L. Kaeppler).

(*a*)

(*b*)

## INDIGENOUS MUSIC

The most important trait of indigenous Australian music is that it is mainly vocal. Sung texts are the primary locus of indigenous literature. Specially sung languages employ poetic techniques and vocabularies that do not occur, or occur in altered forms, in ordinary spoken language. Special knowledge is required to interpret their words. The lyrics of genres primarily consisting of vocables are uninterpretable.

Most indigenous songs are sacred, or at least refer to sacred realms. Performances often occur in restricted contexts, when only women or only men may be present, or only the initiated may hear them. Some songs are intended purely for entertainment, or to accompany dancing (figure 2), or to comment on scandalous behavior. The indigenous uses of songs include initiation and mortuary ceremonies, ceremonies for managing conflict, religious ceremonies that link communities over a wide area, healing and bewitching, attracting a desired member of the opposite sex, and inducing rain (Wild 1988).

### Music of Aboriginal peoples

Australia has two main indigenous traditions: Aboriginal and Torres Strait Islander.

FIGURE 2    On Saibai Island, Torres Strait, men dance *adhi buin*. Photo by Jeremy Beckett, 1960. Courtesy of the Pictorial Collection of the Australian Institute of Aboriginal and Torres Strait Islander Studies.

FIGURE 2    On Saibai Island, Torres Strait, men dance *adhi buin*. Photo by Jeremy Beckett, 1960. Courtesy of the Pictorial Collection of the Australian Institute of Aboriginal and Torres Strait Islander Studies.

Nothing has survived of Tasmanian Aboriginal music except a few wax-cylinder recordings made in the 1890s, too few for definitive generalizations.

### Southeastern Australia

The delineation of a southeastern regional style is made difficult by historical changes there. Available recordings are of solo singers or a dominant singer accompanied by another singer in the background. Little reliable documentation of indigenous dance in the southeast survives, but the songs encode dancers' cues, suggesting that the recordings of solo singing are not merely the result of the loss of a group-singing tradition. Evidence of a device that enabled singers to extend songs indefinitely also suggests a soloistic tendency (Donaldson 1987).

### Central Australia

Central Australian Aboriginal music has been much more fully documented. It is essentially a group-singing tradition with rhythmic accompaniment. Women and men have separate musics and musical occasions, in addition to jointly performed ones. Commonly, male singers accompany themselves by beating clapsticks; women accompany themselves by striking their bodies.

Short songs, each lasting less than a minute, are arranged in series of sometimes hundreds, each song sung to the same melodic contour. A series (also called a songline) refers to the creative activities of a totemic ancestor as it traveled across the countryside. It is known by the name of that ancestor, such as Kangaroo, Rain, and Lizard. Taken together, the series map the spiritual landscape of Central Australian peoples.

The texts of individual songs, and the rhythms to which they are set, are fixed and can be varied only in minor ways. Because the songs follow an ancestor's track, they must follow the same order on each occasion. Most are believed to have originated anciently, but provisions for receiving new songs from spirits exist (Ellis 1985; Wild 1987).

### Northeastern Australia (Cape York)

Northeastern Australia is unique in its use of membranophones. In western Cape York, singing is performed by a solo singer in a tense style and a narrow vocal range, sometimes on a single tone, punctuated by a chorus of clapsticks, rattles, claps, shouts, and calls. Eastern Cape York belongs to the region of *bora,* initiatory songs and rituals, which extends down the east coast, where singing is more relaxed and melodic ranges are wider (Moyle 1968–1969, 1977a).

FIGURE 3    A tortoiseshell mask from Torres Strait. Museum für Völkerkunde, Berlin.

FIGURE 4    At the Pacific Festival of Arts, Torres Strait Islanders perform to the accompaniment of an hourglass drum. Photo by Adrienne L. Kaeppler, 1996.

### Northern Australia (Arnhem Land)

Arnhem Land occupies north-central Australia, where solo singing accompanied by clapsticks and a didjeridu is the predominant musical ensemble. In the whole of Arnhem Land, singers are specialists, who travel around the country performing for ceremonies (Clunies Ross and Wild 1982, 1984; Elkin and Jones 1953–1957; Marett and Barwick 1993; Moyle 1964; Stubington 1978). The Gulf of Carpentaria is a transitional area, with musical traits and genres in common with those of bordering groups in southern Arnhem Land and Central Australia.

### Northwestern Australia (Kimberleys)

The style and genres of western Arnhem Land extend into northwestern Australia, including the Kimberleys, to the west coast. This style coexists with one closely related to Central Australian music. In the late twentieth century, people and ceremonial exchanges have moved between Central Australia and the Kimberleys, resulting in a mixture of musical styles and occasions in the northwest (Keogh 1989, 1990; Moyle 1977b).

## Music in the Torres Strait Islands

Torres Strait Islanders occupy the islands between the northeastern tip of Australia and New Guinea. Most of these islands are under Australian sovereignty, though local culture, including music, was more oriented toward New Guinea than the Australian mainland (Beckett and Jones 1981). The use of drums, log idiophones, flutes, and tortoiseshell masks (figure 3) testifies to this connection.

From the mid-1800s, the strait was missionized, mainly by the London Missionary Society, which brought religious workers from Polynesia and Melanesia to transform local culture. The music that emerged combined Protestant hymnody and its Polynesian offshoots with indigenous music. Today, Torres Strait Islanders' music and dance have distinctive styles, which Aboriginals of the Cape York Peninsula have adopted.

## INDIGENOUS MUSICAL INSTRUMENTS

Indigenous songs in Australia are typically accompanied by musical instruments, mostly idiophones. Used over most of Australia are various concussion sticks, locally called clapsticks, of which the most noteworthy are paired boomerangs. Holding the center of a boomerang in each hand, a player taps the extremities of the boomerangs together, usually simultaneously, but sometimes rapidly alternating the taps at each end. Boomerang clapsticks may be played by many performers in unison, creating stunning effects. Other idiophones include rasps and rattles.

Membranophones in the form of waisted or cylindrical open-ended wooden drums, held horizontally and struck by hand, occur only on Cape York Peninsula and in the Torres Strait Islands (figure 4). Most drums used in the strait are made in Papua New Guinea.

The remaining instrument of note is the didjeridu, a conical wooden trumpet with no fingerholes, usually measuring between 1.5 and 2 meters long [see MUSICAL INSTRUMENTS: AEROPHONES]. Technically simple, it can demonstrate considerable musical virtuosity in a skilled performer's hands. In the late twentieth century, it has become a widespread symbol of Aboriginality, and is often played solo (Moyle 1978).

The didjeridu is typical of music in Arnhem Land, where it accompanies singing and is played in three subregional styles: eastern, central, and western. In *eastern* Arnhem Land, much musical excitement is generated by the rapid alternation of the fundamental tone and an overtone about a tenth above it. Singers' melodic ranges tend to be quite narrow (ranges of seconds, thirds, and fourths are common), linking the musical styles of eastern Arnhem Land and western Cape York. Performances have a strong element of improvisation, melodically and textually. In *central* Arnhem Land, the alternation of fundamental and overtone is much slower, and melodies, texts, and subjects are more fixed. Some melodies have a wider range, though most have ranges resembling those of eastern Arnhem Land. The dominant style of *western* Arnhem Land differs markedly. The didjeridu plays only the fundamental, leaving musical interest to be generated by variations in timbre and other techniques, like humming into the instrument while buzzing the lips, creating acoustic beats and resultant tones. Vocal melodies commonly have a wider range, an octave or more; songs are relatively fixed, musically and textually.

## POPULAR MUSIC

Popular music can be regarded as including folk, country, and what is conventionally called popular music, or pop. This categorization, though not fully satisfactory, differentiates folk, country, and pop from indigenous music and more self-consciously artistic music. Each of these terms covers a wide range of styles, whose boundaries are often fuzzy.

### Folk

In the late twentieth century, Australian folk is mostly performed in urban clubs and at festivals. Musicians often play it on city streets. In rural areas, Aboriginal musicians in southern Australia have been among the main keepers of folk song and music-hall traditions (Sullivan 1988). Folk-oriented clubs hold dances and weekend workshops.

Annual folk-oriented festivals occur throughout the nation. These include the National Folk Festival, held in Canberra on Easter weekend. The largest festivals have become multicultural events, incorporating the musics of immigrant communities, though many enthusiasts consider Anglo-Irish traditions to be the core of Australian folk. Fiddles, concertinas, accordions, tin whistles, and banjos are the core instruments, joined by a distinctively Australian invention, the lagerphone, a rod against which attached beer-bottle tops rattle when someone shakes the instrument or strikes it on the floor.

Though folk receives little media coverage, one weekly national radio program stands out as an exception: the Australian Broadcasting Corporation's "Music Deli," which records and broadcasts performances at festivals and concerts. The federal government gives financial support through its Australian Folk Trust.

### Country

In rural areas, Australian folk has been largely replaced by country, particularly among Aboriginals, who, preferring to live in their ancient lands, predominate in some towns. In the 1950s in western New South Wales, Dougie Young composed and performed songs full of bitter and self-deprecating humor about Aboriginal experiences of racism and its consequences in everyday life, including unemployment, alcoholism, and imprisonment for minor offenses (Beckett 1957–1958, 1965, 1993). Later, Aboriginal performers—including Harry Williams and his band, Country Outcasts—achieved national prominence, and country became a feature of Aboriginal radio. Aboriginal singer Isaac Yama was a local celebrity at the station run by the Central Australian Aboriginal Media Association in Alice Springs. By the 1970s, Australian country was reflecting influences from rock. The dominant musical style among Aboriginals can be identified as country-rock.

Australian country is more an industry than is folk. It gets notable broadcast time, particularly in rural areas, and it has well-developed networks for distributing commercial recordings. Like Nashville, Tennessee, it has an industrial center:

Tamworth, a country town in New South Wales. The main venues of country performances are concerts and festivals.

## Rock

Rock is the urban equivalent of country. A national popular-music industry has flourished since the 1940s. International success has come to several Australian popular musicians and bands, including Olivia Newton John, Midnight Oil, and Men At Work. In 1995, the Australian teenage grunge band Silverchair toured the United States, where it played on MTV's Music Video Awards; in early 1996, it broadcast a show from Madison Square Garden; in 1997, it toured the United States again. The federal government has given particular encouragement to the popular-music industry (Paul Keating, prime minister from 1992 to 1996, once managed a band), establishing and funding Ausmusic, a training-and-promotion organization, and encouraging popular-musical training in secondary schools and technical colleges.

Since the 1980s, Aboriginal musicians and bands have had success in rock. The most widely known Aboriginal band, nationally and internationally, is Yothu Yindi, from northeast Arnhem Land. It performs indigenous songs and rock (Stubington and Dunbar-Hall 1994). Other active Aboriginal bands and musicians originated in remote communities and large cities. Rock, country-rock, and reggae are the prevalent styles. Expressing indigenous themes and often using indigenous musical elements, Aboriginal popular music has struck a sympathetic chord among Australians of all origins, particularly young people.

## INSTITUTIONALIZING MUSICAL MATURITY

In the twentieth century, Australian musical culture began to mature, broadening its musical perspective, embracing diversity, and gaining confidence in the validity of homegrown musical experiences and resources. This maturity finds expression in funding for the arts, primarily through the federal government's Australia Council for the Arts, made of up several boards representing different arts (including the Performing Arts Board) and differently constituted boards (including the Aboriginal and Torres Strait Islander Arts Board). The council awards grants to individuals and organizations and creative-arts fellowships to selected artists. It is paralleled by smaller programs at the state level.

## Broadcasting

One of the most important events affecting Australian music in the twentieth century happened in the 1930s, when the federal government set up the Australian Broadcasting Corporation (ABC, originally Australian Broadcasting Commission). Initially established as a national radio network, the ABC expanded its scope to television in the 1950s. It played an influential role in encouraging Australian musical activity of all kinds through broadcasting Australian music, recording and broadcasting musical events, establishing and supporting state symphony orchestras, conducting musical competitions, issuing commercial recordings of Australian music, and creating and broadcasting educational programs about Australian music. It has also been instrumental in establishing indigenous broadcasting organizations, of which the Central Australian Aboriginal Media Association has been the most successful. Other broadcasting initiatives that have affected Australian music have been the expansion of publicly funded community radio stations and the establishment of the Special Broadcasting Service, which has radio and television aspects.

## Education

Since the 1940s, formal musical education at all levels in Australia has expanded. Increased university education in music raised standards of performance, composition, and scholarship, and broadened musical knowledge and interest in the general population. Indigenous institutional needs in music education began to be met in 1975, when Catherine J. Ellis established the Centre for Aboriginal Studies in Music (CASM) at the University of Adelaide (Ellis 1985:161–185), and in dance education with the establishment of the Aboriginal and Islander Dance Theatre (AIDT, in Sydney), an autonomous dance-oriented college for indigenous students. CASM and AIDT teach old and new forms, and have played a big role in generating new forms of Aboriginal performance.

### Research institutions

A third area of development has been the establishment, since World War II, of national collecting and research institutions and organizations, including the National Library of Australia, the National Film and Sound Archive, the Australian Institute of Aboriginal and Torres Strait Islander Studies, the Australian Music Centre, and the Musicological Society of Australia. As the national repository of Australian music publishing, the National Library of Australia contains a large collection of printed music of the nineteenth and twentieth centuries. The National Film and Sound Archive is the main repository of Australian commercial recordings; the Australian Music Centre is a specialized collection of Australian compositions and recordings of Australian music. Because these collections are recently established, scholars are only beginning to explore their potential. The Australian Music Centre publishes a journal, *Sounds Australian,* which discusses issues concerning Australian music.

The Australian Institute of Aboriginal and Torres Strait Islander Studies sponsors research and collects documentation on all aspects of indigenous culture and history. It has a broad-ranging program of publishing, including a semiannual journal and commercial recordings of indigenous music. It has large collections of unpublished manuscripts, published material, tapes, films, and photos—resources that possibly have had more use than other music collections, but also have major musicological research potential.

State libraries and archives—longer established than their federal counterparts, but narrower in their focus and less fully funded—are also important resources. The Musicological Society of Australia, established in Sydney in 1964, became a national organization with its first national conference in 1976. From the outset, its members have embraced the full diversity of the discipline. The society publishes a newsletter and the journal *Musicology Australia,* holds annual national conferences, and hosts international conferences and symposia.                    —STEPHEN A. WILD

## AUSTRALIAN DANCE IN THE 1990S

As part of Australia's self-description as a creative nation, dance has received special emphasis, ranging from small local groups that perform in converted warehouses to visiting international troupes that perform in the Sydney Opera House. Public and private support for dance has resulted in originating and maintaining myriads of dance companies and the publication of *Writings on Dance,* an Australian-based international journal devoted to dance. The Greenmill Dance Project, a conference devoted to choreography and academic papers, occurs annually in Melbourne. It features Australian choreographers and visiting troupes, including mainstream ballet companies, modern-dance companies, and more esoteric groups, like Korea's Hyonok Kim and Dancers, whose choreography has little to do with Korean dance, but is based on French-German expressionism and surrealism.

Immigrants' dancing is not forgotten; immigrants reinvent themselves in cross-cultural projects such as *The Speaking Tree* (1993) and *Stone the Crows* (1996), ventures that combined old dances into a mix aimed at interethnic understanding. *The Speaking Tree,* directed by the Indian artistic director Dr. Chandrabhanu, preserved but expanded important immigrant values. It politicized the East Timorese great-eagle dance as a symbol for East Timorese liberation. *Stone the Crows* grew out of cross-cultural workshops that explored creating an interethnic movement vocabulary drawn from Melbourne's traditions. Apart from a few protesters, the resident Vietnamese community supported the 1996 visit of the Vietnamese National Theatre, which presented Vietnamese dance in a Chinese-influenced theatrical style, tempered by the influence of Australian choreographer Cheryl Stock.

## The search for uniqueness

The overarching aim of the Australian dance community is to evolve traditions unique to Australia. Inherent in this evolution is the mixing of traits from multiple cultural sources. [For some immigrants' forms of dancing in Australia, see MUSICAL MIGRATIONS; for indigenous forms, see TRADITIONAL AUSTRALIAN DANCE.] Three examples illuminate efforts to create uniquely Australian works.

Exemplifying a unique scenario was the 1996 production of David Williamson's play *Heretic,* based on Australian professor Derek Freeman's attempt to undermine Margaret Mead's Sāmoan research. The onstage Mead, appearing in the play as Marilyn Monroe, Jacqueline Kennedy, and herself (with her trademark forked stick), is credited as being responsible for the sexual revolution that swept the Western world. Interspersed are musical interludes, such as the song "The Age of Aquarius" and Kim Walker's choreography of what he considers to be Sāmoan dancing.

Exemplifying a new style of movement unique to Australia was *But Do You Wanna Buy Some Thongs* (1996), choreographer Leigh Warren's production for the Adelaide Centre of the Performing Arts (figure 5). The dance combines balletic movement with tap dancing in rubber sandals. Ostensibly searching for a serial killer, the tappers lampoon environmental activists by inserting movements from Māori *haka.* They thwack their heels while their toes grip the thongs, but if the slippers fall off, "you just put them back on" (*Melbourne Age,* 30 June 1996).

Exemplifying a unique example of Aboriginal and Western modern-dance fusion are performances of the Bangarra Dance Theatre. *Ochres* (1996), choreographed by

FIGURE 5   Helpmann Academy dancers (*from left*) Catheryne James, Simone Peyroux, Kylie Wright, and Ashley Dolman perform in *But Do You Wanna Buy Some Thongs,* produced by the Centre for Performing Arts, Adelaide, Australia, 1996. Photo courtesy of the Adelaide Institute.

Stephen Page, uses modern-dance crawling movements to evoke the Dreaming, when Aboriginal ancestors created the Australian environment. Symbolic colors of liquid and powdered ochres metaphorically portray past, present, and future, as the dancers perform motifs ranging from indigenous to disco. —ADRIENNE L. KAEPPLER

## REFERENCES

Beckett, Jeremy. 1957–1958. "Aborigines Make Music." *Quadrant* 2:32–42.

———. 1965. "The Land Where the Crow Flies Backward." *Quadrant* 9:38–43.

———. 1993. "'I Don't Care Who Knows': The Songs of Dougie Young." *Australian Aboriginal Studies* 2:34–38.

Beckett, Jeremy, and Trevor A. Jones. 1981. *Traditional Music of the Torres Strait.* Canberra: Australian Institute of Aboriginal Studies.

Clunies Ross, Margaret, and Stephen A. Wild. 1982. *Djambidj: An Aboriginal Song Series from Northern Australia.* Canberra: Australian Institute of Aboriginal Studies.

———. 1984. "Formal Performance: The Relations of Tune, Text and Dance in Arnhem Land Clan Songs." *Ethnomusicology* 28:209–235.

Covell, Roger. 1967. *Australia's Music: Themes of a New Society.* Melbourne: Sun Books.

Donaldson, Tamsin. 1987. "Making a Song (and Dance) in South-Eastern Australia." In *Songs of Aboriginal Australia,* ed. Margaret Clunies Ross, Tamsin Donaldson, and Stephen A. Wild, 14–42. Oceania monograph 32. Sydney: University of Sydney.

Elkin, A. P., and Trevor A. Jones. 1953–1957. *Arnhem Land Music (North Australia).* Oceania monograph 9. Sydney: University of Sydney.

Ellis, Catherine J. 1985. *Aboriginal Music: Education for Living.* St. Lucia: University of Queensland Press.

Keogh, Ray. 1989. "*Nurlu* Songs from the West Kimberley: An Introduction." *Australian Aboriginal Studies* 1989(1):2–11.

———. 1990. "*Nurlu* Songs of the West Kimberleys." Ph.D. dissertation, University of Sydney.

Marett, Allan, and Linda Barwick. 1993. *Bunggridj-Bunggridj: Wangga Songs from Northern Australia by Alan Maralung.* International Institute for Traditional Music. Traditional Music of the World, 4. Smithsonian Folkways CD 40430. Compact disc.

Moyle, Alice M. 1964. *Songs from the Northern Territory.* Canberra: Australian Institute of Aboriginal Studies AIAS 1–5. 5 LP disks with booklet.

———. 1968–1969. "Aboriginal Music on Cape York." *Musicology* 3:1–20.

———. 1977a. *Songs from North Queensland.* Canberra: Australian Institute of Aboriginal Studies AIAS 12. LP disk with booklet.

———. 1977b. *Songs from the Kimberleys.* Canberra: Australian Institute of Aboriginal Studies AIAS 13. LP disk with booklet.

———. 1978. *Aboriginal Sound Instruments.* Canberra: Australian Institute of Aboriginal Studies AIAS 14. LP disk with booklet.

Stubington, Jill. 1978. "Yolngu *Manikay:* Modern Performances of Australian Aboriginal Clan Songs." Ph.D. dissertation, Monash University.

Stubington, Jill, and Peter Dunbar-Hall. 1994. "Yothu Yindi's 'Treaty': *Ganma* in Music." *Popular Music* 13(3):243–259.

Sullivan, C. 1988. "Non-Tribal Dance Music and Song: From First Contact to Citizen Rights." *Australian Aboriginal Studies* 1:64–67.

Wild, Stephen A. 1987. "Recreating the *Jukurrpa:* Adaptation and Innovation of Songs and Ceremonies in Warlpiri Society." In *Songs of Aboriginal Australia,* ed. Margaret Clunies Ross, Tamsin Donaldson, and Stephen A. Wild, 97–120. Oceania monograph 32. Sydney: University of Sydney.

———. 1988. "Australian Aborigines: Aboriginal Culture: Music and Dance." In *The Australian People: An Encyclopedia of the Nation, Its People and Their Origins,* ed. James Jupp, 174–181. North Ryde, New South Wales: Angus and Robertson.

# Traditional Australian Music

*Allan Marett*                    *Tamsin Donaldson*

*Elizabeth Mackinlay*      *Margaret Gummow*

*Grace Koch*                     *Stephen A. Wild*

*Linda Barwick*               *Peter Dunbar-Hall*

*Catherine J. Ellis*

**Northern Australia (Arnhem Land)**

**Gulf of Carpentaria**

**Queensland**

**The Kimberleys Area**

**Central Australia**

**Southeastern Australia**

**Contemporary Trends in Aboriginal Music**

## NORTHERN AUSTRALIA (ARNHEM LAND)

North of a line drawn from the mouth of the Roper River to the Victoria River, Northern Australia supports two musical-cultural areas: Central-Eastern Arnhem Land and Western Arnhem Land. Only the former area lies wholly within the geographical and political boundaries of Arnhem Land. The border between these areas roughly tracks the western boundary of the Arnhem Land Reserve, set aside to protect Aboriginal people from outside interference. A high degree of cultural interpenetration occurs between these areas, particularly near their borders.

All traditional Aboriginal artistic performances in Northern Australia—singing, dancing, executing visual designs—are associated with religious rites. They may occur in nonceremonial contexts, but ceremony remains their fundamental, most potent context. Ceremonies that celebrate ancestral beings' creative activities bear restrictions on who may perform or witness them: many of their songs, dances, and visual designs are secret, never heard outside ceremonial contexts. Public ceremonies, whose songs and dances are associated with spirits of lesser potency than ancestral beings, are common throughout Northern Australia, and performances of their songs often occur in nonceremonial contexts.

In the frequency of ceremonial performances and the diversity of artistic forms associated with them, Northern Australia is unusually rich. Following surveys by A. P. Elkin and Trevor A. Jones (1958) and Alice Moyle (1964, 1974), several detailed studies have been completed. These focus on public genres, including clansongs of Central-Eastern Arnhem Land and individually owned genres of Western Arnhem Land. Detailed musicological studies of clansongs in East Arnhem Land include those by Jill Stubington (1978) and Steven Knopoff (1992). Researchers have studied four Central Arnhem Land song-series: Baratjarr (Stanhope 1991), Djambidj (Clunies Ross and Wild 1982, 1984), Goyulan (Clunies Ross and Mundrugmundrug 1988), and Murlarra (Anderson 1992). Allan Marett has researched western genres (1991, 1992, 1994; Marett and Barwick 1993).

Major anthropological works have focused on Arnhem Land. Some of these—Keen (1978) and Morphy (1984) for East Arnhem Land, and Borsboom (1978) and Hiatt (1965) for Central Arnhem Land—discuss clansongs in detail. No major ethnographic work has been completed for western Northern Australia since that of Stanner (1963), though an ethnography by Rose (1992) contains much of local relevance. For Central-Eastern Arnhem Land, ethnographic films of public ceremonies have been completed by McKenzie (1980) and Dunlop (1979).

## Central-Eastern Arnhem Land

The music of Central-Eastern Arnhem Land (including Groote Eylandt) may be distinguished from that of Western Arnhem Land on the basis of the genre, genesis, ownership, and morphology of songs and associated dances and designs. The people of this area divide their universe between two moieties, Dhuwa and Yirritja. Through affiliation to a moiety, people are associated with the set of totemic species belonging to that moiety. A principal moiety-specific ceremony named Madayin celebrates the activities of ancestral beings who in the Dreaming traveled through Central-Eastern Arnhem Land naming countries and languages, creating clans and waterholes, distributing sacred objects, and singing the songs of this ceremony.

Each moiety owns unique ceremonies and has a set of clapstick-accompanied songs usually called *madayin* (in the northeast, also *bilma*). Because performing and witnessing these and certain other local ceremonies that involve singing or instrumental performance are under restriction, they cannot be discussed here. Such ceremonies include love-magic songs (*djarada*), which occur in series restricted to either men or women, and secret religious ceremonies, including Gunabibi, Yabuduruwa, and Djungguwan. A major ceremony, Ubar (or Ngulmarrk), has not been performed for decades.

The principal elements of social organization in Central-Eastern Arnhem Land are clans. Patrilineal and exogamous, they belong to either of two moieties. Within a moiety, certain clans may share some totems, but no two clans share identical sets. Each clan owns defined tracts of land and ritual property associated with them, including the songs, dances, paintings, and sacred objects that invoke clan-linked totemic species and natural phenomena. Songs, organized into series, are believed to have been created by ancestral beings and to have descended unchanged from generation to generation.

### Musical contexts

Clansongs (*manikai* in northeastern areas of Central-Eastern Arnhem Land, *bunggurl* in southwestern areas) celebrate totemic spirits' activities. They are sung primarily in three public ritual contexts: mortuary rites, ceremonies of ritual diplomacy, and ceremonies associated with initiating pubescent boys. They may also be performed in the public parts of otherwise secret ceremonies and in nonceremonial contexts for entertainment. All three ceremonial contexts require singing and dancing, with visual representations of totemic beings in several media. Totemic designs are painted on Rom poles (figure 1), coffins, and dancers' bodies. Carvings, sculptures in sand, and objects made from feathers or leaves are also used.

### Mortuary ceremonies

These are the principal contexts for the performance of clansongs. The disposal of the dead formerly had three stages. The first, primary burial or exposure, occurred soon after death; it consisted of burying the body or exposing it on a wooden platform. The second occurred months later, after the body had partially decayed; the bones of the deceased were cleaned and put in a bark cylinder, which for months or years relatives carried with them. The third stage, the most complex, involved constructing a hollow log coffin and placing the bones in it.

In some areas, as a result of Christian influence, the first stage has become the

FIGURE 1    Accompanied by clapsticks and a didjeridu, the Bararra and their Nakkára kinsmen,
led by the renowned ceremonial leader
Anabarrabarra, approach the prepared ground in
the main camp on the last day of dancing in the
Rom, a diplomatic ceremony. Photo by Axel
Poignant, 1952.

principal element of the ceremonial complex. In northern East Arnhem Land, the
second and third stages are rarely or never performed. Emphasis has shifted to primary burial, six months after which a second major ceremony (*dadayun* 'rag'), involves
destroying the deceased's belongings or purifying them with smoke; this ceremony is
an important element in mortuary customs throughout Northern Australia. In other
areas of Central-Eastern Arnhem Land, the third stage remains the principal one. In
the film *Waiting for Harry* (McKenzie 1980), some persons decorate the coffin with
totemic designs; others perform the associated songs and dances. Crushing the bones,
placing them in the coffin, and carrying the coffin to its point of sepulture require
specific songs and dances. In northern Central Arnhem Land, the stages of the ritual
require the performance of songs and dances associated with the clan of the deceased
and his mother.

Mortuary practices in Eastern Arnhem Land appear to differ fundamentally
from those elsewhere in the region. Funerals mark the soul's journey from the place
of death to the deceased's clan's lands. Ancestral events associated with the country
through which the soul travels are ceremonially reenacted in ritual episodes tracking a
particular set of dances, ritual actions, and songs. Decisions about which songs and
dances to perform and which paintings to produce are made primarily by members
of the deceased's clan and the clan that is in the relationship of mother's mother to
the deceased. Conducting a soul through the deceased's most important country to a
place of repose typifies mortuary ceremonies on Groote Eylandt (A. Moyle 1964;
Turner 1974). A mortuary ceremony from Eastern Arnhem Land has been documented on film (Dunlop 1979; Morphy 1984).

### Other ceremonies

Ceremonies of ritual diplomacy (Marradjiri, Rom) are widely practiced (Borsboom
1978; Wild 1986). These involve presenting to a distant group a tall pole, elaborately
decorated with totemic designs, through singing and dancing.

Ceremonies of circumcision confer social manhood on boys, marking membership in a clan and affirming connection with particular spiritual beings (Hiatt
1965:60–63). In Eastern Arnhem Land, these ceremonies may involve a symbolic
journey in songs and dances similar to those of mortuary ceremonies (Keen
1978:187).

Another public genre, extremely popular in northeastern Arnhem Land, consists
of *djatpangarri* (also *djedbangari*), didjeridu-accompanied songs sung by young
unmarried men, often in writing called fun songs. The texts are formulaic, mainly

"nonsense words" (A. Moyle 1974), but the songs are associated with everyday topics, including the first Disney cartoons seen locally. Most *djatpangarri* follow the same melodic pattern (Waterman 1971).

### Musical ownership

In Central Arnhem Land, series of clansongs are known by proper names specifying the subject of the series, or by the name of the owning clan. In East Arnhem Land, these series appear to be named by reference to the owning clan and the subject. Since clan-owned totemic species vary from clan to clan, the totemic spirits about which songs are sung vary from clan to clan. The Murlarra (Morning Star) series, belonging to the Rembarrnga-speaking Balngara clan of Central Arnhem Land, covers sixteen subjects: four birds (brolga, ibis, lotusbird, snipe), four fish (perch, saratoga, longtom, shark), three other animals (butterfly, python, wallaby), two plants (stringybark, yam), two forms of spiritual beings, and the morning star. Other clans also own Murlarra, but their subjects differ. The Murlarra of one Djinang-speaking clan shares five subjects (brolga, ibis, butterfly, wallaby, morning star) with that of the Balngara clan, but has fourteen other subjects (Anderson 1992:1:69–73). In Central Arnhem Land, each clan normally, though not exclusively, owns just one series of songs, but in East Arnhem Land, clans appear to own more than one: men can sing the songs of their clans, their mother's mother's clan, and any clan having the same series.

### Musical performance

Clansongs are sung by one or more men accompanying themselves on clapsticks, with a didjeridu. Any performance thus has three main musical elements: song, clapsticks, didjeridu. Women do not perform alongside men, but in funerals and related circumstances may engage in ritual wailing. Men and women's dancing may accompany the performance of clansongs; such dancing affects the musical performance.

In a typical performance, a particular subject is sung several times, followed by the singing of another, and so on. Throughout the area, subjects involve two environments: dryland and wetland. In Central Arnhem Land, subjects of both types occur in one series; in East Arnhem Land, songs associated with the sea often form a series different from those associated with the land. In Murlarra, the implied environment plays an important role in structuring performances: several subjects from one environmental type are sung; and then, if the performers wish, they move to subjects from the other, often making a comment such as "We'll go down (or up) now." They never interweave subjects of the two types: the sequence of stringybark (dry)–longtom (wet)–wallaby (dry) never occurs (Anderson 1992:1:74).

In Central Arnhem Land, subjects may be sung in several styles. A major distinction is between performances featuring no fixed metrical relationship among voice(s), clapsticks, and didjeridu, and those in which these elements follow the same meter. Rembarrnga-speaking owners of Murlarra cite these styles respectively as *ngarkana* and *djalkmi*. Only nine of Murlarra's sixteen subjects are sung in *ngarkana*, but all subjects may be sung in *djalkmi*. Dance, too, falls into these categories. In *ngarkana*, structured movements are unmetered and uncoordinated with musical elements; dances continue through several musical items. In *djalkmi*, dancers perform in time with the music; each dance corresponds to a single musical item. In northern Central Arnhem Land, a similar distinction appears to apply to the series Djambidj. An "elaborate dance," in which several musical items whose sounded elements display complex metrical relationships accompany a single dance, contrasts with "formal dance," in which each dance is performed in time with a single song in the same meter (Clunies Ross and Wild 1984).

*Djalkmi* also show a distinction between musical items in which the tempo of the clapsticks is fast (*djurrkdjurrkna*) and those in which it is slow (*burlpurlna*). Certain subjects may be sung with fast and slow beating. The fast mode represents the adult phase or a large manifestation of a subject; the slower mode, an immature phase or a small manifestation of the subject. Performance realizes any such subject as one or more items in the fast mode, followed by one or more in the slow mode. When musical items are realized in *ngarkana,* they precede those in *djalkmi.*

### Structure of a musical item

Throughout Central-Eastern Arnhem Land, measured songs commonly have three parts: an introductory section, the body of the song, and an unaccompanied coda (figure 2). The introductory section may present each of the auditory components. The lead singer establishes an appropriate clapstick pattern. He may quietly sing a few vocables, convey to other performers information about the song, comment on something unrelated to the music, or begin singing lines of the musical text. Other singers present begin tapping their clapsticks in time with his. The didjeridu enters, typically on two or three short tones, after which it sets up a rhythmically patterned drone. In the introductory section, it may add overblown notes, roughly a tenth above the fundamental.

The body of the song consists of sung text, accompanied by clapsticks and didjeridu. At the start, the singer usually leaps to the highest note of the first of several vocal descents that form the main melodic material of the item. In figure 2, each descent is marked as a numbered vocal section. In Central Arnhem Land, one melody sometimes serves for all items in the series; for other series, such as Djambidj, several melodies serve. A clear relationship apparently exists between the melody or set of melodies and the series. The relationship between melody and clan is clearly defined: in East Arnhem Land too, each of a clan's series has its melody or melodies, though for some songs singers may use other clans' melodies.

As a singer performs, he draws from a memorized pool of apt textual phrases. Improvisatorily, he fits these to the melody. Textual units are measured in relation to clapstick and didjeridu patterns. Textual units frequently consist of a semantically meaningful word, followed by vocables to fill out the meter. The order in which textual units occur varies from performance to performance, so the texts of no two performed items are likely to be identical.

Clapsticks and didjeridu articulate the metrical framework of songs. To articulate internal divisions within songs, both may vary. Each series normally has a range of associated clapstick patterns. Particular subjects often use contrasting alternatives. Figure 2 exhibits four clapstick sections: the first and third show even beating in quarter notes; the second and fourth show even beating in half notes. Figure 2 also has four didjeridu sections, of which the second and fourth feature an overblown hoot.

The beginning of the coda is signaled by a cadential pattern from the didjeridu, ending on the overtone and variant clapstick patterns. A short hiatus frequently occurs before the singers begin a coda. In figure 2, the performers sing a few more textual formulas, often to the lower notes of the descent, in freer delivery; two singers performing together often differ markedly in text and melody.

## Western Arnhem Land

In Western Arnhem Land, ceremonial complexes intersect in varying ways in different places. Since ceremonies associated with reenacting the Dreaming are secret, no discussion of these can be undertaken here.

FIGURE 2
"Saratoga," an item in the Murlarra song-series: *part 1,* an introductory section; *part 2,* the body of the song; *part 3,* an unaccompanied coda. Transcription by Gregory Anderson. (1992:1:121–123)

The principal public genres are *wangga* (also *walaka, ngindingindi, djungguriny*) and *lirrga* (also *lirra, gunborrg, gunbalanya*), which mark celebrations of the social dimensions of life. Singers sometimes give proper names to a set of songs. In the east, where this area borders on Central Arnhem Land, *wangga* and *lirrga,* more commonly known there by the Gunwingguan term *gunborrg,* are often performed in ceremony alongside *manikai* and *bunggurl.* In the west (around Port Keats), and in the eastern Kimberleys, they may be performed alongside public series (like *djanba*) that extend into the Kimberleys, or even with series from Central Australia.

The principal criterion for distinguishing between *wangga* and *lirrga* appears to be the language and the tribal affiliation of the songman who owns them. Songmen who speak Batjamalh, Marrisyebin, Marritiyel, or Ngalkbon sing *wangga,* but speakers of Marrengarr, Mayali, or Ngan'gityemerri sing *lirrga.* The two genres share many formal features, but the key to formal differences between them lies in the movements associated with them.

FIGURE 2
"Saratoga," an item in the Murlarra song-series: *part 1,* an introductory section; *part 2,* the body of the song; *part 3,* an unaccompanied coda. (*Continued from page 423.*)

### Musical contexts

The main performative contexts for *wangga* and *tirrga* are boys' circumcision ceremonies (public, witnessed by the whole community); ceremonies for the disposal of dead people's belongings and other mortuary rites; semiceremonial contexts, as for college graduations and the opening of social clubs or cultural centers; and informal contexts, as for entertainment.

Before being circumcised, a boy was educated by being led around his clan's country. The boy's father selected the genre to be performed. After the ceremony, the boy took the name of this genre, and maintained special links with the singers and dancers who performed for him.

Ceremonies for disposing of dead people's belongings are the major mortuary rituals in Northern Australia. Usually performed between one and two years after a death, they involve burning the deceased person's belongings in a pit, which people subsequently fill in and dance on, confining potentially dangerous spiritual effects. In some areas, the dancing precedes the participants' purification by water.

FIGURE 2 (*continued*)

### Musical ownership

*Wangga* and *lirrga* are given to individual songmen (and occasionally to women, who pass them on to male singers) by spirits, usually when recipients are dreaming. Song-giving spirits take various forms, including the ghosts of deceased songmen (whom the recipients may or may not have known), animals, or semihuman beings (such as the dwarflike *walakanda* of the Daly area); these spirits occupy a realm between the everyday world and the Dreaming, with connections to both.

Songs may be inherited from a father or an uncle; a few popular songs by deceased singers continue to be performed. How songs come into being—and the way in which no effort (comparable to that made to maintain Dreaming songs, or even *manikai* and *bunggurl*) is made to preserve them after a singer's death—reflect a stronger association of these songs with the everyday world than with the Dreaming. Most accounts of musical composition say a spirit sings to a songman in dream, often

*Wangga* and *lirrga* are performed by one, two, or three male singers. Women rarely perform alongside men. *Wangga* melodies consist of descents that cadence on a final whose pitch corresponds to that of the didjeridu.

in association with a picture reflecting a textual theme. Singers then practice the song and fix it by singing it at a corroboree [see COMPOSITIONAL PROCESSES: Australia].

### Musical performance

Some texts of *wangga* and *lirrga* consist solely of vocables. Primarily a vehicle for rhythmic, timbral, and melodic interplay, these texts are not used like those of Dreaming-originated songs, whose correct interpretation is controlled by knowledgeable performers. Other texts resemble statements that could be made in spoken registers, perhaps more than in any other traditional Aboriginal Australian songs. The following *wangga,* by Bobby Lane (1941–1992), has two lines. The first occurs five times over a single melodic descent, which terminates with wordless humming on the tonic; the second is sung over a second smaller descent:

> Rak badjalarrmaka banganyung.
> Winmedje ngandjinyene ngami.
>
> I am going to sing a song for the sake of my father's country.
> I am sitting eating oysters.

The text refers to the singer's eating oysters and thinking of his ancestral country, Badjalarr (North Peron Island).

*Wangga* and *lirrga* are performed by one, two, or three three male singers. Women rarely perform alongside men. Singers accompany themselves on a pair of clapsticks, accompanied by a didjeridu and singing either to accompany dancing or without dancing. *Wangga* often have accompanied sung sections that alternate with purely instrumental sections. Their melodies consist of descents that cadence on a final whose pitch corresponds to that of the didjeridu. Some singers use widely various melodies, but others maintain the same basic melody for all songs in a set. Some descents may be unstable; some consist almost entirely of a vocal glide.

TRACK 28 — Each of Alan Maralung's performances differs as he fits a varying text onto the melodic contour, adjusting the relationship afresh, moment by moment. Thus, as with clansongs from farther east, no two performances of a song are the same. In melodic and textual structures, other singers maintain a stricter, but by no means an absolute, musical stability. Habitually danced songs may have stabler structures than those that are not. In danced contexts, songs may provide a more fixed structure, against which structured movements play.

Singing is accompanied by a didjeridu and the metrical beating of sticks, or by didjeridu alone. Singing unaccompanied by sticks is often unmetrical, though variations of timbre and amplitude in the didjeridu may articulate a metrical framework. Most singers can perform metrical and unmetrical songs.

FIGURE 3  In the Nawaiyu Nambayu community, Daly River, Northern Territory, Jimmy Numbertwo performs a *lirrga,* accompanied on didjeridu by Robert Ilyerre Daly. Photo by Linda Barwick, 1995.

When *wangga* accompany dance, formal dancing usually occurs only in the instrumental section, where clapsticks and a didjeridu set up regular rhythms. Men and women dance, in markedly different styles. Singers signal formal divisions by beating special patterns, often giving dancers important cues. *Wangga* usually divide into two segments, but *lirrga* usually maintain a single style of beating (figure 3). *Wangga* and *lirrga* tolerate a high degree of variability in music and dance. For singers and dancers, this tolerance permits a degree of freedom that is possibly unique in Aboriginal performance. Toleration of variety reflects the role of musical genres in mediating nonreligious aspects of life.                    —ALLAN MARETT

## GULF OF CARPENTARIA

The southwest coast of the Gulf of Carpentaria supports four cultural groups, differentiated primarily by language: Garrawa, Gudanji, Mara, and Yanyuwa. Local music is largely vocal; despite a trend toward modernization, commodification, and Westernization, it is still an oral tradition, which may be performed by one, two, or several singers, in a style described as semiunisonal (A. Moyle 1973:239). Aboriginal trading of songs and material culture in this area is well documented. It continues to occur. For example, the Yanyuwa received the didjeridu, parrot-feather armlets, and stone tools from the Mara.

Musical ownership varies according to ascribed origin. Songs of the Dreaming are believed to have been composed by ancestral beings as they traversed the countryside, naming topographical features (J. Bradley 1994:3). Ownership of these songs reflects social divisions into moieties or semimoieties. As in Central Australia, each series has a ritual owner and a ritual manager, belonging to opposite kin categories: the manager ensures that ritual obligations are met, and the owner directs ceremonial performances. Newly composed songs may be composed by humans (in which case they commonly refer to recent events and are individually owned), or received from spiritual beings by individuals while dreaming (in which case ownership, though often by individuals, relates to moiety or semimoiety affiliation).

The main musical instruments of the area are idiophones. Performers beat rhythms by clapping and slapping their skin, and by striking boomerang clapsticks or paired handsticks together. When clapsticks or handsticks are not available, performers may improvise by flicking a fingernail against a tobacco tin, or tapping a stick on

FIGURE 4 Excerpt from a newly composed or "little-history" song, performed by Yanyuwa-Garrawa women at Borroloola. Text, rhythm, and melody repeat cyclically. Transcription by Elizabeth Mackinlay.

a plastic bottle. The didjeridu (locally *ma-kulurru*) is less important in musical performance than in Arnhem Land.

### Genres of song

The Yanyuwa call sacred songs big-history songs (*kujika*). These are clan, religious, and moiety songs, whose performances at rites of passage are often restricted by gender, age, or both. *Yarrangijirri* are performed for boys' circumcisions. Mortuary songs (*jawala*) help the spirit of the deceased reach the spiritual world. Love-magic songs are restricted by gender: *yawalyu* for women, *jarrada* for men.

Secular songs, performed for entertainment, may be termed fun songs or little-history songs, and may be sung by anyone at any time. Here too distinctions may be made by gender: men compose and perform *walaba,* but women compose and perform *a-kurija.* The musical traits of songs from the Gulf of Carpentaria and the Roper River area somewhat hybridize the often improvisatory style of Arnhem Land and the highly structured vocal style of Central Australia.

Performances of the Yanyuwa-Garrawa, located at Borroloola, typify the musical style of the Gulf of Carpentaria. Much of their music contains syllabic rhythm, which exhibits short and long rhythmic patterns concluding with a long note. Sung rhythm closely matches spoken rhythm. Songs usually have a descending melodic line, culminating in a repetition of the tonic.

A newly composed or "little-history" song performed by Yanyuwa-Garrawa women at Borroloola (figure 4) relates the story of a woman who has heard that a man likes her. Not knowing him well, she sits and thinks about responding. The song features cyclic repetition of text, rhythm, and melody. It exemplifies the opportunity provided through the medium of music for women to express their emotions.

—ELIZABETH MACKINLAY

## QUEENSLAND

The second-largest state in Australia, Queensland consists of 1,727,200 square kilometers of land, ranging from arid desert to lush tropical forests. Of more than a hundred indigenous languages spoken within the area before 1788, only fifteen are thriving (Schmidt 1991:47).

Two major indigenous cultures meet in Queensland: Aboriginals on the mainland, and Torres Strait Islanders to the far north. Within the strait, peoples of the eastern islands share cultural features with peoples of New Guinea, partly from trading and warring with those who lived in the Trans-Fly [see PAPUAN REGION OF PAPUA NEW GUINEA]. On the Australian mainland, musical style distinguishes three groups: northeastern (Cape York), southeastern (coastal areas of central and southern Queensland), and Central Australian (western Queensland).

Throughout indigenous Queensland, music is a vocal art. Instruments function as accompaniments only. Mainland instruments are idiophones, and a membranophone is used in Cape York. Peoples of the eastern Torres Strait favor aerophones: flutes, panpipes, and a single-reed instrument of New Guinean origin.

## Torres Strait

More Torres Strait Islanders live along the coast of Queensland than in the islands themselves, and their music and dances are known throughout Queensland. Island dances—music and movement—came as early as 1871, when London Missionary Society missionaries from West Polynesia began teaching their hymns, songs, and dances to replace indigenous traditions (Black and Koch 1983:158). European administrators and church officials favored island dances because their lack of a mythological base made them a safe alternative to premissionary arts (Chase 1980:361). Island-dance music is in two- or three-part harmony; its melodies encompass a range of an octave or more, ending on a unison or an octave. Its instruments may be guitars or ukuleles, drums, and rattles made of strung segments of the matchbox bean.

Dancers sing as they dance, either in a massed, military formation, or as one or two soloists, moving more or less in unison. Sometimes members of the audience march between rows of dancers, sprinkling talcum powder on the backs of certain dancers, showing relationship and support. Dancers decorate themselves with palm-leaf strips and usually wear headbands. For some songs (such as "*Taba naba norem*"), seated singers gesture from the waist up. Topics deal with historical events (such as the landing of the supply boat *Cora*) or the performers' wishes, sorrows, and aspirations. Island-dance plays—featuring processionals, a game, and recessionals—are also popular.

Traditional music of Torres Strait had mostly been replaced by music for island dances in 1898, when the Cambridge Expedition to the Torres Strait recorded and filmed in the strait. Secular dance-songs (*wed*) often employed a five-tone scale, laments employed sustained notes with ornamental flourishes, and the melodies of religious songs (*malu-bomai*) occasionally included microtonal wailing (Beckett and Jones 1981:8–9).

Dances consisted of highly stylized movements, some of which were mimetic. Dancers, usually male, performed secular works in a semicrouching posture, skipping on the tips of their toes. In varying sequences, they performed fifteen or more named variants of their basic step. Decorations, including animal and anthropomorphic masks, accentuated the dancers' movements. The Cambridge Expedition filmed a segment of dancing in which a performer wore a halo-like white-feather headdress (*dari*), which now graces the Torres Strait Islander flag.

## Cape York

The music and dance of Cape York has been documented in more detail than that of any other area of Queensland. The earliest recordings, made by Ursula McConnel in 1934 on the western coast near the Holroyd, Archer, and Embley rivers, are of songs and stories pertaining to myths about ancestral voices, a string bag, and ghosts.

Music of Cape York can be divided into cult-owned, clan-owned, and individually owned songs. The first are for special rites; clansongs belong to specific totemic groups; and individually owned songs often require virtuosic dancing, known as shake-a-leg, an energetic solo dance, in which the (male) performer holds his legs wide apart and moves forward without lifting his feet off the ground. Excluding initiatory songs (*bora*), ceremonial songs are sung in a strained timbre within a melodic range as narrow as a major second, often punctuated by calls. *Bora* melodies, performed with a more relaxed quality, often in a low vocal register, have a wider range. Accompaniment, from clapping, boomerang clapsticks, or a drum (figure 5), consists of strictly even beats. If two nonmelodic instruments perform together, they relate in the proportion of one to two (Dixon and Koch 1996). The people of Cape York also perform island dances, country, and popular music.

FIGURE 5   At Jumbun, North Queensland, Ida Henry provides musical accompaniment by striking a drum between her legs, under her skirt. Photo by R. M. W. Dixon, 1983.

Songs and dances in Cape York relate to the land, often to specific sites, and must be performed by the proper persons. Placing performers and spirits into juxtaposition, they express identity in terms of historical, mythological, and proprietary acts. *Wanam* is danced within a tight circle by carefully designated participants. The Kugu-nganhcharra (western Cape York) see songs as potentially less dangerous than dances. Singing invokes a spirit, but dancing demonstrates its presence; therefore old men say they must protect initiates or newcomers from the power of the dancing. Ceremonial owners offer this protection by invoking spirits and rubbing onto initiates the scent of their armpits (von Sturmer 1987:69).

Cape York dancers may wear anthropomorphic masks. An area is carefully prepared with props, such as carved totemic objects or massed leafy branches. Since the mid-1960s, festivals for dancing have drawn Aboriginal people from Queensland and other areas. They have changed by incorporating competitions and attracting tourists (Williams 1988).

### South, central, and western Queensland

Though isolated commentaries exist from as early as the 1850s, no researchers have systematically studied music and dance in the area immediately south of Cape York. Margaret Gummow (1992, 1994, 1995) has studied songs from the Bundjalung and Gidabal areas, extending from southern Queensland into northern New South Wales. The earliest recordings of music from southern Queensland (Winterbotham 1949–1950) included songs and discussions by Batjala, Dungidjau, Kabi Kabi, and Waka Waka men and women; these people also sang songs from towns farther north. Most of their recorded melodies spanned an octave; about a third of them were accompanied by concussed boomerangs. Performers mentioned dancing in two contexts: *bora* and corroboree. One man talked about the stepping-out (or "the old walk"), when men formed a protective ring around initiates; another discussed making his own corroboree, where he created song-and-dance movements.

Few recordings of songs have been made in central and western Queensland; songs from Mornington and Bentinck Islands, in the Gulf of Carpentaria, have been recorded since 1960. Woomera, the Mornington Island troupe, received funding from private enterprise for touring; since the early 1960s, they have appeared in schools and concerts.

Instruments may be paired clapsticks or boomerangs, a drum, and possibly a didjeridu (A. Moyle 1968–1969:12–13). By repeating on one tone strings of syllables that may last as long as the singer's breath allows, and by having the range of a major sixth to an octave, songs from Mornington Island show a closer musical affinity with songs of Central Australia than with those of Cape York. Women's songs, for easing a birth or lulling a baby, use smaller ranges. In contrast, Bentinck Islanders use melodic ranges approaching a perfect fourth; songs, sung in tense timbres, consist of short sections punctuated by breaths.

Dancers of Bentinck and Mornington islands paint their bodies much as do Central Australian performers; even their conical, hair-string hats resemble Warlpiri hats. Dance functions as the language of story and argument, imparting knowledge and resolving disputes. A woman is expected to dance whenever her husband dances (McKnight 1967:1). One Bentinck Island dance (A. Moyle 1977b:9), during which men abduct boys for initiation, has no singing.                                     —GRACE KOCH

## THE KIMBERLEYS AREA

North of the Great Sandy Desert in Western Australia, the Kimberleys area is bounded on the east by the Ord River Basin, and on the south and west by the Fitzroy River Basin and the Dampier Land Peninsula. Considerable trade of ritual and material goods occurs eastward into Western Arnhem Land and southward into the Western Desert (Akerman 1979a, 1979b; Berndt 1979). Linguistically, Kimberley languages are distinct from Western Desert and Arnhem Land languages (Stokes 1982; Vaszolyi 1979).

## Musical contexts, genres, and ownership

The distribution of musical genres differs by area. Central Australian genres occur along the southern edge of the Kimberleys, from La Grange to Halls Creek; at the eastern boundary, Northern Australian genres entail different practices. Kimberleys genres are most strongly present from Dampier Land to Kalumburu; through ritual exchange, they have spread into contiguous areas of Northern and Central Australia.

Singing is a feature of rituals accompanying major personal events (initiation, burial); it serves important roles in maintaining lands and species and entertaining audiences. Many ceremonies, especially those dealing with the Dreaming, bear restrictions on who may participate in and witness them, restrictions that apply especially to the most powerful Dreaming performances, including the major traveling-Dreaming cults and so-called love-magic ceremonies. Many restricted genres form part of a ritual-exchange complex with neighboring groups in Central and Northern Australia (Akerman 1979b; Wild 1987).

Dreaming-related ceremonies are commonly owned by moieties or otherwise defined descent groups, but many public genres are individually owned. Public genres, bearing no restrictions on who may witness them, are often performed for entertainment and accompaniment for public sections of rituals, including initiations and mortuary ceremonies. Some public genres may be performed by mixed-sex groups.

The most widely documented public genre is known by different names in different locations: *nurlu* in southern Dampier Land and contiguous areas (Dyabirr Dyabirr, Dyugun, Ngumbarl, Nyigina, and Yawuru languages), *ilma* in northern Dampier Land (Baardi and Nyul Nyul), *djunba* in central north Kimberley (Ngarinyin, Warrwa, and Wunambal), *maru* in the southwest (Garadyarri), and *dyudyu* in the south (Mangarla, Walmadyarri) (Keogh 1989; A. Moyle 1977a). Spirits of deceased kin (*balangan*) or agents of conception (*ray*) reveal songs and associated dances to dreaming individuals. Men's boomerang clapsticks (Nyigina *garli*) and women's clapping or slapping the lap accompany the songs, whose texts, set to a flexibly descending melody, convey a Central Australian musical style. Men and women may sing, but only men dance.

*Balga* (also known as *balganya, balgan,* or *dyuanbanya*) is distinguished from the *nurlu* complex by being owned by moieties, rather than individuals, and accompanied by clapsticks, rather than boomerangs. This genre is mainly performed in the central-north parts of the Kimberleys. The cognate genre, *djanba*, accompanied by clapsticks (men) and slapping or clapping (women), occurs in the south and east Kimberleys, and has extensions into Western Arnhem Land.

*Lilydyin* or *ludin*, a genre of individually owned songs concerning topical events, performed by men of northern Dampier Land for entertainment and without dancing, is said to be individually composed. Of similar origin and treating similar subjects, *dyabi* or *yabi* songs performed in southwest Kimberley, have a unique accompaniment: serrated sticks, producing a rasping sound when rubbed together (Keogh 1981; A. Moyle 1977a; von Brandenstein 1969).

The performance of didjeridu-accompanied *wangga* songs generally conforms to that in Western Arnhem Land, where the genre originates and whence performers frequently travel into the east Kimberleys for ceremonies. Songs are performed by one or two men accompanying themselves on paired clapsticks to the accompaniment of another man playing a didjeridu. In Kimberley *wangga,* performers often do not know the meanings of the texts (originally in Daly-area languages); they frequently classify *lirrga,* which also originate in Western Arnhem Land, as *wangga.* This classification may reflect stylistic similarities between *wangga* and *lirrga,* and the coincidence that the term *lirrga* has another song-related meaning in west Kimberley languages, where it denotes a song in a *nurlu* series immediately preceding a dance-song. Another genre originating in Western Arnhem Land performed in the east Kimberley is the didjeridu-accompanied *djirri djirri.*

## Musical performance

A west Kimberley performance of a *nurlu* illustrates important aspects of musical performance (Keogh 1990, 1995). The series named Bulu consists of seventeen songs and three dances owned by George Dyunggayan, a Nyigina-speaker, who lived on pastoral stations near the lower Fitzroy River, east of Broome. Many of the songs originated around 1925 from Dyunggayan's dreamed experiences with the spirit of his deceased father, Bulu, and several *ray;* the songs describe a journey undertaken by the group through Nyigina and Warrwa country, around the lower Fitzroy River basin. The other songs, which appeared after 1925, also describe events in the spiritual world, but do not reenact a dream-spirit journey. Frequent references to the weather, especially to rain and clouds, reflect Dyunggayan's status as a doctor, believed to hold special powers in relation to spirits and the weather. In 1985, Raymond D. Keogh recorded several performances of Dyunggayan's *nurlu.* On one occasion, Dyunggayan sang with the Nyigina singer Butcher Joe Nangan (figure 6).

In the first text in the Bulu series (figure 7*a*), the beating—by boomerang clapsticks and clapping, the former twice as fast as the latter—has a set relationship to the text, whose linguistic structures illustrate common features of Aboriginal lyrics: the words mix everyday Nyigina, suffixes added for rhythmic purposes, and one term of unknown meaning. The suffixes *-mirri* and *-dyina* occur only in musical texts, where they end everyday words for rhythmic purposes. The meaningful parts of this phrase are *Wanydyal,* the name of a waterhole, and *yingany,* meaning in everyday Nyigina 'he was there'. In the second phrase, the word *mindi* has no known meaning, and the word *yarrabanydyina* in everyday Nyigina means 'we (exclusive) saw him'. A gloss given by George Dyunggayan and Paddy Roe clarifies the text: Bulu and his *ray* come out from the waterhole Wanydyal and contemplate where they will go; Dyunggayan is with them, dreaming (Keogh 1994). Subsequent songs in the Bulu series name other sites passed in the journey, aurally mapping it (Keogh 1990).

The singers may begin and end at any point in the textual cycle, which over the course of an item repeats up to seven times; in figure 7*b,* they begin in the middle of the first line and end in the middle of the second. Certain points within the melodic contour align with the beginning of a textual line; one of these points occurs at the drop from the upper tonic (C) to the descending passage starting on the sixth (A) at the beginning of the third bar of figure 7*b* (Keogh 1995). These and other features of the musical setting are consistent with descriptions of Central Australian musical style (Barwick 1989; Ellis 1985; R. Moyle 1979).     —LINDA BARWICK

FIGURE 6     In the Kimberleys, Butcher Joe Nangan sings a *nurlu* and accompanies himself on boomerang clapsticks. Photo by Ray Keogh, 1983.

## CENTRAL AUSTRALIA

Aboriginal cultures have been in Australia for not less than ten thousand years, possibly about forty thousand. In that time, people learned to value the fragility of the continent's ecosystems and work in harmony with its rhythms. In contrast, European settlers imposed onto the environment their culture, laws, and values, often with devastating results. Their music replaced much of a musical tradition that had been intensely stable without being static, continuing intact while being recreated and renegotiated in performance.

In the central area of the continent, several major language groups survive. Researchers have done the most work among the Alyawarra, Antikirinya, Aranda (Arrernte), Pintupi, Pitjantjatjara, Warlpiri, and Yankunytjatjara, groups that have many similarities, though performers emphasize minor differences (Wild 1975:12).

The central region divides into two major linguistic areas: Central Australia, in which Arandic languages are spoken; and the Western Desert, in which Western Desert languages predominate. Five Arandic dialects and some forty Western Desert ones have been documented. Many once-listed groups (Tindale 1974) no longer have surviving speakers or singers. In this entry, *Central Australia* denotes the entire desert region of the continental center.

In music, Central Australians may "show the other side," allowing structural ambiguities to be perceived from many angles. The Pitjantjatjara call the alteration from quantitative to qualitative rhythm of the same short-long distribution in the rhythmic pattern *inma kampa kutjupa*. In the Western Desert, *inma* denotes the concept that encompasses music, dance, and ceremony, *kampa* denotes 'side', and *kutjupa* denotes 'another' or 'a different one'. The other side of a rhythm can be heard in performances, using the identical text and short-long disposition, but realized with different durations of long notes and a regular pulse (figure 8).

Most specific musical terms have an everyday meaning, which often reveals the conceptual process of the music. In Pitjantjatjara, the general term *inkanyi* can mean 'to have fun, to play, to laugh'; but when used with *inma*, it means 'to sing'. Likewise, the word for ritual wailing, *ulanyi*, when used without being prefixed by *inma*, means 'to cry, to weep'. Another basis for musical terminology is onomatopoeia: the sound of women's slapping their thighs is often denoted by the same term (*tukul*) as that used for the call of the emu.

FIGURE 7    Verse 1 of the Bulu series: *a*, text and rhythmic setting (after Keogh 1990:92, 165); *b*, performance by George Dyunggayan and Butcher Joe Nangan in 1985 (after Keogh 1990:215–218). The circles represent accompanimental clapping or slapping of the lap. Boomerang accompaniment typically occurs at twice this speed.

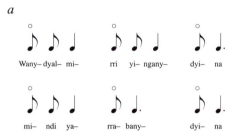

The sensory essence of an ancestor reveals itself in the sounds of a song the ancestor composed. By correctly performing an ancestor's songs, a descendant can reproduce the ancestor's sonic signature.

FIGURE 8
Pitjantjatjara rhythmic transformations: *a,* a typical rhythm; *b,* its "other side," in which a stick-beating accompaniment marks a pulse every five eighths. Transcription by Catherine J. Ellis.

Performers do not segregate musical elements from their everyday correlates, nor do they understand music as the sum of physical components. The concept of unity within the Dreaming combines in one term the separate features of music, dance, and ceremony, which performers subdivide with specific detailed terminology, including the Pitjantjatjara terms *inkanyi* 'to sing'; *pakanyi* 'to rise, to dance'; *mayu* 'melody'; and *timpil* 'beating' (song accompaniment with sticks); other words denote claps, slaps, and other actions.

## Musical structures

Central Australian singing is primarily vocal. Throughout the desert, the preferred style is unison singing, sometimes in octaves to accommodate male and female ranges. Departures from unison are usually understood as mistakes ("noise"), but in some areas these variants are optional, or occur accidentally, through slightly different timing of intervallic leaps.

Central Australian melodies move in a series of terraced descents from a high pitch to a low pitch, with upward leaps to begin new descents; melodies end quietly on a tonic, with reiteration of the lower pitch for several cycles of the text. Melodic ranges extend from an interval of a second to more than an octave.

A typical Central Australian melody can be schematized in three boxes (figure 9), each containing the shape and direction of the melody as it occurs in each full presentation of the text (not shown), which controls the duration of each section. The vertical dotted line in melodic section 2 shows a subdivision of the melodic contour on the basis of the upward leap; the horizontal dotted line in melodic section 3 shows that the melody fades at different points in different performances. The sequence of higher and lower notes must remain constant throughout any song that maps an ancestral journey, regardless of the performed lengths of texts related to each site being sung. Strict rules, known by good performers, govern the interlocking of text and melody.

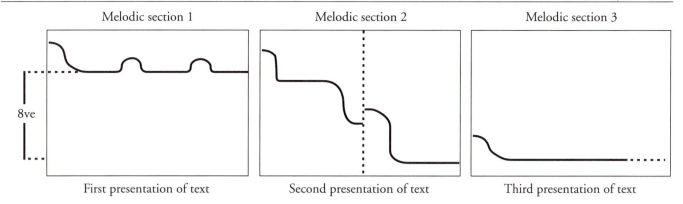

FIGURE 9 Schematic view of a typical Central Australian melody: each box contains the contour of the melody as it occurs in each full presentation of the text. Drawings by Catherine J. Ellis.

Melodic ornamentation includes elaborate glides and microtonal oscillations of pitch, deliberate overemphasis of certain pitches, and anticipatory slides, all in solo and collective singing. To achieve unison, women commonly sing at the low end of their range, and men sing at the high end of theirs. Vocal timbres range from low and sonorous to a harsher, nasal quality. Women use ritualized wailing as a vocal mechanism for expressing grief.

Not surprisingly in a hunting-and-gathering society, ancestral personalities are mainly represented in music through scent or taste, both known in Pitjantjatjara as *mayu*. The sensory essence of an ancestor reveals itself in the sounds of a song the ancestor composed. Each ancestor has its own scent, embodied in musical structure. By correctly performing an ancestor's songs, a descendant can reproduce the ancestor's sonic signature. Differentiation among ancestral scents is partly based on the pitch-based distance between the pivots in the descent, and partly on the length of time spent at each of these points. Specific locking of text to melody may affect this identification (Barwick 1989), as may exact or proportional duration within identifying melodic sections (Ellis 1970; Tunstill 1987).

Aboriginal Australians consider musical knowledge the highest achievement possible: no one can achieve high status without thoroughly understanding relevant local songs (Ellis 1964:20; Payne 1984:269). By correctly interlocking musical structures, a person can gain power over animate and inanimate objects. Musical performance is a process of effecting change: the singer is singing a song, but the recipients of that song may be said to have been sung (Ellis 1983:143).

### Texts and syllabic rhythm

Central Australians receive the texts of songs by direct communication from an ancestor. These texts may remain stable, unaffected by change over time, though the spoken versions of myths are believed to be variable. Texts of songs that Carl Strehlow recorded before 1910 and Catherine J. Ellis recorded in the 1960s show almost no change.

Texts usually have two lines, which make similar statements with minor differences, or say the same thing in different dialects; or the second line may balance the first, making a fuller statement. The following text, from a song performed to commemorate an ancestral lizard as he warms himself by a fire, expresses one idea in two ways: the first verse uses *waṟu* 'fire' and *ngaṟanyi* 'to stand'; the second verse complements these with *pupingka,* derived from *puyu* 'smoke'.

Waṟungka ngaṟanya, waṟungka ngaṟai.
Pupingka ngaṟanya, pupingka ngaṟai.

The rhythmic setting is syllabic. The resultant pattern repeats until the end of the melody. This format, AABB, is the most common textual structure, but variants occur, including AAB, AABC, ABC, and ABCD. Because syllabic patterns closely connect with given texts, rhythms sometimes acquire textual meanings. The structure of rhythmic patterns resembles that of texts, with two main sections corresponding to the verses, which may be identical or similar in rhythm, or balanced with retrogrades, inversions of long and short units, retrograde inversions, or contrasting rhythms. In some examples, rhythm alone conveys semantic meaning.

Sung language differs from spoken language: highly symbolic, it gives mere suggestions of meaning. Texts therefore can have many layers of interpretation, depending on the level of learning reached by the recipient of the explanation. Here again, rhythm seems important, since common rhythmic structures, such as rhythms using three adjacent short notes, often convey related meanings. By stressing phonemes and morphemes not ordinarily stressed in speech, combining and splitting words, and adding the second half of one word to the beginning of the next, performance disguises words and their meanings.

Adults never tell children the secret meanings of texts, but teach them simplified versions. The ceremonies in which children take part involve their community; participants perform and understand the music at their own level. In closed ceremonies, the esoteric meaning of texts gradually unfolds to appropriately initiated adults.

## Women's dancing

Women's dancing of Central Australia has two major classes: formal, which is subdivided into painted dances and painted closing dances (Ellis et al. 1990:101–136), and informal. During formal performances, dancers' bodies bear painted designs relating to the Dreaming being celebrated. Informal dancing can occur outside the formal framework, rendered as introductory sections and interludes, which require no paint.

Women may perform informal dances spontaneously in front of singers, but formal dancing requires strict control in hiding painted dancers until the singing begins, creating a simultaneous revelation of structures of songs, dances, and painted designs. During breaks in the singing, the dancers turn their (usually unpainted) backs toward the singers. On the ground, dancers' tracks create designs believed to hold prodigious power; women conclude important secret ceremonies by obliterating these tracks, lest a man see them and sicken.

## Musical accompaniments

The music of Central Australia involves no melodic instruments; the main accompaniment of singing is concussive or percussive. Boomerangs (Pitjantjatjara *karli*), predominantly weapons of hunting, serve in pairs as clapsticks for musical concussion. In some areas, people discard clapsticks after musical use; in others, they keep them specifically as percussive instruments. Forms of rhythmic accompaniment include clapping, stamping, beating a mound of earth with a rounded stick, rapid beating of alternate ends of a pair of boomerangs, and slapping the thighs, an exclusively female practice.

Other musical instruments of Central Australia are the swung slat and the *ulbura,* a wooden trumpet made from a hollow log about 60 centimeters long and 5 centimeters in diameter. In ceremonial settings, these instruments symbolize ancestors' voices. The didjeridu is not indigenous to Central Australia.

## Functions of songs, roles of performers

Within ceremonies, songs have several functions. Singers sit apart from where the dancers are being painted, but they must sing certain songs while the paint is being applied. In specific songs, the singers and the painters communicate on the dancers' state of readiness. Early in the process, a leader sitting with the singers starts these songs; as the time for dancing nears, the painters start songs until the dances start.

Special songs accompany dancing; others are for returning power to the soil after performances. Some dances are fast, with percussive accompaniment; other dances may be slow and unaccompanied. During a ceremony, women responsible for preparing the ceremonial ground also sing special songs. At the end of a performance, to return to the soil the power raised by the ceremony, the leader begins a closing song.

Differing roles of ceremonial participants reflect differing ownership and ritual responsibility, and distinguish classes of performers, such as lead singer, singer, and dancer. People can access the power inherent in these songs only by performing them correctly; consequently, leaders must maintain the accuracy of their songs. By ensuring that songs are sung in their correct order, starting and finishing each song, introducing the correct beat, and understanding deeply the symbolism and power of each song, the leader controls the singing. The leader usually opens each item with a short solo; and when others are sure of the text and the beat, they join in. Many young people also need to follow the melodic contour given by the leader until they know it for themselves. The leading of the group by an unknowledgeable singer will not produce the desired effects.

The leader also plays an important role in relation to conflict. The structure of songs depends on the correct interlocking of text and music, often in several ways. Good leaders display many contrasting settings when they begin successive small songs within a long series. Some performers may misinterpret this; by emphatically singing the correct structure, the leader repairs any resulting lack of unison.

In ceremonial contexts, singers present the words spoken by the ancestor at the creation of the ceremony, while dancers, by portraying the ancestor's actions, present the parallel physical manifestation. Whenever possible, songs are performed at the actual sites through which the ancestors passed at the beginning of time. The major role of the owner of a ceremony is to portray the ancestor. No ceremony can be performed without owners' presence and permission. The hereditary owner of some women's secret songs is a man, who may not sing the songs in public, but has the right to grant women permission to sing them. The manager prepares the site, paints the dancers, provides food and gifts for the owner, shouts instructions to the singers and the dancers, and cleans up afterward (Wild 1975:54).

## Secret songs

Education involves strict control of powerful, highly secret, material. Supreme knowledge, which comes from years of initiations and ceremonial performances, is confined to the oldest and wisest persons. Central Australia has three basic types of performance: open, educational, fun ceremonies, in which children learn ancestors' stories and laws; gender-specific erotic songs; and gender-specific secret ceremonies, containing power-laden songs, closed to all but initiated men or women.

More published information is available on Australian men's secret songs than on women's. Many researchers are men, to whom Aboriginal women prefer not to reveal their secrets. Consequently, controversy has arisen over the existence of women's esoteric songs of power. In the 1930s, the information that senior Aranda men gave Strehlow persuaded him of the existence of such songs, but he did not verify it. Since the 1940s, Diane Bell, Catherine Berndt, Catherine Ellis, Helen Payne, and others uncovered a vibrant culture of women's ceremonies. Male researchers had viewed with doubt the idea that women owned anything of worth, but the library of

FIGURE 10 The melody of a short song from a long Honey Ant series, sung by women of Central Australia (Ellis 1964:205); the original is a semitone lower. Its structural traits—melody, rhythm, syllabification—resemble those of men's songs. Transcription by Catherine J. Ellis.

research on men's and women's secret songs is now more balanced.

Men's and women's secret songs follow similar structural principles (figure 10). Women's songs are often narrower in range, with less rhythmic complexity, but the rules of melodic movement differ: for men, the extent that particular tones are repeated appears governed by poetic meter; for women, it often reflects divisions of the duration of the melodic line. A comparison of structures in men's and women's songs at Laverton shows that women are more consistent in pitch at the start of melodies, use more ornamentation, and sing in octaves and triple meter; men's songs are faster, in duple meter (May and Wild 1967:216–217).

Women interact in many men's secret ceremonies, though with limited participation; in contrast, women's secret ceremonies rarely allow interaction with men. Notions that including women in men's ceremonies is purely a way of further alienating them from sacred information by making them ignorant and passive, deceiving them, and excluding them from the understanding of ritualized sights and sounds (Hamilton 1980:17) do not take into account women's musical knowledge and their capacity to comprehend information encoded in musical structures. Researchers who do not understand the structural abstractions of Aboriginal music may overlook basic levels of interaction.

A major form of women's esoteric songs of power is love-controlling magic, respected and feared by its target, men. Secrecy in women's ceremonies is more likely to entail more overt eroticism than in men's. In Aboriginal communities, power derives from ritual, physical interaction with ancestors and their sites. Women gain status and power by asserting "my country is good country" (Bell 1979:22). It is politically important for men and women to have ritual access to the sacred sites of their ancestral songs; residency therefore has basic importance to social status.

Inheritance determines access to control and power. By removing women from their homeland, marriage undermines women's power. It little affects men, whose residence is usually their birthplace: they inherit the ceremonies and the land, and during their upbringing, they get a full education about the land of their Dreaming; women, relocated by marriage, must renegotiate for the rights to ritual material at their new residence, but the power gained by negotiation does not enjoy the same status as the power gained by birth and inheritance. To compensate for this situation, women in the 1960s, at different rates in different places, began returning to the land of their Dreaming, sometimes coercing their partners and children into accompanying them. This return asserted their right to choose a residency and reinherit the power of their bloodlines.

Barwick's and Ellis's studies of musical structure and its relationship to knowledge and power show that men's and women's ceremonies contain highly developed encodings. Only persons knowledgeable enough to understand the structures can access them. Analyses prove that a system of absolute pitch is operating, and exact reproduction of pitch and duration is basic to performers' definition of a good performance. By perceiving these details through analysis, Ellis discovered codes based on rhythm, accentuation, proportional divisions of duration, and modulation within arithmetic scalar structures (1984, 1991). These processes show different sides of an ancestor's scent or taste.

—CATHERINE J. ELLIS

## SOUTHEASTERN AUSTRALIA

Southeast Aboriginal Australia may be considered to consist of what is now New South Wales, southern Queensland, Victoria, southeastern South Australia, and Tasmania. The reasons for treating it as a distinct musical region are the shared consequences of a similar colonial history more than the shared features of indigenous musical pasts. After 1788, when British colonization began, the major cities of what became the most densely populated part of Australia sprang up along the southeastern continental rim: Adelaide, Brisbane, Melbourne, Newcastle, and Sydney. All but Newcastle became state capitals, extending urban influence inland in a widening fan. In most of the region, indigenous people faced new forms of disruption and death earlier and often more intensely than elsewhere. Aborigines of Tasmania experienced a genocidal invasion. Each of these states today has a vigorous population of people of mainly southeastern Aboriginal descent. New South Wales and Queensland have the largest Aboriginal-identifying populations in Australia. Each has about 25 percent of the total.

Mapped state boundaries in the west and north of the region are conveniently linear, but they arbitrarily ignore features previously important to Aboriginal societies. They roughly enclose the area bounded on the west (and north) by the Darling River system (some Aboriginal languages give the name Paawan to the Barwon and Darling rivers), a natural boundary that more or less coincided with the western limits of some cultural features, including certain male-initiation practices (tooth evulsion, but not circumcision), religious preoccupations (with sky-dwelling beings), and linguistic features.

Within the region were several groupings of linguistic communities, whose members tended to have language names constructed on the same etymological principles: the names of some repeated a word for 'no', and the names of others used a word for 'no' plus a suffix glossable as 'with'. Along the Murray River lived speakers of the no-no languages Wembawemba, Yitayita, and others; west of the Great Dividing Range, north of the river, lived speakers of the no-with languages Kamilaroi (Gamilaraay), Wiradjuri, and others. South of the river lived speakers of languages whose names ended in *wurung* 'lip'. In Tasmania, linguistic, geographical, social, and cultural relationships at the time of colonization are far less well understood. Tasmania became an island about eight thousand years ago. Available evidence neither proves nor disproves connections between Tasmanian languages and those of the mainland.

Questions of linguistic culture are important when considering to what extent the southeast may have been a coherent musical region in precolonial times. All that survives points to a texted vocal music. But singing recorded in Southeast Australia in the 1960s may only slightly have resembled singing formerly prevalent in the region (A. Moyle 1966:43). How closely the recorded music resembles music sung locally a century before is unknown.

## Evidence for "the old songs"

The only recorded performances of Tasmanian vernacular songs are Fanny Cochrane Smith's wax-cylinder recordings, made in 1899 for the Royal Society of Tasmania. In 1972, Smith's granddaughter recorded what she remembered of one of these songs, but the meanings of the words have been lost (Crowley and Dixon 1981:398). Southeastern Aboriginal recordings housed in the Australian Institute of Aboriginal and Torres Strait Islander Studies (AIATSIS) consist largely of solo songs performed by elderly people, often sung incidentally in the course of other projects, such as recording languages. These singers remembered songs as keepsakes of customs and gave limited information about earlier musical meanings and contexts.

Early twentieth-century accounts of singing and dancing come from anthropologists and travelers, most notably A. W. Howitt (1904) and R. H. Mathews (1904). There are pictures of performances by the nineteenth-century Aboriginal artists Barak, Tommy McRae (Sayers 1994), and Mickey of Ulladulla, and pictures by outsiders [see ENCOUNTERS WITH "THE OTHER": figure 1, p. 8]. There are also photographs of ceremonies. Available evidence leads to certain conclusions about the range of performative elements, participants' roles, musical instruments, painted designs, and so on. Commonly, women beat a possum-skin pillow resting in their laps, men clicked paired boomerangs, and male dancers wore leaf rattles tied to their legs.

### Ceremonial and other special-purpose songs

Throughout New South Wales by 1905, regular ceremonial activity, which continued longer in the north of the region, was drawing to a close (Beckett 1978:6). Only a handful of recorded songs are ceremonial in origin or have powers to heal, control weather, and the like. Even those who remembered them would have been reluctant to sing them out of religious contexts or in the absence of authority to invoke their powers. In the 1950s, George Dutton, reportedly the only surviving ritual leader of the extreme north and west of the region by the 1930s, recorded performances relating to initiation. A. R. Radcliffe-Brown (1929) and R. M. Berndt (1947) accumulated details of hunting-related songs in the northeast and contexts for singing by "clever men" in central-western New South Wales, respectively.

### Corroborees and occasional songs

Long after ceremonial life had ended, secular occasional and informal songs continued to be composed in some languages of the region. The texts of such songs in the AIATSIS archive consist mainly of evocative words, phrases, and sentences, conveying scenes, characters, and events, as in this song, about a child lost in Ngiyampaa (Wangaaypuwan) country in 1932:

> Ngathi pakaa kurraarr kayi purraay nungkal thirramakaanhthi.
> Kuwayupu na yanawanha.
> Mukarri paa na kurunhi.
> Kurraarr na nganaay.

Palunhipa yaama na.
But your child was a long way over there in the hills.
He's still going.
He went into the porcupine grass.
He's away to blazes.
He might have died.

As here, narrative density creates vivid impressions. These songs are often so allusive as to permit various interpretations. As songs traveled from one language to another, meanings and interpretations were often learned separately from texts.

Many short solo fragments are described by their singers as corroboree songs. *Corroboree* originates in a Sydney-region word, *garabara,* denoting a particular dance. It entered English via pidgin to mean any Aboriginal dancing (Troy 1994). This etymology raises two questions: Were fully contextual performances of these songs longer? If so, what were the conventions for extending them?

A comparison of seven recordings of various lengths by different singers of the song quoted above—including one by its composer, Fred Biggs—showed that Ngiyampaa corroboree songs had two sections, one dominant and often more widely remembered than the other. The first section led either to a second section or to its own repetition. Biggs's performance, by variable melodic movement on one word of the first section (*thirramakaanhthi* 'in the hills') revealed which section would be sung next, making possible a prolonged performance with cues for other participants, dancers' stepping, and so on (Donaldson 1987).

Songs with two sections and flexibly repetitive patterns were widespread in the region of the no-with languages and beyond. That traces of it remain among the Wembawemba in the no-no language area (Hercus 1986) and elsewhere is hard to prove in the absence of multiple recordings of the same songs. Margaret Gummow's research in Bundjalung and Gidabal country reveals much about musical practices that flourished longer there than farther south. In the notation of a 1955 recording of Dick Donnelly's singing a nonritual song performed with dancing (figure 11), the meaning of the words is not apparent, and no interpretation has been passed down, possibly because the song was from Gangari country (Gummow 1992, 1994).

### Reactions to introduced music

Southeastern Aboriginal people have long welcomed, and even traveled large distances in search of, new songs and languages, so their enthusiasm for introduced music is unsurprising. In 1794, when Goethe was remarking that "the French tune of Malbrook" was pursuing travelers wherever they went, coastal Aborigines were singing it while paddling their canoes (Donaldson 1995:144).

As gatherings for ceremonies declined, and with them singing and dancing at corroborees, other forms of recreational music grew up in the communities where Aborigines lived. Claypan dances, on riverine flats or banks, became popular. Instruments played included fiddles, accordions, harmonicas, zithers, banjos, and

FIGURE 11 The beginning of the first section of a corroboree song, as sung by Dick Donnelly; clapsticks (not shown) sound on the first beat of each measure. After Gummow 1992: 462–463.

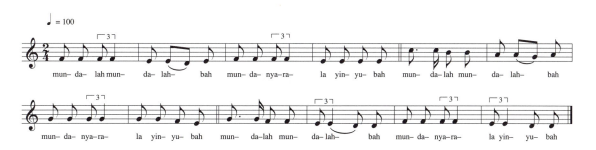

In the old musicians' spirit, the hillbilly-inspired songs of Dougie Young make fun of personal quirks: "You might do something wrong—they'd make a song out of you straightaway!"

guitars (Sullivan 1988). A highlight of the new music was gumleaf bands, which flourished in the 1920s and 1930s [see POPULAR MUSIC: Musical Ensembles: Gumleaves]; their use of leaves differed from customary uses of leaf whistles (K. Bradley 1995).

Since the people of what is now Sydney first began adopting songs from Europe, Aboriginal people in the southeast have responded to and appropriated various vocal and instrumental music. Their main kinds of songs have been hymns and gospel songs, ballads, popular songs, American popular and country music, rock, and reggae. Aborigines often marked introduced songs as theirs by translating the texts into their own languages and including foreign-language words in their own compositions in new styles. Their preferences in choosing new styles partly reflected opportunities available for using them for traditional social purposes. In the old musicians' spirit, the hillbilly-inspired songs of Dougie Young (1994) make affectionate fun of personal quirks: "You might do something wrong, they'd make a song out of you straightaway!" (after Donaldson 1984:250).

### Music in the southeast in the 1990s

In the southeast region, the switch from speaking ancestral languages to speaking English has long been completed in all but exceptional circumstances in a few locations. Because Aboriginal social circumstances have changed, the contexts for interest in the old songs and dances have changed.

Elders with memories of the old songs and dances have begun to use new technology to record their memories independently of anthropologists, linguists, and musicologists. In 1970, with no knowledgeable women present, Jimmy Barker recorded himself singing men's and women's parts (Donaldson 1987:24). In 1991, Bill Reid had a video made of himself giving a solo performance of a collective dance while singing a Gamilaraay song (Donaldson 1993). Some young people have been researching their heritage to preserve, celebrate, and sometimes reintroduce aspects of what they learn. Lorraine Mafi-Williams, a Bundjalung, produced a film (1988) showing Millie Boyd explaining mythology and singing songs, including one that Boyd had received from her deceased aunt (Gummow 1995:122). Some central New South Wales people have been reviving any ancestral songs they can trace as *yuwaay* songs, naming them after the shout that signaled the end of any performance. Revived songs and dance-style elements sometimes become part of Aboriginal children's activities.

Against this background, organizations in urban centers in the southeast are tapping traditions from all over Australia to provide training and schedule performances for Aboriginal and Torres Strait Islander musicians and dancers. Since the mid-1970s at the Centre for Aboriginal Studies in Music (CASM) in Adelaide, central Australian musicians have been training urban Aboriginals in ancestral ways. At about the same time in Sydney, the National Aboriginal Islander Skills Development Association

(NAISDA) started introducing Aboriginal students and communities to each other's dancing. The company associated with NAISDA, the Aboriginal and Islander Dance Theatre, tours Australia and the world. Bangarra Dance Company, formed by some NAISDA graduates, also has national and international standing.

Translocal, intercultural displays of Aboriginality now form part of the mainstream of public musical life in the southeast. Many popular-music groups are participating in international trends, based mainly in metropolitan centers. A newer development is the staging of indigenous musical theater. The most prominent example is the show *Bran Nue Dae*, which originated in Broome, Western Australia, and was later performed in Newcastle, now a center for Aboriginal people mainly from northern New South Wales.

—TAMSIN DONALDSON, with MARGARET GUMMOW and STEPHEN A. WILD

## CONTEMPORARY TRENDS IN ABORIGINAL MUSIC

Though people of Australian Aboriginal ancestry continue to create music in old styles, their music that receives the most widespread public exposure is contemporary popular music—Aboriginal rock. Since the mid-1970s, as the number of recordings made by Aboriginal popular-music performers has increased, this genre has undergone a period of broadening activity and recognition [see POPULAR MUSIC: Music in Place: Aboriginal Rock].

Several factors have led to this situation. Perhaps most importantly, Aboriginals have set up radio and television stations and more than twenty media associations, of which the chief is the Central Australian Aboriginal Media Association. Established in 1980, it began producing records in 1984. Based in Alice Springs, it is the main record-releasing company through which Aboriginal bands of the central and northern regions of Australia record and issue music.

Also important is Aboriginal students' new freedom to enroll in postsecondary courses in music, from which numerous bands have emerged. The most important postsecondary music course for Aboriginal students has been at the Centre for Aboriginal Studies in Music (CASM), founded in 1975 at Adelaide University, an outgrowth of the Program of Training in Music for South Australian Aboriginal People, begun there in 1971. CASM has been the birthplace of several prominent bands, including Aroona, Kuckles, No Fixed Address, and Us Mob.

Other factors in increasing the number of Aboriginal recordings include the national and international success achieved by Aboriginal popular-music bands and soloists (including Archie Roach, Coloured Stone, Kev Carmody, No Fixed Address, and Yothu Yindi); the higher profile nationally accorded to indigenous arts since 1988, when Australia marked the bicentennial of British colonization; Aboriginal performers' regular staging of festivals; Aborigines' increased desire to utilize music, alongside other arts, to explain Aboriginal cultures and political stances to non-Aboriginal Australians; and a rise in Aboriginal women's commercial recordings.

### Styling the music

Contemporary Aboriginal popular music includes several musical styles. Alongside international rock, country has been a favored style for decades, and reggae and calypso have been accepted as important influences (Breen 1989; Castles 1992; Narogin 1990). All these styles remain in the foreground. Additionally, Aboriginal musicians work in folkloric styles, often for social criticism or political protest. Artists in this category include Kev Carmody, Ruby Hunter, Bob Randall, Archie Roach, and the female group Tiddas. A common theme of these performers' songs is criticism of legalized injustice.

In socially critical songs, issues central to contemporary Aboriginal identity and the handling of minorities by the police and the government are typical. Bob Randall's "Brown Skin Baby" and Archie Roach's "Took the Children Away" denounce the bureaucratic practice of removing Aboriginal children from their parents for assimilation into the larger society—a practice that continued into the 1970s. "Malcolm Smith," by the Melbourne-based group Djaambi, describes the death of a young man in police custody—a familiar event of Aboriginal life. Many songs by Kev Carmody treat issues of wide social application, including the plight of street children, capitalist politics, and dispossession. Songs by Tiddas and by Ruby Hunter address problems of family life. Most of Hunter's songs address these issues from a woman's perspective, discussing the situation of the children of separated parents ("Let My Children Be"), prostitution ("Who's To Blame?"), and domestic violence against women ("A Change Is Gonna Come").

Another important stylistic trend is that Aboriginal performers are working in ambient styles. Aboriginal didjeriduists collaborate with other instrumentalists, some of whom perform on instruments from diverse cultural backgrounds. This collaboration has led to performances and recordings of combinations such as didjeridu and Tibetan flute, didjeridu and shakuhachi, and didjeridu and synthesizers.

### Language

Bands such as Kulumindini Band and Yothu Yindi (figure 12) record songs in Aboriginal languages, but this practice has occurred only since the mid-1980s. In the 1960s, the most widely known Aboriginal recording artist was Jimmy Little, who sang ballads, gospel, and country; his lyrics were in English and paid no cognizance to his origins.

In 1984, the Warumpi Band released "*Jailanguru Pakarnu*" ('Out From Jail'), the first commercially released recording in an Aboriginal language (Luritja). Since then, the practice of setting lyrics in Aboriginal languages, including Kriol and Aboriginal English, has become common. Often songs employ more than one Aboriginal language (as do some indigenous songs), or contain alternate sections of an Aboriginal language and English. The musical use of Aboriginal languages is a statement of Aboriginal identity and a means by which Aboriginal languages, many of which are moribund, can be preserved and taught (Dunbar-Hall 1997).

FIGURE 12    While one member of Yothu Yindi sings, others play a didjeridu and clapsticks.

### Lyrics

In common with popular music around the world, the lyrics of contemporary Australian Aboriginal popular music explore issues of romance, though in Australia, those are not the prevalent topics. Instead, political issues, such as Aboriginal rights to land and self-determination, prevail. Some Aboriginal songs are about health, a subject of high local importance. Instructive examples promote ways of ensuring children's health and alert listeners to the dangers of AIDS. Admonitory examples caution Aboriginal youths about problems of sniffing petrol and warn adults about the effects of abusing alcohol.

Another lyrical source is the Dreaming, whose stories and descriptions of personages and events give rise to spiritual knowledge. In accord with the importance of land and personal connections with it, many songs invoke sites and their significations or vent nostalgia for a former home. Firm expressions of Aboriginal identity, often through proclamation or demonstration of the ability to speak a specific language, and hence of belonging to the culture implied by it, also occur.

### Politics

Some Aboriginal musicians use music for voicing social criticism and political comment, but others use it for expressing notions of Aboriginality. Some groups from central Australia (including Kulumindini Band, North Tanami Band, and Wedgetail Eagle Band) produce songs that restrict themselves to localized situations. A song may be about a site, a group united by language, a totemic figure, or a locally understood subject. Often such bands, little known outside their communities, distribute their recordings as cassettes, in small numbers.

Yothu Yindi have had national and international exposure. Their success reflects their musicianship, sponsorship by Mushroom Records, and receipt of prestigious recording-industry awards. They admit to having an agenda: using popular music, including videos, to teach non-Aborigines about Aboriginal cultures in general and their own culture (Yolngu) in particular. Other bands, like the Warumpi Band in the 1980s and in subsequent revival appearances, have managed to gain local and national exposure while attracting a public following.

## Manipulating songs and albums

Though Aboriginal rock ostensibly uses songs, some groups have modified the genre in line with Aboriginal canons of musical form. Yothu Yindi's album *Tribal Voice* (1989) pays homage to earlier performers from the area of the band's origins, and to a local genre of music, the *djatpangarri* (Stubington and Dunbar-Hall 1994). It integrates into rock the melodic shapes and the ethos of *djatpangarri*. In songs by the Warumpi Band (from Papunya, Northern Territory) and by Blekbala Mujik (from Gulin Gulin, Northern Territory), traits of the formal structures of local songs can also be traced.

Some Aboriginal bands include sections of traditional singing within the formal structure of songs. In "Treaty," Yothu Yindi sing a section in traditional style with an Aboriginal text and didjeridu-and-clapstick accompaniment over the band's drums and bass guitar. Similarly, bands have adapted the album, a concept of Western commercial popular music, as an expression of Aboriginal identity, or as a composite statement of issues relevant to Aboriginal communities. The bands that conceive of albums in this way have strong attachments to communities in the central and northern parts of Australia, where old customs flourish.

In Yothu Yindi's albums, clues to the Yolngu cultural system are present in the topics, lyrics, and sequencing of songs. Some of Yothu Yindi's songs cite or allude to totemic subjects that relate to membership in the clans from which the band's performers come.

The Kulumindini Band (from Elliott, Northern Territory), in their first album, *Kulumindini Band: Marlinja Music,* sang songs in Aboriginal languages of the area from which the band originated, in conjunction with topics about specific sites owned by the local Aboriginal community. This combination of language and lyrical subject makes the album a statement of ethnic identity.

Locally spoken languages, specific topics (including the abuse of alcohol, the need for cultural survival, and contemporary customs), and significant sites accumulate throughout the Warumpi Band's albums, creating the impression that their creative productions are a series of pieces of information relevant to their home community.

Another set of Aboriginal bands consists of those living and working in towns and cities. *Love,* an album by the Sydney-based band Mixed Relations, treats interracial relations, urban Aboriginal existence, the status of Aboriginal women, and Aboriginal historical perspectives. With musical clues to the performers' backgrounds, it establishes a cumulative Aboriginal ethos.

Contemporary performers also construct albums by mixing songs in traditional styles and rock, the material in traditional styles deriving from the communities from which the performers originate. Albums by Blekbala Mujik, Sunrize Band, Tjapukai Dance Theatre, Yothu Yindi, and others show this practice. On these groups' albums, music links traditional material and rock—an important trend in contemporary Aboriginal popular music. These links include borrowing melodies, patterning the didjeridu, rhythmicizing the boomerangs or clapsticks, and formal structuring.

## Employing Aboriginal instruments

An important trend among contemporary Aboriginal performers is to integrate elements of Aboriginal traditional music with international rock. This trend can most easily be heard in the use of indigenous instruments. Some bands use seed or shell rattles and swung slats. More usually, bands use concussed clapsticks or paired boomerangs. Often clapsticks or boomerangs produce rhythms that non-Aboriginal listeners associate with those of drums, especially the backbeats typically played on snare drums.

The most used instrument associated with Aboriginal cultures is the didjeridu. Long used in part of Northern Australia, it has spread throughout the continent as a component of Aboriginal musical ensembles, performing rock and other styles. It takes a range of musical roles: in some bands, it is a soloist, replacing guitars in a solo section; in other bands, it recalls one of its roles in traditional music by serving as a drone and providing antiphonal effects against vocal parts.

In a departure from custom, some bands use more than one didjeridu, and female performers have begun playing it. Women's performance is controversial and not fully accepted in communities where gender-based ownership of cultural representation continues. In indigenous Northern Australian genres, only men play the didjeridu in public. A widespread but erroneous urban myth holds that in Northern Australian societies, women are forbidden to touch or play the instrument, but the situation is merely a conventional matter: in public ceremonies, men usually play musical instruments, while women slap their skin or clap.

Studio technicians amplify, distort, electronically alter, and digitally sample the sound of the didjeridu; its fundamental pitch sometimes sets the key of a song or is fitted to the key. Through the introduction of a slide mechanism, inventors have altered the instrument to allow it to change pitch; for the instrument created in this way, musicians have coined names like *didgebone* and *tromdoo.* Through such alteration, the didjeridu enters the tonal contexts of rock, becoming available for songs that rely on modulatory chordal patterns. This use differs from the use of the didjeridu in traditional music of Arnhem Land, where the pitch of the instrument may have no relationship to those of voices performing with it.

Comparison of the didjeridu's areas of traditional use with its adoption in Aboriginal contemporary music across Australia leads to ambiguities in the instrument's significance. For bands from areas where traditional music requires the didjeridu, its use in rock may represent cultural continuity and innovation. For bands from nondidjeridu-using areas, it is an innovation, often interpreted as a national symbol of generalized Aboriginal culture.

—PETER DUNBAR-HALL

## REFERENCES

Akerman, Kim. 1979a. "The Renascence of Aboriginal Law in the Kimberleys." In *Aborigines of the West: Their Past and Present,* ed. Ronald M. Berndt and Catherine H. Berndt, 234–242. Nedlands: University of Western Australia Press.

———. 1979b. "Material Culture and Trade in the Kimberleys Today." In *Aborigines of the West: Their Past and Present,* ed. Ronald M. Berndt and Catherine H. Berndt, 243–251. Nedlands: University of Western Australia Press.

Anderson, Gregory D. 1992. "Murlarra: A Clan Song Series of Central Arnhem Land." 3 vols. Ph.D. dissertation, University of Sydney.

Barwick, Linda. 1989. "Creative (Ir)regularities: The Intermeshing of Text and Melody in Performance of Central Australian Song." *Australian Aboriginal Studies* 1989(1):12–28.

Beckett, Jeremy. 1978. "George Dutton's Country: Portrait of an Aboriginal Drover." *Aboriginal History* 2(1):3–31.

Beckett, Jeremy, and Trevor Jones, ed. 1981. *Traditional Music of the Torres Strait.* Canberra: Australian Institute of Aboriginal Studies. LP disk and notes.

Bell, Diane R. 1979. "The Pawurrinji Puzzle." Report to the Central Land Council, Alice Springs. Typescript. Library of the Australian Institute of Aboriginal and Torres Strait Islander Studies, Canberra.

Berndt, Ronald M. 1947. "Wuradjeri Magic and 'Clever Men'." *Oceania* 17:327–365, 18:60–86.

———. 1979. "Traditional Aboriginal Life in Western Australia: As It Was and Is." In *Aborigines of the West: Their Past and Present,* ed. Ronald M. Berndt and Catherine H. Berndt, 3–27. Nedlands: University of Western Australia Press.

Black, Paul, and Grace Koch. 1983. "Koko-Bera Island Style Music." *Aboriginal History* 7(1–2):157–172.

Borsboom, Adrianus P. 1978. *Maradjiri: A Modern Ritual Complex in Arnhem Land, North Australia.* Nijmegen: Katholieke Universiteit.

Bradley, John J. 1994. "Some Yanyuwa Songs." In *Little Eva at Moonlight Creek and Other Aboriginal Song Poems,* ed. Martin Duwell and R. M. W. Dixon, 3–67. St. Lucia: University of Queensland Press.

Bradley, Kevin. 1995. "Leaf Music in Australia." *Australian Aboriginal Studies* 1995(2):2–14.

Breen, Marcus, ed. 1989. *Our Place, Our Music: Aboriginal Music: Australian Popular Music in Perspective.* Vol. 2. Canberra: Aboriginal Studies Press.

Castles, John. 1992. "Tjungaringanyi: Aboriginal Rock." In *From Pop to Punk to Postmodernism: Popular Music and Australian Culture from the 1960s to the 1990s,* ed. Philip Hayward, 25–39. Sydney: Allen & Unwin.

Chase, Athol. 1980. "Which Way Now? Tradition, Continuity and Change in a North Queensland Aboriginal Community." Ph.D. dissertation, University of Queensland.

Clunies Ross, Margaret, and Johnnie Mundrugmundrug. 1988. *Goyulan the Morning Star: An Aboriginal Clan Song Series from North Central Arnhem Land.* Canberra: Aboriginal Studies Press. Cassette and book.

Clunies Ross, Margaret, and Stephen A. Wild. 1982. *Djambidj: An Aboriginal Song Series from Northern Australia.* Canberra: Australian Institute of Aboriginal Studies.

———. 1984. "Formal Performance: The Relations of Music, Text and Dance in Arnhem Land Clan Songs." *Ethnomusicology* 28:209–235.

Crowley, Terry, and R. M. W. Dixon. 1981. "Tasmanian." In *Handbook of Australian Languages.* Vol. 2, edited by R. M. W. Dixon and Barry J. Blake, 395–427. Canberra: The Australian National University Press.

Dixon, Robert M. W., and Grace Koch. 1996. *Dyirbal Song Poetry.* St. Lucia: University of Queensland Press.

Donaldson, Tamsin. 1984. "Kids that Got Lost: Variation in the Words of Ngiyampaa Songs." In *Problems and Solutions: Occasional Essays in Musicology Presented to Alice M. Moyle,* ed. Jamie C. Kassler and Jill Stubington, 228–253. Sydney: Hale & Iremonger.

———. 1987. "Making a Song (and Dance) in South-Eastern Australia." In *Songs of Aboriginal Australia,* ed. Margaret Clunies Ross, Tamsin Donaldson, and Stephen Wild, 14–42. Oceania Monograph 32. Sydney: University of Sydney.

———. 1993. "The Curlew's Love Song—and Dance." *Australian Aboriginal Studies* 1993(2):134–135.

———. 1995. "Mixes of English and Ancestral Language Words in Southeast Australian Aboriginal Songs of Traditional and Introduced Origin." In *The Essence of Singing and the Substance of Song,* ed. Linda Barwick, Allan Marett, and Guy Tunstill, 143–158. Oceania monograph 46. Sydney: University of Sydney.

Dunbar-Hall, Peter. 1997. "Site as Song—Song as Site: Constructions of Meaning in an Aboriginal Rock Song." *Perfect Beat* 3(3):55–74.

Dunlop, Ian. 1979. *Mardarrpa Funeral at Gurka'wuy.* Sydney: Film Australia. Film.

Elkin, A. P., and Trevor A. Jones. 1958. *Arnhem Land Music (North Australia).* Oceania monograph 9. Sydney: University of Sydney.

Ellis, Catherine J. 1964. *Aboriginal Music Making: A Study of Central Australian Music.* Adelaide: Libraries Board of South Australia.

———. 1970. "The Role of the Ethnomusicologist in the Study of Andagarinja Women's Ceremonies." *Miscellanea Musicologica: Adelaide Studies in Musicology* 5:76–208.

———. 1983. "When Is a Song Not a Song? A Study from South Australia." *Bikmaus* 4(3):136–144.

———. 1984. "Time Consciousness of Aboriginal Performers." In *Problems and Solutions: Occasional Essays in Musicology Presented to Alice M. Moyle,* ed. Jamie C. Kassler and Jill Stubington, 149–185. Sydney: Hale & Iremonger.

———. 1985. *Aboriginal Music: Education for Living.* St. Lucia: University of Queensland Press.

———. 1991. "Exactitude d'intonation et précision de l'ensemble dans la musique de l'Australie Centrale." *Cahiers de musiques traditionnelles* 4:207–226

Ellis, Catherine J., Linda Barwick, and Megan Morais. 1990. "Overlapping Time Structures in a Central Australian Women's Ceremony." In *Language and History: Essays in Honour of Luise A. Hercus,* ed. Peter Austin, R. M. W. Dixon, Tom Dutton, and Isobel M. White, 101–136. Canberra: Australian National University.

Gummow, Margaret. 1992. "Aboriginal Songs From the *Bundjalung* and *Gidabal* Areas of South-Eastern Australia." 2 vols. Ph.D. dissertation, University of Sydney.

———. 1994. "The Power of the Past in the Present: Singers and Songs from Northern New South Wales." *The World of Music* 1:42–50.

———. 1995. "Songs and Sites/Moving Mountains: A Study of One Song From Northern NSW." In *The Essence of Singing and the Substance of Song,* ed. Linda Barwick, Allan Marett, and Guy Tunstill, 121–133. Oceania monograph 46. Sydney: University of Sydney.

Hamilton, Annette. 1980. "Dual Social Systems: Technology, Labour, and Women's Secret Rites in the Eastern Western Desert of Australia." *Oceania* 51:4–19.

Hercus, Luise A. 1986. *The Languages of Victoria: A Late Survey.* Revised edition. Canberra: Pacific Linguistics.

Hiatt, Lester R. 1965. *Kinship and Conflict.* Canberra: Australian National University Press.

Howitt, A. W. 1904. *The Native Tribes of South-East Australia.* London: Macmillan.

Keen, Ian. 1978. "One Ceremony, One Song: An Economy of Religious Knowledge among the Yolngu of Northeast Arnhem Land." Ph.D. dissertation, Australian National University.

Keogh, Raymond D. 1981. "The Two Men: An Aboriginal Song Cycle from the Kimberleys." B.Mus. thesis, University of Sydney.

———. 1989. "*Nurlu* Songs from the West Kimberley: An Introduction." *Australian Aboriginal Studies* 1989(1):2–11.

———. 1990. "*Nurlu* Songs of the West Kimberleys." Ph.D. dissertation, University of Sydney.

———. 1994. "Some Nurlu Songs from Broome." In *Little Eva at Moonlight Creek and Other Aboriginal Song Poems,* ed. Martin Duwell and R. M. W. Dixon, 72–87. St. Lucia: University of Queensland Press.

———. 1995. "Process Models for the Analysis of Nurlu Songs from the Western Kimberleys." In *The Essence of Singing and the Substance of Song: Recent Responses to the Aboriginal Performing Arts and Other Essays in Honour of Catherine Ellis,* ed. Linda Barwick, Allan Marett, and Guy Tunstill, 39–51. Sydney: University of Sydney.

Knopoff, Steven. 1992. "Yuta Manikay: Juxtaposition of Ancestral and Contemporary Elements in the Performance of Yolngu Clan Songs." *Yearbook of the International Council for Traditional Music* 24:138–153.

McKenzie, Kim. 1980. *Waiting for Harry.* Canberra: Australian Institute of Aboriginal Studies. Film.

McKnight, David. 1967. "Outline of Subjects Investigated During Field Trip to Mornington Island." Manuscript. Canberra: Library of the Australian Institute of Aboriginal and Torres Strait Islander Studies.

Mafi-Williams, Lorraine, producer. 1988. *Eelarmarni.* Sydney: Australia Film Institute. Film, video.

Marett, Allan J. 1991. "*Wangga* Songs of Northwest Australia." *Musicology Australia* 16:37–46.

———. 1992. "Variability and Stability in *Wangga* Songs of Northwest Australia." In *Music*

*and Dance in Aboriginal Australia and the South Pacific,* ed. Alice Marshall Moyle, 193–212. Oceania monograph 41. Sydney: University of Sydney.

———. 1994. "*Wangga:* Socially Powerful Songs?" *The World of Music* 36(1):67–81.

Marett, Allan J., and Linda Barwick. 1993. *Bunggridj-Bunggridj: Wangga Songs from Northern Australia by Alan Maralung.* International Institute for Traditional Music: Traditional Music of the World, 4. Smithsonian Folkways CD 40430. Compact disc.

Mathews, R. H. 1904. *Ethnological Notes of the Aboriginal Tribes of NSW and Victoria.* Sydney: F. W. White.

May, Elizabeth, and Stephen Wild. 1967. "Aboriginal Music on the Laverton Reservation, Western Australia." *Ethnomusicology* 11:207–217.

Morphy, Howard. 1984. *Journey to the Crocodile's Nest: An Accompanying Monograph to the Film Mardarrpa Funeral at Gurka'wuy.* Canberra: Australian Institute of Aboriginal Studies.

Moyle, Alice M. 1964. "*Bara* and *Mamariga* Songs on Groote Eylandt." *Musicology 1: The Proceedings of the Musicological Society of Australia,* 15–24.

———. 1966. *Handlist of Field Collections of Recorded Music in Australia and Torres Strait.* Occasional Papers in Aboriginal Studies, 6; Ethnomusicology Series, 1. Canberra: Australian Institute of Aboriginal Studies.

———. 1968–1969. "Aboriginal Music on Cape York." *Musicology* 3:3–20.

———. 1973. "Songs by Young Aborigines: An Introduction to North Australian Aboriginal Music." In *The Australian Aboriginal Heritage: An Introduction Through the Arts,* ed. R. M. Berndt and E. S. Phillips, 238–268. Sydney: Australian Society for Education Through the Arts, with Ure Smith.

———. 1974. "North Australian Music. A taxonomic Approach to the Study of Aboriginal Song Performances." Ph.D. dissertation, Monash University.

———. 1977a. *Songs from the Kimberleys.* Canberra: Australian Institute of Aboriginal Studies 13. Notes to LP disk.

———. 1977b. *Songs from North Queensland.* Canberra: Australian Institute of Aboriginal Studies. Notes to LP disk.

Moyle, Richard M. 1979. *Songs of the Pintupi: Musical Life in a Central Australian Society.* Canberra: Australian Institute of Aboriginal Studies.

Narogin, Mudrooroo. 1990. *Writing from the Fringe: A Study of Modern Aboriginal Literature.* Melbourne: Hyland House.

Payne, Helen. 1984. "Residency and Ritual Rights." In *Problems and Solutions: Occasional Essays in Musicology Presented to Alice M. Moyle,* ed. Jamie C. Kassler and Jill Stubington, 264–278. Sydney: Hale & Iremonger.

Radcliffe-Brown, A. R. 1929. "Notes on

Totemism in Eastern Australia." *Journal of the Anthropological Institute of Great Britain and Ireland* 59:399–415.

Rose, Deborah B. 1992. *Dingo Makes Us Human: Life and Land in an Australian Aboriginal Culture.* Cambridge: Cambridge University Press.

Sayers, Andrew. 1994. *Aboriginal Artists of the Nineteenth Century.* Oxford: Oxford University Press, with the National Gallery of Australia.

Schmidt, Annette. 1991. *The Loss of Australia's Aboriginal Language Heritage.* Canberra: Aboriginal Studies Press. Institute Report Series.

Stanhope, Paul T. 1991. "Baratjarr: A Preliminary Analysis of a Central Arnhem Land *Bunggurl* (Clan Song Series)." B.A. thesis, University of Sydney.

Stanner, W. E. H. 1963. *On Aboriginal Religion.* Oceania monograph 11. Sydney: University of Sydney.

Stokes, Bronwyn. 1982. "A Description of Nyigina, A Language of the West Kimberley, Western Australia." Ph.D. dissertation, Australian National University.

Stubington, Jill. 1978. "Yolngu *Manikay:* Modern Performances of Australian Aboriginal Clan Songs." Ph.D. dissertation, Monash University.

Stubington, Jill, and Peter Dunbar-Hall. 1994. "Yothu Yindi's 'Treaty': *Ganma* in Music." *Popular Music* 13(3):243–259.

Sullivan, Chris. 1988. "Non-Tribal Dance Music and Song: From First Contact to Citizen Rights." *Australian Aboriginal Studies* 1988(1):64–67.

Tindale, Norman B. 1974. *Tribal Boundaries in Aboriginal Australia.* Berkeley: University of California Press.

Troy, Jakelin. 1994. "The Sydney Language." In *Macquarie Aboriginal Words,* ed. Nick Thieberger and William McGregor, 61–78. Sydney: Macquarie Library.

Tunstill, Guy. 1987. "Melody and Rhythmic Structure in Pitjantjatjara Song." In *Songs of Aboriginal Australia,* ed. Margaret Clunies Ross, Tamsin Donaldson, and Stephen Wild, 121–141. Sydney: Oceania Publications.

Turner, David H. 1974. *Tradition and Transformation: A Study of the Groote Eylandt Area Aborigines of Northern Australia.* Australian Aboriginal Studies, 53; Social Anthropology Series, 8. Canberra: Australian Institute of Aboriginal Studies.

Vaszolyi, Eric. 1979. "Kimberley Languages: Past and Present." In *Aborigines of the West: Their Past and Present,* ed. Ronald M. Berndt and Catherine H. Berndt, 252–260. Nedlands: University of Western Australia Press.

Von Brandenstein, Carl G. 1969. "Tabi Songs of the Aborigines." *Hemisphere* 13:28–31.

von Sturmer, John. 1987. "Aboriginal Singing and Notions of Power." In *Songs of Aboriginal Australia,* ed. Margaret Clunies Ross, Tamsin Donaldson, and Stephen Wild, 63–76. Sydney: University of Sydney.

Waterman, Richard A. 1971 [1955]. "Music in Australian Aboriginal Culture—Some Sociological and Psychological Implications." In *Readings in Ethnomusicology,* ed. David McAllester, 167–174. New York: Johnson Reprint Corporation.

Wild, Stephen A. 1975. "Warlbiri Music and Dance in Their Social and Cultural Nexus." Ph.D. dissertation, Indiana University.

———, ed. 1986. *Rom: An Aboriginal Ritual of Diplomacy.* Canberra: Australian Institute of Aboriginal Studies.

———. 1987. "Recreating the *Tjukurrpa:* Adaptation and Innovation of Songs and Ceremonies in Warlpiri Society." In *Songs of Aboriginal Australia,* ed. Margaret Clunies Ross, Tamsin Donaldson, and Stephen A. Wild, 97–120. Sydney: University of Sydney.

Williams, Drid. 1988. "Homo Nullius: The Status of Aboriginal Dancing in Northern Queensland." *Journal for the Anthropological Study of Human Movement* 6(3):87–111.

Winterbotham, Lindsay P. 1949–1950. Wire recordings. Archive of the Australian Institute of Aboriginal and Torres Strait Islander Studies, Canberra.

Young, Dougie. 1994. *The Songs of Dougie Young.* Canberra: Australian Institute of Aboriginal and Torres Strait Islander Studies and The National Library of Australia. Compact disc.

# Traditional Australian Dance

*Drid Williams*
*JoAnne Page*
*Andrée Grau*
*Fiona Magowan*
*Megan Jones Morais*
*Ronne Arnold*
*Adrienne L. Kaeppler*

**Wangga of Northwest Australia**
**Tiwi Dance, Northern Territory**
**Yolngu Dance, Arnhem Land**
**Yanyuwa Dance, Gulf of Carpentaria**
**Wanam of Northeast Australia**
**Warlpiri Dance, Central Australia**
**Photographing Performance in Australia**

Transcending mundane concerns, dance and song in Aboriginal Australia were venerated as sources of power and prestige: "The song invokes the spirit, the dance demonstrates its presence" (von Sturmer 1987:71). Tied to geographical sites and localities, ceremonies and rituals were transmitted from cultural heroes and heroines to particular groups of people. The concept of "traditional Aboriginal dancing" includes singing:

> To approach, embrace, and become part of their land and its animals and plants they had but their wits, their imagination, their will to be masters under the ancestors who had left it all for them. They learned the land, its plants and its animals. . . . Through dance and ceremony, rituals, mutilations, masks, decorations, and the secrets handed down from their ancestors, they could enter for awhile into the very being of kangaroo, wallaby, emu, turtle, eagle, crow. . . . As they moved into the thunder, the lightning, the rain, clouds, so these, inevitably, moved into them. (Burridge 1973:62)

Something was being *said*. People "humanized their natural environment" (Berndt 1987:170). They were Crocodile *Man,* Taipan *Man,* Wallaby *Man,* Echidna *Woman.*

Understanding the spatial features of indigenous dancing—the directions of ancestral tracks in relation to the land and the Dreaming—is crucial to understanding the movements. Danced and ritualized spaces are often oriented on directional axes. At Warlpiri circumcisions, performers of Traveling Women dance toward geographical east; at Warlpiri fire ceremonies, performers face north as they follow the track of Rock-Wallaby Man or Owl Man (Wild 1977–1978). The connection between cultural heroes, surrounding landscapes, and sites of significant events from the mythical past formed the basis of Aboriginal peoples' identities:

> The concept of the Dreaming, the organizing logic of so much of the symbolism of Aboriginal art, is . . . unlike the foundational concepts of most other religious systems. The Dreaming is not an idealized past. The Dreaming, and Dreaming Beings, are not the products of human dreams. In most Aboriginal languages the

concept referred to in English as the Dreaming is not referred to by words for dreams or the act of dreaming, even though it may be through dreams that one sometimes gets in touch with the Dreaming. The use of the English word "Dreaming" is more a matter of analogy than of translation. (Sutton 1989:15)

Dances, for those who owned them, closed spatial-temporal gaps between past and present. Bringing these dances into alignment with Western conceptions of dancing is difficult because Western dancing, and the models of learning and knowing attached to them, provide no clues. Dancing done by Aboriginal troupes on Western stages does not conform to Western conceptions. Performances in Aboriginal contexts are less representations of events, where dancers assume roles different from their social roles, than revelations of participants' being-in-the-world, affirming their inner identities.

People of the Western Desert believe that when a person is in an altered state of consciousness, the person's spirit may leave the body and travel in the spiritual world (Tonkinson 1978:109). Individuals may see spirits performing songs and dances that can be brought back to the ordinary world. The person who brings these items back owns them, is their boss, and has rights over their use and display; other people may not perform them without permission.

*Nurlu* of the Kimberleys are recent (Coate 1966). Their composition is attributed to supernatural beings: spirits of deceased kin (*balangan*) and agents of conception (*ray*). Butcher Joe Nangan [see TRADITIONAL AUSTRALIAN MUSIC: figure 6] attributed more than fifty *nurlu* to Dyabiya, his mother's sister's spirit, whom he met in a dream; these songs and dances portrayed this spirit's release from its body and travels in the spiritual world (Keogh 1989:3). Dances of the Kimberleys featured ornate headgear, worn or carried by dancers, which represented rainbows, pelicans' bills, shields, *balangan,* and other entities (Keogh 1990). These paraphernalia are built from bark, wooden pegs, and twisted strands of grass and wool. From tip to tip, they can sometimes, as in headgear representing a rainbow, reach nearly two meters. They gain symbolic significance when seen in motion against the horizon.

Throughout Australia, ritual performances mediated between the past and the present because life and all good things come from ancestors and creators. In Arnhem Land (Borsboom 1978), Cape York (Arnold 1991), and the Kimberleys, among the Tiwi (Goodale 1971:300–305, 323–329; Grau 1983:32–44) and Pitjantjatjara (Tunstill 1987:122–124), and in Central Australian women's ceremonies (Ellis, Barwick, and Morais 1990), dances seek to bring dancers, spirits, and dreamings into juxtaposition and being. Dances incorporate socially mandated relations between living people and spatial and gestural-action signs meant to signify "the marvels" (Stanner 1966).

In contrast to still-living traditions, as in the Western Desert, few twentieth-century "initiatory and restricted ceremonies" occur in the southeast (Donaldson 1987:23), where outside knowledge of indigenous dancing comes from linguistic and musical research undertaken since 1970, notably by Tamsin Donaldson (1987) and Margaret Gummow (1985, 1992). Because the ritualization of men's life-cycle stages is elevated and hidden, dancing, even more than singing, was vulnerable to social changes resulting from colonization.

In some areas, particularly Central Australia, "women's business" is carried on (Bell 1983). Men and women see each others' performances only in carefully negotiated, arranged circumstances. In Cape York and during some Central Australian rituals, women's roles are chiefly confined to supportive dancing. In Arnhem Land, women dance only when men do, though their steps and patterns, unlike women's steps and patterns in Cape York, are distinctive.

Not much is known about children's dancing, but children probably participated in adults' performances. Children participate now more than before because they are seen as the keepers of a cultural heritage that will otherwise die out. In the past, their participation was limited to open, unrestricted ceremonies—play-about dancing, as it is called in Cape York. Children began to participate seriously in adult dances during and after puberty. Boys' participation began with initiatory ceremonies and led to graded inductions into male ceremonial life. Girls' entry into women's ceremonial life, furthered by childbearing, was less spectacular. In Central Australia, Pitjantjatjara prepubescent children learn simplified versions of adult songs, but Alyawarra, Pintupi, and Warlpiri children apparently have no separate songs and dances (Wild 1988:178).

Dance is more vulnerable to social change than music. In Cape York, singing controls, but dancing does not; singing regulates, but dancing can deregulate. The power of dancing and the powers generated by dancing are no less in other parts of Australia, which always had more songs than dances, whose "performances, being more infrequent and performed in highly restricted contexts, were a more marked form" (von Sturmer 1987:73). Throughout Australia, dances have changed in different degrees in different localities, and little has been documented about any of the processes involved. Not much is known of indigenous dancing before 1788. Drastic adaptations to colonial occupation occurred. Christian churches had strong influence. In much of Aboriginal Australia, Christian songs and dances coexist with older forms and styles of dancing. Hymns and gospel music are major parts of Aboriginal danced events in rural and urban Australia.

Because of the proximity of the Torres Strait Islands and different kinds of music and dancing there, syncretic forms of dancing, as in the culture of Cape York Peninsula, have existed for at least two centuries (Beckett 1972, 1987). Exchanges between mainlanders and islanders resulted especially from mother-of-pearl trade and islanders' migrations to the mainland.

Attempts to forge contemporary expressions of Aboriginal life into new expressions of Aboriginality have occurred, motivating and inspiring Aboriginal troupes of the 1990s, notably the Aboriginal and Islander Dance Theatre and the Bangarra Dance Company, both based in Sydney.

Generalizations about Aboriginal dancing must be qualified with reminders about differences:

> The bodies of dancers are usually decorated, with specific features varying from region to region. Commonly, patterns of red and yellow ochres, white pipeclay and charcoal are applied on greased torso, arms, legs and face. In some areas, particularly in the central region of the continent, male dancers may be decorated with finely chopped feathers or the fluffy efflorescence of certain plant species, . . . coloured by powdering with ochre (or left naturally glistening white) and glued with blood on torso, legs, arms and face in patterns representing the subject of the dance; the decoration often continues upward over a high conical head-dress. Many sorts of head-dresses are worn, mainly by men. They are generally fashioned out of grass and sticks, bound into shape by human-hair string, and covered by coloured fluff in particular designs. Women dancers frequently wear headbands that hold bunches of feathers. Most dancers carry ritual or ritualised objects, sometimes no more than decorated boomerangs, shields, spears, or fighting or digging sticks; at other times the objects are manufactured specifically for the occasion. (Wild 1988:176)

Meager research exists on dances and sign languages (Kendon 1988), especially kinship-designating gestures. In Cape York, knowing kin and clan signs means knowing who are performing together. In Aboriginal dances lie deep stratifications of meaning, expressed in everyday signs, which convey messages based on the theory that meanings attach to sensations in parts of the body. These aspects of Aboriginal dancing differ from Western conceptions of gesture and embodiment.

Among the ceremonial contexts where dancing occurs, religious ceremonies involve sorcery and magic. Major life-cycle rituals usually require dancing. Many rituals reflect beliefs that locate the sources of the performances in the Dreaming. Not all ceremonies are restricted from outside viewing. The openings of houses, where spirits of deceased persons are encouraged to vacate their residences, allowing the living to get on with ordinary life, are unrestricted ceremonies.

Ceremonies that maintain the fertility and productivity of the country are less prevalent in the 1990s. Since the land links singing, dancing, and people, those who follow old customs feel responsible for maintaining the natural order of things by contributing to ancestors' and creators' powers. Performances of music and dance usually occur

> . . . on a specially prepared ground either in the living area or some distance away, depending on the context of the occasion. A bough-shade, sometimes one for each sex, is usually erected on the side of, or near, the performance ground. . . . From a non-Aboriginal viewpoint preparations take much longer than the actual performance, but from an Aboriginal viewpoint they are an integral part of it. Songs belonging to the subject of the performance are sung to summon spirits or spiritual power to ensure the efficacy of the event, and stories are told to explain the meaning of the occasion. . . . Performances are frequently held at night and fires have to be readied at strategic points. . . . When everything is ready and the musicians are in position on the ground, they signal . . . the dancers, who may appear dramatically from behind a screen of trees, boughs or smoke. (Wild 1988:176)

By firelight, the dancers' movements, formations, sounds, and decorations may combine to reveal what Wild calls a genius for dramatic effect.

At festivals, which last two or three days, bosses and managers try to duplicate these conditions in performances of unrestricted dances. When festivals occur by day, sunlight minimizes what would be the dramatic effects of performances at night. Shelters are constructed; by singing songs and discussing myths, participants remind themselves of themes to be enacted; necklaces and headdresses are prepared; and the dancers' bodies are painted.

Time is organized so everyone may perform. Formerly, a ceremony could take months and include customs and protocols of welcome, exchanges of gifts, and farewell. In late-twentieth-century festivals, that sense of timelessness is missing, especially if, besides the dancing, competitive events—throwing boomerangs, throwing spears, lighting fires—are interspersed (Williams 1988).     —DRID WILLIAMS

## *WANGGA* OF NORTHWEST AUSTRALIA

*Wangga,* public dance-songs of the northwest regions of Northern Territory and northern Western Australia, are performed in ceremonial contexts and for entertainment [see TRADITIONAL AUSTRALIAN MUSIC: Northern Australia]. In ceremony, they are often performed alongside examples of other genres, including *lirrga,* with which they share many features, and *djanba* [see TRADITIONAL AUSTRALIAN MUSIC: Kimberley area]. Performative details vary by location, song, and occasion. The following discussion focuses on *wangga* owned by Marrisyebin people, whose country lies at Nadirri, near the mouth of the Moyle River (Marett and Page 1995).

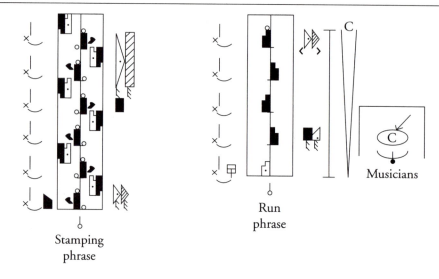

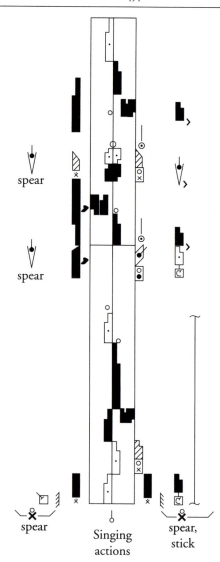

FIGURE 1    Excerpts from a Nadirri men's *wangga*. Transcription in Labanotation by JoAnne Page.

## Structure and style

Nadirri *wangga* have three kinds of movement: men's, women's, and textually accompanied actions. One dance serves for the lyrics of all *wangga*. Movements derive their connection to songs through actions depicting the spirits from whom the songs came. Vocal and instrumental sections of *wangga* alternate. Men's and women's dancing usually coincides with instrumental sections; the actions coincide with vocal sections. Elsewhere, mimetic dancing and other formal arrangements of vocal and instrumental sections occur (Marett and Barwick 1993).

In Nadirri *wangga,* men's dancing, the most elaborate (figure 1), has four phrases: a preparatory walk, in step with the rhythm of the sticks; a run, when dancers establish their positions on the central part of the ground; a stamped phrase; and a terminal phrase of idiosyncratic movements, when performers display exceptional agility.

Dances can begin when dancers choose to join with instrumentalists, but they end with the end of the beating of clapsticks. Women dance during instrumental and vocal sections. They define the space by moving slowly along its circumference. During the singing, they perform an undulating side step, taking the rhythms in their bodies and arms; alternatively, some travel a few steps, stop, and perform digging-like motions to the side. As clapstick beats begin, they stop traveling, and to each beat perform a sharp bounce with their legs and arms, the accents down and in toward the torso. Sometimes during vocal sections, senior men perform solo actions, including approaching people and looking for footprints on the ground. Such actions may recall the behavior of the spirits from whom the songs came.

### Structured movements of wangga

*Wangga* posture for men and women is bent slightly forward at the hips, legs rotated outward, knees relaxed. Women gaze at the ground; men look toward the singers or other dancers. Women's dynamics are more fluid and rhythmic than men's, but men's steps, even their runs, are light and agile, with sharp, discrete movements. The apparent simplicity of the actions, as in other Aboriginal dances, masks agility in the dynamics of movement.

The stamps of different regions of Australia are distinct. *Wangga* stamps include even steps, using alternate legs; a sharp rebound from the ground; no bouncing of the body, the head remaining at a constant height; legs folded close under the pelvis, especially by expert dancers; and stamping in place. Stamps connect the dancers to the ground, but the action is light, with an energetic rebound. This lightness results from how the feet contact the ground: curled, so soles can scoop up sand as they lift, raising a cloud of dust. Arms do not perform specific actions or patterns, but follow the energy and rhythm generated by the stamps.

### Relationship of dancing and singing

To herald the beginning of a dance, male dancers often form a tight, inwardly facing circle, with heads together, bowed toward the ground. A senior dancer initiates a one-syllable call, which the other performers join. The circle breaks up, the dancers fill the space, and clapstick beats begin. Calls punctuate the performance, usually as dancers' and singers' signals cueing the ends and beginnings of phrases. The dancing and musical phrasing are tightly intertwined. Phrases of the dance and the music coincide only at the terminal phrase, which begins within a five-beat break at the end of the clapstick phrases. The beating and the dancing end together.

—JoAnne Page

## TIWI DANCE, NORTHERN TERRITORY

The Tiwi homeland is the islands of Melville and Bathurst, just north of Darwin, Northern Territory. Formerly, Tiwi were hunter-gatherers, and their environment provided an abundance of food. They divide their islands into several so-called countries, inherited patrilineally, with fluid boundaries. After 1911, when the first Roman Catholic missionaries arrived, the church and the government induced the Tiwi to settle in villages. In the late twentieth century, a movement urging a return to older ways began. Though the Tiwi now lead Westernized lives, they maintain hunting-gathering and reenact rituals that reinforce links with the Dreaming.

Tiwi dance (*yoi*) challenges analysis because its elements are seemingly contradictory: one part of it, seen as having been choreographed by named individuals, is the result of a creative process exemplifying intellectual power; another part is seen as belonging to every Tiwi's psychology. The Tiwi classify certain combinations of gesturing and singing as songs, but classify other combinations as dances (Grau 1983). Individuals own dances and bequeath some of them patrilineally. Thus, though distinct sets of dances exist, variations or particular movements that do not belong to a lineage also occur. Other dances are owned by everyone, but can be performed only on specified occasions by certain individuals. Kinship-derived rules govern people's participation, yet strong individuals can twist the rules or invent new ones (Grau 1994).

Dance exemplifies sex divisions found in the society at large. With few exceptions (as husband and wife performing a duet), men and women dance apart. They share dances, but use named feminine or masculine styles. (Men sometimes dance in the feminine style.) Men and women can change roles: men can dance as if pregnant or nursing a baby; women can dance to find spiritual children, a task men can undertake only while not dancing (Grau 1993).

Between 1980 and 1984, during nineteen months of observation, two or three formally danced events occurred each week. The Tiwi formerly danced almost exclusively for mortuary rituals, linked over a year or more. In the twentieth century, celebrations for birthdays, marriages, graduations, and so on started to occur, and most involved dancing. The Tiwi model these ceremonies on mortuary rituals. Rather than perform for a dead person, dancers perform for someone sitting before them; the old terminology and structure serve for the new ceremonies.

Dance is a feature of daily living. It represents a way of life. Every Tiwi person takes part in it according to socially set conditions. Some duties people have toward their relatives include dancing. From birth, Tiwi babies encounter dancing. Tiwi society recognizes individuality in many spheres of life: each child has a unique name, and each dancer finds a niche as a unique individual. Children do not have separate dances, but participate in most ritual activities, sometimes only as spectators. By the time they reach adolescence, all Tiwi can dance acceptably, and the notion of a non-dancer is alien to them. To be human is to dance. Dancing is as essential to survival as breathing.

## The dances

Tiwi society had a single set of dances, in which every member of the society had rights, though not everyone was eligible to perform any dance on any occasion. Tiwi society encouraged the creation of new dances. In theory, men and women could compose dances and their associated songs, but by the early 1980s, few women were doing so. Composing dances and songs had mainly become the prerogative of middle-aged men and old women. Individuals in their early thirties sometimes presented tentative creations. Old women were knowledgeable about ritual matters; their creations were as well received as men's. Musical texts and choreographies belonged to their creators and their patrilineal descendants; only members of the patrilineage were entitled to perform them. Responsibility for organizing, choreographing, composing, and paying for specific performances depended on kinship, which determined the order of performance during a single event.

Tiwi dances were differentiable mainly by the usages of the arms. The dancing body was relaxed. The knees had a slightly bouncing quality. The head stayed at the same level. Women kept their feet parallel, with head slightly bent, or eyes looking downward, and one foot completely flexed off the ground on the beat; they followed a regular tempo. Men danced with their knees slightly turned out, head straight or slightly bent back, and feet on the ground on the beat; their tempos increased, almost doubling near the end of performances.

All danced events had a main dance and an accompanying one. Songs were composed by and for soloists, who, alone or in small groups, performed the main dance in the center of the arena. When soloists performed in a small group and a dance was being choreographed, one dancer usually took charge of the choreography, but others added variations that the rest of the group might take up. These soloists were helped by their close relatives, especially spouses or potential spouses, who usually performed another dance off to the side, starting a few beats later. Every Tiwi was sometimes soloist, sometimes accompanist. Men danced alone and in small groups; women preferred to dance in small groups. Ordinarily, men performed the accompanying dance only to support their spouses, but women helped most of their relatives, especially husbands, children, and siblings.

## Classification of dances

Indigenous conceptualizations of Tiwi dances classified dances by ownership rather than movement. Dances were either "my property" or "not my property." This classification distinguished dances that belonged to specific lineages from those that had common ownership. Choreography of the latter had come from the heroes of the Dreaming. The former group subdivided into dances that were "my Dreaming" and those that were "just a song." Never choreographed, the Dreaming-based dances were within the dancers' bodies: an individual whose Dreaming was, say, crocodilian naturally had knowledge of how to move like a crocodile. In addition to movements that intrinsically marked the Dreaming, every dancer had the opportunity to personalize the dance by adding variations.

Through the just-a-song dances, dancers showed off their skills in choreography and poetry. These dances were usually made for mortuary rituals, when new items were requisite. Enjoyed items were retained as possessions of the choreographer's lineage. Some such dances performed in the 1980s could be traced back to the mid-1800s; most old dances have disappeared.

An analytical classification would further subdivide the commonly owned dances. Among them are kinship-based dances (Goodale 1971:300–306). The Tiwi divide the body into specific parts, each representing a kin: the legs represent matrilineal siblings; the shoulders, mothers-in-law; and so on. By emphasizing these parts, a dancer can show a kin relationship with the person for whom the ritual is held. Among commonly owned dances are several that mark sections or junctions in the ritual.

In dance, the Tiwi express the belief that they belong to a unitary order of existence, linking human beings, plants, animals, geographical features, and natural phenomena (Grau 1992). Spiritual, social, and ecological worlds coexist in all human bodies, but become explicit in dancers' bodies. The sun-woman Imunga, who created the Tiwi world, is a force in the lower abdomen, from where the low-down breathing used for singing and dancing emanates. Through kinship-based dances, the social world enters dancers' bodies. Most dreamings are animals; many are inanimate concepts, including rainbows, fruits, and rocks.                                —ANDRÉE GRAU

## YOLNGU DANCE, ARNHEM LAND

Yolngu ritual performances blend voices, instruments, and movements, elements that influence, and are influenced by, four main aspects of Yolngu life and cosmology: social relationships, political power, spiritual power, and ritual contexts. Yolngu men and women live in complementary ritual worlds, with varying degrees of access to musical knowledge and its sacred power. Access is differentially marked at birth: each person automatically belongs to either of the patrilineal exogamous moieties, Dhuwa or Yirritja, which own the animals, plants, birds, and landscapes depicted in songs and dances.

Knowing how and what to sing are among the most important Yolngu skills. From an early age, boys and girls experience "outside" meanings of songs, which detail the shapes of the plants and animals around them. After initiation and maturity into adulthood, Yolngu are increasingly privy to "inside" meanings, which encode ideas of human conception, birth, and death. As knowledge increases with age, so does an awareness of political, spiritual, and reproductive power.

### Ancestral stories in song

Each song depicts a primordial ancestral being who journeyed across the Yolngu landscape fashioning important topographical features. These beings then went underground, where their essence remains. Stories relate their creative acts in Dhuwa and Yirritja ecological zones. Dhuwa beings created Dhuwa lands and followed Dhuwa ocean currents, but they crisscrossed Yirritja lands and seas, and vice versa. Thus, though songs are specific to moieties, the songs of either moiety can incorporate names of the other moiety's ancestral beings. Cooperation between moieties extends to practical ritual details: people of one moiety who relate as sister's sons to people of the other may act for them as workers, play the didjeridu, lay out and prepare the ground, and provide practical assistance (Morphy 1984, 1991).

The interlinking of Dhuwa and Yirritja identities is illustrated through the ritual construction and meaning of a sequence of songs that narrate the events of an ancestral journey (figure 2). Two of the Dhuwa moiety's myths, Thunderman (Djambuwal) and Shark (Mana), show how the conceptualizing narratives in performative contexts produces ritual meaning (Groger-Wurm 1973:61). Thunderman dwelled in rain clouds. An expert fisherman, he used his sacred spear (larrpan) to spear fish. The two creative sisters of the Dhuwa moiety traveled by canoe and sang

The shark and rain, they're all connected. The Thunderman stirred up the wind and the waves. The water in which the shark lies became muddy. He was twisting and turning from side to side, making the creek.

FIGURE 2   Yolngu men perform a shark dance, their bodies twisting from side to side in a representation of the shark's movements. Photo by Fiona Magowan.

about him. Muwarra, in 1990 the eldest man of the D̲atiwuy clan, recounted the relationship between Thunderman and Shark:

> Dhuwa men were pointing their spears to the various places where the shark stays. He was floating with his head and fin just showing. That's the place they call Bukulandjipa or Galapunggarri. That's where the song of the shark comes from, but different clans can sing it. They'll also sing about Djambuwal: the shark and rain at those places, they're all connected. Yolngu heard the roar of the Thunderman in the clouds as it started raining over at Marapay and the creek where the shark lies. The Thunderman stirred up the wind and the waves, and the water in which the shark lies became muddy. He was twisting and turning his head from side to side, making the creek. The clans who sing it are Djapu, Ngaymil, D̲atiwuy, Rirratjingu, Marrakulu, Golumala, Gälpu, Djambarrpuyngu, Barrarrngu, Barrarrparrarr, and Mälarra.

Thus, the members of all Dhuwa clans have the right to dance the ancestral dances.

As Yolngu sing and dance Thunderman and Shark, they embody these ancestors' power. Because the Yolngu perceive the parts of human bodies to be analogous to those of sharks (figure 3), dancers' movements replicate and evoke Shark's creative actions and power.

### Ritually delineating ancestral space

The site of ritual dancing becomes a microcosm of the ancestral routes of Arnhem Land and a theater for reenacting the ancestors' travels. It is ordered around a ritual focus such as a funeral shelter or a sacred tree. Dancers depict ancestral travels by moving toward, around, or away from this focus.

FIGURE 3   The human body (with spear) as ancestral shark: physical outlines show analogies the Yolngu make. Drawing by Fiona Magowan.

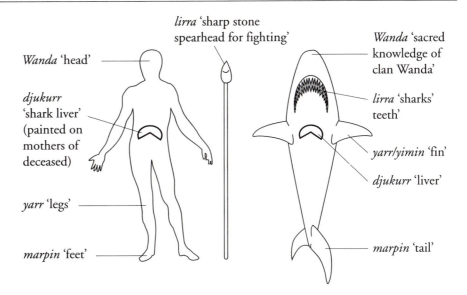

*Wanda* 'head'

*lirra* 'sharp stone spearhead for fighting'

*Wanda* 'sacred knowledge of clan Wanda'

*djukurr* 'shark liver' (painted on mothers of deceased)

*lirra* 'sharks' teeth'

*yarr/yimin* 'fin'

*djukurr* 'liver'

*yarr* 'legs'

*marpin* 'feet'

*marpin* 'tail'

The lead singer decides on an individual's relational links, and composes main (*yindi*) and subsidiary (*nyumukininy*) songs in order of place and event. A possible combination of main subjects may begin with Thunderman's song and be followed by those of the canoe and the shark. Interspersed among these can appear subsidiary subjects, like seawater, driftwood, and flatfish.

In formations of circles and lines, men's and women's dances depict the progression of songs. Certain formations of Djambarrpuyngu dances depict the mythology of Thunderman and Shark in funeral contexts. The dancers move slowly toward the shelter, spears raised overhead, pointing to Thunderman's sacred sites in Arnhem Land (figure 4*a*).

As they approach the shelter, they increase the tempo, indicating the confluence of clans approaching sacred places associated with the deceased. Terms that describe the tempo of verses include *bulnha* 'slow', *märr bondi* 'a little faster', and *ganydjarr* 'quickly, powerfully'. Eventually the dancers reach and circle the shelter, holding their spears overhead until the song tells that rain is starting to fall.

Some songs later, men and women form two lines, dancing the song of the canoe. They paddle slowly at first, increasing in speed and dynamism as they advance (figure 4*b*). When they again reach the shelter, the song changes to the shark, which the leader of the clan and the closest patrilineal relatives of the deceased dance near the shade while other clansmen approach them (figure 4*c*). The men hold spears and sticks in an interlocking line; the women dance with one arm behind their backs: both styles represent the fin. From side to side, the dancers twist and turn their heads and bodies, evoking Shark's creative actions, which gouged out the creek. Eventually, the lines merge, symbolizing the integration of the deceased's soul with its shark-identified spirit.

The shelter and its contents—the corpse, with sacred ritual objects—are the focus and embodiment of ancestral and human spiritual identities. Songs and dances enable those knowledgeable in utilizing ancestral power to approach the "inner reality" of the spiritual realm (Rudder 1993). Dancers become vessels through which structured movements realize musical power. This power has ambivalent qualities, harmful and beneficial. It determines who may sit near the shelter, touch the corpse, offer food to relatives, and perform in the ritual.

Male leaders exert restrictions over who may sing, depending on the networking of clans that own and share the ancestral tracks (Keen 1978). Thus, Yolngu ideas of social and political organization mark ritual singing and dancing. Consequently,

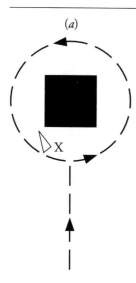

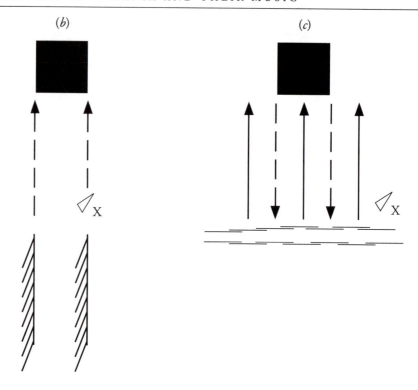

FIGURE 4    Plans of three Yolngu dances, for which the square represents the shade, the arrows show the direction of travel, the triangle is the man playing the didjeridu, and the X is the lead singer with clapsticks: *a,* in Thunderman (*Djambuwal*), dancers approach the shade and circle it; *b,* in Canoe (*Lipalipa*), in parallel lines, dancers approach the shade (the hatched lines show the position of stick-carrying dancers); *c,* in Shark, dancers in the bottom two lines move forward and backward toward the shade. Drawings by Fiona Magowan.

Yolngu performance encapsulates generational histories: by recreating and regenerating a timeless canvas of ancestral action through ritual drama, it details the interweaving of clan-based relations and their rights and obligations.  —FIONA MAGOWAN

## YANYUWA DANCE, GULF OF CARPENTARIA

Yanyuwa country includes the Sir Edward Pellew Islands and nearby coastal areas. About two hundred Yanyuwa, most of the tribal population, live in or near the town of Borroloola. Their social organization sorts individuals among four exogamous patrilineal units, which researchers call semimoieties (Bradley 1992:31).

### Styles of dancing

Most dances begin at sunset or after dark, in a cleared area. Clothes are casual; sometimes designs and ritual paraphernalia are applied to dancers' bodies before performances. Ceremonial dances, having originated in the Dreaming, are owned and passed on by totemic ancestors' descendants. Of dances performed for entertainment, some have been received from spiritual beings by sleeping humans, some have deliberately been composed, and some have been borrowed from neighboring cultures.

#### *Ceremonial dances*

The Yanyuwa perform dances for funeral rites called Yalkawarru and Kulyukulyu and initiatory rites called Marndiwa and Kunapipi. A celebration of Yalkawarru that occurred in 1994 marked the deaths of persons of one moiety who had died within the previous few years; it took three weeks to complete. Performative roles were determined by semimoiety affiliation and gender. On the last night, men and women performed simultaneously but apart, doing essentially the same movements, modified with gender-specific nuances (figure 5). The ritual ended when male owners made a dramatic display of throwing flaming bundles of bark stripped from paperbark trees (*Melaleuca* spp.).

A circumcision ceremony for boys in 1994 lasted seven days. Performative roles were determined by gender and participants' kinship with the initiate. Men and

FIGURE 5   Benesh Movement Notation shows how Yanyuwa men's movements (lower lines) use more space than women's: the men tilt their bodies more, bend their knees more, have a wider stance, lift their legs higher, and call out on beats. Transcription by Megan Morais.

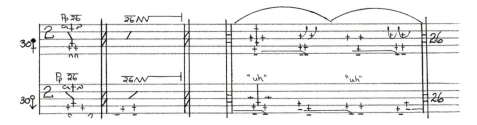

women mostly danced apart; neither gender was permitted to observe the other's dances. On the penultimate night, the women danced until dawn; on the final night, the men did, and then the initiates were circumcised.

### Nonceremonial dances

For entertainment in 1994, dances were usually performed at night near someone's house. They lasted two to three hours. Some of the audience provided singing and rhythmic accompaniment. Performances ranged from singers focusing on one song and moving their hands, to fully painted dancers singing and performing most of the items they knew.

Borroloola is a focus for "Aborigines living east of the Roper River to Queensland and throughout the Barkly Tablelands" (Avery 1985:1). The effects of this focus manifest themselves in entertainment-oriented dances, many of which exhibit differences in musical accompaniment, structure, lyrics, patterns of movement, and dancers' formations. All songs but "Buffalo Dreaming" are accompanied with clapsticks.

*Ngadiji,* with texts in Wakaya, tell of mermaids' meetings with tableland women. Sequentially and separately from performing women, boys (not men) perform gender-specific movements. The women's and girls' movements of their arms sometimes resemble those of Warlpiri women. A similar dance, *kalwanyarra,* differs mostly in movements of the arms. Sometimes dancers reenact the movements of a male spirit ("devil-devil"); the texts, sung in Yanyuwa, tell of his travels.

Other dances, performed to Yanyuwa texts, include island songs and *nguyul-nguyul.* The former, usually accompanied by a didjeridu, end with a repeatedly trilled sung phrase. Lined-up men and women dance simultaneously in place, men on one side and women on the other. Their movements are the same, but they show gendered nuances: men's knees are more bent and turned out at the thigh. Movements of performers' arms are often mimetic, as when imitating sea turtles. *Nguyulnguyul* usually deal with human exploits; some have texts in Gudanji. Dancing to *nguyulnguyul* takes the form of an anyway corroboree (also called just dancing), or of a dramatic reenactment.

Some Yanyuwa songs and dances come from neighboring areas. *Malkarri,* from the Queensland area, were danced (and never only sung) by boys and men. Some include a question-and-answer discourse in Kriol, between singer and dancer. Often dances end with deft and agile individual variations, which lend themselves to competition. "Buffalo Dreaming," a Mara dance-song, is sung in Alawa and Nung-gubuyu, accompanied by short clapsticks and a didjeridu. A change in the rhythmic pattern marks the end of the danced phrase. In 1994, only young girls danced it; the basic movement of their legs and feet differed from other Yanyuwa movements. An item called the airplane dance, sung in Yanyuwa, relates events surrounding the crash of a B-24 bomber in 1942. The dancers sometimes represent the biplanes used to search for the wreckage.

### Dance in society

Ceremonies include all members of the community, even infants. Through observation, participation, and vocal and manipulative guidance, usually in camp during an evening's entertainment, children learn to dance. Yanyuwa dancers, proud of their knowledge and abilities, regularly participate in Aboriginal ceremonies and festivals throughout the Northern Territory. In 1995, the Lijakarda Festival, the first Aboriginal festival in the area, occurred at Wandangula, an outstation. Participants performed old and new dances and songs, some presented by locals and some by visitors. Aborigines, non-Aboriginal Australians, tourists, and representatives of state and federal governments took part (Margaret Sharpe, personal communication).

Research among the Yanyuwa has informed two doctoral dissertations (Avery 1985; Baker 1989). Several governmental agencies encourage and financially support Yanyuwa dance. In 1994, the Australian Research Council and the Australian Institute of Aboriginal and Torres Strait Islander Studies funded Yanyuwa-approved documentation of dances performed by the Yanyuwa-Garrawa in the Borroloola area. At that time, dancing for entertainment regularly occurred at Wandangula, usually inspired by visitors' arrivals. —MEGAN JONES MORAIS

## WANAM OF NORTHEAST AUSTRALIA

The forms and styles of dancing in Cape York Peninsula were once as diverse and numerous as the societies that inhabited the area. Of these societies, inland speakers of Wik-Munkan were the largest and most important. Their culture was more homogeneous than those of coastal peoples, who borrowed cultural traits from the Torres Strait Islands and New Guinea. Because the inland peoples maintained a seemingly undisturbed existence, it was on them that anthropological research first concentrated (McConnel 1930, 1935).

Conditions have altered drastically: some of the old societies are represented by just one or two people. Of the societies that remain in strength, this entry focuses on *wanam* families of the Kugu-nganhcharra. For these families, the *wanam*—a ceremony that occurs at Thaa'kungadha, at the mouth of the Holroyd River—is "the symbol and expression" of identity (von Sturmer 1987:67). Like many indigenous practices in Aboriginal Australia, it is on the verge of extinction because people born after the 1960s prefer Western forms of music and dancing and avoid old customs and ways.

*Wanam* families live in the towns of Aurukun and Edward River, on the west of the peninsula. The country containing the sacred sites for their dances lies roughly south of the Kendall River, north of Christmas Creek, on the eastern coast of the Gulf of Carpentaria. After the 1960s, to salvage or revive flagging traditions, *Wanam* families made some restricted dances available for viewing by non-Aboriginal audiences and Aboriginal people other than the members of the families and clans who owned and managed them. These dances were, and still are, mediums for representing and experiencing the history that emanates from two cultural heroes, the Kaa'ungken brothers.

### The story of wanam and its effects

One version of the story of *wanam* is this. In the old-old days, in "the beforetime," the Kaa'ungken brothers traveled south to the Holroyd River, singing songs about what they saw and did, and creating dances, which they taught to the people they encountered. At the river, they stole fish, and people pursued them. Carrying the fish, the brothers fled southward to Wallaby Island, in the mouth of the Mitchell River. Mosquitoes plagued them there, so they returned to the Holroyd River. Throwing boomerangs, they cleared the coastal plain of trees, leaving salt pans that still remain. Finally, they arrived at Thaa'kungadha, where they instituted the *wanam* for future generations.

Performances of such dances as the wallaby dance (*minha punka*) and the string dance (*kugu-nga'a-wu*) join the present to the past, the fountainhead of all good things. Kugu-nganhcharra believe dances have the power to demonstrate the presence of ancestors' spirits: through *wanam,* people realize their religious and historical beliefs.

*Wanam* allude to ancient events and characters, whose travels, deeds, adventures, and doings created landscapes and formed the identities of the people to whom they belong. Dance-associated myths link the creative activities of ancestors, divine heroes, sites, and rituals, which in turn create precedents for the present form of dances. These rituals were not recitals of the original creative activities or events taking place at a site. Instead, they reflected relationships among ancestors, divine heroes, sites, and people. Totemic dances represent an individual's relationship with a particular phenomenon, such as an animal, a bird, or a cyclone.

The naming of a person automatically associates him or her with the traits of that phenomenon. In the bonefish dance of the lower Archer River (*winychinam* tradition), the senior clansman hunts his totem at night from a bark canoe. In the *taipan*-snake-versus-the-blue-tongued-lizard dance of lower Knox River (*aaplatj* tradition), the conflict is recreated between the two totemic reptiles. *Wanam* are structured around social—mainly genealogical—networks and organizations, made explicit at various levels of political affiliation within and between clans.

## Ceremonial performance

The wallaby dance starts in a circle of seated people, symbolizing Kugu-nganhcharra society. The circle divides into two camps, each headed by a boss. Some singers have more spatial freedom: they get up, walk around, and go where they please; others stay put. Next, the bosses pretend to abuse and fight each other. Their antagonism throws everything into chaos; everyone stands up and mills around, acting confused.

After the bosses' feigned fight, which ends when a spear is broken, the men form two lines facing the bosses, who carry spears, symbolizing hunters. The men in lines now crouch low to the ground and hop like wallabies. Depending on occasion and circumstance, the hunters may lead these wallabies around a bit, but the hunters finally stop and turn to face them. Each hunter stands with legs widespread so each crouched man can pass between them. A performance witnessed in 1988 featured one hunter and one line of wallabies; performances would once have had two hunters and two lines of wallabies. The crouching and hopping men are symbolically animals and therefore nonhuman, but passing between the hunters' legs transforms them into humans, and they stand up again. They are to be understood as having been eaten and excreted by the hunters; their labor and energy have been consumed by the clans and the bosses.

The Kugu-nganhcharra people themselves are like the fish in the Kaa'ungken brothers' story. Another version of the myth recalls that the brothers threw the spoiled fish into the river. The fish revived and swam away—meaning that without allegiance to leaders, and without the story, the people would be nothing but rotten fish. Metaphorically, the Kugu-nganhcharra are consumed and transformed by the brothers and the myth.

Because most of the peoples of Cape York were patrilineal and the dances celebrated men's business, women and children did not formerly participate in the main ceremonial dancing. The string dance was an exception. Women danced alongside men, each woman with her own string or rope. Women took part in the general aspects of *wanam* myths and rituals, either "warming up" the dance before the men started, or complementarily moving alongside the men, with their arms and hands held in positions specifying their kinship with the men. This kind of dancing was peripheral. Women had no secret ceremonial dances of their own, but did have a special dance, *wuungk,* prominent throughout the central peninsula. It pertained to mortuary ceremonies.

### Concepts in transition

Unlike some other traditions in the cape, *wanam* ceremonies were tied to specific sites. They were not composite ceremonies where clans brought in their own separate dances. The whole *wanam* ceremonial, including many rituals and dances, followed established formats, inextricably linked with sites appointed by the Kaa'ungken brothers.

In 1972–1975, to preserve peninsular traditions, Cape York Dance Festivals were set up. In these festivals, Aboriginal peoples gathered in Aboriginal-controlled contexts. They became acquainted with each other, performing, strengthening, and preserving their heritages. Communities participated enthusiastically. By the mid-1990s, the festivals had become tourist attractions. They added competitive events: throwing spears, building fires, selling artifacts, and playing didjeridus (instruments not indigenous to the cape). As a result, old styles of dancing are subject to becoming contrived forms of "primitive dance," faking reality to suit the tastes of ignorant outsiders.
—RONNE ARNOLD

## WARLPIRI DANCE, CENTRAL AUSTRALIA

Warlpiri dance occurs mainly within ritual contexts, reenacting Dreaming events and maintaining the Warlpiri world. Sexually segregated rituals that incorporate dance occur sporadically throughout the year: men's rituals (*panpa*) focus on totemic increase; women's rituals (*yawulyu*), on the physical and spiritual growth and maintenance of land and people. Other rituals, which may partly exclude either sex, or in which both sexes participate, occur in summer (September through February): annual rituals provide circumcision for pubescent males; *kajirri* provides initiation to adulthood; fire-based ceremonies (*ngajakula, jarriwanpa*) resolve conflict; and *purlapa* publicly entertain.

Warlpiri people sometimes present dances at extraneous events, as in 1980, when a women's troupe from Ali-Curang performed at elementary schools in Canberra, and in 1988, when it performed at the Festival of Pacific Arts in Townsville. After Christian missionaries arrived, new dances in old styles began to develop: at Christmas and Easter, some Warlpiri perform the public dance *Jesus Purlapa,* focusing on Jesus's life.

All Warlpiri dances originate in the Dreaming, but some *yawulyu* and all *purlapa* are newly received from ancestral spirits in dreams. Dances pertain to totemic sites; with few exceptions, descendants of totemic ancestors own those ancestors' dances and pass them on. The Warlpiri borrow dances from neighboring cultures; they may have borrowed the circumcision-related dance from the Pitjantjatjara.

Women classify dances and movements primarily by the dreamed focus (land or totemic ancestor); secondarily, by the involved implement, song, activity, or part of the body. Men classify dances and movements by their actions, including dancing on all fours and quivering the torso.

### Settings and styles

Dances usually occur at sunset or night, in a clearing. Older, ritually knowledgeable, experienced adults perform them. Clothes are casual. Dancers go barefoot. Participants who bear a certain kinship relation to the dances or the Dreaming apply totemic designs to dancers' upper bodies, and to symbolically multireferential paraphernalia, which the dancers wield or emphasize. To activate the power of the Dreaming, those applying the designs sing appropriate songs. Men's and women's dances are segregated. For some rituals, men and women dance simultaneously in a common area, but only men do the singing.

Each sex has two styles of dancing: one shared, the other sex-specific. The Warlpiri call women's dance *wirntinjaku karntakarnta-kurlangu* (a term that includes both styles), and men's dance *milimili wirntimi* 'shared style' and *walaparimi* 'sex-specific style'. Shared-style dances maintain families, symbolizing fertility and nurturance; roles reflect interpersonal relationships, and dancers represent generalized ancestors. Sex-specific-style dances maintain the cosmos, symbolizing relationships between land and people; roles reflect relationships to totemic ancestors and the concepts of owner and manager.

By inheritance, a person owns one's father's Dreaming (which serves as one's own Dreaming) and manages one's mother's Dreaming. As manager, a person is guardian of the Dreaming. The owner, in movements that may be representational, symbolic, or allusive, mimes the ancestor's behavior. Qualified by experience and ability, a person functions in either role, according to the Dreaming manifested. Now and then after a dance, in exchange for transmitting sacred knowledge, owners give managers payment, such as money or cloth; occasionally, roles extend to opposite patrilineal moieties.

### Shared style

Women use this style mainly during sexually mixed rituals; men use it on other occasions, as by managers in men's rituals, or by clowns in religious rituals. Each dance, which lasts several minutes, consists of an upper-body motif combined with a sliding bounce, feet apart and parallel, with bent knees making a together-apart movement (figure 6). Some dances repeat for hours, with a few differing upper-body motifs; sometimes dancers utter calls synchronously with the bounce.

### Sex-specific style

Overall choreography differs notably between the sexes, but men's and women's dances include comparable movements: quivering of legs and torso; alternating side-stepping; looking behind, ahead, or from side to side; and kneeling. A dance in the sex-specific style sometimes manifests more than one Dreaming.

#### Women's dances

Usually performed during *yawulyu*, these dances last about half an hour. A participatory audience of performers and observers provides vocal and rhythmic accompaniment. Dancing begins immediately after the singing starts: the singing sets the rhythm; physical movements reinforce the pulse. Songs and accompanying actions end simultaneously. Dances focus on a ritual stick: to open the dance and Dreaming, a few managers plant it and "awaken" the painted owners, who stand in single file.

The managers flank the owners on each side; they demonstrate the movements, calling out instructions. The owners dance toward the stick, encircle it, and return to sit with the audience; they may sing. Then certain managers dance toward the stick, pull it up, bring it toward the audience, and hand it to seated managers. Dancers periodically stop to catch their breath. At the end, random claps occur. Women usually perform variations on this plan (Dail-Jones 1984:107).

#### Men's dances

On bodies and headdresses, one or more owners (rarely more than five) usually wear plant or animal-down designs, applied by managers with blood let from their arms.

The Warlpiri do not learn dances by rote and rehearsal; they recreate them. Skilled dancers are agents of change, and audiences judge new dances to decide whether to perform them again later.

FIGURE 6   Shared styles of Warlpiri dance: *a*, in Benesh Movement Notation; *b*, in Labanotation. Transcriptions by Megan Morais.

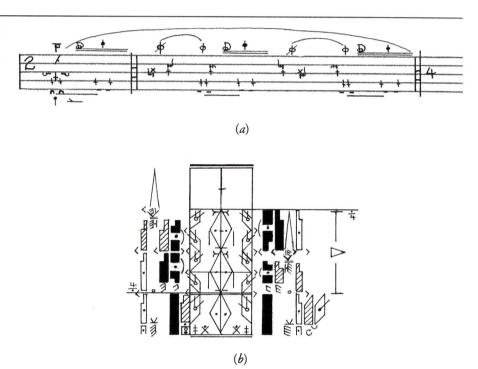

(*a*)

(*b*)

For a few minutes, they dance on a sand painting, destroying it. Some dances require only percussive rhythms (such as beating on shields), but seated dances also require singing. Dancers never sing.

Men have two performative styles. In one (*kujingka*), owners and novices sit in a compact circle while managers stand around them. All sing. Then all stand while the owners dance. At the climax, managers touch the dancers' designs and remove their headdresses. In the other style (*kumpalja*), which schematically emphasizes traveling, owners and managers sing, shuffling in procession. They make several variations on this theme: the singers step in place; a few singers circle the others; two groups sing songs from one Dreaming, not in unison.

### Dance in Warlpiri society

Ritual training begins early: children watch until old enough to participate. During rituals for boys' circumcision, girls and women dance in the shared style. In the 1980s, girls performed as owners in modified *yawulyu* dances while older women performed as managers. As girls grow, they increasingly participate in *yawulyu*; at first menstruation, a small-scale ritual marks sexual maturity (Bell 1983:152).

For boys, circumcision marks initiation into men's rituals; but as junior novices, they may not yet dance. Three or four years later, they undergo subincision and may then dance in the shared style as clowns during cult rituals. A year later, they become senior novices. After undergoing several inductions, they may wear designs created in fluff. After a man receives a design (associated with his own or his mother's descent group), he may dance as owner or manager, in a role determined by the Dreaming; he receives designs until he marries (Wild 1975:127–133).

The Warlpiri do not learn dances by rote and rehearsal; they recreate them, based on evidence shown by singing, myths, and managers' directions. They aim for choreographic conservatism, but not in details. Dance in sex-specific styles is the medium of expression most saturated with artistic communication and aesthetic evaluation. Skilled dancers are agents of change: audiences judge new dances to decide whether to perform them again later.

Because of a taboo on speaking a dead person's name (with a consequently shallow genealogical memory), the Dreaming goes back only two generations. Reclassification of new *purlapa* into sacred classes is one way the rituals of all classes change (Wild 1987). It is also a way of uniting both sexes in expressing the Dreaming. Increased mobility and the breakdown of tribal boundaries have changed the dances, as when a resurgence of ritual activity by the Pintupi of the Western Desert extended to the Yuendumu Pintupi and thence to the Warlpiri.

The Aboriginal Land Rights (Northern Territory) Act of 1976 enables many Warlpiri to claim legal ownership of customary lands. Dances are the primary evidence tying personal relationships to lands. Several governmental agencies, local and national, encourage and financially support the continuation of ritual dancing: in Yuendumu in the 1970s, the Aboriginal Arts Board funded separate buildings for men's and women's ritual activities.    —MEGAN JONES MORAIS

## PHOTOGRAPHING PERFORMANCE IN AUSTRALIA

Aboriginal Australians do not always welcome photography. The witnessing of many performances of music and dance is restricted to ritually qualified audiences, and a widespread taboo on naming the recently deceased includes making and showing visual images (Michaels 1991). Some performances, however, are public, and with changing community attitudes photography is becoming acceptable. Especially notable public performances are Rom ceremonies, presented to clinch and herald amicable relations [see MUSIC AND THEATER: AUSTRALIA].    —ADRIENNE L. KAEPPLER

## REFERENCES

Arnold, Ronne. 1991. "A Structural Analysis of Two Dance Idioms: The Wanam (Cape York Peninsula) and Black Jazz Dance (Philadelphia, U.S.A.)." M.A. thesis, University of Sydney.

Avery, John. 1985. "The Law People: History, Society and Initiation in the Borroloola Area of the Northern Territory." Ph.D. dissertation, University of Sydney.

Baker, Richard M. 1989. "Land Is Life: Continuity through Change for the Yanyuwa from the Northern Territory of Australia." Ph.D. dissertation, University of Adelaide.

Beckett, Jeremy. 1972. "The Torres Strait Islanders." In *Bridge and Barrier: The Natural and Cultural History of Torres Strait*, ed. D. Walker, 307–326. Canberra: Australian National University Press.

———. 1987. *Torres Strait Islanders: Custom and Colonialism*. Cambridge: Cambridge University Press.

Bell, Diane. 1983. *Daughters of the Dreaming*. Melbourne, Sydney: McPhee Gribble, and Allen & Unwin.

Berndt, Ronald. 1987. "Other Creatures in Human Guise and Vice-Versa: A Dilemma in Understanding." In *Songs of Aboriginal Australia*, ed. Margaret Clunies Ross, Tamsin Donaldson, and Stephen A. Wild, 168–191. Oceania monograph 32. Sydney: University of Sydney.

Borsboom, Adrianus P. 1978. *Maradjiri: A Modern Ritual Complex in Arnhem Land, North Australia*. Nijmegen: Katholieke Universiteit.

Bradley, John J. 1992. "Warnarrwarnarr-barranyi (Barroloola 2) Land Claim." Darwin: Northern Land Council.

Burridge, Kenelm. 1973. *Encountering Aborigines: Anthropology and the Australian Aborigines.* Sydney: Pergamon Press.

Coate, Howard. 1966. "The *Rai* and the Third Eye: North-West Australian Beliefs." *Oceania* 37(2):93–123.

Dail-Jones, Megan. 1984. "A Culture in Motion: A Study of the Interrelationship of Dancing, Sorrowing, Hunting, and Fighting as Performed by the Warlpiri Women of Central Australia." M.A. thesis, University of Hawai'i.

Donaldson, Tamsin. 1987. "Making a Song (and Dance) in South-Eastern Australia." In *Songs of Aboriginal Australia,* ed. Margaret Clunies Ross, Tamsin Donaldson, and Stephen A. Wild, 14–42. Oceania monograph 32. Sydney: University of Sydney.

Ellis, Catherine J., Linda Barwick, and Megan Morais. 1990. "Overlapping Time Structures in a Central Australian Women's Ceremony." In *Language and History: Essays in Honour of Luise A. Hercus,* ed. Peter Austin, R. M. W. Dixon, Tom Dutton, and Isobel White, 101–136. Canberra: Australian National University.

Goodale, Jane. 1971. *Tiwi Wives: A Study of the Women of Melville Island, North Australia.* Seattle: University of Washington Press.

Grau, Andrée. 1983. "Sing a Dance—Dance a Song: The Relationship between Two Types of Formalised Movements and Music among the Tiwi of Melville and Bathurst Islands, North Australia." *Dance Research* 1(2):32–44.

———. 1992. "Danses rituelles Tiwi." *Cahiers de musiques traditionelles* 5:205–206.

———. 1993. "Gender Interchangeability among the Tiwi." In *Dance, Gender, and Culture,* ed. Helen Thomas. New York: St. Martin's Press.

———. 1994. "Dance as Politics: Dance as a Tool for Manipulating the Social Order among the Tiwi of Northern Australia." In *Study Group on Ethnochoreology: 17th Symposium: Nafplion, Greece, 2–10 July 1992: Proceedings,* 39–44. Nafplion, Greece: Peloponnesian Folklore Foundation and International Council for Traditional Music.

Groger-Wurm, Helen M. 1973. *Australian Aboriginal Bark Paintings and Their Mythological Interpretation.* Canberra: Australian Institute of Aboriginal Studies.

Gummow, Margaret J. 1985. "Cueing in Several Performances of a Song from the Bandjalang Tribal Area of NSW." Paper presented at the Ninth National Conference of the Musicological Society of Australia, Monash University.

———. 1992. "Aboriginal Songs from the *Bundjalung* and *Gidabal* Areas of South-Eastern Australia." 2 vols. Ph.D. dissertation, University of Sydney.

Keen, Ian. 1978. "One Ceremony, One Song: An Economy of Religious Knowledge Among the Yolngu of Northeast Arnhem Land." Ph.D. dissertation, Australian National University.

Kendon, Adam. 1988. *Sign Languages of Aboriginal Australia: Cultural, Semiotic and Communicative Perspectives.* Cambridge: Cambridge University Press.

Keogh, Ray. 1989. "*Nurlu* Songs from the West Kimberley: An Introduction." *Australian Aboriginal Studies* 1989(1):2–11.

———. 1990. "*Nurlu* Songs of the West Kimberleys." Ph.D. dissertation, University of Sydney.

McConnel, Ursula. 1930. "The Wik Munkan Tribe of Cape York Peninsula." *Oceania* 1(1):97–104.

———. 1935. "Myths of the Wikmunkan and Wiknatara Tribes." *Oceania* 6(1):66–93.

Marett, Allan, and Linda Barwick. 1993. *Bunggridj-Bunggridj: Wangga Songs from Northern Australia by Alan Maralung.* International Institute for Traditional Music: Traditional Music of the World, 4. Smithsonian Folkways CD 40430. Compact disc.

Marett, Allan, and JoAnne Page. 1995. "Interrelationships Between Music and Dance in a *Wangga* from Northwest Australia." In *The Essence of Singing and the Substance of Song: Recent Responses to the Aboriginal Performing Arts and Other Essays in Honour of Catherine Ellis,* ed. Linda Barwick, Allan Marett, and Guy Tunstill, 27–38. Oceania monograph 46. Sydney: University of Sydney.

Michaels, Eric. 1991. "A Primer on Restrictions on Picture-Taking in Traditional Areas of Aboriginal Australia." *Visual Anthropology* 4:259–275.

Morphy, Howard. 1984. *Journey to the Crocodile's Nest: An Accompanying Monograph to the Film Maṁarrpa Funeral at Gurka'wuy.* Canberra: Australian Institute of Aboriginal Studies.

———. 1991. *Ancestral Connections: Art and an Aboriginal System of Knowledge.* Chicago: Chicago University Press.

Rudder, John. 1993. "Yolngu Cosmology." Ph.D. dissertation, Australian National University.

Stanner, W. E. H. 1966. *On Aboriginal Religion.* Oceania monograph 11. Sydney: University of Sydney.

Sutton, Peter, ed. 1989. *Dreamings: The Art of Aboriginal Australia.* Ringwood, Australia, and London: Viking Penguin.

Tonkinson, Robert. 1978. *The Mardudjara Aborigines.* New York: Holt, Rinehart and Winston.

Tunstill, Guy. 1987. "Melody and Rhythmic Structure in Pitjantjatjara Song." In *Songs of Aboriginal Australia,* ed. Margaret Clunies Ross, Tamsin Donaldson, and Stephen A. Wild, 121–141. Oceania monograph 32. Sydney: University of Sydney.

von Sturmer, John. 1987. "Aboriginal Singing and Notions of Power." In *Songs of Aboriginal Australia,* ed. Margaret Clunies Ross, Tamsin Donaldson, and Stephen A. Wild, 63–76.

Oceania monograph 32. Sydney: University of Sydney.

Wild, Stephen A. 1975. "Warlbiri Music and Dance in Their Social and Cultural Nexus." Ph.D. dissertation, Indiana University.

————. 1977–1978. "Men As Women: Female Dance Symbolism in Walpiri Men's Rituals." *Dance Research Journal* (CORD) 10(1):14–22.

————. 1987. "Recreating the *Jukurrpa:* Adaptation and Innovation of Songs and Ceremonies in Warlpiri Society." In *Songs of Aboriginal Australia,* ed. Margaret Clunies Ross, Tamsin Donaldson, and Stephen A. Wild, 97–120. Oceania monograph 32. Sydney: University of Sydney.

————. 1988. "Music and Dance." In *The Australian People: An Encyclopedia of the Nation, Its People and Their Origins,* ed. James Jupp, 174–181. Sydney: Angus & Robertson.

Williams, Drid. 1988. "Homo Nullius: The Status of Aboriginal Dancing in Northern Queensland." *Journal for the Anthropological Study of Human Movement* 6(3):87–111.

# New Guinea

Rhythmic sounds from log idiophones, hourglass-shaped drums, swung slats, paired flutes, shaken rattles, and leaves are complemented by the visual impact of costumes with moving parts, while bodies of men and women move up and down or side to side. Sounds and movements imitating waterfalls and other natural phenomena and learned from birds and other animals pervade the traditional music of New Guinea.

Success in life depends on working with spirits, nature, and kin. Musical sounds are spirits' voices. Performances validate the identities of individuals and families, and affirm communal feeling in gender relations, trade, warfare, and parliamentary debate. Traditional musics are transformed into modern ones, while modern musics are transformed into traditional ones.

Preceded by men playing hourglass drums, performers carry elaborate constructions of feathers and plant materials. Hansa Bay, Madang Province, Papua New Guinea. Photo by A. B. Lewis. Field Museum, Chicago.

# The Music and Dance of
# New Guinea

*Adrienne L. Kaeppler*
*Don Niles*

**Past and Present Cultures**
**Musical Instruments**
**Musical Contexts**
**Words in Musical Settings**
**The Preservation and Analysis of Performances**
**Dance**

The landmass of New Guinea is a maze of sociocultural groups, with a long prehistory of cultural challenges and a checkered history of colonial influences. Global politics of the 1800s and 1900s resulted in political boundaries that do not match cultural or social boundaries. Irian Jaya, the western part of the island, is politically a province of Indonesia. The modern political entity of Papua New Guinea, an independent member of the British Commonwealth, includes not only the eastern part of the island of New Guinea, but large and small islands—New Britain, New Ireland, Manus, the Trobriand Islands, Bougainville, and others—whose cultures are in some cases only distantly related (map). When dealing with the arts, it is appropriate to use cultural rather than political boundaries, yet politics influences how the peoples of New Guinea construct their past.

Many societies on both sides of the political divide of New Guinea have features in common, including social organizations centered around leaders who attain power and renown primarily by individual or family achievement, rather than chiefs, born (as in Polynesia) to ascribed positions of leadership. Each tribal grouping, and in some cases each village, differs in important ways from others. This diversity manifests itself in hundreds of dialects and languages, details and underlying concepts of political structures and social relationships, the fabrication and use of material culture, the use and exploitation of the natural environment, religion and ritual, clothing, lore, poetry, music, and dance.

In New Guinea, large political units were rare. The effective sociopolitical grouping was often a single village, sometimes with as few as a hundred people. Larger groupings—clans and tribes—cooperated among themselves during wars, ceremonies, and the local production of crafts, and for exchanges of pigs, shell ornaments, and spouses. In many other ways, they were not politically united. Political power was often in the hands of a leader who achieved his position by ability and personality, and acquired temporary status by developing a following.

The people of many areas favored elaborate rituals and dramatic ceremonies, often connected with the building of men's houses (structures in which men spent time and kept ceremonial objects), rites of initiation and puberty, wars, and funerals. These were occasions for spectacular displays: dressed in elaborate costumes and

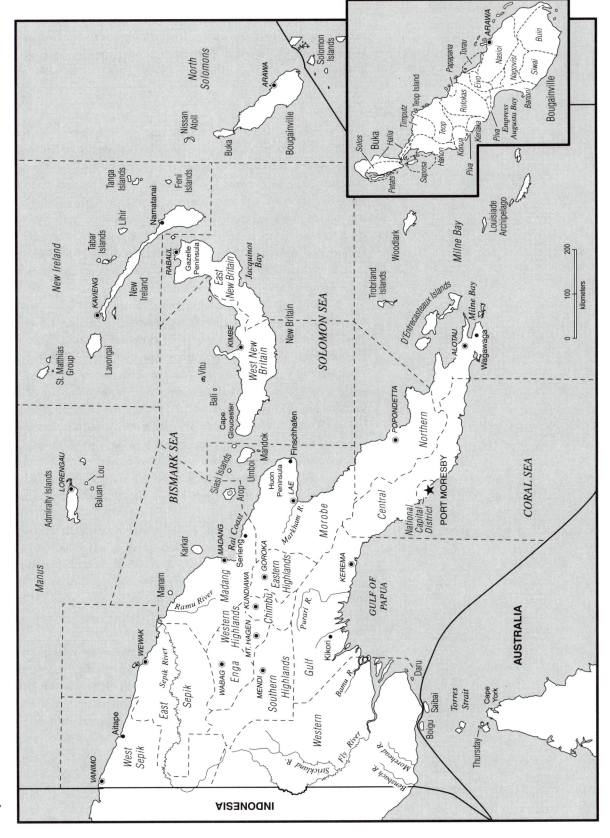

Papua New Guinea

painted in characteristic designs and colors, participants wore or carried carved and painted figures and ceremonial boards. To the accompaniment of singing, drumming, and dancing, huge masks, representing spirits, totems, and ancestors, made their appearance. In stylistic details and underlying concepts, each area, tribe, and even village differed from others.

—ADRIENNE L. KAEPPLER

## PAST AND PRESENT CULTURES

Evidence along the Huon Peninsula suggests people first entered this part of the world about fifty thousand years ago, when the environment was much colder and New Guinea and Australia were connected by land. A "general resemblance" (Laycock 1973:58) between log-idiophone melodies sung by speakers of languages of the Ndu family of East Sepik Province and didjeridu melodies sung by Australian Aborigines, plus other cultural and genetic similarities, could prove links between arts of the Purari River basin and those of the Australian Aborigines. Because New Guinea and Australia have been separated from Asia for about fifty million years, local animals are distinct from those of Asia, and the first local people must have come by sea.

About thirty-five thousand years ago, people from New Guinea started visiting New Ireland, from which, after about twenty-eight thousand years ago, others visited Buka. By fourteen thousand years ago, snow and ice on the high mountains of New Guinea had begun to melt, permitting easier settlement farther inland. By ten thousand years ago, people had settled all the main interior valleys of New Guinea, and settlements existed in New Britain and some islands to the east. About nine thousand years ago, in the uplands, some of the first gardening in the world occurred. By five thousand years ago, the inhabitants were growing Asian varieties of yams, taros, and bananas, and were raising pigs. Possibly about the same time, people speaking Austronesian languages began arriving. They moved up the Markham River, pushing earlier inhabitants inland, and into New Britain and New Ireland (Wurm et al. 1975). About thirty-five hundred years ago, people began to move out to other islands of the central Pacific.

Papua New Guinea is one of the most linguistically complicated nations on earth. Current estimates range between seven hundred and eight hundred distinct languages. Since the 1960s, linguists have sorted most of these languages into larger groupings (Wurm and Hattori 1981). In this cultural complexity, researchers have sought relations between language groups and genetic markers, but genetic affiliations probably reflect geographic proximity, rather than linguistic similarity (Hill and Serjeantson 1989).

In the late twentieth century, three languages are widespread in New Guinea: English, promoted by the educational system; Tok Pisin, also called New Guinea Pidgin; and Hiri Motu, also called Police Motu. It is uncertain how the distribution of indigenous languages relates to the distribution of musical styles, instruments, rituals, and other musically important aspects of human experience. Linguistic diversity does not mean that neighboring groups did not communicate. People learned neighboring languages. They married, fought, and traded with their neighbors. In coastal and inland areas, extensive trade-based networks helped diffuse and popularize musical instruments and dances.

### History and government

European contact with the area began in the 1500s, with visits by Portuguese ships; Indonesian and Chinese contacts may have occurred earlier. In the 1600s and 1700s, Dutch, English, French, and Spanish explorers made increasingly frequent visits.

Shipping between Australia and Asia took vessels through or near local waters. In 1828, the Dutch formally annexed the western half of New Guinea.

In 1884, Germany proclaimed a protectorate over northwest New Guinea and the Bismarck Archipelago, and Britain proclaimed a protectorate over southeastern New Guinea and adjoining islands. In 1906, the federal government of the Commonwealth of Australia took responsibility for British New Guinea. In 1914, at the outset of the Great War, Australian troops occupied German New Guinea. Later, the League of Nations gave Australia a mandate for its administration. From 1921 to 1942, Australia administered separately the Australian Territory of Papua (formerly British New Guinea) and the Mandated Territory of New Guinea. During World War II, Japanese troops conquered part of the former and much of the latter. After the war, Australia again became the controlling authority. In 1945, the two territories administratively merged, forming the Territory of Papua and New Guinea. The first nationally elected legislature met in 1964.

On 16 September 1975, Papua New Guinea attained independence as a sovereign state within the British Commonwealth. Its constitution vests power in a one-chamber national legislature and executive authority in a prime minister. A governor general represents the British Crown. Though numerous changes of government have occurred, political transitions have followed strictly constitutional procedures. Party affiliations remain fluid, and regionalism influences the formation of governments.

## Cultural regions

For descriptive convenience, Papua New Guinea divides into four regions: Papua, Highlands, Mamose, and Islands. Among these regions, cultures overlap; within these regions, much cultural variation occurs. Several provinces make up each region. Provincial distinctions and boundaries more often reflect colonial policy, rather than ethnographic reality.

The geographical untidiness of cultural diversity in Papua New Guinea makes any nationwide overview of music and dance suspect. Exceptional cases nearly always contradict general statements. Scholars have not done enough research to define "musical areas" or make other useful geographical distinctions, but to anyone familiar with New Guinea and the islands near it, certain patterns are clear. In some places, researchers find value in contrasting dances performed inside a house and those performed outside, dances performed by males and those performed by females, and instrumentalists who dance while playing and those who do not.

Four Tok Pisin musical terms—*garamut, kundu, singsing, susap*—occur widely in speech and writing in the area, even in communications among people fluent only in English. Their anglicized plurals—*garamuts, kundus, singsings, susaps*—are standard in Papua New Guinean English, and appear as such in this volume.

## MUSICAL INSTRUMENTS

The distribution of musical instruments in New Guinea reflects distinctive ethnological patterns. Some of the present-day distribution of instruments is attributable to trade, geography, and environment, just as these factors figure in the distribution of languages and other cultural traits. Some instruments correlate with musical contexts and genres (Fischer 1986; Kunst 1967; McLean 1994).

### The garamut

The garamut, a hollowed log idiophone, takes its name from a common indigenous name for *Vitex cofassus,* the tree from whose wood men commonly hew the instrument. Societies in much of the Mamose and Island regions use it. In addition to accompanying songs and dances, it often serves for intervillage communication.

Men play garamuts with either of two techniques: jolting, when they hit the instrument with the end of a stick; and striking, when they hit it with the side of a stick. By far the more common technique in New Guinea is jolting.

### The kundu

A widely distributed instrument is the kundu (figure 1), a drum, most widely played by men, but in some areas commonly played by women. It is absent in certain inland areas of the mainland, and in many societies of the Island Region. Because it is widespread, its absence is possibly more revealing than its presence (Niles 1983a).

The kundu has the shape of an hourglass, or sometimes a cylinder or a cone. One end is open, and the other holds a membrane. In one hand, a player holds the instrument (sometimes by a handle), and with the other, strikes the head. Materials of construction vary. The body is normally wood—often *Pterocarpus indicus,* but sometimes *Vitex cofassus, Litsea* spp., and *Intsia bijuga.* Bamboo and clay variants occur. In lowland areas, the membrane is usually from a monitor (*Varanus* sp.) or a snake; in mountainous areas, it may be the skin of species of cuscus, ringtail, wallaby, or other marsupial; in some areas, it may be the skin of a megapode, a bird that lays eggs in mounds of debris.

Players often tune the kundu by attaching to the membrane blobs of beeswax (from stingless bees, *Trigona* sp.) or gum from trees. Tuning involves heating the membrane over a fire, adjusting the blobs, and testing the sound. Some peoples along the Rai Coast and in inland areas tune the instrument by pasting clay on the membrane.

A common accompaniment to singing, kundus usually serve nonreligious purposes. Their rhythmic patterns often give clues about the performers' geographical origins. Researchers distinguish between peoples that play kundus synchronously (with obvious coordination in sonic motion) and those that play kundus asynchronously (with little or no such motion). The former peoples are more numerous. They subdivide into those that use repeating, unvarying rhythms, and those that use different rhythms to structure music sectionally.

### Other instruments and their social implications

Probably the most widespread musical instrument in New Guinea is the susap, an orally resonated lamellaphone, usually played by males, though seldom associated with male religious activity. Its ordinary use, as an instrument of self-entertainment, gives it less social importance than other, less widely distributed, instruments. For signaling, men in coastal areas sound conchs or garamuts. Flutes and trumpets, voice-modifying tubes, rattles, and miscellaneous idiophones also occur in New Guinea. The forms and materials used for their construction vary widely.

The distribution of sound-producing instruments conspicuously parallels the distribution of languages. The number of linguistic groups increases from south to north on the mainland, and so does the variety of instruments: in the Mamose Region, ensembles of variously sized and pitched flutes, garamuts, trumpets, and voice-modifying tubes are typical, but in much of the Papuan Region, the only musical instruments are a rattle, a kundu, a conch, and an end-blown flute. Besides the mere presence or absence of an instrument, other factors—indigenous names, constructional materials, performative usage, distinctive rhythms—prove useful in understanding relationships among cultural groups in New Guinea. Comparative work along such lines has focused on why the garamut is absent from the Papuan Region (Niles 1983b).

FIGURE 1 A Boazi man holds an exceptionally large kundu, Western Province. Photo by Don Niles, 1984.

## MUSICAL CONTEXTS

A useful Tok Pisin term for which English has no convenient word is *singsing*. This term can refer simply to any performance of a song, but it often denotes an important context: purposeful singing and dancing by decorated performers. Purpose, song, dance, and decoration intertwine: particular occasions demand particular dances, which, in turn, require appropriate decorations and preparatory rituals. Dancers, singers, and instrumentalists may perform separately, but singsings require their simultaneous participation.

Music and dance highlight various occasions: birth, initiation, first menstruation, courting, mourning, first haircut, construction of a house or a canoe, exchange-related ceremonies, religious activities, welcoming, farewelling, fighting (before, during, after), séances, communication, games, general amusement. Such contexts vary by culture and area. People often regard "dance" as an integral part of a performance; to separate it from "music" is often a Westernism, foreign to local concepts of effective performance.

Sounds highlight events. In many areas, sounds appease ancestral spirits by proving that traditions are continuing according to familiar notions of correct procedure. But sounds also serve other purposes: sending messages between lovers, evoking emotional states, ordering uninitiated persons away, and so on.

### Male initiations

Music in New Guinea importantly occurs in association with male initiation. Instruments often play a prominent role, either as creators of a spirit's voice (Tok Pisin *tambaran*), or as objects that even males must not play or see until they have undergone the rituals that transmit or authenticate esoteric knowledge and guarantee social responsibility (Gourlay 1975). Uninitiated persons—boys and females—fear the sounds, and must not learn that men create them. For learning this secret, women have been put to death, despite widespread belief in myths that women once held such knowledge, which men took from them. Paired, side-blown Sepik and Highland flutes are the most thoroughly studied examples of secret instruments, but men employ other instruments: voice-modifying tubes and vessels, swung slats, end-blown flutes, piston flutes, vessels inserted into water or mud, rubbed idiophones, ensembles of trumpets or side-blown flutes, and so on.

These instruments often produce continuous sounds, rather than sounds subject to interruptions (such as inhalation), or they change the quality of human vocalizations. By setting sounds apart from ordinary experience, acoustic continuity fosters the illusion that the sounds emanate from nonhuman sources. Continuous sounds may inhere in the instrument (like swung slats), or result from a specialized technique (like playing in alternation, common with flutes and trumpets). Men modify their voices by singing through bamboos, gourds, and conchs.

### Christian missions

In the 1800s and early 1900s, missionaries reacted harshly against indigenous music, especially music associated with non-Christian religious practices. Most missionaries, in the light of their own morality, considered indigenous music and dance the results of moral darkness:

> The worst excesses arose in connexion with the immoral dances of the district. The nature of these may be judged from the fact that while the wife, as being so much private property, was not allowed to be present, the unmarried girls were present and became the centre of uncleanness. . . . Some of the old practices must

go, such as the dances referred to, and it is our bounden duty to put Christian festivals in their place. (Lenwood 1917:166–167)

The "bounden duty" to make Christian substitutions led to the rise of new styles of singing and dancing, dependent in part on the music of the missions concerned. Some missionaries banned indigenous dancing completely; others allowed dances to be modified, or Polynesian choral styles to be substituted. Some missionaries made Christian men prove their faith by disrespecting the old ways, particularly by revealing to women and uninitiated youths the secret instruments. Missionaries everywhere banned dances that promoted sexual activities.

In the second half of the twentieth century, most churches with long histories in Papua New Guinea championed some aspects of local culture and sought out indigenous contributions to Christianity. Since it was neither possible nor worthwhile for many peoples to revive abandoned practices, revised versions have been created.

### Other contextual influences

In some areas, whether people perform inside or outside a house is significant. In the Highland Region, the location of a performance is a distinguishing feature between courting parties and formal distributions of wealth. In the central Highlands, main singsings occur outside; in areas that fringe the Highlands, they occur inside.

*Ancestors.*—In many parts of New Guinea, traditions maintain music that ancestors had created or transmitted, and people appease ancestral spirits by performing their traditions. For such occasions, they do not perform new compositions, nor do they compose them. This trait often occurs in association with traditions of secret initiation. By contrast, in parts of the Islands Region and the western section of the Highland Region, some cultures highly value the composition of new songs.

*Communication.*—Songs and instruments can aid communication. Where garamuts are present, people communicate by signaling on them. The sounds are audible for kilometers, but the messages conveyed are few, and the signals often have tight structures (Zemp and Kaufmann 1969). Messages commonly announce a person's death or visitors' arrivals, or call people to gather. On the coast, people signal with conchs; in the mountains, people call out in stylized forms, often yodeling.

*Display.*—Performances of music and dance often enable personal display. By appeasing spirits, correct presentation and execution assure the prosperity of people, the growth of crops, and the health of communities. In the beauty of costumes and postures, performers display to people of the opposite sex, suggesting sexual liaisons. They effectively display to people of the same sex, proving their maturity and skill.

*Local shows.*—The early 1950s saw the rise of new occasions for performing old genres: local shows, displays of agricultural and industrial development. Musicians and dancers participated competitively. Judges awarded cash prizes. Troupes performed apart from customary contexts, alongside unrelated troupes. In 1952, the first Kokopo Show occurred; about the same time, the Papuan Agricultural, Industrial and Cultural Society hosted the first Port Moresby Show. Other shows, in other towns, followed. In the 1990s, many shows—Port Moresby Show, Tolai Warwagira, Hiri Moale Festival, Madang Festival (formerly Maborasa Festival), Morobe Agricultural Show, Goroka Show, Mount Hagen Show, Malanggan Show, and others—attract residents and tourists.

## WORDS IN MUSICAL SETTINGS

Indigenous musical texts have been little studied, but completed work proves the importance of certain commonalities and contrasts. Texts often employ archaic terms. Metaphoric language, different from everyday speech, is common everywhere. Songs provide an aural representation of myths and legends—a striking feature where stories of ancestors' actions are taught to youths during initiation, especially in the Sepik area. In a Manambu (East Sepik) song about a failed marriage, the composer's lover uses her elder sister's totemic name, Ramakwarawindjəmbanəmbər, identifying with the subclan that owns it (after Harrison 1982:69–69):

> Aiya, nəmandəmb
> Langgwunlanggwun karəndatəkwa!
> Wunakəl Ramakwarawindjəmbanəmbər,
> Nyənda-ka'asa Apawuluwita'akw-ma'am,
> Wuka varana.

> Hey, stop pulling
> At my breasts so hard!
> My Ramakwarawindjəmbanəmbər elder sister,
> The middle-vine Apawuluwi-woman,
> Is coming.

*Nyənda-ka'asa* 'middle-vine' is an epithet specific to this clan, referring to the clan's hereditary right to have a special vine attached to the gable of its ceremonial house during yam-harvest rituals; *Apawuluwita'akw* is an epithet for women of this clan. Such devices transpose the event "into the landscape of the totemic ancestors, creating a poetically effective intersection of myth and mundane life" (Harrison 1982:16).

An important metaphoric process is the use of singing to map ancestral actions and migrations (Wassmann 1991). Places cited in musical texts often evoke nostalgia for individuals, events, or eras (Feld 1990a). The order of songs, which can determine the correctness of performances, may play out against segments of day and night (Lewis 1980).

## THE PRESERVATION AND ANALYSIS OF PERFORMANCES

Visitors to New Guinea occasionally commented on performances of music and dance, but the invention of devices for recording sounds and images helped researchers study music and dance more scientifically (Niles 1992). In 1898, the Cambridge Expedition to the Torres Strait made the first recordings of music in New Guinea. Many important collections from the German colony of New Guinea resulted from German expeditions: the Deutsche Marine Expedition of 1907–1909, the Hamburg Südsee-Expedition in 1908–1910, and the Kaiserin-Augusta-Fluss Expedition in 1912–1913. Important collections of recordings come from the work of Emil Stephan in 1904, Richard Thurnwald in 1907 and 1933–1934, Richard Neuhauss in 1908–1910, F. Börnstein in 1909–1913 (?), and Ernst Frizzi in 1911. In contrast, research in British New Guinea was rarer. Early collectors were Charles Seligman in 1904, Gunnar Landtman in 1910–1911, Diamond Jenness and Andrew Ballantyne in 1912, and Bronislaw Malinowski in 1914–1918.

In the late 1800s and early 1900s, the foundation of aural archives in Europe encouraged recording and made equipment even more available. From 1904 to 1906, the Vienna Phonogrammarchiv equipped the Austrian ethnologist Rudolf Pöch with discs for visits to German and British New Guinea. For the Phonogramm-Archiv Berlin, the missionaries Joseph Winthuis in 1908–1909 and Heinrich Zahn in 1928–1932 made important collections of cylinder recordings.

In 1918, when the territories of Papua and New Guinea came under Australian administration, music-recording activity declined. Frank Hurley in 1920–1923 and

New Guinean systems of structured movement—though having elements in common—differ from area to area. They have an elemental basis in rhythm. This feature contrasts with Polynesian dancing, whose elemental basis is poetry.

Paul Wirz in 1927 and 1930–1931 made exceptional recordings. Only after 1945, with the invention of magnetic tape, did most researchers in New Guinea have access to a convenient means of recording sounds.

### Academic studies

In the 1960s, an important change in methodology occurred: researchers began spending extended periods living among local peoples to study music. Vida Chenoweth (1974, 1979) produced the first doctoral dissertation on New Guinean music studied in this way. Previous researchers had written dissertations on local music, but none had collected the materials themselves. Regis Stella (1987, 1990) produced the first thesis written by a Papua New Guinean on the music of a Papua New Guinean people. After the 1970s, international interest in researching New Guinean musics grew. Researchers came from Australia, Austria, Canada, Germany, Japan, New Zealand, Switzerland, the United Kingdom, and the United States. Despite the efforts of scores of researchers, much work remains to be done.

In the 1940s and 1950s, staffers of Papua New Guinean governmental bodies, including the Education Department and radio stations, engaged sporadically in research and recording. In 1974, the founding of the Institute of Papua New Guinea Studies systematized this work. Its music department employed full-time musical researchers (including Charles and Frederic Duvelle, Ilaita Gigimat, Clement Gima, Les McLaren, Don Niles, and Filip Lamasisi Yayii), who developed a music archive, issued publications, and networked with interested parties. This institution moved among various government ministries and in 1988 joined other research bodies to become the Cultural Studies Division of the National Research Institute. In January 1996, it was reestablished separately as the Institute of Papua New Guinea Studies.

The Faculty of Creative Arts of the University of Papua New Guinea (once the Creative Arts Centre, and later the National Arts School) has had a music department since its inception, in 1972. Its faculty, though teaching the elements of Western classical and popular musics, has always offered courses on local music. Goroka Teachers College, the main institution for training high-school teachers, has offered courses on local music and has collaborated with the Institute of Papua New Guinea Studies in producing publications for school use.

*The Papua New Guinea Music Collection* (1987) contains more than three hundred examples of music, from every province. The largest and most representative collection of indigenous recordings, it provides a foundation for future research. Many local cultures, with hundreds of languages and millions of people, still await their first musical recordings and their first systematic writings on music.

—DON NILES

## DANCE

New Guinean systems of structured movement, though having elements in common, differ from area to area. Throughout New Guinea, they have an elemental basis in

FIGURE 2    Papua New Guinean dancers at the Pacific Festival of Arts. Photo by Adrienne L. Kaeppler, 1980.

rhythm. This feature contrasts with Polynesian dancing, whose elemental basis is poetry.

Traditionally, ritual movement was often the province of men. Women might perform at the end of a line, or near the men, or as observers. Whether part of rituals or social activities, dancing was usually participatory, rather than presentational. Performances may not have a specific facing; performers arrange themselves in a circle, or in lines or groupings. These positions may be static, or may shift as performers move. At some occasions, two or more groups perform different dances simultaneously. Each group focuses on itself, rather than on any spectators who may be present; and they do so even when ranged in a single line or column. Dancers often form a moving group, which may take participants from one area to another.

When performers are arranged in a circle, each may move in a circular direction, or the whole circle may move in one or another direction. A common choreographic pattern is arrangement in two columns, which move in one direction by pairs. The first pair, followed by the others, makes a half-turn outward, and then moves in the opposite direction until two lines are formed going in that direction; then they reverse again. Or dancers may be arranged side by side in one or more long rows facing in one direction for one sequence of movements, and then, perhaps, facing the opposite direction for another (figure 2). In many cases, dance is realized as movement only after the introduction of a regular rhythm set by the beating of a kundu (or occasionally a garamut) or the jingling of rattles. Changes in instrumental rhythms may trigger changes in movements. In some areas, melodic instruments, such as panpipes, furnish the aural dimension.

FIGURE 3 At the Pacific Festival of Arts, performers from Madang Province wear shredded leaves, feathered headdresses, boars' tusks, and shells. Photo by Adrienne L. Kaeppler, 1980.

The most characteristic movements are up-down bouncing of legs and body. The torso typically serves as one vertical unit: the hips do not usually move separately or break at the waist, even when a dancer sways from side to side. The body may be held straight, or it may be inclined forward slightly at the hips. The vertical movements are often created by alternately bending the knees and lifting the heels in place, or by step-bend-step-bend progressing, forward or backward.

Often, performers carry kundus, sometimes carved or painted or both. The open end may have the form of an open jaw, or bear designs based on a human face. Sometimes the kundu represents a mythical animal with sacred characteristics and a sound all its own. When the performers are masked, they too may represent ancestral or totemic spirits. Singing may involve vocables (such as *yo-o yo-o*) or short texts, which may or may not convey narrative meaning.

A leader begins by bending and straightening his knees. The others down the line join in or circle until the whole group moves up and down together, in place or in a prearranged choreographed pattern. Costumes emphasize this rhythm. They consist primarily of attachments, most of which are mobile. Bird-of-paradise plumes and other feathers extend from headdresses, backs, bustles, or arms. Hanging rattles of seeds or shells are attached to legs or costumes, or are held in the hand. Cuscus skin ripples like vertical waves, and shredded leaves and fibers cascade and bounce (figure 3). In some areas, penis coverings (of gourd, shell, or bark) are curved forward and upward to emphasize the up-down movement of the penis. All accouterments of dress contribute to making a mass rhythmic statement (figure 4), and it is difficult to discern if costumery aims at emphasizing rhythm, or if rhythm is a way of showing off costumery.

These are not the movements of everyday life elaborated for a stage; they are movements of the supernatural and the ceremonial world, or movements to project hostility, warfare, and leaders' rise and fall. The visualization of rhythm manifests underlying equivalence-based cultural principles: villages are equivalent, tribes are equivalent, individuals are equivalent; yet, like leaders, they all rise and fall, each having equal access, each in its own time.

Movements, costumes, instruments, and sounds are in some areas aimed at dis-

FIGURE 4   At the Pacific Festival of Arts, Gogodala dancers and musicians perform. Photo by Adrienne L. Kaeppler, 1988.

play, sometimes decorative, sometimes forceful. In other areas, costumes and movements depict or evoke birds, which in turn relate to spirits of the dead, projecting sadness and pathos. Among fringe-highland groups including the Kamula and the Kaluli, movements and music are calculated to make audiences cry.

How rhythm is made visual communicates important information about the deep structure of local culture. Some of these principles deal with political equivalence, sexual antagonism, and the bipolarities of nature-culture and natural-supernatural.

FIGURE 5   A *hevehe* dances on the beach with its escort, a "flock of mountain birds" (after Williams 1940: plate 51). By permission of Oxford University Press.

## Dance in Papua New Guinea

Opportunities for dancing differ greatly among the areas of the country. Space permits only a sampling of available information.

### Lowlands

#### The Papuan Gulf

Some of the most spectacular ceremonies of the country were characteristic of the area of the Papuan Gulf (Williams 1940). Here, long cyclical ceremonies, centered on sea-dwelling spirits that manifested themselves at certain stages during the building of a men's house, connected with the ceremonial initiation of boys into manhood.

Huge *hevehe,* masks constructed of rattan and covered with cloth made from bark, appeared when the house was completed. Some were more than six meters high (figure 5). At sunrise, mask after mask emerged from a never-before-opened door. To a rhythmically drummed accompaniment, clansmen joined these masks, and the spirits danced their way back to the sea. *Eharo,* masks representing totemic creatures or mythological characters (or purely fanciful creations), appeared in dances at specific points in the cycle. Other conical masks, *kovave,* served in ceremonies connected with boys' initiations.

That the masks were supernatural beings, difficult to move in, influenced the dancers' movements. Stylized walking and rhythmic changes in elevation were important. Arms of the sea-dwelling spirits might be covered and used to steady the masks. The masks were joined by their clansmen, who carried and played kundus, creating a massed rhythmic environment of sound and motion.

*West Sepik Province: the Umeda*

In many societies of New Guinea, men and women inhabit separate cultural worlds, manifested as sexual dissociation, and even as antagonism. This separateness is beautifully illustrated in the film *The Red Bowmen* (Owen 1976), which shows the *ida* ritual among the Umeda (Gell 1975, 1985). Basically, women sway from side to side; men make up-and-down movements, emphasizing their genitalia.

Men realize their vertical movements through deep kneebends, but the amount of bend and placement within the movement motif imparts more subtle information than simply that the performer is male. The uninhibited primordial state, associated with cassowary birds, is realized in a series of leaps preceded by deep kneebends and thrusts, which cause each dancer's penis-gourd to click against his abdominal belt. At the other end of the continuum is the bowman, the embodiment of culture: though the movements are still up-and-down, the motif is a stride, and the penis is bound. Leaps associated with the cassowary emphasize the back of the foot; the bowman's strides emphasize the front of the foot. Aimed at biological and social regeneration, the series of dances encapsulates the formalized opposition between the sexes and among groups of men at different stages of life.

### Highlands

In the high interior of New Guinea, each grouping of people, including Enga, Huli, Kaluli, Maring, and Mendi, emphasizes a unique combination of elaborate feather headdresses (often including bird-of-paradise, cassowary, or cockatoo feathers), painting of the face and body, leaves and vines, fur, shells, bones, beads, pieces of clothing (such as aprons, long or short), and implements that performers carry in their hands (arrows, axes, bows, drums, shields, spears). Dances of courtship, widespread in the Highlands, are usually performed by seated boys and girls; movements focus on turning the head from side to side and bending the torso until heads touch.

*Western Highlands and Madang Provinces: the Maring*

In movement, the Maring of the Bismarck Mountains make visual the equivalence of their political groupings (Jablonko 1968, 1991). *Kaiko,* a cycle of warfare based on war, truce, and peace, joins Maring clans into a ritual network. As an expression of solidarity between allies and an expression of equivalence between groups that can become antagonists, the movement system encodes this equivalence and hostility.

Often, groups of men perform simultaneously, synchronizing steps and drumbeats only within their own group, and moving in curved paths back and forth across the arena. Only rarely does one group become a focal point. Some men play drums, while others carry bows and arrows, axes, or long wooden spears. Groupings are similar for dancing and fighting; only the goal is different. Before entering a battle or a ceremonial ground, a man's legs are rubbed with gray clay to make them strong in battle or tireless in dance.

There are four main movements of the legs: a bounce, performed by flexing the legs while head and torso remain rigid, with arms hanging at the sides or beating a drum; a flat-footed, walking step, used when a group moves in a column; a stoop, which brings all the men of a group to a motionless position; and a "display" step, in which the trailing leg thrusts backward, or bends up toward the buttocks during a leap. An axe is wielded, or a spear is passed from one hand to the other above the head. Displaying hostility, this step is used only occasionally, and then by only a few men. The vertical linear movements use the torso as one unit.

*Western Highlands Province: the Melpa*

Dancing among the Melpa is a rhythmic analogy of human and bird-of-paradise lives

(Strathern 1985). The birds mature by growing the famous tail plumes, lost by molting after their sexual display. Men's dances at festivals of exchange demonstrate the maturity of the leader holding the festival. Men dance for the climax of the event; they then molt their dance, putting it away until the next festival.

The common element of dancing is rhythmically concerted movements. Those of *mörl,* a dance presented by kundu-beating rows of men facing an audience, consist of rising on the toes, holding shoulders and back straight, with knees bent in a downward movement to make long aprons move in unison as a graceful forward sweep in rhythm with the bouncing of the feathers. This rhythmic unison presents the performers as a unified group of undifferentiated men at the height of their communal existence. But they are not equal: some have more elegant feathers and costumery, and some perform better; thus, they embody underlying principles of equivalence and nonequivalence. *Werl,* the women's corresponding performance, adds to the rhythmic bending of the knees a side-to-side sway with knees together.

### Southern Highlands Province: the Kaluli

Dancing among the Kaluli north of Mount Bosavi consists of genres that differ by choreography, number of performers, costumes, instruments, and kind of song (Feld 1988, 1990b; Schieffelin 1976). Usually performed at night in a communal longhouse, the songs evoke images of the past. Their aim is to make observers cry—and when this happens, anger drives the observers to use torches to burn the dancers on the back and shoulders. The performers then give those who cried small presents in compensation for their anguish.

The primary movement motif is up-and-down bouncing, which recreates the movement of the giant cuckoo dove, which mythically taught the Kaluli to dance. The performer represents this bird's singing and dancing at a waterfall, and accentuates its movements by the bouncing of feathers, streamers, and rattles attached to his costume. The sound of the streamers represents the sound of the waterfall, and the performer's voice represents the sound of the bird's singing.

The Kaluli consider only one genre, *gisalo,* indigenous. It is performed by four men wearing cassowary-feather headdresses. Each performer in turn sings a long song while tapping a mussel-shell rattle on the floor, and then proceeds through the center of the longhouse and back. At each end of the longhouse, men sing refrains. The introduced genre *iwɔ* is a series of forty-five songs, each of which is begun by two men as they burst into a house and bang axes on its floor; twenty men, forming a dancing chorus, follow. *Kɔluba* is performed by paired men, facing each other at one end of the house, then at the center, and then at the other end. Dancing in place, they sing overlapping parts; after five statements of the music, they move to the new position. After every ten songs, the whole group sings and parades through the house. *Heyalo* is all-night singing, drumming, and hopping sideways around the edges of the longhouse. *Sabio* consists of two lines of men, who face each other bouncing up and down in place, tapping a stick on the floor, singing alternate lines. *Ilib kuwɔ* is a processional and prelude, in which one to six performers, beating drums and rattling crayfish claws at the rear of their costumes, move up and down in place, and then skip from one end of the longhouse to the other.

### Trends of the 1990s

Contemporary popular music in Papua New Guinea accompanies new styles of dancing. String-band music in coastal Central Province often includes imitation of Polynesian elements: movements of hands, feet, and hips, and skirts made of long strips of cut rice bags. Power bands—electrified guitars, drums, and microphoned singers—perform in hotel bars, or for special dances. Dancing in those venues is usually based on equivalent Western styles. Because the clientele of bars are mostly males, dancing by males without a female partner is common.

## Dance in Irian Jaya

Large and culturally complex, this area of some one million inhabitants has given rise to dances that remain among the least-studied in the world. Researchers have published only passing references to performances of structured movement. In 1975, Soedarsono, a specialist in Javanese dance, spent two weeks researching dance in the area. In a short article (1985), he classified indigenous performances into three categories: traditional dancing, for ceremonial or ritual purposes; and two "fairly recent developments," dancing for personal pleasure and dancing as an art.

In the interior of Irian Jaya, some ritual choreographies use imitative movements (hunting, fighting, procreating); others involve performers arranged in single or double circles, believed to have the power of protecting individuals from evil spirits. In such a dance among the Ekari (Kapauku) of the Central Mountain Range, a mother holds a newborn child in the center of the circle while adults dance around them. In Biak, after a boy's circumcision, adults dance around him. In contrast, Ekari dances for a proposal of marriage require two parallel lines, in which the suitor's kin face those of the courted woman: if the proposal is accepted, the members of the woman's family stretch out their arms with upturned palms; if the proposal is rejected, the palms face forward. In urban areas of Irian Jaya, social dancing includes popular genres: the *mapia,* the *gale-gale,* the *yosim,* and the *pancar.*

### Presentational dances

In the 1970s, residents of towns in Irian Jaya began choreographing dances for presentation to audiences (Soedarsono 1985:64). Troupes stage such performances for national holidays, such as Independence Day of the Republic of Indonesia, 17 August.

The Indonesian government has sponsored dancers' travel. In 1991, in conjunction with exhibits of Indonesian art, a troupe consisting primarily of Dani and Asmat performed at four museums in the United States (figure 6). The Asmat, accompanying their performances with hourglass drums and wooden trumpets, emphasized circular rotations of the hips in a horizontal plane. The torso moved as a block; the

FIGURE 6   Performers from Irian Jaya at the Baird Auditorium, Smithsonian Institution. Photo by Adrienne L. Kaeppler, 1991.

movements did not break at the waist. Bent knees (one or both simultaneously) moved in and out, and the feet slid across the floor. These movements were said to represent shorebirds and cockatoos. The Dani of this troupe, using uncommon vocal techniques and lamellaphones, made side-to-side hip movements, again using the torso as a block; with flexed knees, they strode from one side of the stage to the other. In the film *Dead Birds* (Gardner 1961), the Dani used similar movements, proceeding from one place to another and counterclockwise in a circle.

Like some of their Papua New Guinean counterparts, men of Irian Jaya wear elaborate costumes with attachments and headdresses (often of bird-of-paradise feathers) that emphasize the rhythms of their performances.

—ADRIENNE L. KAEPPLER

## REFERENCES

Chenoweth, Vida. 1974. "The Music of the Usarufas." 2 vols. Ph.D. dissertation, University of Auckland.

———. 1979. *The Usarufas and Their Music.* Publications, 5. Dallas: Summer Institute of Linguistics Museum of Anthropology.

Feld, Steven. 1988. "Aesthetics as Iconicity of Style, or 'Lift-up-over Sounding': Getting into the Kaluli Groove." *Yearbook for Traditional Music* 20:74–113.

———. 1990a. "Aesthetics and Synesthesia in Kaluli Ceremonial Dance." *UCLA Journal of Dance Ethnology* 14:1–16.

———. 1990b. *Sound and Sentiment: Birds, Weeping, Poetics, and Song in Kaluli Expression.* 2nd ed. Publications of the American Folklore Society, New Series. Philadelphia: University of Pennsylvania Press.

Fischer, Hans. 1986. *Sound-Producing Instruments in Oceania.* Edited by Don Niles. Translated by Philip W. Holzknecht. Boroko: Institute of Papua New Guinea Studies.

Gardner, Robert. 1961. *Dead Birds.* 16mm. Cambridge: Harvard University.

Gell, Alfred. 1975. *Metamorphosis of the Cassowaries.* London: Athlone.

———. 1985. "Style and Meaning in Umeda Dance." In *Society and the Dance,* ed. Paul Spencer, 183–205. Cambridge: Cambridge University Press.

Gourlay, Kenneth A. 1975. *Sound-Producing Instruments in Traditional Society: A Study of Esoteric Instruments and Their Role in Male-Female Relations.* New Guinea Research Bulletin, 60. Port Moresby and Canberra: New Guinea Research Unit.

Harrison, Simon. 1982. *Laments for Foiled Marriages: Love-Songs from a Sepik River Village.* Boroko: Institute of Papua New Guinea Studies.

Hill, Adrian V. S., and Susan W. Serjeantson, eds. 1989. *The Colonization of the Pacific: A Genetic Trail.* Research Monographs on Human Biology, 7. Oxford: Clarendon Press.

Jablonko, Allison. 1968. *Maring in Motion.* Ph.D. dissertation, Columbia University.

———. 1991. "Patterns of Daily Life in the Dance of the Maring of New Guinea." *Visual Anthropology* 4:367–377.

Kunst, Jaap. 1967. *Music in New Guinea: Three Studies.* Translated by Jeune Scott-Kemball. Verhandelingen van het Koninklijk Instituut voor Taal-, Land- en Volkenkunde, 53. The Hague: Martinus Nijhoff.

Laycock, Donald C. 1973. *Sepik Languages: Checklist and Preliminary Classification.* Pacific Linguistics, B 25. Canberra: Australian National University.

Lenwood, Frank. 1917. *Pastels from the Pacific.* London: Oxford University Press.

Lewis, Gilbert. 1980. *Day of Shining Red: An Essay on Understanding Ritual.* Cambridge Studies in Social Anthropology, 27. Cambridge: Cambridge University Press.

McLean, Mervyn. *Diffusion of Musical Instruments and Their Relation to Language Migrations in New Guinea.* Kulele: Occasional Papers on Pacific Music and Dance, 1. Boroko: Cultural Studies Division, National Research Institute.

Niles, Don. 1983a. "Diversity as Unity: The Drum in Papua New Guinea." In *Documents: 6th Asia Music Rostrum and Symposium,* 115–120. Pyongyang: Democratic Peoples Republic of Korea.

———. 1983b. "Why Are There No Garamuts in Papua?" *Bikmaus* 4(3):90–104.

———. 1992. "Collection, Preservation, and Dissemination: The Institute of Papua New Guinea Studies as the Centre for the Study of All Papua New Guinea Music." In *Music and Dance of Aboriginal Australia and the South Pacific,* ed. Alice Marshall Moyle, 59–75. Sydney: University of Sydney.

Owen, Chris. 1976. *The Red Bowmen.* 16mm. Boroko: Institute of Papua New Guinea Studies.

*Papua New Guinea Music Collection.* 1987. Edited by Don Niles and Michael Webb. Boroko:

Institute of Papua New Guinea Studies IPNGS 008. 11 cassettes.

Schieffelin, Edward L. 1976. *The Sorrow of the Lonely and the Burning of the Dancers.* New York: St. Martin's Press.

Soedarsono. 1985. "Dance in Irian Jaya: A Preliminary Report." *CORD Research Annual* 15:62–66.

Stella, Regis N. 1987. "Forms and Styles of Traditional Banoni Music." B.A. honors thesis, University of Papua New Guinea.

———. 1990. *Forms and Styles of Traditional Banoni Music.* Apwitihire, 1. Boroko: National Research Institute.

Strathern, Andrew. 1985. "'A Line of Boys': Melpa Dance as a Symbol of Maturation." In *Society and the Dance,* ed. Paul Spencer, 119–139. Cambridge: Cambridge University Press.

Wassmann, Jürg. 1991. *The Song to the Flying Fox.* Translated by Dennis Q. Stephenson. Apwitihire, 2. Boroko: National Research Institute.

Williams, F. E. 1940. *Drama of Orokolo: The Social and Ceremonial Life of the Elema.* Territory of Papua, Anthropology Reports, 18. Oxford: Oxford University Press.

Wurm, Stephen A., et al. 1975. "Papuan Linguistic Prehistory, and Past Language Migrations in the New Guinea Area." In *New Guinea Area Languages and Language Study, Vol. 1: Papuan Languages and the New Guinea Linguistic Scene,* ed. Stephen A. Wurm, 935–960. Canberra: Australian National University.

Wurm, Stephen A., and Shiro Hattori, eds. 1981. *Language Atlas of the Pacific Area.* Pacific Linguistics, C 66. Canberra: Australian Academy of the Humanities and the Japan Academy.

Zemp, Hugo, and Christian Kaufmann. 1969. "Pour une transcription automatique des 'langages tambourinés' mélanésiens (un exemple kwoma, Nouvelle-Guinée)." *L'Homme* 9(2):38–88.

# Papuan Region of Papua New Guinea

*Don Niles*
*Virginia Whitney*
*John D. Waiko*
*Vida Chenoweth*
*Wolfgang Laade*

**Central Province**
**Gulf Province**
**Milne Bay Province**
**Oro (Northern) Province**
**Western Province**

The Papuan region includes the provinces along the southern coast: Western, Gulf, Central, Milne Bay, and Oro (Northern). This area roughly corresponds to the former British New Guinea, control of which passed to Australia in 1906. Five years later, the Papua Act changed the name of the possession to *Territory of Papua.* Port Moresby, the capital of Papua New Guinea, lies in this region, within the National Capital District. The region accounts for 43 percent of the area of Papua New Guinea and 21 percent of its population, though without the population of the National Capital District, the latter percentage would drop to 15.

Much of the region lies south of the central mountains. Large expanses of lowlands and plains gradually narrow toward the east. The largest river in the country, the Fly, dominates Western Province; it is navigable more than two-thirds of its 1,200 kilometers. In Gulf Province, the Purari River has an extensive delta at its outflow into the Gulf of Papua. Farther east, foothills often reach down to the sea. By the ratio of height to width, Goodenough Island (Milne Bay Province) is one of the most mountainous islands in the world.

South of Western Province is the Torres Strait, which separates New Guinea from Australia. Until about six thousand years ago, this strait was dry land. Trade has occurred extensively throughout the strait, sustaining many cultural relations and traits, including rattles, songs, and dances. The presence of the kundu in the Cape York area of Australia probably reflects influence from New Guinea.

Non-Austronesian languages of the Trans–New Guinea Phylum dominate the region. The only major exceptions are Austronesian languages spoken in Central and much of Milne Bay provinces; Yele, a non-Austronesian language of the East Papuan Phylum, spoken on Rossel Island (Milne Bay); and a couple of unclassified languages. Throughout the region, Hiri Motu, a pidginized form of a language spoken around Port Moresby, is widely understood; but with the spread of Tok Pisin, it is becoming less important.

## Ceremonies and epics

In many western coastal areas of the region, especially in Western and Gulf provinces, initiatory ceremonies were important. Swung slats, associated with such initiations, are played in central parts of Oro, where men play side-blown flutes in pairs—flutes resembling those of the Sepik-Ramu area, but geographically isolated from them.

The Orokolo (coastal Gulf Province) once conducted ceremonies in which swung slats related physically and conceptually to large masks worn by male dancers (Williams 1940). Formerly, masked dances occurred from Gulf Province westward; by the 1990s, coastal people no longer performed them. Clan-specific ancestors' movements are important in Western and Gulf Provinces. The Orokolo sing epics in parallel fifths, to the accompaniment of a rattle (*kalai*) consisting of a piece of cane split at one end; in a steady rhythm, a singer strikes this end against a leg. The Kiwai sing of ancestral movements in the land of the dead, naming places and mentioning associated events.

As in most parts of coastal Papua New Guinea, extensive networks supported trade. The *hiri* trade (see below) linked the Motu people with parts of Gulf Province; the Motu exchanged clay pots for Gulf sago. Without lessening the individuality of any areas, extensive networks encouraged the spread of songs and dances. While visiting traders exchanged dances, groups remained culturally distinct; some, such as the Mailu, borrowed dances from others. Songs often addressed such trade and magically helped performers get desired items.

## Musical instruments

In most of the region, kundus are important dance-accompanying instruments. The only Papuan area where kundus are absent is the territory of certain Anga peoples (northeastern Gulf Province). In western coastal areas, people carve the open end of a kundu into shapes resembling a mouth, often described as crocodile jaws; similar instruments occur in the Torres Strait Islands. In most lowland Papuan areas, the membrane is the skin of a lizard; in southern Western Province, the skin of a water-dwelling snake, *Acrochordus* sp., serves this function.

For ceremonies, the Gogodala (Western Province) make massive *diwaka,* kundus that may be more than 3 meters long. Men tune them by inserting wedges between the skin and the rope that binds it to the body of the instrument—a common technique in Irian Jaya, but highly unusual in Papua New Guinea. *Diwaka* are distinctive because clans, instead of individuals, own them. Because of their size, they are stationary: seated players hit the skin with their fists (Crawford 1981:350–351). The Boazi (Western Province) make other large kundus; to attach the head to the body, men use a mixture of lime and penis-drawn blood. In Milne Bay and Oro provinces, Aeka, Binandere, Duau, Kilivila, and other ensembles use differently sized kundus.

To cue dancers' movements, leaders play special rhythms on small kundus; other drummers play less intricate rhythms on larger ones. In the Trobriands (Milne Bay), mnemonic vocables help players recall rhythmic sequences on the small kundu. To dramatize local incidents in Oro Province, the Aeka, Binandere, Orokaiva, and others perform dance-dramas (Schwimmer 1979; Waiko 1982; Williams 1930). In parts of Milne Bay Province, dancers imitate the movements of animals.

In most of the region, drummers also dance; but in areas of Milne Bay Province (Bwaidoga, Dobu, Kilivila), drummers are a separate group (Fortune 1932; Jenness and Ballantyne 1920; Malinowski 1916). Goodenough Islanders divide into moieties: the *modawa* 'drum' and the *fakili* 'comb, spear', require different decorations, demeanors, totems, and so on. Drum-moiety men go to spear-moiety villages, where they sing while beating combs on gourds; spear-moiety men go to drum-moiety villages, where they sing while beating drums. In both cases, hosts supply food to guests.

In Oro Province, to accompany collective singing and dancing, performers stamp bamboo tubes on the ground. Individuals play smaller tubes, open at both ends. They hit one end against a thigh, and the other against the palm of a hand.

A distinctive instrument is a struck wooden bowl, played in the Yonggom area of Western Province. Another is a wooden disk used in the Pawaia area (northern Gulf Province): the player holds the disk against his belly and hits it with a stone; his abdomen resonates the sound.

## Dancing

A favorite dance in the Papuan region is the so-called Kiwai dance (locally, *taibubu* or *taibobo*), of Western Province (figure 1). It may have come from Rotuma via the Torres Strait. The Kiwai and most other coastal peoples of the province perform it. Male and female dancers move in place in parallel lines, apart from male and female singer-instrumentalists, who play kundus, rattles, and small bamboo garamuts. These features distinguish this dance from local indigenous dances, in which each dancer holds a kundu, dancing in a group that moves around.

A favorite dance of Central Province is the *kitoro,* which relates news and discusses events; probably original to the Rigo area, it has spread into many areas of the province. Young people of the Trobriand Islands are known for making sexual movements in dances performed at harvesttime and for school shows. Trobriand lyrics have been the object of much translation (Baldwin 1945, 1950; Kasaipwalova and Beier 1978); many treat *kula* voyages (see below), intertwined with religious beliefs.

In the Goilala area (inland Central Province), the Fuyuge construct "dance-villages" for major dances, in which costumed dancers play kundus. Contrary to Jaap Kunst's skepticism (1967:108), unaccompanied songs in falsetto, harmonized in thirds, appear indigenous. In parts of coastal Central Province and among the Wedau (Milne Bay Province), where special houses are built for dancers and guests, dancing occurs on platforms. For many dances in Milne Bay Province, mainly in the Trobriands and on Rossel Island, male dancers wear women's skirts.

In several areas, dancing occurs in the men's house or a communal longhouse. The Polopa (inland Gulf Province) dance inside the men's house at competitive feasts. Along the coast at Kerewo and westward among the Awin, Beami, Gebusi,

FIGURE 1 Kiwai dancers compete at the Port Moresby Show. Photo by Don Niles, 1982.

FIGURE 2 Decorated with paint and feathered headdresses, Roro men perform at the Pacific Festival of Arts, Port Moresby. Photo by Don Niles, 1980.

Gogodala, Kiwai, and Purari, dancing inside longhouses during initiations formerly preceded headhunting.

## Local contrasts

Stark contrasts in music and dance between neighboring groups are unusual in Papua New Guinea, but in the Papuan Region, notable instrumental dissimilarities occur: in contrast to the Austronesian Motu, the non-Austronesian Koita have distinctive dances with stamped bamboo tubes. The Goilala contrast sharply with their Austronesian neighbors, the Mekeo and Roro (figure 2): the Goilala sing polyphonically with wide ranges, but the Mekeo sing basically in unison within a range of a major third or narrower; the Goilala also lack flute-accompanied singing, common among their neighbors. On another point of contrast, the people of Rossel Island differ from those of nearby Austronesian-populated islands: they sing in distinctive polyphony, and do not play kundus.

## Singing and composition

Throughout the region, groups or sometimes individuals own songs, but the Managalasi consider songs the property of the owners of places described in their texts, rather than the composer's property (McKellin 1980:264–267). The Hamtai, an Angan people (inland Gulf Province), often sing of the surrounding limestone outcroppings; each performer sings a unique, independent melody and text.

In the Trobriands, to learn new songs, composers go into trance and travel to Tuma, the land of the dead, where spirits teach them new pieces. Trobriand songs have syllabic phrases descending to a tonal center. Sections continually repeat; hummed sections usually precede sung ones. The Gebusi (Western Province) sing during spirit-medium séances, in a practice resembling that of their Kaluli neighbors. Young Ok women (northern Western Province) compose songs about their environment and men they have seen. In Oro Province, Binandere and Managalasi women compose and perform dirges.

## CENTRAL PROVINCE

On the southeastern mainland of Papua New Guinea, Central Province surrounds the National Capital District. Both entities share the administrative center of Port

In large vessels (*lagatoi*), Motu men sailed 400 to
500 kilometers northwest to exchange armshells
and pottery for sago. Voyages were occasions for
performing *ehona*, songs sung by men to the
accompaniment of a struck bamboo idiophone.

Moresby. In 1990, 141,195 people lived in the province. Austronesian languages are
spoken along much of its coast and lowlands; inland areas are mountainous, inhabited primarily by non-Austronesians.

### Motu

About forty thousand Motu live in villages around the National Capital District and
along the nearby coast. They speak an Austronesian language, whose pidginized version (Hiri Motu) has become widely spoken in the Papuan Region. The Motu divide
into seven western villages, four eastern ones, and three independent of the rest and
each other. The western and independent villages formerly engaged in *hiri*, an activity that has become a symbol for the Motu people (Dutton 1982). In large vessels
(*lagatoi*), Motu men sailed 400 to 500 kilometers northwest to exchange armshells
and pottery for sago to supplement their food between yam harvests. The people they
traded with spoke non-Austronesian languages, especially Orokolo, Purari, and
Toaripi (all in Gulf Province). *Hiri* voyages occurred in October or November, with
the southeast tradewind; the men returned in late December or January, with the
northwest monsoon.

As the *hiri* has become an icon of the Motu generally, so each *lagatoi* was an
emblem of the clan whose men planned its construction and voyage. The most
important men worked in pairs. During the planning, building, and voyaging, the
crew abstained from certain activities of ordinary life, including sexual relations. Each
*lagatoi* bore its clan's name; if a *lagatoi* represented two clans, half the vessel bore one
name, and half the other. The signs of these names were badges that decorated the
vessels (figure 3).

*Hiri* is part of a wider linkage of ceremonial and economic activities undertaken
by seagoing peoples, extending into the *kula* of the Trobriands. The Motu also traded
with their inland neighbors, the Austronesian Doura and Gabadi, the non-
Austronesian Koiari and Koita, and coastal groups to the southeast.

### *Music of the hiri*

The *hiri* were occasions for performing *ehona* (or *hehona*), songs sung by men to the
accompaniment of a bamboo idiophone (*sede*). One node was left intact, the other
removed. A tongue-like projection, cut out of the side of the bamboo and extending
beyond the open end, was hit with a stick. Men returning from a successful voyage
stood on the *lagatoi* and sang while hitting their *sede*. *Ehona* were also sung at wakes;
hence, they seemed suitable for times of danger or grief, as when men were facing
death, or had just died.

Back in the village, women have their own songs and dances. They perform
*upara* to strengthen people remaining in the village and those on the *hiri*, keep the
*hiri* leaders' wives from worrying, save the voyaging men if their *lagatoi* is overdue,
and welcome the men home.

The Motu have not made *hiri* voyages since the 1970s, but during the annual Hiri Moale Festival in Port Moresby, they reenact the building and sailing of their *lagatoi* (figure 4). Aside from the display of Motu traditions, this festival has become an occasion for peoples of other parts of the country to present dances.

### Other Motu music

One means of resolving powerful men's quarrels was hosting a dance-feast, which displayed the host's wealth, the number of kinsmen and allies owing allegiance to him, and the power of his clan (Groves 1954). At such events, the Motu performed kundu-accompanied songs (*gaba anedia*). They also performed songs for catching dugongs. *Ehona* differ musically from other Motu music, such as *upara* and *gaba anedia*. Aside from distinctive use of *sede,* they are more melodically active. Many texts in all these genres contain archaic or foreign words.

### The Motu and missionaries

The Motu were one of the first peoples in Papua New Guinea to undergo a sustained missionary presence. In 1872, missionaries from the London Missionary Society (LMS) made first contact. Soon the base for their effort in the Papuan Region was near Port Moresby. They fretted about Motu dances, which they thought occasioned adultery, so people who maintained the old dances could not belong to the church.

LMS missionaries introduced hymns in Motu sung to Western melodies. The first hymnal printed in a Papua New Guinean language was published in Motu (1877). Eventually local choirs developed. Formed in the early 1930s, the Poreporena Village Choir, led by John Spychiger of the LMS and performing in Motu and English, was, before World War II, one of the first choirs to be broadcast on radio.

Missionaries recognized a need for substitutes for music they opposed. LMS Polynesian teachers working in several Motu villages gradually introduced Christian singing based on their own traditions. Songs in the introduced style, now known as

FIGURE 3    Associated with songs called *ehona,* clan badges decorated vessels built for *hiri,* the trading voyages that epitomized Motu culture; from the nautilus shell hang meter-long strips of leaves (Barton 1910:105).

FIGURE 4    At the Hiri Motu Festival, as passengers sing, beat bamboo idiophones, and dance, a Motu vessel built for long-distance trading sails, surrounded by motorboats. Photo by Don Niles, 1991.

prophet songs (*peroveta anedia*), feature unaccompanied independent melodic parts for women (*pere* 'treble') and men (*maru* 'bass')—terms with Polynesian roots. A principal promoter of *peroveta* was the LMS teacher Ruatoka (1846–1903), from Mangaia, Cook Islands (Crocombe 1982). Texts were originally in Polynesian languages, but new ones were composed in Motu. Texts often allude to biblical stories. Today, *peroveta* are a strong Motu tradition. They have spread to other areas of the region, where they are performed at church functions and competitively at the Hiri Moale Festival.

Because the Motu have been living near the national administrative center and have long had contact with missionaries and other outsiders, they participated in the early development of chordophone-based bands (Lohia and Vele 1977). With the assistance of studios based in Port Moresby, Motu-language songs spread widely throughout the region and remain influential.                    —DON NILES

## GULF PROVINCE

Gulf Province occupies an area bounded by about 300 kilometers of Papua New Guinea's southern coast. Its northern boundary lies in mountainous terrain 50 to 150 kilometers inland. In the west, the mouths of the Purari, Kikori, Turama, and other rivers form an alluvial fan, with sloughs and inlets on which people have built villages and camps, accessible only by canoe. A virtually uninhabited coastal plain ranges from less than 20 kilometers wide (near Kerema), to more than 110 (northwest of Kikori); especially in the east, this plain has kept mountain peoples culturally separate from coastal peoples.

The largest provincial towns are Kerema (the provincial center) and Malalaua. Smaller towns—Ihu, Baimuru, Kikori—dot the coast. Each town has government offices, a handful of stores, a hospital, one or more schools, and an airstrip. Many workers at these facilities come from outside the province. Forming a middle class between rich expatriates and poor farmers and urban squatters, they lead what villagers consider desirable lives. The mountains have government stations staffed by outsiders, mostly workers who stay only until posted to more desirable locations. The 1990 population of the province was 68,737.

About thirty languages are spoken in the province. The coast has three prominent linguistic families: in the west, Kiwai; in the east, Eleman and Purari. Linguistic isolates, including Porome and Rumu, occur. Officials drew the northern border of the province without respect to linguistic boundaries; most dialects of the Folopa language (in the west) and languages of the Angan family (in the east) are spoken in the provinces to the north.

Augmenting or supplanting indigenous technology, Western technology affects all levels of local life, even ceremonies central to the culture. Some people know only their own music; others know music of the wider world. The more isolated a village, the more its people perform indigenous music in precontact cultural contexts.

After the 1960s, the National Broadcasting Commission recorded traditional music nationwide. In the Gulf Province, more than 75 percent of the recordings came from lowland areas. The commission has tried unsuccessfully to record music from outlying areas.

In the music of this province, rhythmic pulses occur steadily throughout songs, but singing is nonmetrical: the pulses do not usually group into "regularly recurring accents" (Chenoweth 1972:99).

### Coastal peoples

Before Western contact, the Motu (Central Province) traded throughout Gulf Province. Their language, Hiri Motu, was widely understood, but by the early 1990s,

FIGURE 5
"Horohito," a song from Gibi Village, in the Kope language: *a,* a slow glide; *b,* a faster glide; *c* and *d,* up-and-down glides. Tape library, National Broadcasting Commission. Transcription by Virginia Whitney.

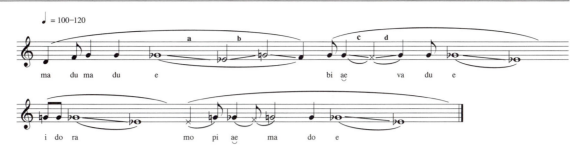

with the rise of public education, English was supplanting it. By then too, Western clothing and technology (such as machetes) had become universal among coastal dwellers.

With residents of towns, radios are common. At least one radio station run by the national government broadcasts to all parts of the province all day; the provincial station broadcasts for two hours in mornings and seven hours in evenings. These stations play a mix of Western music and string-band music, plus about an hour of indigenous music each day.

For middle-class urbanites born after the 1950s, frequent exposure to Western music (on radio and videos, in schools and churches) makes the practice of indigenous music unimportant. On national holidays and during church- and school-sponsored cultural-awareness celebrations, they perform traditional music and dances, but often with costumes that mix Western and traditional clothing and materials, and always apart from contexts that would give the performance traditional meaning. As a result, indigenous music is a reminder of a life left behind.

Churches encourage indigenous music. The United Church, the largest Protestant denomination in the province, sponsors Torchbearers, organizations of youths who perform traditional music and dances. In mountainous parishes, the Roman Catholic Church adds the vernacular language to imported styles of music.

Some coastal groups sing in harmony. Lowland melodies have smaller ranges, usually a third or a fourth. Coastal singing uses a small melodic range: one-step melodies are common, and harmony often occurs.

### Eastern coast

Toaripi-speakers and Orokolo-speakers are the most influential populations of this coast. Their melodies move mostly stepwise, in a range of a third or a fourth. Groups usually sing to drummed accompaniment, stressing the beat. Harmony commonly occurs in parallel fourths or fifths, sometimes doubled an octave above or below. The part conceived to be the melody is the lower member of a fourth or a fifth.

### Western coast

The Kerewo (centered on Goarabari Island) and Kope languages are members of the Kiwai family, which dominates this area. Local melodies typically range over a third. Rhythmic patterns are less regular and pronounced than in eastern coastal music. The outstanding feature of the songs of the western coast is melodic ornamentation, sung on one vowel: in figure 5, at point *c,* the quick downglide ends at the F, but the following upglide (point *d*) begins on an indeterminate tone.

About a thousand people in two villages at Aird Hills, near the mouth of the Kikori River, speak Porome. Their typical musical genre features responsorial phrases. After a rising major second, the first half of the phrase, the question, ends abruptly; joining the lead singer on repeated unisons, the chorus answers. With each new phrase, this structure repeats.

Rumu has several dialects north of Kikori and along the Omati and Turama

The most striking Angan musical trait is coordinate monophony: an Angan chorus is a crowd of soloists, simultaneously singing their own melodies at idiosyncratic tempos. They base their melodies on a shared tonal center.

rivers. A unique feature of a local musical style is that phrases end with the harmony of a major second, often approached from a third.

## Mountain peoples

After about 1960, mountain people's contacts with outsiders intensified. Apart from persons who lived near government stations, the population (of about ten thousand) maintains customary marriage, religion, medicine, and other contexts. In every family, at least one male owns matches, machetes, and store-bought cloth; but about half the people do not own enough Western clothing for everyday wear.

The sharpest musical contrast between the mountains and the coastal areas is that most of the young people in the mountains know and perform their music. As travel to urban centers becomes easier, more young people leave the villages, and the proportion of those who know only indigenous music decreases. Indigenous music remains dominant in the mountains.

### Angan peoples

Inland, the groups most available for study have been those of the Angan family of languages, of which four (Akoye, Ankave, Tainae, Kamea) appear in the province. Each of the first three languages has a thousand or fewer speakers, spread out in less than a dozen villages per group. The Kamea number more than thirty thousand, living in hamlets from Kerema to Wau (Morobe Province).

*Angan singings*

Angan singings mark the end of mourning. As host and honoree, the closest male relative of the deceased gathers and dries meat for distribution on the last day of the singing. When he returns from that work, families from neighboring hamlets, and even neighboring languages, begin preparing for the singing, which lasts from dusk to dawn, every night for a week to a month. Men prepare headdresses; women prepare the incidentals needed for the journey. Each headdress is a 2-meter-long pole, topped with a bird-of-paradise effigy and strapped to the dancer's back. A plank of wood tied with a headband or rope braces and anchors it above his forehead. Halfway up the pole, a sprig of leaves protrudes 3 to 6 decimeters forward and upward. Attached just below the bird of paradise, a cape drapes over the dancer's head and shoulders, giving the effect of a man's torso with an oversized conical head. Also attached below the bird of paradise is a pair of meter-long poles; on the end of each, one large cockatoo feather protrudes parallel to the ground. An hourglass drum completes the outfit. Women in attendance may carry branches of a tree whose leaves serve in magic; they wear "grass" skirts, but no special decorations.

Most performers arrive, usually grouped by clan, after about 10:00 P.M. Performers sing and dance idiosyncratically. Men bob their heads, bending their knees in time with their drumming, so the movement of the cockatoo feathers describes a semicircle from above the headdress almost to the ground. Women may hold branches in either hand while swiveling their hips—a motion their skirts exaggerate. Early in the night, women walk along a circle 5 to 10 meters in diameter, exaggerating the motions of their hips. As performers' energy dissipates, men sing less frequently and dance less vigorously, until, near dawn, the remaining dancers are either plodding forward or simply standing in place. The walk also provides an opportunity for girls to flirt by stepping behind favored boys. At sunrise, the party breaks up.

The day after the last night of the feast, the host rehydrates, cooks, and distributes the meats he has gathered; the distribution discharges debts incurred during bereavement. At sundown, after he has distributed the meats, he dons ceremonial belts. For about ten minutes, he dances—first alone, then with his wife (or wives). Onto a bonfire, people toss green stalks of bamboo, which explode with a bang. The celebrants then shoo the spirits of the deceased, and the singsing ends.

### Angan musical style

The most striking Angan musical trait is coordinate monophony: an Angan chorus is a large group of soloists, simultaneously singing their own melodies at idiosyncratic tempos. They base their melodies on a shared tonal center.

Solo singing is by far the most common Angan music. The Akoye have two styles: *ayaake* is spontaneous, often improvised singing; *oimae* is music for singsings, usually accompanied by a steady beat on a drum. Angan melodies often span an octave, and sometimes a tenth, commonly leaping by thirds, fourths, and fifths. An Angan song often consists of two sections, each with its own tonal center; the second section presents new melodic material. In figure 6, the first two phrases end one section of the song, and the tonal center is D; the second two phrases begin a new section, with the tonal center an octave lower.

Inside houses, where traditional singing occurs spontaneously, a husband and wife often sing duets, consisting of differently texted melodies in the same style, sharing one tonal center. Angan phrases end in long notes. Often, as one singer holds a note, the other singer begins a new phrase; when the second singer reaches a cadence, the first begins a second phrase; and so on. Sometimes the duet resembles the choral style, with the performers simultaneously singing different songs.

## String bands

Urbanites have access to videos. Many own radios and cassette players. Other than Western popular songs, the music they most commonly hear on these devices is string-band music. The musicians are men under the age of about forty; church-based groups occasionally include female singers. Since the population of eligible musicians is highly mobile, bands are short-lived. Most play chords that function as tonic, subdominant, and dominant, often with an added sixth or seventh; urban bands have a larger tonal vocabulary. Parallel thirds and sixths frequently embellish vocal lines, but open fourths or fifths are common, particularly at the beginnings and

FIGURE 6 An excerpt from an Angan two-section melody, sung by Waiketa, of Waikuna Village, 1983. Transcription by Virginia Whitney.

endings of phrases. These harmonies echo sonorities favored in the coastal areas, from which most bandsmen come.      —VIRGINIA WHITNEY

## MILNE BAY PROVINCE

Milne Bay Province occupies the southern tip of the New Guinea mainland and many widely scattered islands, including the D'Entrecasteaux Islands, Trobriand Islands, and Louisiade Archipelago. The 1990 population was 158,780. Residents speak Austronesian languages, except in the interior of the mainland, and on Rossel Island. Many traditionally engaged in interisland trade, the most famous of which, *kula,* involved an extended network of participants.

Instruments used to attract members of the opposite sex include raft panpipes, an end-blown flute (made of a papaya branch, played by opening and closing the far end), and a one-stringed zither (made of a midrib of a sago frond). Conch trumpets serve for signaling. A lime gourd, struck with a lime spatula or a comb, often accompanies singing. On many islands, one moiety is named for the kundu and one for the gourd. Songs associated with feasts after deaths are common.

On many islands, ensembles of differently sized kundus accompany dancing. A leader plays a small one, cueing changes in drummed patterns and danced movements. On Rossel Island, kundus are absent, possibly reflecting the relationship of the language to languages and cultures far to the east, in North Solomons Province.

### The Trobriand Islands

The people of the Trobriands annually stage a yam-harvest festival (*milamala*), in which families and villages show off their yams and other valuables (figure 7), and people indulge in communal visiting, singing, dancing, and partying (Malinowski 1916). Songs sung at this festival and during mourning are in *biga baloma,* the language of the spirits of the dead. They poetically and erotically describe the life the spirits lead on Tuma Island, making it easier for such spirits to leave. Solo or collec-

FIGURE 7 Wearing white cockatoo feathers in their hair and carrying shields (*kaidebu*) used only for dancing, men of Yalaka Village, Trobriands, perform (Malinowski 1922).

tive songs of many stanzas with elaborate melodic phrases ending on a repeated tonal center tell of *kula* transactions or historical events.

In contrast to many other parts of the region, performers in the Trobriands do not use feather headdresses, but put white cockatoo feathers, red feathers, and black cassowary feathers in their hair. Some dancers hold a painted shield, while others hold pandanus streamers. Men usually wear women's "grass" skirts.

Typically, drummers and singers stand in a cluster. Dancers move around them in a counterclockwise circle. Only three men dance the *kasawaga*, usually to the accompaniment of drumming; they mime the movements of animals, including wallabies, crabs, crocodiles, dugongs, white herons, and lizards.

Within the past few decades, young people at *milamala* have begun to perform the *mweki*. Girls enter from one direction and boys from another. Each party carries yam-filled baskets, sings erotic lyrics about the opposite sex, and makes thrusting hip movements. Throughout Papua New Guinea, students perform *mweki* on high-school cultural days, calling it the tapioca dance (Tok Pisin *tapiok*); but Trobriand elders, believing its lyrics lack the poetic allusions of older local genres, do not regard it highly.

## ORO (NORTHERN) PROVINCE

Oro (Northern) Province, with a 1990 population of 96,491, is on the northeast coast of the mainland of the Papuan Region. The administrative center is Popondetta. The Owen Stanley Range forms the southwestern border with Central Province. Oro saw heavy fighting during World War II, especially at Buna and along the Kokoda Trail, where the Japanese advance halted. In 1951, the eruption of Mount Lamington caused much damage to property and loss of life. All but a couple of languages in the province are non-Austronesian.                    —DON NILES

### Binandere: the *ario*

About five thousand Binandere people occupy the lower reaches of the Mamba, Gira, and Eia rivers, within Binandere Census Division. In family gardens, they grow bananas, manioc, sweet potatoes, and taro. In inland waters, they catch fish; and in the forest, they hunt wild animals (pigs, lizards, cuscus).

The principal Binandere dance, the *ario*, dramatizes a story, a legend, or an experience. It is a complex dance-drama, an abstract art, whose movements convey highly aesthetic meanings. Its presentation follows conventional formal sequences. The Binandere observe and abstract simple actions of humans, animals, birds, and insects. In music and movement, composers and choreographers devise ways for dancers to express these observations. Each sequence has a title that describes how it derives its name from the observed movement. The art behind these sequences has its origins in how the Binandere see and perceive the activities of hornbills or birds of paradise, or even the motions of logs in water:

> An old man sits and stares at the water. A tree trunk drifts past: at certain intervals it rises to the surface and then sinks again, always with the same motion. The old man reaches for his drum and softly takes up the rhythm that he has discovered. While he beats the drum, the image of a dance takes form in his mind. So the Orokaiva . . . express the process among themselves. The rhythm must be discovered; then the dance arises, which imposes it on the environment, . . . drawing the environment into the movement. (Winslow 1977:499)

The essential elements of the *ario* are the art, style, and sequence the choreographer teaches the dancers during rehearsals.

Like hawks in flight, crossing each other's paths and clashing their wings, the dancers swoop as if catching rats. The head pair move toward the tail end, cutting back and forth across the column.

For performing the *ario* in public, five pairs of dancers are the minimum number. The first pair is the head (*kopuru*); then comes the neck (*dubo*), behind which stands the middle pair (*toropu*). The "tail's neck" (*ambo da dubo*) follows, and the last pair forms the tail (*ambo*). Any number of middle pairs—usually from one to six—can perform.

### The acts of the dance

In sequence, the *ario* has twelve acts. To define and explain their meaning, I give each act its title in Binandere.

1. *Gugu gaiari.* *Gugu* is the noise produced when water in a clay pot overboils onto the fire; *gaiari* is 'to piece'. Thus, *gugu gaiari* is the sound of the *tataun,* the 'special small drums' like the *gugu,* making the sound of the froth as it overflows. In the dance, *gugu gaiari* is the stage when the performers emerge from an enclosure in the center of the village or the bush. The head pair is the most spectacular and graceful: this couple acts like a butterfly about to alight on a flower. The other pairs, moving forward while beating their drums, face each other, turn to bump their backs, and alternately bend their knees. After emerging in such a manner, they repeat this routine until they reach the center of the arena, where they pause for several minutes, standing in place. To show appreciation, some onlookers beat large wooden drums (*euku*), clap hands, and shout; others weep for joy. During each act, female relatives of the dancers sometimes join in, imitating and following them.

2. *Bebeku yaungari.* The meaning of *bebeku* is unclear, but *yaungari* is 'to split in the middle'. The pairs in the column of dancers remain in place, beating their drums to the rhythm of the *gugu gaiari.* Passing outside the column, the head pair dance to the rear; then, moving inside the column (between the members of the other pairs), they return to the front.

3. *Deoga* is an archaic word, whose meaning is unclear. The actions derive from watching hawks in flight: they cross each other's paths, clashing their wings. The dancers swoop like hawks catching rats: the head pair move toward the tail end, cutting back and forth across the column; they return to their position and repeat the sequence.

4. *Biama giri* 'hornbill's noise' is the sound the bird makes when it hops from branch to branch. The dancers tap their drums with the tips of their fingers, exactly imitating the bird's call. In time with the tapping, the dancers hop about or move forward.

5. *Batari* refers to the sound of the drum of one member of the head pair. All but one of the dancers beat their drums in a single rhythm, syllabified as *purou;* one of the head pair cuts in against it, beating the rhythm *purotou purou,* or even *purototou purotou purou.* The head and the tail pairs carry out extremely complex physical actions.

6. *Dabibiro* means 'to slip', and the head pair do just that. Both slip and dance backward, again outside the column, until they reach the tail; with varying movements, they then dance inside the column, back to their initial position.

7. *Warawa gatari*, or *ambe atoro*. *Warawa* is a tree; *gatari* is 'crack (to collect grubs)'; *ambe* is a sago tree; *atoro* is the 'hard layer', which protects the pith, beaten to extract sago. The names of the movements refer to actions reminiscent of cracking open pieces of wood, or of pounding sago.

8. *Otara doratugari*. The *otara* is an orange leaf-cutting ant. *Doratugari* describes what people do when ants crawl over their skin: they brush them off. *Otara doratugari* is precisely what the performers do: paired dancers move toward each other, bend down to put their drums on the ground, and go backward, brushing their skin as if to knock ants off; then they return to pick up the drums.

9. *Woiwa tembari*. Flowering sago and coconut attract red parrots (*woiwa*); *tembari* indicates 'crossing', as two birds sometimes cross their legs and hop on the palms. Each dancer elevates the right leg, which crosses that of his partner; facing each other, the pair swap places.

10. *Gagi dari*. The *gagi* is a pandanus whose fruit turns yellow when ripe. Men or women pick and boil the fruit, and then in a wooden bowl crack the core, crush it, and pour coconut milk over it. They drink the juice and throw the waste to the pigs. In the context of the drama, the actions follow what happens when a person beats the *gagi*: the beating drives the nuts from one end of the bowl to the other. Thus, the head pair push the rest backward, and then the neck pair chase the head forward, so the column shifts back and forth.

11. *Woduwa* 'side'. One of the head pair takes the lead, and his partner follows; the rest trail after them, in single file. The leader wheels the column in a circle, to meet the back of its tail pair. The dancers then move randomly toward the center, beating their drums.

12. *Tugata* is a standard form of an address, delivered at the end of every performance. From the center, one dancer begins a song that tells the story behind the presentation. The other members of the troupe join in. As the song fades away, the dancers disperse and the performance ends. After applauding, the audience scatters.

### Analysis of the dance

The *ario* has two main elements. First, the plot recounts a legend or real-life experience, observed and structured into an abstract form; in a concentrated idiom, the reenactment transmits the theme. Second is the standard set of nature-derived artistic expressions. The Binandere abstract into human movement the actions of birds, insects, and animals, which the dancers express through the art of the drama. This abstraction is a culture-bound process. Though the anthropologist F. E. Williams (1930), a sympathetic observer, praised the *ario,* he did not understand the Binandere language enough to appreciate the subtleties of its drama. The outsider's ear is closed to the allusions of the poetry (Waiko 1990).

The art of the *ario* highlights the difficulties met in using an etic viewpoint to analyze non-Western music (Chenoweth 1968–1969:218). Binandere culture provides an example that has been emically deciphered by a Binandere. The analysis shows how art sets up conforming relationships with the people's natural surroundings.
　　　　　　　　　　　　　　　　　　　　　　　　　　　　—JOHN D. WAIKO

### Managalasi

Just south of Popondetta, about four thousand Northern Managalasi inhabit small, agrarian villages at an altitude of about nine hectometers. In 1966, at Numba and

FIGURE 8   Managalasi dancers of Northern Province. Photo by Don Niles, 1981.

Siruvani, I researched their music. Linguists Jim and Judy Parlier, who spoke the language and reduced it to writing, indispensably helped my research.

### Communal singing with dancing

Managalasi singsings are social events that typically occur at night, featuring dancing, singing, drumming, and rattling (figure 8). At a singsing I witnessed, twenty drums began the performance. Spectators brought bamboo firebrands. Male performers wore loincloths that hung to the ground at the back, floating gracefully as they moved. The dancers moved their feet subtly: with a slight hop backward and a flexing of the ankle, the weight-bearing foot shifted. The men periodically raised their drums over their heads. Any of half a dozen men began a song. All drums and voices joined in, and the men started dancing. With the singer-dancers aligned in two columns, men walked rhythmically, two at a time, from one end of the column to its opposite end. When all had taken a turn, the columns circled once and returned to the original formation.

Women played peripheral roles. Shaking rattles, they entered the columns, each girl between two men, just in time to make the circle. When the original configuration reformed, the girls walked to the sidelines. Close to their bodies, in both hands, they clasped rattles, which, with a quick movement of a wrist, they sounded on the offbeats of the rhythm played by the drums.

Textual themes for singsings deal with attachment to home, thirst, dancing, or important events. Attachment to home is clear in the text of a song that expresses homesickness for Usije, "whose treetops are visible through the fog." Another example laments: "Our house in Siruvani, our house, our house, our house is there alone, with no one to take care of it, our house." The name of a spring can symbolize thirst. Events important to the composer may relate a time when he scolded his wife or girlfriend; they may be as mundane as "While I was asleep, rats ate my basket."

To cause excitement, women and girls perform a dance with stamped tubes. On one occasion, dressed in foliage and some wearing wigs of cassowary feathers, they maneuvered with bamboo poles, each thumping one on the ground while singing, "I am pounding the ground with this stick." Boys jeered, but older women chased them away.

A few people remember old dances. Reru, an old man, demonstrated how adults danced and sang for adolescents' tattooing. Into the back of his loincloth, he stuck a long branch, which arched above his head. Then he began to sing. Bent forward, he took running steps, first in one direction, and then in another. Periodically, he would straighten up, still running, and then bow forward, so the branch would wave up and down. Standing in place, he bent at the waist from side to side, from front to back, and around in a circle. He performed the dance of joy when elders celebrated new initiates' appearance. The boys emerged from dark huts, where, for months, they had hidden from sunlight so their skin would fade, giving contrast to the tattoos they were to receive. Gracefully leaping about, he held his hands up, arms slightly bent at the elbow, and fingers pinched together as if holding a feather upright.

### Communal singing without dancing

The most distinctive Managalasi songs are *itiuri,* songs for mixed voices with stamped tubes. In the 1960s, only old people knew these songs. *Itiuri* are responsorial, sung in a soft falsetto, and quicker in tempo (basic beat = 80–82) than most Managalasi drum-accompanied songs (basic beat = 50–75). A second or third part may join in. In translation, the text of one *itiuri* goes: "Planting and cooking, / Planting and cooking, / Planting and cooking. / This ground was cursed, / And our bellies are loose." The curse came from someone's uttering a dead man's name; the last line means the ground will not produce, leaving the people hungry.

Before the 1940s, when tribal warfare was rife, men sang to menace their enemies. A tremolo on a sustained tone over a reiterated glottalized vowel (*'o*) worked this effect. In battle, warriors sang to build up their spirits. Unique to their songs was a grunt from the belly, as men lunged forward to spear.

Nowadays, after a death, the wife or mother of the deceased composes a lament. Only women sing; men sit quietly. As the singer proceeds, the voice develops a vibrato on sustained notes (Chenoweth 1968:417–418).

### Musical instruments

The main Managalasi musical instruments are the four played for collective singing. A kundu (*chaja*) is made from a burned-out log. It has a snakeskin head, tuned by the affixion of heated resin pellets. This is the drum that male singer-dancers play at singsings. A women's bundle rattle (*kiji'i*) is made of several seedpods, about 15 centimeters long. The *itiuri* is a hollow bamboo tube, some 30 centimeters long; it accompanies the set of songs named after it. Each singer, seated, holds a tube in the left hand and hits its top with a cupped right hand, popping the open end against the thigh. *'Urutu* are bamboo tubes, stamped by women to accompany women's dance-songs.

The Managalasi have two solo instruments, a flute and a susap. The flute (*hurisia*) is a piece of cane more than 30 centimeters long, with a diameter of about 2 centimeters and two holes near its closed end. The player holds it vertically, puts the open end at the corner of his mouth, and blows gently across the rim. In 1966, Kovai, of Numba, was an undisputed master of this instrument: he played skillfully, in long, flowing lines, without the triple rhythms prevalent in singing. The susap (*pupuaha*) is made of bamboo. Young men make and play it; adults do not think it a serious instrument.

### The Managalasi music system

Songs of the singsing show harmonic flexibility: the chorus can divide temporarily into two or three parts. Improvisation is minimal. In *itiuri,* melodic ornamentation commonly occurs between phrases. Textual improvisation may alter melodic

Managalasi choral singing is in two or three parts, sometimes doubled at the octave. When a part enters—whether above or below the melody—it consists of two tones. At cadences, all parts converge on the melody.

rhythms, though the melody remains recognizable. The tones of laments move within simple skeletal frames.

Communal singing has two dynamics: softly controlled, and loudly unrestrained. In *itiuri,* the vocal quality is calm and quiet: men sing upper parts in falsetto; women sing in unison, with either the principal voice or the part below it. The falsetto voice is not always higher than the principal, but its quality can give this impression. Parts may cross. Vocal quality in the singsing is tense.

### Tonal inventories

Melodies, usually in undulating contours, use three to six main tones. The leader sings an introduction, which may contain more tones than occur in the body of the song.

Five tonal inventories appear in the corpus of songs collected in 1966 (figure 9). These inventories help define five classes of song in the Managalasi music system. A change in tonal inventory signals a change in class. In figure 9, tones in parentheses are auxiliary: they ornament the main tones, and do not occur on rhythmically strong beats. The principal tone below the tonal center is crucial to defining the inventory. In each of the inventories, the tonal center and the principal tone below it form a different interval. Tonal inventory *a* is the commonest, followed by inventory *b.* Inventory *c* involves only laments: excluding the final phrase, a minor second below tonal center typically ends phrases. Inventory *d* includes dance-songs. Inventory *e* is rare; it occurs in older songs, known only to one or two elderly singers.

### Musical form

Managalasi songs usually have two phrases, A and B, which occur in variation, as in the seven examples of the following table, read across. Phrase $B_a$ derives from phrase A.

| A | B | | | | | |
|---|---|---|---|---|---|---|
| $A_1$ | $A_2$ | $B_a$ | $B_1$ | | | |
| $A_1$ | $B_a$ | $A_2$ | $B_1$ | | | |
| A | B | B | A | | | |
| A | $B_1$ | $B_2$ | $B_3$ | | | |
| $A_1$ | $B_1$ | $A_2$ | $B_2$ | $A_1$ | $B_3$ | |
| $A_1$ | $B_1$ | $B_1$ | $A_2$ | $B_2$ | $B_3$ | $B_4$ |

A song may also consist of one phrase and its repeated variation, as in $A_1A_2A_3A_4A_5$.

### Melodic shape and rhythm

Managalasi melodic intervals rarely exceed a fourth. No more than three continue in

FIGURE 9   Five Managalasi tonal inventories. Transcriptions by Vida Chenoweth.

a common direction; hence the undulating contour. Dance-songs have wider intervals than others. Perfect fifths and minor sixths are usually the widest leaps.

Melodies have ornamental configurations describable as trills, quick alternations of a tone and the tone immediately below it, and embellishing tones preceding a main tone. A phrasal ending featured in many *itiuri* consists of a downglide from tonal center to a fourth below, followed by a return. Just before a cadence, singsing melodies typically shift from triple to duple rhythm.

Repeated tones form more than half of most Managalasi melodies, but rhythmic variety vivifies them. There is a preference for triple rhythms, as seen in the repeated use of eighths in groups of three. Danced songs superimpose a drumbeat, favoring the triple rhythm of a quarter and an eighth.

*Phrasing*

Four considerations define Managalasi phrases. Musical and textural phrases have a schematic similarity, so understanding the syntax is the most direct method of identifying a musical phrase; some phrases set a single word, but others set a complete sentence. Textural contrast between a single voice and the chorus marks the ends of phrases. Polyphonic parts reduce to unison or octaves at cadences. Elaborate treatment of a phrase-final vowel in a voice other than the principal signals the juncture of two phrases.

*Harmony*

Managalasi choral singing is in two or three parts, sometimes doubled at the octave. When a part enters, whether above or below the melody, it consists of two tones, which vary among a major second, a major third, and a perfect fifth. When the part occurs above the melody, its featured tone is typically that of a major third or an octave above tonal center; though this tone may alternate with one or two others, the vocal line is not elaborate. When a part enters below the melody, it frequently focuses on the tonal center, or on a featured tone a perfect fourth or fifth below tonal center; from the featured tone, the vocal line alternates with one or two others. At cadences, all parts converge on the melody.

Parts move together in rhythm. Some harmonic intervals do not occur melodically. Harmonic motion is more parallel than contrary. Managalasi born after the 1940s harmonize in thirds and sixths, the local tokens of innovative musical styles.

—VIDA CHENOWETH

## WESTERN PROVINCE

Western Province, in area the largest province of Papua New Guinea, had a 1990 population of 110,420. To the west is the international border with Irian Jaya; to the south, across the Torres Strait, is Australia. Steep mountains distinguish the northern part of the province, but the lower two-thirds are lowlands, through which runs the

Fly River, the longest in the country. Only non-Austronesian languages are spoken here. The administrative center is on Daru Island. In the north, the Ok Tedi Mine, which began producing gold and copper in 1984, is a principal earner of revenue for the nation.

—DON NILES

## The Trans-Fly

The Trans-Fly, the coastal area between the border of Irian Jaya and the mouth of the Fly River, is flat, muddy country, with mosquito-ridden forests and mangrove swamps, interspersed with savannas. In 1843–1845, H.M.S. *Fly* surveyed the coast. In 1871–1872, from the Torres Strait Islands, members of the London Missionary Society visited the coast, where they stationed teachers. In 1872, John Moresby claimed the coast for Britain. In 1875, the Italian explorer Luigi d'Albertis made the first ethnographic report on the area (d'Albertis 1880). In the late 1800s, trepang and pearls were collected from local waters (Beardmore 1890), missions grew, and more explorers came. By 1901, surveyors had fully mapped the coast, and outsiders (Beaver 1920; Landtman 1917, 1927; Williams 1936) had begun learning about the inhabitants.

The people of the Trans-Fly have exogamous moieties and totemic clans. They subsist chiefly on yams, manioc, sweet potatoes, sugarcane, bananas, papayas, and coconuts. In lagoons and rivers, they use poison to catch fish; on reefs, they spear fish. With bows and arrows, men hunt cassowaries, wallabies, and wild pigs; for feasts, they raise pigs. To make crops flourish, protect them from pests, and secure success in fishing and hunting, people recite charms; every village has specialists, who, by singing spells, make rain or fair weather. After the late 1800s, customary rites of passage and associated ceremonies vanished.

### Ethnographic history

Tugeri groups calling themselves Marind inhabit the west of the province, from the Bensbach River to sites deep in Irian Jaya. In dugout canoes, they used to punt along the coast, up the Morehead River, or farther east to the Strachan Island Delta, hiding in the mouths of the Wasi Kussa (Agöb *kussa* 'river') and Mai Kussa, from where they would attack sleeping villagers. In 1886, they raided Mawatta; six years later, they marauded eastward as far as Mabaduan, but by 1900, a combined Dutch and British operation had defeated them.

At Mari and Jarai, between the Morehead River and the Wasi Kussa, live speakers of Dorro and Peremka, respectively. Between the Mai Kussa and the Pahoturi (Owera *turi* 'river') live Agöb-speakers whose most prominent coastal villages are Buji and Sigabaduru, opposite Boigu and Saibai islands, respectively; their most important inland villages are Ngao (Gnao) and Kibuli, on the central Pahoturi. Owera, a Kiwaian language, is spoken along the coast east of the river, from Mabaduan to Daru Island. Long stretches of coastal land belonged to the people of Mawatta (Mawat), who in 1918 settled Mabaduan, but gradually abandoned old Mawatta and founded New Mawatta, Masingara, and Tureture.

Farther inland are other populations and languages: Ende (east of the Pahoturi), Bine (between the Ende and the Gizra), and Gizra and Gidra (between the Binaturi and Oriono rivers). By 1900, the trade language Hiri Motu had spread over most of the south coast, where newly composed songs continue to use it. People of the Trans-Fly sing foreign songs, even without understanding a word. Trade-oriented visits and voyages to the Torres Strait Islands involved feasting and dancing, when people of different languages exchanged songs and dances.

People of the coast traded with Torres Strait Islanders, who needed wood and bamboo for making canoes, drums, spears, bows, arrows, mats, stone for clubs and axes, and feathers for headdresses. In exchange, the islanders gave seashells, valued as ornaments and money. The people of Buji, Mabaduan, and Sigabaduru still visit their insular neighbors on Boigu, Dauan, and Saibai, 3 to 6 kilometers away.

The Parama Islanders traded with many peoples. On outrigger canoes with mat sails, they took their goods to the central and eastern Torres Strait. Mawatta and Parama received goods from people living inland and along the rivers. They visited the islands at the beginning of the northwest-wind season and returned when the southeast monsoon began to blow; between those times, trade, feasts, and marriages occurred.

With worldly goods, coastal religious elements found their way southward. Legends speak of heroes who crossed the strait, scattering over the central and eastern islands and reaching the northern tip of Cape York Peninsula (Laade 1970). Each set up a religious center: Sigai on Yam Island, Kulka on Aurid, Seo on Masig, Malo on Mer. Sido imported garden plants. Waiet settled first in Mabuiag, where he established secret rites; he crossed the strait and lived finally in Dauar (Murray Islands).

### Songs and dances

In August and September, when crops are plentiful, people celebrate the harvest. Into an enclosure, a leader heaps food. Others compete to provide the most, singing songs without dancing and song-dances with drums. Villages formerly invited each other alternately to feasts that featured singing and dancing. The area also has solo songs, songs in tales, and charms.

For the Tugeri and eastward to the Pahoturi, *badra* is the most popular indigenous dance. A mixed group, or men only, stand in the open air, clustering around drummers. They bob up and down, flexing and unflexing their knees. They wear fiber skirts, loincloths, or shorts, with plaited armlets and leglets and palm-leaf decorations hanging from their necks. Sometimes, special headpieces extend their movements. Fast and slow *badra* alternate, each usually sung twice. The Owera of Mabaduan have adopted the *badra*. People at Mawatta also know the genre, but Gizra- and Bine-speakers do not. Its Kiwaian equivalent is the *mado*, traditionally performed in longhouses (Landtman 1917: no. 275).

Island dances came from the Torres Strait, where they originated around 1901. Their themes, using English terms (like *navy play, army play, football play*, and *tennis play*), show Western influence; their style shows Melanesian and Polynesian influence. Adapted to local taste, they rapidly became popular throughout the Trans-Fly. Typical dress is a T-shirt and shorts, or a loincloth with a thin palm-leaf skirt over it. The dancers stamp heavily, flexing their knees and gesturing. Uniformly in two or three lines, they turn, bow, kneel, and rise. Each dance has a one-stanza song, repeated as long as the dancers continue. After a break, they repeat the song and the dance before moving on to the next.

*Badra* stylistically resemble island dances. Most melodies have scales transcribable as A–C–E–G–A, A–C–E–F–A, and G–A–D–E–G. The island dances of Daru and Parama sound much like those of the Murray Islands.

Early missionaries in the Trans-Fly prohibited local dances, but let their congregations perform songs and dances from other areas. In the 1880s and 1890s, Rotumans imported *tautoga*, which developed into *taibobo* in the strait (Niles and Webb 1987:92) and spread to New Guinea. Today they are commonly called Kiwai dances, though the Kiwai are not the only people who performed them.

### Sound-producing instruments

*Badra* and island dances require beating on kundus (Dorro *dundu*, Agöb *búrubur*,

For island dances, a struck bamboo joins the kundus.
In the late 1890s, boatmen imported it from Fiji—
replacing the rolled mat, imported from Sāmoa. The
standard struck-bamboo rhythm is now usually
played on empty kerosene tins.

Owera *gáma*; according to Duvelle 1978, Gizra *walep*, Bine *warpe*). The drumhead is
the skin of a monitor (*Varanus indicus*) or a large, brown, water-dwelling snake.
Makers moisten the skin with water, glue it to the body of the drum, and secure it
with a cane ring. The weight of beeswax lumps, applied to the middle of the drumhead, makes the skin vibrate with a booming timbre.

People east of the Pahoturi used an older drum, *gagóma,* with a bellied body and
an open end, carved in the shape of a mouth, probably that of a crocodile (Fischer
1958 [1986]: fig. 216). The body bore decorative carvings, cassowary feathers, and
seeds of *gora* (*Pangium edule*). The center of its manufacture was Mawatta; it went by
export to the Torres Strait Islands, whose people called it *warup.* The last specimens
date from about 1901.

For island dances, a struck bamboo (*marap, marep*) joins the kundus. In the late
1890s, boatmen imported it from Fiji, replacing the rolled mat, imported from
Sāmoa. In the Trans-Fly, the standard struck-bamboo rhythm is transcribable as a
measure of eight eighths, the first and fifth stressed; since the 1960s or before, percussionists have usually played this rhythm on empty kerosene tins. Performers sometimes rhythmically shake bundle rattles, named for seeds: in the west, *kúlap* (sword
bean, *Entada gigas*); in the east, *gora.*

Swung slats (Agöb *wagra*) once accompanied initiatory ceremonies. According
to a widely known tradition, a woman invented the instrument: when she bent down
to sweep, it came from her vagina; men killed her and took it for their secret instrument.

### Solo instruments

Other instruments serve exclusively for solo use; unmarried boys and men play them
to put girls and women into an amorous mood. A bamboo lamellaphone (Agöb
*dárombi,* Gizra *darumbere,* Owera *begube*) has a lancet-shaped frame, 18 to 30 centimeters long, and an elastic tongue. With the left thumb and forefinger, the player
holds the pointed end. A string, fastened to the bottom of the frame and its open
end, passes over the outstretched thumb, with the knot lying on the joint of a finger.
The thumb knocks the knot rhythmically against the tongue of the instrument, making it vibrate. Beeswax fixed to the tip of the tongue of the instrument also affects its
sound.

An end-blown flute (Agöb *burári,* Owera *túru*; according to Duvelle 1978, Gizra
*tatarore*), with both ends open, has one hole for fingering, about a hand's breadth
above its lower end. Seven specimens collected in 1964–1965 range from 60 to 75
centimeters long. The preferred material is *patér,* a thin-walled bamboo. The sound
of the flute is said to resemble the song of the *obukobu,* a bird that sings in the rainy
season, the favorite time for playing; the music consists of the melodies of songs
(Laade 1971). A bundle panpipe (Agöb *tátaro*) occurs west of the Pahoturi. Also
made from *patér,* it consists of six to eight bamboo pipes of different lengths, tied

TRACK 20

together. The pipes do not touch the player's lips: he blows lightly over the upper openings.

### Recordings

The first musical recordings in the Trans-Fly are probably those made during Laade's research in the Torres Strait Islands in 1963–1965. A selection of music from the area appears on one album (Laade 1971); another is available on compact disc (Laade 1993). These collections present music mostly of the Agöb and the Owera, but include songs in other languages. One album (Duvelle 1978) documents Gizra and Bine music. More musical examples from the area appear on a cassette (Niles and Webb 1987) and two records (Anderson n.d., 1971).　　—WOLFGANG LAADE

## REFERENCES

d'Albertis, Luigi Maria. 1880. *New Guinea: What I Did and What I Saw.* 2 vols. London: Sampson, Low.

Anderson, James L. N.d. *This Is New Guinea: A Recorded Sound Picture.* Hibiscus Records HLS 19. LP disk.

———. 1971. *Primitive Sounds: An Authentic Sound Picture of New Guinea.* Hibiscus Records HLS 31. LP disk.

Baldwin, B. 1945. "Usituma! Song of Heaven." *Oceania* 15:201–238.

———. 1950. "Kadaguwai: Songs of the Trobriand Sunset Isles." *Oceania* 20:263–285.

Barton, F. R. 1910. "The Annual Trading Expedition to the Papuan Gulf." In *The Melanesians of British New Guinea,* ed. Charles G. Seligman, 96–120. Cambridge: Cambridge University Press.

Beardmore, Edward. 1890. "The Natives of Mowat, Daudai, New Guinea." *Journal of the Royal Anthropological Institute* 19:459–473.

Beaver, Wilfred N. 1920. *Unexplored New Guinea.* London: Sealey, Service.

Chenoweth, Vida. 1968. "Managalasi Mourning Songs." *Ethnomusicology* 12(1):415–419.

———. 1968–1969. "An Investigation of the Singing Styles of the Dunas." *Oceania* 39:218–230.

———. 1972. *Melodic Perception and Analysis.* Ukarumpa, Papua New Guinea: Summer Institute of Linguistics.

Crawford, Anthony L. 1981. *Aida: Life and Ceremony of the Gogodala.* Bathurst: National Cultural Council and Robert Brown & Associates.

Crocombe, Marjorie Tuainekore. 1982. "Ruatoka." In *Polynesian Missions in Melanesia,* 55–78. Suva: University of the South Pacific.

Dutton, Tom, ed. 1982. *The Hiri in History: Further Aspects of Long Distance Motu Trade in Central Papua.* Pacific Research Monograph 8. Canberra: Australian National University.

Duvelle, Frédéric. 1978. *Papua New Guinea, Western Province: Traditional Music of the Gizra and Bine People.* Larrikin Records LRF 031. LP disk.

Fischer, Hans. 1958. *Schallgeräte in Ozeanien.* Sammlung Musikwissenschaftlicher Abhandlungen, 36. Strassburg: P. H. Heitz.

———. 1986. *Sound-Producing Instruments in Oceania.* Edited by Don Niles. Translated by Philip W. Holzknecht. Boroko: Institute of Papua New Guinea Studies.

Fortune, Reo. 1932. *Sorcerers of Dobu.* New York: Dutton.

Groves, Murray. 1954. "Dancing in Poreporena." *Journal of the Royal Anthropological Institute of Great Britain and Ireland* 84:75–90.

Jenness, Diamond, and Andrew Ballantyne. 1920. *The Northern D'Entrecasteaux.* Oxford: Clarendon Press.

Kasaipwalova, John, and Ulli Beier, eds. 1978. *Yaulabuta: The Passion of Chief Kailaga; An Historical Poem from the Trobriand Islands.* Port Moresby: Institute of Papua New Guinea Studies.

Kunst, Jaap. 1967. *Music in New Guinea: Three Studies.* Translated by Jeune Scott-Kemball. Verhandelingen van het Koninklijk Instituut voor Taal-, Land- en Volkenkunde, 53. The Hague: Martinus Nijhoff.

Laade, Wolfgang. 1970. "Notes on the Boras at Lockhart River Mission, Cape York Peninsula, North-East Australia." *Archiv für Völkerkunde* 24:273–309.

———. 1971. *Music from South New Guinea.* Folkways AHM 4216. LP disk.

———. 1993. *Papua New Guinea: The Coast of the Western Province.* Jecklin-Disco "Music of Man Archive" JD 655-2. Compact disc.

Landtman, Gunnar. 1917. *The Folk-Tales of the Kiwai Papuans.* Acta Societatis Scientiarum Fennicae, 47. Helsinki: Societas Litterariae Fennicae.

———. 1927. *The Kiwai Papuans of British New Guinea.* London: Macmillan.

Lohia, Simon, and Raka Vele. 1977. *Central Guitar Songs.* Boroko: Institute of Papua New Guinea Studies.

McCarthy, Frederick D. 1939. "'Trade' in Aboriginal Australia, and 'Trade' Relationships with Torres Strait, New Guinea and Malaya," part 3. *Oceania* 10:179–195.

McKellin, William H. 1980. "Kinship Ideology

and Language Pragmatics Among the Managalase of Papua New Guinea." Ph.D. dissertation, University of Toronto.

Malinowski, Bronislaw. 1916. "Baloma: The Spirits of the Dead in the Trobriand Islands." *Journal of the Royal Anthropological Institute of Great Britain and Ireland* 46:353–430.

———. 1922. *Argonauts of the Western Pacific.* London: Routledge.

Niles, Don, and Michael Webb. 1987. *Papua New Guinea Music Collection.* Boroko: Institute of Papua New Guinea Studies IPNGS 008. 11 cassettes.

*Papua New Guinea Music Collection.* 1987. Edited by Don Niles and Michael Webb. Boroko: Institute of Papua New Guinea Studies IPNGS 008. 11 cassettes.

Ray, Sidney H. 1923. "Languages of the Western Division of Papua." *Journal of the Royal Anthropological Institute* 53:332–360.

Schultze-Westrum, Thomas G. 1965. "Anthropological Research in the Western District of Papua New Guinea." *Bulletin of the International Committee on Urgent Anthropological and Ethnological Research* 7:45–61.

Schwimmer, Erik. 1979. "Aesthetics of the Aika." In *Exploring the Visual Art of Oceania,* ed. Sidney M. Mead, 287–292. Honolulu: University of Hawai'i Press.

Seligman, Charles G. 1910. *The Melanesians of British New Guinea.* Cambridge: Cambridge University Press.

Waiko, John Douglas Dademo. 1982. "*Be Jijimo*: A History According to the Tradition of the Binandere People of Papua New Guinea." 2 vols. Ph.D. dissertation, Australian National University.

———. 1990. "'Head' and 'Tail': The Shaping of Oral Traditions Among the Binandere in Papua New Guinea." *Oral Tradition* 5(2–3):334– 353.

Williams, Francis Edgar. 1930 [1969]. *Orokaiva Society.* Oxford: Clarendon Press.

———. 1936. *Papuans of the Trans-Fly.* Oxford: Oxford University Press.

———. 1940. *Drama of Orokolo: The Social and Ceremonial Life of the Elema.* Oxford: Clarendon Press.

Winslow, J. H., ed. 1977. *The Melanesian Environment.* Canberra: Australian National University.

Wirz, Paul. 1922 and 1925. *Die Marind-Anim von Holländisch Süd-Neuguinea.* Abhandlungen aus dem Gebiete der Auslandskunde, 10 and 16. Hamburg: Friederichsen.

# Highland Region of Papua New Guinea

*Don Niles*          *Vida Chenoweth*

*Allison Jablonko*          *Paul W. Brennan*

*Andrew J. Strathern*          *Jacqueline Pugh-Kitingan*

*Edward Gende*

**Western Highlands Province**

**Chimbu Province**

**Eastern Highlands Province**

**Enga Province**

**Southern Highlands Province**

This region, deriving its name from its altitude in the central mountains, includes Enga, Western Highlands, Southern Highlands, Chimbu, and Eastern Highlands provinces. With only 13 percent of the country's area, it contains 36 percent of the population, but has fewer languages than the other regions. Some of its languages are spoken by tens of thousands of people. All belong to the Trans–New Guinea Phylum of non-Austronesian languages.

The highest point in Papua New Guinea, Mount Wilhelm (4,509 meters), lies in the region, which humans have settled for about fourteen thousand years. About three hundred to four hundred years ago, the introduction of sweet potatoes permitted gardening at higher altitudes, the domestication of more pigs, and the rise of pork-based feasts, replacing feasts of ceremonial puddings.

Culturally, the region has a core and a fringe. Core peoples (such as Benabena, Chimbu, Enga, Fore, Melpa, Mendi, Usarufa, Wahgi) occupy the central areas; highly populous, they base their social organization on direction by self-selected leaders, who mobilize others to take social action. Fringe peoples (Baruya, Dadibi, Fasu, Foe, Hewa, Kaluli, "Sambia"), living on the outskirts, have more egalitarian social organizations. Comparative works on the ethnography of the region (Brown 1978; Feil 1987) have appeared, but few anthropologists have paid attention to its music.

## Musical contexts

The east—Eastern Highlands, Chimbu, the eastern areas of Western Highlands—emphasizes initiatory ceremonies, in which boys learn secrets of paired, side-blown bamboo flutes, played by initiated men. Players vary pitches by overblowing; by opening and closing the far end of these instruments with the palm of a hand, they produce the harmonics of closed and open tubes. Paired players sound their flutes in quick alternation, paralleling performance in the central Mamose Region. Though such flutes may have entered the region along the Yuat and Jimi Rivers (Wirz 1952:12), the absence of the instrument along much of the upper route of these rivers suggests they entered the region up the Ramu River, where such flutes also occur. Terence E. Hays (1986) offered valuable theories about ceremonial activity in this region; on the distribution of instruments, Vida Chenoweth (1976) assembled useful data, supplied by workers of the Summer Institute of Linguistics.

Fringe Angan peoples in southern Eastern Highlands, including the Baruya and the "Sambia," use a secret ensemble of end-blown flutes with the far end closed. Men play them in pairs and in alternation, but individual instruments seldom produce more than one tone. These flutes have a strong association with male-male sexual activity (Herdt 1981). Eastward, in Morobe, other Angan peoples, including the Menya, use similar flutes publicly; some, including the Angaataha, who appear to have no secret male flutes, play panpipes in ensembles.

In the Eastern Highlands, a swung slat is another important initiatory instrument. Its importance diminishes in the west: it is absent or unimportant in Chimbu and the Western Highlands, and absent farther west. Most southern fringe peoples use it; but again its ritual significance diminishes in the west, and in some areas it may be an import.

Also distinctive of Angan peoples, in contrast with neighboring core peoples, is the lack of kundus, recently introduced elsewhere in the core. Reports from Eastern Highlands peoples such as the Fore and the Usarufa suggest the kundu entered this area only after about 1900. Its use here—for nonunison drumming—seems to imitate a rattle, exemplifying idiophonic imitation on a membranophone.

In Chimbu and Wahgi, sections of nonunison drumming contrast with unison single beats. Farther west, drumming often provides a steady beat to dancing and singing. In Melpa performances, an initial section, with words, has a slow kundu beat; but the terminal section, sung with vocables, features a more active kundu part, at twice the original tempo.

In the area of Mount Hagen and westward, initiation is no longer important, and the use of secret instruments has disappeared. Instead, people focus on large exchange-based festivals, including the Enga *tee,* the Melpa *moka,* and the Mendi *mok-ink.* At these events, music and dance play varying roles, but have the highest importance and variety at *moka,* where performers distinguish themselves by age, sex, instrument, dance, decoration, and text (figure 1).

Courtship is an important ceremonial activity in much of the region, especially in Chimbu, Enga, Southern Highlands, and Western Highlands. The forms of these activities vary widely. Around Mount Hagen, boys may collectively visit a girl's house, where each performs a seated dance with a female partner, while other males sing. Pairs dance by touching cheeks, holding hands, and turning their heads. Westward, in Enga and parts of the Southern Highlands, youths sing, but without dancing. In the Huli area, to communicate with lovers, youths recite poetic verses and play an orally resonated bow or lamellaphone.

A striking feature of many songs in the region is a preference for composing new texts, as opposed to repeatedly performing archaic ones. This trait may relate to the lack of elaborate initiations, especially in the west of the region.

### Inside and outside

A contrast between indoor and outdoor performances differentiates the core and the fringe. The latter, such as the Fasu, Foe, and Kaluli, perform many dances inside communal longhouses. Dancers may bounce shell rattles on the floor, or beat kundus. The Baruya, an Angan people, sing *daata* in unison while seated inside, and sing during ceremonies of healing indoors. To inaugurate a new house, the Hewa, a fringe people at the border of Southern Highlands and the Sepik provinces, perform a *yap.* All night, they dance around a central housepost, while two elaborately decorated lead singers play megapode-skin kundus. After a leader opens the text, other singers

FIGURE 1    A female Melpa performer wears fin-
ery of feathers, shells, paint, plaited fibers, and
beads. Photo by Andrew J. Strathern.

overlap with the same text. Previously, only men performed *yap,* but women are now joining in with the larger chorus.

Core peoples conduct courtship rituals inside and ceremonial exchanges outside, where dancers can more readily perform for visitors. For these peoples, outdoor dances vary greatly. In Enga and Melpa performances, kundu-holding men may face onlookers in a long line, with girls or women occasionally joining them. Performers bob up and down, bending their knees in synchrony with kundu beats. Dances from the Mendi area, and from parts of Enga and Hagen, include numerous rows of men, perhaps four or five abreast; carrying axes, they stamp while moving forward. Huli dancers form two rows: facing inward, all performers simultaneously jump to a kundu beat. Wahgi and Chimbu dancers distinctively shuffle in and out from the center; men and women dance together or separately. In the Eastern Highlands, male dancers carrying kundus may wear on their backs large, clan-specific emblems; men and women sing together with asynchronous beating of kundus.

### Texts

Texts often contrast lexical items (words) with nonlexical items (vocables), which local languages often specify in terms meaning 'leaves' and 'trunk', respectively. Long sung stories (*kang rom* in the Hagen area) take related forms among the Duna, Enga, Huli, and Ipili. They feature rapid, solo singing and minutely descriptive texts, contrasting a slow-paced story with a fast musical tempo.

The Kaluli have developed a musical theory that metaphorically links musical sounds to those of birds, places, and waterfalls (Feld 1981, 1985, 1990, 1991). As with Kaluli music, Foe poetry involves the recreation of geography and landscape for listeners (Weiner 1991).

Several collections of musical texts represent peoples of the region: the Enga (Talyaga 1973, 1975), the Kewa (Franklin 1970; Josephides 1982), the Melpa (Strathern 1974; Koyati 1979), the Usarufa (Chenoweth 1974), and the Wiru (Paia and Strathern 1977).

## WESTERN HIGHLANDS PROVINCE

Western Highlands Province, in the center of the region, had a 1990 population of 336,178, the most populous of the region and the second most populous in the country. The province contains numerous broad valleys, where the main population lives. The province is the nation's largest producer of coffee and tea.

Just outside the provincial capital, Mount Hagen, is Kuk Swamp, where archaeological research has uncovered a network of drainage ditches dating back about nine thousand years and suggesting that horticulture developed here about the same time as in southeastern and western Asia—making New Guineans among the first gardeners in the world. All languages indigenously spoken in the province are non-Austronesian. Local societies have leader-based organizations and elaborate exchange ceremonies.

—DON NILES

### Maring

The Maring, about seven thousand horticulturists inhabiting the Bismarck Mountains (including populations in Madang Province), were first studied in the 1960s, when anthropologists described and analyzed their world (Jablonko 1968a; Rappaport 1968). Movement that many Westerners might consider "dance" was integral to the articulation of relationships among territorially independent, patrilineal clans.

The most inclusive Maring terms referring to structured movement were two: *kaiko* and *kanant,* the names of nonoverlapping patterns of movement, musical accompaniment, personal participation, and social circumstance. *Kaiko* was part of each clan's ritual cycles, covering periods of interclan peace, warfare, and truce; *kanant* was a central element in forming interclan connections through clan-exogamous marriage.

### The kaiko

*Kaiko,* the final stage of each clan's ten-to-fifteen-year-long ritual cycles, lasted about a year, while clansmen fulfilled obligations to the allies and ancestors who had aided them in battle. They cleared and leveled an arena where they periodically entertained visitors from allied clans. Hosts distributed vegetable food to guests and joined visiting male troupes in nightlong dancing. These events provided opportunities for visual and aural communication regarding the size of clans, the virility of warriors, the extent of wealth, and the solidarity of allies.

During the first part of this ritual year, men accompanied their dancing with *wobar,* songs also used to mark the first stage of hostilities, when enemy clans, with the possibility of reconciliation still open, would arrive at an agreed-upon place carrying bows and arrows. The second part of the *kaiko* year echoed the second stage of hostilities, when hope for reconciliation had faded, and warriors, some carrying axes (used in hand-to-hand combat), arrived singing *de* songs. During this stage of *kaiko*, men accompanied themselves with drums, and sang *wobar* and *de*. On days when no visitors were present, girls would sometimes dance for their own amusement, with only children as spectators. The concluding ceremony, the *konj kaiko* (when hosts gave pork to their allies), lasted three days and was the occasion for the largest assembly of Maring that ever occurred—as many as a thousand participants (Jablonko 1968b).

Throughout the *kaiko*, movements were similar. Each contingent of performers, alternating between bouncing in place in a rough clump and stepping forward in a column (two, three, or four men wide), moved back and forth, or meandered around, singing with full voice in loose synchrony. The more contingents present, the more they had to interweave, since each contingent retained its own pathway. Local and visiting women and children lined the edges of the arena, shouting in excitement.

The predominant movement was an up-and-down bounce, either in place or stepping forward. Performers bent both knees and rocked their torsos back and forth, setting their headdresses swaying in the sagittal plane. Coordination of drumming among the men resulted in a pulsing flow of beats, which complemented the ebbing and flowing of the songs (Jablonko 1968c: roll 50).

Feathered headdresses visually accentuated the movements, and costumes acoustically accentuated the singing and drumming. Leaves tucked into the back of wide belts rustled. On each bounce, long loincloths tasseled with fur and set with rows of shell fragments clattered and rattled. The most elaborate movements were performed by those at the head of each contingent, especially while entering the arena. Instead of drumming, they wielded axes or spears over their right shoulders, as they traced looped pathways on the ground.

### The kanant

The *kanant* gave young men and women of different clans an opportunity to meet in more intimate circumstances than the *kaiko*. Communities arranged *kanant* at any time, when young men or women of different clans passed through, trading goods or visiting relatives. It usually occurred at night, in the house of an older woman, who acted as chaperon. The house—no more than 1.5 meters high, 3.5 meters wide, 4.5 meters long, and lit by a fire in a central hearth—was an apt venue for interactions that emphasized tactile communication.

The young people sat in a row, males and females alternating, so close that their legs and hips touched. In soft falsetto, one person started a song, and the others gradually joined in. (Local people thought that the lyrics, not in the Maring language, had come from the south.) After a while, participants began swaying gently. Male-female pairs touched foreheads and noses, turning their heads from side to side (Tok Pisin *kukim nus* 'cooking nose'). The rhythm of the movements was independent of the singing: each person would start with an idiosyncratic rhythm, which, though it eventually matched the partner's rhythm, was independent of others' rhythms (Jablonko 1968c: roll 35, 1991:372).

Diphasic patterns of movement were basic to *kaiko* and *kanant* as they were to many everyday activities, such as chopping wood, sharpening knives, and bouncing babies to comfort them (Jablonko and Kagan 1988:160). Asynchrony of movement, reflecting the individualism of action in Maring society, was more pronounced in *kanant* than in *kaiko*. Each genre emphasized a different spatial dimension: vertical and sagittal in the *kaiko*, horizontal and side-to-side in the *kanant*.

As major organizing events and concepts in Maring society, *kaiko* and *kanant* reverberated throughout everyday life, where they were frequently visible in "movement quotations." Little boys used the *kaiko* bounce to taunt one another and celebrate their use of a bow and arrow to shoot a lizard, a bird, or an insect. Adults used the *kanant* turn of the head and falsetto voice while playing with infants; adolescents enjoyed it in moments of reverie.

—ALLISON JABLONKO

## Melpa

About eighty thousand Melpa-speakers live around Mount Hagen township. Intensive horticulturists, they grow sweet potatoes as their staple and coffee for cash. For compensation payments, ceremonial exchanges, and bride-price presentations, they rear pigs. In a system of patrilineal descent, they divide into tribes, which subdivide into two to ten exogamous clans, usually allied in pairs. Under flexible rules of residence and affiliation, some persons belong to clans by nonpatrilineal ties. Men dominate politics—as orators, settlers of disputes, and legislators (Strathern 1971, 1972).

Europeans entered the area in 1933, mainly searching for gold. They brought colonial controls, economic and political changes, and Christian denominations: Roman Catholic, Lutheran, and Seventh-Day Adventist; later, charismatic evangelical sects (Baptists, Apostolics, Assemblies of God). Despite much cultural change, the Melpa still perform many of their precontact genres of music and dance, albeit less frequently. Pastors have translated Christian songs into Melpa, and participants in the church compose songs with guitar accompaniment, but the indigenous genres are expressively unmatched by the introduced genres.

### Social contexts

The Melpa most commonly voice feelings in songs of courtship and songs based on melodies and images similar to these but directed toward kin, friends, or enemies. Public songs are composed for and performed at dances, which accompany ceremonial exchanges (*moka*). Funeral songs, sung solo or in concert, lie midway between the personal and the public; composed by individuals of either sex, they emerge in the process of grief and mourning.

#### Courting

Since about 1980, courtship-related songs (*amb kenan*) and the occasions on which people perform them have become a casualty of radios, cassettes, and the introduction of Christian music and values. Traditionally, people sang these songs at night. Decorated with feathers, marsupial furs, and facial paint, suitors would visit a house where one or more girls were expecting them, chaperoned by a senior woman. To encourage the girls to emerge from the rear (sleeping) compartment, the suitors would begin singing. After a while, a girl would come out and kneel, facing the fire. At her side, a suitor would sit. Accompanied by spectators' singing, he would sway his head toward the girl until his forehead touched hers. After a few quick rotations of the neck, with noses pressed together, the pair bobbed their heads in unison to the floor three times or so, and then brought them up for a fresh round. After a while, another suitor would replace him beside the girl, who during one evening might "turn head" with up to six youths. All partners moved in synchrony to the musical rhythms.

The text of an *amb kenan* from the 1960s runs (after Strathern 1974:26):

| | |
|---|---|
| Mbarat o a rokl ile, o e: | Along the road, *o e:* |
| Na nanom a köu mbi nda, o e? | Must I go alone, *o e?* |
| Nggap Thres, a konta mbukl, erol, | Thres from Gap, let's go together, *erol,* |
| Erol paiye paiya. | *Erol paiye paiya.* |

| | |
|---|---|
| Na mep a Rut pamb, o e, | Let me take you to Mbukl, *o e,* |
| Rut ken a ou tan, o e, | And there you alone will tend, *o e,* |
| Ou tan a palka tan, erol, | Will tend and mind my love-magic plants, *erol,* |
| Erol paiye paiya. | *Erol paiye paiya.* |

The boy tells the girl he is lonely. He asks her to walk with him back to his place, where she will have charge of the plants he has used to make himself sexually attractive. He pledges himself only to her.

*Amb kenan* express love-driven sentiments of confidence, amusement, pleasure, doubt, loss, or despair:

Okla köi nikint a por pokla ila nga
Öi walinga ronom, ndo we na.
Kandep ku moklmba we,
Nomba mering e mering ponom, ndo we na.

Wö tenda mong, e a,
Nggoklnga ot ropa pukl ile wat elmba we,
Temet mara pona ila,
Kona mana onom, ndo we na.

Up there the red parrot
Swings its tail, *ndo we na.*
I'll stay and watch it,
As it pecks at fruit and moves away, *ndo we na.*

I'm alone, *e a,*
Waiting to shoot an arrow at the base of the tree,
Waiting in the *mara* grove,
And rain falls down, *ndo we na.*

The girl is like a parrot, which swings its tail and moves through trees. The singer waits, with his arrow ready; but rain falls, dampening his vigil.

An evening of courting could lead to elopement, but the seriousness of paying a high bride-price, with its attendant risk of failure, always loomed, as this song (after Strathern 1974:46) laments:

| | |
|---|---|
| Konde moklp, a, kant mel, a, | Here at Konde, *a,* I see, *a,* |
| Wande kopa ropa wone ninim, a, | How the mist spreads out at Wande, *a,* |
| Le pa win a, pa wa ye. | *Le pa win a, pa wa ye.* |
| | |
| Kng e korond, a; mel e korond, a. | I'm seeking pigs, *a;* I'm seeking shells, *a.* |
| Pren, nim kandep, a; kond enem, a, | My girl, looking at you, *a,* I feel sorry, *a,* |
| Le pa win a, pa wa ye. | *Le pa win a, pa wa ye.* |

The singer is sorry because he has not yet assembled the needed goods, so he cannot marry the girl he wants. The mist separating him from the girl symbolizes his regret at being cut off from her.

Melpa musical texts cite places to evoke emotions between the singer and the desired one, and use vocables to end phrases or stand as independent phrases. Lines may divide in half, as shown by a vertical bar:

**amb kenan** Melpa courtship-related song, formerly sung while a boy and a girl, with noses touching, bobbed and turned their heads

**ka** Melpa lament, usually sung by large numbers of mourners, praising the dead or accusing them of deserting the living

**kang rom** Melpa ballad, performed solo at night mostly by men, telling stories of heroes and heroines and often using archaic expressions

**moka** Melpa ceremonial exchange, in which partners in allied groups alternately at intervals of months or years give each other pigs and Papua New Guinean currency

**mölya** Melpa lighthearted song, performed by men, women, or mixed groups, often informally in private

**mörl** Melpa men's dance in a line, with each man holding a spear or playing a kundu and singing words usually evoking feelings of loss on a clansman's death

**werl** Melpa married women's dance in a line, with each woman playing a kundu and singing words resembling those of *mörl* or detailing young men's activities

| Konde | moklp | a | | kant | mel | a | |
|-------|-------|---|---|------|-----|---|---|
| Konde | staying | *a* | | I-see | as | | *a* |
| | | | | | | | |
| Wande | kopa | ropa | | wone | ninim | a | |
| Wande | mist | striking | | spread | says | | *a* |

A further gloss shows how syntax emphasizes a word by putting it first in a phrase; texts often mention objects first, feelings second.

| Kng | e | korond | a | | mel | e | korond a | |
|-----|---|--------|---|---|-----|---|----------|---|
| Pig | it | I-seek | *a* | | thing | it | I-seek | *a* |
| | | | | | | | | |
| Pren | nim | kandep | a | | kond | enim | a | |
| Friend | you | seeing | *a* | | sorrow | it-makes | *a* | |

The vocable *a* ends every verse but the refrain, itself a string of vocables. Other common vocables are *e* and *o*. In songs of courtship, the phrase *o e* marks a downward sweep of the head.

*Ceremonial exchanges* (moka)

To partners in allied groups, men give pigs and Papua New Guinean currency. By surpassing gifts received earlier from the other side, they try to display superiority. A crowd of spectators gathers to rate the wealth handed over and the dancers' decorations. For these exchanges, leaders compose songs, which hosts perform for guests. The texts comment on political relations, subtly revealing states of hostility or alliance, ironically deprecating the collective strength of their singers, and obliquely announcing intentions to fight or make peace. Men and women dance in separate companies, each with its own song. On the same occasions, young people of both sexes convene informally to perform dances and songs that have humorous or sexual connotations.

Most men dance the *mörl,* for which they wear feathered headdresses; black, white, and red facial paint; long-stringed aprons, netted by women; and at their backs, bunches of fresh cordyline leaves (figure 2). In a long row, holding spears or kundus (*nditing*), they face the spectators. Their song wafts up and down the line, as lead drummers and singers take it up in turn and bend their knees to the drumbeats. Rather than expressing triumph over their competitors, *mörl* often evoke feelings of loss on the deaths of clansmen, whose absence from the dancers' line reduces its length. Most texts have just one stanza, which performers repeat many times, sometimes singing of themselves collectively in the first person singular: *Ndekene moklp noint ndop a / Kant mel a. / Kana rapa kröu ronom. / Ang nim elpa mak rolna, / Rokl e kawa ndonom* 'Here at Ndekene, I look / Across the river. / The men's house at Kana

FIGURE 2    Melpa men perform the *mörl,* wearing feathered headdresses, paint, and long-stringed aprons. Photo by Andrew J. Strathern, 1976.

is cold. / My brother, you made another mark, / And our tall man is missing'. Here, to one of their tribesmen, they impute wrongdoing that resulted in the death of a tall, handsome man. Concealed intentions to pursue revenge underlie such sentiments of grief and loss. They add counterpoint to the formal speeches made after the dancing ends—speeches that usually proclaim alliance and peaceful intent.

For *moka,* married women perform *werl,* slow dances in place. Wearing ornaments and feathers, they keep time by beating kundus (figure 3). Their songs repeat the topics of *mörl* or detail the activities of young men of the community into which they have married. One begins by recalling that for tethering pigs, women weave

FIGURE 3  At the 1989 Port Moresby Show, married Melpa women perform the *werl*. Tuning pellets, affixed to the drumheads, are clearly visible. Photo by Don Niles.

FIGURE 3  At the 1989 Port Moresby Show, married Melpa women perform the *werl*. Tuning pellets, affixed to the drumheads, are clearly visible. Photo by Don Niles.

ropes: *Okla ndop kant e, o e, / Kora Manda wi, o, / Weng kan kanem, o e: / Werl ro* 'I look up and I see, *o e*, / Up there Manda from Kora, *o*, / Is weaving a rope, *o e*: / Strike *werl*'. In the second stanza of this song, the women recall that to decorate their heads for dancing, they mount scarab beetles within orchid fibers: *Noint ndop kant e, o e, / Kora Korlopi noi / Morok rom ronom: / Werl ro* 'I look across and see, *o e*, / Over there Korlopi from Kora / Sings to the scarab beetle: / Strike *werl*'.

### Lighthearted songs (mölya)

*Mölya* (or *mörli*) are lighthearted, flirtatious, mischievous, challenging, exuberant. Crowds sing them at dances. Friends sing them on more private occasions, in gardens, or on pathways. The texts voice feelings and opinions, often protesting or threatening others, or praising them. When at war, the Melpa sang songs promising to kill individual enemies. Persons of both sexes, particularly young people, freely compose *mölya*. Others may repeat them, but neighbors recognize the composer and the circumstances behind their composition.

### Funerals

For funerals, people compose and teach *ka,* highly stylized and expressively simple songs, which praise the dead or accuse them of deserting the living. This example honors a Mokei man who died in 1971 in a car accident: *Mbarat o rokl nile / Kokela ond o. / E e e ye e. / Wö kuki ndaep nile nga, / Korop nint o. / We e e e e* 'I have just come / Along the road. / *E e e ye e.* / My fine-skinned man, / I search for him, I say. / *We e e e e*' (after Strathern 1974:96). Smeared in orange or yellow clay, a massed choir of male mourners performed the song. They marched onto the arena where the body was on display, circled it counterclockwise many times, and sat at the edge of the grounds. Other *ka* receive similar performances.

Women sing funeral songs that highlight a kin relationship to the dead, as in a song from 1982:

Ta, Ndakla mbraun omong ile raep ndonom.
Ta, na petem kona na köneimb, e.
Ta, na morom kona na könamb, e.
Ta, na wak rolna, namba ukl itimb nda?

Father hides in coffee-tree leaves at Ndakla.
Father, I want to see where he lives, *e.*
Father, I want to see where he is, *e.*
Father, you've left me; what am I to do?

The funeral was for an old, respected man, buried among his coffee trees. The expression *na wak rolna* 'you've left me' is typical: the living see the dead as having left them to join the company of the other dead, rather than ceasing to exist.

### Recreational music

For casual entertainment, persons of either sex play susaps (*tembakl*) or four-holed end-blown flutes (*koa pela ming*), in both cases using melodies associated with tales. A flutist may accompany a singer or sing the song after playing the melody. Because of the availability of radio and cassettes, skill at playing these instruments is declining. Individuals of the same sex may play them in duets.

The words of recreational songs might evoke warfare, as in this flute-accompanied song: *Mökö kep ile, e e, / Reipö rönt e monom* 'On the banks of the Mökö River, *e e,* / Shields are massed.' Or texts might pose a question to creatures of the forest: *Köi nde nduin mam rakl ninembil, e: / Namba ninembil nda?* 'The *nde nduin* bird and its mother, *e:* / What do the two of them say?' Or texts might express a philosophical point:

| | |
|---|---|
| Amb o rua nde-nga öngin, rol nde rol, | Woman is like the banana tree, *rol nde rol,* |
| Ek nimba mana on, | That fruits and dies, |
| Kik ile kröyö kanem. | Grows cold. |
| | |
| Wö nde ui-nga öngin, rol nde rol, | Man is like the holm-oak tree, *rol nde rol,* |
| Ui-mel mun etepa | That puts out shoots and |
| Kont kont mondop ond e. | Shows itself fresh again. |

### Ballads

Ballads (*kang rom*) are important items of sung entertainment. They are performed mostly by men, though some women know them. Often using archaic forms of expression, they tell stories (also preserved in certain tales) of the doings of heroes and heroines. Performing them is a challenge, because the singer should complete a piece without a break—inhaling at the end of each couplet, but continuing to sing—for hundreds of lines. Singers perform at night, mostly in men's houses, for a circle of kin and visitors. In payment, listeners present small gifts.

A famous tale tells how Miti Krai, the love-magic man of Miti Mountain, courts and marries the woman Rangmba of Ambra Hill, dies in a fight, and returns as a ghost. Joseph Ketan and Andrew Strathern have collected versions of this and other ballads: in 1965, Oke-Korpa sang a version having more than five hundred lines; in 1982, a Kawelka Kundmbo clansman sang another, of 386 lines; longer versions exist. Each couplet completes a thought, often expressed in parallel syntactical structures. Each line divides in half, as in this excerpt:

| | |
|---|---|
| Miti kang, \| Krai nam, o; | The Miti boy, \| Krai, *o;* |
| Mukl Miti \| rona murum, o. | Was up \| on Miti Hill, *o.* |
| Ndip i ya \| wurlung nggöröm, o; | Fire blew \| to the west, *o;* |
| Ndip i ya \| arlung nggöröm, o. | Fire blew \| to the east, *o.* |
| "Niminga wamb \| kae namin?" o, | "Who are \| your good people?" *o,* |
| Nimba kumb, \| kelpa purum, o. | He said, \| and he departed, *o.* |

Pei kang e | rui purum, o;     The boys | envied him, *o;*

Amb ralt nt e, | romborong, o,     The girls, | they sought to have him, *o.*

Ambra amb, | Rangmba, na     The Ambra girl, | Rangmba, *na,*

Mukl Ambra | rona murum, a.     Was up | on Ambra Hill, *a.*

### Adaptations

In the 1960s and 1970s, the broadcaster-singer Andrew Dokta restyled the melodies and topics of *amb kenan* and *mölya,* accompanying himself on a harmonica. In the 1980s, younger Kawelka men imitated his style. In a song played in 1982 by a Kawelka clansman, a suitor likens himself to the red parrot:

Mina köi nikint, o e,     At Mina the red parrot, *o e,*

Por pukl ile tinim, o e,     Turns around, *o e,*

Öi walinga ronom, o e.     And swings its tail, *o e.*

Mul kona ile morom, o e,     He's there at home, *o e,*

Le pa win.     *Le pa win.*

Amb wentep pren,     That girl, my girlfriend,

Wamb mur ile ponom.     She goes into the throng of men.

Namba mel mat ngur ndo e?     What have I given for her?

Kond mat enem, o e.     I'm just sorry, *o e.*

Ro el, le pa win, o e.     *Ro el, le pa win, o e.*

Like the parrot, the suitor advertises himself, but in vain: another youth will make a bride-price payment and marry her. How sorry he feels!     —ANDREW J. STRATHERN

## CHIMBU PROVINCE

The word *Chimbu,* sometimes pronounced /simbu/, derives from the Kuman word *sipu-u* 'thank you'. Despite high mountains and deep valleys, the province is densely populated: in 1990, it was home to 183,849 people. All languages indigenously spoken in the province are non-Austronesian. Kuman is the dialect of the Chimbu language spoken by the most people; other dialects include Chuave, Nomane, and Sinasina. In the south of the province, people speak languages unrelated to Chimbu.

Chimbu people share many musical traits. Among their instruments, aerophones and membranophones predominate; idiophones are next in importance, and chordophones lowest. In the north of the province, people sometimes perform music purchased from other areas. Since the introduction of Western music, indigenous Chimbu music has been in decline, but individuals and organizations are trying to preserve it. The province has musical variation, but Kuman music is homogeneous.

### Kuman

For dancing, singing, and playing musical instruments, Kuman society recognizes five important occasions: a pig-killing ceremony (*bugla yungu*), a food-exchange ceremony (*mokna bir*), a women's song-dance (*ambu yungu beglkwa*), initiation, and formal courting. The main accompanying instrument is the kundu (*ongun*), for which people may substitute bows and arrows, except in women's song-dances; on downbeats, they strike the bowstrings.

#### Pig-killing ceremonies

Pig-killing ceremonies honor ancestral spirits. To begin them, men play bamboo flutes (*kuakumba*), often called birds of life. The far end is cut open, and the near end is left closed by a node; the hole for blowing lies about 15 centimeters from the closed end. A performer changes pitch by covering and uncovering the open end with his palm. Flutes are played in pairs, of similar sizes and lengths (about 60 to 70 centimeters). Kuman believe ancestral spirits dwell in the flutes, and disaster will strike families if mothers, girls, or uninitiated boys see or touch them. Boys first see the flutes during their initiation. The flutes are kept in specially made cases, hung in the corners of houses.

Each composition for flutes has several patterns, which, for a complete performance, follow a set sequence. Each family maintains an ancestrally bestowed flute piece. The same music is performed every time a pig-killing ceremony occurs. Each family plays its melody and may not play other families' melodies. Though new compositions are possible, men advise initiates to play only the ancestral patterns, of which some popular names are *gandia* 'cry of a baby cuscus', *bongre* 'bark of dogs while chasing a cuscus', *nere bare* 'butterfly', and *dingi goglm* (a kind of tree); other patterns imitate the cries of pigs and babies.

In the second part of the ceremony (*indaun die singwa* 'trimming the roofs of new houses'), men and women sing unaccompanied songs, dancing with spears, sticks, clubs, bows, and arrows. In a martial mood, they move collectively around new houses. Hosts then distribute food to friends, guests, and families.

The third part is the core of the ceremony. Music lasts for an extended season—sometimes months, with the same items reiterated. Appropriate music is *bugla gende,* dancing and singing accompanied by many instruments, especially kundus, rattles (*minge sumugl,* hung from an apron), and seashell necklaces (*aringai mongo,* which clink in the dance). Dancers' attire features a headpiece of long, black plumes, taken from Stephanie's astrapia (*Astrapia Stephaniae*), a bird of paradise. People of any age may dance in *bugla gende,* but males predominate. Dancers arrange themselves in an oval formation, which can stay in place or move around. Dances occur by night and by day; at night, bonfires around the dancers give light and warmth. After the *bugla gende* season, men club forty to fifty pigs to death, and everyone consumes the pork.

The fourth part of the ceremony, *nnde gamba yungum* 'sorrow and revenge', then occurs. It has little music. Participation is optional, but people of all ages usually take part. With black mud and white ashes rubbed on their bodies, participants chase undecorated people, trying to get mud on them. They fight with anyone who tries to avoid getting marked with mud. While this is going on, people sing songs, but do not dance or play instruments.

### The food-exchange ceremony

Lasting one to two months, the food-exchange ceremony is less comprehensive than the pig-killing ceremony. Its preparation may take two to four months. *Mokna owa,* its music, is an important feature, whose musical instruments, songs, dances, and costumes resemble those of the pig-killing ceremony. Only men compose *mokna owa.* They rehearse in the men's house at night. Wanting as many good songs as possible, they discard bad ones and retain fifty to sixty for the performance.

### The women's song-dance

This occasion is obsolete. In a circle, women danced as for *bugla gende* and *mokna owa.* They decorated themselves in their best ornaments. They used few musical instruments. The performance, which often coincided with the pig-killing ceremony, presented a drama: while some danced, others acted. Only women composed the songs.

### Initiation

Kuman boys and girls undergo separate initiations. Male initiation (*kua ombuno dingwa*) occurs about every five years. One day, elders gather the adolescent boys (about ages thirteen to eighteen), and tell them it is time to see the *kua* (the "bird" of the *kuakumba*). To the accompaniment of hidden flutes, they lead the boys to riverbanks, where they reveal the flutes, whose secrets the boys study as they learn the social rules a man should know. For weeks, each boy practices on his family's flutes. After the elders approve, a actual ceremony occurs. Pigs are killed and cooked. The young men dress up. Elders play the flutes, and declare that the initiates see the *kua*. Afterward, initiates may revisit the riverbanks, practicing until they master the melodies.

Female initiation (*ambai yungugl pangwa*) is for one girl at a time. When a girl first menstruates, preparations begin. She stays indoors, attended by other girls and close female relatives. At night, young men and women sing songs to her. Until the two last nights, she studies everything about domestic economy a woman should know. Finally, she dresses in full costume; one or two similarly dressed girls accompany her into the daylight. Pigs are killed and cooked. After a distribution of pork and vegetables, everyone returns home.

### Formal courting

Songs of courtship (*kaungo*) have three styles of performance. For the first (*ambai dangro dingwa*), a boy sits next to a girl and touches her with his side. The pair often sing together, their hands joined with intertwined fingers; they cross their legs, usually one of each girl's legs over a boy's. While singing, they sway from side to side. At the end of each song, for six to eight seconds, they formally giggle. Most of the singing and giggling is in high falsetto (*nunguno giglti* 'high neck'), which contrasts with normal singing (*nunguno yoko* 'normal neck').

TRACK 10

The second style is *giglang dingwa* 'singing the songs of courtship'. These items are performed as are those in the first style, but the boys and girls number from eight to twelve, boys usually more numerous. The girls sit along a wall; the boys sit near the fireplace, in a line parallel to the girls. Most of the singing is in falsetto. The first four stanzas illustrate common features of Kuman song. Vocables establish the melody in the first stanza: *E yo yara waya, / Yo yara waya, / Yo yara waya, u we: / Yo yara waya, / Yo yara waya, / Yo yara waya, / U we-e-e-m-m saya-m.* Meaningful text begins in the fourth line of the next stanza:

| | |
|---|---|
| E-u-e, yo yara waya, | *E-u-e, yo yara waya,* |
| Yo yara waya, | *Yo yara waya,* |
| Yo yara waya, u we-i: | *Yo yara waya,* but: |
| Moro Kuni Peni yo, | Young girl Kuni Peni, |
| Moro Kuni Peni yo, | Young girl Kuni Peni, |
| Moro Kuni Peni yo, | Young girl Kuni Peni, |
| U we-e-e-m-m saya-m. | *U we-e-e-m-m saya-m.* |
| | |
| E-u-e, moro Kuni Peni yo-i! | *E-u-e,* young girl Kuni Peni! |
| Moro Kuni Peni yo-i, | Young girl Kuni Peni, |
| Moro Kuni Peni yo, u we-i: | Young girl Kuni Peni, but: |
| Nono kwi dmun ba-i, | It's good to talk and chatter together, |
| Nono kwoia dmun ba-i, | It's good to talk and chatter together, |
| Nono kwi dmun ba, | It's good to talk and chatter together, |
| U we-e-e-m-m saya-m. | *U we-e-e-m-m saya-m.* |

| | |
|---|---|
| E-u-e, nono kwi dmun ba-i. | *E-u-e,* it's good to talk and chatter together, |
| Nono kwoia dmun bai-i, | It's good to talk and chatter together, |
| Nono kwi dmun ba, u we-i: | It's good to talk and chatter together, but: |
| Yugu mo imbara i aglo ne, | The place up there, where's this place? |
| Kamno imbara i aglo ne, | The place up there, where's this place? |
| Yugu mo imbara i aglo ne, | The place up there, where's this place? |
| U we-e-e-m-m saya-m. | *U we-e-e-m-m saya-m.* |

The third stanza refers to the previous one and continues. With similar repetitiveness, this pattern of linkage, a common Kuman structural device, leads to ten more stanzas.

The third style, largest in scope but seldom performed, is *kuanand* 'bird-song singing'. A month or two before, boys of a village different from the girls' village set a date. The event occurs in a longhouse, warmed by fires about 3 meters apart. On the appointed date, in formal attire, the boys approach it, where the girls are waiting, also properly dressed. About 6 meters from the house, the boys begin an introductory song, *kaungo tom singwa*; still singing, they enter and sit facing the girls, so each girl has a partner. The performers may number fifty to sixty. Mothers, fathers, and children enjoy watching. Procedures are the same as the other styles of courtship, but *kuanand* start at the beginning of the boys' line; then everyone joins in, so the song flows down the lines to the end. After a few songs, partners change; the process repeats until all possible pairings have occurred. As they sing, the boys and girls turn their heads vigorously from side to side, rub noses, and sway. After a session ends (about 1:00 to 2:00 A.M.), some girls may follow boys home. Others, usually those who had been courting during *giglang* and *ambai dangro dingwa,* may join select boys in trial marriages. After two or three weeks, girls who do not wish to stay married return home.

### Purchased music

Kuman perform music from elsewhere. Those living near the border of Madang and Chimbu trade their music with the Bundi (of Madang Province), usually paying with pigs, dogs, and cassowaries, but sometimes using money, traditional or modern. The purchased kinds of music are *kundu kaima* and *kanam.* Persons who buy the music receive the rights to the pertinent dances and decorations. Later, in their own language, they may add new texts to the melodies.

For performing *kundu kaima,* men carry 6-to-8-meter-long bamboos on their backs. From kitelike masks at the top hang three or four ropes, each pulled by a woman while dancing around the man. Participants move in a circle, accompanied mainly by kundus. *Kanam,* also performed in a circle, have many similarities to *kundu kaima,* though without the masks. Performers dance with bent backs; at the end of each song, they stand up straight. Outside the circle, moving in rhythm to the drums, men enact little dramas: they take comical turns, as when a man tries to pinch a woman's buttocks and she reports it to her husband, who charges at the culprit—who may actually be a man dressed as a woman.

### Recreational music

Several musical instruments entertain leisure time. The most salient are raft panpipes (*perurupe*), which young men make of bamboo. From each pipe, they sever one node, leaving the other intact. The minimum number of pipes is four; the maximum, more than twelve. The pipes are arranged from shortest to longest, fastened with cane or other twine. Anyone may play them, though not for accompanying vocal music.

Bamboo susaps (*tambagle*) are kept off the ground and in dry places; if carefully

At night, men kidnapped boys and took them into the forest—where they disciplined them in ordeals such as letting blood and piercing the nasal septum. Men sang while bleeding the boys and swatting them with nettles.

maintained, they can last for years. People of either sex may play them, but males do so more often. The player puts the instrument between his lips. One hand supports it; the other uses an attached string to vibrate the tongue of the instrument. To get different pitches and combinations of overtones, the player controls the pace of inhaling and exhaling, and adjusts the position and tension of his lips and vocal tract.

The *pumingi* (*pu* 'blow', *mingi* 'container') is an end-blown bamboo flute with both ends open. Near the far end, it has four holes. Anyone may play these flutes, though mostly men do. People play them at any time, but often at night, around 9:00 to 11:00, and in the early morning, around 4:00 to 6:00. The performance tells fortunes, cures illnesses, drives away evil spirits, and simply entertains. In the early 1980s, some flutes were made of plastic or metal pipes. *Pumingi* are usually played in twos, threes, or fours. For preservation, as with susaps, people keep them inside houses, plunging them into the walls so they remain dry.          —EDWARD GENDE

## EASTERN HIGHLANDS PROVINCE

In 1957, this province had sparse contact with Australian patrol officers, missions (chiefly Lutheran), and traders. Most data cited here came from Kainantu Subdistrict, home of most Usarufa-speakers. This account also covers the music of nearby peoples: Agarabi, Asaro, Awa, Baruya, Benabena, Binumarien, Fore, Gadsup, Gahuku, Gimi, Kamano, Kanite, Kosena-Awiyaana, Siane, and Tairora.

### Performative contexts

Eastern Highlanders use music to appease ancestral spirits, make gardens and pigs grow, and reinforce ceremonies for attaining physical attractiveness. Major ceremonies formerly occurred every few years. Male initiation began when several boys were between the ages of eight and twelve years; a girl's coming of age depended on menarche, so its celebration was individual and immediate. Communal feasts occurred only when pigs were in abundance. The singsing held in late December and early January, when food was abundant, marked the year.

Into the 1960s, men of the Eastern Highlands preoccupied themselves with preparing for battle, either to defend themselves and their land or to satisfy grievances against other villages. Strangers were a threat, not only for potentially stealing land and other possessions (pigs, wives), but for controlling sorcery.

### *Male initiation*

Initiations instructed boys in the ways of their people, frightened them into subjugation to their elders, and subjected them to painful practices that would make them virile, admirable, and responsible. In stages, boys learned secrets allowed only to initiated men.

At night, men kidnapped boys and took them into the forest, where they blackened their bodies with charcoal and put initiation skirts on them. To emphasize the seriousness of events to follow, the men roughly disciplined them for the first time in their lives. Two key persons eased a boy's fears and physical ordeals: one was usually his mother's brother, who comforted him during ordeals such as letting blood and piercing the nasal septum; the other was a coinitiate, who endured the initiation alongside him. Coinitiates would become inseparable friends; in playing secret flutes together, they would share one musical pattern.

After the physical ordeals, the men began to instill pride in the boys, whom they decorated, slipping onto their foreheads, arms, and legs finely woven bands, into which they inserted colorful foliage while singing *ibóáq-ímá,* whose texts related the kidnapping, mentioned the initiatory belt, and detailed the decorative foliage. Men also sang while bleeding the boys and swatting them with nettles.

The next day, a feast occurred. The village gathered, singing *amuq-ímá,* songs whose texts, relaying the happiness engendered by the boys' maturity, cited initiatory activities, preparations for feasts, articles of costumery, and perfection in the weaving of bands from yellow-orchid fiber. Speakers of five languages—Fore, Kamano, Kanite, Kosena, Usarufa—sang the same initiatory songs and interacted in ceremonies. Indigenous musical classes lend themselves to borrowing, as about two-thirds of texts are vocables, and what literal texts exist are elliptical. Thus, musical form and intent carry more meaning than sung words.

Schooling continued for years, and boys reached adolescence before the final stage, when, from the front of the boys' belts, men suspended two secretly crafted tassels. In back, they hung a narrow, colorfully painted bark-cloth streamer, ending in a braided tassel that nearly touched the ground. Effort went into creating the streamer: with the painting of each design on it, men sang songs to give it power. Its attachment signaled the end of initiation and the making of a warrior.

### Girls' coming of age

Women in the Eastern Highlands are providers. They typically spend their days in gardens—planting, weeding, and harvesting vegetables. Girls garden with their mothers, submitting early to the community's needs. When a girl begins to menstruate, she and her girlfriends gather to enjoy a five-day party, when they sing songs called *ígárú-aimma* and her mother prepares and serves them food.

The girls sit cross-legged on the floor, bobbing their knees and swinging their shoulders. Their songs are distinct from songs sung by men or mixed ensembles: the tempo is quicker, the phrases are shorter, and rhythmic calls name places, foods, and kin. The texts address topics broadly sorted in four sets: *daily routine,* recalling netted bags (made by all women), sores (irritated by flies), and pleasure over good food (grown or gathered); *unusual events,* like sighting a helicopter, European missionaries' arrival, and death in a hospital; *desires,* including the romantic, with meanings often hidden in metaphor, but also the adventuresome, like wanting to ride in a vehicle; and the *coming-of-age performance itself,* speaking of dancing together, laughing together, and becoming adults. Some songs, having unglossable texts, fit into no set.

On the last day, the girls energetically dance around the village, flaunting their freedom before resuming their gardening. Men studiously ignore the celebration as something that "belongs to the women." A girl receives no villagewide recognition until her marriage—an event that lacks joy and music.

Girls' coming-of-age songs are most prevalent in the central mountains of the province. In data collected during the 1960s, Awa girls produced many new songs. The Awa and the Fore had some form of female initiation. Girls' nasal septums were pierced like those of the boys. The Kamano, Kanite, Kosena, and Usarufa girls had a hole bored through the tip of the nose, where they wore a bat's bone.

### Courtship

Adults vividly recall the "chin-rubbing ceremonies" (Usarufa *timaaíkaq tótó yare-qtareq-yátááré*) that marked youths' formal courtship—parties that ceased in the 1950s. These events allowed the only socially acceptable physical contacts between boys and girls. Older brothers or cousins accompanied girls to the host village, where they, with some fathers, chaperoned and directed the activities, taking note of which couples were compatible. Such information would help men arrange their children's marriages.

One village provided a house. Inside, parallel lines formed: boys sat in one, and girls sat opposite them. Facing partners leaned forward and rubbed their chins together. As the night wore on, the boys' line repeatedly shifted position, so each girl and boy would meet. During feasting and socializing that occurred over two days, participants sang songs whose texts recount preparing for the event. One recalls how the girls washed and oiled their skin and in their armbands put flowers and plaited leaves, and how the boys plaited leaves for their armbands, decorated themselves with red paint, and atop their headdresses stuck two feathers. Another notes a brother's inviting his sister to go with him to the party. Some texts have only two or three words, like "joining" and "courting," or "I danced for you" (Chenoweth 1974).

Knowledge of the songs extends across the northern half of the province. As people borrowed magic and efficacious ceremonies, they borrowed such social activities as chin-rubbing ceremonies. Only the intent of the activity was intelligible: people sometimes sang a quasi-translation of the lyrics, but performed foreign songs with little or no lexical understanding.

### Purification after a birth

After a woman has borne a couple's first child, a purificatory rite restores her husband's strength. As he stands motionless, his mother's brother holds a fire-heated stone in cupped hands, spits on it, and blows the steam onto the new father's headdress, focusing on the cassowary bone in the headband (figure 4). Attending men sing in unison a song to purify each part of the anatomy: mouth, chest, belly, genitals, legs, and feet. The man undergoing purification does not sing. The Usarufa sing the texts of purificatory songs in Fore, Kamano, Kanite, Keyigana, and Kosena-Awiyaana whenever native speakers of those languages are present.

### Marriage

Throughout the province, weddings have two features: the ceremony involves only the woman, and it is a sad occasion. Four peoples—Awiyaana, Binumarien, Fore, Kanite—have songs for weddings. They usually sing them in the bride's house the night before the ceremony, when elders admonish her to forsake adolescent thoughts. Usarufa weddings involve only songs cried by the bride's mother, who surveys the guests and laments losing her daughter.

Other names for a wedding are glossable as 'skirt-tying ceremony' and 'becoming a woman', for it is then that the bride begins to wear the woman's skirt, bark strips suspended from a belt to encircle the hips. (The girl's skirt consists of separate panels, which hang in front and back, leaving the outer thighs bare.) Each of the bride's maternal aunts makes a skirt, which they tie about her waist, one atop the other. As the mother-in-law leads the bride away, her girlfriends follow. Pausing, she gives them cooked pork to take home. If her husband lives far away, this may be the girl's last farewell to her friends and family.

### Sweating

In the 1950s, most men of the province ceased dwelling apart from women and chil-

FIGURE 4    A young Usarufa initiate wears in his headband a cassowary-bone needle, used for letting blood during his initiation. Courtesy of Vida Chenoweth, 1969.

dren. Before then, men had slept in large, oval, grass-roofed houses, heated by fires. During intertribal warfare, the sanctity of the men's house helped maintain the secrecy of military strategies and activities that empowered men over enemies and women. Wives, if related to an enemy clan, were a particular threat, because their allegiance was frequently to their fathers and brothers.

Also within the men's house, adolescent boys lived with the men. There they practiced making arrows, carving wooden bowls, weaving decorations including tiny bands ornamenting their bows, and fashioning bark hoops (worn around men's waists), fringed belts, headbands, armbands, legbands, and feather headdresses. There too they learned their heritage through singing and storytelling.

The men's house was the site for formal sweating, which lasted four to eight weeks. The Fore, Gimi, Kanite, Kosena-Awiyaana, Tairora, and Usarufa practiced it, all in the central and eastern areas of the province. It went out of use when men ceased dwelling apart from women and children. The length of the confinement required the men to gather large amounts of firewood. Boys helped, as they helped collect the raw materials for men's crafts; they also gathered nettles, with which men would swat them, to subordinate and strengthen them.

Participating men assumed a specific pose. Each sat by the fire with legs outstretched and arms extended. He put the palms of his hands flat on the floor or sat upon them, rested against a special wooden support, and tilted his head back. The aim was to sweat profusely, so perspiration running down the face and onto the chest would form symmetrical patterns, a sign of beauty and virility. The first few days, the men consumed no water or sugarcane; for salt and moisture, they licked the perspiration from their arms. Later, women brought them bamboo tubes of water, and as they quenched their thirst, the sweat cascaded down their bodies. Women also brought food in bowls, which they handed through the door. Men believed eating ginger, salt, certain leaves, and bark stimulated perspiration.

While sweating, the men sang. Their songs differed conspicuously from danced songs: they had no refrains, and the texts were longer. Their subjects had a nostalgic character, highlighting women, homesickness, dead loved ones, and their lands—the same songs often sung at wakes.

### Healing

The central part of the province has no known sung ceremonies of healing. Kosena and Usarufa healers formerly called on spirits and blew smoke over the sick one; but, from about 1960, with the arrival of medical dispensaries, the practice dissipated. Binumarien and Tairora peoples had collectively sung healing-related songs, but such musical activities mainly occurred in the southeastern part of the province. From the Baruya, linguist Richard Lloyd collected thirteen *naare* 'healing-songs'; mud or clay, rather than smoke, was the curative agent (personal communication). The texts recount ailments. One says: "Going off main track, going off main track, cassowary biting fish, holding down." This text relates an incident in which a man veered from the path to impale a fish, but while he stood in the grass, an adder bit him, so he went to a healer for help; because he was "hard like a cassowary," he survived.

### Singsings

Singsings often occur in a reserved building or tract of land (Chenoweth 1969:219). They are elaborate affairs, for which participants dress up. Men assemble headdresses made of stiff feathers, taken from parrots and pigeons; they put the feathers in a headband, to tilt slightly forward, framing wearers' faces. Kosena and Usarufa animate their headgear by putting pairs of white cockatoo feathers onto springs, making the feathers snap together in the dance. (Bird-of-paradise plumage belongs more to peoples south, east, and west.) Men also don bark-cloth bibs, painted with red designs and edged with shells; on opposite corners at the top, they attach a white cowrie.

Singers and dancers move in concentric circles around a bonfire, singers in the inner circle, dancers in the outer one. All able-bodied men, women, and children participate. Some men carry kundus, accompanying themselves; others brandish bows and arrows. The climax occurs after midnight, when featured dancers enter, wearing large bark-cloth emblems mounted on poles tied to their backs. Dancers barely raise their feet off the ground. After ten paces or so, they pause, keeping time by bending their knees, and turning their heads from left to right; then they retrace their steps, but with fewer paces, so the circle eventually works its way around the fire. The foliage tucked in armbands and waistbands rustles; and seed necklaces, pigs' tusks, and shells strung at the back of girls' skirts clink. Mixed voices sing songs for dancing (*yaa-ánama*). A leader begins, and a mixed chorus and drums join him. The chorus sings only vocables, with women's voices an octave above the men's. Repeatedly throughout the night, cooks separate about a dozen performers from the pageant and feed them local greens, sweet potatoes, and rice seasoned with pork or tinned fish. The festivities conclude at daybreak.

During intertribal wars, which continued into the late 1960s, the peoples of the province engaged in fight-singsings, feasts that called for songs of aggression and sometimes celebrations of victory. An account translated by linguist Doreen Marks, who lived twenty-five years with the Kosena-Awiyaana (personal communication), says only men performed singsings. Wars lasted up to ten months, until both sides agreed to stop. Kosena hamlets would then exchange pigs. One hamlet after another reciprocated with hosting the singsing and repaying with pork. For months, between one-week periods of rest, the singsings continued.

In the 1990s, singsings included old war-related songs; but subjects were mainly local events and feelings. The events were social, though vestiges of ancestral veneration or spiritual appeasement remained. Typical texts go: "I'm hot and thirsty; rain, come and cool me" (Awa); "I come to see the young men dressed up in their bird-of-paradise feathers" (Awa); "A young man had a vision after he ate the sap of a certain tree" (Awa); "A man runs from a spirit with a flat nose" (Kamano); "Sweet potato! O come, my pig, and eat it" (Kamano); "Look up there at your land" (Kamano); "A small hawk flies at daybreak" (Kamano).

## The Eastern Highlands music system

The Eastern Highlands music system extends throughout the province and into Morobe, where Waffa-speakers share it. In the southeastern area of the province, Baruya music differs slightly: it uses many repeated notes and favors rapid tempos. To the north, the Binumarien sing more slowly than others; phrases end in extremely long holds. Siane musical instruments reflect the usage of the Chimbu, west of them. Only in the northwest, among the Asaro, Siane, and others, do men of the Eastern Highlands sing in high falsetto, a timbre more characteristic of Chimbu and the Western Highlands. Siane and Gahuku melodies contain many microtones; an augmented fourth may be an emic interval to the Siane, but nowhere else in the province.

Eastern Highlanders believe the most pleasing public music is choral, and unison singing (with women doubling men at the octave), executed forcefully and without errors in text or melody, makes good singing. Adolescent boys play alone on panpipes or susaps—an activity that adults consider unserious (figure 5). In boys' and girls' respective periods of puberty, singing reinforces personal identities. In wartime,

FIGURE 5    A Baruya man constructs elaborate journeys by plucking varied rhythmic and melodic patterns on a lamellaphone; Eastern Highlands Province. Photo by Don Niles, 1982.

it frightens enemies. Mixed participation helps unite communities, and when someone dies, it spurs the catharsis of grief.

## Musical instruments

Eastern Highlanders are principally vocalists, and their important instruments involve the human mouth (Chenoweth 1979:80). Their sacred flutes are famous. Kundus accompany their singsings, but did not always do so: around the 1930s, kundus from the coast supplanted shaken gourds. Other musical instruments serve in men's secret ceremonies or attract members of the opposite sex. The simplest local idiophones are those that make the rhythmic pulse explicit (Chenoweth 1976:ii). Stringed instruments are not indigenous to the province.

### Idiophones

Before people played drums in the province, women used to shake gourds, or sections of bamboo filled with seeds saved from crops planted the preceding year. Susaps, kept secret from women, occur throughout the province; since boys may speak the name of girls as they play, adults regard susaps as courtship-oriented instruments. Another men's instrument is an unadorned, flat, oblong plank about 35 centimeters long, threaded through one end by a cord. Men swing it in circles overhead; some believe its sound will magically strengthen them.

### Membranophones

Kundus accompany dances at singsings except among the Angan in the south, where kundus are absent. Kundus seldom have decorations, but makers give their bodies a smooth finish by rubbing them with sandpaper-rough leaves. The animals whose skins serve for drumheads are possum (the most common), snake, and lizard. The manufacture of kundus is a social event, for which men stop other work. For days, the village commons is strewn with blocks of wood, knives, adzes, and scraped hides. At the finish, men tune the drums by heating and attaching to the drumhead small pellets of resin. Dancers do not step to the rhythm of kundus: drumbeats and singing continue in one meter; dancers do their steps in another, concurrently with the singing and drumming, but without matching the beat.

### Chordophones

Two-stringed mouth-resonated bows were formerly played in the northeast and as far south as the Kainantu area. Men and women made and played these instruments for entertainment. Holding the bow at one end, the player put the other end in his or her mouth. Plucking the strings with the fingertips, the player changed pitches by flexing the bow slightly. The only other chordophone found in the province was a bamboo tube zither. It was more typical of East Sepik Province.

### Aerophones

Aerophones are the principal instruments of the province. Chief among them are the paired bamboo side-blown flutes commonly known as sacred flutes, though they are more secret than sacred. Only initiated males may see or play them. Women and children, afraid of their sound, hide in houses to keep from seeing them. Men play them only at night. The secrecy surrounding them adds to the mystery of their sound—mellow, haunting, and baffling to the listener, who does not know the source or the location. The sound is like no other in the culture; men tell women it is a bird. Also adding to the mystery is the unbroken continuity of the sound, achieved by the skill of paired men, who alternate parts so smoothly as to resemble a single voice.

People dub flute-sharing men "twins". At a partner's death, "his flute is silent": one of his flutes is broken and buried with him; the other is given to his son, as only a son may play a man's flute and melody. Initiated men identify a man by either his melody or his name. For them, playing flutes achieves a social and personal goal, but it has a communal purpose. People say the sound of the flutes directly influences pigs, which grow large because the sound pleases them. The Usarufa say gardens prosper at the sound.

Unlike flutes of peoples along the Sepik River, flutes of this province are simple, with no holes for fingering. Men cut bamboo to about 50 centimeters long; for contrast of pitch, they cut another, 2 to 3 centimeters longer. They do not otherwise tune the tubes. A hole for blowing is cut in the side near the joint, the closed end; the opposite end is open. Each pair of flutes has a proper name, whose phonetic rhythm forms the rhythm played (figure 6). Each pair of men practice their pattern until they can vary it while increasing the tempo.

### End-blown flutes

During important feasts, only initiated men once played end-blown flutes (Kamano *yubíremma,* Kanite *kabufane,* Usarufa *kaapáumma*), which came in three sizes: the largest was 38 centimeters long and 5 in diameter; the midsize was stored inside it, with the smallest fitted into the midsize. The Binumarien and Kosena-Awiyaana also

FIGURE 6 An example of the paired-flute melody *íqtabebe,* one of thirty-nine known; to the first syllable, rhythmic intonation adds a glottal (*q*). After Chenoweth 1979:181–190.

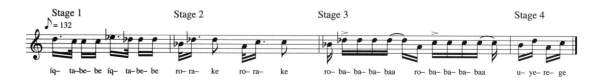

| Stage 1 | Stage 2 | Stage 3 | Stage 4 |

♪ = 132

íq– ta–be– be íq– ta–be– be   ro–ra– ke   ro–ra– ke   ro–ba–ba–ba–baa   ro–ba–ba–ba–baa   u–ye–re– ge

eq–   táá   kaa– yo– náá

FIGURE 7 Excerpt from an Usarufa performance on end-blown flutes, showing how musical shape follows verbal rhythm. Transcription by Vida Chenoweth.

had such flutes, which men played while women gathered and cooked food. The men sounded these flutes by blowing across the rim. Some men had only one flute; others carried in either hand a flute of contrasting pitch.

While sounding these flutes at feasts, men marched around the village in a procession that fell into ranks of two to four men abreast, led by the most prestigious, who had contributed the most pigs. With each step, they bent one knee and blew one flute. As the knee straightened before the next step, they blew a flute with contrastive tones. The result was harmonic cacophony, since actual tones were unimportant. As with secret flutes, tuning played no part in making and playing the instrument. The names of the patterns, like those of the secret flutes, set the rhythm. In figure 7, the tonal contour copies the rhythm of the words: *táá* and *náá* as spoken are high-pitched syllables, so the highest musical tone moves upward.

*Panpipes and other aerophones*
Adolescent Usarufa males play a row of four panpipes graduated in length from about 7 to 12 centimeters. No two sets sound alike. Males play variations on the name of the instrument (*porétépoqa*), and all tones in the melody proceed to an adjacent tone. The syllables *ré* and *té,* high pitches in this language, are rendered melodically as tones above *po.* Boys freely add a girl's name, which they play in its ordinarily spoken rhythm. Adults treat panpipes as toys and do not play them.

Other aerophones occur as isolates. For personal entertainment, a few men play solo a rim-blown vertical cane pipe with a small bore and two or more holes for fingering. These instruments range from 45 centimeters long (as played by Binumarien, Gadsup, and Kosena-Awiyaana men), to 91 centimeters long (as played by the Siane). The Gadsup say coastal missionaries introduced the instrument, and the Siane say theirs came from Chimbu Province.

The Asaro and Fore play vessel flutes made from a round fruit. The Siane play clay whistles, also believed to have originated with the Chimbu. To announce the killing of enemy warriors, Binumarien men once buzzed their lips into a section of bamboo; a similar trumpet, with a gourd amplifier attached to the end, summoned Siane leaders. Conch trumpets, gotten from the coast, are widely used for summoning villagers to Christian services. Near Goroka, the Benabena have a double side-blown flute, with a hole for blowing cut on either side of the closed joint of the bamboo and both ends left open; this configuration allows people to play from either side. —VIDA CHENOWETH

## ENGA PROVINCE

About two hundred thousand Enga, the most numerous people of Papua New Guinea, live in scattered hamlets in the mountains and valleys north and west of Mount Hagen. They speak a single language, differentiated into nine dialects. Throughout the province in the late twentieth century, singsings became a business, especially at Christmas. Hosts charge admission and sell food and drink. Attendees pursue politics and social affairs: they may arrange marriages, negotiate trades, exchange pigs, and pay compensation to a murdered man's relatives.

### Musical styles
For eight social settings, the Enga maintain distinct styles of singing. To meet evolving cultural needs, they have modified some of them. In particular, the musical style of songs for courting serves for newly composed songs, whose subjects include astronauts, nationhood, and Christian themes. The New Guinea Lutheran Mission and Wabag Lutheran Church have documented and promoted Enga music.

Enga dancing is famous for its line of men with interlocked arms. Standing in place, they bend their knees to a slow and steady drumbeat—making their skirts flip, like a waving curtain. On offbeats, they hiss.

### Dancing

The Enga perform dance-songs (*mali lyingi*) at singsings. Enga dancing is famous for its line of men with interlocked arms (figure 8). Standing in place, dressed in long skirts, they bend their knees to a slow and steady drumbeat, making their skirts flip in unison, like a waving curtain. On offbeats, they hiss. Photographers attending the Mount Hagen Show (held in alternate years) often concentrate on the men of Wabag, whom a postage stamp has featured.

Another famous trait of the costume is a wig, circular and black, worn by each dancer to symbolize strength and handsomeness. Speakers of each dialect use a distinctive style of wig. Each man's wig is made of cuttings of his own hair, kept since adolescence. Inserted in it, bird-of-paradise plumes or long, black feathers evoke an imposing height. On noses and foreheads, men often wear paint, which identifies clan and status. They wear kina shells as breastplates. Girls and women occasionally join the line, standing beside a relative or friend.

The Enga have two other dances. In semicircles, three or four singer-dancers link arms over their shoulders, performing unaccompanied. Larger ensembles, with individuals not touching, focus the performance on a prospective spouse.

### Courting

Adolescents meet at parties organized by adolescent girls, with married aunts or sisters as hosts and chaperones (Duvelle 1974). Invited boys approach the designated site, announcing in songs that they will see the girls at sundown. They pass by,

FIGURE 8    Kundu-playing Enga men dance in a line. Photo by Don Niles, 1986.

singing. At dusk, they return, joking and singing. They enter silently and sit on the men's side. The hostess and her husband serve them food, and the husband and his sons then leave. The girl who organized the party goes to get her girlfriends; in her absence, the boys sing songs of courtship (*enda lakungi*). The girls arrive and sit on the women's side. They too begin to sing. Boys, a few at a time, go over to them. As the singing continues, each boy whispers into the ear of one girl. Girls' songs alternate with boys' songs. Near dawn, both sides sing jointly. Then, while the girls sing, the boys leave.

### Mourning

The Enga musically express grief over a loved one's death. Relatives daub their bodies with white mud and gather at the home of the deceased. Almost in unison, touching the body of the deceased, they wail laments demonstratively, using words of relationship like *father* and *brother*. They sing the final syllable of the word, with the addition of the vowel /o/, on a sustained, diminishing tone. Fearing retaliation from an offended ghost, they avoid using the dead person's name. They usually sing laments in large gatherings, where wailing continues for days.

### Initiation

Male initiation (*sanggai, sandalu*) formerly prepared adolescents for manhood. Five to ten males retreated to a secluded part of the forest, where respected elders taught them magical techniques to counter women's contaminating influences. The elders encouraged them to dream about the clan's future. Emerging from these rites, the initiates celebrated their maturity. Standing shoulder to shoulder with eyes closed, bodies oiled, faces blackened, and wigs adorned with special plumes, they sang initiatory songs (*kongali*), whose texts metaphorically related a boy's love for a girl whom he hoped to marry and told of his aspiration to clan-based leadership and responsibility. The dreamed song about the clan was highly important. With rapt attention, relatives strained to hear each nuance of the sacred lyrics, for they forecast the clan's future.

### Miscellaneous settings

Marriage is an interclan contract. To secure the alliance, the bride's clan gives gifts (pigs, cassowaries, axes, shells, money), and makes speeches of praise and promise. During the transaction, the groom's clanswomen sing nuptial songs (*akali lakungi*).

Songs of victory (*akali konjo lenge*) have two contexts: warfare and exchanges of pigs. After victory in battle, men—usually the younger and more aggressive ones—sing these songs. They stand on promontories overlooking enemy territory, often in the presence of retreating warriors. To impress or intimidate trading partners at exchanges of pigs, they boast of wealth and generosity.

In remote areas, male and female specialists practice sorcery, focusing on sickness, famine, and lost property (Brennan 1977). Its songs (*yainanda palima pingi*) appeal to supernatural forces. To avoid retribution, other songs (*yalyu*) praise offended ghosts.

Apart from the foregoing settings, informal activities invite the performance of other songs. Journeys, men's work (like building houses), and women's work (like gardening) are typical themes. The songs are mostly extemporaneous, though examples called *pindita wee* have retained popularity for generations.

## Poetry

Many Enga lyrics are direct. One, sung by the clan of the deceased to the people who have given compensation, says: "We are brothers, and we thank you for the pigs from Wabag." Others common at singsings in the 1990s include these: "We gathered feathers for decoration; now we are singing; some of the feathers will be broken";

"Though some of our people have died, we still have a healthy community, and we have young men who are growing up"; "When the government comes, land disputes are settled, but we don't always know who will get the best part"; "Our mothers did not give us food because we disobeyed them and went off to fight; we were hungry when we came to Irelya."

Other texts have hidden meanings (Brennan 1970). The text "When I went to *sanggai,* it was cold near the gate; I throw away my things and come home" might mean "You jilted me; you accepted gifts from another." The text "The house shines; when I see it, I want to come: why don't you hide the shining?" might mean "Your body is beautiful; it attracts me: why don't you cover it?" The text "While we came down the hill, we picked some leaves, so you separate them on the rain cape" might mean "We girls gathered together, so now you men come and choose us." Dance-songs praise one's clan, citing pigs, cassowaries, and kina shells.

### The music system

The Enga recognize that certain people have an ability to compose and prefer that performers have strong, resonant voices. Skilled singers, usually elders, strategically position themselves in the line of dancers. A clan's reputation and influence in part depend on the quality of the music it performs. The Enga admire composers who can extemporize imaginative lyrics.

Men's songs have a narrow range and distinctive glides. Informal songs are responsorial, with a leader and a chorus; each phrase varies the initial one. A typical text is a women's song about building houses: "Now I am working; someday I will sleep in a good house; now I am not concerned about these things." Young women sing this before their marriage. These songs have in common an inventory of four essential tones, C–D–E–F or D–E–G–A, of which the lowest is the tonal center.

### Musical instruments

The most important Enga instrument is the kundu (*laiyane*). With hot coals and knives, men hollow out a hardwood log, scraping away the excess until a shell of about 1.5 centimeters remains. The drumhead is the skin of a lizard or a pig, wetted and stretched onto the rim, and sealed there by sap. Tuners stick to its center several pellets of heated resin. In dance-songs, each man grasps his drum at its middle, steadily beating its head with his free hand.

Informally, Enga soloists play end-blown bundle panpipes (*pupe*) and bamboo flutes (*kululu*). The latter have three to five holes for fingering, and measure some 40 centimeters long, with a 3-centimeter bore. Both instruments are commonest in the Kandep area. For amusement, young men play bamboo susaps (*olaiyole*).

—PAUL W. BRENNAN, VIDA CHENOWETH

## SOUTHERN HIGHLANDS PROVINCE

Southern Highlands Province, with a 1990 population of 317,437, lies in the southwest of the region. Mendi is the provincial capital. Colonial powers joined part of the province to Papua, to the south. Its northern and central cultures have many ethnographic parallels with other upland cultures; peoples along its southern and western borders share some traditions with lowland cultures (figure 9). All peoples speak non-Austronesian languages. From the country's first oil well, the Kutubu Petroleum Project pipes petroleum to the southern coast of Gulf Province, where tankers receive it for export.

—DON NILES

### Huli

Culturally and linguistically homogeneous, more than one hundred thousand Huli inhabit the Tagali River Basin and surrounding areas. Their land covers roughly

FIGURE 9   Wearing paint and headdresses typical of lowland cultures, Erave women of Southern Highlands Province dance in a circle. Photo by Don Niles, 1986.

5,200 square kilometers, mainly at altitudes of 1,500 to 2,400 meters. Sweet potatoes are the Huli staple.

The Huli language is a subfamily-level isolate of the West-Central family of East New Guinea Highlands stock of the Trans–New Guinea phylum (Wurm 1977:469). It displays three contrastive speech-tone patterns: low-rising, high-falling, and mid-level. Sentence-terminating intonation marks verbal affixes; marks indicate tonal positions of first syllables (Rule 1977:10; Rule and Rule 1970a, 1970b), and a line under a vowel shows nasalization.

Huli society is egalitarian, with cognatic descent expressed in the formation of clans. In scattered settlements, males and females occupy separate houses. Young men withdraw to the forest to develop survival skills and grow their hair, symbolizing masculine strength and purity. Some join the organization of celibate bachelors, receive magical ginger plants, and wear crescent-shaped ceremonial wigs. After passing tests, they receive common, rounded wigs and panpipes. Some remain bachelors, but most marry.

Sweethearts show affection through poetic stanzas articulated with a two-stringed musical bow (*gáwa̱*) and a susap (*híriyùla*). A man marries by paying his in-laws about fifteen pigs. The couple postpone consummating the marriage for months, but begin gardening and raising pigs. Spouses occupy separate houses, but meet in their gardens. Most marriages are monogamous. Polygynists court additional wives at nocturnal gatherings (*dáwanda*), which only married men and single women attend; the men sing clan-identifying songs (*ū, dáwanda ū̱*), enabling the women to choose their partners.

Huli spirits include God (Datagaliwabe, also named Dataliwabe and Dapobe), departed human spirits, and demons. Myths (*bí hēnene* 'true stories') record Huli history, including the development of language, yodeling, and musical instruments. Ritual practices include mass sacrifices of pigs to avert catastrophes and promote healthy crops, animals, and humans. In the *màli*, a ritual celebrating successful sorcery, kundu-playing men dance; by the 1970s, this genre was commemorating Independence Day and religious celebrations (Pugh-Kitingan 1979a, 1981:11–148).

### Relationships with surrounding cultures

Traditionally, the Huli traded with only their immediate neighbors: the Obena, west-central peoples to the east (Kewa, Mendi, Wage, Wela) and northeast (Ipili, Paiela); the Duna (Yunua) to the northwest; the Duguba, small Papuan Plateau peoples to the south (Beda'muni, Etoro, Kaluli, Onabasulu), of the same language stock as the Duna; and Hewa 'Foreigners' (Fasu, Foe), of Lake Kutubu. Huli in fringe areas sometimes intermarry with the Duna and the Obena.

Social institutions like courtship-related parties and bachelor seclusion also occur among Obena, but their music differs. The two-stringed musical bow, though occasionally found among fringe Duna, seems uniquely Huli. Panpipes and susaps occur throughout west-central peoples, but tunings and music vary. The Huli, the Kewa, and the Samberigi articulate susap performances similarly (Pugh-Kitingan 1982).

Within the area, rituals are traded, adapted, and discarded when ineffective. The *tēge* came from the Obena, but *tēge púlu* from the Duna. The Huli purchase sorcery from the Duna, but *màli* dancing came from the Obena. Some bachelors' rituals also originated with the Obena, and spread from the Huli to the Duna. Some exorcistic practices, costumes, and *yūlu málai* drums were adopted from the Kaluli, modified, then passed on to the Ipili and the Paiela.

Christianity helped unify the area. From 1973 to 1976, some indigenous churches experienced a spiritual revival, starting among the Foe and spreading to the

Wage and the Wela, then to the Huli and the Duna, and finally back to the Huli. It produced outpourings of new Christian songs (some displaying non-Huli melodic sources), which developed into a distinct Huli musical genre.

### Music systems

The Huli have no term for any comprehensive concept of "music." Most perform many vocal and instrumental genres, mostly solo; performers spontaneously compose pieces. Besides magic-controlling recitations (learned from older practitioners), aspiring musicians receive no instruction; to develop skills, they watch and practice.

In musical expression, language is paramount. Apart from drumming (*bà* 'hit'), all vocal and instrumental performance employs the mouth, and is signified by *là* 'speak', as in *hìriyùla là* 'speak with the susap, play the susap'. Poetic articulation characterizes all performances on the double-stringed musical bow and the susap: while the vocal cords remain inactive, the oral cavity reshapes the acoustical energy of the instrument. When men play long panpipes, they often whisper phrases.

Huli poetry develops the imagery of parable words (*bì yōbage*). Stanzas typically consist of multiple repeated lines, each containing a changing noun. Alternating names of places and clans identify individuals or express yearning for one's homeland. The Huli say thoughts form in the heart, rise in breath from the lungs to the mouth, and roll off the tongue as words. Language determines musical structure: linguistic tones affect melodic tones, and linguistic articulation determines musical pace and rhythm. Where context or instrumental technique disallows linguistic articulation, music imitates yodeling—the precursor of human speech, according to Huli myths (Pugh-Kitingan 1977, 1984, 1992).

Pitch is described as *dìndiha* 'underneath', *dòmbena* 'in-between', or *dāliga* 'above'. Various expressions—*lō pòdo ìri dāli* 'break the speaking up and down' and *lōpodopoda* and *lōpodalu* 'going up and down'—describe melodies. *Lō pòdo* (also *lō pòda*) 'breaking the speaking' denotes pauses and codas. Another expression, *gīlinine òre pōdolene* or *pōdolene*, implies breaking a decorated length into pieces. *Gīlini, gīli,* and *gīligili* (zigzag patterns in using cane to bind artifacts) suggest movement up and down. Men's singing on a level pitch below melodies, the continuous sound of the outer *gáwa* string below inner-strand melodies, and the underlying pitch of the longest bundle panpipe blown in passing to surrounding tubes, are denoted *lā āmuhà* 'speak, stand toward *āmu* direction'. This direction lies along a valley, or horizontal; musically, it means 'going along straight' (Pugh-Kitingan 1979b:6–9).

For melodic structure, each genre utilizes a characteristic cell. The simplest is the major third, occasionally condensed to a minor third or inverted as a minor sixth; it occurs widely in yodeling, magic, and legal declamations. Other common cells, expressed in numeral notation, include: 134 for *ū* and *gáwa*; 127 or 127♭ for stories and some magic; 321 for laments. Panpipe music uses combinations of cells.

### Vocal music

Huli vocal music encompasses solo and collective yodeling [see UNDERSTANDING MUSIC: TIMBRE], solo laments of love, collective singing, laments, storytelling, legal declamations, and magic-controlling recitations.

#### Singing

The Huli describe two genres as singing (*ìba gàna* 'trickling water'): men's collective songs (*ū, dáwanda ū*) and hymns (*Ngōdenaga ìba gàna* 'God's songs'). Men sing *ū* in falsetto using three pitches, the upper two lying a major third and a fourth above the lowest. Any man starts a stanza by creating the first line, using the higher pitches. The penultimate line contains only two words, a name and a word glossable as 'and'. Some men sing continuously on the lowest pitch. Lines begin with an upward then downward glide caused by contracting abdominal muscles after inhalation. During interlinear pauses, the soloist says the changing name for the next line. These names, referring to places or clans, identify individuals present.

During the religious revival of 1973–1976, the indigenous church created hymns, which men and women, sitting separately, now use in worship. As with *ū*, some people sing continuously on a tonic. Five-tone melodies among upper pitches follow a repeated two-phrase pattern derived from non-Huli sources, including Foe Christian singing and string-band music. A free translation of a typical hymn is: "When Jesus comes, he'll bring two rewards. One is eternal life; the other, death. That's when we'll receive the reward of eternal life, so let's stand strong."

*Pīlipè*

The term *pīlipè* denotes an end-blown flute and a musical genre performed by a young unmarried man abandoned by his sweetheart. He sits outside, wailing loud, spontaneous, falsetto stanzas, punctuating ends of lines with blasts on the flute. Linguistic tones determine small-scale melodic patterns, with terminal intonation producing cascading contours. Three main descending pitches are used, separated by a tone and a semitone. A text illustrates the poetic style of the genre.

| | |
|---|---|
| Nògo māmarume, | Pig's mother many. |
| Nògo māmarume. | Pig's mother many, |
| Lài lī wīaga yàgo. | Lài flood might put down. |
| Mánda bìalu bībe. | Think do, do it, |
| | |
| Nògo māmarume, | Pig's mother many. |
| Làngobi lī wīaga yàgo, | Làngobi flood might put down, |
| Mánda bìalu bībe. | Think do, do it. |
| | |
| Nògo māmarume, | Pig's mother many. |
| Tīgawi lī wīaga yàgo, | Tīgawi flood might put down, |
| Mánda bìalu bībe, | Think do, do it, |
| Māganeao. | Darling [lit. 'niece']. |
| | |
| Nògo māmarume | Pig's mother many, |
| Tùmane ìbali wīaga yàgo, | Tùmane flood might put down, |
| Mánda bìalu bībe. | Think do, do it. |
| | |
| Àli laro. | Àli, I'm saying. |
| Gàgali ìbali wīaga yàgo, | Gàgali flood might put down, |
| Mánda bìalu bībe. | Think do, do it. |

A free translation explains contextually understood meanings: "Make up your mind, darling. My mother and female kin have many pigs for your bride-price. If you desert me, the Lài, Làngobi, Tīgawi, Tùmane, Àli, and Gàgali rivers (from my mother's clan's lands) might flood: my female kin (with whom you'd live if you married me) might vent their anger against you."

*Crying*

Crying (*dùgu*) includes all genres cried by Huli women while mourning, such as *ō*, *kīabudugu*, and *dùgu* for a dead child. Walking together to the crying house (*dùguanda*), where the body of the deceased is laid out, women cry *ō*, whose vowel, sustained on a level pitch, traverses the countryside as other women repeat it, announcing the death. Any woman walking alone to the *dùguanda* cries her own poetic lament for the deceased. Men, barred from the *dùguanda*, stand guard outside.

Inside the *dùguanda*, a skilled soloist cries *kīabudugu*, a loud, impassioned lament, recounting events surrounding the death. She uses three pitches, each a tone apart. Linguistic tones determine melodic patterns. Lines use the higher pitches before falling to the lowest at the ends, when other women join in crying *ō*. These pieces are not cried for a child's death, which women commemorate only by crying *ō*. Recalling a child months after its death, the mother may cry a poetic lament.

### Magic-controlling recitations

People of either sex learn magic-controlling recitations (*gāmu*) from older practitioners or from spirits. Context allows for wide stylistic variations, from secret mumbling to loud performing. Women use *dàgia gāmu* to help their daughters obtain desirable husbands; when painting girls for dances, this is named *hàre gāmu* (from *hàre* 'ochre facial paint'). Mothers with sickly babies can pay an older practitioner to perform *wāneigini gāmu* ('children magic'). After removing a child from its mother's hearing, the old woman mutters her *gāmu* while rubbing clay and spittle on its body. Women perform *húbibi gāmu* to make men appear invisible to their enemies in battle; *húbibi gāmu* also protect a husband from another woman's charms.

Men also use magic. Bachelors perform *mānda gāmu* to make their hair grow and perform *ìba gìya gāmu* to receive their ginger plants. Both genres use falsetto, with melodic structures that resemble those for telling stories. During initiation rituals, specialists loudly perform *lìruali āwa* for healthy crops, pigs, and initiates. Male exorcists perform *bílogua* while performing farewell *dáwe* (*dáwe bílogua*) and hitting their long *dìndanao tàbage* drums.

### Other genres

Huli tales (*bí tè*, combining *bí* 'talk, words' and *tè* 'story') are melodic prose recitations, told at night in men's and women's houses. They use three main pitches: the highest lies a tone above the central pitch, which functions like a tonic; the lowest lies a semitone or tone below the middle one. Periodically, to assist the flow of the story, listeners interject *é* 'yes' on the central pitch. Tales sometimes feature historical characters, but they are invented stories, not myths.

In heightened speech, eminent male genealogists make legal declamations (*dámba bí*). During interclan legal disputes, an orator stands between opposing parties. Turning from side to side, he recites facts, silencing debate.

### **Musical instruments**

Huli instruments include a susap, three drums, three musical bows, and three panpipes. Apart from drumming, which accompanies men's dancing, these instruments are played solo.

### Susap

The susap (*híriyùla*, also *híliyùla*, *híliyùle*, and *yùlambe*) is cut from wild bamboo and shined by being passed through ashes. Twine is affixed to the basal end. Holding the instrument between the lips, the player jerks the twine to vibrate the tongue of the instrument. Men and women play the susap in contexts used for the musical bow. Its performance features poetic articulation. Inarticulate interstanzaic sections imitate Huli collective yodeling (Pugh 1975; Pugh-Kitingan 1977, 1980). The stanza in fig-

FIGURE 10 Excerpt from Amele's performance on a Huli lamellaphone (*híriyùla*) at Bebenete in 1978. Transcription by Jacqueline Pugh-Kitingan.

ure 10 uses cloud imagery punctuated by the phrase *àyago nēdò* 'I am in a state of having experienced sorrow'.

### TRACK 11    Drums

Kundus (*tàbage, làyano tàbage*) have undecorated, somewhat hourglass-shaped bodies of *làyano* wood, with single heads of cuscus (*tía bàlena*) skin. Held in the left hand, they are hit with the right open palm. The *tòmbena tàbage* sounds *dòmbeni* or *tòmbeni* 'in-between'; the long *dìndanao tàbage* sounds *dìndiha* 'underneath'.

Male dancers play the common *tòmbena tàbage* at *màli* celebrations. In two facing rows, wearing ceremonial costumes with crescent-shaped red or black wigs, they jump sideways while hitting their drums in a simple syncopated rhythm.

Only male mediums play *dìndanao tàbage*. During exorcisms, two or three exorcists, wearing feathered headdresses and women's skirts, run around a bonfire beating their drums; they stop periodically to perform *bílogua* into the fire. Their comical attire and running supposedly make malevolent demons laugh, and *bílogua* stanzas suggest the demons should go far away. Exorcists sometimes use the rare decorated *yūlu málai* (or *málai*), which sounds *dàliga* 'above'; with a fishtail-shaped body and a lizard-skin head, it was formerly imported from Papuan Plateau peoples.

### TRACK 18    The two-stringed bow

The *gáwa* is a two-stringed, orally resonated, strummed bow, through which performers articulate spontaneously created poetry. It has a soft, clear, shimmering sound. The Huli consider its performance the supreme artistic achievement.

Makers pass a strong, flexible piece of wood through hot ashes. The bowstring and plectrum are traditionally *tùgubili*-vine root; from the 1970s, makers also used wire, strummed with *ígibu* cane or bamboo. The bow is mouthed at its shorter end. The left hand holds the longer end, while the right hand strums the bowstring with a plectrum near the mouth. The inner string sounds a major third higher than the outer; when stopped by the left thumb, the inner pitch rises a semitone.

Men and women play two-stringed bows. The structure and technique of playing vary by sex. The woman's bow spans 20 to 30 centimeters. Its string hooks around the shorter end; both strands pass under the longer arm and wind up to the tip. A woman holds it horizontally or with the longer arm pointing downward [see MUSICAL INSTRUMENTS, figure 1c]. While stopping the inner strand with the thumb from above, she strums the strings with a plectrum. The man's bow, spanning 50 centimeters, is held with the longer end pointing upward. Its strands wind along and pass under the shorter arm together, and cross over the longer arm before winding up to the tip. A player holds the plectrum below the string, strumming while stopping the inner strand with his left thumbnail from below.

Performance on two-stringed bows features the articulation of poetry. The most audible pitches are the fundamentals and first partials of the open strands. Linguistic tones determine inner-strand melodies, while the outer-strand pitch sounds continuously below. Inarticulate introductions, interludes, and codas use upper partials of the open strands, imitating Huli collective yodeling. Texts are figurative: a text expressing a woman's love for her husband is: "I am being wetted by rain from Ìbai, Àluya, Àndama, Gúrubu, Gàngabu, and Màndalo"—her husband's clans.

### The one-stringed bow

The *hìbulu báralu* is a one-stringed symmetrical bow, 50 to 60 centimeters long. It is played by men and boys as a pastime. It does not serve to articulate poetry. It is rare, almost obsolete. If the string is loose, tuning nooses of twine are tied around wood and bowstring, separating a central length from end sections. For resonance, the player holds the bow downward, with the string in front of his mouth. The right thumb activates the string from above, and the left thumbnail periodically stops it from below, raising its fundamental a major third.

*Hìbulu báralu* music imitates *màli ìwa* yodeling, with two techniques: *hìbulu* involves alternately blowing and sucking air across the bowstring, suggesting *tàbage* rhythms; *báralu* involves softly resonating string upper partials. Performances containing some *hìbulu* sections are in *hìbulu* style; those without, in *báralu* style.

### The hunting bow

To pass time on the hunt when other instruments are unavailable, men play the hunting bow (*dānda*). It has a strong blackpalm bow, spanning 1.5 meters. Plaited-cane binding affixes a split-bamboo string to the bow. The arrows are about 1.3 meters long. During warfare or when hunting, men clutch bows and arrows in their left hands, holding single arrows in their right to shoot. The *dānda* becomes a musical bow when a man orally resonates the string like the *hìbulu báralu* while hitting it with the blunt end of an arrow. The *dānda* only imitates *màli ìwa*. Loud crashing sounds of arrow hitting bowstring suggest *tàbage* rhythms, while the *ìwa* is freely imitated among resonated upper partials.

### Bundle panpipes

Huli men play bamboo bundle panpipes, of three kinds: the common, medium-sized, seven-tubed *gúlupòbe*; the rare, longer *gùlungùlu* (also *ngùlungùlu*); and the short, eight-tubed *púlugèla* (also *wélagèla* or *gèlagi*). Their sound is soft and breathy (Peters 1975). Men play common *gúlupòbe* and *púlugèla* by day, on long journeys; they keep *gùlungùlu* at home for playing at night. They play *gúlupòbe* and *gùlungùlu* upon reaching adulthood and wearing wigs. They carefully tune and personally label the pipes. The longest pipe of a *gúlupòbe* measures about 60 centimeters; that of the *gùlungùlu* reaches about 90 centimeters. Both instruments have seven pipes, the shortest closed by a bamboo node. Pipes are cut from *bè hàraya*, bundled with the longest pipe in the center and bound with twine or grass. In numeral notation, the tuning is 1345713 or 13457♭13. The closed pipe has pitch 5.

FIGURE 11
Excerpt from Dambago's performance on the Huli small bundle panpipe (*púlugèla*), imitating the Huli genre *màli ìwa*; at Bebenete, 1978. Transcription by Jacqueline Pugh-Kitingan.

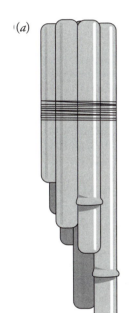

(a)

Playing *gúlupòbe* or *gùlungùlu*, men alternate breaths utilizing pipes 1, 3, 4, and 5 with those using higher-pitched pipes. Tone 1 functions like a tonic below melodies of other lower-range tones. Men sometimes whisper courtship-related words as they blow. The lyrics are short fragmented statements, unlike those of other Huli sung poetry.

A man plays the short *púlugèla* only after he has fathered children. Its performance imitates *màli ìwa* and *gèla* styles of yodeling (figure 11). Consisting of four open and four closed pipes, about 25 centimeters long (figure 12), it is held in the right hand with the three longest (closed) pipes against the fingers and the three shortest (open) pipes against the thumb. Its tuning varies. Discordantly breathy timbre enhances the imitation of yodeling.

—JACQUELINE PUGH-KITINGAN

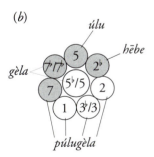

(b)

FIGURE 12    The Huli small bundle panpipe in front view and cross section; the shaded pipes are closed. Drawings by Jacqueline Pugh-Kitingan.

## REFERENCES

Brennan, Paul W. 1970. "Enga Referential Symbolism: Verbal and Visual." In *Exploring Enga Culture: Studies in Missionary Anthropology: Second Anthropological Conference of the New Guinea Lutheran Mission,* ed. Paul W. Brennan, 17–50. Wapenamanda: New Guinea Lutheran Mission.

———. 1977. *Let Sleeping Snakes Lie: Central Enga Religious Belief and Ritual.* Adelaide: Australian Association for the Study of Religions.

Brown, Paula. 1978. *Highland Peoples of New Guinea.* Cambridge: Cambridge University Press.

Chenoweth, Vida. 1969. "An Investigation of the Singing Styles of the Dunas." *Oceania* 39:218–230.

———. 1974. "The Music of the Usarufas." 2 vols. Ph.D. dissertation, University of Auckland.

———. 1976. *Musical Instruments of Papua New Guinea.* Ukarumpa, Papua New Guinea: Summer Institute of Linguistics.

———. 1979. *The Usarufas and their Music.* Museum Series, 5. Dallas: Summer Institute of Linguistics.

Duvelle, Frédéric. 1974. *Enga Traditional Music.* Institute of Papua New Guinea Studies. LP disk.

Feil, D. K. 1987. *The Evolution of Highland*

*Papua New Guinea Societies.* Cambridge: Cambridge University Press.

Feld, Steven. 1981. "'Flow Like a Waterfall': The Metaphors of Kaluli Musical Theory." *International Council for Traditional Music Yearbook* 13:22–47.

———. 1985. *The Kaluli of Papua Niugini; Weeping and Song.* Bärenreiter-Musicaphon BM 30 SL 2702. LP disk.

———. 1990. *Sound and Sentiment: Birds, Weeping, Poetics, and Song in Kaluli Expression.* 2nd ed. Philadelphia: University of Pennsylvania Press.

———. 1991. *Voices of the Rainforest.* Rykodisc RCD 10173. Compact disc.

Franklin, Karl J. 1970. "Metaphorical Songs in Kewa." In *Pacific Linguistic Studies in Honour of Arthur Capell,* ed. Stephan A. Wurm and Donald C. Laycock, 985–995. Pacific Linguistics, C 13. Canberra: Australian National University.

Hays, Terence E. 1986. "Sacred Flutes, Fertility, and Growth in the Papua New Guinea Highlands." *Anthropos* 81(4–6):435–453.

Herdt, Gilbert H. 1981. *Guardians of the Flutes.* New York: McGraw-Hill.

Jablonko, Allison. 1968a. "Dance and Daily Life

among the Maring People of New Guinea: A Cinematographic Analysis of Movement Style." Ph.D. dissertation, Columbia University.

———. 1968b. *Maring in Motion.* 16 mm. College Park: Pennsylvania State University.

———. 1968c. "Maring Film Project." Human Studies Film Archives 84.14.1. Washington, D.C.: Smithsonian Institution.

———. 1991. "Patterns of Daily Life in the Dance of the Maring of New Guinea." *Visual Anthropology* 4:367–377.

Jablonko, Allison, and Elizabeth Kagan. 1988. "An Experiment in Looking: Reexamining the Process of Observation." *The Drama Review* 32(4):148–163.

Josephides, Lisette. 1982. "Kewa Stories and Songs (Southern Highlands Province)." *Oral History* 10(2):1–86.

Koyati, Peandui. 1979. "Traditional Songs of the Baiyer River." *Oral History* 7(2):42–106.

Paia, Robert, and Andrew Strathern. 1977. *Beneath the Andaiya Tree: Wiru Songs.* Boroko: Institute of Papua New Guinea Studies.

Peters, Bronwyn L. 1975. "Huli Music: Its Cultural Context, Musical Instruments and Gulupobe Music." B.A. thesis, Monash University.

Pugh, Jacqueline. 1975. "Communication, Language and Huli Music: A Preliminary Survey." B.A. thesis, Monash University.

Pugh-Kitingan, Jacqueline. 1977. "Huli Language and Instrumental Performance." *Ethnomusicology* 21:205–232.

———. 1979a. "The Huli and Their Music." *Hemisphere* 23:84–89.

———. 1979b. "Analogy in Huli Ethnomusicology." Paper presented at the Third National Conference of the Musicological Society of Australia, Monash University, Clayton.

———. 1980. "Language Articulation Using Musical Instruments in the Southern Highlands of Papua New Guinea." Abstract of paper presented in the "Structured Session on Acoustical Aspects of Australasian Music." *Tenth International Congress on Acoustics* 1:151.

———. 1981. "An Ethnomusicological Study of the Huli of the Southern Highlands, Papua New Guinea." Ph.D. dissertation, University of Queensland.

———. 1982. "Language Communication and Instrumental Music in the Southern Highlands of Papua New Guinea—Comments on the Huli and Samberigi Cases." *Musicology* 7:104–119.

———. 1984. "Speech-Tone Realisation in Huli Music." In *Problems and Solutions: Occasional Essays in Musicology Presented to Alice M. Moyle,* ed. Jamie C. Kassler and Jill Stubington, 94–120. Sydney: Hale & Iremonger.

———. 1992. "Huli Yodelling and Instrumental Performance." In *Sound and Reason: Music and Essays in Honour of Gordon D. Spearritt,* ed. Warren A. Bebbington and Royston Gustavson, 64–124. St. Lucia: Faculty of Music, University of Queensland.

Rappaport, Roy A. 1968. *Pigs for Ancestors.* New Haven, Conn.: Yale University Press.

Rule, W. Murray. 1977. *A Comparative Study of the Foe, Huli and Pole Languages of Papua New Guinea.* Oceania Linguistic Monograph 20. Sydney: University of Sydney.

Rule, W. Murray, and Joan E. Rule. 1970a. *Statement of the Phonology and Grammar of the Huli Language.* Tari: Asia Pacific Christian Mission.

———. 1970b. *Huli–English, English–Huli Dictionary.* Tari: Asia Pacific Christian Mission.

Strathern, Andrew J. 1971. *The Rope of Moka.* Cambridge: Cambridge University Press.

———. 1972. *One Father, One Blood.* Canberra: Australia National University Press.

———, ed. 1974. *Melpa Amb Kenan.* Port Moresby: Institute of Papua New Guinea Studies.

Talyaga, Kundapen. 1973. *Eda Nemago: Meri Singsing Poetry of the Yandapo Engas.* Papua Pocket Poets, 40. Port Moresby: no publisher.

———. 1975. *Modern Enga Songs.* Boroko: Institute of Papua New Guinea Studies.

Weiner, James F. 1991. *The Empty Place: Poetry, Space, and Being among the Foi of Papua New Guinea.* Bloomington: Indiana University Press.

Wirz, Paul. 1952. "Die Enga." *Zeitschrift für Ethnologie* 77(1):7–56.

Wurm, Stephen. A. 1977. "Eastern Central Trans–New Guinea Phylum Languages." In *Papuan Languages and the New Guinea Linguistic Scene,* ed. Stephen A. Wurm, 915–924. Canberra: Pacific Linguistics.

# Mamose Region of Papua New Guinea

*Don Niles*

*Richard Scaglion*

*Vida Chenoweth*

*Gordon Donald Spearritt*

*Yoichi Yamada*

*Robert Reigle*

*John R. Kelsey*

*Alice Pomponio*

**East Sepik Province**
**West Sepik Province**
**Madang Province**
**Morobe Province**

FIGURE 1   A mask from the Siasi Islands, covered with bark cloth and mounted with cassowary feathers. Hamburgisches Museum für Völkerkunde.

The Mamose Region (sometimes called Momase) includes the provinces along the northern coast of New Guinea: West Sepik, East Sepik, Madang, Morobe. Its name derives from parts of the names Madang, Morobe, and Sepik. With 31 percent of the national area, it supports 16 percent of the population.

Most of the region is north of the central chain of mountains. In the west, the Sepik River, the second longest in the country, drains the western part of the central depression. To the east of its mouth is the Ramu River; farther east, near Lae, is the Markham River. The Torricelli Mountains, near the border with Indonesia, run west to east, in West Sepik Province. On the border of Madang and Morobe, the Finisterre and Saruwaged ranges rise to about 4 kilometers.

Linguistically, the region is complex. Non-Austronesian languages predominate, in several phyla: Trans–New Guinea, Sepik-Ramu, Torricelli, Sko, Kwomtari. Austronesian languages, which dot the coast, go deeply inland only in the area of the Markham River.

## Singsings

Several areas of the region have distinctive types of singing. In the Teptep area (on the border of Morobe and Madang), the Yupno and other peoples perform *konggap,* personal melodies sometimes sung simultaneously to the unison beating of kundus. Distinctively too, these people tune drumheads by smearing moist clay on them (Niles 1992b). People of the Middle Sepik area sing clan-specific songs (Wassmann 1982); a related people, the Manambu, have men's songs with texts that recall failed sexual affairs (Harrison 1982): in both cases, understanding the meanings of the songs is possible only for those who know the mythological stories of creation.

As in the Papuan Region, the northern coast had trade-based networks and routes. In one, Siasi Islanders joined mainlanders with people of New Britain, trading many artifacts, including kundus, songs, dances, and masks (figure 1). Their status popularized the *sia,* a dance ordinarily performed at night. Decorated with triangular headdresses, men perform intricate mimetic choreography, accompanied by kundu-beaten patterns and their own singing; on the periphery, women dance and sing in pairs. The *sia* has become a symbol of the region. Nationwide, children perform it at school festivals. It has spread throughout Morobe, coastal West New Britain, and parts of Madang. Its origin is obscure, but Tami Island and the Siasi Islands are likely sources.

*Kanam,* another important regional song-dance, is popular farther west. It apparently originated on Karkar Island, but has spread through much of western Madang and into East Sepik. Owners may sell the rights to perform certain *kanam*; they appoint teachers to make buyers follow correct procedures. *Kanam* frequently imitate the movements of animals. The adoption of dances of other areas reaches particular importance among the Arapesh (East Sepik Province), described as an importing culture, which changes dances and rituals according to the availability of new forms (Mead 1938).

## Musical instruments

Instrumental ensembles have ritual importance in the region, particularly for male initiations, but their distribution and traits vary (Niles 1992a). The following ensembles, distinctive of various parts of the region, assist in defining subregions. The most conspicuously distinguishing regional musical instruments are flutes.

### Flutes

#### End-blown

At the near end, some end-blown bamboo flutes have a projection, on which the player, always a male, touches his lips, directing air down to the opposite rim. These flutes have no holes for fingering. Their far end is closed. In initiations, people of the West Sepik coast, across the border in Irian Jaya Province of Indonesia, use an ensemble of such flutes (Kunst 1967:130, fig. 18; Oosterwal 1961:228–237; Sande 1907:307, pl. 29). In the Wutung-language area, people play these flutes in large ensembles: in the *bö chu* ensemble, paired flutes of the same length and pitch share a name; men play the pairs in alternation. Many coastal peoples who speak languages of the Sko phylum favor such ensembles.

At the coastal border of Madang and Morobe, men do not use synchronized instrumental ensembles to create spirits' voices (*tambaran*). Instead, they play *tambaran* instruments individually or asynchronously. They also play long, end-blown, bamboo flutes with holes for fingering.

#### Side-blown

Side-blown flutes, a famous feature of *tambaran* music in the region, have received much attention (Graf 1950; Spearritt 1979). Along the coast, such instruments occur from Sissano (in the west), past the mouth of the Ramu, to Hatzfeldthaven (Madang Province). To the south, the border of the distribution of such instruments runs along the mountains of the highlands. Isolated areas of paired-flute ensembles occur along the Rai Coast and in south Morobe Province.

Speakers of many languages in the Sepik-Ramu Phylum use paired side-blown flutes, averaging 2 meters long. Playing exploits many of the natural harmonics of the tubes. The fundamentals of a pair often vary by a tone. Players usually sound their instruments in alternation, creating intricate melodies.

These flutes often play unaccompanied. In the Lower Sepik area, they accompany singing. The Iatmul join them with other instruments during clansongs (*namoi*). Though highly important in Iatmul society, they are absent from the Abelam, a neighboring, linguistically related people. The word *wapi,* used by the Iatmul to name flutes, is used by the Abelam to name long yams; therefore, *wapi* may psychologically mean "symbol of male prestige in phallic form" (Forge 1971:313). These flutes are much longer than their counterparts in the eastern and central Highland Region, but similarities in technical methods and secret associations occur between them. They possibly entered the highlands along the Ramu River.

Ensembles employing more than two side-blown flutes occur in a few areas along the Sepik River, but they are much more common in the south, especially in the area of the Karawari and Korosameri rivers, where up to fourteen flutes are employed. Peoples that use flutes in ensemble also have paired flutes. Flutes played in ensembles are often shorter than paired instruments, less than a meter long. Such sizes are somewhat longer than those of highland peoples to the southeast, but Sepik peoples do not vary pitches by covering and uncovering the far end of the instrument, as is standard in the highlands.

*Piston*

In parts of the Huon Peninsula and the Rai Coast, piston flutes produce the voice of *tambaran.* A man inserts a thick stem into the far end of an end-blown bamboo flute; while blowing into the flute, he pushes the stem upward, shortening the air column in the tube to raise the pitch.

### Trumpets

Two contrasting ensembles of trumpets appear in close geographic proximity. End-blown wooden conical trumpets, played only by men, are not secret. They occur only in the western Sepik area, from Bewani southward to Green River. Paired instruments, widely distributed throughout the border area, commonly announce the killing of a pig or a cassowary; in some rituals, the beating of kundus joins in the sound. Ensembles of five trumpets, with one to three optional bass trumpets, occur only in the Waina-language area and in adjacent villages of the Amanab-language area, where they ritually serve in the Waina *ida* and the Amanab *yangis* (Gell 1975; Juillerat 1992; Sanger and Sorrell 1975).

In contrast to the open use of wooden trumpets, ensembles of bamboo trumpets, occasionally with one trumpeter also beating a kundu, are an important part of *tambaran* activities. The far end of such instruments is open. The node of the near end is partially bored or cut out, to create a hole for blowing. Such ensembles extend from about the Kwanga in the west, through the area of the Mountain Arapesh in the north, eastward to the Kamasau. Ensembles vary from two to nine instruments. Each instrument produces one pitch (Tuzin 1980).

### Garamuts

The people of much of the region use garamuts. Just across the Indonesian border, these instruments disappear; and even on Papua New Guinean territory near the border, in the Sko phylum area, garamuts are more usually suspended, hardwood beams than hollowed-out logs. Continuing east, garamuts occur along the coast up to the Madang-Morobe border, where they suddenly disappear; they sporadically reappear at Lae and on New Britain Island (Niles 1983). Inland incursions of garamuts follow major riverine basins, especially those of the Sepik and the Ramu. In most of the region, one player jolts a garamut with a long stick. In the Middle Sepik, one player jolts it with short sticks held in each hand, alternating with another player.

### Voice-modifying instruments

From about the Korak-language area eastward to Saidor (Rai Coast), voice-modifying instruments create the voice of *tambaran.* Most are of gourd or bamboo. Inaccurate reports abound: these instruments are not trumpets (in which the player forces air through vibrating lips); nor are they megaphones (which merely amplify voices), or

FIGURE 2    In the *ida* ritual of Punda Village, West Sepik, men play end-blown wooden trumpets while masked dancers perform. Photo by Don Niles, 1986.

flutes (in which the player directs air against an edge): instead, the player sings or shouts into these instruments, modifying his voice (Niles 1989).

Gourd instruments—played with voice-modifying bamboos with split sides, kundus, garamuts, and voice—are the distinctive components of the *tambaran* ensembles of the Saidor area. Men play other, longer, voice-modifying bamboos separately. Voice-modifying instruments also occur around Maprik (East Sepik Province), where men insert the far ends of the tubes into headless kundus, laid on the ground (Tuzin 1980).

### Other instruments and ensembles

The preceding ensembles, though prominent within the region, are not the only important instruments there, nor must all peoples in the region fit into one of these classes. Any people that uses a secret instrument is likely to use the swung slat, which occurs in much of the region. All peoples of the region use kundus. Perhaps uniquely for Papua New Guinea, in the Ok-speaking area (along the border between West Sepik and Western), youths during initiation gain knowledge of playing kundus and susaps, considered small equivalents of kundus (Brumbaugh 1979:241–244, 360–378). In other areas, kundus have no link with initiation. The Adzera, of Morobe, make a distinctive clay kundu (May and Tuckson 1982:143–144).

In the Imonda and Amanab area, north of the Ok, each male dancer in the *ida* and the *yangis* wears a mask, symbolic paint, a belt with a pig's bone embedded in it, and a gourd attached to his penis. By thrusting his pelvis, he flips his penis upward so the gourd clicks against the bone. The clicking accompanies an ensemble of wooden trumpets (*fuf*) (figure 2).

## EAST SEPIK PROVINCE

East Sepik Province derives its name from the Sepik River, which runs its length. The administrative headquarters is Wewak. The 1990 population, of 254,371, live along the river and its tributaries, and in the Torricelli and Prince Alexander mountains to the north, and the Hunstein Range to the south. The fame of wooden carvings made in the province has attracted tourists. Austronesian languages are spoken in only a

few coastal areas and on offshore islands. Many of the non-Austronesian languages belong to the Sepik-Ramu and Torricelli phyla, and many smaller peoples are represented.
   —DON NILES

## Abelam

About sixty thousand Abelam speak intergraded dialects of Ambulas, a non-Austronesian language of the Ndu family. The Samukundi Abelam, on whom this sketch concentrates, densely populate the foothills of the Prince Alexander Mountains (Scaglion 1997).

Abelam musical performances usually occur in either of two places: for male initiations, within the ceremonial house; for public rituals and social occasions, on the ceremonial ground in front of it. At the center of this ground lies the moonwoman (*baapmutaakwa*), a smooth, roughly spherical white stone about 20 centimeters in diameter, on which social dancing, to songs called *bira*, focuses. A ring of men, each carrying a kundu in one hand, circles it counterclockwise. With the palm of the free hand, they strike the drumheads. Drummers take turns, but the best play longest. The meters are irregular, in patterns that mark out sung phrases. The tempo starts slow, and repeatedly accelerates and decelerates.

Dancers of both sexes, often with linked arms or hands, circle the drummers counterclockwise in a normal gait. A chorus of women stand inside this circle, facing the moonwoman. Performances are casual; individuals come and go at will. Each event lasts all night, with only short interruptions; it ends at daybreak. At large celebrations, singing and dancing may fill several nights.

Festivals involving the long yam (*Dioscorea alata*) are momentous Abelam occasions. Male prestige hinges on success in growing large tubers, which may exceed 3 meters long. Men display their finest tubers, which intervillage rivals inspect and measure. Later, the growers give the tubers to the rivals, who try to return yams as large as or larger than those received. (Returning a like-sized yam ends the rivalry; returning a larger one continues it.) After the inspection and measuring, men take turns walking the ceremonial ground, brandishing spears, giving brief speeches, and performing songs called *minja*. When the yams are unusually large, initiated men hold a *kaangu* ceremony, which noninitiates may not attend; texts of its songs focus on sacred ancestors.

Singsings of many types accompany male-initiation ceremonies. In stylized and symbolic motifs, costumes combine shells, feathers, flowers, and paint. Particularly distinctive are men's headdresses, woven from split cane and adorned with colorful feathers. At successive initiatory stages, headdresses increase in size. For the final stage, they tower 3 to 6 meters above dancers' heads.

### Musical instruments

Most Abelam instruments serve ceremonial functions. Two idiophones, the susap and the garamut, are exceptions. People play susaps infrequently, according to whim; the instruments do not have high cultural significance. Garamuts (*mi*) have utilitarian and ritual functions. Hollowed from hardwood logs (usually *Vitex cofassus*), they adorn most main Abelam hamlets, summon people to meetings, signal important occasions (deaths, harvests, feasts), and accomplish certain tasks (calling home a person or a lost pig, warning a rainmaker or sorcerer to desist). Intricately carved garamuts stay hidden inside the ceremonial houses, where only initiated men may see them. These instruments form trios: the lead garamut (*maama mi*) has the lowest pitch; the second (*kwaté mi*), an intermediate size and pitch; the third (*nyégél mi*), the highest pitch.

In ritual contexts, people play several aerophones: swung slats, vessel flutes (carved from nuts), conch trumpets, and bamboo aerophones. With carved wood and other objects, these instruments form a class of sacred items (*mayéra*), displayed to initiates during initiations and called spirits' voices; later, men teach initiates how to play.

The only Abelam membranophone is the kundu (*kaang*), carved from one piece of wood. Stretched lizard skin covers one end of it. To control the pitch and timbre, the center of the head bears waxy pellets.

### Musical genres

The Abelam have two basic genres of song: *minja,* normally performed solo by men; and *bira,* performed by mixed-sex ensembles. Solo singing ordinarily occurs during yam festivals, village meetings (to resolve conflicts or help heal individuals), and the performance of myths and tales. Typically, men perform in turn, each singing one song.

In the context of yam festivals, the performances of *minja* become musical duels. Texts recount incidents in veiled, metaphorical diction: a leaf floating on water may represent the body of an enemy, killed near a river. The performer may sing of birds or flowers, but most adult listeners grasp his hidden messages. The following text names only the *nyaamio* 'pigeon', but informed adult listeners would know the singer alludes to his clansmen, whose totem is the Victoria crowned pigeon (*Goura victoria*).

> Nyaamio apwi yénayéyéna wakwe,
> Me me saapé Yaangéwaaru Bawungaalé du.
> Wakwe yu wutkéndiyau pwiya kén dé:
> Vetik dé vi ya, kwupuk dé vi ya.

> Men of the Crowned Pigeon clan,
> Go and tell of Bawungaalé of Yaangéwaaru.
> Talk about this decorated warrior:
> He speared his enemies by twos and threes.

These songs, routinely meant to insult, are frequently answered with rejoinder *minja,* relating other incidents.

An important genre of solo song, the *ngwayé kundi* 'stopping talk', can interrupt fighting or warfare. The singer hoists in the air a leaf of the *naaréndu,* a symbol of peace. He sings the song and gives a short speech. While he is performing, people must suspend hostilities. *Ngwayé kundi* also herald the settlement of disputes.

Mixed-sex singing, *bira,* associated with yam festivals and male-initiation ceremonies, occurs typically at night. At yam festivals, *bira* have polyphony in two parts: one for male singer-drummers, and one for a chorus of women. Vocal lines alternate and overlap. Melodies, which usually descend about an octave, freely repeat, with bridges between statements. The most distinctive features of the music are the extent of its repetition and the irregularity of its rhythms.                    —RICHARD SCAGLION

### Abelam: a musical view

Some songs performed for lining the yams are lengthy. Men and women inexactly repeat a cycle of parallel fourths in a spoken style with phrases sung alternately (figure 3). Accompaniment is a steady beating of kundus, from which the only deviation, at the peak of excitement, is a doubling of the pace.

The tonal inventory uses as a frame a perfect fourth in two vocal parts, frequently moving in parallel. Fillers within the frame are a major second, a minor second, and a major second. In the men's part, an additional semitone (C♯ in figure 3) acts as

FIGURE 3 Excerpt from an Abelam song for lining the yams, sung by men and women. Kundus (not shown) sound on every quarter beat. Transcription by Vida Chenoweth.

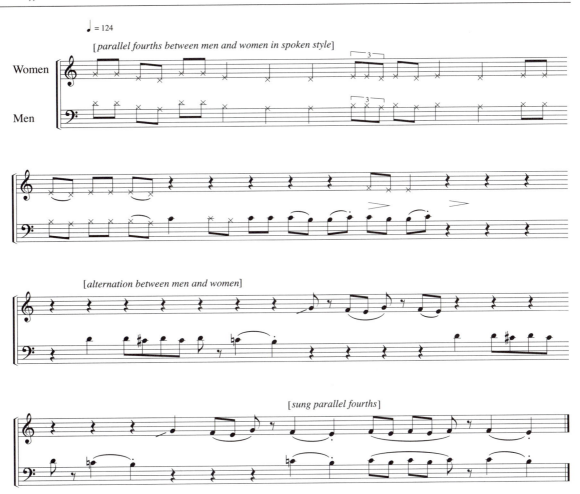

a neighboring tone. In both parts, a melodic change occurs after the tempo alters: E becomes E♭ in the women's part, and B becomes B♭ in the men's. As men and women sing, they walk counterclockwise in a circle and a garamut spasmodically joins the beat.

In a singsing sung and danced by kundu-playing men, a major third forms the melodic nucleus, with its lower tone the tonal center. Long phrases contrast with short ones. The tempo relentlessly accelerates. A typical cadence is a leap a major sixth upward on the syllable *pu.*

At the singsing after the judging of the yams, paired dances occur. First, male dancers cluster around several singer-drummers. In time to the drumbeats, some dancers bend their knees; others shuffle one foot forward (left, right, left, right); younger ones kick a foot high off the ground as they bring it forward. The other dance then begins. The tempo quickens. The drummers make parallel lines, facing each other. Other participants follow randomly behind the drummers. With a quick, prancing step, the lines back away from each other, only to reconverge; they continue this oscillation until the song ends.

### Initiatory ceremonies around Maprik

Like some other peoples in the area, Ambulas-speakers around Maprik retain the practice of male initiation. As a crowd of men and prospective initiates approaches the ceremonial house to begin the rites, men play vessel flutes. Their performance warns women and children to flee: they must not see the procession. In 1965, during an initiation at Maprik II Village, only males participated (Norm Draper, personal

The youths could neither speak nor see. Their eyes were sealed shut with a thick, yellow paste. On one side of the initiates' backs, men incised small cuts, making patterns of scars believed to resemble the hide of crocodiles.

communication). After lining the yams, men led youths out of the house. The youths wore fresh foliage, with leg-tied rattles. They could neither speak nor see, for their eyes were sealed shut with a thick, yellow paste. The singsing went on for hours. Wild shouting marked the finish of a ritual stage when, on one side of the initiates' backs, men incised small cuts, scarifying a pattern believed to resemble the hide of crocodiles.

The singsing resumed, led by Yamikum Village, using the same drums. Gifts of yam and pork arrived. Vessel flutes again sounded a warning, and the crowd moved to Maprik I Village. Carrying spears, the men of Maprik I circled a post within a secluded area, bordered by a fence of sago leaves. A mock-battle between about two hundred fifty participants ensued. Singing loudly, men from Bainyik Village entered the arena. All formed a large circle, making space for an exodus from the ceremonial house. Singing, some men tore the sago fence down. Others emerged from the house, leading the initiates in pairs. As at the first venue, men had painted yellow paste on the youths' eyelids and noses. While they led the youths around for all to admire, other males, symbolizing a bond of friendship, removed the red *tanget* leaves covering the initiates' bird-of-paradise headdresses.

Twenty-three youths underwent initiation. Ornamenting them took all day. Ceremonies lasted all night until daybreak. On banana-leaf trays, men displayed wealth in the form of rings made from giant clamshells. When the youths reentered the house, leaders permitted them to see carved wooden spirits (*tambaran*), and all the men entered the ceremonial house.

*Musical instruments*

Garamuts usually sound in a set of three. Each player jolts his instrument with a beater, hitting one side of the slit. Some kundus have carved decoration, painted with ochre. Only adult males play aerophones. From a dried fruit the size of a tennis ball, men make vessel flutes. Aside from an aperture for blowing, the body bears one hole. Open-ended bamboo trumpets are played in an ensemble of three sizes (*kaaparak, kagale, makapa*). These trumpets, with or without other instruments, serve in special ceremonies, including invoking ancestral spirits at initiations.

—VIDA CHENOWETH

## Iatmul

The name *Iatmul* has come to apply to about ten thousand people inhabiting about twenty villages on or near the shores of the middle reaches of the Sepik River. They share a common language. Their neighbors are the Sawos (on the grasslands north of the river, speaking a language similar to Iatmul) and the Chambri (to the south, speaking a different language). The Sepik flows eastward to the Bismarck Sea. Even 400 kilometers from its mouth, it bulges to half a kilometer wide. During the wet season (October to April), it often floods.

The vegetation of its basin includes swamps, bushlands, and forests; reeds line its banks. It forms many lagoons, with islands of matted grass. Fish abound in the river and its tributaries, and birds exploit the marshes; especially in the wet season, mosquitoes swarm. Crocodiles have economic and symbolic importance; the forest provides marsupials and swine. The staple diet is sago (obtained largely by trade or exchange with neighboring peoples), supplemented by fish and produce. To tourists, the Iatmul sell carvings and pottery, but cash is scarce. People travel by canoe or foot. To counter flooding, houses rest on stumps. Women do most of the fishing and much of the gardening; in Aibom, they make pottery. Men do the heavier work of building houses, raising fences, and making canoes. While a few men also garden or carve, many spend time smoking, chewing betel, arguing, preparing for ceremonies. A few men provide transport by long canoes, powered by outboard motors.

Social structure hinges on patrilineal descent. Moieties—*nyame* 'mother' and *nyoui* 'sun'—reflect "important totemic emblems, the vulva and the sun" (Bateson 1931–1932:256). Each moiety has several clans; across the division of moieties and clans cuts an age-grade classification. The focal point of village life is the men's house, a ceremonial structure or compound; its site, within an avenue of palms, largely determines the layout of the village. A man, his wives, and his children use a single house, but sometimes two brothers and their families share one. Marriage is virilocal. Leaders arise, often with the help of friends and relatives, by demonstrations of wealth, character, and mythological knowledge.

The Iatmul believe ancestral spirits hold power over the living. The most forceful are *wagin.* Nonhuman spirits, mostly evil, inhabit the water and the forest; these are mainly crocodiles, fish, water-dwelling snakes, eels, birds (including cassowaries), fruit-eating bats, and pigs. All ancestral spirits play important parts in Iatmul mythology (Wassmann 1991). Each clan takes a plant or an animal as a totem.

The Iatmul build striking ceremonial houses, for which they carve posts, gables, stools, hooks, and garamuts; they also carve masks, wooden trumpets, water-stamped idiophones, ornamental ends for flutes, and prows for canoes. Among the items Aibom potters produce are fireplaces, cookware, and sago-storing jars, often elaborately painted. Women and children make baskets and traps for fish.

### Musical contexts

Music enhances most Iatmul feasts. Because mythology concerns village clansmen (particularly leaders of clans and subclans) and informs musical activity, the men's house is often a focal point for musical performance. Sometimes it has an upper story, where men keep sacred objects and hold ceremonies. To prevent women and children from seeing secret ceremonies, the lower story, where men keep garamuts and other ceremonial objects, usually has a fringe of natural materials. Most musical performance occurs at night, when men are at leisure and women and children are less likely to spy on them.

For feasts, each Iatmul village has an idiosyncratic pattern of performance. The following outline portrays the ceremonies at the village of Kandingei (on a lagoon just south of the Sepik River), as practiced in the 1970s. Clan-specific ceremonies commemorate a person's death and celebrate the completion of a new house or a new canoe; other ceremonies, including initiations and treatments for sickness or malaise, are in the communitywide repertory.

### Death-marking feasts

Feasts known as *kitagamat* usually occur between one month and three months after a burial. The music is a *sagi,* a long series of texts, recited mainly by a soloist, but

FIGURE 4    In a Iatmul village of the Middle Sepik, men play paired flutes. Photo by Gordon Donald Spearritt, 1975.

with intermittent choruses of men, accompanied by a kundu and a split bamboo beater. The texts relate ancestors' exploits and list totemic names. The ceremony, which occurs in the dead person's house, often lasts sixteen hours or more, beginning at sunset. Sometimes the playing of a pair of *wabi kain* (long, side-blown bamboo flutes) accompanies textual recitations; at those times, Iatmul call the ceremony *minjango*. The flutists stand inside the house, in an area screened by banana leaves and fronds of sago and coconut palms. If a family cannot afford an elaborate feast, the flutes may not be present.

Each clan has unique paired flutes and sets of pieces for them (*sagi*, figure 4). At Kandingei, the shortest of these sets lasts six and a half minutes; the longest, twenty-nine. The flutists must know the order of *njangit* (melodically and rhythmically differentiated sections of the piece) and how the instrumental parts fit together. When the flutists have finished playing an appointed piece, they rest and then repeat it; and so on, throughout the night. They do not try to coordinate their playing with the singing. Adult female relatives of the deceased, often with painted faces and bodies, usually sit and quietly weep. Other women may dance around the screened area. In some villages, including Aibom, ceremonies with flutes usually occur in the men's house.

*Mariuamangi* is typical of the pieces accompanying a *sagi*. One flute begins, soon followed by the other, whose fundamental tone is a second lower. After a few slow, pensive measures, the tempo speeds up and the meter becomes more regular (figure 5). A single performance may have as many as twenty alternately slow and fast segments. Usually after every five segments (slow, fast, slow, fast, slow), the players take a few seconds' rest. The piece ends with long notes played simultaneously (MacLennan et al. 1981). A recorded excerpt from this piece is being carried by the U.S. spaceship *Voyager* (Niles 1990).

FIGURE 5 Excerpt from *Mariuamangi,* for two long side-blown flutes, kundu, and men's voices; Kandingei Village. Transcription by Gordon Spearritt.

*Feast for a new house or canoe*

A similar *sagi* graces certain other feasts. For a new house, the ceremony occurs inside; for a new canoe, it usually occurs in the men's house, or close to the stream or lagoon where the canoe was built. Again, screens hide the flutists.

*Initiations*

At initiations, music is critical. Formal scarification requires musical accompaniment. For a month or two thereafter, new initiates learn men's secrets and how to play flutes and garamuts. The evening before the operation, the old initiates of the village, painted and decorated with leaves, headdresses, ankle- and wrist-tied rattles, and shell necklaces, dance processionally along the avenue. They wave palm fronds or sheaves of reeds, calling the names of ancestral crocodiles. One or more kundus usually accompany them. Out of sight, in the men's house, others may play garamuts and flutes. Women and children may watch the dance—but not, on the following morning, the cutting of the skin.

*Feast in time of sickness or trouble*

To appease spirits believed to be causing malaise, the leading men of the village might decide to stage, in the ceremonial house, a spirits' feast (*wagin mbangu*), which requires two huge garamuts to sound continuously for more than twelve hours, sometimes for days. Men decorate the garamuts and enclose them in a screened area. The garamuts play rhythmically ordered patterns in a strict sequence, memorized by the drummers at their initiation. A complete cycle may take up to ninety minutes, after which the men begin it again (Spearritt 1984). It requires precise coordination and considerable concentration. Without breaking the rhythm, paired players change every twenty minutes or so. A performance that lasts several days requires many skilled drummers, periodically spelling each other.

Music in other Iatmul villages may take other forms. In Aibom, the ceremony in time of sickness or trouble, Yumanwusmangge, requires seven side-blown flutes and a kundu. It usually lasts from twelve to sixteen hours, beginning at sunset. Named in honor of a goddess of pottery, it follows well-ordered patterns. The drummer largely determines the rhythm. The flutes form into three pairs and one single. Each has a predetermined melodic line and place in the ensemble. The drummer normally plays a *njangit* four times before starting the next; after a minute or two, the drummer summons the flutists to get ready again (Spearritt 1990). Aibom is the only Iatmul village that favors an ensemble of so many flutes—probably an influence of similarly sized ensembles in neighboring villages near Lake Chambri.

*Mwai*

Young initiates used to enact this ceremony. After donning full-length masks with carved wooden faces, they danced in pairs near the junior ceremonial house. Dancing, they sang through short, voice-modifying bamboos, hidden inside the masks; they shuffled forward for a space, then backward. Moving and singing coordinated closely (Schlenker 1984). Mwai has almost disappeared from Iatmul villages.

*Recreation*

In addition to ceremonial music, the Iatmul have recreational forms, including lullabies, songs of love, children's songs, and work-accompanying songs. They sing them in gardens or canoes, or at home. The texts, which often show the influence of songs heard on radio, usually deal with sentiments and feelings: love, sorrow, joy, anger. They often concern relationships between villagers. They normally have no accompaniment, but sometimes use a kundu, a ukulele, or a guitar.

Recreational music also includes a man's or woman's spontaneous playing of a susap while sitting in a house or walking along a path. People also play a musical bow, in either of two forms: a mouth-resonated bow, and a string stretched over the aperture of a small canoe or garamut put on the ground. The player sounds a rhythm by tapping the string with a short stick.

### Musical instruments essential to the performance of ceremonies

The largest Iatmul instruments are garamuts. Teamed men hew them from hardwoods: formerly, they chose *garamut* trees; often in the late 1900s, they prefer *kwila* trees. Hewing out the trunks with axes, a team might take several months to make a pair of these instruments. Their length at Kandingei (which in 1975 had three pairs) varied from 2.8 to 4.2 meters; the outer diameter, from 53 to 84 centimeters; the thickness of the shell, about 2.5 centimeters. Carvers usually shape the head of the drum like the snout of a pig, a crocodile, or another totemic emblem. Standing on chocks of wood, the drums resonate freely. In the dead of night, their sound carries up to 18 kilometers.

Water-stamped idiophones are used in pairs at initiations. These instruments have handles projecting perpendicularly as much as 5 decimeters. Players plunge each instrument into water. As it breaks the surface, it makes a thud. A different water-sounded instrument is occasionally used. It is an oval-shaped hardwood board, about 75 centimeters long, 37 wide, and 11 deep. Ropes attach to each side; the undersurface is concave. The board hits the water with a bang.

Sepik men fashion kundus from hardwood trunks. These drums are usually about 5 to 6 decimeters long. Elaborately carved and painted, they often serve as a totemic or ancestral figure, whose nose is the handle. Over one end of the drum, men stretch a lizard's skin, which they glue to the perimeter. To improve the timbre, they sometimes add drops of wax to the skin. As a player holds a drum at an angle with one hand, he beats rhythms with the fingers of the other.

Iatmul flutes are bamboo instruments. Most, especially the paired flutes, usually from 1.8 to 2.5 meters long, have no holes for fingering. Shorter flutes sometimes accompany pieces for long flutes; they may have one or two holes for fingering. The flutes in the Aibom ensemble vary from half a meter to a meter in length. None has holes for fingering. When flutes decay, men cut bamboos to make replicas. To coordinate the performing, paired flutists face each other, about a meter apart (figure 6). The fundamental pitches of each pair are usually about a tone apart; favored partials are from the third to the sixth. Except during simultaneous playing near the end of a piece, players blow alternately throughout the performance.

Wooden trumpets rarely appear in Iatmul villages. Men formerly carved them from hardwood; about 4 decimeters long, usually decorated with shells and paint, they were open at one end. To sound them as warriors returned with prisoners, paired men blew through a hole about halfway along the body of the instrument. Each trumpet sounded only one note and was paired with a trumpet that sounded a different note.

FIGURE 6 Facing each other, Chambri flutists put their forefingers onto the edge of the hole into which they blow. Photo by Robert MacLennan, 1995.

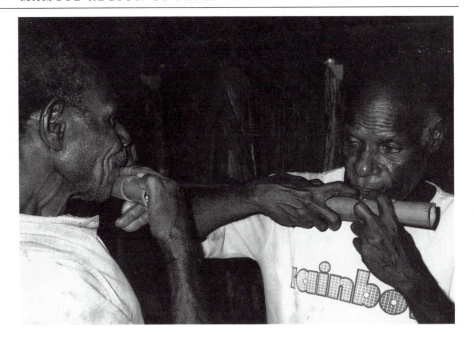

### Musical symbolism

Each pair of flutes usually bears the name of an ancestor, whose voice the sounds of the flutes represent. But these sounds also represent the voices of birds (*wabi*); a flute-accompanied *sagi* is a *sagi wabi*. The sounds of garamuts are also ancestral voices, but some *njangit* are identified with totemic figures. This is an ambiguity; but in many Iatmul myths, ancestors turn themselves into birds, fish, or other creatures.

At initiations, the sounds of water-stamped idiophones simulate the crocodile's swallowing of initiates before he vomits them back. Incisions on youths' backs and chests are marks of the crocodile's teeth. Similarly, the humming of swung slats, heard constantly for weeks after an initiation, proves the crocodiles are hungry.

Duality informs Iatmul music as it does Iatmul society. Two moieties, a clear division between male and female roles, an alternating age-grade system, initiatory death (swallowing) and rebirth (vomiting)—all have parallels in the use of paired instruments: flutes, garamuts, water-stamped idiophones, trumpets, voice-modifying bamboos, and musical structures (Spearritt 1979). —GORDON DONALD SPEARRITT

## Sepik Hills

The Sepik Hills lie north of the central range and south of the Middle Sepik River. They support populations speaking about twenty-five languages, many of them in the Sepik Hill Language Stock. The main peoples of the Sepik Hills are the Alamblak, Bahinemo, Kapriman, Karawari, Sanio, Waxei (Watakataui), Yabio, and Yimas. Individual populations range from less than a hundred to not more than two thousand (Dye, Townsend, and Townsend 1969; Laycock 1981).

Most inhabitants of the hills are sedentary hunter-gatherers, whose staple food is sago starch. In the forests they hunt pigs, marsupials, and birds; from the rivers they take fish, turtles, and shrimp. They cultivate taro, bananas, pandanus, and breadfruit. Their social organization is based on patrilineal clans, each of which holds a mammal, a bird, or a plant as its progenitor and totem. People with the same totem believe they share a common origin, even if they speak different languages. Social networks link people and music in every part of the Sepik Hills. Within these networks, a musical culture unique to each language has arisen.

In musical style, the Sepik Hills divide into an eastern-central area and a southern-western area. Notable musical traits in the former are polyphonic singing by men and women; a men's ensemble of short, side-blown, bamboo flutes; and in many communities a strong relationship between music and religious beliefs. Musical instruments in this area include an eight-to-twelve-instrument set of short, side-blown bamboo flutes without holes for fingering, half a meter to 1.5 meters long; a pair of long, side-blown, bamboo flutes without holes, 2 to 3 meters long (the same as the so-called Sepik flutes); a bamboo tube used as a vocal modifier, 0.8 to 2 meters long; a garamut; a kundu with a lizard-skin membrane; and a bamboo susap with a string.

Notable musical traits in the southern-western area are: singing in rounds, in which several men repeat short phrases in turn; the absence of independently performed instrumental music; and a weak relationship between music and religious beliefs. Musical instruments in this area include only a kundu with a marsupial-skin membrane and a bamboo susap without a string.

## Waxei

About three hundred Waxei live along the Middle Korosameri River, which flows into the Sepik amid the East Sepik Hills. They are the only Sepik-Hill people among whom intensive musical research has been done (Yamada 1991, 1997). Waxei music (*windioqom*) includes polyphonic vocal and instrumental genres, performed for male initiations, or for feasts celebrating the completion of a dwelling or a large canoe. After a performance, the sponsor (the novice's father, or the owner of the house or the canoe) and his kin exchange cash and clothes for food. All Waxei musical genres originated outside Waxei society.

### Vocal music

The Waxei recognize three genres of polyphonic vocal music: songs of Guxaj (*Guxaj windioqom*), songs of Agriq (*Agriq windioqom*), and manhunt songs (*ima tegate windioqom*), all performed by mixed choruses. Songs of Guxaj are the oldest. The people believe these songs came in mythical times from the Alamblak, living along the Karawari River. Guxaj is a powerful spirit, dwelling in specific riverbed rocks, or in trees along rivers. He supposedly appeared in Waxei territory in the form of a crocodile. He introduced male initiation, whose main procedure is to make cuts along novices' shoulder blades, representing his bites. The texts of these songs depict mythical contexts and motifs, such as the origin of initiation, an image of death, and a battle between men and Guxaj. Dynamic movements of the men's low voices and women's high voices express the variety of Guxaj's powers (figure 7).

Songs of Agriq are believed to have originated from Agriq, a male supernatural spirit, who lives in a cave in the mountains. The Waxei say Agriq sang beautiful songs with a fascinating voice, luring women into the cave, where he ate them. When the Waxei sing songs of Agriq, they recall that Agriq is a tremendous being, whose

FIGURE 7   In a melody from the Sepik Hills, dynamic movements of men's low voices and women's high voices express the variety of Guxaj's powers. Transcription by Yoichi Yamada.

strength they desire. This genre supposedly came from the Wombio, who speak a dialect of Alamblak.

Manhunt songs originated with the founder of the eagle clan. An intrepid fighter, he transformed himself into a giant eagle; from the sky, he killed and ate his enemies. When he succeeded in his hunt, he sang celebratory songs, citing his names or the names of sites where he caught his enemies. Such songs are prototypes of manhunt songs, formerly sung at celebrations of victory in intertribal war. Because the eagle clan is part of Gaidio-speaking society, whose language belongs to the East New Guinea Highland stock, manhunt songs supposedly came from the Gaidio people.

### Instrumental music

The Waxei recognize three genres of polyphonic instrumental music: Sagais's songs (*Sagais windioqom*), Igofnemis's songs (*Igofnemis windioqom*), and Songus's songs (*Songus windioqom*). These genres are performed by bamboo flute ensembles, played by men.

A set of bamboo pipes of Sagais (*Sagais kunu bogonim*) consists of ten to twelve bamboo flutes without holes for fingering and with a node left unpierced in one end. Their lengths range from 5 to 9 decimeters. Each has a name: the longest is *togo bogoniq* 'head pipe', four or five are *uyagu bogonim* 'man pipes', four or five are *toganu bogonim* 'woman pipes', and the shortest is *gemxaidai bogoniq* 'edge pipe'. These flutes supposedly came from the Alamblak.

The Waxei say that Sagais's songs are produced by Sagais, a female spirit, dwelling in bamboos near the rivers. She is called by men to the human world and dwells in the flutes. The Waxei believe that men merely blow into the flutes. It is Sagais who makes the sound, a sign of her power. On the origin of these songs, a myth records that Sagais appeared in a Waxei woman's dream and gave the set of flutes exclusively to women, who got so absorbed in performing, they let their men go hungry. The men then stole the flutes. Waxei men continue to conceal from Waxei women esoteric knowledge of the meanings of the songs of Sagais.

A set of bamboo pipes of Igofnemis (*Igofnemis kunu bogonim*) also consists of ten to twelve bamboo flutes without holes, but they are 4 to 8.5 decimeters long. The names of these flute differ from those of the bamboo pipes of Sagais: the longest is *wayuwa bogoniq* 'through pipe', four or five are man pipes, four or five are woman pipes, and the shortest is a child pipe. Igofnemis's songs differ from Sagais's songs in the order of blowing the flutes, the combinations of the sounds, and their mythical meanings. Igofnemis is Agriq's wife. She produces her songs when men call her from her cave. Like the songs of Agriq, these flutes supposedly came from the Wombio.

The bamboo pipes of Songus (*Songus kunu bogonim*) are a pair of flutes 1.6 to 2.2 meters long. The longer is the man pipe; the shorter, the woman pipe. Duets using these flutes are Songus's songs, considered productions of a female supernatural spirit, Songus, who dwells at the inlets of rivers. Men call her to dwell in the flutes. A myth says that when she emerged from the river to make her distinctive sounds, her brother, Songuq, entered a wooden statue carved for him, and it began dancing.

The Waxei assert that the bamboo pipes of Songus came from the Sogofa, an extinct people who lived along a tributary of the Karawari River. A myth describes the spread of the flutes from the Waxei to the Iatmul. Possibly, therefore, this type of paired flutes, widely known in the lowland area along the Sepik, spread not from there southward to the hills, but northward from the Karawari River.

### Musical instruments and other music

The Waxei garamut (*nogus*), about 2 meters long and 6 decimeters high, rests on the ground. To send signals or accompany songs, a man strikes it with a wooden stick.

Ritual singsings energized intertribal fighting.
During responsorial singing, the leader twanged his
bowstring and pranced at the head of a column of
marching villagers, who tilted their heads forward,
animating the feathers of their headdresses.

This instrument supposedly came from the Alamblak. For accompanying songs, the Waxei use a kundu (*waguq*), about one meter long, with a handle in the middle. They learned to make and play it about 1970, from the Kapriman, living along the lower Korosameri River. Local susaps (*taimbagos*), which came from the Kapriman with kundus, are thin, flat versions, about 2 decimeters long, with a string to hold and strike near the base of the vibrating tongue. They serve for personal entertainment; players imitate birds and reproduce melodies.

The Waxei have a lighthearted polyphonic genre (*lefen*), which in the late 1960s two Waxei men learned from the Sumariup, living along a tributary of the Karawari River. People often gather in a house at night to sing it, accompanied by kundus.

—YOICHI YAMADA

## WEST SEPIK PROVINCE

On the northwestern part of the mainland, West Sepik or Sandaun (Sundown) Province had a 1990 population of 139,917. Low mountain ranges separate the coast from the low area around the upper Sepik River. South of the Sepik are the high mountains of the central chain. The province is linguistically complex: five Austronesian languages are spoken along the coast; members of non-Austronesian phyla (Sko, Trans-New Guinea, Torricelli, Sepik-Ramu, Kwomtari, and numerous isolates) make up the remainder. The administrative headquarters is Vanimo. To escape fighting between Indonesian troops and separatist rebels, refugees from Irian Jaya Province of Indonesia have crossed the border into West Sepik.     —DON NILES

### Karkar

About twelve hundred Karkar (sometimes called Yuri, not to be confused with Karkar Island in Madang Province) inhabit villages in Papua New Guinea and Irian Jaya beside a silicone desert, where the terrain changes abruptly to rivers and forests. Sustained by sago, they live in thatched houses built on posts to allow the air to circulate. Information on Karkar musical practices comes from linguists Dorothy Price and Veda Rigden; I studied Karkar music at Auya Village, Green River.

#### *Musical contexts*

Before the 1950s, ritual singsings energized intertribal fighting. During responsorial singing, the leader twanged his bowstring and pranced at the head of a column of rhythmically walking villagers, who tilted their heads forward, animating the feathers of their headdresses.

About 1947, the Karkar began using a singsing to heal the sick. Circling the patient, dancers sang, brandishing bows and arrows or playing played kundus. This singsing originated in Amanab, center of the Anggor people, just north of where most Karkar live.

Performance of the *aum* singsing guarantees success in the hunt. Its songs are *nonkor*, whose texts focus on persons. One song metaphorically tells of a man's attrac-

FIGURE 8   Tonal relationships in Karkar *nonkor*: *a*, tonal flows; *b*, a typical cadential formula. Transcriptions by Vida Chenoweth.

tion to a girl. Another honors a deceased father. Another deals with the burial of a man's skull; after its flesh wastes away, people decorate it with red ocher and bury it in a cave. In song, a hunter may enlist the help of his deceased father, exhibiting not only a strong filial link, but vivid recollections of a man whose spirit might provide aid. Another subject is the ground-dwelling spider that at sundown climbs into trees, where it makes the sound *wa' wa-o wa-a-o wa,* assimilated into the sung text.

The Karkar used incantations to manipulate the forces of nature. Uttered in rhythmic speech, these items sought health, safety, and success in gardening, hunting, and warfare. People believed such songs ensured the sturdiness of roofs, the productivity of gardens, and the strength of children. They regarded these songs as inherently causal, addressed to the target of the action. They also sang to exert influence over circumstances and objects: to empower a trap for pigs, a singer addressed the sago palm where he had set the trap and the pig he expected to catch.

### Musical style

*Nonkor* recorded solo are in falsetto voice; collective singing may produce parallel minor seconds. *Nonkor* usually consist of two couplets. Their most typical structure is AABB; other common structures are ABAB and ABCC. The melody of each has four tones or more. The tonal inventory includes an optional minor second below the tonal center, a major second and a major third above, and an optional minor third above (Bureau 1983). These tones flow as in figure 8*a*, where arrows above tones show reversible movement; arrows below show movement in one direction only. The motif in figure 8*b* typifies cadences; it alternately supports the vowels /e/ and /o/, or the syllables *we* and *wo.* Phrases normally descend from the highest pitch to the lowest; the compass is narrow. Vocal tones glide into one another. Melodies end on the tonal center.                                                        —VIDA CHENOWETH

## MADANG PROVINCE

Madang Province lies between Morobe and East Sepik provinces. Its 1990 population was 253,195. Madang is also the name of the provincial headquarters. The main islands in the province are, from west to east, Manam, Karkar, Bagbag, and Long. The Ramu River marks the western border, and then turns and runs parallel to the southwest border. The Adelbert and Finisterre ranges provide rugged terrain, contributing to the presence of many languages, spoken by small numbers of people: Madang has the greatest number of indigenous languages of any province of Papua New Guinea. Austronesian languages are spoken mostly in coastal regions. Most languages in the province belong to the Trans–New Guinea phylum. Around the Ramu, Sepik-Ramu phylum languages predominate. The Ramu Sugar Company produces all the sugar consumed in the country. Other important provincial products are timber, cigarettes, and tinned meat.                                    —DON NILES

### The Rai Coast

The Rai Coast extends some 105 kilometers, from Bongu Village eastward to Morobe Province. A linguistically rich area, it supports dozens of languages, spoken by peoples ranging in population from fifty to several thousand. This diversity has influenced the spread of musical genres, musical instruments, and spiritual beliefs. The Finisterre Mountains, rising from a narrow coastal plain to heights above 4 kilometers, form natural boundaries, limiting and shaping the spread of cultural ideas.

#### Music and spiritual beliefs

Traditionally, music functioned as the embodiment, symbol, and reminder of *tambaran,* a system of beliefs in male dominance based on men's control of spirits' voices.

The word *tambaran* has several possible glosses: 'spiritual system of beliefs; musical instrument used in the system; sacred song; spiritual voice; spirit'. Spirits cause sickness, restore health, ensure good crops, and help with love-controlling magic. Performances of sacred music try to accomplish these acts, or set them in motion.

The exact boundaries of the precontact *tambaran* area are indeterminate. In the early 1990s, the knowledge and practice of *tambaran* were concentrated in the coastal area to altitudes of about 900 meters, usually no more than 25 kilometers inland, extending far beyond the Rai Coast in the west and ending a few kilometers east of Saidor.

Every village formerly had a spirit house (*haus tambaran*), off-limits to females and uninitiated boys. In it, men stored sacred instruments, paraphernalia, and (in some areas) carvings. They used it for initiations, secret work, and meetings. Many villages no longer have one. Instead, some clans have a boys' house (also forbidden to females), which contains the sacred instruments and serves as a lodging for youths.

Women of childbearing age are forbidden to know about the sacred instruments, but old women may know about them. This prohibition comes from a belief that if a woman sees a sacred instrument, the spirits will make her future children sicken and die. The situation would never reach that point, because if a woman sees a sacred instrument, her village must be destroyed, as one may have been, as recently as the turn of the twentieth century: near Biliau, I photographed some human bones that purportedly confirmed such a massacre. Allegedly with the knowledge and consent of the offending village, the men of surrounding villages would meet and arrange an attack. The most important men of the offending village would dress in their finest decorations. Younger men would encircle them, surrounded in turn by women and children. Thus, the oldest, most important men would die last. A few children might escape, to be adopted in another village.

### Sacred instruments

In the coastal strip, from near Saidor westward to the Guabe River (and formerly farther), the most important musical instruments are voice-modifying gourds. About a meter long, they usually have two or three sections, glued together with sap; they may last more than forty years. Only an old woman may plant and harvest the gourds, but a man may tend the growing plants. A weight attached to each gourd makes it grow in the right shape. In Nekeni (which Z'graggen 1975 calls Nekeni Neko and Nekgini), voice-modifying gourds are *kaapu naing* 'spirit's mother'. They are played in pairs, so if one performer is weak or errs, women will not discover that men make the sounds. These instruments came from near Gabumi Village, about 11 kilometers inland, just east of the Mot River. Legends say they first belonged to women, but the house was full of refuse and feces. When women tried to play the instruments, the sounds were bad. Taking the instruments (with the women's consent), men forbade women to see them.

Men make voice-modifying bamboos (Nekeni *kaapu simang* 'spirit's child') from a piece of bamboo about 3 meters long, with the nodes removed. With one or both hands, the singer holds the instrument to make an airtight connection with his mouth. The bore is too big to fit between his teeth, so he rests the end against his teeth and gums, puts his lips around it, and sings in falsetto.

Inside a *haus tambaran,* garamuts are sacred; under a house, in public view, they are secular. Secrecy and ritual surround their construction, which women are forbidden to watch; nor may women see one before it is officially available for public viewing. Garamuts span less than 1 meter to more than 2 meters; the larger ones are more common. Unlike those used near the Ramu and Sepik rivers, most garamuts in the Rai Coast have little or no carved decoration, though men may paint them for their unveiling. In addition to their use in some sacred music, garamuts serve to communicate messages, within a radius of several kilometers. The signal for a particular man may be a rhythm taken from a song his clan owns.

Also found in the Rai Coast are several instruments that, though treated with respect and secrecy, play a lesser role. Used less frequently and for a shorter time than voice-modifying gourds and bamboos, they include a coconut vessel flute (Nekeni *kwarising*); a swung slat (Nekeni *fungewangewang*); a medium-length voice-modifying bamboo (Suroi *inom*); a tree-pod rattle (Ngaing *parangaing sakuing* 'old woman'); paired side-blown flutes (Nekeni *pakung*); a piston flute (Ngaing *ilainggaring* 'black cuckoo shrike', *Coracina melæna*); a banana leaf (Nekeni *kakeo*); and a short voice-modifying bamboo, made from a single node, with cracked sides (Nekeni *tereri*). People of Somek Village believe the sound made by men stamping on the ground is a spiritual sound, as clapping and stamping are in Sorang Village and humorous conversation spoken in falsetto is in Yeimas Village.

### Secular instruments

The most common secular instruments in the Rai Coast are kundus; vertical flutes (Nekeni *suupi*), which may have one or more holes; conchs (Nekeni *pung*); susaps (Nekeni *tukin*); and small bamboo idiophones (Nekeni *kongkong*). Rattles, including tree pods (Nekeni *asaalu*) and stone-filled bamboos (Nankina *gawum*), may be either sacred or secular. Dancers may wear leg-tied rattles (Malalamai *kapapa*). Bonga and Kasu villagers have a rare instrument (Malalamai *kerker*, Morafa *sat*): two pieces of wood, 8 decimeters long and 1 wide, carved like two giant combs, bound together and struck.

### Performance

Believing that an error or incomplete preparation could result in misfortune or death, men perform sacred music with instruments only after the village has completed ritual preparations. Several weeks before a singsing is to occur, boys who will carry heavy decorations during the performance stop drinking water; they eat only food cooked in the fire, with no soup. This food cannot have come into contact with a female, whose touch would contaminate it, preventing them from performing correctly. Older men, who will be leading the singing, may limit the severity of this diet to one day or a few days before the event.

The evening of the singsing, men secretly carry the voice-modifying gourds to where a spirit lives or originated (usually a stream), where they wash them. Each participant chews a piece of ginger and spits it onto the gourds. The man who will lead the singing asks his ancestors to ensure the success of the singsing. He speaks so quietly that even men standing nearby cannot hear him. A man breaks a coconut above the gourds and pours its milk over them. Before the men may carry the instruments back to the village, they warn women and uninitiated boys to stay inside and not to look out, lest they break the taboo. The spirits must receive pork to eat; otherwise, becoming angry for having been summoned without compensation, they may cause sickness or other misfortune.

A typical performance may begin with a melody played on a banana leaf; the singers suck their breaths in, producing a high sound, whose pitch is difficult to control. They then sing the melody through two or more voice-modifying gourds. Performers usually consider one man, who knows the song well, their leader; in unison with simultaneous melodic variations, one or more others, also singing through gourds, follow him. Others may then join in, using short voice-modifying gourds. Next, men begin playing kundus, each entering when he likes, with a pattern that may not be in sync with the established tempo. Finally, unmodified singing begins,

564 PEOPLES OF OCEANIA AND THEIR MUSIC

while those singing through gourds continue. Women, singing a melody different from the men's, may join the singing in the first, second, or third stanza. Typically consisting of six to twelve stanzas, songs last fifteen to twenty minutes.

Singsings begin after dark and end at dawn. The secret instruments are played within a circle of men, out of the view of women and uninitiated boys. In addition to feathers, bark, and paints, males wear leafy branches on their backs, often secured by large wooden frames, designed to hide the secret instruments. For about forty-five minutes, performers sing two or three songs; they then take a break of about fifteen minutes. During breaks, the decorated dancers usually stand in place; they must be careful not to expose the instruments. About ninety minutes before dawn, the performers begin sending away the spirits of each song. They gradually shift to the edge of the arena, where they send the spirit back to the forest. For each spirit invoked in the singsing, they return to the arena and repeat the process. Besides singsings, men play sacred instruments during boys' initiations, the main occasions for performing on long voice-modifying bamboos.

### Songs

Clans own songs; several clans, including clans in different villages, may own songs jointly. Leaders, usually the oldest males, have the right to trade songs, sell them, or give them as gifts. They may retain the right to perform it; if they do not, they charge a higher fee. Most songs pass from generation to generation within clans. Someone who performs a song without ownership or permission must pay the owner a pig— one of the most serious punishments.

Songs are dreamed, not consciously composed. They are controlled by deceased leaders' spirits, invoked by performance with sacred instruments. Musical texts treat diverse topics: the sound of a stream, wind blowing dead leaves off a tree, a frog sitting on a stone, an airplane.

Above or below a melodic note, skillful singers add embellishments consisting of one or two short tones, which they may color by singing with the glottis nearly closed; for the main note, they switch back to a normal voice. Singing through a voice-modifying gourd or bamboo, skillful performers use the tongue and the jaw to change timbres.

#### Songs of Serieng Village

Serieng has five clans and a population of about 150. Its residents own twenty-eight songs: fifteen voice-modifying-gourd songs (*kaapu naing*; the same term denotes the song and the instrument), seven long-voice-modifying-bamboo songs, three songs for performance with either instrument, two paired-flute songs (and one whose name is known, but melody forgotten), and one secular song. Kundus are not used in some of the long-voice-modifying-bamboo songs. A few songs call for garamut accompaniment.

About half the sacred songs have nonlexical titles, which villagers say are spirits' names, though these names are not those of ancestors or anything tangible. Lexically titled songs bear the names of animals, birds, places, yams, and other entities. One, "*Uru*," is named for the *uru,* the hooded butcher-bird (*Cracticus cassicus*), whose call the melody imitates, but the imitation is more impressionistic than realistic.

The Serieng text "*Ngainba*" ('White Cockatoo', in Nekeni) exemplifies the lexically titled genre. In the translation, the italicized phrases are vocables: in the first verse, they imitate the bird's cry; in the second, they imitate the sound of the bird's wings.

FIGURE 9 Excerpt from "*Kwapang Sang*" ('Tree Leaf'), a Serieng piece for flutes, played in hocket on the fundamentals and the first three overtones, 1991; original a semitone lower. Transcription by Robert Reigle.

Yooo! saran-gipo! nge-nge-nge-nge-nge eeee!
Yooo! saran-gipo! worok worok worok worok worok!
Yooo! saran-gipo! yain: kelang-kelong.
Yooo! saran-gipo! yain: gupo-gupo-gupo, yoooo yooo aeeee!

*Yooo!* white! *nge-nge-nge-nge-nge eeee!*
*Yooo!* white! *worok worok worok worok worok!*
*Yooo!* white! hole: the bird is looking in.
*Yooo!* white! hole: clear [the debris], *yoooo yooo aeeee!*

The hole—in the trunk of a tree—is where the cockatoo lives.

*Tonal organization*

Voice-modifying-gourd songs typically begin with a held note at the bottom of the male vocal range. This leads into a skip up to the main tone of the song, often about a fifth higher. Many songs use three or four main tones, transcribable as C–D–F and C–D–F–G, which they may embellish with other pitches, slides, or harmony, typically fifths or octaves. Most melodic activity occurs above the tonal center.

The songs sung through long bamboos are melodically similar to the songs sung through gourds; some use either instrument. Unlike performances with gourds, songs with bamboos are sung in falsetto, never performed at singsings, rarely accompanied by unmodified singing, and sometimes sung with a drone.

Paired side-blown flutes, found only around Masi Village, are tuned a major second apart. The longer is male; the shorter, female. Men play them in hocket, using the first four partials (figure 9). The players stand facing each other; each holds a flute to his right. As a note sounds, the player twists the top half of his body to the left; breathing in, he twists back to the right. As one player blows, the other breathes in, moving in the opposite direction. The players must coordinate their movements: if one erred, they would collide. Since the flutes are sacred, men play them only inside a *haus tambaran,* or at camp during initiations.

**Late-twentieth-century transitions**

The introduction of Christianity set in motion major cultural changes. In some villages, people no longer hide the secret instruments. The musical life of the Rai Coast includes Christian music (mostly Roman Catholic and Lutheran) and popular songs, learned from radio, or composed by local string bands. For most people, these musics, heard several times a week, are eclipsing indigenous music, heard only a few times a year, but for middle-aged and older people, indigenous music retains its power: when they hear songs associated with relatives, spirits, and experiences, they sometimes weep.

—ROBERT REIGLE

## MOROBE PROVINCE

At the northeastern part of the mainland, Morobe Province had a 1990 population of 380,117, the largest of any province. The administrative headquarters is Lae, Papua New Guinea's second-largest city, connected by road to Madang and the highlands via the Okuk Highway. Main offshore islands include Umboi and smaller islands collectively known as the Siasi Islands. The Markham River cuts the province in half; on both sides, plains give way to mountains.

On the coast of the Huon Peninsula in the northeast is the earliest known archaeological evidence of human occupation in New Guinea, dating from about forty thousand years ago. Austronesian languages are found in numerous coastal regions in the north, and inland along much of the Markham; the remaining languages are non-Austronesian.

Lutheran missionaries began work in Morobe in 1886. Goldfields were developed at Wau and Bulolo in the 1920s and 1930s. Morobe was the scene of heavy fighting during the Pacific War (1941–1945).

—DON NILES

### Buang

Along the Snake River live people who speak three dialects of Buang, an Austronesian language: one dialect is spoken at the headwaters; a second, in the central valley; and a third, in the lower valley. Many Buang work and live in towns. Bruce Hooley, who studied the Central Buang language (which has about 4,500 speakers), collected the following data, assisted in 1982 by Beth Gathman.

At singsings, women follow men, in a circle. They strike the ground with one foot while kicking the other backward. Men merely bend their knees, their weight resting on the balls of their feet. Two singers begin by dancing in place. After the first stanza, with kundus sounding, they lead the dancers halfway around the arena; after the second stanza, the line completes the circle. Being celebratory, dancing is discontinued during periods of mourning. Buang men's headdresses consist of three vertical sections on a cane framework, adorned with bird-of-paradise plumage.

In the 1990s, few Buang perform indigenous Buang dances. Youths employed in towns return to the village with amplifiers and generators to accompany their imitations of Western dancing. No Buang music is being composed in traditional genres. Attracted to the guitar and commercial music (as heard in towns, on radio, and on cassettes), young people have not continued the indigenous repertory; nor are Christian hymns being composed in local styles: instead, the Buang are singing Jabêm music of the Finschhafen area (Huon Peninsula) and Western hymns.

Buang musical texts show the poetical use of parallelism, one form of which is to substitute synonyms and antonyms from different dialects. Textual ellipsis is common to lyrics in the area; extra vowels vary or complete phrases. Deeper meanings often underlie metaphorical expressions (Hooley 1987:446–448).

The Buang play kundus of four sizes. From smallest to largest, they are *avuuk atov, kuung kuung, koong koong,* and *ketuk* (Chenoweth 1976:54). Some receive proper names. In *sengii,* other drums (*ggageng*) and nut rattles (*döleng*), played by anyone, accompany dancing.

### Musical genres

The Central Buang have five distinct indigenous genres of singing; a sixth has disappeared from use. *Tarot*, originally courtship songs, may commemorate special events or express personal feelings, like pride in harvesting one's food. Composed by women, most are sung by adolescent girls, who formerly challenged "the young men of a village to come out and fight," or entered villages "singing these songs and beating up the young men, claiming them as husbands. It is not clear whether these claims actually resulted in marriage" (Hooley 1987:449). Only older women remember these songs. Examples taped by Hooley in 1971 and 1975 are of two types, the first possibly older than the second. Songs of type I emphasize a tonal center, with an occasional move to other tones. The noncentral tone may be a minor second below, a minor third below, a minor second above, or a major second above. Songs of type II have a scalewise inventory of four or five tones: a major second and a minor second, followed by either a major third or two more major seconds, whose highest tone occurs only in unstressed position. Centric and one-step melodies tend to be freer in form, but three-step melodies are repetitive, with minimal melodic variation. Each phrase joins two sections of about the same length; the tonal center rises to a fourth, third, or second, and returns scalewise.

*Sengii* accompany dancing. They have strophic texts, sung loudly in falsetto, as a duet by two men, or occasionally two women. Carrying kundus, the singers lead the dancers and other drummers. Subjects include histories, legends, territories, weather, hunting, and gardens. The musical texture of *sengii* is in two parts. The second voice, which enjoys some freedom from the first, enters after a delay. Both voices move in imitation. Phrasal development heightens the intensity by alternating consonance and dissonance, as harmonic thirds or unisons alternate with seconds. Final phrases conclude in unison of pitch and rhythm, resolving the microdrama. A metronomically steady pulse on kundus underlies the singing. In some performances, a mixed chorus responds to a leader.

During intertribal warfare, the Buang sang and danced songs of victory (*bahil*) before consuming their enemies' corpses. Some men blew conch trumpets. The victors intended their noise to belittle any surviving enemies. *Bahil* are one-step melodies sung by a mixed ensemble. In a recorded example, an auxiliary pitch (C#), occurring only in weak rhythmic position, ornaments the tone D. Phrases share a single shape, with slight melodic variation. During the performance, a conch sounds periodically. After a death, survivors compose and sing solo laments (*susën*). Periods of weeping interrupt the singing; hence the name *crying songs*. This custom is all but lost. Laments have several distinguishing features. The tones have unstable pitches, but the melodies can be analyzed as one-step melodies. Though most Buang phrases terminate on a sustained tone, here they tend to fall in a long downglide, whose end is barely audible. Despite consisting mainly of two tones, phrases are unalike, probably the result of textual improvisation. *Tahi köök*, a call intended to be heard far away, uses two tonal areas in the manner of a one-step melody, and ends with a shout.

—VIDA CHENOWETH

## Irumu

Near the headwaters of the Irumu River, at elevations of 900 to 1,400 meters on the southern slopes of the Saruwaged Mountains, about fifteen hundred Irumu inhabit seven villages: Aret, Dahäman, Däku, Garämbon, Gumia, Uyaŋget, Zuepak. The Irumu language, in four dialects, is non-Austronesian, of the Trans–New Guinea phylum. By 1975, English had locally become the language of formal education. In the 1990s, the school in Zuepak was the only school in the valley where students regularly read and spoke English.

English-language religious songs mark the start of
school. During assemblies, held outside once a week,
schoolchildren stand at attention, pray, sing a song
of thanks, salute the flag, and sing the national song.

The first missionaries settled at Finschhafen in 1886 and reached Wantoat in
1929; Australian colonial patrol officers arrived in the 1940s. Carl A. Schmitz recorded Irumu music in 1955; thirty-four years later, people recognized pieces he had
recorded. For intercultural communication, missionaries introduced Kâte, a language
spoken near the mission at Finschhafen. In Kâte, the Irumu sing from a hymnal
(*Lutheran Gae Buk* 1960) and read from the Bible. In primary schools at Gumia,
Dahäman, and Uyaŋget, Kâte is the language of instruction.

### Language and song

In church, Irumu sing songs in Kâte. The *Gae Buk* contains texts for 470 hymns
(*gae*), responsorials (*nareŋ gareŋ gae*), and liturgical instructions. Papua New
Guineans and missionaries adapted or composed the hymns. Seminarians memorize
the melodies and teach them in churches. Some hymns use free rhythm. Most have
five-tone scales within the major-minor system; others, like the scale of hymn 220
approximately (B–D♯–E–F♯–A), are outside that system.

Tok Pisin songs treat biblical or commonplace topics. Nearly all scholastic songs
treat Christian themes. Boys organize string bands, whose repertories include sacred
and secular pieces. In churches, preservice singing, sometimes accompanied with guitars or drums, serves to *pulim i kam* 'coax [to church].' English-language religious
songs mark the start of school. During assemblies, held outside once a week, schoolchildren stand at attention, pray, sing a song of thanks ("Father, We Thank You"),
salute the flag, and sing the national song.

Local people speak and write Irumu, Kâte, Tok Pisin, and English, whose
orthographies derive from the English alphabet, but *j* represents [ĵ] in Tok Pisin, [dz]
in Irumu, and [j] in Kâte. Kâte letters are "phonetic in the popular sense of the word"
(Flierl and Strauss 1977:xiv); Irumu and Tok Pisin letters are phonemic (Mihalic
1971; Webb and Webb 1990). By the 1990s, Irumu phonology and Tok Pisin
orthography prevailed; linguists and biblical translators were helping the Irumu learn
to read.

### Musical contexts

Nocturnal singsings include performances of ancestral song-dances. Around a fire,
performers make two concentric circles: in the inner one, men move clockwise, bob
up and down, and play kundus in unison; in the outer one, women move counterclockwise. All sing loudly, about a hundred short pieces, each with a brief text and
vocables. Women's musical role is that of singers, rarely of instrumentalists.

A chorus often repeats a verse, changing dialect for one of the textual elements.
A typical stanza is monophonic, with percussive accompaniment, asymmetrical
meter, and change of dialect (figure 10). Its first line is in Uyaŋget dialect; its second,
in Gumia:

Nambitna ŋamani piŋ kukät kukät.  I'm planting my red yams.

Nakna ŋamani piŋ kukät kukät.  I'm planting my red yams.

Singsings that formerly accompanied initiation, curing, and planting included feasting, decorative dressing, and applying aromatic substances to the body. Accouterments for dancing included a mobile: fastened to a man's back, a masklike painting on bark hung from the string of an archer's bow, fixed horizontally on a pole; the dancer bobbed, setting the mask in motion. Another dance-appropriate object was a *yawik* (Schmitz 1958), a 3-meter plank, half a meter wide, carved as a fantastic face, topped by a meter-tall male figure (figure 11).

The Irumu recognize eight genres of song: *aka, bäri, beŋgo, gäragära, iwuŋ, kap karoɲi, min, omboroŋ.* Though some have names in two dialects, the meanings are lost. Determinants of genre include meter, melodic shape, and closing signal on kundus. The Irumu borrow a few other singsings. All songs performed at a given singsing belong to one genre.

Singsings arose in ancestors' dreams. The *singsing omboroŋ,* an exception, came from Sililik, a spirit, who sometimes appears as a snake. *Singsing bäri* relate to tribal fighting (no longer practiced); in the late 1990s, people still sang them. Old-timers recall hearing of the *singsing beŋgo* but forget actual songs. In the mid-1990s, singsings celebrated the opening of a building or the visiting of officials. They continued for a day or more but omitted dancing. The genre was in decline; children often watched in silence.

Multilingual singing is common. At assemblies, schoolchildren sing "My God Can Do Anything" in English, Tok Pisin, and Irumu:

My god can do anything, anything, anything.
My god can do anything.
He made the world, he loves us all, and I know he's my friend.
My god can do anything.

God b'long mi ken wokim samting, samting, samting.
God b'long mi ken wokim samting.
Em wokim graun, em wokim yumi, na yumi save.
God b'long mi ken wokim samting.

An'tunin 'maka 'maka täŋpek, täŋpek.
An'tunin 'maka 'maka täŋpek.
Kome ŋo täŋkuk, nin tämbäŋ nipmaŋkuk, unita nin andäkamäŋ.
An'tunin 'maka 'maka täŋpek.

The words change to fit the melody. In the Tok Pisin stanza, *samting* 'something'

FIGURE 11    Utjämba holds a *yawik*-topped plank for dancing. Photo by John Kelsey, 1990.

replaces "anything," and occurs only twice (the more correct *olgeta samting* would not fit). From *em i wokim,* the particle *i* disappears; *bilong* contracts to *b'long.* In the Irumu stanza, *täŋpek* 'whatever' also occurs fewer times than "anything." *Anutunin* 'my god' contracts to *An'tunin,* and *imaka* contracts to *'maka.*

Local cargo cults took inspiration from such outsiders as Miklouho-Maclay (1975) and the military forces of 1939–1945. Participants seek "cargo," material goods from overseas (Lawrence 1964). As part of the ritual to get these goods, the Irumu redirected singsings. Though local leaders forbade cargo cults, they arose sporadically as recently as 1992.

### Musical instruments

While courting, young men play a bamboo susap, *biŋgoŋ,* held so its tongue faces rearward. The player taps it with the wrist from behind (figure 12). To dedicate it as a charm, he breaks off the tip of its tongue while whispering the desired girl's name; if the charm fails, that susap cannot serve again as a charm. While reading from the *Gae Buk* and mouthing a melody, some males play hymns on susaps.

Garamuts are locally absent. In a map of their geographic distribution, Jaap Kunst (1967) includes the Irumu area; finding a correspondence between Austronesian languages and garamuts, Don Niles (1983) correctly excludes the Irumu area.

Formerly, men shaped kundus (*waŋgäm*) with stone tools and burned out the interiors; now, they carve them with steel. A kundu has two conical ends, connected by a cylindrical middle, where the player holds it. Skin covers one end; attached wet, it is tuned when dry. To adjust its timbre, tuners press wax pellets onto it. So mutual reinforcement will increase amplitude and duration, tuners match the fundamental frequency of the membrane and the cavity of the drum. Men reportedly tried to make the sound of a drum resemble the name of a girl whose favor they sought (Schmitz 1963:91). Kundus come in three sizes: *jinäm,* up to 12.5 decimeters long; *tsarot,* midsized; *biniŋ,* 5 decimeters long. In contrast with their coastal counterparts, these drums have no decoration. The *biniŋ* is unique to the area. Its head is 3 decimeters in diameter; its open end, 8 centimeters. It has an arc-shaped handle, but no cylindrical segment.

An idiochord musical bow (*ehat waŋgäm, ende waŋgäm* 'bamboo') comes in pairs of bamboo segments, each with both septums intact; the string is a strip of bark raised by tiny sticks, which, for tuning, are shifted along its length. The center of each bamboo has a hole for resonance. A slip of wood (8 centimeters by 1.25 by 0.25) split at one end is pushed onto the string and secured with the free end over the hole. The player taps the string with two sticks.

The *uhuwep,* an end-blown reed flute with two holes for fingering, is 6 decimeters long and 2 centimeters in diameter. One hole is slightly below the middle; the other, between it and the far end. Players use mostly the second through fourth overtones, but flutists rarely close only the lower hole. They usually improvise, but at least one man plays the hymn "Amazing Grace." To announce Christian services, funeral processions, and (in Gumia) school, men blow a conch (Tok Pisin *taur,* locally [tawɛl]), traditionally a shell of *Charonia tritonis* (Mihalic 1971:193). Fischer (1983:116), citing Schmitz (1956:237), places panpipes among the Irumu. By the 1980s, panpipes (*beŋgo*) and the gourd trumpet (*womat*) had fallen into disuse.

Uyaŋget's string band uses a set of sixteen tuned bamboo tubes (Tok Pisin *mambu*). The tubes, with septums removed, are arranged in four rafts. Each produces four tones, transcribable as an ascending scale of G–C–D–E; paired rafts sound an octave apart. The smaller two rafts lie on the ground, one atop the other. Over them stands a player, who, with a rubber sandal in each hand, simultaneously strikes unison pairs

FIGURE 12   Jiŋama, a young Irumu man, twangs his susap left-handed. Photo by John Kelsey, 1990.

of tubes, end-on. The larger two rafts are tuned an octave lower; each has its own player. The tubes furnish arpeggiated chords as a bass.

### String bands

The Irumu tune guitars by function: lead, rhythm, and bass. There is neither a standard instrumentation nor a single system of tuning, but most Irumu ensembles have at least one two-stringed bass guitar, which provides triadic roots and fifths. A rhythm guitar, with three to six strings, rapidly strums chords. The lead guitar's lowest four strings, tuned to tones transcribable as C, E, F, and G, are played open. The major mode is more common than minor modes. In *kwaia* 'harmony', the highest two strings add a descant, which may feature added sixths. Some young men own electric guitars and bass guitars, which they play through battery-powered amplifiers.

Irumu singing with string-band accompaniment often incorporates a high falsetto, sometimes sung extremely quietly. A single kundu, a plastic container, or an inner tube stretched over a 15-liter drum supplies a basic pulse. The texts, often social commentaries, bewail the performers' plight, tell a story, or sketch a vignette. Bands repeat single songs at length.     —JOHN R. KELSEY

## Komba

Some twelve thousand Komba live in hamlets scattered through mountainous terrain. The remoteness of the hamlets may explain the conservatism of Komba musical style. Data supplied by Australian linguists Neville and Gwyneth Southwell, who lived with the Komba for sixteen years, inform the study of Komba music. Neville served as interpreter for Karen Hudson and Vida Chenoweth in 1983, when they documented music in Ununu and Konge hamlets.

### Musical genres

The Komba name seven genres of songs, based on function, rather than stylistic traits. *Muŋgep* have kundu accompaniment and a wide range of subjects. Some concern feasts, for which the gift of one or more pigs fulfills social obligations. Some are for male initiations, including initiation in hunting and killing in warfare. Some moralize about a disobedient son. Examples identified with particular composers are nonceremonial. *Han* are for initiations and telling of spiritual beings. To perform them, singers sit on the floor, accompanying themselves by beating sticks on it. *Kirâm* tell of feasts involving pork, citing facets of the event, such as an admired headdress or food-preparing activities. *Bunam,* dating back to times of intertribal warfare, are songs appropriate for fighting. *Zumzem* are women's songs. In the only recorded example, women call out for the hunted animals to come and be killed. After they finish singing, they close the door of their shelter; no one goes out, lest the magic fail. *Seru,* associated with magic, invoke spirits' help, but they may serve as laments. *Aiyon* are singsings with kundu accompaniment. Many are current and topical; men and women create them.

### Musical system

Komba music is monophonic. Melodic rhythms derive from textual rhythms. In the transcribed recordings, melodic intervals seldom exceed a fifth. Semitones are not a recognized interval. Phrases typically begin above the tonal center, toward which, in a wavy line, they descend. As with most highland music, a sequence of more than three tones in one direction seldom occurs.

Songs are through-composed. Each phrase may include material from the preceding one ($AB_aC_bD_c$). Contrastive phrases may or may not have variations ($A_1B_1A_1B_1$ or $A_1B_1A_2B_2$). Variations may quote or develop one phrase, borrowed from an initial phrase ($AB_aC_aD_aE_a$).    —VIDA CHENOWETH

## Siasi Islands

These islands lie 40 or more kilometers off the mainland of New Guinea, with a population of about twelve thousand. The main islands are Arop to the northwest and Umboi to the southeast. Siasi Islanders are famous as intrepid maritime entrepreneurs, who connect participants as far apart as Madang, Kilenge, and Finschhafen (Harding 1967) in a system wherein people trade goods, services, and important kinds of knowledge, including songs and dances.

The performance of *sia,* the trademark singsing of the Siasi Islands, usually honors firstborn children at their first singsing. It is the most melodic and colorful Siasi dance. For these reasons, Siasi Islanders often choose to perform it at regional shows and teach it to schoolchildren as part of their curriculum. It also serves as a context for arranging trysts—a trait that has elicited comment from all sorts of outsiders, from the first missionaries to mainland New Guineans. For this and other reasons, early missionaries tried to eradicate all dance-related feasts, and Siasi Islanders who converted to Lutheranism did abolish them. Of the small islands of the archipelago, only Mandok maintains its feasts; its people became Roman Catholics precisely because the priests of that religion did not insist on abolishing cultural practices of this kind. Aromot Island, partly Lutheran and partly Roman Catholic, is divided on the subject.

Siasi Islanders can be distinguished as sea people and land people. A typical example of the former are the people of Mandok Island, a 4-hectare coral islet (population around five hundred), whose people speak Mutu, an Austronesian language. Mandok lies just off the south coast of Umboi, whose inhabitants are mostly land people.

### Mandok Island and the sia

The *sia* originated on Arop. Its mythical origins have been recorded in the sacred historical myth of the legend of Namor (Pomponio 1992:27–53), and in genealogies. The name *sia* comes from the Arop word for 'bird'. The dancers' movements often imitate the motions made by birds, especially in the principal dance, that of the golden-crested cockatoo. Performances occur at night. Other dances, performed by day, are called *kai*.

Men, the featured dancers, demonstrate their talents for style, motion, and endurance. They move in different formations at different periods of the day, following a complex sequence over many days. After they perform, village elders clear the central plaza to make way for dancers who imitate scenes from nature in popular skits that include a man hunting a wild boar, a cockatoo crossing an open space to peck at bananas, and two birds traveling together along a branch to a desired location. The most talented dancers wait until nightfall to perform solos. While they perform, they hold pigs' tusks in their teeth. In the dark, their white hats (*ruum sia*) and other white decorations, picking up the soft light from fires and pressure lamps, seem to glow.

From the sidelines, women sing in tense falsetto, soaring above the male voices' melodic lines. Women dance in twos and threes, arms linked in a rhythmically bouncing walk, swinging special pandanus baskets in their hands. For *kai*, women hold the baskets high; for *sia*, women swing them from a lower position. Women scrutinize the men, perhaps to slip a betelnut into a dancer's basket as he passes—an invitation for a tryst.

### The sia as an index of change

Over time, to accommodate individual creativity and current fashion, songs have been added to the *sia*, and costumes have been altered for it. Its form, function, and meaning have remained core features of Siasi life, and stand as testimony to the continuity of Siasi Islanders' values and culture.

When performed for firstborns, the *sia* can last for years, at a cost of thousands of dollars. The primary objects of exchange were formerly pigs and locally carved bowls, up to 1.2 meters long. The child's parents and grandparents gave these valuables to a ritual-exchange partner in the village, or to their overseas-trade partner, as appropriate. The partner's family distributed the pork and other valuables, with food for the feast—betel, manioc pudding, sweet potatoes, taro pudding, tobacco. After persistent European contact, and especially the introduction of a market economy and industrially manufactured goods, the processes and functions of exchange and feasting remained, but the actual goods in play changed to reflect the hosts' financial means, including resources from urban relatives and wage employment.

In addition to goods for distribution, sponsors give gifts to relatives and present special gifts to kin who help them with stages of the feasts. Often these latter gifts are responses to specific requests, or to their recipients' known desires. They might include wristwatches, pressure lamps, cassette radios, tapes, batteries, saucepans, pots, nails, can openers, vegetable peelers, bedding, towels, clothing, children's toys, running shoes, soccer balls, guitars, guitar strings, and other merchandise (Pomponio 1992:115–116).

Costumes have changed while maintaining the themes of the dance. Precontact male dancers wore bark cloth obtained from New Britain through trade partnerships; today's dancers may or may not have this cloth, but they do wear shorts, and possibly a wristwatch or sunglasses (figure 13). The materials of men's hats have changed from real feathers to white paper, with the occasional cereal-box logo when available. An important part of the costume is white armbands and legbands, today supplied by sterile gauze—a fact that becomes a source of contention with medical dispensaries, whose personnel view this use as wasteful. Women's costumes have changed to

FIGURE 13    Adorned with hat, pigs' tusks, armbands, wristlets, anklets, sunglasses, and other ornaments, a man of Mandok plays a kundu and dances the *kai*. Photo by Alice Pomponio, 1987.

include 2.5-meter sarong-like strips of cloth, bras, baby powder, face-and-chest splash, and store-bought paint and colored feathers for the hair. —ALICE POMPONIO

### Umboi and its music

Umboi, the largest of the Siasi Islands, has a population of about ten thousand. Its musical traits are typical of an area extending westward through the Siasi Islands to the coast of the Huon Peninsula. A people of the southeastern coast of Umboi speak Mbula (also known as Mangap), an Austronesian language; elsewhere on the island, other Austronesian languages and one non-Austronesian language are spoken.

The people of Umboi perform several precontact songs and dances: laments (*tingiizi*); old songs (*kon ninngana*); magic-controlling songs (*naborou*), including those for planting crops and inspiring love; and songs in tales (*ngger*), by which adults lull children to sleep.

Feasts involve songs and dances of several kinds, each with a generic name, whose change marks a fresh text, drumbeat, and choreography. Generic distinctions reflect choreographic differences, not musical ones. *Sia* occur at night. Subtypes are *sia sangga* and *sia mangga*; in the latter, two young men, between two columns of male dancers, dance virtuosically in mirror image with each other. *Kai,* with subtypes *kai gomlongan* and *kai bok,* occur by day. In *tooro* 'spirit', a dancer in the guise of an eagle dances a solo. *Lou,* a slow-paced dance, survives from precontact days; in *lou iizi,* one or more men carry spears. *Abutun* are songs of male initiation, no longer practiced. *Lelang ainu* features women, while men sing and play drums. In *kanaaza* 'ants', the choreography incorporates distinct positionings of kundus: near the end of the performance, the men put their drums in a circle on the ground and dance around them; with their hands free, they scratch their legs as if bitten by ants. Women usually dance on the periphery. Their gait animates their bustles, made of grass. The interplay of vocal parts, drumbeats, and choreography sets up a style of performance admired by visitors and nationals. Dancers sometimes perform for pay and to raise money for a Christian church.

A celebration for a woman who has given birth to her first baby is an all-female party at the river. After bathing her, women decorate her with shell armlets, armbands, and foliage. They dye her hair with red paste; they paint white streaks onto her forehead and nose. Older women act as clowns. The party howls in laughter at jokes about men. Later, the women parade into the village, where they enact a singsing before the celebrant's house, merrily mocking the men's singsing.

Other ancient songs for feasts exist, as do songs for hunting pigs or canoeing at sea. Since the 1970s, a new kind has come into existence: prayer-songs (*mboe sungngana kana*), which have new melodies, with texts deemed suitable for Christian worship. Children play a variety of games: in one, singing accompanies the rhythm of coconut shells, which children strike on the ground; in another, children sing while jumping into the river.

### The Siasi musical system

The people of the archipelago know hundreds of songs and dances, but many melodies follow a predictable format. An above-average dancer introduces each song: by singing, drumming, and shouting cues, he coordinates the others. Other men then join in. Women then take their cue from the men, adding their part an octave higher.

In a typical *kai sangga* (figure 14), the women finish phrase $A_1$ alone, after which damped drumbeats begin. Stepping in rhythm, men with kundus lightly tap the drumhead with their fingers (figure 15); they stifle resonance by resting the palms of their hands on the membranes. By contrast, the resonant drumbeat (to follow) will

FIGURE 14 Excerpt from a Siasi *kai sangga* in a typical format: the voices enter in a standard order. Transcription by Vida Chenoweth.

be dramatic. The drummers sometimes hoist their drums vertically, grasping the drum's waist in one hand and resting its rim just above their knees. In the second melodic phrase (A$_2$, a variation of the first), the entrances follow suit: leader, men, women. As before, the women secure their octave from the men's part and complete the phrase. The drums then break the quiet with a stylized rhythm, after which they play a muffled, one-handed flutter-roll. Then phrase three (A$_3$) begins. The leader sings portions of the first phrase. Midway, the singers shout mightily, ending their phrase in a downglide; the women complete the phrase. The leader begins a final phrase (A$_4$, not shown), and the men join him briefly. As before, the leader continues until the women enter. The men give a shout, which glides downward with a rapid series of glottalized syllables, *aʻ aʻ aʻ aʻ*, and so on. A four-beat cadence and a shout by the leader close the performance.

*Tonal resources and progressions*

Melodies typically use four tones: a tonal center, a minor third below, and a major second and a perfect fifth above. These are the tones found in indigenous songs; the tones of some dance-songs differ. One nuclear interval is common to many Siasi songs: the minor third whose higher tone is the tonal center. Historically, this interval may have been the basis of one-step melodies whose inventory gradually expanded. All sampled men's songs have three tones in common: a tonal center, a minor third below, and a major second above. The perfect fifth below a tonal center occurs optionally in danced songs, defining a tonal inventory transcribable as G, B, D, and

FIGURE 15    Stamps, a postmark, and a specially
printed envelope celebrate the music of Papua
New Guinea. Philatelic material courtesy of
Don Niles.

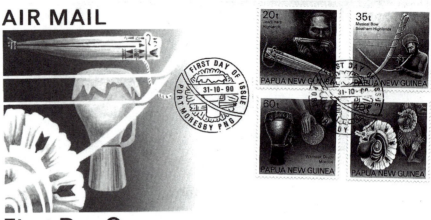

FIGURE 15    Stamps, a postmark, and a specially printed envelope celebrate the music of Papua New Guinea. Philatelic material courtesy of Don Niles.

E, with D the tonal center. The women's part contains the same tones, but with the
D on the bottom and a different tonal center, G. A sequence of these tones can be
heard as either a root-position major triad with an added sixth (the men's part), or
the same chord in second inversion (the women's part). In addition, the women's part
contains a minor triad: E–G–B. Despite the illusion in outsiders' ears, triadic harmony is not an indigenous concept; the governing rule is simultaneous melodic variation.

—VIDA CHENOWETH

## REFERENCES

Bateson, Gregory. 1931–1932. "Social Structure
of the Iatmül People of the Sepik River." *Oceania*
2:245–291, 401–455.

Brumbaugh, Robert. 1979. "A Secret Cult in the
West Sepik Highlands." Ph.D. dissertation, State
University of New York at Stony Brook.

Bureau, Claire. 1983. "The Karkar Music
System." Paper submitted as an academic requirement, Wheaton Graduate School.

Chenoweth, Vida, ed. 1976. *Musical Instruments
of Papua New Guinea*. Ukarumpa: Summer
Institute of Linguistics.

Dye, W., P. Townsend, and W. Townsend. 1969.
"The Sepik Hill Languages: A Preliminary
Report." *Oceania* 39(2):146–156.

Fischer, Hans. 1983. *Sound-Producing Instruments
in Oceania*. Edited by Don Niles. Translated by
Philip W. Holzknecht. Boroko: Institute of Papua
New Guinea Studies.

Flierl, Wilhelm, and Hermann Strauss. 1977.
*Käte Dictionary*. Canberra: Australian National
University.

Forge, Anthony. 1971. "Art and Environment in
the Sepik." In *Art and Aesthetics in Primitive
Societies*, ed. Carl F. Jopling, 290–314. New York:
Dutton.

Gell, Alfred. 1975. *Metamorphosis of the
Cassowaries: Umeda Society, Language and Ritual*.
London: Athlone Press.

Graf, Walter. 1950. *Die musikwissenschaftlichen
Phonogramme Rudolf Pöchs von der Nordküste*

*Neuguineas*. Österreichische Akademie der
Wissenschaften, Rudolf Pöchs Nachlass, B II.
Vienna: Rudolf M. Rohrer.

Hannemann, E. F. 1979 [1935]. "Madang
Dances and Dancing." *Northeast New Guinea*
1(2):37–62.

Harding, Thomas G. 1967. *Voyagers of the Vitiaz
Strait*. Seattle: University of Washington Press.

Harrison, Simon. 1982. *Laments for Foiled
Marriages: Love-Songs from a Sepik River Village*.
Boroko: Institute of Papua New Guinea Studies.

Hooley, Bruce A. 1987. "Central Buang Poetry."
In *Festschrift for Frances I. Andersen's 60th
Birthday*, ed. Edgar W. Conrad and Edward G.
Newing. Winona Lake, Ind.: Eisenbrauns.

Hudson, Karen. 1983. "Analysis of Komba
Music." Senior document, Wheaton College.

Johnson, Ragnar, and Jessica Mayer. 1977. *Sacred
Flute Music from New Guinea: Madang*. Quartz
Publications: !Quartz 001. LP disk.

———. 1978. *Windim Mambu: Sacred Flute
Music from New Guinea: Madang*. Quartz
Publications: !Quartz 002. LP disk.

Juillerat, Bernard. 1992. "'The Mother's Brother
Is the Breast': Incest and Its Prohibition in the
Yafar Yangis." In *Shooting the Sun: Ritual and
Meaning in West Sepik*, ed. Bernard Juillerat,
20–124. Washington, D.C.: Smithsonian
Institution Press.

Kunst, Jaap. 1967. *Music in New Guinea: Three
Studies*. Translated by Jeune Scott-Kemball.

Verhandelingen van het Koninklijk Instituut voor Taal-, Land- en Volkenkunde, 53. The Hague: Martinus Nijhoff.

Lawrence, Peter. 1964. *Road Belong Cargo.* Manchester: University Press.

Laycock, Donald C. 1981. "Sepik Province." In *Language Atlas of the Pacific Area,* ed. Stephen A. Wurm and Shirō Hattori, map 6. Canberra: Australian National University.

*Lutheran Gae Buk.* 1960. Madang, Papua New Guinea: Kristen Pres.

MacLennan, Robert, Gordon Spearritt, Meinhard Schuster, and Gisela Schuster. 1981. *Music of Oceania: The Iatmul of Papua Niugini.* Bärenreiter Musicaphon BM 30 SL 2701. LP disk.

May, Patricia, and Margaret Tuckson. 1982. *The Traditional Pottery of Papua New Guinea.* Sydney: Bay Books.

Mead, Margaret. 1938. *The Mountain Arapesh.* Anthropological Papers of the American Museum of Natural History, 36. New York: American Museum of Natural History.

Mihalic, Francis. 1971. *The Jacaranda Dictionary and Grammar of Melanesian Pidgin.* Milton, Queensland: Jacaranda Press.

Miklouho-Maclay, Nikolai Nikolaevich. 1975. *Mikloucho-Maclay: New Guinea Diaries 1871–1883.* Edited and translated by C. L. Sentinella. Madang, Papua New Guinea: Kristen Pres.

Niles, Don. 1983. "Why Are There No Garamuts in Papua?" *Bikmaus* 4(3):90–104.

———. 1989. "Altérateurs de voix de Papouasie-Nouvelle-Guinée: Où comment la confusion des donnés appauvrit l'organologie." *Cahiers de musiques traditionnelles* 2:75–99.

———. 1990. "Sepik Music in Outer Space." *Times of PNG,* 6 September, 19.

———. 1992a. "Flute and Trumpet Ensembles in the Sepik Provinces." In *Sound and Reason: Music and Essays in Honour of Gordon D. Spearritt,* ed. Warren A. Bebbington and Royston Gustavson, 49–60. St. Lucia: University of Queensland.

———. 1992b. "*Konggap, Kap,* and *Tambaran:* Music of the Yupno/Nankina Area in Relation to Neighbouring Groups." In *Abschied von der Vergangenheit,* ed. Jürg Wassmann, 149–183. Berlin: Dietrich Reimer.

Oosterwal, Gottfried. 1961. *People of the Tor.* Assen, the Netherlands: Royal van Gorcum.

Pomponio, Alice. 1992. *Seagulls Don't Fly Into the Bush: Cultural Identity and Development in Melanesia.* Belmont, California: Wadsworth.

Sande, G. A. J. van der. 1907. "Ethnography and Anthropology [of New Guinea]." *Nova Guinea* 3:1–390.

Sanger, Penelope, and Neil Sorrell. 1975. "Music in Umeda Village, New Guinea." *Ethnomusicology* 19(1):67–89.

Scaglion, Richard. 1997. "Abelam: Giant Yams and Cycles of Sex, Warfare, and Ritual." In *Asia and Oceania,* ed. Melvyn Ember and C. R. Ember, 253–276. Portraits of Culture: Ethnographic Originals, 4. Englewood Cliffs, N.J.: Prentice Hall.

Schlenker, Hermann. 1984. *Auftritt der 'Mai'-Masken in Korogo.* 16-mm. Göttingen: Institut für den Wissenschaftlichen Film.

Schmitz, Carl A. 1956. "Die Initiation Bei den Pasum am oberen Rumu, Nordost-Neuguinea." *Zeitschrift für Ethnologie* 81.

———. 1958. "Die Jawik-Figuren der Pasum in Nordost-Neu-Guinea." *Jahrbuch des Museum für Völkerkunde zu Leipzig* 17:30–51.

———. 1963. *Wantoat: Art and Religion of the Northeast New Guinea Papuans.* Translated by Mrs. G. E. van Baaren-Pape. The Hague: Mouton.

Spearritt, Gordon D. 1979. "The Music of the Iatmul People of the Middle Sepik River (Papua New Guinea) with Special Reference to Instrumental Music at Kandangai and Aibom." 2 vols. Ph.D. dissertation, University of Queensland.

———. 1984. "Problems in Transcription: Drum Rhythms and Flute Music of Papua New Guinea." In *Problems and Solutions: Occasional Essays in Musicology Presented to Alice M. Moyle,* ed. Jamie C. Kassler and Jill Stubington, 32–50. Sydney: Hale & Iremonger.

———. 1990. "The Yumanwusmangge Ceremony at Aibom." In *Sepik Heritage: Tradition and Change in Papua New Guinea,* ed. Nancy Lutkehaus et al., 535–545. Durham, N.C.: Carolina Academic Press.

Tuzin, Donald F. 1980. *The Voice of the Tambaran: Truth and Illusion in Ilahita Arapesh Religion.* Berkeley: University of California Press.

Wassmann, Jürg. 1982. *Der Gesang an den fliegen-den Hund.* Basler Beiträge zur Ethnologie, 22. Basel: Ethnologisches Seminar der Universität und Museum für Völkerkunde.

———. 1991. *The Song to the Flying Fox.* Translated by Dennis Q. Stephenson. Apwitihire, 2. Boroko: National Research Institute.

Webb, Ross, and Lyndal Webb. 1990. "Tuma-Irumu Orthography Paper." Manuscript.

Yamada, Yoichi. 1991. *Rei no Uta ga Kikoeru: Wahei no Oto no Minzokushi* (Songs of spirits: An ethnography of sounds of the Waxei people). Tokyo: Shunjusha.

———. 1997. *Songs of Spirits: An Ethnography of Sounds in a Papua New Guinea Society.* Translated by Jun'ichi Ohno. Apwitihire: Studies in Papua New Guinean Musics, 5. Boroko: Institute of Papua New Guinea Studies.

Z'graggen, John A. 1975. *The Languages of the Madang District, Papua New Guinea.* Pacific Linguistics, B-41. Canberra: Australian National University.

# Irian Jaya Province of Indonesia

*Vida Chenoweth*
*Kathleen Van Arsdale*
*Artur Simon*

---

**Musical Contexts**
**Musical Instruments**
**Musical Systems**
**A Lowland People: the Asmat**
**A Highland People: the Eipo**

---

The easternmost province of Indonesia, Irian Jaya covers the western half of New Guinea Island. Its central mountains ascend more than 5 kilometers, but much of its land is swamp. Its two million inhabitants are clustered in more than 250 distinct groups (Silzer and Clouse 1991). Most interior peoples had first contact with the outside after 1945; even in the mid-1990s, the southern slopes of the central mountains, the northern border with Papua New Guinea, and the Wapoga (Owa) River watershed had experienced no direct contact (Duane Clouse, personal communication).

Politically, the province divides into eight regencies, clustered in four cultural regions (map): the highlands (Jayawijaya, Pania), the north coast and plain (Jayapura, Yapèn-Waropèn), the south coast (Merauke), and the Vogelkop (Sorong, Manokwari, Fakfak). Since provincewide studies of music have not been carried out, available information remains scattered and sketchy.

In the 1990s, Irian Jaya was embracing a new ethos, with status based on the acquisition of material goods. Musical creativity was responding to foreign styles and genres. Indonesian radio and teachers proselytized their own musical culture, as did Christian missionaries, who by the 1980s were fostering innovation. Some governmental officials believe performances of local music and dancing are wasteful practices, but teachers at the University of Cenderawasih (in Abepura) encourage them. As foreign instruments—guitars, ukuleles, harmonicas—enter the culture and young people play them, a rift between the generations widens. Functional tonality increasingly shapes local musical thinking, and leaders are becoming anxious, lest the memory of the old music die.

## MUSICAL CONTEXTS

The peoples of Irian Jaya classify songs mainly by circumstance and manner of performance. The songs of inland peoples favor themes common elsewhere in New Guinea: hunting pigs, initiating boys, conducting intertribal warfare, and dying. Important feasts require pork, a sign of wealth and prestige. Hunting wild pigs and

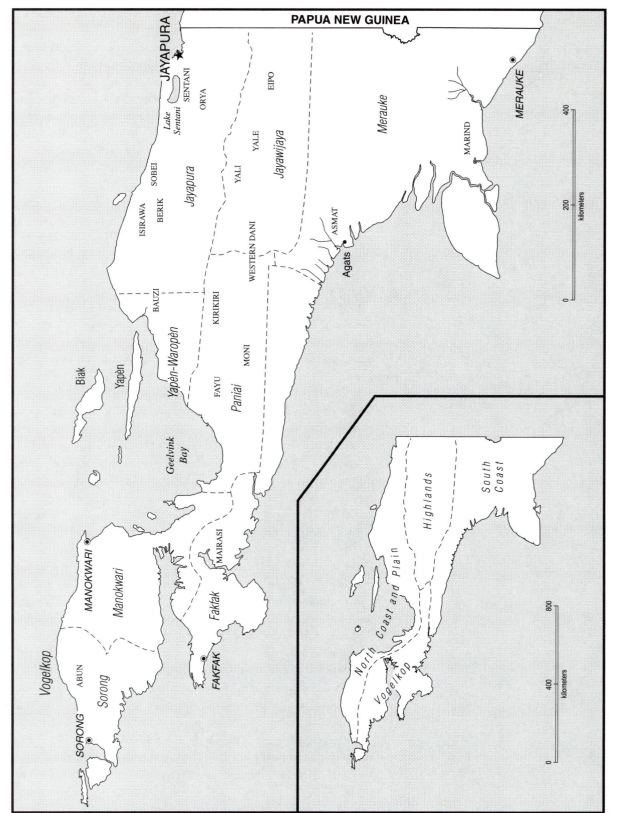

Irian Jaya Province of Indonesia

other animals often follows the singing of a song to ensure success. At feasts, people sing while the pig is cooking. The Yale sing to make domestic pigs fertile, and formerly sang while sacrificing pigs; other Yale songs accompany butchering and distributing the meat. Songs about hunts or feasts are absent from Bismam Asmat and Abun music.

Many peoples of central Irian Jaya east of the Vogelkop, on both coasts, sing during male initiations. The oldest Isirawa genre, *kona,* includes initiatory songs once sung in a secret ceremony, accompanied by paired flutes. People sing and dance to some initiatory songs during celebrations, including those for completing a new men's house, a baby's first outing, and a coconut tree's first bearing. Bismam Asmat initiations are the most elaborate in the province.

In the interior, some songs are vestiges of warfare. Songs celebrating victory are most common; but where fighting has been recent or has played a major social role, songs celebrate the phases of warfare. Two Yali villages may together sing of a desire for revenge; other war-related songs recall battles and their heroes, victories, and making peace. Along the north coast and in the Vogelkop, intertribal warfare is uncommon.

Spontaneously sung laments occur throughout the province. On the north coast, the Sentani dance for a chief's burial. Isirawa laments, first sung by friends and relations while someone is dying, may commemorate the loved one for a year after the death. In customary mourning, the Bismam Asmat roll in mud while improvising laments.

Peoples of Irian Jaya musically celebrate major public projects. Documented instances include songs performed after building a bridge across a river (Yale), putting a roof on a house (Mairasi), making canoes for warfare (Asmat), and building a men's house (Isirawa). In Yali culture, only healers may sing medicinal songs. When sickness was raging, the Yale, in the mountains south and west of the Yali, sacrificed a pig: in the seclusion of the jungle, they offered its fat to evil spirits; when they returned home, they built a fence around their village, believing the sickness-causing spirits could not leap over it. Elsewhere in Irian Jaya, songs of hunting and courting serve magical functions.

Songs often serve as histories (Wilson 1988:34). The Yale record their heritage in lyrics about their first drum and its maker, the coming of their ancestors, the first clearing of their gardens, and the beauty of their mountains. Other Yale songs treat contemporary life: falling on a muddy slope when fetching water, learning how to maintain an airstrip, taking a trip to Womena, where the Yale first saw cars and bikes. The Asmat *bis,* a ceremony involving the carving of effigies, musically commemorates the dead.

Many songs of Irian Jaya complain about men's mistreating women. Asmat women humiliate their husbands, at whom they direct songs of ridicule, which listeners acknowledge with knowing laughter. Sentani women compose and sing songs bewailing the times their husbands have beaten them and made them cry. Yale women compose songs deploring local men's uncleanliness (K. Van Arsdale 1982). In contrast, Asmat men often sing about women's love; men and women, together or separately, sing to children and to express gratitude for daily food or gifts from outsiders.

Throughout the province, people learn to sing by watching and imitating. At home, Mairasi boys may receive vocal instruction from their father or uncle; dancing, however, they learn during public performances (Peckham 1981:59). All children dance, but only boys play instruments. Children do not have their own songs, but imitate those of adults. A longhouse ordinarily serves as a school; for further instruction, proficient students seek teachers, usually lead singers.

FIGURE 1    Playing hourglass drums, dancers
from Irian Jaya perform at the Baird
Auditorium, Smithsonian Institution. Photo by
Adrienne L. Kaeppler, 1991.

## Dancing

In the highlands, dancing by men and women moving in circles and singing responsorially while men play hourglass drums resembles performances of highland peoples
across the international border (figure 1). An example is the *fatiya,* a genre whose
songs originated with the Kwerba, south of the Isirawa. Performed only at night, and
formerly continued until people had devoured their enemies' bodies, it highlighted
weddings and initiations (now discontinued), funerals, and babies' first outings, and
still marks the construction of buildings, New Year's, and feasts for men to publicize
songs they have composed (Oguri 1981:15). Yali adults dance to bellicose songs; Yali
boys and girls dance to antiphonally sung songs of courtship, whose texts express sexual desire.

W*or,* graceful dance-songs accompanied by hourglass drums, spread from Biak
to nearby islands and the coast. In *mon,* dance-songs for healing, people sang and
danced around a decorated bamboo platform while a religious specialist went into
trance to learn the remedy from a spirit. In *walla,* the Alfur of the Misool Islands
stamped metrically on a wooden or bamboo platform. In southern Sorong, dancers

used similar stamps of alternate feet with slightly bent knees, so bodies bobbed metrically. The Moi called this dance *alin*; north and inland, the Karon and Moraid called it *séra* and performed it in a circle, with linked arms. In the Moi *kalenkokla*, women waggled their buttocks while men beat drums and sang (Kunst 1967:125–126).

In Fakfak too, dancing occurs on a platform. The Mairasi sing responsorially to the beat of drums and gongs. Participants, in ranks of two or three (first men, then women, then children), follow two to four drummers and one or two men carrying a gong and a beater. All step mincingly. Rapid drumbeats cue the dancing. For the singing, the tempo slackens; to cue the final phrase, the tempo slows more. Only men play instruments, but whistling or hissing occasionally breaks out. The Mairasi perform these dances at feasts, weddings, changes of leadership, and celebrations of national independence. Daytime performances are more casual: between songs, people sit and converse at tables under temporary shelters.

## MUSICAL INSTRUMENTS

The distribution and playing of musical instruments in Irian Jaya and Papua New Guinea show broad similarities. Aerophones are important, and men play paired flutes, often in secret. Hourglass drums, introduced into the highlands from coastal peoples, are played widely. Irian Jaya differs markedly in the use of idiophones. Though many peoples of Papua New Guinea play struck wooden idiophones, some peoples of Irian Jaya play metal gongs.

### Idiophones

The playing of gongs in Irian Jaya suggests cultural relationships with peoples of Indonesia. In Fakfak, to accompany communal dancing, Mairasi men play bossed brass gongs in rhythm with drums while walking counterclockwise in a circle; the population follows, but only men sing or play instruments. Fishermen of Seram Island may have introduced these gongs (Peckham 1981:58), which come in two sizes: one (*mamonggo*) has a depth of about 6 centimeters; the other (*unguni*), about 11 centimeters. Both are about 35 centimeters in diameter. Each player carries his gong suspended on a cord and hits its boss with a wooden mallet held in his right hand.

In some parts of the province, men who are not dancing may produce a percussive sound by striking arrows against a bow. Isirawa men and others make bamboo lamellaphones, which persons of either sex twang for private amusement; highlanders are reputed to be the best players (Duane Clouse, personal communication).

### Membranophones

The handheld drum typical of Irian Jaya has an hourglass shape, formed by gouging and burning out a meter-long log. The drumhead is made from the skin of a small animal (often a lizard), stretched over an opening 12 to 15 centimeters wide. Men, the only drummers, tauten a drumhead by sticking pellets of wax to its center. This drum accompanies dancing. Though not indigenous to the western highlands (Duane Clouse, personal communication), it has the widest provincial distribution of any musical instrument there. The Asmat version has a decorative filigree above and below the handle.

### Aerophones

On the north coast, secret flutes occur in Jayapura and Yapèn-Waropèn. The playing of Isirawa sacred bamboo flutes (*asiina*) by initiated males once formed part of initiations. The flutes have a rectangular notch cut in the open end. Their names—*asiinaya* (about 1.5 meters), *tiikiire* (about 1.25 meters), and *faafrataya* (about 1 meter)—specify their length and imply the order in which each enters the musical texture. Women are forbidden to know about these flutes: on seeing them, women would be struck by storms and lightning; on playing them, they would die (Oguri 1981:10). People formerly sacrificed animals and birds to the flutes. The Bauzi play similar flutes, held vertically, with the player's hands cupping the mouthpiece. Knuckles of the player's thumbs block leakage of air from the corners of the mouth. In pairs, the players move vigorously, facing each other and sounding their flutes. As a player takes in air, he tilts the flute up; as he blows into it, he forces it downward.

Other aerophones are played in public: for *fatiya*, the Isirawa play short bamboo flutes and conchs, with no restrictions on who may play. Such instruments often sound a rhythm notatable as three eighths and a long-held quarter; to assemble the populace, they sound a rhythm notatable as a half, two eighths, a half, two eighths, and a half. On the south coast, the Asmat headhunting trumpet is made from a bamboo tube open at one end; a small hole pierces the closed end. Its surface bears carved designs.

## MUSICAL SYSTEMS

In Irian Jaya, communal singing is responsorial or unison. Solo singing occurs among the Abun and elsewhere, in the form of laments for the death of a loved one. Not uncommonly, as among the Isirawa, men and women sing different songs simultaneously, in coordinate monophony. Contrapuntal polyphony has been identified only among highland peoples, mainly the Yali. Accuracy in melody and text is important; the timing of vocal entries, less precise. Dynamic variation is of no concern; singers seek a forceful uniformity of sound.

Most ritual songs have fixed texts. To existing melodies, people improvise other songs. Texts often obscure emotional intensity, or with metaphor disguise ulterior meanings. Many songs have more vocables than words; those entirely in vocables carry meaning by association. People do not understand the texts of songs borrowed from others, or songs with archaic texts. The texts of men's secret songs are intentionally obscure. The Bismam Asmat sing ritual songs in a special ceremonial language. Occasionally an elliptical text is informative and well understood: a Mairasi song of that sort names a sequence of reefs, in geographic order up the coast; the text is a tool for finding areas where fish and mollusks are bountiful.

### Highlands

TRACK 35

East of the Moni and Uhunduni (Ugunduni), at Lake Paniai, live the Dani and the Ilu, with the Baliem Valley as their center. Farther eastward, where valleys and populations are smaller, live the Yali, around the mission station of Angguruk. East of the Yali is the large but less populated area of the Mek, and farther eastward, those of the Yale and the Ok.

The most common highland style is responsorial. A leader repeats each phrase with slight variations in rhythm or pitch, to which the rest reply. In nondanced songs, one or two persons softly sing a descant a perfect fifth above the leader's melody (Duane Clouse, personal communication). Melodic ranges rarely exceed a fifth; performances attain a thick harmonic texture, covering two or more octaves, greater than the range of music elsewhere in Irian Jaya.

In responsorial singing, the contrast between leader and chorus helps demarcate phrases. Performances may mark phrases with special effects: the Dani and the Moni produce an audible hiss as they inhale through clenched teeth, usually between a short phrase and its repetition; at the end of textual phrases, Moni performers repeatedly snap their fingers for about five seconds. Moni songs are famous for a thick harmonic texture, with melodies sung in parallel motion on chords using ninths and

FIGURE 2 Excerpt from a Western Dani song; Danau Bira Village, 1984. Later, singers enter with variations of a drone on A below C; all breathe at staggered intervals. Transcription by Vida Chenoweth.

elevenths, transcribable as C–E–G–B–D–F, over a bass drone. A Western Dani song (figure 2) has a melody on a major third over a regular two-note oscillation.

Contrast between leader and chorus is minimal in Yali and Ok dance-songs. The Yali polyphonic style has virtually no lead singer, except at the start of songs (Simon 1978:454). In Ok *yase,* one person may start a song, but the vocal parts are almost equivalent (Royl 1992).

### Yale

Yale melodies elaborate any of three scalar patterns, all of which require at least four tones with F the tonal center. In pattern one, F–(G)–Ab–Aⁿ–(Bb)–C–D (the commonest), tones move freely to adjacent tones. With one exception (four tones ascending), only three tones move in a common direction; reversal or repeated notes check the path. Semitones are never stressed. In melodies where the tonal center leaps to Ab, the latter continues upward to Bb. When Aⁿ is present, the tonal center leaps to C. The tonal center leaps irreversibly to any tone but D. Downward leaps go only from Bb or C to G. Repeated notes are common, to a maximum of seven repetitions.

In Yale pattern two, D–F–G–A–(Bb), any tone may move to an adjacent tone. Leaps from tonal center to Bb, or from G to Bb, are reversible; other leaps are not. In Yale pattern three, (A)–C–(D)–F–G–A, melodies move above and below tonal center; only here do melodies leap over it—from a minor third below to a major second above. Adjacent movement is reversible among D, F, G and A: D proceeds to C, and C to A, but not the reverse. Leaps from C to F, and from D to G, are reversible: leaps from A to G, C to G, and F to A are not. This pattern includes the widest Yale leap: from A to G, a minor seventh. The widest leap in a song is usually a perfect fifth. Contours resulting from these melodic restrictions may be described as an undulating descent. A second voice may sound below the main melody.

### Yali

Yali songs, which resemble those of the Western Dani more than those of the Yale, have contrapuntal polyphony in two to four voices. The vocal lines are of three types: type 1 has a single melodic interval, often a perfect fourth, which varies rhythmically; type 2 has a brief motif, which recurs with a minimal amount of alteration; type 3 is a single tone reiterated in the same rhythm with another voice or independently. An excerpt from a Yali lament illustrates all three types (figure 3).

FIGURE 3 Excerpt from a Yali lament; Lolat Village, 1988. Transcription by Vida Chenoweth.

### North coast

Peoples of this area often sing in unison, accompanied by a hand-held drum. Musical forms are typically variations on a theme, set in a descending melodic contour called tiled music (Kunst 1967:7). Some melodies, including those of Berik and Sobei songs, are through-composed. Berik men's initiatory songs feature a nuclear fourth whose upper tone is the tonal center. Berik women's songs, usually accompanying work, have short, falling, kinesthetically impulsive phrases (figure 4a).

Influenced by Indonesian and Berik popular music, the music of the north coast is changing rapidly. Only Sobei elders sing old Sobei songs; young Berik are composing non-Western Berik songs, mostly religious. In the plains, because of immigrant highlanders' influence, change is also occurring: the tonal inventory has increased, a new emphasis includes the entire village, people who have never had drums are adopting them, and borrowed songs are undergoing adaptations, including increased tempos and omitted harmonies.

### Berik and Sobei songs compared

A comparison of ten Berik songs and ten Sobei songs reveals musical systems with much in common, like dialects of a language. Both are monophonic, with similar forms, contours, and tonal inventories and progressions. Phrases descend only to leap upward and descend again, with a rapid fall broken by up to eight repeated notes. Sobei phrases have fewer repeated notes; in dance-songs their descent has smaller intervals. Both peoples share a tonal inventory and syntax (figure 4b). Arrows show tonal progressions in common; other tones occur, more in Sobei than Berik. D♯ and F turn up consistently in Sobei data, but infrequently in Berik. Upward leaps may not occur. Five tones make minimal Sobei melodies; only three occur in ascent, but four to six occur occur in descent. Sobei melodies flaunt a tritone and a falling major third at cadences, though rarely at the final one. Four tones (A, C♯, D♯, $A_1$) make minimal Berik melodies. Melodic movement is usually to adjacent tones with few leaps, except tones that begin phrases.

FIGURE 4 Berik music: *a,* excerpt from a song for pounding sago, Somanente Village, 1983; *b,* the Berik and Sobei tonal inventory. Transcriptions by Vida Chenoweth.

*a*

*b*

### Sentani

Like the Sobei and the Berik, the Sentani dance to steady drumbeats and sing responsorially, sometimes antiphonally. The syntax of Sentani musical phrases varies from a

One Sentani song is about a hunt. Learning that a boy has killed his first pig, a mother cries. She recognizes that her son will soon reach adulthood and shun her protection.

FIGURE 5    Three Sentani tonal inventories. The third is G–A♭–B♭–B♮–C–D♭–E, with C and D♭ moving only to B♮, and E moving only to C. In all Sentani tonal inventories, B♭ is tonal center. Transcriptions by Vida Chenoweth.

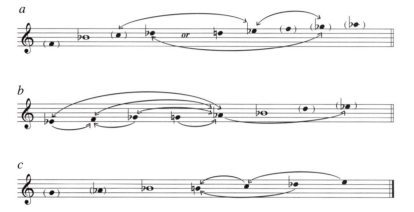

simple structure, such as AB$_a$ (phrase B deriving from features of phrase A), or ABC$_b$, to through-composed structures and variations of compound phrases, of which an example may be abbreviated: $A_1$ (=$a_1b_1$) + $A_2$ (=$a_2b_2$) + $A_3$ (=$a_3b_1$) + $A_4$ (=$a_2b_1$) + $A_5$ (=$a_4b_1$) + $A_6$ (=$a_5b_2$). In this example, phrase A combines two motivic units, a and b, which vary as the song progresses.

In some Sentani pieces, compound phrases reach considerable complexity. In one song, phrase A = abc + y$_a$cyd. Later phrases consider the treatment of each motif: $A_1$ = $b_1b_2c_1$ + ycy. Phrase B omits the first motif entirely; a phrase C consists only of $c_4c_5$ + yy. Development moves from complex to simple. In another song, one compound phrase varies thus: A (=$a_1$bcd$_1$) + B (=$a_2$bcd$_2$d$_1$) + C (=$a_3$bbcd$_3$). Phrase B derives from phrase A, maintaining the contour and essential elements, but varying them by repetition or melodic and rhythmic substitution. Rhythmic variation is largely the result of textual change. Phrase C uses the same devices, but in a different arrangement (DeVilbiss 1989:32).

In a sample of fifteen transcriptions of Sentani songs, three melodic types occur. Tones in parentheses do not always occur; those at the ends of the spectrum (F, A♭) turn up only once in the sample. In songs of melodic type 1 (figure 5*a*), the tonal center precedes any tone except A♭; any tone proceeds to the tonal center, except those above E♭, the optional ones. Adjacent tones move freely from one to the other, but D♭ and D♮ do not occur in the same song. Two-way leaps are E♭ to C, E♭ to G♭, and G♭ to D♭. A single, one-way leap from D to F occurs.

Melodies of type 2 move mainly below the tonal center (figure 5*b*). One song of type 2 is responsorial, with a G♭ in one voice and a G♮ in the other, but never sounding simultaneously. G occurs only in the progression G–A♭–G♭. These melodies ground themselves in a strong fourth: tonal center B♭ and a fourth below. Any interval can approach the tonal center, which can move to any tone except the lowest. Reversible adjacent movement involves only tones between G♭ and C. Adjacent movement in a single direction includes lower E♭ to F, G♭ to F, and G to A♭. Two-way leaps other than to or from the tonal center include lower E♭ to A♭, F to A♭, and G♭ to A♭. Only one leap (A♭ to the upper E♭) crosses the tonal center and immediately returns.

In neither of the first two types does a minor second above tonal center occur, but songs of type 3, laments, have small intervals, often heard in downglides. Most movement occurs above tonal center. Of two transcribed examples (DeVilbiss 1989), one concerns a wife, crying because her husband is beating her: she tells him he should hunt wild pigs instead. The other is about a hunt: on learning that a boy has killed his first pig, a mother cries, recognizing that the son will soon reach adulthood and shun her protection. The minimal Sentani melody of type 3 has three tones (B♭–B–D♭); a maximum of four tones in a common direction occurs, descending only. One recorded responsorial song has nine repeated notes.

### Other peoples

Isirawa melodies use five tones, with no melodic interval smaller than a major second. Melodies descend. To mark the conclusion of a section, Isirawa singer-dancers sustain on one tone the vowel /o/. Between songs, the leader sings episodic material (*sri*) that, being in a water-dwelling spirit's language, has no semantic meaning (Oguri 1981:14).

Kirikiri songs allow the free movement of three tones: a tonal center, a major second above, and a slightly sharp minor third, transcribable as the tones A–B–C⁺; but Kirikiri songs borrowed from peoples to the south (Wano, Dani, Turimo) have a different inventory, E–G♭–A–C⁺, with A the tonal center. In these melodies, only one upward leap (G♭ to C⁺) occurs. The borrowed style is responsorial: a leader sings a short phrase, on the last word of which choral singers enter a minor second lower.

## South coast

Typical Asmat singing is responsorial, with one dynamic level and occasional acceleration. The lead singer often adds a third above the chorus (figure 6). A stylized cadence occurs in the drums, followed by shouts. Farther south than the Asmat live the Marind, Yey, and Kanum. Many of their songs are in ternary meter and have scales of tones arranged in chains of thirds (Kunst 1967:135–176).

## Vogelkop

### Mairasi

Mairasi instrumentalists contrast a slow, even-beat tempo with a fast, uneven-beat tempo. Reversing the positioning of their drums reinforces such changes: they play slow, even rhythms with the drum upside down, hitting the head from below; in a quick tempo with uneven beat, they reverse the drum, hitting the head from above. Six locally named rhythmic combinations exist (Peckham 1981:59). Dance-songs often begin with a rapid drumbeat, slow "to about half that tempo for most of the song" and again halve the tempo (Hughes 1989:3:24).

Songs consist of a single phrase A or phrases AB or ABC, with descending phrasal contours. According to textual demands, phrases require rhythmic substitution, omission, or expansion, and slight melodic alterations. Mairasi structures are through-composed, or show various schemes of repetition, from a simple AB, to complex patterns, including $A_1A_1 + B_aB_1B_1 + A_2B_2$, and even $A_1B_1C_1C_1C_2A_2B_2 + A_3B_3C_4C_5C_5A_1B_4 + A_4A_5C_6C_7C_8A_5B_6 + A_4B_7C_9C_{10}C_{11}C_{12}A_1B_4$. Some form of phrase B ends each song.

Tonal inventories show an obligatory kernel: the tonal center and a major sec-

FIGURE 6    Excerpt from an Asmat song. Transcription by Kathleen O. Van Arsdale.

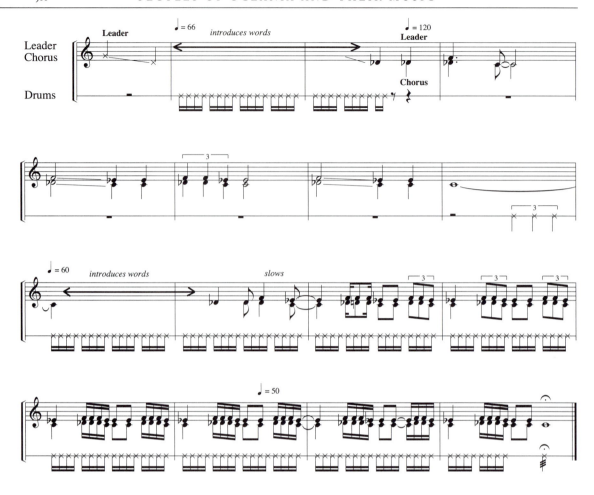

ond and third above (figure 7). Mairasi melodies have four to nine tones: those between C# below the kernel to C# within the kernel move freely to and from adjacent tones; below C#, adjacent movement and all leaps are downward. No semitones occur; G and G# do not occur within the same melody. Melodies move freely between the tonal center and a perfect fourth above and below. Free movement also occurs between the tonal center and the major third and perfect fifth above (C# and E within the kernel). Above the kernel, reversible movement occurs only between F# and G#.

Upward leaps typically include F# a minor third below the tonal center to C# or E; tonal center to C#, E, or an octave above; E above the kernel to G to F#. Downward leaps include $A_1$ to F# or E, F# above kernel to D, F# below kernel to low A, and E below kernel to low A. The significant tones (lowest to highest: A, E, A, C#, E, F#, A) are leapt to. The tonal center is crossed only by an upward leap from the F# below to either C# or E within the kernel. Low A proceeding to E within the kernel may look like a further example, but this interval arises only when a song repeats: in a given song, low A is the final tone, and E the initial. The structural segmentation of

FIGURE 7    The Mairasi tonal inventory and typical melodic motion, in which tones relate to a hypothetical given tonal center (A) and arrows mark upward leaps and irreversible downward ones. Transcription by Vida Chenoweth.

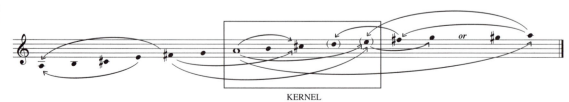

KERNEL

Mairasi songs correlates with their textual tenses: lyrics in the present tense are songs with a single phrase; songs with more than one phrase relate past events (Hughes 1989:3:24–25).

### Orya

The Orya dance to sounds from hourglass drums. A typical song, of the genre *kanang,* displays two phrases, which alternate and vary. Some songs change midway to two other phrases, treated in like manner. Those called *boyo* have antiphony between two voices. In twenty sampled songs, seven tonal inventories occur:

|   |   |   |   |   |   |   |   |   |
|---|---|---|---|---|---|---|---|---|
|   |   | A |   | C | D |   |   |   |
|   |   | A |   | C | D |   | F |   |
|   |   | A |   | C | D |   | F |   |
| A | G | A | B | C | D |   |   |   |
| F |   | A |   | C | D | E | F |   |
| F | G | A |   | C | D |   | F |   |
|   |   |   |   |   | D | E |   | G or G♯ |

The basis of six songs is a minimum of three tones: a tonal center (A), a minor third above, and a fourth above.

In Orya songs with three or four tones, any tone can precede any other, though not in any one song. A tone occurring below tonal center proceeds to and from tonal center alone. Six tones may be the maximal inventory for an Orya melody. In one recorded song, F and G occur below tonal center A, and E is omitted. In six-tone songs, movement to adjacent members is typical. Leaps are small; upward leaps are more prominent than downward. As with other musical systems of the region, no more than four tones succeed each other in one direction; this restriction produces a wavy contour.

### Abun

Abun melodies resemble those of the north coast more than those of the Mairasi. Of local musical genres, the *sukrot* is the least modernized. *Sukrot* melodies have a nucleus of a perfect fourth. A song may consist of only the tonal center and a perfect fourth below; or to these it may add the fifth below. The minor third below, optional and rhythmically weak, normally appends to the fourth below. The melodic structures of the genres *sukne* and *sukba* are similar: to begin a phrase, either makes wide leaps upward to tonal center; a gradual, undulating descent follows, ending typically on tonal center an octave below. Semitones intervene between principal tones; vocal downgliding and unstable tonality also occur. —VIDA CHENOWETH

## A LOWLAND PEOPLE: THE ASMAT

The Asmat, more than sixty-five thousand speakers of a non-Austronesian language, inhabit part of the southwestern coastal swamp and forest of Merauke Province, an area which, though visited by Captain Cook and technically controlled by the Dutch through 1962, has known continuous outside contact since the early 1950s. Formerly hunter-gatherers, the Asmat have settled mostly in villages. Music informs their culture, as revealed in the myth of Fumeripits, the creator, who from wood carved the first Asmat people and drummed them to life.

TRACK 34

### Musical contexts and genres

The most important Asmat music enhances rituals, which demarcate seasons and life-cycle stages, placate and communicate with ancestral spirits, brace villages for battle, and consecrate feasts. Music is part of a sacramental whole, organized by experts who occupy inherited positions of status. Among the most important rituals are *bis, warmoran* (sending spirits of the dead to "the other side"), men's initiations (*emak cem*), sago-palm feasts, longhouse feasts, head-hunting raids, shield-making festivals (*salawaku*), ceremonies of masks and adoption, peace-and-reconciliation feasts, warrior's funerals, canoe-dedicating feasts, and *basu suangkus* ("making visible" the heads of men killed in battle).

*Bis,* the central Bismam ritual, lasts for weeks, when men carve and set up poles, 4.5 to 9 meters high, portraying dead ancestors. Believing death the work of enemies, spiritual and human, people sing songs pledging revenge (Van Arsdale and Van Arsdale 1991:20). Painted, dressed in fur or feather headdresses, boar-tooth or dog-tooth necklaces, and bone or shell nasal ornaments, and carrying spears, men sing and dance during breaks from carving. Women perform simultaneously but apart. The music includes songs celebrating the carving (sample text: "Now I am carving your mouth"), commemorating dead individuals, and recounting history and mythology. In the longhouse at night, men present the nucleus of ritual music: epic cycles lasting up to twenty-four hours. The cycle *Bowep* narrates the villagers' origin, deeds, and journeys. When men haul the trees felled for poles, women attack, in a mock skirmish. Only women sing the myths *Bokpim* and *Cawor. Bis* formerly ended in a head-hunting raid, beginning with embarkation to the sounds of the head-hunting trumpet (*fu*).

Initiations formerly followed head-hunting rituals. Paddling home from a successful raid, men sang songs and sounded *fu*. They ritually washed and scorched the freshly severed head; old men then ate the brains and decorated the skull. Men smeared a mixture of blood and ashes onto the initiate, who contemplated the skull for three days while listening to songs of history and genealogy. Each night, all villagers celebrated, singing with drums and festively eating sago, furnished by women, their arrival announced by head-hunting trumpets.

In evenings, parties sing around a fire. To children, women sing lullabies and nursery rhymes. While working, paddling canoes, gathering wood, fishing, and collecting sago, people sometimes sing or whistle (K. Van Arsdale 1982:55). They use music in courtship and for expressing thanks and appreciation. To commemorate a villager's death, women improvise a lament and throw themselves into mud. Songs of sorrow and complaint provide women with humiliative power, commonly regarding mistreatment, social missteps, failure in battle or hunting, and sexual problems. Anyone may musically express feelings; people employ specialists to use music in bringing about love, luck, health, disaster, and death.

## Music in the mind

The Asmat believe music to be powerful: a given piece can communicate with and appease spirits, drive away disease and suffering, cause death, facilitate a sexual seduction, brace a village for battle, and protect canoeists and the inhabitants of new homes. Many songs are available for all to sing. In ritual performances, men and women function separately, with separate roles, songs, and leaders. Each important ritual song belongs to an individual, who controls its performance. This copyright is heritable and transferable. The Asmat acknowledge ancestors' musical contributions but do not attribute to spirits the source of music. Few compositions have an identifiable composer, and spontaneous composition has value in songs of grief, derision, and courting. Some people compose and perform personal songs, such as pieces recalling a loved one. Many Asmat villages share specific pieces, with associated notions about where and when to perform them.

Asmat musical timbre is relaxed, with unchanging volume. Melodies normally descend, developing motives through thematic repetition. Meter is unvarying, and tempo sometimes accelerates. Choral textures are usually responsorial; at the end of sections and pieces, shouts punctuate cadences. Sometimes a lead singer sustains a major third above a chorus. Large forms have discrete sections, and certain songs chain together into suites. All songs have poetry, sometimes in long, highly organized texts. Most ritual texts employ an ancient, secret, ceremonial language, which has symbolic, magical, and spiritual significance and occurs only in song. Musical elaboration focuses on words, not melodic or rhythmic material.

The Asmat learn music informally, through observation and imitation. In long-houses, boys learn about drumming, dancing, and singing. Certain boys and girls are trained, usually by their kin, to be musical leaders. In the 1990s, schools (run by Christian missions or the government), churches, and mosques teach or sponsor musical performances.

## Musical instruments

From ironwood or hibiscus, Asmat carvers hew hourglass drums, with heads made from the dried skins of iguanas (Leimbach, Dutilleux, and Van Arsdale 1975). A mix of a drum-owning family's blood and ground clamshells attaches the head to the rim, around which is braided a rattan strip. Players tune the drum by heating its head over a fire and attaching to it resinous or waxy blobs. Meant to last, drums become heirlooms.

Asmat head-hunting trumpets are end-blown straight trumpets, without mouthpiece. Made of wood or bamboo, covered with symbols, they are not always carvers' work. The Asmat consider them signaling devices. Residents of the interior play conical trumpets, lamellaphones, and swung slats; children use leaves as buzzers.

## Music in transition

Most Asmat have been in continuous contact with outsiders since 1953. Traders, missionaries, officials, teachers, and corporations have brought outside musics. In 1979, government-sponsored tourism began. Indonesian popular music and non-Asmat indigenous music reach most villages. Issues of introduced language and instruments concern Asmat elders, but young people enjoy music heard on radio and cassettes.

The government and some missionaries have tried to suppress Asmat rituals (P. Van Arsdale 1975:49). The last authentically complete *bis* occurred in 1974. By Indonesian law, musical performance for a *bis* can lead to criminal prosecution; persons wishing to hold a major ritual must seek permission from the government, which views ritual efforts as nonproductive (K. Van Arsdale 1982:74). Some villages perform rituals secretly or in the jungle. Revitalization movements, in which music plays an important part, have appeared, notably in 1976. An important annual celebration is Christmas. Introduced instruments, especially ukuleles, guitars, and harmonicas, are popular.

The Asmat Museum of Culture and Progress, founded by Roman Catholic missionaries and initially funded by the John D. Rockefeller III Fund, has a splendid collection of instruments, with some recordings. The founders intended the museum to help the Asmat retain their cultural identity in the face of worldwide change.

—KATHLEEN VAN ARSDALE

## A HIGHLAND PEOPLE: THE EIPO

The Eipo, speaking a non-Austronesian language, live in the valley along the upper course of the Eipomek River. The climate is cool and wet: trails and paths hardly ever dry off. Larger animals and reptiles seldom visit this altitude; nor do mosquitoes, so

FIGURE 8   Dangan plays a *bingkong* at Munggona. Photo by Artur Simon, 1975.

malaria is unknown. Eipo villages have twenty to 250 inhabitants, mostly dwelling in round huts. The social order is egalitarian, organized into exogamous patrilineal and patrilocal clans. Because local life is ruled by the struggle for food, adults have little leisure: they spend time carving arrows, making axes, building huts, and braiding nets or ropes. Most evenings, rain and cold disfavor public life. People huddle beside fireplaces, women and children in family houses, and men in men's houses. Only rarely does somebody sing. Intervillage feasts resulting from marriage, friendship, and trade are highlights of Eipo culture.

The only indigenous Eipo musical instrument is a lamellaphone (*bingkong*), which, in construction and playing, resembles those found generally in New Guinea, but since bamboo does not grow at Eipo altitudes, instruments are made from *fina,* a local reed, *Miscanthus floridulus.* Boys and men play (figure 8). In scattered areas, rarely at *mot* (see below), men play hourglass drums, imported from lowlands.

In 1975–1976, research was conducted in the southern part of the valley, in Dingerkon, Malingdam, Moknerkon, Munggona, and Talim villages. Since then, disasters have challenged the Eipo world. In 1976, two earthquakes destroyed local villages, among them Munggona; and Christian missionaries began restricting the performance of *mot* to Christmas, or banning them altogether.

## Musical contexts and genres

### Feasts

*Mot* are ceremonial songs and dances performed by men at feasts held to mark an alliance, the end of a war, or the payment of duty or compensation. *Mot* used to be performed at boys' initiations; men perform them after having cleared an area of the forest and cultivated a new garden. Feasts occur about every five years, when the stock of pigs, having been reduced by slaughter for the previous feast, has replenished itself. Men perform *mot* on a sacred ground in front of the men's house, usually in a central location within a village, where women and the sick may not venture, though women may dance on the edge of this space.

The formal structure of the music reflects the choreography, which divides into four sections: position A, static; position A, dynamic, moving counterclockwise to position B; position B, static; and position B, dynamic, moving back to position A (figure 9). The song is performed only in the static sections. In the dynamic sections, the dancers utter alternating rhythmic shouts on the syllables *ae, ha, hu, lo, uh, wo, ya, ye,* or *yui,* or make in-breathed whistling (*kwasekokna, fotfotana*) or gasping (*kolkolana*).

A *mot* is started by a lead singer (*mot winye*), who normally stands at the head of a semicircular row. He improvises a short syllabic phrase. The chorus adds stereotyped melodic movements, sung on vocables, called *mot dem wine gum* 'empty *mot* without a story'. Standing side by side, the men form a line; the first dancer starts running and shouting, and the others follow. They glide like a serpent, coming at last to a standstill, the lead singer now among them. The singing resumes, and the queue unfolds in the opposite direction.

Lead singers' words are hard to understand. They hint at the names of hills, forests, dead people, mythical ancestors, cultural values, plants, animals, or events. They may joke or make ironic remarks about the guests or the missionaries' introduction of new animals (like fowls or ducks); mock unsuccessful hunters, people afraid to fight, or the hosts; mention hunting, mythical ancestors, mythical creators, bringers of culture, voices of spirits, or scenes from war, nature, friendship, and trade; or make joyful expressions. About twenty-five kinds of *mot,* with specific names and tonal structures, exist in the Mek area, fifteen among the Eipo.

FIGURE 9   Men of Munggona perform a *mot.*
Photo by Artur Simon, 1976.

### Gossip

In the morning before going into the gardens, women sometimes gossip, mainly about sexual liaisons, while men make implements. People may sing *dit* during these activities. The occasions behind the creation of many *dit* and the name of the composers, usually women, are known. Most *dit* derive from sexual liaisons. All have an underlying story, though texts may merely evoke natural images or describe sites. A subgenre, *kulub-kulub dit,* hints at sexual intercourse. Some texts concern researchers' arrivals, airplane-dropped goods, and the building of an airstrip; others mock individuals. *Yaltapenang dit* recount the mythical origin of the Eipo. Content-based categories do not differ from each other musically: standard melodic patterns serve for old and new lyrics.

In 1975–1976, the *dit* most often sung was "The Marikla Arrow Song," which circulated in variously texted versions. The people of Marikla, a village in the lower Famek Valley, are enemies of the Eipo. The lyrics damn the war, as in a version sung by Tingteningde from Dingerkon (Simon 1993:66, 166–167):

> Arub tobe debake, tobe obake.
> Kanye dolamle, yo dam-ak.
> Tulum doubnul; tulum bukle buknul; binune, banune.
> Kungkab yo dan-nang aikdam,
> Ek yo bonang aikdam; binune, banune.
> Urye konkona daktinye; tenebre bunman.
> Bon urye konkon bone bobtinye.
> Busikna bobuka daibuktinye; teneniryuk.
> Bung yo bung dabtinye, teneniryuk.
> Bung yo bung bobtinye; tenebre buniryuk.
> Kungake, turune yokmal; obrane bune like,
> Na wicape, na buyape.
> Ublinge burye bobtinye; teneniryuk.
> Kalinge burye daktinye; teneniryuk.
> Kungake yokmal; turune yokmal:
> Tobe obrane dune like.

Eipo curing is described as 'sucking illness from a sick or wounded person'. The therapist recites on a monotone, interrupted by the sounds of sucking, which reinforce the belief that the magic is working. Eipo doctors treat sick pigs similarly.

Today they are still dying, they are still hitting.
It takes the soul away, close to the tree.
The smoke is spreading; the smoke is lying down; I will go, I will go.
Close to the house of them who cook with short pieces of wood,
Close to the house of them who carry fresh wood; I will go, I will go.
I would like to break through the piece of *urye*; I sit thinking so.
I would like to carry the piece of *urye*.
I would like to smash having carried the *busikna*; I must think so again.
I would like to burn the tree with the bark stripped away; I must think so again.
I would like to carry the tree with the bark stripped away; I sit thinking so again.
The *kungake,* the *turune* hangs down, war disgusts me,
My sisters, my friends.
I would like to carry the top of the *ublinge*; I must think so again.
I would like to break the top of the *kalinge*; I must so think again.
The *kungake* hangs down; the *turune* hangs down:
I am fed up with war.

These lyrics use the imagery of trees (*urye, busikna, ublinge, kalinge*) as men, and of grasses (*kungake, turune*) as arrows; the trees grow only in the upper Eipo Valley, where the singer's lover is. Because the lovers belong to opposed camps, they cannot meet.

### Laments

Laments (*layelayana*) are spontaneous expressions of mourning, interspersed with weeping or crying. They begin emphatically and loudly; after some minutes, they end quietly. In 1975, a Munggona man about twenty-two years old died, and his brother lamented his death: *Nun-de kurunang-anye mirin bol bobobbinnamume. / Dib-namum-ate. / Neik-ak mabnanam abmanumwe. / Na niye, na niye-o, fi ubninbinamal-ak. / Na niye, na niye, gum yanamal-ak-e!* 'You wore dark skin, but you were our light. / You departed from us just now. / We just had agreed to sleep side by side [in the men's house]. / Oh, my father, my father, he went irreversibly from us. / My father, my father, he will not come back to us, woe!' (after Eibl-Eibesfeldt, Schiefenhövel, and Heeschen 1989:197).

### Cures

Recitations to cure illnesses are described with a verb that designates a typical cere-monial element, *fungfungana* (also *fuana*) 'suck illness from a sick or wounded per-son'. The sucking is done by a therapist, who recites on a monotone, interrupted by the sounds of sucking, which reinforce the belief that the magic is working. Eipo doctors treat sick pigs similarly.

—ARTUR SIMON

## REFERENCES

Clouse, Duane Allen. 1984a. "A Comparative Study of the Structure of Berik and Sobei Music Systems in Irian Jaya, Indonesia." Master's thesis, Wheaton College.

————. 1984b. "The Music of the Berik: Irian Jaya, Indonesia." Capstone document, Wheaton College.

DeVilbiss, Caryn. 1989. "Analysis of the Sentani Music System." Senior document, Wheaton College.

Eibl-Eibesfeldt, Irenäus, W. Schiefenhövel, and V. Heeschen. 1989. *Kommunikation bei den Eipo: Eine humanethnologische Bestandsaufname.* Beitrag zur Schriftenreihe "Mensch, Kultur und Umwelt," 19. Berlin: Reimer.

Hughes, Valori E. 1989. "An Analysis of Mairasi Music." Senior document, Wheaton College.

Kunst, Jaap. 1967. *Music in New Guinea.* Translated by Jeune Scott-Kemball. The Hague: Martinus Nijhoff.

Leimbach, William, Jean-Pierre Dutilleux, and Peter Van Arsdale. 1975. *WOW.* 16-mm. London: Survival Films.

Oguri, Kiroko. 1981. "The Music of the Isirawa." *Irian* 9(3):1–33.

Peckham, Nancy. 1981. "Day and Night Songs in Mairasi Festival Music." *Irian* 9(1):55–65.

Royl, Ekkehart. 1992. *Untersuchungen zur Mehrstimmigkeit in den Gesängen der Hochlandbewohner von Irian Jaya (West-Neuguinea).* Berlin: author.

Silzer, P., and Clouse, H. 1991. "Index of Irian Jaya Languages." *Irian,* special edition.

Simon, Artur. 1978. "Types and Functions of Music in the Eastern Highlands of West Irian." *Ethnomusicology* 22(1):441–455.

————. 1993. *Musik aus dem Bergland West-Neuguineas (Irian Jaya): Eine Klangdokumentation untergehender Musikkulturen der Eipo und ihrer Nachbarn/Music from the Mountainous Region of Western New Guinea (Irian Jaya): A Documentation in Sound of the Vanishing Musical Cultures of the Eipo and Their Neighbors.* Museum Collection Berlin CD 20, vols. 1 and 2. 6 compact discs.

Van Arsdale, Kathleen O. 1982. "Music and Culture of the Bismam Asmat of New Guinea: A Preliminary Investigation." In *An Asmat Sketchbook,* 8:17–94. Agats, Irian Jaya: Asmat Museum of Culture and Progress.

Van Arsdale, Peter W. 1975. "Perspectives on Development in Asmat." In *An Asmat Sketchbook,* 5. Agats, Irian Jaya: Asmat Museum of Culture and Progress.

Van Arsdale, Peter W., and Kathleen O. Van Arsdale. 1991. "Asmat." In *Encyclopedia of World Cultures,* 2:19–21. Boston: G. K. Hall.

Wilson, John D. 1988. "Scripture in Oral Culture: The Yali of Irian Jaya." Master's thesis, University of Edinburgh.

# Melanesia

Orchestras of log idiophones or panpipes give melodic and rhythmic meaning to public events, friction blocks and swung slats give sounds of fear and wonder, flutes whisper songs of love, spectacular displays of masks and massed bodies bespeak life-crisis feasts and secret-society rituals: Melanesians have created, and still use, a sensational variety of accouterments and musical instruments to complement their singing and dancing.

Influences from the outside world—explorers, missionaries, merchants, immigrants, and media—have expanded the array to include stringed instruments, which have sparked the rise of pan-Pacific pop amid familiar local forms. From ritual to reggae and rock, contemporary performances in Melanesia mix old and new—at work, during ceremonial events, in festivals, and for tourists.

Dukduks, masked otherworldly spirits, perform at Beru Hamlet, Mapiri Village, Nissan, as men playing kundus provide rhythmic sounds. Photo by Steven R. Nachman, 1971.

# The Music and Dance of Melanesia
*Adrienne L. Kaeppler*

Melanesia (from Greek, meaning 'black islands') encompasses an area of the Pacific Ocean roughly west of the International Dateline, south of the equator, and east of New Guinea. The French explorer Dumont d'Urville used the term to describe the skin of the people he encountered. Their physical traits, however, are as varied as their cultural traits, which include classic "Melanesian" societies, Polynesian outliers, and Micronesian outliers. Melanesian societies range from those where power lies in the ability to create a following, to those where power comes from the inheritance of chieftainship. Though the term *Melanesia* is really not helpful, no term has satisfactorily replaced it.

Melanesia, here excluding New Guinea, includes four regions: a series of islands that are part of the nation of Papua New Guinea, the Solomon Islands, New Caledonia, and Vanuatu. The political lines as drawn today do not necessarily match any sociocultural entities of the past (figure 1). The people of these regions have developed separate cultural and musical traditions, which, though related, are distinctive. Traditions particular to parts of Melanesia include elaborate dances and ensembles of panpipes (sometimes joined by wooden trumpets), voice-modifying instruments, and horizontally and vertically placed log idiophones.

Ancestors of the indigenous peoples of Melanesia migrated from the west, bringing various social and cultural traits, which changed over time into general and specific complexes. The most renowned of these complexes involves pottery, once made in most of the region. Examples of it appear in the archaeological record—especially Lapita ware, named after the site in New Caledonia where it was first studied.

Performances in much of Melanesia involved spectacular displays during times of crisis and rituals associated with secret societies and advancement to higher grades in them, warfare, construction of men's houses, funerary and memorial ceremonies, the making and consecrating of log idiophones, or simply reactivating social relationships. Performances often included large and elaborate masks and otherworldly costumes, set into motion by performers moving to sounds from hollowed log idiophones or hourglass drums, flutes, panpipes, or singing (figure 2).

Influences from the outside world—explorers, missionaries, merchants, immigrants, and the media—have brought pan-Pacific chordophones and popular music,

FIGURE 1    Promoting national unity, the currency of Papua New Guinea depicts a kundu with the raggiana bird of paradise (*Paradisaea raggiana*).

FIGURE 2    Ritual clothing of New Caledonia includes wooden masks surmounted by human-hair wigs and feather overgarments. From the National Gallery of Art's exhibition The Art of the Pacific Islands, 1979.

whose rhythmic patterns, melodic lines, and harmonies Melanesians have incorporated into their own musical systems to develop rock and reggae into music expressing lost loves, nostalgia for old ways, commentary on contemporary life, and political protest. Simultaneously, Melanesians have preserved and expanded their traditions in contemporary ways for performances at ceremonial events and festivals, and for tourists.

—ADRIENNE L. KAEPPLER

# Island Region of Papua New Guinea

*Don Niles*
*Gerald Florian Messner*
*Wolfgang Laade*
*Luke Balane*
*Clement Gima*

*Lynn Stewart*
*William R. Thurston*
*Jane C. Goodale*
*Vida Chenoweth*
*Michael Gunn*

**Manus Province**
**New Britain Island**
**West New Britain Province**
**East New Britain Province**
**New Ireland Province**

The Island Region of Papua New Guinea includes Manus, New Ireland, East New Britain, and West New Britain provinces. With North Solomons Province, it contains 12 percent of the area of Papua New Guinea and 16 percent of the national population. It contains islands within the Bismarck Archipelago: Admiralty Islands, New Ireland, St. Matthias Group, New Hanover, New Britain. Austronesian languages are spoken throughout the region; non-Austronesian languages occur on New Britain, New Ireland, and Bougainville.

In some parts of the region, the difference between music produced by Austronesians and music produced by non-Austronesians is striking. On the northern tip of New Britain live the Tolai, an Austronesian people, and inland of them live the Baining, a non-Austronesian people. The Tolai have cultural links with southern New Ireland; within the past few centuries, they have migrated to East New Britain, displacing the Baining. Many traits link Tolai music with that of southern New Ireland, often called the *tumbuan* area, opposed to northern New Ireland, the *malanggan* area.

Tolai and New Ireland dances are often elaborate. Dancers stand apart from instrumentalists, who frequently play kundus and stamp bamboo tubes, or strike pieces of bamboo with a wooden stick. Dancers may wear wooden masks or costumes of leaves. Though Baining dances also separate dancers from instrumentalists, dancers often wear large bark-cloth masks and perform to quickly sung texts, accompanied by stamped tubes; kundus are absent. The Baining are famous for a dance in which, at night, men move through fire (Fajans 1985; Hesse 1982).

## Musical instruments

Kundus, common instruments throughout much of Papua New Guinea, are regionally important only on New Britain and the southern part of New Ireland, where they accompany *tumbuan*-style dances; they occur in scattered localities on Manus and in North Solomons Province. This pattern of distribution suggests that kundus spread from New Britain, but languages of coastal West Sepik Province, the Wuvulu-Aua and Kaniet islands of Manus Province, and Ponape, Kosrae, and the Marshall

FIGURE 1    At the Pacific Festival of Arts, men of Manus strike garamuts with one or two sticks. Photo by Don Niles, 1980.

Islands (Fischer 1986:57) have cognate words for kundus, so the diffusion of kundus may have a complex history.

In much of the region, garamuts have high importance. In New Ireland, northern East New Britain, and parts of North Solomons Province, each garamut is jolted with a stick made of lengths of cane bound together; frequently, two men stand on either side of it, interlocking their rhythmic patterns. In Manus Province, ensembles of six garamuts of various sizes play rhythmic patterns to accompany dancing (Niles 1980).

In contrast to most other parts of the country, the people of Manus often strike garamuts with the sides of two sticks (figure 1). Such ensembles accompany dances for which each man traditionally attached to his penis a white shell (*Ovula ovum*). At rhythmic cues, each dancer either shook his hips, propelling the shell from side to side or up and down, or caught his penis between his legs. Women dance in place at the sides, hopping from one foot to the other. Since the 1960s or 1970s, men, clothed in shorts, have attached the white shells to long rubber-and-tape constructions, suspended from the waist. Dancers shout "*He he he!*" and there is otherwise no singing. Such a dance occurs through most of Manus Province, but styles of singing without dancing vary conspicuously. Titan men, of the southern part of the main island, sing dirges (*ndrilang*) monophonically, but other peoples sing in polyphony that variously features harmonic seconds and large intervals.

TRACK 22, 23

Use of notched flutes extends from Morobe Province through New Britain. People of either sex commonly use them as secular instruments, but in some locations they are secret instruments. Panpipes take various forms: raft and bundle, with far ends open or closed. A rubbed idiophone is distinctive of the *malanggan* area. Voice-modifying instruments, found sporadically in New Ireland and West New Britain, are always men's secret instruments.

## Intraregional areas

Of high significance in the region, especially in East New Britain and New Ireland (as in northern North Solomons Province), is the presence of different dances for each sex—and few, if any, dances requiring both sexes. In such dances as the *malanggan* and *tumbuan,* performers commonly stand apart from instrumentalists, who sit to play. New Ireland Province is famous for the *malanggan* ceremonies of northern parts of the province (Yayii 1983). Also noteworthy in that area is the catching of

TRACK
-36    sharks by observing certain ritual practices: men in boats sing while shaking under-
water a rattle made of coconut shells, strung onto a cane circle.

## MANUS PROVINCE

Manus Province, in the northwest of Papua New Guinea, borders the Federated
States of Micronesia in the north and Indonesia in the west. Its population, 32,840
in 1990, is the smallest of all provinces in the country. In the east are the Admiralty
Islands: Manus and numerous smaller islands, including Los Negros, Rambutjo, and
Baluan. In the west are small islands: from east to west, Kaniet Islands, Hermit
Islands, Ninigo Group, Aua Island, and Wuvulu Island. The administrative headquarters, Lorengau, lies on the eastern part of Manus Island. Some of the western
peoples display Micronesian physical and cultural features. All languages spoken in
the province are Austronesian.

—DON NILES

### Baluan

A volcanic island of about 23 square kilometers, Baluan lies about 50 kilometers
southeast of Manus. It has a population of about four hundred, living in patrilineally
exogamous clans. The fertility of the soil enables the people to get cash from growing
fruits and vegetables. The local language, ŋola(m)banu Okamo, is Austronesian.

Composing means producing new texts stimulated by events while using and
modifying old musical patterns. The proper composition of songs is possible only if
the composer has inherited magical powers, enhanced by the use of ginger, cinnamon, and betel. "Anyone who wants to influence things and events through magic,"
says Konda'i Lipamu, "has to follow all the rules related to the kind of magic he
wants to practice" (Messner 1981:435). Performing songs or recitations, some men
exercise magical power.

Good singers and instrumentalists are treated as specialists. For providing musical services, they receive dogs' teeth, shell money, food, and round wooden dishes
filled with meat, fruits, turtles, and seasonal goods. At festivities, a specialist may
function as master of ceremonies (figure 2). In garamut ensembles and multipart
vocalizing, Baluan music is polyphonic. Flutes, panpipes, and susaps serve only for
expressing soloists' moods and aiding love-controlling magic.

#### Dance

Women's costume for dancing formerly consisted of fine skirts, made from dyed,
braided, fringed, knee-length, raffia strings, held at the waist by a braided belt, covering the front and back to leave the hips free. Preferred colors were red, yellow, and
brown. A woman would wear a braided, dyed, raffia headband about 3 centimeters
wide. A similar braid circled upper arms, upper calves, and ankles. Women wore dog-
tooth necklaces, which, in the late 1990s, they replace with beads of plastic and glass.
They carry a woven fringed shoulder bag. At Christmas, they decorate their heads
and necks with leaves, flowers, or baubles. Most enjoy exposing bras and petticoats.

In all simply structured dances, women stiffly hop up and down on both feet,
which they point outward, parting their legs. Then they shuffle their feet backward
and forward. They shake leaves in their hands, turn their shoulders in countermove-
ment to their hips, puff out their chests, and make their breasts swing. Christian
churches have censored many of these movements.

Men traditionally danced wearing headbands, armbands, legbands, and dog-
tooth necklaces. Each attached to his penis a white shell, which his father or another
close relative had given him at initiation. Performers waggled their penises and made
coital movements. Christian missionaries and directors of the Paliau movement prohibited these dances on Baluan; nowadays, men rarely perform them.

FIGURE 2    The master of ceremonies at the
Christmas festivities of 1979. Photo by Gerald
Florian Messner.

### Vocal music

Baluan musical classification focuses on user and function. Each vocal activity has a context-related term. The term *wokwok* can be glossed 'call out loudly for an announcement' and 'recital of a ritual text'. For some kinds of singing, the term *w(e)ii* denotes the main women's ritual song and men's work-accompanying songs. Used as a verb ('sing'), it is gender-neutral and does not cover all kinds of singing. Older persons say [uii]; younger ones, [uei]. Hence the spelling *w(e)ii*.

Throughout the province, a unique style of vocal polyphony is an important element in religious beliefs. Some songs have more power than others. Songs stand in a hierarchical order: *kolorai,* of highest value; several kinds of *w(e)ii*; and *polpolot,* songs for entertainment, with no ritual value.

Baluan vocal texture has two parts: a lead (*yaret* 'call out') and a second (*isiol* 'join'). For *kolorai,* the lead stands on the left of the second; for *w(e)ii* and *polpolot,* the lead is a soloist, but more than one person may sing the second (Messner 1980:60–63). Singers of *polpolot* position themselves side by side in a line, sitting or standing. By the 1980s, because indigenous social structures were no longer intact, *polpolot* had become the most important genre. *Kolorai* and *w(e)ii* were moribund; older musicians regretted that young people no longer understood Baluan's ancient ritual language, used in those genres.

### The performance of kolorai

Only important and wealthy persons can afford to sponsor *kolorai.* Performances formerly commemorated deceased persons; specialists performed inside the men's house between sunset and sunrise. The texts have a heroic character. Sections in the old ceremonial language are unintelligible; specialists now improvise new texts. The textual rhythm dominates the musical rhythm; interpolated exclamations, sighs, and vocables occur. This text extols the dead man Kelu:

> Oii, yabune ipe si isiuom pirou, pirou rakole.
> Isiuom melasapon.
> Ikenau uru naron ukukasi.
> Kamel isapon urukasi kalouek teli.
> A piŋinteli re kilelip a osok luenem.
> Menau a olasok sapoliemui kilemolaelu kirupulen.
> Kouei Kelu kiru lepelasapon teli en sapon.
> Ironul eimeueimesut keneluiparu kolonpianeireli.

> A tropical laurel is cut at the bottom, a laurel tree.
> Two of his children came into the men's house.
> They came and waited for the man to die.
> On the day he dies, one passes by in front of him,
> And one puts dogtooth necklaces in front of him.
> They remain in front of Kelu. A woman enters to bring food.
> The disease in this men's house will also kill that woman.
> The food remains, but she'll finally die.

The performance proceeds expressively. To intensify emotion, singers sometimes raise a hand. The lead usually starts with the exclamation *oi,* expressing grief at the loss of the person commemorated; it also "opens the voice," as singers say. The second repeats the initial phrase, changing it slightly; it then aids the soloist by singing the main referential notes as a drone. The lead uses cadential formulas, crossing below the tonic and returning above it. This crossing forms the most important simultaneous interval of the style, an interval that varies between 80 to 165 cents. *Kolorai* follow and precede performances by garamuts (Messner 1981:438).

### *The performance of w(e)ii*

*TRACK 37*

The term *w(e)ii* denotes something smooth and quiet; musically, it specifies ritual songs shorter than *kolorai* and having three dependent sections and a coda, without antiphonal features. Specialist singers are women; men sing one solo genre. Five main varieties are known.

1. Women's *w(e)ii*, in two parts; sung at commemoration rituals, outdoors, by day. As in *kolorai*, the texts have a heroic character.

2. Women's *w(e)ii*, in two parts; sung at other functions, notably bride-price-paying, canoe-carving, and garamut-carving ceremonies.

3. Women's *ninen w(e)ii*, a lamentation, based on *ninen* 'crying, mourning, being sad at the loss of a loved one or an object'. These songs have no ritual restrictions.

4. *Yedeŋsame* 'worried', solo songs for persons of either sex. In worry or nostalgia, anyone can perform them, anywhere, alone or in company.

5. Men's work-accompanying songs, performed solo; fit for performance by a man who has inherited power.

*W(e)ii* follow and precede a piece performed by garamuts, the *kileŋ w(e)ii*, to which women usually dance, making restricted spatial movements within scattered formations. They hop, shifting their feet back and forth. Slowly they progress forward. They first move their arms, but then hold them close, repeatedly twisting the torso.

### *The performance of polpolot*

Without restrictions of place or time, people perform *polpolot* for entertainment, introduced by rhythmic patterns borrowed from *w(e)ii*. Texts are in colloquial speech, without ritual value.

### **Instrumental music**

Throughout Manus Province, garamut ensembles (Tok Pisin *planti garamut*) are the most important form of instrumental music (figure 3). Each language names the instruments differently, but the numbers and functions of the instruments within an ensemble mostly remain the same. At high-ranking leaders' weddings, players double every instrument but the lead instrument.

A garamut ensemble has six instruments in four sizes: three *san(t)san*, one *kipou*, one *lolop*, and one *kil*. The *san(t)san*, the smallest, is about 80 centimeters long, with a diameter of 25 centimeters. The *lolop* is about 110 centimeters long and 36 in diameter; in performance, it takes the lead. The *kipou* is 140 centimeters long and 46 in diameter. The most revered instrument is the *kil*, about 2 meters long, with a diameter of 66 centimeters; it rests on the floor. The *kil* may lean against a post or solid wall; it may also rest on a wooden stand.

Men hew garamuts from *sinal*, a tropical laurel (*Calophyllum inophyllum*). Rituals mark selecting and felling a tree, transporting the trunk to a sacred area, and finishing the log, which men cut to size and hollow with fire. Some stages of the process are secret. Finally, men polish and paint the instruments. Unplayed garamuts "have no voice." Especially at Christmas and Easter, men adorn new instruments with leaves and flowers, and carry them on special beds to the feast, where men knock them against a previously played instrument.

Each performer strikes a garamut with wooden sticks. A secret magic spell protects against evil spirits: performers chew ginger, cinnamon bark, and secret herbs

FIGURE 3    With two sticks, men of Baluan strike garamuts; the instrument in front is a *kipou*. Photo by Gerald Florian Messner, 1980.

(sometimes with betel), and spit the mixture into their hands; murmuring the spell, they rub it onto the sticks.

Rhythmic formulas (*kileŋ*) are fast, long, and complex. They never accompany singing. Before and after songs, they accompany dancing. They serve as signals and summonses. In the early 1980s, eighteen patterns were extant. Two experts listed them in the following sequence, which they believed the best conceptual order.

1. *Kileŋ pame(k),* related to the ritual use of betel, is performed during a major feast to remind leaders to cut the nuts.
2. *Kileŋ mosap* governs certain rituals during brideprice-paying ceremonies.
3. *Kileŋ kolorai* introduces and concludes *kolorai.*
4. *Kileŋ w(e)ii 1* introduces and concludes the performance of two-part *w(e)ii.* The patterns of this signal alternate and interlock (figure 4). After a short introductory solo performed on the *lolop,* the other instruments join in. At certain concluding points of a phrase, all garamuts sound in unison. The *lolop* and the *san(t)san* produce stressed and unstressed beats, but the other instruments perform unstressed beats only.
5. *Tuktuk tou,* for one instrument (*lolop*) calls people to assemble at the village center.
6. *Kileŋ puasik,* governing certain mortuary rituals, is appropriate for festivities commemorating important deceased persons at fixed periods after the funeral.
7. *Yalyal,* for one instrument (*lolop*), is performed immediately after someone has died. The repetition of the pattern tells the people the status and sex of the deceased.
8. *Teŋsel,* calls on people to gather and mourn a death.
9. *Kileŋ sinal* is performed by two to three instruments while men fell a *sinal.*
10. *Kileŋ w(e)ii 2.* This pattern differs from the *kileŋ w(e)ii* described above. It repeats many times. It calls on people to gather for the meal during a feast at which *w(e)ii* are performed; during brideprice-paying ceremonies, it calls on the father of the bride to bring the pigs required for the meal; it serves with *kileŋ sinal* as part of the tree-felling ritual, when it is known as *sipian sinal.*

TRACK 29

FIGURE 4 *Kileŋ w(e)ii 1* for garamut ensemble; Parioi, Baluan, 1978. Each line shows one part: the top line is for the *san(t)san*; then follow the *lolop*, the *kipou*, and the *kil*. Transcription by Gerald Florian Messner.

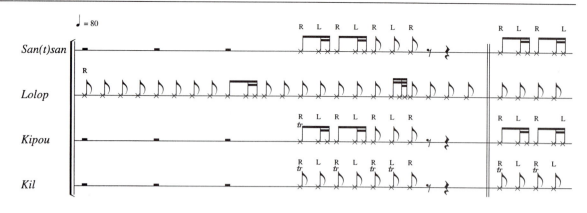

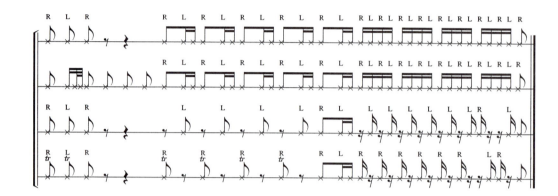

11. *Kileŋ pein* is used when women, after singing, perform a specific dance (*pein*).

12. *Samari* regulate meals at certain festivities; they occur in four patterns, each of which usually repeats four times.

13. *Nununuampou* is performed once only, at the end of an extended feast, before the last and final meal.

14. *Kileŋ boy* is addressed to a much-appreciated fish (Tok Pisin *karua*). When people bring ashore a catch of this fish, the ensemble performs this pattern.

15. *Tendén táki rendén*, a new pattern, marks certain women's ritual activities. It probably came from Lou Island.

16. *Nineŋ dayet* sounds during certain feasts, before and after the song "*Rokrok*" ('Frog').

17. *Lupsambirou* is reserved for the death of the highest-ranking person. It was performed once, while the body of the deceased was lying in state.

18. *Purui* marks the sunset during a festivity, after which the feast takes a different course.

*Other musical instruments*

Several aerophones serve for private expression and love-controlling magic. The *yui*, a raft panpipe, consists of four bamboo tubes, tuned E–F–F♯–G♯. Blowing two adjacent tubes simultaneously yields a narrow second. The *yui* is suitable for performing two-part songs, mainly *polpolot*; only males play it. A notched bamboo flute (*ruŋ*) is about 35 centimeters long, open at both ends, with three equidistantly spaced holes near the far end. Men play it for recreation and love-controlling magic. A nose-blown flute once existed on Baluan, but no one interviewed in the 1970s could play it. From bamboo tubes 15 to 25 centimeters long, people of either sex make and play susaps (*kupu(w)uk, kubu(w)uk*).

*Music in transition*

Baluan supports five churches: Roman Catholic, Lutheran, Seventh-Day Adventist, United Church, and Baha'i. Hymns are similar in all. Based on four-part harmony, they are sung in as many parts as available voices permit; improvised harmonies result in chains of six-three chords. The texts of most Baluan hymns are in the Tolai language. From 1946 to 1954, John Paliau, a charismatic local politician, imposed on the inhabitants of Baluan a modernizing movement (Schwartz 1963), which, by interrupting indigenous sociocultural activities, drastically changed local customs and obliterated much of the people's religious heritage.

Young people informally play guitars and ukuleles, sometimes in bands. Instrumentalists may sing popular songs; others may join in, singing, clapping, humming, and whistling. Many such songs came with missionaries, sailors, and other visitors; some came when local persons returned from work on other islands. Structurally, most resemble hymns.                           —GERALD FLORIAN MESSNER

## NEW BRITAIN ISLAND

New Britain is a crescent-shaped mountain range 600 kilometers long and no more than 80 kilometers wide. Its Whiteman Range and Nakanai Mountains reach a height of 2 kilometers, rising in sharp ridges, cut by deep, narrow, rocky riverbeds. Well into the 1900s, the inaccessibility of the interior protected the island from foreign occupation. Colonizers concentrated on the Gazelle Peninsula, where, from 1886 to 1914, the German colonial government of New Pomerania had its capital. For wages, men from farther south, notably the Sulka, came to the area.

The rest of the island remained virtually unexplored by outsiders till a Roman Catholic mission opened stations at Malmal (Jacquinot Bay) in 1932 and Uvol in 1940. From 1942 to 1945, Japanese troops occupied the island. From 1945 to 1972, it was an Australian trust territory. Since 1973, it has been part of Papua New Guinea. It divides into two provinces: East New Britain, with Rabaul as capital, and West New Britain, with Kimbe as capital. The provinces subdivide into districts.

The music of the Baining was the first music of New Britain studied (Hübner 1935, 1938, 1939). A record produced by Ray Sheridan (1959), besides Baining and Tolai songs, includes songs from peoples of the north, south, and southeast coasts: Makolkol, Sulka, Mengen, and Arowe. Frédéric Duvelle (1977b) further documented Tolai music. Two cassettes of the Papua New Guinea Music Collection of Don Niles and Michael Webb (1987) include musical examples from East New Britain: one song of the Sulka, one of the Kol, two of the East Lote, four of the West Nakanai, and two of the West Mamusi.                  —WOLFGANG LAADE

## WEST NEW BRITAIN PROVINCE

West New Britain Province encompasses the southern part of New Britain and numerous islands, most notably the Bali-Vitu Group. In 1990, the provincial population was 130,190. Austronesian languages are spoken by most residents; at either end of the province, two non-Austronesian languages are spoken. Rugged mountains rise inland; most residents live at lower altitudes. The province is one of Papua New Guinea's leading producers of cocoa, copra, palm oil, and timber.     —DON NILES

### Bali-Vitu

The Bali and Vitu islands lie off the northwest coast of West New Britain. Unea (the local name for Bali) is the largest island in the group; circular, about six kilometers across, it has a curved ridge paralleling the west coast and running across two peaks, of which the higher is about 600 meters above sea level. Garove, the second-largest

After the death of an elderly person, people perform the twenty-five-day ritual. It opens when a relative of the deceased makes special shouts and throws a spear in front of the men's house, proving he has enough pigs.

island, is about 35 kilometers northeast of Bali. The 1990 population for Bali-Vitu was 10,986, including about five hundred plantation workers.

The indigenous inhabitants speak an Austronesian language, of which Vitu, with four inhabited islands, has two dialects (Garove, Mundua), and Bali has a third (Uniapa). Local ceremonies are seasonal. Most songs are monophonic, with instrumental accompaniment.

### Sacred songs

Some songs are sacred (Mundua *tawaua*, Uniapa *tauanga*), a concept referring to serious, solemn, and religious ideas. The opposite concept, secularity, has no indigenous term; but secular music can be called *lingena lupua*, from *lingena* 'song' and *lupua* 'public gathering'.

### Masked dances

On Bali, men and some initiated women perform masked dances (*miri*). Two dancers wear carved and painted masks, crowned with two long canes, covered with chicken feathers. Other dancers rhythmically shake bamboo-leaf bundles (*vuvu*), singing to the accompaniment of six kundus (*kure*). Performance of this dance commemorates the death of an important person or follows boys' circumcisions, if their relatives have pigs ready for slaughter. The masks are named Kive for the Ranggalingga Ke Poi (Seashell For Poi) clan, and Kauho for the Boro (Pig) clan. People who have magic lime, used in chewing betel, learn *miri* songs in dreams; close relatives, such as maternal uncles, pass this ritual down orally.

On Vitu, an analogous dance is *kakaparagha*, combining *kaka* 'person' and *paragha* 'chief' (*gh* represents a voiced velar fricative). Most *kakaparagha* last about six minutes. The ritual takes eleven days. Rehearsals and demonstrations from the first to the tenth day occur in a special enclosure. The final performance starts with two great voicings of a swung slat (Mundua *tambelena kakaparagha*, Uniapa *rurubale*). Then male dancers emerge from the enclosure, followed by two dancers (*base vairukurukur* 'false shields'), and finally the masked dancers, led out by two *base matoto*, men armed with spears and shields. The main dance with the *kakaparagha* and the *base vairukurukur* climaxes the ritual.

The sacred genres do not follow a set order. Elders hold the *kakaparagha* to be the most important. As guardian of chiefly prestige, it fulfills a political function. Legally, it can be invoked to prevent strife and punish offenders. Performance provides an opportunity for circulating items of wealth: household goods, shell ornaments, and pigs.

### Leleki

After the death of an elderly person recognized for devoted participation in customs, people perform the twenty-five-day ritual (*leleki*). It opens when a relative of the deceased makes special shouts (*kamundu* in both dialects) and throws a spear in front of the men's house, proving he has enough pigs to sponsor the ritual.

Hidden from women, men play instruments in a specific sequence. As each instrument is introduced, at five-day intervals, it joins the instruments that people may play at any time. During the first five days, only a special bamboo trumpet (*sina leleki* 'leleki mother') is played, blown into a natural hollow in a tree. During the next five days, in addition to playing this trumpet, men sing through cracked bamboo voice-modifying tubes (Mundua *pasese*). On day eleven, one-holed vessel flutes (*manu karukaru* 'floating bird') join the previously introduced instruments. Days sixteen through twenty add bamboo trumpets (*kure ke Kono* 'drums for Kono'), played inside larger pieces of bamboo, with the far ends closed. On day twenty-one, single bamboo pipes (*pilipili*), 10 to 15 centimeters long, appear. On the last day, a large bamboo voice-modifying tube calls men together; its name, Kaogho, is that of a spirit. An ensemble of single bamboo pipes starts the ritual. Then an ensemble of vessel flutes plays, followed by *balu* ('pigeon', also called *sina-makure* 'drum-mother', because it sounds like a drum) and bamboo trumpets. (The *balu* is a larger version of *kure ke Kono*; both kinds of trumpets are usually played in ensembles of four.) Finally, an ensemble of *pasese* plays.

After these performances, the men form two lines: one represents males; the other, females. Before and after each *pasese* performance, the men in the male line shout *ae,* and the men in the female line shout *aeu.* Next, a pig's bladder is inflated, attached to a stick, and popped against the ground. This is the cue to bring the orchestra to life. At the end of the ritual, the instruments used at the beginning reappear. Songs for *leleki* last about twenty minutes. After the music, relatives and friends of the deceased exchange food and pigs.

In 1998, only two men who knew the magic ritual remained in Vitu. The same ritual occurs in Makiri and Manopo villages, Bali, where, influenced by Christianity, people turned *leleki* into hymns. They perform these hymns in public, using cracked bamboo voice-modifying tubes (Uniapa *patete*), formerly sacred instruments, hidden from females' view, and reserved for *leleki.*

### Talaukanga

Men and women perform these songs at night. The only instruments used are kundus. During the day, men make mischief in the village, wearing any of three kinds of mask: *lakiki,* a tall one, randomly asks people for whatever it wants; *telumbo* or *manga,* another tall one, chases people; and *bakana boroko,* a short mask, also chases people. A person who retaliates against these masks risks the fine of a pig.

### Ngaveo

This is an important ritual, performed by initiated men. Its performance honors a dead person or boys' circumcision. Men sing its songs into *mavela,* voice-modifying vessels made of small coconut shells. They cut off the top third of the shell and put several orchid leaves (*kerekere*) inside. They believe their singing is spirits' singing. They prohibit women from seeing the instruments or the performance.

The ritual requires twenty-five days, a time of peace, when tribal fighting, marital disputes, and picnicking along the beach may not occur. The songs are about twenty-five minutes long; a typical performance of all of them requires some three hours. The ritual originated in Vitu. Two villages on Bali (Palenganikumbu and Penatabotong) own some songs for *ngaveo,* purchased from the Vitu people.

### Tumbuan

These songs, performed in Bali and Vitu, come from the Kombe or Kaliai people of

New Britain, who systematically barter with the Bali-Vitu. Men stand in the middle of the arena, beating kundus and singing while paired women and young girls dance around them. Masked dancers (Mundua *ghulu,* Uniapa *ulu*) take the outer circle, dancing in pairs in the direction opposite that of the females. The dance fosters joy and solidarity. It may precede important rituals, or occur during festive celebrations. The melodies resemble those of *sia.*

### Secular songs

Many kinds of secular singing occur in Bali and Vitu. *Linge urauranga* (Uniapa) 'created melodies' are sung unaccompanied for pleasure, at any time, by anyone. The subjects come from personal experiences or dreams.

*Maghu* is a women's dance. Each clan has its own version. Performances lead up to the main performances of *kakaparaha* and *leleki.* Three to four minutes long, the songs are accompanied on kundus by four to five men, who sing while women dance in two parallel lines. The texts treat miscellaneous subjects, including birds, canoes, and babies. Dancers hold croton leaves in both hands; for long periods, experts execute graceful yet vigorous movements. *Maghu* may be bought and sold. In the mid-1990s, people still performed *maghu* in Bali and Vitu.

*Kewaia* (in Mundua) and *tangiranga* (in Uniapa) are laments. Most last less than three minutes. Relatives of the deceased sometimes arrange to keep the body an extra night before burial, to sing these songs in his or her honor. Slow and sustained, such performances often move friends and relatives to tears.

When a person dies, everyone in the village participates in the death-marking ritual (*mateanga*): adults must not sing or beat kundus, and children must not play. Everyone remains in this state until, to announce the restoration of normality, a member of the dead person's immediate family beats a kundu. Formerly, to restore happiness, people sang *leleki* using *patete.* In the late 1990s, people sang *tangiranga* during the period of mourning.

The *sia* came to Bali-Vitu from the Siasi Islands via the Kove and Kaliai areas of West New Britain. Men dance it in two straight lines, then in a circle. Kundus provide the rhythm. Women sing and dance around the men. Melodies typically move like a fanfare on a four-note scale, G–B–D–F♯ (figure 5). The *kai* likewise is danced by men with kundus in two lines. It also came from the surrounding islands.

Several weeks after an exchange of pigs, the inhabitants of Bali perform *lou.* The term for these songs and the accompanying dance is *vakalitsi a topona boroko* 'rubbing off pigs' blood with the feet'. Everyone joins in the singsing, as there are no taboos. For another dance (Mundua *tarupasia,* Uniapa *tarupoitsianga*), elderly men sing and beat kundus at the center of a circle. Young initiated men, their bodies painted yellow and red, surround the elders and shake rattles tied to the top of long, decorated poles. In pairs, women sing and walk around the men. *Voreanga* are of two types: slow ones, sung with *tarupoitsianga* and *lou,* and fast ones, sung when racing canoes near the finish. Of work-accompanying songs, *linge urauranga* (Uniapa

FIGURE 5    "*Kayau reme,*" a *sia* of Vitu Island. Transcription by Luke Balane and Clement Gima.

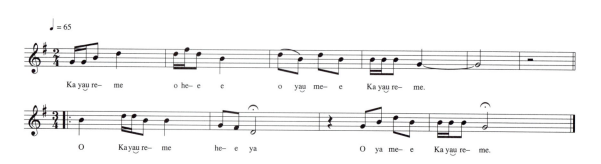

dialect) are sung by one person; *gheromata* and *takuluanga* (Uniapa dialect), by several. Men sing the former while carrying a heavy load; the latter, while pulling a new dugout canoe from the forest to the beach.

Social events often involve music. The *ireki* (Uniapa dialect) is performed when a clan presents to another clan an important person (such as a chief's firstborn child or a bride) or valuables. Everyone participates, singing and dancing to the beat of kundus. Traditional Unean society honored the delivery of a firstborn child, for which the Katutu Maemae clan has a singsing, *totoanga* (Uniapa dialect). It is the only Bali singsing that uses a garamut (locally *garamo*). During weddings or brideprice payings, people perform *potongo,* the same songs as *murmur* of mainland New Britain: dancers stand in a circle or two straight lines, performing to the beat of kundus.

Children especially enjoy singing *sia, tangiranga,* and legendary melodies (*lingena manaka*), songs that show Western influences of harmony and instrumentation. Youths arrange songs for stringbands and Christian choirs.

### Major ceremonies

Three contexts—*roghomo* 'spirit-dwelling house', *tangegeanga* 'canoeing', and *mateanga* 'death-marking ritual' (all in Uniapa dialect)—provide settings for performing traditional songs and dances.

#### Roghomo

Deceased ancestors' spirits dwell in the *roghomo,* the paramount house in Bali-Vitu society. Its construction takes four to six years to plan and celebrate. Public opinion favors undertaking a *roghomo* festival only when pigs and crops are mature and plentiful. Singsings associated with the process of construction employ a swung slat, several kundus, and a peace-symbolizing spear (*diaro buaka*). Performed songs are sacred and secular, indigenous and imported. *Linge urauranga* may be sung at any time; people perform *talaukanga* during the nights of planning and building, when they also perform work-accompanying songs, *leleki, paghanga, maghu,* and *sia.* In the final ceremonies, they perform *lou* singsings in front of the house.

The highlight of a *roghomo* is the performance of *tarupoitsianga* for breaking down the barricade. Men make a tower, consisting of two poles 18 meters or more high. On one side, they build a ladder; on the other, they attach two long vines, stretching to the ground at a sixty-degree angle to the poles. To the vines, they tie a boatlike structure. When men are singing the last songs of the *tarupoitsianga,* several men, who have been fasting for months, emerge from the forest, trembling. Two of them uncover the masks and carvings in front and on top of the house, while the others climb the ladder. Two men get into the boatlike structure, and others release restraints holding it. The structure slides on the vines down to the ground, cheered by a swung slat and the audience. Participants carry the two men into the house, ending the festival.

#### Tangegeanga

*Tangegeanga,* a festival of ceremonies leading up to an important canoe race, occurs only when village leaders decide not to build a *roghomo,* since both events have the same value. As in *roghomo,* different songs come to the fore at different stages of the festival. In addition to *linge urauranga* and work-accompanying songs, *tarupoitsianga* are sometimes sung when men are on the ocean in new canoes, paddling to other villages; they also sing slow, sentimental examples of *lou,* and both kinds of *voreanga.* When all the canoes are ashore, women from the host village bring prepared food. The activities may continue at night, with the singsing *takuluanga.* Leaders then decide which village will host the next festival and when it will occur.

### Twentieth-century transitions

In the 1900s, Bali-Vitu underwent striking political, economic, social, and religious transformations. Music changed, mainly because of the introduction of Christianity. Beginning in the 1930s, missionaries forbade practices they viewed as evil and immoral. Beliefs changed; and in the late 1990s, people were no longer performing indigenous singsings. Young people were blending *sia, tangiranga, voreanga, potongo,* and other traditional songs with the sound of electric and acoustic guitars, ukuleles, and indigenous percussion instruments, and were performing the new versions during the celebrations for Independence Day, the annual end of school, and other occasions.

Translated into local dialects, European hymns are sung in church. To local melodies, Roman Catholic missionaries added biblical texts. In the 1930s, when they set up a mission on Bali, they discouraged many practices; but within decades, they were encouraging people to use traditional elements in church. In contrast to this attitudinal change, Seventh-Day Adventists, members of the other intrusive sect in the area, continued to deplore indigenous ceremonies and discourage their performance. Because of these factors, some of the music discussed here had fallen out of use by the 1950s, especially on Bali.     —LUKE BALANE, CLEMENT GIMA

## Lolo

About twelve hundred Lolo inhabit seven mountain villages in central northwest West New Britain (Stewart 1990). They speak a dialect of Maleu, a Siasi language, belonging to one of three Austronesian language families in the area (Thurston 1987). On the Idne River, toward the south coast, the Idne-Lolo, once thought a separate people (Capell 1962), are distinct only in habitat. On the north coast near Cape Gloucester, administrative center of the Kilenge-Lolo Census District, Lolo who moved from the mountains in the 1960s and 1970s to share in coastal economic development have established four villages.

The Lolo divide into exogamous cognatic lineages, which focus their physical and cosmological concerns in the men's house, a unique architectural feature in each village, which serves as a repository for supernaturally powerful objects, including masks and flutes. It locates the Lolo in time and space, marks a location that links people to their first ancestors, and connects the human world with the spiritual world.

The Lolo consider that more than any other belief or practice, musical performance most clearly separates them from others and embodies most clearly the essence of their culture. To understand Lolo music and performance requires knowledge of the Lolo universe, a world that involves humans, spirits (ancestral, mythical), and spiritual powers (free-flowing energies, which occupy the ground, certain plants, and certain areas). Namor, the being who gave the Lolo a template for ceremonial action, created this world. He bestowed music, instruments, and dances. He gave ancestors the plots of land on which the men's houses stand. For ceremonial performances, he set down guidelines on the distribution of wealth and food, and on the ceremonial interactions of kin.

### Ceremonies for the dead and the firstborn

Lolo music and ceremonies derive power from supernatural sources. Performance lends that power to humans: it is the primary means of reaching the supernatural, and of coherently connecting the ordinary and the extraordinary.

Traditionally, the Lolo had an elaborate ceremonial complex, a cycle of ceremonies (*narogo*) that took about twenty years to complete. The cycle involved two broad kinds of events: ceremonies commemorating the dead and those celebrating the living, especially the firstborn child. The events intertwine—in preparation, performance, and the conception of the relations between the living and the dead.

The cycle has three phases: the mortuary phase, an interim phase (celebrating the dead and the firstborn), and a phase dedicated to the firstborn. Each lineage conducts a cycle for its own members, and each of the constituent performances demands participation from kin and affines, in various capacities. The cycles run continuously among different lineages: at any moment, each Lolo individual is participating in several different cycles, each at different points.

Starting with the mortuary phase, the cycle involves a series of feasts for honored dead, culminating in an exchange of pigs among the affines of the deceased, each of whom represents a different men's house. Once this series of feasts concludes, the interim phase begins.

The first ceremony of the interim phase is *nakamutmut,* celebrating firstborn children and calling for people to amass pigs and other signs of wealth. Masked males and females dance as spirits. The next ceremony is *navoltomare,* performed to raise the central post of a men's house. Old men's houses eventually die. Their resident spirits do not decline, but associated masks and paraphernalia lose their potency. As men reconstruct their house, they rework the masks; *navoltomare* celebrates the birth of the new house and the rebirth of its spirits. The interim phase concludes with an all-night performance of lullabies, honoring firstborn children and concluding the birth of the men's house.

In *vukumu,* the first ceremony of the phase dedicated to the firstborn, people put black woven bands around male firstborns' ankles. The material of the bands is a vine the Lolo consider their emblem, since it grows only on the mountain at Namor's birthplace. After *vukumu,* the people again perform *nakamutmut,* this time celebrating a firstborn boy's circumcision and a firstborn girl's appearance in dance regalia. These events acknowledge the firstborn's reproductive potential; for boys, they begin the process of masculinization. By virtue of the blood seen at menarche, girls naturally grow into fully reproductive beings; boys gain their reproductive powers only by ceremonial contrivance.

The next ceremonies honor specially named firstborn children. The ceremony *vokoi* celebrates any female firstborn named Galiki: it "turns her into a man." Men take her into the men's house, show her the sacred objects, and teach her the lore by which she gains male and female creative and reproductive powers. A performance of *malanggan* turns her back into a woman; this ceremony features some of the Lolo's most frightening masked spirits.

The Lolo perform the concluding ceremony of this phase for any firstborn boy named Natavolo, the term also used for the senior male of the men's house. Natavolo receives female reproductive powers in *naosung,* a ceremony characterized by the appearance of masked spirits. *Naosung* and *malanggan* are no longer performed. In the 1930s, fearing punishment by missionaries, the Lolo burned the masks. The spirits, however, remain. The Lolo speak of them briefly, in hushed tones, not to arouse their anger.

### Musical instruments

Certain Lolo musical instruments derive power from supernatural associations. Some gain power in construction; some, through ritual acts; and some, from substances such as wild ginger.

Kundus (*napareaua*) are the only instruments appropriate for public ceremonies. Played by men, they are instruments of joy and vehicles for tapping extraordinary power. Lolo society puts no prohibitions on storing, handling, or playing them; but when making them, many men follow pertinent rituals. For dancing, drumming guides singers' pitches and rhythms. To sound the tonic with the dominant as an overtone (Feld 1983:81), drummers carefully tune their instruments. On a fire-heated lizardskin head, they adjust blobs of resin. They play rhythms with deliberate and stylized variations. Each song has patterns of regular beats, plus a break, each cued by a leader's whoop.

Conceptually and literally, garamuts (*nakure*) stand at the center of a set of powerful objects. In the men's house, they remain out of women's sight, alongside spirits' masks, flutes, and other ritual paraphernalia. Animated by the senior male of the men's house, they send and receive messages from the world of spirits. In other ritual acts, they ward off evil. They announce deaths and punctuate deliberations for ceremonies. Unlike other areas in Papua New Guinea (Burridge 1969), the Lolo do not have an elaborate system for signaling with garamuts.

In the men's house, the lineage maintains end-blown bamboo flutes (*napiloli*). According to myth, these flutes, women's property, sounded without human aid; stolen by men, they became mute. As female objects in the men's house, they embody female power, which, from surroundings and ceremonies, absorbs male power. Their sounds are spirits' voices, animated by men to masculinize boys. The Lolo also have bamboo bundle panpipes (*nasomsom*), played by fathers when teaching their sons esoteric lore, and by young men working love-controlling charms. Bamboo raft panpipes (*nakerkuli*) serve for love-controlling magic. Flutes and pipes, thought difficult to play, have no set music. They produce quiet sounds, often in scalar sequences, punctuated by trills.

### Musical structures

Each ceremony requires male drummers and a mixed chorus. A senior man takes responsibility for leading. He begins most songs; after the first phrase, the chorus enters. Anyone may lead a song, but in ceremonial performances, leaders are typically male elders, well versed in songs and associated esoteric lore.

Ceremonies divide into segments containing strophic songs, each with its own text. Songs have similar structures: each has responsorial alternation, with the number of repetitions determined by the leader. Phrases overlap, creating polyphony between male and female voices.

Melodies normally stay within an octave, moving stepwise, ascending and descending. Ceremonial songs usually have five-tone scales, whose construction derives from an irregular alternation of intervals of major seconds with occasional minor seconds and minor thirds. The significant tones are the root, third, fifth, and second. Motivic units often use three tones in stepwise progression, with the largest interval a major second.

—LYNN STEWART

### Anêm

Some five hundred Anêm, speakers of the only non-Austronesian language in northwestern New Britain, are surrounded by, and in close contact with, Austronesian-speakers: to the east, Lusi and Kove; to the south, Mouk; to the west, Amara and Kabana. The Anêm share much of their music with these peoples, the Kilenge, the Lolo, and the Siasi. The lyrics of most Anêm songs are in those languages.

Contacts with non-Melanesians began in the late 1800s with German colonial officials, and after 1918 with British and Australians; other outsiders included Japanese and American soldiers (1941–1945) and Australian administrators. In the 1950s, Dutch-speaking Roman Catholics set up a mission nearby. Especially after 1945, men worked on plantations and boats in Rabaul and beyond. These contacts brought Christian hymns (mainly in Tok Pisin), rock (on cassettes), and string-band music.

Most musical performances entail singing and dancing, accompanied by drums. One man usually starts a verse; other men, and then women, join in. All songs and dances are under local copyright: only composers, their heirs, or people who have paid royalties may perform them.

### Musical instruments

Intricately carved from local hardwoods, the kundu (*buamu*) is the primary musical instrument. Only men play it. The drumhead is a monitor's skin; to tune it, players adjust blobs of beeswax on it. For up to a year after a death, all drums are silent; singing quietly, men may rap their fingernails on floorboards.

To signal the killing of pigs at festivals honoring the recently deceased and initiating firstborn children, the Anêm formerly jolted garamuts (*gilamo*). They now sound this signal on conch trumpets (*koni*), which primarily function to call people from their gardens.

A spirit manifests itself in the moan of a swung slat (*êlêŋgî eni*), which men sound in a special clearing, out of women's and children's sight. It is a thin, lanceolate wooden slat, 20 to 40 centimeters long, 5 to 10 centimeters wide. Through a hole at the base passes the end of a 5-meter-long cord, secured to the top of a pole. The player swings the pole in an arc above his head.

Children gain musical skills through imitation, striking coconut shells and empty cans. They also play *taŋguxi,* a bamboo susap (probably brought by Japanese soldiers from Okinawa); *kau,* a bamboo flute; *solpet,* a bamboo panpipe; *siloŋgote,* a bow with a bamboo disk, which vibrates a string by riding it up and down; *seme,* a large beetle, which vibrates when held against the teeth; and *tagxîŋ,* a cicada, tied to a string so it flies around, buzzing.

Dancers' costumes make rhythmic noises. For some dances, men tie strings of rattles (*gilao*) around their ankles. To woven plates of fiber bundles (*didu*), fastened with a belt made from bark, women add cordylines and crotons, which rustle as they bounce. For similar sound, dancing men and women shake bundles of leaves (*iaŋa*).

### Spirits and dances

Anêm society segregates the sexes. Women and children may not enter the men's lodge, where men collectively invoke spirits (*eni*) to preside over initiations, mortuary rites, and settlements of disputes. These spirits are prominent during complex mortuary-initiation rituals (*lêlêxîm*). During these rituals, which include dusk-till-dawn dancing and may last for weeks, children meet the spirit who sanctions the final mortuary rites for their recently dead ancestors.

Several spirits attend dances: Baxku and Makikuol are represented by single masked dancers; Mukmuk, by imitations of birds and frogs; Nabeu, by vocalizations amplified in coconut shells; Aulu, by pairs of masked dancers, whose fringes extend to the ground; Tubuda, by a swung slat. Choreographies attach to Baxku and Aulu; but *boelo, potŋên,* and *sia,* as multifunctional dances, may involve sundry spirits. Since people must be initiated and put to rest by the same spirit, the Anêm sample through the list of spirits over a period of decades. Whichever spirit is active in the men's lodge is available to celebrate public events.

*Boelo,* the only exclusively Anêm dance, may honor a renowned man or a special occasion. A line of men carrying shields and spears swirls through the space bordered by houses. Drumming men and dancing women follow. Apart from a stanza for praising the occasion, the lyrics are vocables.

In *potŋên,* men stand, beating drums and singing; women dance around them. Throughout the night in an ordered sequence, participants shift from one phase of songs and dances to another. Each *potŋên* has seven phases, in this order: *sapopo,*

Throughout the night, groups compete in song. Men beat kundus, and visitors beat spears against their shields. Simultaneously, paired women and young girls dance between the groups, whistling in counterpoint to the melody.

*potŋên* (a special use of the name of the genre), *tikŋên, asingit, aroman, pagunuŋa, lutŋên.* During the sixth phase, the lyrics list trees, vines, animals, and important people.

*Sia,* an imported genre, has a precise choreography, for which men wear elaborate, triangular headgear, fringed and topped with feathers. It is the only Anêm dance in which the company coordinately move their heads, bodies, and drums.

### Laments

To memorialize sad events—the death of a loved one, the departure of a friend on a journey, the failure of a sexual conquest—individuals compose laments (*taŋdaŋa*). The following text, in Kabana, is attributed to a man under the near-fatal charms of unavailable Kabana women he had seen during a festival.

| | |
|---|---|
| Taine-ne-e-e-ne-e-e-e-e Kakasi-o-o-o-o! | Oh, women of the Kakasi River! |
| Taine-ne-e-e-ne-e-e-e-e Kakasi-o-o-o-o! | Oh, women of the Kakasi River! |
| I-vege-e-e-e kaka. | They make me pine. |
| I-vege-e-e-e kaka. | They make me pine. |

A lament, in Anêm, honored a young woman at her marriage; a string band from her village sang it: *O Beronika, tîmnid omên mesekan aled, a neki êbêl, / Kan nin mamêd a nêsîk tauêd, / A mîn mesimîl moul axî agoneŋ* 'Oh, Veronica, let's shake hands, but don't you cry, / For today you have to stay right here, / While we return home without you'. To the Anêm, weddings are lamentable events because they mark the end of carefree youthfulness. People typically compose laments while keening over the body of someone who has died. Short, simple, repetitious, each song is highly affecting. Years later, a composer may sing a lament, weeping in reminiscence.

### Songs in tales

Especially during the rainy season (when travel or work is nearly impossible), the Anêm enjoy all-night sessions in which adults take turns telling *alemge,* stories distinguished from other narratives by short songs, repeated at intervals. The tales feature Galiki, a pig, representing any female human; Akono, a dog, representing any male human; Kumbeku, a bird, representing a troublemaking liar; *eni,* ghoulish, cannibal monsters; and assorted other animals in human roles. Usually, a single song musters the main character's emotions; after each event, the narrator sings it.

In one tale, Kumbeku tricks a Galiki named Lae into killing herself. Heading for the underworld, she seeks her husband. At each stop, she sings the refrain (partly in Kilenge) *Lae-e-e, Lae! Lae-e-e, Lae! / O iomko-o-o, Lae, o Lae-a-o-a-e!* 'O Lae, Lae! O Lae, Lae! / Oh, you there, Lae, O Lae!' In some stories, each of two characters has a distinct song. A successful session of storytelling brims with food and laughter.

—William R. Thurston

## Kaulong

About one thousand Kaulong inhabit the foothills of the central mountains of southern West New Britain. Taro is their staple, but much of their subsistence comes from the forest and streams. They occupy hamlets of less than two dozen inhabitants each. People of different hamlets meet to exchange shells and pork, sing, and sometimes fight. Their language is Austronesian. Their close linguistic and geographic neighbors—Sengseng, Miu, Karore—share with them many cultural traits. In the early 1900s, patrols by German and Australian administrators penetrated only a few kilometers inland. After 1945, patrols reached inhabited inland areas, and a permanent patrol station and two missions, Anglican and Roman Catholic, arose on the coast at Kandrian.

### Contexts: lutŋin

Events that involve pigs (*lut a yu*) are socially the most important. People invite trade partners to come from other hamlets to sing and share pork. Occasions for *lut a yu* include a death, the male-initiation ritual, and the completion of a house. A hamlet schedules performances called *dikaiyikŋin* for various reasons: making the hamlet flourish, resolving disputes between residents, marking residents' travels. All *lutŋin* last from dusk to dawn, with continuous singing for twelve hours.

### Singing with pigs (lut a yu)

Before sundown, men tie up the pigs intended for sacrifice. The hosts begin singing a *dikaiyikŋin*. Visitors arrive well after dark, armed with spears and shields. If asked their mission, they answer, "We go to sing and fight"; of these alternative behaviors, the Kaulong value singing more. Older men wear a pair of boar's tusks (symbols of aggression), hanging from the neck, over the chest or the back. To enhance their sexual attractiveness, young men deck themselves in fragrant leaves and flowers: in the morning, after the singing, they go courting. Young and old women alike wear special skirts.

Throughout the night, groups compete in song. Men beat kundus, and visitors beat spears against their shields (figure 6). A man begins a song, and others of his group join him in the refrain. Simultaneously, paired women and young girls dance between the groups, whistling in counterpoint to the melody. One group sometimes outperforms the other—in volume, length of song, and musical continuity. Such an achievement forces opponents to retreat in shame. The event is competitive; its ritualized attacks may lead to real fighting. At dawn, men kill the pigs, and visitors go home to cook and eat their pork. Feeling sorry for their own pigs, the hosts do not eat the meat.

### The performance and style of Kaulong songs

Intrahamlet performances involve men and women, who sing together, walking counterclockwise around the clearing. Men and women take the lead in singing; the tonal quality of women's voices resembles that of men's. Alone and together, singers compete for fame and honor. Because competition has personal and political importance, children of both sexes begin singing almost before they talk; among adults working on daily tasks, singing is as common as speaking. Song is the supreme Kaulong art, the defining act of being human.

A Kaulong song usually has three stanzas: a variable, improvised list of names within select classes; a nonvariable, set poem; and a concluding word or phrase. A refrain often begins and ends each stanza. In this text, which names palm trees, the refrain is *yia li nok* 'fire sleeps there'.

FIGURE 6   During all-night singsings, Kaulong performers play kundus and strike spears against shields. Photo by Jane C. Goodale, 1964.

| | |
|---|---|
| Yia li nok por egis. | Fire sleeps inside a wild *buoi*. |
| Yia li nok por aiyal. | Fire sleeps inside a type of *limbum*. |
| Yia li nok por kambe. | Fire sleeps inside a little *limbum*. |
| Yia li nok por kahame. | Fire sleeps inside areca palm, |
| Yia li nok por limbum. | Fire sleeps inside edible *limbum*. |
| Yia li nok por ewit. | Fire sleeps inside coconut. |
| | |
| Yia li nok por ewit a kaloh: | Fire sleeps inside a yellow-leaved coconut: |
| Li simhit a kahoh, | A dry branch underneath, |
| Li pohut a kaloh. | A new shoot at the head. |
| | |
| Yia siwoh, yia li nok. | Smoke curls up, fire sleeps there. |
| Yia minmin, yia li nok. | Fire smolders, fire sleeps there. |

Leading singers display their knowledge by singing of famous men and women they know, sites along a road to distant hamlets, crossing streams and rivers, foods that cassowaries love, kinds of women's skirt material, phases of a coconut's growth, kinds of wood for spears. By formulating many lines, an expert singer makes a song last longer than an inexpert singer's.

Kaulong songs are monophonic, with women sometimes singing an octave higher than men. Unusually in the region, women sing with men; but at large, intergroup singsings, only men sing (*lut*), while women dance (*yik*). In list-making songs, a solo singer sings an item; the rest of his group answers with a refrain, and all sing the last two parts of the song. Marked by drumbeats, meters are simple. Drummed timbres are distinctive: at distances of more than three kilometers, the Kaulong can distinguish the sound of one kundu from that of another.

### Introduced genres

The Kaulong enjoy three introduced genres: the *tubuan,* a masked dance, in which young men sing to seduce young women; the *sia,* a masked dance from the Awawe and Siasi Islands; and in some near-coastal areas, a ceremony marking a girl's pubescence. The musical style of these genres differs from that of indigenous genres: they have different structures and tonal systems, and have fixed lyrics.

### Musical instruments

Kundus (*lambu*), usually imported, regularly receive new lizardskin heads. By moving and fixing four or five beeswax pellets in the center, tuners adjust the pitch. Each drum has a distinctive "voice." The Kaulong say garamuts once accompanied singsings held in gardens to make pigs grow, but no examples of garamuts have been documented.

An end-blown flute (*lapulil*) and a raft panpipe (*lawi*) are common instruments, made of bamboo. Women become proficient on the flute; men, on panpipes. (Either sex may choose to play both.) The flute has two holes for fingering. The panpipe usually has six or seven pipes, but may have up to nine. Young people bespell their flute or pipe so their playing will attract someone of the opposite sex.

The bundle panpipe (*larasup*), a man's instrument, mimics natural sounds and human and animal speech and activity. It has six to eight variably lengthed pipes, the longest in the center. The player holds it about 15 centimeters below a stream of air exhaled through his mouth. As he rotates it, it "speaks," evoking familiar sounds: a hornbill's flight, a widow's wail, a butterfly's flutter, a fictional inchworm's remarks on burrowing into the ground, a fictional baby cucumber's response to its mother's call. Learning to make it speak takes years. With it, adept elders tell stories in the men's house at night. In the tale of Asis the Grasshopper, each time Asis sings, the narrator plays (figure 7):

Two women have no husbands. They go to cut firewood. When they return to dump their loads of wood outside the house, they hear the wind.

"What is it?" they ask each other.

Asis cries inside the firewood [the *larasup* speaks].

The women take the sticks of firewood, throw them outside in the rain, look for the origin of the sound, and can't see anything.

Asis sings again [the *larasup* speaks].

The women throw the firewood to the other side of the house, look again, and can't see who sings.

Asis sings again [the *larasup* speaks].

The women break up each piece of wood, and can't find who sings.

Asis sings again [the *larasup* speaks].

They throw away the stick of wood where Asis hides, and Asis sings again [the *larasup* speaks].

They break the stick in pieces, and finally locate Asis.

FIGURE 7 The
song of Asis, played
on a bundle pan-
pipe. Transcription
by Amanda
Weidman.

One woman says to the other, "Sister, here is the one that sings."
They marry Asis.

The wind, the sound of the *larasup,* is the voice of Asis.          —JANE C. GOODALE

## EAST NEW BRITAIN PROVINCE

East New Britain Province includes northern New Britain Island and offshore
islands. The 1990 population was 185,459. Volcanoes are active here: in September
1994, Rabaul was devastated by an eruption. The province has long had contact with
outside traders, missionaries (since 1875), and governments. East New Britain suffered much loss of property and life during the Japanese occupation (1942–1945).
Numerous Austronesian and non-Austronesian languages are spoken in the province.
Tolai (Kuanua) is spoken by the largest number of speakers of any Austronesian language in Papua New Guinea.

—DON NILES

### Lote, Mengen, Mamusi

These peoples are neighbors (Laade 1998). In the west live the Lote; outsiders often
call them and their area Uvol, the name of the local Roman Catholic mission. They
inhabit the coast between Atu in the east and Tavolo in the west, where the swamps
of the Ania River form the provincial boundary with West New Britain. The
Mangseng (Arowe) were traditionally friendly with villages in eastern Uvol. The
Melkoi River separates the Lote from the Mamusi, marking off the administrative
district that bears its name and in 1990 had a population of 6,123.

The Mamusi live in the interior, in Mamusi District, centered on Au'una Village
and covering the mountainous area between the Melkoi River in the south, the
Nakanai Mountains in the north, and the Bairaman River in the east. About 15 kilometers inland, this district meets the Kalamalagi District, formerly joined to it to
form West Pomio District. Some Mamusi live in nearby areas of West New Britain.
The Mamusi homeland is virtually inaccessible except by air. It adjoins the Lote in
the south and the Mengen in the east. Between the Lote and the Mengen, around
Meili Village, Mamusi have migrated to the coast and formed a mixed population,
which has developed a special dialect, Pälaukona. In 1990, the Mamusi census division had a population of 5,412.

Mengen lands extend from Jacquinot and Waterfall bays about 50 kilometers
across the mountains to the northern shore of the island. The people divide into the
Mengen proper, around Jacquinot Bay; Mengen II, in East Pomio Census Division;
and "Bush Mengen," in Inland Pomio Census Division, between the north and south
coast. In the 1990 census for these divisions (West Pomio, 2,560; Central Pomio,
4,371; Inland Pomio, 5,822; East Pomio, 4,608), only the former two are predominantly Mengen. The Mengen share Central Pomio with the Kol, whom they outnumber. The Mengen II share East Pomio with the Sulka. The Mengen proper split
into branches corresponding with cultural and musical distinctions. The Lote,
Mengen, and Mamusi speak Austronesian languages; the languages of the Kol and
Sulka are non-Austronesian.

All peoples discussed here, possibly all peoples living along the southern coast of New Britain, say their ancestors migrated from the mountains. Looking for jobs, Mamusi families are still migrating to the coast and West New Britain. These peoples are chiefly gardeners and hunters. They organize themselves into moieties and clans; leaders sponsor feasts, for which followers donate produce and pigs.

### Musical contexts and intercultural relationships

The central event of local feasts is adolescents' initiation: boys undergo circumcision; girls have their nasal septums perforated so they can wear a white seashell peg. Since no celebration is possible without abundant food, initiations begin at harvesttime and last for months. Around Christmas, they culminate in feasts, for which neighboring villages gather. Initiatory feasts occasion singsings that honor the past year's dead, whose decorated skulls people dance around and then bury. Formerly, boys initiated during the previous year had their teeth blackened; to show nubility, Mengen boys also scarified their cheeks.

The cycle of ritual and social events includes spirits, which appear as masked dancers (*tumbuan*). The forms and names of masks differ interculturally. Mengen examples include netted masks, conical and cylindrical wickerwork headpieces, and large, round, umbrella-shaped masks, also known to the Kol and Sulka. Lote examples are semicircular: some consist of large sheets of bark, with painted eyes and mouths, covering the heads and shoulders of certain *tumbuan*; others have painted, spindle-shaped wooden parts, mounted on conical headpieces and relating to masks of the Kandrians area. These relationships touch other cultural property and show historical ties. By canoe, the Kandrian used to visit certain Lote villages. Besides other articles, they traded kundus, said to have come from Siasi Island. They were allies in war; Lote villages encouraged intermarriage with them.

Lote group singing corresponds with Mamusi group singing. Mengen unison singing corresponds with that of the Kol and the Sulka. In certain Central Pomio villages (including Marmar and Olaipun), the Mengen language borrows heavily from Kol. Mengen customs, songs, and musical terminology are influenced by Kol culture; some genres, including circumcision-accompanying songs, are purely Kol. The easternmost Mengen, in turn, adopted songs from the Sulka.

The western Lote adopted Mangseng songs and dances. From the eastern Lote, the western Mengen adopted the *sasanga,* a mimetic dance. The Lote and the Mengen have adopted much Mamusi music, with texts in pure Mamusi, a blend of Mamusi and Lote, or Mamusi and Mengen. In all described instances, musical culture absorbed sets of songs, not individual items.

### Dances

Most indigenous songs are choral and accompany social dances. Lote and Mamusi choral singing is polyphonic, but Mengen, Kol, and Sulka choral singing is unison, or in octaves. Women perform most dances. A mixed group of singers and drummers stands in the center (Lote), or in front (Mengen). Two, three, or four of the singers, men or women, play drums. Lote performance requires a garamut, on which the player sits, striking it with a heavy stick. He leads the music, and with it the dance. The Mengen no longer use garamuts.

Dressed in fiber skirts and decorated with scented leaves, Lote dancers move in pairs or threes around singers and drummers. They hold each other around the neck or waist, shuffling forward and back, mostly counterclockwise in a circle. In some places, notably Maso Village, the circle may break into complex formations. Mengen dancers usually appear in two or four files, which, through the dancers' turns and intertwining lines, form varying patterns. Men's dances include war-related dances and *sasanga*, which pantomime various themes: catching bats, collecting seafood, fighting with spears and shields. In war-related dances, blasts from conchs punctuate the singing and drumming.

*Tumbuan* dances stand apart. Maskers appear singly or collectively, depending on the nature and function of the spirits they represent. With melodies that end in drawn-out notes (Lote and Mamusi *utunga*; Mengen *baingasuari, taninglel, tantaning, tonga*), women call them from the forest. Decorated men lead them. To the sound of drums and a conch, they sing special songs (Mengen *kangaole*). For a while, as the men approach the village, the women's songs blend with theirs. The maskers wear anklets of strung nutshells. When they reach the village center, they begin dancing, some accompanied only by the rattling of the anklets, others with a new song. At various stages of initiations, they reappear.

### Musical genres

Other than women's lullabies, little indigenous solo singing occurs. Magic spells (Lote *milang*, Mengen *walu*)—charms for controlling love, gardens, weather, hunting, and fishing—are sung by whoever uses them. During initiation, in the men's house, men teach love-controlling charms to boys; every adult male knows them. Other spells, including those for hunting, fishing, and gardening, belong to individuals, who can give them to a relative (son, son-in-law, brother-in-law), or sell them for shell money or some other valuable object. After chewing ginger and rubbing scented leaves on the body, men sing these incantations in a low voice. Sometimes after the death of its owner, a charm becomes public property and serves as a social dance-song. A special kind of tale (Lote *poponing*, Mengen *nanang*) includes solo songs, slow and lyrical. At intervals, the narrator repeats a song, sometimes joined by the audience.

People sing few group songs without drumming or dancing. An exception is women's *tumbuan*-calling songs; originally, they were laments, mostly composed by women, memorializing a dead relative. Composition usually involves inspiration in a dream, often about a composer's relative. The texts, in local vernaculars, belong to the few intelligible classes. The Lote sing them privately, as personal laments. "It is just like crying," they say.

In the house where *tumbuan* are prepared, men sing other songs (Lote *milang*, Mengen *baungalol* or *baungapite*) unaccompanied. Such songs make the masks shinier and more beautiful—so attractive, the men hope, the *tumbuan* will "strike the hearts" of the onlookers, mostly women. Men sing such songs for each part of the *tumbuan*: headpiece, feather decoration, leaf cloak.

Most songs are sung for dancing by a mixed chorus with drums. The Mengen names differ from area to area and from subsection to subsection (Laade 1992). Some songs belong to a particular clan, who alone have the right to perform them; if paid for permission, the clan may allow another clan to perform.

Dance-songs divide into two classes. One (Lote *hototinga, kanggata, koko, loploping, lumbura, mangoila, sasanga, talivota*; Mengen *baungaleglege, baungamanna, gagata, kumento, lapulilo, lumbura, pälaukona, upupunga*) is choral from beginning to end. The other (Lote *maenge, mala, manna, poule, popo, pumpumunga, ungalele*; Mengen *balingpis, bingor, kangaole, kulung kulung, kumuri, magoegoenga, pangkamala, pupungalel, pututunga*) has a solo introduction for each stanza. In each stanza, the soloist must change a principal word, usually the name of a village, a hill, a river, a person, a clan, an animal, or a plant; in English, local people call this process counting. Some dances have fast and slow songs (Lote *maenge, mala, manna, poule, ungalele*; Mengen *upupunga*), sung and danced alternately and begun with a marching-in song (Lote *mololinga*; Mamusi *ongake*; Mengen *ilo* or *lolong*, depending on the kind of dance it introduces), sung when the group arrives. Mamusi songs and dances (*gagata, lapolilo, loso, mititi, ongalele, suluko, taninglele*) are firmly integrated into Lote and Mengen music. The *kanggata, mangoila,* and *talivota* come from the Mangseng, adopted by the Lote of the extreme west.

Most dance-songs are of unknown origin, have unintelligible texts, and are accompanied by drums. In a long singsing, people sing some songs (Mengen *baungaleglege, pututunga*) before midnight; then they sit down and continue to sing without dancing (Mengen *taranga*). Other dances and songs (Lote *manna,* Mengen *iso* and *pänanale*)—the most important, maybe the oldest—continue through the night in a prescribed order: people must not mix them with other songs. Many dances occur at set times during events. Some songs and dances belong to the sequence of initiatory rituals, the days and weeks before and after the operations on boys and girls, the preparation and bringing out of the masks, and the terminating rites and final feast.

### Sound-producing instruments

To denote the sound of musical instruments, the Lote and Mengen borrow the English term *cry.* Fischer 1986 [1958] describes all musical instruments mentioned here.

#### Nonmelodic instruments

Of idiophones, the garamut is a hollowed-out trunk, about 8 to 10 decimeters long, with a slit on the top, cut into a tongue in the center. The instrument lies on the ground; the player sits on it, striking the tongue with a heavy stick. Men make and play the instrument; women must not touch it. Large garamuts announce to neighboring villages the death of a leader (male or female), meetings, feasts, and the number of pigs killed for a feast. Rattling anklets (Lote *polpolo,* Mengen *gargar,* Mamusi *kege*) are string-threaded nutshells, worn by *sasanga* and *tumbuan* dancers A lamellaphone (Lote and Mamusi *milollo,* Mengen *inue*), though widely known, has lost popularity. It is a lancet-shaped, forked bamboo frame, 23 to 30 centimeters long. The player, holding it near his open mouth, strikes its tongue with a knotted string attached to the base of the frame. Only men play, chiefly to attract women. Skilled players produce myriad rhythms and timbres.

Local membranophones are of two kinds: kundus (Lote *ario,* Mengen *paro*), and older, mortar drums (Lote *kovong,* Mengen *sirolai,* Mamusi *kurumiso*), with or without handle. Lumps of beeswax on the drumhead make the skin vibrate with a booming sound. Holding kundus with the left hand, men strike the heads with the right. Men hold mortar drums upright, with the drumhead down and the open end up, leaned against the left shoulder.

Various instruments produce sounds interpreted as spirits' voices. In secret forested places, when men preparing masks are hungry, they make these instruments wail; women who hear the sound send food. The ribbon reed (Lote *ilimo kanna* or *ilimo tut,* Mengen *saya,* Mamusi *koko*) is the most common of these instruments. Only the Lote of the interior use the piston flute (*sivisivi*). The swung slat (Lote *uvuvu,* Mengen *romrom,* Mamusi *säya naname*), once a spiritual voice, has gone out of use.

From the shell of *Charonia tritonis,* men make a side-blown trumpet (Lote *tangailu,* Mengen *pula* or *bu,* Mamusi *poponga*), which serves for signaling and accompanying war dances and *tumbuan* appearances.

For toys, children play leaf buzzers (Lote *chareräch,* Mengen *ngo*), whirring nuts (Lote *akau,* Mengen *gongorau*), and spinning tops (Lote *aum,* Mengen *mä kanna,* Mamusi *lelepo*).

At night a boy wanting to court a girl may sneak to her house. Nearby, he plays his flute. On hearing the music, she will come to him.

*Melodic instruments*

The only melody-producing instruments in southeast New Britain are flutes and panpipes. Their generic name is that of their constituent bamboo (Lote *iu,* Mengen and Mamusi *isong*). A notched flute (Lote *opeopeo,* Mengen *kannakenna*), about 5.5 to 6.5 decimeters long, has two holes near its lower end, closed by the node. In common parlance, the sound of the flute is love-controlling magic, which attracts women.

Two local panpipes—Mengen *isong akakä* 'daytime bamboos' and *isong akarigo* 'nighttime bamboos'—are in use. The former are raft panpipes of seven to ten tubes, with names referring to tunings or the music played; some have names that show whether the far ends of the tubes are open or closed. A rattan string fastens the tubes with a simple ligature near the upper ends and a stepped ligature at the lower.

Men play raft panpipes only while walking to and from the gardens, usually in the hills. They say breathing during the ascent is easier while playing. They make a further association: "If you go up a mountain and you play it, there will be a woman who likes the man who plays it; she will go follow him."

The Lote, Mengen, and Mamusi associate different panpipes and their music with either a married or an unmarried man (Lote), or the player's moiety (western Mengen). One Mengen raft panpipe calls the spirit of a newly dead person, letting it reveal the cause of death. Spirits give certain panpipes to people, mostly on the way home in evening twilight, when one should not play panpipes because playing may attract a spirit.

The bundle panpipe consists of ten (Lote) or nine to ten (Mengen) tubes of different lengths, open at both ends, bound with one string in the upper part and another in the middle. The largest pipe is the father; the others are the children. The player holds the instrument in both hands, with the biggest pipe pointing away. He moves the upper end in circles, about 10 to 15 centimeters from his mouth; with pouted lips, he blows air against the edges of the upper openings. The resulting tone is feeble, yet the instrument serves for communication. A young man wanting to court a girl may in the night sneak to the house where she and her parents live. Beside the house where she is sleeping, he may play his flute; on hearing the music, she will come to him. An old man said this panpipe did not originally exist in southeast New Britain, but came "from the west."

Different bundle panpipes have names said to specify their tunings. The Lote name seven, of which the *ämuku,* the *rora,* and the *chamateitei* are the only ones actually made and played. The first is the most common; the second and third are rare. The Mengen know the *rora* and give instruments six more names, including *marmasisi* and *mangini*—names also of raft panpipes. In both cases, *marmasisi* signifies that the ends of the tubes are open; *mangini* refers melodies played on both types.

By pushing the two smallest pipes of the *ämuku* down in the binding, the player can mute them, effectively making a ten-tube instrument an eight-tube one. To alter the tuning of the Mengen *marmasisi,* the player can exchange the two smallest pipes; he cannot produce all required tunings by changing or muting pipes on one single instrument.

Some Lote and Mengen bundle panpipe melodies have no names; some have merely the names of genres. Since the bundle panpipe is an instrument of the night, people also play lullabies on it. Lote and Mengen sometimes fluttertongue it. The Lote call fluttertonguing fruitbat style; they say *pianga ngawa hur* 'fruitbat eats banana'—while the animal eats bananas, it flutters.

The maker tunes the tubes by size. He begins with the longest tube. From this to the next, and to the third, the difference in length is the joint of one forefinger each; from tube three to four and four to five, it is two joints each; from five to ten, again one joint each. Thus, he consecutively constructs smaller pipes, ending with the smallest. The tuning of bundle panpipes is difficult to determine because the sound is full of overtones and noise. With the slight vagueness of the B and B♭ and the f⁺ (a high f) left aside, all tunings of Lote instruments show the same scales: A–B–C–d–e–f⁺–g–a–b♭–c (*ämuku*), A–B♭–C–d–e–f–g–a–b♭–c (*rora*), A–B♭–C–e–f–g–a–b♭–c (*chamateitei*). The tones of these scales appear in different arrangements on different panpipes.

### Music in the 1990s

In the season culminating at Christmas, villages still hold feasts, combined with songs and dances. Girls have their septums perforated. Boys undergo circumcision, but they no longer have their teeth blackened or their cheeks scarified. Preparations begin as usual, in September, with the making of new headdresses and the repairing of masks. Most traditional genres of songs and dances survive. Mengen singsings associated with a particular site or clan (the *iso* of Rovan, the *rai* of Malakur, the *kulung kulung* of Galuwe) will probably vanish. People still play indigenous instrumental music, notably that of notched flutes and some raft and bundle panpipes.

Christian ritual music came into local cognizance with missionaries. It largely consists of traditional melodies supplied with Christian texts in the vernacular. Beside them, in every service, people sing English hymns. In Rabaul, where many Christian sects have taken root, American gospel songs and spirituals fill chapels for hours.

The principal nonindigenous instrument is the guitar. With it have come string bands and guitar songs, with texts in the local language or Tok Pisin. Every large village has a string band. In 1988, the Mengen had bands in several villages; the Lote had but one. Children sing Western songs, but only in school; in a mission school in 1988, they sang "*Frère Jacques*" every morning. All schools in the area have annual cultural festivals with competitive dancing. Students perform dances learned from village elders, under whose supervision they sometimes practice for weeks. At these festivals, *tumbuan* appear, usually in an authentic form. Thus, schools help maintain the cultural heritage.

A dance that began before 1914 among ethnically mixed boatmen and laborers is the *solomon.* Working on plantations in the Gazelle Peninsula, the Sulka learned it from New Irelanders; the Mengen adopted it and passed it to the Lote. Men or women dance it, usually to the sound of bamboo idiophones struck with two sticks. Dancers wear nutshell anklets. A whistle, blown by the lead dancer, cues movements. Dancers usually march or skip in double file into the arena, where they make various formations. They wear a special costume: around the waist, a skirt made from colored plastic fibers; on the head, painted wooden effigies of birds, fishes, and other animals. The *solomon* is a favorite in schools, where male and female groups perform it competitively, and at cultural festivals.

—Wolfgang Laade

## NEW IRELAND PROVINCE

In the northeast of Papua New Guinea, New Ireland Province had a 1990 population of 86,999. Its largest island, New Ireland, is a long, narrow landmass, extending from northwest to southeast. Other islands important in the province are Lavongai (New Hanover), the St. Matthias Group (Emira, Mussau), Djaul, and the Tabar, Lihir, Tanga, and Feni groups. The administrative headquarters, Kavieng, lies at the northwestern tip of New Ireland Island. Apart from Kuot (Panaras), all languages spoken in the province are Austronesian.     —DON NILES

### Sursurunga

Some eighteen hundred Sursurunga-speakers live on the mideastern coast of New Ireland, where the narrow, northern peninsula begins. By 1875, contact with Europeans had begun. After the introduction of Christianity and the training of local pastors in English, the Sursurunga abandoned some traditions.

In 1981, Vida Chenoweth collected data from Sursurunga-speakers, with linguist Don Hutchisson interpreting. The usual venue for the investigation was Tekedan, a village about 70 kilometers south of Namatanai airstrip. Adult men listed eleven functional classes of song, sorted primarily by the performers' sex.

#### Men's songs

These are often in soft falsetto. *Garan liki* are nondanced songs that use kundu accompaniment and sometimes a conch trumpet. The latter hailed the arrival of the *mone,* an outriggerless canoe, whose cargo consisted of food given by non-Sursurunga people in exchange or for paying off an obligation. *Inngas* is a dance sung at the celebration of a payback feast. A special table is heaped with food; one song mentions a man dancing on it. The occasion is happy, with singing accompanied by a kundu and a small garamut. *Kamkarwas* are danced and accompanied by the same instruments; originally, songs of this class invoked evil spirits. *Pidik* are danced and accompanied in the same manner as the two previous classes, but the performance occurs in secret; the nature of these songs was not revealed.

#### Songs for mixed voices

*Kubak* were formerly sung for a girl's initiation. In 1981, the Sursurunga still confined girls before their marriage. For weeks, a nubile girl stayed concealed in a hut so small she could barely stand up. When she emerged for her marriage feast, she was too weak to walk without help. Being so long in the dark, her skin paled; deprived of exercise, she became plump. (Light skin and physical weakness are believed desirable in a young woman about to marry.) The blowing of conchs inaugurated the feast. A typical *kubak* (figure 8) has two sections. A leader and a chorus sing section A responsorially the first time; on subsequent repeats, all sing it. Only the leader sings section B.

*Wágin* are danced with kundus at a funeral feast or the opening of a new men's house. *Gar* resemble *wágin,* but are accompanied only by garamuts. *Tiko,* guessing-game accompaniments, are danced without kundus. In two facing lines, participants try to guess the identity of a man dancing behind a mat, hidden from view. When he is identified, he throws the mat down and returns to his line; a member of the identifiers then takes a turn. *Kángkáng* are lighthearted, unaccompanied songs, danced for fun. *Pepe,* believed to have a spiritual quality (*tanyan*), are not danced or accompanied.

#### Women's and miscellaneous songs

One class, *seráu,* belong exclusively to women. Formerly sung at a girl's initiation,

FIGURE 8 "*Kumgu*," a Sursurunga song for a girl's initiation (*kubak*), performed the night before the initiate leaves her confinement; original a minor third lower. Transcription by Vida Chenoweth.

they have been adapted to social or political celebrations, and in one instance for the opening of a new church. Garamuts and kundus accompany the women, who dance holding coconut leaves.

Of other Sursurunga genres, *ngoingoi* are sung after a person's death, though not as laments or eulogies. One example sings of hiring a car to go to the wake; another recalls that the man's mother-in-law, the deceased, was always angry with him. Songs for love-controlling magic have fallen out of use; the melody of one, having gained a new text, has become acceptable for use in church. Some *seráu* have been transformed into Christian songs; at least one new hymn has been composed.

### Musical instruments

The Sursurunga play two aerophones. One is a short bamboo flute (*khi*); the other, a conch trumpet, announces important events. A kundu and a small garamut accompany singing; large garamuts play for dancing.

### Music system

The Sursurunga know many Tolai songs, but the melodic compass of Sursurunga songs is wider and the tonal inventory more extensive than in most Tolai songs. Sursurunga melodies may have five consecutive rising tones, or up to seven descending tones. Melodies may have from five to nine tones. A prevailing contour is that of a high tone early in the phrase, cascading gently down. Dotted rhythms are common.

Sursurunga melodies employ either of two basic tonal inventories, (E)–(G)–(A)–C–D–E–G–(A) and G–(A)–C–D–F–G–A, both with tonal center C. Because examples of both inventories occur within a single class, the choice of tones apparently does not relate to function, nor do rhythmic patterns help define classes, with one possible exception: *seráu* sung with accompanimental clapping have more complex rhythms than the beat provided by garamuts and kundus: clapping mixes two patterns unpredictably. Melodic intervals include approximations of major seconds, minor thirds, perfect fourths, perfect fifths, and a major sixth. The sixth is ascending only; the other intervals are ascending and descending. Large intervals occur only between phrases.

Influenced by practices of the United Church, the Sursurunga try to harmonize. Songs, notably those whose texts reflect Christian beliefs, are often sung with one man supplying harmony under a melody sung by a chorus, as in the song commemorating George Brown, the famous Wesleyan missionary (figure 9). In other songs, such as *ngoingoi,* a lower voice may be present, but with harmonic uncertainty.

—VIDA CHENOWETH

FIGURE 9    In an excerpt from the Sursurunga song "Dr. Brown," a man supplies harmony below a choral melody. Original a semitone lower. Transcription by Ruth Colgren.

## Tabar Islands

Tabar, three islands (Simberi, Tatau, Big Tabar) lying off the northeast coast of New Ireland, is populated by about twenty-five hundred people, who cultivate sweet potatoes, catch fish, and operate important ritual ceremonies. Before 1884, when a German administration arrived, residents had a reputation for repelling outsiders—renown enhanced by reputed skill in the arts of death. But trade was an intrinsic part of the people's place in the world: Tabar joined a network that linked the coastal islands to villages on the mainland.

### Songs of the malanggan traditions

In ritualized contexts in northern New Ireland, songs are used most notably in the *malanggan* complex of ceremonial activity, centered on funerary rites and the commemoration of dead relations. Other ritual contexts that use songs include the removal of broken taboos, sorcery, hunting sharks, and the relationship between a person and his or her totemic shark. Songs also induce supernatural assistance during medical treatments, for gardening, and in fishing.

In Tabar, songs are an integral part of more than twenty *malanggan* traditions, each of which has its own character, ritual sites, ritual behavior, history of ownership and context, names, and music. Each tradition can include forty or more songs, which all owners of *malanggan* may perform in a ritual context related to the song's specific tradition. If a *malanggan* ceremony is held in a ritual site belonging to the Kulepmu tradition, Kulepmu songs are sung during the ceremony; if *malanggan* sculpture belonging to the Malagacak tradition is then also used, Malagacak songs are sung at the appropriate juncture.

*Malanggan* songs can be sacred, sung only by men in the *malanggan* ritual site, or secular, sung by all owners of *malanggan* (men, women, children) during *malanggan*-related activity held in the open. Nonsacred songs are most usually sung at funerals while the participants are sitting on the ground in the village plaza. These songs are part of the traditions to which the deceased person belonged. If he or she had owned *malanggan* rights in, for example, Valik, Deŋenasi, and Kulepmu, then during the night after the death, mourners would sing the entire known corpus of secular songs of all three traditions.

Most sacred songs accompany *malanggan* activity or mark sections within a ceremony. During the construction of a ritual house, activity-specific *malanggan* songs serve for hauling logs, attaching sago leaf to laths, attaching laths to the framework, and so on. These songs are sung by all the participating men and boys, who may be sitting, standing, or even hanging 8 meters up in the rafters. Other sequences of songs recount the history of the *malanggan* copyrights being used. The first song in the Malagacak tradition travels from one ritual site to the next; bringing each location to mind, it presents the circumstances when the ownership of that set of *malanggan* had changed hands. The second song in this tradition closes the gate of the ritual site, breaking the connection between the sacred *malanggan* world and the secular world.

### Musical instruments

Unique to northern New Ireland, the three- or four-tongued friction block is used in ritual contexts as a dominant feature of the *malanggan* tradition called Lunet (or

FIGURE 10    Sengseng children sing and play kundus; Suvulo Village, West New Britain Province, Papua New Guinea. Photo by Don Niles, 1981.

Lounet) on Tabar. This instrument is colloquially called a bird (*ma*) because its cry is birdlike and much of the ritual in the Lunet tradition involves bird-related imagery. But on mainland central New Ireland, where the instrument was apparently invented, it has been documented as *nunut, leinuat, livika,* or *lapka.* According to current belief, it was originally made in the image of a bird by men living high up in the forest plateau of central New Ireland. A man initiated into the Lunet tradition would hide in a conical "nest," either suspended from a tree over the graveyard, or resting on a table made from an inverted trunk with its roots forming the platform. Hidden inside this nest, at night and in the early morning before the *malanggan* ritual, he would rub both hands and the instrument with leaves of cordyline (*Taetsia fruticosa*), and then play the instrument by rubbing the tongues in sequence. Women and the uninitiated were told that its sound was the voice of spirits of the dead.

Another instrument locally restricted to the ritual context of *malanggan* is the swung slat, made from segments of bamboo and sounded during funerary ceremonies. Conch trumpets (*tavuri, tuwir*) are restricted to certain types of *malanggan* ritual. They formerly announced success on shark-hunting expeditions. Other aerophones used on Tabar include an end-blown bamboo flute (*katoŋuŋu*) and bamboo panpipes (*potoviso*), both of which serve in breadfruit-fertility ceremonies and other secular activities. Men use panpipes to attract and seduce women.

Tabar Islanders use three percussive instruments: garamuts, bamboo idiophones, and kundus. Garamuts are used in sacred contexts at ritual sites, and in secular contexts, such as the social event called rounding the garamut, which occurs in the village plaza at night. The bamboo idiophone is much lighter; women use it during their fertility rituals and in other ceremonial activities where women play a dominant role. Kundus, evidently an import from elsewhere in Papua New Guinea (figure 10), mainly accompany vigorous dances.

Rattles, used in ritualized and secular contexts, include the *leŋaleŋa,* made from seed cases or shells and played mainly during *malanggan* rituals; and the *tobo* (which evidently originated on mainland New Ireland), resembling the *leŋaleŋa* but having dog's-tooth clappers.

—MICHAEL GUNN

## REFERENCES

Burridge, Kenelm O. L. 1969. *Tangu Traditions: A Study of the Way of Life, Mythology, and Developing Experience of a New Guinea People.* Oxford: Clarendon Press.

Capell, Arthur. 1962. "Oceanic Linguistics Today." *Current Anthropology* 3(4):371–428.

Fajans, Jane. 1985. "They Make Themselves: Life Cycle, Domestic Cycle and Ritual Among the Baining." 2 vols. Ph.D. dissertation, Stanford University.

Feld, Steven. 1983. "Sound as a Symbolic System: The Kaluli Drum." *Bikmaus* 4(3):78–89.

Fischer, Hans. 1958. *Schallgeräte in Ozeanien.* Sammlung Musikwissenschaftlicher Abhandlungen, 36. Strassburg: P. H. Heitz.

———. 1986. *Sound-Producing Instruments in Oceania.* Edited by Don Niles. Translated by Philip W. Holzknecht. Boroko: Institute of Papua New Guinea Studies.

Hesse, Karl, and Theo Aerts. 1982. *Baining Life and Lore.* Boroko: Institute of Papua New Guinea Studies.

Laade, Wolfgang. 1992. "East New Britain: Catalogue of Tape Recordings Made 1 August to 11 October 1988." Manuscript. Auckland: Archive of Maori and Pacific Music.

———. 1998. *Music and Culture in Southeast New Britain.* Bern: Peter Lang.

Messner, Gerald Florian. 1980. *Die Schwebungsdiaphonie in Bistrica: Untersuchungen der mehrstimmigen Liedformen eines mittelwestbulgarischen Dorfes.* Wiener Veröffentlichungen zur Musikwissenschaft, 12. Tutzing.

———. 1981. "The Two-Part Vocal Style on Baluan Island Manus Province, Papua New Guinea." *Ethnomusicology* 25:433–446.

Niles, Don William. 1980. "The Traditional and Contemporary Music of the Admiralty Islands."

M.A. thesis, University of California at Los Angeles.

Schwartz, Theodore. 1963. *The Paliau Movement in the Admiralty Islands, 1946–54.* Anthropological papers, 49. New York: American Museum of Natural History.

Stewart, Lynn. 1990. "Our People are Like Gardens: Music, Performance, and Aesthetics among the Lolo, West New Britain Province, Papua New Guinea." Ph.D. dissertation, University of British Columbia.

Thurston, William. 1987. *Processes of Change in the Languages of North-Western New Britain.* Canberra: Pacific Linguistics. Series B 9.

Yayii, Phillip Lamasisi. 1983. "Some Aspects of Traditional Dance Within the Malanggan Culture of North New Ireland." *Bikmaus* 4(3):33–48.

# Solomon Islands

*Adrienne L. Kaeppler*  *Jill Nash*
*Don Niles*  *J. W. Love*
*Steven R. Nachman*  *Jared Tao Keil*
*Vida Chenoweth*  *Ryūichi Tai*
*Regis Stella*  *Hugo Zemp*

**North Solomons Province, Papua New Guinea**

**Western Province**

**Isabel Province**

**Central Province**

**Guadalcanal Province**

**Malaita Province**

In 1568, hoping to find gold to rival that of the biblical King Solomon's mines, the Spaniard Alvaro de Mendaña visited and named the Solomon Islands. Louis de Bougainville in 1768 determined the extent of the archipelago, and gave his name to its largest landmass.

Bougainville, Buka, and several small islands form the North Solomons Province of Papua New Guinea, home to some 130,000 people. The rest of the archipelago forms the independent nation of the Solomon Islands, with a population of about 260,000 (map). Several Polynesian outliers are located in the Solomons. The archipelago, especially Guadalcanal, are known for the fierceness of fighting that occurred there during World War II.

Musically, the Solomons are known for their panpipe ensembles, still used in traditional ways and styles, including polyphony in several parts, sometimes doubled, tripled, or even quadrupled at the octave. Details of this polyphony vary geographically. Panpipe ensembles are also formed into contemporary bands, which play Western-inspired pop. A famous dance, in which men in lines carry wicker shields (figures 1 and 2), is said to derive from Nggela Island, but is performed by men of Guadalcanal.
—ADRIENNE L. KAEPPLER

## NORTH SOLOMONS PROVINCE, PAPUA NEW GUINEA

As the name implies, the culture of the North Solomons Province of Papua New Guinea has strong cultural affinities with that of the rest of the Solomon Islands. In both areas, panpipe ensembles are important. The absence of the hourglass drum (kundu) in Buka and Bougainville, in contrast to most other parts of Papua New Guinea, is also a strong parallel with the Solomon Islands, though the kundu occurs only sporadically in much of the Island Region of Papua New Guinea. Even within the province, the absence of the kundu is not universal: the people of Nissan use it, proving their cultural links with southern New Ireland. Most peoples of Buka and Bougainville practice polyphonic singing as the norm. They consider the susap a men's instrument and the musical bow a women's instrument (figure 3). In a given language, both instruments usually share one name.

Probably the most distinctive type of musical context in Buka and Bougainville

Solomon
Islands,
Vanuatu,
and New
Caledonia

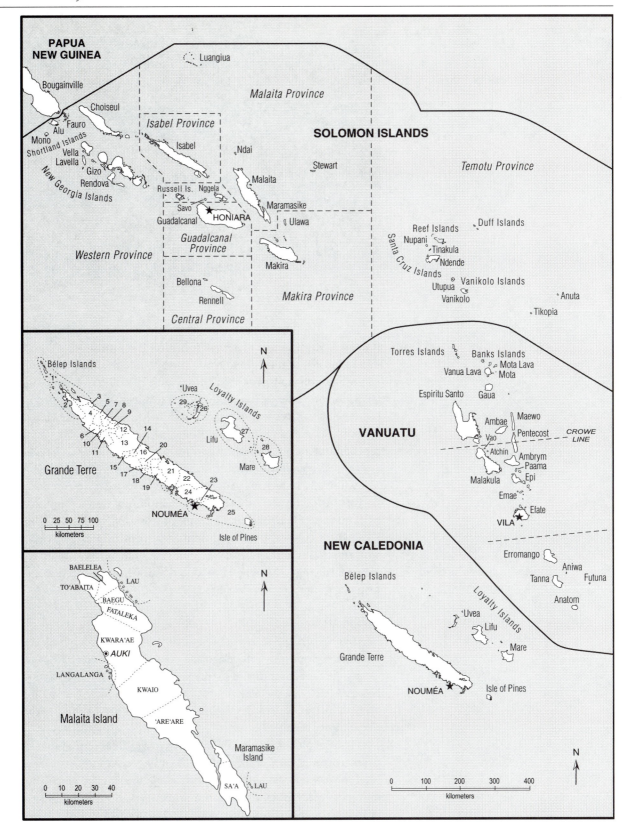

FIGURE 1   Men of Longgu Village, Guadalcanal, perform a dance with wicker shields. University of Sydney. Photo by H. Ian Hogbin.

TRACK 38   is dancing to the music of aerophones (Tok Pisin *singsing kaur*). An orchestra commonly consists of several differently sized double-row panpipes (one row with distal ends closed, one row with open ends), several end-blown bamboos tied together like a raft, and an end-blown conical wooden trumpet. While performers dance in a concentric circle, this ensemble accompanies polyphonic singing with vocables. Such an ensemble, common in Buka and Bougainville, is a recent introduction to the Buin area of southern Bougainville, where panpipe ensembles usually resemble those of the rest of the Solomon Islands, employing single-row panpipes without trumpets.

Musically important geographical divisions characterize the province. In the north, musical texts are short, many repetitions of text and music occur within the performance of one song, and men play hollow log idiophones (garamuts) singly or in small groups. In the south, musical texts are often poetically elaborate and change with repetitions of the music. Garamut ensembles often include ten or more instruments. Dancing to aerophone-produced music has features that inform the musical mapping of the province (Vatahi 1989).                                    —DON NILES

## Nissan Atoll

Nissan (Nehan) and its companion atoll, Pinipel (Pinipir), form the Nissan Group, linking the Bismarck Archipelago and the Solomon Islands. Known for dukduk and tubuan performances (figure 4), the people also play garamuts and kundus. In 1971, Nissan Atoll had a population of 2,551 persons, in fifteen autonomous villages. The local language, Nehan, is Austronesian, a member of the Northwest Solomonic Group (Ross 1988:217).

The people subsist mainly on starchy vegetables (taro, yam, sweet potato) and fruits (coconut, breadfruit). They fish and for ceremonial consumption raise pigs. Men succeed their fathers to civic leadership; they confirm their succession by sponsoring mortuary feasts. Trade with Anir (off New Ireland) and Buka once fostered the introduction of new customs. Since 1900, especially since the 1940s, islanders have visited Rabaul and New Ireland, where they have learned songs, dances, and dance-controlling magic. Radios, Roman Catholic missionaries, and expatriate and indigenous schoolteachers bring further musical innovations.

On Nissan Atoll, individuals rehearse songs for upcoming feasts, repeat songs they have heard, and—as women do with small children—turn everyday speech into

FIGURE 2    Wicker shield of the Solomon Islands. Smithsonian Institution. Photo Smithsonian Institution.

song. Songs (*kereker*) include short indigenous items, usually sung informally; guitar songs, based on nonindigenous, often Western, styles; songs introduced in Roman Catholic worship, some in English, some in Nehan; and songs composed on Nissan or nearby islands and sung in connection with mortuary feasts. Men and women sing (men sometimes in falsetto), but only men play musical instruments and compose songs.

### Songs at feasts

To commemorate the recently deceased, a hamlet or village periodically holds a feast under the direction of its leader. By presenting pork, survivors pay debts arising from the relatives' deaths—and thus, while confirming their claims of inheritance, officially "forget" the dead. Visitors from neighboring peoples attend to receive major presentations of pork and enjoy the prevailing hospitality. A successful feast enhances the prestige of the hosts.

The mortuary feast follows a series of *tigul* 'nocturnal sessions of singing'. At these sessions, which occur over a period of several months, the sponsor and his associates present visitors food. The hosts or a group of guests take the lead in starting songs; all present then join in. By extension, the word *tigul* denotes structured movements with drumming, the accompanying song, and the session itself. As men, women, and children walk around a *Myristica fatua* pole standing in the plaza of the feast-hosting hamlet (often before the sponsoring leader's house), they sing *tigul* in series. Garamuts, played in the men's clubhouse, accompany them. Islanders do not consider this promenade a dance. Begun long after dark, the session continues until midnight or later, even until dawn. At its conclusion, the hosts distribute food and the crowd disperses.

Each village has multiple *tigul*. Some songs from precolonial times tell of heroic feuds and cannibalistic feasts; others are newly composed. In a few villages, by adding lyrics to fixed melodies, men still compose *tigul*. Each song, ancient or modern, consists of several stanzas: six-, seven-, and eight-stanza *tigul* are common. Different stanzas of one song, sometimes the work of different persons, may develop unrelated topics.

A *tigul* is composed by the person from whom the owner (the man whose history it draws on) has commissioned it. The composer teaches the song to its owner and his relatives, who can bequeath it to their descendants. None of these persons has exclusive rights to it, for anyone who remembers a *tigul* may sing it and teach it to others. People who commission songs are usually those most interested in preserving and singing them. They understand the hidden meanings. An owner may not tell a composer the connotations of the events a commissioned song recounts, but may simply require that the text mention such-and-such a place. The owner understands the reference, as do certain other persons, including those whom the owner may wish to shame. Consequently, *tigul* are composed and forgotten according to changing intents and memories of events. Some *tigul* survive, though their meanings may not be entirely clear. Villagers call *tigul* their newspapers; when they speak of events, they often cite appropriate verses.

*Tigul* deal primarily with two subjects: shame and escape from death. They describe recovery from illness and rescue from calamity. They bear witness to quarrels and bad feelings between persons. Their intent is frequently to shame individuals, never by name or description, but by hints and clues. An owner may be a disputant (often a victim) who has chosen to publicize his humiliation. Many *tigul* include stanzas or verses that evoke the act of composition. They may portray a man standing on the beach, waiting for inspiration to float in from the sea, like driftwood. Composers may declare in song they are unworthy to compose:

FIGURE 3    A woman of Teabes Village, North Solomons Province, Papua New Guinea, plays a mouth-resonated bow. Photo by Don Niles, 1982.

Iairiwi, iambomi lele ro la lih?
Kami obioboro tane talipenio.
Io tada tigi ran antar langit!
Keme lum tane talipenio.
Io banga tunula dohi Hois,
Keme lum tane talipenio!
Ku kakatupa tun matuk la welhir poluk.
Iu suge tabilane.

Iairiwi, but where is a road I may traverse?
Trees were felled to block me.
O look up at the sky!
Darkness surrounds me.
O look truly toward Bougainville,
Whence darkness comes upon me!
I am unable indeed to fetch it [the sun] again.
I sit bowed.

In this stanza, a villager complains that rivals, thwarting his magic, have brought rain.

Two songs created by Tomunsai of Balil illustrate the composition of *tigul*. He composed one for another Nissan man when the two worked together on a boat in Sohano. One stanza indirectly referred to the time when that man went to Rabaul for false teeth. Because his relatives had not accompanied him to the boat, he wished to shame them in the song. Tomunsai composed a second stanza at the request of a crewman who, having overheard Tomunsai in the act of composition, had asked him to describe his sadness at leaving Nissan to go to a hospital. Yet another Nissan crewman asked for a stanza that implied his family did not care for him. The original buyer then requested a stanza containing the question, "Why are you angry at me when you summon me to make it rain?" A final stanza, composed for the entire crew, described a wind that had almost destroyed their boat.

On Nissan, Tomunsai composed a *tigul* for a villager who, with another man,

FIGURE 4    At Beru Hamlet, Mapiri Village, Nissan, dukduks and tubuan perform as men with kundus watch. Photo by Steven R. Nachman, 1971.

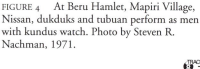

had found and eaten a blowfish discarded by fishermen. Because the two had not prepared the fish properly, they became ill from its poison. On recovering, one of them commissioned two stanzas. At another's request, Tomunsai composed a stanza describing a drought, in which the trees on the atoll had shed their leaves. Another stanza recalled a villager employed by a Tolai man in Rabaul: the villager had gotten lost, and the text celebrated his rescue. A final stanza for a Balil man described his nearly drowning while working on a boat. He had thrown overboard a bucket on a line, which had dragged him into the sea. The melody of this song uses a semitoneless five-tone scale.

### Sua

Another kind of *tigul* is *sua,* comic songs, sung toward the end of a *tigul* (session). These are musical insults, intended to evoke laughter. *Sua* are archaic, their texts not fully understood, but the insults are usually obvious. To heighten the humor, singers insert living persons' names. No *sua* have been composed since about 1900. Their melodies and drumming, known as *sua* beats (*tuktukung sua*), differ from those of conventional *tigul.*

### Tiko

On Pinipir and the northern villages of Nissan, people may perform another type of entertainment during a *tigul* (session). This is *tiko,* a game in which people sing and guess at the identity of a person holding and dancing behind a coconut-leaf mat. *Tiko* songs are short and humorous. Some are in Nehan, but most are in Tok Pisin or the languages of Anir, Tanga, the Siar area of Southern New Ireland, and the Gazelle Peninsula. Since about 1900, only a few islanders have composed *tiko.*

### Tigul from Buka

At *tigul* sessions, people may perform *tigul* from Buka. These are faster than indigenous ones. Dancers sing lively melodies, stamping bamboo tubes on the ground. They may hoot and whistle. Accompaniment may include garamuts, kundus, and sometimes whistles.

### Bot

At *tigul* sessions, people may also perform dances called *bot.* With a blunt stick, a drummer beats a small garamut, set in the center of the ensemble. In a series of concentric circles, dancers move around this instrument; men and women walk slowly together. Some *bot* are in Nehan, but many are in the same languages as *tiko* often are. *Bot* appeared on Nissan in the late 1800s, when they were most popular; after the 1940s, islanders rarely composed them. Gabriel of Balil composed this humorous *bot* in Tok Pisin and Nehan:

> Mi silip long maien bet;
> Tumasu i kilim mi, kilim mi man long biknait.
> Mi no moa silip gut alonep bong.
>
> Bai mi silip olsem wanem?
> Sikin i hat nogut pinis.
> Mi ron i go daun long paranda.
>
> I sleep on my bed;
> Bedbugs are killing me, killing me at midnight.
> I no longer sleep well at night.
>
> How can I sleep?
> My skin is insufferably hot.
> I rush down to the veranda.

FIGURE 5   At New Camp Hamlet, Mapiri Village, Nissan, a man performs movements of the *tinoia: a,* holding plant fibers at chest level; *b,* opening his arms and facing to the left diagonal. Photo by Steven R. Nachman, 1971.

(a)     (b)

Gabriel recounts his experience sleeping in a village apparently notorious for its infestation of bedbugs.

### Choral dances

Most choral dances (*tinoia*) occur on the day of a feast. All villages represented, including that of the hosts, compete. Each performs two *tinoia:* a men's and a women's. A company of fifteen to twenty-five dancers performs before an audience for about half an hour. (If four or five villages are attending the feast, the show fills most of an afternoon.) Wearing decorative costumes, a company parades into the arena in two or three columns behind a leader. The dancers perform in rows but sometimes make circular promenades. To the accompaniment of stationary male drummers beating kundus, they sing while executing a series of coordinated, stylized, usually nonrepresentational movements (figure 5). Then they leave, remove their costumes, and rejoin the spectators. Each company tries to execute *tinoia* more flawlessly than those of others (figure 6). Success partly depends on magic: the dance realizes magical power in a field of contending powers.

Most current *tinoia* have come from abroad. Since about 1900, men have returned with them from visits to Anir and Rabaul. Dancing in lines has become increasingly popular since the 1940s, when islanders began to import dance-controlling magic, named for a betel-related ingredient important in it: *buai* (Tolai) 'areca nut' (Nehan *makih*). Men visiting Rabaul purchased instruction in *buai* from magicians there, and then taught the magic to their fellows. Men and women also perform *tinoia* at *tigul* sessions and celebrations of national and Christian holidays and the building of new stores and chapels.

Each kind of *tinoia* has a typical combination of movements, rhythms, and ornaments. In creating new dances, artists try to follow this combination. Though they create new *tinoia* modeled on introduced types, they do not create new types of *tinoia.* Performers sing loudly the songs to which they dance, but they sing with little effort to communicate the sense of the texts. The words, usually the least important aspect of the pieces, are frequently the most original. Even those composed locally are

FIGURE 6    Men of Beru Hamlet, Mapiri Village, Nissan, rehearse the *tinoia*. Photo by Steven R. Nachman, 1971.

often in Tolai or languages of New Ireland. Without knowing the precise sense of the words, Nissan composers use them to give their compositions the authenticity of foreignness. Such words may mention the activities of the dance-magic societies. Sometimes the words are the names of spirits.

The texts of *tinoia* composed in Nehan are hard to translate. Some have no continuity of sense from one phrase to another. All are idiosyncratic: by a word or two, a composer alludes to a personal incident; the next words may allude to an unrelated event. Many texts are unglossable without the composer's help. The composer mentally foregrounds the melody; considerations of meaning, syntactical structure, and morphemic construction are often secondary. For melodic or rhythmic purposes, some texts have vocables; occasionally, a composition consists entirely of them.

### Warmong and warabat

As part of *buai* rituals, islanders sing *warmong* and *warabat*. At night, during the weeks before a performance, men may gather to sing *warmong* (or *paragas,* an older variant); they sing loudly, to the accompaniment of a kundu. Women dancers sing women's versions of the songs. For a public performance, as *tinoia* performers enter the feast-sponsoring hamlet, they may sing other *warmong* before they begin the *tinoia. Warmong* are songs of joy, which enable participants in a dance or ritual to focus their minds. They attract helpful ghosts and spirits. Many have magical themes, particularly the seduction of women; some cover the events of daily life. Lemak of Tanamalit composed a *warmong* that boasts of his knowledge of magic ritual: *Reg laia, reg labum; / Ke tungara wom tar miog; / Ke tungara toro lug* 'My *laia,* my *labum*; / It already sprouts from my tongue; / It sprouts from my head'. The *laia* and *labum,* varieties of ginger, are important magical plants.

Men sing *warabat* to summon *buai* spirits into their bodies, either as part of initiation into a society of magicians, or as preparation for performing *tinoia* at a feast.

'I am ashamed of the ways of the elders; / They chased me away when I played the ukulele. / I am sorry to be living on Nissan; / I am sorry to be living at Balil'.

—from a Nissan song

They sing softly, in a secluded area. They also perform *warabat* for other magical purposes, particularly the seduction of women. Various ritual actions—consuming magical coconut oils, chewing and spitting betel—may accompany the singing. Many *buai* songs remain in Tolai or languages of New Ireland, but some are in Nehan. One *warabat* composed in Mapiri consists of two stanzas. The first refers to the eating of vegetable ingredients as part of the ritual. The second calls on a spirit to enter the singer's stomach. This stanza begins with a cry, to make the spirit feel sorry for the singer.

### Other songs

Indigenous, often one-stanza songs unconnected with feasting but sung informally according to individual mood include *kirkiring* and *lilili*. Islanders do not use these terms consistently. They sometimes use them, or the generic word *kereker,* to classify songs they cannot readily categorize. In the early 1970s, they still sang these songs, but rarely composed new ones. These songs also occurred as story songs (*kerekereng kiwkiw*), which reinforce events in tales (*kiwkiw*), or form bridges between them.

*Kirkiring* (from *kiring* 'cry, mourn') derive from the rhythmic keening of female mourners at funerals and departures of loved ones from Nissan. A woman keens, "Sorry, my son," or "He has left [so-and-so] alone." Such laments inspire people to compose *kirkiring*. Lemarias of Mapiri composed an example about a woman whose three sons have left Nissan to work; she laments that if she dies, no one will be around to bury her: *Iu kirkiring tatamiwomur tantowon rung huliwpe ane togwo. / Iu rikin tun tar rigu mat; / Ra enir huet, ra enir lo. / E welhireper sitori kaweke tang tinom* 'I cry for the three of you who left me here. / Truly, I lie here in my illness; / Pigs will eat me, dogs will eat me. / For the story says to look after your mother'. The story (Tok Pisin *sitori*) may be the biblical injunction to "honor your father and your mother" (Exodus 20:12).

*Lilili* describe escape from death and danger, allude to personal humiliations, and treat other events. One, composed by Tomunsai, describes his visit to Rabaul, where in a dream he saw his father's ghost; the ghost told him to compose a song. People also once sang *lilili* to insult enemies, possibly as a prelude to warfare. In the early 1940s, Kiabig of Siar composed a *lilili* in which he tells women to wait for the "workboys" (laborers, working for Allied troops), to give them grass skirts to sell. The song highlights these women's vanity, as they flaunt items they get in exchange for the skirts: "The women, indeed, flaunt their loincloths; / Their baskets are full of handkerchiefs. / They are showoffs; they are really showoffs." Some *lilili* begin with the sound that names the genre.

### Songs for pastimes and various contexts

Islanders once sang songs that accompanied pastimes and other activities. Some activities had a single song; for others, men could compose new songs. Songs accompanied games of hiding and games in which players tried to identify a person in disguise or to locate a hidden object. Ragi of Mapiri composed the following *sisiak,* which people sang as they jumped (*siak*) from diving platforms into the sea: *Bangatig tasir sela ra hamamas tabil iran totor simbumuna Maiwara. / Tabil iran tasir beu; mu wakwakes taro butwan gero kokoro wahung i sarang ion* 'Look up at the sailors who sit happily atop the boom of *Maiwara. /* [I] sit atop the *beu* [tree]; you all watch the waves as they come ashore on the beach'. The text includes words from Tok Pisin: *amamas* 'happy' and *sela* 'sailor'; *simbum* may denote a 'jib boom'.

Islanders continue to perform magical rituals to cure or cause illness, or to insure the success or failure of any important activity. Only people who own such rituals perform them. The rituals usually include songs known as *ker* (the root of *kereker*), delivered in a monotonous, slurred voice. Performed so quietly others cannot overhear, a *ker* states the purpose of a ritual, either directly or in figurative language. Because the diction of *ker* is archaic and telegraphic, performers and audiences are unable to translate some of them.

As voyagers to Anir or Buka approached the shore, they sang special songs, (*ma*)*mai,* often in the Anir language. Other kinds of songs had semimagical intent, including those performed to summon a high tide (*kiladudud*), sung by women collecting *Canarium indicum* nuts (*kerekereng sir lueh*), sung by children washing in the rain to make it fall more heavily (*kerekereng panghuan*), sung to chase away whirlwinds (*kerekereng solihang*), and performed on capturing a sea turtle to secure a plenteous supply of meat (*kerekereng won*). For a cargo cult on Nissan in the 1940s, islanders composed songs imitating those sung in church.

### Guitar songs

After 1945, the playing of guitars and the singing of guitar songs became popular. Imitating Western practices, young people hold parties at which they dance to these songs. Guitarists and singers often repeat songs heard on the radio. These songs come from abroad, mostly from elsewhere in Papua New Guinea and the Pacific Islands. Western missionaries and islanders teaching in Nissan schools bring new songs, some of which teachers learn from songbooks.

Local lyricists fit new words to introduced melodies. Their lyrics, combining Nehan with words and phrases from other languages (including Tok Pisin and English), treat men's travels and homesickness, quarrels, insults, sexual affairs, and women's inconstancies. Peto of Balil composed this text for a guitar song: *Ku matala tun tar pasin tasir mahoh; / Ka weltul la io ru sarape toro kulele. / Weldelomoio ru wangolpe doh i Nehan; / Weldelomoio ru wangolpe doh i Balil* 'I am ashamed of the ways of the elders; / They chased me away when I played the ukulele. / I am sorry to be living on Nissan; / I am sorry to be living at Balil'. Other documented songs tell of a man who drowned in the lagoon during a storm, a nun who dispensed medicine to a young male patient, and a bat that devours bananas unpalatable to humans.

### Musical instruments

The most important musical accompaniments are percussive. Each men's clubhouse contains garamuts (*tuk*). Hewn from a local hardwood (*Vitex cofassus*), they rest lengthwise in the open area of the house. With a bound rattan-stem beater, each percussionist jolts the lip of a garamut. Combinations of long and short beats mark feasts and other communal events, and accompany *tigul* processions and one kind of *tinoia.* Each garamut sounds a single pitch, and the ensemble produces various pitches.

Most *tinoia* are accompanied by stationary drummers beating kundus. The skin of the monitor, *Varanus indicus,* covers the opening at one end. Holding a drum with one hand, a performer strikes the membrane with four fingers of the other.

Another percussive device is a hand-held section of bamboo (*rawat*), beaten with a stick. Dancers carry it for one type of *tinoia* and a form of *tigul*. In rehearsals of *tinoia*, it substitutes for a kundu.

Other indigenous instruments, rarely seen, include bamboo susaps (*pagur*), raft panpipes (*wek*), and side-blown flutes (*tulal*). Fritz Krause (1907:143–147) describes and illustrates some of these. A respondent said men formerly wooed women by playing a susap outside women's houses. Sailors signaled their approach to shore by blowing conchs (*tuil*). Since 1972, other instruments that have reached the atoll are electric guitars and keyboards and Western drums.          —STEVEN R. NACHMAN

## Halia

About thirteen thousand Halia-speakers inhabit the east coast of Buka Island. Rainfall is scarce. The people sometimes move from coral-cliff villages to camps on the beach, 60 meters below. There, when the tide is out, freshwater springs well up from under the coral. The Halia grow food in gardens, and get fish and shellfish from the sea. They buy imported food in Buka Town.

The Halia have had contact with outsiders for nearly a century. Some of their music is no longer current, but singsings remain important. Local schools educate children in their own language. In the mid-1980s, the people were beginning to seek outside help in finding ways to preserve their music. Data for this account were gathered in the Halia villages of Hagus, Tohatsi, Hanpan, Hanahan, Eltupan, and Hahalis; Thomas Tohiana of Hahalis provided valuable aid, and Tim Cooley recorded songs (Richardson 1986).

### Musical contexts

Halia people sing in many contexts. On the water, rowing from Buka to the Carteret Islands, they sing while waiting for the sun to set; at daybreak, they sing when light permits going ashore. Women traditionally performed bride-price songs and laments. Current songs treat subjects like Christian faith and soldiers at war.

By organizing and hosting a singsing, a Halia man gains prestige. The evening before the event, he sponsors a rehearsal, like one witnessed at Hanahan. In a counterclockwise-moving circle, men played pipes and bamboo trumpets. Songs were accompanied by garamuts, pipes, or both. Girls danced in a line, arms hooked together, rocking forward with their weight on the left foot, then leaning back with weight on the right foot while tilting the pelvis. As the night progressed, all other participants were circling in a walking step; only the girls performed formal steps.

The singsing featured nine songs. According to experts Betsin and Kahia (interpreted by Maurice Koesana), the first song celebrated the host. It had three parts: singing with pipes and trumpets, instruments only, and return of the first part. The second song celebrated the singers; performed with the aerophones, it repeated thrice. One group sang the third song to overpower the music of another, singing simultaneously; people sang it thrice unaccompanied, then twice with aerophones. The fourth song, sung with aerophones, was repeated. Five songs followed. People sang song 5 for enjoyment; it was accompanied by two garamuts and repeated five times, with a text of vocables only. Song 6 sometimes expresses jubilation at catching tuna; people sang it five times unaccompanied, then twice more with garamuts. People sometimes sing song 7 when going to the garden; it was accompanied by garamuts, and repeated once. Song 8 expressed happiness about singing in front of the garamuts; it repeated nine times. Guests sang song 9 as they departed; accompanied by garamuts, it repeated three times.

At Hahalis, a leading political personage hosted a party for his son's birthday. Three singsing pipe and trumpet ensembles performed simultaneously while boister-

FIGURE 7 Excerpt of Halia singing with aerophones, Hanahan Village, 1984. Transcription by Vida Chenoweth.

ous crowds danced and others prepared food. Late in the afternoon, hired schoolgirls in traditional dress arrived to perform dances. The format for this singsing was similar to that heard at Hanahan. The first song expressed appreciation to the host; Hanpan and Eltupan villagers sang it after feasting. They sang the second song in competition with another group, singing simultaneously; Hanpan and Eltupan competed with Hahalis and Hanahan villagers. In the third song, Hanpan villagers sang: "We are coming to celebrate the birthday of the chief's son." The fourth song was the hired performance. By blowing a whistle, a male teacher directed the schoolgirls; accompaniment came from a small garamut. The women and girls sang: "We are coming to dance at Hahalis."

### Musical instruments

In communal dancing and singing with aerophone accompaniment, singers take their pitches from those of aerophones, two kinds of which accompanied dance-songs: bamboo panpipes, bound in rows of four; and bamboo trumpets, bound in rows of three, the longest of which extended about a meter. At the beginning of a song, a low E♭ sounded. The players, all men, were all but hidden in the crowd. Occasionally, they raised the long pipes skyward as they sounded them, their cheeks puffing. Some pipes played G♭ and A♭ somewhat sharp, but the consensus in vocal and instrumental parts was G♭ and A♭ unsharped. Voices entered contrapuntally: first the instruments, then the singers (figure 7). Men may play garamuts singly or in pairs, accompanying singing and dancing. Garamuts also serve for signaling.

### Music system

Phrasal form in Halia songs consists of two to eight phrasal types, which analysis reduces to three minimal prototypes: A, AB, and ABC. Later phrases derive from these. Variations consist of slight modifications: melodic substitution, expansion, contraction.

Halia performances are polyphonic. A typical song with garamut accompaniment (figure 8) has no text. A male leader sings an introduction on the vowel /o/, until at phrase B, a men's chorus enters singing /oa/, and women enter at phrase $B_2$, singing /ae/. Three beats before $B_2$, two garamuts enter. This is a simpler pattern than that of other songs in the cycle, which insert eighth-note pairs, plain or dotted, between triplets. The tonal center of voice two is G an octave lower than in voices 1 and 3. A pattern of more than three successive tones in a common direction is atypical.

In Halia polyphony, some parts are obscure, especially when the entry of one vocal part dovetails with and eclipses the phrasal ending of another part. At phrase $B_2$ (figure 8), the garamuts are distant and unclear. On a weak beat and drawn upward

FIGURE 8  A Halia song with garamut accompaniment, Hanahan Village, 1984. Downward stems denote the smaller, higher-pitched drum. Transcription by Vida Chenoweth.

to D on a stronger beat, the B♭ in voice 1 is sometimes sharp. Wide leaps upward, particularly in the women's part, begin with an upglide. Two phrases, A and B, occur in the following order: ABB, BAB, BBB, BAB; only voice one sings the unvaried phrase A. The kernel inventory of tones in this song is D–G–A–B♭, plus D–G an octave higher and tonal center G. The tonal flow of voice one differs somewhat from that of the other voices. Three motifs produce simultaneous variations, sounding above irregular punctuation by garamuts. The smaller drum marks the pulse, while a larger drum embellishes it at a lower pitch, mainly interjecting sixteenth- or eighth-note pairs, plain or dotted.

## Teop Island

This island can be circled on foot in about an hour. The population speaks Teop, a member of the Tinputz family of Austronesian languages. The population probably numbers less than five hundred. The closest mainland village is Saba, in northeastern Bougainville. From an airstrip there to Teop takes about twenty minutes by outrigger.

Songs sung by mixed voices and accompanied by stamped tubes are *siguru*. Samson Purupuru, to whom Queen Elizabeth II awarded the Order of the British Empire for his diplomatic service, organized a performance of these songs in 1984. Songs that provincial broadcasters had previously recorded on Teop are songs of

FIGURE 8
(*continued*)

another people, the Nagovisi. For the performance of 1984, the radio station requested songs in the local vernacular.

Before singing got under way, young men started a noisy generator to power
large amplifiers, on which they played cassettes of popular music. In connection with
copper-mine jobs, they had spent time in Arawa, a town populated by Australians
and others. They had not undergone initiation in their cultural traditions, including
singsings. To be out of range of the amplifiers, the performers—older people, who
had retained traditional knowledge—moved down to the beach, where in moonlight
they sang *siguru*. Their voices were quiet. They stamped bamboo tubes for their first
several songs, and then laid them aside. The youths whose noise had caused the withdrawal drifted to the beach, where they sat in shadows—to listen, perhaps for the
first time, to their ancestors' songs.

### Music system

The people of Teop sing in simple harmony, not unlike the linear harmony found in

Santa Isabel [see SOLOMON ISLANDS: Isabel Province]. Now and then, imitation occurs. Vocal entries, syncopated against the main pulse, heighten rhythmic interest. The tonal inventory of *siguru* does not fit neatly into a particular scale or scheme. In 27 percent of the recorded corpus of these songs, two perfect fourths are linked: P4–P4 plus an optional major second. Older songs tend to surround a minor third or a perfect fourth with smaller intervals: M2–m3–M2 or m3–P4–M2. Other, more elaborate inventories occur. Patterns composed of fourths divided into a minor third and a major second constitute another 27 percent of these data.

### Texts

Some *siguru* are old, their composers unknown. Two of them relate to male initiation; one was sung when the ceremonial hat was put on the boy. Placing a tall, colorful, cylindrical cap on the initiate's head is a custom vaunted by the Rotokas people, in east-central Bougainville. Postage stamps have celebrated these hats. Of other songs, one was about Dane, a man who while fishing from his canoe had a vision of a dead man singing a song; the text was not in Teop, but Dane remembered the melody and taught it to others.

About half the recorded *siguru* express feelings. In one, a man laments having been abandoned by his betrothed, who has left him for a man of another village, "and never even said goodbye." Men sing of women they desire, or vent unrequited emotions. One of the most moving songs (as interpreted by Samson) was that of a man who, realizing he will not recover from his sickness, asks his mother to take care of his two little boys—"and then he died." Only living composers, and those whom people remember having seen, are remembered for their songs. A song of the 1980s by Enoch Botoa tells of a new and thrilling sight: fishing from his canoe at night, he sees electric lights reflected in the harbor.          —VIDA CHENOWETH

### Banoni

About fifteen hundred Banoni-speaking people inhabit the shores of Empress Augusta Bay. The Banoni language is Austronesian, a member of the Northwest Solomonic Group (Ross 1988:217). Much Banoni music resembles music elsewhere in Bougainville. Banoni musical genres occur among the Hahon (Spearritt, Lulungan, and Renssy 1983:56–66), and especially among the Nagovisi, the Piva, and the Siwai. In Banoni life, music is important: everyone participates, as performer or listener. Music adds aesthetic value to public events, but musical meaning lies within private experience.

### Musical contexts and genres

Before important feasts, groups plan and rehearse their music. Certain individuals play the role of musical critic. Groups collectively compose *dare,* but composers in other genres do not usually receive public acknowledgment or payment. As a repository of important customs and information, each song (*tabe*) has a function. In the twentieth century, some musical genres lost their original functions, and new musical styles blended with old ones.

#### Singsings

At all-night feasts, when the populations of several villages assemble in one village, people sing songs of two kinds, *tsigul* and *roori.* The bulk of the music consists of *tsigul* and pieces played on panpipes. *Tsigul* came from Buka, where Banoni workers learned it in the 1950s. Adapted to local musical norms, it became a Banoni genre, and by the 1980s, for performance at feasts, it had become one of the people's favorite musical types. The texts of most *tsigul* are short and simple, as in the following, recorded at Marabono in 1987: *Waia, waia, / Ko regha wano? / Ko reghe karana-man* 'Where, where, / Did you see me? / You are jealous of us'.

Cautionary songs (*roori*) convey social commentary or ridicule. People compose them to point out that the host of a feast has failed to meet his obligation to provide a pig and other gifts. When a group sings one, everyone listens carefully to the words; and if expedient, the person at whom the first group has directed their song makes a reply, in the form of another.

Unlike the texts of other Banoni genres, those of *roori* are metaphorical. In the following example (recorded at Mabesi in 1983), each stanza ends with the sigh *e! e!* (not shown).

| | |
|---|---|
| Na ko ta tanisita. | I will cry. |
| Ta tanisi, tagowa | I will cry, because |
| Ke ta puke ghususa | I'm always catching |
| Pau tetapoisi. | All kinds of illnesses. |
| | |
| Pau tetapoisi | All kinds of illnesses |
| Kemata ghau koweya. | Are coming to me. |
| Na ko banatsi nana. | I'm already old. |
| | |
| Sawana! Ghena, | Poor me! Previously, |
| Mo boghi tatsuwan, | In the olden days, |
| Ko pipito gheusa | I used to cut down |
| Kare me mapisi na, | The big trees, |
| Na maragu wena | To plant |
| Ghe pada namara. | My food. |
| | |
| Witana ghena wawasi Katsuna | But I'm only saying |
| Na tsito pisai dara | I cannot change |
| Na ke darai na Kobonara. | What God has said. |
| Na kewaina | He told me |
| Tobona na ta banatsi gero; | The young will grow old again; |
| Saneu ta buta nga. | Then they'll die. |

The translation gives the figurative meaning, not the literal. The first metaphor, *ke mata ghau koweya,* describes how a thief creeps toward a target. The second, *na ko banatsi nana,* describes a leaf going brown; it means a person is growing old. The third metaphor, *ko pipito gheusa,* can be glossed 'stepping on big trees and the trees falling'. The fourth, *tobona na ta banatsi gero,* describes a plant; it means the young plant will wither and die. Finally, *saneu ta buta nga* depicts a log: having been on the ground a long time, it is wet.

*Roori* fall into three classes: *roori na daka,* sung on arrival at a host village; *roori na pisi,* sung in ridicule, as on catching people having sexual intercourse; and *roori na watetanisi,* sung in self-pity. The example given above falls into the third class.

*Funerals*

A person's death leads to formal mourning. Survivors voice their feelings in one of a small set of laments (*tanisi*). Performing near the corpse, they wail and sob. They often add stylized rhythmic swaying. Against the ground, they stamp their feet or hands.

The texts of laments are short. Mourners repeat them many times in succession. When two groups, each relating differently to the deceased, are present, the simulta-

Banoni dance has simple basic movements, on which each dancer may improvise: women move with restraint; men move more vigorously. The usual procedure is to form two concentric circles. As the dancers sing, the circles rotate clockwise.

neous performance of two laments occurs. When relatives of the deceased come from different tribes and speak different languages, such performances can involve two languages.

In a recorded performance of a lament (at Matsunke in 1987), mourners repeated the following text several times. The lines end in the same vowel because Banoni poetry has rhyme. After each line, singers pause: *O wawine ghena! / Ghera wawine ta! / Na kami kota nana! / Na mata na Rogasa, / Kenewa pitoi ta / Burina Puruata! / O wawine ghena!* 'My poor sister! / Our poor sister! / You are really dead now! / Children of Rogasa, / Who brought us / To Puruata! / My poor sister!' From Banoni audiences, laments elicit tears; people say it is hard to cry in silence.

### Babysitting

To comfort children when their mothers are away (usually during the day, or in the early evening), a Banoni babysitter, usually a woman, may sing a lullaby (*watetamasi*). Crooning softly, she cuddles the child until it calms down or goes to sleep. In the following example (recorded at Mamarego in 1982), the first line names the child; the last line repeats ad libitum: *Esam, Esam, / Tetanisa na tsuma, / Ke kena ritoa. / Tamau! tamau!* 'Esam, Esam, / Always cries for its child, / Taken by a bird. / Hush! hush!' By the 1990s, with the introduction of baby-bouncing nets and other child-care products, lullabies were dying out.

### Tales

For amusement on moonlit evenings, children of both sexes sing *wakekena*, unaccompanied songs relating to legends and myths. Examples are many. They have short texts, which covertly teach ethics and norms. Some of them are in archaic diction, as in this example: *Ne pau, ne pau. / Tsiwa raragu tenge mi dare. / Na tenge mi para kadaken. / Ke tsiba kepea na wanoi.* The Banoni do not understand such texts, and can provide no translations for them. Before the children sing, an adult—usually an older woman—may narrate a tale.

*Wate* (an archaic term), a subset of *wakekena,* are songs that children perform while swimming and playing games. This example (from people of Matsunke in 1979) also has archaic diction: *Simiai moro ee. / Apam buabua. / Apam buabua.* Songs of this sort do not relate to tales. The texts are obscure, but people get some sense out of them.

### Traditional baptism

*Dare* 'happy' are songs for children's traditional baptismal ceremonies (no longer held). Only a chief's child received the rites. Until it reached the age of two or three, it stayed indoors. Then, the chief hosted a feast. Singing *dare,* women escorted the child around the village, showing it sites of interest. By the 1940s, Christian baptism had supplanted the traditional rites, and adults of both sexes performed *dare* for general entertainment. The songs have long texts, sometimes in the Piva language, and sometimes in the Kenasiu dialect of Banoni.

### Dance

Dance (*ganini*) is an integral part of Banoni music. It has simple basic movements, on which each dancer may improvise (Stella 1990:25). For all kinds of music, Banoni dances are similar. The kinetic force varies by sex: women move with restraint; men, more vigorously. The usual procedure is to form two concentric circles, women in the outer one. As the dancers sing, the circles rotate clockwise.

### Musical instruments

Though Banoni music is mainly vocal, people play several instruments, of which the most important ensemble, the *kowi*, uses three (Stella 1990:38): panpipes, a wooden trumpet (*ruumau*, with a coconut-shell mouthpiece), and a pan-trumpet (*tsugha-nato*). Panpipes are tubes of bamboo, cut in various lengths. The longest pipe is on the player's left; the shortest, on the right. The pipes form double rafts: one row of closed pipes, and one row of open pipes. Instruments come in three basic sizes: *wikewike* or *piore* (the shortest set), *bughau*, and *tsinna kowi* (the longest set). Their combination yields various pitches and timbres. The wooden trumpet sounds a single note as a rhythmic bass. The pan-trumpet doubles notes of the panpipes. Ensembles produce a melody and harmonies; the melody often sounds in three octaves.

For the performance of *dare*, stamped bamboo tubes (*makau taposa*) form an ensemble. Players strike the tubes against a long plank (*tatatsuwe*). For *tsigul*, other stamped tubes, some with split tops acting as rattles (*tarasa*), accompany singing and dancing. Banoni instruments also include a susap (*bekuru*), a mouth-resonated bow (also *bekuru*), a conch trumpet (*tsughini*), rattles, and garamuts.

### Twentieth-century innovations

In the early 1900s, Roman Catholicism reached the Banoni; by 1930, conversion was effectively complete. For worship, the people learned to follow texted rituals and sing alien hymns in Latin. After the second Vatican Council (1963–1965), priests and catechists conducted services in English and local languages. In the 1960s, largely from foreign influence, Banoni music underwent many changes. No new *wakekena*, *wate*, or lullabies came into existence, but people composed new *tsigul*, *roori*, and *dare*.

—REGIS STELLA

## Nagovisi

Most Nagovisi live on alluvial plains, or in the foothills of the Crown Prince Range, south-central Bougainville. They perform music mainly on ceremonial occasions, usually those linked to funerary observances. Outside influences, notably music from Radio Bougainville, have increased the popularity of new musical styles. The major all-night singing (*sira*) is the *lawanda*, which marks the end of mourning. It follows daytime feasts, consisting primarily of distributions of food, which involve no singing. Ideally, it occurs a year after a person's death, but temporal variation occurs.

To host the *lawanda* is a duty of the deceased person's relatives. At a person's death, a complex pattern of rivalries among relatives by marriage develops; these rivalries reflect the balance of affinal debts and credits, which mortuary observances discharge. To the *lawanda*, guests and hosts alike wear their best clothing. In the morning, at the end, guests receive pieces of pork to take home for cooking.

Men and women dance in separate, counterclockwise-moving circles. At only one cremation did I see a mixed group. Dancing consists of a shuffling march. Dancers usually carry an instrument (panpipes or trumpet), or an item to manipu-

late: men carry sticks, spears, axes, bunches of arrows, or stalks of ginger; women carry fans, folded mats, or furled umbrellas. All ordinarily use the right hand, so as not to brush their implements against other performers.

### Vocal music

*Ko:ma,* unaccompanied vocal music, is the most pervasive musical style, appropriate to many situations. In one common practice, men affront their rivals by singing insults. On hearing these, people sometimes become emotional, but the normative reaction may be a studied, deliberate calmness. In 1969–1974, the text of one recorded insult was: "You people think you're putting on a good feast, but you can't put them on the way Laukaka [our relative] did." Another, for a different occasion, was: "You claimed to have given us a good fat pig, but that pig consisted of nothing but vagina." The most effective texts exploit rhetorical flourishes, involving veiled speech, double entendres, and archaic terms.

At wakes and cremations, people of either sex wail stereotyped dirges (*marimari* 'kinship'). A person's connection to the deceased influences the lyric he or she uses. The underlying formula requires the singer to state a kin term for the deceased and one for the singer, with the vocables *e-e-e*. A son addresses a dead father: *Mma e-e-e, loli e-e-e* 'Father *e-e-e*, (I'm) your son *e-e-e*'. From several available kin terms, unrelated mourners choose appropriately decent ones. A mourner might address an older, opposite-moiety man as father, or a coeval, same-moiety woman as older sister. The formula is syllabic (figure 9*a*), and the mourner repeats it over and over. The dances and songs at mortuary occasions are the same as at other singsings, but their demeanor is sad at the former and happy at the latter.

Adults sometimes sing lullabies (*wate*), whose texts—nonsense, archaic, or non-Nagovisi—are obscure. Children sing songs they have heard on the radio program "*Singsing Blong Ples*" ('Village Songs'); they do not often understand the lyrics.

### Musical instruments

At singsings, the two primary instruments are bundle panpipes (*busi*) and wooden trumpets (*kunkun, bugau*). Panpipes consist of several unequal lengths of bamboo, prepared by males for playing certain songs at a particular singsing; afterward, performers discard them. They supposedly came from the area around Mount Bagana, inhabited by Rotokas-speakers. In the distant past, a Nagovisi man, having seen them at a singsing near the Jaba River, introduced them to the Nagovisi.

Only men play panpipes and compose panpipe-accompanied songs. To enhance the surprise of new music, they rehearse in seclusion, away from the village. Sometimes, they brush up favorites from past events. Typical compositions use three notes (figure 9*b*). Performers usually play while walking to the village that hosts the singsing. There, the effect is pleasant: hosts hear faintly the sound of distant panpipes; as guests approach, the music grows louder. Panpipes accompany dancing. Their music is ideally in unison, but different tones often sound simultaneously.

The *kunkun* or *bugau* consists of a hollow log, about a meter long and 15 to 20 centimeters in diameter, with half a coconut shell capping one end. A hole drilled in the shell serves as the mouthpiece. Trumpeters play and dance simultaneously, supporting the instrument with a twisted or folded length of cloth.

Another instrument is the bamboo susap (*bekura, tagowande*). For private recreation or entertainment, youths play it solo at night, often in connection with courtship.

The log idiophone (*tui*) announces prominent people's doings, but does not accompany dancing or singing. A set of these idiophones usually has seven or nine instruments, of differing sizes. In precontact times, the ensemble often played at the cremation of an important person. Its rhythmic patterns convey messages, like "the pigs are being brought into the clubhouse," and a count of the number of pigs. In 1969–1974, people said there were far fewer extant drums than formerly.

Two obsolete instruments suggest parallels of gender. People recall the woman's *bekura,* which they describe as a mouth-resonated bow. They also speak of the woman's *tui,* a struck plaque (*tagum*) resting over a three-chambered hole in the ground near the entrance to the clubhouse; women danced and stamped on it.

### String bands

Guitarists, ukuleleists, and singers form string bands, which provide entertainment essential at parties (Tok Pisin *pati*), all-night festivities of dancing, singing, playing instrumental music, drinking alcoholic beverages, and eating European-style foods. Most of these groups are based in villages. Young men are the principal affiliates; women belong to their husbands' bands, but are unwilling to attend every party. Hosts pay string bands for performing. Their music, learned from radio and other bands, differs sharply from older styles of Nagovisi music.          —JILL NASH

## Buin

About twenty thousand Buin-speakers inhabit the southern end of Bougainville, in three distinct geographical areas: lowlands, middle lands, mountains. The Buin and Siwai languages form the Buin family, a non-Austronesian grouping. Buin music is known for its use of garamuts and panpipes; men play the latter while dancing (figure 10).

FIGURE 10   Carrying weapons and playing raft panpipes (*takamasi*), men of Kukurina Village, North Solomons Province, Papua New Guinea, dance. Photo by Don Niles, 1982.

In the twentieth century, Christian missionaries influenced Buin music and culture. The most effective were those of the United Church of Christ, who admitted little indigenous music into their services; Roman Catholic missionaries of the Society of Mary allowed more use of indigenous music. In the 1980s, solo singers still used traditional texts, but choirs often sang biblically derived texts, in performances that imitated Western singing in parts. Radios and stereos competed with traditional music. Adolescent men, unschooled in the old musical culture, sought outside ways, seen and heard in Arawa, where they met men from other areas mining copper. Buin villagers began viewing videotapes, which further challenged their inherited values.

Buin music received intensive study by the German ethnologist Richard Thurnwald during visits in 1908–1909 and 1933–1934. Results of his work are primarily in collections of musical texts and general descriptions of musical performance (1912, 1936, 1941). He made hundreds of wax-cylinder recordings, some of which Erich M. von Hornbostel analyzed (1912). Derived from research in 1938–1939, valuable information on Siwai music appears in an ethnography by Douglas L. Oliver (1955). In 1966, Donald C. Laycock, an Australian linguist, began a study of the Buin language; taking an interest in musical texts (Laycock 1969a–c), he made numerous recordings. In 1971–1973 and 1982–1983, Jared Tao Keil worked in villages north of Tabago mission, where he recorded music of several genres. In 1984, Jeffrey T. Meyer recorded music; with Vida Chenoweth, he analyzed songs from these recordings and tapes dubbed at the North Solomons Cultural Centre, Kieta. Chenoweth and Meyer used information from Buin musicians Karapo and Langapai, translated and discussed by linguist Margie Griffin.     —J. W. Love, Don Niles

### An anthropological view

Of particular importance in the music of the Buin people north of Tabago mission are the musical instruments, singing, and dancing, associated with festive and ceremonial contexts. Some of these, especially men's songs (*akaru*) and women's songs (*ruumpii*), also occur in everyday contexts.

At all-night performances during major ceremonies, while beating garamuts, men sing songs that usually relate to the pigs they will give or receive at the upcoming feast, or to the event itself, or to the generosity of guests or hosts. Men sing similar songs when they carry pigs or new garamuts and engage in tasks connected with feasts and ceremonial occasions—and formerly, with fighting. Often, texts tell of the difficulty of the work involved, and therefore of the glory due to workers and host. Sometimes texts make analogies with ancient events. *Akaru* involve repetition of parts of lines or whole lines, and alternation between soloist and chorus. Some have additional generic names: for example, pig-carrying songs are *tarenke*.

At certain ceremonies, including *unu* (the major political event), men enter the area ceremonially, in a line. With upraised spears or stalks of plants, they strike threatening poses, shuffling their feet in the dance *aabi*. At some of these ceremonies, men who dance also sing. Women most often sing together at *remuremu*, ceremonies celebrating children's proper growth and achievements. At most other ceremonial occasions, women sing and dance apart from men. In 1971–1973 and 1982–1983, the most popular *ruumpii* was the song "*Keako*" (or "*Kiaku*"), a term that also denotes a parrot. Women sing together. Trumpeting on a conch (*uugiŋ*) may punctuate their singing. While they sing, they dance (*ture*), hopping from foot to foot, sometimes almost in place, sometimes in a circle. Some dance while holding in their hands a pandanus mat, which they move from side to side, or above their head.

Other songs are sung solo. The most common are laments (*pia*), sung to remember and praise a dead person, and charms, recited to induce sexual attraction. For past injustices, including insufficient compensation or spurned attraction, some songs ridicule or humiliate people; these songs, for which no generic terms exist, are being replaced by local forms of country music and the music of string bands.

To soothe babies, or to ease them into sleep, the Buin also sing lullabies. Recorded examples cite the sun, the moon, and fruitbats. Lullabies might once have had mythological meanings, but by the early 1970s, only children sang them.

When men went to fight, women sang songs to guarantee success. For *kukuinu,* women struck two hard nuts and a piece of coconut shell against each other, producing loud clicks. Simultaneously, they sang a song that began *Kugurakuraku* 'You will catch the spears [of the enemy]'; by 1971, this had become a children's game.

### Musical instruments

At ceremonies and feasts, the loudest, most important sound-producing instruments are garamuts (*tuiruma*), hollowed-out sections of the tree *moikui* (*Vitex cofassus*), resting on wooden slats (*kaa*). Men manufacture garamuts in lengths varying from about one meter to three, with diameters from about 3 decimeters to 12. Performers jolt a wooden pole against the side of each instrument, just above the slit. The resulting sound is a deep boom, audible throughout the surrounding communities.

Garamuts are kept in men's houses (*abaito*), usually associated with leaders (*mumira*). For women and children to enter these houses, where men planned killings and wars, was once taboo. By the 1970s, villages often celebrated feasts and ceremonies in them. Each men's house contains a set of six garamuts, of different sizes. The ensemble can send messages, communicating rhythmically coded information. Many of the rhythms have names, such as *turioto, aukoto, tuntuŋ, aarare,* and *uŋkonu.* The messages include information about the nature and timing of feasts, the number of pigs to be distributed or killed at feasts, illness or death, and formerly an attack. For major occasions, men jolt garamuts at various stages of preparation, and usually for the entire night beforehand. In 1971, they did not know the name or message of some of the rhythms they were playing. To some rhythms, they sang songs.

Most notably at *remuremu,* women stamp bamboo tubes (*tsinguru*) on the ground as they dance. These instruments are long, single, and open at each end. Stamping them produces a low boom. To add a high buzz, women sometimes split the upper edge of the tube.

Mostly at feasts and ceremonies, especially *remuremu,* men play raft panpipes (*takamatsi*), eight or ten differently lengthed bamboos (*kauru*), bound in two rows. On similar occasions, men blow wooden trumpets (*kururu,* also denoting thunder), which produce a low, loud note. Men usually play panpipes and trumpets together, in polyphony.                                                    —JARED TAO KEIL

### A musical view

Buin melodies have a structural peculiarity, a polar fifth, consisting of a tonal center and one other tone, either a perfect fifth above or a perfect fourth below. All documented Buin songs (except *pempam,* noted below) begin and end on one member of this fifth. Phrases have undulating contours. Some songs, especially of the genre *pempam,* require singers to warm up by getting their "measure" (a word that denotes the measuring of a house) by singing vocables.

Apart from a tonal center, no tone appears in every genre of Buin song, but several intervals make up an inventory. In order of frequency, from most to least, these are M3H, P5H, m3L, P4L, and M2H. Rare intervals are P5L, M6H, m3H, M9H, and P8H; rarer still are M3L, m6L, M7H, P4H, m7L. The tonal inventories of individual songs often divide into two sets: tones in a higher range and tones in a lower one. These sets may have tones in common. Individual tones have degrees of versatility; the ten most versatile tones (from most to least versatile) are tonal center, P5H, M3L, P4L, m3L, M2H, P5L, m3H, M6H, and M2L.

Buin musical phrases are often compound: two smaller phrases make up one large phrase, which repeats, either exactly or with variation. The number of repetitions is limitless. More variation usually occurs in the first of two phrases; as the cadence approaches, phrases become more alike. Rarely, a single phrase within a song begins on a tone other than the polar fifth. Pulse is usually strict; rhythmic groupings within a pulse consist of five or eight beats, organized as 2+3, or 3+2+3.

### Musical genres

A large family of songs, the *tuamiru*, includes several genres: *pitonopi, uninomi, kiakuu, pia,* and *pempam.* The word *pitonopi* denotes 'that which resembles the water in a whirlpool interrupting a flowing stream'. Refrains of vocables distinguish these songs, whose texts mainly concern relations between the sexes, gossip, gifts, marriage, obstacles, and rejections. A sex-based view often drives the text (Laycock 1969b). The internal shape of phrases is undulant, but the polar fifth is inactive. A *pitonopi* melody consists of five tones: three below tonal center and one above. In smaller phrases, ranges do not contrast. Larger phrases never repeat exactly. Succeeding initial phrases may not resemble the original, except at cadential points. The last few notes of a phrase, which create a cadential pattern and refrain, stay constant through every verse. The main melodic movement progresses in thirds and major seconds.

*Uninomi* are commemorative songs, which mourners sing around a cremating fire. *Uninomi* resemble laments, but their performance displays less emotion. Their melodic contour consists of a short, undulating phrase, followed by another short phrase, which rises and falls in an arc. *Uninomi* and *pitonopi* include a minor third above tonal center, instead of a tone a major third above (as in other Buin melodies). The third below tonal center is major, instead of the usual minor.

A *kiakuu* is a song sung at specific ceremonies, usually celebrating boys' and girls' maturation and often marking the lifting of taboos on food. In all documented examples of *kiakuu,* the refrain remains the same, but the text of each verse changes for different ceremonies (figure 11*a*). A polar fifth occurs between the tonal center and P5H. The tonal inventory includes four or five tones. Each large phrase has two smaller phrases; in one (A), the text changes; in the other (B), the word *kiakuu* continues the refrain. Owing to textual variation, phrase A has more variation; phrase B may not change at all, or if it does change, it returns to its original form in later verses. Phrases A and B develop a perfect fifth, the one (D to A) alternating with the other (B to F♯). When a word repeats, the corresponding tones and rhythms repeat. Every large phrase ends with the word *kiakuu,* set to the same tones and similar rhythms. Textual settings are syllabic, but where the word *kiakuu* occurs, two notes per syllable are possible. As an appendage to the main text, the word *kiakuu* occurs several times in each phrase.

A *pia* is a lament in lyric poetry (Hornbostel 1912). A woman may sing one for a relative or a child; inspired during a cremation, a close relative of the deceased may later compose one. As in most Buin songs, melodic movement of *pia* is undulant and the polar fifth is clear (figure 11*b*). One pole may be the center of a melodic grouping in a small phrase, or both poles may create the outer boundaries of a melodic grouping. A melody consists of either of two sets of tones. One set occurs primarily above tonal center; the other, primarily below. As in *kiakuu,* phrase B repeats more or less exactly from stanza to stanza. In contrast, phrase A may vary or change thoroughly; melodies that show few differences between phrases A and B have a single phrase with a recurring cadential pattern. Melodic movement includes an even mix of sec-

FIGURE 11 Buin melodies that divide into two phrases: *a*, a *kiakuu*, with polar fifths D–A and B–F♯; *b*, a *pia*, with polar fifths G–D and C–G; *c*, a *pempam*, with tonal centers C and A. Transcriptions by Jeffrey T. Meyer (1985).

onds and thirds, with few fourths and fifths. All fifths ascend. Normally, the larger intervals ascend more than they descend.

*Pia* textually divide into verse and refrain. Uniquely in them, verses undergo a process of backward looping: the text of each new verse incorporates the last thought of the preceding verse. The refrain interrupts the textual flow, but with each new verse, the topic reasserts itself. The only consistent repetition is a tone hummed on /n/ or /m/ at cadences.

*Pempam* are panpipe-accompanied songs whose texts treat political and sexual topics: overtures, gifts, hindrances, rejections, injuries, marriages. Each first complete stanza has vocables—*pim, pem, pam, pom*—which imitate the piped sounds. To ensure aural perception of the right pitches, men sing the first verse only after the panpipes have played the song through. The melodic contours of *pempam* are jaggedly undulant; upward leaps are more frequent than downward leaps. The direction continually changes. Few repeated notes and little stepwise motion occur. Most melodic movement is by thirds, with two or three sometimes linked in a common direction. Typical melodic contours have a quick leap upward and a slow descent in smaller intervals.

Like *pia*, a *pempam* consists of two sets of tones (figure 11*c*). The tonal inventory ranges from eight to twelve tones. Uniquely among Buin songs, the compass of a phrase may reach a perfect eleventh. Larger phrases usually consist of two smaller phrases, which may last longer than in most other Buin songs. Smaller phrases alternate in range between high and low. Little variation occurs between phrasal repetitions. A *pempam* may have up to four phrases. Performers pipe and then sing a verse with *pempam* vocables, repeating the larger phrases three or four times. Breathing defines phrases. Imitating piped pitches, *pempam* contain wide melodic leaps, even beyond a seventh. Unpiped Buin songs have restricted ranges, usually within a fifth. Large downward leaps are rare. In a phrase of an unpiped song, melodic movement typically uses three or four notes; but in a piped song, it uses five to ten.

### Panpipes

Buin panpipes (*takamasi*) consist of a single row of bamboo pipes. They are also known as *takiia*, the name for the smallest set of pipes. Other sizes, from small to large, are *kukuro, marou,* and *uruku*. The *kukuro,* ten pipes grouped in two sets of five, are the most common. The largest pipe is about 40 centimeters long; the smallest, about 13 centimeters. The pipes of each set are arranged from largest to smallest; the second set is smaller than the first. The two sets are unpaired. The pipes of the largest are about 2.5 centimeters in diameter; those of the smallest, about 1 centimeter.

Because notions of west and east are central to Buin thought, Buin panpipes have directional symbolism. Moving from largest to smallest, whether within a set or between sets, is moving westward; moving from smallest to largest is moving eastward. Each pipe, reflecting the importance of family relationships, has a name: from largest to smallest in the first (and larger) group, the pipes are *okou* 'large' (also a name for a big garamut) or *mumira* 'chief'; *paaromoru* 'his-younger-brothers' (also a name for a second garamut); *numaturu* 'he-became-breathless'; *pere* 'side, stem'; and *pumpum* 'his-child'. Some of the second group of pipes are *urotumana* 'chief-of-the-smaller-group'; *uumo* 'brainless'; and *maasi* 'female cross-cousins, sisters-in-law'. Legendarily, two brothers at Tonolei Harbor invented the pipes. After their mother's death, they planted her head in a garden; from the grave grew the first coconut tree.

—VIDA CHENOWETH

## WESTERN PROVINCE

### Choiseul: Sirovanga

About one thousand Sirovanga live in the northwest of Choiseul Island. Their original language is Vagua, but Varisi has become dominant. Their staples are taro and yams, supplemented by *Canarium indicum* nuts, fish, and shellfish. The land and property of each kinship unit is controlled by the head of the clan (*batu*), who formerly functioned as commander in battle and sponsor of feasts. Politically, the Vano Sirovanga Association is a self-governing body.

#### Musical contexts

Public musical performances include *kelo,* feasts that formerly occurred on return banquets for assistance received and as rewards for participating in battle, murder, or magic, and feasts for the dead, occurring about one year after cremation (for these, Christians substitute burial). Especially for the latter, competitive performances of panpipe and trumpet ensembles accompanied women's dancing. Another women's dance, *venga ria golero,* performed for a political leader's inauguration, is treated as important and therefore public. Songs of love, lullabies, and other instrumental music are treated as private. In the 1990s, the Sirovanga make Christian holidays the main occasions for performance.

Formerly, most singing and dancing were done only by women; men played panpipes and trumpets. Since the 1950s, after the introduction of new styles of musical performance, guitars, and ukuleles, men started singing popular songs in named styles: *kela boru* in the 1950s, and *piku, piku sunrise, cyclone,* and *gongala* in the 1960s. In most of these, men sing and play guitars while couples—in some performances, same-sex couples—circle them [see POPULAR MUSIC: Music in Place: Solomon Islands].

#### Songs

The Sirovanga sort musical experience into five classes: songs (*kela*), instrumental music (*pata giso* 'something to play'), dances (*venga*), Christian music, and guitar-accompanied songs for dancing. The last class shows influence from Western and Polynesian music since the 1950s. Sirovanga songs subdivide into crying songs (*kela dae,* from *dae* 'cry'), including laments (*dae lei* 'cry for dead') and songs of love (*dae tamatūra* 'cry for loved person'); lullabies (*tangotango sāle* 'to rock a baby [on one's legs]'); and topical songs (*kela giso,* from *giso* 'play'), treating events of everyday life. Most Sirovanga songs are sung only by women, in a three-part unaccompanied cho-

FIGURE 12   Decorated for the dance and resting an ax on his shoulder, a Sirovanga man plays a side-blown bamboo trumpet, 1990. Photo courtesy of the MABO Project.

rus (*kapisa zukazuka* 'three roads') involving a leader (*kekīnaga* 'person who starts'), a high part (*lele suka* 'small melody'), and a low part (*lele lavata* 'big melody').

### Musical instruments

An ensemble of panpipes and trumpets is the most important Sirovanga ensemble. The panpipes are raft panpipes (*shengo*), combining in two rows eight to ten bamboo tubes. For resonance, the tubes of one row are open. For blowing, those of the other are closed. Each instrument comes in two sizes, as does the bamboo trumpet (*langama*) (figure 12). Ensembles combine two parts (*kalo zukazuka* 'two roads'): the *sasai* is the basic melody, using the high-pitched set of panpipes; against this melody, the *vuduvudu* moves in counterpoint, using the low-pitched set. Most melodies played by this ensemble memorialize dead people.

A side-blown conch trumpet (*kubili*), played in war, continues to be played for feasts. Musical instruments played for self-entertainment include a musical bow (*kongo*), a side-blown bamboo flute (*bosabosa*), an end-blown papaya-stem flute (*vijivijuku*), a humming top (*kilakōla*), and an insect buzzer (*kalebuli*).

### Dances

Women's dances include the *venga shengo* (accompanied by panpipes) and the *venga ria golero* 'dance of women'. In the former, particular to Choiseul Island, dancers in four columns cross their hands in front of their chests, gracefully moving their elbows up and down (figure 13). In the latter, wearing wreathlike or skirtlike headdresses, dancers form columns; they may kneel, putting their palms together. The spirits' game-dance (*vaga manuru*), played on moonlit nights, features spirits (*buki*) and children of both sexes.

## Shortland Islands

The Shortland Islands include the bigger islands of Alu, Mono, and Fauro. Maleai, a village I studied in detail, is on the eastern part of Magsaiai, a small island near Alu. The language and culture of Alu, Magsaisai, and Mono are similar. In the late 1800s, the ancestors of the people of Alu and Magsaisai came from Mono as conquering settlers.

Maleai has about 950 people, who cultivate taro, yams, and manioc; for feasts, they prepare sago as ceremonial food. Men fish with nets and traps. Formerly, hunting wild pigs with dogs and spears and hunting cuscus for funerals were popular. The people get cash from selling trochus shells, copra, and sea cucumbers.

The power of local chiefs is stronger than in other parts of the Solomons. Maleai has three ranked chiefs. One holds the most political power: he regulates cultivation,

FIGURE 13   Four columns of women dance the Sirovanga *venga shengo,* 1990. Photo courtesy of the MABO Project.

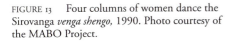

assigns work, supervises meetings, maintains order, and sponsors entertainment, including dance and sports. Because ordinary people must show respect to chiefs, songs that honor a chief are especially important. The chief's sister plays important roles in women's activities. Maleai society consists of eight extended families, each of which elects one elder and an assistant elder to serve on a council that advises the chiefs, whom it can restrain from authorizing radical political action.

### Musical contexts and genres

Great feasts (*gatu*), the most important occasions of musical performance, are held for any of several reasons: *gengegete* pay respect to an injured or ill chief; *gatu sairare* celebrate friendship between men and women; *hainamate* commemorate dead persons; *evā* mark weddings of chiefs or their relatives; *nunuke* formalize housewarmings. On these occasions, musical performance plays a leading role. People say *gatu* cannot rightly occur without songs (*ēla*), dances (*tōlia*), and instrumental sounds; they also say games (*tiale*) may require musical performance.

Current musical genres are *iloilo*, songs of respect from an ordinary person to a chief; *asipa*, songs formally sung in respect for a chief, accompanied by women's stepping on a board; *'a'anana hasuelenria*, lullabies; *otioti*, songs whose texts concern love; *ēla tiatiale*, songs that accompany certain games, such as manipulating string figures and diving; island-dance songs; and *lotu elena*, Christian hymns. In addition to these, funereal weeping (*ta'aha*) has songlike qualities, but the people do not class it as *ēla*. The singing of *asipa*, especially in women's chorus, is in four parts (*tābe*): a basic part (*ikuna*, sung by a leader and others) and three ornamental parts (*tābesue* 'cross', *hēsū* 'counter', *silikoshi* 'highest').

In common with games, dancing involves physical actions, but the Maleai recognize it as standing plus actions. It can be added to all songs except Christian hymns. Local dances include the *asipa*, a female dance; male (sometimes female) dances accompanied by a panpipe ensemble; the *sāgini*, a women's dance, performed after a chief's death; the *singuru*, a men's and women's circular dance, introduced from Bougainville in the 1950s; the *gongala*, a dance by couples, introduced from Choiseul in the 1970s; and a dance in Polynesian style, introduced in the 1960s.

### Instrumental music

Two kinds of aerophone, raft panpipes and trumpets, are locally important. The panpipes (*ehu*) [see MUSICAL INSTRUMENTS: figure 12*a*] combine open and closed bamboo tubes in two rows. The trumpets include a bamboo trumpet (*mavū*) and a side-blown conch trumpet (*siburi*). Each panpipe, consisting of five to twelve tubes, comes in two sizes, as does the bamboo trumpet.

A panpipe and trumpet ensemble has seven named parts: *ehuna*, basic melody (two to four players); *ngkana*, hocketed ornament (two to three players); *kilolina*, high-pitched ornament, said to weep (one player); *ihunasi* or *hannashi* 'to extend', a drone on selected tones (two to four players); *ihusogo* 'to blow shortly', tonguing selected tones (one player); *ihurupu*, combining *ehuna* and *ngkana* (one player); and *silikosi*, mid-pitched counterpoint, said to "battle with other parts" (one player). This ensemble sometimes accompanies panpipers' dances, of men armed with bows and arrows, and of women. It resembles those of Bougainville.

Log idiophones (*okou*)—large and small, of five types—were formerly played, with one stick, at the announcement of the start of a meeting, a great feast, a battle, and for a chief's death. Each occasion had a special pattern. The instruments were kept in the men's house (Ribbe 1903:133–134). Other instruments include a musical bow (*makomako*); a bamboo lamellaphone (also *makomako*); a semicircular plaque (*tubitubi*), placed and struck over an earthen pit (figure 14); and a set of bamboo

FIGURE 14   Men of the Shortland Islands lower a struck plaque (*tubitubi*) over an earthen pit, 1991. Photo courtesy of the MABO Project.

instruments for bamboo bands (*lohe*), introduced from New Georgia in the 1940s [see POPULAR MUSIC, figure 13]. Children formerly played a *cricri:* they cut a tongue in an empty galip nut, which they clicked (Ribbe 1903:160).     —Ryūichi Tai

## ISABEL PROVINCE

Santa Isabel is a long, narrow island. The interior has forested mountains; along the coast, coral reefs jut into the sea. Outside a few lagoons, coastal waters are rough. About once a week, an interisland freighter calls at Buala, the port. Several times a week, planes land on a nearby coral atoll, from which cargo and passengers go by canoe to Buala.

### Blablanga

On the central northeastern coast live about six hundred Blablanga. They subsist on sweet potatoes and other garden crops, supplemented by imported foods: rice, tea, biscuits, canned meat. A few local coconut plantations produce copra. People earn cash from collecting trochus shells; ships take burlap bags full of these to Honiara, where Japanese traders buy them for making buttons, jewelry, and paint. Blablanga houses have bamboo walls, verandas, and sago-leaf roofs. A village in the foothills may have a related village on the edge of the lagoon. In 1982, musical data were obtained at Hovukoilo and its related village, Popoheo.

#### *Musical contexts and genres*

On the water, Blablanga women sing unaccompanied songs. Other songs include a song of welcome, plus songs dealing with the familiar, such as sea turtles and dogs. Choirs of mixed voices sing in contrapuntal textures, but only men sing songs that originated in warfare. Children are carefree. A favorite pastime for boys is to paddle toy canoes. Older children attend a secondary school at the southern end of the island. Traveling on interisland freighters, they return home for holidays.

*War-related dance*

As performed by men of Hovukoilo, war-related dances (*ragi māgana*) display physical grace and control. Singing, the men move slowly and serenely. Back and forth, keeping in tempo, each man swings a shield supported on his left arm. In his right hand, he holds an ax, which he leans against his right shoulder. As the leader calls out instructions, the dancers' bodies rotate to the right and left. When each body rotates leftward, its right leg slowly lifts, kicking to the left; when the body rotates rightward, the left leg slowly lifts, kicking to the right.

The leader cues every change in choreography. At a given call, the men crouch; in synchrony, they may bob up and down. Simultaneously, each man continues to swing his shield, but now holds it flat on the forearm, instead of vertically. At another cue, they rise and begin to step forward, one leg crossing in front of the other. Before weight goes onto the foot in action, the foot gently taps the ground several times. Throughout, the knees bend in time with the beat.

A typical dance begins with men in three columns, facing forward. A leader sings a musical introduction (figure 15). As some men join his vocal part, others sing a countermelody above it. The only text sung is the vocable *e* or *he*. After introductory intervals, the pitches stabilize. The melody, derived from a scale whose tones are alternately a major second and a minor third apart (G–A–C–D–F–G) has a wavy contour. This composition has two motifs, A and B. After the leader's introductory passage (derived from A), both motifs occur simultaneously, followed by their chiasmus and a repeat of A. The original texture, B over A, recurs, followed by a convergence on A instead of the chiasmus. Motif B then reenters below A, and that texture repeats. This pattern continues until the dance ends, without formal cadencing.

FIGURE 15 The start and basic pattern of a Blablanga war-related dance, performed by men of Hovukoilo in 1982. Transcription by Vida Chenoweth.

### Dances with aerophones (gragi nifu)

Men also dance while playing bamboo trumpets (*bubu*) and panpipes (*nifu*). Each man wears a loincloth or shorts, white designs painted on his face, chest, and back, and a shell disk through his nasal septum. A large slice of shell in a half-moon shape hangs from his neck.

The music begins with trumpets [see UNDERSTANDING MUSIC, figure 19]. When the panpipes enter, the dancing begins. Facing inward in a circle, players slowly step left and bend the knee. By pivoting on one foot while lifting the other, they turn to face outside the circle. They continue playing. The circle gradually turns in a clockwise direction, as they again step left. Dancers with midsize trumpets begin a movement that resembles scooping the earth with their trumpets, while the bass trumpets continue to sound.

Performances of 1982 used thirteen trumpets, of two sizes. Eleven were of medium length, about five decimeters and sounding a pitch lower than F a twelfth below middle C. Men played the long trumpets in alternation, acting as drones. The melody and tonal inventory of ceremonial dances draw from the same scale as warlike songs, but with E♭ as tonal center. They have no vocal parts, but each dancer plays an aerophone. In addition to the trumpets, men play three sets of panpipes: small, medium, large, two of each set. The small instruments have about eleven pipes, the longest about 13 centimeters. The large instruments consist of about twelve pipes, the longest about 50 centimeters. The texture is harmonic, though the performers conceive the parts linearly. Harmonic seconds sometimes occur as voices cross. All phrases end on the same tone, with octave duplications. A pattern that emerges at phrasal endings strengthens the sense of a greater tonal center in association with a lesser one, reminiscent of a tonic-dominant relationship.

### Women's songs

Women sing as they travel by canoe, and musically welcome visitors. Often when they sing, a man positions himself as their leader. Canoe-related songs, like other

FIGURE 16 The beginning of a Blablanga canoe-paddling song, performed by women of Popoheo in 1982. Transcription by Vida Chenoweth.

Blablanga songs, are contrapuntal. In a song performed in 1982 (figure 16), the vocal parts are rhythmically identical. The uppermost voice in the transcription and that assigned to its own staff below are similar. Each part is equally prominent, so the tonal center (D♯) is less obvious. The tones, D♯–F♯–G♯–B–C♯–D♯, are a string of minor thirds and major seconds. Variation comes from minimal melodic substitution.

### Musical instruments

Only Blablanga men play musical instruments. The production of sound for panpipes involves blowing across the upper rim of the pipes. Men play straight trumpets by buzzing their lips into an aperture at one end of a bamboo tube. The people of Buala have one log idiophone, which sits in a cradle about a meter off the ground. Instrumentalists stand to play, using short, thick sticks, one in each hand. Its call develops two patterns, used only for signaling.                    —VIDA CHENOWETH

## Maringe, Hograno, and San Jorge Island

The Maringe and Hograno areas are in the southeast of Isabel Island—Maringe on the north coast, Hograno on the south. The provincial capital, Buala, is in the Maringe area. Cheke Holo is spoken in these areas. The local staples are taro, yams, and manioc, supplemented by coconuts, bananas, papayas, and canarium almonds (*Canarium indicum*). Local performative genres are dancing (*ḡraḡi*, from *raḡi* 'to dance'), singing (*khoje*, from *koje* 'to sing'), instrumental music (*ḡlepo ḡlalahu*), games (*ḡlalahu*, from *lalahu* 'to play'), and theater (*thukma*, from *tukma* 'to perform').

### Dancing

Dances provide several contrasts: men's (*ḡraḡi nalha'u*) and women's (*ḡraḡi ḡa'ase*), standing (*ḡraḡi kheḡra*) and sitting (*ḡraḡi gnhokro*), traditional (*ḡraḡi kastom*) and entertaining (*ḡraḡi ḡlalahu*), old (*ḡraḡi thiamifa*) and new (*ḡraḡi majagani*). These dances are a circular dance (*ḡlegi*) by men and women, or only by women; a men's ax-wielding dance (*ḡraḡi khila* [*kikile*]); a men's club-wielding dance (*ḡraḡi khodo pheko* or *ḡraḡi sesele*); and a women's dance with long sticks (*siakole*). Other recognized dances are a men's dance with arms extended to imitate bird's wings (*ḡraḡi khame*), a men's dance with a split bamboo tube (*ḡraḡi du'e*), a women's dance with ornamented sticks (*saleolo*, figure 17), a women's dance while seated (*ḡraḡi gnhokro*), a women's

The oldest and most important dance was performed during big feasts and sacrificial rituals. In a circle, men and women danced together hand in hand. In the sacrificial ritual, women danced, kicking the victim's neck.

FIGURE 17    Carrying decorated wands, women of Koisisi Village, Isabel Province, dance the *saleolo,* 1993. Photo courtesy of the MABO Project.

dance with clapping (*ḡraḡi proaprosa*), and a women's bamboo-tube dance (*ḡraḡi du'e*); their styles are new, invented in the twentieth century.

The oldest and most important dance was the *ḡlegi,* performed during big feasts and sacrificial rituals (*fafara*). In typical performances, the distinction between men's and women's movements is strict, but *ḡlegi* were exceptions: in a circle, men and women danced together, hand in hand. When it was performed in the sacrificial ritual, women danced, kicking the victim's neck. Dances with axes and curved clubs were performed when warriors practiced on the way to actual battles, and when they returned in triumph. *Siakole* and *saleolo* are similar; the latter develops the style of the former. *Saleolo* and *ḡraḡi khame* have become the most typical dances of the island.

Newer dances include a mixed adults' dance (*ḡraḡi famaemahe* 'funny dance', or *ḡraḡi lalahu* 'playful dance'), a children's dance (*ḡraḡi ḡro sua* 'dance of children'), and a dance with guitar accompaniment (*ḡraḡi guitar*). For these dances, the style of movement is not so strict as for indigenous dances.

### Singing

Songs are classified as traditional songs (*khoje kastom*), new songs for entertainment (*khoje glalahu* 'song for play'), and Christian songs (*khoje blahi*). Traditional genres include tree-cutting songs (*khoje ḡrave* 'stone-ax song'); mallet-pounding songs (*khoje tuge*), bonito-fishing songs (*khoje ḡria*); turtle-catching songs (*vae*), canoe-paddling songs (*khoje valuha* or *khoje balu ḡorha*), thanksgiving-presenting songs (*thautaru*), lullabies (*khoje fatutu sua* or *fameomeḡo*), legendary-giant songs (*khoje ḡoigoli*), swing songs (*khoje siuli*), war-related songs (*khoje maḡra*), and laments (*papado*, not strictly recognized as songs).

People sing tree-cutting songs when they cultivate virgin soil; the performance magically appeals to spirits. In ritually fishing for bonito and catching turtles, people sing when they have a big catch. They sing *thautaru* for ritually giving gifts; when children thank their fathers on the occasion of the property-distribution ritual (*faghamu thaego*), the recipients (the fathers) and the givers (the children) sometimes cannot continue singing because the performance has moved them to tears. Lullabies have several types, defined by the age of the children—a feature uncommon elsewhere in the Solomons. War-related songs include pieces that recall events of the Pacific War (1941–1945).

New genres for entertainment include songs of love (*khoje namha* or *khoje keakepa*, often sung by people at work); songs in a local language (*khoje cheke holo*); songs in English or local pidgin English (*khoje english, khoje pijin*, or *khoje cheke waka* 'white-language song'); and guitar songs (*khoje guitar* or *khoje ḡlalahu*).

Christian music distinguishes between genres sung inside a church (*khoje lamna suga tharai*) and genres sung outside (*khoje kosi suḡa tharai*). These include hymns (*khoje tarai* 'prayerful song', or *khoje ka buka* 'book-related song', or *khoje blahi*), songs sung in Sunday School (*khoje sade-sikol* 'Sunday-school song'), and other religious songs (*chorus,* including *khoje toatokuma*, songs with gestures).

### Instrumental music

No term covers all musical instruments. If forced to choose, people use a term like *ḡlepo ḡlalahu* 'something to play'. A frequently heard term, *nifu*, denotes aerophones except conch trumpets, or more particularly, panpipes. To play aerophones is *ifu* (as in *ifu pophosa* 'blow panpipes').

Local idiophones include a lamellaphone (*kuleru*), a log idiophone (*belo*), and an introduced iron bell (*kulekule*); the last two are used in Christian services. The only local chordophone is a musical bow (*khodili*). Conch trumpets (*khufli*), blown to call people and symbolize political leaders, are of two kinds: side-blown conchs (*khufli*) and end-blown conchs (*pheopeo*). Flutes include bamboo raft panpipes (*nifu*), played solo by people walking alone, or played in ensemble during feasts; a side-blown bamboo two-holed flute (*filiŋji*); and an obliquely held bamboo flute (*kuleru*).

In much of Santa Isabel, indigenous musical instruments have gone out of use. Panpipes are played only in Hovukoilo, on the northeast coast, in the Blablanga area. These panpipes, with tubes in one row, come in four varieties, each in two sizes. Bamboo tubes (*bubu*) in two sizes are played with panpipes in ensemble; their numbers are almost the same as those of panpipes. Players blow them while moving clockwise in a circle, kicking backward and forward. This ensemble and dance were performed before battle. The numbers of panpipes and bamboo tubes, and the circular movement with kicks, make the style of Hovukoiko unique among panpipe-playing styles in the Solomons.

### Other contexts

Games with songs and gestures include water-sound games (*kotio*, figure 18), string figures with songs (*sisi'oke*), and hide-and-seek games (*kikidi*). Typically several variations of the water-sound game occur: two groups may play in hocket, and they may add claps and songs, traits not heard in similar games of other areas in the Solomons.

Local theatrical performances commemorate persons and events. Many presentations recount the introduction of Christianity at Buala, on 24 August 1905. Each year, Buala people take the roles of prominent persons, including Hugo Hebula (d. 1931), a catechist from the Bugotu area, and Chief Getu and his people, who migrat-

FIGURE 18   Women of Koisisi Village, Isabel Province, play a water-sound game (*kotio*), 1993. Photo courtesy of the MABO Project.

ed from Maringe to Bugotu, fleeing an attack from the western Solomons. The performance has three acts: the attack, the arrival of Christianity, and the propagation of the faith (White 1991).

The most conspicuous occasions for musical performance were formerly feasts (*g̃ag̃amu* or *eg̃ano*) and big feasts (*diklo*); for the latter, people danced on a special field. Since about the 1920s, Christian holidays have been the prime occasions for feasting. On these occasions, people usually dance first and sing later. Performers group themselves by sex, age, and residence, distinguished between hosts and guests.

## CENTRAL PROVINCE

### Russell Islands

About one thousand people inhabit the Russell Islands. They speak Lavukáleve, a non-Austronesian language. The population divides into four matrilineal clans, each having a political leader (*kua o sulum*) and a totemic animal. Ownership of land descends through women, but rights over coconuts and betel descend through men.

In 1905, Anglican missionaries began preaching Christianity locally. Roman Catholic missionaries soon made converts on Loun Island. Establishment of foreign-owned coconut plantations on Namutin and Banika forced local residents to abandon their ancestral homes there. By 1950, settlers from Malaita, Santa Isabel, and Tikopia had begun arriving. The indigenous population resides mainly on Karumulun, Loun, Mane, and Maruloun.

### *Dancing*

The people of the Russell Islands divide their musical performances into four classes: dancing, singing indigenous songs, playing instrumental music, and singing Christian hymns. They devalue pure instrumental and vocal music in favor of dance (Tai 1990). Dancing formerly occurred at ceremonies and feasts, including a political leader's inaugural ceremonies, ceremonies for the completion of a political leader's house or of a men's house, and weddings.

Tours and competitions were once the most important performative occasions, organized by political leaders to acquire prestige. After months of practice, a men's troupe would go on tour, spending weeks visiting a series of localities. Troupes from all over the archipelago participated in competitive dancing. Before competitions, men prepared dance-controlling magic (*sauru*). By applying to their skin a mixture of ginger and leaves, they believed they would feel no fatigue, their steps would become light, and their performance would excel, attracting shell money and women.

The last large-scale competition occurred on Loun Island in 1948. Troupes from Hae, Karumulun, and Maruloun competed in nightlong performances. To the winners, the political leader of Loun gave pigs, shell money, and Australian dollars. By the 1980s, most local occasions for dancing were religious holidays, such as Christmas and the Feast of Saint Matthew (21 September).

Personnel who perform within an ensemble vary: interested persons assemble around a leader (*ragi o vatu* 'head of dance'), who directs other dancers (*ngasive sava* 'following persons') by shouting cues (*aitauli*). In the West Russell Islands, each dance belongs to an owner (*ragi anubem*), who does not dance, but has the right to permit and organize performances; the right is hereditary, usually along patrilineal lines.

Relationships among the Russell Islands and other islands (especially Guadalcanal, New Georgia, and Santa Isabel) have influenced local styles of dancing. Local *ragi* resemble the *ḡraḡi* of Santa Isabel, local *mana* resemble dances of the northwest Solomons, and local *vivi* resemble dances of the central Solomons. Local dances retain several distinctive original traits: condensed temporality, synchronized movement, and imitation of incidents of human and animal life.

### Men's dances

Men perform two kinds of dances: *mana* and *ragi*. In both, they move synchronously in two columns. Apart from an item sung for *mana*, the only vocal accompaniments are leaders' shouts and dancers' grunts ("*e, he, he*"). Another accompanying sound is the rattling of nuts, which, to execute *ragi*, performers attach to their ankles.

The performance of *mana* requires an ax (bearing the figure of a snake), a shield (bearing the figure of a shark, a frigate bird, and a snake), and a bark-cloth loincloth. With lime-and-water paste, performers paint their faces, chests, arms, and legs, in designs imitating tattoos, shell money, and stone ornaments. The basic movement of *mana* is shaking the ax and the shield left and right, stepping, and jumping sideways. Holding an ax in the right hand and a shield in the left, each performer makes warlike movements, staging scenes of battle and triumph. To obtain power, men in olden times performed *mana* before battles and after victories; otherwise, performance was taboo.

*Ragi* imitate the movements of people and animals. Each independent segment lasts thirty to sixty seconds. On Loun, each dancer wears a shell-money headdress, a shell necklace, clamshell coins, tassels of fragrant leaves, a loincloth, a sago-palm skirt, ankle-tied rattles made of nuts, and sago-palm arm-tied and knee-tied ornaments.

In the basic position (*belama o runai* 'frigate-bird wing'), performers stretch their arms out and imitate the frigate bird's movements. They move their arms to other positions, but return to this one. To excel, they must maintain this position while moving and jumping "as high as their skirts are rolled up." When they meet these conditions, spectators shout *joreo* 'marvelous as a frigate bird', or *lakomu* 'cry'.

### Women's dances

Women's dances are of two kinds: one while standing (*ragi* or *sale*) and one while sitting (*vivi*). All women's dances have songs accompanied by the sounds of a nut rattle (*sesel*), which a leader wears or holds.

In *ragi* or *sale,* women wield a decorated baton (West Russell *bao,* East Russell *ba*) or a grass-and-leaf bundle (West Russell *saful,* East Russell *vekevek* and *malemal*). They form three columns. Alternately shifting batons or bundles from left to right (or at various angles), they step frontward and rearward. In the west, the baton is a bamboo tube bearing white cockatoo feathers; in the east, it is a wooden stick bearing cockatoo feathers and painted with designs recalling frigate birds, sea horses, and *kilkil* birds.

There are two types of dance while sitting. On Maruloun, women sit facing each other; in their right hands, they hold bamboo tubes (*tukumal*), which they strike on the ground, move toward and away from their bodies, or shake. On Mane, women sit in one row, with outstretched legs, shaking their hands alternately on their right and left sides.

### Singing

Some local songs (*linga*) accompany dances. Others, including laments (*tatal*), lullabies (*guario*), songs of love (*roku*), and women's humming while paddling, ordinarily do not. For nighttime entertainment (*baile* 'talk at night'), narrators sing songs in tales and jokes.

### Musical instruments

Indigenous musical instruments are a conch trumpet (*buku*), a hollowed log idiophone (*makut* 'wood'), and a paddle (*kereve,* used to make regular sounds in paddling, but only by the people of Maruloun Island). In June and July, the dry season, men blow trumpets to announce the number of turtles they have caught. On Pavuvu, men hunting pigs for a feast formerly blew trumpets to announce the number of wild pigs they had caught. The log idiophone is a little more than 1 meter long and half a meter wide; it is struck with a stick (*vui*) about 30 centimeters long and 4 centimeters in diameter. The instrument on Maruloun—bought in 1928 from its maker, Jack Manigaro of Guadalcanal—is beaten at sunrise and sunset to signal the start of Christian services. Mnemonic vocables (*kuku tom*) name the rhythms.

—Ryūichi Tai

## GUADALCANAL PROVINCE

The largest and highest island of the nation of the Solomon Islands is Guadalcanal, about 150 by 40 kilometers. Several peaks of its mountains rise more than 1800 meters. On the south coast, the mountains plunge to the sea; on the north, they slope gently, giving way to hills and a coastal plain several kilometers wide. On this plain is the seaport of Honiara, the national capital, which has more than thirty-five thousand inhabitants, mostly Melanesians from Guadalcanal and other islands of the Solomons, but also residents from Polynesian outliers and other regions of Oceania, mainly Micronesians from Kiribati.

The northern plain supports coconut plantations, the breeding of cattle, and the cultivation of rice. The people of Guadalcanal, other than those who live and work in the industrialized zone around the capital, live in villages and hamlets. For cash, coastal dwellers produce copra, but like inland peoples, they subsist on garden produce, particularly yams, taro, and sweet potatoes.

The indigenous languages of Guadalcanal belong to the Melanesian branch of the Austronesian family. All but 'Are'are, spoken in the southeast tip of Guadalcanal by an immigrant population from Malaita, are closely related. Most of the people are Christians. Evangelization has heavily influenced music. For many years, aeolian flutes (wind-sounded aerophones), once associated with indigenous funeral rites,

FIGURE 19   U.S. Marines with The Jungle Rhythm Boys, a string band of Guadalcanal, Solomon Islands, 1944. Photo National Archives, U.S. Marine Corps.

have no longer been set up, and Christian hymns have replaced women's funeral songs (Zemp 1971b).

The disappearance of old music is most marked among followers of the major Protestant churches—South-Sea Evangelical Church (SSEC), Seventh-Day Adventist, United Church (Methodist)—some of whose European leaders believe that ancestral customs, including music, are incompatible with Christianity. The Anglican and Roman Catholic churches encourage the islanders to maintain indigenous music.

Songs accompanied by guitars and ukuleles are popular everywhere. Young people become acquainted with them in town, or on plantations where they work. A strong influence was foreign soldiers' activity during World War II (figure 19). Despite some Christian denominations' prohibition on the performance of pagan music, and in the face of broadcast and cassette-played international music in religious and secular styles, older music survives, even in villages near Honiara.

—J. W. LOVE

## Guadalcanal

The music of Guadalcanal is fairly homogeneous. On the north coast, festival music is essentially vocal; in the mountains, it is instrumental, played by panpipe ensembles, which commonly use whistles and bamboo trumpets as drones, producing a continuous tone.

The vocal music of Guadalcanal also uses a drone, above which two solo parts interweave melodic lines. In the Nginia language, a person may say that the first voice opens (*hihinda*) the singing, the second follows (*tumuri*), and the drone growls (*ngungulu*). In women's singing throughout the island, the growl is a continuous drone, like that of the panpipe ensemble. Nginia is spoken only in a few hamlets of one valley of the area Honiata, about 15 kilometers west of the capital. The Nginia ensemble of panpipes (*rihe mumu*) and women's songs (*rope*) exhibit typical musical traits of the island (Zemp 1973c).

In three-part instrumental or vocal polyphony of Guadalcanal, the melodic parts at the end of stanzas and pieces join the tone of the drone, so all parts cadence in unison or at the octave. Besides this type of polyphony, the songs of Guadalcanal feature two solo vocal parts having wide ranges and frequent and rapid change of register, a kind of yodeling. In Marau, off the extreme east of the island, panpipe ensembles play in the typical Guadalcanal style (with a harsh sound and a drone) and the 'Are'are style of Malaita (Zemp 1994).

## Savo

Savo is a volcanic island six kilometers in diameter, 19 kilometers off the northwest point of Guadalcanal. It has about fifteen hundred inhabitants, whose language, Savosavo, is non-Austronesian. Many people of Savo no longer speak it; they use instead a Melanesian language, that of the northwest coast of Guadalcanal, or that of Nggela, several islands 40 kilometers eastward. They maintain relations with these islands by traveling to them in canoes, sometimes on musical tours.

The music of Savo resembles that of Guadalcanal, but is purely vocal. The parts, by using a drone that supports interweaving soloists, recall instrumental textures of Guadalcanal (Zemp 1978b). The vocal parts of Savo are the before (*nyagogu*), the after (*buringa*), and the backgrowl (*salanguru*), which usually enters after a stanza, often one or two tones above or below the drone. People say the soloist "takes the low" (*neo laua*) when singing with a chest voice, and "takes the high" (*tago laua*) when singing in falsetto. Singers alternate between these timbres, but at a slower rate than on Guadalcanal.

On Savo, the word *linge,* apparently borrowed from Nggela, denotes all songs, some of which may be danced. The term *dele* denotes dancing in a circle, several columns, or seated rows. The major movements are those of the upper part of the body.

—Hugo Zemp

## MALAITA PROVINCE

Malaita Province consists mainly of the islands of Malaita and Maramasike. Its people, numbering about eighty-five thousand, are mostly Christians. The administrative capital is Auki, at the northern end of Langalanga Lagoon. The main exports are copra and timber. Coastal dwellers of northern Malaita are famous for making artificial islands by assembling coral blocks in lagoons and adding compost (Ivens 1978 [1930]); they build houses and live on these islands, but maintain gardens on the mainland.

The music of northern Malaita, the more heavily populated part of the province, is more homogeneous than that of southern Malaita and Maramasike. Many musical genres distinguished by people of northern Malaita occur farther south, varying locally. The distinctive musical instruments of Malaita are bamboo panpipes, made and played in varying sizes and sets, in sacred and secular contexts. The musical scale most frequently used by panpipe ensembles divides the octave into seven equal intervals (Zemp 1973a).

The most extensive musical research in the province has been done by Hugo Zemp, who in 1969 and the 1970s worked with the 'Are'are (Zemp 1978a, 1979, 1981, 1994, 1995a, 1995b; Zemp and Coppet 1978), and surveyed other music of Malaita (Zemp 1971a, 1972) focusing on the Fataleka and the Baegu (Zemp 1973b) and the Kwaio (1982). David Akin has worked with the Kwaio and others, conducting anthropological research that included the study of musical performances and concepts.

—J. W. Love

## 'Are'are

About ten thousand 'Are'are inhabit southern Malaita. Most formerly inhabited the interior of the island, some occupied coastal lagoons in the southwest, and others lived beside the Maramasike Strait; during the twentieth century, new coastal villages sprang up. Other 'Are'are villages are at Marau, the eastern tip of Guadalcanal. 'Are'are staples are taro, yams, and sweet potatoes, supplemented by pigs at ceremonies, and saltwater fish.

The 'Are'are area divides into two zones: the south has hereditary chieftainships;

in the north, leaders seek prestige by giving funeral feasts, in which participants exchange pigs, taro, shell money, and music. These zones have musical implications: the north has only one kind of men's vocal music, songs of divination; but the south has that and three others—songs for paddling, for pestling, and with struck bamboos.

By the mid-1970s, at least 90 percent of the 'Are'are had become Christians. One half adhered to the South-Sea Evangelical Church (SSEC); the other half, to Roman Catholic and Anglican churches. The SSEC teaches that because ancestral spirits are devils, traditional music is diabolical; consequently, the only music the SSEC allows are North American Protestant hymns and pan-Pacific pop songs.

The radio plays string-band songs, which 'Are'are youths sing for recreation, often in pidgin, but also in 'Are'are. These songs are international in style, with no specifically indigenous traits. The 'Are'are call Christian hymns and secular songs Europeans' songs (*nuuha ni haka*) and Europeans' music (*'au ni haka*). They call 'Are'are traditional music customary music (*'au ni tootoraha*), customary songs (*nuuha ni tootoraha*), and music of the land (*'au ni hanua*).

### Thinking about 'Are'are music

For "music," the 'Are'are have four concepts. *'Au* 'bamboo' denotes all musical instruments made of bamboo—and by extension, the music these instruments produce. Log idiophones (*'o'o*) are played solo to send messages and in ensembles at feasts (Zemp 1997). Water-based games (*kiro ni karusi*) consist of women's rhythmic splashing in water. *Nuuha* include three kinds of women's songs and four kinds of men's songs (Zemp and Coppet 1978:115).

The 'Are'are distinguish between blown bamboos (*'au kia ka uuhi*) and struck bamboos (*'au kia ka 'ui*). Blown bamboos, apart from four panpipe ensembles (*'au rokoroko*), include four instruments for one person to play: a side-blown flute, two kinds of bundle panpipes [see MUSICAL INSTRUMENTS: Aerophones], and one raft panpipe. Struck bamboos include a mouth-resonated zither and tapped tubes, played solo or by three persons.

Women's songs (*nuuha ni keni*), include laments, lullabies, and songs expressing feelings for a boy, as in this excerpt (after Zemp 1995b:91–92).

'O oomo kaesi nau hana rapeku, 'arei hoe.
'O nono kaesi nau hana rapeku, 'arei hoe.
'Au oorioori ru'u, maani nau, 'arei hoe.
'Au oorioori ru'u, oorioori ru'u, 'ewa'ewa hu'a!

'Au oorioori ru'u, maani nau, rohomakoi nau.
'Au nono kaesi nau hana rapeku; oorioori ru'u.
'O ma kaesi nau hana rapeku, 'arei miiwau.
'O nono kaesi nau; oorioori ru'u, maani iinau!

You enlace me with lies to have my body, O friend.
You embrace me with lies to have my body, O friend.
Go away, far from me, O friend.
Go away, go away, forever!

Go away, far from me, man with the flat stomach.
Don't embrace me with lies to have my body; go away.
Don't tell lies to have my body, my good man.
You embrace me telling lies; go away, far from me!

Fataleka divinatory songs are performed by a men's choir seated in two facing rows, each singer holding a rattle. One man flicks his wrist to sound his rattle continuously; the others sound theirs on downbeats.

By contrast, men's songs (*nuuha ni mane*) often have ritual goals. Men's and women's songs are in two-part polyphony, usually based on semitoneless five-tone scales, disposed in strophes performed by two singers. The lead singer usually sings the words; the second singer often hums.

### Fataleka and Baegu

About four thousand Fataleka and five thousand Baegu inhabit northern Malaita. Their most highly valued ceremony is the funeral series (*maome*), organized after an important person's death and consisting of an eight-year-long set of rituals. Panpipe ensembles perform during particular rituals. During some, men perform narrative songs (Baegu *'ainimae*, Fataleka *kana*), to the accompaniment of concussed sticks.

The Fataleka play solo bundle panpipes (*tala 'au, susuku*) only during the funeral series, but the Baegu also use *susuku* for entertainment in nonritual contexts. The Baegu instrument has seven pipes in a bundle; the Fataleka instrument has nine pipes in a trapezoidal bundle, in rows of two, three, and four pipes, respectively. The Fataleka associate rattle-accompanied songs (*uunu* in both languages) with divinatory sessions, but the Baegu sing them at festivals and ceremonies including those of the funeral cycle.

### *Songs*

Fataleka divinatory songs (*uunu*) form a subgenre of *'aukwee*, items that include *nguu 'oio*, songs associated with warriors. Characteristic of *'aukwee* in both variants is singing in two parts, *na'o* and *buli*, performed by a men's choir seated in two facing rows, each singer holding a rattle. One man flicks his wrist to sound his rattle continuously; the others sound theirs on downbeats. The men hum, but sometimes take up the lead singer's words. They perform on nights when they must make big decisions. They believe their leader sees lights representing ancestral spirits, whose appearance he interprets.

Narrative songs, relating myths and histories, are sung at night during certain rituals of the funeral series, and at weddings. Some continue for hours. Sitting in two facing rows, men beat concussion sticks as they hum in two parts, *buli* and *bola nguu*. In the middle of the *bola nguu* row sits a soloist (*sili*), who alone sings words. When he stops for breath, the singer of the *tali nguu*, seated on his left, relieves him, singing without words. These songs divide into sections, each of which has a melody, sung several times to accommodate its words.

Before playing panpipe music, Fataleka and Baegu musicians sing an introductory song (*mae'au*). Sitting in two facing rows, they sing in two parts. With a sudden crescendo, they stand up. They repeatedly stamp their right feet on the ground, sounding rattles tied to their ankles.

Women and girls sing *roiroa* in unison for entertainment; the singer who best knows the melody and the words leads while the others hum. A child's older sister may sing lullabies (*rorogwela*). The words of a typical example refer to such a situation: the elder sister asks the baby not to cry, saying its parents are dead and no one else is around to hear it.

### Musical instruments

#### Idiophone-aerophone

Struck and blown tubes (*sukute*), played for private entertainment by Baegu women and girls (and sometimes boys), consist of two pieces of bamboo, 25 and 28 centimeters long and open at both ends. The lower end of a tube held in the right hand is tapped against the left thigh. The other tube is held in the left hand, its upper end tapped alternately against the left cheek and the right palm; between these movements, the player blows into it. The player may use the left tube alone.

#### Chordophone

The musical bow (*kwadili*), played only by Fataleka and Baegu women, has two strings attached to a bamboo tube open at both ends. Bridges may be inserted to raise the strings off the tube. The player holds the bow in her left hand, puts the tube between her lips, and plucks the strings with a plectrum or the end of the fiber from which the strings are made, obtaining two fundamental sounds. She sometimes presses her left thumb on the strings to shorten their vibrating length, raising the tone. Resonance of her oral cavity and throat amplifies select harmonics.

#### Aerophones

The Fataleka bundle panpipe consists of nine variously sized bamboo tubes, open at both ends. Holding the tubes in place, the player moves his head to blow into specific pipes.

The Fataleka panpipe ensemble (*'au sisile*) has six musicians, who play for the funeral series. Four like-sized instruments—*safali, ufi buri, sui, sili*—each have fifteen pipes; the other two, *life na'o*, have three pipes, pitched lower. The musicians stand in two facing rows, with the players of three-pipe instruments in the middle of each row. On their right ankles, all musicians wear rattles made of dried husks.

The Fataleka ensemble *'au sango*, with the same instruments as *'au sisile*, involves dancers, wearing rattles on their right ankles and standing on each side of the musicians. It plays four pieces: *Safali Fuli 'Au, 'Ae 'Au, Faa Sungu*, and *Faa Sasaka*. Between pieces, dancers change sides. During the fourth piece, instrumentalists change places while playing. Dancers carry in their right hands flat carvings painted black, white, and red, depicting a hornbill (figure 20). One dancer shakes a rattle, whose sound is brighter than that of the ankle-tied rattles.

The end-blown flute (*sukwadi*), played only by Fataleka and Baegu women, is a bamboo tube open at the lower end, with a circular mouthpiece in the node that closes the upper end. It has no holes for fingering. The player opens and closes the lower opening with her right forefinger. In addition to two fundamental sounds, she obtains harmonics by overblowing.

The panpipe ensemble (*'au ero*) ordinarily consists of twelve musicians, but the number varies. Each musician plays a nine- or ten-pipe instrument. Complementary sets of pipes produce a scale of seven equidistant tones: odd-numbered tones from the *buli* 'behind' instruments, and even-numbered tones from the *na'o* 'front' instruments. The musicians arrange themselves in two facing rows, the *buli* on one side and the *na'o* on the other. *Na'o* and *buli* are also the names of the two main polyphonic parts.

—HUGO ZEMP

FIGURE 20 At a chief's installation, Baelelea men carry flat, painted carvings of hornbills and other birds. Panpipe players form a cluster behind the dancers. Photo by Adrienne L. Kaeppler, 1976.

## REFERENCES

Chenoweth, Vida. 1972. *Melodic Perception and Analysis: A Manual on Ethnic Melody.* Ukarumpa, Papua New Guinea: Summer Institute of Linguistics.

———. 1979. *The Usarufas and Their Music.* Dallas: Summer Institute of Linguistics Museum of Anthropology.

Hornbostel, Erich M. von. 1912. "Die Musik auf den Nord-Westlichen Salomo-Inseln." In *Forschungen auf den Salomo-Inseln und dem Bismarck-Archipel,* vol. 1, ed. Richard Thurnwald, 461–504. Berlin: Reimer.

Ivens, Walter G. 1978 [1930]. *The Island Builders of the Pacific.* New York: AMS Press.

Krause, Fritz. 1907. "Zur Ethnographie der Insel Nissan." *Jahrbuch des Städtischen Museums für Völkerkunde zu Leipzig* 1:44–159.

Laycock, Donald C. 1969a. *Akaru.* Port Moresby: Papua Pocket Poets.

———. 1969b. *Sublanguages in Buin: Play, Poetry, and Preservation.* Pacific Linguistics A-22; Papers in New Guinea Linguistics, 10. Canberra: Australian National University.

———. 1969c. "Buin Songs." *Kovave: A Journal of New Guinea Literature* 1(1):5–8.

Meyer, Jeffrey T. 1985. "An Analysis of Buin Music." Senior document, Wheaton College.

Oliver, Douglas Llewellyn. 1955. *A Solomon Island Society: Kinship and Leadership among the Siuai of Bougainville.* Cambridge: Harvard University Press.

———. 1973. *Bougainville: A Personal History.* Honolulu: University Press of Hawai'i.

Ribbe, Carl. 1903. *Zwei Jahre unter den Kannibalen der Salomo-Inseln.* Dresden: Blasewitz.

Richardson, Susan. 1986. "An Analysis of Halia Music." Document in ethnomusicology, Wheaton College.

Ross, Malcom D. 1988. *Proto Oceanic and the Austronesian Languages of Western Melanesia.* Pacific Linguistics, C-98. Canberra: Australian National University.

Spearritt, Gordon, Thomas Lulungan, and Pio Renssy. 1983. "A Preliminary Report on the Traditional Music of Petspects Villages (Hahon Society) of N. W. Bougainville." *Bikmaus* 4(3):56–66.

Stella, Regis. 1990. *Forms and Styles of Traditional Banoni Music.* Boroko: National Research Institute.

Tai, Ryūichi. 1990. "Song and Dance of the Russell Islands: A Preliminary Report on the MABO Project in the Russell Islands." *O'o: A Journal of Solomon Islands Studies* 2(2):27–38.

Thurnwald, Richard. 1912. *Forschungen auf den Salomoinseln und dem Bismarck-Archipel.* 2 vols. Berlin: Reimer.

———. 1936. *Profane Literature of Buin, Solomon Islands.* Yale University Publications in Anthropology, 8. New Haven, Conn.: Yale University Press.

———. 1941. "Alte und neue Volkslieder aus Buin." *Zeitschrift für Ethnologie* 73:12–28.

———. 1971a. "Instruments de musique de Malaita (I)." *Journal de la Société des Océanistes* 30:31–53.

Vatahi, Albert. 1989. "Panpipe Ensembles of the North Solomons." Manuscript. Institute of Papua New Guinea Studies Music Archive.

Zemp, Hugo. 1971. "Un orgue éolien de Guadalcanal." *Objets et Mondes* 12(3):221–226.

———. 1972. "Instruments de musique de Malaita (II)." *Journal de la Sociétee des Océanistes* 34:7–48.

———. 1973a. "Échelles équiheptaphoniques des flûtes de Pan chez les 'Aré'aré." *Yearbook of the International Folk Music Council* 5:85–121.

———. 1973b. *Fataleka and Baegu Music: Malaita: Solomon Islands.* Philips 6586018. LP disk.

———, ed. 1973c. *Musique de Guadalcanal: Solomon Islands.* Ocora OCR 74. LP disk.

———. 1978a. "'Are'are Classification of Musical Types and Instruments." *Ethnomusicology* 22(1):37–67.

———. 1978b. *Polyphonies des Îles Salomon (Guadalcanal et Savo).* Le Chant du Monde LDX 74663. LP disk.

———. 1979. "Aspects of 'Are'are Musical Theory." *Ethnomusicology* 23(1):5–48.

———. 1981. "Melanesian Solo Polyphonic Panpipe Music." *Ethnomusicology* 25(3):383–418.

———. 1982. "Deux à huit voix: polyphonies de flûtes de Pan chez les Kwaio (Iles Salomon)." *Revue de Musicologie* 68(1–2):275–309.

———. 1994. *Solomon Islands: 'Are'are Panpipe Ensembles.* Le Chant du Monde LDX 274961.62. 2 compact discs.

———. 1995a. *Écoute le bamboo qui pleure: récits de quatre musiciens mélanésiens ('Are'are, Îles Salomon).* Paris: Gallimard.

———. 1995b. *Solomon Islands: 'Are'are Intimate and Ritual Music.* Le Chant du Monde CNR 274963. Compact disc.

Zemp, Hugo, and Daniel de Coppet. 1978. *'Are'are: un peuple mélanésien et sa musique.* Paris: Éditions du Seuil.

# New Caledonia

*Jean-Michel Beaudet*
*Raymond Ammann*
*Véronique Nagiel*

**Musical Contexts and Genres**
**Singing on Grande Terre**
**Musical Instruments**
**Music in the Loyalty Islands**
**Kanak Dance**

The New Caledonian archipelago includes Grande Terre (the mainland) and surrounding islands: to the south, the Isle of Pines; to the east, the Loyalty Islands; to the north, Belep. Extending over 80,000 square kilometers, it has reef constructions (lagoons, atolls) and a mountain range that divides Grande Terre into a narrow, heavily rainwashed, coastal strip on its east side, and broad and dry coastal plains on its west. The prevailing climates are tropical and temperate. A hot season with deep atmospheric depressions alternates with a cool winter. The natural vegetation—mangrove, shrub, savanna, forest—supports many endemic species.

About thirty-five hundred years ago, a people whose descendants call themselves Kanaks first settled New Caledonia. A few Polynesian migrations, of which the last reached Ouvéa in the 1700s (Bensa and Rivierre 1982:355–359), contributed to the process of linguistic diversification. In the late 1700s, when European explorers reached the archipelago, more than thirty languages were locally spoken.

The French government claimed the territory in 1853. Waves of European immigrants followed, and Kanak life underwent violent changes. In 1989, of the 164,000 inhabitants in New Caledonia, seventy-four thousand were Kanaks, fifty-five thousand were Europeans, and thirty-five thousand were peoples from Ouvéa and West Futuna, Tahiti, Vanuatu, Indonesia, and Vietnam.

The Kanaks are horticulturists, who augment their diet with fish and game. They widely consume commercial foodstuffs (rice, sugar, tea), but yams retain ancient religious connotations, and are still the staple, the most highly prized source of nourishment (figure 1). As the basis of ceremonial exchanges, yams have forged Kanak communities into a "yam civilization" (Haudricourt 1964).

The exchange of goods follows routes between coastal communities and groups living at higher altitudes, and even between the inhabitants of one slope and another. Social organization, tightly bound to the vagaries of space, is marked hierarchically by a subtle and complex balance between the symbolic power of a chief and the decisive power of landowners: seniority on the land is the basis for social legitimacy.

Twenty-nine aboriginal languages are spoken in the archipelago. In contrast to linguistic diversity, however, cultural practices (including music) exhibit comparative

FIGURE 1    Behind a pile of plantains and yams, guests from Bondé arrive in Hienghène. Photo by Wayenece Wayenece, 1984.

unity. The largest difference occurs between Grande Terre and the outer islands, which have absorbed cultural traits from Polynesian settlers.

Within the two main practices, cultural homogeneity yields to minor stylistic differences, which help define each locality, centering cultural life on a relationship between unity and diversity. Thus, the organization of music and dance follows just a few distinct forms; repertories easily circulate, while affirming the specific traits of each locality.

## MUSICAL CONTEXTS AND GENRES

Vocal genres of music divide into two classes: a body of more intimate music, linked to the household; and a body of communal music, performed at major ceremonies of exchange. The former class includes lullabies, games of noisemaking and singing, melodies for flutes, and curative and religious invocations. The last class includes rhythmic speeches, mimetic dances, men's songs—and since the end of the 1800s, the music of mixed choirs, cast in the mold of Protestant hymns, a European musical genre, which New Caledonians call *pilou-pilou,* denoting any kind of Kanak communal music.

Since the Europeans' arrival, the islands appear to have adopted more flexible musical practices, and have accepted the modification of certain musical elements of old forms, such as the tendency to use the tempered scale and sing in unison. The musical life of Grande Terre, however, seems to have been more rigid, more secretive, and less equipped to face the vectors of change: censorship by Christian priests, broadcasting on radio, and recording on tape.

### Intimate music

Throughout the country, intimate music, with its corresponding instruments, is disappearing more quickly than ceremonial music. Lullabies are the only kind of private music still thriving. On Tiga, in the Loyalty Islands, some of them are slow, soft versions of important collective dances. Others talk about sleeping, closing eyes, and quietness, like this one, from the extreme north of Grande Terre, sung in the Yuaga language by Noel Pwanee Pwahalu (Bondé, October 1986; translated by Kaloonbat Tein).

*Torohiia, Torohiia:—*
Na yu gi, na yu caaxo, *Torohiia, Torohiia.*
Na yu mani, na yu nool, *Torohiia, Torohiia.*
Mani! ma koi nyanya, *Torohiia, Torohiia.*
Mani! ma koi caaya, *Torohiia, Torohiia.*
Wana gele du a gele da, *Torohiia, Torohiia.*
Gele du pwaala ni dono, *Torohiia, Torohiia.*
Wana gele du mwa Pwaaluben, *Torohiia, Torohiia.*
Gele mwaju Pwaxeraan, *Torohiia, Torohiia.*
Gela kale bwa thaavan, *Torohiia, Torohiia.*

*Torohiia, Torohiia:—*
You cry, and you stop, *Torohiia, Torohiia.*
You sleep, and you wake, *Torohiia, Torohiia.*
Sleep! mom is not here, *Torohiia, Torohiia.*
Sleep! dad is not here, *Torohiia, Torohiia.*
Maybe they went down, or up, *Torohiia, Torohiia.*
They are in the canoe far at sea, *Torohiia, Torohiia.*
They are down at Pwaaluben, *Torohiia, Torohiia.*
They come back from Pwaxeran, *Torohiia, Torohiia.*
They are fishing on the bare reef, *Torohiia, Torohiia.*

Lullabies name persons and places; they often detail historical events, maintaining a social memory within the household. Many abound in metaphors, and are subject to the endless unwrapping of adults' exegesis and commentary. In the Hienghène Valley, two long lullabies form a diptych that traces the history of a rebellion. The second ends metaphorically: *Duudup hai kuun:* / *Daalok hai hwan* 'Triton conch with many mouths: / *Cymatium* conch with many points'. These shells name the valley's high chiefs, who in 1917 led an unsuccessful rebellion. The mouths and the points represent the chiefs' alliances; the text blames these chiefs for the rebellion and the deaths it caused.

## Communal music

Different collective forms of music may be performed in different circumstances, including those linked to contemporary transformations: cultural and political events, Christian celebrations, marriages, shows for tourists. The most important events are the festival for the first yam of the season, the investiture of a new chief, and above all, the ceremony that ends the period of mourning for a chief, a year after his death. Its musical genres are described below, in the order of their appearance in this ceremony.

### The ceremonial speech

The mourning feast lasts several days, and may involve the gathering of hundreds of people. It follows the pattern of a large, complex exchange between representatives of paternal and maternal lines of descent. The exchange may include food, cloth, bead money, relics, and words. Members of the family on the paternal side host the ceremony.

Once the paternal hosts have met and collected the goods they intend to offer, a man steps up to a podium; as his people display the gifts, he delivers a ceremonial speech. His words introduce the gifts, recalling the real and symbolic journey made by those who have come to offer their wealth; he may mention alliances, or be more historical. "The clan past is not viewed in linear fashion as a series of epochs; it appears as a group of scenes, set out on a single plane in hierarchical order, but obeying a spatial dimension, in accordance with a policy that seeks communal security, cohesion, and survival" (Tjibaou 1976, trans.). This form has become fixed, and offers a highly poetic polysemy, mixing many levels of metaphors (Beaudet 1990).

On Grande Terre, a speech—uplifting, yet highly formalized—may last half an hour, depending on the orator and the circumstance. Naturally, the content of the speech varies with the region and the local history of alliances, but all over Grande Terre the staging remains the same: the orator, on a raised platform, is surrounded by men of his clan, who utter rhythmic hushings, and tread the ground as a sign that they are a people on the move.

The speech follows an introduction declaimed by a person other than the orator; this, too, is almost identical in every region: *wa titititi . . . waya wasika! waka!* The speech is delivered in full voice, with as few interruptions as possible; the basic criteria for an aesthetic evaluation are speed and constancy of tempo. The orator is a specialist, accredited after a ritualized apprenticeship. In the islands, where formal oratories are plentiful, rhythmic speeches are nonexistent; the orator stands on the ground, and the speech follows no set rhythmic pattern.

### Mimetic dances

According to tradition, birds taught Kanak people how to dance. In certain regions, the gray fantail, which hops ceaselessly (elsewhere, the *notu,* a big and beautiful pigeon, which struts powerfully) gave the inhabitants a love of rhythmic movements. This kind of dance tells a story through figurative and stylized gestures, performed by a company in synchrony. It consists of a series of segments, each executed twice.

The choreographic narrative of dances in the north (area of Hoot ma Whaap) may be a legend, or it may recount historical events, or describe the building of chiefs' houses or the cultivation of yams. In the rest of Grande Terre, the main subject of dances is warriors' exercises, such as attacking and defending with traditional weapons. The dancers arrange themselves in rows or lines while one or two leaders dance at the side, or weave among the rows. In the Loyalty Islands and on the Isle of Pines, these dances are more often led by a mixed choir of men and women, who simultaneously and rhythmically strike leaf parcels and bamboo tubes. On the mainland, an ensemble placed behind the dancers accompanies them; the Paicî area uses no instrumentalist at all.

Painted black, the dancers hold bunches of pandanus root or straw, emphasizing their movements. The basic action, from which all the actions evolve, is a series of vigorous stamps, broken up by a light hopping on the supporting foot. The main rhythm of mimetic dances in the north of Grande Terre involve, in 4/4 time, a repeating pattern of eight eighths, of which the second and sixth are stressed.

Some mimetic dances are done exclusively by men, and some exclusively by women, who move more smoothly, with a less athletic display. Since the early 1900s on Grande Terre, most women's dances have disappeared. In the north, where they were called *cero,* they involved women from the maternal side of the ceremony, who sang and danced together. The *cero* (or *ceto*) is still performed by women in the area around Poyes.

On Grande Terre, as each troupe of mimetic dancers makes its entrance into the central area of the village, it is ritually shielded by accompanists carrying branches, while a leader dances in front, to divert spectators' attention. These acts supposedly protect the magic powers that favor dance, and consequently prevent accidents. Before starting, the dancers offer a gift of allegiance to the male representatives of the maternal line in the ceremony. These dances are transmitted through formal apprenticeship.

In the islands, people classify dances into many subgenres, which vary from one community to another. Several distinct dances may be performed in one day. Mimetic dances, with their choral support, are far more important to the economy of a feast than on the mainland. Until the early twentieth century, each hamlet had its own dance. Imbued with a strong sense of communal ownership, these dances are handed down patrilineally.

After the changes of around 1900 and the tendency to "globalize the Kanak," the search for cultural identity in the 1980s led to a more local, more differentiated characterization of Kanak culture, and this tendency has been strengthened by the resurgence of mimetic dances. The comments that accompany these dances carry many references to authenticity; the dances are spectacular productions, and for that reason are most subject to self-conscious change and folklorization.

## SINGING ON GRANDE TERRE

On Grande Terre, two-part men's singing is held in higher esteem than other kinds of music, as the testimony of a great northern singer makes clear: "People come because of alliances. We sing to mourn the death of our chiefs. Nothing, nobody is left out. Our song is over and above all else. It is a tool of our civilization. It gives each one of us weight" (Pierre Pwaili, personal communication, 1986).

Throughout Grande Terre, the accompanying dances—called round dances or outdoor dances, according to the area—follow the same pattern, a human wheel in motion. Two singers stand at the hub, surrounded by a dozen musicians, who stamp bamboo tubes on the ground, clash bark-clapper beaters, or scrape palm spathes. With rhythmic shouting, calling, whistling, and hushing, they urge the singers on. Finally, everyone attending dances counterclockwise around the orchestra, joining in the medley of sounds with jokes and exclamations. The dance itself is simple: people sway along, stamping, walking, or trotting, depending on how close they are to the center. It invariably lasts all night, sustained at the center by successive pairs of singers.

All over Grande Terre, the tempo of any single song is constant and unchanging, but the paces of different songs may differ. For rhythm, the ensemble splits in half. Each half has the same number of musicians and the same combination of instruments, power, and pitch. One half is said to mark the main beat; the other, to "cut" or "pierce" it.

The first singer leads each repeat, imposing pitch and tempo. After a short segment, the second singer answers, as the ensemble joins in. The paired singers share each melody, divided into three or four segments, which sometimes cross and meet in true counterpoint. The effect of this duo is that no room remains for silence. The orchestra supports the singers, maintaining the tempo and vigor of the ensemble. The singers do not strictly follow the beat of the clappers. By the accuracy of the melodic interweaving, singers brook no interruption or slackening in phrasing. These qualities make up the main aesthetic criterion for this song, which "must be spirited," or "must not drop"—literally, "must be sung pushing ever higher, as if two men were chasing each other up a hill."

Thus, the song finds its structure in named dualities: the instrumental beat, organized in two sections, and the vocal melody, organized in two parts. The melodies draw their thematic material from the uncultivated world (the forest, the sea), while the words relate to the world of culture. These dualities correspond to general practices of exchange in Kanak society, but they may also be understood as a musical choice, which energizes melody and rhythm.

TRACK 40　　Intensity of phrasing comes from simple counterpoint, where the two voices alternate or double each other in parallel. One of the voices systematically supports

FIGURE 2 Excerpt from a song from Koné (*Kanaké* 1984 [1975]:B1), showing typical two-part men's singing of Grande Terre, accompanied by concussive clappers [see figure 5]. Transcription by Jean-Michel Beaudet.

the other with marked stresses or short elaborations on one syllable, or again, prepares the tension of the liaisons between the melodic segments by a progression of tones independent of the other voice. The themes often build on small intervals, but the overlapping of long and short segments enhances melodic contrast. Rather than producing an alternation of the voices themselves, the intertwining favors close and rapid alternation in the mutual support and autonomy of the parts (figure 2).

Forms are stanzaic, with each line sung twice. Melody, rhythm, and poetic meter are largely independent of one another. Texts are altered by common techniques: shortening or lengthening of syllables, and morphological or semantic ellipsis. Even in the tonal languages, as in the Paicî area, where the same words can fit different melodies, the language adapts to the music. In many Kanak languages, the words are "the content, the root of the song."

Texts can be as long as about forty lines. The lead singer divides them as he wishes, taking a few lines, then, for some words, substituting a coded formula, the syllables *aeae* in the north, *caea* in the Paicî area. Beyond marking a pause at the end of the melodic theme, this pattern has no significance. Then all participants shout together, and the song comes to a momentary halt, only to start again, a few minutes later, with the repetition of the last line sung.

Drawing widely on the names of places, lyrics recount historic events, such as interclan wars, alliances, or colonial episodes. They define social areas and relations with the natural world; they sometimes tell stories of love. The singers often perform borrowed songs, the words of which they do not understand. During most of the performances, because of the noise, the crowd dancing around the singers cannot hear the sung words; with coded gestures, the singers cue them. Thus, in performance, the words are secondary.

In musical style, the farther south in Grande Terre, the quicker the tempo. The main local differences stressed by musicians concern the style of the counterpoint: in the Hienghène Valley, the voices *heun kot himō* 'remain together'; but on the west side of the central chain, voices *kot hnāle pe hyele* 'go more separately' (Damwet Yanhunit, personal communication in the Nemi language, 1985). In the north, the men's song divides into several subgenres. One includes *cada*, in a quick tempo and a vigorous style, with words referring to important historical events. Another includes *ayoii*, slower (whether light or melancholy), all usually sung to the same melodic contour, recounting recent events. Verbal innovations are much more frequent in *ayoii* than in *cada*. A third subgenre, *ayoiicada*, is a hybrid, particular to Thanghène, a tiny area of the Hienghène Valley. Another subgenre, *ayoiini*, is known only by the singers of one local group in the valley.

Throughout Grande Terre, the form of this song is the same: "There are different ways of singing, different words from north to south, but all that makes one song" (Pierre Pwaili, personal communication, 1986). The ease with which the music travels, and the frequency of the borrowings (a song of Kanala is in the Ájië language, songs of Hienghène originated in Koné), prove the musical unity.

## The dissemination of songs

Musicians often talk about festive nights, when singers from different regions dance together, answer one another in singing, listen to one another, and exchange their pieces. In fact, besides the official renderings of their song, the singers perform in many informal gatherings that favor borrowing, innovation, and transmission. They do not stress any genealogical line, or any formal way by which they have learned how to sing; but speaking warmly about elders from whom they have learned, they define a style of singing, an independent musical kinship, of which they are proud to be the "juice" (Nemi *peween*).

The following song, an *ayoiicada* sung in Fwâi, tells the story of a burned-down tree set up as the central pole of a chief's house. A metaphor of the alliance between chiefdoms, the tree is also Kaavo and Hixé, the elder and the younger daughters of the giving chiefdom (sung by Theoury Wanyman and Hwâdo Pulawa, Thanghène, April 1985; translation by Kaloonbat Tein and Bealo Wedoye).

| | |
|---|---|
| Wo Kaavo le Thiro; | I am Kaavo from Thiro; |
| Wo Hixé le Théévaac, | I am Hixé from Théévaac, |
| Kaavo le we Gaalowé, | Kaavo from the Gaalowé water, |
| Hixe le pu doofhala. | Hixé from the Joinvillea bush. |
| Ye ra vhai wo ru Yao, | Yao, he who gets me hot, |
| Ye uu wo ru unengen, | The sun, who wakes me up, |
| Vhai toavi hulong, | He gets me hot and loaded me with sugarcane, |
| Vhai tobune hure hyung, | Gets me hot and cuts my arm, |
| Vhai po theen le jiong. | Gets me hot up to the womb. |
| Taa tai wâ diuut, | He goes up to tear off the *Dioscorea* liane, |
| Time thao o ji noong. | And goes down to tie it around my womb, |
| Thaa nem bwala le noong. | And goes down to tie it on my throat. |
| Thaa ne daween thung, | He ties it between my breasts, |
| Daween thung ka kohia, | Between my pretty breasts, |
| Hwe maa kuun daalhook. | Pretty like the apex of a conch. |
| Hido ga taa tho nanhua, | Then he calls grandfather, |
| Hua Daobwat hweena, | Grandfather Daobwat, |
| We time thoi thaba. | To go down and catch *thaba* fish. |
| Pweli ra pweli ceegi, | Pulled, pulled like a tree, |

Mixed four-part choral songs, sung all over the archipelago, derive from Protestant hymns brought at the end of the 1800s. Though the harmony of these songs is completely European, the scalar gliding is characteristically indigenous.

| | |
|---|---|
| Pweli wo o ga Loohwê, | Pulled on to the Loohwê peak, |
| Pweli o pa Cibahup, | Pulled on to the Cibahup stone, |
| Pweli ra pweli ceegi, | Pulled, pulled like a tree, |
| Pweli tiwo le Haxu, | Pulled and led to Haxu, |
| Na le Haxu Doonceek. | To Haxu Doonceek. |
| Kuun we Hiavhehnook. | At the spring in Hiavhehnook, |
| Pweli wo le ne Thedalik:— | Pulled to Thedalik:— |
| Ye pweli wo hen hiri lek. | He pulled me to the sacred place. |

In this text, assonance (as in the line-ending words *hulong, hyung, jiong, noong,* and *thung,* and again at the end, *Doonceek, Hiavhehnook, Thedalik,* and *hiri lek*) is probably not accidental.

Mixed four-part choral songs (*temperance*), sung all over the archipelago, derive from Protestant hymns, brought at the end of the 1800s. Though the harmony of these songs is completely European, the scalar gliding, especially on the final stress, is characteristically indigenous. In local terminology in colloquial French, this genre divides into two subforms: one, the most measured, called *do* (after a sol-fa name of the note C), and one called *temperance.* The repertory of these songs is extensive; it grows at periodical tournaments, where competing choirs define themselves spatially according to their localities. The words, initially biblical, have since covered the whole field of social activities: historical events, secular commemorations, ceremonial exchanges.

Music for the community has economic aspects. On the mainland, during ceremonies, singers are given a symbolic gift of cloth, but performers of mimetic dances receive nothing: it is they who make a gift to the opposite line. In the islands, during the performance, the spectators give money and cloth to individual dancers. On Tiga in 1986, in one short but appreciated performance, twelve dancers received nearly twenty pieces of cloth and 40,000 Central Polynesian francs (in 1998, about US$400). As a consequence, islanders are sensitive to the business of royalty and copyright.

In 1986, of the four radio channels of New Caledonia, two did not broadcast any Kanak or Pacific music, and the other two broadcast no traditional Kanak music, 1 percent modern Kanak music, and 0.9 percent Pacific music. By contrast, they broadcast 1.1 percent Western classical music, 22 percent French popular music, and 75 percent pop music of the rest of the world (Weiri 1986). Modern Kanak music, edited on cassettes, has developed within the Western music system; but in the 1980s, young musicians, perceiving the gap between their music and their parents' music, tried to compose songs incorporating old rhythmic patterns and sequential exclamations.

In the islands, two localized dances occur: *bua,* a men's dance, which seems to be an imitation that mixes the speech and the song of Grande Terre; and *cab,* a playful round for men and women, performed informally at feasts, or to support cricket teams.

At most gatherings, whether minor feasts or major ceremonies, different musical productions coexist: music of the same genre, such as the music at the feast marking the death of Jean-Marie Tjibaou (in 1989), when three pairs of singers, with their three "outdoor dances," were performing at the same time in the central place of Hiedanit, his home; music of different genres, as on Tiga in 1986, where at night, after the dances of the day and the collective meal, one could simultaneously hear reggae from one man's radio, the sounds of another man's guitar, a *temperance* choir, short *cab* games, and a medley of exclamations, shouts, and laughs.

## MUSICAL INSTRUMENTS

Musical instruments of New Caledonia fall into two main classes: instruments of entertainment, including musical toys; and instruments associated with dances and ceremonies. These classes overlap: during dances, certain toys (whistles, lamella-phones) sometimes serve to punctuate sequences, or to highlight the rhythm and excite the dancers; and under the censorship of Christian missionaries, ceremonial instruments (such as panpipes) have become children's toys.

Most of these instruments are still in use. Instruments of European origin, sold commercially, include metal whistles (*vesel*) and harmonicas (popular in the early 1900s), played during dances in the islands. Guitars turn up everywhere, usually in young people's hands.

Apart from concussive stones (Garnier 1871:160), the conch, and a crab-shell clapper, the materials of all New Caledonian instruments come from plants. These materials are easy to find, though a person may need to seek permission from the owner of some plants before cutting them down. Most plant-derived instruments, because they dry out and lose their shape, last no longer than a few days; after the ceremony for which they were made, people sometimes destroy them.

### Instruments of entertainment

These are various small objects, easy to make and not durable. On the east coast of Grande Terre as in the Loyalty Islands, lamellaphones are made from a strip of coconut foliole and held between the musician's teeth or lips, with a segment of the midrib of a green foliole, which, when hit by the hand twangs the leaf. A whirring disk is made from *Cycas* fruit, pierced by two strings. A coconut-leaf whizzer (Pijé *maguk* 'bee') resembles one found in Vanuatu (Fischer 1983:196–197).

### *Flutes*

A piston flute is made from rose laurel, but it can also be made from a native shrub. In the water-struck flute of the islands, "smaller pieces of cane, made up at one end, and filled with water, according to the pitch of the tone desired, were blown; these *hoho* produced a sound somewhat resembling that of Pan's pipes" (Hadfield 1920:134).

An obliquely played end-blown flute comes from the petiole of the papaya; open at both ends, it measures roughly 30 centimeters. Played mainly in gardens and on the paths leading to them, it is often associated with courtship. A typical melody (figure 3) is in D major, and uses only diatonic tones of the scale. To its tune can be sung this couplet: *Muto, muto in, / Eko ma muto, muto i sengone* 'Sheep, sheep mine, / You're not the sheep, sheep of another'. The reference to sheep and the use of this scale suggest that the tune postdates European colonization.

A side-blown flute found on the mainland is made of a reed (*Phragmites* sp.), or of a thin, native bamboo. Closed at both ends, it has a hole for fingering at the end

FIGURE 3 End-
blown flute solo:
"*Muto, muto in*"
('Sheep, sheep
mine'), as played by
Hoilane Walles of
Tiga in 1984.
Transcription by
Jean-Michel
Beaudet.

opposite the hole for blowing. It is curved, extending roughly 1 meter, with a diameter of 2 centimeters [see MUSICAL INSTRUMENTS: Aerophones: Side-blown flutes of New Caledonia]. Whether or not the bamboo version was a nose-blown flute is controversial, but a nineteenth-century description seems precise enough to be reliable: "the natives play equally as easily with the nose as with the mouth, blocking one of the nostrils with the thumb" (Rochas 1862:189).

On the Isle of Pines, a duct flute roughly 60 centimeters long is made from the petiole of the papaya tree, cut transversely at the lower end, and beveled at the upper. Into this mouthpiece fits a strip of petiole, forming a deflector, which conducts the air onto the lateral orifice. Holding the flute horizontally, the player uses the lower end as a hole for fingering.

In the Kanala region (central mainland), a panpipe made from two bamboo pipes was played in a children's orchestra in the early 1900s. Named *bèchöö* 'piece of reed' (*Arundo donax*), it also served to punctuate some dances, and in this use substituted for metal whistles.

### Other aerophones

Children make a simple, free-reed aerophone by holding a blade of grass between their thumbs. The blade can be fixed in a frame made from the stem of a fern (*Phymatosorus grossus*). On Tiga, this instrument takes the name of the fern *shukeli*; people play it by drawing breath in and blowing out again, while holding the instrument between the lips. Another clarinet, found on Lifu, is made from a papaya petiole, open at both ends; the reed is a coconut-leaf strip, inserted into a beveled mouthpiece.

The people of New Caledonia use three kinds of oboe. They make one from a flat, hollow grass: when its base is blown, it swells up; the air whistles as it escapes (figure 4). People of the central mainland make a similar one from a fine bamboo, split lengthwise and given a beveled mouthpiece; as air escapes under pressure through the slit, it vibrates. For the third oboe, two reeds are made from coconut-leaf strips; they are entwined with another strip, forming a conical bell. This oboe is usually about 10 centimeters long; but on the Isle of Pines, where it has the same name as the local conch trumpet, it can reach 30 centimeters in length.

A side-blown trumpet of the islands is made from the petiole of a papaya; the upper end is naturally sealed, its hole for blowing is rectangular, and it is nearly 60 centimeters long. It is now out of use, but probably served for signaling.

### Ceremonial instruments

### Idiophones

Stamped bamboo tubes—*wau* 'bamboo' in the Xârâcùù and Ájië languages of the central mainland, and *duu hyavic* 'real bamboo' in languages of the north—are primarily an instrument of the mainland. They contribute to the rhythmic support of

FIGURE 4 A man of New Caledonia plays a leaf oboe.

FIGURE 5    A man of Gööpä, Paicî area, strikes bark clappers together. Photo by Wayenece Wayenece, 1984.

two-part men's songs and mimetic dances. They measure from 1 to 1.5 meters long, and are between 7 and 25 centimeters in diameter. They are normally made from a thin native bamboo. (In the islands, where bamboo does not naturally grow, musicians use tubes brought from Grande Terre, or, as a substitute, plastic pipes.) Women sometimes stamp tubes, but in important ceremonies, only men do. Stamped tubes also appear in the islands.

Two-part men's songs are highly valued. They follow a rhythmic beat set mainly by concussive clappers made from the bark of a fig (*Ficus habrophylla*), stuffed with dried grass and the thin bark of a melaleuca (figure 5). Clappers are usually about 30 centimeters long, one held in each hand. This instrument is called *cinfwe* 'fig-tree bark' in the north (Paicî *jépa*, Xârâcùù *dööbwè*), where people say it was originally made of the shells of crabs. Apparently an isolated instrument in Oceania, it occurs only in Grande Terre.

As part of the most important musical context, these clappers are highly valued, and they bear important connotations of ceremonial exchange and competition: old people say that when these clappers "are well played, the force of their rhythm causes a strong wind to arise, lifting coconut fronds, and causing coconuts to fall"—which could well be a metaphor for aggression against the chief hosting the ceremony. Alternatively, it might be an image of pleasure, the enthusiasm of the chief who dances and gives his fruits (offers his daughters). In response, the hosts may fill their clappers with magical leaves, which, as they say, "will awaken everybody, lift the dance, bring down the opposing singers, and calm the guests' greed and aggressiveness." A subgenre of these songs can have the accompaniment of a forest-palm spathe, as much strummed as hit. It turns up everywhere on the mainland, but can be replaced by a mat for sitting or a cardboard box.

The rhythmic support of mimetic dances comes from idiophones specific to each region: in the Paicî region (central mainland), the only sound-producing instruments for these dances are the ornaments the dancers wear: garters and skirts of coconut leaves or straw. People on the mainland sometimes make leg-tied rattles from the dried fruit of *Cycas,* or more rarely the fruit of a spiky liane (*Caesalpinia* sp.) from the forest; in the islands, people make them from a set of rings fashioned from young palm leaves. In the north, the dancers have the backing of stamped tubes, a little log drum, or a bamboo idiophone. In the islands, rhythmic support comes mainly from leaf parcels; these leaves, which come from a tree frequently found by the sea (*Macaranga vedeliana*) are piled on top of one another, knotted with ribs of the coconut foliole. They are also made of pieces of paper, stuck together with adhesive tape. Accompanying dancers with singing, men and women hold one instrument in one hand and strike it with the other. Formerly on Ouvéa, some dances had the accompaniment of struck crab shells.

Formerly at Kwenyii, Isle of Pines, near the navigators' house, the wind caused two suspended plates (*waypülü*) to whirl and hum. These instruments, oblong in shape, were made of *bourao* wood (*Hibiscus tiliaceus*); hooked onto a rod, they supposedly served as weathervanes.

### Aerophones

Throughout New Caledonia, the conch is the most symbolically charged instrument. The shell is usually the larger triton (*Charonia tritonis*), less frequently the smaller (*Cymatium lotorium*). With one exception, these are end-blown trumpets without mouthpiece (Fisher 1983:135); exceptionally in Oceania, one observed side-blown conch has the hole for blowing on the side opposite the opening of the shell.

An instrument of the chieftainship the conch summons people to meetings and ceremonies. After being turned into a trumpet (figure 6), it must undergo ritual

FIGURE 6    A young chief of Hienghène blows a conch. Photo by Martine Paris, 1987.

washing with magical plants, which give it the power to summon; then, for safekeeping, it goes into a special basket, high in the chief's house.

Each hamlet formerly had its own conch, with its own rhythm: "the conch is the voice of the chief," people would say. Set as a sculptural element atop the pole of the chief's house, it becomes a symbol of the chief's power and alliances. It once had a more religious meaning: men blew it to call and petition gods, and its sound marked important steps of agrarian rites (Leenhardt 1935:85–86). A northern myth links the conch with the aerial power of thunder and the mineral power of mountains.

—JEAN-MICHEL BEAUDET

## MUSIC IN THE LOYALTY ISLANDS

The four main Loyalty Islands—Lifou, Maré, Ouvéa, Tiga—are situated on a line parallel to Grande Terre, the main island of New Caledonia, 110 kilometers away. Grande Terre and the Loyalty Islands were first inhabited sometime between 1200 and 1000 B.C. (Sand 1994:248–258). Many different migrations occurred later, making the Loyalty Islanders of today a mixture of Melanesians and Polynesians. The Melanesians arrived from Grande Terre and Vanuatu; the Polynesians, from Sāmoa, Tonga, 'Uvea, and Futuna.

Ouvéa is the only island in the Loyalties that has two languages: Fagauvea, a Polynesian language, is spoken in the north and south; Iaaï, a Melanesian language, is spoken in the center. Social intermingling has made Ouveans bilingual. The language spoken on Lifou is Drehu, and the language of Maré is Nengone; both languages have Polynesian, Melanesian, and English elements, the last from missionaries of the London Missionary Society. Maré and Lifou have a linguistic register (on Lifou, called Minji; on Maré, Wateno) reserved for addressing high chiefs. The population of Tiga is bilingual, speaking Nengone and Drehu.

The combination or coexistence of Polynesian and Melanesian elements occurs not only in language, but in other cultural dimensions. Houses resemble those of Grande Terre, but canoes resemble those of Sāmoa and Tonga. Music and dance, too, reflect multiple sources.

### Musical instruments

The leaf parcel, the musical instrument used throughout the Loyalty Islands to accompany dance-songs, is likely of Melanesian origin, and is used on one of the

Solomon Islands (Zemp 1978:37–67) and in Vanuatu. Also of Melanesian origin are the rhythms of dances accompanied only by percussion. These rhythms are played on leaf parcels, and on stamped tubes brought from Grande Terre. The leaf parcel (Drehu *itra pwe,* Faga and Iaaï *bwinj-bet,* Nengone *ae be*) is a round, flat pile of leaves about 20 to 30 centimeters in diameter and 10 to 15 centimeters high. A sinew wrapped around it preserves its shape. The singer holds it in one hand, beating it with the palm of the other.

### Dance and music

Most dances of the Loyalty Islands are accompanied by the singing of a mixed choir. The singers, who beat a leaf parcel while singing, sit on the ground behind or beside the dancers. Each dance-song usually consists of a short musical sequence, repeated as many times as performance requires. In old dance-songs, the melodic range does not exceed the interval of a perfect fourth; two voices may move in parallel, and a drone may occur.

Dances created in the twentieth century are either exclusively women's dances (*wahai* on Maré, *wahaihai* on Ouvéa), or mixed dances. Dancers stand in two or three lines. Synchronized movements of their upper bodies and arms portray events mentioned in the lyrics. Women keep their feet together; men stand with their legs apart and bent. All the dancers move their legs only rarely.

The diction of twentieth-century dance-songs is that of ordinary daily life. But lyrics have layers of meaning, and only the composer, the lead dancer, and maybe a few other informed persons understand them all. For example, the dance *yewakedrera* (of Maré) mimics the hunting of crabs. The dancers portray the action of catching crabs and putting them into a bucket; but the crabs escape, again and again. This representation is understood by all who watch the dance and understand the language of the lyrics. To appreciate it on a second level, one needs to know that the crabs stand for girls, and that the hunter is a man whose girlfriend keeps running away. On this level, the dance deals with girls' infidelity. The information on a third level is understood only by close friends of the composer, who refers to his personal experience with specific girls when he was a young man.

In the choreography of old dances (dating from before the mid-1800s), the Polynesian or Melanesian elements were transformed into the individual style of each island. Revered and protected, such dances belong to high chiefs. The words of old songs are no longer fully intelligible; but oral traditions and words whose meanings are clear show that the lyrics refer to important historical events, such as wars, famines, and migrations. On Maré, such dances are *be ko be* and *be be nod*; and on Lifou, *fehoa* and *bua.*

The dance *bua,* belonging to high chief Bula of Lösi District, Lifou, is performed mostly by men of the village of Kedeng, whose chief, Wanyamala, is responsible for its performance. The dancers, with blackened upper bodies and faces, holding a club in one hand, form two lines marching in concentric circles in opposite directions. When the first dancers of each line meet, all dancers make warlike movements, such as attacking and defending with the club. The first dancers of each line engage in attack and defense, and the dancers behind them portray a fight against an invisible enemy. A short pause follows these actions, and then the first two dancers of each line change places. Again the dancers walk in their circles, and when the leaders next meet, they carry out a different action. In the center stand two singers, who beat a percussion box with two sticks; the words of their songs have lost their meaning.

Dancers of the district of Wetr on Lifou have asked themselves how to present an old legend in a dance so everybody understands it. In their dances *Capenehe e Hlemusese* and *caee* (both created between 1992 and 1994), the performers become

actors, for their dance is a music-accompanied skit. Before these dances receive off-island performance (figure 7), a participant explains the legend in the language of the audience (Ammann 1994:54–65).

### Music apart from dancing

On each of the Loyalty Islands, young people have songs that do not accompany dances. They sing those songs when working together in fields, or during feasts and the celebrations of weddings. On Maré, these songs, called *waueng,* are textually romantic and sometimes provocative: therefore, the singers, usually men, never perform *waueng* in public; during weddings, they sing them in a nearby forest. On Lifou, young people of both sexes sing similar songs, called *wejein,* whose words, though possibly also romantic, are less provocative; some even have proverblike structures. *Waueng* and *wejein* are polyphonic and unaccompanied. When performing them, young people feel happy, and sometimes the singing collapses into shouting and laughing.

On Ouvéa, songs of a genre called *seloo*—originally sung by young people, but today mostly sung by elders—differ from *waueng* and *wejein. Seloo* may refer to events in a composer's life, historical events, or biblical themes. They have several stanzas, whereas *waueng* and *wejein* are short, consisting of one part only. But it is polyphony that makes *seloo* special: the voices are set so that, to outsiders' ears, harmonies sound dissonant. *Seloo* are unique to Ouvéa (Ammann 1995).

—RAYMOND AMMANN

### KANAK DANCE

Carved in stone in the cave of Bhraghra (at Ponérihouen, Paicî area) are reliefs of human figures, including a woman and her child. Possibly a sacred site, the cave may have been devoted to fertility-promoting rites. Its cosmological universe asserts an earthly element, to which Kanak philosophy attaches itself. These reliefs may imply that the earliest Austronesian dancing in New Caledonia began as the distillation of emotion, the first human language.

In Kanak mentality, masculine and feminine elements, integral to the sociopolitical organization of clans, ceaselessly meet in the flux of life. As agriculturalists, Kanaks derive the basic element of their dancing from contact with the earth. Conventional Kanak botanical symbolism treats yams as male and taros as female. Expressed in dance, these analogies link two worlds in complementary dualities of masculine and feminine. The bond between dancers and earth reinforces human bonds of exchange, such as alliances between maternal and paternal clans.

## Genres and clans

Kanak dancing takes various forms. Some are collective. None is exclusively for a soloist. Most involve men. In the dance most frequently performed on Grande Terre, the round dance (*la spirale*), everybody can participate. In another dance (*faimanu*, of Hienghène, Fwai-Nemi area), participants form two sex-specific lines, making a metaphor for sex-based tasks, which Kanak society apportions between maternal and paternal lineages.

In Kanak life, the paternal group offers the clan's primary expression, on which the maternal group bases its feelings. Thus, with certain funeral ceremonies (as in Hienghène, Fwai-Nemi area), the maternal group receives the paternal group of the deceased. Responsible for the clan's equilibrium, men emphasize contact with the earth, whose space, the arena set aside for dancing, ritually matches and opposes their activity with that of women, from whom come the waters—metaphorical blood, showing that to be feminine is to give life.

### Women's performance

Rarely does Kanak dancing feature the maternal clan's contribution to social organization. Kept apart from rituals, women do not speak in public or participate in the rituals around which their clan's social organization revolves. Numerous dances, however, are reserved for them.

The dance *wahai* (originally from the Loyalty Islands), often described in print, takes various forms, each particular to where it is performed. The women of any single clan perform it. From their village, they go to a secluded spot where, hidden from observation, they perform various rites. The step of the *wahai* simply consists of the movement of one foot over the other, either in place, or with one foot behind the other; women sometimes perform this movement with children. Despite numerous social interdictions imposed on women, this dance plays an important role in the sociopolitical structure of clans. The dance of women of Pénélo (Maré, Nengone area) suggests the presence of an allied clan, of maternal neighbors, protectors of places. The dance mimics the movements of a buzzard, the totem of the clan, as it flies over the island.

## Angularity and aesthetics

The motions of Kanak dancing make angular patterns: bodily postures and movements often take the form of angles. The angular aesthetic, reinforced by strong contact of feet against earth, favors bent-knee positions, reinforced by movements of the arms. Dancers' steps, with their feet stamping on the ground, are warlike, heavy, and harsh (figure 8). The rhythm is binary, sustained by the beats of stamped bamboo tubes and concussed leaf parcels, marked by sonorous footfalls.

FIGURE 8 In angular positions and stamping their feet, dancers perform with clubs to welcome guests at Hienghène. Photo by Wayenece Wayenece, 1984.

The paternal clan usually expresses authority over the maternal clan. To simulate the ritual workings of this relationship, companies of Kanak dancers divide in half. Since dancing symbolizes men's functions, it uses few movements thought to be feminine.

From place to place throughout Grande Terre and in the Loyalties, choreographies differ drastically. In some ways, however, the *basic* choreographies hardly vary: individual dancers use little personal space, seldom touching even each other's hands or shoulders, and their passage through larger spatial dimensions follows precisely structured forms. Kanak choreography allows few isolated or improvised movements: its ideal unites all postures and actions in one ensemble. This ideal allows some steps to be in place, or in back or at the sides. It permits few turns and leaps, movements it allows mostly in martial and masculine idioms.

## Totems and rhythms

Some rhythms for dancing vary by clan and geographic area. A performance can identify a clan by revealing its totem, the emblem of a maternal or paternal clan. Some dances, originating in connection with a totem, trace the clansmen's function through the symbolic signification of the totem, just as the sociopolitical role of this totem informs sessions of exchange between maternal and paternal lineages. The totem gives each man his identification within the clan. A typical dance of this sort is the dance of the frigate bird, performed by Kwêêniji-speaking people of the Kapumé area, Isle of Pines.

The totem represents two worlds—the invisible, where mythical values rule, and the visible, where social constraints do. Rancid smells permeate the ancestors' world, a realm of black land and ashes. Nothing can venture into it without having acquired these smells (Leenhardt 1979:48–50), which human beings can wear like a second skin, assimilating themselves to it. Accordingly, dancers plaster themselves with layers of earth and ashes, as if such adornments will attract maternal clansmen's attention. (In fact, the ancestors' power is perceived as restoring the dancers.) This aspect of Kanak choreography reflects a conceptual duality: dancing retranslates the function of human beings and totems. On the Isle of Pines, Kwêêniji-speaking people of the Kapumé area perform the dance *yaace trii khôrô* 'of the ancient ones [devils, fisherghosts]', which mimics the action of mullets (*ngêre*). In an alliance of maternal and paternal clans, this dance strengthens the totemic bonds between mullets and seaweed, symbols of the union of the clans.

Each totem exerts complementary functions against the other. The paternal clan usually expresses authority and superiority over the maternal clan. To simulate the ritual workings of this relationship, companies of Kanak dancers divide in half, with all the dancers of each half belonging to the same (maternal or paternal) clan. Since Kanak dancing symbolizes men's functions in promulgating social rules and building gardens, it uses few kinetic elements locally viewed as feminine.

—VÉRONIQUE NAGIEL, translated by J. W. LOVE

## REFERENCES

Ammann, Raymond. 1994. *Les danses kanak, une introduction.* Nouméa: Agence de Développement de la Culture Kanak.

———. 1995. *Chants et Musiques, Iaaï . . . Drehu . . . Nengone.* Collection Musiques Kanak, 1–3. Nouméa and Maré: Centre Culturel Yéiwéné and ADCK. 3 cassettes.

Beaudet, Jean-Michel, Kaloonbat Tein, and Lionel Weiri, eds. 1990. *Chants kanaks: Cérémonies et Berceuses.* Le Chant du Monde LDX 274 909. LP disk.

Bensa, Alban, and Jean-Claude Rivierre. 1982. *Les chemins de l'alliance.* Paris, Selaf.

Fischer, Hans. 1983. *Sound-Producing Instruments in Oceania.* Edited by Don Niles. Translated by Philip W. Holzknecht. Boroko: Institute of Papua New Guinea Studies.

Garnier, Jules. 1871. *La Nouvelle Calédonie.* Paris: Plon.

Hadfield, Emma. 1920. *Among the Natives of the Loyalty Group.* London: Macmillan.

Haudricourt, André-Georges. 1964. "Nature et culture dans la civilisation de l'igname: l'origine des clônes et des clans." *L'Homme* 4:93–104.

*Kanaké.* 1984 [1975]. Recording of Melanesia 2000 Festival. Nouméa: Office Culturel. Cassette.

Leenhardt, Maurice. 1932. *Documents néo-calédoniens.* Paris: Institut d'Ethnologie.

———. 1935. *Vocabulaire et grammaire de la langue de Houaïlou.* Paris: Institut d'Ethnologie.

———. 1979. *Do Kamo.* Translated by Basia Miller Gulati. Chicago: University of Chicago Press.

Rochas, Victor de. 1862. *La Nouvelle Calédonie et ses habitants.* Paris: Sartorius.

Sand, Christoph. 1994. "La préhistoire de la Nouvelle-Calédonie: Contribution à l'étude des modalités d'adaption et d'évolution des sociétés océaniennes dans un archipel de Sud de la Mélanésie." Ph.D. dissertation, University of Paris 1.

Sarasin, Fritz. 1929. *Ethnologie der Neu-Caledonier und Loyalty Insulaner.* Munich: C. W. Kiedel.

Tjibaou, Jean-Marie. 1976. "Recherche d'identité mélanésienne et société traditionnelle." *Journal de la Société des Océanistes* 32:281–292.

Weiri, Lionel. 1986. "La musique *kanak* dans les radio de Nouméa." *Nouméa: La Case, Patrimoine Kanak* 7:19–24.

Zemp, Hugo. 1978. "'Are'are Classification of Musical Types and Instruments." *Ethnomusicology* 22(1):37–67.

# Vanuatu

*Adrienne L. Kaeppler*
*Peter Crowe*
*Vida Chenoweth*
*Lamont Lindstrom*

**Northern and Central Areas**
**Mota, Banks Islands**
**Southern Area**

The nation of Vanuatu comprises scores of islands with a population of about 170,000, speaking more than 100 languages. First visited by the Portuguese Pedro Fernandez Queiros in 1606, these islands remained little known to the wider world until the late 1700s, when Captain Cook surveyed it and named it the New Hebrides. Traditional society focused on autonomous villages in which men's power and position depended on the purchase of levels in graded societies. Wealth in the form of pigs was particularly important. The performance of music and dance featured masked rituals and the sounds of log idiophones, which often gave voice to ancestral spirits, represented by human images carved in stones or tree ferns (figure 1). These spirits issued commands. Through conventional rhythms, they incited the living to dance. Their placement reflected social structures: sometimes in areas that traced descent through the mother's line, they lay horizontally, whereas in areas that traced descent through the father's line, they often stood upright.

—ADRIENNE L. KAEPPLER

## NORTHERN AND CENTRAL AREAS

Colonization of Vanuatu began about four thousand years ago, when successive waves of Austronesian-speakers, possibly with a few non-Austronesian-speakers, proceeded south from Santa Cruz. Indications of ancient music and dance may be inferred from archaeology and the ethnographic record. Southeast Asian metallurgy never arrived; nor did the weaver's loom, known only as far east as Santa Cruz. Drills for shell money were known only as far south as the Banks Islands. Musical instruments were readily biodegradable, barring any of shell or pottery. No archaeological evidence of lithophones survives, though stones are now employed as instrumental adjuncts—to scratch upon, beat with, and so on. Ancient tombs orient skeletal ornaments in ways that suggest that their makers preferred a counterclockwise direction in circular dances.

Lexicostatistics indicates two local groups of Austronesian languages: Eastern Oceanic, with open syllables and few consonant clusters, and a so-called Other Melanesian, with complex phonology. This distribution may correspond to the presumed waves of migration, Other Melanesian now being found south of a line

FIGURE 1    Ancestral figures carved in tree ferns
stand at the edge of a dance ground on Ambrym
Island, Vanuatu. Photo courtesy Field Museum,
Chicago.

between Espiritu Santo and Malakula, south of Ambae, cutting through central
Pentecost at Melsisi (Apma-speakers). This classification correlates with the presence
of planted, giant, log idiophones (not found north of this line) in the Other
Melanesian area, which may well be the elder linguistic stratum.

Lapita and Mangaasi pottery is known from many sites. Only Wusi (west coast
of Espiritu Santo) still makes pottery, and it is the only site in Oceania where arrows
are feathered. Pottery vessels may have been at the origin of Malakula vocal modifiers
(*temes nainggol* 'ancestral voices', nowadays hollowed wooden cylinders, used to
amplify bamboo aerophones). In 1972, on a visit to Fiji to attend the inaugural
Pacific Festival of Arts, Malakula musicians saw resemblances between the playing of
these instruments and the blowing of Australian didjeridus.

Myths, song, the names of places, and linguistic features make a case for Maewo
as the springboard of a first eastward migration toward Fiji, known locally as
Mamalu. Origin-recording myths sometimes even seem to correspond with recent
scientific work, such as the three successive appearances of Maewo in the recent geo-
logical past (twenty-five million years)—but how could this have been known? Myth
states that Maewo is now in *maran'a rua* 'second rebirth'—an idea retained in song-
dance forms like the *bulu* 'union of the sexes'. The prehistoric record of Vanuatu
seems almost to be there: as though embedded in mythology, it permeates references
in musical texts, and is shown in gestures, the ritual calendar, and ideas about prereq-
uisite elemental presences for human existence. Maewo men say the favorite topic of
discussion in a kava-drinking session is history, inferring reinterpretation of myth.

### Historical records

In 1606, Queiros and Torres thought they had found Tierra Australis del Espiritu
Santo (Holy Ghost Land on English maps of the 1700s). Their accounts hint at
struck log idiophones, conchs, and dancing, but lack useful precision. Bougainville in
1768 reported hearing log-idiophone ensembles on Ambae, taking their music for
"native messages." Captain Cook in 1774 noted similar things. After 1800, adventurers and sandalwood traders began to exploit the islands.

In 1839, the first Christian missionaries began their proselytizing, later to be followed by sailors who kidnapped islanders to sell them into slavery. This was when

Bislama, the national pidgin, began its development. Some missionaries left useful records of indigenous rituals, and the best of them did remarkable work in ethnography and linguistics (Codrington 1891; Codrington and Palmer 1896), work that aided pioneering anthropologists. Of particular musical interest among the latter are the works of John Layard (notably that of 1942, based on fieldwork in 1914–1915) and a book by A. B. Deacon (1934, based on fieldwork of 1926–1927). After World War II, a series of ethnographic studies by Jean Guiart appeared, emphasizing social organization, politics, arts, and material culture. Much of the bibliography on Vanuatu has relevance to contextual studies of music and dance.

The first recordings of Vanuatu music were made by Layard in 1914–1915 (Clausen 1958). Deacon, when discussing the southwest Malakula *temes nainggol* ensembles, bemoaned his lack of equipment:

> The total effect is unlike anything l have ever heard, except some Japanese records of Japanese orchestral music. . . . So far I have found it hopeless to try and record [notate] the music. It is altogether too unlike anything l am used to; moreover, it is orchestral in character and therefore really needs a phonograph to do anything with it. It is a powerful form of art. (1934:392)

Few properly thought-out musical studies of Vanuatu have been published, and the discography remains scant and obscure.

## Musical mysteries

Anthropological and musical scholarship in Vanuatu, though particular only to several specific areas or peoples, has shown enough of the generally underlying musical systems of Vanuatu as to reveal several musical mysteries, involving musical and social aspects of artistic performance. None has satisfactorily been solved, and all are worth further research.

### Apparent absence of polyphony

Virtually no traditional polyphonic choral singing is heard in Vanuatu, and nobody can be sure if such a style was ever extant. This situation contrasts with parts of the Solomons and New Caledonia. Was vocal polyphony lost en route in the ancient migrations? Some singing in parallel thirds from Paama has been adopted into customary Ambae song-dances, like the *sawagoro* form, but Layard (1942) notated some parallel thirds in Atchin songs.

Few polyphonies occur in homogeneous ensembles, where combining sonorities are musically regulated, but many kinds of ensembles or orchestral musical spectacles, embodying principles of synchronization and specificity in the parts, demand a quasi-polyphonic performance. These principles are present in the music of log-idiophone ensembles, whose polyrhythms are ordered by contrasting pitches.

Some panpipe music in Espiritu Santo and northern Malakula may have been polyphonic, but it now appears to be forgotten. The ensemble music with *temes nainggol* heard by Deacon included singing and hand-action songs, which he thought were like part-songs, and in which the cylinders burst into musical pyrotechnics, with trills punctuated by hornlike notes on the small, high-pitched cylinders and backed by repeated low-pitched notes on the larger ones, interrupted now and then by scale-like passages and sometimes rising to a prolonged climax, in which all the cylinders merged into a drawn-out harmony or discord (Deacon 1934:391–392).

Simultaneous performance of different diapasonal (unison) songs and song-dances in quasi-random combinations may be heard on Ambae and Maewo, and in the Banks Islands (and possibly elsewhere), as competitive performances, or to cover the texts of taboo-related songs, creating a sort of polyphony of spectacle. One song, the culture-hero Tagaro's farewell to Maewo to sail in search of Mamalu, may be sung in two- or four-part canon, provided the singers are dancing. In an experimental session, the same singers, when seated, could not synchronize to their satisfaction a performance of that song. This is the sole example of the kind so far known outside local communities.

Ni-Vanuatu, the people of Vanuatu, sing four-part Christian hymns and choruses, from numeral notation or by ear, often with choral precision, so no cultural or inherent incapacity prevents them from singing polyphony. But nearly all the traditional musical forms heard today are monophonic. Was it always thus?

### Restricted distribution of upright log idiophones

In all of Oceania, upright log idiophones are unique to central Vanuatu. Tall—up to six meters above the ground—and vertically planted, they were once used in an area defined on the north by the Crowe Line and on the south by the strait between Efate and Erromango. Nineteenth-century pictures—the sketches of Miklouho-Maclay and early photographs—often show them in groups. Specimens from Efate, Malakula, and Ambrym have reached museums worldwide, though as artistic carvings, rather than practical musical instruments. Despite widespread interisland voyaging, the idea of making such instruments was not pursued outside central Vanuatu, neither in the neighboring northern islands nor in the southern ones, where log idiophones are not used, and the only struck idiophones are handheld bamboo tubes.

In border areas in the north of the distribution, some longish log idiophones may be used horizontally and then propped up for specific ritual purposes, as for women's ululations in South Pentecost circumcision-related ceremonies. In central Vanuatu, the wooden, upright, planted instruments are usually played with smaller, portable ones oriented horizontally. An exception to the north of the Crowe Line is Maewo, where for certain ritually special purposes performers hold portable wooden instruments upright while playing.

### Preference for counterclockwise directionality

This mystery parallels the frequency of the incidence of circular formations of dancing, wherein directional movement follows the right-hand side, and according to local explanation, it relates to ideas of male hardness versus female softness. The principle extends to the playing of log idiophones of all kinds, which performers always strike on the right-hand side, a position that is obvious when the instruments are standing upright. Horizontal log idiophones are turned with the slit facing a seated player, who strikes the upper lip. Such instruments are seen as if they were toppled trees with the roots (earth) to the right and the crown (sky) to the left: the upper lip conveys message; communications from the lower (left-hand) lip would be nonsense. Orientation of this kind is less observed today, thanks to acculturation. Younger ni-Vanuatu need to learn the idea of correct direction. Their need is shown in children's dances and games, where participants tolerate clockwise directionality, but only up to a certain age.

### Coincidence of scales and chains with pivots

The simultaneous presence of stepwise scales, chained thirds, and chained (pendulum) fourths with microtonal pivots, all found in a particular area (as Maewo), may well be unique in Oceania. It is unusual in traditional music, implying an ability to swap systems, and puts in doubt conventional notions of scale.

### Origins of singing and dancing

Ni-Vanuatu tell myths about the origins of songs, dances, and instrumental resources, but researchers have not studied these accounts comparatively. George Boe of Maewo believed that women anciently quieted suckling babies by rocking them at the breast, murmuring on an oscillating minor third. Then they stepped to and fro, in short-short-long rhythms, and gave vowels to the hummed sounds, so semitoneless five-tone tunes emerged,

> in the form now called *turimarani* 'bringing to light'. Men were pleased with the tunes the women had thus invented, and decided to add words to give meaning and significance, to make song. The act of adding texts thus created true song. . . . Now when you hear a solo flute melody, though you don't listen to an actual text, you know one is held in the player's mind, because the sounds can pull women to come and make love. When we hear a song whose words we can't follow, we sometimes know what place that song comes from by the melody, the women's invention. (Crowe 1992)

On the basis of this evidence and other information, it is possible to postulate matriality in melodies and patriality in texts, with a tacit local hierarchical contrast of nature and nurture.

## Renewable resources

People and musical instruments are renewable resources. Singing, dancing, and playing instruments are continually renewed through the application of mnemonic formulas. Nonliterate ni-Vanuatu have prodigious memories. George Boe of Maewo claimed to know more than a thousand songs and two hundred myths—and proceeded to record a great number of them. Rather than being conservative (unchanging), Vanuatu oral tradition is dynamic and adapting. An operating principle is to get away with breaking the rules—referring to a deeper rule, the capacity to reinvent, which the people much admire. Thus, over time, ritual forms can undergo gradual, but visible, alteration.

Repertories are retained in units, as songs with fixed texts; but their uses, as in ritual sets, may involve changing plans. Rigidity of form is more apparent where custom is in jeopardy, as with the development of a cash economy. Potential capacity to lead singing or dancing, also to be seen as creativity (as in contracts to perform), is as much valued as the possession of a stock of specific items (as in a repertory).

A common act preparatory to the revival of a song or dance or instrumental item is straightening it in the performer's mind. This process involves the revision of the text and the context appropriate to the coming performance. For these reasons, traditional music and dance is in a state of change, and the antiquity of an item is shown, not by any specific and notable shape (sonorous or gestural), but by contextual position.

What seem to be permanent are the formulas for rituals and the basic structures of their units, while superficial permutations, like styles of singing, may rapidly and radically alter. The presence or absence of polyphony or the steps of a favored scale are unreliable as marks of antiquity in a given repertory. Many children's songs have fanfarelike melodies using the tonic, third, and fifth of a major scale.

### Instrumental resources

With neolithic technology and natural materials, ni-Vanuatu produced many blown and struck instruments, but they produced only one or two plucked or scraped instruments. Most Vanuatu instruments are biodegradable because they are made of vegetable or animal material. Stones, shells, bones, ivory, and pottery are the most durable materials. The following list, a necessarily incomplete one, approximates indigenous classifications.

## Wood

For manufacturing log idiophones, empirically known relative hardnesses of trees determine the selection of species. In the upright area, trunks are dressed to the shape of regular cylinders; through a slit, they are hollowed out, and their surfaces are ornamentally carved. In the horizontal area, makers retain natural irregularities to exploit any resulting variations in pitch; these instruments usually bear carved ornamentation only on their handles.

Myths say a primordial woman invented log idiophones, but failed to produce sonorous meaning or beauty from them, so men took them over to show what could be done. Psychological implications of associating a slitted cavity and a phallic shape are not lost on the ni-Vanuatu.

Beaters (drumsticks) are selected for size, balance, and weight, from hardwoods or softwoods, or from the woody ends of coconut fronds. Vocal modifiers are made from softwoods, but in performance they become activated in association with blown bamboo tubes. A membrane drum (possibly resembling a kettledrum) has been reported from the Banks Islands and Maewo, but it is a secret instrument. The buttress roots of trees are carved into concussion plates, struck by bamboo tubes.

## Bamboo

Diameters and internodal lengths of different species permit varied products from small hand-sized panpipes to medium-sized multivoiced log idiophones of two or more nodes, too big to dance with, but handheld log idiophones of one node are frequently carried and played by lead dancers. The people of Maewo recall using a portable five-tone xylophone, but no playable specimen remains. In accompaniment to Ambae dances, split and dried lengths of bamboo, bundled on forked supports, may be struck by several players for a rattling rhythmic effect.

Bamboo aerophones are known everywhere in Vanuatu, in several guises: a V-notch, one-node, end-blown flute, having two or three holes near the bottom, played with arms and hands fully extended to the waist; a two-node, centrally blown "bamboo to satisfy two women at once," wherein the mistuning of a melody (caused by the slightly different lengths of nodes to the player's left and right), played the same on both ends, is joked about as "no two women are quite alike"; a 1.4-meter side-blown shoulder flute, formerly in use on Ambae; panpipes; and a side-blown trumpet, substituting for a conch.

People of Maewo and Mota Lava suspend notched bamboos from the upper branches of a banyan tree to whine in the wind as the voices of ghosts. People of Malakula and the Banks Islands used similar tubes for the same purpose (Deacon 1934). Stamped bamboo tubes, usually about 1.4 to 1.8 meters high, are sometimes tuned by the removal of internal nodes and the burning of holes or the cutting of notches.

## Leaves, stems, fruits, roots

On Mota, scraping dried umbrella-palm fronds on stone makes the sounds of tabooed spirits (*tamate*). To imitate fowl, Apma-speakers of Pentecost roll coconut-leaf fronds into a simple oboe. Handheld seed-pod rattles are used at Naviso. Ankle and coconut fiber rattles are made with *pangium* pods and coconut fiber. Ambrym's musical bow employs a vine cord. Humming tops are made from seed pods. Halved coconut shells are clopped on the ground in games. The use of shark rattles of cane loops strung with halved coconut shells came to Vanuatu via Santa Cruz.

*Shells and stones*

In the Torres and Banks groups, dancers use rattles of sea snails, cowrie, and other small shells. Conch trumpets are made from several genera in various sizes, blown through a hole in the apex or on the side. Stones and shells were carvers' tools for manufacturing struck log idiophones and struck plaques; stones may provide a base for making musical sounds by friction, and they may have percussive and concussive functions.

## Endangered resources

Under the pressures and demands of modern life, the indigenous human and environmental resources of Vanuatu are endangered. Knowledge of, and adaptation to, the particular biocultural environment of Vanuatu has depended on its oral and gestural transmission in song, dance, and ritual. In 1976, recognizing that old people brought up traditionally ("before school came") might take vital pieces of knowledge to the grave, the Vanuatu Cultural Centre established a conservation-oriented program, and by 1992 it was sponsoring forty-three staffers, who used audiovisual recording devices in villages throughout the country.

An array of material, much of it musical, awaits study; but academic analysis will not stop changes in rural areas—customary changes wrought by modernization, attrition, and homogenization. For export and tourists' consumption, the denaturization of music, dance, and art—and colorful rituals, like the land diving of South Pentecost—is increasing.

### Environmental resources

In Vanuatu, dangers from earthquakes and volcanic eruptions have always been present. As the global ozone layer depletes and temperatures rise, freeing and melting ice in polar glaciers, low-lying islands of Vanuatu, especially in the Torres Islands, risk inundation from a rising sea. Harvesting trees from virgin forests, mining mineral resources, and fishing in the ocean are diminishing.

A tendency to agricultural monoculture locally reduces the variety of resources available for fully enacting rituals. Cash cropping of coconuts on Western Ambae (Nduindui District) led to difficulties in raising pigs—a major factor in abandoning the huge pig-killing grade rites as early as the 1930s. But log-idiophone ensembles there have maintained a huge repertory; Radio Vanuatu uses one such item, *surara,* as its broadcast signature.

## Ritual life

Secret societies were once widespread in Vanuatu (Codrington 1891). Major events centered on the taking of grades: working within competitively organized systems, men killed tusked boars and became leaders (Layard 1942). Women sometimes also became leaders. Ceremonies of culmination provided spectacles permeated by dances and music, where log idiophones joined in the punctuation and accompaniment of orating and singing, often themselves accompanied by dancing. From birth to death, rituals marked important moments of life. On Maewo in the 1970s, at least six secret societies maintained special rites (Crowe 1994). These societies celebrated customary power or esoteric knowledge by sponsoring public spectacles, where they made elaborate displays of polyphonic music and dance (Crowe 1981).

Drinking kava, participating in the network of customary debts, and killing pigs for conspicuous consumption are anathema to fundamental Christian sects (though replaced with their own unacknowledged systems of debt), but the desire to mark with rituals the opening of new buildings and the completion of public works is entrenched in ni-Vanuatu minds. The singing of seemingly innocuous Christian choruses is heard everywhere, and string bands often perform subversive popular songs with deadly texts, so that, despite bland appearances, in the savor of customary life, the confession of the notion of "sorry"—fate, vulnerability—persists. To rediscover the persistence of tradition, curious persons must dig.

## Traditional musical systems

### Forms and structures

In most musical forms of music in Vanuatu, the idea of symmetry in design is omnipresent. A high degree of redundancy shows in the use of repetitions or balancing phrases in songs and instrumental pieces. Thus, verses and litanies are recurrent. They depend on the repetition of gestures, as in dance in a limited area, and the concepts of self-contained lines (textual) and phrases (melodic). A textual line or a melodic phrase may represent the formalization of moras and rhymes and the effects of physical constraint, such as the maximum duration of a breath. Iterative forms may result from a required ordering (as with lists of names) or the priority of significance, whether temporal (present against past) or ranked (higher against lower).

Free or continuing variation, comparable to Wagnerian-Schönbergian endless melody, is a formal tendency only in certain long narrative songs, such as the banned *tanurnwe* of Ambae, wherein the narrated or sung events may be fairly unpredictable, and transcribed melodies are difficult to segment because of an apparent lack of repetitions in lines. Here is a finesse of formal conceptualization. The *tanurnwe* deals with technical incest, locally defined as sexual relations between people of the same moiety whose degree of kinship is more distant than cross-cousinhood. Such songs are usually long, often ten minutes. Their melodies seem rather unrhythmic. Performers adopt a floppy, relaxed style, with a deliberate avoidance of marked posture. But these are felt to be highly affecting songs of "sorry," and their performances, partly because they are rare, attract profound local attention.

If one may take a holistic view, rather than a segmental one, rhetorical and narrative structure is also a determinant in the symmetrical structures of longer songs. To illustrate this, consider the *sawagoro,* the *bolo,* and the *lenga,* as these forms are sung and danced on Ambae, Pentecost, and Maewo. A different kind of *sawagoro* also exists, on Mota and the other Banks Islands (Codrington and Palmer 1896). Nondanced versions of all these songs are also performed.

### The sawagoro

The text of a *sawagoro* recounts a hero's (mis)adventures without naming him at first. In the penultimate stanza, a floral metaphor identifies him, and his proper name comes out only in the final verse. This plan employs suspense and rising excitement, paralleled by increasing speed and volume, until the final eruption.

A performance begins with the men stamping their feet (right feet on downbeats) and clapping on the halves of beats, about ninety-six to the minute, until someone launches the opening phrase of an item. The stanzas are typically quatrains, and lines are tossed among solo singers up to the point where the whole company cuts in with a repetition of that stanza, cued by a double clap, and the stanza may be repeated yet again if someone puts in another double clap. As the song proceeds, feet stamp harder, and the clapping gets louder. In culminating crescendos of choral repetition, the tempo accelerates, to finish at around 140 beats a minute.

Dancers form columns behind a leader, known as the great hawk. They are led into labyrinthine patterns, which unwind to finish neatly where they started. Some women and men peel off and "fly as hawks" around the line.

This form originated on the southwestern Maewo coast, where a female ghost inhabiting a nearly 2-meter-high phallus-like stone asked men to surround her, singing and dancing. For any performance today, men stand in a circle, or, if many are present, in concentric circles. Around the men, women and children may run in counterclockwise circles with their right arms raised, making joyful noises with hoots and cries. Participants hope that by looking smart they will later receive sexual favors from admiring bystanders.

A *sawagoro* session lasts from sundown to sunrise, so in about ten hours of dancing, one hundred fifty to two hundred different items are performed. For marriages and other events, shorter sessions occur during the daytime. The size of the repertory is impressive, especially when one adds other popular forms, such as *na bolo,* to the quantity of memorized knowledge ni-Vanuatu believe a performer ought to hold.

### The na bolo

The term *bolo* and its cognates, used in much of the area, can mean any of several specific forms of dancing. *Na polo,* the version of central Espiritu Santo, is sung by a stationary circle of men who with bamboo poles beat a struck plaque put over a hole, while women and children circle them counterclockwise. It appears related to the all-night Maewo session called *waswastarnhla* 'hitting the plate', in that the texts are richly varied, while the gestural aspect is rotating. *Bolo* songs of central Santo typically have five-tone tumbling strains, often in the form of versified epics.

The *bolo* of Ambae (*bolo tambae*) is now favored on Maewo, and finds its analog in South Pentecost bungee-jumping rites. In this form, repetitive movements, backward and forward in short-short-long steps, at the moderate pace of about eighty beats per minute, are done in moving lines. Around the singing, stepping company, well-wishers may make counterclockwise circles.

This dance is as much for women as *sawagoro* is for men. A principle of reciprocity seems to be shown in the sexual symbolism of the gestures: the *sawagoro* grasps, the *bolo* pierces. This interpretation, if expressed in public, is shocking to many ni-Vanuatu, though in private they often accept it. Throughout the night to celebrate a wedding on Ambae (where custom still counts), the bride's line will dance *na bolo tambae* and the groom's line *sawagoro.* Persons of either sex may perform *na bolo,* and groups are usually mixed.

### The na lenga

The foregoing examples may illustrate principles like yin and yang, but what of a form where directionality is unclear, as with the form of a wriggling, coiling serpent? Dances called *na lenga* are performed on Malakula and many points north. They are performed as long cycles. Chosen for timeliness and appositeness, their songs have similar rhythmic and textual features, but sometimes a narrative plan lies behind the ordering of the items, which superficially tend to run on and on, but may fundamentally reveal a mythic continuity.

At the start, the dancers form several columns behind a leader, known as the great hawk. Keeping in line, they are led into labyrinthine patterns, which unwind to finish back neatly where they started. The dance seems to contradict the principle of counterclockwise directionality, but perhaps it goes this way and that intentionally, to end up "as you were," or to neutralize all directional pulls. *Na lenga* and serpentine symbolism sometimes serve as a medicine for technical incest. The dance may be done by both sexes. It is sometimes performed by an all-female company. Some women and men have the right to peel off the group and "fly as hawks" around the phalanx, not seeming to obey any obvious directionality during such flights.

### Pitch

Conventional classification by scales shows a familiar pattern: fanfare-like triadic melodies; high incidence of semitoneless four- and five-tone scales; and widespread usage of six- and seven-tone scales, which effectively map the tempered diatonic scale. Chained thirds, with alternations of minor and major, are frequent in sets of three intervals on four notes, as A–C–E–G. Some South Pentecost bungee-jumping *bolo* (*gol bolo*) have chains of four thirds on five notes, with two lower narrow thirds, as F♯–A–C–E–G with F♯ 25 cents sharp and A 12.5 cents sharp, and C a central scalar pivot.

The presence of chained perfect fourths is notable on Maewo, where a clear pivot occurs around a semitone step, sometimes seemingly cut into tones 25 cents apart, but this conclusion needs testing for emic status. This situation exists alongside the scales mentioned above. Because few instruments other than flutes have fixed pitches, these tones refer mainly to songs. Maewo is said to have a V-notch flute adapted to chains of fourths of the kind mentioned.

Chains of distances exceeding one-tone intervals puts the notion of steps into doubt, especially when the intervals become as large as fourths, giving an impression of aural pendular motion. One might speak of melodic templates. Research is needed on whether steps and gaps are emic in ni-Vanuatu musical cognition, assuming some real distinctions are waiting to be discovered.

### Rhythm and tempo

Body-based binary pulsation dominates Vanuatu dancing, subdividing in twos or threes. Solo song, without regular gestures, sung in a sitting position, tends toward additive groupings in combinations of twos and threes, in parlando rubato. In passages involving a six-beat measure, some log-idiophone pieces of Ambae and Raga play with a two-against-three relationship. As Raymond Clausen has demonstrated (personal communication) for Walarano log-idiophone-raising rituals, Malakula ensembles employ elaborate codings for long sets of rhythms, which on first hearing may seem random. Sets of rhythms are often in ostinatos as extensible subsets. Some unpredictable rhythmic combinations occur in crossover passages from one subset to another.

In northern and central Vanuatu, a wide range of tempo is in use, from adagio to presto. Controlled acceleration is frequent; less often, slowdowns occur. Some songs may be sung slowly in a briefly variable tempo in one context, but sung or danced quickly in a steady tempo in another: in the first, text dominates, and the singer says he or she is "pulling the song" or the text; in the second, the spectacle dominates.

Elasticity of rhythm may be heard on solo handheld log idiophones. Performers take liberties for the exact duration of long notes. At the ends of lines and finals in chorally sung hymns, a dominant singer uses a glottal stop or a brief downward slide to signal the ends of prolongations. Especially in rural areas, ni-Vanuatu show as much rhythmic skill, flexibility, and invention as they show to compositional creativity.

### Timbre

Aesthetic principles apply to preferred sonorities, as in the quality of the resonance of log idiophones, the preferred manner of singing (variable according to district and repertory), and a player's skill in sounding a flute. No systematic description and analysis of ni-Vanuatu timbral preferences has yet been attempted, but it should probably be construed with local ways of appreciating the overall excellence of a performance.

### Ensemble

Despite allowed variables, mostly in rhythm and pitch, the idea of being together, in sync, and of performing with good style is important. The people of Mota had more than three hundred terms of critical appraisal and appreciation. Examples: *liñai* 'sound, voice, taste, way of life, manner'; *nunuai* 'the mental impression of sound or force . . . taken to be real'; *sito*' 'the cry in the *mago* to mark the change in the song which the dancers are singing to themselves'; *qaui* 'knee, a turn in a song', thus *qau as*' 'be behind at the turn' (Codrington and Palmer 1896).    —PETER CROWE

## MOTA, BANKS ISLANDS

In the Banks Islands of northernmost Vanuatu, Mota forms a triangle with Vanua Lava and Mota Lava. It is accessible only by boat. A steep, 150-meter mountain, rising like the peak of a sombrero, dominates its center. On a low plateau encircling it, people live and garden. They speak Mota and understand some English. Mariu Village, where I obtained most of the data discussed below, is populated by the sons of one woman and their families. The sons run the village, keep order, and oversee activities of the local Anglican parish.

Music and dance marks the annual celebration of Pentecost (Whitsunday). On 4 June 1995, a three-hour service began the event. As two men at one side of the sanctuary struck solid posts and a bamboo idiophone, four pairs of boys dressed in white came down the aisle. The first pair carried feathered sticks, associated with local dances; the next pairs brought the elements of communion: first the wafers, and then the wine and chalice. The boys wore feather headdresses. Around their ankles, seed-pod rattles sounded as they stepped. Bowing low the whole time, they progressed to the altar. After the service, a feast for hundreds of people, featuring yams and cow, was laid out on the grassy mall that centers the village. After a speech by Chief Dean, women prepared for their dances. Individual villages performed separately.

### Traditional dancing

The generic local term for a dance is *lakalaka*. At feasts, women's dancing (*lega*, pronounced /leŋa/) usually precedes men's; songs sung for it may be sung at other times.

#### Women's dancing

For a typical sequence of dances, strokes of a bamboo idiophone set a pace of about 120 beats a minute. To this beat, girls and women begin walking. Singing begins, and the percussion changes to a motif transcribable as two sixteenths and an eighth per beat. The dancers stress downbeats by accenting one footfall. To finish, the singer sustains the vocable *hē* while the dancers run in place, doubling their tempo. With each step, they scrape their feet in a backward kick, keeping alert for the singer's staccato utterance of *hē*, which signals the cadence; on hearing this cue, all shout the vocables *ai yai yo* on the next two beats, and the dance ends [see COMPOSITIONAL PROCESSES: Vanuatu].

Sometimes the girls weave in serpentine fashion, in single file; or they present themselves in two lines facing each other, alternately approaching and retreating; or they form a tight pack, circling the lead singer—who calls out directions, at times ordering a backward looping in the serpentine file, or a reversal of direction when the entire group is circling. Though admired when done energetically and without error, these performances are not taken so seriously as men's, nor do these women—busy mothers, gardeners, homemakers—have much time to invest in it. For them, it is fun and entertainment, though observers wait to ridicule any flaws in performance. It abodes no mysteries and makes few demands on its audience.

### Men's dancing

Men's dancing is usually called *lakalaka sala goro* 'tabu-place dancing', referring to where men prepare to perform. Only those who have joined the men's society may participate there. Men's songs and dances (*kokoa,* also denoting the hats the men wear while dancing) are performed on special days in accordance with the calendar of Christian saints' days. Precontact ceremonies were sources for these activities.

Men of the host village do not perform. Only guests dance. An unseen crier announces their entrance. They approach backward, with a demeanor of respect and deference, which they sometimes intensify by crouching and stepping extremely slowly. All is quiet until men start striking a wooden plaque and bamboo idiophones.

In the festivities of 1995, the first and final men's dances were canceled because they had not received proper respect when last performed. The chief decided their performance would be suspended for four years. Linguist Dan Garst has described the dances of an event of 1994, and a recording of it has been studied. These are what men of Tuqetap Village performed; the order of the dances is probably the standard order of men's dances at any feast.

1. *Mai* (pronounced /ŋmai/) 'sea-dwelling snake' is so named because of white and black rings painted on the dancers' legs, the markings of the snake. Beating on solid posts and singing precede the entry. The dancers enter backward, moving slowly, and then kneel. The singing for all dances is responsorial. Cadences have a contrasting percussive rhythm.

2. *Marawa* 'spider' is danced to rhythms of a struck bamboo, mounted on two supporting sticks so the percussionist can play standing. Dancers carry in one hand a three-pronged wand, ornamented with white feathers.

3. *Tamat memegel,* said to have come from Gaua Island, has a name related to spirits or ghosts, but the same term can denote the hats the dancers wear. The text is archaic and untranslatable, and its meaning is secret. Dancers enter the arena in parallel lines. Crouching, they move backward (figure 2). Finally, the beat changes. They rise and turn to dance. It is a moment of high drama when these men suddenly face the audience, stern and magnificent. In the last section of the dance, they mime the paddling of canoes, the action with which they exit.

4. *Nonou* is identifiable by the piercing yell of a male crier. In two parallel lines, the dancers face forward when they enter. They go around the idiophones in a circle, which gradually widens. The yell, which seems to emanate from nowhere, gives cues for reversing direction and performing other movements. The crier's skill in striking an E a tenth above middle C after intervals of silence and physical exertion is impressive. He signals the end of the dance with the pattern (in equal beats) note–rest–note–rest–note–rest–note–note–note. From a wide circle, the dancers break away into a line and exit.

FIGURE 2    Performing *tamat memegel* on Mota, crouching men slowly move backward. Photo by Dan Garst, 1995.

FIGURE 2    Performing *tamat memegel* on Mota, crouching men slowly move backward. Photo by Dan Garst, 1995.

5. *Maptoa* refers to weeding and cutting grass. The dance is regarded as music for coming and going, a sociable affair: the music continues, though some may tire out and others join in. Unlike the other so-called men's dances, women may participate. This dance has a different cadence: *e-e-e-e!* in a crescendo, and an accented *a-a-a-a!* in a decrescendo.

### Songs without dancing

Solo songs often cover one's dreaming about a deceased relative or friend. The crashing of waves against the reef is a frequent background for songs—not surprisingly, since this sound is a trait of island life. Some songs recount legends. Some treat historic events, as when a seaplane landed near the shore during World War II. Several speak of seaside caves. Expressions of hurt and rivalry are important; lyrics mention moonlight, birds, nearby islands, chickens, and pretty girls.

A typical solo song consists of two phrases, A and B, with others optional. Phrase A is varied, and phrase B is more likely to remain constant. Men's dance-songs have two contrastive phrases, though they may add several new phrases. Cadential patterns sometimes feature a minor third ascending and descending on the vocable *hē*. Other songs may cadence in a men's grunted *uh-uh-uh-uh,* with the mouth open or the lips closed.

Some indigenous songs have been adapted for use in Christian worship. The liturgical format, introduced by Anglican missionaries in the late 1800s, remains that of the Church of Melanesia. A song about flying a kite off the cliff and calling for wind to come and lift it is the melodic source of the Sanctus (figure 3).

### Tonal analysis

Of the men's dance-songs investigated, two patterns emerge. The first, $N_1$, has an obligatory nucleus of tonal center and a major second and third above it, with no optional tones, formulaically: $N_1 = TC + M2H + M3H$. This nucleus is accompanied by either of two sets of additional tones. The second pattern, with a five-tone nucleus, emerges in men's songs recorded by Garst in 1994: $N_2 = M6L + M3L + M2L + TC + m3H$. All these songs were old.

Women's songs may also be sung by men, but men never dance women's dances. Some women's songs are traditional ("custom music"), but others are recently composed. Some intervals—tonal center and four tones above it (major second, minor

FIGURE 3    The melody of a Mota song about a kite, serving for the Sanctus. Transcription by Vida Chenoweth.

third, perfect fourth, perfect fifth)—are common to men's and women's tonal inventories. In most women's songs, one to four tones occur below tonal center. The most common are a major second or a minor third, or both. A perfect fourth below tonal center is rare, and peripheral tones—such as fifths and sixths—usually progress to and from an adjacent tone.

In a documented contemporary setting of a traditional song, a leading tone appears, as does a perfect fourth above tonal center. These features reveal European influence, causing a change from a five-tone inventory to a major scale. The perfect fourth above tonal center occurs in the present-day singing of two older women, Ada and Legas; the former sang a song dreamed by Noel, with archaic words.

### Tonal movement

Men's and women's melodies have leaps in a single direction, such as two fourths ascending in men's songs, or a fourth and a minor third, after which, in both cases, the direction reverses. No leaps wider than a perfect fourth occur. The most consecutive tones in a single direction are five (E–D–B–A–F♯) in men's songs, but six (G♭–E♭–D♭–C–B♭–A♭) in women's. Ascending movement, with three tones in a common direction in men's songs and four in women's, is more restrictive than descending. In men's songs, a melody seldom crosses tonal center, but such crossing occurs frequently in other songs. When a melody crosses tonal center, it usually returns immediately to it.

In men's songs with $N_1$ nucleus, tonal center precedes any tone within the leap of a perfect fourth. A major second, a major third, and a perfect fourth above tonal center proceed to any tone above tonal center, whereas a minor third below tonal center proceeds only to tonal center, or to a fifth below. Peripheral tones a fifth or sixth below tonal center proceed to adjacent tones only. In men's songs with $N_2$ nucleus, tones move freely, with two exceptions: no crossing of tonal center, and a minor sixth below tonal center is approached and left only by a major third below.

### Musical instruments

The people of Mota dance to the sounds of rattles and percussion idiophones. All are important to men's dances.

### Rattles

Rattles are worn on dancers' ankles as part of the costuming. They come in two varieties.

1. Rattles of dried seeds from *Pangium edule*, a tropical vine.—The pods are flat and sectional. Each is about 3 decimeters long and 1 wide. It has four sections, each of which houses a fig-shaped seed, whose shell, though hard, is cut with a sharp knife. The pulp is scraped away, and a hole is burned through the top edge for stringing the seeds.

2. Rattles made from sea-urchin spines.—These are spikes of rocklike hardness, the size of a 1-decimeter nail, thicker at one end. They are grooved at the thicker end, to be tied with a cord and bundled together. These rattles produce much higher pitches than those made from seeds.

### Percussive ensemble

Mota dancing requires an ensemble of percussion idiophones, centered in the arena and decorated by branches and transplanted bananas. The branches bear fruits the size and color of oranges. At least five players participate, two or three on a struck plaque, one or more on struck bamboo idiophones, and two on a struck log idiophone.

1. Struck plaque (*taqasrah*, sometimes pronounced /ta'asrav/, 'earthdrum').—According to Garst, the word *taqas* denotes a pit dug into the ground, as that made for cooking. The hole is covered with a lid made from the buttress root of a tree (*Elon vitiense*), said to be the largest in Vanuatu. Men secure the lid in place by stuffing leaves around its edges and driving stakes around it. Standing, players beat rhythms on it with solid wooden posts 1.2 to 1.5 meters long and 7 to 10 centimeters wide.

2. Struck bamboo idiophone (*vat ge uro* 'hollowed log', with *vat* a shortened form of *vatiu* 'log').—This is played in alternating strokes with two short sticks. Considered an expedient substitute for a log idiophone, it joins the latter for men's dances. It can easily be made in a few minutes. Players mount it on supporting posts so they can stand to play it.

3. Struck log idiophone (*vat ge uro*).—Though called by the same name as the preceding, the log idiophone is larger and much harder to make. It also is mounted for playing.

—VIDA CHENOWETH

## SOUTHERN AREA

Vanuatu's five southernmost inhabited islands—Tanna, Erromango, Anatom, Aniwa, Futuna—in 1989 had a population of 22,423, of which 90 percent lived on Tanna. The languages of Tanna, Anatom, and Erromango are a subfamily of Oceanic languages (Lynch 1978). Speakers of Proto–South Vanuatu arrived three thousand to four thousand years ago. Aniwa and West Futuna are Polynesian outliers. Available evidence of human occupation on West Futuna dates back about seventeen hundred years, and oral-historical evidence recounts continuing accidental or deliberate voyaging and contact between southern Vanuatu and West Polynesia (Irwin 1992).

Cultures of southern Vanuatu differ from those of the rest of Vanuatu. Horizontal and upright log idiophones, the latter a hallmark of central Vanuatu, are absent in the south. Mythology, social structure, and musical styles suggest Polynesian borrowings. Mwatikitiki, the Polynesian Mautikitiki, is an important Tannese spiritual figure. Unlike northern Vanuatu, where people pound or grind kava, the Tannese process it by chewing the root, as did most Polynesians. Tanna has a version of dual chieftainships (sacred and oratorical), and a moiety system possibly borrowed from or modeled after that of Polynesia.

### Tannese musical performances

Tannese ritual-exchange festivals feature dancing and singing, which take either of two principal forms. *Nupu* 'dance, song' are circular dances, performed at life-cycle

FIGURE 4    Men of Tanna dance in a circle at the Pacific Festival of Arts, Port Moresby. Photo by Adrienne L. Kaeppler, 1980.

feasts and other exchanges (figure 4). Six other genres of dance, and accompanying songs, are associated with *nakwiari* (or *nekoviar*), large, irregularly organized festival exchanges. These dances are *toka* (which in touristic writing have become eponymous with *nakwiari*), *nau*, *kosusiva*, *kouasi*, *nirup*, and *kauas*. Four of these are line dances, with deft mimetic movements. Dancers in all the festival genres wield clubs or other implements.

### Nupu

The dances and songs of *nupu* celebrate events. To mark personal life-cycle points—birth, naming, first words, first haircut, circumcision, first menses, marriage, death—families may exchange food and other goods. People also dance *nupu* at annual firstfruits exchanges and *nieri* festivals, wherein two communities exchange foods magically associated with fertility-promoting stones.

Exchange of goods occurs typically in the afternoon at *imwarim*, ritually important circular clearings, which serve as grounds for meeting, drinking kava, and dancing. At dusk, men prepare and drink some of the kava exchanged that day. When kava intoxication abates, singing and dancing begin. The hosts and guests dance in turn, each team singing its local songs. Hosts may invite one or more teams from neighboring communities to dance. Each team performs in sequence while others rest, but near dawn, all teams may crowd onto the arena.

Everyone on Tanna dances *nupu*, but in many local varieties. Famous southern varieties are *katiham*, *iapwas*, *kepui*, *kesa*, *kurkurau*, *kwatukros*, *nupu ikou* 'crooked dance', *suvirpig*, and *tarakini*. These are counterclockwise dances. (In one *kouasi*, each man, while walking backward, rotates clockwise.) Men form a circular mass; women, typically in pairs, perform on the circumference. The mass of men contracts and expands, rotating counterclockwise, while the periphery of skipping women spins. This procedure echoes Tannese spatial aesthetics: the center connotes masculinity, culture, high status, and speech; the periphery evokes femininity, nature, lower status, and silence.

A *nupu* begins with a formulaic opening, *katiham* (this word also denotes formulaic closings): a clap, a pause, two claps, a pause, and two claps. Then the core of dance begins. It lasts about forty to 110 claps, and has a pause and a final clap. Male dancers, massed in the center of the clearing, next stamp the ground three times. The

A festival begins as women march across the arena. Each team sings songs that match the number of pigs their community will exchange. To determine how many pigs must die, people in the audience count songs.

circle expands, men stamp, and the circle contracts. After two stamps, a dozen or so claps, a pause, a clap, a pause, two stamps, and two claps, the circle expands and contracts a final time. With hands clasped, each man for about fifteen beats assertively swings his elbows from side to side, and then claps twice. The dancers' line begins to circle counterclockwise. Dancers skip for ten beats, clap twice, and stamp four to six beats. The *nupu* then ends in a formulaic closing: men trot to keep up; women, on the periphery, move even faster. Terminal circling lasts thirteen claps; on the final one, dancers sing the *kova* 'babbling, humming', a two-note rising glide on the vocable *hui*; they stamp thrice, pause, and end with a double stamp.

Songs have structural connections with these movements. A typical *nupu* lasts 145 to 200 beats. Before the first stamp, its tempo proceeds at about 120 beats per minute; afterward, it slows to about ninety-five. A *nupu* turn usually lasts one and a half to two minutes. A short *nupu* song may occupy only one turn, but many have multiple stanzas; with each stanza, dancing begins anew. The singing for each turn begins with the final verse of the preceding turn. (If in one turn the people sing verses 1–4, they resume in the next by singing 4–7.) The formulaic opening occurs only with the first stanza of songs; turns that accompany other stanzas omit most of the *katiham.*

During the first *nupu* turn, men hum the melody. This is the spirit or shadow (*nanumun*) of the song. They begin singing lyrics (*nipran* 'body') during the second turn, but in this and later turns, words and humming alternate; humming occurs at the beginning, again when dancers swing their elbows, and at the end, when the circle rotates faster. The women's part and voices complement the men's. Women join in after men's initial nasalized *nanumun,* and they join the song's *nipran*; in *nanumun* sections, they outline the melody with a clear, melodic vocable *e-e-e* above male nasal humming.

After one or two minutes of rest between turns, almost any adult male dancer may begin a song. Men with extensive musical and textual knowledge ordinarily control the selection. Someone starts a *nanumun,* and men who recognize it join in, with women following. Many women are musically knowledgeable; their voices may predominate, particularly in little-known songs. Dancers who do not know texts may hum. At a performance, usually lasting from about 10:00 P.M. to 7:00 A.M., each team may perform more than a hundred stanzas—about twenty an hour, over a four- or five-hour stretch. Individual dancers may participate, given links of kinship and friendship, or abundant energy, in several community teams. Everyone who has received goods exchanged that day must dance, as must those from communities where the event's hosts have visited to dance at their own exchange-related feasts.

### Festivals (nakwiari)

To celebrate longstanding linkages between areas, Tannese communities organize *nakwiari* (Guiart 1956:17–36). To balance a previous exchange, often several generations ago, wherein today's hosts had been yesterday's guests, one locality invites a second to participate. The hosts, who dance *nau* and *kosusiva,* and the guests, who dance *toka* and *kauas,* recruit other communities to participate, so a festival may attract more than a thousand dancers, male and female. *Nau,* symbolically being female, feeds the gathered crowds; *toka* is male. During the main exchange, each person who has danced *nau* presents a pig and a large kava root to a guest who has danced *toka.* About four weeks later, dancers of *toka* reciprocate with pigs and kava, but enough debt purposefully remains to require more festivals.

The three festival-defining male dances (*toka, nau, kosusiva*) and the female *nirup* are line dances. (*Kouasi* is a circular dance of hosts and guests.) In *toka* and *nau,* dancers form pairs of facing parallel lines; in *kosusiva,* dancers form single files that march across the grounds. During festivals, men and women perform separately. The *toka* also occurs on West Futuna (Thomas and Kuautoga 1992), where it may have diffused from East Futuna (Crowe 1993:96). It may therefore be a Tannese borrowing from Polynesian voyagers. In southern Tannese mythology, festivals started in (now depopulated) Iankahi, a ridge near the island's active volcano, on the island's east coast, from which West Futuna and Aniwa are visible. People call festival teams canoes. As each team brings its pigs into the arena, a vine encircling it represents its gunwales. For a *kouasi,* three men stand next to the dancers' circle, representing steersmen.

After hosts have scheduled a festival, teams begin six or more months' practice. Members must not miss rehearsals, and must undertake ritual taboos, including the avoidance of sexual activity. As the date of the festival approaches, rehearsals move from one kava-drinking ground to the next, along ritual-exchange relationships (*suatuk* 'roads'), which lead to the site of the exchange. Festivals spark collateral exchanges that strengthen the island's network of "roads."

A festival begins as women dance *nirup,* marching in lines across the arena. They heartily beat rectangular baskets filled with dried leaves. In some performances, women kneel in lines; in others, they portray geometric figures: squares, stars, and parallel lines, viewed from above. Women elaborately paint their faces and wear barkcloth skirts, brightly colored with imported dyes (figure 5). Each team of women sings songs that match the number of pigs their community will exchange. To determine how many pigs must die, people in the audience count songs.

FIGURE 5   Women of Tanna perform a *nirup* during the first day of a *nakwiari* festival on Tanna. Photo by Lamont Lindstrom, 1978.

Women dance through the following night, but rowdy groups of men dancing *kauas* join them. This is a time of license. Male dancers try to force their way through and disrupt the *nirup* dancers' lines, protected by a ring of male guards. Some men stand near the women and purposefully sing off key. Some grab at women and mimetically hint at trying more. Carrying branching clubs (*tapau,* many carved into phalluses), some shout obscenities, like "my testicles!"

At dawn, teams of *toka* dancers, heralded by blasts of conch trumpets, move onto the arena. They carry feathered poles (*kaio apomus*) up to 6 meters long, made of the central ribs of coconut fronds lashed together and decorated with chicken and harrier feathers. When the guests have finished dancing *toka,* hosts enter the grounds to dance *nau* and *kosusiva.*

As *toka* dancers perform, they carry *nesko,* hook-shaped implements, 1.5 meters long, made from the trunk and root of a small tree, dyed white, yellow, or black. *Nau* dancers carry bundles of wild cane (*mai nig*), or 1.8-meter lengths of bamboo they twirl and pound on the ground. *Kosusiva* dancers carry crescent-shaped clubs (*tinaprau* or *kwaruvinari*), often painted with abstract or pictorial designs, as of birds or fish; in the dance, they slap them together and flick them back and forth. During *nirup,* some women may dance with *tinaprau.*

Besides *kauas,* the four other men's dances (*toka, kouasi, nau, kosusiva*) involve mimetic actions by dancers who, by ones or twos, present in pantomime the theme of the song the others are singing. Often, one dancer emerges first and "pulls" a mimer from the group, as if he were a fish. Many mimers are young men or boys. They imitate a wide range of actions, including landslides, seabirds flying, cocks fighting, fishing, boxing, cutting grass, fetching water, and gathering honey. Movements during pantomime consists of rapid hops, three or four on one leg and then the other, as a mimer circles around the massed dancers. In the pantomime, dancers sometimes use their club. To the audience, they toss gifts, including tapa belts (*toti,* which formerly held up men's penis-wrapping fibers), chewing gum, cigarettes, and matches.

### Other contexts and genres

Of other Tannese dances, one carries the part-Bislama name *tanis asori* 'big dance', suggesting twentieth-century origins. A circular dance, it accentuates rotations and circular contractions, and sometimes substitutes for *nupu.* In *tieksas* 'Texas', a risqué dance, which originated between 1942 and 1945, men and women dance in couples. More common is free-form dancing to string-band music, with males and females performing in separate areas.

At New Year's celebrations (*ponane,* from French *bonne année*), groups of singers visit friends and kin in neighboring villages. They enter a village singing, and perform Christian and secular songs. They sometimes specify one person as the recipient of their performance. In return, hosts give money and other gifts, and pat visitors' faces with talcum powder. During this foolery, singers try not to miss a beat, despite the ludicrousness of being dusted white.

The Tannese are expert yodelers. Walking in the forest or working in the gardens, men (and sometimes women) yodel to attract the attention of others, who may be several ravines away. Men yodel just for the fun of making themselves heard. Yodels are distinctive, though not personally unique; by sound alone, people can easily identify a yodeler.

### Tannese music as history

Each area has a musical treasury, which serves as an historical archive, preserving ancestral names and deeds. Copyrights or patents protect valued knowledge of all sorts, including songs, myths, histories, genealogies, herbal cures, and artistic motifs. Dancers need permission to sing *nupu* belonging to neighbors.

Songs store information of personal names, places, and events. On West Futuna, songs chronicle "experiences and values, which therefore remain as watermarks in people's emotional recollection" (Thomas 1992:229). Tannese songs chronicle experiences of World War II (Lindstrom and White 1993). Songs stand within cultural contexts of common understanding and mythic narrative, to which people turn for elucidating lyrical elisions and metaphors. Legends and stories often encapsulate songs, as characters in a narrative sing about important topics. To knowledgeable people, songs say just enough to cue appreciation of their subjects.

Tannese songs also recount journeys. These geographic songlines, as Bruce Chatwin (1987) has called them, are common in many Pacific musics. Lyrics may link sites that have meaning within a cultural landscape, as in these *nupu* verses:

Riskamter ia tina imwamiaha,
Mipi irapw pehe Ripunuman,
Muvehe muveraha, men mivi teter i,
Mamesi nari nehev rapomus,
Mipi irapw pehe Iakurakau mata kwanamrig.
Narari mirkuri irapw *gavman rod* uei Iakwarumanu,
Ierema ruta i mamakurkure ikin uei Iankuru.
Tik murkurau mavahi uta paha misansani.
Hinarari mesi iraha me mhuvin mho *kona,*
Minamrai uvehe uta kwanpri nahakw.
Havehe irapw; mhamini mhiuvare.
Rinua, "Iou me nepwun, iakinapou.
Pwah suvin pam a mhirukwi irapw nari uei Isiui
Iankwanau apomus, Nari Iamnesu, Ianekomatua,
Iankwaneinipik Rerin."
Mivi teter i mhipi irapw pehe.
Kasavavehe mhino *trabol,* mhamakurkure tukwe ia rukwasikar.
*Pos* rinamakwein *polis* me hinamo *rere.*


He begins at your land,
And comes through Ripunuman,
Walks seaward, goes on level ground,
Follows the long valley,
Comes out at Iakurakau, but there is nobody there.
Turns and comes up to the government road at Iakwarumanu,
Where the ancestral spirit rose to sit there at Iankuru.
Dick passed by, and lifted up his ax and showed this.
They turned and followed together and made the corner,
And began to climb up the small hill.
They emerge; they say they go landward.
He says, "My friends, I'm tired.
Let's all go through to Isiui
Iankwanau apomus, Nari Iamnesu, Ianekomatua,
Iankwaneinipik Rerin."
They walk along on level ground, and come through.
They come because of the problem, and are sitting in the sun.
The boss begins to call the police to make ready.

This song follows Dick and his neighbors down trails that link claimed sites. Each time performers sing it in public, they reassert these claims. Many in an audience, understanding its allusions, would recall the events it reports. During disputes about ownership of land, a debater may sing *nupu* that document his claims.

## Musical instruments

Tannese dancing seldom requires sounds from musical instruments. As dancers sing, they clap their hands and stamp their feet. The soils of Tanna, being volcanic, reverberate with almost ringing tones, and the island itself serves as an immense drum, on which people dance. *Reri* 'voice' also denotes 'heart, desire, emotion, innards'.

### Idiophones

In certain dances, men carry clubs and sticks, which they strike together and on the ground. Women dancing *nirup* beat their right hands in unison on rectangular baskets filled with dried leaves. *Nirup* is the only local dance that accompanies instrumental sounds.

People—often children—make lamellaphones from the leaves and central spines of coconut fronds. In 1923, Felix Speiser described these instruments on neighboring Futuna (1991:379). That the Tannese call them by the Bislama word *susap* suggests they may be a recent diffusion to Tanna. Speiser also located horizontally held drums on Tanna. In the late 1990s, the Tannese did not use them; nor did they use rattles, which elsewhere in Vanuatu dancers wear on their arms and legs.

### Aerophones

From bamboo, people make raft panpipes (*tarheinau*) and flutes (Kwamera *kwataratara*, Lindstrom 1986). They sometimes use the former to practice tunes (*Traditional Music of Vanuatu* 1980 has an example). Typically, panpipes have seven, or sometimes eight or more, tubes, tuned to scales running within an octave. The lower end of each tube is closed.

End-blown bamboo flutes about 75 centimeters long, with two or three holes in the lower section, are rarer. Some families have rights to flute-played melodies associated with summoning ancestral spirits, who may inspire further compositions. Unlike flutes from northern Vanuatu, Tannese instruments are not commonly incised or otherwise decorated.

To signal the start of dancers' rehearsals and other important events, men play side-blown trumpets (*kisip*), made from shells of *Charonia tritonis* and *Bursa* spp. Trumpet blasts are ubiquitous from May to September, the circumcision season. After undergoing the surgery, boys (five to twelve years old) are secluded in special houses roughly constructed near *imwarim*. They ritually bathe twice a day in local springs and pools. Along trails in the forest, they and their attendants walk in a single file. Several blow conchs in sequence. The sound warns women and girls, who must not look upon recently circumcised boys until they officially rejoin society—an event marked by an exchange of goods, a feast, and a dance, linking each boy's family with his mother's brothers' families. In conch ensembles, three to five conchs are usually played in turn like a fanfare. On reaching the site of the ritual bath, the conchs harmonize on long chords.

In the 1800s, the Tannese played trumpets for medical purposes. They believed illness stemmed from malevolent sorcery, based on contagious magic. A sick man called another

> to blow a shell, a large conch or other shell, which, when perforated and blown, can be heard two or three miles off. The meaning of it is to implore the person

who is supposed to be burning the sick man's rubbish and causing all the pain to stop burning; and it is a promise as well that a present will be taken in the morning. (Turner 1884:321)

By the 1980s, the Tannese had abandoned musically accompanied techniques of sorcery.

## String bands

Tanna has many string bands, formed by teenagers who play guitars and ukuleles. Bands may play together for years. Singing with these bands, males often use falsetto, recalling traditional yodeling. To celebrate a circumcision or other life-cycle ceremony of exchange, a string band may furnish music, to which celebrants dance all night. Steps associated with this music are free and individual. Men and women usually dance in separate areas. Only the most avant-garde dance *tieksas,* in mixed-sex couples. Alcohol replaces kava as the drink of choice.

Songsmiths rely on inspiration to compose string band–accompanied songs in a local language or Bislama. These include songs poking fun at troublemakers and songs commenting on national events (elections, censuses), burdensome taxes, and AIDS-awareness drives. In studios in Vila, some of Tanna's most popular bands, including Noisy Boys (1982) and Nahabau (n.d.), have produced commercial cassettes.
—LAMONT LINDSTROM

## REFERENCES

Bitter, Maurice, ed. N.d. *Musique Folklorique du Monde: Les Nouvelles-Hébrides.* Musidisc 30 CV 1273. LP disk and commentary.

Chatwin, Bruce. 1987. *The Songlines.* London: Cape.

Clausen, Raymond. 1958. "A Musicological Study of the Layard Collection of Recorded Malekulan Music in Its Sociological and Ritual Setting." Bachelor's thesis, Oxford University.

Codrington, R. H. 1885. *The Melanesian Languages.* Oxford: Oxford University Press.

———. 1891. *The Melanesians: Studies in Their Anthropology and Folklore.* Oxford: Oxford University Press.

Codrington, R. H., and J. Palmer. 1896. *Dictionary of the Language of Mota, Sugarloaf Island, Banks Islands, with a Short Grammar.* London: Society for the Propagation of Christian Knowledge.

Crowe, Peter. 1981. "Polyphony in Vanuatu." *Ethnomusicology* 25(3):419–432.

———. 1990. "Dancing Backwards?" *The World of Music* 32(1):84–98.

———. 1992. "La naissance du chant à Maewo: étude d'une musique mélanésienne." *Cahiers de musiques traditionalles* 5:183–204.

———. 1993. Review of Thomas and Kuautoga 1992. *Pacific Arts* 7:96.

Crowe, Peter. 1994. *Vanuatu: Custom Music: Singsing-Danis Kastom.* Geneva: Musée d'Ethnographie, AIMP XLVIII. VDE 796. Compact disc.

Deacon, Arthur Barnard. 1934. *Malekula: A Vanishing People in the New Hebrides.* Edited by C. H. Wedgwood. London: Routledge.

Gray, William. 1892. "Some Notes on the Tannese." *Report of the 4th Meeting of the Australasian Association for the Advancement of Science* 4 (Section G):645–680.

Guiart, Jean. 1956. *Un Siècle et Demi de Contacts Culturels à Tanna (Nouvelles-Hébrides).* Publications de la Société des Océanistes, 5. Paris: Musée de l'Homme.

Inglis, John. 1887. *In the New Hebrides: Reminiscences of Missionary Life and Work, Especially on the Island of Aneityum, From 1850 Till 1877.* London: T. Nelson and Sons.

Irwin, Geoffrey. 1992. *The Prehistoric Exploration and Colonisation of the Pacific.* Oakleigh, Victoria, Australia: Cambridge University Press.

Layard, John W. 1942. *Stone Men of Malekula: Vao.* London: Chatto & Windus.

Lindstrom, Lamont. 1986. *Kwamera Dictionary—Nikukua sai Nagkiariien Nininife.* Pacific Linguistics, C 95. Canberra: Department of Linguistics, Research School of Pacific Studies, Australian National University.

———. 1990. *Knowledge and Power in a South Pacific Society.* Washington, D.C.: Smithsonian Institution Press.

Lindstrom, Lamont, and Geoffrey M. White. 1993. "Singing History: Island Songs from the Pacific War." In *Artistic Heritage in a Changing Pacific,* ed. Philip J. C. Dark and Roger G. Rose, 140–148. Bathurst, N.S.W.: Crawford House Press.

Lynch, John. 1978. "Proto-South Hebridean and Proto-Oceanic." In *Second International Conference on Austronesian Linguistics: Proceedings, Fascicle 2, Eastern Austronesian,* ed. Stephen A.

Wurm and Lois Carrington, 717–779. Canberra: Department of Linguistics, Research School of Pacific Studies, Australian National University.

Nahabau. N.d. *Radio Vanuatu and The Sound Centre.* Alain Gault Productions. TC AGP 17. Cassette.

Noisy Boys. 1982. *Noisy Boys: Fes Tua.* Alain Gault Productions. TC AGP 10. Cassette.

———. 1986. *Noisy Boys: 1986 Tanna Inta Distrik Gems.* Vanuata [sic] Production (Société de Promotion de Musique Mélanésienne) VP 24. Cassette.

Speiser, Felix. 1991 [1923]. *Ethnography of Vanuatu: An Early Twentieth-Century Study.* Translated by D. Q. Stephenson. Bathurst, NSW: Crawford House Press.

Thomas, Allan. 1992. "Songs as History: A Preliminary Assessment of Two Songs of the Recruiting Era Recently Recorded in West Futuna, Vanuatu." *Journal of Pacific History* 27:229–236.

Thomas, Alan, and Takaroga Kuautoga. 1992. *Hgorofutuna: Report of a Survey of the Music of West Futuna.* Occasional Papers in Pacific Musicology, 2. Auckland: Archive of Maori and Pacific Music, Department of Anthropology, University of Auckland.

*Traditional Music of Vanuatu.* 1980. Vanuatu Cultural Centre. Cassette.

Turner, George. 1884. *Samoa a Hundred Years Ago and Long Before.* London: Macmillan.

# Micronesia

Singing and moving for gods of the sea, storms, sacred creatures, and spirits of the deep; conveying aural assistance to guide tattooers' hands and lessen the pain of tattooing; performing for welcomes and farewells; dancing to ensure fertility—all gave aesthetic enhancement to Micronesians' lives.

Some of these traditions are only memories; others have been culturally reconstituted in original and altered forms: modern gods require new styles and sites of musical performance; musical ideas and concepts are imported from colonial and influential countries. During generations of change, Micronesians have transformed old and new into musical traditions specific for each community, yet ready to meet the challenges of the twenty-first century.

*Dancing on Canoes in the Harbor of Pohnpei.*
Detail of a lithograph by V. Adam after a drawing by A. Postels, from Lütke's voyage (1835). Photo by Smithsonian Institution.

# The Music and Dance of Micronesia
*Barbara B. Smith*

---

**Origins, Settlements, Cultures**
**Musical Instruments**
**Responses to Foreign Commerce and Empires**
**Responses to Christian Missionaries**
**Music and Dance in the Late 1990s**

---

The name *Micronesia* (from Greek, meaning 'tiny islands') was first used by Europeans in the 1830s for mapping the islands that lie east of the Philippines, north of Melanesia, and west of Polynesia (see maps). The name is an appropriate description for more than two thousand islands having only about 3,000 square kilometers of land. Micronesia includes three archipelagos (the Caroline, Gilbert, and Mariana islands), two parallel chains (the Marshall Islands), and two solitary islands (Banaba [Ocean Island] and Nauru).

Geologically, Micronesia contains three kinds of islands. Its high islands—the Marianas and five insular complexes in the Carolines (from west to east, Palau, Yap, Chuuk, Pohnpei, Kosrae)—are mostly volcanic in origin, with extensive natural resources. Its low islands—most of which lie in seventy-two coral atolls in the Carolines, Marshalls, and Gilberts—are smaller, with limited land-based resources, but bountiful marine resources in atoll lagoons. Its raised coral islands—Banaba, Nauru, and some scattered elsewhere—are intermediate in size, but have, or formerly had, phosphate deposits, useful to foreign interests.

Politically, Micronesia includes the Commonwealth of the Northern Mariana Islands, the Federated States of Micronesia, Guam (an unincorporated U.S. territory), and four republics (Kiribati, the Marshall Islands, Nauru, Palau). Some boundaries correspond roughly to indigenous settlement at the time of European contact; some resulted from foreign involvements; and Kiribati's resulted, in part, from twentieth-century geographic expansion to accommodate the growth of the population.

Some of these political entities sustain communities of extraneous Micronesians, including the survivors of a natural disaster on Lamotrek Atoll (central Carolines), who in the early 1800s resettled on Saipan (Northern Marianas), and people from Palau and the Federated States, who in the late twentieth century moved to Guam. Micronesian communities exist abroad: Banabans relocated to Rabi (Fiji Islands) after the phosphate covering the surface of their island had been shipped overseas; Gilbertese settled in Guadalcanal (Solomon Islands) to relieve population pressure in their homeland; and Chuukese, Kosraens, Marshallese, and others migrated to Hawai'i and California for advanced education and other opportunities.

The population of Micronesia is less than five hundred thousand, but its density

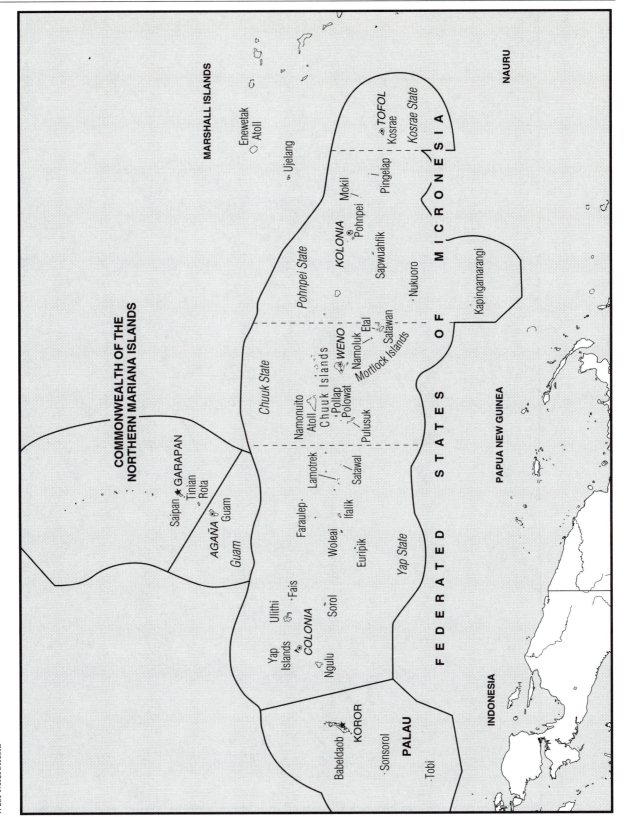

West Micronesia

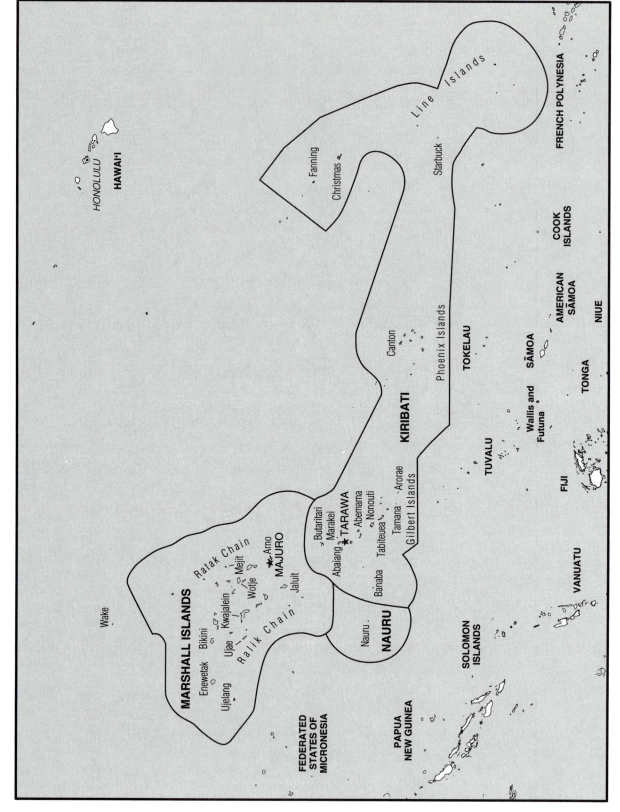

East Micronesia

in some urban centers is high: on Majuro, capital of the Republic of the Marshalls, it is about fifteen hundred persons per square kilometer; Ebeye, an islet in Kwajalein Atoll, has nearly twenty times that density.

The terms *Micronesia* and *Micronesians* also have narrower applications. Colonizing foreigners used them to denote the islands and peoples administered by their governments: Germans, Japanese, and Americans in turn used them to refer collectively to the Carolines, the Marshalls, and the Northern Marianas; and the British used them to specify the Gilberts, or collectively Banaba, the Gilberts, and Nauru. When political self-determination led to the establishment of the Federated States of Micronesia (often abbreviated to *Micronesia*), islanders and foreigners began using that designation to specify that government and the islands and peoples of its states. In this encyclopedia, *Micronesia* refers to the whole region designated in the 1830s; and *Micronesians,* to the peoples indigenous to it, except those of two islands (Kapingamarangi and Nukuoro), of Polynesian origin and culture.

## ORIGINS, SETTLEMENTS, CULTURES

The roots of the Micronesian peoples lie in Southeast Asia, but Micronesians were, and are, diverse in physique, social organization, language (at least twelve mutually unintelligible languages are still spoken), and many other aspects of culture, including music and dance. Their diversity can be attributed to differences in routes and dates of migrations, accommodations to the natural resources of the islands on which they settled, post-settlement contacts with other Micronesians and other peoples of the Pacific, and internal changes during periods of isolation, which, as for Nauru, were of long durations.

Some high islands in western Micronesia (Guam, Palau, Yap) were settled more than three thousand years ago by Austronesian-speaking peoples from islands now known as the Philippines and Indonesia. Some eastern Micronesian islands (Gilberts, Kosrae, Marshalls, Pohnpei) were settled more than two thousand years ago by peoples of a branch of Austronesian-speakers from Melanesia, probably some directly from islands now known as Vanuatu and others progressing through West Polynesia. The central Carolinean atolls were probably settled last, by peoples who had sailed westward from the eastern Carolines until they reached Palau and Yap, which had already been inhabited.

Most Micronesian societies were matrilineal. The inhabitants of the Marianas and each of the high islands in the Carolines had a uniquely hierarchic social organization, language, and other aspects of culture (including music and dance), with local variants owned by specific villages, clans, or persons. Similarly, the people of the low islands of each archipelago or chain had a distinctive social organization (highly stratified in the Marshalls, more egalitarian in the Carolines), language (or several related languages), and culture.

By the time of European contact, the people of some high islands no longer made long voyages, but the peoples of the low islands continued to sail, not only among islands of an atoll, but among atolls. The central Carolineans regularly voyaged to the Marianas, and occasionally—sometimes unintentionally—to the Marshalls and the Philippines. The central Carolineans are the world's only people with an unbroken tradition of open-ocean, noninstrumental navigation, a skill that in the 1970s a respected navigator from Satawal shared with Hawaiians eager to replicate ancient Polynesian voyages.

Ceremonial musical performance preceded departures for long voyages; feasting and dancing welcomed voyagers on their return. Sometimes when visiting an island for peaceful purposes, voyagers and hosts performed for each other—a custom that continues in new contexts. Occasionally, new songs with dancing recounted the events of a voyage. Micronesians had many reasons to undertake long voyages, among them war (to expand a chief's domain or exact revenge for a battle), refuge (after a typhoon or a drought had devastated local resources), and trade. The most extensive interisland trade flourished before the 1800s within the so-called Yap Empire. People from the atolls west of Chuuk periodically voyaged to Yap, where, as an item for exchange, usually called their tribute, they gave a dance to the chief of a Yapese village. That item became highly valued property of that village, was learned by an appropriate group of villagers (the text maintained in the language of origin), and was performed when the chief required.

## MUSICAL INSTRUMENTS

Throughout Micronesia, the human voice was, and continues to be, the predominant musical instrument. In the language of musical texts and some aspects of musical style, the vocal musics of each Micronesian culture differed from the others. The genres of each culture were differentiated by textual content, musical style, and manner of performance—whether solo or collective, and if collective, whether in unison or in multiple parts.

Among the indigenous vocal musics performed today, melodic shapes depend on linguistic contours or genre-based prescriptions; textual articulation ranges from fast and crisp to sustained and flowing; multipart relationships are prescribed and well defined; tones usually lie within a narrow range, those less specifically defined often encompassing a wide range; musical phrases have uniform lengths, or are contrastive, or follow the pattern of their text; tempo and duration vary; rhythmic relationships are mostly duple or nonmetric; loudness of vocal projection (and, in some cases, preferred timbre) varies by genre; and small, individualistic variations in ornamentation are acceptable in much solo performance. Most vocal music was, and much still is, owned by a specific person, clan, or village, and was performed only in specific contexts for specific purposes.

Percussion involving the human body—stamping feet, clapping hands (with flat or cupped palms), clapping one hand over the hollow formed within the bent elbow of the other arm when pressed against the chest, slapping hands on thighs or chests— is a major auditory component of many Micronesian musical performances. Skill in dancing the most highly valued genres was essential to attaining adulthood. Except, perhaps, for the food at feasts, synchronized performances by groups of men or women (in most Micronesian cultures, not together), were the principal presentations on prestigious occasions. Other genres were performed in less formal contexts; and in some islands, young men and women danced together while making love.

Instruments external to the human body served for music, signaling, and other purposes. With rare exceptions, they were idiophones or aerophones, made from a single material, used for a single purpose, and limited in geographic distribution. Important exceptions included the conch trumpet, used throughout Micronesia primarily for signaling. Sticks were widespread as implements used in dancing (figure 1). In some cultures, they were of bamboo; in others, of wood (figure 2). In a few cultures, they were ornamented with plaited leaves or feathers. Most stick dances were stylized enactments of combat. A few were training exercises for combat: dancers in parallel-facing lines rhythmically and vigorously executed complex stick-clashing patterns, and frequently interchanged positions within and between the lines.

The only Micronesian membranophone was a single-headed drum, resembling drums of some Melanesian peoples. In the eastern Carolines (where only men played it) and the Marshalls (where only women played it), it was shaped like an hourglass. In Nauru, its body was more nearly cylindrical.

FIGURE 1   Yapese women perform a stick dance in a space bordered by stone valuables (*rai*). Photographer and date unknown. Courtesy of Hamilton Library, University of Hawai'i.

Two indigenous instruments are of special interest. A reed flute with an external duct—similar to those of some Filipino peoples, but different from the other flutes of Micronesia and elsewhere in Oceania—was played in Palau and Yap. A stone instrument, valued in Pohnpei for its sonority, was used in preparing the ceremonial beverage *sakau* (known as *seka* in Kosrae): striking fist-sized stones against large, sonorous basaltic slabs of different pitches, young men pounded kava roots in prescribed sequences of interlocking rhythms.

A few easily made instruments serve as children's toys. The conch trumpet serves for signaling (in Kiribati) and occasionally in theatrical presentations. Only sticks remain essential to the performing arts. Micronesians abandoned drums and other instruments when missionaries proscribed their use, and reed flutes and other instruments when they adopted Western instruments.

## RESPONSES TO FOREIGN COMMERCE AND EMPIRES

For most foreigners who went to Micronesia to engage in whaling, trade, or other commerce, or to administer the islands and peoples for their country or an international body, the musics and dances of their homelands were incidental to their reasons for being in the islands. Apart from members of military bands, they were not professional musicians, but some of them occasionally entertained Micronesians by informally performing secular musics and dances. Islanders sometimes imitated these performances, often parodistically. By combining foreign and indigenous elements, they created new genres of singing or dancing, which they added to, or in some cases used to replace, indigenous genres.

The Hispanic-Chamorro heritage was developed during the first 150 years of Spanish colonial rule (1668–1898), when Guam was a port of call for galleons sailing between Mexico and the Philippines. The Chamorro, much of whose culture was devastated in the Spanish encounter, composed Chamorro-language musical texts and combined indigenous stylistic features with Spanish, Mexican, and Filipino songs and dances they learned from ships' crews and foreign settlers, creating a heritage that flourished into the early 1900s and is being revived in Guam and the Northern Marianas as a symbol of Chamorro identity.

### Dances

Marching dances were created during the German colonial period, from the late

FIGURE 2    Micronesian stick dances old and new: *a,* in 1909, dancers from Yap pose with carved wooden sticks (photo by Elisabeth Krämer, Institute of Ethnology, University of Tübingen); *b,* in 1971, men of Namoluk Atoll, Chuuk, perform with bamboo sticks (photo by Mac Marshall).

(*a*)

(*b*)

1800s (beginning on different dates for different islands) to 1914. Dancers form one or more forward-facing rows. Some sections imitate military drills: marching in place, legs moving forward (sometimes with an upward flick of the foot), arms swinging forward and back with elbows straight and torsos vertical (or even slightly inclined backward), and cadential patterns of stamping feet and slapping thighs. These alternate with sections of flexible, indigenous-style structured movements—with knees and elbows bending slightly, arms moving in various patterns (mostly in front of slightly forward-tilting torsos), and hips swaying gently or vigorously, sometimes exaggerating for humorous effects. Some marching dances incorporate steps of foreign dances.

In addition to the sounds of bodily percussion, the swishing of leaf skirts, and intermittent shouts, the marching sections have calls like those of military drills, with words identifying left and right legs, and the indigenous-style sections have Western melodies played on harmonicas, or songs in postcontact styles sung in an indigenous language or a mixture of languages. Men sent from various islands to mine phosphate on Anguar (in Palau) and Nauru enjoyed marching dances, which they disseminated when they returned home; other interisland contacts circulated these dances further.

The Yapese sing songs of a marching-dance genre they created between 1918 and 1939; after the mid-1960s, some islanders changed the movement for the call for "left" from lifting the left leg to stepping on the left foot. In the 1990s in most of the Carolines, marching dances, in culture-specific variants of content and name, are frequently performed by teenagers for school and community events and foreign audiences.

In Pohnpei, when the German administration curtailed the frequency of feasts (where *sakau* was prepared and drunk, and long, narrative, historical recitations and dances were performed), four dances that had been performed separately, each to its own text, were coordinated for simultaneous performance to one text. Since then, in performances at home and abroad, two dances for men (one with gestures, one with paddles) and two for women (one with gestures, one with short sticks) are performed by forward-facing rows of dancers arranged in two or four tiers, men (or, in the late twentieth century, more often boys) standing in back, and women (or girls) seated in front. Sometimes only two of these dances are performed together [see WEST MICRONESIA, figure 4].

### Songs

Songs with nonindigenous melodies and harmonies, secular and religious, constitute by far the largest body of postcontact Micronesian music. Some songs composed in each of the colonial administrations continue to be sung solo or by a group, in unison or in parts (in adult mixed choirs and choruses, usually in four-part harmony), often accompanied by guitar or ukulele, or (in urban centers in the late twentieth century) by electric guitar, electronic keyboard, and drums.

New popular-song genres and pieces, many about love, were created during Japanese colonial rule (1914–1945), especially in Palau, the center of Japanese administration, where indigenous vocal timbres resemble those used by Japanese for singing popular songs. From 1941 to 1945, new songs and dances recounted the hazards and hardships of war. People forcibly relocated by the Japanese military (as Nauruans to Chuuk) composed songs to express love of home and longing for loved ones.

During the United Nations trusteeship, administered by the United States (from 1945 to different terminal dates for the new political entities), songs incorporating stylistic features of country music and other American popular styles were created. Government-controlled radio stations broadcast American popular songs of the 1940s and later decades. When small, battery-operated cassette players and cassettes (American, and later Filipino, especially in the Marianas, and Japanese, especially in Palau) became readily accessible, favorite songs could be heard whenever desired. The growth of tourism and the anticipation of political self-determination also stimulated local creativity.

Except while occupied by Japanese forces during the Pacific War, Micronesians in British-administered areas—the Gilbert Islands with the (Polynesian) Ellice Islands (1892–1976), and Nauru (1914–1968)—created new genres and songs. Though each was stimulated in part by American popular musics, some developed in virtual isolation from each other and from simultaneous creative developments in American-administered areas. Brass bands became established in some areas.

### RESPONSES TO CHRISTIAN MISSIONARIES

For Christian missionaries who went to Micronesia to convert the islanders, the music of their particular denomination was intrinsic to the practice of their faith. The music they introduced, and the songs composed by Micronesians in these styles and styles derived from them, are major components of music in Micronesia.

The Chamorro converted to Roman Catholicism and adopted the music of

Because the visual components of dancing are readily recognized, dancing is an effective cultural identifier. Therefore, teams of dancers often represent Micronesian peoples and governments—abroad, as at the Pacific Festivals of Arts, and in civic events at home.

Spanish Jesuits, who in 1668 established a mission on Guam. The peoples of Yap and the western Carolinean atolls rejected early-eighteenth-century efforts at conversion, but in the late 1800s began accepting Roman Catholicism and its music. The Yapese, while incorporating Christianity into their heritage, retained their dancing, and set biblical texts to the music and body-movement style of an indigenous genre of dancing. Dances with indigenous movements are performed in Roman Catholic churches in Kiribati.

The peoples of eastern Micronesia (eastern Carolines, Gilberts, Marshalls) had their first experience with Christian missionaries in the mid-1800s, when the American Board of Commissioners for Foreign Missions (Congregational) expanded its work in the Pacific, westward from Hawai'i. These missionaries abhorred not only the liquor and behaviors that whalers had introduced, but all customs integrated with indigenous beliefs. In their view, dancing was sinful, and performing music—except Christian hymns—was a waste of time, so they prohibited their converts from participating in these activities.

The missionaries quickly learned local languages, translated hymns, and taught the islanders to sing. In schools, they taught musical notation. Micronesians soon began composing religious songs in hymnodic styles (later also in gospel-music styles), and choral singing became a communal activity, within and outside the church. Choral competitions and festivals, which became major events, continue in some islands. Kosrae has village-choir competitions, and Kosraeans from the whole island and several overseas communities gather at one church every four years to celebrate Christmas. Musics of other denominations—the London Missionary Society, the Liebenzell Mission, the Congregational Church of Japan—as adopted and adapted, added to Micronesian styles and genres.

During the colonial period, nativistic religious movements arose among several Micronesian peoples. Of these, Modekngei, which originated in Palau during the Japanese administration, contributed to the perpetuation of the precontact Palauan heritage through its songs in indigenous musical style. Musics of Shinto and Buddhist rituals, introduced during the Japanese administration, made little or no continuing contribution to local music.

Of the sects and denominations that entered Micronesia during the latter part of the American administration, the Church of Jesus Christ of Latter-Day Saints (Mormons) has proselytized most successfully and extensively. Throughout Micronesia, the Mormons use the same hymns (with texts translated into local languages), favor a "sweet" vocal timbre (in contrast to the intense vocal production favored by some islanders of other denominations), and rely on the accompaniment (or, more accurately, support or leadership) of Japanese-made electronic keyboards.

In a few islands in the late 1990s, locally composed hymns and religious songs remain the predominant music, and collective singing remains a major public activity; but in other islands, especially those in which the population divides among com-

FIGURE 3 Kiribati women dance in a line in front of men, who sing, clap their hands, and perform movements. Pacific Festival of Arts. Photo by Adrienne L. Kaeppler, 1980.

peting faiths, these songs and their singing have lost much of their former importance.

## MUSIC AND DANCE IN THE LATE 1990S

Popular songs, foreign and locally composed, are heard extensively on radio, and as live or recorded commercial entertainment in urban centers (Guam, Majuro, Palau, Saipan). In addition to performing for local people and tourists, Micronesian performers and composers seek fame and money by distributing cassettes of their music. Many contemporary songs about love, personal and environmental problems, and other topical concerns have texts in an indigenous language, with musical features that identify them and specific places or people; others, especially those with English-language texts, sharing enough traits to be enjoyed beyond political boundaries, are considered pan-Micronesian. This identity does not embrace the popular music of Nauru or Kiribati; apparently, popular musics have not bridged a long-standing boundary between foreign administrations.

Traditional arts, especially dancing, have enjoyed a renaissance. To negotiate relationships with other peoples and governments, each new government needed to define its people. A powerful statement of sociocultural identity—and of collective commitment to a village, an island, or a nation—can be made by a large troupe of performers in a rehearsed presentation, whether of an old dance or of a new one with genre-specific movements, set to a text newly composed for a particular event. Because Micronesian cultures value dancing highly and the visual components of dancing are readily recognized (even if the text is not understood), dancing is a particularly effective cultural identifier. Therefore, teams of dancers often represent Micronesian peoples and governments, abroad (as at the Pacific Festivals of Arts) and in civic events at home (figure 3). Some Micronesians have recreated what they appreciate as ancient music to identify themselves more closely with their natural environment and neighboring islanders, and to represent themselves in civic, national, and international events.

FIGURE 4 Schoolchildren of Awak, Pohnpei, dance and sing of local history. Photo by Glenn Petersen, 1974.

In some islands, to build self-esteem and pride in cultural identity, schools teach traditional dances to children (figure 4), often with less limitation to clan affiliation than in precontact times. For twentieth-century Micronesians, as for their ancestors, indigenous performing arts are not merely reflections of culture (as many outside writers describe their own arts and those of other peoples), but active determinants of people's places in the world.

# West Micronesia

Adrienne L. Kaeppler
Faustina K. Rehuher
Eve C. Pinsker
Deirdre Marshall-Dean
Mac Marshall
Larry Gabriel

Joakim Manniwel Peter
Juliana Flinn
Glenn Petersen
Karen L. Nero
Judy Flores

**Palau**

**Federated States of Micronesia**

**Mariana Islands**

## PALAU

Palau (Belau), though part of the Caroline Archipelago and culturally related to Yap, is politically separate from the Federated States of Micronesia. Established in 1980, the Republic of Palau consists of high volcanic islands (including Babeldoab and Koror, the capital) with dramatic hills sculptured into terraces, many small islets, and the southwest coral islands of Tobi, Sonsoral, and others, with a population of about sixteen thousand [see MUSIC AND INGESTED SUBSTANCES: Alcohol].

The origin of Palau is mythically traced to a child with an insatiable appetite, who was tied up and set on fire. In a struggle, the child's body fragmented into more than three hundred pieces, which form the islands of Palau. Sometimes, this originator is said to be a giantess named Chuab. These events are recounted in songs.

Divided into two paramount chiefdoms based on matrilineal descent, Palauan society has been overlaid with an American-style administration. Oceangoing vessels once sailed the sea, and spectacular structures (*bai*) dotted the landscape. *Bai* are profusely decorated with carved and painted interior beams and gables, illustrating events and symbolizing wealth.

An indigenous currency, known as men's money, is thought by some to derive from Asian porcelain that found its way to Palau through the Philippines, and by others to derive from glass beads and bracelets from Chinese sources. This currency consists of a limited number of named pieces of opaque glass and other materials not found in the Pacific Islands, formed into beads and bars. Elaborate behavioral postures accompanied their use, and women sometimes wore them as necklaces to exhibit wealth, or during pregnancy and after the birth of a first child. Pottery, which turns up in archaeological contexts, was still being made (by the coiling method) in the 1700s.

Palauan arts have received little outside attention. Apart from an eighteenth-century explorer's accounts of musical events (Keate 1788), the Südsee Expedition monographs (Krämer 1926), and research by Hisakatsu Hijikata (1993 [1941], 1995, 1996), Hisao Tanabe (1935), and Osamu Yamaguti (1968, 1973), few publications are available. Local music and dance exist primarily as systems of knowledge in the heads of known bearers of traditions.

### An eighteenth-century description

The shipwreck of British Captain Henry Wilson on *Antelope* in 1783 brought Pelew, as it was then known, to the attention of the outside world. After an intertribal skirmish,

> in the evening our people were entertained with a dance of the warriors, who were just then returned, which was performed in the following manner:—The dancers have a quantity of plantain leaves brought to them, which they split, and sliver into the form of ribbands, these they then twine and fix round their heads, wrists, waists, ankles, and knees, and the leaves being of a yellowish hue, so prepared, have not an inelegant effect when applied to their dark copper skin. They make also bunches or tassels of the same, which they hold in their hands. When drawn out, they form themselves into circles of two or three deep, one within another. In general an elderly man amongst them begins, in a very solemn tone, something like a song, or long sentence, for our countrymen could not discriminate which it was, and when he comes to a pause, or what we should call the end of a stanza, a chorus is struck up, and the dancers all join in concert, still continuing their figure. Their dancing does not so much consist in capering or agility, as in a particular method they have of balancing themselves, and this frequently very low sideways, singing together all the while; during which, they will flatten their circles, so as to bring themselves face to face to each other, lifting up the tassels they hold in their hands, and giving them a clashing, or tremulous motion; after this there will be a sudden pause, and an exclamation from every voice, *Weel!* Then a new sentence or stanza is repeated, and danced to as before, and the same ceremony continued, till every man who is engaged in the dance has in his turn had his repetition and chorus. (Keate 1788:116–117)

At performances in the 1990s, an appropriate collective shout, possibly a descendant of that eighteenth-century "exclamation from every voice," is *o hui!*

### Musical concepts

Palauan music was primarily vocal; flutes and lamellaphones were also known. Melodic contours and rhythms were formulaic; clear pronunciation and the ability to sing long phrases with decorative figures were admired; the terminal tones of each textual line were stressed by the addition of phonetic elements. Long texts told of people and events that served as subjects of incised and painted *bai* rafters (Yamaguti 1973).

Yamaguti (1968) recorded Palauan conceptions of music and a taxonomy, noting that the Palauan conception of music is differentiated from nonmusical sound by tonal heights, rhythms, and accents. In an elaborate taxonomic diagram, he divided music into classical and contemporary, and gave a chronological dimension to each genre.

### Traditional music and later influences

Palauan music included songs performed at council activities, funerals, festivities, and daily life (figure 1). Council activities included songs of devotion, heroism, address, and other activities. Funerals included primary and secondary dirges. Festival music was mainly various kinds of dances performed by men or women standing, sitting, or with sticks, and children's festival songs. Music from daily life included wishful and resentful songs, lullabies, quarreling songs, and game songs. Other kinds of structured sound not considered music included incanting and reciting, singing work songs and racing songs, playing lamellaphones, and signaling with conchs.

FIGURE 1 Girls of Ngatpang, Palau, dance and sing a *matmatong*. Photo by Yoshiyasu Morikawa, 1945.

Religious music, new music for dancing, and European and Japanese songs profoundly influenced Palauan music. *Matmatong,* marching songs, developed around 1900 from the sight of German soldiers marching; in them, boys and girls dance together in verse-refrain alternation, featuring traditional Micronesian movements alternating with a marchlike refrain. Japanese secular songs influenced Palauan songs before World War II, introducing concepts still current. Added into the modern mix of Palaun music are contemporary sounds and Christian religious music from Japan and America, performed by Palauans for themselves and tourists.

—ADRIENNE L. KAEPPLER

## Palauan performing arts (*ngloik*)

Imagine you are in the Palau Islands, back in the 1700s. A full moon is shining, and a feast to dedicate the completion of a new *bai* is in progress. Tall and A-framed, the structure towers over the villagers, who move around, distributing baskets of food.

Suddenly, people hush. Dancers are about to perform. They have been in seclusion for months—fed, massaged, and exempted from work. Having practiced to perfection, they emerge. As they move into a long line on the platform in front of the *bai,* their song, slow and melodious, rings out. Their bodies sway in subtle movements to its rhythms, with hypnotic voices broken only by an individual dancer's high-pitched call. Poised and regal, the dancers move in perfect unison as they sing of hallowed events, relaying important messages about heroes, ancient battles, and loved ones lost or gained. Onlookers sit, listen, and watch in awe and respect.

According to the Palauan historian Ngiraklang Malsol, Palauan music deals with the lives of people interacting with their community and environment. In ancient Palau, everyone knew the community's techniques and styles of performing. Songs and dances graced various occasions, often on a platform in front of a *bai* (figure 2).

*Ngloik* served several functions: to dramatize stories (one or more storytellers made tales rhythmic and visual); to inaugurate a newly built *bai*; for people of either sex to express their feelings; magically to make hunting and fishing, planting, and harvesting successful by stimulating the regenerative powers of nature; to encourage warriors, before and after battle; to direct a newborn child or an ill or dying person; to ease a family through critical times by giving them strength; to free children from the rigorous subordination in which they were habitually kept; and to provide entertainment during feasts and other public gatherings.

Dances and recitations were performed to appease the gods if an important person was ill, to honor a chief's wife, and to earn income. A song invoking the spiritual being Obilngesul includes this stanza:

FIGURE 2    On a platform in front of the *bai* at
the Belau National Museum, students perform
the *delal a ngloik "Surech me a Dulei,"* telling the
story of two lovers. From inside the *bai*, other
students look on. Photo by Simeon Adelbai,
1994.

FIGURE 2    On a platform in front of the *bai* at the Belau National Museum, students perform the *delal a ngloik "Surech me a Dulei,"* telling the story of two lovers. From inside the *bai*, other students look on. Photo by Simeon Adelbai, 1994.

Obilngesul, cheang! kede du el merrael e mei.
Me ka dechedal a ika ng; me ka el belaud a ika ng—
Ng di bad, me a ralm, me a bad er a ngeasek,
A merredel er a chutem, iang!

Obilngesul, oh! we both migrated here.
We are not related to this land; this is not our home—
Only rocks, and water, and the core of the earth
Are the owners of the land, right!

This text implies that everything on earth comes from nature; we may use it, but we must take care of it for future generations. As here, Palauan dances embody Palauan beliefs. They record and preserve communal events, activities, histories, and genealogies (Rehuher 1995). The respect given to dancers and the care taken in preparing dances show the importance of dance in Palauan culture.

### The aesthetics of Palauan dancing

Palauan dances must be performed in pairs, like other living things. Each paired dance (*ulekbut el ngloik*) has a mother dance (*delal a ngloik*) and a humorous dance (*beluulchab*) to accompany it. The mother dance conveys serious, important messages; it requires earnest performance by dancers and complete attention by audiences. The *beluulchab* allows dancers to make fun and joke about current events.

Dancers usually perform in pairs; if more than ten dancers perform, they stand in two rows. Their movements include gestures, facial expressions, steps, and turns, executed with exactness and elegance; some movements are pantomimic. A loud, penetrating call opens the performance. The singing is slow, in a high-pitched vocal range, with little melodic variation.

Aesthetically, three elements make up a well-staged performance: *besiich,* describing a performer's physical appearance and impact; *kldachelbai,* referring to the composer-choreographer's artistic creativity; and *cheldecheduch,* describing the content to be conveyed. These concepts concern the physical, mental, and artistic elements that combine to generate the whole of a performance.

—FAUSTINA K. REHUHER

## FEDERATED STATES OF MICRONESIA

The Federated States of Micronesia (FSM) is a multicultural nation with a population of about 110,000. From 1947 through 1986, it was administered by the United States as part of the U.N.-designated Trust Territory of the Pacific Islands. In 1986, the FSM, as a sovereign republic with a constitutional government, entered into a compact of free association with the United States, to be in force through 2001.

The FSM consists of four states: Yap, Chuuk, Pohnpei, and Kosrae. The last contains only the island of Kosrae, a high, volcanic island. The others include high islands and atolls. Land areas in the FSM range from Pohnpei's 334 square kilometers to atolls of less than 1 square kilometer.

Most lagoons in the western and central FSM are larger than those east of Pohnpei; most western atolls have more than one major inhabited islet, which, for some purposes, are regarded as distinct communities. Chuuk Lagoon, the main island-complex of Chuuk State, includes separate high islands, with recognized differences in dialect and customs, surrounded by a large fringing reef.

Internally recognized divisions in the FSM partition islands further. Most inhabited atolls and all the high islands, including those within Chuuk Lagoon, subdivide into sections or districts. On the high islands of Yap and Pohnpei, these districts, corresponding to contemporary municipalities, again divide up into distinct communities: on Yap, villages (*binaew*); on Pohnpei, sections (*kousapw*).

### Dance

Indigenous levels of political organization and recognized communal identity in the FSM enter into the production and performance of dances. Before the mid-1800s and the arrival of outside traders, whalers, missionaries, and colonial powers, the most important contexts for the production and performance of dances were probably feasts, for which sections or villages competed in presenting dances and exchanging goods (figure 3).

In the late 1980s in the FSM, new governments and increasing tourism began providing contexts for reviving and revitalizing dance. This trend continues. Japanese tourists frequently ask to see traditional dancing, and provide economic incentives for performances. Exposure to dance elsewhere in Oceania—through participation in the Pacific Festival of Arts, access to VCRs, and student and government travel—has yielded new motifs for dancing, including disco moves and fast hip movements, blended into older styles.

#### *Contexts involving exchange*

Some contexts show a close link between dance and exchange, as in the *täyoer,* a genre of the high-island complex of Yap. *Täyoer* is sometimes called a begging dance

FIGURE 3 *Caroline Islands: Dance of the Natives.*
Engraving by Jacques Arago, 1825. Photo by
Bishop Museum.

because each of a pair of villages competing in a ritualized exchange (*mitmiit*) is represented by a troupe that performs to recitations asking the other village for particular items. Goofalan, an expert living in Choqol Village, Maap' Municipality, Yap, in 1986 recalled a *täyoer* he had seen about 1918. Small girls from Wocholaeb Village, paired with Choqol, performed a dance directed to Goofalan (representing Choqol men), asking them to give each of the girls ten bottles of liquor for their fathers. Goofalan and his father gave Wocholaeb ten cases of liquor, with forty-eight bottles each and some loose bottles on top. Their one-upmanship, by which their gifts exceeded the request, was made possible through messengers sent to watch rehearsals of the dances, which had continued for three or four months.

In 1986, Goofalan and his wife, Rualath, demonstrated the movements: *täyoer* performed by little girls and women of mixed ages typically included a slow part and a fast part. The basic posture is posterior out, knees bent, feet forward. In the slow part, outstretched arms gracefully moved up and down, and hands waved, grasped (in movements associated with asking for goods), and clapped. The fast part included stamping the right foot to the back and the side while swishing the hip frontward and back, and swinging and clapping the hands.

Most dancing in the FSM has far less hip movement than dancing in East Polynesia. Yapese dancers use their hips more than performers elsewhere in Micronesia. Yapese skirts, made of colorfully dyed hibiscus fibers, have additional short layers on the top, dramatically emphasizing the movements of performers' hips.

Contemporary examples of dance used in competitive exchanges in other parts of FSM have included an event held to commemorate the new municipal constitution of Sapwuahfik (formerly Ngatik), an atoll in Pohnpei State. Displays of coconuts and taro, and presentations of dances, represent sections of the main islet during friendly competition in performative skill and horticultural abundance. The difference between this event and earlier contexts demonstrates a development common throughout the contemporary FSM: an emphasis on more encompassing levels of community. The emphasis at the Sapwuahfik ceremony, shown by speeches and introductions to the dances, is less on the separate sections and more on the presentation of Sapwuahfik as a whole—a presentation to outsiders from elsewhere in Pohnpei State and the FSM. Similarly, in Yap, *mitmiit* and associated competitions between paired villages have become increasingly rare. The most extensive display of dances is now seen in the Yap Day celebrations, sponsored by the state annually on 1 March. Troupes usually represent whole municipalities, rather than individual villages.

### Contexts involving change

People of the FSM associate different genres of dance with different historical periods, outside influences, contexts, and movements. Genres seen as more recent in origin are also more productive: new dances are still choreographed within these genres; older, more archaic genres may be performed or revived, but are not generating new choreography.

Goofalan of Maap' listed eight genres of Yapese dance: *gabngeg,* an old genre, with melodic formulas in archaic, no-longer-understood diction; *barug,* performed for the completion of a men's house, typically in competition between villages (a genre said to originally come from the atolls to the east); *par u buut,* a dance including seated recitations with movements of the head, the torso, and the arms; *tey,* for men (the others can be performed by groups of women or men), primarily done in the southern part of Yap proper; *täyoer,* mainly performed by women; *gaslaaw,* erotic-themed dances, performed with pelvic thrusts; *gamel',* where the dancers' rhythmic collision of bamboo sticks is accentuated with movements of the hips; and *maas* 'march', dating from the later part of the Japanese administration and said by Goofalan to be the only genre men and women may perform together.

In 1986, a performance for a visiting Japanese consul in response to his request to see local dancing included a *par u buut,* a *gamel',* and a *gaslaaw* (the last performed by prepubescent boys, to minimize the eroticism). Goofalan himself continued to choreograph dances: he composed the songs and movements for the so-called unity dance performed by Yapese and Yap outer-islander male employees of the FSM government at the 1989 Independence Day and Dedication ceremonies at the FSM capitol at Palikir, Pohnpei (Pinsker 1992).

People of Chuuk also recognize various genres and associate them with historical origins and appropriate contexts. Similarly for Pohnpei, Kim Bailey (1985) lists local genres: *wehn,* a dance of standing males, and *kehnsar,* a more energetic and audience-pleasing accompaniment to *wehn,* done by men or women; *kepir,* done in place by males who stamp, turn, and strike ornamental paddles against a railing in front of them; *sapei,* a dance by seated females using hands on a lapboard, a plank placed across the lap; *dokia,* a dance by seated performers using sticks on a lapboard (figure 4); and *lehp,* a march using movements said to derive from Spanish and German military exercises, hornpipes, and other sources. The older genres, excluding the *lehp,* are often now performed together by rows of dancers, the women seated in front, the men standing in back. *Lehp* remains productive. A contemporary favorite of performers from the Palikir area of Pohnpei, where the children of the Pohnpeians who rebelled against the Germans in the Sokehs Rebellion of 1910 settled, was choreographed as a *lehp* by Joseph Aldiss to a song composed in the 1920s about the rebellion (Petersen 1992; Pinsker 1992).

FIGURE 4   Representing Pohnpei at the Pacific Festival of Arts, seated women perform a dance using sticks on a lapboard while standing men perform different movements behind them. Photo by Mary Jo Freshley, 1985.

From Boston in the mid-1800s, Congregational Protestant missionaries came to Kosrae and frowned on dancing. Kosrae became strongly Congregational, indigenizing the church as its population rebounded from a disease-induced decline, to one-tenth its former level. Kosrae custom today is the custom of the Kosrae church. It does not include dancing, though choral singing is highly developed, encouraged through church-sponsored competitions.          —EVE C. PINSKER

## Yap

Yap State comprises the closely grouped islands known as Yap and the atolls of Ulithi, Fais, Ngulu, Sorol, Euripik, Woleai, and Lamotrek. The Yap Islands (orthographically Waqab), are distinct from the others, which, despite strong historical and political ties with Yap, have cultural affinities with Chuuk. Yap first experienced contact with European cultures in the mid-1800s. From 1886 to 1979, contact took the form of colonial administration, in four historical periods.

In 1885–1886, the Spanish government established a colonial administration on Yap, which Germany also claimed. Arbitrating the dispute, the Vatican ruled for Spain, but granted Germany exclusive rights to trade. In 1886, Spain built the first Christian church and set up a Roman Catholic mission, whose ritual music was plainsong. The missionaries urged the Yapese to renounce their ancestral totems and spirits, and to attend church and school. In 1899, to raise capital for war against the United States, Spain sold Yap to Germany. German administrators mostly concerned themselves with overseeing local trade: they built a station that by undersea cables linked Shanghai, Guam, and the Philippines. They tended not to get involved in local issues.

The first essay on Yapese performing arts, written by a German doctor stationed on Yap (Born 1903), anecdotally surveyed local music, poetry, and dance. Later ethnological surveys, by various authors, documented the island's culture and society. At least one of these authors made recordings. Sixtus Walleser, a Capuchin missionary on Yap for six years, noted (1915) the beginnings of cultural loss; he listed eight genres of dance-songs and four genres of personally expressive music.

Germany withdrew from Yap in 1914. Within months, the Japanese government had set up a local administration, which expelled the German priests in 1919. At the request of some Yapese, it invited the Roman Catholic Church to send missionaries from a neutral country; in 1921, the pope appointed Spanish Jesuits to serve in Yap.

In 1936, during the Bishop Museum's Micronesian Expedition (1935–1936), the anthropologist Iwakichi Muranushi recorded local music. The expedition spent two weeks on Yap, based in the capital, Colonia. Muranushi made recordings in Balabat, the village closest to Colonia. Most of the songs were *churu'*. An exception is the first recorded example of a *teempraa* (see below). Probably not the first recordings of Yapese music, Muranushi's are the earliest commercially available ones.

In 1944, U.S. troops captured Ulithi Atoll and Yap. Three years later, the United Nations declared Yap a part of the United Nations Trust Territory of the Pacific Islands, and gave the U.S. control of the region. By the mid-1960s, all of Yap and the atolls had embraced Christianity, and American Jesuits had built churches on each atoll. In the late 1960s, priests began conducting liturgies in local languages; for decades, they had already permitted the singing of vernacular hymns. English became a common second language, which children studied in elementary school. By 1979, television was introduced; it mostly broadcast programs from videos provided by California-based stations.

In 1979, Yap joined the FSM. Under self-government, the preservation of Yapese culture became an important concern. On Yap Day (1 March), celebrations

"I went to see Budweiser. We went to see San
Miguel. We all arrived at Asahi's. Now it's dawn and
I'm home."

—Yapese song

feature dance-songs, which cultural-awareness classes study in municipal elementary schools. WSZA, the local radio station, airs local genres, especially *teempraa* and dance-songs. It features local bands (which cultivate a popular keyboard-and-vocal idiom) and transmits the Voice of America.

### Vocal music

All surviving Yapese music is vocal. It falls into two classes, each with a distinct context: performances of personally expressive songs (*tang*) occur in private; rehearsals and performances of dance-songs (*churuq*) occur in public, including Christmas Eve celebrations of Mass. Yap is in the diocese of the Caroline Islands, whose see is on Pohnpei; most of its priests and deacons are from Yap and the outer islands.

Instrumental music did not feature highly in Yapese culture. The earliest surveys cited aerophones: *ngal*, end-blown bamboo flutes; *uchif*, leaf oboes, made from rolled coconut leaves; and *yubul*, conch trumpets. These instruments are no longer in use.

#### Private songs

From precontact times, two genres of *tang* have survived: songs of love (*dafael'*), dealing with lovers' personal experiences, and songs of abuse (*t'aay*), recounting situations in which one party has supposedly injured another. Songs of abuse are a culturally legitimate means of social retaliation. Typical recipients of musical abuse are chiefs and former lovers. The word *t'aay* can also be glossed 'rust, filth, bilge, excrement'—senses that well describe the content of the texts. By local criteria of propriety, the subjects of *tang* made them unsuitable for public performance. Because the singer often sat under a pandanus tree, the songs became known as *taan e chooy* 'under the pandanus'.

During the Japanese period, a new genre developed: *teempraa utaa* (or *teempraa*) 'songs in mixed languages' combined Japanese melodies with Yapese and Japanese words. After 1945, this genre included songs based on American and European melodies, with mixed Yapese and English words. In an example that dates from the late 1940s or early 1950s (figure 5), the character singing is the composer's husband. The text gives a tongue-in-cheek account of his reasons for disappearing for several days on a binge:

> Chaaneyi Budweiser rebo fager nib athib,
> Nib felifela ligun kum nangi paingega n'ug.
> Ngeyani n'ageg ngabayang nike buchbuch yaag;
> Nge pangig nge lingug nge thilig make mil rog.
>
> Meni ruw dalip fanag mawor guguye tobin.
> Gura sul nga un fitheg mugub gu ana thilig.
> Guburom ku Budweiser; gubowurom ku San Miguel;
> Gutaw gad ku Asahi: make taran ma kaf ni gub.

FIGURE 5
"Budweiser," a *teempraa utaa,* as sung and translated by Raphaela Tinaan; original an octave lower. Transcription by Deirdre Marshall-Dean.

This Budweiser is a sweet friend,
Who also knows how to win me over.
He'll take, and I'll go along;
Then he leaves me alone when I'm not well.

Two or three days later, I haven't been home.
After I get home, I tell my story:
I went to see Budweiser; we went to see San Miguel;
We all arrived at Asahi's: now it's dawn and I'm home.

This text names the brands of beer most popular on Yap: Budweiser, San Miguel, and Asahi.

### Public songs

*Churuq* are monophonic, strophic songs, with narrow ranges. Melodic phrases curve upward. Most are in duple time. Older texts are about historical events, wars, and mythology, but newer texts frequently have biblical themes. Melodies and texts are often interchangeable.

    Yapese dancing and singing are inseparable. Men dance only with men; women, only with women. Children learn from adults of their own sex. Performances begin with a solo introduction, whose text apprises the audience of the story or sense of the dance.

Of the musical genres performed on the island, dance-songs are the most valued. As a social and communal obligation, their performance reinforces the sense of belonging to the community and helps confirm and define relationships, satisfying individual and social needs. In contrast, Yapese regard solo performances as personal expressions, which do not meet public needs (Carmen Chigiy, personal communication).

A group rehearses privately for several weeks. For approval, it then performs for its village. When the planned occasion has passed and the group has performed, the group performs again for the village. That performance is the *penga lan* 'hanging up'—a term that refers to the hanging up of valuables (including shell money) in the rafters of the meetinghouse (*pebai*). These practices hark back to the 1800s, when villages danced competitively.

In the late 1990s, Yapese *churuq* include dances by seated or standing performers, dances with bamboos, and marching dances.

### Dances

TRACK 42

*Par-nga-but* are line dances by seated performers wearing grass skirts and arm-and-head decorations made from coconut leaves and flowers. Movements of the upper body and arms illustrate the texts, which usually deal with events or people. Dancers' clapping accompanies a solo vocal introduction. A call from a soloist cues the start of unison singing, marked by another round of clapping.

#### Dances by standing performers

Many Yapese recognize four genres of dances by standing performers. For one, called *barug* by women and *tey* by men, dancers perform in a row. Among the oldest *churuq,* they are rarely performed. In style and subject, they resemble the dances by seated performers.

*Tam'* are funeral dances, whose movements resemble those of *barug.* Only women perform them, in honor of the dead.

In *täyoer,* women may proclaim a person's good deeds, reminding that person of his or her social duties; for the proclamation and performance the dancers then request payment (figure 6). Because this dance often serves to praise chiefs or persons of high status, people call it chiefly. After the line *Ga ira l'awe,* whose meaning is unknown to the translator, Carmen Chigiy, an example (figure 7) goes: *Padre Thall, o, gamade, / Liyol e kogbod, / Ningad fangicho gadi / Kefel!* 'Father Thall, oh, we / The girls are here, / For us to say / Farewell'. The text continues:

| | |
|---|---|
| Padre Thall, o, ngam | Father Thall, oh, you |
| Ma kammagar, | Are leaving, |
| Ko gubine a pigpig a ni | And we thank you |
| Kam tayu daken a yu, | For the service you provided, |
| Waab nayu ihi. | Here on Yap Island. |
| | |
| Padre Thall, o, mu tay i lim! | Father Thall, oh, listen! |
| Ngam man o ma, | You are leaving, |
| Gam nange wonoma da ni. | And you should know our minds. |
| Nga ma kumuh | We wish for |
| Ya ngar gu falan gadi. | Your return someday. |
| Padre! Kefel! | Father! Goodbye! |

FIGURE 6  Yapese children dance a *täyoer*. Photo by Deirdre Marshall-Dean, 1990.

| | |
|---|---|
| Padre Thall, o kefel! | Father Thall, oh, farewell! |
| Ke magar e Kan ni Zozup, | And we are thankful for the Holy Spirit, |
| Ke go mingo nag dad, u donap nayi, | Which has prepared us on earth, |
| Me waliy dad nga langi. | And will guide us to heaven. |
| Padre! Kefel! | Father! Goodbye! |

The text is in short phrases, set to music that uses a scale transcribable as E–G–A♭–B.

An erotic dance, *kuziol* (women's version) and *gasalaew* (men's version), has movements that suggest coital positions and techniques. The texts cite the erotic shortcomings of the opposite sex. The dance is also called *umman,* a term that denotes the thrusting of hips.

### Other dances

In *gamal',* paired dancers face each other in sets of four. On downbeats, each strikes a meter-long tube of bamboo against her partner's tube. When the dance becomes too vigorous for the performers to keep singing, a separate singer or group backs them up. Yapese believe *gamal'* traveled as payments of tribute from Woleai to Ulithi, and then to Yap. The texts are not in Yapese. Marching dances (*maas,* from English 'march') may have come from Pohnpei after 1945. No comprehensive study of these dances in the Carolines has been done.          —Deirdre Marshall-Dean

## Chuuk

One of the Federated States of Micronesia, Chuuk consists of about two dozen inhabited islands and atolls, on which about fifty-five thousand people live. Most of the following information comes from two locations: Namoluk, an outer-island atoll,

FIGURE 7  Excerpt from "Girls' Farewell for Father Thall," a *täyoer*, composed by Elvira Tinag in 1990. Transcription, from a performance at Colonia in 1990, by Carmen Chigiy.

FIGURE 8  Seated girls dance, Weno, Chuuk. Photo by Elisabeth Krämer, 1909. Institute of Ethnology, University of Tübingen.

southeast of Chuuk proper; and Weene (Weno, also called Moen), Peniyesene District. Most orthographical conventions follow those in Goodenough and Sugita 1980 and 1990. Throughout the state, people recognize two major classes of music: vocal and purely instrumental, usually played on a guitar.

### Vocal music

The oldest known vocal art, now moribund, is *ngor* 'recitation' ('sing' in Goodenough and Sugita 1980). *Ngor* survive as the texts of seated dances (figure 8), dances in lines (figure 9), and dances with sticks. Recitation was an important part of Chuukese lore (*rong*), a concept that included oral history, navigational instructions, and medicinal practices.

Vocal music (Mortlockese *kkéél*) on Namoluk divides into four genres: island songs (*kkéélún fénú*), hymns (*kkéélún fáál*), ballads and laments (*asangut*), and songs of love (*akinákun, ngorupapa*). Chuuk proper may have three genres: *emweyir, engi,* and *kéénún Seetan* (Goodenough and Sugita 1980 and 1990). Namoluk probably has no analog for *emweyir,* locally glossed 'song sung while carrying *mwatún* to present to the district chief'.

### Island songs

These are composed in commemoration of a communal event, location, or mood, or of a combination of these. They formerly served in interisland diplomacy and conflict resolution, and continue to provide a means of public comment and behavioral control. Most residents of a community know that entity's *kkéélún fénú.* Some island songs operate as an oral history, though chronicling is not always their primary purpose. Large mixed groups typically sing them in public meetings or musical competitions, where a musical expert (*sowukkéén*) leads. Performances are vocal, but small groups may use the accompaniment of guitar (*kitar*) and ukulele. Mortlockese can readily identify specific *kkéélún fénú* as the cultural property of one community or another: these songs operate as markers of communal distinctiveness and identity.

### Hymns

Christian hymns, translated into the languages of Chuuk, are sung by mixed choirs on Sundays in church, and on other church-sponsored occasions. Though often in

FIGURE 9    Men of Namoluk Atoll, Chuuk, celebrate Micronesia Day. Photo by Mac Marshall, 1971.

four-part harmony, hymns have taken on a local imprint or flavor; nevertheless, they come precomposed from abroad, and probably no one in Chuuk has composed any. The American Board of Commissioners for Foreign Missions and other Christian missions have produced hymnals in the language of Chuuk (originally in Mortlockese, now in Nomwoneyas dialect).

On Namoluk from 1969 to 1971 and on Chuuk in 1976 and 1985, people sang *kkéélún fáál* unaccompanied. During a Protestant service on Weene in August 1993, however, cassette-recorded instrumental music and an electronic keyboard provided accompaniment. This phenomenon is likely widespread in Chuuk State.

### Ballads and laments

*Asangut* may be the Mortlockese equivalent of what Goodenough and Sugita (1990), for the language of Chuuk Lagoon, give as *engi* 'song of lament (in love or mourning)', and of what are called *wur* in the western atolls of Chuuk State. As with *kkéélún fénú,* these songs are locally composed. Prestige accrues to *chóón fféér kkéél,* people who compose music and lyrics.

*Asangut* on Namoluk fill a niche much like country music: they are songs of sadness, pining, homesickness, lost love, unfulfilled passion, and occasionally of blame. Their themes frequently involve a person's departure for a destination outside Chuuk State. Such a person may be a spouse, a lover, a child—or even, during the 1920s and 1930s, male conscript laborers, taken by the Japanese to work in phosphate mines on Angaur. As on many Pacific Islands, departures on Namoluk are important events, and *asangut* that mark them are emotion-laden and highly evocative. Firmly grounded in community and place, *asangut* tell of longing, unrequited love, and fears the one who has gone away may never return. Hearing *asangut* taped in 1969–1971 has brought tears to the eyes of adults from Namoluk visiting in the United States.

In specificity and identification with named communities in Chuuk, *asangut* resemble *kkéélún fénú.* Small groups, of six or fewer (male or female), sing them, usually accompanied by string band, guitar, or ukulele.

### Songs of love

By 1950, these songs had gained Western melodies, foreign words, and reduced lengths (Fischer and Swartz 1960:218). In the late 1990s, composers continued producing new examples. In Chuuk, people call these songs *kkéénun lukun* 'nonreligious songs'. In 1976 and 1985, they were often called *itenipwin*—a term that denotes nighttime activities: dancing, singing, serenading, lovemaking, and murdering (Goodenough and Sugita 1980).

Since the 1960s or before, the local radio station has played tapes made by groups of youths from around Chuuk who compete to have their songs aired. Groups of unmarried young men (*aluel; anuon* in Chuuk), between the ages of about twelve and twenty-five, sing *akinákun* in falsetto, accompanying themselves on guitars or ukuleles, or on combinations of those.

Songs of love are structurally repetitive: melodies have narrow ranges; instrumentalists strum the same chords over and over. The lyrics, highly variable, usually extol the beauty and virtues of a particular young woman, and express longing for her affection. They frequently express self-deprecation, protestations of unworthiness, and masochism (Fischer and Swartz 1960:221, 223).

Young men often sing of dejection because their sentiments are unnoticed, unreciprocated, or rejected. By day, they practice *akinákun* alone; only after dark, sitting in a tight circle outside a young woman's house, do they perform in earnest. Against the quiet of the night they raise their voices. The object of their appreciation appears at her door, with other members of her family. A lyric popular in 1997, with even-numbered lines rhyming *abba*, was:

| | |
|---|---|
| Tong mi fat mi nimienimech ningen | As beautiful as clear water |
| Tongom me rei. | Is my undying love for you. |
| Esop usun tongei me remw mi chok— | Unlike your faded love for me— |
| Pinekunek. | A pool of murky water. |
| Met lomotan awomw an apasa pue tong | Your often whispered words of love |
| Nge ua silei a rik omw ekiek. | Cannot hide that you no longer love me. |
| Ua chimweta ne ua kan ne kekechiw, | In the morning I awake crying, |
| Pwe a keukitiw poren sechaulei. | For I realize you only reject me. |

As the serenade unfolds, the young woman and her female kin step down from the house and sprinkle the singers with fragrant coconut oil or water, or with imported hair oil and aftershave.

### Instrumental music

Instrumental music has one lexically labeled form: *polka*. As the word suggests, it is a postcontact introduction, as are the instruments on which people play it: usually a six-stringed acoustic guitar, sometimes a ukulele, and especially nowadays a keyboard. Performed solo, *polka* requires skill. The performer plucks the strings rapidly. By contrast, when guitars and ukuleles accompany other forms of singing, the performers strum the strings. Using a wider range of notes than songs of love, *polka* come across as lively, energetic, "happy" pieces. Like *kkéélún fénú* and *akinákun,* they are locally composed, and WSZC radio often plays them.

Europeans and Americans who had early contact with the islanders of Chuuk State mentioned few musical instruments. Goodenough and Sugita (1990) present *nikattik* or *nikettik* as a generic word for 'any musical instrument; whistle'.

One instrument that has disappeared was a nose-blown flute, *aangún* or *nikaangún* (Goodenough and Sugita 1990). A photograph of a young man playing one appears in Damm and Sarfert (1935). Chordophones do not appear to have been used, nor were drums in evidence, except possibly in the Mortlocks (Fischer 1970 [1957]:203). Performers emphasized rhythms by slapping themselves in synchrony, and during stick dances by cracking together sturdy wooden poles (*kurukur*).

In the late twentieth century, U.S. popular music—on cassettes and CDs, sold in stores and broadcast on radio—became widespread in Chuuk. Many people owned VCRs and had access to cable TV, which offered new avenues for U.S. music to penetrate the culture. In the early 1990s, in areas where homes had electricity, young people began to play electric guitars and keyboards.

—MAC MARSHALL, LARRY GABRIEL, JOAKIM MANNIWEL PETER

### Dance

In Chuuk State, dancing is called *pwérúk* (Goodenough and Sugita 1980:294; 1990:92). The term *pwaay* is common on Polowat, in the Western Islands (Elbert 1972:137), and on Satawal, a culturally related island in Yap State. Descriptions appear in Ishimori (1987) and Damm and Sarfert (1935). The material presented here is based on work on Pollap and Namonuito atolls, and among Pollapese on Weno.

Much Chuukese dancing has disappeared because missionaries prohibited dances they considered immoral or pagan, though they allowed dances they thought promoted strength and agility (Fischer 1970:207; Flinn 1992:61). Pollapese talk of stick dances learned through possession by spirits; connections between Chuukese dancing and gods or spirits appear in Bollig (1967:195), Ishimori (1987:249), and Krämer (1935:96–97, 151; 1968 [1932]:434). The German government prohibited dancing because it robbed time from work (Krämer 1968 [1932]:442).

Pollapese describe their older dancing, which persisted longest in the (less acculturated) Western Islands, as consisting of daily and specially celebratory dances. When breadfruit were ripening, men performed in a vigorous style, promoting physical strength for the work of harvesting. Performers began seated, and stood to execute more strenuous dances. During the lean season (when, to conserve resources, chiefs limited the harvesting of coconuts and taro), dancing occupied the people and kept them under watchful eyes. Dances celebrated large catches of fish, navigators' initiations, and interinsular gatherings.

Dancing remains a part of festivities and celebrations, including those at Christmas and Easter, visits from dignitaries, dedications of churches, and gubernatorial inaugurations. Dances include selections from the old corpus of seasonal dances, newly composed examples (especially by women honoring relatives and dignitaries), *maas* (marching dances), *pwérúken fáán maram* 'dances under the moon' (celebrating romance), and other, borrowed genres.

All Pollapese, even small children, participate. Individuals may achieve recognition as experts, but the Pollapese deem everyone capable of dancing. Furthermore, dancing is a collective endeavor: performers dance with others of the same gender and sometimes with those of similar age. I once saw women briefly join men, and was told that men may dance with women as a way of showing pride in them; the appearance was spontaneous, not choreographed. Performers focus on onlookers, who may shower dancers with perfume and other gifts; such actions warded off magic from "ill-disposed spectators" (Bollig 1967:199).

### Aesthetic components of dancing

Recognized aspects of danced performance are lyrics, melodies, and movements, which may combine independently. Men and women sometimes use the same melody and movements but different lyrics. Dancers perform similar movements in synchrony, accompanying their own singing but without instruments. Percussion and rhythm are supplied by clapping, slapping thighs and arms, stepping, and, in some dances, clashing sticks.

Men are associated with mobility, bravery, sea—women with stability, nurturance, land. Women garden and care for homes and children. Men leave their natal homes, fish, and sail to other islands.

Typically, men or women march in with a dance and sit in rows: two if only a small group, more if larger. A few may briefly stand to dance, not as solo performers, but singing and moving with the rest. The point is to enhance the dance as a whole, not to bring attention to oneself. Eventually, all rise and dance standing.

Clothing and bodily ornaments enhance the movements, especially swaying when standing. Decisions about dress are typically made in advance. Dancers dress as similarly as possible, with no single dancer outshining the others, and with little gender-specific costumery distinguishing the sexes. Men wear a loincloth and women a skirt, of which the finest are colored woven cotton; otherwise, dancers wear lengths of cloth, with red a favorite color. They usually wear an overskirt of young coconut leaves, a mantle of coconut leaves on the upper body, one or more beaded necklaces, and a garland on their heads. They sometimes tie young coconut leaves around their upper arms, wrists, and middle fingers. Women traditionally danced with no other upper-body covering, and still do in many of the outer islands. Since the 1980s, however, Pollapese women have been opting to wear halters when they dance publicly on Weno. Garlands are made of flowers, fragrant leaves, young coconut fronds, or sometimes imported flowers and fabric. Belts, usually of black and red beads, are other options. Performers may smear paint, including turmeric, on their faces and upper chests. The rustling of coconut-frond skirts and mantles (and formerly the sound of shell jewelry) and the smell of flowers enhance the beauty of the presentation (Steager 1979:351–352).

Some melodies of dance-songs are Western; others are of older and indigenous styles. Chuukese borrow dances from each other, sometimes influenced by foreign administrations. Lyrics are sprinkled with English, German, and Japanese phrases; older lyrics, because their diction is figurative and symbolic, tend not to be widely understood. Islanders freely adapt lyrics: they may change the lyrics of a *pwéruken fáán maram* to honor the bishop; they may borrow a melody and lyrics but maintain their own movements.

These dances reflect cultural notions about appropriate behavior (Flinn 1992, 1993). The emphasis on the group and similarity highlights a cultural focus on concern for kin, rather than individualism. Pollapese dance with those of the same gender, just as they work and socialize with them. They say women compose dances that highlight caring and nurturance (locally interpreted as female traits), but men's dances extol strength, bravery, fishing, navigation, and warfare.

This dichotomy dovetails with beliefs about gender: men are associated with mobility, bravery, sea; women, with stability, nurturance, land. Women garden and care for land, homes, and children, the resources of matrilineal descent groups. After marriage, women remain in their natal homes. Men leave their natal homes, fish, sail, and travel to other islands. Women are expected to compose songs and dances that honor their kin by expressing feelings of concern; men's songs and dances invoke the past, vaunting adventures of travel.

—JULIANA FLINN

## Pohnpei

Pohnpeian music is mostly vocal, performed with or without instrumental accompaniment. When heard in public, it is usually choral; solo singing is done primarily for small children, or privately in courtship. The most common occasions for singing are kava-drinking sessions, religious services, religious activities, and broadcasts. Singing sometimes accompanies collective or communal projects, including fishing, cutting brush, and processing copra. It is an integral part of most dancing, and choirs may perform in the absence of dancers.

John L. Fischer (1970 [1957]) described "native-style" songs having two-tone melodies marked by shifts in rhythm and syncopation; by the 1950s, only the oldest Pohnpeians remembered these songs. Instrumental music of the 1990s is mainly that of string bands, but immigrants and visitors from Pingelap and Mwokiloa atolls have an important percussive repertory.

### Diffusion in Pohnpeian musical history

Songs and dances have much in common throughout the eastern and central Caroline Islands, reflecting ancient patterns of regional integration and frequent interisland contacts, despite the distances between adjacent islands—in some cases, 325 kilometers or more. Forms of social organization, mythological themes, agricultural and economic activities, and political processes, with singing and dancing, provide clear evidence of long-term diffusion among these populations.

Dances with sticks are known on almost every island in the Carolines (on Pohnpei, paddles replace mock-spears), as are certain styles of choral singing. Interinsular relationships have disseminated to every island in the eastern Carolines the choral styles introduced in the mid-1800s by missionaries from the American Board of Commissioners for Foreign Missions. Simple four-part harmony is common to all these traditions.

The earliest European visitors to Pohnpei described formal songs (*koul*) and dances (*kahlek*), performed in houses built on raised platforms, which served as stages (O'Connell 1972 [1836]). Pohnpeians speak of their ancestors' dancing in floating canoes while twirling paddles. Many Pohnpeian communities (*kousapw* 'local chiefdoms') support casually organized troupes, which rehearse for performances on special occasions. At the island's Roman Catholic sodality conventions and intercongregational Protestant convocations, many of these troupes perform. Some items they perform are old; these include the lengthy song and dance that recount the history of the rebellion of the Sokehs chiefdom against the German colonial administration, in 1910 (Petersen 1992:23–24). Other items introduce new styles. Often male clowning plays a role in otherwise quite decorous performances.

Interinsular cultural diffusion has enormously affected Pohnpeian musical styles and themes. Most public singing is in four-part harmony. Melodies are continually appropriated from hymns and popular tunes. Songs transcribed by the German ethnographer Paul Hambruch (1932–1936) reflect these influences. The Japanese ethnological expedition that traveled throughout Micronesia in 1936 recorded at least one Japanese song, a *bon* dance (Tatar 1985). In the 1940s, Fischer collected songs that included lyrics and melodies borrowed from Japanese songs. Today, Pohnpeian lyrics are often set to the music of English-language popular songs. In the mid-1970s, a local version of the Beatles' "Ob-la-di, ob-la-da" delighted listeners.

### Pohnpeian musical genres

In many communities, young men play guitars in string bands, sharing and composing songs. Some string bands record their music on cassettes, which circulate among appreciative audiences; some reach the island's Pohnpeian-language radio station,

WSZD, which features daily programs of local music, mainly in the early evenings, when many Pohnpeians convene to drink kava (*sakau*). These songs typically have romantic themes (especially of beautiful young women), but some comment on current events or offer lightly veiled commentary on, or criticism of, individuals or events. Many melodies are continually recycled with new lyrics.

At feasts (especially large formal feasts, where paramount chiefs are present), successively larger kava plants are sometimes carried in procession and stacked in the center of the house. As each plant is placed in position, a master of ceremonies sings a line from an ancient recitation (*ngis*). These occasions are almost the only times ancient recitations are now heard in public; historians (*soupoad*) may recite them to recount the island's history. At the same feasts, kava is ritually prepared. The pounding of stone on stone eventually becomes regularized into metrical pounding (*tempel*), which may continue for five minutes or so. Sometimes during this pounding, older women spontaneously mount the platforms that line three sides of the interior of the house, and improvise movements to the beat of the pounding.

Songs of love (*koulin sampah*) are sung in private contexts. A comparative study found that Chuukese and Pohnpeian examples relied on stereotyped themes and borrowed melodies, and were sung softly, so as not to be overheard. Chuukese songs tended to dwell upon death, pain, and sacrifice, but Pohnpeian songs included more emphasis on aggression, boasting, and self-assertion, as in the following translation (after Fischer and Swartz 1960:222).

| | |
|---|---|
| I would like to return to you | How punishing for you to sin |
| But this is what I regard as punishing: | And not keep it secret from me! |
| For I pity my name | For this is what I suffer from: |
| Becoming classed with an old person. | My name has been destroyed because of you. |

—GLENN PETERSEN

## Kosrae

Kosrae comprises one high island and a few nearby islands, historically and prehistorically in communication with Nauru, the Marshall Islands, and Pohnpei. Kosrae has four main populations: Utwe, Malem, and Tafunsak on the high island, and Lelu Island, ancient and modern seat of government and site of a monumentally stone-walled, canal-crossed compound, home of the paramount chief, the Tokosra (figure 10).

### Music and society

Because the first Europeans who wrote about Kosraean music knew little but European harmonies, the music sounded dissonant to them. In 1824, René Primevère Lesson, on the first European vessel to visit Kosrae, wrote: "The singing of the natives has nothing agreeable about it. There are sorts of sentences without rhyme, pronounced with a slow and monotonous tone" (Ritter and Ritter 1982:69).

Before the earliest European visits, the population had declined, apparently from a typhoon and warfare—losses accentuated in the 1800s by exposure to foreign diseases, which resulted in a plunge to fewer than three hundred people. As the survivors then embraced a Protestant Christianity that considered dancing and singing anything but Christian hymns immoral, drastic cultural transformations followed.

The most hierarchical Carolinean society, Kosrae was united under the Tokosra. The major deities were Sinlaka, a female associated with breadfruit and typhoons, and Sitel Nosrunsrap, a male identified with thunder, lightning, and turtles. With feasting, dancing, and singing at Lelu, Kosraeans honored Sinlaka in an annual breadfruit festival. Sitel Nosrunsrap may originally have been an ancestral spirit of

FIGURE 10   Two men dance in front of a Kosrae chief's house. Lithograph after a drawing by A. Postels, from the voyage of Lütke (1835). Photo Smithsonian Institution.

the lineage of the Tokosra, with whom he was associated in a recitation collected by Fyedor Petrovich Lütke in 1827, during the second European visit: *Talaelem séka mai. / Sitel-Nazuenziap. / Rin séka. / Naïtouolen séka. / Seouapin séka. / Chiechou séka. / Mananziaoua séka. / Kajoua-sin-liaga séka. / Kajoua-sin-nionfou séka. / Olpat séka. / Togoja [Tokosra] séka* (1835–1836:1:394, after Ritter and Ritter 1982:130).

The word *mai* was vocalized on a drawn-out tone. This text prefigured late-twentieth-century practices of intoning the names of important persons or places as mnemonics for transmitting history. It names the god's wives and sons, ending with the Tokosra; each phrase concludes with a word probably to be taken as *sekau,* the kava plant. Today's presentational styles, which may reflect that of the 1820s, would require a descent at the end of each phrase and a response by listeners.

Members of the Südsee-Expedition arrived nearly fifty years after the population had reached its nadir. Among them, Ernst Sarfert (1919, 1920) recorded vocal music of several kinds, based on a two-tone scale (Segal 1989:141). John L. Fischer, writing later, described this music:

> Native songs had a range of only a few notes, sometimes only two, and complexity was introduced by rhythm and syncopations in the shift from one note to the other. It is surprising how subtle and difficult a two note song can be to a Westerner used to less complex rhythms and more regular tone shifts. (1970 [1957]:204)

### Music and dance

Reciting, singing, and dancing were intertwined. A long music-dance sequence began with a women's recitation (*usok*), followed by a *mulmul,* a song using a two-tone scale, animated by clapping and graceful twists and bends. The line dance (*ra*) that followed was more active, with slapping and brisk movements of arms and feet; the men wore shell bracelets and wreathed ferns and flowers (Segal 1989:31). This sometimes led into an *alul,* in which women seated in a circle sang, and men, each sometimes with his arms on the neck of the next, moved in synchrony, swinging an arm and stamping their feet. Sarfert observed children's games, including *oakoak kekajo*, which mimics these movements, and three dances with sticks (*unin sak*) and associated music. Lesson reported a children's clapping game that appears to have been practice for stick-dance movements (Ritter and Ritter 1982:203). *Nepe* is a seated women's dance. At the end of festivities, to drumbeats only, the *salsal* was apparently danced by chiefs, in twos or threes.

A critical principle of performance involving movement is synchrony:

> Some men get in a line one behind the other, slowly execute in the same place some movement of the feet and move their hands in different ways which apparently lack system. This is done with an exactitude so surprising that in looking at the column from the back, one would think that these were robots moved by a single movement. (Lütke in Ritter and Ritter 1982:126)

At a dance in the mid-1800s, performers would "stand erect, all except the drummers, their bodies leaning forward, backwards, sideways, stooping halfway down, raising up, arms to right or left, above the head or pointing down, in perfect keeping with each other, as perfect as machinery" (Cordy 1993:46).

Kosrae had several kinds of recitation: historical, religious, and instrumental, including those to move stones from the mainland for construction at Lelu. Struck stones, blown conchs, and certain recitations communicated with deities and spirits. The *bas* was a song that builders of houses and canoes used for moving logs. Before roofing, the *amela* was sung by one man at each corner of the house. The *supsup* was sung on a raft towing a sugarcane offering to the Tokosra. Burial, honorific, and other offering recitations have been documented.

Some songs helped with work and love. Lütke became the focus of the latter as he walked along the seashore during a moonlit evening, the usual place and time of courtship: the girls "sought to conquer me with their gaiety; they laughed, they sang songs in which my name was repeated" (Ritter and Ritter 1982:103).

### Musical instruments

At Okat harbor was a huge basalt stone that priests struck to call Sitel Nosrunsrap. A stone at Lelu, struck at a royal birth, figured in a children's game, indicating its more general use as a signal. Daily, sacred kava was rhythmically pounded on stones. Other musical instruments included conchs (*ukuk*), used in religious ceremonies. An hourglass drum (*asig*) was apparently imported from the Marshall Islands in association with Marshallese dances (Fischer 1970 [1957]:203). A hollowed-out log served for percussion (Haley 1948:158–159), as in Pohnpei today.

### Traders and missionaries

By the mid-1800s, Kosrae had become a major station for U.S. whalers. The first trading schooner arrived in 1830. By 1852, whalers were visiting regularly. Because of these encounters, sailor's hornpipes played on harmonicas have locally become important musical pieces.

In 1852, the U.S. missionaries Benjamin Snow and his wife, with the Hawaiian missionary Opunui and his wife, arrived and taught Christian hymns in four-part harmony. They and later missionaries banned indigenous music and dance. Later U.S. missionaries, the Baldwin sisters, were so intent on protecting Kosraeans from unseemly influences, they destroyed 250 phonograph records donated from Boston (Price 1936).

### *Music of the 1990s*

Today's music, including U.S. country and pan-Micronesian songs translated into Kosraean and performed by indigenous artists, is strongly influenced by hymns, which form the bulk of religious services. Choirs primarily sing unaccompanied. Christmas, the major festival, is observed with feasting and long processionals, which wind into the church in a manner recalling Kosraean dancing of the early 1800s. Songs and marches are composed and arranged for the occasion, and every four years overseas Kosraeans return to join in.

After a century of disuse, Kosraean recitations, songs, and dances are being reinstated and reinterpreted. At state occasions, including the opening of the Kosrae airport-dock complex in 1983, men standing in ranks performed a hornpipe (Fanshawe 1995); each man occasionally rested his arms on the shoulders of the one in front, blending Kosraean and sailors' styles. At the 1988 Pacific Festival of Arts, Kosraean dancers recreated stick dances.

—KAREN L. NERO

## MARIANA ISLANDS

The Marianas Archipelago includes the U.S. territory of Guam (the largest island in Micronesia) and the Commonwealth of the Northern Marianas, including Saipan, Tinian, Rota, and other islands. During the 1600s, the indigenous people, now called Chamorro, were ravaged by war and disease. The present population is a mixture of Chamorro, Filipinos, and others.

Archaeological excavations have revealed an important ceramic tradition, Marianas Redware (pottery having a thin red slip), radiocarbon-dated to about 1800 B.C. and related to similar pottery in the central Philippines. This tradition locally evolved into Marianas Plainware and later died out.

The Chamorro built impressive architectural sites, some of which date to about a thousand years ago. These sites consist of double rows of megalithic columns (*latte*) with upturned hemispherical capstones, which served as bases for large wooden structures. The remains of the House of Taga on Tinian, depicted by George Anson on his visit in 1742, included twelve stone columns 5 meters high, part of a site that ran parallel to the coast and included large stone platforms; even by Anson's visit, however, the site was not in use. Wooden houses may have resembled Palauan high-gabled *bai,* built on *latte* and housing chiefs and their families. The *latte* sites are associated with the Marianas Plainware tradition.

Little is known of the indigenous arts of the Marianas, including music and dance, and few objects are found in museums. In the Pacific Festivals of Arts, performers from the Marianas often present plays based on reconstructed traditions (figure 11), and performances based on the manipulation of sticks. Introduced music includes that of brass bands, string bands, and modern styles popular throughout the world.

—ADRIENNE L. KAEPPLER

FIGURE 11 At the Pacific Festival of Arts, performers from the Northern Marianas celebrate their past. Photo by Adrienne L. Kaeppler, 1996.

FIGURE 12    Guitar and piano provide music for European-inspired ballroom dancing in the Mariana Islands, 1945. Photo U.S. National Archives.

## Guam

European explorers of the 1600s noted that the Chamorro were fond of singing and highly esteemed their poets. Their songs apparently had the instrumental accompaniment of handheld rattles, made by encasing seashells or seeds in woven pouches. Steps and gestures accompanied certain songs, but these did not survive Spanish colonial influence (1668–1898). Historical references to a circle of women who sang and danced to the sounds of handheld shells have become the basis for latter-day recreations of indigenous dances. In the *bailan uritao* 'bachelors' dance', 2-meter-long sticks are struck and moved in intricate rhythmic patterns.

Dances within living memory are European genres, adapted to fit indigenous systems of structured movement (figure 12). They include a local polka (*so'tis,* sometimes spelled *sohtis*), a local waltz (*batsu*), and a Philippine dance with sticks (*bailan fayao*). In the coconut-shell dance (*bailan a'iguas*), while making *so'tis* steps, performers rhythmically clap shells together. Since the 1950s, the cha-cha has been popular on Guam.

### The chamorrita

A genre that probably evolved from aboriginal culture is the *chamorrita,* whose text is a series of improvised quatrains, with the second and fourth lines rhyming (Bailey 1981). With slight variations, one melody sets all quatrains. Singers use a nasal timbre, most extremely on Rota. A lively melody, "*Lelulelu*" (figure 13), repeated after each quatrain, reflects musical influences from the Spanish colonial period.

Adults formerly sang *chamorritas* in groups while working. Performances were responsorial and competitive. Listeners rated singers by their skill in improvising responses appropriate to an opponent's quatrain. Sessions could last for hours. They often began with several soloists, called *kantot* (male) and *kantora* (female), but ended with two competitors, as less skilled improvisers dropped out to join the chorus. Only elders now sing *chamorritas.* By the 1990s, young people were ignoring the genre; having incomplete knowledge of the Chamorro language, they responded mainly to rock.

FIGURE 13   The melody of the nonsense refrain "*Lelulelu*," showing Spanish musical influences.

Texts of *chamorritas* relate the romance of courting couples, the ridicule of social rivals, and the humor of sexual acts. They richly play on words, often conveying layered meanings. An example sung by a man to his woman uses stock phrases, known by most singers:

| | |
|---|---|
| Ti gumadi yu' put ti'ao; | I'm not casting my net for little fishes; |
| Na gumadi yu' put hagu. | I'm casting my net for you. |
| Yan hu chechit hao tres biahi, | When I whistle three times, |
| Yuti' gadi' ya-un falagu. | Throw your net and run. |

Each line has eight syllables, some of which consist of two moras. The strophe rhymes *abcb*. The text makes romantic innuendos, most obviously in the second line. One sense of the first couplet is that the singer declares he loves his woman to the exclusion of others, the "little fishes." The second couplet has at least two senses: when the singer whistles three times, the woman should run to him; and she should fix her love exclusively on him.

### Popular music

Local popular music resembles country, which has influenced local composers since the 1930s, when the U.S. naval administration brought in cowboy movies. Possibly because of the practice of improvising lyrics for existing tunes (as in *chamorritas*), musicians of the 1990s often compose new lyrics for the music of old songs. This practice is exemplified in the song "You Are My Sunshine," translated into Chamorro and adopted as a local musical icon: a common change in its translation is the first line, *Hagu i flores* 'You are the flowers', rather than the Chamorro equivalent of 'You are my sunshine'.

### Musical instruments

The principal Chamorro musical instrument is the *belembaotuyan,* a struck chordophone, which appeared in Guam during the Spanish colonial period, brought by sailors in the galleon trade, or by whalers. It came from Brazil, where its prototype, the *berimbao,* had developed from African origins. In the Chamorro version, a two-meter-long bow secures a string noosed near its midpoint by a steel wire, whose location sets the tuning; half of a gourd, affixed to the middle of the bow, provides resonance. The player holds the open end of the gourd against his belly (*tuyan*) and strikes the string with a pencil-thin piece of bamboo, held in the right hand. Between the string and the board, the left-hand fingers rise to touch the string while the bamboo strikes it, producing two tones. Photos from the early 1900s show players lying on their backs with the resonator placed on their bellies. Performers now play sitting.

The *belembaotuyan* accompanies a singer or other instruments, including harmonicas, button accordions, and guitars. Chamorro lore recalls a lamellaphone (*belembaopachut*), probably made of bamboo, but nothing of its music has survived.

### Local resources

The Guam Council on the Arts & Humanities Agency, established in 1982, serves the Territory of Guam. It receives state-grant monies from the National Endowment for the Arts, and awards them to applicants for local projects. Its mission is to encourage and assist the development of all arts, especially traditional arts. It has

***bailan a'iguas*** Chamorro dance in which performers take polka steps while rhythmically clapping coconut shells togethr

***bailan fayao*** Philippine stick dance, popular in Guam

***bailan uritao*** Chamorro dance in which men strike 2-meter-long sticks and rhythmically move them in intricate patterns

***batsu*** Chamorro waltz

***belembaotuyan*** Chamorro musical bow, whose string, struck with a pencil-thin piece of bamboo, produces two tones by the use of a tuning noose and the player's variable touch with his fingers

**Chamolinian** Countrylike blend of Chamorro and Carolinian music performed by Saipan-dwelling immigrants from Yap and Chuuk

***chamorrita*** Chamorro strophic song with textually improvised quatrains, of which the second and fourth lines rhyme

**Chamorro** The indigenous people of Guam

***so'tis*** Chamorro polka

---

published a video documenting the history of the *belembaotuyan,* including interviews with two surviving masters of the instrument (Soliwada 1980). It has released a cassette illustrating the sounds of the *belembaotuyan,* religious songs, *chamorritas,* and songs of love (Flores 1992).

Members of the Carolinian community—founded by immigrants from Yap and Chuuk, who for generations have lived on Saipan—have contributed their musical heritage to the music of Guam. Their blend of Chamorro and Carolinian music has been called Chamolinian by those who compose it. Strongly influenced by country, it gains a unique identity by combining ukuleles and guitars with rich vocal harmonies.

—JUDY FLORES

---

**REFERENCES**

Bailey, C. R. Kim. 1981. "Chamorrita Songs: A Surviving Legacy of the Mexican *Verso?*" Micronesian Area Research Center Archives, University of Guam.

———. 1985. "Acculturation and Change in Ponapean Dances." *Dance Research Annual* 15:122–130.

Bollig, P. Laurentius. 1967 [1927]. *Die Bewohner der Truk-Inseln: Religion, Leben und kurze Grammatik eines Mikronesiervolkes.* Translated for the Yale Cross-Cultural Survey in connection with the Navy Pacific Islands Handbook Project. New Haven: Human Relations Area Files.

Born, L. 1903. "Einige Bemerkungen über Musik, Dichtkunst und Tanz der Yapleute." *Zeitschrift für Ethnologie* 35:134–142.

Cordy, Ross. 1993. *The Lelu Stone Ruins: Kosrae, Micronesia.* Honolulu: Social Science Research Institute, University of Hawai'i Press.

Damm, Hans, and Ernst Sarfert. 1935. *Inseln um Truk.* Vol. 2. Ergebnisse der Südsee-Expedition, 1908–1910, ed. Georg Thilenius, II.B.6. Hamburg: Friederischen, de Gruyter.

Elbert, Samuel H. 1972. *Puluwat Dictionary.* Pacific Linguistics, C 24. Canberra: Linguistic Circle of Canberra.

Fanshawe, David, ed. 1995. *Spirit of Micronesia: Traditional Music Recorded between 1978–1984: Chants, Hymns, Dances from Kiribati, Marshall Islands, Kosrae, Pohnpei, Chuuk, Yap & Palau.* Saydisc Records SDL-414. Compact disc.

Fischer, John L. 1970 [1957]. *The Eastern Carolines.* New Haven: Human Relations Area Files Press.

Fischer, John L., and Marc J. Swartz. 1960. "Socio-Psychological Aspects of Some Trukese and Ponapean Love Songs." *Journal of American Folklore* 73:218–224.

Flinn, Juliana. 1992. "Pulapese Dance: Asserting Identity and Tradition in Modern Contexts." *Pacific Studies* 15(4):57–66.

———. 1993. "Who Defines Custom? Dance and Gender in a Micronesian Case." *Anthropological Forum* 6(4):557–566.

Flores, Judy, ed. 1992. *Musikan Guahan.* Agaña: Guam Council on the Arts & Humanities. Cassette.

Freycinet, Louis Claude de Saulses de. 1825. *Voyage autour du monde . . . pendant les années 1817–1820.* 2 vols. and atlas. Paris: Pillet Aîné.

Goodenough, Ward H., and Hiroshi Sugita. 1980. *Trukese-English Dictionary.* Memoir 141. Philadelphia: American Philosophical Society.

———. 1990. *Trukese-English Dictionary: English-Trukese and Index of Trukese Root Words.* Philadelphia: American Philosophical Society.

Haley, Nelson. 1948. *Whale Hunt: The Narrative of a Voyage by Nelson Cole Haley, Harpooner in the Ship Charles W. Morgan 1849–1853.* New York: Ives Washburn.

Hambruch, Paul. 1932–1936. *Ponape.* Ergebnisse der Südsee-Expedition 1908–1910, ed. Georg Thilenius, II.B.7. Hamburg: Friedrichsen, de Gruyter.

Hijikata, Hisakatsu. 1993 [1941]. "Palauan Dances." In *Society and Life in Palau,* ed. Hisashi Endo, 191–197. Collective Works of Hisakatsu Hijikata. Tokyo: Sasakawa Peace Foundation.

———. 1995. *Gods and Religion of Palau.* Edited by Hisashi Endo. Collective Works of Hisakatsu Hijikata. Tokyo: Sasakawa Peace Foundation.

———. 1996. *Myths and Legends of Palau* Edited by Hisashi Endo. Collective Works of Hijikata Hisakatsu. Tokyo: Sasakawa Peace Foundation.

Ishimori, Shuzo. 1987. "Song and Cosmology on Satawal." In *Cultural Uniformity and Diversity in Micronesia,* ed. Iwao Ushijima and Kenichi Sudo, 241–253. Osaka: National Museum of Ethnology.

Keate, George. 1788. *An Account of the Pelew Islands . . . Composed from the Journals and Communications of Captain Henry Wilson.* London: privately printed.

Krämer, Augustin F. 1926. *Palau.* Ergebnisse der Südsee-Expedition 1908–1910, ed. Georg Thilenius. Hamburg: Friederichsen, De Gruyter.

———. 1935. *Inseln um Truk.* Vol. 1. Ergebnisse der Südsee-Expedition 1908–1910, ed. Georg Thilenius, II.B.6. Hamburg: Friederichsen, de Gruyter.

———. 1968 [1932]. *Truk.* Translated for the Yale Cross-Cultural Survey in connection with the Navy Pacific Islands Handbook Project. Ergebnisse der Südsee-Expedition 1908–1910, ed. Georg Thilenius, II.B.5. New Haven, Conn.: Human Relations Area Files.

Lütke, Frédéric [Fyedor Petrovich]. 1835–1836. *Voyage autour du monde.* 4 vols. Paris: Firmin Didot.

O'Connell, James. 1972 [1836]. *A Residence of Eleven Years in New Holland and the Caroline Islands.* Honolulu: University Press of Hawai'i.

Petersen, Glenn. 1992. "Dancing Defiance: The Politics of Pohnpeian Dance Performances." *Pacific Studies* 15(4):13–28.

Pinsker, Eve C. 1992. "Celebrations of Government: Dance Performance and Legitimacy in the Federated States of Micronesia." *Pacific Studies* 15(4):29–56.

Price, Willard. 1936. *Pacific Adventure.* New York: Reynal & Hitchcock.

Rehuher, Faustina K. 1995. "The Museum As a Guardian of Tradition: Authenticating Performing Arts." In *Pacific History: Papers from the 8th Pacific History Conference,* ed. Donald H. Rubinstein, 447–453. Mangilao: University of Guam Press.

Ritter, Lynn Takata, and Philip L. Ritter, ed. and trans. 1982. *The European Discovery of Kosrae Island: Accounts by Louis Isidore Duperrey, Jules Sebastien César Dumont D'Urville, René Primevère Lesson, Fyedor Lütke, and Friedrich Heinrich von Kittlitz.* Micronesian Archaeological Survey, report 13. Saipan: Office of the High Commissioner.

Sarfert, Ernst. 1919. *Kusae.* Vol. 1. Ergebnisse der Südsee-Expedition 1908–1910, ed. Georg Thilenius, II.B.4. Hamburg: Friederichsen.

———. 1920. *Kusae.* Vol. 2. Ergebnisse der Südsee-Expedition 1908– 1910, ed. Georg Thilenius, II.B.4. Hamburg: Friederichsen.

Segal, Harvey Gordon. 1989. *Kosrae: The Sleeping Lady Awakens.* Pohnpei: Good News Press.

Soliwada, Lee, ed. 1980. *Belembaotuyan.* 30 mins. Agaña: Guam Council on the Arts & Humanities Agency. Video.

Steager, Peter W. 1979. "Where Does Art Begin on Puluwat?" In *Exploring the Visual Art of Oceania: Australia, Melanesia, Micronesia, and Polynesia,* ed. Sidney M. Mead, 342–353. Honolulu: University Press of Hawai'i.

Tanabe, Hisao. 1935. "Māsharu oyobi Karorin guntō ni okeru ongaku to buyō" (Music and dance in the Marshall and Caroline Islands). *Minzokugaku Kenkyū* 1:258–276.

Tatar, Elizabeth, ed. 1985. *Call of the Morning Bird: Chants and Songs of Palau, Yap, and Ponape, Collected by Iwakichi Muranushi, 1936.* Honolulu: Bishop Museum, ARCS–2. Booklet with cassette.

Walleser, Sixtus. 1915. "Die Tanzgesänge der Eingebornen auf Jap." *Anthropos* 10:654–659.

Yamaguti, Osamu. 1968. "The Taxonomy of Music in Palau." *Ethnomusicology* 12(3):345–351.

———. 1973. "Music as Behavior in Ancient Palau." In *Nihon Ongaku to Sono Shuhen,* ed. Fumio Koizumi, Akira Hoshi, and Osamu Yamaguchi, 547–568. Tokyo: Ongaku no Tomo Sha.

# East Micronesia
*Mary E. Lawson Burke*
*Barbara B. Smith*

**Marshall Islands**

**Nauru**

**Kiribati**

## MARSHALL ISLANDS

The Marshall Islands consists of twenty-nine atolls and five raised coral islands, in two parallel chains running northwest to southeast. These chains, called Ralik (Sunset) and Ratak (Sunrise), display minor cultural and dialectal differences. The land, about 180 square kilometers, supports a population of about fifty-five thousand, of whom two-thirds live in urbanized areas of Majuro and Kwajalein. A republic in free association with the United States since 1986, the islands were previously administered by Germany (1886–1914) and Japan (1914–1944). A period of U.S. trusteeship (1947–1986) followed. Changes introduced by successive administrations, missionaries, and other outsiders have profoundly affected local society and culture.

### Musical contexts

The observance of Christmas (Kirijmoj), is probably the most prominent occasion for musical performance. Intrainsular and interinsular celebrations include singing, dancing, and feasting. Protestant churches are especially active. Choirs (*jebta*) begin rehearsing and composing new songs as early as October, concentrating on musical presentations through which each church vies for recognition.

Line dances (*biit*), accompanied by singing and guitars or electronic keyboards, are a recent introduction. In long, moving chains, participants repeat simple steps and sometimes clap, wave, and whirl. Easter is celebrated with special songs, but line dancing is not considered appropriate for them. Roman Catholic, Mormon, Assembly of God, Seventh-Day Adventist, and Baha'i groups celebrate events with hymns or songs.

By performing music and dance, schools, religious groups, women's associations, and other organizations celebrate festivals, the launchings of boats, dignitaries' visits, school events, major governmental events (especially the opening of the Nitijela, the national legislature), and Liberation Day (varying from atoll to atoll), the anniversary of the date when U.S. troops arrived in 1945. On Majuro, the annual cultural festival of the Alele Museum is a focal point for local performance. Rallies, especially of youths, occasion choral singing, line dancing, and the presentation of religious and

FIGURE 1 At the Alele Festival, members of Youth to Youth in Health perform. Photo by Mary E. Lawson Burke, 1988.

secular songs by bands, acoustic or electric. Church-affiliated adult and youth choirs rehearse regularly throughout the year, and present hymns (*alin jar*) in Marshallese and other religious songs at church and civic events.

Occasions with ties to precontact practices include *kamlo,* feasts welcoming and honoring visitors through orating, dancing, and singing. Appropriate for these feasts are *alin kamlo* 'kamlo songs' and *alin karwainene* 'welcome songs'. *Kemem* are occasions associated with children's first birthdays.

Periodically, youths form bands to entertain at festivals and parties, and popular bands have recorded cassettes for commercial distribution. Local versions of popular music in international styles include topical songs in Marshallese and imported songs in English. Musical instruments, electric or acoustic, include guitars, ukuleles, drums, and electronic keyboards. Costumes range from contemporary Western clothing to fibrous skirts, floral wreaths, and armbands. Youth groups associated with official organizations, including the Ministry of Health, compose and perform songs and dances for public occasions, and spread their messages through song (figure 1).

Public organizations for the elderly sponsor and participate in events featuring performances of traditional and syncretic songs and dances. On Majuro and Kwajalein, where individuals from various islands live close together, these events afford opportunities for interinsular teaching and sharing—a situation that would not have occurred in precontact settings.

### Contemporary songs and dances

Contemporary songs appropriate for public and private events exhibit Western musical traits, often with accompaniment from guitars or ukuleles. Many, especially songs of love or commemoration, circulate among villages and islands, surviving for years. Genres include *alin kamlo, alin karwainene, alin Kirijmoj, alin bwebwenato* 'historical song', *alin emlok* 'song of remembrance', *alin buromoj* 'song of sadness', *alin wa* 'song for launching a new boat or canoe', *alin mweina* 'private song of love', *alin lokonwa* 'sad song' (especially associated with departures), *alin mij* 'song for a dead person', *alin kaubowe* 'cowboy song', and *alin kelok* 'song of flying away'. The last genre includes songs composed by individuals whose souls are lost ("flown away") in grief, inspired by spousal death or forsaken love, as in excerpts from a text by Jebwen Hax (b. 1903) of Wotje Atoll, after his wife had left him:

Jera, emloke wöt mantin oñ ko am,
Kwön raak töm oñ tok.
Aö ememej eok ilo an tön raantak raan en an irooj. . . .
Ij jañ, im kötoor dännin meja etoor kon eok.
Am tum wöt ñe erup bamin menono e aö.

Lover, I miss the way you were and long for you,
When you were close to me and longed for me.
I have memories of you in the early-morning hours. . . .
I cry, and tears fall from my eyes because of you.
My heart will miss you until it stops beating.

*Alin kelok, alin bwebwenato, alin wa, alin mij, alin mweina,* and other genres probably existed before missionization. Older people remember Japanese songs, learned during the Japanese occupation.

Imported styles of dancing, favored by young people at clubs and social dances, include *tewij* 'twist' (fast dancing, partners not touching) and *tanij* 'dance' (slow dancing, partners touching). Bands or recordings provide the music. Modern Marshallese dances, blending Western and Marshallese elements, include the *eb* (Ralik dialect) or *leep* (Ratak dialect) and the *taidik*. All emphasize simple steps, sways, and turns, performed in columns by men and women (figure 2). Variations incorporate other introduced dances, including waltzing, and present stories or imitate daily tasks. In the flying-fish dance (*bobo*), women and men imitate with nets the motions of fishing. For *letin* 'using the tin' (developed by the 1890s, popular through the 1940s, but rare in the 1990s), dancers swing cracker tins around, striking them with sticks.

*Ebjijet,* danced by seated persons, usually women, feature gesturing. These genres include a fan dance (*deelel*), one using coconut shells as rhythmic instruments (*iukkure n lat*), and several that imitate household tasks. A famous example treats revered aspects of Marshallese culture: mothers, fishing nets, and pandanus-pounding stones.

Lyrics are labeled by genre; for example, *alin kajojo* 'song for the flying-fish dance', *alin deelel* 'song for the fan dance', *alin letin* 'song for using the tin'. Songs and dances of various kinds may link together to tell a story (*iukkure*).

### Extant traditional dances

Precontact dances considered fully or partially traditional persist, though some have undergone changes in the style of singing and moving. The staff dance (*jebwa*), the most important of these, is a national treasure, a symbol of Marshallese identity. Originally revealed by mythical beings (*noonniep*) in a dream on Ujae, it survives there in what is believed to be an unadulterated form. Only men perform it. Rehearsals and performances are strictly controlled by appropriate chiefs. Presentations occur only on the most prestigious occasions, including cultural festivals abroad. In rows of quartets, dancers interweave and strike their staffs against those of their partners. A caller (*du*) leads the singing. The dancers respond, accompanied by one or two men playing a modified indigenous drum. Formerly, a female caller and female singers and drummers provided the music; today, women only maintain the costumes and decorations on the staffs. For this and other dances, a superior performer is physically fit, able to "feel the music," and expert at drawing attention to himself; he inspires enthusiasm and moves lightly.

*Jiku,* a women's dance with sticks, is sometimes performed by young girls and boys. *Lemade* 'using the spear' was originally another men's dance with sticks, accom-

TRACK 41

panied by a chorus of women, but different from *jiku* and *jebwa* in that the dancers' lines did not interweave. Today, both these dances are performed almost exclusively by older men and women, accompanied by guitars and ukuleles, rather than traditional singing.

In *jimökmök*, women sit in facing rows. Each holds two short sticks, which she strikes against those of her opposite number. The song for *jimökmök* survives in an early and a late version, with modernized music.

*Jurbak* 'jitterbug' is commonly acknowledged as a new version of an older dance, *bwijbwij,* from Mejit Island. Widely popular, *jurbak* reportedly received its new name with an expanded repertory of footwork learned from American servicemen during World War II. The version of the 1990s—an enthusiastic execution of rapid stamping, shuffling, and turning, performed by columns of boys—resembles Mejit laborers' performance of *"budjebudj,"* which Augustin Krämer (1906:381–382) witnessed on Jaluit in 1898. As with other dances, singers with guitars and ukuleles have replaced the chorus of women who sang while beating drums.

### ⦿TRACK 44  *Extant traditional songs*

Elders remember traditional singing not associated with dancing, but apart from songs about fishing and love, this style no longer has much relevance. Old genres include *alin mur,* an inspirational song to impart strength in strife or crisis; *alin jerakrök,* a navigational aid, integrating knowledge of stars and places; and *roro,* which, increasing spiritual strength, summon exertion for warfare and heavy tasks, and attract fish, as in this excerpt, from the family of Toromon Bujen of Arno Atoll:

> Moñä o o, moñä im kamnönö mömaan in wa in waam,
> Bwe ewadikdik lok wöt.
> Jitto, jitto, em malto.
> Jitto in kein ni; jitto wöt jene.
> Moñä im kenlik eö, bwe ijamin enlik.
> Moñä im iö, bwe ijamin towaj.

> Eat *o o,* eat and make the man in your canoe happy,
> For you must because it's getting late.
> Point west, point west, and look west.
> Point west like a coconut trunk; point west and stay.
> Eat and pull the line from me, for I will not grow weaker than you.
> Eat and pull from my canoe, for I will not fall out.

Some older people perform historical narratives (*bwebwenato*), interspersed with brief *roro* highlighting important moments in the story. Another navigational song, *alin meto* 'maritime song', serves as a mnemonic aid, combining stories from oral and religious knowledge.

*Alin lejoñjoñ* are sung by adults and children while juggling stones, lemons, balls, or small coconuts. Other songs accompany boxing and ball games, and include lullabies (*alin kakiki*) and songs to accompany culinary tasks, like pressing pulp from pandanus. Songs to anger others (*alin kalulu*), possibly an obsolete category, were composed for competition or from jealousy.

### Musical transmission and education

Emphasis on Marshallese traditions varies among the media. WSZO, the main AM radio station, features an eclectic playlist of Western, Marshallese, and other Oceanic popular music, but neither FM station stresses local traditions. WSZO promotes Marshallese cultural awareness by broadcasting a weekly show of stories, songs, and proverbs produced by the Alele Museum. Cable television, available on Majuro for a fee, features U.S.-derived entertainment. The Alele Museum show is free of charge; like its radio counterpart, it focuses on Marshallese culture. Cultural events receive coverage in the local newspaper.

## Music in interethnic perspective and history

Early written sources—especially the expeditionary records of Otto von Kotzebue (1821, 1830), who visited the Marshalls four times between 1817 and 1825—provide the most valuable information on indigenous contexts and performances. These sources describe music, dance, and gymnastic performances or pantomime with songs (*eb*), presented to entertain guests. Grand presentations, described as artless operas, consisted of a series of songs and dances (including dances with staffs), accompanied by a chorus of female drummers; a conch trumpet was blown to signal sections of the plot. Possibly this form is the source of *iukkure*.

Music enhanced religious activities, domestic life within villages or chiefly households, and interclan or interinsular warfare. Dances, performed sitting or standing by commoners, nobles, and chiefs, reenacted historical events and commemorated individuals. Songs educated young people in the histories of their clans and islands. Accounts of dancing from the early 1800s through the 1880s report zealous, enthusiastic, animated performance, marked by bodily contortions, especially of the upper body and arms, and convulsive grimacing and rolling of the eyes.

Feasting and dancing occurred on a woman's release from seclusion after her first menstruation or the birth of her child. Other festivities honored visiting chiefs and their retainers, traveling among the islands for firstfruits celebrations and to collect tribute. Tattooing songs (*alin eo*) strengthened the participants in tattooing, whose rituals occurred during the breadfruit harvest. After a death, especially that of a chief, laments were sung and drums played. Religious rituals included a supplication to quell high surf, with singing, drumming, and beating the waves with fronds.

Warfare, frequent before about 1900, inspired music and dance. Men's dances based on martial movements occurred before and during battles, heartening warriors and menacing their opponents. The blowing of conch trumpets animated troops and signaled charges. Warfare highlighted women's role as the mainstay of society; during battles, women sang and beat drums to inspire their men, formed the second line of defense, and helped negotiate peace. Dances recreating battles also existed.

In addition to whalers, traders, and administrators, missionaries of the American Board of Commissioners for Foreign Missions, who began arriving in 1857, altered the people's social and religious lives. They banned indigenous attire, dances, drumming, and singing, and introduced new, less ebullient, songs and dances, with mixed choral singing and dances in a circle.

By the 1880s, some Marshallese dances had been suppressed and hymns were being sung by Christian converts, but the German ethnographer Otto Finsch witnessed dances by seated performers (with and without sticks), a men's dance with staffs (*jorañ*) similar in description to *jebwa,* and a dance called *rrumm:*

> The girls participating wore a mat, one end of which was pulled between the legs and fastened by a string around the hips, but in the course of the performance they let this covering fall, and then appeared completely naked. Besides the familiar rolling of eyes to the accompaniment of singing and clapping by the women's chorus, this production . . . consisted principally of a vibrating motion of the low-

er belly and wiggling the buttocks, thus an imitation of coitus, in which the motions of the man were also represented. (Finsch 1961 [1893]:389–390)

In the late 1890s, dances by seated performers, men's dances with staffs, and *bwij-bwij* were still performed, but dances incorporating tin idiophones, songs with church-influenced melodies, imported clothing, and a peaceful demeanor began to prevail.

### Composition and style

Composers of the 1990s use three methods to record their songs: cipher notation, introduced by missionaries and still used in hymnals; notation on five-line staffs, learned in school; and writing out the text and memorizing the melody. The melody for a new text need not be newly composed, or even Marshallese in origin. A song may have more than one set of associated movements. The lyrics of some dances, like *jurbak* and *lemade,* describe the movements of the feet and arms; most incorporate poetic imagery and symbolism.

Early sources reveal little about indigenous compositional practices, but Marshallese say the composition of music and dance was assisted by spirits, often while the composer slept. *Bwijbwij, jiku,* and *jebwa* were originally obtained in dreams from specific spirits or historical personages. Some individuals, claiming to compose in indigenous ways, say songs that come easily to composers and maintain a wide popularity are proof of supernatural assistance. Other composers attribute their songs to the Christian deity.

The music and dance popular in the 1990s fuse old and new elements. The most obvious adopted musical trait is chordal harmony in three or more parts, based on nineteenth-century Protestant hymnody. Vocal lines use diatonic scales. New and old melodies often have simple duple meter and distinctive phrasal endings. Most are through-composed in two or more sections of text with associated music, repeated in performance. Hymns are strophic.

Extant traditional melodies have a narrow range, predominantly stepwise movement, many repeated pitches, and irregular phrases. Many religious songs are unmetered. Some songs, especially those associated with certain dances, are responsorial. Songs described by early researchers began slowly and softly, and gradually rose in pitch, loudness, and tempo, and ended with a shrill cry.

### Musical instruments

Acoustic and electric guitars, mandolins, ukuleles, drums, and electronic keyboards are among the musical instruments (*kojañjañ*) that accompany most Marshallese songs and dances. The trend is toward dancing to recorded accompaniment.

Musical instruments extant in the early 1800s included a single-headed hourglass drum (*aje*), a conch trumpet (*jilel*), and concussive staffs and sticks. *Aje* were almost exclusively women's instruments (figure 3); one or more accompanied dance-dramas, pantomimes, and dances with sticks. Constructed from the wood of *lukwej,* a tropical laurel (*Calophyllum inophyllum*), *aje* were between 60 and 80 centimeters long, with a smooth, undecorated surface and a head fashioned from a shark's stomach, bladder, or possibly throat. The original hourglass form was used on some islands until about 1900; one specimen remains in the Marshalls, exhibited in the Alele Museum. Women no longer play drums, and men play modified *aje* to accompany *jebwa.* Conch trumpets, in end-blown and side-blown forms, signaled the beginning of sections of longer dances and alternations between male and female or solo and choral singing. Conchs and *aje* were sounded during battles and to keep canoes together at night. Beginning around 1900, struck tins (*turam*) supplanted

FIGURE 3 *Inside of a House in the Radack Islands,* lithograph by I. Clark after a drawing by Louis Choris (Kotzebue 1821). At the far center stands an hourglass drum; at right, a woman plays another. Photo by Smithsonian Institution.

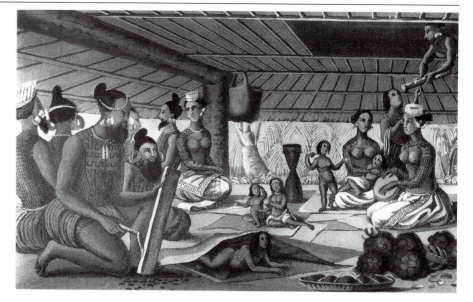

hourglass drums for some dances; until the 1950s at the earliest, tins accompanied singing and the dances *letin* and *leep.*

Implements used for some surviving indigenous dances are of two lengths. Male dancers wield decorated staffs about 1 meter long, representing weapons. For *jimokmok,* sitting women strike pairs of sticks, 18 to 20 centimeters long, against the ground and each other's sticks.
—MARY E. LAWSON BURKE

## NAURU

About ten thousand people inhabit Nauru, a 21-square-kilometer coral island, surrounded by a reef. Most of the land is a plateau, covered by phosphate rock until twentieth-century mining reduced it to jagged limestone pinnacles. Nauruans are descendants of twelve tribes, represented by a twelve-pointed star on the national flag. The first settlers of each tribe arrived by canoe, from islands now known as the Carolines, the Gilberts, the Marshalls, and the Solomons. The largest number came from the Gilberts, directly or via Banaba. They settled on fertile land around the plateau and along the shore of an inland lagoon.

Nauru's first inhabitants were confined by the reef, which prohibits passage of oceangoing canoes. They believed frigate birds to be spirits, and made them an integral part of their culture: men still compete in catching and training wild birds, women once wove pandanus-leaf mats with frigate-bird designs, and young people, chant about the birds while realizing choreographies based on their movements.

Some tribes have maintained part of their heritage. Respect for its ownership continues, even as a sense of national cultural identity has developed. Parts of tribe-specific heritages have become so consolidated their sources are difficult to identify. Only a few elders understand old linguistic forms. Other than Nauruans, a few residents—Pacific Islanders, Asians, Europeans (mostly from Australia)—work for the Nauru Phosphate Commission and the government, a republic since 1968.

### Early outside contacts

Contact with the West began in 1798 with the British ship *Hunter.* From the 1830s, whalers stopped for supplies, and Nauru became a beachcombers' haven. As Nauruans acquired alcohol, tobacco, and firearms (first from visiting ships, and after the 1850s from resident foreign traders) and learned how to ferment coconut toddy (from Gilbertese who about 1872 reached Nauru via Banaba), intertribal competition became deadly.

In 1888, at German traders' request, Germany intervened in local warfare. The gunship *Eber* arrived, and some of its personnel (including the ship's band) marched around the island to assemble the chiefs (Fabricius 1992:228). Under threat of their chiefs' deportation, Nauruans turned in their guns, and Germany took Nauru into its Marshall Islands Protectorate.

German interest in Micronesia was primarily in copra, but during German rule (which lasted until 1914, when British forces captured the island), foreigners with other interests arrived: Protestant and Catholic missionaries to convert the Nauruans to Christianity, and British engineers to mine phosphate.

## Historical perspectives

No comprehensive survey of Nauruan musics exists, but certain features are apparent. Nauruans put vocal music into either of two classes: *iruwo* and *iriang*. These, when speaking in English, they respectively call chant and song.

Stylistically, *iruwo* range from what might be described as vigorously articulated rhythmic speech to long phrases of sustained, rhythmically organized text, utilizing a few tones within a narrow range, with extensive tonal repetition and set phrasal beginnings and endings; some have rhythmically based phrases with more varied contours. *Iruwo* include aboriginal chants (of old dances); long, narrative chants, some composed between 1900 and 1950, about heroes and voyages on European ships to Australia and the Marshall Islands; celebratory introductions of honored leaders whose actions culminated in the founding of the republic; and short items for string figures, children's games, and lullabies.

The stylistic determinant of *iriang* is that their melodies are in the Western tonal system. *Iriang* include hymns, secular songs (sung in Nauruan, unaccompanied or instrumentally accompanied), and European children's songs (sung in English or Nauruan). Nauruans use the word *ekeong* 'cry, sound' to denote instruments in contexts where popular hits are played.

Instrumental music is primarily brass-band music. Other instruments—ukuleles, guitars (formerly acoustic, now more frequently amplified), electronic keyboards, synthesizers—are usually played for modern hits and *iriang* that have become quasi-traditional. Most Nauruans, thanks to their phosphate royalties, own high-quality equipment for playing tapes and CDs.

### *Views of music*

Most indigenous Nauruan music was intrinsically affiliated with dance. Ernest Stephen, marooned as a boy on Nauru before German colonial rule, later wrote letters describing Nauruan life. He said the only Nauruan musical instruments "were a drum made out of a hollow pandanus log covered over at the end on which they played with the skin of a shark's stomach, which they beat by using their fingers as drum-sticks for a tattoo at their dances; and a toy trumpet made out of the leaf-stem of the pandanus tree" (1936:38). He also wrote that the band of a German man-of-war (undoubtedly *Eber*) had frightened Nauruans, who asked:

> "What is the matter with the white man now? Why does he make that noise? What have we done wrong?" They objected to the reed instrument, as it squealed like a pig when being killed; the kettle-drum made too much noise, but they were pleased with the big drum and one old man wanted to look inside to see what made the noise. (1936:38-39)

*ekeong*　Musical instruments played, often with electric amplification, in the performance of popular music on Nauru

**frigate-bird dance**　Nauruan dance in which singers perform structured movements depicting frigate birds and actions by which people catch them

*Iriañ in Evangelium*　The Nauruan hymnal, containing 252 hymns notated for four voices, first printed in 1936; reprinted and still in use

*iriang*　Nauruan music in the Western tonal system, including hymns, secular songs (sung in Nauruan, unaccompanied or instrumentally accompanied), and European childen's songs (sung in English or Nauruan)

*iruwo*　Nauruan recitational singing ("chanting"), varying from vigorously articulated rhythmic speech to long phrases of sustained, rhythmically organized text utilizing tones within a narrow range

By 1910, Nauruans must have come to like such music, because Paul Hambruch, ethnographer with the Südsee-Expedition, said they strongly desired music, and had a band capable of performing excellently on flutes, cornets, French horns, tubas, and drums (1914–1915:190).

Hambruch wrote that drums and sticks were the only indigenous musical instruments, harmonicas (introduced by Europeans) were played, and conch trumpets served for signaling. He said he had not seen drums because Nauruans no longer used them. The drum described to him was a hollow cylindrical pandanus trunk about one meter long, with a sharkskin head, fastened with coconut-string wrappings. Seated men and women beat it for rhythmic accompaniment. Dance sticks were of two kinds: those about 1 to 1.5 meters long (photos show each dancer holding one), and those about 20 centimeters long, used in pairs; both were ornamented.

Several Westerners who described Nauruan life in the early 1900s wrote that Nauruan children and youths played most of the time. Aloys Kayser, a Roman Catholic missionary, listed twenty-four activities as play and seven as sports. Among the former was a party to which young, unmarried men of one district invited young, unmarried women of another district. All began singing, with men seated in one row, facing women seated in another. The women eventually crossed over to the men's row. Each woman sat in the lap of the man opposite her, who, to hold her firmly while she swung her arms in accompaniment to the song, placed his arms across her breasts. This amusement continued day and night, the visiting women often staying in the district's communal house for two or three weeks and on departure inviting the men to come to their district for similar activities (1921–1922:706–707). After the colonial administration banned these sessions, Christian hymns served as songs for collective singing.

Teaching hymns was an important component of Protestant missionary endeavor. In 1899, soon after arriving, Philip A. Delaporte, who with his wife represented the American Board of Commissioners for Foreign Missions, began translating hymns and teaching Nauruans to sing them. Singing was one of seven subjects taught in the school he built; the others were the Bible, reading, arithmetic, writing, geography, and German (Delaporte 1907:10).

Translating hymns and biblical passages, Delaporte was assisted by Timothy Detudamo, a chief's son. From 1902, missionary presses (first in Kosrae, later on Nauru) printed hymnals; the earliest had texts only, but later editions added musical notation. To gratify colonial administrators' interests, Delaporte published a German hymnal and a songbook that included German chorales ("Ein' Feste Burg"), secular songs ("Loreley"), and patriotic songs ("Dem Kaiser"). After leaving Nauru, Delaporte and Detudamo (1936) completed *Iriañ in Evangelium,* a book of 252 hymns, notated for four voices; in its original printing and a reprint, this hymnal is still used in services of the Nauru Congregational Church.

Choral singing occurs in church-sponsored competitions—with judges, numerical scoring, and publication of results. Some competitions are for singing hymns, some for singing secular songs (most often those that express love of Nauru), and some for composing new songs. Choral singing is especially important around Christmas. About 18 December, carolers begin visiting and entertaining elderly people, sick people in hospitals, and distinguished people. In churches, people sing carols and exchange gifts. The Menen District Protestant congregation sponsors carol-singing competitions every year, and the Independent Church puts on Christmas concerts.

### Views of dance

Nauruan dance was first ethnographically described by Antonie Brandeis, who, before 1907, must have observed one of the large events that she reported were held almost every year. She wrote that most dances had been introduced by Gilbertese and were pantomimes. The administration encouraged these events, but American missionaries had forbidden their followers to participate in them. About forty dancers in each "division" performed with precision; to emphasize the words, a chorus of men, who began the dances, beat their hands against mats they wore.

Brandeis listed six kinds of dances: a war-related dance; a dance in which participants struck little sticks together in various patterns; a dance in which seated persons gestured with their arms and hands; a dance that women performed alone, with men standing in rows behind them; a dance in three seated rows, with one man and one woman making various patterns; and a dance with women seated in rows, flanked on either side by a row of men, with various movements of the arms (1907:73). She mentioned instruments (sticks, drum, conch trumpet), dancers' attire and ornaments (some being family heirlooms), and facial painting (each family having its own design).

Hambruch, who went to Nauru later, wrote that he did not see indigenous dances because they were no longer performed—except on the kaiser's birthday, after weeks of rehearsal. Therefore, in his ethnography of Nauru (1914), he copied Brandeis's material. He added texts of some chants, with extensive descriptions of dancers' attire.

Describing Nauruan dancing, Stephen wrote that it consisted of marching and stamping; seated performers synchronously swayed and moved their arms. Dancers would sometimes take about six weeks to circle the island, "accompanied by friends who carry presents to be given and those which will be received. They are entertained by the various villages they pass through. The dancing is generally done in the cool of the evening or on moonlit nights" (1936:60–61). For the frigate-bird dance, he added,

> The performers had green leaves in their hands and went through the motions of catching the bird while chanting all about the process. They were led by an old woman marching forwards and backwards, facing the audience all the time, occasionally stamping with one foot which made a noise like a drum, then turned quarter round and repeated the recitation. (1936:61)

Most of this description could apply to Nauruan dancing as performed at the Pacific Festivals of Arts (figure 4).

Stephen briefly described a men's dance with sticks and a dance he called Gilbertese (1936:61–62). His identification of the latter by place of origin may suggest that, though some Nauruan tribes originated there, this dance came with people who arrived later. He and other early writers mentioned dancing at a young woman's

FIGURE 4   Girls from Nauru perform at the Pacific Festival of Arts, Townsville, Australia. Photo by Mary Jo Freshley, 1988.

FIGURE 5    Nauru boys demonstrate string figures at the Pacific Festival of Arts. Photo by Mary Jo Freshley, 1988.

coming-of-age festivities; those for a chief's daughter involved a parade around the island.

## Approaches to, and use of, music and dance

Nauruans' facility and enjoyment in improvising, imitating, teasing, and competing have ancient roots. In notes compiled while on Nauru in 1888, the imperial commissioner of Germany, Franz Sonnenschein, wrote that "the women compose little ditties at every opportunity and on the most trivial subjects" (1889:24, trans. in Fabricius 1992:221). Of girls too, another German report states: "Their merry disposition soon inspires one of them to compose a ditty about the latest novelty, and by evening they are all singing it together" (Senfft 1895:105, in Fabricius 1992:269).

In string figures (many illustrating chants), Nauruans "instead of endlessly repeating traditional patterns . . . possessed the originality and expertize to construct entirely new patterns . . . to depict what interested them in their changing environment" (H. E. Maude in Maude 1971:xviii). Sometimes composition of the music preceded that of the figure. Patterns were displayed in competitions attended by "everyone on the island" (1971:xxiii). Interest in string figures declined during World War II, when Japanese officials sent many of the people to Chuuk and those remaining on Nauru felt extreme deprivations. Children still make string figures, which they display at cultural events, at home and abroad (figure 5).    —BARBARA B. SMITH

## KIRIBATI

The Republic of Kiribati encompasses the Gilbert, Line, and Phoenix Islands and Banaba—thirty-three scattered islands with an area of 811 square kilometers. Most of the country's seventy-six thousand people live in the Gilberts, sixteen low coral islands known as Tungaru; a third lives in the urban center of Tarawa, an atoll. The Gilberts were under British rule from 1872 to 1975, united with the Ellice Islands (Tuvalu). In 1979, they gained independence as a member of the British Commonwealth.

The culture of the Gilberts shows Polynesian influence resulting from ancient Sāmoan contacts and joint colonial administration. The Gilbertese (I-Kiribati) are renowned for their pride in indigenous skills and customs (*te katei*), including music and dance. Traditionally, the nine northern islands divided into several stratified societies under chiefly control; the southern islands, more egalitarian, were ruled by councils of male elders. Through the 1800s, warfare and factional fighting appear to have been common except on the two northernmost islands, Butaritari and Makin.

## Musical contexts

Many old genres are still performed, as are new and syncretic styles of sound and movement. Important social activities and discussions occur in meetinghouses (*maneaba*), affiliated with churches, schools, civic organizations, and performing troupes. Social gatherings include farewell parties, ceremonies associated with a new *maneaba*, gatherings to welcome or entertain visitors, and newer celebrations, including civic holidays and festivities associated with schools and churches. Rooted in custom and etiquette, such gatherings require feasts and artistic performances, as of oratory, music, and dance.

Singing often occurs when family and friends gather or travel, and for individual relaxation. "Island nights" are social dances, which feature live or recorded Kiribati and other Oceanic music, rock, or country. Hymns and religious songs are important to all religious sects; special presentations occur on Christmas and Easter. While cutting toddy in coconut trees, men sing to coax sap from the tree—and to announce their presence to unwary people below.

### Social groups and music

Music and dance are important markers of I-Kiribati identity. Traditionally, all the singers and dancers of any troupe came from one descent group, a body that, with its associated lands and heritage, defines its members' social place. Skills associated with musical composition and performance (*kainikamaen*) were valuable clan property, as were ancestral spirits and historical narratives. Performances in *maneaba* were the most public and communal display of the strength of this knowledge.

In the late 1800s, beliefs and social concepts introduced by missionaries and the colonial government challenged the vigor of descent groups. With changes in the structures of music and dance came a broadened concept of social affiliation. Performance now marked events relating to governments, churches, schools, and holidays. On Tarawa, groups developed solely for singing and dancing; now serving a quasi-kinship function, they include resident outer-islanders and Tarawans, and vie to be chosen to perform at public events.

### Competition in musical performance

Competition filled Kiribati life. It permeated games, musical performance, rivalries between descent groups, and warfare. Before battle, to encourage warriors, communities sang and danced. Victories in battle and in dance had similar effects: both proved the superiority of a clan's knowledge of supernatural powers. At least in the southern islands, I-Kiribati connect one's (lineage-determined) seat in the *maneaba* with one's role in fighting and dancing: people who defended the village in battle took the leading positions in performance.

Formal competitions included contests (*kaunikai*) between rival troupes and matches (*uaia*) between individual dancers. Both called for supernatural intervention and psychological motivation through public and private rituals. Ostensibly a contest of singing and dancing, *kaunikai* were actually competitions between bodies of knowledge. Apart from social occasions and entertaining guests, performances were not merely for enjoyment. When more than one troupe performed, people seethed with antagonism and tension, as the rivals, ritually strengthened and protected, faced each other from opposite ends of the *maneaba*. At stake were the health and lives of the composer, his assistants, and the lead singer.

A contest began with a challenge, frequently the result of gossip about the abilities of a musically specialized priest (*tia-kainikamaen* 'skillworker'). Protective words and phrases guarded against one's own inadvertent errors and one's rivals' dangerous phrases. In a song that begins *Tabekan toa nikunau aio Rurubene ma Nareau, te riki teuana* 'The raising of my song is from Rurubene and Nareau, who are united', attributing the text to prominent deities gives it strength and vitality. A declaration like *E I tabukibuki ngai ao I taebaeba* 'O I am hilly and like a gust of wind' asserts the composer's invincibility. *N na katea rabanau te nang roro* 'I will build my defense of thick dark clouds' is a protective phrase, symbolizing a wall of protection against enemies, as dark clouds block the burning rays of the sun.

Supported by supernatural power, songs made rivals falter, sicken, or die. In the text *Ti ibeia baani kana natin bakoa* 'Hammer the distant rocks into pieces for the food of baby sharks', the beginning invokes an opposing group's turmoil; the reference to sharks adds insult. Through the imagery of slumber with a deity, the phrase *be anoiko Nei Tinanimone ba ko na matu ma ngaia* 'for Nei Tinanimone sees you and you will sleep with her' threaten's a composer with death. To harm or kill selected targets, participants surreptitiously pointed ritually prepared sticks at them.

Musical contests required ritual preparations, which encouraged spirits to work through the singers and dancers, making them fit, inspired, exciting, and safe. Ceremonies protected troupes and individuals, and enhanced the protective power of

FIGURE 6    At a *mamira* ceremony on the beach at Betio Islet, Tarawa Atoll, the troupe ItitinKiribati performs a Polynesian-influenced dance, accompanied by log idiophones and a bass drum. Photo by Mary E. Lawson Burke, 1985.

costumes. *Mamira,* ceremonies not limited to competitions, bestowed blessings on a song to enhance its appeal and its composer's fame (figure 6).

Pressure from the colonial government and missionaries, who considered the passion of competitions unhealthy and unproductive, resulted in modifications. The goals of competition became less malevolent, as rivals tried merely to undermine the success of each other's performance. With decreased emphasis on the descent group has come a change of name: from *kaunikai* to *kaunimaneve* 'competition with musical texts' (*maneve*). With proclamations of superiority in artistic skill, songs tease and provoke rivals. Involving village or social groups rather than lineages, formal competitions are more closely associated with choral singing (*kuaea*) than with dancing (*maie*). This change probably resulted from suppression of dance-associated rituals; eventually, ritual aspects resurfaced in more efficient forms. Choral singing as a genre became institutionalized in the 1960s, concurrent with a resurgence of interest in artistic skill. Outstanding performances display forceful singing, with precision in diction. A trend of the 1990s is that competitions are advertised—and winners receive cash prizes.

Despite these changes, competition still frames Kiribati dancing, and awareness of its impact guides rehearsals. Competitions are judged on the precision of singing and dancing, the attractiveness and appeal of songs and choreographies, and the excitement experienced by the audience. Occasionally, composers conduct *mamira* for dancing and choral singing, though large communal rituals are rare. On radio and cassettes, successful songs carry composers' fame throughout the nation and beyond: to I-Kiribati settlements in Fiji, Nauru, and the Solomons.

### The power of performance

A dramatic potential of performance is an ecstatic state (*angin te maie* 'the power of the dance'), brought on by the event in combination with psychological factors of social identity, sexuality, and shyness. This state is shown by dancers' labored breathing, vigorous movements, trembling, and screaming, and by singers' vocalizing more loudly, increasing the tempo or tonal level of the song, and moving with greater force. Transferred from the dancing, this state can be seen in singing when participants vocalize and play instruments fervently, often with their eyes closed.

I-Kiribati believe the ecstatic state displays the power of *kainikamaen,* as spirits work through the performers. Participants ensure that performers not lose control and cry, faint, or make mistakes. Elements of the music and dance are consciously

(a)

(b)

FIGURE 7    Solo dancers in character-istic poses: *a,* seated with diagonal arms, a Kiribati dancer performs a *bino* in Tanimaiaki Village, Abaiang Atoll (photo by Mary E. Lawson Burke, 1985); *b,* standing, with typical positions of the arms in northern-movement style, a Kiribati dancer performs in Nanikai Village, Tarawa Atoll (photo by Mary E. Lawson Burke, 1981).

TRACK 16

TRACK 45

structured to create tension. One or more exciters (*tani-kaunga*) roam among the singers to encourage them to sing enthusiastically, inspiring the dancers.

## Musical systems

Indigenous Kiribati dances are usually called *ruoia.* They vary slightly from island to island, but usually include the *kawawa,* a warm-up dance; the *arira* or *katika ne bee,* dances for men to fasten their mats; the *wanibanga;* the *wantarawa;* the *bino,* performed seated; the *kamei* or *kabuti;* and in some areas, more obscure forms, *tie, tarae,* and *kamaototo.* On Butaritari and Makin, battles between chiefs were celebrated with danced suites, such as *ietoa* and *nantekei,* in which the performers divided into opposing groups, named after legendary canoes. Each dancer carried a stick decorated and tapered at each end, representing a weapon.

*Ruoia* are performed by a line of one to six dancers (*tia-maie,* pl. *tani-maie*), who execute choreographed sequences of flowing movements, interspersed with poses and abrupt movements of head, hands, and arms. Stylized walking, swaying of the hips (for females), and bending of the knees are features of certain dances. Dancers in a single line (*un*) are of the same sex and approximate age, but mixed dancing formerly occurred. Movements and positions are based on actions of birds, fishing, martial arts, sailing, and canoes. Dancers do not interact with onlookers, but maintain a fixed aloofness (figure 7).

Located behind the dancers are the singers (*tan-uboubo* 'those who clap'), arranged in lines, or more traditionally, in a canoe-prow formation. With rehearsed precision, they sing, clap, and move with the principal dancers, stamping their feet and slapping their skin. Dancers and singers alike sing initial dances.

The music uses a five-tone scale, roughly analogous to the tempered tones D–E–G–A–B. Melodies are syllabic, conjunct, and through-composed in one to three sections, each of which may immediately repeat. Within each section, rhythmic activity often goes from free meter to duple meter. In free-metered sections, the chorus performs choreographed movements accented with clapping; in metered sections, it provides steady stamping, clapping, and slapping. Concluding the song and the dance is a climactic cadence (*motika*), often shouted.

Each dance has its music. *Kawawa* may use from one to three pitches, but *wantarawa* and *wanibanga* often consist of melodies on one tone, which gradually rises through the performance. The *kamei,* danced by men or women, consists of two or three sections, as does the *kabuti,* an analogous women's hip-shaking dance. The music in each section begins with a freely rhythmic melody centered on the minor third E–G, and ends in a *ruruo,* a passage in duple meter, centered on A, and accompanied by choral clapping. Each succeeding section has proportionately lengthier *ruruo,* and often the last consists almost entirely of *ruruo.*

The *bino,* considered by many I-Kiribati to be their most elegant dance, is also sectional. Based on a five-tone scale, the first section (*rabata* 'body' *bino,* or *binona* 'real' *bino*) is rhythmically free; a seated chorus mirrors the dancers' movements. The second section (*ruoiana, karuoiana,* or *uboana*) is in duple meter with choral clapping.

Each section of a *ruoia* has a distinctive solo cue (*akeia*), which gives the starting pitch of the melody. The lead singer then begins; at a designated spot, the chorus joins in. Though the music may contain passages of harmony in thirds, fourths, or fifths, the singing is usually in unison, with men and women an octave apart and simultaneous variants provided by the lead singer.

### New and borrowed genres

The term *maie* denotes dancing and associated singing. *Maie* and *batere* also denote dances that incorporate traits of outside music or dance, and *batere* denotes the

FIGURE 8    On Tarawa, Kiribati, members of the troupe ItitinKiribati perform a Polynesian-influenced dance. Photo by Mary E. Lawson Burke, 1985.

Tuvaluan *fatele,* from which the term derives. The *kateitei,* the *kaimatoa,* and the *buki* are *ruoia*-derived dances with percussion-box accompaniment. Their melodies, and those of contemporary dances from the northern islands (*kainimeang* 'northern movement'), have Western musical traits, including diatonic major scales, functional harmonies, and duple meters. Typical patterns of clapping (different from those of *ruoia*), steady acceleration of tempo (borrowed from Tuvaluan *fatele*), and costume are hallmarks of several of these dances, which probably developed around 1900. *Kakibanako* and twentieth-century *bino* incorporate sections of older and later musical styles. *Ruoia*-derived dances have a different starting cue (*nako we*); the chorus, seated, provides only rhythmic clapping or percussion-box accompaniment. *Ruoia*-derived dances include most recent compositions, but new movements are sometimes composed for a *ruoia* song.

Foreign dances have been performed in the Gilberts since missionary times. The *taubati,* which features Polynesian-style movements and costumes, developed from styles introduced by Sāmoan missionaries in the southern islands as a substitute for *ruoia* dances. The Tuvaluan *fatele* (*bātere*) has become established as light entertainment in many islands. Dances from Sāmoa, Tahiti, the Cook Islands, and Tonga have become popular, as have Polynesian-influenced styles (*maie ae bou* 'new dancing') developed in the I-Kiribati community in the Solomon Islands (figure 8).

### Other genres

Two games with sticks are occasionally presented at formal performances of dances. Performers of *karanga,* dances with interweaving lines of players, strike meter-long sticks against others' sticks. To play the *tirere,* participants, seated in opposing rows, strike two short sticks against those of the players directly and diagonally across from them. For both games, the music formerly consisted of intonations centered on two main tones about a minor third apart, with the entire melody rising one or more semitones during a performance.

The *kabure* (*karuo*) is a game played by quartets of seated individuals, who in complex patterns slap their own and each other's hands and bodies. The music is a three-tone melody in duple meter.

TRACK 46    Vocal genres include *kuaea,* accompanied by guitars and ukuleles (occasionally electronic keyboard), using functional tonal harmonies, duple meter, narrow melodic range, monotonic passages, and typical cadences. *Kuaea* are associated with youth, civic, or religious organizations, but unaffiliated groups have formed since the early 1980s. Though usually composed of males and females, some *kuaea* are for males only, with the highest one or two of the (four to six) vocal parts sung in falsetto. An important genre, the *kuaea* incorporates many of the rituals and compositional methods of the *kainikamaen.*

Songs called *anene* are sung informally in a late-twentieth-century local style, incorporating Western musical elements. Lacking the drive of *kuaea,* they are in the repertory of amplified bands, which entertain at weddings, social dances, and other events. *Te katake,* a historical song, is sung by one or two individuals as informal family entertainment.

Hymns (*kairi*), sung in three to four parts, are important in Protestant and Roman Catholic services; other religious songs are sung by Baha'i, the Assembly of God, and other sects. The Roman Catholic church allows indigenous melodies, costumes, and movements in special masses.

### Musical instruments

Indigenous Kiribati musical instruments were few. Bodily percussion was the main accompaniment to singing, and conch trumpets (*bu*) served for signaling and assem-

FIGURE 9   Kiribati children entertain guests by performing a *ruoia* with arms in typical diagonal placement. Photo by Mary E. Lawson Burke, 1981.

bling people. Percussion on *baoki,* a large, flat, wooden box borrowed from Tuvalu, supplements bodily percussion as accompaniment for *ruoia* and *bātere.* Since the early 1980s, some troupes have used bass drums and small log idiophones. Electronic keyboards, acoustic guitars, and ukuleles often accompany *kuaea,* and guitars or ukuleles may accompany the casual singing of *anene.* Bands that provide music at social dances often use electric instruments and Western drums.

## Intercultural perspectives

Music and dance formerly marked events in *maneaba.* For boys and girls, dancing and feasting celebrated the end of puberty-related rituals. Training to become warriors, boys underwent ritual education in dancing and esoteric lore. Girls were kept inside houses for bleaching; while their skin lightened and they studied domestic rituals, they were bespelled to make them attractive and fertile. On their emergence, they were the featured dancers at large celebrations. At nuptial ceremonies in some areas, the newly wedded couple danced. A funeral (*bomaki*) included dance-songs, laments (some of which had been composed for the deceased individual), and wailing (R. Grimble 1972; Wilkes 1844).

Entertaining guests with music and dancing was an important component of Kiribati etiquette (figure 9). Interisland voyages formerly took months because travelers had to stop at every intermediate island to be welcomed and entertained (Coulter 1847; Finsch 1961 [1893]; Parkinson 1889; Stevenson 1900). Feasting and dancing occurred at taro-weighing competitions, ceremonies associated with constructing new *maneaba,* and lunar-cycle festivities.

### Missionaries

The first resident Christian missionaries were Protestants of the American Board of Commissioners for Foreign Missions, who arrived in the northern islands in 1857. Lack of major progress led to their withdrawal in 1917, but not before they had introduced hymns and musical training in the mission school. In the early 1870s, Protestant missionaries from the London Missionary Society (LMS) began working in the southern islands, where they more effectively established their churches as centers of social activity. LMS schools taught hymns and musical notation. Beginning in 1888, Roman Catholic missionaries founded churches in the northern islands. They taught their own singing, music theory, and notation, but tolerated some indigenous practices; hence the persistence of older artistic genres in the northern islands.

In the southern islands by the 1890s, LMS missionaries had promulgated regulations that restricted most aspects of daily life. Believing indigenous dancing to be evil, they included it in their prohibitions on the old religion, gradually weakening the power of the *tia-kainikamaen.* Though they introduced new, Sāmoan-derived dances, which they considered more appropriate for Christians, they eventually forbade all dancing when the enthusiasm for the new styles, which quickly filled the vacuum left by the suppression of indigenous customs, became uncontrollable.

Colonial administrations took a more moderate stance. Recognizing the importance of dancing, they regulated merely when and where dancing could occur, forbidding only public events aimed at harming individuals. From about 1900 to 1940, this difference in approach resulted in a running debate between the mission and the government (A. F. Grimble 1989:314–333). Eventually, new genres of music and dance developed: some were borrowed; others, such as the *kaimatoa,* derived from older forms, but incorporated new traits.

TRACK 47

### Other outsiders

In the 1800s, traders, whalers, and laborers returning from overseas exposed I-Kiribati to foreign social concepts and material goods. Beads, cloth, crepe paper,

***anene*** Kiribati song sung informally in a late-twentieth-century style incorporating Western musical elements, sometimes including the use of electric amplifiers

***bātere*** Kiribati version of the Tuvaluan *fātele*, performed as light entertainment; loosely, any outside-influenced Kiribati dancing

***bino*** Elegant Kiribati seated men's or women's dance in two sections, the first rhythmically free and the second in duple meter with choral clapping

***kabure*** Kiribati game played by quartets of seated individuals, who in complex patterns slap each other's hands and bodies while singing a three-tone melody in duple meter

***kairi*** Kiribati hymn, sung in three or four parts in Protestant and Roman Catholic services

***kuaea*** (from English 'choir') Kiribati guitar- and ukulele-accompanied choral singing, using Western harmonies in duple meter

***maneaba*** Kiribati formal house, used for village meetings and in the twentieth century by churches, schools, civic organizations, and performing troupes

***ruoia*** Kiribati traditional dance, realized in versions that vary slightly among islands but have sections started by a distinctive solo cue

---

yarn, and costume jewelry became incorporated into performative costumery, replacing plant fibers, shells, and animal teeth. Cultural contacts between I-Kiribati and the Tuvaluans, in the phosphate mines of Nauru and Banaba, and on Tarawa, deeply affected the musical evolution of Kiribati; they resulted in the adoption of new traits of music and dance and the *bātere*.

During World War II, Japanese troops occupied the Gilberts. Songs and dances memorialize the people's wartime hardships and their liberation by U.S. forces. Present-day settlements of I-Kiribati in the Solomon Islands and Nauru, and of Banabans in Fiji, have opened avenues of cultural exchange, including dancers' and composers' reciprocal visits.

—MARY E. LAWSON BURKE

## REFERENCES

Brandeis, Antonie. 1907. "Ethnographische Beobachtungen über die Nauru-Insulaner." *Globus* 91:57–62, 73–78.

Coulter, John. 1847. *Adventures on the Western Coast of South America and the Interior of California: Including a Narrative of Incidents at the Kingsmill Islands, New Ireland, New Britain, New Guinea, and Other Islands in the Pacific Ocean.* London: Longman's.

Delaporte, P. A. 1907. "Nauru As It Was and As It Is Now." *The Friend* 64(6):6–7, 64(7):13–14, 64(8):7–8, 64(9):9–11.

Delaporte, P. A., and Timothy Detudamo. 1936 [1915]. *Irian in Evangelium.* Melbourne: Specialty Press.

Fabricius, Wilhelm. 1992. *Nauru 1888–1900.* Edited and translated by Dymphna Clark and Stewart Firth. Canberra: Division of Pacific and Asian History, Research School of Pacific Studies, Australian National University.

Finsch, Otto. 1961 [1893]. *Ethnological Experiences and Materials from the South Seas.* Translated by Benjamin Keen. New Haven, Conn.: Human Relations Area Files.

Grimble, Arthur Francis. 1989. *Tungaru Traditions: Writings on the Atoll Culture of the Gilbert Islands.* Edited by H. E. Maude. Pacific Islands Monograph Series, 7. Honolulu: University of Hawai'i Press.

Grimble, Rosemary. 1972. *Migrations, Myth and Magic from the Gilbert Islands: Early Writings of Sir Arthur Grimble.* London: Routledge and Kegan Paul.

Hambruch, Paul. 1914–1915. *Nauru.* 2 vols. Ergebnisse der Südsee- Expedition 1908–1910, ed. Georg Thilenius, II.B.1. Hamburg: Friederichsen.

Kayser, Aloys. 1921–1922. "Spiel und Sport auf Náoero." *Anthropos* 16–17:681–711.

Kotzebue, Otto von. 1821. *A Voyage of Discovery, Into the South Sea and Beering's Straits, For the Purpose of Exploring a North-East Passage, Undertaken in the Years 1815–1818.* 3 vols. London: Longman, Hurst, Rees, Orme, and Brown.

———. 1830. *A New Voyage Round the World in the Years 1823, 24, 25, and 26.* 2 vols. London: Colburn and Bentley.

Krämer, Augustin. 1906. *Hawaii, Ostmikronesien und Samoa.* Stuttgart: Strecker und Schröder.

Maude, Honor. 1971. *The String Figures of Nauru Island.* Adelaide: Libraries Board of South Australia.

Parkinson, Richard. 1889. "Beiträge zur Ethnologie der Gilbert-Insulaner." *Internationales Archiv für Ethnologie* 2:31–48, 90–106.

Senfft, Arno. 1896. "Aus dem Schutzgebiete der Marshall-Inseln: Die Insel Nauru." In *Mittheilungen von Forschungsreisenden und Gelehrten aus den Deutschen Schutzgebieten,* vol. 9, ed. Freiherr von Danckelman, 101–109. Berlin: Mittler und Sohn.

Sonnenschein, [Franz Leopold]. 1889. "Aus dem Schutzgebiete der Marschall-Inseln: Aufzeichnungen über die Insel Nauru (Pleasant Island)." In *Mittheilungen von Forschungsreisenden und*

*Gelehrten aus den Deutschen Schutzgebieten,* vol. 2, ed. Freiherr von Danckelman, 19–26. Berlin: Mittler und Sohn.

Stephen, Ernest. 1936. "Notes on Nauru," ed. C. H. Wedgwood. *Oceania* 7(1):34–63.

Stevenson, Robert Louis. 1900. *In the South Seas.* London: Chatto and Windus.

Wilkes, Charles. 1844. *Narrative of the United States Exploring Expedition: During the Years 1838, 1839, 1840, 1841, 1842.* 5 vols. Philadelphia: C. Sherman.

# Polynesia

Poetry, sung and danced; chiefs, honored and entertained; families, made and defined; the creation of gods, islands, and people; the celebration of love, the joy of birth, the solemnity of war, the dignity of death—this is Polynesian music.

At the core of Polynesian music lie words, for music is primarily a vehicle for conveying poetry. Words are the basic and most important feature of Polynesian musical performance. Rendered melodically and rhythmically, words impart hidden meanings through metaphors, whose allusions can be interpreted on multiple levels. Performers are storytellers, who sing to communicate messages by moving their hands and arms while keeping the beat by moving their hips, feet, and legs.

Stamped bamboo tubes accompany the *Night Dance by Men in Hapaee*. Detail of an engraving after a drawing by John Webber in 1778, from Captain Cook's third voyage. Photo by Smithsonian Institution.

# The Music and Dance of Polynesia
*Adrienne L. Kaeppler*

**Understanding Polynesian Music and Dance**
**Performers and Audiences**
**Continuity and Change**

Polynesia (from Greek, meaning 'many islands') comprises a large number of islands mapped roughly as a triangle with Hawai'i at its northern apex, Rapa Nui at its southeast, and Aotearoa at its southwest. Culturally, Polynesia has three subdivisions: West Polynesia, East Polynesia, and Polynesian outliers west of the triangle. The ancestors of the Polynesians originated many generations ago in Asia or Southeast Asia, and they developed a maritime culture as they migrated through eastern Melanesia to West Polynesia. However, they cannot be considered Polynesian until they arrived in the Polynesian area, where the culture they brought with them evolved.

Traditionally throughout Polynesia, prestige and (usually) power resided in chiefly offices. Political regimes were long and enduring, and succession to chiefly office was by genealogical rules. Rank, based on descent from gods, was a distinctive social feature, which often resulted in pyramidal social structures, with the highest chief at the apex and commoners at the base; relative rank within the pyramid influenced social relationships.

Music and dance paid allegiance to rank-based sociopolitical systems by validating and helping construct the systems of social distinctions and interpersonal relationships that characterized each island group. Specialists composed poetry, added music and movement, and conducted rehearsals. Music and dance were, and still are, composed to be performed for audiences, which bring to performances a critical aesthetic appreciation. In addition, the order of pieces within a performance, and performers' placement and clothing, imparted important information about the performers, the occasion, and the sociopolitical system.

## UNDERSTANDING POLYNESIAN MUSIC AND DANCE

Polynesian music requires multidimensional analyses in an historic perspective that encompasses the study of poetic text, melody, rhythm, movement, and sociocultural context. Poetic texts, based in metaphor and allusion, formed the basis for most Polynesian music: essentially, music and dance were aural and visual vehicles for conveying oral literature. Rendered melodically and rhythmically, words suited the contexts in which they were performed, and were often accompanied by movements that contributed to the telling of stories.

Indigenous ceremonial contexts included funerals, weddings, investitures, and celebrations of historic and contemporary events. Social structure and religion were often the motivating forces behind aesthetic productions, but the performances, though serious in intent, were often occasions for entertainment. Less formal music included work, game, and love songs, and songs deriding or praising people and places. The variety of functions ranged from criticizing social institutions (as with the 'arioi of the Society Islands, with performers breaking ordinary social rules), to paying allegiance to the sociopolitical system (as with formal *faiva* in Tonga, with performers honoring chiefs).

To understand Polynesian music and dance, performers and audience must understand the spoken language, have an aesthetic appreciation of the rhythmic and melodic rendering of the poetry, grasp the allusions of the texts and the movements, and fathom relevant sociopolitical contexts and cultural philosophies.

Music was, and still is, primarily vocal. Nonvocal sounds, including claps and slaps, emphasized rhythm, often with contrasting timbres; but they seldom emphasized melody. The only distinctive Polynesian melody-producing instrument was the nose-blown flute (figure 1), made from a joint of bamboo and played by blowing through a nostril. With the introduction of European-derived instruments, especially ukuleles and guitars, instrumental melody became more important, though a primary function of these instruments was often rhythmic.

Before 1940, Edwin G. Burrows examined Polynesian music from a cross-cultural perspective. Polynesian vocal music, he said,

> is largely either formal declamation (recitative) or little songs built on couplets. Rhythm is governed mainly by the words, and is irregular except where responsive couplets or dancing give it symmetry. Tonality is simple, with narrow compass and emphasis on one tonic. The commonest melodic lines are level and arched. Structure consists most often of simple progression, varied repetition on one motive, or alternation of two contrasting motives. Singing in two parts is found in most of the islands, usually in the form of bordun [a relatively unchanging vocal line, with one or two more melodic lines that move above it] or heterophony. (1940:338)

Burrows observed inconsistencies in pitch: one of his 'Uvean informants sang successive performances of the same song with tonal variations of as much as a fourth. Though pitch varied widely, consistent rhythm was essential (1945:3, 86).

Polynesian meter is usually duple; tempo change is usually acceleration. Songs often end in a downward trailing off. Intensity or loudness is not varied for effect, as this would inhibit understanding the poetry. This trait confirms the nondramatization of storytelling, a trait also visible in the movements of Polynesian dance, dramatization being an index of modern aesthetics. Performers do not become characters in a dramatic interchange, and stylized gestures do not correspond to words or ideas put together in a narrative sequence.

## PERFORMERS AND AUDIENCES

Performances are usually by large or small groups, in which all performers do the same sequence of choreographed movements. Sometimes the men and women do separate sets of movements simultaneously. Many performances occur seated (figure 2). When standing, the legs and hips add rhythmic and aesthetic dimensions, but do not usually advance a story. Most important are the movements of the hands, wrists,

FIGURE 1    A Fijian nose-blown flute collected by the U.S. Exploring Expedition, 1840. Photo by Smithsonian Institution.

FIGURE 2 Singing and movements of the arms and hands are the important dimensions of Polynesian music and dance. Lapaha, Tonga, 1975. Photo by Adrienne L. Kaeppler.

and arms. The rotation or turning of the lower arm, flexion and extension of the wrist, curling of the fingers, flexion at the knuckles, and placement of the upper arm in space are significant dimensions. The combination of two bodily complexes—the amount and velocity of movements of the hips and legs, and the interplay of movements and placements of the hands, wrists, and arms—give each Polynesian movement tradition its distinctive style.

Polynesian audiences were interested in hearing stories and accepting a composer's challenge to understand the deeper meaning embodied in the poetry and movements. Performances were informative and aesthetic, but without knowledge of the language, and specifically the conventionalized text-and-movement allusions, the lack of dramatization makes following a story impossible, and today some audience members may not realize that a story is being told. Though melodically, polyphonically, and rhythmically engaging, the rendering of the poetry made the musical dimensions secondary and often repetitious. Similarly, Polynesian dance was the visual dimension of this poetry, with metrical lower-body-movement motifs and text-tied arm movements. Postcontact Polynesian music has changed in the direction of more melodic and rhythmic variation, and dance has become more pantomimic; nevertheless, poetic texts remain the basis for most music and dance.

## CONTINUITY AND CHANGE

Polynesian music has considerable variety, within a society and among societies. This variety has gone largely unrecognized because dimensions important to Polynesians are not the melody and the harmony (dimensions important to European analyzers), and analyses have often resulted in simplistic categories of "indigenous" and "acculturated," based on tonal elements apparent to outside observers. It is a mistake to consider Polynesian music acculturated simply because Polynesians adopted Western tonal intervals and harmonies, for these substitutions may be only irrelevant changes in "decoration." Polynesian music can be considered Polynesian if the structure and sentiment have not changed or have evolved along indigenous lines, or new musical concepts have been incorporated into old musical systems. This approach, however, poses the problem of indigenous function, for not many genres have the same function today as in earlier times.

## REFERENCES

Burrows, Edwin G. 1940. "Polynesian Music and Dancing." *Journal of the Polynesian Society* 49:331–346.

———. 1945. *Songs of Uvea and Futuna.* Bulletin 183. Honolulu: Bishop Museum.

# West Polynesia

Adrienne L. Kaeppler
David Goldsworthy
Dorothy Sara Lee
Wendy M. Ratawa
J. W. Love

Tialuga Sunia Seloti
Raymond Mayer
Alan Howard
Allan Thomas
Dieter Christensen

**Fiji**

**Tonga**

**Sāmoa**

**'Uvea and Futuna**

**Niue**

**Rotuma**

**Tokelau**

**Tuvalu**

West Polynesia includes Fiji, Tonga, Sāmoa, 'Uvea, Futuna, Niue, Rotuma, Tokelau, and Tuvalu (see map). Each archipelago is socially distinct, but all share basic cultural and linguistic patterns. Research on the prehistory of the West Polynesian societies shows that the Lapita cultural complex, derived from Melanesia and marked by distinctive dentate-stamped pottery, was once important in the region. West Polynesian voyagers maintained a trade-based network that included the importation of chiefly spouses and prestige items. The interisland movements of certain raw materials, lacking in some areas, linked utilitarian necessities (such as wood from large trees for canoes and basalt for adzes) to ritual necessities (such as colored feathers and special plaiting materials), and to marital partners and warfare.

During the 1400s to 1600s, Tonga dominated West Polynesia, under what is known as the Tongan Empire. Tongan overlords and warfare were tied to fertility-oriented rituals associated with the sacred Tu'i Tonga dynasty, whose originator was a descendant of the sky god Tangaloa. These rituals required the presentation of first-fruits and other tribute, but they also served as outlets of exchange, including the sexual unions that introduced variety into local gene pools.

Edwin G. Burrows, in a work analyzing music of 'Uvea and Futuna (1945:79–106), found that in melodies, the predominance of a single tone allowed this tone to be regarded as a tonic, and that whole songs were sung essentially on it. The tone next in importance was a dominant, a fourth below the tonic, fairly accurately pitched. A variable cluster of tones a second below the tonic often completed the scale, or one or two tones might occur above the tonic. Melodic or polyphonic intervals were usually a major second, a variable third, or a fourth. The most usual scales had two to four tones, a range of less than a fifth, and a level melodic movement with a prevailing monotone.

Musical instruments important in West Polynesia are hollowed log idiophones, stamped bamboo tubes, struck wooden plaques, mat idiophones, nose-blown flutes, and conch trumpets. Contemporary instruments include ukuleles, guitars, electrically amplified stringed instruments and keyboards, and the aerophones used in brass bands.

An analysis of West Polynesian movement systems reveals a torso usually

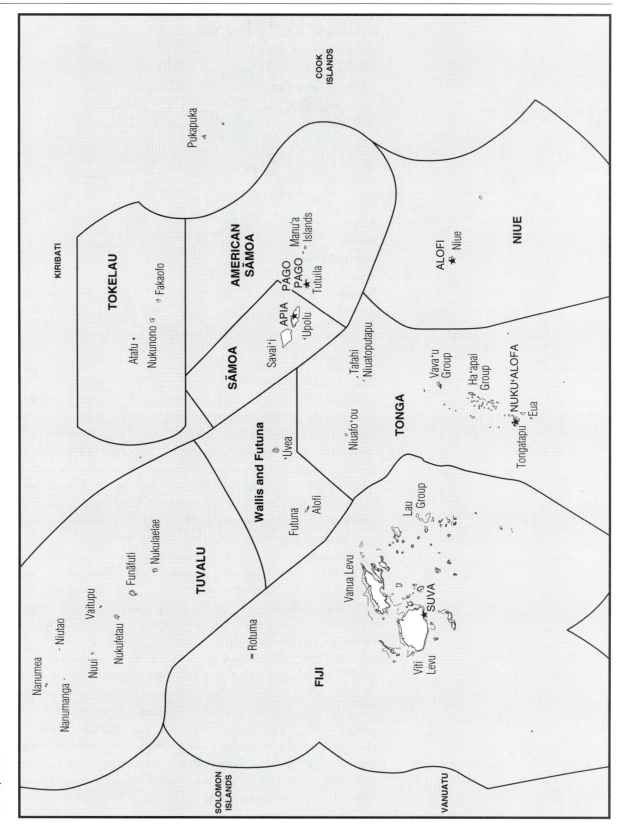

West Polynesia

FIGURE 1 At the Pacific Festival of Arts, men of Futuna perform a *tākofe*. Photo by Adrienne L. Kaeppler, 1992.

upright, shoulders that do not move, and an emphasis on hand-arm motifs that enhance the texts. Within these conventions, movements vary with gender: men perform "virile" movements, often with the legs parted, open to the sides; women perform "graceful" movements, with the upper legs parallel and close together. Movements of the hips—subdued, often hidden by voluminous costumes—are not a significant dimension. Distinguishing features are the complexity of the interplay among turning the lower arm, bending the elbow, extending and flexing the wrist, and curling the fingers. Dance implements such as paddles, clubs, and long staffs (figure 1) are found throughout the region. Sometimes struck, they may make artistic patterns in space.

## FIJI

An independent nation of about 320 islands in eight groups, Fiji lies at the confluence of Melanesia and Polynesia, sharing cultural and physical affinities with both. Much of its music and dance, however, should be considered Polynesian because of its similarity to the music and dance of West Polynesia.

Fiji has an area of about 18,000 square kilometers and a population of about 700,000, about half of whom are Asian Indian, the descendants of indentured laborers imported to Fiji to cultivate sugarcane. Other immigrants include Chinese, Europeans, Micronesians, and Polynesians. In the 1800s, the Fijian people put themselves under British colonial influence, at least partly to be free of Tongan authority and attacks.

The main islands, Viti Levu and Vanua Levu, show distinct cultural differences between coastal peoples and those that live in the interior. Most villages recognize lineage-based distinctions between land people and sea people. Even the smaller islands in the Lau Archipelago, on the eastern reaches of Fiji, observed the land-sea distinction. Other main groups are Kadavu to the south, and the Yasawa Islands to the west.

Social groups related through kinship held land in common, and these groups combined into larger political federations. The leader or chief of each group was the closest descendant of a common ancestor. The spirit of this ancestor was consulted and worshipped in a temple (*bure kalou*), where the spirit descended by means of a piece of bark cloth. Second- and third-rank descendants were executive officers of the chiefs and *matanivanua* (mouthpiece or "herald" of the chief and social unit), and served as repositories of information on tradition and protocol.

—ADRIENNE L. KAEPPLER

FIGURE 2 Backed by a seated male chorus, seated Fijian women perform a *meke* at the Pacific Festival of Arts. Photo by Adrienne L. Kaeppler, 1992.

FIGURE 2 Backed by a seated male chorus, seated Fijian women perform a *meke* at the Pacific Festival of Arts. Photo by Adrienne L. Kaeppler, 1992.

## Fijian music

Fijian music may be divided into three broad categories: indigenous music, Christian religious music, and popular music [see POPULAR MUSIC: Music in Place: Fiji].

### Indigenous music

The mainstays of Fijian music are *meke,* sung narrative texts with instrumental and dance accompaniment, performed in ceremonial and social contexts by men or women (rarely mixed) in lines or blocks, standing or sitting (figure 2). Movements, usually synchronous, emphasize collective excellence, rather than individual achievement. Men's movements are vigorous; women's, graceful and controlled.

Fijians subdivide *meke* into named genres, distinguished from each other by the dancers' gender, position (sitting or standing), movements, and accouterments. Genres include men's dances with spears (*meke wesi*) and clubs (*meke i wau*), dances with fans (*meke iri*), a standing women's dance (*seasea*), standing men's dances (*ruasa, liga*), and the ever-popular *vakamalolo,* done by seated men or women. The *meke ni yaqona* is a ceremonial song, performed by men while making ritualized movements of their arms and clapping their hands during formal kava-drinking ceremonies [see MUSIC AND INGESTED SUBSTANCES]. The genres of *meke* are performed with varying frequencies in different areas. On Taveuni and Kadavu, the *vakamalolo* predominates.

Performances of *meke* fulfill various social functions. Apart from entertainment, they encourage social interaction and solidarity, and establish cultural identity, which may be local, like the spear dance of Vanua Levu (Kubuabola et al. 1978:18). *Meke* may have an enculturative or didactic role, and frequently serve as a record-keeping medium. Though the significance of performance has changed with the society, *meke* remain an important part of festive and official occasions, such as religious conferences, weddings, and official visits by political dignitaries. Some genres, like *vakamalolo,* are more popular than others. Some support competitive dancing. Some survive by altering their functions, as men's dances with spears and clubs have become vehicles for entertainment on festive occasions or in *meke* competitions.

Vocal accompaniment for Fijian *meke* usually comes from singers who sit in a tight, circular formation, with the leaders near the center. The most important person in the performance of any *meke* is the composer (*dau ni vucu*), "responsible for every aspect of the *meke*—poetry, music, dance, accompanying instrumentation . . . and costume" (Thompson 1971:19). The composer of the lyrics, male or female, is usually known by name. Composers teach their *meke,* and may lead the singing.

Performances of *meke* exhibit the Polynesian emphasis on the primacy of a text, usually composed by an individual and rendered musically by a company. Lyrics usually divide into stanzas, each of which may repeat. The number of lines in a stanza, and the number of words in a line, vary. The ends of lines usually rhyme on an identity of two vowels, regardless of any intervening consonant. Recounting historical events, lyrics often use archaic words and structures.

Some *meke* have a prelude (*ucu*), sung without dancing. The *meke* proper (*matana*) consists of several stanzas, and often includes a refrain (*taletale*), sung after a series of stanzas. *Meke*-style singing without dancing is called *vucu*. Usually in three or more vocal parts, *vucu* may chronicle events, praise deeds or individuals, or lament a death. They are usually sung by men for relaxation at night, with or without instrumental accompaniment.

Fijian musical theory distinguishes vocal parts or roles by name. The *laga* 'to sing' usually leads, closely followed by the *tagica* 'to cry, to chime in', sung above the *laga*. Parts called *druku* 'bass' are sung in several levels in chordal harmony. In effect, *laga* and *tagica* are high solo parts, and *druku* constitute a harmonizing chorus. Earlier *meke* developed melodies within narrow ranges, and employed a great deal of tonal repetition. They used static harmonic clusters of seconds and fifths. Modern *meke*, taught in schools, use the standard harmonies of functional tonality. Most *meke* use triple divisions of the beat.

*Vakalutuivoce* 'dropping the oar', an ancient style of unaccompanied Fijian singing, survives in some areas. Formerly, two people rowing or rafting down a river sang songs in this style. Their voices moved in close counterpoint, emphasizing the harmony of a major second.

Apart from *meke, vucu,* and *vakalutuivoce,* the principal forms of musical expression in old Fiji were lullabies, game songs, and work songs. Like *meke,* these genres survive in Fiji, but their frequency of performance has decreased, and some are moribund. Lullabies, sung to children by parents, or more commonly, grandparents, have narrow melodic ranges. Game songs include juggling songs, sung by women, and various children's songs; these pieces often have a defined and regular beat, in 3/8 or 6/8 time, fitting the actions, and a narrow-ranged melodic contour with a nondiscrete tonal structure. Men's javelin-throwing songs (*meke ni veitiqa, sere ni veitiqa*) are almost extinct. Special songs formerly accompanied fishing, planting, and other kinds of work.

### Christian religious music

Fijian biblical songs (*same* 'psalms') bridge the precontact and Christian periods. They are sung in Methodist churches by mature women. Their texts are based on Fijian-language biblical passages, of which the Song of Solomon and the parable of the prodigal son (Luke 15:11–32) are favorites. Musically, *same* derive from *meke* and owe nothing to outside influence. Their vocal parts are *laga, tagica,* and *druku,* the same as in *meke*. In all parts, the melodic movement is minimal, and the range is narrow. The *laga* and the *tagica* sing in a two-part texture, utilizing close harmonic intervals, mainly thirds and seconds, sometimes converging on unisons. The choral parts (*druku*), providing tonal repetitions within narrow contours, feature block chords consisting of seconds, thirds, fifths, and octaves. *Same* use syllabically set texts with an indefinite musical meter and a strophic structure.

The catechism (*taro*) is another unaccompanied religious genre. It is usually sung responsorially from the Fijian hymnal, with the leader speaking the questions and the congregation answering in a musical style like that of *same.*

*Polotu,* a form of worship with distinctive singing and accompaniment, is associated with Tongan people in the Lau Islands and has spread to other Fijian regions. A

FIGURE 3   At the Polynesian Cultural Center in
Lāʻie, Hawaiʻi, Fijians stamp bamboo tubes.
Photo by Adrienne L. Kaeppler, 1964.

triangle, or a beaten rod or plate, keeps time for melodic and harmonic triadic structures.

Choral polyphonic singing of religious texts is extremely popular in Fiji. These pieces, *sere ni lotu,* range from simple hymns to ambitious choral arrangements, using common-practice tonal harmonies.

### Musical instruments

The most common musical instruments that accompany *meke* are *lali ni meke,* small log idiophones, played with two wooden sticks, and *cobo,* clapping with cupped hands. To these, the performers in some areas add bamboo tubes (*derua*) of various lengths, which they stamp against the ground (figure 3).

Other indigenous musical instruments are a large log idiophone (*lali*), often used in pairs for summoning people to church, and a conch trumpet (*davui*), used for signaling. In a performance by two large *lali* filmed in Baidamudamu (Kadavu) in 1986, one instrument played an ostinato while the other played interlocking patterns. The playing of panpipes and bamboo nose-blown flutes, once common in Fiji, is now almost extinct.

Introduced musical instruments mainly include guitars, ukuleles, and mandolins. These instruments may occasionally accompany modern-style *meke,* but their primary use is for popular music.                    —DAVID GOLDSWORTHY

## Music and dance in Naloto

Naloto, a village on the eastern coast of Viti Levu, Tailevu Province, has three patrilineal tribes, which local history says settled the Naloto Peninsula in specific locations: Qalibure, the chiefly lineage, occupies the south side, facing land; Saraviti, the fishermen's lineage, occupies the north side, facing the sea; Mataisau, the carpenters' lineage, shares the north side with Saraviti. Lineages in this region have close ties to those of the Lau Archipelago—which, in turn, has received influence from Tonga.

The people of Naloto divide music into two classes: things that are *meke,* and things that are not. *Meke,* usually glossed 'dance', form the most important musical genre. Though visitors to Fiji may take home memories of elaborately costumed, carefully rehearsed dancers performing with a *lali* and a chorus, people emphasize that *meke* provide opportunities for reaffirming social, political, and supernatural relationships.

### Musical concepts

Naloto people describe music in social terms. Singers in ensembles interact musically in diverse ways, determined by vocal quality and part. Two Fijian verbs translate the English verb "to sing": *sere* 'to sit and sing' denotes the act of singing alone, or at least singing outside the context of ensembles, which characterize major Fijian performances; *laga* denotes the act of beginning a melody or leading voices in an ensemble (the individual who leads is by extension a *laga*).

### Vocal textures

Performances of *meke* are a structured ensemble of vocalists (*vakatara*), who sing the text and add layers of percussive accompaniment to the texture. Aurally and spatially, the group has two components: the inner voices, consisting of the *laga,* the *tagica* (the one who follows the lead), and the outer voice, or *druku.* Naloto performers say these parts comprise the core of Fijian vocal texture. The *laga* sets the pitch and tempo, but is not expected to be heard above the rest of the group; the prescribed timbre for this voice, as for the *tagica,* is light, soft, and small. Together, these voices furnish rhythmic and melodic cues for the rest of the ensemble.

Singers of the *druku* sit in a dense, irregular circle around singers of the inner voices, enveloping them with sound. Though singing *druku* requires the least amount of skill, anyone, without attending rehearsals or even learning the words, can sing the part. Performers consider it to be the most important voice. With a basic knowledge of the structure of Fijian music, those singing *druku* can watch the faces of the two principal singers, gauging the impending end of a verse to synchronize with a unison close. In rehearsals, *druku* may outnumber those singing the inner voices. The sheer number of their voices ensures that the words will be heard and understood clearly. They add weight and substance to the other voices, and the prescribed vocal quality for the voice is heavy (*bibi*).

### Instrumental textures

The fundamental organizing layer of rhythm is provided by a *lali ni meke,* a small log idiophone. Performances in Naloto rely on one of the principal singers to beat the basic rhythm on a *lali.* To the basic beat, master musicians add conventional decorations: *ukuuku,* for the *lali*; *geregerea,* for the voice. Each genre has its identifying rhythmic pattern, complemented by percussive layers in the ensemble: stamped tubes (*derua*), which, though not tuned to a specific pitch, produce deep booms; and two kinds of clapping, *cobo* (cupped clapping, which has a deep, hollow sound) and *sausau* (flat, lengthwise clapping, which has a bright, sharp quality). The texture receives further enrichment as dancers slap their hands against fans, brush their hands and arms against leafy wrist ornaments, or stamp their feet.

For the genres *taralala* and *sere ni cumu,* Western instruments—guitar, one-stringed bass, ukulele—provide underlying rhythms. Secondarily, these instruments contribute a harmonic structure to the vocal framework, cueing pitches, sections, and harmonic changes. In other contexts, concussed spoons provide a forum for virtuoso instrumental performance.

### Verbal structures

Most *meke* have several stanzas (*qaqana ni meke* 'small part of the meke'), each of which may consist of lines (*yatu ni vosa* 'rows of words'). For supernaturally composed *meke,* larger formal divisions distinguish one genre from another, and in part organize the major sections of the choreographed movement. In general, the large formal divisions include one or more introductory verses (*ucu ni meke* 'nose of the meke'), which may be distinguished from the other stanzas by differences in melody, tempo, the dancers' position, or the absence of movement; the main body of the *meke* (*lewe ni meke* 'inner flesh of the *meke*'); and a closing verse (*kena i oti* 'its end'), whose text often signals that the *meke* is ending. So watchers can appreciate multiple facets of the dance, the performers may repeat any of these verses several times.

Couples dance side by side, inner arms crossed behind partners, with one partner's hand resting on the other's outer hip, outer arms hanging loosely at the side. The couples two-step at a fast walking tempo.

Other formal divisions are specific to particular genres. These include a refrain (*vakatale* 'come again'), which sometimes graces *taralala* and *vakamalolo*; an antiphonal phrase (*ie sasa* [Bauan *sausau*] 'to answer'), which characterizes the *seasea*; and the turn (*vuki*), which graces several genres, but in Naloto is typical of *vakamalolo*.

Naloto performers identify two kinds of poetry: *serekali,* poetry that is usually not sung; and *vucu* or *meke,* poetry sung as part of a *meke.* In everyday speech, these terms are often interchangeable. Fijian poetry rhymes, emphasizing phonetic agreement on the penultimate syllable of lines. All lines in a stanza must agree (*ra bose vata* 'come together'). To fit a particular rhyme, words can gain or lose syllables. For example, the name *Jesus* translates into Fijian as *Jisu,* but in the following excerpt, it gains the syllable *ya* to rhyme with the next verse: *Siga ni Sucu i Jisuya: / Sa sucu na yacana Ko Jiuta* 'The day of Jesus' birth: / He was born in a place named Judea'. Most genres have a distinctive verbal meter (*veineireyaki* 'the way things fall'), which interweaves the melodic rhythm with the linguistic rhythm. In emic analysis, four syllables involving reduplication (as in the word *wasawasa,* from *wasa*) might count as two, so the etically analyzed number of syllables per line is flexible.

Early observers quickly recognized the complexity of Fijian poetic forms. In a report on Fijian ethnology and philology, Horatio Hale, philologist on the U.S. Exploring Expedition, devoted a section to poetry:

> A poet of Viti . . . must not only possess a good knowledge of music, as it is understood by his countrymen, and be acquainted with the principles on which their dances are regulated, but in the composition of his song he has to adapt it both to the tune and the dance,—and he must do this while fettered by a complicated system of rhythm and rhyme peculiar, so far as we know, to his language. (1846:383)

Buell Halvor Quain, writing about an epic cycle of Vanua Levu, noted: "Ancestors chant the songs as they teach so that the rhythms implicit in the language are qualified by a musical style which can freely reduplicate syllables to change the stress in words" (1942:14).

When performers intone a stanza, they stress the rhymes, slightly pause, and shift the intonation at the ends of lines. When they sing the same stanza, the ways they highlight the rhymes and the meter are different. Hale thought the sung text bore little relation to the poetry: "The words in their singing, or rather chanting, are divided according to the tune, without any reference to the sense—a pause not unfrequently occurring in the middle of the word" (1846:384). Local understanding contrasts recited poetry and sung verse: recitation is usually solo, but singing is collective. In *vakawelegone* and *vakalutu i voce,* this ideal produces a flexible, near-improvisatory style, which matches more fluid melodies to less adaptable texts. For *meke* utilizing large ensembles, aesthetic emphasis on the massed textures of sight, sound, and movement gives the music precedence over its text.

### Music associated with Christianity

In addition to the standard Methodist musical repertory, which consists principally of hymns and composed anthems (*sere ni lotu*), *taro* and *same* blend Christian themes and indigenous musical style and performance. These genres are sung by women, in church and at casual gatherings.

*Taro* 'questions' are excerpts from the Methodist catechism, as the text appears in the back of the Methodist hymnal. One woman recites the question, chosen from a section of the catechism containing questions appropriate to the daily lesson; the ensemble sings the response. Typically performed just before the start of the Sunday service, *taro* can serve as an anthem during the service.

Adaptation of the texts of *taro* follows precise structural conventions. The ends of textual lines and the corresponding musical phrases are marked by the practice of *solosolo* (*vakasoloba* 'to cut off, surround') or *laqa yarayara* 'trailing voice', in which the bass drops out for the last two syllables, leaving only the *laga* and *tagica* audible. The *druku* rejoins the two inner voices on the first syllable of the next line. Because Fijian music requires a continuous sound, the practice of *solosolo* allows the *druku* to take a breath (*vakacegu*); the two inner voices take quick breaths just after the bass joins in.

Similar to *taro* in vocal quality and musical structure, *same* are instructive religious songs, based on biblical episodes and themes. They can be sung just before or during the service. Unlike *taro,* they are composed by women. Though the composers of *same* in Naloto are dead and their names are no longer remembered, their compositions are still active in the repertory. The texts of *same* use plain expressions, eschewing metaphorical embellishment.

### Popular traditions

In Naloto, European or European-derived popular song sung in Fijian is known as *sere.* Many songs survive from World War II, when soldiers from America, Aotearoa, and Australia interacted extensively with Fijians. Other songs are adaptations of popular songs from any era. *Sere* can be performed solo, with guitar accompaniment, or in small ensembles. Some singers employ vibrato, a vocal production rare in most indigenous genres, and distinct from the deliberately decorative shaking of the voice (*geregerea*).

Western-styled popular songs (*sere ni cumu*) with romantic or supernatural texts, form a large part of young people's music in Naloto. Singers accompany themselves with guitars, ukuleles (*ukalele*), spoons, and one-stringed basses (*wa dua*), constructed of a broomstick, a string, and a large biscuit tin or metal bucket (players vary the pitch by fretting the string and changing the angle of the broomstick). Young women play guitars and sing popular songs in private, but only young men form string bands and play in public.

In *sere ni cumu* and the related *taralala,* voices are pitched higher and exhibit greater vocal tension than in older Fijian music. *Sere ni cumu* are slow, matching the introspection and melancholy of their texts. They employ the three principal vocal parts: *laga, tagica,* and *druku.*

*Taralala* (possibly from English *tra-la-la*) are contemporary alternatives to indigenous Fijian dances, and they are the only mixed couples' dances performed in Naloto. Of European origin and inspiration, the genre arrived locally before 1900. Couples dance side by side, inner arms crossed behind partners, with one partner's hand carelessly resting on the other's outer hip, outer arms hanging loosely at the side. The couples two-step at a fast walking tempo in a circle clockwise around the floor, women flexing alternate knees so their hips sway slightly. Occasionally, prompted by one or more experienced couples, the entire circle might vary the basic forward progression by pivoting sharply to one side, then the other, turning in place, or backing up for several beats and then moving forward again. This dance does not require special skill: anyone may participate, regardless of ability.

*Taralala* are in duple meter, with a lively tempo and cheerful texts. Early examples were performed without guitar, using indigenous vocal ensembles, but new instruments, harmonies, and songs have come into vogue. Since elders remember the *sere ni cumu* and *taralala* of their youth, emerging string bands must learn their parents' and grandparents' songs. Naloto's popular songs include musical styles fashionable just after the Great War (1914–1918) and those current on radio.

*Taralala* provide opportunities for public dancing in mixed-sex pairs. Women also dance in pairs to clown around. Older women sometimes use *taralala* to enliven informal gatherings, when they dress in men's clothes, lunge aggressively at spectators, and lampoon musicians by seizing instruments and pretending to play them.

—Dorothy Sara Lee

## A local view

From a Fijian point of view, music subdivides into two classes: *meke,* formal music, which enhances social life as part of ceremonial occasions; and *sere,* informal music, an expression of play and entertainment. In text, style, and context, *meke* focus on social structures implied in chieftainship, place, and precontact religion. *Sere* relate to place, kinship, informal entertainment, introduced religion, and holistic Fijian identity. *Meke* and *sere* connect closely with the land (*vanua*), "the social and cultural aspects of the environment" (Ravuvu 1988:6).

Fijians once belonged to small, autonomous, kinship-based communities, with allegiance to local clans. Under British colonial administration (1874–1970), they expanded their social universe. Christian missions (mostly Wesleyan) appeared, travel became easier, and the economy changed. Looking to a holistic identity, Fijians redeveloped their concepts of land.

### *Meke*

Fijians danced during rites of passage, exchanges of goods, rituals for visitors, entertainment, farewells, and seasons of taboo and license. For these contexts, some of which remain important, performative genres included dances with implements and standing women's dances (*seasea*). New contexts are school bazaars, fund-raising events for provincial and ecclesiastical conferences, and festivals (figure 4).

FIGURE 4    Backed by a seated men's chorus, standing Fijian women with fans perform a *meke* at the Pacific Festival of Arts. Photo by Adrienne L. Kaeppler, 1988.

Some genres are for men only. These include the songs and declamations associated with the formal preparation of kava. Only men dance with spears or clubs, and only women dance *seasea,* but the chorus may include men and women.

A close relationship once linked vocal music and spiritual dimensions of life, as in the songs and declamations associated with kava. Taboo and mana had their usual Pacific connotations: performers feared to make errors. In the late 1990s, musical performances still mediate social relations, but performers no longer fear death from transgressing mana.

Fijian music included taunts sung by women on the beach when men who had been trying to catch turtles returned. The melodic movement was pendular (a style locally associated with taunting), and the lyrics included sexual innuendos, disguised in metaphors.

### Sere

Within twentieth-century Fiji, internal migrations—for constructing buildings, mining, planting, and trading—diffused languages and musical ideas. Colonial and post-colonial networks brought new cultural concepts, modernization, textual themes for songs, multivocal parts, musical instruments, and international popular music.

In hymns (*sere ni lotu*), Christian perspectives became subsumed into indigenous culture. Hymns substituted for abandoned rituals, like singing before a temple or during the rebuilding of a temple. Fijians sing hymns at intercommunal festivals, conferences, bazaars, and competitions.

In eastern Fiji, *sere* include *polotu,* songs derived from Tongan music and exploring Christian topics. Unlike standard four-part harmonizations of hymns, they have flexible voicing, which lets singers improvise. A triangle or other metallic object provides accompaniment.

Fijian custom reserved the formal drinking of kava for chiefs, but twentieth-century democratization led to the informal drinking of kava by commoners. This change occurred gradually, but accelerated during the years 1941 to 1945. With it came a new genre, *sere ni cumu.*

Under British rule, patriotic songs (*sere ni vanua*) developed. Contexts for their singing included New Year's observances, community functions (such as school bazaars and Independence Day), and in the period of the military coups (1987), political protests and roadblocks. An excerpt from a patriotic song (figure 5) recalls the year 1835, when Wesleyan missionaries arrived in Lakeba:

| | |
|---|---|
| Lotu sa tadu mai, ki Viti e daidai. | The church came here, to Fiji this day. |
| Dua walu tolu lima, yaco ma kina. | In 1835, it came here. |
| Jisu sa loko mai. Vaka e vakilai | Jesus comes here. Understand |
| Ko Rosi kei Kakili yaco mai. | The Rose of Galilee comes here. |
| Sa yaco mai ki ke na Lotu Wesele. | The Wesleyan Church comes here. |
| Viti, sa lotu dina ne. | Fiji, the true church. |

The texts of some *sere* are in local languages and dialects, but most are in standard Fijian (Bauan dialect), which offers the widest geographical base for intelligible presentation.

### Tourists, immigrants, innovations

*Meke* and *sere* occur in tourist-oriented performances, particularly on the western side of Viti Levu and in the urban centers of Suva and Lautoka. Rather than honoring the land, performances typically emphasize energy, surprise, and humor. Good humor balances formal rules of responsibility for the land. Calendrically set periods of

FIGURE 5   Excerpt from "*Lotu sa tadu mai,*" a Fijian patriotic song (*sere ni vanua*). Transcription by Wendy M. Ratawa.

behavioral excess enable the members of society to deal with the prescribed behavior of respect for chiefs and the changing circumstances of a pluralistic society. Fijians use vocal music as play, especially in the *taralala,* an informal dance for couples, which had no precedent in old Fiji, though it continues the clowning and joking of women's erotic dancing.

Asian Indians have lived in Fiji since the 1870s. They make up about half the population, but ethnic Fijians have borrowed little musical material from them. The two musical systems do not interact, though many Fijian children attend schools that emphasize Asian Indian culture. On rare occasions, a Fijian performer may sing a Hindustani text—and even, by intentionally using a high register and vibrato, sing in the Indian style of solo narrative or religious song (*qawwali*).

Besides formally taught songs, Fijian children create their own songs at play [see MUSIC AND EDUCATION]. Though these songs may refer to specific local environments and cultural traits, they have traits that may belong universally to children.

Fijian playground songs (*veiqito*) have recurring textual-rhythmic patterns, based on duration, assonance, and rhyme. The inclusion of Hindustani and English songs in Fijian children's repertories shows the influence of the curriculum. As Fijian and Indian children mature, they become less likely to sing in languages other than those of their ethnic background.

—WENDY M. RATAWA

## TONGA

The kingdom of Tonga consists of 172 islands, totaling 748 square kilometers; thirty-six are inhabited by about one hundred thousand people. The people and culture are closely related to those of Sāmoa, Niue, 'Uvea, and Fiji. Tonga is a small society, rooted in a genealogically stratified social structure. As a British-protected state, it easily absorbed the British monarchical mystique. Titles bestowed on certain chiefs came to define hereditary nobles with landed estates. These concepts codified ideas that had been present in precontact times.

Music is, and probably always has been, an important element in the life of the Tongan people. No event is complete without music (and often dance), and what is remembered about an event is often the music performed in it. Music defines an event by giving voice to its purpose.

New compositions were, and are, composed for any important public or private event. Major compositions, such as *lakalaka* (see below), are often restaged for appropriate contemporary events. The restagings commemorate the event for which the *lakalaka* was composed, and may recall other events at which it has been performed. Analyses of musical compositions help decode cultural ideas about values; rather than simply reflecting these ideas, however, Tongan musical compositions help construct and restructure them.

### Thinking about Tongan music

Modern Tongan music is a composite of multiple strands of sound and movement, evolved from precontact Tongan performances under a variety of influences—from the Western world, from other Pacific islands, and in the late twentieth century, from the Caribbean. It has followed its own lines, retaining the importance of poetic texts.

Indirectness (*heliaki*) is an aesthetic concept through which Tongans construct meaning in their lives. It finds its most important outlet in music, where metaphors emphasize the centrality of oratory to social activity and hierarchy. Using metaphors, composers select concepts and information that will be sung, remembered, and usually accepted by the populace, especially if the composer is a genealogically important person, or a member of the royal family.

### *Poetry*

An important activity in Tongan life is the performance of oratory and poetry. Rendered melodically, and sometimes accompanied by percussive instruments and sounds and movements made by human bodies, poetic texts are often complex. Their functions are primarily secular: composed mainly for specific occasions, they honor individuals, social groups, villages, and events. They also chronicle the history and values of the Tongan people.

Poetry is basic and composed first. Lyrics receive a melody, often a preexisting one; or a composer invents a new melody, or improvises a melody. When performed for a subsequent occasion or event, melodies may undergo major changes, but Tongans believe poetry in such settings should undergo only minor changes. Adding music to a new poetic composition, composers often take melodic motifs from old songs, or combine parts of melodies of several old songs. Composers also borrow other Polynesian or Western melodies, altering them to fit local tastes.

### Polyphony

Vocal and instrumental polyphony has long existed in Tonga. Ensembles of stamped bamboo tubes and struck log idiophones accompanied danced poetry. Eighteenth-century accounts report that voices were harmonious and melodious, and state that Tongans sang in parts. Singing in parts, though no longer the same as that described by eighteenth-century visitors, remains conceptually similar. The most important part is the *fasi,* the leading part or melody, often conceptualized as fitting with a lower part (*laulalo*), a movable drone. These parts could receive decoration from others, described in 1793 as accompanying a simple melody "with different modulations," featuring a countertenor audible above the others (Labillardière 1802:133, 137–138).

According to elderly and knowledgeable musicians in the 1960s, precontact Tongan singing had as many as six parts. The leading part (*fasi*) was usually sung by men. Two women's parts were described as high and low. *Lalau* was described as a men's part that could cross above the melody. *Ekenaki,* another men's part, was sung lower than the melody. Finally, *laulalo* was a low men's part, conceptually like a drone (Shumway 1981: example 4b). According to Tongan views, *fasi* and *laulalo* were the essential parts; the others were decorative.

This six-part texture seldom occurs in Tongan performance, having been replaced by Western-derived harmony, with up to three parts each for men and women. In the newer form, men and women may each sing a *fasi* (the women's *fasi* is sometimes known as *solo,* the Tongan word for soprano), the same melody an octave apart. Women have one or two lower parts (*kanokano* and *'oloto*), similar to a high and low alto, though some singers say these parts are the same. Some men sing tenor (*tenoa*), which may cross above the *fasi,* and the *laulalo.*

Though the evolved style of singing in parts resembles the old, its tonal intervals are based predominantly on those of Western music. The bass is more melodic, and women have an added soprano part (*fasi* or *solo*), sung an octave higher than the men's *fasi* or a separate part. In the older and the evolved styles, the parts are not consistent, and often collapse into two or three: *fasi, laulalo,* and a decoration of the *fasi.*

Sung poetry is primarily a group activity, rendered in several parts. A leader may sing a few introductory notes to set the pitch and tempo, and then others join in. On each repetition, the parts and ornamentation may differ slightly.

### Polykinetics

Tongan structured-movement systems are based on three parts of the human body. The legs and feet serve primarily to keep the rhythmic pulse, often a series of side-to-side steps, executed nearly in place; in seated dances, one foot may keep a metrical pulse. For women, movements of the feet and legs are small, in keeping with the stricture of always having the upper legs parallel and close together. Men's movements are larger, with more bodily actions—including kneeling on one knee, striking the ground with feet or hands, and even lying or rolling on the ground.

The movements of hands and arms are most important and form complex motifs that have three functions: to allude to selected words of the text, or to concepts arising from the poetry; to form beautiful movements, which decorate or complete textual and musical phrases; and to form dividing motifs, which separate stanzas or sections of poetry. Motifs of the arms are based on flexible wrists and lower-arm rotations with various movements of the fingers and positions and facings of the palms, occurring in a limited number of arm positions. These motifs are known by the general term *haka.* Some motifs have specific names, such as *milolua,* a movement that derives from the wringing of kava. Women's arm movements are soft and graceful, while men's involve stiffer wrists or clenched fists. A tilt of the head to the side (*fakateki*), though sometimes choreographed, is primarily an aesthetic element added by the performer to express *māfana,* an inner feeling of exhilaration.

### Aesthetics of performance

Concepts useful in studying Tongan aesthetics are *faiva* 'skill'; *heliaki* 'indirectness'; *faka'apa'apa* 'respect, humility'; and the integral association of verbal and visual modes of expression. Though "art" was not a category of Tongan culture, the concept implied by the incorporation of *faiva* is important for understanding Tongan aesthetics. *Faiva* denotes any work, task, feat, trade, craft, or performance requiring skill or ability. The incorporation of *heliaki* requires skill based on extensive cultural knowledge. *Heliaki* is manifested in metaphor and layers of meaning, developed by skirting a subject and approaching it repeatedly from different angles. Hidden meanings must be unraveled layer by layer. An observer cannot understand a performance by simply examining it from the outside, on its surface. The performing arts incorporate social philosophy, forming the basic structure of the aesthetic system [see COMPOSITIONAL PROCESSES].

## Musical contexts and genres

Based on context, function, musical setting, bodily movement, and textual structure, Tongan sung and moved poetry can be categorized into six main performative types. Tongan performances are often concerned with the metaphorical validation of hierarchical social forms, important in the analysis of the poetics and politics of presentation and representation.

Planned and composed by culturally and aesthetically knowledgeable individuals, delivered in an aesthetically charged atmosphere, sung and moved by aesthetically motivated men and women, received and evaluated by receptive audiences, performances bring politics into the poetic domain. Study of these presentations reveals how Tongans represent themselves to themselves and the outside world, and suggests that metaphor and indirectness are keys to Tongan thought and cultural forms. The following discussion arranges genres primarily by events and functions, though categories cross and intermix. Each major genre, and many subgenres, appear to have existed in some form in precontact times.

### Laments and eulogies (tengihia)

Death in Tonga is an important rite of passage, and mourning dictates the kinds of music that can be performed, and by whom. The verbalization of grief is the duty of high-ranking individuals (usually women) as part of specific social events. The general term for this verbalization (*tengihia* 'to weep for') encompasses two poetic forms, *tangi* 'to cry' and *laulau*. Spontaneous weeping in stylized, pitched, rhythmic form with improvised or preset texts at a wake is *tangilaulau,* or simply *tangi*. On such occasions, individuals formally cry, explaining why they are sorry the deceased has died. More thoughtful poetic creations in praise of one departed are *laulau,* in which individuals explain with a memorial poem what is in their hearts.

Laments involve texted weeping in straightforwardly pitched rhythms; eulogies, characterized by genealogical metaphors in poetic verse, are manifestations of the composer's knowledge of genealogy and its expression as metaphor in culturally appropriate forms of indirectness. Metaphors use the names of places, flowers, and birds to refer to high-ranking individuals. Especially important are references to floral mixtures, which serve as metaphors for the mixtures of bloodlines that produced the elevated genealogy of the deceased.

The content of *tangilaulau* often includes a remembrance of things past, including what the lamenter was doing at the time of the person's death. Sometimes the

Men and women of Tuʻanuku dragged a huge pig and kava root through the ritual area. The presentation of the *tauʻaʻalo* combined the lineages of Tuʻanuku, the giving of gifts, metaphor, and straightforward speech into a unique aesthetic form.

lamenter scolds the person for dying, or asks to be left alone (with or without the dead person), to contemplate and ponder what he or she will do now that the dead person is gone. Occasionally a *tangi* serves as a public airing of animosity between factions or individuals, or expresses an individual's personal distress about life and has little or nothing to do with the dead person.

An extension of *tangi* is its use in selected parts of narrations. Such applications are called *fakatangi* 'in the manner of *tangi*'. *Fakatangi*, some of them passed down for generations, preserve important and unchanging elements of famous stories (*fananga*). The narrative is usually told in recited prose, but the *fakatangi* part is intoned melodically, often to tell the part of the story about death, mishap, or unrequited love.

### Work songs (tauʻaʻalo)

*Tauʻaʻalo* (from *ʻaʻalo* 'paddling') were sung during work that required coordinated movements, such as rowing, dragging a boat, and pulling a pig for presentation. The term *tauʻaʻalo* expresses the essence of paddling together, a metaphor for coordinated effort. Usually short, these pieces are sung repeatedly until the task is done. In ritual performances, they serve to confirm indigenous ceremonies and transform modern ceremonies into traditional ones.

William Mariner, who lived in Tonga from 1806 to 1810, uses the term *tow alo* (Martin 1818:2:320), which, he says, "are mostly short songs, sung in canoes when paddling, the strokes of the paddle being coincident with the cadence." Charles Wilkes, visiting Tonga in 1840, saw the canoe of certain chiefs

> advancing slowly over the calm sea by the efforts of its scullers, and was filled with men, all . . . keeping perfect time and making excellent music. . . . To this they sing any words, but generally such as are applicable to the mission of business or pleasure they may be on; and although the air and bass are heard most distinctly, the four parts are all sung in the most perfect harmony. From the fact that the tenors and basses sing parts of a bar, alternating with each other, and come in perfectly, it would seem that they cultivate music in their own rude way, producing a wild but agreeable effect (1845:3:20).

A *tauʻaʻalo* sung in 1990 for the ritual investiture of ʻUkulālala, chief of Vavaʻu, shows how Tongan verbal and visual expressions interconnect. The poetry, composed for the occasion by Sunia Tuineau Pupunu, received a formulaic musical-rhythmic setting, which the village of Tuʻanuku sang in numerous repetitions:

Haʻa Ngata, e tuʻu keta ō.
O fuataki atu e katumanō.
Kuo toe hā, kuo toe hā,
Fetuʻu ne puli he sotiakā.

Koe kie ena 'o 'Utukaungá,
Moe katuafe 'o Makapapá,
Mo e lauteau 'o Toloá.
Ko e 'uma'ā ke taká.

Ha'a Ngata, stand up and we shall go.
Carry onward the *katumano* [countless spans of mat].
It appears again, it appears again [as the new 'Ulukālala)].
Star that disappeared from the Zodiac [the previous 'Ulukālala].

That is the *kie* [fine mat] of 'Utukaunga,
And the *katuafe* [200 spans of mat] of Makapapa,
And the *lauteau* [enormous bark cloth] of Toloa.
The reason or purpose is needless to say.

The poetry, mentioning the four lineages of Tu'anuku and their gifts to the ritual, makes metaphorical references to the previous 'Ulukālala and the new one.

While singing about the women's mats and bark cloth, the men and women of Tu'anuku dragged a huge pig and kava root on sledges through the ritual area as representatives of the men's presentations of food, already laid out on the ceremonial ground (*mala'e*). The presentation of the *tau'a'alo* combined the lineages of Tu'anuku, men and women and their gifts, metaphor, and straightforward speech into a unique aesthetic form.

### Game songs and pleasurable pastimes

Game songs or intoned rhymes (*hiva vá'inga, mé a fakatamaiki*) are sung by children while playing a variety of games—and sometimes by adults in games of gambling (for other games, see Moyle 1987).

### Juggling

*Hiko* is a game in which small fruits, stones, or green candlenuts (*tuitui*) are juggled, usually by girls. It is performed to a short rhythmic text (which the players do not fully understand), intoned usually on one or a few pitches. An example of a *hiko* text is:

Alipate hala ki langi kia 'afu tapu ta'ane mata
Tangi ka hu langivalu tangi hoatu tangi hoate
He siale ko pili ko vaivai manu lele.

At the end of the recitation, the player says "*Ulu,*" proving she has gone through the stanza once. She keeps juggling and repeating the text until she reaches a previously agreed-upon number of repetitions, or until she misses. Girls use at least three balls, but often manage six; as many as twelve are said to have been juggled.

E. E. V. Collocott quotes two long *hiko,* and notes the supernatural connotations of the game. Playing *hiko* at night, he says, was taboo: the god Fehuluni "would be angry, and come and take the offender's eyes, and play *hiko* with them" (1928:100). Though this taboo is becoming less important, I have heard mothers caution their daughters about juggling at night, especially inside a house.

The game has been incorporated into a dance of the *tau'olunga* type, accompanying *hiva kakala* (see below). During this dance, the performers juggle; the one who keeps the juggling going the longest is the winner. Though any *hiva kakala* can accompany this performance, the preferred one is "*Fuofua,*" based on an old *hiko* text (Collocott 1928:101).

*Tapu lea*

In the game *tapu lea,* children sing a rhyme on one or two tones. Participants forbid themselves certain actions, such as moving, laughing, or making noise. The conclusion of the song starts the period of prohibition.

| | |
|---|---|
| Tapu lea ki 'Uvea, | Don't speak to 'Uvea, |
| Ki he motu'a kava tea. | To the white-bearded man. |
| Fai 'ene 'uku 'umea | Wash his hair with clay |
| 'I he vai pelepela. | In the muddy water. |
| 'Oua e ngū, 'oua e lea, | Don't make noise, don't speak, |
| Takapau tetea. | Coconut mat. |
| Faka'osi ki Velenga. | The last to Velenga. |
| Ngūngū tapu. | Noise is taboo. |

Though this appears to be a game of no great importance, it may derive from a taboo against moving or speaking during rituals associated with Tu'i Tonga, the highest-ranking chief. While Tu'i Tonga was in sight, no witness dared walk or stand: everyone, "man, woman, or child, instantly uncovered to the stomach and sat down, and crossed his hands and legs, and remained in this posture till he had passed by" (Vason in Orange 1840:162).

### Narrative songs (fakaniua)

*Fakaniua,* an indigenous medium for conveying historical and mythological tales, might be described as rhythmic-melodic recitation. The tales, usually *tala a e fanua* 'tales of the land', recount commonly known places and events, rather than stories about individuals or genealogical recitations. Since European contact, *fakaniua* have often related famous places, events, lore, and biblical stories, like those about David and Goliath, and about Satan's deceptions.

*Fakaniua* are accompanied by clapping, often syncopated to form complex rhythmic patterns. William Mariner (in Martin 1818:2:319–320) described them as

> descriptive of scenery, but some of these are descriptive of past events, or of places which are out of their reach, such as *Bolotoo* [Pulotu, the Tongan afterworld] and *Papalangi* [Europe]: the accounts they give of the latter place are ludicrous enough. The poet describes, among other things, the animals belonging to the country, stating that in the fields there are large pigs with horns, that eat grass, and . . . there are houses that are pulled along by enormous birds. The women are described to be so covered with dress, that a native of Tonga coming into a house takes a lady for a bundle of *Papalangi gnatoo,* (linen, &c.) and accordingly places it across his shoulder to carry it away, when to his great amazement the bundle jumps down and runs off. One of these songs describes the principal events that happened during Captain Cook's visit, and which, excepting a little exaggeration, is tolerably correct: another describes the visit of Admiral d'Entrecasteaux: another the revolution of Tonga, and the famous battle that was there fought, &c.

How these *fakaniua* might have sounded is hard to guess, but Mariner says they were "pieces of recitative," in contrast with singing that had "a considerable variety of tone" (Martin 1818:2:322). Today, the musical setting is often in a style adapted from Roman Catholic religious music. One of the most popular pieces of the 1960s, composed by Atu of Longoteme, told of Satan's wearing a necklace of burning coals.

### Sung speeches with choreographed movements (faiva)

Though the word *faiva* basically denotes the application of skill or cleverness, it can denote, in a more restricted sense, genres describable as sung speeches with choreographed movements. These *faiva* usually occur during ceremonial occasions known as *kātoanga,* featuring the performance of music and structured movements as complex verbal, rhythmic, and visual theater. Village-, community-, or school-based *faiva* in the current repertory include *lakalaka, māʻuluʻulu, meʻetuʻupaki, faʻahiula, sōkē,* and *kailao.*

##### TRACK 14

### Lakalaka

The most important of these types, a key to understanding Tongan cultural and social values, is *lakalaka.* Here, history, mythology, and genealogy influence contemporary events, and the values it imparts deal primarily with social structure and the people of rank through whom that structure operates. Though this genre is considered a late-nineteenth-century innovation, it appears to be an evolved form of the *meʻelaufola,* an indigenous genre (Kaeppler 1967a, 1976b, 1970).

The poetry of a *lakalaka* is a series of concepts and references, rather than a complete story, and is usually composed for performance at a specific event. Poetic allusions often evoke mythology and genealogy, usually in roundabout ways. Many are understood by everyone, but others are understood only by other poets, and the desire is often to take old allusions and transform them into something new. The references are often common knowledge, but observers must make associations to proceed to an understanding of successive allusions. The figurative language and allusive movements elevate the king and the chiefs, paying them high honor, while honoring the dancers and their villages.

The performers of a *lakalaka* are men and women, often two hundred or more, arranged in two or more rows facing an audience. The men stand on the right half (from the observer's viewpoint), and the women stand on the left [see MUSIC AND GENDER, figure 2]. Men and women perform different sets of movements, consistent with the Tongan view of what is suitable and appropriate for each. The movements of the arms allude to the lyrics.

Each *lakalaka,* in a structure derived from that of formal speeches, has three sections: an introductory *fakatapu,* which acknowledges the important chiefly lines relevant to the occasion; the main section (sometimes called *kaveinga*), which conveys information about the occasion, genealogies of relevant people, the history or mythology of the village performing, and other information; and the closing *tatau,* a counterpart of the *fakatapu,* in which the performers say goodby, again deferring to the chiefs. One stanza may be a *tau,* a section that expresses the essence of the performance, during which the performers do their best to compel the audience to pay strict attention.

This structure forms the outline of a *lakalaka.* The overall design, and thus the meaning of any specific composition, however, need not be apparent until the end. The meaning reveals itself as each verse—through verbal, musical, and visual allusions—builds on those that have gone before, mediated through the aesthetic principle of *heliaki.*

### Māʻuluʻulu

Another appropriate performing medium during *kātoanga* is *māʻuluʻulu,* a group speech with choreographed movements, performed sitting. On semiformal occasions, *māʻuluʻulu* are often performed as showpieces, without a strict formal structure; when performed for *kātoanga,* they incorporate the formal divisions of *fakatapu* and *tatau.* The overall structure has either of two forms: a through-composed form, resembling

its prototype (the seated *'otuhaka* section of a *fa'ahiula*), or a stanza-refrain form, adapted from Christian hymns. In the latter (now the more usual), the refrain is the *tau,* containing, as in *lakalaka,* the essence of the composition. Though strophic in form, the stanzas need not have the same melody or the same number of phrases per stanza.

Seated cross-legged in one or more rows, or with rows gradually elevated in various ways—kneeling, sitting (on chairs or benches), standing (figure 6)—the performers are accompanied by one or more membrane drums (*nafa*). The movements of the arms, though resembling those used for mixing kava and for performing *lakalaka,* are more varied and precise. The sung poetry is preceded and followed by *haka fakalongolongo*—silent *haka,* textless sections, performed to patterned drumming. As in *lakalaka,* the tilt of the head arises from inner feelings of exhilaration, and emphasizes that the performance is directed to an audience. Usually the performers are all of one sex, often the students of a sex-segregated secondary school. A subtype, *tafi* 'sweep', is often performed first, metaphorically to clear the ceremonial ground for the subsequent performances.

### Me'etu'upaki

In *me'etu'upaki* 'dance standing with *paki*', men use *paki,* lightweight implements with a flat blade and a cylindrical handle. The blade serves as an extension of the lower arm, and recurrent movements consist of striking one palm to the blade in a manner resembling a flat clap (*pasi*) and twirling the blade by rolling the shaft between the hands. The movements are bigger than usual Tongan movements of the arms, but are always graceful and dignified.

Men standing in several rows, or in two or more groups, execute turns and twirls of the *paki* and skillfully rearrange themselves. In one section, they divide into three groups, simultaneously singing three sets of words with different melodic contours, each having different lengths and different sets of movements. The other sections (or songs) of the *me'etu'upaki* are sung in unison, with women's voices an octave higher than men's.

The grace of the movements is striking. The movements of the feet include steps in place, small steps in a circle, small jumps, and touching one toe in front of the other foot. The tilt of the head is performed in prescribed places, and is added when the dancers feel *māfana.* In addition to the dancers' singing, a group called *lolongo,* comprising male and female singers and male drummers, conveys the poetry and sets the timing (figure 7). One or more *nafa* are beaten. This *nafa* is a hollowed-out log,

FIGURE 7    At celebrations honoring the coronation of King Tupou IV in July 1967, male
dancers, male and female singers, and male
drummers perform a *me'etu'upaki*. Photo by
Adrienne L. Kaeppler.

from which drummers obtain different tones. In former times, Tu'i Tonga himself
sometimes beat the *nafa* while lesser chiefs danced.

The poetry of *me'etu'upaki,* which Tongans can no longer translate fully, is
through-composed in several stanzas. Each stanza is performed two or more times,
and a short interval usually separates stanzas. Before each stanza, the dance leader,
standing at one side, shouts, "*Tu ki hoki.*" Stanzas end with a shout (*tu!*), as the performers flourish their *paki*. The stanzas and the number of their repetitions are at the
leader's discretion.

This dance, performed for ceremonial occasions such as the firstfruits ceremony
(*'inasi*), has come down from ancient times. Paying tribute of food and valuables, villages from Tonga and elsewhere brought their dances to honor Tu'i Tonga and themselves. Futunans brought *tapaki.* It appears that the *tapaki* of Nuku Village, in
Futuna, entered the Tongan repertory. It probably required more people than could
travel from Futuna for the ritual presentations. A company of Futunans probably
taught the dance to the ceremonial attendants of Tu'i Tonga and other members of
his village, Lapaha. The Tongan dancers memorized, but did not necessarily understand, the poetry.

The *tapaki* continued as a dance to honor Tu'i Tonga; eventually the movements
of the legs became indigenized, but the movements of the paddles were passed on as
learned. In the late 1700s, the dance was described in the journals of Captain Cook's
voyages and was illustrated by John Webber during Cook's third Pacific voyage.

During the 1800s, civil wars and conversion to Christianity resulted in lesser
chiefs' attaining more power. Converts to Wesleyanism, these chiefs acquired guns.
Tu'i Tonga's line lost power but retained its status, and its heirs converted to Roman
Catholicism. This line has preserved the *me'etu'upaki*, which it performs to demonstrate its rank and prestige.

### Fa'ahiula

*Fa'ahiula* is the inclusive term for an ancient suite of women's dances. Though not
usually performed during a contemporary *kātoanga,* they are the women's *faiva,*
equivalent to the men's *me'etu'upaki.* The term *fa'ahiula* can be used for the whole
suite, or for the seated section of the suite, though the latter is often called *'otuhaka.*
*'Otuhaka* (from *'otu* 'row of') describes the performance. Performed standing, the
second section of a *fa'ahiula* is usually known simply as *ula.*

Singing is done by the dancers and those who play the *tafua,* an idiophone, consisting of one or more lengths of bamboo wrapped in a mat and struck with one or two beaters. Occasionally a mixed chorus sits behind them. Some texts are performed responsorially, the call being given by one or more individuals, and the response by a larger number; or the call may be given by the singers, and the response by the dancers. Dancers sometimes divide into two or more groups, which sing alternately or polyphonically, and the groups' movements may differ. *'Otuhaka* are often through-composed, but *ula* typically have multiple repetitions. Percussion usually begins, simply to set the pulse, but it becomes increasingly complex, adding a rhythmic counterpoint to the melody.

The structure and poetry of the two sections of this *faiva* differ, but the movements of the arms and the musical traits are similar. The pulses are usually organized in four or eight, though occasionally the *ula* is in six. Some *'otuhaka* have phrases with eight pulses each, followed by a phrase with a different number of pulses. The poetry of *fa'ahiula,* usually known as *langi,* has a narrow tonal range, usually within a fifth, though larger intervals occur in vocal slides, and sometimes when parts switch.

Singing is often in unison; but harmonic seconds, thirds, fourths, or fifths may occur sporadically, or in continuous sequences. The tempo usually increases, and a climax may highlight the end. Rhythm is sometimes simple and regular, and sometimes complex and varied, usually resulting from syncopated accentuation of weak beats. Structured movements and words may begin on a weak beat and carry through a strong beat, creating duple or even triple rhythms.

## Sōkē

*Sōkē* is the present Tongan name for the *eke,* introduced from 'Uvea and used by Roman Catholics. It formerly had three sections. In one version, the first section (*taki*) was an entrance, with poetry about Moses leading his people with Pharaoh in pursuit (Exodus 14:5–9). In the second section, the performers, with one hand on their hearts, sang of the Virgin Mary crying to God the Father. In the third section, quartets of performers struck sticks in intricate patterns while jumping to different positions, accompanied by rapid rhythms beaten on empty biscuit tins; the poetry was about Noah's ark and the flood (Genesis 7–8).

Late-twentieth-century versions, performed by women and men, usually use only the third section. The sticks are longer, and the texts resemble those of other *faiva.* The first stanza is performed by sets of four performers. The second and succeeding stanzas are variations in which the quartets of performers combine into eights, sixteens, and finally the entire company, which may consist of a hundred or more performers. In the last section (*heke loa*), the performers move to a different place after each repetition of the stanza; after numerous repetitions, they return to their original positions. On important occasions, the *sōkē* follows a *taki* and a stanza of poetry, sung without movements.

## Kailao

Also said to have come from 'Uvea, the *kailao* is a vigorous men's dance, involving the manipulation of wooden clubs and the striking of a metal container. The performers, of any number, wear fanciful costumes, decorated with crepe paper and ankle rattles (of large seeds, *vesa pa'anga*). *Kailao* are unlike other Tongan dances: they have no associated poetry, the movements are accompanied by rapidly beaten biscuit tins, and the movements of the feet and the legs differ from those of all other Tongan dancing. The boys of sex-segregated schools often perform them as their *faiva.*

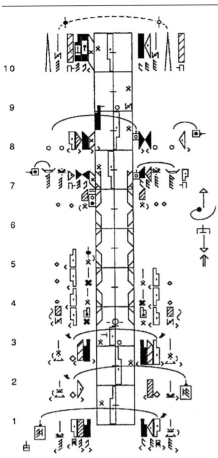

FIGURE 8　The beginning of a *tau'olunga* performed by Tu'imala Kaho to music of the song "*Hala Vuna*," choreographed by Vaisima Hopoate. Labanotation by Judy Van Zile.

## Hiva kakala

*Hiva kakala* 'sweet song, fragrant song' is one of the major Tongan musical genres of the twentieth century, the musical genre most often composed and sung. Its thousands of compositions are evidence of the thoughts and values of the Tongan people. The genre derived from *pō sipi*, poems recited spontaneously during informal kava-drinking gatherings. *Pō sipi* consisted primarily of allusions to the (female) mixer of the kava, made on behalf of one of the young men in attendance, either by one of his friends, or by a ceremonial attendant (*matāpule*). Allusions to flowers and the names of places referred to the individual without naming her. During the 1800s, melodies were added to the poetry, often in the form of verse-chorus alternation, borrowed from the structure of Protestant hymns.

*Hiva kakala* are usually played and sung by gatherings of men or women or both, forming string bands of ukuleles and guitars; sometimes a bass, electronic keyboards, violins, and accordions are added. Movements are then added. The word that describes them, *tau'olunga*, is the word Tongans use to gloss the English word *dance*; it does not include the sense of 'ballroom dancing', which Tongans, building on a Hawaiian term, call *hulohula*. The movements of *tau'olunga* need not make consistent allusions to the poetry, but may focus on the creation of beauty. They have been composed and choreographed by some of the most famous choreographers of the twentieth century—Queen Sālote [see COMPOSITIONAL PROCESSES, figure 6], Vaisima Hopoate, and Tu'imala Kaho (figure 8).

Several subtypes of *hiva kakala* have evolved. These are *hiva sō* 'true love song', *hiva hanu* 'complaining love song', *hiva 'ofa* 'song that honors individuals or places', and *'ūpē* 'aristocratic lullaby'.

The sentiment expressed by the poetry of *hiva kakala* usually focuses on an individual or a place. Movements may also be choreographed spontaneously (figure 9). They are not set into a planned sequence. They are widely known motifs, which in other performing genres often serve as fill-in motifs. The *heliaki* of the poetry and the movements may allude to the performer, the text, or the overall concept of the composition.

Most modern examples have stanza-refrain alternation. Sometimes each stanza is sung twice before the refrain, and sometimes the refrain precedes the first stanza. Melodies and their accompanying harmonies may come from hymns, Western secular songs, and earlier *hiva kakala*.

## Musical instruments

Several important indigenous Tongan musical instruments served percussively to accompany danced poetry (see above). Indigenous melodic musical instruments were nose-blown flutes [see MUSICAL INSTRUMENTS, figure 1*d*], panpipes, and conch trumpets; Western contact brought instruments used in brass bands and string bands [see POPULAR MUSIC: MUSICAL ENSEMBLES].

### Idiophones

Two kinds of lamellaphone—the *'ūtete*, made of a coconut-leaf midrib, and the *mokena*, made of bamboo—served as toys. In the 1960s, the former were remembered by older people, who recalled having played them as children, obtaining myriad sounds by playing two or more at the same time.

Human bodies also serve as sound-producing instruments. Skin strikes skin in several named movements: a high-pitched flat clap (*pasi*); a low, cupped clap (*fū*); clapping the back of one hand to the other open palm; snapping the fingers (*fisipā*), the thighs (*pāpātenga*), and other parts of the body.

To awaken chiefs was bad manners, except with a nose-blown flute. In 1953, during the Tongan visit of Queen Elizabeth II, such a flute roused the slumbering monarch.

FIGURE 9    A *tau'olunga* accompanies a *hiva kakala* in Tonga. Photo by Adrienne L. Kaeppler, 1967.

### *Aerophones*

#### *Panpipes*

Raft panpipes (*mimiha*) served mainly for amusement, but are important because they have preserved indigenous intervallic relationships, providing clues for understanding Tongan musical aesthetics. No aboriginal panpipes remain in Tonga; several survive abroad, in museums. Most were collected in the late 1700s (Kaeppler 1974:102–128). Bound with twisted coconut fiber, most of these consist of ten bamboo pipes (some have nine or five), closed on the lower end by a node, open at the top. Both sides of the top are beveled, probably to facilitate moving the instrument along the lips while blowing, and to control the direction of the airstream.

Though some observers have claimed that the pipes were "placed promiscuously" (Forster 1777:2:456) or "without regular progression" (Beaglehole 1967:2:940), surviving instruments show a definite pattern with three important intervals. A nine- or ten-pipe instrument had two sets of four pipes each. A set consisted of three tones, with a repetition of the middle tone. One of the sets was slightly higher in pitch than the other. Finally, there was a high note, and sometimes a low note; these notes do not seem to have been essential, but varied from panpipe to panpipe, and may have been considered decorative.

Many panpipes in museum collections are cracked, but some can still be sounded. Two, taken to England on Captain Cook's second voyage, were examined in the 1770s by a musician, who notated the pitches and superimposed the pitches on a drawing of one of the instruments (figure 10). This intervallic structure is essentially the same for all complete extant eighteenth-century panpipes, many of which, dating from Cook's second voyage, can be considered to incorporate indigenous Tongan tonal structures. This intervallic structure may exemplify the aesthetic principle of *heliaki*, repetition expressing musical concepts at slightly different tonal levels.

#### *Conch trumpets*

Conch trumpets (*kele'a*) served for amusement and signaling. Fishermen blew them when returning to shore, announcing that they had caught fish. Blowing conchs also served to announce the approach of an important person. Today, when the king approaches, a fanfare on brass instruments replaces the blasts from *kele'a*. Three *kele'a* may often have been blown at a time, sounding a minor triad in simply syncopated rhythms (McKern n.d.:788); since the 1880s, conch ensembles have been played at cricket matches (Moyle 1975:98).

#### TRACK 19    *Nose-blown flutes*

Nose-blown flutes (*fangufangu*) may also have provided musical amusement. According to William Anderson on Cook's third voyage, flutes of different sizes were played polyphonically; and David Samwell, also on that voyage, said "About sunset they play upon their Flutes . . . before their Houses" (Beaglehole 1967:2:1036), implying that people played such flutes as a pastime at the end of the day.

One of the primary uses of the nose-blown flute was to *fangugangu* 'awaken gradually or gently' a person of high rank. To awaken chiefs was bad manners, except with a nose-blown flute. In 1953, during the Tongan visit of Queen Elizabeth II, *fangufangu* roused the slumbering monarch. Today, they are seldom played, but they can be heard each day at the radio station's opening and closing (figure 11).

Unlike some Polynesian nose-blown flutes, the Tongan *fangufangu* is closed by nodes on both ends and can be played from either end. It has six holes (five on the upper surface, one below), but only four tones are obtained, using the holes at the far end and the first from the hole for blowing. These tones are open, first hole, far-end hole, and both together. Thus, from flute to flute the scales are similar, but the pitches, set by the diameter and length of the bamboo, differ.   —ADRIENNE L. KAEPPLER

## SĀMOA

The Sāmoan archipelago divides into two political units: Savai'i, 'Upolu, and two small inhabited islands, Apolima and Manono, united as the independent nation of Sāmoa; and Tutuila, which, with a cluster of little islands known as Manu'a, are a territory of the United States. The population of the western islands is about 170,000; that of American Sāmoa, about forty thousand.

Sāmoan society is a hierarchical system of chiefly titles, most of which symbolize and govern extended families. Succession to most titles follows an election in which the candidates represent different lineages; the electorate is the family. Other principles of succession, which sometimes bring candidates into conflict, are that titles should rotate among lineages within the family, persons who have conspicuously served the previous titleholder have an advantage, and descendants of the sister(s) of the first titleholder have extra electoral weight.

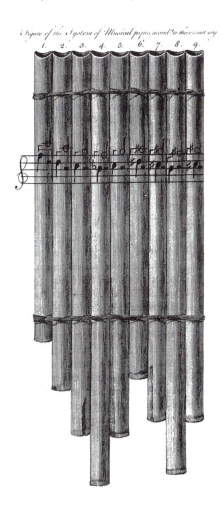

FIGURE 10   A Tongan raft panpipe of about 1770 (after Steele 1771:76).

Archaeological evidence suggests that Polynesians had settled Sāmoa by about three thousand years ago. Into the 1800s, Sāmoans maintained sporadic contact with parts of Fiji, Tonga, and 'Uvea. Centuries before the 1500s, Tongans exercised political influence in Sāmoa. Eventually, a system of chieftainships uniting villages into districts and larger entities developed. One's village (*nu'u*) was one's country (also *nu'u*), but intervillage alliances crosscut such affiliations, and political structures were more fluid than suggested by tidy charts now printed in books.

Sāmoa presented a typical high-island Polynesian pattern of reliance on taro, breadfruit, yams, and other plants, supplemented by fish, shellfish, and fowl, and on formal occasions by pork. International commerce has changed this pattern. Bagged rice comes from Asia; frozen mutton, from Aotearoa; and boxed, bottled, and canned goods, from many countries. The most prestigious imported foods are corned beef (*pīsupo* 'pea soup') and canned herring. The main exports are copra and cocoa; both Sāmoas gain income from tourism.

The first European to view Sāmoa was Jacob Roggeveen, whose expedition sighted Manu'a in 1722. Other distinguished explorers who visited the islands were Louis de Bougainville in 1768, Jean Francis de La Pérouse in 1787, and members of the U.S. Exploring Expedition in 1839 and 1841. In 1830, the Rev. John Williams brought the first missionaries of the London Missionary Society (LMS). Only weeks before their arrival, supporters of an alliance of villages had assassinated a rival, whom the missionaries, rejoicing in their timing, promptly labeled a devil. High chief Mālietoa took up the new religion, and the rest of the populace followed. Old rivalries then began working themselves out through differential affiliation with Christian sects, Mālietoa supporting the LMS, and his rivals becoming Roman Catholics and Methodists. Late in the twentieth century, Mormonism grew in fashion.

FIGURE 11 Beginning of a melody played on a Tongan nose-blown flute by Veʻehala in the 1970s. Transcription by Elizabeth Tatar.

## Thinking about Sāmoan music

Verbalization, intonation, and movement combine to create many Sāmoan genres. The union of words, music, and motion is evident in songs designed for public presentation; but even in private, performers may spontaneously move their arms, or rise to involve their legs. A narrator may gesture to enhance critical actions or moments in a tale.

Sāmoan musical genres do not fit into a neat hierarchical structure, but the language has names for select kinds of singing and dancing. In reaction to Christianity, genres of indelicate dancing have disappeared, and the ordinary processes of cultural change have led to such a turnover that few musical genres popular in the mid-1800s are performed today, at least under the same names.

Nineteenth-century musical texts, written by insiders and outsiders, offer glimpses into Sāmoan musical thinking before the indigenous system responded to the world beyond West Polynesia. As transcriptions, they lead analysis toward thinking of performance as a product, but this approach is serviceable because Sāmoans say sounded words are the most important element of performance. The preserved texts vary systematically in the average length of their lines, setting up musical classes that apparently subdivided into genres (*ituʻāiga*), many of which had names. An alternate analytical process (Moyle 1988), rather than focusing on sounded words, focuses on worded sounds, resulting in a system that classifies songs as entirely or predominantly solo, unison, responsorial, responsorial with dance, and polyphonic. This system is incompatible with the word-based one, and neither would perfectly match a system based on music as a process; word-based analysis, however, because it emphasizes the aspect of performance that Sāmoans say is most important, proves useful in sorting the repertory.

### The vocabulary of music

Sāmoan lyrics bind words (*ʻupu*) into lines (*fuaʻiʻupu, fuaʻitau*), which usually end in rhyme. The words once had a meter (*fua*) possibly based on the length of vowels, which, in some genres, percussive stress may have overridden. The basis of Sāmoan music is the human voice (*leo*). Two verbs, *lagi* and *pese,* cover the idea of 'sing'; for songs in tales, Sāmoan adds *tagi* 'cry'. The idea of 'compose' is *fatu,* or less precisely *fai* 'do, make'. Two terms, *siva* and *ula,* commonly cover the concept of 'dance', for which the special terms *saʻa* and *tulei* imply an element of dignity or elegance, as when a high-ranking person performs.

FIGURE 12 A Sāmoan melody popular before the twentieth century, showing the division into *usu* and *tali*. Transcription by J. W. Love.

*Singing*

Most singing in Sāmoa is choral. Leaders (*usu*) are the few singers who begin phrases; the chorus (*tali*) are the many singers who finish phrases. Sometimes these parts engage in dialogue, as in a song popular before the 1900s (figure 12), shown with *tali* phrases indented:

| | |
|---|---|
| Aue, toli mai pua mōtoe! | *Aue,* O pluck and bring budding gardenias! |
| Tala lava ‘oe. | Open them yourself. |
| Aue, toli mai pua mātala! | *Aue,* pluck and bring opening gardenias! |
| Tala i le vasa. | Open them at the groin. |

In 1838, songs mostly consisted of "two short strains, repeated alternately, the first by a single individual, the second by several" (Wilkes 1845). Texts transcribed in the 1800s show that the singers of the *usu* launched into the refrain, sometimes cueing and overlapping with the *tali*.

Wilkes published three notated songs of two vocal parts each. The rate of alternation of voices varies. The first song, which accompanied dancing in ‘Upolu, begins with an alternation of individual measures, later changing to an alternation of a four-measure phrase. The second consists of alternations of pairs of measures, with a quarter-note overlap; the notation seems to lack a concluding measure. Though notated in cut time, the third song resembles, in its alternation, the second half of the first.

TRACK 9

Each section of many dance-songs, often a couplet, probably recurred for minutes, making a long song out of short material. In 1861, the missionary George Turner said, of dancing at "the night assemblies," the music "is a monotonous chant of a line or two, repeated over and over again, with no variety beyond two or three notes" (1861:210–212). Later, an American journalist in Sāmoa spoke of "humdrum music" and "singing in high-pitched notes" (Whitaker 1889:20). In 1890, the historian Henry Adams supposed, "Their songs are mere catches; unmeaning lines repeated over and over" (1951:143). A tourist who spent three days in the islands said "the singing became monotonous . . . after they had sung the same verse over two hundred times" (Wheeler 1907). Though these descriptions reveal their writers' cultural ignorance, they confirm that some Sāmoan performances repeated short segments many times.

*Dancing*

Some Sāmoan musical performances involving dance begin with a formal introduction, the *laulausiva.* Since the 1800s, the term has changed its meaning. It once denoted a man who gave ‘out a song verse by verse’ at a dance held at night, and it probably derives from the verb *lau* ‘give out a song verse by verse’ (Pratt 1911). *Laulausiva* also included instrumental playing before a series of dances: "usually called *tālesiva,*" it meant "the first dance isn't sung, but is accompanied only by beating of the mats" (Krämer 1903:322, trans). When all had assembled, "the performance commenced with the *Tafua-le-fala,* which consisted of beating a roll of matting as a substitute for a drum. After this one of the performers commenced singing a song, the rest of the company joining in the chorus" (Stair 1897:133).

In the 1800s, the initial accompaniment to dancing was a rolled-up mat; *tafua* can be glossed ‘to beat a mat rolled up as a drum, preparatory to commencing a night-dance' (Pratt 1911). After a song sung with the dancers in place, the mats were beaten again, and another song was similarly performed; the whole series of items were "introductory songs" (Stair 1897:133). In the 1920s, a tourist observed similar percussive sounds at the start of a dance:

> The "music" starts. It consists of a rhythmic clapping of hands in a steady timing, with the beating of folded mats with sticks, just twice as fast as the handclapping. The dancers keep the same time with their feet as the chorus does with its hands. (Calnon 1926:88)

In the 1970s, percussion still opened the show at the main hotel in Apia; but the instruments were kerosene tins and small log idiophones (*pātē*).

### Polykinetics

Sāmoan structured-movement systems combine the activity of three parts of the human body, roughly seen as legs, arms, and head. The upper body is inactive, with the back straight and the hips not making large movements. For humorous effects, and formerly in lascivious dancing, performers emphasize side-to-side movements of the hips.

The feet and legs follow the beat. In a typical men's stance, the knees are bent, the body's weight is on the balls of the feet, and the heels metrically move outward and inward. Seated dancers (figure 13) may use their feet or knees to keep a metric pulse. Women's foot-and-leg movements are small; men may make larger movements, with more muscular involvement. In the excitement of dancing, men and women may seize and wave objects, and shake or bounce against furniture, houseposts, and walls; men may kneel, strike the ground with their forearms and hands, and roll on the ground.

The hands and arms make complex movements (*tāga*), which have multiple functions: to allude to sung words, comment on implied concepts, and decorate and connect musical phrases. *Tāga* use flexible wrists. Movements and positions of fingers and palms occur in a limited number of arm positions. Men's and women's hand-and-arm movements may be soft, but men's may use stiffer wrists or clenched fists, and may be faster and freer.

The head and face mask or express emotion. When a ceremonial virgin performs the last dance (*taualuga*), she fixes her facial muscles into a weak smile, maintaining

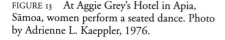

FIGURE 13   At Aggie Grey's Hotel in Apia, Sāmoa, women perform a seated dance. Photo by Adrienne L. Kaeppler, 1976.

an aloofness that onlookers interpret as dignity. Men and women clowning around featured soloists may show animation, including frequent tilts and turns of the head, variable facial expressions, and darting eyes. They may grunt, shout, and whoop.

## Musical contexts and genres

Artful performances grace many aspects of Sāmoan life. Chiefly councils require rhythmically and intonationally marked orating and poetical reciting. Services in Christian churches use several kinds of singing, sometimes with instrumental accompaniment. Marriages, visits, and wakes require singing, and some events invite dancing. Because music helps define events, performances need apt music, and newly composed pieces are much in demand. Highly important, however, are older items: some are the points of departure for new compositions; others, by metaphorically linking the present event to a past one, lend historical authenticity to an occasion, and so are performed intact, or as close to bygone styles as modern interpretation permits.

### Storytelling

Storytellers entertained children and adults with tales (*fāgono*), many of which contained sung sections (*tagi* 'cries'), usually representing a character prominent in the plot. Skilled storytellers received fame beyond their own villages; a few maintain the tradition. Since the late 1800s, the classical repertory has become diffuse, accommodating prosaic narratives (*tala*), whose characters may have nonindigenous names, undertake nontraditional activities, and recount biblical stories.

Performing a *fāgono,* a narrator takes standard plots, and within limits that vary from tale to tale and from moment to moment within a tale, improvises the diction. The *tagi* have structures more set and less variable than the words of the narration. They often take the form of an outburst when a character, on an emotional high, releases feelings. The change in the narrator's tone of voice—from speech to song—underscores this release. In response to exciting events in the plot and stirring moments in the *tagi,* an audience freely exclaims the word *'aue,* and may add other conventional responses.

Syntactical clarity, in which each clause occupies one line, makes the verbal processes of *tagi* simple, but narrative terseness contrasts with the style of colloquial discourse. The vocabulary sometimes becomes complex. Terms heard infrequently in daily discourse abound.

### Texts with no refrain

Many *tagi,* especially short ones, resemble *solo* in having lines of approximately equal length, arranged in regular succession. In some tales, short *tagi* repeat. Older examples set simple rhyming phrases to simple melodic formulas (figure 14*a*), concluding in a nonformulaic section. These pieces tend to elaborate a scale transcribable as B–D–E–F–G, with D and F the principal tones, E a passing tone (and sometimes a final), and B and G pickups or auxiliaries. In contrast, a twentieth-century formulaic melody (figure 14*b*), though monophonic, may imply a major key and the standard relationships of functional tonal harmony.

### Texts with a single refrain

In some *tagi,* the refrain begins and ends each line or stanza; in some, it merely ends the line or stanza. Of texts whose refrain ends each line, performances tend to be quite variable, to the extent of unpredictably adding and deleting lines. In this sense, they may reveal improvisation; but similarities between performances imply that the

FIGURE 14
Excerpts from
melodies of Sāmoan
*tagi: a,* a nine-
teenth-century
melody, showing
traditional tonality;
*b,* a twentieth-cen-
tury melody, imply-
ing standard rela-
tionships of func-
tional harmony (the
words may predate
the melody).
Transcriptions by J.
W. Love.

improvisation has limits, fixed by a memorized core. In support of this possibility, many lines rhyme just before the refrain, as in the following excerpt.

| | |
|---|---|
| Lupe, tā ō ia, *Lūpē.* | Dove, let's really go, *O Dove.* |
| Tā moemoe solo, *Lūpē,* | Let's sleep about, *O Dove,* |
| I Le-Tiʻalu-ma-le-Togo, *Lūpē.* | At The-Tiʻalu-and-the-Togo, *O Dove.* |
| Tā ō ia, *Lūpē.* | Let's really go, *O Dove.* |
| Na fai le faiva, *Lūpē,* | The fishing was done, *O Dove,* |
| O Sā Levavau, *Lūpē.* | By Sā Levavau, *O Dove.* |
| Na tuʻuaina ai ʻita, *Lūpē,* | They left me behind, *O Dove.* |
| ʻUa taʻa ʻi le faiva, *Lūpē:* | The catch was plundered, *O Dove:* |
| E ʻato iva iʻa, *Lūpē.* | Nine baskets of fish, *O Dove.* |
| Momoli mai ʻita, *Lūpē,* | They arrested me, *O Dove,* |
| ʻI le mao ʻai iva, *Lūpē.* | For the nine were scavenged, *O Dove.* |

Here, Sina cries to her brother, visiting her in the form of a dove. Line 1 rhymes with lines 4, 5, and 7 through 11; the second rhymes with the third; and only the sixth has no rhyme.

The refrain may begin and end each line or stanza. An excerpt from the middle of a *tagi* shows how the refrain stretches the story out.

| | |
|---|---|
| *Īlae, Īlae,* | *O Ila, O Ila,* |
| ʻUa ʻou fāifai mao lava, | I've really acted by chance, |
| *Īlae, Īlae,* | *O Ila, O Ila.* |
| | |
| *Īlae, Īlae,* | *O Ila, O Ila,* |
| ʻOna ʻua sui ʻo lona suafa: | Because he changed his name: |
| *Īlae, Īlae,* | *O Ila, O Ila.* |
| | |
| *Īlae, Īlae,* | *O Ila, O Ila,* |
| ʻ"O Sugaluga-opea-mai-vasa," | "Driftwood-floating-from-sea," |
| *Īlae, Īlae.* | *O Ila, O Ila.* |
| | |
| *Īlae, Īlae,* | *O Ila, O Ila,* |
| ʻUa fānau ai laʻu nei tama. | By whom I've borne this my child. |
| *Īlae, Īlae.* | *O Ila, O Ila.* |

Through a skilled singer's voice, the ponderousness of the plot, slowed by the repetitions of the refrain, can evoke an entrancing atmosphere. More practically, these repetitions give the singer time to recall or plan upcoming lines.

### Texts with multiple refrains

These items achieve a higher degree of structural complexity. The following stanza shows a conversation between the man Tāla-ʻi-solo-mamao and the woman Lātū-tama.

| | |
|---|---|
| "Lātū-tāmae, | "O Lātū-tama, |
| ʻO le ā le mea ʻua faʻī?— | What's the reason it's unmade?— |
| Faʻī ai le moega nei? | For which this bedding's unmade? |
| *Lātū-tāmae.*" | *O Lātū-tama.*" |
| "ʻĪoe, e moʻi lava, e moʻi, sē! | "Yes, it's really true, it's true, *sē!* |
| Na mā soloia ma Aliʻi-mai-Fīti ē, | O I mussed it with Fellow-from-Fiji, |
| *Tāla-ʻi-solo-mamao,* | *Tāla-ʻi-solo-mamao,* |
| *Le mānaia o Toga Mamao.*" | *The beau of Distant Tonga.*" |

Each stanza contains a question and an answer. In a more taxing pattern, some *tagi* have stanzas that gain lines, one by one, until, by the end of the piece, the structure severely tests singers' faculties of recall and listeners' powers of concentration.

### Exchanging women's goods

Certain goods manufactured from natural objects by women are known as *tōga*. Their formal bestowal, accompanied by a range of performed language (orating, citing conventional phrases, singing), has important social implications, some of which involve music. At weddings, funerals, the paying of civil penalties, and other contexts that imply reciprocity, ceremonial mats (*ʻietōga*) are the cardinal medium of exchange. Etiquette requires the recipient of such a mat, or even a person who catches sight of one, to make a public response, especially with the formula *sāō! faʻalālelei!* To plait mats, women work for months, usually in cooperative associations. On completing an association's mats the weavers, helped as necessary by their kin, parade the mats around the village (figure 15), receiving refreshments served by chiefs. This parade (*fuataga*) authenticates the mats so they may enter the system of exchange. On catching sight of the mats along the route, onlookers spontaneously shout the standard formula and join the singing.

Two musical genres relating to *tōga* have fallen out of use. The *sula* was a song in praise and solicitation of a ceremonial mat. The name of the *ʻailao* relates to the

FIGURE 15   Sāmoans authenticate new mats by parading them around the village, singing and dancing as they go. Photo by J. W. Love, 1972.

Most Sāmoan couples began cohabiting without public fuss, but the unions of high-ranking persons, especially ceremonial virgins and official beaus, ordinarily entailed elaborate formalities. Weddings occurred in the bride's village. Men from the bridegroom's side arrived exclaiming nuptial cheers.

terms 'ailaopulou 'give thanks for property or good news; putting the gift on the head' (Pratt 1911), and 'ailaopulouina 'acknowledge a present (by proclaiming the giver's name and placing the gift on one's head)' (Milner 1966). It may not relate to a homonym referring to a surviving performative genre—'ailao 'the act of fencing with, or flourishing, a club; to brandish the club' (Pratt 1911), 'twirl, flourish a hooked knife (specially used for that purpose, a Samoan game of skill)' (Milner 1966).

### Visiting

Intervillage visiting (*malaga*) is a long-standing institution, with cognate activities elsewhere in Polynesia. In varying numbers, but ideally in tens or scores, people travel for overnight visits, sometimes circling an island and stopping at receptive villages en route. These events may involve the youthful members of a church, or the women of a village or neighborhood, or many other affiliation-based groups. Interactions may involve competitive activities, like orating and the playing of games. The hosts provide food and lodging, and the guests provide entertainment.

The distinction between guests and hosts plays itself out in the orating, playing, feasting, singing, and dancing associated with the visit. Usually, the drinking of kava (with its attendant oratory and poetry) precedes the feast, and the musical performance follows. Inside a house, the guests take one side and the hosts the other, forming seated choruses, facing each other. Between the choruses, individuals or small groups from one side stand to dance while the rest of their company sings. One side performs and then yields to the other, and the sides alternate through the event. Set phrases mark the shift from one side of the house to the other. These include sung statements, such as *'ua alu atu le afi* 'the fire has gone to your side', recalling the practice of illuminating performers by torchlight. The last number of an event is the *taualuga,* the dance of the hosts' ceremonial virgin. Formerly, when unmarried men went on *malaga,* this dance paired the ceremonial virgin with the guests' ceremonial beau. Before the late nineteenth century, the event might then have broken down into lascivious dancing, but Christian prudery ended most such displays.

### Soa

In the 1800s, *soa* honored visitors. The name denotes a suite of dances, a 'concert where some sing seated, and others standing' (Violette 1879, trans.). By the 1890s, *soa* were obsolete. They were "performed by a hundred or more persons standing in the open, who slowly raise and lower their outstretched arms; at great ceremonies, deaths of chiefs, and so on" (Krämer 1903:315, trans.). Not all the sentiments in extant texts are solemn, but some are somber. *Soa* may ordinarily have been performed at night; a temporally marked term, *aosoa,* denotes their performance by day.

A suite called *soa* had at least four sections performed in a set order, each possibly entailing distinct gestures or performers. The sections for which texts survive are:

the *ta'i* 'lead', the first item; the *si'i* 'lift'; the *tatū* 'stamp'; and the *sā'aga*, the last item (Love 1991:154–155). It is tempting to regard the lift as referring to the arms, especially in the light of Krämer's description, and the stamp as emphasizing the feet. The *soa* possibly developed into the genre known since the late 1800s as *mā'ulu'ulu,* in which singer-dancers ideally performed in three tiers: the front row sat cross-legged, the middle row knelt, and the back row stood. Sāmoan performers sometimes still arrange themselves this way, but the term *mā'ulu'ulu* has come to denote popular songs presented to an audience from a stage.

### Having kava

At a kava-drinking ceremony, the person who will announce the order of drinking recites a *solo*—a word unrelated to the English (Italian) homonym. With the possible exception of Christian hymns, more material relating to this genre survives in print than for any other kind of Sāmoan musical performance [see MUSIC AND INGESTED SUBSTANCES].

The Sāmoan word *solo* derives from a root connoting movement; its nonpoetical glosses include 'procession . . . parade . . . stroll . . . line . . . row . . . landslip' (Milner 1966). The focus is on a progression or flow; in referencing performed poetry, the term may indicate the sequence by which equally extended units, the lines, pass through time. The words praised chiefs by naming and describing their lands, but some *solo* treated diverse topics, drawn from myth, legend, and history.

Poems called *solo* seem to divide into two categories: *solo* proper and *solo'ava,* the latter standing out as being especially fit for recitation in kava ceremonies. (Their texts allude to the beverage.) In style and content, *solo'ava* of the late twentieth century differ from those of the 1800s: so different are they from *solo* and *solo'ava* of proven age, they can be considered a new and distinct genre. Constraints on meter and rhyme are usually tighter in nineteenth-century *solo'ava* than in *solo* proper; but in contemporary *solo'ava,* these constraints are looser.

An excerpt from a longer text illustrates the style of nineteenth-century examples: *Ifo i Li'u, a'e i Fuiono; / Lau o le fiso, lau o le tolo: / 'Ua ala-e-tasi le Maugaiolo* 'Descend at Li'u, ascend at Fuiono; / Leaf of the *fiso,* leaf of the *tolo:* / There's one road at the Maugaiolo'. The reciter said this text is appropriate for oratorical use in unifying opposed parties. Its images emphasize the underlying sameness of different-looking things: Li'u and Fuiono are the southwest and northeast sides, respectively, of a large hill in northwest Savai'i, where the Maugaiolo, a small mountain, rises; the *fiso* and the *tolo* are kinds of sugarcane, superficially distinct, but essentially the same.

### Celebrating weddings

Most Sāmoan couples began cohabiting without public fuss, but the unions of high-ranking persons, especially ceremonial virgins and official beaus, ordinarily entailed elaborate formality. Weddings occurred in the bride's village. Men from the bridegroom's side arrived exclaiming nuptial cheers (*tini,* or anciently *tautapa*) [see LANGUAGE IN MUSICAL SETTINGS: Metaphor and Symbolism]. Preserved nineteenth-century texts of these shouts have lines lasting about ten moras (short syllables). The first two lines name the bridegroom and the bride respectively; the remaining lines convey delight. A text preserved in a nineteenth-century manuscript goes: *Tiatia ē! Le Lauto'elau ē! Mimisā ē! mimisā ē! Apa ē! apa ē! Aitu, aitu, āitu ō!* 'O Tiatia! O Le Lauto'elau! O urination! O urination! O cleave! O cleave! Spirits, spirits, O spirits!' (Penisimane 1860s:27). The "urination" was the blood of the deflowered bride, collected on a white mat and paraded around the village as a token of honor. The phrase "O cleave!" may refer to sexual intercourse. Women still salute sexually forward males as spirits (*aitu*).

### Lulling babies

Sāmoan caregivers sometimes hush children by singing. The concept of a lullaby occurs only in circumlocution: *le pese e faʻamoemoe aʻi le pepe* 'a song with which to lull a baby'. Several references to the action of singing for an infant appear in tales, which themselves can serve to lull children. Few Sāmoan songs are specially marked as lullabies. Babysitters sing any song that suits them, or they let music on the radio do the job.

### Playing games

Songs accompany all sorts of Sāmoan games, but two kinds of songs—cheers and formulas for juggling—bear generic names.

#### Cheering, jeering (lape)

Use of the noun *lape* is known from the twentieth century, when texts so called have constituted "music and dancing organized by the members of a cricket team and their supporters, to encourage the players who are batting" (Milner 1966). Earlier use of the term was only as a verb: 'sit and wish bad luck to the opposite party' in the game of *tāga-a-tiʻa* (Pratt 1911). In the late 1800s, cricket replaced *tāga-a-tiʻa* as the favorite sport at large gatherings: whenever a player struck the ball, "there was a beating of drums, a clapping of hands, and a shrill chorus of voices to add to the excitement of the moment" (Keeler 1903:715).

Social settings suitable for jeers and cheers still occur. At cricket matches near Apia in the 1970s,

> those not batting or fielding sit together in the shade singing and dancing. When their captain blows his whistle, those fielding leap into the air with a whoop, somewhat like a Thai boxer who calls to his spirits before the fight. The Samoans flutter like birds, spin on their heels like tops, perform somersaults, all according to the number of blasts. (Eustis 1979:89)

In 1989, at an impromptu cricket match on the Mall in Washington, D.C., competitors displayed similar antics, making similar shouts, cued by a whistle. In such games played in rural Savaiʻi in the 1970s, cueing from a whistle occurred, but the fielders moved with more restraint. The predominant sound was the singing of songs, whose sources and musical traits were diverse.

#### Formulas for juggling (palo)

Under the heading *palo,* a term that ordinarily bears the sense 'puzzle, riddle', Sāmoans collect songs performed to accompany juggling (*ʻaufua*), an ancient form of Polynesian competition. For the game, a member of the U.S. Exploring Expedition obtained a variant term, *tuaë-fuä* (Jenkins 1890:205), as did a French geographer: *tuai fua,* "played by five or six, with balls or oranges tossed into the air, each player keeping six or eight oranges in motion at once, according to the example of Indian jugglers" (Marques 1889:58, trans.). The texts of *palo* often consist of rhyming lines of near-equal length.

Most surviving *palo* contain numerical references, as in the following example, sung entirely on a monotone; here, written accents mark heavily stressed moras:

| | |
|---|---|
| Láugapā túu i le vao: tási laʻu ao. | Fern grows in the woods: my collection's one. |
| Láugapā túu i le vao: lúa aʻu ao. | Fern grows in the woods: my collection's two. |
| Láugapā túu i le vao: tólu aʻu ao. | Fern grows in the woods: my collection's three. |

And so on, to ten. Another example exhibits a similar pattern: *Váe 'avi'i, váe 'iao: tási la'u ao* 'Sandcrab leg, honeyeater leg: my collection's one', and so on. Because *palo* mark time to measure jugglers' success, they have a regulated, singsong quality.

### Conducting funerals

In a procession to where an important adult's corpse lies in state, chiefs and orators responsorially exclaim a text honoring the deceased. The performers, the procession, and the text are each known as the *'āuala*. Nineteenth-century missionaries observed

> an ancient custom, which is that, when a chief dies, whether of Savai'i or Upolu, to [sic] carry about the corpse from place to place, and for persons to cry out during the procession, "*Tuimanu'a e, lo'u alii*," "O my chief, Tuimanu'a!" (Powell 1886:153)

*'Āuala* of the late twentieth century honored chiefs with the stock phrase *Tulouna a le lagi* 'Acknowledgment of the sky'; other phrases are available for the deaths of ranking personages. An old man of Savai'i said the following shout was appropriate for the funeral of a chief of Manono: *Maile, Mailē! / Ē! ta fia tāue! / Maile, Mailē!* 'Dog, O Dog! / Ē! I want to fight! / Dog, O Dog!' (Persons of Manono took the honorific term *Maile* 'Dog'). Several persons of Savai'i, interviewed between 1971 and 1974, recognized the text of an *'āuala* of the Fāgaloa area of 'Upolu, documented by Buck (1930:597).

Christian burial sometimes follows a procession of mourners bearing the body from the church or house (where a pastor, a priest, or a deacon has led a service) to the grave. Some Roman Catholics are buried in cemeteries maintained by the church, but most Protestants are buried on familial land. The placement of graves gives indisputable support to territorial claims by descendants of the deceased.

While a body is lying in state, people of the village, or of nearby villages, may come in groups to offer their voice (*'ave le leo*) by singing Christian hymns. As one group sings, others may sit outside the house, listening. Each visitation may entail the giving of orations—an expression of condolences by the singers' representative and a response by the bereaved family's representative. The groups usually sing unaccompanied, but a choir may bring the organ from its church.

## Musical instruments

Musical instruments enhance Sāmoan vocal performance. In the twentieth century, several began to be required for certain genres. The action of the human body is a primary musical instrument. Skin strikes skin in several named movements: a high-pitched flat clap (*pati*), a low-pitched cupped clap (*pō*), the snapping of fingers (*fiti*), and the slapping of other parts of the body. These and other actions occur in *fa'ataupati* (figure 16) and *sāsā* (figure 17), songless movements performed by a company in synchrony. Their sounds combine with stamps and vocal clicks and grunts to make a favorite aural mix. Formerly, putting one hand under the opposing armpit and moving the opposing bent arm up and down (the action called *sāsāfi'a*) augmented movements of *sāsā* and possibly other genres. The collective rubbing of palms (*mili*) makes a sound used mainly in introductory sections.

### Idiophones

Old Sāmoa had several struck idiophones. A common accompaniment to dancing was percussion on a rolled-up mat (*fala*), sometimes with a bamboo tube inserted into its hollow, when the instrument was called a *tu'itu'i*. The *fa'aali'i* is probably the instrument named in a poetical text: *Pe ni fa'aali'i 'ua tātā?* 'Are *fa'aali'i* being

FIGURE 16 At the Pacific Festival of Art, men of Sāmoa perform a *fa'ataupati* with movements resembling those observed by the U.S. Exploring Expedition around 1840 [see ENCOUNTERS WITH "THE OTHER": figure 10, p. 20]. Photo by Adrienne L. Kaeppler, 1996.

played?' (Love 1991:162); the implication in the source is that the *fa'aali'i* accompanied the dancing of *soa*. Such an instrument may have been the *nafa*,

> formed by hollowing out a part of a log, leaving a narrow longitudinal mouth. It is now rarely seen, but is closely copied in the *longo*, an instrument derived from *Tonga*, excepting that the Tongan instrument is longer. When beaten, the *Nafa* was struck with two short sticks, the drum itself being laid on its side and bedded upon cocoanut-leaf mats, by which means contact with the ground was prevented, and a better sound produced. (Stair 1897:135)

Introduced log idiophones, in increasing order of size, are the *pātē*, the *lali*, and the *logo* (Moyle 1974).

Another struck idiophone, the *fa'aali'i lāiti*, also called *pulotu*, was "an instrument formed of a loose slat fitted into a board, on which they beat time with two sticks" (Wilkes 1845:2:134). This instrument

> was formed by fitting loosely a thin slip of board into a bed of close-grained wood. It was beaten with two small sticks, and although the sounds produced could not have been very pleasing, it was used exclusively by the higher chiefs. (Stair 1897:135–136)

FIGURE 17 At the Pacific Festival of Arts, the Sāmoan contingent presents a *sāsā*. Photo by Adrienne L. Kaeppler, 1985.

FIGURE 18    Ropati plays his ukulele, homemade from wood, a five-pound corned-beef tin, and nylon line. Photo by J. W. Love, 1972.

TRACK 48–49

How the rhythms played on it fitted with those of the words is unknown. For private amusement, individuals played lamellaphones (*utete*).

### Chordophones and aerophones

Ukuleles and guitars commonly furnish accompaniment for private, informal singing by individuals and groups of friends. Ukuleles are available for purchase, but boys take pride in making their own (figure 18). Indigenous aerophones included conchs (*pū*), whistles or pipes (*faʻaili,* a term based on the verb *ili* 'blow'), and a nose-blown flute (*fagufagu, siva-a-ʻofe*).

—J. W. LOVE

## A local view

Sāmoan music has two eminent sectors: secular and Christian. More than half of the secular sector, like the culture of which it is a part, consists of orally transmitted songs, contingent for planned occasions or random occurrences. Most planned occasions culminate in performed entertainment, including precomposed singing.

Sāmoan choral songs are descriptive and narrative pieces of poetry that express situational opinions and feelings. They include poems recited by orators. Public occasions that have produced such songs include the eruption of a volcano in the first decade of the twentieth century, a rebellion that in the 1920s involved the whole archipelago, the dedication of churches, and school graduations. Remaining secular forms of singing are personal songs, musical creations on the basis of personal incidents, expressing an individual's thoughts and feelings: love, grief, approval, animosity, an attempt to clear a misunderstanding between friends, the remembrance of someone's birthday. They sometimes admire a flower, a place, and so on. Secular songs can be about almost anything. The most common formalize grief on the death of a loved one.

Each kind of event calls for a unique type of composition—in wording, melody, and style. The style of choral songs at flag-day celebrations follows that of Sāmoan oratorical speech. Its diction comes from composers' repertories of legends, proverbial sayings, myths, history, and the Bible; the figures of speech reflect composers' preferences. Personal compositions, by not following a set format, allow for greater variety of texts and melodies, to the extent the composer's ability allows. For each form of music, audiences inevitably encounter differences in the perception of cultural values.

If the rhetoric of a song entertains Sāmoans' sensitivity to language, or if a melody provides more than momentary pleasure during its initial performance, it will be sung again. If the rhythm of a new song is fit for Sāmoan dancing, it may join the repertory of songs popular at gatherings. In that manner, a song works its way into the canon of popular culture. As a social product, it may eventually be forgotten as other songs enter the canon. Few songs composed for special events go through this cycle, and fewer become popular on all the Sāmoan islands. Many songs, choral and personal, have a regional distribution, wherein only residents of certain sites fully understand the import of the music. Most songs are soon forgotten. When a new occasion calls for a composition, the composer—usually a gifted individual from a family noted for musical talent—will create a new product.

TRACK 5–6

Sāmoans keep Christian religious singing strictly within the confines of churches, pastors' houses, and family devotions. Each church has a four-part choir on the Western model—soprano, alto, tenor, bass. Most Christian religious songs are translations of hymns in English and American hymnals. Choral singing is usually accompanied by an organ and occasionally by a piano, though it is done well unaccompanied. A clarinet or a trombone may join the organ.

FIGURE 19    At the Pacific Festival of Arts, a Sāmoan brass band performs. Photo by Adrienne L. Kaeppler, 1996.

### Technological changes

With the influx of modern technology, Sāmoans are changing their attitudes toward the instrumentation and place of religious music. They accept guitars in church, especially for young people's singing. Electric organs that imitate other instruments have made the sounds of drums and guitars available, and in services, most choirs use their organ's drums and other sounds. The radio plays recordings of hymns daily, and public places with amplifying systems rebroadcast the recordings.

Technology affects Sāmoan music in other ways. With modern recordings, personal secular songs and religious songs are becoming more developed. Studios record songs (original and unoriginal) by individuals, groups, and choirs, and manufacture hundreds of cassettes. At gatherings for leisure and work, the sounds on these recordings are replacing singing. In these productions, various musical instruments and arrangements accompany singers. In other contexts, brass bands furnish music (figure 19).

Some successful musical artists have made recordings a livelihood. As a result, an eclectic contemporary wave of popular Sāmoan music has arisen. Its components include Christian hymns and gospel music, country, rock, and jazz. From most of these sources, local musicians borrow melodies; leaving the arrangements unchanged, they interpolate Sāmoan words into the texture. The texts of some songs borrowed in this manner are word-for-word translations. From some sources, musicians adapt melodies to suit local preferences.

Choirs in churches are encouraging modern training, which leads musically inclined Sāmoans to adopt more Westernized traits, including the reading of staff notation. As singing from the diaphragm replaces traditional nasality, vibrato arises and becomes prominent; choirs then produce soloists who attain Western timbres. This training is subtly adapted into cultural performances: two- and three-part textures have yielded to that of the quartet. Some persons fault the adaptation of traditional singing, but others, perceiving that change is irreversible, help develop a new decorum.

—TIALUGA SUNIA SELOTI

## 'UVEA AND FUTUNA

An overseas territory of France, 'Uvea (Wallis Island) and Futuna (Hoorn Island) cover about 153 square kilometers, with a population of about 15,000. Archaeological excavations indicate that these islands were receivers of the Lapita cultural complex and the Polynesian tradition of plainware pottery. After a series of invasions and wars, 'Uvea and Futuna received heavy Tongan influence. Among the firstfruits and tribute sent to Tonga was a series of important dances, including the *tāpaki,* the *kailao,* and the *'eke,* all still performed in both areas.

'Uvean social structure, culture, language (Biggs 1980:124), and history (Campbell 1983) relate closely to those of Tonga, while Futunan social structure, culture, and language relate closely to those of Sāmoa. 'Uvea and Futuna were missionized by Roman Catholics, and the people have been Roman Catholics since the mid-1800s. That Tonga and Sāmoa are predominantly Protestant gives a superficial modern difference to basically similar cultural traditions. Paramount chiefs (*hau* in 'Uvea, *sau* in Futuna) rule local social life.

## 'Uvea

'Uvea has about ten thousand inhabitants in nineteen villages, the main spatial points of reference and context. Every village supports at least one composer (*māu*) and one lead dancer (*pulotu*). There is a saying that each place has its own composer: *takitahi te ki'i tolofue mo tona kalae* 'every little liane [vine] has its purple swamphen'.

### Musical contexts

A month before a feast, a village council brings to a composer a *mau-kava,* a gift of kava—or, since the 1960s or before, imported alcoholic beverages. Composers usually work only on request. For entertainment, a village provides specialized singers and instrumentalists and recruits as many singer-dancers as possible.

Outdoor performances in which all dancers sing occur on each important religious holiday (*aho lahi*), including *katoaga* (feasts, with distribution of food). These holidays attract the populace toward one of the four main ceremonial centers (*mala'e*), open places near the four parish churches, on 1 May (St. Joseph, feast at Mala'efo'ou), a variable Sunday in June (Sacred Heart, at Tepa), 29 June (Saints Peter and Paul, at Vaitupu), 15 August (Assumption of the Blessed Virgin Mary, at Matautu).

Songs by specialized singers, and indoor dances, are performed in informal *maholo,* evening entertainments and familial feasts. Bastille Day (14 July) is nowadays the yearly occasion when the rarest and most ancient songs and dances are performed.

### Text and melody

The common denominators of 'Uvean vocal music are *fasi* and *kupu*. *Fasi* is a melodic, rhythmic pattern. The word can be glossed 'segment' or 'sequence', referring to elements to be arranged and assembled. Part of a *fasi* may repeat or vary. The same *fasi* may serve in a historical song, in a *lakalaka,* or in a *sāsā*. Binary rhythm is usual in *fasi* used in dances.

*Kupu* is to *fasi* as 'text' is to 'melody'. Secondarily, *kupu* is opposed to *fakatauga,* as 'stanza' to 'refrain'. Stanzas musically contrast with refrains: the latter takes a faster tempo, and occurs twice at every reprise. This distinction also occurs in movement: stanzas use clapping motifs, and refrains use various movements.

The relationship between *kupu* as text and *fasi* as melody is metrical, and linguistic rhythm reinforces musical rhythm. *Fasi* usually have four measures per verse. In a *lakalaka* performed in 1970, stanzaic verses are cut into four-syllable units, with rhythmic stress (here marked with an acute accent) on the third syllable of each unit:

The time of his inhumation: / Then the whole Lano (seminary) / Comes in procession. / It is only to honor his body; / It is only to honor his body: / For he was taken to heaven by Mary.    —'Uvean song

Fakatápu | kau fái || ki te háo | kua tóka, ||
A si'í ka- | -u alíki || mo oná fa- | -kafofóga. ||
Kae áu | fia fái || haku kí'i | talanóa ||
Ki te lótu | ne'e mái || mai lóto | Eulópa. ||

In other texts, verses divide into three syllabic units, and rhythmic stress falls on the first.

'Uvean singing has several voices: *fakafoa* and *kī* are high voices; *'ekenaki,* accompaniment; *'ekenaki elemuhu,* a bass; and *leo kanokano,* a full voice (Bataillon 1932:206). The last word indicates that vocal quality may be more relevant than harmonic position. Songs usually start in unison, climb, and end in polyphony.

### Sung genres

'Uvean music comprises several sung genres and many danced genres. *Hiva,* the most general term for singing and genres of song, includes dancing-singing, *hiva o te mé'e* 'song of the dance'. More generally, it implies a range of traits, including polyphony, poetry, and instrumental accompaniment. It may be masculine, feminine, or both. In all *hiva,* accompaniment is conceived as essentially rhythmic. 'Uveans call playing the guitar *tā ukalele* 'strike the guitar' and danced *hiva* has percussive accompaniment. In all *hiva,* compositions follow a stanza-refrain construction. Texts are numerous and diversified in thematic content, but they use a small number of *fasi* (Mayer and Nau 1973:85).

*Hiva tau'ine* 'farewell songs' are defined by content rather than by tonal features. A *fasi* lasts for two verses, and the poetry is composed in several quatrains, but only one refrain. *Hiva foli fenua* 'island-touring songs' are devoted to the natural beauty of the island. They highlight the names of famous places, and indirectly focus on female beauties. These traits appear in texts of *sāsā,* where metaphors move from village to village (Mayer 1987:141).

### Hiva as dirge

Dirges do not take a specific term, but are specifically titled with the Christian name or the nickname of the deceased person: a *hiva o Fiu* is a 'song for Fiu' (Mayer and Nau 1976:152). The following dirge, "*Hiva o Pātele Tominiko*" ('Song for Father Dominic'), dates from 1956:

| | |
|---|---|
| Te matagi tana hifo momoko, | The wind coming down fresh, |
| Mokomoko i pelepitelio | Fresh on the presbytery |
| O hage he aisi momoko. | Like a fresh piece of ice. |
| Pātele ne'e mole takoto; | Father was not abed; |
| Pātele ne'e mole takoto: | Father was not abed: |
| Ne'e tō fakafufu ifo. | He was struck suddenly. |

| | |
|---|---|
| Fetu'u e fia na tau maofa? | How many stars fell? |
| Te peau na hake i Faioa, | The wave came up at Faioa [Islet], |
| O hage e ina fakailoga | So as to announce |
| Te aposatolo na teu fagona. | The apostle was preparing his travel. |
| | |
| Hoko pe ki tona avaifo: | The time of his inhumation: |
| Pea katoa fuli ko Lano | Then the whole Lano (seminary) |
| O haele fakapolosesio. | Comes in procession. |
| Ko te ofa noa ki tona sino; | It is only to honor his body; |
| Ko te ofa noa ki tona sino: | It is only to honor his body: |
| Ka kua ave ia e Malia ki selo. | For he was taken to heaven by Mary. |
| | |
| Ha'u la, Patita o fakaamu | Come on, Baptist, and mourn |
| Ki tau tamai tapu, kua alu. | Your sacred father, who has gone. |
| Pea ofa pe keke toe ma'u | May you be given |
| Te fua o tau faifekau. | The fruit of your service. |

Father Tominiko Galuola, an 'Uvean priest, died suddenly. The blowing wind, shining stars, and crashing waves metaphorize his death. Faioa Islet (stanza 2) is on the reef opposite the presbytery of Mu'a, where he died. He was about to fell a tree to build a canoe. He had been teaching at Lano seminary (stanza 3). The text calls on Baptist, his servant, as a witness. The *fasi*, an eight-bar pattern, is performed three times in the first stanza (figure 20).

### Songs in tales

A *tagi* 'cry, shout' is a short sung part of a tale (*fagona*), sung unaccompanied. It is a solo genre, unlike all others. Structurally, it can be taken as an archetype of *fasi*, for it repeats for each line of the text, as in this example: *Ko au ko Masina'afi'afi, / Ta'ata'a ia si'i va'eva'e lagi. / Mo'oa si'i a Lagakali; / Gata peau Simatalea* 'I am Masina'afi'afi, / Wandering on the edge of heaven. / I have nothing to do with Lagakali; / Nobody else for me, except Simatalea'. In 1,292 'Uvean narratives, more than twenty *tagi* appear (Mayer 1976:107–111).

### Laulausiva 'dance-opening song'

*Laulausiva,* where *siva* must be taken as an imported form of *hiva,* is linked with danced genres. For a troupe, *laulausiva* is an opening song, as *hiva tau'ine* is a closing song. It may be defined as a dance without movement, as it opens a series of dances with obeisance to King Lavelua and the customary authorities of the island. It is sung unaccompanied before the first dance. Musically, it has the polyphonic form of a *hiva,* but the unaccompanied performance of a *fo'i lau.*

### Hymns

Christianization has produced a musical genre known as *katiko* (Latin *canticum*), neither Roman Catholic nor indigenous. After the Second Vatican Council (1962–1965), Gregorian plainsong went into disfavor, and by adding new texts to old *fasi,* 'Uveans created the *katiko* (Mayer 1973:84–86). The polyphony matches that of *lakalaka* and *sāsā. Katiko* were originally sung unaccompanied. Then the

FIGURE 20 An 'Uvean melody: the first stanza of "Hiva o Patele Tominiko" ('Song for Father Dominic'), a lament. Transcription by Raymond Mayer.

'Uvean contrabass known as *fo'i poe* (string and pole attached to a kerosene tin) and electric guitars were added, especially on feasts. By the 1980s, the genre had disappeared from 'Uvean religious services.

*Other sung genres*

*Hiva o te me'e* 'dance-songs' were *hiva* for dancing texts developed from *lakalaka* and *sāsā* and set to one or several *fasi,* in a two- or four-verse contour. The 'Uvean expression *fo'i lau* 'male old songs' denotes old men singing old songs and the songs themselves. These songs are sung unaccompanied, in contrast with other *hiva.* Instead of blending-voice qualities (preferred for polyphony), a leading-voice quality is preferred, and *tuli* 'vocal breaks' end many musical lines. Textual themes are hagiographies, remembrances of wars, and moralizing stories.

Songs for juggling and other games, and children's songs, appear in the inventory of 'Uvean musical genres (Burrows 1932). In the mid-1800s, *tau'a'alo* were sung when paddling, "or elsewhere" (Bataillon 1932: 362), and *lave* were concerts of instrumental and vocal music accompanied with movements (Bataillon 1932:239). No living genres correspond to these terms.

### Danced genres

It is a puzzle whether *hiva* 'song' and *me'e* 'dance' differ musically. There is at least one definitely contrastive musical trait: *me'e* implies percussive rhythm. The 'Uvean term for performing dances is *tā me'e* 'beat the dance'.

*Kailao*

A men's dance simulating battle, the *kailao* is the masterpiece of 'Uvean dances. On formal occasions, it is the main opener or closer (figure 21). Its performance occupies the greater part of the *mala'e,* where spectators on each side (*alofi*) leave space for dancers' lines to spread out.

The *kailao* is a double exception in the system of danced genres. It is performed without song, accompanied by a metallic idiophone instead of a wooden one or a mat. The precontact accompaniment could have been a wooden gong (Burrows 1937:151). Nowadays, it is beaten on imported kerosene barrels. All *kailao* use a basically binary rhythmic pattern (Burrows 1945:88). The dancers divide into two groups, which face and then approach each other, rhythmically twirling clubs.

FIGURE 21  On the feast of Saints Peter and Paul (29 June), men of Vaitupu Village, Hihifo District, perform a *kailao.* Photo by Raymond Mayer, 1982.

In the *kailao tokotoko* (no longer performed), the implement was a pole, *tokotoko*. The genre was seen by Burrows in 1932. Photos of it survive from the 1950s. The *kailao hele* seems to be a later version of it, but a machete replaces the pole in a solo performance, and musical accompaniment comes from an orchestra consisting of guitars, a struck bamboo pole, and sometimes repetitive songs. The *kailao afi,* a dance performed at night, uses a baton, with one or two ends lit with fire. The performer twirls it, like the machete of the *kailao hele.* The common feature among these genres is dexterous handling of a sticklike implement.

### Lakalaka

The *kailao* and its subgenres may be taken as *meʻe tagata* 'male dances', performed standing and moving. At the opposite end of the spectrum are *lakalaka.* Though the etymological meaning is 'step forward', *lakalaka* in the 'Uvean system is a *meʻe nofo,* a dance by seated women. The spatial disposition allows for several rows of dancers to be surrounded by a semicircular standing line of mixed dancers.

The structural difference between men's and women's dances is the difference between movement and text. Movement is considered male; text, female. A *lakalaka* text is composed to tell a story. It is the first text danced by a village, to show gladness. It is in quatrains with refrains, under one or several *fasi.* All dancers sing the text. An ensemble, beating mats and playing guitars, joins them. Stanzas use one *fasi,* and refrains use another. Danced movements are usually repetitive sequences of clapping (*fū*) for stanzas, and diversified sequences (*haka*) for refrains.

### Sāsā

The *sāsā* is said to have come from Sāmoa. On 'Uvea, it has split into two major forms, one of which has become the most performed genre in the island: in 1982, sixty-six known sung *sāsā* were performed. The *sāsā fakalologo* 'silent *sāsā*' (also called *sāsā fakamāfana* 'warming *sāsā*') is a subgenre that seems closer to the imported form. It was the only one Burrows observed (1937: table 5). Its rhythmic formula differs little from that of the *kailao.*

The *sāsā* can be performed with singing. *Sāsā* and *lakalaka* differ in the order of performance and the content of texts. In a performance, the *lakalaka* comes first, and the sung *sāsā* comes second. The text of the *lakalaka* is descriptive and solemn; the text of the *sāsā* is metaphoric and entertaining. More than thirty themes are in use (Mayer 1987:142), including *sāsā aka* 'soccer *sāsā*', *sāsā inu-kava* 'kava-drinking *sāsā*', and *sāsā inu-kafe* 'coffee- drinking *sāsā*'.

Musically, a sung *sāsā* takes the same shape as a *lakalaka.* Stanzas share one *fasi,* and refrains share another. Movements, alternatively on the left and the right, mainly portray narratives. *Fū* cover stanzas, and *haka* cover refrains.

### Soāmako and niutao

This is locally the most appreciated genre. It is said to have come from Futuna. The *soāmako faka-'Uvea* is considered more female; the *soāmako faka-Futuna,* more male. One melody serves for all *soāmako* texts, which are short and repetitive, as are texts and melodies of *niutao* (or *faka-Niutao*), whose tempo usually increases. Each *niutao* has a specific *fasi* and specific movements. Burrows collected texts in 1932. Twenty-eight *niutao* are studied in Mayer 1987. The ensemble (*lologo* 'noise, report, news') performs in front of the dancers (figure 22). It includes instruments and voices.

### Dances with implements

Three villages specialize in performing the *'eke* or *sokē* 'dance with sticks', using almost the same rhythmic formula as in *kailao* and *sāsā fakalogo.* The word *sokē*

FIGURE 22   To welcome the French governor, young people of Ha'afuasia Village, Hahake District, perform a *niutao* in front of the king's palace, Matautu. On the ground in front of them, percussionists play bamboo *lali*; others play guitars and a ukulele. Photo by Raymond Mayer, 1971.

comes from the interjection ending *'eke* stanzas. Dancers sing short monophonic ritornello stanzas and strike sticks together. The *tāpaki* 'dance with paddles', common to Futuna, 'Uvea, and Tonga, has a vocal accompaniment.

### Other dances

The *leti* 'children's dance' is an imitation of any local or imported genre, like a New Caledonian *pilu*. The *mā'ulu'ulu* is a seated dance, in 1932 described as "the most popular of present-day dances" (Burrows 1937:152). 'Uveans have abandoned its name, but the genre survives as the *lakalaka*. The *me'e Fisi* 'Fijian dance' has entered 'Uvean tradition. The *me'e tokotahi* is a solo dance performed standing; the *me'e fakahuahua*, a joyful *sāsā*; the *takitaki*, an introduced dance built on a *niutao*, a *soāmako*, or other dances. Dancing in couples (*tauhoa*), the cha-cha (*lakalua*), and disco (*tisikō*) are popular.

### Musical instruments

The prime 'Uvean musical instrument is the human voice, *leo*. Sung genres, including female danced genres, are based on the voice; male danced genres are based on percussion, the next commonest timbre. The typical percussive instrument is a log idiophone, *lali*. Percussion is specific to dance, and melody is often molded on rhythmic patterns. Beating mats and striking a wooden plaque also seem genuinely 'Uvean. Beating pieces of iron on fuel barrels is new, as is playing a double bass with a string on a kerosene tin. In dances, ukuleles, Spanish guitars, and other stringed instruments serve less for melody than for rhythm. They are mostly strummed, not picked.

## Futuna

A French protectorate since 1888, Futuna lies 220 kilometers southwest of 'Uvea. Its population is about five thousand. Before 1970, when a local airfield opened, distance kept both islands distinct in linguistic, cultural, and to some extent political history. Futuna has two kings (*sau*), heading rival districts, Sigave and Alo, whose last war was in 1839 (Rozier 1960). Futunans have been French citizens since 1960. Futuna was entirely converted to Roman Catholicism in 1842, the year after St. Peter Chanel's martyrdom there.

Broadcasts from 'Uvea—radio since 1979, television since 1996—have transformed the ways Futunans hear music. Often aired are the recordings of Polikalepo Lautoka, a Futunan resident of New Caledonia; his orchestral arrangements of

Futunan music have made him a star. In the 1980s, disco (*tisikō*) invaded Futuna, and rock is now performed in local nightclubs, appealing to teenagers and young adults.

### Musical contexts

Musical performances have moved from indigenous observances to those of the Roman calendar—feasts associated with patron saints of villages and districts. In each village, these saints have replaced local divinities, but are not strictly an imported Christian form (Gaillot 1962). On the feast of the patron of each village and parish, an important ceremony (*aso lasi*) occurs, featuring three important components: kava, *katoaga* (distribution of food), and *mako* (the performance of integrated poetry-music-dance).

On the eve of St. Peter Chanel's feast (27 April) at Poi, where the missionary was killed, the districts have a joint musical and oratorical competition (*taulau*). At various times throughout the year, visits of Futunans from New Caledonia inspire fund-raising events (*kelemesi*) for local churches and other public purposes. Besides these events, informal gatherings with singing and dancing (also called *taulau*) are part of everyday life. Elderly people prefer singing, while young people prefer dancing to the music of guitars and ukuleles. Hymns, laments, and songs about history, land, and love, blend into an evening of entertainment. Finally, during communal labor—rowing, hauling a canoe to shore, making cloth from bark—people lighten their efforts by singing (Mayer and Nau 1982:31).

### Musical repertories

As in 'Uvea, the Futunan musical framework comprises a text (*kupu*) and a melody (*fasi*), a melodic-rhythmic vehicle for conveying the poetry. The texts and melodies of some genres (including *tāpaki* and *tākofe*) have remained in the repertory without essential change, passed on orally for generations. Compositions in other genres (including *lakalaka* and *sāsā*) may be performed only once, for a specific event, and then forgotten.

Musical terminology in Futuna differs from that of 'Uvea, though the concepts are similar. Thus, for 'Uvean *hiva* 'to sing, song', Futunans use the terms *sua* 'to sing' and *sua lau* 'song'. The Futunan term *mako* includes movement and the melodic and rhythmic rendering of poetry.

Futuna has two distinct performative genres: *tākofe* 'strike the bamboo' and *tāpaki* 'strike the *paki* (a short, broad, paddle-shaped implement)'. *Tākofe* is a specialty of the villages of Fiua and Alofitai in Sigave and Alo, respectively, and can be performed only by men from these villages. The performers stand in rows that move and interweave. They strike on the ground 2.7-meter-long bamboo poles, decorated with a tuft of leaves and a streamer of white cloth. They raise the poles into the air, manipulating them in various patterns. They are accompanied by rhythmic beating on a *lologo pāpā*, or a wooden body like an overturned canoe. The texts of *tākofe* are fixed: examples collected by Burrows in 1932 (1936:215) are the same as those collected by Manuaud in 1979 (1983:378). In a related dance, *lau taimi,* men singing *tākofe* texts swing coconut-frond implements horizontally.

*Tāpaki* are performed by several villages, each having its own text (Burrows 1945:39–48; Manuaud 1983:379–381). A company of men, interweaving their columns in various patterns, twirl, slap, and toss their *paki*. This dance occurs in 'Uvea, Tonga, and elsewhere, but it seems to have originated in Futuna.

The ritual *tū* mimes warfare, accompanied by shouts. It occurs during a ceremonial procession for the investiture of a *sau,* when men point long lances to form a triangle over the chief's head. As he and his retinue approach the places where kava will

FIGURE 23   At the Pacific Festival of Arts, men of the Wallis and Futuna contingent perform a *soā mako.* Photo by Adrienne L. Kaeppler, 1996.

be mixed and served, men in warlike garments feign attacks on them (Likuvalu 1977:219).

*Sosoāmako,* a men's dance without implements, repeats a four-measure text over and over, faster and faster. Though texts may change, the movements and their order do not vary from one text to another. As *soāmako faka-Futuna,* this genre has been exported to 'Uvea (figure 23) and other islands. A formally related genre is *faka-Niutao,* said to derive from the island of Niutao, Tuvalu; women may join in. *Faka-Niutao* also have short, repetitive texts and melodies, but specific movements go with specific texts.

*Kailao* is an 'Uvean dance with implements, based on the manipulation of long wooden staves (see figure 21). It has no text and uses rhythmic beating on a 200-liter kerosene barrel.

Contrasting with these dances, *lakalaka* and *sāsā* are performed by mixed companies of seated dancers from a specific village. The texts, composed for the occasion, treat current events, metaphorically using themes like picking flowers, making necklaces, fishing, and playing soccer. *Lakalaka* and *sāsā* are usually performed to raise funds.

### Musical instruments

Typical West Polynesian instruments were once part of the musical landscape. These included a nose-blown flute (*fagufagu*), a lamellaphone (*ūtete*), and a log idiophone (*nafa*). Today, percussion comes from beating a mat (*tāfala*) or a log idiophone (*lali*) and playing imported chordophones. The word *ukalele* denotes any ukulele or guitar. Guitarists pick the strings for songs and strum them for dances; ukuleleists aways strum.

—RAYMOND MAYER

## NIUE

Since 1974 a self-governing island in free association with New Zealand, Niue is a raised coral island of 263 square kilometers, inhabited by about two thousand people. Located about 480 kilometers east of Tonga, Niue is closely related in culture and language to Tonga and Sāmoa.

The first known European visitor was Captain James Cook, who in 1774 called Niue Savage Island because he received a hostile reception there. The London Missionary Society was the exclusive Christian church in Niue from the mid-1800s until 1952, when Mormons arrived; they were followed by Roman Catholics in 1955.

Events that featured the performance of music and dance included feasts, investitures, circumcisions, javelin-throwing contests, and funerals. In addition, there were prayers, charms (as to bring rain), and game songs. Today, events include celebrations of national independence (on 19 October), a boy's first haircut, Christian holidays and meetings, dignitaries' visits, and festivals abroad. War dances have evolved into pregame challenges in preparation for rugby matches.

Apart from short recording trips (Moyle 1985), little research has been done on the music and dance of Niue. Edwin M. Loeb (1926) published an ethnography that included contextual materials, musical texts, and descriptions of performances. During the 1960s, I worked with a Niue composer and choreographer, Mata Smith (Kaeppler 1983), and have analyzed performances from Pacific Festivals of Arts.

Niueans qualify and categorize *lologo,* the word for vocal music, and *koli,* the word for dance, by descriptive terms. Thus, *lologo tagi* (or just *tagi*) are laments, and *koli ngesi niu* are dances that use coconut shells. Songs and dances are distinguished by poetry and intended use, rather than musically. Most vocal music incorporates tonal intervals, melodic sequences, and harmonies borrowed from Western music; however, dances with long paddlelike implements and other performances for special events are based on older systems of structured sound and movement.

In addition to clapping, instruments included log idiophones (*logo, nafa*) and nose-blown flutes (*kofe*). In the 1920s, tins and accordions were used; today, string bands and brass bands, modeled on the usage of Sāmoa, Tonga, and New Zealand, are popular.

Vocal production was recitational, with little melodic movement. A leader (*uhu*) began, and others joined in. Sitting cross-legged, performers might face each other in two or more rows while swaying from side to side and moving their arms. Some performances imitated animals, including rats, owls, and bats. Loeb (1926:122) classed performances into four main genres: *tame,* singing and dancing at daytime feasts; *tafeauhi,* nighttime performances around a fire; *takalo,* war dances; and a drama in which the god Limaua—a "merman, with streaming hair, and a fish's tail" (Loeb 1926:125)—was speared and then mourned.

Nonindigenous performances of the 1990s styles of music and dance are borrowed from Europeans and other Polynesians and adapted to local taste; for example, the abolitionists' song "John Brown's Body" has become the basis for a single-file dance while exiting the arena.

Most musical performances are for entertainment and hospitality. An example, composed in the 1960s by Mata Smith for high-school students to perform for visiting dignitaries, is sung, played by a string band, and danced by a group of boys and girls, who make patterned rhythms and movements with coconut shells (Kaeppler 1983:101–110).                    —ADRIENNE L. KAEPPLER

## ROTUMA

Near the intersection of Polynesia, Micronesia, and Melanesia, Rotuma borrowed heavily from its neighbors—in music as in language. Rotumans have long claimed that all their songs and dances but the class known as *tautoga* are imports (Gardiner 1898:488). By blending borrowed and indigenous traits, Rotumans have generated a unique musical repertory.

A volcanic island of approximately 43 square kilometers, Rotuma rises to about 215 meters. It lies 500 kilometers north of Viti Levu, from where, in the late 1990s, biweekly flights were scheduled; government and private shipping provided additional, though irregular, transportation between Fijian ports and Rotuma.

Mythology attributes the creation of the island, and the founding of the society, to Raho, supposedly a Sāmoan chief. Early in the 1700s, Ma'afu, a Tongan chief from Niuafo'ou, reportedly conquered Rotuma (Churchward 1937:255). Legends portray him as an oppressor, killed by rebelling Rotumans; nevertheless, the title *Maraf,* an obvious cognate, remains the premier title.

In 1791, H.M.S. *Pandora* became the first European ship to visit Rotuma.

Music forms an integral part of playtimes. On the grounds of selected houses, youths sing and dance to the accompaniment of guitars and ukuleles. In reward, residents sprinkle them with perfumed powders and spray them with cologne.

Christianity arrived in 1839, when John Williams assigned two Sāmoan teachers to the island; but they were unsuccessful, and in 1841, Tongan Wesleyans replaced them. In 1847, Roman Catholic missionaries arrived. Sectarian antagonisms mounted, culminating in 1878 in a war won by the numerically dominant side, the Methodists. Continuing unrest led the paramount chiefs of the seven districts to petition Britain for annexation. In 1881, the year of cession, Rotuma became administratively part of Fiji. In the late 1990s, the population on the island was about twenty-six hundred; but three times as many Rotumans lived on Viti Levu, mainly in Suva.

## Performative contexts

At special occasions, no major gathering occurs without performances for which groups compose (*hạ̄i*) celebratory songs and dances. Depending on the size of a festival (*kato'aga*), performances range from an hour of informal singing around a few guitars (*kitā*) and ukuleles (*ukalele*), to daylong sessions in which rehearsed groups formally sing and dance. At domestic ceremonies, such as weddings or the raisings of gravestones (*höt'ạk hạfu*), songs honor featured persons. When a group from one village or district performs at another location, it presents songs to honor its hosts: texts reference local chiefs, pertinent events, and outstanding features of the community or landscape. Annual events (such as Cession Day, and the Methodist Church Conference), and specially scheduled events (a high dignitary's visit, the dedication of a new building), spur groups to polish their performances. In Suva in 1974, at the dedication of Churchward Chapel, groups presented songs praising C. Maxwell Churchward (Methodist missionary), for whom the congregation named the building; songs also praised the architect, and likened the structure to a spaceship.

On some occasions (like the Methodist Church Conference), performances occur within a competitive framework. Judges rate presentations by unity, degree of difficulty, and appearance (costume, stance, expression). At these performances, audiences enthusiastically receive successful innovations.

During celebrations, public musical performances occur where convenient: for a religious occasion, in or next to a church; for a wedding, near the bride's home; for a feast, at the host's house. To receive guests, some villages maintain open public spaces (*marä'e*), where they erect sheds for protection from rain and sun. Informal singing or dancing may precede the serving of kava and food; but formal presentations routinely follow feasting, with performers facing the high chiefs and featured guests.

Music forms an integral part of playtimes (*av mane'a*), periods set aside for socializing. Most notable is the four-to-six-week period during December and January, when few people work. On the grounds of selected houses, youths sing and dance to the accompaniment of guitars and ukuleles. In reward, residents sprinkle them with perfumed powders and spray them with cologne; if adequate supplies are on hand, hosts also dispense soft drinks and food.

In premissionary times, nubile youths frequented houses set aside for dancing

and played beachgames (*mane'a hune'ele*), including singing and dancing, which provided culturally controlled frames for courtship. Missionaries, fearing immorality, curbed such gatherings. In the current version of beachgames, young people informally gather around a guitar, often under the auspices of the church, to perform hymns and other religious songs (figure 24). In the 1980s, activity began to give way to passivity—listening to cassette recordings. Guitars, ukuleles, and cassettes are unavailable for purchase on the island, but returning sojourners bring them home.

Composers are known as *manatu*; with lead singers, they are known as *purotu*. Several persons have attained local reputations as composers. Some older people keep musical texts in notebooks, which, to consult while planning performances, they sometimes bring to meetings. A few Rotuman bands (*päne*) have composed and recorded songs in popular Polynesian styles.

No survey of indigenous musical instruments remains, though Rotumans said in 1932 they had once had a nose-blown flute and a panpipe (MacGregor n.d.). By the mid-1900s, rhythmic beating on a pile of folded mats had become the only normative accompaniment to *tautoga*; it may have replaced striking a log idiophone (Eason 1951:23). Metallic idiophones, made from bicycle bells, bullet casings, or other hollow metal containers and struck with a nail or metal strip, accompany a new kind of hymn, *mak pel* (from English *bell*).

## Indigenous songs

At the time of European intrusion, Rotuman music included recitations, dances with paddles, and *tautoga*.

### *Recitations*

Mosese Kaurasi (1991) distinguishes three types of Rotuman recitation: texts composed for dances and songs with movements; texts intoned before battles or wrestling matches; and *temo,* performed during a chief's funeral, or at a reception for a visiting chief.

Songs with movements commemorate special events or occasions, including war-provoking incidents, the deaths of notable persons, successful seafaring ventures, and festivals involving two or more communities. Their sentiments vary circumstantially, in moods from solemn to exultant. In 1926, the Reverend Kitione, a Wesleyan minister, composed the following text to mark the end of festivities involving groups from Faguta and Motusa (Kaurasi 1991:143).

| | |
|---|---|
| Hanis 'e soro te Faguta! | Pity the troupe from Faguta! |
| Hauen ava la a'u'ua, | The time to stop has come, |
| Fufui ne is Moitaua | For the flock of Moitaua Point |
| Orsio ka hanua la malua. | To rest and yarn as the sun sets. |

To mobilize sentiment and muster courage (*mäeva*), the songs and dances performed before battles were textually belligerent and kinemically aggressive (Kaurasi 1991:147):

| | |
|---|---|
| Kaf se' po', | Clap your folded arm, |
| Hula hula majei tato. | And wrestle in pairs till darkness falls. |
| 'Apsi' la' kel hula, | Stroll to watch the wrestling match, |
| To' filo'ua le' herua. | And witness the snapping off of wrestlers' heads. |

In form, such songs resembled songs for wrestling matches (*hula*), though the latter, usually tempered by good-natured teasing, alternated in exchange between hosts and guests.

*Temo* praise deceased individuals, respected chiefs, and special places. Before Christianization, mourners sang them at funerals. Leaders chose a tempo and started the singing; they sat close to selected others, facing inward, and the rest of the company sat around them. The leaders performed in sets of four: the first three *temo* were slow and subdued; the fourth, quick and bright, with clapping. The chorus accompanied by humming (*verea'aki*) a drone.

The melodies of *temo* usually have a range no larger than a perfect fourth, plus indefinitely pitched notes wailed in high registers. By about a semitone, singers depress the pitches of notes, and then slide back up again. *Temo* end in a downward slide, with diminishing volume. In 1932, their volume was "so low that one feels that those outside the circle are not supposed to hear or understand the words. The clapping too is very soft. The best chanting of *temos* resembles the singing of toothless old men" (MacGregor n.d.). By 1960, *temo* had fallen out of use.

### Dances with paddles

People performed dances with paddles (*mak pąki*) within the ritual cycle associated with the offices of *sau* and *mua,* spiritual representatives of the unified polity. Because the dances originated in pagan worship, they fell into disuse after the 1870s, when Christianization had become complete.

In 1865, a missionary witnessed a dance of "mostly elderly men": each performer held a paddle, and

> the sau and the mueta [*mua*] stood together, all the rest squatted down near them. Rising up, they commenced a song, raising the legs alternately, and brandishing the paddles. The song over, they rushed, one half one way, and one half the other way, and meeting in the centre of the square, stood in two lines, the sau and the mueta being in the centre of the front line. A man sat before a native drum to beat time, and lead the chanting. All joined, moving the legs, and gently brandishing the paddles, now giving them an oscillating movement on the front of the head, and again striking them gently with the tips of the fingers of the left hand. At intervals, the back line dividing into two went round and joined again in front of the line, where stood the sau and the mueta, which line in its turn divided, and

FIGURE 25   Rotumans perform a *tautoga*. Photo by Alan Howard, 1960.

passed to the front. In each song these evolutions were gone through five or six times. The whole may have lasted about half an hour. (Fletcher 1866; letter, 4 November 1865)

Severed from their original context by the 1880s, dances with paddles continued in secular settings, where they highlighted special celebrations.

### Tautoga

Reserved for large festivals, these songs and dances embody late-twentieth-century Rotuman taste. Men and women arrange themselves in rows, men on one side, women on the other (figure 25). Movements occur in synchrony: men's are vigorous and coarse; women's, restrained and delicate.

Costumes include lavalavas (*ha̗fali*), usually of uniform color and design: women wear theirs down to the ankles; men, to just below the knee. Over the lavalavas, from the waist, hang ti-leaf skirts (*titi*). Dancers adorn themselves with garlands (*tefui*) made from young coconut-palm leaves, supplemented by sweet-smelling flowers, tied together with colorful wool. Men's skirts and garlands are more elaborately decorated than women's. Women usually let their hair down, as a "mark of respect and deference" (Hereniko 1991:133).

In form, a complete *tautoga* is a suite of pieces in three types: from one to three *sua*, one or two *tiap hï'i*, and two or more *tiap forau*; in a complete performance, at least one example of each type occurs. For *sua* and *tiap forau*, elders provide accompaniment: with wooden sticks, several people beat on a pile of folded mats; they begin each dance by introducing the song, and take responsibility for sustaining the rhythm and the tempo. In *sua* and the *tiap hï'i*, each of the first three rows of dancers takes its turn in front; after completing a set of verses, the dancers in the first row drop back, and the row behind them comes forward (Hereniko 1991:128–130).

### Sua

For *sua,* dancers stand in place: men, with their feet apart; women, with their feet together. The basic movement involves lifting the hands from the sides, clasping them together in front of the waist, and releasing them to the sides. Dancers repeatedly bend and straighten their legs.

*Sua* normally consist of four-verse stanzas, whose texts allude to the occasion.

FIGURE 26 Rotuman songs recorded in rehearsal in Oinafa Village, 1989: *a* and *b*, two *sua*; *c*, a *hï tägtäg*. Transcriptions by J. W. Love.

The music consists of a single phrase in duple meter, repeated many times. One recorded performance (figure 26*a*) ended during the twentieth statement of the phrase. The performers sing a melody in parallel fifths, with women on the upper part. Sometimes (as at the beginning of figure 26*b*), singers sound other notes, creating three- or four-note harmonies.

### Tiap hïi

After *sua* come *tiap hïi*, dances of two kinds. In one, *hï tägtäg* 'languid drone', women sing *hïïe, hïïe, hïïe, hïïe*, while men grunt *hüü, hüü, hüü, hüü* (figure 26*c*). The performers focus on a major triad: men sing the root; women, the third and fifth. A subdominant triad serves as an auxiliary. The performers clap their hands on downbeats. The transcribed performance has thirty-seven statements of the indicated phrase; after the nineteenth, the tempo begins to increase sharply. In the other kind of *tiap hïi*, the *hï sasap* 'sustained drone', the men drag out their *hü*. In both subgenres, some singers breathe while others vocalize, so the performance spins a continuous thread of sound.

Performances of *tiap hïi* mark the contrast between feminine constraint and masculine freedom. Women stand in place, as in the *sua*; they confine their movements to graceful, subtle motions of the hands and arms. Men may jump from side to side, or in circles. In one version, men maintain a textless drone, while women sing four or eight verses, recounting legends.

### Tiap forau

Unlike *sua* and *tiap hïi*, which have a temperate character, *tiap forau* feature the exuberance of yelping and clowning; spectators may spontaneously join in. During the dance, the back row splits: the men come down one side of the group, the women down the other, until they meet in front, replacing the first row; the process continues until each row has had its turn in front. The texts usually acknowledge distinguished personages (especially chiefs acting as hosts), and praise people whose labors have contributed to the event (Hereniko 1991:130–131). Many *tiap forau* are in duple meter, transcribable as 2/4 time; some are in a triply compound meter, transcribable as 6/8 time.

### Twentieth-century developments

Wesleyan and Roman Catholic missionaries introduced hymns, which are central in Rotuman sacred contexts, and even occur in secular ones. In 1927–1928, C. M. Churchward prepared the Rotuman Wesleyan hymnal, *Him Ne Rot Uesli;* others revised it in 1986–1989. It contains 405 Rotuman hymns in sol-fa notation.

Performances of hymns take two styles: one is based on four-part harmony; in the other, *mak pel,* a struck metal idiophone keeps time. Gatherings of the Methodist Youth Fellowship sing religious songs in English and Rotuman, sometimes between skits on biblical themes.

Rotumans have adopted foreign styles of singing and dancing as they have come to know them through travel, films, radio (mostly Fijian stations), and video. In the 1990s, many Rotumans knew of the Sāmoan *māʻuluʻulu* (via its Tongan analog) and *sāsā,* the Fijian *vakamalolo,* and dances from Tahiti, Kiribati, and elsewhere. Pan-Polynesian harmonized music is popular, with Rotuman words often substituted for the originals. The favorite foreign musical genre is Rarotongan, introduced by Rarotongans who in the late 1940s visited Rotuma for months. Rotumans associate Rarotongan-style dances with playtimes.

—ALAN HOWARD

## TOKELAU

The atolls of Tokelau are nearly 500 kilometers north of Western Sāmoa. Fakaofo, Nukunonu, and Atafu, though out of sight from one another across 80 kilometers of ocean, share much history and culture. Each atoll supports a single village, concentrated on an islet on the west (lee) side of a lagoon. The combination of small size and geographic isolation has made the indigenous populations vulnerable to foreign influence.

With a mass exodus (to ʻUvea), wholesale religious conversion, kidnapping, epidemics of fatal diseases, and large-scale alienation of land and settlement to immigrant Europeans, the demographic history of the islands was miserable (Hooper and Huntsman 1973:385). In the 1860s, slavers removed more than half the population of Fakaofo and Nukunonu. The remainder, demoralized by novel diseases and natural disasters, adopted a new cultural order, based on Christianity. The London Missionary Society, which dominated Atafu and Fakaofo, discouraged traditional forms of expression: it prohibited old dances and (in church contexts) the Tokelau language, and lent its prestige to Sāmoan missionaries' introduction of Sāmoan tales, music, and dances, and the Sāmoan language. Only in Nukunonu, in the sphere of Roman Catholic dominance, did the old arts find a secure place in the new order. Though Tokelau bears the marks of contrastive missionizing groups, the atolls increasingly share their musical genres.

The music of Tokelau owes much to the connections it had in the 1800s and early 1900s. ʻUvea was the nearest missionizing headquarters of the Roman Catholic Church. From the 1910s to 1925, Tuvalu was the center for Tokelauan administration by the Gilbert and Ellice Islands Colony. After 1925, ʻUpolu (the most populous Sāmoan island), headquarters of the Protestant mission, was the site of New Zealand's Tokelauan administration.

Several times in the twentieth century, storms devastated Tokelau. The 1966 disaster prompted the administration to begin a program of resettlement in New Zealand. At first, the government approved as migrants only young married couples; later, to set up complete communities, it included those of all ages. By the 1970s, Tokelauans had communities in several centers—Hutt Valley (Wellington), Porirua, Taupo, Rotorua, and Auckland—where they maintained a Tokelauan identity in performing, going to church, and having community-based events. Despite this migration, depopulation of the Tokelau Islands did not occur; and since the 1970s, the numbers on each atoll have remained about the same.

In 1962, to investigate the chance of political union or association with another Pacific state, Tokelauan representatives visited Western Sāmoa and the Cook Islands. They chose to keep their ties with Aotearoa. Tokelauans are citizens of New Zealand, with free entry into the country, and the Tokelau Islands are internally self-governing.

The 1980s saw Tokelauans take all positions of responsibility in the administration of their islands. Interinsular cooperation increased markedly—even between islands that through much of the historic period had been enemies. This cooperation led to the publication of *Matagi Tokelau* (1991), an extensive book on indigenous history and traditions. The book required cooperative debate on competing versions of history.

## Musical contexts and genres

The people of Nukunonu sing *tuala* while a newly married couple parade around the village, and funeral laments (*haumate*) while mourning over a body. On these occasions, they may use examples of other genres (hymns, modern dances); but, for funerals and weddings, they maintain and value the old songs. At occasions perceived to be momentous, such as major interinsular councils (*fono*), they use them as treasured historic icons. In the 1980s, schools began including them in the curriculum.

*Tuala* and *haumate* are distinct musical genres. Their variations suggest a more extensive repertory of types in the past. In *tuala* (also called *hoa*), the voices move without a break from one line to the next. A fast tempo associates *tuala* with dance-songs (*hiva hahaka*) and dances with paddles (*tafoe*).

*Haumate* (also called *vale*) have a distinct verse-and-refrain construction. Their singing proceeds slowly and solemnly. After each verse (*patiga*) comes a refrain (*tali*), which in figure 27 is "*mo ia ē.*"

Vonu e, Vonu, Vonu, te lagi maohaoha.
Ni aua, ni aua hē tanu kelekelea,
Kae tanu, kae tanu ki kāpiti te kamea.
Ni aua, ni aua hē paepae fatua,
Kae pae, kae pae ki lei e fualima,
Kae pae, kae pae ki lei e fuaiva.
Ni aua, ni aua hē putu atu ki uta,
Kae putu, kae putu fonu toho ma ulua.
Ni aua, ni aua hē tagihia ki mata,
Kae tagi, kae tagi ki pu e ganagana.
Vonu e, vonu, vonu, te lagi maohaoha.

O Vonu, Vonu, Vonu, the sky is too high.
Don't, don't bury him in the ground,
But bury him, bury him in the turtle's safekeeping.
Don't, don't line the grave with stones,
But line it, line it with fifty pearlshells,
But line it, line it with ninety pearlshells.
Don't, don't let it happen on land,
But bring, but bring good luck to the people.
Don't cry, don't cry with your eyes,
But cry with the voice of the grave.
O Vonu, Vonu, Vonu, the sky is too high.

FIGURE 27 The beginning of "*Vonu e,*" a Tokelau funeral lament; sung by Fafie Pahelio, Iohefo Perez, Apolo Ioakimi, and Kotelano Kele, in November 1986 (after Thomas et al. 1990:22–23).

Vo— nu  e,   Vo— nu,   Vo— nu, te  la— gi mo— o—ha—o— ha,  mo  i— a  ē.

The invocation to Vonu probably refers to the turtle as a god. After some repetitions, a *haumate* concludes with the words *outou tino,* a terminal downglide (*fakalā*).

### Celebrations

Celebrations (*fiafia*) include all gatherings that involve singing and dancing: religious festivals, nuptial feasts, meetings, receptions. The most common items at a celebration are *fātele,* songs created in the first decades of the twentieth century, resembling the Tuvaluan dance of the same name. For celebrations, people rehearse *fātele* assiduously, but they sing them spontaneously in many settings: working, traveling, and playing cricket, in which the side batting entertain themselves with music (*lape*). For Tokelauans living abroad, *fātele* evoke strong reminiscences of Tokelau (Thomas 1996).

The text of each *fātele* is short, usually two to four lines:

Amutia mua koe e mamoe te fāhua e, Fāhua.
Ka ko kita nei e hē mamoe te fāhua e.
Taeao, te fakatinoga o ilāmutu e!
Taeao, te fakatinoga o mātua e!

You're really lucky to doze like a clam, Clam.
But I myself don't doze like a clam.
Tomorrow, O the children's performance!
Tomorrow, O the parents' performance!

A typical performance repeats such a stanza, usually three to six times. After the first statement of the stanza, the pitch of the music rises, and the tempo begins to accelerate. A box drum (*pōkihi*) controls the pace. The singers and other instrumentalists sit with the *pōkihi,* behind the dancers. Distinctive traits of the *fātele* are the gestures (*taga*) and dancing in a progressively lower stance (*koli ki lalo*) as the tempo accelerates.

With *fātele* occur several short dances accompanied by song or rhythm. The most elaborate of these, *hui-unu* 'changing lines', may last longer than the performance of the *fātele*; it lets the front line be replaced by another row. The most frequently performed short dance, the *tuku,* vigorously concludes the performance of a *fātele,* and continues the acceleration and heightened dynamics of the final portion of the dance. *Tuku* may end any *fātele* and are a troupe's stock in trade for a particular occasion, often having been created by the dancers. (*Tuku* often exploit movements that would not be acceptable in the *fātele* itself.) The *tū,* a short rhythmic burst, allows the dancers to stand together; it may be performed with any *fātele.* One short dance is performed only with its companion *fātele.* This is the short introductory *taki,* an infrequently performed item. The *taki* is created by the composer of the *fātele.* When several short dances are associated with a *fātele,* the result is a suite with textual, melodic, tempo, and dynamic contrasts.

If the occasion is right, celebrations may include old dances and new ones, like the *pehe lagilagi,* a choral composition modeled on the Sāmoan *laulausiva:* a sitting choir performs it, guided by a standing and dancing conductor. Celebrations usually require competitive singing, which alternates between two groups of performers, sta-

Shininess comes from oiled skin, the surfaces of leaves, and bright, colorful plastic occasionally substituted for flowers or treated fibers. It is visual and kinesthetic, implicating costume and dance.

FIGURE 28   At the Pacific Festival of Arts, similar costumes adorn Tokelau men and women: *a,* men perform movements with paddles; *b,* in a *fātele,* members of a mixed group perform a characteristic arm movement in outstretched diagonals. Photos by Adrienne L. Kaeppler, 1996.

(*a*)

(*b*)

tioned at either end of the house, or (in Aotearoa) in a school or church hall. Besides elders who oversee the proceedings, all present take part in the singing and dancing. The audience for one performance will be the performers in the next. At the end of each *fātele,* to cue the other side to begin performing, the singers declaim the phrase *ō fanatu ē* 'going over there'. The choice of songs, the jokes and entertainments, the costumes, the excitement of the singing and dancing, the appearance of new or beloved compositions, the provocative speeches—all add to the mood. But the competition is informal: seldom are there judges or the awarding of prizes. The winner is by common consent the side that gains ascendency through the evening.

The Tokelau dance costume shows preference for color, fragrance, and shininess. While uniformity is often the goal (figure 28), room remains for individuality in floral ornaments and other features. Shininess, which Tokelauans designate *gigila,* comes from oiled skin, the surfaces of leaves, and bright, colorful plastic, occasionally substituted for flowers or treated fibers. *Gigila* is a quality that shines and moves. It is visual and kinesthetic, implicating costume and dance. Personal decorations—garlands of flowers, leaves, or fibers, placed around the head and neck—emphasize the Tokelauan concept of the sacredness of the head. Close attention is paid to the skirt-and-waist ornament (*titi*).

### Games

Many indigenous games (*tafaoga*) contain short songs, some of which resemble those of neighboring West Polynesian islands. In the children's game *tulituli* appear aspects of games from Sāmoa and Tuvalu. In the Tokelau game, the players squat in a circle, making a tower of fists, with the index finger vertically extended. In turn, each hand grasps the index finger below. For each tower, they recite this rhyme.

| | |
|---|---|
| Tulituli, pakilagi, | *Tulituli*, low on the horizon, |
| Tautafa mai ke potipoti: | [Flapping near me:] |
| O le mumea ma le fagamea. | Either that fish or this fish. |
| Famo la le ki a [——], | Therefore go to [someone named], |
| Ke hogi la ki tona kaokao. | To smell his armpit. |

When the rhyme ends, the player whose hand is on top lifts the hand from the tower, smells it, and places it behind his back. The first player to remove both hands is the winner (Thomas 1995).

Major sports include wrestling (*fāgatua*) and casting darts (*tagātika*, also called *velo*). In the latter, contestants single out the one whose dart has gone the shortest distance, humiliating him with a rhyme: *Keinā omaiā! / Takaho te fale, / Te fale o Meto* 'Come on! / Roof the house, / Meto's house'. This recalls a tale in which, for winning at *tagātika*, Alo must marry the repulsive woman Meto.

### Tales

Tokelauans have a repertory of tales (*kakai*) by which older narrators entertain audiences, mainly at night. At high points in the narratives, short songs (*tagi*) occur. Listeners who know a *tagi* join the narrator in singing. Many people, young and old, know examples. *Tagi* are among the simplest pieces of music in the Tokelauan repertory, but they have been little studied (Vonen 1992).

## Composition

Besides the discursive *pehe lagilagi* and several types in the historic repertory, late-twentieth-century Tokelauan songs are short. Listeners cannot fully understand them without an accompanying story—a tale, an historic account (*tala anamua*), a biblical story, or another narrative. To the *fātele*, composers (*pulotu*) adapt old texts, especially of *tagi* and *hiva hahaka*. Performers may compose *fātele* for a particular occasion, but composers known as *pulotu* are older men or women who have a high reputation (Thomas and Tuia 1990) [see COMPOSITIONAL PROCESSES]. Musical texts may be in Sāmoan (especially for the *laulausiva* and *māuluulu*), Tuvaluan (for *fātele* or *mako*), or other languages.

An important feature of local music and dance is typological innovation. Adapting several Pacific genres, Tokelauans have created new local items: the *hake*, a texted dance with sticks, from 'Uvea; the *māuluulu*, a choral dance, from the Sāmoan *māuluʻulu*; and the *upaupa*, a lively dance, brought from Pukapuka in the 1920s.

## Musical instruments

Most organological interest in Tokelau concerns a reference to a drum the U.S. Exploring Expedition saw in the 1830s. Without acknowledging a source, Gordon MacGregor (1937:75) described a Tokelau drum (*pasu*) made from *kanava* wood.

FIGURE 29  In front of drummers playing struck plaques, Tokelauan dancers move *televalevale*—in whichever direction they please. Photo by Father MacDonald, 1960s.

Makers burned one end of a section of trunk, which they hollowed to a depth measuring from the fingertips to the elbow. Over the open end, they pulled the dried skin of a shark and lashed it under the rim. In the 1980s, Tokelauans did not use or remember such an instrument.

Of much importance is the struck plaque (*papa*), which makes a light, brittle sound. With it, elders direct the historic dances (*hiva hahaka, tafoe*) and other old songs. It is an ordinary mat-weaving board (*papa fai lalangi*), which players beat with two *gagie*-wood sticks. Several such plaques once accompanied dancing (figure 29); but by the 1980s, dances required only a single instrument.

For postcontact dances (*fātele* and others), Tokelauans use the *pokihi*, a specially constructed box drum, sometimes with a tin (*apa*) that once held thick, hard biscuits. They play the *pokihi* with palms of their hands; several performers around the box add to the accompaniment. In other contexts, people use other instruments: in cricket, an empty tin; in some introduced dances, a rolled mat (*fala*) and a handheld log idiophone (*pātē*); in church, a *pātē* for accompanying hymns (*pehe lotu*).

The *logo,* a log idiophone, gives signals. It marks the opening of village councils and the announcing of legislative decisions, made by the local police, in a formal *vakai* 'shout'. A bell rings for Christian services and meetings of the congregation. Several other instruments—whistle, gas bottle, tin drum, bugle—summon community groups. Children's playthings include an orally resonated lamellaphone (*ūtete*) and leaf whistles (*pū lau, pū launiu*). A *fagufagu* is a papaya-stem whistle. A *tagihuhu* is a hollow-eyed coconut, wailing or moaning when it is thrown.   —ALLAN THOMAS

## TUVALU

Tuvalu consists of nine low coral islands on the northwestern margin of Polynesia. Known as the Ellice Islands when it was part of a British protectorate (1892) and colony (1916–1974), it became an independent nation in 1978. Inhabitants of all its islands (other than the part-Micronesians of Nuui) are Polynesian. The total national population does not exceed ten thousand, but differences among the musical practices and repertories of the islands reflect differences in historical experience. Only the musics of Niutao, Nanumanga, and Nukufetau have been studied in detail.

Little is known of the lifeways of Tuvalu before the mid-1800s, when representatives of the London Missionary Society (LMS) began to take an interest in the archipelago. Their observations speak of "heathen . . . [performing] incantations to prevent the introduction of disease" (Gill 1885:19), "crowds of men . . . besmeared with ashes mixed with oil, each wearing the sacred leaflet on the left arm, with necklaces and flowers, . . . dancing and performing their wild incantations to the gods during the night" (Gill 1885:22, for Nanumanga), and "meat-offerings . . . laid on the altars, accompanied by songs and dances in honour of the god" (Turner 1884:292, for Nanumea).

Other sources of facts about precontact musical culture are oral histories, which name and tell of several kinds of songs and dances associated with ritual practices. On Funāfuti, *taanga* were sung in the cult of certain gods, and as part of the ceremonial presentation of turtles' heads to the high chief (*aliki tutu*), as were *teletele*:

> On hearing the cry, '*Ulufonu! Ui e! E!*', the *aliki tutu* would come from his dwelling to sit on a mat with the *malae* between him and his subjects. From the crowd would come a song, called the *taanga,* and some would dance towards the *aliki tutu*. A *taanga* was customarily a chant commemorating some feat of renown by a warrior of the island. The actual delivery of the turtle's head to the *aliki tutu* was made during a dance, a *teletele,* performed by either a man or a woman from one of the fighting families. . . . The *teletele* would be danced by a man if the offering were the head of a male turtle, or by a woman if the gift were the head of a female turtle. (Roberts 1958:412).

Such reports provide some terms related to poetry, music, and dance, but the resulting picture is vague, and can be filled in only by historical reconstruction based on later data.

Between 1862 and the late 1870s, the population of Tuvalu converted to Christianity, mainly through the efforts of Sāmoan evangelists, who imposed their own standards of conduct and spread Sāmoan musical influence. The forced abolition of indigenous religious practices and changes in social organization—in particular, in the chief's ritual status—made indigenous ritual songs and dances obsolete. Sāmoan pastors also suppressed dances they deemed obscene; for instance, they stopped the people of Funāfuti from dancing on their feet, because in Sāmoa such dancing sometimes had connotations of sexual license (David 1899:67).

The missionaries introduced choral religious singing patterned after Sāmoan and European models, and supported nonliturgical singing and dancing in praise of the new religion and its protagonists. Nevertheless, older practices of singing and dancing survived into the 1960s, when the German ethnographer Gerd Koch undertook a musical survey as part of general ethnographic research. He predicted that the old songs would disappear with the elders who remembered them; however, in 1990, some of these resounded anew, perhaps triggered by ethnographers' interest, and fostered by pride in the achievement of national sovereignty. The following sketch of the music of Tuvalu, based largely on materials collected by Koch, draws on analyses of performances recorded in 1960–1961 and 1963, with verbal data collected at the time (Christensen 1964).

## Indigenous traditions

As was or is the case in much of Polynesia, the presentation of poetry through vocalization, movement, and ornamentation was in Tuvalu the main purpose of making music. For the men's dance (*fakanau*) of Niutao and Nukufetau, men would sit in a circle, accompanying the words of a song with movements of the hands, arms, head, and upper body; or they would perform kneeling or standing, but without moving about. Women would similarly perform *onga*. Performers of either dance might be joined by members of the opposite sex. Instrumental sounds, apart from those of log idiophones (*pātē* on Niutao, *nafa* on Nanumanga), beaten mats or fans, and clapping, were ancillary.

Three distinct styles of vocal delivery are part of practices that predate European-Christian influences: choral rhythmic recitation of poetry without fixed tones (parlando recitative), rhythmic recitation on one tone without any melodic movement (monotone recitative), and the singing of poetry on the tones of a triad. The two types of recitation resemble each other in all regards but the use of fixed tones: faithful reciting of the poetry appears to be the main concern. In some recorded instances, the same text is performed either way, or both ways combine in one performance (Christensen and Koch 1964:32–33). Typically, the tempo of the reciting increases over multiple repetitions, as does the volume, and the whole performance ends with a shouted formula (Linkels 1994: tracks 5, 6, 8).

The examples recorded by Koch on Niutao, Nanumanga, and Nukufetau were performed by elders who had learned them decades earlier. Performers usually said the poetry was old. The examples from Niutao were described as dance-songs of three genres (*fakanau, fakatapatapa, onga*), or as game-related songs, all of them considered old. On Nanumanga, equivalent genres are the *utu tanga,* the *fakahuahua,* the *tī,* and the *mako mo tahaonga.* On Nukufetau, such genres are the *mako manea* and the *mako tafao*—dances and songs that in the 1960s lived only in fading memory.

Triadic songs—short strophic pieces, whose melodies move exclusively or mostly on the steps of a triad—are documented for Tuvalu only on Niutao, but have parallels elsewhere in Oceania. These melodies are performed mostly in a much slower inner tempo. The melodic shape seems to prevail over the need to enunciate the poetry clearly. Some items (*fakanau* and *onga*) are performed in this style, which appears distinct from the recitational ones, but shares with them the use as dance-songs and the shouted or spoken endings (Linkels 1994: track 18).

### Sāmoan influences

Apparently from Sāmoa came a musical style that has remained popular throughout Tuvalu. A soloist sings a text on a melody that uses a five-tone scale, or emphasizes five tones in a six- or seven-tone scale; the melodic range often exceeds an octave. A chorus then answers with a different melodic phrase. In strophic repetitions, the melodic lines of soloist and chorus overlap to produce a distinctive form of polyphony (Linkels 1994: tracks 13–17). In contrast to recitations (which focus on a clear enunciation of the poetry), these songs often put extended melodic turns over single syllables, and have strongly differentiated rhythmic patterns, favoring musical elements over verbal ones.

The five-tone responsorial style is associated in Niutao and Nukufetau with the genres *mako fakaseasea* and *mako fakatangitangi,* dances considered old in the 1960s, but mostly postdating the Sāmoan missionaries' arrival. Standing, men and women, gestured with their hands and arms, or clapped on main beats. They took only occasional steps. The texts usually refer to new experiences, datable people, and later events—such as tobacco from Germany, Sāmoan pastors, and the construction of a church on Niutao about 1910. Though details of how this style spread from Sāmoa to Tuvalu are sketchy, there is little doubt that it was popular from the late 1800s to about 1950—a period when it affected genres other than the two categories of dances, increasingly incorporated elements of Western styles, and on Funāfuti served as a vehicle for singing hymns (David 1899:20):

> After the prayer came a hymn. . . . One man started and got through half a line, when all others joined, in harmony, such a weird savage harmony, but still harmony. . . . The natives sang in many parts, from the high-pitched nasal reedy treble to deep thunderous bass . . . and such perfect time. . . . Instead of decreasing the pace, when coming to the end of a song or hymn, the Funafutians always increase it considerably; and just as you think you are going on at express speed—stop!

With Christianity and the formation of churches initially led by Sāmoan pastors came the singing of LMS hymns in their Sāmoan versions, and since the 1950s, Tuvaluan-composed hymns in syncretic styles. Four-part harmony and trained choirs in turn influenced secular singing in such topical genres as *fātele* and *vīki,* based on Sāmoan imports. Since the 1960s, young people have followed Western and Oceanic models of popular music, with the use of guitars—and since the 1980s, electronic instruments.

An increasing sense of national identity, participation in Pacific Festivals of Art, and the value placed by foreign researchers on old styles and genres, have contributed to the revival, in some instances in self-conscious and folklorized forms, of practices that in the 1960s seemed moribund. Innovations include abolition of old distinctions of gender (such as women's singing of fishing-magic songs, once a male prerogative), the organization of troupes to represent Tuvalu abroad, and an increased competitive spirit, manifested musically in faster tempi and the periodic raising of pitches during performances, until singers reach the upper limits of their vocal ranges.

—DIETER CHRISTENSEN

## REFERENCES

Adams, Henry. 1951. *The Selected Letters of Henry Adams.* Edited by Newton Arvin. New York: Farrar, Straus & Young.

Bataillon, Pierre. 1932. *Langue d'Uvea (Wallis): Grammaire uvea-français, Dictionnaire français-uvea-anglais.* Paris: Librairie Orientaliste Paul Geuthner.

Beaglehole, J. C. 1967. *The Journals of Captain James Cook on His Voyages of Discovery: The Voyage of the Resolution and Discovery 1776–1780.* Cambridge: Hakluyt Society.

Biggs, Bruce. 1980. "The Position of East 'Uvea and Anutan in the Polynesian Language Family." *Te Reo* 22–23:115–134.

Buck, Peter H. 1930. *Samoan Material Culture.* Bulletin 75. Honolulu: Bishop Museum.

Burrows, Edwin Grant. [1932.] Notebooks W1 and W4. Bishop Museum, Honolulu.

———. 1936. *Ethnology of Futuna.* Bulletin 138. Honolulu: Bishop Museum.

———. 1937. *Ethnology of 'Uvea (Wallis Island).* Bulletin 145. Honolulu: Bishop Museum.

———. 1945. *Songs of Uvea and Futuna.* Bulletin 183. Honolulu: Bishop Museum.

Calnon, William Lee. 1926. *Seeing the South Sea Islands.* New York: Frederick H. Hitchcock.

Campbell, I. C. 1983. "Imperialism, Dynasticism and Conversion: Tongan Designs on 'Uvea (Wallis Island), 1835–52." *Journal of the Polynesian Society* 92(2):155–167.

Christensen, Dieter. 1964. "Old Musical Styles in the Ellice Islands, Western Polynesia." *Ethnomusicology* 8:34–40.

Christensen, Dieter, and Gerd Koch. 1964. *Die Musik der Ellice-Inseln.* Veröffentlichungen des Museums, Neue Folge 5, Abteilung Südsee 2. Berlin: Museum für Völkerkunde.

Churchward, C. Maxwell. 1937. "Rotuman Legends." *Oceania* 8(2):247–260.

Collocott, Ernest Edgar Vyvyan. 1928. *Tales and Poems of Tonga.* Bulletin 46. Honolulu: Bishop Museum.

David, Edgeworth, (Mrs.). 1899. *Funafuti or Three Months on a Coral Island: An Unscientific Account of a Scientific Expedition.* London: Murray.

Eason, William. 1951. *A Short History of Rotuma.* Suva: Government Printing Department.

Eustis, Nelson. 1979. *Aggie Grey of Samoa.* Adelaide, South Australia: Hobby Investments.

Fletcher, William. 1866. Letter from Rotuma. *The Wesleyan Missionary Notices,* 37. Sydney: Australasian Wesleyan Methodist Conference.

Forster, George. 1777. *A Voyage Round the World in His Britannic Majesty's Sloop* Resolution, *Commanded by Capt. James Cook.* 2 vols. London.

Gaillot. Marcel. 1962. "Katoaga et danses à Futuna." *Missions des Iles* 114:63–66.

Gardiner, J. Stanley. 1898. "Natives of Rotuma." *Journal of the Royal Anthropological Institute* 27:396–435, 457–524.

Gill, W. Wyatt. 1885. *Jottings from the Pacific.* London: Religious Tract Society.

Hale, Horatio. 1846. *Ethnology and Philology.* Vol. 6 of *Narrative of the U.S. Exploring Expedition.* Edited by Charles Wilkes. Philadelphia: C. Sherman.

Hereniko, Vilsoni. 1991. "Dance as a Reflection of Rotuman Culture." In *Rotuma: Hanue Pumua (Precious Land),* ed. Anselmo Fatiaki et al., 120–142. Suva: Institute of Pacific Studies, University of the South Pacific.

Hooper, Antony, and Judith Huntsman. 1973. "A Demographic History of the Tokelau Islands." *Journal of the Polynesian Society* 82:366– 411.

Jenkins, John Stilwell. 1890. *Adventures in and Around the Pacific and Antartic* [sic] *Oceans.* New York: Hurst.

Kaeppler, Adrienne L. 1967a. "Preservation and Evolution of Form and Function in Two Types of Tongan Dance." In *Polynesian Culture History: Essays in Honor of Kenneth P. Emory,* ed. Genevieve A. Highland, Roland W. Force, Alan Howard, Marion Kelly, and Yosihiko H. Sinoto, 503–536. Special Publication 56. Honolulu: Bishop Museum.

———. 1967b. "The Structure of Tongan Dance." Ph.D. dissertation, University of Hawai'i.

———. 1970. "Tongan Dance: A Study in Cultural Change." *Ethnomusicology* 14:266–277.

———. 1974. "A Study of Tongan Panpipes with a Speculative Interpretation." *Ethnos* 39:102–128.

———. 1983. *Polynesian Dance, With a Selection for Contemporary Performances.* Hawai'i: Alpha Delta Kappa.

Kaurasi, Mosese. 1991. "Rotuman Chants, Sports and Pastimes." In *Rotuma: Hanue Pumua (Precious Land),* ed. Anselmo Fatiaki et al., 143–152. Suva: Institute of Pacific Studies, University of the South Pacific.

Keeler, Charles. 1903. "My Friend Leóta: A Samoan Sketch." *Out West* 18:569–578.

Krämer, Augustin. 1903. *Die Samoa Inseln.* Vol. 2. Stuttgart: Nägele.

Kubuabola, S., et al. 1978. "Poetry in Fiji: A General Introduction." In *Essays on Pacific Literature,* ed. Ruth Finnegan and Raymond Pillai, 2:7–19. Suva: Fiji Museum.

Labillardière, J. J. 1802. *An Account of a Voyage in Search of La Pérouse . . . Under the Command of Rear-Admiral Bruni D'Entrecasteaux.* London: Uphill.

Likuvalu, Apeleto. 1977. Cérémonie d'investiture de Tuiagaifo, roi d'Alo (île Futuna), le 20 avril 1974." *Journal de la Société des Océanistes* 33(56–57):219.

Linkels, Ad. 1994. *Tuvalu: A Polynesian Atoll Society.* PAN 2055CD. Compact disc with notes.

Loeb, Edwin M. 1926. *History and Traditions of Niue.* Honolulu: Bishop Museum.

Love, Jacob Wainwright. 1991. *Sāmoan Variations: Essays on the Nature of Traditional Oral Arts.* New York and London: Garland.

McKern, William C. N.d. "Tongan Material Culture." Manuscript. Honolulu: Bishop Museum Library.

MacGregor, Gordon. N.d. "Field Notes on Rotuma." Honolulu: Bishop Museum, manuscript SC MacGregor, Box 2.11.

———. 1937. *Ethnology of Tokelau Islands.* Bulletin 146. Honolulu: Bishop Museum Press.

Manuaud, Suzanne. 1983. *Futuna: Ethnologie et actualité.* Publications, 33. Nouméa: Société d'Études Historiques de la Nouvelle-Calédonie.

Marques, A. 1889. "Îles Samoa: notes pour servir à une monographie de cet archipel." *Bulletin de la Société de Géographie de Lisbonne,* 8th series, 1 and 2.

Martin, John, ed. 1818. *An Account of the Natives of the Tonga Islands.* 2 vols. London: Constable.

*Matagi Tokelau.* 1991. Apia and Suva: Office for Tokelau Affairs and Institute of Pacific Studies, University of the South Pacific.

Mayer, Raymond. 1973. "Éléments de la tradition orale de Wallis et Futuna." Thesis, University of Lyon 2.

———. 1976. *Les transformations de la tradition narrative à l'île Wallis ('Uvea).* Publications de la Société des Océanistes, 38. Paris: Musée de l'Homme.

———. 1987. "Les codes de la danse à l'île Wallis ('Uvea)." Doctorat d'État dissertation, University of Paris, Sorbonne.

Mayer, Raymond, and Malino Nau. 1973. "Un millier de légendes aux les Wallis et Futuna et divers éléments de la tradition orale." *Journal de la Société des Océanistes* 38:69–100.

———. 1976. "Chants funèbres de l'île Wallis: Description, analyse, commentaire." *Journal de la Société des Océanistes* 51:141–184, 52:271–279.

———. 1982. "'Talatuku o le Puke' ou ethno-politique de l'île Futuna." *Oceanic Studies* 11:23–31.

Milner, G. B. 1966. *Samoan Dictionary.* London: Oxford University Press.

Moyle, Richard M. 1974. "Samoan Musical Instruments." *Ethnomusicology* 18(1):57–74.

———. 1975. "Conch Ensembles: Tonga's Unique Contribution to Polynesian Organology." *Galpin Society Journal* 28:98–106.

———. 1985. *Report on Survey of Traditional Music of Niue.* Working Papers in Anthropology, Archaeology, Linguistics, Maori Studies, 67. Auckland: Department of Anthropology, University of Auckland.

———. 1987. *Tongan Music.* Auckland: Auckland University Press.

———. 1988. *Traditional Samoan Music.* Auckland: Auckland University Press.

Orange, James. 1840. *Life of the Late George Vason of Nottingham.* London: John Snow.

Penisimane. 1860s. Manuscript. Sydney: The Mitchell Library, manuscript A1686-25.

Powell, Thomas. 1886. "A Samoan Tradition of Creation and the Deluge." *Journal of the Victoria Institute* 29:147–175.

Pratt, George. 1911. *Pratt's Grammar & Dictionary of the Samoan Language.* 4th edition. Edited by J. E. Newell. Malua, Western Samoa: Malua Printing Press.

Quain, Buell Halvor 1942. *The Flight of the Chiefs: Epic Poetry of Fiji.* New York: J. J. Augustin.

Ravuvu, Aselele. 1988. *Development or Dependence: The Pattern of Change in a Fijian Village.* Suva: University of the South Pacific.

Roberts, R. G. 1958. "Te Atu Tuvalu: A Short History of the Ellice-Islands." *Journal of the Polynesian Society* 67:394–423.

Rozier, Claude. ed. 1960. *Écrits de S. Pierre Chanel.* Publications de la Société des Océanistes, 9. Paris: Musée de l'Homme.

Shumway, Larry V. 1981. "The Tongan *Lakalaka:* Music Composition and Style." *Ethnomusicology* 1981(3):467–479.

Stair, John B. 1897. *Old Samoa, or Flotsam and Jetsam from the Pacific Ocean.* London: Religious Tract Society.

Steele, Joshua. 1771. "Account of a Musical Instrument, Which was Brought by Captain Furneaux from the Isle of Amsterdam in the South Seas to London in the Year 1774, and

Given to the Royal Society, and Remarks on a Larger System of Reed Pipes from the Isle of Amsterdam, with Some Observations on the Nose Flute of Otaheite." *Philosophical Transactions of the Royal Society* 65:67–78.

Thomas, Allan. 1995. *Tokelau Tafaoga: Games.* Wellington: Asia Pacific Archive, School of Music, Victoria University of Wellington. Video.

———. 1996. *New Song and Dance from the Central Pacific: Creating and Performing the Fātele of Tokelau in the Islands and in New Zealand.* Dance & Music, 9. Edited by Wendy Hilton. Stuyvesant, N.Y.: Pendragon Press.

Thomas, Allan, and Ineleo Tuia. 1990. "Profile of a Composer: Ihaia Puka, Pulotu of the Tokelau Islands." *Oral Tradition* 5(2–3):267–282.

Thomas, Allan, Ineleo Tuia, and Judith Huntsman, eds. 1990. *Songs and Stories of Tokelau: An Introduction to the Cultural Heritage.* Wellington: Victoria University Press.

Thompson, Chris. 1971. "Fijian Music and Dance." *Transactions and Proceedings of the Fiji Society* 11:14–21.

Turner, George. 1861. *Nineteen Years in Polynesia: Missionary Life, Travels, and Researches in the Islands of the Pacific.* London: J. Snow.

———. 1884. *Samoa a Hundred Years Ago and Long Before.* London: Macmillan.

Violette, Louis-Théodore. 1879. Dictionnaire Samoa–Français Anglais – et Français–Samoa–Anglais précédé d'une Grammaire de la Langue Samoa. Paris: Maisonneuve.

Vonen, Arnfinn Muruvik. 1992. "A Tokelau Folktale." In *Kupu Mai Te Tūtolu,* ed. Ingjerd Hoëm, Even Hovdhaugen, and Arnfinn Muruvik Vonen, 89–168. Oslo: Institute for Comparative Research in Human Culture, Scandinavian University Press.

Wheeler, William Webb. 1907. *A Glimpse of the Isles of the Pacific.* N.p.: no publisher.

Whitaker, Hervey W. 1889. "Samoa: The Isles of the Navigators." *Century Magazine* 38:12–25.

Wilkes, Charles. 1845. *Narrative of the United States Exploring Expedition: During the Years 1838, 1839, 1840, 1841, 1842.* 5 vols. Philadelphia: C. Sherman.

# Polynesian Outliers

*Niko Besnier*  
*J. W. Love*  
*Michael D. Lieber*  
*Barbara G. Moir*  
*William Donner*  

*Jane Mink Rossen*  
*Raymond Firth*  
*Richard Feinberg*  
*Allan Thomas*

**Kapingamarangi**

**Takuu**

**Luangiua**

**Sikaiana**

**Bellona**

**Tikopia**

**Anuta**

**West Futuna**

The Polynesian outliers comprise about eighteen communities scattered along a northwest-southeast arc across Micronesia and Melanesia (see map). The people of these communities all speak Polynesian languages, in contrast to the people of surrounding societies, who speak non-Polynesian Oceanic languages. In social structure and culture, outlier societies have few traits in common, and other than for classificatory convenience, they do not form a distinct cultural area. Archaeological investigations, conducted in about half the outlier communities, have found evidence that prehistoric patterns of settlement were comparable among them.

## Geography

The northernmost Polynesian outliers are the tiny atolls of Nukuoro and Kapingamarangi, which lie south of the Caroline Islands and are politically integrated into the Federated States of Micronesia. Farther south, Nukuria, Takuu, and Nukumanu, all atolls, are in the Northern Solomons Province of Papua New Guinea. Nukumanu is geographically, culturally, and linguistically close to the large atoll of Luangiua, though the latter falls under the political jurisdiction of the Solomon Islands. Also in the Solomons are the atoll Sikaiana, the larger islands of Rennell and Bellona, Pileni in the Reef Islands and the culturally related Taumako in the Duff Islands, and Tikopia and Anuta, whose populations have long maintained close ties with one another.

Outliers politically integrated into the Republic of Vanuatu include two villages at the eastern end of Emae (Mae); Fila (Ifira), a small island in the middle of the harbor of Vila, and the village Mele, nearby; and Futuna and Aniwa, small islands near Tanna. Finally, Heo and Muli villages at the opposite ends of 'Uvea, an atoll in the Loyalty Islands (under the administration of New Caledonia), are inhabited by speakers of a Polynesian outlier language. To distinguish Futuna and 'Uvea from the islands of the same name farther east, linguists customarily call them West Futuna and West 'Uvea, respectively.

People from several outliers have set up migrant communities on larger Pacific islands. For example, a Kapingamarangi community lives on Pohnpei, and Tikopia settlements are in Honiara and the Russell Islands.

Polynesian
Outliers

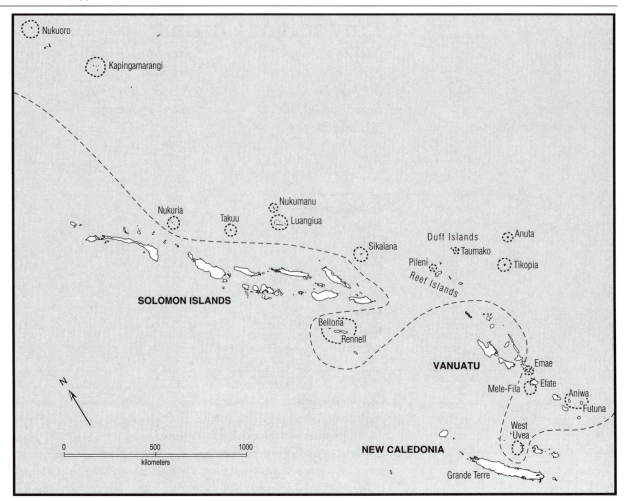

## Language

Language is the one undisputed criterion justifying the identification of Polynesian outlier islands and villages with the rest of Polynesia, rather than with their Melanesian and Micronesian neighbors. Though the structure and vocabulary of many Polynesian outlier languages (especially Mele-Fila, West Futunan, and West 'Uvean) have received strong influence from nearby non-Polynesian Oceanic languages, all outlier languages have features that identify them uncontroversially as Polynesian. Most outlier languages are poorly documented: lexicons and dictionaries have been published only for Anuta, Kapingamarangi, Nukuoro, Rennell-Bellona, Tikopia, West Futuna, and West 'Uvea; grammatical descriptions—none detailed—are available only for Luangiua, Nukuoro, Rennell-Bellona, and West Futuna.

These languages form two distinct subgroups, neither of which is made up exclusively of outlier languages: Ellicean (after the Ellice Islands, the former name of Tuvalu), which comprises languages spoken on all outliers north of Sikaiana, plus Tuvaluan; and Futunic, which includes all other outlier languages, plus East Futunan. The evidence for the unity of the former subgroup is stronger than for the latter. Because languages and their speakers do not always have the same history, archaeologists beware of drawing from the linguistic evidence inferences about prehistoric settlement and cultural development.

## Archaeology

Little archaeological research has been conducted on Polynesian outliers because many are small and hard to reach, and many are geologically unstable atolls—which means that finding and interpreting archaeological records are exceptionally difficult tasks. However, since Janet Davidson (1971) demonstrated that archaeology on atolls was possible, archaeological data from about half of the outlier communities have become available. They show that the prehistories of outlier Polynesian societies broadly shared some traits, but diverged significantly in others. As summarized by Patrick V. Kirch (1984), the settlement of several outliers, including Tikopia, Anuta, and Taumako, dates to about 1,000 B.C., roughly the same time as the settlement of West Polynesia. Some outliers appear to have been inhabited discontinuously over time, as the population may have been wiped out, perhaps repeatedly, by natural disasters, like hurricanes, tsunamis, and famines.

The settlement of the outliers was not a unique event, but the product of successive voyages, originating from different points. On most or all outliers, the Polynesian influence, which in all cases brought language and in some cases brought culture and a consequential population, was a later phenomenon. The linguistic evidence, and in some cases the cultural evidence, indicate that this influence originated in West Polynesia, though it is unknown whether the Polynesian settlers traveled directly from there or via other outliers or non-Polynesian islands. On several outliers, archaeologists have found evidence of sustained contacts with neighboring non-Polynesian societies. In every instance, the history of settlement exhibits great complexity.

## Society and culture

The society and culture of one outlier community, Tikopia, is the subject of a large corpus of writings by Raymond Firth, who conducted initial work on the island in the 1920s, when Tikopians still practiced indigenous religious rituals. The documentation of life on Tikopia presented in these writings (notably in Firth 1936) remains matchless for its scope, detail, and theoretical sophistication, and has made Tikopia one of the best-documented societies in the world. In contrast, little ethnographic information is available on other outlier communities. Exceptions are Luangiua (Hogbin 1934); Rennell and Bellona, investigated by a team of Danish ethnographers over several decades; and Anuta (Feinberg 1981). Other outliers are known through a handful of scholarly articles each, while virtually nothing has been published about some outlier communities, like West 'Uvea.

The extent to which the structure of outlier societies resembles typically Polynesian configurations depends largely on the extent to which the Polynesian settlers remained distinct from any non-Polynesian populations already established at the time of the Polynesians' arrival. At one extreme, the political and kinship systems of the Polynesian-speaking villages on West 'Uvea are indistinguishable from the social arrangements of the non-Polynesian-speaking inhabitants of the atoll, which follow patterns attested throughout the Loyalty Islands. At the other extreme, Tikopia closely resembles the high islands of West Polynesia in its chiefly system, kinship structure, economic life, and cultural underpinnings, including the elaboration of such concepts as mana and tabu.

The sociopolitical organization of outlier societies exhibits the same variation in the relative elaboration of hierarchy as occurs elsewhere in Polynesia—variation that according to Marshall Sahlins (1958) relates to such factors as the amount of resources to be managed and distributed, the size of the population, the amount and quality of cultivable land, the importance and complexity of religious rituals, and the importance and nature of emigration. At one extreme are outliers like Luangiua, where hierarchy was minimal and chiefly authority diluted, as is typical of small atolls elsewhere in Polynesia, including Tuvalu and the Tuamotus. At the other extreme is Tikopia, where chiefly authority is considerable, society is hierarchically ordered, and ascription is more important for chiefly rank than achievement, as is typical of Tonga.

Because contemporary outlier societies fall under the political jurisdiction of various nation-states (with different colonial histories), they vary in their access to economic resources and tokens of modernity, the mobility of their populations, and their relations to the polities of which they are part. Tikopians perceive themselves as significantly distinct from their Solomon Island compatriots, and despite the presence of Tikopian enclaves elsewhere in the country, they insistently maintain their cultural autonomy. In contrast, Polynesian-speaking West 'Uveans do not see themselves as significantly distinct from other groups in New Caledonia and the Loyalty Islands; in fact, they are at the forefront of a movement for Kanak independence.

—NIKO BESNIER

### Performing arts

Like other Polynesian music, that of the outliers is a voice-based system, with little instrumental elaboration. Indigenous songs are usually monophonic. Melodies sometimes move in parallel octaves, sometimes with simultaneous tonal variations. Rhythms usually stress downbeats, with little or no syncopation from singers or the typical accompaniments of clapping hands or striking a wooden plaque or a rolled-up mat. Some songs require the immediate repetition of stanzas. Texts typically tell or imply stories, often with conspicuous metaphors. In two textual traits, the outliers contrast with much of West Polynesia: the music systems allow words to have shapes phonemically different from their shapes as ordinarily spoken, and the ends of phrases or lines do not regularly rhyme [see LANGUAGE IN MUSICAL SETTINGS]. Musical genres and tonalities resemble those of West Polynesia, but dances combine elements typical of West Polynesian and nearby Melanesian cultures.

—J. W. LOVE

### KAPINGAMARANGI

Kapingamarangi has a population of five hundred people, called Kapinga, who fish and garden. For most of its history, it has been one of the most isolated Pacific atolls. Colonial contact began in 1877, and the people converted to Christianity—Roman Catholic and Congregational—in 1917. On Pohnpei in 1919, Kapinga founded the resettled village Porakied (1998 population about 750). Anthropologists of the Südsee-Expedition studied the music in 1910, and Kenneth Emory (1965) used it to reconstruct the ancient religion. In 1965, when I began research, older people recalled the religious music but considered it sinful, an embarrassing leftover from "the time of darkness."

Kapinga people recognize two classes of music: *daahili* and *langa*. Certain *langa* were performed without instrumental accompaniment, but included dance (*koni*)—moving knees and feet in place with arms outstretched while standing or, in the ritual celebrating the birth of a child, with women sitting.

From visitors in the 1890s, Kapinga teenagers adapted the Scottish-Highland reel, but the population ceased dancing after conversion to Christianity. Kapinga learned to sing Japanese popular music before World War II and American popular music thereafter, accompanied by ukuleles, guitars, and harmonicas. Young people compose songs in Western major keys and 4/4 time, mixing English and Pohnpeian words with their own language, often as euphemisms.

## Daahili

Precontact songs were one-line phrases that alluded to events in a person's life—being jilted by a lover, being treated unjustly, accusations of theft, getting caught in a tryst, and the like. Victims of others' delicts or callousness composed their own songs, singing them to close friends, who would sing them to others. Songs about thievery and buffoonery could be composed by anyone who knew of the events.

*Daahili* were ephemeral and short (four or eight beats at moderate tempo), with one line—such as *Di budala ne kae go ai?* 'Who stole the taro pudding?'—repeated until people tired of it. Songs were a playful form of gossip, meant, like other gossip, to flow through networks of friends and kin until they reached a perpetrator. As Kapinga learned Western dances, young people began having parties for dancing, modifying songs to fit the rhythm of the steps.

## Langa

*Langa* were serious pieces, with standards of rhythmic tension and variation, textual fit, and lyric grace. They included religious and secular items, distinguished by content, not by separate terms.

### *Religious langa*

Religious *langa* were classified by their places in particular rituals, and these places corresponded with distinctive rhythmic patterns. While new pandanus-leaf mats were being installed in the temple, melodies had a distinctive duple rhythm at moderate tempo, with texts like the following.

| | |
|---|---|
| Gei lakeia go di Mangodahola. | Then Mongodoholo put on his regalia. |
| Hoogouda e malidu, | He later mounted upon, |
| Lima dugu ee! lima gai ee! | Put his hands down *ee!* ate *ee!* |

The transformation of the name normally spoken as *Mongodoholo* exemplifies an important trait of Kapinga musical performance [see LANGUAGE IN MUSICAL SETTINGS: Sonics].

Melodies praising a particular god, occurring later in the rite, had a rhythm subdivided further: the first beat of every line was accented, and every syllable thereafter got a single beat, performed as fast as the performer could errorlessly mouth it, as with this text:

| | |
|---|---|
| Hongo di damana aligi! | At his place, the priest-father! |
| Le ge he udua, le ge dogo-dala-uda, | A promontory, a rock-stretching island, |
| Le ge mau senua, dogo-dala-uda! | Holding firm the land, rock-stretching island! |
| Le ge di ado Louwou le ge dagu haeha, | The descendants of Loua are my care, |
| Le ge tongiaa uda i dai. | The resounding of wood inland near shore. |

The "resounding of wood" came from the work of adzes as men hewed timber.

Ritual vocalizing was performed by the high priest (figure 1), other priests alone or in groups, other religious functionaries, or the congregation, depending on to whom the piece was directed and who was representing which sector of the community. Some males of the priestly class, eligible by descent (through females) to occupy the high priest's position, were selected young for training, which lasted for years. Before being selected to succeed to the high priesthood, trainees usually held lower positions in the panel of twenty priests.

FIGURE 1    Tawera wears the ceremonial clothing of a Kapingamarangi high priest (*ariki*): a hibiscus-bark loincloth and young coconut-leaf necklet, armbands, and headdress. Photo by Kenneth P. Emory, 1947. Bishop Museum.

### Secular *langa*

Secular *langa* were poetic accounts of events in people's lives. Commonly memorialized events were expeditions for catching fish, particularly collective netting expeditions. Competitive *langa* were composed by young men in the men's communal houses, where collective fishing and competitions for the largest catches and most spectacular feats of fish-catching finesse were organized. Competitions included songfests (*hagamada*). Affiliates of one men's house, having composed and practiced a set of pieces, competed with those of a rival house. The elders of the competing groups judged the quality of the pieces and the performances. Criteria included the fit between rhythmic patterns and lyrics, the ingenuity by which lyrics combined the clarity of the memorialized event and the artistic masking of the words by phonemic shifts, and the importance of the event. These compositional factors are denoted by the term *lee* 'sound', which denotes vocal pitch, timbre, tempo, and rhythm. Aural quality could be secondary to verbal content. A mediocre rendition of fishing for culturally important fish (like rainbow runners) was rated higher than a well-composed rendition of netting for unimportant ones (like small reef-dwelling fish). For entertainment, people sang competitive *langa* near the end of wakes.

Another large class of secular *langa* is *hehenga*, referring to sex and love. *Hehenga* are variable in length and rhythmic patterning, some as short as three lines, and others with eight stanzas of four lines each. The content of most is sexual activity, including metaphoric accounts of getting an erection, engaging in intercourse, and having specific sexual trysts. The bawdiest were sung mainly by men, usually in groups. The subtler ones were sung by men and women for ceremonies including those that closed major rituals, such as repairing the temple. Some recounted a couple's love with no explicit reference to sexual activity, invoking familiar images, like an item of clothing or a favorite piece of jewelry. Their slow tempos and gentle reflections on how one sees, hears, and remembers a lover contrast with the exuberance of other *langa*. Males or females sang them, sometimes at a loved one's wake.

Laments (*langa tangihangi*) are a small but important class of *langa*, usually composed by a person for a relative to sing at his or her funeral (Lieber 1991). Thereafter, they become family property, to be sung at the wakes of the composer's kin.

—MICHAEL D. LIEBER

## TAKUU

Takuu is an atoll of about twenty islets. About eight hundred people live in a single village, subsisting by gardening and fishing. For most social activities, kinship is the organizing principle. *Mako* 'songs (words and melody)' have two important classes: songs for dancing celebrate or narratively commemorate; incantations enlist the aid of ancestral spirits (*aitu*).

## Songs for dancing

Of genres that involve singing (*fua*) and dancing (*anu*), *tuki* are most frequently performed. *Tuki* recount feats of daring, prowess, and perseverance. Men perform some; women, others. Staged at community gatherings in the main street, they entertain and instruct. Participants wear new waistcloths, leaf garlands, and bead necklaces; between dances, relatives sprinkle talcum powder and cologne onto performers. *Tuki* last five to fifteen minutes, but in series may continue for hours, till the dancers collapse in exhaustion.

Performances are usually competitive: in style, energy, and difficulty, each of two groups (drawn from five lineages, or the halves of the island) tries to outdo the other. After one group performs several *tuki,* another counters with more. To improve the execution or respond to an enthusiastic reception, performers may repeat a *tuki* several times. When one group performs at length, fatigued or inexpert dancers drop out, and fresh ones join in. Women's competitive dancing makes a land-based parallel to men's competitive fishing: while men from one end of the village are trying to catch more fish than those from the other, their female counterparts are vying in dance. Weary fishermen return to a welcome from exhausted women, who teasingly compare the catches and divide up the fish.

Individual *tuki* belong to the lineages in which they arise. Each tells a tale associated with a relative, usually long deceased; most are several generations old. The antiquity of *tuki* that tell of the lineage-founding gods is uncertain. Most adults do not remember all the *tuki* of their lineage. Encyclopedic knowledge is the province of *purotu*, respected persons recognized as living repositories of musical material; learning the melodies, lyrics, and movements (*aauna*) can extend over many years. For little-known *tuki*, people consult *purotu* on points of accuracy.

In formal settings, *purotu* from all the lineages provide accompaniment, which consists of singing and using wooden drumsticks (*kaisamu*) to strike hollow log idiophones (*tuki*) and five-gallon tins. The lead musician determines the order of the *tuki,* each of which he announces by calling out the first few words. Seated facing the dancers, the instrumentalists play and sing slowly; the dancers respond with singing and movements. The tempo increases until the performance reaches a frenzied pace. Dancers may rhythmically clap their hands, slap their chests, and stamp their feet. Performances occur on a surface of fine coral gravel, and their last moments make a rousing blur—of bodies swaying, arms flailing, and feet kicking gravel into spectators' ranks.

A special variety of *tuki* is the boast (*afu*), whose texts typically proclaim the singer's or an ancestor's prowess at fishing. People perform *afu* competitively at village gatherings, and fishermen perform them on return from successful outings: the sound of the singing alerts waiting villagers to the results of a contest or the quantity of a catch. If a *purotu* is in a canoe, he leads the song. As the flotilla returns, successful fishermen stand in their canoes, dancing in triumph.

### Typical dance-song structure

The structure of a *tuki* links several sections: a prelude (*vvoro*), a lead (*usu*), and at least four stanzas: *puku mua* 'first stanza', *soa te puku* 'pair to the stanza', *toru naa puku* 'third stanza', *puku fakaoti* 'terminal stanza'. Each section ends in a refrain (*fati*). This structure is clear in a *tuki* that came to Takuu with a nineteenth-century immigrant from Luangiua. The languages spoken on Takuu and Luangiua may be regard-

The structural elements of *tuki*, Takuu songs for dancing, accompanied by hollowed log idiophones, with texts recounting feats of daring, prowess, and perseverance:

*fakamau fua*  A verse stated twice in the lead (*usu*) and in each stanza

*fati*  Refrain, ending the prelude (*vvoro*) and each stanza

*puku fakaoti*  Terminal stanza

*puku mua*  First stanza

*soa te puku*  "Pair to the stanza," second stanza

*usu*  Lead, following the prelude (*vvoro*) and its refrain (*fati*) and preceding the first stanza (*puku mua*)

*vvoro*  Prelude, ending in a refrain (*fati*)

ed as dialects of a single language (Howard 1981:101). In this text, Takuu singers make minor phonetic shifts, retaining most of the original vocabulary and syntax. The song chronicles a struggle with a shark: before the fisherman killed it, it had broken the canoe's outriggers, nearly capsizing the vessel. The term *onopupu* denotes an unidentified species of large shark, reported to attack canoes; *Peelau* is the local rendering of *Peilau*, a village of Luangiua; *Areahu* may be the shark's ritual name.

| | |
|---|---|
| *vvoro* | Taku tamana, |
| | Te vaka raa ee lanakina te ika ee fakamataku. |
| *fati* | Taha-te-uila, |
| | Teara raa ee lanakina te ika ee fakamataku. |
| | |
| *usu* | Kii sorokina taku vaka kaa fano ki tua. |
| | Te vaka raa ee lanakina te ika ee fakamataku. |
| | Kii sorokina *Kailopo* kaa fano ki tua. |
| | Te vaka raa ee lanakina te ika ee fakamataku. |
| *fati* | Taha-te-uila, |
| | Teara raa ee lanakina te ika ee fakamataku. |
| | |
| *puku mua* | Kii tuu varoina te ika ee kkofu mai, |
| | Te vaka raa ee lanakina te ika ee fakamataku. |
| | Kii tuu varo ifo ko uta i ana kofu, |
| | Te vaka raa ee lanakina te ika ee fakamataku. |
| *fati* | Taha-te-uila, |
| | Teara raa ee lanakina te ika ee fakamataku. |
| | |
| *soa te puku* | I taku ika raa see tau ki tana kau. |
| | Te vaka raa ee lanakina te ika ee fakamataku. |
| | I taku onopupu! ta-taaofi rima. |
| | Te vaka raa ee lanakina te ika ee fakamataku. |
| *fati* | Taha-te-uila, |
| | Teara raa ee lanakina te ika ee fakamataku. |
| | |
| *toru naa puku* | I naa te fenua ee seesee nifo mai. |
| | Te vaka raa ee lanakina te ika ee fakamataku. |
| | I naa Peelau ee seesee nifo mai. |
| | Te vaka raa ee lanakina te ika ee fakamataku. |
| *fati* | Taha-te-uila, |
| | Teara raa ee lanakina te ika ee fakamataku. |
| | |
| *puku fakaoti* | I fakasaaerea te nifo i tana soa. |
| | Te vaka raa ee lanakina te ika ee fakamataku. |
| | I fakasaaerea te nifo i Areahu. |
| | Te vaka raa ee lanakina te ika ee fakamataku. |

*fati*          Taha-te-uila,
               Teara raa ee lanakina te ika ee fakamataku.

               My father,
               The canoe was lifted out of the water by the fearsome fish.
               Taha-te-uila,
               Teara was lifted out of the water by the fearsome fish.

               My canoe was dragged out to sea.
               The canoe was lifted out of the water by the fearsome fish.
               *Kailopo* was dragged out to sea.
               The canoe was lifted out of the water by the fearsome fish.
               Taha-te-uila,
               Teara was lifted out of the water by the fearsome fish.

               Thrust upward by the fish as it struck the water in clouds of
                    spray,
               The canoe was lifted out of the water by the fearsome fish.
               Thrusting down and shoreward in its clouds of spray,
               The canoe was lifted out of the water by the fearsome fish.
               Taha-te-uila,
               Teara was lifted out of the water by the fearsome fish.

               O my fish did not hang from its hook.
               The canoe was lifted out of the water by the fearsome fish.
               O my shark! I caught it in my arms.
               The canoe was lifted out of the water by the fearsome fish.
               Taha-te-uila,
               Teara was lifted out of the water by the fearsome fish.

               O everyone is coming to ask me for [shark] teeth.
               The canoe was lifted out of the water by the fearsome fish.
               O the people of Peelau are coming to ask me for teeth.
               The canoe was lifted out of the water by the fearsome fish.
               Taha-te-uila,
               Teara was lifted out of the water by the fearsome fish.

               O the tooth is being torn away from its mate.
               The canoe was lifted out of the water by the fearsome fish.
               O the tooth is being torn away from Areahu.
               The canoe was lifted out of the water by the fearsome fish.
               Taha-te-uila,
               Teara was lifted out of the water by the fearsome fish.

A feature of all *tuki* is the *fakamau fua,* a verse stated twice in the lead and in each stanza.

### Fula and sau

Since the 1970s, to celebrate homecoming from high school (on Bougainville), females—usually girls and younger women—have sung and danced *fula,* primarily at impromptu family gatherings. In a circle, each dancer faces the back of another, moving her hands, arms, hips, and feet. Any young person with a guitar or a ukulele may add accompaniment, using three or four chords. *Fula* begin at a slow tempo, but quicken suddenly, when the musicians shout "*Fula! fula!*"

*Sau* are unaccompanied songs, performed by either men or women during a funeral and the subsequent period of mourning. Lyrics recount significant events in the lives of the deceased person's ancestors and ancestral gods, whose spiritual world he or she has entered. Motions and vocalizations are slow and solemn. Relatives of the deceased dance, often for hours.

### Incantations

At stages of ritualized fishing, men perform *kavai,* songs to ancestral spirits and Pakeva, goddess of the sea. The texts ask the spirits to protect the fishermen, make their canoes attractive to fish, and prevent poisoning; songs to Pakeva thank her for a bountiful catch, and ask her to favor future efforts. *Kavai* are heirlooms, handed down through successive generations of males, who keep them secret within the lineage and normally sing them in a whispered voice. Most are performed for magic (to make the canoe and the fishermen attractive to fish), purification (to cleanse the canoe and crew), and veneration (to honor fish recognized as the children of Pakeva).

During ritualized fishing, men may intone other incantations: *sere,* addressed to a school of tuna as it rises through the water toward the bait, exhorting the fish to linger until the fishermen fill their canoes; *fakamasike,* asking ancestral spirits to intercede with Pakeva so she will send sharks or sailfish; *uka,* an alliterative song calling the above species by their ritual names, luring them to the hook; *taa manoo,* sung to a shark (*manoo*) fighting the hook, to calm its struggles; and *ppui,* a spiteful call on ancestral spirits, to bring another fisherman bad luck. *Fakamaumau* invoke the aid of ancestral spirits; their incantation occurs in the context of fishing (to ensure success), funerals (to beg refuge for the spirit of the deceased), and other activities susceptible to supernatural influence. *Lluu* are laments, sung during funerals as relatives of the deceased prepare the body for burial. The texts speak of irrevocable loss and lives unfulfilled.

### Miscellaneous genres

For several dances, Takuu songs take other forms: *fakatuu, filipoe* (introduced), *manokofo, manu, paki* 'dance using a wooden fan', *rue, sea, siva* (brought from Sāmoa), *tofa* (developed after the Great War of 1914–1918). Other styles of dancing include *suamere, takere, takitaki,* and *vori.* For *oriori,* people stamp bamboo tubes on the ground. Other kinds of songs are *lani* and *poti.* By the 1980s, the specifics of many of these terms had passed out of common knowledge and use.

Tales (*kkai*) recount ancient contests betwen animals, between people and *tipua* 'bogeys, monsters', and between *tipua* and animals. Some retell myths about early Takuu and their interactions with *naa tama te lani,* people who lived in the heavens.

—BARBARA G. MOIR

## LUANGIUA

Luangiua is an atoll of more than one hundred islets set around a C-shaped lagoon about 60 kilometers long. It has about 8 square kilometers of land. Polynesians have settled in two villages: about one thousand people on Luangiua, and about five hundred on Peilau. They cultivate crops on those islands and several islets (Parkinson 1986 [1897]; Sarfert and Damm 1929, 1931).

In 1643, Abel Tasman, captain of the first European expedition to visit Luangiua, named it Ontong Java. In 1904, evangelists from Sāmoa and Tonga landed. In 1910, a Wesleyan missionary began a year's stay. Later, the Melanesian Mission (Anglican) set up regular visits.

## Musical system

Indigenous music of Luangiua is mainly vocal. For Hugo Zemp (1971), a ritual leader sang some items solo, but all other songs are choral, sung by men, women, or mixed choirs. Older musical styles included one-note recitations, with rhythms deriving from those of the words. Responsorial polyphony, usually in two parts, sometimes occurred; the secondary part was repetitive and dronelike. Western-influenced styles include Christian hymns and secular songs.

Musical instruments accompanied singing: small log idiophones (*samu*), struck with two sticks; pieces of wood or bamboo, complementing or replacing log idiophones; fans, struck against the palms of hands; and stamped tubes, one singer per tube. Men blew conchs to accent the annual parade of naked virgins (Johnson 1945:134–135). By the 1940s, men of Luangiua were familiar with pan-Pacific popular songs: forming the crew of the colonial district officer's launch, some had "a guitar, a few ukuleles, and gramophone records to help them" (Mytinger 1942:268).

### Songs for the sanga

The people of Luangiua assembled for an annual celebration, the *sanga,* which required extraordinary activity: serving food to carved images of deities, racing canoes, feasting, and the parade of naked virgins. Unisex groups of singers traversed the village, accompanying a procession of two wooden gods and singing *langi,* whose texts, frequently derisive, made sexual allusions. (They also sang *langi* at other times, to enliven leisure and work.) In the late 1940s, the people discontinued the *sanga.*

Several genres of song occurred only during the celebration. Mixed choruses sang *papasau,* songs for inaugurating a new temple; the performers clapped in a steady tempo. On the evenings before canoe races (held for several days), mixed choruses sang *olioli,* songs whose texts treated techniques of fishing and invoked maritime divinities, accompanied by the stamping of bamboo tubes. For *sea,* some men sang while others danced, and each stanza accelerated. Mixed choruses sang *lopu,* featuring bamboo tubes, which singers stamped on the ground while others danced around them.

### Other songs

*Lue* are sung by women while men dance, or by men while women dance. Some singers clap; others strike log idiophones or bamboo tubes. As in *sea,* each stanza has a section in which the tempo increases. *Ku'i* celebrate the birth of a couple's first child: mixed choruses sing in various sites around the settlement, each singer beating a fan against the palm of a hand (Hogbin 1930:108–109). At wakes, mixed groups sing laments (*huakanga* and *sa'a*), and women sing formal cries (*kangi*), which otherwise serve as lullabies.

## Dances

Dancers formerly wore special attire. Over cloth wraparounds, they draped strips of pandanus or sections of fronds, secured with belts of multicolored beads. They smeared their bodies with turmeric and coconut oil. They put wreaths on their heads, and hung garlands of leaves, flowers, beads, and buttons around their necks. For dances and rituals, men wore tortoiseshell ornaments suspended from their nostrils, and girls affixed mother-of-pearl pendants in the cartilage of their noses and shells in their earlobes (Collinson 1926:49).

The most common entertainments were beachgames (*kahao vakai*) at night, when men and women played in the surf, danced on the beach, or sat in clusters, singing (Johnson 1945:127–128). Girls entertained each other, sitting and moving their hands, or standing and moving in lines; individuals sometimes paired up, patting each other's hands (Zemp 1972a, 1972b). These entertainments attracted revelers:

> A man or woman would leap into the centre of a cluster and give a solo performance while the others sat and watched with great interest, clapping their hands or chanting. Every now and then a girl or boy would hop in beside the dancer, do a few steps or wriggles, and retire. Even the old people joined in. . . .
>
> The men excelled at dancing and were always showing off to the women. A handsome young Adonis would do all sorts of acrobatics before the girls, giving special attention to one, and the girls would applaud wildly and beg for more. (Johnson 1945:128)

Organized group dances at these events were in two parts: first, a slow and steady section, performed in place; then, a fast and accelerating section, when the dancers approached the singers.

—J. W. LOVE

## SIKAIANA

The resident population of Sikaiana is about 250; about five hundred live elsewhere in the Solomon Islands. In the mid-1800s, whalers and traders visited Sikaiana. In 1929, Anglican missionaries arrived, and within a decade had converted the populace to Christianity. Many rituals and practices, unperformed since the 1940s, are only vaguely remembered.

Young people attend schools elsewhere in the Solomons, some attain secondary-level educations, and a few attend colleges and universities. Most Sikaianans born since 1929 have spent time abroad, in school and at work. In addition to Sikaianan, they speak Solomon Islands Pidgin, and some speak English.

### Musical contexts

Before conversion to Christianity, music had an integral place in sacred events, special ceremonies, and informal entertainments; after conversion, many indigenous rituals and ceremonies fell into disuse. During one festival, the *puina,* men and women formed separate companies: one went to the western islets (Muli Akau) while the other stayed on the main islet (Hale); thus apart, each company developed songs that taunted the other (figure 2). Rejoining on the main islet, each company presented its songs. A similar festival, *hakatoo pakupaku,* occurred on the main islet without the retreat to Muli Akau. Because the *puina* praised extramarital heterosexual activity, the missionaries discouraged it.

In the 1940s, a modified form of the *puina,* the *uiki hakamalooloo* 'holiday week' occurred during school vacation. A similar festival was performed in 1969, ostensibly

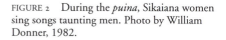

FIGURE 2 During the *puina*, Sikaiana women sing songs taunting men. Photo by William Donner, 1982.

FIGURE 3   For an important visitor's arrival, Sikaiana women sing and dance. Photo by William Donner, 1980.

celebrating the lunar landing. The men's song praised the beauty of a woman who lived on the moon; the women's reply claimed that such a woman would have no desire for the men of the earth (that is, Sikaiana), because of men's behavior.

Musical performance intensifies from late November to early January, a festive season. The local Anglican Church commemorates St. Andrew, the island's patron, on 30 November. Sikaianans celebrate Christmas and New Year's for two weeks, when the church prohibits most labor and expects people to participate in drinking, singing, and dancing. Most spontaneous performances occur when people drink toddy (*kaleve*) or imported alcoholic beverages: men say they prefer to be at least slightly inebriated when performing. Sikaianans claim, however, that as recently as about 1960, they celebrated festivals by dancing and singing for long hours into the evening without such stimulation.

Sikaianans rehearse for special presentations, such as the arrival of an important visitor—the Bishop of Malaita, for example, who visits every year on St. Andrew's Day. Early in 1982, when the populace prepared for the arrival of the national prime minister, they rehearsed several songs, including *kaitae hakatele, suamele,* and *mako o te henua*. Women often rehearse dances for performance at special feasts, or at the visit of an important official (figure 3). Many of their dances came from residents of other islands. In 1980–1981, a Gilbertese woman married to a Sikaianan man organized rehearsals and presentations of dances from Kiribati. Dancing also occurs during customary exchanges that accompany marriage. The families of the bride's and groom's mothers exchange goods, as do the families of the bride's and groom's fathers. When members of each family make their presentation, they perform drum-accompanied dances.

In performing songs and dances, and in rehearsals and presentations for important visitors to the island, women participate more actively than men. Perhaps because custom restricts their opportunities for consuming alcoholic beverages, they are more enthusiastic participants when sober.

## The vocabulary of music

The English concept of "sing" glosses three Sikaianan terms: *pese,* the most general and frequently used term; *lani,* which specifies the reciting of a certain prayer, the *kaitae;* and *tau,* which specifies the reciting of a certain ritual, the *mako mahamaha.*

At festivals and dances, enthusiastic singing is described by the verb *too*: before a performance, persons may call out "*Hakatoo!*"

The word *anu*, as a noun and a verb, covers the structured-movement systems that can be glossed 'dance'. Some dances I witnessed had instrumental accompaniment, and many involved singing. In the 1980s, older Sikaianans used the word *mako* to denote 'song with gestures or motions'; for younger persons, however, the term denoted all sung performances, including songs without gestures and music for guitar.

To compose a song is *hatu*, of which an archaic form, *hatusei*, can be glossed 'speak slowly, as when trying to teach the words of a song'. To teach or learn a new song is *ako mako*, a phrase built on *ako* 'teach, learn', whose reduplicated form, *akoako*, means 'to practice', but also denotes a section of certain songs. In keeping with the common Polynesian distinction of alternate possessives in *a* and *o*, a Sikaianan refers to *tana mako* 'his or her song' if he or she composed it, or *tona mako* 'his or her song' if others composed it about him or her.

Motions and gestures are *aauna*; the causative form, *hakaauna*, can be glossed 'practice, teach, or make gestures'. The term *hakapepele* describes the motion of twisting and lowering the body by bending the knees—a frequent movement in girls' dances. An organized dance is an *anumana*, a nominalized form of *anu*; such dances are accompanied by guitars after an evening feast or party (*kai*). On festive occasions, such as Christmas, youths make progressive presentations (*hakamolimoli*), dancing first in one neighborhood, and then in another.

Musical genres said to be composed include *makohakatanitani, olioli, saka, sau, siva, tani, tuki*, and guitar songs. Sikaianans attribute most such songs to a specific composer or group of composers; the texts concern specific events or individuals. Genres not associated with a particular composer include those with ritual significance (including *kaitae* and *suamele*) and genres that originated in other islands. Some songs associated with ritual ceremonies contain words whose meanings, once known only by ritual leaders, are not now understood. Several Kiribati songs, notably *kalana* and *mau tolotolo*, are sung on Sikaiana.

## Musical genres

The following list defines musical genres known in the early 1980s. Several are no longer performed, and respondents differed in describing them.

*Kaitae* include ritual prayers sung to specific spirits. The *te-ika-lle* ritual was performed when a large fish or a whale washed up on the reef; as the carcass was being taken ashore, people sang *kaitae* to spirits who inhabited the reef. They sang other *kaitae* in the island's central ritual house. *Kaitae hakatele* 'dedicatory *kaitae*' is a prayer, sung as part of the *manea*, a ritual for rebuilding that house. *Tau* were formerly sung in ritual houses for a ritual known as *kunaaika*. *Tuki* are also songs of ritual significance; mediums sang them in the ritual houses to summon ancestral spirits.

*Mako hakatahao* are sung for amusement. *Mako hakatanitani* 'imploring songs' are about sex and love. *Mako o te henua* 'songs of the land' include exogenous songs with gestures. In some, the words are Polynesian, but not always Sikaianan; in others, the words could be Sikaianan, but their meanings are obscure. The oldest woman I encountered remembered having learned and sung these songs informally in the evenings, about 1910. They are nowadays performed on festive occasions.

*Naha* include songs that recount a legendary invasion of people from "Tona." This event, which occurred about twelve generations before the 1980s, supposedly resulted in a massacre of Sikaianans, whose modern descendants associate the invaders with Tongans.

*Olioli,* composed in a style different from that of *sau, siva,* and *saka,* are performed without dancing at *puina* and other secular occasions. A recorded example uses a scale transcribable as D–F–G. Also presented during *puina* were *sau.* They are still sung, especially by persons who have been drinking; new examples are still composed. During *puina,* a *siva* followed each *sau,* in a faster tempo.

*Saka* lasciviously praise a secret sweetheart or lover. Old *saka* are still performed, especially by people when drinking. Missionaries have discouraged the composition and performance of *saka.* Because the songs are ribald, they are thought unsuitable for performance in mixed company, especially in the presence of opposite-sex siblings.

*Suamele* are performed with gesturing and clapping at holiday festivals, for the arrival of important visitors, or on other special occasions. The words are archaic and not fully understood. *Suamele* were appropriate for performance toward the end of *te-ika-lle.* Along the shore, men and women divided into separate groups, faced each other, and executed a series of *suamele* at different locations.

Laments (*tani* 'cries') commemorate a deceased person's life. They are no longer composed, but some are still known, and a few are quite popular. An excerpt from a lament composed before 1940 recalls a man whose canoe-racing enthusiasm comes to his brother's mind.

> E ni naenae ko nau; te taaina nei e hahano mai.
> E ni moe ko nau; te taaina nei e hahano mai
> E taaua vaka e ki mua.
> E taaua mahi i o taaua hoe,
> Ko ki taaua e naatahi.
>
> I was tired; my brother woke me.
> I slept; my brother woke me
> To make our canoe first.
> Our strength is in our paddles,
> So that we're together.

*Tuuhoe* include a pair of songs associated with long-distance voyaging. The texts recount feats of the legendary heroes Semalu and Kaetekita, who traveled in outrigger canoes, about twelve generations before the 1980s.

*Ttani kkai* are short, sung parts of tales (*tala*). The melodies are sung by the narrator or someone appointed as singer; some melodies serve for songs newly composed in other genres.

*Mau tolotolo,* the name of a song that Gilbertese immigrants brought to Sikaiana late in the 1800s, is part of a ceremony involving fosterage. An assemblage of people moves toward the house of someone who has a foster child, singing the song as they approach. If they perform correctly, they may demand labor or material goods from the foster parents, who, to prove their love for the child, must comply. *Kalana,* a song with gestures that depict combat, came with immigrants from the Gilbert Islands in the 1800s, and is rarely performed.

### Miscellaneous genres

Hymns (*aasi*) are in Mota, which until the late 1930s served as Anglican missionaries' official language. *Hakateletele vaka* 'dedicating boats' are songs sung ritually to aid sailors and commemorate long-distance voyages; a respondent claimed one example was a *kupu* associatied with Savaiki, one of the ritual houses. (*Kupu* 'word' is a set of prayers associated with the ritual houses.) *Mako mahamaha* are songs suitable for *te-*

Performers dance in a circle or a line, facing the
audience, who sit. For some dances, they carry
clubs or green branches. Audiences intently follow
movements, imitate gestures, laugh at drolleries,
and sing along.

*ika-lle. Olitana* 'swaying' was said to be a weather-controlling prayer. *Sea* were learned
from the people of Luangiua.

### Musical instruments

A small log idiophone (*puloto*) is beaten during some dances; biscuit tins also serve
for percussion. Sikaianans have some ukuleles (*ukalele*), but prefer guitars (*kitaa*).
Both instruments are played in a manner described as *lliki* 'strike with handheld
object'. A conch (*puu*) is blown (*ili*) on special occasions and for announcements; the
text of one recorded song contains the phrase *ka tani te puu* 'the conch must sound',
applying the verb *tani* 'cry' to the performance. One tale mentions a musical instrument called *pahu*, which some said was a twanged lamellaphone, and others said was
a bamboo flute.

### Outside influences

Since the 1930s, several musical styles have been introduced. In church, congregations sing English hymns from an Anglican hymnal, and children sing Sunday-school
songs. Local men, when drinking, sing old American and British songs, including
"You Are My Sunshine," "Pack Up Your Troubles in Your Old Kit Bag," "The U.S.
Marines Marching Song," and "There's a Church in the Valley."

The guitar, introduced in the late 1960s, has become a preferred means for
unmarried young men and women to enjoy music. Sikaianans consider guitar-
accompanied singing more suitable for unmarried persons than for married ones.
Public performances occur at dances, held several times a month. Intersexual dancing
came to the island in the 1970s: formerly, men and women did not dance as couples.
Parents complain that guitar-accompanied music and dancing are breaking down old
rules of sexual conduct. Many adults disapprove of guitars, whose playing they call a
*mea pio* 'foolish thing'.

Young men like to sing to guitars while inebriated, though they sometimes sing
sober. Young women also enjoy singing to guitars. Groups of young people record
guitar songs on cassettes for posting to friends and relatives abroad. Sikaianans listen
to the Solomon Islands Broadcasting Corporation, which programs popular music in
international styles; they also record and play this music on cassettes.

—WILLIAM DONNER

## BELLONA

Bellona (Mungiki) is a coral island, 30 meters at its highest, 11 kilometers long, and
1,500 meters wide. Along its length runs a main trail, from which paths lead to each
of seven villages, in which about six hundred Bellonese live. With Rennell, Bellona
shares one language, most closely related to that of Futuna (Elbert 1967:271).

Bellonese clans are a patrilineal, patrilocal groups, whose members trace descent
from the same immigrant. Two of the original clans survive; they divide into sub-

clans, which divide into lineages, whose members help each other in clearing, planting, fishing, hunting, building canoes and houses—and, formerly, fighting other lineages. Twenty-one lineages exist. The landholders of a lineage rank equally, but seniority and skill may enable one of them to claim a position of highest responsibility as lineage elder. A man's leadership in performing music and organizing performances helps him improve his status.

## Musical contexts

On Bellona and in the Bellonese colony in Honiara, musical performances occur in front of a house. The performers dance in a circle or a line, facing the audience, who sit. For formal presentations, dancers wear a turmeric-dyed bark-cloth loincloth, a headband, a mat with a fan tucked in back, and plaited armlets. For some dances, they carry clubs or green branches. Audiences, even small children, intently follow movements, imitate gestures, laugh at drolleries, and sing along.

### Rituals

Before Christianization, Bellonese presented music on occasions such as feasts of distribution and tattooing. Rituals were for two sets of gods: those of the outdoors or sky, and those of the house or district. These gods' respective domains were nature and culture; men distributed raw food for the former, and cooked food for the latter.

Each landholder's home stood in a circular clearing, bordered by coconut palms. Rituals occurred in the larger half of the clearing, between the house and the main trail, and highlighted the seasonal cycle and human life-cycle events. At rituals for the gods of the sky, dancing followed a distribution of food; at rituals for gods of the district, one of these deities might speak through a medium, who would reveal songs the deity had composed.

Men's lives more frequently involved rituals than women's. About age sixteen, a boy would undergo initiation as an assistant priest, and his father would hold a distribution for him. The next year, he would become a secondary priest-chief; a few years later, a full priest-chief. A man held distributions whenever his gardening or fishing could gain him enough food to certify his skill and generosity; he also conducted rituals for a large canoe's first voyage, noosing a shark, and harvests. Nowadays after a harvest, Bellonese summon family and friends for distributing food and, since the 1950s, singing Christian hymns.

At least once in his life, a prominent man would try to organize a visit-marking dance (*mako saʻu*) to a high-status person in another village, or preferably in Rennell. To enhance his prestige, he would get a chest tattoo, whose completion occasioned elaborate musical displays in festivities that could last a month. A prominent man's wife would have a women's dance (*muʻaabaka*). When she was older, she might receive around the waist the *taupito,* a rare tattoo. Most men and women would try to compose and lead songs for the occasions they sponsored, thus documenting the history of lineages and rationalizing the social structure.

## Performative concepts

Bellonese distinguish several performative classes and many musical genres and poetic types. Religious songs (*ongiongi*) and collective dancing and singing (*tauʻasonga*) illustrate the main contrasting styles. Alone or with assistants, the ceremonial leader delivers formal addresses and *ongiongi,* which, delivered as a dedication at the beginning of every ritual, honor and thank the gods for the food. The texts praise and offer comfort to deities or people; some entreat protection or other favors.

Large feasts dedicated to the gods of the sky involved *tauʻasonga.* Compound genres of this class contain several kinds of song in a set series and many individual

FIGURE 4   A Bellonese melody: the first stanza of "*Te Pese a Kaitu'u*" ('Kaitu'u's Clapsong'), with clapping marking most beats. After Rossen 1987:2:34.

songs of each kind. Several events and occasions have their repertory of songs, performed by a group, often in all-night sessions. Like the dances, several types follow in strict order, each with many individual songs. Song-session occasions included the harvest ritual, when people performed clapsongs (*pese*, figure 4), songs by seated singers (*mako noho*), and laments (*haingaa tangi*) [see LANGUAGE IN MUSICAL SETTINGS: Metrics]. Some tales include short songs (*tangi*). Adults formerly played musical games, some of which have children's versions. Clapping accompanies some game songs (*babange 'anga*).

Composition confers high prestige; by composing poetry for public performance, singers may achieve renown—for themselves and their descendants. Members of the composer's family often perform the composer's song. They keep it in memory and may relate "the story of the song," which tells about the circumstances of composition and first performance. The poet's name lives in the title of the poem, which specifies the name of the poetic type and the musical genre. The poet's deeds are sometimes the subject. Old people compose songs in indigenous genres, including *tangi* and songs for the *pati* dance, though they seldom perform these in public. Young people compose new songs, which they accompany with ukulele and guitar. Composers perform their own compositions, and may lead a group to present them.

## Music systems

Bellonese music is vocal, often with dance, based on poetry—a form epitomized in some religious songs recited on one note. Songs are usually strophic; some songs for dancing consist of a freely repeated couplet. Leader and group, often responsorially, repeat lines or parts of lines, sometimes with variations. The length of a performance depends on the number of songs included in each genre.

Choral singing involves three possible textures: two-part polyphony with simultaneous melodic variations; drone-based polyphony with recitation on two levels; and three-part polyphony, of a soloist and two subsidiary parts (*mua* 'front', *mungi* 'back'). A double chorus sings *pese* and parts of the *suahongi*, sometimes performing two pieces of music simultaneously.

Except in accelerating *huaa mako* of the *papa* dance, tempo holds steady, and meters are simple, whether accompanied or not. Many melodies take their rhythms from their verbal rhythms. Most Bellonese melodies employ two to five tones or more, often in semitoneless scalar configurations; many have four- and five-tone scales. Common melodic and harmonic intervals are a major second, a minor third, a perfect fourth, and a perfect fifth.

Several timbres, including speech-song, are used; many songs end in shouted cadential formulas. Falsetto occurs in several contexts: rehearsing (*pungotu*) all songs, performing personal songs (*kananga*), and singing some songs of the *papa* dance. For dancing, a struck plaque sometimes accompanies vocal music. Many genres have tranquil dynamics. In *pati,* the singer produces a slow vibrato on the long tones of vocables.

Singers vary rhythms and melodies. Multiple singers simultaneously produce different intervals, accepting them as correct. Omission of a stanza is unacceptable, as are incorrect rhythms in clapping and incorrect numbers of segmental repetitions.

FIGURE 5   In Honiara, as men of Bellona perform a *mako tu'u,* Jason Ngiusanga beats a struck plaque. Photo by Jane Mink Rossen, 1974.

### Interrelationships of music, language, and movement

Songs and dances present composed poetry. In circles or lines, singing dancers perform set movements in synchrony. Outstanding dancers achieve renown, and song-poetry praises them. There are far more terms for movements of the arms (*'aaunga*) than for leg-and-foot movements (*mako* 'dance, run, movement of legs'). When a text mentions the word for a movement, such as *mongi* 'leap like a porpoise' and *sua* 'to paddle', the dancer executes the movement. The designation *tengetenge* denotes vocalizing and the accompanying *mako* (Rossen 1987:1:147–163; Rossen and Colbert 1981).

Bellonese recognize that people have different voices (*nge'o*). The result when they sound together is *mou hatingaa nge'o* 'variation of voices', a concept that grants performers considerable tonal and rhythmic freedom. Singers purposefully vary rhythms, and augment and diminish tonal intervals using several kinds of ornamental intervallic variation (*okeoke* 'swing back and forth').

## Musical instruments

A struck plaque (*papa*) accompanies certain dances (figure 5). The only indigenous Bellonese instrument, it has a loud, penetrating sound. It consists of a flat, crescent-shaped board, about 110 centimeters long, 40 centimeters wide, and 4 centimeters thick. A man (*tipa* 'beater') beats it with two stout, tapered sticks (*kau tipa*); to provide resonance, he wedges its convex edge against a pin in the ground, and props the concave, beveled edge up on his feet.

During the 1930s, from papaya-leaf stalks, people made notched and fipple flutes, which they used for courting and personal entertainment. Adapted from flutes used on other islands in the Solomons or used by fishermen on Japanese ships, these were popular for about a decade, but are no longer common. Children play a mouth-resonated bow, as adults formerly did.

## Musical transmission and education

In school, Bellonese children learn songs from elsewhere in the Pacific. Hymns are the most commonly performed items; the churches favor versions with English texts. Many adults keep notebooks of lyrics and dance-related movements, but transmission is primarily aural. Bellonese who listened to my audio-video recordings most frequently requested *suahongi, papa,* and *tangi.* The most common genres still composed are *tangi, pati, kananga,* and modern songs (figure 6).

Men compose songs of all classes. Women primarily compose laments, often in praise of a husband's skill in fishing, gardening, and dancing. Men perform most dances; women do two kinds of *pati,* alone or with men. Householders organize gatherings at which they distribute food and lead the singing; formerly, they also led the dancing. In the center of a circle of dancers, or in front of a line of dancers, the beater leads the songs that require struck-plaque accompaniment. A singer or the clapper (*pese*) leads unaccompanied songs. The *suahongi* requires four leaders: two for singing, two for dancing. Composers often sing stanzas; a group adds the refrain (*'umenge*). In songs without a refrain, the group can echo (*ta'o muna*) the leader's start.

## Music and history

West Polynesians settled Bellona and Rennell. Traditions say the ancestors of the present population, in search of land, emigrated from 'Ubea (probably 'Uvea) twenty-five generations before the 1960s, bringing songs and dances (Elbert and Monberg 1965). One of these dances, the *suahongi,* is considered their most important cultural legacy.

On arrival, the immigrants composed songs that still grace the repertory, but comprehensive translations are impossible. Only the texts of songs composed after about 1880 are fully intelligible. Some song-dances were introduced in the early 1900s by castaways from Tikopia and Taumako.

After 1939, when the Rennellese evangelist Moa converted the Bellonese to Christianity, the religious basis of musical performance began to change. Using English letters in an orthography of his own invention, Moa translated Seventh-Day Adventist hymns into Bellonese. During World War II, indigenous singing and dancing began to revive, but in 1947, the first missionary from abroad, a Solomon Islander, spent several months on Bellona. He gathered the people into villages around a church, and forbade performances of indigenous music.

Since 1947, missions of the Seventh-Day Adventist Church and the South Seas Evangelical Church have barred the performance of indigenous songs and dances, which, however, have regained importance in the search for identity that ensued after 1978, when the Solomon Islands became an independent member of the British Commonwealth. International festivals and visits by dignitaries provide opportunities to perform; other opportunities occur on national radio and at national festivals, held biennially in Honiara. Festival presentations draw from the old repertory, a primary cultural storehouse. Designed to interest tourists, the programs consist only of dances, mainly those with strongly marked rhythms. Leaders omit genres that have tranquil dynamics or feature poetry in varying meters.

In 1933, the Templeton Crocker Expedition made recordings on Rennell; of these, Burrows published one transcription (1934). In 1957–1968, anthropologists Torben Monberg and Samuel Elbert made further recordings. After fieldwork in 1974 and 1977, Jane Mink Rossen has written on indigenous songs. The Solomon Islands Broadcasting System (Honiara) and the Danish Folklore Archives (Copenhagen) house copies of these recordings.    —JANE MINK ROSSEN

## TIKOPIA

A small, isolated island of volcanic origin in the eastern Solomon Islands, Tikopia has a Polynesian population of fewer than two thousand, engaged in agriculture and fishing. After the 1940s, its people founded settlements elsewhere in the Solomons. Throughout the country, in government service and commerce, they hold a range of jobs.

The Tikopia political system is notable throughout the Solomons for its internal government by four ranked chiefs, each the head of a clan and formerly its major priest in the worship of ancestors and gods. Chiefs are responsible for important decisions on social affairs, and are treated with great respect.

### Traditional music

Tikopia music is largely indigenous in style. From the 1920s, gradual conversion to Christianity brought Christian hymns to the culture. Guitars, ukuleles, and recordings of Polynesian and Western popular music supplement older-style performances. Indigenous Tikopia music was orally transmitted. Basically vocal, it required for accompaniment only percussion: handclaps, or beating on a struck plaque (*tā*), a timber slab, struck with two sticks or a coral stone. Ritual laments were accompanied by *ū sēru,* a swishing rattle of dried palm-leaf ribs, or by a stamped bamboo tube (*lopu*), with palm-leaf fiber tied over its mouth. The percussive sounds varied little in pitch, but much in rhythm.

Most Tikopia song is choral. Solo singing occurs in some tales and ritual procedures, and in laments when, for emotional release, a person privately mourns or farewells a friend or relative. Teaching a new song, a choral leader may sing alone. But there is no virtuoso singing by a soloist to an audience. Nor does much importance attach to vocal timbre, which is often somewhat nasal and tense. People prize vocal power, plus the knowledge of songs and appropriate gestures.

#### Composition and repertory

Songs (*pese*) are often identified with named composers, as "a lament by So-and-So," or "a song for dancing by So-and-So." Each song is a poem in musical form; its music has a uniquely ordered set of intervals, but these conform to general types, and it is the wording of the song that has aesthetic salience. Most songs whose composer is known are the work of men, but women also compose songs, and some are remembered as composers.

Since a song may endure for several generations, it may give a clue to history, as in the doings of a chief or a noted ancestor. But songs may not only enshrine memory; they can reflect a continually changing cultural scene. Composers produce new songs for every communal festival and every funeral of a major social figure—not highly original, but acceptable as a novel contribution to the occasion. Songs whose crispness of phrase, aptness of allusion, and catchiness of melody earn consensual approval tend to enter the public repertory. But since many songs are produced, many are soon forgotten, so the repertory has continually been in flux. In musical poetics, Tikopia tradition was essentially a changing tradition—not a static one, handed down intact from time immemorial. What remained fairly constant, or changed more slowly, was the general style of musical performance.

### Kinds of song

Tikopia music has two major divisions: songs for dancing (*mako*) and laments (*fuatanga*). To some extent, another category, *pese,* crosscuts these. *Pese* is the general term for singing of any kind, but applies specifically to a few ritual and narrative songs that are neither dances nor laments. *Pese* also covers various twentieth-century productions, including hymns and popular songs, indigenous and imported.

Songs for dancing and laments are usually short. Each piece conventionally divides into two or three stanzas (*kupu*). If there are three, the first stanza is the *tafito,* 'base, entry'; the second is the *kupu i roto* 'middle stanza'; and the last is the *safe,* which has an alternative meaning of 'flower-bearing stem' or 'fruiting bunch of bananas', and so may figuratively imply the fruition of the song. Each stanza divides into sections. Musical diction often involves reduplication of initial syllables of words. Medial- or final-vowel modification commonly turns what would be a spoken /a/ into a sung /o/.

### Topical content

The themes of songs vary. *Fuatanga,* usually melancholy, express sadness at the absence or death of a relative or friend. *Mako,* usually cheerful, express pleasure in dancing or another technical skill, and comment on travel, natural features, or wildlife. Some are trenchant: on a beach in the moonlight, unmarried young men and women, in separate groups, sing formal taunts, each sex making slanderous allegations about the other. Such songs, commonly roared out while dancers tramp up and down, serve as a poetical means of sexual titillation, an introduction to secret affairs.

In the words of the following *mako,* the composer, an expert seaman, praises the speed of his canoe. As is common in such songs, it has two stanzas, a *tafito* and a *kupu.*

| | |
|---|---|
| Te uru manongi o Takarito! | The fragrant leaftip of Takarito! |
| Faofao i toku rā | Enclosed in my sail is |
| Te matangi rongo muri. | The wind blowing from the stern. |
| | |
| Tautā te naio ka rere. | Swiftly the garfish will swim. |
| Te kipara ka kai poa, | The tuna will swallow bait, |
| Kae au i toku miromiro. | And follow in my wake. |

Composed by a principal chief in the late 1800s, this song remained in his grandson's memory fifty years later. The first stanza is figurative: it says the sail-billowing wind is a fragrant scent from an aromatic plant; coming from the site of a temple, it empowers the canoe. The second stanza raises images of fast-moving fish, which the rushing craft nevertheless outstrips. Such songs, danced with verve, vividly express a sense of movement.

### Musical style

Scalar intervals in Tikopia music correspond inexactly with tempered values. Most Tikopia songs use four- or five-tone semitoneless scales. Some laments have scales with semitones. Most melodic movement focuses on a tonal center, which usually ends the song.

All Tikopia music has meter. Differences in rhythm produce three major kinds of song. *Matāvaka,* generally of steady tempo but often increasing to a rapid pace, may be unaccompanied, but commonly have guidance from a struck plaque. *Ngore* are slow-tempo songs, accompanied only by clapping. *Matāvaka* may often be sung as *ngore.* Of a distinctly different sort are *fuatanga,* laments, often funeral dirges, sung extremely slowly, with many long-held notes. The singing of *fuatanga* is often broken by wailing, solo or in unison, *ē, auē!* 'oh, alas!', in a long, dying musical cadence.

### Music and social activity

Tikopia music is rarely performed as a purely musical occasion; it is usually part of some social activity, accompanied by bodily action. Men sing while paddling a canoe across the lake; women sing while washing turmeric roots for processing into pigment.

To express emotion, a *fuatanga* at a funeral is accompanied by raising and lowering palm-leaf fans, and beating the breast with the fist. Formerly, men cut the forehead with a knife, but because Christian baptism involves making a sign of the cross there, they have abandoned the pagan bloodletting. Women, however, may still tear their cheeks with their fingernails.

The duration and intensity of singing a *fuatanga* indicate the rank of the deceased; mourning for a chief may extend over several months. Timing in singing a *fuatanga* also shows what kind of relationship the singer has to the dead person.

### Traditional dancing

The performance of songs for dancing entails vigorous gestures (*āunga*) and hand-and-arm movements (*sava*), swaying, and stamping (for men) or shuffling (for women). Men wave arms or brandish clubs or paddles (*paki*), which they manipulate in patterned ways. Women are more restrained, but use fans to emphasize their gestures (figure 7).

Tikopia dancing included an annual cycle of four days and four nights of formal religious performance, dedicated to ancestral gods, with unique posturing dances,

FIGURE 7   At the Pacific Festival of Arts, Tikopian women emphasize their gestures with fans. Photo by Adrienne L. Kaeppler, 1996.

When a person dies, the populace divides into small choirs of about twenty members. After rehearsing, each choir proceeds to the house of the deceased and spends up to an hour singing over the body. Sobbing punctuates the singing.

some of an archaic, erotic nature. Some of these dances were restricted to one gender or the other. Some songs for religious dancing were the property of particular chiefs, and only their clans performed them.

Of secular dances, there were formerly nearly a score, most of which are still performed. They show much variation in structure, musical accompaniment, use of accessories (such as sticks or fans), and individual display of expertise. *Matāvaka* are simple dances, loosely organized. To the rhythm of a refrain, assembled in ragged lines, performers traverse the arena. Their performance often ends with a rally on the struck plaque and a shout. For hours, they raise fresh songs. Men, women, and children join or leave as they wish. By contrast, the *mori* is a complex, phased, spectacular dance of men only, in which, with clubs or paddles, leader-soloists execute intricate movements and gestures.

Decoration for a dance is elaborate. Leaves and flowers, drawn from about thirty kinds, are set in hair or pierced earlobes, or are worn around the neck or waist. Traditionally, dancers also wore shell armbands, beads, and breast-decorating pendants. In adornment for dancing, colors—especially red, yellow, white, and black—are important.

—RAYMOND FIRTH

## ANUTA

Anuta, supporting a resident population of about two hundred, lies 116 kilometers from its nearest neighbor, Tikopia. Anutans collect most of their music under the term *pete* 'song'. The human voice (*reo*) is their principal musical instrument; accompaniments to singing and dancing are percussive and concussive. They distinguish between two dynamic levels: loud (*pete ki runga* 'sing upward'), and soft (*pete ki raro* 'sing downward', also *pete maarie*). To compose is *pete te mako pou* 'sing a new song' and occasionally *patu* 'make something up'. To dance is *pai aaunga* 'make gestures'. Composers, choreographers, and lead dancers are known as *purotu*.

### Musical contexts

For several nights or weeks before a celebration, people assemble on the beach for a rehearsal (*pete-mako* 'dance-sing'). Contexts for performance include rites of passage (particularly marriage and initiation), celebrations marking Christian holy days (Christmas, Easter, and other feasts), competitions, funerals, storytelling, and children's and young adults' informal parties. At celebrations, dancing lasts several hours after collective meals. Young adults do most dancing; others watch, chat, and participate in singing.

*Tauaangutu* are competitions that occur between mixed groups of men and women at informal parties and at major festivals. Competitions require a chief's approval. Married men and unmarried women make up one company, the paternal side (*tau tamana*); unmarried men and married women form the other, the maternal side (*tau pae*). One company performs, the other answers, and this alternation continues until the participants agree to defer completion of the contest, which may last for months.

When a person dies, the populace divides into small choirs of about twenty members. After rehearsing, each choir proceeds to the house of the deceased, and spends up to an hour singing over the body. Sobbing punctuates the singing. At the end of stanzas, the mourners cry out, "*Ei, aue!*" and emit a long, loud, falsetto wail. After one choir has finished, it may linger to listen to the next.

Short solo songs occur in *tangikakai,* spirit-related stories, whose performance lasts from five minutes to an hour and recounts events occurring in *Nga Rangi* 'The Heavens'. Adults tell them primarily to lull children to sleep.

## Genres of music and dance

Anutans classify songs into *mako* 'dance, dance-song', and *puatanga* 'lament', both ideally performed by a large group. Many examples of the former exist, distinguished by musical style and textual content; examples of the latter are few, distinguished mainly by textual content.

### *Dances and songs for dancing (mako)*

*Mako* are of three main kinds: dances featuring hands (*mako nima*), paddles (*mako raakau* 'wood dance'), and clubs (*pua taa* 'strike dance'). Dance-songs are described as inoffensive (*rerei* 'good', songs about various activities, and those descriptive or laudatory of specific persons' traits and accomplishments) and "about something bad" (*tauaangutu* 'war of words', personal invective intended to embarrass, sometimes expressed as good-natured teasing and sometimes as genuine hostility, often conveying sarcasm). Both kinds are metaphorical, and listeners must know the stories behind them to understand what their texts imply.

#### *Dances featuring hands (mako nima)*

The most frequently performed *mako nima* are *mataavaka* 'bow of a canoe' (but any association between the dance and the vessel is obscure), and occur in formal dances. They make up almost exclusively the musical resources of young people's informal dancing.

To perform a *mataavaka,* the dancers line up in straight rows, file forward in a stiff gait, incline their upper torsos slightly forward, and swing their arms loosely from side to side, swaying sideways as they advance. After moving straight ahead for about fifteen steps, they turn around and with the same gait move back to the start; then they turn around again and repeat. In stepping and gesturing, all execute the same motions at the same time. A struck plaque sets the beat, and everyone present—drummers, dancers, and observers—takes part in the singing.

*Uru teenongi* feature the linking of arms and certain dancers' rotations. *Taki* are dances in a circle, performed in synchrony by a large group. Performers make intricate movements, which become increasingly faster and more forceful. The drummers are the principal singers. In *mataavaka,* movements are routine, giving little opportunity for improvisation.

In *pakapaapine* 'women's-fashion', women perform the actions of the dance, and men furnish clapping (instead of beating a struck plaque). The texts center on fishing, sometimes from a woman's point of view, portraying a woman's pining for a lover overseas. Stanzas end in a formulaic refrain. There are four sections, performed in unvarying succession: *uru* 'entrance'; *oa,* in which dancers stand in a circle and follow a leader, frequently clapping; *tipa* (sometimes pronounced [tipo]); and refrainless items called *tungaunu,* in which women perform in four rows while one person beats the struck plaque as for the *mako nima.* Figure 8 transcribes a *tungaunu* with this text:

FIGURE 8  The melody of an Anutan *tungaunu*; original a fourth higher. Transcription by J. W. Love.

Kaatoa te penua kua uruuru;
Poki, kaatoa te taranga na
Kia ko au, ko te nea varea:
Ko au ko te tama kaia!

Kua rua te taranga au ake
Kia ko au i te taka:
"Aute i mate matou roto.
A e aa ke pakapepea, ee?"

Kua maanava kita te taranga:
Oku muna rangomia ee!
Oku tuatina mai Muri ee!

The whole island has gone;
Also, everyone has entered that discussion
About me, the foolish thing:
Myself, the thieving child!

Twice the word came forth
To me among the young folk:
"Don't destroy our inner being.
O why do you despise me?"

I've put the discussion to rest:
O my message-relaying words!
O my uncles from Muri!

The poet's boast reaches its climax on the phrase *muna rangomia* 'message-relaying words', the most intricate point of the melody: a rhythm of eight successive quarters create a prolonged syncopation.

*Teru* end funerals, using the text and music of a *puatanga*, but with clapping. They can also be performed on other occasions: in one observed daytime ceremony, the *teru* featured a lone male dancer, who stood in the center of a crowd, rapidly shaking his arms, head, and torso. Other *mako* include *makorangi*, to cleanse a dying person's mind or for general entertainment; and three dances typically performed in a set order in a circle (*tuoko, neepuru,* and *tua,* which tends to be the last item of a celebration, called *te pakaeva o te mako* 'the jumping of the dance'); *tatao,* in triple time; *pakararokoa,* with swinging the arms from side to side; *ngongore; aukeu* or *pakararo,* performed in a circle; *mako rati* 'big dances'; *tumarekau*; and *taritari pua*, performed without clapping.

### Dances featuring paddles (mako raakau)

After *mataavaka*, the dances most frequently performed on ceremonial occasions belong to a complex that can be called *mori*. These items feature paddles (*mori*), meter-long pieces of wood, carved into handled planks that dancers move in various patterns. Alternatively, dancers may use plaited fans (*iri*), which, holding in one hand, they wave and strike against the body.

For all dances with paddles, percussionists beat the struck plaque in the same pattern, increasing the tempo. All dancers execute the same motions simultaneously. Dances called *mori* share a metrical avoidance of duple (or quadruple) time. *Mori* proper are in five, as are *mori tuu-popora* 'spread-standing *mori*'. *Rau o te mori* 'blade of the *mori*' have the metrical complexity of a vocal line in 3/4 sung against a percussive line in 6/8. The use of these meters gives *mori* temporally distinctive movements; but these meters are not unique to this genre. Texts of *mori* and *mori tuu-popora* include one-verse refrains (*pakataurangi*), which end in the word *ue*. *Mori* address topics that include voyaging and the demigod Motikitiki's pulling Anuta up from the ocean.

*Taa* resemble *mori* in using paddles and refrains, but instead of lining up in rows of four or five persons as in *mori*, the dancers form one line, behind a leader, whose movements they imitate in an action called *manumanu o te mako*; the stepping is slower than in *mori*. A performance may begin with a *taa* 'strike', continue with a refrain, and end with an *iki*. For *taa-vakai*, the struck plaque is said to be beaten as in dances with paddles. The music of *taa maarie* 'gentle strike' differs; the meter of a recorded example is in five. The melody of a recorded *taa-taviro* is distinctive for having several rests. In *taa-tuu* 'stand-strike', the leader sings the stanzas, and the followers respond with a one-word refrain. The *taa-nopo* 'sit-strike' has no *taa* and no *iki*, but is beaten and danced as in *mako raakau*: dancers divide into two groups; during the refrain, one group kneels, while the other, which remains standing, sings the text. The word *veia*, a Tikopia genre and possibly an exclamation, begins most verses. In *pakapungaarei*, two groups sing verses in alternation. The meter of one recorded example is in five.

### Dances featuring clubs (pua taa) and other genres

Anutans rarely perform *pua taa*, men's dances in which performers in rows manipulate clubs (*raakau taua*), meter-long pieces of hardwood, with surfaces sometimes scored in crosshatches. The dancers form two lines of equal numbers. A climax occurs after the men of one line have turned their backs on those of the other; they suddenly turn around, and each man strikes his club against his opposite number's club.

Other examples include *pua taa paka-Tonga* 'Tongan-style *pua taa*' and *pua taa paka-Taamoa* 'Sāmoan-style *pua taa*', both using the struck plaque beaten as in *mataavaka*; *pua taa paka-Uvea* 'Uvean-style *pua taa*', with texts in Anutan; *reirei ao*; and *mako kairao*, an analog of the Tikopian *mako kailao*, abandoned on the advice of chiefs who reasoned that the violence of the dance does not conform with ideal Christian peaceableness.

Other Anutan songs and dances include *pakatapeepe*, in two stanzas and steady tempo, with dancers in two parallel lines; *toa* 'friend, warrior', performed during the funeral of an unmarried young person, with clapping; *vetu*, with clapping; *pakatamaaroa*, while functionaries are decorating a deceased person's body; and *tea*, featuring words identified as foreign or archaic.

### Laments (puatanga)

By content and context, Anutans differentiate laments: funeral lament (*puatanga o te tangata mate* 'a dead person's lament'), farewell lament (*puatanga pakamaavae*), and lament for a canoe (*puatanga o te vaka*). The most numerous of these are funeral laments, composed for specified persons—*puatanga o te pa* 'father's lament', *puatanga o te taina* 'parallel sibling's lament', *puatanga o te toa* 'friend's lament', and so on. A composer may create laments for siblings, cousins, relatives by marriage, children, and even grandchildren; and a composer may have died before the person whose loss the lament considers.

In contextual performances, waverings and glides add microtonal variations to melodies, though for discussion, soloists sing without such elaborations. The lyrics of one *puatanga o te pa* poignantly recall the father as a provider of food:

| | |
|---|---|
| E teteva saele i te ara, | Walking hungrily in the path, |
| Poi ou o tangi kai atu: | I go crying for food: |
| Pe ki ai? Pa kua poi. | To whom? Father has gone. |
| Puku mai te mau ou rima. | Give me the sustenance from your hands. |
| Taku rangi mamapa pakaoti raa, | My heavy foodbasket is empty, |
| I oku perenga mai ou rima. | My tokens of love from your arms. |
| | |
| Taripaki ko au ke oko mai: | I wait for him to arrive: |
| Pa ee, i mata o aamonga. | O Father, [with our] load of food: |
| Tuku mai o repe mai ki ou sei, | Give it to be divided among your children, |
| E riikopi tou titi manongi. | Your sweet catch, who sit in a circle with food. |
| | |
| Tona roto raa, toku tamana: | His mind there, my father: |
| I ou rima kai kua pakaoti raa. | O your food-bearing arms are finished. |
| Kau maanatua i te monoopo, ee! | I think of the family, *ee!* |

Anutans may also sing *puatanga* at feasts and celebrations, when the *pakaporepore* may be danced. Three or four persons rise to their feet from a seated crowd, which starts clapping: these persons try to "stand against a spirit," which, by entering them, causes their bodies to tremble; they run madly about, shaking uncontrollably. Raymond Firth reported (1954:100) a similar Anutan dance, the *makomako tapu* 'sacred dance'.

## Musical instruments

Aside from the voice, the main musical instrument used on Anuta in 1972–1973 was a struck plaque (*napa*), played for dances, but not rehearsals. For signaling, Anutans blow a conch (*puukaa*): about fifteen minutes before Christian services, a man or boy blows three blasts; after about ten minutes, he repeats the set. Children make a hollow reed or stem into a whistle; they also blow onto a blade of grass or a leaf, held between the thumbs of cupped hands to make a buzzing sound; they use rattles as toys.

## Outside influences

Since the 1970s, Western music has made inroads on Anuta, mainly through the influence of Christianity, to which Anutans converted under the auspices of the Melanesian Mission of the Anglican Church, reportedly in 1916. Initially, Anutans sang Christian hymns in the slow tempo and "heavy" timbre of laments; by 1983, they sang in standard functional harmony, with synchronized rhythms. In addition to hymns, they sing Christmas carols of the international repertory. Predominant secular musical influence is North American and Australian country, resulting from residence overseas—on Tikopia, Guadalcanal, and the Russell Islands.

—RICHARD FEINBERG

## WEST FUTUNA

West Futuna is a rocky island with steep sides and little habitable land. About four hundred people live in three districts along the perimeter of the island. They speak a Polynesian language (Dougherty 1983), do excellent craftwork (Keller 1988), and have unique songs and dances. The districts, once at war among themselves, enjoyed an autonomy that made conversion by missionaries dangerous and slow. John Williams's final missionary voyage touched the island in 1839, but the people accepted their first resident missionary only in 1866. Between these dates, they killed Sāmoan missionaries who landed. The northern district, the last to accept Christianity, retained more precontact music than the others.

Missionary activity, late-nineteenth-century slavers, colonizing governments (British, French), and participation since 1980 in Vanuatu affairs, brought West Futuna into contact with a world abroad. By the late 1900s, the people had within their cultural forms little that was obviously archaic. They still knew tales and legends that alluded to a Polynesian origin, though none related specifically to East Futuna.

### Musical contexts

The coming of Christianity changed or ended most indigenous contexts of musical performance. Missionary William Gunn (1914) wrote of festivals that featured songs and dances, often connected with religious and seasonal observances. A remnant of them survives in presentational displays of food, as at the all-Vanuatu Presbyterian Church synod, held in West Futuna in 1988, and in Christmas festivities and memorial gatherings.

Most people remember an extensive ritual that preceded communal distribution of a catch of kingfish and tuna: it entailed a distinctive dance, the *pohpokiga,* performed by fishermen around displayed fish, first on the beach, and then on the village center (*marae*). The text frequently contained bawdy references—which may be why the missionaries disapproved of the genre. The dance takes its name from the clapping (*hpo*) that occurs in it. Before fishermen brought the catch to land, they sang songs of paddling (*hgorohgorosaki*). They gave special musical shouts, alerting other fishermen and people on land.

In 1990, the singing of hymns was the most pervasive musical practice. The local hymnal, translated in the late 1800s, reflects various sources of texts and melodies. West Futunans sing hymns in unaccompanied four-part harmony, close to that of their European models, with the addition of a timbral quality that outsiders characterize as harsh. In the 1980s, missionaries introduced hymns in Bislama, Vanuatu pidgin. New churches, the Assemblies of God and Holiness Fellowship, favor guitar accompaniment for hymns.

At Christmas and New Year's, the people gather for extended singing and dancing, and West Futunans living in Tanna and Port Vila visit the island. Services in church, sports, light entertainments, music, and dancing, may occupy Christmas Day and two or more days after. *Punani,* a continuation or resumption of the festivities, occurs on New Year's: bearing gifts and singing newly composed songs and old favorites, people move from house to house. In much of the dancing at the festivities, dancers' hands express or decorate the meaning of the words.

Memorial gatherings (*kaitarua*) occur about a year after a death. They mark the end of mourning and the completion of the gravestone. For these gatherings, relatives commission a song to recount the life of the deceased. Such a song, though in contemporary style (choral or accompanied by a string band), continues the memorial function of older songs.

West Futunan songs began as commissioned or inspired works. A spirit could inspire a composer; the resulting song might reveal how a person died. For a commissioned work, a family would supply the composer with fitting biographical details (*ujia*). Gunn gave a glimpse of this system when he said a man who had commissioned a composer "brought a basket of flowers and leaves to him, that their names might be introduced into the song" (1914:23).

## Genres of music and dance

The principal West Futunan instrument is the human voice (*reo*); the paramount musical activity, singing for dancing. Natural imagery is common in texts, which often hide meanings in metaphor. A text of the genre *bau* tells the story of the hewing of a canoe, its launching, and its loss in the reef-crossing channel:

> Tavaka fou a maua, *ruerue yangrinia.*
> Saua ma htatu ifo, *ruerue yangrinia.*
> Kojikai ta ekeiai, *ruerue yangrinia.*
> Kojikai ta fakapani, *ruerue yangrinia.*
> Tatu ifo tafoi takere, *ruerue yangrinia.*
> Kerovau i ata seuseu, *ruerue yangrinia.*
> Heio heiowa heioweiya gaeae, *ruerue yangrinia.*
>
> Our new canoe, *ruerue yangrinia.*
> Cut it and let it fall, *ruerue yangrinia.*
> Nothing will stop it, *ruerue yangrinia.*
> Nothing to lean against, *ruerue yangrinia.*
> Complete the canoe base, *ruerue yangrinia.*
> Cry in the channel, *ruerue yangrinia.*
> Drowned in the channel, *ruerue yangrinia.*

Local people believe this canoe is metaphorically a person under a curse to die.

*Tagi* are songs that recount historical incidents or events in an individual's life. West Futunans think the most recently composed *tagi* honored a man who died in 1976. Accompanied by *kafa,* people sing *tagi* in unison. *Tagihkai* are short songs in tales (*hkai*). They mark dramatic moments within the narrative. West Futunans know many, which form an extensive corpus. *Hgororagina,* a festive dance, contains a distinctive call or shout. *Kaimata* and *hgorohgorosaki* are genres associated with fishing.

Games often have short songs of teasing or timekeeping. Figure 9 shows a song from a game in which players, after making a stack of hands, pinch the skin on the upper surface of the hand below them in the stack.

| | |
|---|---|
| Niginigi tona, | Pinch the lump, |
| Niginigi tona. | Pinch the lump, |
| Ojikai a tona, | Nothing to its lump, |
| Tona reu ma tona fatu | Its wart and its callus. |
| More kea tam rama. | Pray it will go to the moon. |

The melody, the same as that used in another game (Thomas and Kuautoga 1992:20), ends in a spoken line with a downward slide. Apparently archaic, these features do not appear elsewhere in the music of West Futuna.

FIGURE 9    The game "*Niginigi tona*" as performed by school-children on West Futuna in 1990, with cadential words in spoken rhythm. Transcription by Allan Thomas.

## Musical accompaniments

In the late 1800s, West Futunans commonly sang to the accompaniment of a struck idiophone: "At night men and women ranged themselves in the square [*marae*] on either side of a log which they struck with a slow, regular beat, and sang, shouted, and yelled their native heathen songs until dawn" (Gunn 1914:210). This instrument, the *kafa,* a log of wood or bamboo, takes its name from coconut husk, whose fibers people roll into string. At performances observed in 1990, all participants sounded a basic pulse, which in the last section of songs accelerated. The drummers sang while others danced. Unlike log idiophones, the *kafa* is not a constructed instrument, but terms for beating it (*hta kafa*) and a name for the beaters (*kane*) exist.

Other local instruments are conch trumpets (*pŭ*) and panpipes (*fagovava*). Children's musical toys (often called *fago*) include a twanged lamellaphone, a rolled leaf, a struck bamboo tube (*fagoigoi*), and a leaf whizzer (*ragohpa*).

## Participation in festivals

Festivals within Vanuatu and abroad have played decisive roles in the continuation of old artistic forms. The first extrainsular event in which a West Futunan troupe participated was the visit of Queen Elizabeth II to Vila, in 1974. This occasion included a presentation of the old dances by young people. The same troupe performed at the first national Arts Festival (1979) and at the Independence Festival (1980), which showed the national government's commitment to traditional arts as a contemporary expression of national identity. In 1988, the troupe represented Vanuatu at the Pacific Festival of Arts in Townsville, Australia; the Australian Expo in Brisbane; and a festival in Japan.

These undertakings guaranteed intensive training in the arts, provided income for young people, and afforded opportunities for travel. The troupe's repertory includes the *toka,* a Tannese circular dance, and the *namauia,* a festive dance. The most distinctive genre is the *pohpokiga,* though it is not performed in its original context. The text of figure 10 refers to four plants that grow on West Futuna and other islands, including those of West Polynesia; the song is about Majijiki, the cultural hero elsewhere known as Maui.

Through commercial cassettes, broadcasts on radio, and festivals, people of Vanuatu know about West Futuna's string band, Fatu'ana, which has a distinctive sound, including the clinks of what they call a bottle-piano, a row of bottles filled

FIGURE 10    "*Eiau*," a *pohpokiga,* sung by dancers on West Futuna in 1990. People clapped on the downbeats of each bar. The text refers to the *futu* (a tree, *Barringtonia asiatica*), the *fue* (the common convolvulus), the *fau* (a shrub, *Hibiscus tiliaceus*), and the *sinu* (the wild almond, *Terminalia catappa*). Transcription by Allan Thomas.

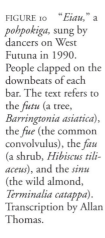

with water and struck with sticks. At the celebrations of the tenth anniversary of the political independence of Vanuatu (held in Tanna in 1990), Fatu'ana won the national string-band competition.

—ALLAN THOMAS

## REFERENCES

Burrows, Edwin G. 1934. "Polynesian Part-Singing." *Zeitschrift für Vergleichende Musikwissenschaft* 2:69–76.

Collinson, Clifford Whiteley. 1926. *Life and Laughter 'Midst the Cannibals.* London: Hurst and Blackett.

Davidson, Janet. 1971. *Archeology on Nukuoro Atoll, a Polynesian Outlier in the Eastern Caroline Islands.* Auckland Institute and Museum Bulletin 9. Auckland: Auckland Institute and Museum.

Dougherty, Janet. 1983. *West Futuna—Aniwa: An Introduction to a Polynesian Outlier Language.* University of California Publications in Linguistics, 102. Berkeley: University of California Press.

Elbert, Samuel H. 1967. "A Linguistic Assessment of the Historical Validity of Some of the Rennellese and Bellonese Oral Traditions." In *Polynesian Culture History: Essays in Honor of Kenneth P. Emory,* ed. Genevieve A. Highland, Roland W. Force, Alan Howard, Marion Kelly, and Yosihiko H. Sinoto, 257–288. Special publication 56. Honolulu: Bishop Museum.

Elbert, Samuel H., and Torben Monberg. 1965. *From the Two Canoes: Oral Traditions of Rennell and Bellona Islands.* Copenhagen: Danish National Museum.

Emory, Kenneth P. 1965. *Kapingamarangi: Social and Religious Life of a Polynesian Atoll.* Bulletin 228. Honolulu: Bishop Museum Press.

Feinberg, Richard. 1981. *Anuta: Social Structure of a Polynesian Island.* Lāʻie and Copenhagen: Institute for Polynesian Studies and The Danish National Museum.

Firth, Raymond. 1936. *We, the Tikopia.* London: George Allen & Unwin.

———. 1954. "Anuta and Tikopia: Symbiotic Elements in Social Organization." *Journal of the Polynesian Society* 63:87–131.

———. 1990. *Tikopia Songs: Poetic and Musical Art of a Polynesian People of the Solomon Islands.* Cambridge: Cambridge University Press.

Gunn, William. 1914. *The Gospel in Futuna.* London: Hodder & Stoughton.

Hogbin, H. Ian. 1930. "Transition Rites at Ontong Java (Solomon Islands)." Journal of the Polynesian Society 39:94–112, 201–220.

———. 1934. *Law and Order in Polynesia: A Study of Primitive Legal Institutions.* London: Christophers.

Howard, Irwin. 1981. "Proto-Ellicean." In *Studies in Pacific Languages and Cultures,* ed. Jim Hollyman and Andrew Pawley. Auckland: Linguistic Society of New Zealand.

Johnson, Osa H. 1945. *Bride in the Solomons.* London: George G. Harrap.

Keller, Janet D. 1988. "Woven World: Neotraditional Symbols of Unity in Vanuatu." *Mankind* 18(1):1–13.

Kirch, Patrick V. 1984. "The Polynesian Outliers: Continuity, Change, and Replacement." *Journal of Pacific History* 19:224–238.

Lieber, Michael D. 1991. "Cutting Your Losses: Death and Grieving on a Polynesian Atoll." In *Coping with the Final Tragedy: Cultural Variation in Dying and Grieving,* ed. Dorothy and David Counts, 161–190. Boston: Baywood Press.

Mytinger, Caroline. 1942. *Headhunting in the Solomon Islands around the Coral Sea.* New York: Macmillan.

Parkinson, Richard. 1986 [1897]. "Ethnography of Ontong Java and Tasman Islands with Remarks re: the Marqueen and Abgarris Islands." Translated by Rose S. Hartmann. Introduced and annotated by Richard Feinberg. *Pacific Studies* 9(3):1–31.

Rossen, Jane Mink. 1987. *Songs of Bellona (Na Taungua o Mungiki).* Language and Culture of Rennell and Bellona Islands, 6. Copenhagen: Kragen, Danish Folklore Archives.

Rossen, Jane Mink, and Margot Mink Colbert. 1981. "Dance on Bellona, Solomon Islands: A Preliminary Study of Style and Concept." *Ethnomusicology* 25(3):447–466.

Sahlins, Marshall D. 1958. *Social Stratification in Polynesia.* American Ethnological Society Monographs, 29. Seattle: University of Washington Press.

Sarfert, Ernst, and Hans Damm. 1929. *Luangiua und Nukumanu: Allgemeines Teil und Materielle Kultur.* Ergebnisse der Hamburger Südsee-Expedition 1908–1910, II.B.12, vol. 1. Hamburg: Friedrichsen, De Gruyter.

———. 1931. *Luangiua und Nukumanu: Soziale Verhältnisse und Geisterkultur.* Ergebnisse der Hamburger Südsee-Expedition 1908–1910, II.B.12, vol. 2. Hamburg: Hübner, Friedrichsen.

Thomas, Allan, and Takaroga Kuautoga. 1992. *Hgoro Futuna: Report of a Survey of the Music of West Futuna, Vanuatu.* Occasional Papers in Pacific Ethnomusicology, 2. Auckland: Department of Anthropology, University of Auckland.

Zemp, Hugo. 1971. *Polynesian Traditional Music of Ontong Java (Solomon Islands).* Vogue LD 785. LP disk and notes.

———. 1972a. *Musique de Luangiua: Atoll d'Ontong Java.* Musée de l'Homme. LP disk and notes.

———. 1972b. *Polynesian Traditional Music of Ontong Java (Solomon Islands).* Vogue LDM 30109. LP disk and notes.

# East Polynesia

*Adrienne L. Kaeppler*  *Kauraka Kauraka*  *Jennifer Shennan*
*Jane Freeman Moulin*  *Kevin Salisbury*  *Jan Bolwell*
*Amy Kuʻuleialoha Stillman*  *Kaʻala Carmack*  *Keri Kaa*
*Takiora Ingram*  *Allan Thomas*  *Juan Pablo González*
*Jon Tikivanotau Jonassen*  *Te Puoho Katene*
*Helen Reeves Lawrence*  *Te Ahukaramū Charles Royal*

**Society Islands**

**Austral Islands**

**Tuamotu Islands**

**Mangareva**

**Marquesas Islands**

**Cook Islands**

**Hawaiʻi**

**Aotearoa**

**Rapa Nui**

East Polynesia includes the Cook Islands, the Society Islands, the Austral Islands, the Tuamotu Islands, Mangareva, the Marquesas, Hawaiʻi, Rapa Nui, Aotearoa, and the Chatham Islands (see map). Aotearoa and the Chatham Islands form an independent nation, New Zealand. Rapa Nui is a dependency of Chile; Hawaiʻi is a state of the United States of America; the Cook Islands have a special political relationship with New Zealand. The Marquesas, Societies, Australs, Mangareva, and Tuamotus constitute an overseas territory of France known as French Polynesia.

East Polynesians share with their West Polynesian and outlier cousins similarities in musical concepts and contexts, especially the importance of sung poetry. Polyphony took different forms, and in some islands (Hawaiʻi and Aotearoa) was absent from indigenous practice. In postmissionary times, thickly textured harmonic forms became typical, especially of French Polynesia and the Cook Islands.

The inventory of musical instruments varied widely from that of West Polynesia. Membranophones of different sizes, made of a sharkskin-covered hollow wooden cylinder and called *pahu,* replaced or supplemented log idiophones; mouth-resonated bows were found in the Marquesas, Australs, and Hawaiʻi; mouth-blown flutes and wooden trumpets are known from the Marquesas and Aotearoa; varieties of idiophones (rattles and clappers) were used in Hawaiʻi, the Marquesas, and Aotearoa; *poi* (weighted balls, attached to strings) create visual designs and audible rhythms as they strike the body.

East Polynesian movement systems emphasize hand-and-arm movements, upright torso, lack of shoulder movements, restricted locomotion, and linear formations. Various combinations of wrist flexion and extension and the rotation of the lower arm result in characteristic movement motifs. Lower arm rotations in conjunction with a rather stiff wrist are characteristic for Tahiti, while a hand quiver with stiff wrist is characteristic of New Zealand. In Hawaiʻi a flexion and extension of the wrist in conjunction with bending at the knuckles and curling the fingers are characteristic. In East Polynesia, lower-body movements have been elaborated into complex motifs that differ according to gender. The lower-body motifs usually keep the time, while the arm movements convey the poetry. A combination of two main elements—

East Polynesia

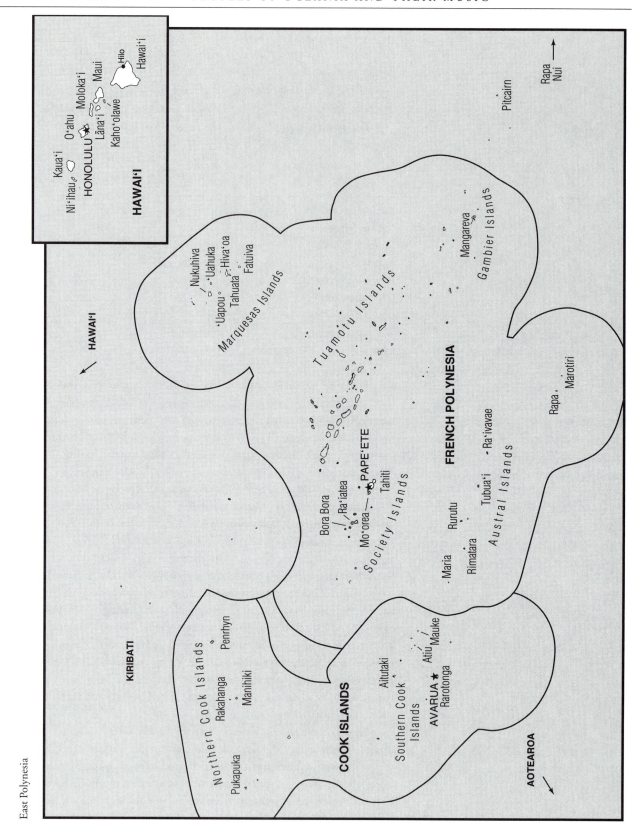

the arm-wrist movements and the interplay of leg-and-hip movements—gives each Polynesian dance tradition a distinctive style.          —ADRIENNE L. KAEPPLER

## SOCIETY ISLANDS

The Society archipelago includes windward islands (Tahiti, Mo'orea, Mai'ao, Tetiaroa, Mehetia) and leeward islands (Ra'iatea, Taha'a, Huahine, Bora Bora, Tupai, Maupiti, Maupiha'a, Manuae, Motu One). The term *Tahitian* applies to the shared language and culture typical of the archipelago. In referring to the language and revived customs, the term *mā'ohi* 'indigenous' is increasingly popular.

About two hundred thousand persons live in the Society Islands—more than 85 percent of them on the windward islands. The largest concentration of people inhabits the town and environs of Pape'ete, seat of the territorial government and economic hub of French Polynesia. During the economic boom of the 1960s and 1970s, tourism and French nuclear testing increased the number of urban jobs, attracting immigrants from elsewhere in French Polynesia. These immigrants formed communities that retain their languages and traditions.

### Music and dance in Tahitian life

Beginning in the 1950s, French Polynesia experienced intense, accelerated social transformation. Islanders responded by adapting their performances to common artistic values, expectations, and aesthetics. Outsiders sometimes reproach Tahitians for supposedly commercializing the arts during this period; Tahitians, however, portray these years as ones when they restored the beauty and dignity of their music and dance, established these traditions in a global world, and searched for authenticity. An understanding of the social, political, geographical, and artistic factors that influence performance helps place late-twentieth-century arts in perspective.

As prominent symbols of cultural identity, music and dance are vehicles for expressing nationalistic feelings and ethnicity. Tahitians who espouse *mā'ohi* values and practices embrace an identity that looks to the past, but carries social and political overtones in the present.

Musical events reveal changing sociopolitical currents, and Tahiti's annual music-and-dance competitions provide prime examples. For more than a century, these competitions celebrated Bastille Day (14 July), the French national holiday. In the mid-1970s, local political involvement increased, reinforcing nationalistic feelings and recognizing Tahitian as the official language on 30 November 1980. The competitions reflected the redefinition of the political association with France. In 1985, Tahitians celebrated July (*Tiurai*) as La Fête de l'Autonomie Interne, and moved the opening ceremonies from Bastille Day to 29 June. In 1986, they renamed it Heiva i Tahiti, reinforcing the Tahitianness of the event by incorporating the Tahitian word *heiva* 'dance, amusements'.

Though new ideas and practices from Tahiti eventually reach the other islands, Pape'ete sets the trends in fashion, politics, and culture. Performers on other islands look to Tahiti for innovation, but maintain what Tahitians consider older styles of performance. Tahiti savors creativity and innovation. The 1980s brought rapid changes in music and dance, as Tahitians chose selectively from their own past, absorbed compatible elements from their neighbors, and incorporated innovative ideas from outstanding choreographers. Change continues, and the Heiva serves as an arena for exhibiting the new and imaginative. Sometimes, innovations shock the audience: entering a stage on motorcycles, performing a modern dance choreographed by a Frenchman, or mocking consumerism by wearing skirts made from old tin cans and garbage—all were tossed off as outlandish, or viewed as single-instance social statements, not to be repeated. Other new ideas are accepted. By 1995, introductions from 1989 to 1992—new techniques of drumming, women's demi-pointe dancing, men's hip movements—had become standard features.

Though Heiva highlights the year, performances occur year-round. Occasions include presentations by professional troupes and those representing districts, schools, and churches; shows for tourists; official receptions; local balls and club-sponsored celebrations; and impromptu musical performance among friends and family. Religious services, Bible-study meetings, the March fifth celebration of the arrival of Christianity, and meetings of churchwomen's associations are important musical occasions. Visiting troupes from other Polynesian islands are enthusiastically received.

### Non-Polynesian performances

Chinese immigration dates from 1865, when 329 Chinese laborers arrived in Tahiti to work on a cotton plantation; another 681 soon followed. When the plantation failed, these workers settled throughout the Society Islands, where they set up businesses that led them to financial success. Chinese stores are landmarks on all islands, and only since the mid-1980s have non-Chinese entrepreneurs successfully challenged them. Chinese residents created Chinese associations in Pape'ete, and schools established by Kuo Min Tang, Kuo Men Tong, and Chun Fa Fui King (or Association Philanthropique) still teach Chinese the language. Other Chinese associations include Si Ni Tong (a religious, charitable, and social organization, which organizes events featuring Chinese culture) and Wen Fa (dedicated to integrating Chinese into the cultural life of French Polynesia). Parallel and probably linked to the Polynesian quest for identity, an interest in Chinese arts has grown in Pape'ete and 'Uturoa (on Ra'iatea). Cultural ties among French Polynesian Chinese extend to such activities as dances for the Chinese New Year, the Festival of the Moon (February and September), festivities held at Tahiti's T'ai Kung Ch'ong temple, a Chinese presentation at the Pacific Festival of Arts in 1985, and dance-centered competitions. Some Chinese families sponsor singing groups, and families recognized for their musical talent perform at public celebrations [see MUSICAL MIGRATIONS].

Western musical presence in French Polynesia has gradually increased, especially with the arrival of satellite television (1977). Concerts, recitals, and musical theater are more frequent in the 1990s. Some non-Tahitian theatrical presentations include Tahitian music and dance. Musique en Polynésie, a concert-producing society, presents an annual series of seven or eight concerts or recitals by artists visiting from Europe, South America, and the United States. Pro Musica, an amateur vocal and instrumental ensemble, offers concerts of Western classical music; it sometimes includes musicians from the local conservatory and the Régiment d'Infanterie de Marine du Pacifique, the French military band. These concerts attract an audience composed mostly of Europeans and mixed-blood Tahitians (*demis*).

### Musical instruments

Musical instruments in Tahiti are associated with specific forms of singing and dancing. Guitars (electric and acoustic), drums, electric bass, and synthesizers accompany songs for entertainment, religious songs in popular styles (played by young people), couple dancing at local hotels and bars, fashion shows, and theatrical events. Guitars and ukuleles, a requisite for informal music, also accompany large groups of dancers. Around 1993, locally made eight-stringed ukuleles in unusual shapes came into vogue.

Instruments that accompany Tahitian-style dancing include a log idiophone, *tō'ere,* played with one stick (two-stick playing, *tā'iri piti,* is an importation from the

FIGURE 1    The double-membrane *pahu* (foreground), the single-membrane *fáatete* (right rear), and the struck log idiophones *tō‘ere* (left rear) are the primary instruments in the Tahitian percussion ensemble. Photo by Jane Freeman Moulin, 1995.

Cook Islands); the one-headed *fáatete,* a short drum, played with two sticks; and the two-headed *pahu,* with origins in the European bass drum (figure 1). In the mid-1980s, performers began to use the *ihara,* a bamboo instrument in which raised lengths of the bark are struck with sticks; by 1995, it had become a regular member of several instrumental ensembles. Nose-blown flutes (*vivo*), played until the early 1900s, made a quiet comeback after an appearance in a Heiva performance (1976) by the troupe Te Maeva. At the same performance, Te Maeva resurrected the one-headed *pahu tupa‘i rima,* a tall, hand-struck drum, which gained popularity during the 1980s and is now an accepted addition to the standard ensemble (of *tō‘ere, fáatete,* and *pahu*). The conch trumpet (*pū*) is often sounded to accent the start of a dance.

The reappearance of, and renewed interest in, such instruments as the *ihara,* the *vivo,* and the *pahu tupa‘i rima* emphasizes issues of identity. The disappearance of these instruments caused a break in the tradition; their revival reflects contemporary views, and provides a model for revalidating aspects of their history. A key to understanding is not to look for a pure, unchanged tradition, but to enjoy how Tahitians bring tradition into the present.

### Scholarship on music and dance

The earliest known recordings of choral singing in the Society Islands were supervised in 1906 by Henry Crampton, a biologist. In 1923, at the Bastille Day competition, anthropologist E. S. Craighill Handy recorded the choir from the district of Fa‘aone, Tahiti, and took photographs of performances. Edwin G. Burrows (1934b) analyzed Handy's recordings and notes. In 1986, Raymond Mesplé completed a master's thesis based on work with two choirs in Pape‘ete. In 1987–1988, Amy Ku‘uleialoha Stillman documented choral singing in Protestant churches (1987b).

References in popular and academic publications have touched on Tahitian dance, but Patrick O'Reilly's overview of historical and contemporary dancing (1977) was the first monograph to deal with the subject. Jane Freeman Moulin's research and experience as a professional dancer in Tahiti (1973–1977) provided the basis for her detailed description of dance from a dancer-scholar's point of view (1979).

—JANE FREEMAN MOULIN

### Choral music

British missionaries arrived in the Society Islands in 1797. To describe introduced Christian hymns, they transliterated the English term *hymn* into a Tahitian form, *hīmene* (figure 2). By the late 1800s, the term *hīmene* covered all choral singing, Christian or not. It adjectivally specifies choirs (*pūpū hīmene*) and describes events (like *tātá ura‘a hīmene* 'choral competition') in which choral singing is a major component (Stillman 1991).

Tahitian choral singing is comprised of named styles differentiated by musical criteria, and of named repertorial categories differentiated by nonmusical criteria, such as poetic content, the performers' ages, and whether or not the text appears in a printed hymnal. At the broadest level, Tahitians differentiate two categories of musical performance, based on the perceived origins of the music: styles of reputedly indigenous origin are *hīmene mā‘ohi* 'true *hīmene*'; styles of reputedly foreign origin are *hīmene pōpa‘a* 'foreign *hīmene*'. Musical traits differentiate five styles: *hīmene nota, hīmene puta, hīmene rū‘au, hīmene tārava,* and *hīmene tuki.* The first two are of foreign origin, the last two are of Polynesian origin, and the third, originally of foreign origin, is considered indigenous.

FIGURE 2    Directed by a woman, a group sings a *hīmene* in a competition at the Fête Nationale, 14 July 1923. Photo by R. H. Beck. Courtesy of the Department of Library Services, American Museum of Natural History.

### Genres of choral music

#### Hīmene nota

These are equivalent to three- and four-part Western choral singing, whose origins are clearly nonindigenous. The vocal parts bear the French names for choral parts: *première voix, seconde, ténor,* and *basse,* corresponding in English to *soprano, alto, tenor,* and *bass.* The term *nota* (from English *note*) refers to the notated arrangement of a *hīmene,* usually in published hymnals. Tahitian-language texts are composed and written by hand below the notes in place of the original text, which choristers cover with liquid whiteout.

Arrangements of *hīmene nota* incorporate musical motion beyond simple note-against-note harmonization. Calls and responses may occur between subdivisions of vocal parts, and in passages where one or more parts perform patterns rhythmically different from the principal part. No part takes a completely subordinate role throughout a *hīmene*; each part can be assigned the lead or some section with melodic interest.

#### Hīmene puta

The term *puta* transliterates the English word *book*; hence, *hīmene puta* are hymns whose texts appear in printed hymnals. Three Protestant Tahitian-language hymnals are in use. The *Buke Himene Tahito* (first printed in 1909, most recently reprinted in 1979) contains a mixture of repertory carried over from nineteenth-century imprints, with Sunday-school repertory from around 1900. The *Buke Himene* of 1974 contains Sunday-school repertory exclusively. A third hymnal, also titled *Buke Himene,* was issued in 1983, and includes material drawn from updated English and French hymnals.

Despite the tendency of *hīmene puta* to denote hymns in printed hymnals, the term implies specific musical traits that designate a style of performance—that of late-nineteenth-century American Sunday-school hymns, known primarily through the *Buke Himene* of 1974. A primary melody is harmonized note-against-note with a subordinate chordal accompaniment. *Hīmene puta* either repeat strophes exactly (all stanzas sung to one melody) or alternate stanzas and a refrain. They have three vocal parts, named according to gender: first women (*vahine hōʻe*) sing the melody; second women (*vahine piti*) harmonize the melody, usually at a third or sixth; and men (*tane*) sing a bass of root chordal tones.

#### Hīmene rūʻau

The term *rūʻau* 'old' has been variously applied to the reputed age of the orally transmitted melodies, or to the age of the singers who take particular pleasure in singing them. *Hīmene rū'au* apparently emerged out of the earliest introduced English hymns; many devotional texts sung to the melodies of *hīmene rū'au* appeared in print in Protestant hymnals between 1814 and 1909. Though their inclusion in printed hymnals permits their classification as *hīmene puta,* they differ from those of the printed hymnals.

Vocal parts may number from two to five, depending on particulars of melody and form. Women sing the primary melody, which some of them harmonize; some refrains require a high part. Men sing a bass, above which may be a tenor. Vocal parts in *hīmene rū'au* are named, but inconsistencies among the names reveal more casual conceptions than inform *hīmene tārava.* Some singers simply use the gender-based terms *vahine* and *tane,* but other singers borrow terms from *hīmene tārava,* such as *fa'aaraara* for the woman who begins the performance, and *marū* for the main melody or the men's harmonizing part.

The melodies of *hīmene rū'au* consist of highly structured norms of melodic organization. Melodic motion in the primary melody among chordal tones is step-wise, or with stereotyped patterns of upper or lower decorative auxiliaries. Melodic contour and register are balanced: an ascending line in one phrase invites a descent in the next; likewise, a phrase in one vocal register (section of a singer's range) invites a phrase in another. Cadential harmonization is entirely idiosyncratic. All women reach the tonic on or before the final syllable. The men approach the dominant, which they hold momentarily on the final syllable against the women's tonic before resolving to the tonic. The result is a tonic harmony in second inversion, which resolves to a unison at the octave.

### Hīmene tārava

Singers agree that the term *tārava,* a verb meaning 'to lie horizontally', denotes the drawn-out cadence at the end of stanzas. *Hīmene tārava* are indigenous in origin. They flourish in French Polynesia in three regional styles, whose differences appear in the number of named vocal parts and their musical content. *Hīmene tārava Tahiti,* the style practiced in the windward islands, usually has five to seven vocal parts. *Hīmene tārava raromata'i,* the style practiced throughout the leeward islands, averages seven to nine or ten parts. Society Islanders collectively call the styles practiced in the Austral Islands *tārava Rurutu.*

*Hīmene tārava* have a detailed vocabulary by which singers distinguish the vocal parts and articulate various aspects of singing procedures. The number and musical contents of vocal parts vary among choirs. In general, each vocal part takes one of three ascribed functions: textual declamation, melodic decoration, and rhythmic punctuation. Some are for women (w) and some, for men (m):

| General function | Windward Islands | Leeward Islands |
|---|---|---|
| Textual declamation | *fa'aaraara* (w) | *fa'aaraara* (w) |
| | _____ | *haruharu* (w) |
| | _____ | *parauparau* (w) |
| | _____ | *huti* (w) |
| | *marū* (w, m) | _____ |
| | *marū tāmau* (m) | *marū tāmau* (m) |
| Melodic decoration | *perepere* (w) | *perepere* (w, m) |
| | *marū teitei* (w, m) | *marū teitei* (w, m) |
| Rhythmic punctuation | *hā'ū* (m) | *hā'ū* (m) |
| | *marū hāruru* | _____ |

*Hīmene* are an integral part of the two major devotional activities: worship and Bible-study meetings. During worship on Sundays, *hīmene* separate major components of the service—confession of sins, reading from the Bible, a sermon, an offering, and, on the first Sunday of each month, communion.

Vocal melodies are narrow, and the melodic configuration that results from combining individual parts is the musical basis for locally distinguishing *hīmene tārava.*

In a typical *hīmene tārava,* a female lead singer (*fa'aaraara* 'to awaken') commences, giving out the first line in a strong, confident, often piercing voice. Other singers find their own niches at their own pace, some entering almost simultaneously with the leader, others taking as long as the entire first line of text. A successful start is described as rising (*mara'a*); conversely, when singers fail to catch (*haru*) onto the leader, the *hīmene* is said to fall (*topa*). Once the performance is under way, at least one soloist (usually a woman) ascends to the *perepere,* the high decorative part. At the back of the choir, young men and teenaged boys perform grunting (*hā'ū*). At the end of the stanza, the singers consolidate together on the tonic. There is a moment of anticipation while they hold the tonic in unison. If someone restarts the stanza, the cycle repeats, either until everyone is exhausted and no one gives out the beginning line, or (in the case of presentational performances) until the end of the final repetition of the final stanza.

Though no evidence on the birth of *hīmene tārava* has turned up, the genre undoubtedly has links to the local establishment of Protestantism, in the early 1800s; travelers' accounts document its practice since the 1870s. Its music probably emerged from indigenous styles, revitalized in the 1830s and 1840s, for some of its traits correspond to those of performances reported by eighteenth-century explorers.

### Hīmene tuki

Tahitians describe the *hīmene tuki* as a Tahitian rendition of the Cook Island equivalent of *hīmene tārava.* The word *tuki* is the Rarotongan term for the guttural grunting performed by the men in short periods near the ends of phrases or stanzas. This style is sometimes called *hīmene raroto'a,* referring to the Rarotongan-language texts and to Rarotonga, principal island of the southern Cook Islands. The texts come from two sources: the current Cook Islands Protestant hymnal and Cook Islanders living in the Society Islands.

*Hīmene tuki* are through-composed, and each normally consists of three or four sections of music. Tahitians observe the conventions of repetition by repeating the final one or two lines of text within a section, then repeating the entire section, but they like to combine different sources into one *hīmene tuki.* As performed in the Society Islands, *hīmene tuki* have two vocal parts, named by gender: women sing the primary melody in unison; men dwell on grunting, to an extent that Cook Islanders find excessive.

Singers in the Society Islands perform *hīmene tuki* only on special occasions, not normally in regular Sunday worship. Women sit on the floor, in straight or semicircular rows. Older men sit behind them. Younger men, who stand around the others in a horseshoe-shaped row, bend inward and outward in synchrony, and perform scissorlike movements of the legs (*pā'oti*) during the grunting.

### Performance venues

Choral singing in the Society Islands flourishes in two contrasting domains: Christian worship and civil celebrations. It emerged out of Tahitian Protestantism, established by 1819. Christian denominations established in later decades (Hodée 1983) have adopted musical styles associated with Protestant worship and devotional activities. *Hīmene* are an integral part of the two major devotional activities: worship and Bible-study meetings.

During worship on Sundays, *hīmene* separate major components of the service—confession of sins, reading from the Bible, a sermon, an offering, and, on the first Sunday of each month, communion. The congregation sings the opening and closing *hīmene,* and set *hīmene* during the confessional and the offering. The other *hīmene* are performances prepared by the choirs within a parish. *Hīmene* performed during services in church are only in the styles of *hīmene pōpaʻa, hīmene puta,* and *hīmene rūʻau. Hīmene tārava* are not sung inside a church, and *hīmene tuki* are performed there only on special occasions, such as the annual May collections.

Bible-study meetings are held in *fare putuputuraʻa,* halls maintained by parochial groups, whose membership is determined by locale within the parish. Each meeting is devoted to interpreting one assigned biblical verse, delivered within a Tahitian oratorical framework. The singing of *hīmene tārava* occurs between spoken remarks. The texts are short, four to eight lines in a stanza, and normally only one stanza; they usually paraphrase biblical episodes relating to the verse under study. In Vaitoʻare, Tahaʻa, the meeting discussed the verse "Where is he that is born King of the Jews? for we have seen his star in the east, and are come to worship him" (Matt. 2:2), and sang a *hīmene tārava* with this text:

| | |
|---|---|
| Taʻata faʻaroʻo ʻo Iosua rā: | Joshua is a faithful man: |
| I te tapeʻa raʻa i te mahana, | At the setting of the sun, |
| Mai te mea atu rā te mahana, | When the sun sets, |
| E tariʻa tona e faʻaroʻo. | His keen ear listens. |

Children acquire competence in singing *hīmene tārava* by simply absorbing the style; by their late teens or early adult years, those with musical aptitude develop a niche in one of the solo parts.

Choral singing is also an integral part of civil festivities surrounding the French national holiday, observed annually since in 1881, following French annexation of the Society Islands, with precedents in festivities commemorating the birthday of the French Emperor Napoleon III in 1859 and 1875. In the 1880s, these festivities featured choral-singing competitions. Participants emphasized *hīmene tārava,* for which judges awarded the largest prizes. Organizers offered smaller prizes for *hīmene pōpaʻa,* and sometimes only for *hīmene tārava.* In 1979, *hīmene rūʻau* became a compulsory category in the competitions.

*Hīmene* sung in competitions at the Heiva come from indigenous legends, myths, and historical chronicles, which collectively form a record of important places, people, and events. When delivered in oratory or recited in poetry (as with *hīmene tārava*), these traditions are *paripari fenua,* 'praises of the land'. Texts have at least six stanzas. To maximize the impact of the presentation, choirs rehearse *hīmene tārava* carefully before performing them in competitions.

—AMY KUʻULEIALOHA STILLMAN

## Dance

In Papeʻete and its environs, people attend presentations of Polynesian dances, recognizing differences in dances of the Society, Tuamotu, Marquesas, and Austral Islands.

They see Western dances, including contemporary popular styles, ballet, and modern dance. Occasionally, they see Chinese dances. They see the national styles of visiting troupes, participate in school church, district, and professional troupes, take formal classes in imported and Tahitian dances, and dance the night away at hotels, bars, and discos.

Beyond the cosmopolitan life of Pape'ete, dance participation consists of couple dancing using imported or Tahitian movements and group dancing. Dancing in couples is participatory, improvisatory, and spontaneous; dancing in groups is presentational, choreographed, and rehearsed. In Pape'ete, dancing occurs nightly; in outlying districts and on the other islands, it is less frequent, and may consist of a weekly Tahitian show at a hotel and weekend dancing in couples to a local band's music. Communal and ecclesiastical events that include dancing dot the calendar and animate village life.

### Couple dancing

Most couple dancing follows Western models. The Tahitian waltz, a standard waltz with Tahitian text, is a perennial favorite. Young people follow new crazes from abroad, and older people prefer the dances of their youth. Dancing is the expected activity at large gatherings, such as balls for Bastille Day and New Year's Eve; events organized by clubs and sports associations; and evenings in Tahiti's bars and clubs. During weekends, hotels have live music for local people. The music features internationally known compositions and local creations, with texts in Tahitian or French, and Westernized melodies, harmonies, and rhythms. Tahitians prefer live music, especially electric bands, using guitar, bass guitar, synthesizer and drums.

Some couple dancing uses Tahitian dance movements, and couples shift from Western to Tahitian movements depending on the music. Typical songs are short, with repeated verses and driving rhythms. Overall melodic contours are mainly level; when melodic movement occurs, prevalent intervals are minor thirds at the start of phrases and major seconds above the main tone near the endings of verses.

Tahitian movements accompanying these songs are gender-specific, featuring movements of the lower torso and legs. Women revolve their hips, with legs slightly flexed and feet flat on the ground; men open and close their knees (*pāʻoti* 'scissors'), with legs bent and feet close together (figure 3). Women and men keep the upper torso erect and stationary; arms move primarily above the waist. The man faces the woman and may circle her, defining a shared space.

The older, proper way of referring to this style of dancing is 'ori tahiti, but in the 1950s, *tāmūrē* emerged as a popular term. A popular Tahitian song repeatedly employed this word, which became applied to the movements. *Tāmūrē* has sexual connotations, denoting a fish that lives among corals, sticking its head in and out of its hole. In Tahiti, dance is associated with joy and pleasure. Proto-Polynesian glosses of the word *\*'ori* include 'move pleasurably', 'joy, happiness', 'play, divert, amuse; wag the tail' (Walsh and Biggs 1966:36).

Couple dancing may exhibit flirtatious interplay: dancers move as close as possible without touching, the man adding small, forward pelvic thrusts, the woman adding large, sideways swings of the hips, aimed at her partner's pelvis, and urging his gaze toward her hips. Non-Polynesians interpret this as overt sexuality, but fail to understand that sexuality is neither the purpose nor the intent of all Tahitian dance.

### Group presentational dance

In group dancing, a community displays the skill, physical beauty, and stamina of its young, reconfirms its identification with Tahitian culture, solidifies group affiliation and pride, marks the importance of an occasion, and presents a spectacle of coordi-

nated movement, dynamic music, and beautiful costuming. Its purpose and focus are communal, and favor perfect coordination of a large troupe over virtuosic solos.

Group dancing has roots in traveling companies of *ʻarioi,* a graded sect of sacred, privileged, ceremonially initiated musicians, dancers, and actors, consecrated to the god ʻOro, and dedicated to pleasure and entertainment (Oliver 1974:913–964). The arrival of the *ʻarioi* began a period of festivity, with feasting, athletics, oratory, and performances by elegantly costumed performers.

Protestant missionaries deprecated the worship of ʻOro; legislation restricted dancing, and even forbade it. Penalties for dancers and audiences did not stop surreptitious dancing, which included nighttime performances in valleys, far removed from missionaries and administrators. Choreographed Tahitian dances were introduced to the Marquesas in the 1880s, confirming a continuity that neither the government nor the church approved.

Because of the drunkenness and impropriety of bar-girl dancers in Papeʻete, dance from the 1920s to the 1950s had a stigma that prevented widespread participation, particularly for women. In 1956, to restore beauty and dignity to Tahitian dance, schoolteacher Madeleine Mouā created a professional troupe, Heiva. Several of her dancers started their own troupes, of which the most famous was Te Maeva, formed by Coco (Jean Hotahota) in the late 1960s. Judged the best male dancer in the Bastille Day competitions, Coco became the most important creative force in twentieth-century Tahitian dance.

Professional troupes attract young people because they afford an opportunity to dance regularly, enjoy the company of friends, and travel abroad. Troupes negotiating contracts in France, Guam, or Japan are well paid in comparison to their counterparts at home, where dance is seldom a viable career. Troupes may enlist more than a hundred dancers (fifty-five is the minimum for the Heiva competitions), under the direction of a director (*raʻatira,* of either sex). Most hotel shows have smaller troupes—ten to twelve dancers, five or six musicians. Attracting teenagers and young adults, they focus on the physically mature, active, and fit. Amateur troupes representing districts, churches, or schools flourish throughout the archipelago.

Occasions involving dance include official receptions, entertainment for balls or banquets, feasts, competitions, festivals, presentations, events at schools and churches, visitors' arrivals, and shows in hotels. The repertory draws from four basic genres: *ʻōteʻa, ʻaparima, pāʻōʻā,* and *hivinau.* The first two are a standard part of virtually all performances. The last two occur mainly in competitions and festivals, or when dancers want to show the breadth of Tahitian traditions.

## 'Ōteʻa

Danced in "grass" skirts (*more*) to drummed rhythms, the ʻōteʻa is, for outsiders, the stereotypical image of Pacific dance. This image—primarily female, sexual, infused with fantasy—traces its roots to Western imagination more than to local practices. For Tahitians, a well-done ʻōteʻa crowns a presentation, and displays the choreographer's creativity, the dancers' and drummers' stamina, the troupe's knowledge and understanding of appropriate interplay between drumming and movement, and the physical beauty of dancers and costumes. The proper execution of gender-specific movements reaffirms acceptable male and female behavior.

As performed in the twentieth century, ʻōteʻa represents a possible mixing of two genres. Though early sources describe dances for which females employed revolving movements of the hips, the term ʻōteʻa as the name of a dance does not appear until the late 1800s, when it was described as a men's dance and a warriors' dance. Since the 1950s, ʻōteʻa are choreographed for mixed groups. Remnants of the older practice remain in the inclusion of separate dances for men and women.

ʻŌteʻa may develop a theme, such as the mythical Hina's clam, a fan, or a star; or it may relate a local legend or event. The movements, however, are mostly abstract. Movements of the arms, hands, head, and upper torso function in isolation from the movements of the legs and lower torso, as if an invisible line horizontally divides the body at the waist. Symmetrical and asymmetrical usage of the arms occurs; asymmetrical positions or movements usually repeat on the opposite side. Lower-body movements are the same as ʻori tahiti.

The basic formation consists of parallel same-sex columns, or formations that relate to a chosen theme (figure 4). By the 1920s, changes of formation had become features (Handy 1923:308). Since the late 1970s, they have occurred more frequently, with greater emphasis on variety of patterning.

An ensemble of male musicians provides musical accompaniment: three *tōʻere,* one *faʻatete,* and one *pahu* are standard. Important occasions call for many dancers and an expanded orchestra, adding hand-struck, one-headed membranophones (*pahu tupaʻi rima*), a bamboo struck idiophone (*ihara*), and additional *tōʻere* and *faʻatete.* Coco reintroduced the *pahu tupaʻi rima* in 1976 and the *ihara* in the 1980s.

Musical accompaniment draws from a repertory of repeating rhythmic patterns (*pehe*): the lead instrument (*tōʻere ʻarataʻi*) introduces the initial pattern, one or more *tōʻere tāmau* provide the basic rhythm, and a smaller, higher-pitched *tōʻere tāhape* improvises. The *pahu* provides the basic pulse, coordinating the other performers; the

FIGURE 4   At the Heiva festival, female dancers perform an ʻōteʻa. Photo by Jane Freeman Moulin, 1995.

FIGURE 5   At the Heiva festival, female dancers perform an *'aparima*, using expressive movements of their hands to accompany and elaborate a sung text. Photo by Jane Freeman Moulin, 1995.

*fa'atete* plays rapid subdivisions of this pulse, interjecting dotted rhythms and syncopation. The ending may use a standardized formula (*toma*).

*'Ōte'a* costumes worn on important occasions exemplify the skill and creativity of local handiwork with fibers and shells. *More,* skirts made from strips of the inner bark of the *pūrau* tree, are topped with fibrous belts ornamented by shells, seeds, mother-of-pearl, and feathers. Skirts are also made of *'autī* leaves and other plant materials, or strings of flowers or shells. A large headdress and an upper-body covering (fabric, fiber, shell, or coconut bras for women; shawls or sashes for men) coordinate in color and design with the belt. Necklaces of shells or flowers and optional whisks of *pūrau* fibers complete the costume. For ordinary events, crowns, garlands, and belts of flowers, ferns, or leaves, provide fragrant and pretty costumery. Dancers may carry spears, fans, torches, or other props relating to the theme of the presentation.

### *'Aparima*

Performed by large groups, *'aparima* tell stories through an expressive use of hands (figure 5). They are of two basic types: *'aparima vāvā* 'mute storytelling dances' and *'aparima hīmene* 'sung storytelling dances'. The former tell a story by miming everyday activities, such as making *po'e* (a pudding of cooked fruit or root vegetables), grating coconuts, and fishing, and are sometimes described as dances done *i raro* 'in a low position'—kneeling or sitting. A percussive ensemble accompanies them, the rhythms differing subtly from those of *'ōte'a*. Rather than serving as a force that shapes the choreography, the drumming underscores the mime with less virtuosic, more repetitive patterns, intended to coordinate the dancers' movements.

*'Aparima hīmene* ('sung *'aparima*'), usually called *'aparima,* have texts and string-band music. Texts cover many topics, but many express love (for a person or place), or describe the physical features and beauty of a favorite locale. A text of greeting or formal acknowledgment of those present is commonly the first dance. The final dance is often slow and peaceful, closing the presentation with a feeling of repose. Dancers and instrumentalists sing the melody and improvise inner parts, guitars and ukuleles provide the chordal structure, and the *pahu* reinforces the pulse. The drummers usually provide the chordophonic accompaniment, and occasionally an outstanding singer, male or female, joins them.

*'Aparima* emphasize movements of arms and hands, rather than those of the lower torso and knees. Lower-body movements include sideways steps, taps of the heel, and slowly revolving hips. Gestures underscore key words in the text: a hand to the eyes conveys the idea of 'looking'; hands over the navel symbolize the homeland, referring to the Tahitian practice of burying a newborn's placenta under the house. Ornamental gestures include waves, decorative claps, and other nontextual movements, added for sight or sound. Performers may also make mimetic gestures.

*'Aparima* may alternate with *'ōte'a,* or can occur as a series of items in a separate portion of a program. Separate segments of *'ōte'a* and *'aparima* allow dancers to change costumes and perform the *'aparima* in *pareu* (a wraparound cloth, tied into pants for males and a skirt for females), with garlands for the neck and head. As in the *'ōte'a,* dancers may carry story-related props, including fishing poles, hats, and fans.

### Pāō'ā

Tahitian cultural experts say this dance began in making bark cloth, a women's task. One or two women would rise to lighten the work with improvised singing and dancing, accompanied by the rhythm of the pounding. In the twentieth century, when cloth manufacture waned, *pāō'ā* became a dance and permitted the inclusion of male participants. Texts refer to old legends, particularly when performed for competitions. For less-formal occasions, texts about hunting and fishing, with sexual implications, are favorite subjects. The leader recites a short section of text on a single tone, or in heightened speech (*pāta'uta'u*); the group answers, in unison. The answer may repeat the soloist's line, provide comment, elaborate on his statement, or exist as a set phrase unrelated to the preceding text. The last two lines of the answer typically begin with an ascending minor third to the tonal center, and end with the shouts *hī* and *hā,* as in

| | |
|---|---|
| Ehe, e manino te miti, hī! | *Ehe,* the sea is calm, *hī!* |
| Aha, e manino te miti, hā! | *Aha,* the sea is calm, *hā!* |

A complete performance, only forty to sixty seconds in duration, may repeat immediately.

A mixed male-female group sits cross-legged in a circle around the leader and musicians, accompanying the recitation by striking their hands on their knees or, less commonly, on the ground in front of them. As the leader and group sing, a solo female dancer or a mixed couple rise from the group and improvise, drawing movements from the vocabulary of *'ori tahiti,* but emphasizing mobility within the circle. With a temporary halt in movement and an abrupt change in the placement of the arms (such as throwing both hands high above the head with the palms facing forward and upward), dancers accent the shouts. Drumming adds rhythmic interest to the pulse of the clapping, matching the lengths of textual phrases. Strong accents punctuate the syllables *hī* and *hā,* emphasizing the end of a textual unit and reinforcing the visual accents of the movements. The *pāō'ā* is usually part of the *'ōte'a* portion of a program.

### Hivinau

This dance, whose name derives from the *heave now!* shouted by sailors on nineteenth-century ships, is for a mixed group. Tahitians trace its origin to the Tuamotu Islands, where sailors and local people, assembled on deck in lighthearted celebration before departure, jointly raised the anchor. In the 1930s on Bora Bora, people performed *hivinau* for a social mixer at feasts and on Friday nights. Like *pāō'ā, hivinau* became a presentational dance after 1950. Troupes perform it primarily at competitions and festivals.

In two concentric circles, usually facing opposite directions and surrounding a leader and drummers, the *hivinau* consists of a short line of leader's text, followed by a choral response. The leader's text, delivered in heightened speech or on a reciting tone, often concerns fishing and the sea, and has secondary meanings. The response is *'Āhiri 'ā ha'aha'a,* a nonsense phrase that conveys a sense of happiness. Using a stylized walk during the leader's recitation, the dancers move forward in their circles. As they shout their response, they pause to dance briefly with a person in the opposite circle; each pause brings a new partner. The complete dance, usually lasting less than a minute, repeats immediately. In a community setting, the *hivinau* was a spontaneous, fun-filled dance, in which everyone participated. As a presentational dance, it is often linked with *pā'ō'ā* in the *'ōte'a* portion of a performance.

*Dances of non-Tahitian origin*
Learned from immigrants, Tahitians who have lived abroad, or visiting troupes, these include Hawaiian *hula 'auana,* Māori *poi,* a Sāmoan dance with fire, and dances from the Tuamotu, Marquesas, and Cook islands. Tahitians seldom acknowledge the origin of non-Tahitian compositions.

### Innovations after the 1970s

After the 1970s, innovation was emphasized. Changing floor patterns (within a dance and between dances), expanded gender-specific lower-body movements (pelvic movements for men, scissorlike knee movements for women), and emphasized sexuality (open stance and forward pelvic thrusts for women, dancers touching their bodies) challenged concepts of what is Tahitian. *'Aparima* were influenced by Hawaiian *hula:* softer, suppler movements of the hands overshadowed the tapping and flicking that distinguish earlier Tahitian styles; the Hawaiian *kāholo,* the step that Tahitians call *hura* and perform with deeply bent knees, resulted in lower level and increased mobility. Choreographers experimented with new formations for *pā'ō'ā* and *hivinau.* Adding *pahu tupa'i rima,* and *ihara* changed the timbre and texture of the drumming. Choreography became more complex, with fewer repetitions. Locomotion changed: rather than a means of moving to a new stationary position, it became a feature in itself. Change was most apparent among professional troupes in Tahiti, where competitions promote novelty and choreographers receive praise for creativity.
—JANE FREEMAN MOULIN

## AUSTRAL ISLANDS

Stretching across 1,450 kilometers of open sea, the Austral Islands include five high, volcanic, inhabited islands (Rimatara, Rurutu, Tubua'i, Ra'ivavae, Rapa) and two uninhabited islets (Marotiri, Maria). Rurutu lies about 500 kilometers southwest of Tahiti. The southernmost island, Rapa, lies well south of the tropics. The population of each island numbers no more than several hundred. Throughout the islands, the Tahitian language is spoken, but local phonemic and dialectal deviations occur, especially on the remote southern islands, Ra'ivavae and Rapa.

The Austral Islands have figured little in the colonial history of French Polynesia. Difficult anchorages and a lack of marketable resources deterred encroachment from abroad. Evangelization began in 1821, initially with Tahitian catechists from missions in the Society Islands. The archipelago officially became part of French Polynesia in 1880.

With a minimum of distraction from extraneous options, Austral Islanders maintain customs that have disappeared in the Society Islands. Television broadcasts

Protestantism enjoys a monopoly on all the Austral Islands except Tubuaʻi, which hosts an assortment of Christian denominations. Village social life is virtually synonymous with parish activities.

run several hours daily, and video-movie selections change with twice-weekly flights on Rurutu and Tubuaʻi and twice-monthly visits of supply ships to other islands. To benefit from economic and educational opportunities, many émigrés have settled on Tahiti. Protestantism enjoys a monopoly on all the Austral Islands except Tubuaʻi, which hosts an assortment of Christian denominations. Village social life is virtually synonymous with parish activities.

Little is known about local precontact traditions. Archaeological research was carried out as part of the Bayard Dominick Expedition in the 1920s. Anthropologists have done research in the islands, beginning with work by F. Allan Hanson (1970) on Rapa in the 1960s. Alain Babadzan's research in the 1980s focused on syncretism in religious beliefs on Rurutu. Compared to the wealth of written accounts available for Tahiti, descriptions of music and dance from travelers' accounts are rare. The only musical research is that of my surveys of Tubuaʻi, where I spent one month in 1985, and the other inhabited islands, which I visited for two weeks in 1988.

**Music for dancing**

Dances performed throughout the Austral Islands are those performed in Tahiti, retaining their Tahitian names, with full cognizance of their origins: ʻōteʻa, hivinau, pāʻōʻā, and ʻaparima. Musical ensembles that accompany dancing are identical to those used in Tahiti. The three drum-accompanied dances use an ensemble of tōʻere, faʻatete, and pahu. For ʻaparima, the accompanying instrumentation consists of ukulele (usually with a coconut-shell body), guitar, and pahu.

Troupes from Rurutu participate frequently in the Heiva and have toured internationally. In 1985, the troupe Tamariʻi Manureva no Rurutu represented the Austral Islands in the Pacific Festival of Arts, in Papeʻete. Tahitians respect Rurutuan troupes, and consider Rurutuan costumes particularly beautiful examples of handiwork.

Performances by these troupes include Tahitian ʻūtē. Poetic texts are frequently commentaries on daily life, and the liberal use of innuendo can be entertaining. They may treat mythical or legendary themes, or topicalize them, as in an example of a Rurutuan text prepared for the July festival, which in the Austral Islands is still called fête nationale:

| | |
|---|---|
| ʻAʻatupu rā ʻoe Māui tāne | The man Māui gives |
| I tītaʻi Tiurai raʻi, | A large July festival, |
| ʻŌroʻa raʻi ʻanaʻana, | An event of honor, |
| E tōna atoʻa ʻētiʻi. | And all the family. |
| Tītau mai nei i te vaʻine a nuʻa | You seek a woman from the east |
| E tāpiti ʻaʻaʻō. | To accompany you. |
| Ia oti tā ʻoe Tiurai, | When the July festival is over, |
| ʻAʻaʻoʻi iaʻu i taʻu ʻare. | Return me to my house. |
| E aroʻa pauroa tātou | We'll exchange farewells |
| Ia tae te taime reva raʻa. | As the time to depart approaches. |

The main melody of *ʻūtē* is performed by one singer, or by two singers who alternate lines or phrases. A lead singer (*ʻaʻamata* 'to begin', also *ʻarataʻi* 'to lead') and a second singer (*māpeʻe* 'to follow') are accompanied by an ensemble of guitars and ukuleles, with interjected vocables (*marū* 'calm'). In the late 1800s and early 1900s, the accordion was a favorite accompanimental instrument.

## Choral singing

Styles of choral singing stem from the performance of Protestant hymnody. Evangelization was effected by Tahitian catechists from missions in the Society Islands; conversion to Christianity was accomplished by the end of the 1820s. Choral singing is an integral part of regular worship and devotions, including daily services in the early mornings, three services on Sundays (early morning, midmorning, afternoon), Sunday school, and weekly Bible-study meetings. Special occasions, which prompt new compositions, extensive rehearsals, and elaborate preparations, include New Year's and annual offerings taken in late April or May. Choral singing also highlights the *fête nationale,* celebrated on each island in July.

Despite close ties to the Society Islands, distinct practices in choral singing have locally emerged. One such practice is in the naming of choral styles. On Rapa, Rimatara, and Rurutu, *hīmene piana* 'piano' denotes three- or four-part arrangements in note-against-note harmonization (*hīmene nota* in the Society Islands). *Piana* refers not to an instrumental accompaniment, but to islanders' conceptualization of the singing of hymns with keyboard accompaniment. *Hīmene taʻata paʻari* 'old people's hymns' serves on Rapa for what elsewhere are called *hīmene rūʻau.* This term refers to old people, who prefer singing these hymns, and avoids the ambiguity of the term *rūʻau,* meaning 'old' (of either the singers or the hymns). The style is essentially identical to that in the Society Islands. It includes an indigenized melody sung by women, harmonization in parallel or similar motion by women, and a men's bass that uses highly patterned melodies. Cadences are formulaic: men hold momentarily on the fifth scalar degree, and then resolve to the tonic in unison with women.

Rapa Islanders use the term *hīmene atiu* to denote the Cook Island style of choral singing. Elsewhere in the Society and Austral Islands, that style is called *hīmene tuki* and *hīmene rarotoʻa.*

## Hīmene tārava

Throughout the Society Islands, all *tārava* from the Austral Islands are known as *tārava rurutu.* On musical grounds, however, this designation is unacceptable to Austral Islanders, for each island has a distinctive style of singing *tārava,* and accordingly qualifies *tārava* by its own name. The distinctions lie in the number, names, and content of the vocal parts, whose functions are identical to those identified in singing *tārava* in the Society Islands: textual declamation, melodic decoration, and rhythmic punctuation.

The functions of women's parts—four on Tubuaʻi, five on Rimatara and Raʻivavae, six on Rapa, seven on Rurutu—include:

1. A soloist (*faʻaaraara* 'to awaken' on Tubuaʻi, *vahine haʻamata* 'woman who begins' elsewhere) begins.
2. Most women (either *vahine tāmau* 'woman who makes fast' or *parauparau* 'to speak') perform the text.
3. A soloist (the *māpeʻe, māpehe* on Rapa, *tārere* on Rimatara and Rurutu) performs a partially texted decorative part
4. A soloist (*pēpere* 'to fly,' *perepere* on Tubuaʻi and Raʻivavae) performs a vocable-texted decorative part.

5. A woman (*haru* on Rimatara, *tauturu ha'aaraara* 'assist the leader' on Ra'ivavae) assists the leader by "catching" her lead.

Two other functions reported on Rurutu and Rapa are those of *arata'i hīmene* '*hīmene*-leader' and *arata'i turu* 'assistant leader'. Islanders say these parts are not merely alternate names for the lead woman and her assistant, but have corresponding musical contents.

The function of men's parts—four on Tubua'i, five on Rimatara and Rurutu, six on Ra'ivavae, seven on Rapa—include:

1. Some men, either *marū* or *parauparau,* perform the text.
2. Some men, either *hā'ū* 'grunt' or *marū pua'atoro* 'calm bull', primarily perform a pitched rhythmic grunting.
3. Soloists, all of whom add melodic decoration, include *'auena* 'response' (on Ra'ivavae), *māpe'e* (*māpehe* on Rapa), *marū teitei i ni'a* 'high tenor above' and *marū teitei i raro* 'high tenor below', and *tuō* 'to call'.

In the Austral Islands, *tārava* sung in Bible-study meetings use a textual format distinct from devotional *tārava* sung in the Society Islands. Biblical or religious texts contain two stanzas of unequal length. The first stanza, containing four or six lines, is performed twice; the second stanza, *harura'a* 'grabbing', containing six or eight lines, may be repeated as often as singers wish. On festive occasions, one *tārava* may last an hour or longer.

A typical biblical *tārava* involves counterpoint among many vocal parts (figure 6), distributed in staggered phrases moving over a drone. Its text, in the Rurutuan language, alludes to Belshazzar's feast (Daniel 5:1–31):

| | |
|---|---|
| 'Oa rā 'o Beletatara | Belshazzar rejoices |
| I te fa'atupura'a i te 'oro'a, | At the great banquet, |
| I te mau 'ohipa tana e rave | At his deeds he does |
| Te fare o te Atua e. | The Lord's house. |
| Na te Atua rā tā'iri noa mai | The Lord will punish |
| Te 'arai i roto iā 'oe e. | The pride within you. |
| | |
| 'Auē rā, Beletatara, | Alas, Belshazzar! |
| Te rave a te Atua e! | The work of the Lord! |
| Tu'uhia to tino i te faito rā | You are judged |
| Tēnā i mua iā 'oe ē: | By that which is before you: |
| 'Etoru numera tei patahia mai. | Three signs are written. |
| Na Daniela i tātara e. | Daniel will interpret them. |
| E tātara, Daniela, | Interpret, Daniel, |
| Te rahi a tēnā numera e. | The meaning of those signs. |

The three signs are the words of the handwriting on the wall.

—AMY KU'ULEIALOHA STILLMAN

## TUAMOTU ISLANDS

The Tuamotu Archipelago includes some seventy-five atolls and the raised coral island of Makatea, lying in a northwest-to-southeast crescent east of the Society Islands. Close cultural relationships are with the Society Islands and Mangareva. Tuamotuan arts included poetry (with its attendant music and dance), canoes sewn out of planks, elaborate headdresses (which included tropic bird tail feathers), shell

FIGURE 6 Beginning of the second stanza of "*Te 'oa'oa Beletatara*," a *hīmene tārava,* as performed by the parochial group Siloama, parish of Moera'i, Rurutu (*Pupu Himene no Rurutu 2* 1980:A2). Transcription by Amy Ku'uleialoha Stillman.

ornaments, tattooing, finely plaited loin girdles and belts, and twined pandanus skirts.

Kenneth Emory and J. Frank Stimson did research in the Tuamotus in 1929–1931, when they recorded on wax cylinders some 350 chants and songs, which Edwin G. Burrows (1933, 1934a) analyzed. Emory did further research in 1934, especially in Napuka (Emory 1976). During his first visit, he introduced the guitar and its music to the Tuamotus, and Tuamotuans are said to have preserved his way of playing. Since 1934, little research has been carried out, except in 1976 and 1979, when Emory and I worked with Tuamotuans living in Tahiti.

Though social organization was less elaborated than in some Polynesian areas, prestige derived from genealogical connections that Tuamotuans traced back to gods. Genealogies were recounted in melodic and rhythmic form, as were epics and tales detailing the exploits of gods (such as Rogo and Rū, propping up the sky with posts) and heroes (such as Maui and Tahaki), and serving as odes to important objects, including Rogo's red-feathered girdle. Besides the surface meaning of poetic texts, hidden meanings often referred to fertility, sexual desire, and fulfillment, as in an example honoring the royal girdle (Burrows 1933:13, Stimson's translation):

> Royal girdle of the close-set rippling weft!
> The cherished possession.
> A venerated crimson treasure—exquisitely soft, beloved flaming plumes!
> Beating with lifted wings, the bird flashes into flight.
> O cherished possession!
> It is the royal girdle—
> It is the royal girdle of Rogo!
> Twisted beneath,
> Wound round the back,
> Firmly fastened in front—
> The cherished girdle!
> It is the royal girdle of Rogo,—
> Rogo, invested with the royal girdle on Mount Nokunoku.
> Venerated treasure.

Analyzing traditional vocal production, Burrows found that texts were begun by a recognized leader (male or female), who sang the first solo passage (*hua* or *pepenu*); this singer was joined by another, the *maro,* usually on a different tone, which became the upper part of a two-part song, and they were joined almost immediately by a chorus (*rena* or *popoki*). The tonal plan included singing primarily on one tone, varied occasionally by a slight rise or drop, or in some songs a larger leap, often a fifth. Vocal quavering (*fakatukutuku*) was common, and some styles of singing featured rapid enunciation (*patakutaku*). Melodic movement was essentially horizontal, and polyphony consisted of two simultaneous melodies that often resulted in a lower part primarily on one pitch and a more melodic upper part. Units of sound were repeated to give each piece a "definite pattern, a decorative design to appeal to the ear somewhat comparable to the decorative designs on pots or mats which appeal to the eye" (Burrows 1934a:79).

Tuamotuans had many indigenous musical terms, some known throughout the archipelago and others varying from island to island, but it is unclear if the terms refer to the social function of the pieces, the vocal quality, or the manner of performance on a particular occasion. An important category was *fagu,* sacred or solemn songs, including songs to or for gods and spirits, laments (*fagu tutagi*), and songs for events such as superincision ceremonies (*fagu kiri*), for honoring virginity, and for objects used on important occasions, such as a chief's investiture girdle. Songs of an endearing or topical nature were *koivi* or *teki*. Songs praising a place (*fakataratara*) or a person (*fakateniteni*) were delivered in recitative (*pehepehe*). Various terms, including *papa ruta, kapa, haka, kotaha, kihau,* and *koke,* specified dances and songs for dancing.

Dancing (*kori*) was a group activity, often in a two-line formation (one line of men, one of women), the lines facing each other or an audience. Moving around, a leader directed the choreography from between or in front of the lines (figure 7). The lower-body motifs included stamping, stepping in place, and moving the hips from

FIGURE 7  At Vahitahi Island, Tuamotus, a leader stands at the front of two lines, directing the choreography. Photo by Kenneth P. Emory, 1930. Bishop Museum Archives.

side to side. Upper-body motifs emphasized fluttering the arms and hands, often alluding to frigate birds. Sometimes performers held branches and moved them about.

As elsewhere in Polynesia, laments were an important category. They included dirges used in grieving for the dead (*fagu tutagi*), eulogies in honor of the dead, and songs for absent loved ones. With the coming of Christianity, these songs and others were recomposed as *hīmene*.

A genre of comparative Polynesian interest is *rorogo* or *rongorongo* 'resounding, fame'. Sung in honor of an individual's exploits or in praise of his girdle or other insignia of rank, it bears unmistakable similarities to *rongorongo* of Easter Island, where *kohau rongorongo,* the so-called *rongorongo* boards, rendered *rongorongo* chants into visibly memorable form; in the Marquesas, knotted cords served a similar purpose.

In the late twentieth century, Tahiti and the Tuamotus influence each other in sounds and movements. Tuamotuans circulate between their home islands and Tahiti, carrying influences in both directions and combining Tahitian and Tuamotuan languages, musical instruments, vocal styles, and dances.

—ADRIENNE L. KAEPPLER

## MANGAREVA

The largest of four high volcanic islands and several reef-fringed rocks that comprise the Gambier Islands, Mangareva lies at the southeastern end of the Tuamotu archipelago. Europeans first sighted it in 1797, when *Duff* and its band of Protestant missionaries from London passed it on the way to Tahiti. In 1826, Captain F. W. Beechey (1831) of H.M.S. *Blossom* made the earliest firsthand written description of the inhabitants. Three Roman Catholic priests landed in 1834, and by 1838 had converted the islanders. In the late 1990s, 99 percent of Mangareva's inhabitants are Roman Catholic, but only about 65 percent participate actively in worship.

Local musical traditions were first documented by the Bishop Museum's Mangarevan Expedition (1934). During two months' residence, Sir Peter Buck

(1938) collected more than two hundred musical texts and made fourteen wax-cylinder recordings of the last known musical expert (*pou kapa*). In 1985, for the Territorial Survey of Oceanic Music, Amy Kuʻuleialoha Stillman and Monica Paheo did research on Mangareva (Stillman and Paheo 1985).

Musical traditions in Mangareva can be grouped into three broad domains: indigenous Mangarevan genres, introduced Tahitian genres, and Roman Catholic practices. The indigenous musical instruments Buck enumerated, including shark-skin drums (*paʻu*), a log idiophone (*kereteta*), flutes (*pū koʻe*) and conch trumpets (*pū*), were obsolete by the time of his visit. He based his descriptions of them on exemplars in collections around the world, and derived his discussions on their use from descriptions by nineteenth-century voyagers. In the mid-1980s, the only instrumental accompaniment for performing dramatic enactments (*peʻi*) was a kerosene tin (*tini*), beaten with two sticks; Tahitian *tōʻere* accompanied performances of Tahitian dances.

## Indigenous genres

Mangarevan traditions distinguished poetic types from musical styles. Extant indigenous Mangarevan genres recorded in 1985 are *akatari peʻi, kapa,* and *tagi.* These genres are associated with *peʻi,* enactments of episodes from legends and historical narratives (*atoga*), incorporating movement, mime, and song. Performances are staged annually on the French national holiday. Organized by locale of residence, troupes compete for prestige and prizes. They may also prepare performances for special occasions, such as dignitaries' visitations.

The performance of a *peʻi* begins with an *akatari peʻi* while the dancers file into view. Once they are in place, actors mime the chosen episode, to rhythmic accompaniment on a tin. Mimed episodes alternate with *kapa,* which provide commentary. *Tagi,* performed at the conclusion, summarize the action. In the context of the *peʻi, kapa* known to be choreographed or performed previously in *peʻi* are called *peʻi,* rather than *kapa.*

The term *kapa* carries general and specific meanings. It serves as a generic term for 'song', including the poetic text and its melodic rendition. It denotes poetic texts in alternating stanza-refrain form, in contrast to through-composed incantations. It denotes a style of musical performance. It serves generically as a verb glossable as 'to sing'. It is also a style of recitation, contrasting with other named styles.

### Poetic types

Mangarevan traditions recognize five categories, distinguished by poetic themes.

1. *Porotu.*—Buck (1938:392) defines this as "a laudatory song regarding rank and synonymous with *keko.*" The term *porotu* describes something beautiful or lovely, often a person. Thus, specific characters in *atoga* may be *porotu.* Songs of this category celebrate renowned people and their exploits.

2. *Rogorogo.*—Buck (1938:392) defines this as "a chant used by the *rogorogo* orators, [showing] their knowledge of past history, and the classics." All three examples he cites (pages 152, 332, 392) are in the stanza-refrain form of *kapa*; they are *rogorogo* by virtue of their subjects. *Rogorogo* as a thematic category contrast with incantations sung by chanters and priests (*taura*). Texts preserved in manuscripts from the 1850s are not in stanza-refrain form: containing archaic vocabulary and diction, they are associated with practices that disappeared after Mangarevans' conversion to Christianity. Singers interviewed in 1985 could not understand the structure and content of the incantations, and had no idea how to perform them.

3. *Tagitagi.*—The reduplicated form of the term *tagi* 'to sing' carries a different meaning from that of the basic word. A *tagitagi* is a sentimental poem, "a chant or

song . . . generally of an amorous or libidinous character" (Tregear 1899:98). The sentimentality is rendered by the *tagi* musical style.

4. *Tau* and *akareimarū.*—Buck defines *tau* as "a lament . . . to express grief" (1938:389). When included within a *pe'i* danced at funerals, *tau* become *akareimarū,* the dance being the sole distinguishing feature.

5. *Uga.*—These were "songs to embellish a speech" (Buck 1938:393). Singers recorded in 1985 performed Buck's poetic text as a *tagi,* an *akatari pe'i,* and a *pā ō 'ā magareva.*

Three basic textual techniques that produce parallelism in Mangarevan poetry are question-and-answer, substitution, and enumeration. Some patterns include posing a question in the first stanza and responses in subsequent stanzas, or alternating a question in one stanza with a response in the next. Substitution, where one or several components vary within one verse, often combines with enumeration. In the following song, from the Mangarevan legend of Toga-te-huareva, the stanzas engage question-answer and substitution procedures. Each question asks "for whom is" and itemizes a chiefly possession—sovereign rule (*ao*), land (*kaiga*), house ('*are*), people ('*ū*), and fresh water (*vai*):

> To kō toku ao mo ai?
> Mo koe 'oki, e te tama e.
>
> To kō toku kaiga ko Tutuira mo ai?
> Mo koe 'oki, e te tama e.
>
> To kō toku 'are ko Hapai-a-pua mo ai?
> Mo koe 'oki, e te tama e.
>
> To kō toku 'ū ko Tuarau mo ai?
> Mo koe 'oki, e te tama e.
>
> To kō toku vai ko Te Vai-raromea mo ai?
> Mo koe 'oki, e te tama e.
>
> For whom is my sovereign rule?
> For you of course, O son.
>
> For whom is my land of Tutuira?
> For you of course, O son.
>
> For whom is my house named Hapai-a-pua?
> For you of course, O son.
>
> For whom are the people of Tuarau?
> For you of course, O son.
>
> For whom is the fresh water of Te Vai-raromea?
> For you of course, O son.

Topics favored for enumeration include legendary characters, environmental features, and named places. Enumeration lengthens a text: the more items to enumerate, the more stanzas. An increase in the number of stanzas increases the number of times the refrain must be sung—a process that enhances the singers' enjoyment.

### Musical styles

The Mangarevan musical system recognizes four styles, distinguished by performance-related criteria.

In Sunday worship adults lead unaccompanied, harmonized singing in Tahitian or Mangarevan. Youths with electric guitars and a portable electric organ accompany hymns in French or Tahitian.

FIGURE 8    *"E Te Tumu Ē,"* a *kapa,* recorded by the Mangarevan Expedition in 1934 (Bishop Museum Archives). Transcription by Amy Kuʻuleialoha Stillman.

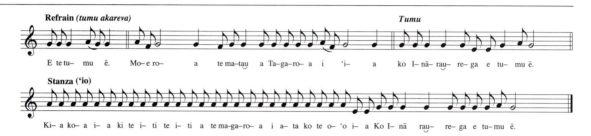

1. *Akatari peʻi* are metered renditions of texts thematically related to *kapa, tagi,* and *atoga.* They provide a rhythmic pulse while the performers dance into view at the start of dramatic enactments. The texts are sung to composed melodies.

2. *Kapa* consist of alternating stanzas (*io*) and a refrain (*tumu* 'source'). The refrain often contains an inner refrain (*tumu akareva*). The *tumu* is the essential phrase, performed at the end of each stanza. If it is brief or grammatically incomplete, the *tumu akareva* may repeat between stanzas. Otherwise, the *tumu akareva* occurs in only the first and last statements of the *tumu* (figure 8). The musical performance is conceived as recited formulas, rather than fixed melodies. *Kapa* use two principal reciting tones: one in the refrain and a different one in the stanza, a minor or major second above. At the end of a stanza, the return to the principal tone is via descent through a lower auxiliary, most often on the penultimate syllable of the verse.

3. *Tagi* involve a slower tempo than *kapa,* with deliberate and sustained textual delivery. The literal gloss of the word, 'to cry', is reflected in the vocal style: one woman leads, projecting the text in a high, strident, clear, vibratoless timbre, akin to Mangarevan weeping and crying. The *tumu* is performed solo, and the troupe enters for the *tumu akareva.* In the stanza, the soloist lines out the first few syllables, and the troupe enters at a prearranged point in the text.

4. *Keko* involve delivery of the text on a monotone, in an even and steady rhythm, and at a tempo similar to or slightly faster than *kapa.* No secondary reciting pitch sounds. The style of *keko* is closer to that of speech than to that of *kapa.*

Musical styles can be arranged on a continuum from speechlike to sustained wailing: a song may be recited (*keko*), sung (*kapa*), or cried (*tagi*). Musical styles can also be associated with particular genres: Mangarevans consider *keko* appropriate for *porotu; kapa* appropriate for *kapa, porotu,* and *rogorogo;* and *tagi* appropriate for *kapa, tagitagi,* and *tau.*

### Introduced Tahitian genres

Of Tahitian genres sung and danced through much of southeastern Polynesia, only two are frequently performed in Mangareva. Both retain Tahitian nomenclature. *Pǎ ō ʻǎ magareva* are equivalent to their Tahitian models, except that texts are in the Mangarevan language, and for rhythmic accompaniment performers slap the floor, rather than their thighs. *'Aparima magareva* are equivalent to their Tahitian models, with texts in Mangarevan. Composed on the themes of *kapa* and *pe'i,* they are performed separately after the conclusion of the *pe'i,* and are not considered part of the *pe'i* proper and its performance. No movement traits distinguish Mangarevan from Tahitian *'aparima.*

### Music in the Roman Catholic Church

Musical practices associated with Roman Catholic worship and devotions have developed music extensively. Mangarevan-language catechisms and books of prayers were issued beginning in 1837. Of publications used in 1985 that include Mangarevan hymns, the two most recent are *E Katekimo Katorika no Magareva* (second edition, 1898) and *Na mau purega me te takao kiritiano aka Magareva me te mau himene* (1908).

Before 4 December 1963, when the Second Vatican Council permitted bishops to grant priests the freedom of using a vernacular translation of the Mass, Mangarevan priests had conducted the liturgy in Latin, though local parishioners had performed certain devotions (including the singing of hymns) in Mangarevan. Since then, the archdiocese of Tahiti has advocated the use of French and Tahitian. The teaching of catechismal classes in French, the use of Tahitian in worship and devotion, and the speaking of Mangarevan in secular contexts, have established multilingualism.

Mangarevans classify hymns (*īmene*) by language. *Īmene magareva,* Mangarevan-language hymns (some of which appeared with melodic notation in 1908), are transmitted orally, and variants have developed. The sung melody of some concurs with the notated melody, and that of others matches the contour, but not the rhythm or meter, of the notated melody; in still other cases, sung and notated melodies are entirely different. *Hīmene tahiti* and *īmene française* were introduced after the 1960s. Those known on Mangareva are local versions of American gospel hymns, and do not include the polyphonic choral singing associated with the Tahitian Protestant Church. *Īmene latino* are Gregorian chants, performed in the liturgy before the reforms of the Second Vatican Council. In a Latin Mass recorded in 1985, chants of the ordinary (Kyrie, Gloria, Credo, Sanctus, Agnus Dei) were sung in unison, but cadences were harmonized, in plagal or authentic progressions. *Akamagareva* are sacred counterparts of *kapa,* with which they share terminology for structural components. More than a hundred devotional texts appeared in *Na mau purega me te takao kiritiano,* which described the structural components of *akamagareva* with the same terminology used for *kapa.* However, *akamagareva* incorporate greater melodic variety than *kapa,* and the refrain is a distinct, fixed melody, specific to one particular text.

In Sunday worship the singing of hymns alternates between adults and youths. Adults lead unaccompanied, harmonized singing in Tahitian or Mangarevan; youths with electric guitars and a portable electric organ accompany hymns in French or Tahitian, singing in unison or harmonizing mainly in parallel thirds.

—Amy Ku'uleialoha Stillman

## MARQUESAS ISLANDS

The Marquesas Archipelago includes twelve high, volcanic islands lying about 1500 kilometers northeast of Tahiti. About 7,500 mainly Polynesian people inhabit six islands, comprising a northern-leeward group (Nukuhiva, 'Uapou, 'Uahuka) and a southern-windward group (Hiva'oa, Tahuata, Fatuiva). Dialectal and cultural differences distinguish these groups. Since the early 1960s, emigration from the archipelago, sparked by increased chances of employment on Tahiti, has resulted in an immigrant Marquesan community in Pape'ete. Immigrants' continued contact with their home islands fosters the movement of ideas in both directions, maintaining a sense of Marquesan identity.

Since the late 1970s, Marquesans have felt a need to break free from Tahitian cultural hegemony and emphasize their identity, producing a climate favorable for revitalizing music and dance. Large-group presentations are infrequent, but occur as part of events that combine communal resources for a special reason, such as church-oriented celebrations, official receptions, the Ko'ina Rare festivities, and archipelago-wide festivals (begun in 1987). Even the informal making of music is not a daily occurrence. Beginning in 1985, the cultural organization Motu Haka and local communities worked to involve youths in traditional music and dance and to pass on the body of knowledge that remained.

Finding a suitable vocabulary to bridge insiders' and outsiders' conceptualizations of the performing arts is challenging. In Marquesan performance, music and movement fuse to the point where some kinetic component—limited or elaborate, improvised or choreographed—accompanies most types of vocal music, and precludes differentiating sound and movement into separate concepts. Marquesans usually distinguish performative genres by textual content, function, stylistic traits and important features, rather than by the presence or absence of movement. A *rari*, for example, is a combination of words, melody, and movements of the hands. Marquesans do not call it poetry, or music, or dance, for it is a sum of these elements. In local discourse, one does not recite a *rari*, sing a *rari*, or dance a *rari*; one *rari*s a *rari*.

The term *mea kakiu* 'ancient things' denotes traditional arts and customs, including music and dance. (Because these items have texts and use vocal techniques and melodies that Marquesans distinguish from songs, I call them chants.) The term for exogenous genres is *mea hou* 'new, imported things', including music. The term *haka* refers to a style of movement characterized by extended arms, weight supported mainly on one foot, and a feeling of gentle verticality (resulting from repetitively bending and flexing the knees, sometimes momentarily leaving the ground). *Haka* followed by a modifier, as in *haka manumanu* 'bird dance', may specify a composition that features *haka*. When Marquesans speak of dance in a general sense, or of the movements of imported dances, they employ the Tahitian word *'ori*, or the French word *danse*.

## Mea kakiu

Marquesans recognize at least thirteen kinds of *mea kakiu*, listed below in alphabetical order. *S* or *N* after a term denotes a southern or northern locus of the word's usage; an island-specific name designates terminology particular to that island. Where more than one name exists, I list the southern word first and use it throughout the discussion. Musical research in the Marquesas has focused on the southern group, the more remote area, where the people retain a greater variety of *mea kakiu* and have a reputation among Marquesans as the guardians of tradition (Handy 1923; Handy and Winne 1925; Moulin 1989, 1991a, 1991b, 1994). Preliminary observations in the northern group reveal close parallels with many traits of the southern islands.

*Ha'anaunau* (Hiva'oa), *anaunau* (N and Fatuiva), designates a nonmetrical, declamatory style of unaccompanied intoned declamation, and pieces performed in the style; Marquesans today define the genre by musical features. Men and women perform solo, but brief responsorial sections may occur. Consisting of spells, charms, invocations, and announcements employed in a variety of situations (tattooing, fish-

FIGURE 9  A
Marquesan invoca-
tion to the god
Tana'oa. Elicited
recording of Rupena
'Āvae'oru, 12
November 1976 at
Pape'ete, Tahiti. The
performed words dif-
fer slightly from
orthographic words
glossed in the text.
Each × above the
staff marks a hand-
clap. Transcription by
Jane Freeman
Moulin.

ing for turtles, performing surgery), *ha'anaunau* are a standard part of large-group performances. In the twentieth century, contexts for performing *ha'anaunau* changed, but Marquesans still believe in the power of efficacious performance. The following *ha'anaunau,* an invocation to the god Tana'oa, was documented in 1930 by Handy (1930:91–92) and in 1989 by Jane Freeman Moulin (figure 9). The leader begins:

| | |
|---|---|
| Na ueue te tumu. | The base shakes. |
| Te aka te tumu o te fenua. | The roots, the base of the land. |
| Vevau ho'i, to fenua nui, Tana'oa. | Vevau indeed, your great land, Tana'oa. |
| | |
| Tana'oa e. | Tana'oa. |
| E aha to 'ahu a? | What is your robe? |
| He Tiu to 'ahu a. | The northwind is your robe. |
| Metani to 'ahu a. | The wind is your robe. |
| 'Ahu a te Tiu. | Robe of the northwind. |
| Me te afa i uta? | With what do you come inland? |
| To va'a nui, Tana'oa. | Your great canoe, Tana'oa. |

The leader's longer lines then contrast with choral exclamations: *Tana'oa i te rau kaki. / Huia! / Te rau kaki. / Huia! / Te rau kaki. / Huia!*

Performers employ definite pitch (usually a reciting tone, often with the minor third below it) or heightened speech, often in combination. Speech-dominated rhythm characterizes the style. Other features include a tendency toward lengthened penultimate syllables and a descending contour at endings of phrases and sections. A solo performer may enliven a performance with improvised movements, but the non-metrical rhythm is unsuitable for *haka.* Marquesans interchangeably use the terms *ha'anaunau, mauta'a, tapatapa,* and *vakahoa* (also *va'ahoa*), and do not agree on qualities that differentiate them.

*Hahi* (S), *mave* (N) 'welcome calls' are unaccompanied, solo greetings, ad-libbed by women at occasions of communal importance: receptions honoring official visitors, ecclesiastical celebrations, formal music-and-dance presentations, weddings.

Texts may include genealogical references, identify the performers' valley of origin, greet the audience, or acknowledge important persons' presence. Delivered in a high, strong voice, *hahi* consist of a phrase of rapid parlando and a sustained tone ending in a drawn-out, downward slide. A performer may bend forward in place, or walk around the arena waving greenery.

*Haka manumanu* (from *manu* 'bird'), a genre of bird-related dances, refers to performances that feature distinctive elements, including *haka* and the wearing of feathers attached to a ring on the middle finger of each hand. Many older Marquesans regard *haka manumanu* as the most beautiful Marquesan dance. Drawings duplicated from nineteenth-century sources, and the exhibition of a historical costume at the Musée de Tahiti et des Îles in Pape'ete, have made younger Marquesans more aware of this dance and its revival, often with innovations.

*Mahitete* was defined as a type of chant around 1900. In 1989, I found only one polyphonic composition, from the village of Puama'u, Hiva'oa. This example featured a mixed vocal group, accompanied by clapping, drumming, and striking bamboo idiophones.

*Mahohe* (S), *maha'u* (N) is a choreographed, large-group dance often called the pig dance. Arranged in two or more columns, males perform strongly accented arm movements, which mime ordinary activities (preparing breadfruit paste, cracking coconuts, bathing in a stream), adding claps, bodily percussion, and sometimes erotic movements. Though people throughout the archipelago perform, Nukuhivans are the acknowledged specialists, and Marquesans attribute the origin of this dance to Nukuhiva. Northern islanders say the dancers imitate the actions of pigs; Southerners say the dancers imitate the sound of pigs, but mime actions of daily life. Texts consist of short rhythmic sequences of rehearsed vocables (figure 10), which men deliver as strong, husky, rumbling, rhythmic grunts. The dance may include women, arranged in one or more columns between men. Women do not vocalize; standing or squatting with their hands on their hips, they sway their hips gently, in rhythm with the underlying pulse.

*Matatetau* 'genealogies' are recited in rapid, rhythmic speech; when accompanied with juggling, they are called *pei*. Before about 1925, women gathered informally in the village and held friendly competitions, reciting genealogies while juggling fruits, nuts, pandanus-leaf balls, or hand-sized packets of breadfruit paste (*pei*). By the early 1990s, only a few elders knew the genealogies.

*Mauta'a.*—A declamatory solo. See *ha'anaunau.*

*Putu* is a large-group chant performed by men (by men and women together in Puama'u, and on 'Uahuka) in an inward-facing circle surrounding one or two standing male leaders. Performances by men of Atuona, Hiva'oa, are especially admired.

A small body of *putu* forms the core of a fixed repertory, performed on occasions calling for the presentation of music and dance. These pieces have no standardized textual content, though a secondary sexual component is clear in most. Handy and Winne (1925:42–43) transcribed an honorific piece, still performed in Atuona. The following text reveals the kinds of change that mold Marquesan texts over time, including new words, substitutions of names to make composed items fit a new occasion or a new troupe, and the deletion of material (Moulin 1991b:275).

FIGURE 10　Rhythmic vocables used in the Marquesan *mahohe*. Transcription by Jane Freeman Moulin, from performance in 1989.

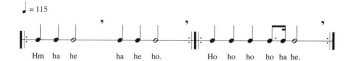

| Leader | Pa'a'oa e, |
| Chorus | Pa'a'oa-titi'a, tu'u tama |
|        | Mei te moana. |

| Leader | 'E'i nui, |
| Chorus | 'E'i nui tau, |
|        | Te po'ea mei Vevau. |

| Leader | E Tiu e! |
| Chorus | O ai te putu nei? |
|        | Na'iki ho'i te putu nei. |

| Leader | Ma 'una! |
| Chorus | Ma 'una o na mou oho, |
|        | Mou oho no te motua. |
|        | Motua, motua o Piua, 'ei nui. |

Dolphin,
My beloved dolphin, my son
From the sea.

A great whale's tooth,
A great whale's tooth disembarks,
The handsome youth from Vevau.

Oh you Tiu!
Who are these *putu*?
These *putu* are certainly the Na'iki.

Up!
Up on the heads,
The heads of the uncles.
The uncle of Piua, a great whale's tooth.

Most *putu* are in binary form: a responsorial section in speech-dominated rhythm with leader-group responses yields to a unison declamation with a regularly recurring pulse and clapping. In the 1970s and 1980s, these chants were sung in unison, but a 1963 recording made in Atuona has two-part chanting in the first section of one *putu*. The part no longer performed is a drone at the interval of a perfect fourth below the tonal center. The leader may improvise movements and incorporate *haka* as he dances inside the circle; group movements are choreographed and do not draw on *haka*.

*Rari* (S), *ru'u* (N) are strophic, topical songs, performed in unison by either an all-female or mixed group. The most popular and frequently performed indigenous Marquesan genre, they appear in any presentation of traditional music and dance. The repertory encompasses old and new compositions. As topical songs, *rari* record major events in village life: communal celebrations, important visitors, islanders who left, details of amatory liaisons. *Rari* often have several stanzas (*kio*), each announced by a solo female voice; some also have a refrain (*'ave*). The sweep of the poetry and the practice of repeating stanzas make *rari* among the longest of late twentieth-century Marquesan chants. Performers sit cross-legged in lines, a circle, or a semicircle, swaying from side to side in rhythm with the music, or moving their hands to decorate the poetic text. Melodies undulate gently, emphasizing the tonal center and the third below it, either major or minor.

*Tapatapa.*—A declamatory solo chant. See *ha'anaunau.*

*Tapeʻa* (also known as *rikuhi*) usually signals the end of a presentation. Following the *rari,* women stay in place while men often kneel on one knee. Melodies recall the intervals and general melodic contour of the *rari,* but several unique features distinguish it as a separate genre. Unlike the dreaminess, occasional melancholy, and moderate tempo of *rari,* the *tapeʻa* is fast and energetic, with claps or body slaps reinforcing a strongly accented, regularly recurring pulse. Men may rhythmically interject grunts and accented gestures, adding an erotic element. Rather than the extended poetry of *rari, tapeʻa* consist of short textual lines (often mentioning the names of important people in the audience), answered by a refrain, whose incorporation of the meaningless words *rikuhe* and *rikuhi* gives rise to the secondary name of the genre.

*Uē tūpāpaʻu* 'cries for the dead' (also *uē tūpāpaku; uhaki; puhi nui* 'wails', Hivaʻoa).—Until the late 1800s, Marquesans performed elaborate rituals of mourning, chanting to accompany the stages of passage to Hawaiki, the afterworld. Elders living in the 1990s remembered having witnessed abbreviated forms of these rituals; a few recalled traditional laments. Performed mainly on one tone with an initial rise of a minor third at phrasal starts, these cries employ a stylized wail, reflected in long strings of repeated syllables at the end of textual lines.

*Vakahoa* (also *vaʻahoa* and *hoavaka*), a declamation, apparently derives its name from a former association with arriving canoes (Handy 1923:340) and ceremonies for launching canoes. See *haʻanaunau.*

In addition to the foregoing, research in the southern islands reveals nonclassified performances: the *haka o te kuku* 'dance of the *kuku* (bird)'; the *tuharara,* for bringing dancers forward into an arena; and the *haka paʻaʻoa* 'dolphin dance'. The *haka pahaka* 'leaning dance', earlier considered a men's dance, denotes a style of dancing wherein people perform *haka* with the torso tilted sideways. Lullabies and children's game-playing songs complete the list of *mea kakiu.* Older women still know these pieces, but children prefer French songs learned at school. The term *pipine,* earlier used for a eulogistic song in honor of a young woman (Handy and Winne 1925:23, 38–39), denotes a game-playing song that Marquesans in the 1980s did not consider a *mea kakiu.*

## New things

Imported music and dance are called new things (*mea hou*)—a distinction that implies a strong differentiation of "the other." By the 1890s, important political and religious changes, including the imposition of French rule (1842), had made France, the Roman Catholic Church, and Tahiti the dominant sources of external influence. Most *mea hou* have roots in Tahitian music and dance. The Tahitian *ʻaparima, hivinau, ʻōteʻa* (locally known as *tapriata* and *tapiriata*), *pāʻōʻā,* and *ʻutē* have widely known and often performed Marquesan counterparts. Physical and cultural distance from Tahiti fosters a cultural lag, making Marquesan styles dated versions of Tahitian ones. Compositions may undergo Marquesan alterations, resulting in differences from Tahitian practice.

The word *hīmene* as used in the Marquesas refers to singing, and is applied to a variety of sacred and secular pieces. Prayer-conveying songs (*hīmene pure*) are sung in all churches. People throughout the archipelago once enjoyed Tahitian *hīmene tārava,* but when intervalley musical contests became intensely competitive and the Roman Catholic church eliminated Tahitian elements from Marquesan worship, their popularity faded. In the 1990s, this polyphonic choral tradition rests primarily with local Protestants. Songs of entertainment (*hīmene ʻekaʻeka*) and the road (*hīmene ʻaʻa nui,* sung by young people along roadsides), ingredients requisite for informal music, are popular songs in pan-Pacific style, accompanied by guitar or other plucked stringed instruments and sung in various languages. At monthly gatherings in Hivaʻoa, a band

FIGURE 11   Marquesan single-headed hand-struck drums (*pahu*): *a,* a nineteenth-century instrument (Institut für Völkerkunde, Göttingen); *b,* an instrument in Atuona, Hiva'oa (photo by Jane Freeman Moulin, 1989).

FIGURE 12   A Marquesan wooden trumpet (*pū 'akau, pū rohoti*); Omoa, Fatuiva. Photo by Jane Freeman Moulin, 1989.

(*a*)                                                      (*b*)

provides music for dancing in couples, which also occurs, to recorded music, throughout the islands on such occasions as Ko'ina Rare, the July festivities marking Bastille Day.

## Musical instruments

To accompany performances of *mea kakiu,* Marquesans use traditional musical instruments. The *pahu,* a hand-struck, one-headed membranophone, provides a simple rhythmic foundation (figure 11). Marquesans also use two trumpets: *pū,* a side-blown or end-blown shell trumpet, and *pū 'akau* (*pū rohoti,* N), a wooden trumpet about 70 centimeters long, with a bamboo mouthpiece (figure 12). Their function is signaling, but the *pū* may also provide an elaborating element. Clapping is important; in some *mea kakiu,* it is the sole aural accompaniment.

Imported Tahitian dances require other instruments. *'Aparima* require a string band and *pahu* (either one-headed or two-headed); *tapriata, hivinau,* and *pā 'ō 'ā* require a standard Tahitian ensemble: two or three struck log idiophones (*tō'ere*); a *fa'atete,* a short, one-headed drum, struck with two sticks; and a two-headed *pahu,* struck with a padded stick. Some villages use a biscuit or kerosene tin, which Tahitians replaced with the *fa'atete* in the 1950s. These instruments are played by men. Women play only guitar, though seldom for presentations by large groups.

Men and women play musical instruments for private amusement. Elders remember several: the nose-blown flute (*vivo*), the musical bow (*tita'apu*), and the single-reed aerophone (*pū hakahau*); but these had disappeared from use by the 1980s. Only a bamboo lamellaphone (*tioro,* Fatuiva; *tita'apu,* Hiva'oa) remains; and only a few older women can play it well. Children's amusements provide contexts for homemade noisemakers: a struck bamboo idiophone (*kohe*), a leaf oboe (*pū*), a

Women sing when pounding arrowroot to make starch, preparing food for feasts, pounding bark into cloth, and plaiting mats and hats. Men sing when building canoes.

whirled coconut-leaf aerophone (*pinao*), and bamboo or *pititu*-wood whistles (*kī, kī kohe puru*).

Imported guitars and ukuleles combine with the locally made *'ukarere,* a fretted, plucked chordophone featuring one-piece construction and a goatskin membrane. For informal music, a homemade one-stringed bass (*tura*) may join in. Atuona's band, Hiti Marama, uses electronic instruments: guitar, synthesizer, and drums. Most liturgical music is unaccompanied. To attract young people to church, some priests permit music in popular styles, accompanied by guitars and sometimes by electronic keyboards. —JANE FREEMAN MOULIN

## COOK ISLANDS

The fifteen Cook Islands are widely scattered, with only 241 square kilometers of land, spread over thousands of square kilometers of ocean. In 1990, the population living in the Cook Islands was eighteen thousand; forty-five thousand lived overseas, mainly in Aotearoa. The official language is Cook Islands Māori (Rarotongan), but each island cultivates a different dialect or language; English is spoken widely.

### Southern Cook Islands

According to genealogies and archaeological evidence, voyagers from what is now French Polynesia settled Rarotonga about A.D. 1100. Legends say later waves of settlers were led by Tangi'ia from Tahiti and Karika from Manu'a (Sāmoa), possibly about A.D. 1250. Captain Cook sighted one of the southern islands in 1773 and landed in Atiu in 1777; within a few decades, the Russian explorer Krusenstern had named the group after Cook. From 1901 to 1965, the Cook Islands were a protectorate of New Zealand. Since 1965, the islands have enjoyed with New Zealand a relationship that allows for autonomy in all political sectors except defense.

Social and cultural structures within the Cook Islands are hierarchical, based on descent. Paramount chiefs (*ariki*) take the highest level; chiefs of major lineages (*mata'iapo*) come next, followed by chiefs of minor lineages (*rangatira*), heads of branches of minor lineages (*kiato*), heads of households (*metua*), and commoners (*unga*). This system continues, largely because access to land and communal identity remains a function of descent.

Music has a highly public role in Cook Islanders' lives (Gill 1876). It enhances ceremonial, ritual, and festive occasions, including the investure of leaders, religious ceremonies, children's christenings, marriages, and funerals. It enhances political leaders' stature, and it rallies support for political parties. Songs have been composed about all political leaders prominent since 1965.

In the postcolonial period, music became an important medium for developing a national identity. Celebrating love of country and environment, musical ensembles pay tribute to people, places, islands, indigenous trees, plants, and flowers. Some songs extol the virtues of a particular island, district, clan, or chiefly line. Others commemorate great voyages of discovery and sensational current events. The lyrics of many local songs employ environmental themes to liken the loved one to the mountains, the ocean, the moon, the stars, a special tree, a plant, a flower, or a bird.

Music often accompanies economic activities. Women sing songs (*pe'e*) whenever groups gather for productive purposes, such as pounding arrowroot to make starch, preparing food for feasts, pounding bark into cloth, and plaiting mats and hats. Men sing when building canoes. Mothers sing lullabies; children use lullabies to accompany games, such as hide and seek (*pinipini ta'ae*).

Though the people of each island speak a unique dialect, most music in the Cook Islands is composed and sung in Rarotongan, interspersed with dialectal words. To borrow words from Tahitian is prestigious, or at least popular. Terminological variants among islands serve as evidence of localized musical practices.

### Vocal music

Vocal music has two basic classes: secular and religious. The most common form of secular music is suitable for dancing. Christian missionaries, led by John Williams, arrived in 1823. From then until the end of the colonial era, missionaries and the colonial government discouraged traditional music, and a split between religious and "drinking" songs occurred. The latter, often accompanied by the consumption of kava (and later, alcohol), were sung away from settled areas. Drinking songs differ from religious songs in melody, lyrics, and tempo. They are lighthearted and fun; many are about love and sex, but some are about sadness and tragedy.

#### Secular music

Cook Islanders sang many songs about ships, their captains, and their voyages. At least one song ("*Pai rere Sunderland*") was composed about the flying boats that in the 1950s and early 1960s serviced the islands; jets, which began local service in 1974, have not inspired the composition of songs. Previously songs were composed to accompany the paddling of canoes, but they have almost disappeared with the canoes. In the 1990s, a resurgence of voyaging in canoes has led to a renaissance of canoe-paddling songs.

Commemorative songs are popular. Many touring parties compose a song for themselves. The opening of a meetinghouse, athletic competitions, election victories, and individual achievements are also occasions for composing songs.

Choral secular music includes an unaccompanied vocal form called *ūtē,* performed by a mixed chorus. Another choral form of Cook Islands music is the *pe'e,* performed by unaccompanied mixed groups on more formal occasions. *Karakia* are poems, myths, and prayers.

The archipelago has two radio stations. One of them, government-owned, plays local songs and American pop, interspersed with music from other parts of Polynesia. In seven restaurants and hotels on Rarotonga, live music is played. Music in local nightclubs mixes American pop and indigenous styles.

The choice of music relates to age. Younger people enjoy new, Western pop, while those of middle age or older enjoy a mixture of vernacular-language songs and Western pop. This situation is reflected in the music played at social parties, where the participants' ages are a major factor in determining the music.

#### Religious music

Local religious music has two forms: Sunday-school hymns and traditional hymns. Religious music is sung in churches (*'are pure*), in communal houses, at the opening and closing of governmental ceremonies and conferences, and at major rituals, including marriages and funerals.

FIGURE 13   At the Pacific Festival of Arts, the Cook Islands National Dance Company performs. Photo by Adrienne L. Kaeppler, 1985.

Sunday-school hymns (ʻīmene apiʻi-Sāpati) are sung unaccompanied, using texts translated into Rarotongan by early missionaries, especially Aaron Buzacott. These texts are printed in a hymnal published by the Cook Islands Christian Church. Other churches, including the Roman Catholic Church, the Church of Jesus Christ of Latter-Day Saints (Mormon), and Seventh-Day Adventist churches, have their own hymns. The mid-1980s saw the development of another form of religious music—Southern Baptist gospel music, based on a newly introduced fundamentalist Christianity, the Apostolic Church. The melodies and style of singing are gospel, but the lyrics are often in Cook Islands Māori.

Traditional hymns (ʻīmene tuki) are polyphonic and more complex than the simple harmonies of Sunday-school hymns. The people believe that ʻīmene tuki are the remains of the music their ancestors performed to worship deities: the harmonies survive, but the lyrics now incorporate Christian doctrine. Indigenous religious music survives in the form of karakia, songs performed on important occasions like chiefly investitures. Music is presented at religious festivals, including annual pageants (nuku) and Pentecost (Ririanga Vaerua). Secular competitions, including the annual Constitution Celebrations, Dancer of the Year, Singer of the Year, Tangi Kaʻara (a drumming competition), and other festivals (figure 13), present opportunities for performing.                                          —TAKIORA INGRAM

### Instrumental music

Played individually or in ensembles, musical instruments in the Cook Islands accompany recitations, prayers, dances, and songs (figure 14). On special occasions, they perform without singing. Individual instruments may bear names that mark their importance to their owner (Jonassen 1991).

### Idiophones

The most important traditional musical instrument is the struck log idiophone. In museum collections, old examples from Mangaia reveal exquisite carving, with the slit in the shape of a figure-eight. These were said to announce war and peace.

Small log idiophones called tōkere or tōʻere are widely used today. A straight hardwood branch 50 centimeters long and about 12 centimeters wide, free of smaller branches, ideally makes the best instrument. The carver sets the wood lengthwise on

FIGURE 14    Tutonga, Tom Lindsay, Andrew Andrew, and John Lindsay sing and play. Photo by Jon Tikivanotau Jonassen.

the ground, and along one part of the surface cuts a 5-centimeter longitudinal slit, leaving about 8 centimeters uncut at both ends.

Through the slit, the carver hollows the interior. Parallel to the first slit, he cuts a second slit from one end, working 2.5 centimeters inward, leaving 5 centimeters of unremoved wood between the slits. He cuts the other end the same way, and then hollows out the end slits, taking care not to break the septum of unremoved wood. Since the amount of wood hollowed out from the center slit determines the pitch and timbre of the instrument, experienced carvers consider this the most important part of their work.

The *tōkere* is played with two 30-centimeter sticks, usually made from the roots of ironwood (*toa*). Each stick is 5 centimeters in diameter at one end, tapering to a point at the other. Holding the thicker end, a player strikes the side of the central slit; for special effects, he hits the end slits. To strengthen and add weight to the sticks, players sometimes soak them in mud for days before a performance.

Carvers cut *pātē*, slightly larger log idiophones, from a big branch of a hardwood tree, and occasionally from the trunk. The carving resembles that of the *tōkere*, but the ends are often left intact. The length of a *pātē* varies from 70 to 90 centimeters, depending on the pitch and timbre desired. If three pitches are needed, a carver makes three *pātē*, of varying sizes. Players ordinarily use one 30-centimeter stick, hitting the side of the central slit or the side of the body of the instrument.

*Ka'ara*, made from the trunks of trees, are about twice the size of *pātē*. A carver hollows an instrument by a process resembling that of the manufacture of *pātē* and *tōkere*, but giving the slits the form of a triangular figure-eight. The top of the *ka'ara* has decorative lines incised in cross-hatching, sometimes with painted patterns in black. The size and shape of the slit give the instrument at least three different pitches. The triangular openings are connected by a middle narrow slit. When struck, each triangular side and the central narrow slit produces a specific tone.

A player uses two 30-centimeter sticks, which vary from those used in playing the *pātē* and the *tōkere*. Instead of hardwood, the wood is cut from a coconut frond. Softer, it has the effect of eliciting from the *ka'ara* a haunting, mellow sound.

Specialized noisemakers include gourds, shells, coconuts, woodblocks, bamboo, cloth beaters, mat drums, and rocks. To the sounds of log-idiophone ensembles, these instruments add subtle rhythms and timbres. Even the human body, through slaps,

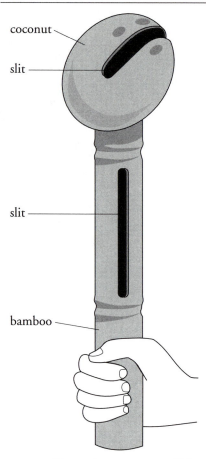

coconut

slit

slit

bamboo

FIGURE 15   The *tangianau*, a compound idiophone, is made from a coconut and a bamboo tube. Drawing by Jon Tikivanotau Jonassen.

claps, and vocalizations, adds musical sounds. In the spirit of using natural resources, modern-day ensembles sometimes include spoons, forks, and bottles. A coconut-leaf lamellaphone (*kikau akatangi*) has a midrib held across the mouth and twanged with a finger. The *tangianau,* named after Tangianau Tuaputa, who reintroduced the instrument in 1989, is a slit coconut shell attached to a slit bamboo (figure 15). With a thin stick, the player alternately strikes the bamboo and the coconut.

### Membranophones

Drums of the Cook Islands are usually made from the trunk of a tree or a large round piece of wood. Carvers hollow them out and cover their opening or openings with the skin of an animal or a shark. The skin covering distinguishes two basic types of drums: the *pa'u* and the *pa'u mangō* (or simply *mangō*).

*Pa'u* are made from several kinds of wood. The trunk is cut to the desired length, ranging from 1.8 to 2.4 meters. The maker hollows out the inside of the log, leaving a circular outer strip at least 7 centimeters thick. The work of hollowing out large drums formerly involved many people, who with fire burned out the interior; alternative techniques are now available, but the task remains arduous. The openings are covered with dried skin, bound with rings and cords. The cords were formerly lengths of coconut fiber, passing from holes in the skin down to slots, through which they were fed for tying around the woodwork between the lower corner of the base and the bottom of the slot. Players use a round, 30-centimeter beater, usually of wild hibiscus (*'au*). Many villages formerly had communal drums. For playing, these were hung from trees. The diameter of such drums reached one meter.

The *pa'u mangō* has a tongue (*arero*), carved on the inside of the top portion. It is not usually hollowed out completely: the carver leaves a septum between the top and bottom sections. One old kind of *pa'u mangō,* hollow throughout, with skin covering one end, has gone out of use. Another kind, with the tongue, is in common use; it has one skin, ideally of shark. A third kind, resembling the second, bears carved figures for religious, decorative, or historical reasons. Players use two thin, 30-centimeter beaters, or strike the drumhead with their hands. To improve the sound of the instrument, players often heat the drumhead with fire or in the sun. The skin commonly used today is goatskin.

### Chordophones

Stringed instruments include the guitar, the string bass, and the ukulele, all introduced in the early twentieth century. These instruments are often made from local materials. In the twentieth century, the banjo and the mandolin joined musical presentations, but their use has been limited.

The guitar (*kitā*) was most likely introduced into the Cook Islands via Hawai'i. Cook Islanders who worked on whaling ships or as phosphate miners overseas also encountered the Spanish guitar. At least three ways of tuning the strings came into local use. Coupling with a common Polynesian free style of strumming and picking, a sound peculiar to the Cook Islands developed.

The guitar was usually accompanied by the ukulele (*ukarere*). The version typical of the Cook Islands is made from coconut shells and specially shaped hibiscus or local mahogany. Based on the Hawaiian *'ukulele,* it is smaller, with a much higher pitch. It is usually strummed, adding timbral depth to the sound.

The string bass (*umupa*) is the third element in a typical string band of the Cook Islands. Made from a tea chest, a string, and two pieces of thin timber, it furnishes the heartbeat of the musical presentation, reminiscent of local drumbeats.

*Aerophones*

Precontact Cook Islanders used wind instruments of two kinds: a nose-blown flute (*vivo*) and a conch trumpet (*pū*). The former was made of bamboo, hibiscus, or hardwood (such as *tamanu, tira,* or *pua*); bamboo and hibiscus were particularly common. The bamboo variety had a tube about 30 to 60 centimeters long, with one end kept closed and the other end open. The player blew air from one nostril through a hole placed near the closed end. Two or three small holes were made near the middle of the bamboo, in a straight line about 5 centimeters apart. Makers applied the same technique to a non-bamboo instrument, hollowing out a piece of wood but leaving one end blocked. Hibiscus required a special approach in creating the hollow: the bark, rather than the wood, was used.

The flute is associated with love and ceremonial events. On Mangaia, it was played near the house of entertainment (*are karioi*) to send signals from the player to a woman inside. It is mentioned in stories centered on the *are karioi*. This association possibly discouraged its use during the strict Christian period, beginning in the 1820s.

A conch trumpet is made by cutting off the apical whorls of the shell *Cornis rufo.* Sometimes the maker puts a hole on the side near the closed end of the shell. The trumpet announces meetings, marks the beginning of ceremonies and performances, welcomes special visitors, or simply declares that bread has finishing baking. It formerly warned warriors to mobilize. Often it was sounded with a *ka'ara.*

An aerophone associated with children's games is the *pu'i kikau,* made by rolling the green part of a coconut leaf into a close spiral, with one end smaller than the other. The player blows through the smaller end, producing a strident sound. Another aerophone associated with children's games is a whistle (*pu'i nita*), made from a papaya-leaf stalk. The stem end is cut straight, and the leaf end is left on; the player makes a small slot just stemward of where the leaf develops, and blows through it.

During the 1930s, brass trumpets were introduced into traditional musical formats to play bridges between melodic phrases; accepted in the presentation of much local music, they remain a novelty. Brass bands are popular, and harmonicas have also found a place in local music. An old aerophone is a stone sling (*maka*); when swung in the air, it makes a haunting hum, which formerly enhanced the sound of warlike songs.

*Percussive ensembles*

Percussive ensembles are an important part of Cook Islanders' national identity. The drumming of traveling Cook Islands entertainers—Araura, Betela Dance Troupe (figure 16), the Cook Islands National Arts Theatre (CINAT), the Cook Islands Youth Council, Muriavai, Ta'akoka, Te Ivi Māori, Tereora, Tupapa Maraerenga—is admired by attentive audiences.

Typical drumming of the Cook Islands uses five kinds of instrument: the *ka'ara,* the *pātē,* and the *tōkere* combine with the *pa'u* and the *pa'u mangō.* The *pa'u* keeps a basic one-one beat, interrupted by the *pa'u mangō,* which, because its pitch is higher, gives out distinctly perceptible rhythms. The *pātē* sets a basic rhythmic pattern, which the high-pitched sound of the *tōkere* plays against. To that, the *ka'ara* adds percussive complexity by stressing offbeats.

## Dance

In the Cook Islands, dances reflect expressions that linger in traditional musical forms: each island has unique forms or variations. Some dances are performed solo; more often, dances are performed in ensembles, which can be all-male, all-female, or a mixture of males and females.

FIGURE 16  The Betela Dance Troupe in Tokyo: Fiji Wilson Snowball, *pa'u*; Ota Tuaeu, *pa'u mangō*; Jon Tikivanotau Jonassen, *pātē*; Mataio Nielson, *tōkere*; Teinakore Tuake'u, *pātē rua*. Photo by Diya Moana Jonassen, 1971.

### Ura pa'u

*Ura pa'u* are the most famous dances of the archipelago. They portray activities of everyday life—fishing, cooking, and building—through movements of each dancer's face, hands, hips, and legs, and through combinations of movements from multiple dancers.

Dancers' movements follow beats from a variety of instruments, played in unison or individually. Log idiophones (*tōkere* and *pātē*) direct the movements of the face, hands, and legs, while membranophones (*pahu*) direct the movement of the hips and knees. Anciently, *ura pa'u* were performed in ceremonies and festivals. The *ka'ara* controlled the dancers' motions. Presentations would include war-related songs, with dancers manipulating weapons and other implements.

During the 1800s, women and men danced the *ura pa'ata* on platforms. In response to pressure from missionaries, costuming (leaves and cloth) yielded to long dresses for women and white shirt and black trousers for men. In the twentieth century, as churches relaxed their controls on dancing, aspects of the old dances and the associated costuming were reintroduced.

### Kaparima

*Kaparima*, songs with gestures, were once performed to recitations and the nose-blown flute. Today, they are accompanied by guitar and ukulele, and have incorporated introduced movements, sometimes portraying modern situations, but the storytelling remains paramount.

### Other named dances

There are three types of teasing dance (*ura tatiaeae*)—those that tease to anger, for fun or comedy, and to entice. The dances identify individuals and villages or islands. They can be performed at any time, with or without musical accompaniment. *Ura tamataora* are impromptu unplanned dances, done by one or more persons. The term also describes dances performed for informal entertainment, but usually implies that the movements are not preset. *Ura tamataora* utilize all kinds of music. The scaring dance (*ura tamataku*), probably common before the 1800s, can be disciplinary or part of the enactment of a story. Movements of insects, fish, animals, and ghosts are imitated by a soloist, usually unaccompanied. A playful dance (*ura kanga*), resembling *ura tamataora,* is easily recognized as a nonsense dance, intended to attract laughter and often performed at sports events, usually unaccompanied.

The pageant (*nuku*) combines all types of entertaining activities, based on a historical period important to the group making the presentation. It involves large numbers of people, and the total performance can last for hours. This is still performed, with modern religious themes.

The *ura piani* (sometimes called the *ura takapini* after the 1950s, when the harmonica was introduced) is an impromptu performance, usually accompanied by percussion, and having subtle sexual connotations.

The tool dance (*ura penu*)—a term invented by Kauraka Kauraka—derives from the Pukapukan word *penupenu* 'object'. A group dance, it highlights a weapon, a tool, or a household utensil, and takes its theme from that tool. Men and women perform it. A special kind of tool dance is the women's fan dance (*ua taʻiriʻiri*), symbolizing peace.

A martial-arts dance (*ura pia*) is associated with the island of Aitutaki, where men perform it to display their skills in balance and fitness. It involves exercise-like movements, and accompanies percussion. Another popular dance associated with Aitutaki is the stilt dance (*ura rore*), which men perform on stilts, showing off their balance and strength; it accompanies percussion. In the abdominal dance (*ura kopu*), men roll their abdominal muscles upward and downward in repeated waves; only a few can do it.

The top dance (*ura topi*) is performed to assist the spinning of a top. Playing with tops was once common among Cook Islands men. Whole villages performed this dance during festivals, but it has now almost disappeared. The *ura pua* resembled the *ura topi,* but it featured the *pua,* a small, flat, round piece of wood, used for rolling. The objective was to see who could roll it the farthest, and the performance involved dancing to guide the *pua* on its way. It, too, has almost disappeared.

Fire has often appeared in arts of the Cook Islands. The torch dance (*ura rama*) was once done in ceremonies using coconut leaves, but it has since developed into an entertaining dance with bamboo torches or candles held inside coconut shells. Movements are based on flames, accompanied by percussion and singing. The fire dance (*ura aʻi*), showing influences from Sāmoa and Tahiti, involves twirling a stick lit with fire at both ends, accompanied by percussion.

Dances to praise (*ura akamori, ura akapaʻapaʻa*) feature movements that honored traditional gods, but have been adapted into Christian worship. Accompanied by hymns, they now have little or no movement of the hips; instead, movements of the face and hands dominate.

The legend-telling dance (*ura peu tupuna*) tells legends in combination with chants, speeches, and staged displays. In *haka,* men in unison perform warlike actions of the legs and hands. Accompanied by recitation and the *kahara,* it is a feature of Cook Islands dancing, usually seen now only in the outer islands. Anciently, a spear dance (*ura korare*) was performed by men, performing aggressive movements to accompany recitations.

—JON TIKIVANOTAU JONASSEN

## Northern Cook Islands

### Manihiki

People collectively called Manihikian inhabit Manihiki and Rakahanga, atolls separated by 40 kilometers of open sea. The population of Manihiki in 1991 was 666, and that of Rakahanga was 262. These atolls are inhabited by a single people, who see themselves as differing historically and culturally from other Cook Islanders.

Popular songs are accompanied by guitars and ukuleles. Bands may add a harmonica, a button accordion, drums, and metal spoons. Most youths prefer to dance to the sound of imported records.

Low-lying, with a central lagoon, each atoll has porous, infertile, coral soil, mainly supporting coconut palms. The diet consists largely of seafood and coconut, supplemented by imported foods. The main exports are pearls and copra (dried coconut meat). Since 1987, an airstrip on Manihiki has eased travel and communication. Diesel-generated electricity was introduced in 1983. Each village—one in Rakahanga, two (Tukao, Tauhunu) in Manihiki—has stores, churches, infirmaries, a school, and a post office. Tauhunu, the administrative center, has governmental offices and a courtroom.

Manihikians trace their descent from two male ancestors, Matangaro and Hukutahu, believed to have been the first settlers' sons. Senior and junior lines of descent from each ancestor give structure to four major lineages. The chiefs, Te Fakaheo and Te Faingahitu, served priestly functions (Buck 1932:45), which they lost when missionaries converted the people to Christianity; after 1901, when Britain annexed the Cook Islands to New Zealand, their secular powers weakened.

Landholding and residency reflect seniority and juniority among lineages (Matheson 1987:170–172). Thus, the village of Tauhunu has four sections, whose members form teams that compete in sports and dancing. Whole villages may compete against each other. For national competitions in Rarotonga, teams may represent Manihiki or Rakahanga.

### Musical contexts

The term *tārekareka* 'entertainment' denotes public performances, which may include secular music, dance, oratory, sports, and theater. Most forms of Manihikian music imply physical movements, which Cook Islanders recognize as stylistically unique, though they share many traits with dancing elsewhere in eastern Polynesia. Extant genres of dancing are secular only.

Dancing serves many functions. Performances grace feasts (held to honor visitors, farewell atoll residents, and open communal buildings) and major festivals, such as New Year's and Gospel Day, held annually on 26 October, commemorating the arrival of the first missionaries. Many performances enhance the public giving of gifts. Some mark major life-cycle events: boys' first birthdays and haircuttings, twenty-first birthdays, marriages, and deaths.

Most choreographed dances are either songs with gestures ('*aparima, kaparima*) or dances with percussion (*fōtea, hupahupa*). Manihikians rarely perform '*aparima* and *fōtea*; they believe *kaparima* have come from Rarotonga, but *hupahupa* have arisen locally.

The *hupahupa*, the most popular genre of dances in Manihiki, is a choreographed dance of young men, young women, or mixed groups, accompanying an ensemble of log idiophones (*kōriro*), a tin (*tini*), one or two upright, footed drums (*pahu matatahi*), and one large two-headed drum (*pahu matarua*). Drummers prefer percussive rhythms to be distinct and clear; hence, they beat *kōriro* with one stick, not two, as drummers often do in the southern Cook Islands. Similar troupes dance the *kaparima,* accompanying guitars, ukuleles, and one *pahu matarua.* The dancers usually sing; sometimes they dance while only a chorus sings.

Each village has a club that organizes young people's activities, including watching videos, volleyball matches, and social dances. The president of each club is usually an older person, whose permission authorizes such activities. Each club sets its code of dress and behavior, whose breach may result in the cancellation of activities. Perhaps once or twice a year at social dances, British and American dances (*hura pupu*), including square dances, are performed; the most popular is the waltz, performed by young and old alike.

Song-dance genres include the *ūtē,* introduced from the Society Islands, and the *pātahutahu,* in which a solo dancer improvises, using stereotyped movements. Other improvised solo dances occur at events and ceremonies where presentation is important.

### Religious music

Most Manihikians are Protestants belonging to the Cook Islands Christian Church (CICC), which developed from the church established by the London Missionary Society. Each village has one CICC building, made from coral blocks and lime. In 1908, Roman Catholic missionaries converted some local people, who built a church in Tauhunu and another in Tukao. The smaller village, Tukao, has the larger number of Roman Catholics. Seventh-Day Adventists have one church, built in the 1980s in Tauhunu. Missionaries from the Church of Jesus Christ of Latter-Day Saints (Mormon) have unsuccessfully tried to convert the population and establish a church in Tauhunu.

Religious music is entirely vocal. Youths sing evangelical songs to guitar accompaniment; hymns are unaccompanied. Manihikians distinguish two hymnodic genres: a simple, harmonic, Western style (*hīmene āpī-Sāpati*), and a complex, polyphonic, local style (*hīmene tuki tapu*). Congregations sing the latter more frequently, as loudly as possible, for the local musical aesthetic equates loudness with liveliness.

A secular vocal genre similar to the *hīmene tuki tapu* is *hīmene tuki tārekareka.* Both forms of *hīmene tuki* feature male singers' pitched guttural vocables (*tuki*), a woman's introductory phrase (*tumu hīmene,* starting each stanza), and one or two singers' improvisatory parts (*perepere*). These forms differ in text and performance. Percussive rhythms, from a drum or the singers' clapping, and impromptu solo dancing may accompany *hīmene tuki tārekareka.*

### Secular music

Manihikians no longer perform ancient compositions frequently, and several nineteenth-century genres are obsolete. The *kapa* was a recited song with gestures; the *pehe,* a choral or solo recited song without gestures. At special events, people still perform the latter, but they have largely replaced it with a modern song (*atu pehe*), often used as an introduction to dancing. A *pehe* proper more frequently serves as a component of percussion for dancing: percussionists may sing one as part of their performance, or they may use it as a reminder of the rhythms; the lead percussionist may call out its name or first line.

Young people call their popular vocal music *hīmene māpū.* These songs are accompanied by guitars and ukuleles. Bands may add a harmonica, a button accordion, drums, and metal spoons; but most youths prefer to dance to the sound of imported records.

FIGURE 17    Tokorua Teaurere blows his *pū nīnītā*, newly made from a papaya-leaf stem. Photo by Helen Reeves Lawrence, 1987.

### Musical instruments

Log idiophones (*kōriro*) are usually made from branches of *fano* (*Guettarda speciosa*), hollowed inside through a lengthwise slit; the sticks, from branches of *ngangie* (*Pemphis acidula*). The player of a tin uses two flat sticks of lightweight wood. A player of a *pahu matatahi* plays barehanded, or with paired wooden sticks resembling those used for playing a European side drum. A player of the *pahu matarua* uses a single, large, wooden mallet with a bulbous end. The body of a *pahu* is normally made from the trunk of a palm, but sometimes from the wood of other trees, such as breadfruit. Until the 1970s, drumheads were usually of sharkskin; since then, they have been of goatskin, imported from the southern Cook Islands.

For two small idiophones, *titāpū,* the human oral cavity serves as resonator. One is a coconut leaflet held across the mouth and struck with part of the midrib of another leaflet. The other consists of two cylindrical wooden sticks, one slightly smaller than the other: the player, usually a young boy, holds the larger stick beside his mouth, and strikes it with the smaller. The mouth serves as another instrument, the *pahu ngutu,* for which the player taps each cheek with a finger. Children use nearly all these instruments.

Adults usually play musical instruments in ensemble, but sometimes signal with solo instruments: a conch trumpet (*pū*), a log idiophone (*kōriro*), and imported metal whistles (*pīpara*), which drummers blow for cues during rehearsals. The ringing of bells—some of them ships' bells, salvaged from wrecks—calls worshipers to attend CICC and Roman Catholic services; for the same function, Seventh-Day Adventists in the late 1980s used a log idiophone.

Other aerophones in use in Manihiki include a slitted tube (*pū nīnītā*), made from a hollow papaya-leaf stem (figure 17); leaf oboes (*pū nikau, pū raufara*), made from coconut leaflets or pandanus strips, respectively; and a fipple flute (*vivo*), made from the hollow stem of *ngahu,* a tropical shrub (*Scaevola sericea*).

Manihiki supports one brass band: the Boys' Brigade Band, which plays processional music at weddings and the church parade, a monthly Protestant event. About ten members play imported drums (bass drum, side drum, tenor drum) and several brass instruments (trumpets, cornets, euphoniums). In addition to the foregoing instruments, the human body provides music with percussive accompaniment in the form of clapping (*pōkara*) and slapping.        —HELEN REEVES LAWRENCE

### Manihiki: a local view

Manihiki music resembles the music of the rest of the Cook Islands, with influence from Rarotonga, but it has unique features. Christian missionaries arrived in 1849, and their descriptions provide clues about precontact musical styles. The range of sung notes was narrow. Singing in parts extended from Christian hymns to secular songs at beer parties (*putuputuhanga inuinu*), mostly attended by men.

Like other northern islands, Manihiki's modern styles lag Rarotonga's. Manihiki uses fewer minor chords, which Rarotongans have adopted for playing guitars and choral singing. Men traditionally led singing; later, women began to take leadership roles. In the late twentieth century, female voices have taken the lead for singing *ūtē, hīmene tuki,* and *hīmene āpī-Sāpati;* the *hīmene māpū* is led by male or female voice.

As a result of Christian influence, music since the 1850s has taken inspiration from biblical stories. The sound is local, but the messages are Christian. The music changed as people resorted to more secular pastimes, such as drinking beer and composing bawdy songs. The introduction of brass instruments, the button accordion, and the harmonica added musical diversity.

### Performance

The drum-accompanying dance (*hupahupa*) is the major dance in which men and women participate. Men and women alike covet the position of lead dancer, but each troupe's director is a man. Directors formerly blew a whistle to signal the beginning and ending of a dance, but by the 1980s, performers deemed this cue unnecessary, and most cues are verbal or musical.

Other dances include *kaparima,* in which the dancers move their limbs to guitar- and ukulele-accompanied singing; and a combination of *hupahupa* and *kaparima.* Guitars are often of the Yamaha brand, made in Japan; ukuleles are locally made. Some dances involve the use of portable objects, including wooden boxes and spears, but the dance remains the same. Women sway their hips from side to side, and men scissor their legs in and out. The choreography dictates the movements of the arms.

The locations of musical performances depend on the purpose of the occasion. *Hīmene tuki* and *hīmene āpī-Sāpati* are performed in church. The older members of the congregation lead the singing of the former, but younger members, forming the Sunday-school section of the church, lead the latter. When *hīmene tuki* and *hīmene āpī-Sāpati* are sung outside of churches, they are in the formal section of a program. They may be part of ceremonies welcoming dignitaries at a feast in the public plaza in Tauhunu, opening the observance of Parents Day at local schools, celebrating Gospel Day at the CICC pastor's residence, and conducting marriages and funerals.

*Hupahupa* and *hīmene māpū* are usually performed at the plaza, as at New Year's. The village divides into halves, which perform items alternately for about three hours. After each item, the audience shows appreciation by donating money. If the event is organized by the church, the donated money goes to support the church. The club of village youths also raises funds by presenting dances. The music for *hupahupa, hīmene māpū,* and *ūtē* may be called secular. Cassette-supplied disco music with European lyrics is popular among young people; Tahitian songs are popular on cassettes.

To welcome visitors to the island, ensembles usually begin a sequence of songs with a performance of the following text, an *hīmene māpū* in Rarotongan, with a few words in Manihikian:

| | |
|---|---|
| Hakarongo mai e te au manuhiri! | Listen, oh visitors! |
| Ko matou, teia tamariki Manihiki e, | This is us, the children of Manihiki, |
| Te tu atu nei i teia ra ki runga i te tahua e. | Standing before you today. |
| E no reira e te au manuhiri, | Oh, visitors, |
| Tapiri mai, ka ruru rima tatou e. | Welcome, let us shake hands. |
| Na runga mai koe i te moana uriuri, | You have come across the deep ocean, |
| Te moana tua tea e. | The white-foamed seas. |
| E no reira e te au manuhiri, | Oh, visitors, |
| Tapiri mai, ka ruru rima tatou e. | Welcome, let us shake hands. |

There is little difference between Manihikian and Rarotongan, the national language; in this text, *hakarongo* would be *akarongo* in Rarotongan. The singing is usually accompanied by guitars and ukuleles for about eight minutes, usually played by men. The singers vary in age from ten to fifty years. The last two lines of the lyrics often repeat to signal the ending of the song. There are no minor chords in the music, and usually four beats to the bar. It is in a moderate to fast speed, with a deceleration on the last two lines before the ending. Some songs speed up toward the end, and members of the audience may join the dancers.

Some *hīmene māpū* are just for listening, as when, in 1984, the group Marokaipipi of Rakahanga played at the Tangaroa Restaurant in Rarotonga. As in other islands of the Cook Islands, love is their most frequent theme. They may quote from legends. In general, they are favored and sung by young people, and *hīmene tuki* by older people.

### Collective styles

Manihiki styles resemble other styles of the Cook Islands, and can be categorized similarly: dances with percussion (*hupahupa*), songs with gestures (*kaparima*), *ūtē*, *hīmene tuki*, and *hīmene āpī-Sāpati*. The content, however, differs. The lyrics of *hīmene tuki* and *ūtē* are in Manihikian, whose vocabulary differs by about 20 percent from Rarotongan, which all Cook Islanders speak after progressing through governmental schools.

One special feature of Manihiki dance is percussion on an empty biscuit tin with two wooden sticks. This practice is typical of northern *hupahupa,* but in the southern islands the tin was replaced, about the 1960s, by a small log idiophone (*pātē*). The use of the tin is a post-European innovation, but it has remained a feature of Manihiki *hupahupa.*

Manihiki songs with gestures often accompany the harmonica. A common brand of harmonica used is Blessing, manufactured in China. Players repeatedly press their tongues onto the holes to triple or quadruple the notes per beat. No bending of notes occurs. Totini Pukerua (b. 1910), Takai Ngatipa (b. 1933), and Ngaro Taverio (b. 1939) are expert local players of harmonicas.

How Manihikians perform *hīmene tuki* and *hīmene āpī-Sāpati* resembles that of the rest of the Cook Islands, but this music is usually sung at a higher pitch. It uses Christian texts for lyrics, whose language is usually Manihikian for *hīmene tuki* but Rarotongan for *hīmene āpī-Sāpati.* Occasionally, stories or customs become the content of *hīmene tuki,* but *hīmene āpī-Sāpati* have biblical themes. An example of the former, "*Kua aruru te 'enua kātoa,*" is commonly sung by congregations; an example of the latter, "*E 'aere rekareka mai,*" is frequently sung by younger members of the church. The hymn "*E tuku ua mai te au tamariki*" is always sung for baptisms.

At Christmas, carols of the international repertory come into vogue, sung mostly in English. During the main service on Christmas, "Silent Night" is sung, in the form translated into Rarotongan by E. R. W. Krause. While waiting for midnight on

Christmas Eve, most affiliates of the church gather at the pastor's house, singing *īmene tuki* one after the other. At midnight, the party breaks up, and people greet each other with a kiss, saying in English, "Merry Christmas"; young men and women visit relatives, who may greet them with "Merry Christmas" also. A reprise of this practice occurs on New Year's Eve, but most young people prefer to stay home to sing *hīmene māpū* while drinking imported beer.

### Copyright

Formerly, a musician would declare that he or she had composed a piece of music before it was premiered. Relatives, friends, and performers would support the composer's rights over the composition. In the 1980s, however, composers began experiencing musical thefts—problems that increased as people became aware that they could earn money from owning and recording songs. A composer can secure a musical copyright by registering the music with SPACEM (Société de Protection d'Auteurs et Compositeurs d'Éditions Musicales) in Tahiti. Two local composers, Mr. Nipu Nipu (b. 1941) of Rakahanga and Mr. Tauraki Tokarahi (b. 1948) of Manihiki, have joined SPACEM to secure their musical rights further. Manihiki music is not specifically protected by registration with SPACEM or the Australasian Performing Rights Association (APRA) in Australia, but protective legislation stems from the New Zealand Copyright Act of 1913. Older music, based on oral traditions, is mostly anonymous. Manihiki composers such as Mehau Karaponga (b. 1920), Tutai Pukerua (b. 1921), Ben Ellis (b. 1934), and Nipu Nipu have contributed much, and many of their works are recorded for sale.

### Musical instruments

The Manihikian *kōriro* is a log idiophone, beaten with a single stick to give time to dances, and to signal public announcements. Other instruments include conch trumpets and coconut-leaf rattles. Upright, footed drums are made with goatskin membranes (Buck 1932:203).

In the twentieth century, Manihikians began using an increasing variety of instruments. More traditional ensembles consisted of a large *kōriro,* beaten with one stick; a smaller *kōriro,* beaten with two sticks; a sharkskin drum; a large drum; and an extra *kōriro* or two, beaten with one stick. Later instruments include the guitar, the ukulele, the button accordion, the harmonica, and brass instruments. Occasionally an off-island band brings electric guitars, an organ, and modern percussion. In 1986, Tauraki Tokorahi brought his electrified band to celebrate the opening of the palace for the chief of Manihiki.      —KAURAKA KAURAKA

### Pukapuka

A 5-square-kilometer atoll about 1,200 kilometers northwest of Rarotonga, Pukapuka has a population of about 750, with about a hundred others on Nassau (65 kilometers southeast). Here developed a distinct language and culture, more closely related to Sāmoa and Tokelau than to the rest of the Cooks, though showing signs of ancient links with islands to the east, including Manihiki and Rakahanga. Traditional music and dance blend features from East and West Polynesia. The Pukapukan terms *mako* 'dance-chant' and *nawa* 'log idiophone' have cognates only in languages to the west; and anciently, the use of the sharkskin drum extended no farther west than Pukapuka and Tokelau.

After the mid-1800s, many aspects of Pukapukan culture and language received heavy influence from the southern Cook Islands, and locally favorite musical genres are now those common throughout the Cooks; nevertheless, old musical genres have survived more completely than on others of the Cook Islands, largely because of geographic isolation. Since the 1960s, some Pukapukans have migrated to New Zealand and Australia. In 1997, more than a thousand live in Auckland, and more than 350 in Wollongong and Brisbane.

### Musical contexts

By residence and commensality, the population of Pukapuka clusters in three villages, which, for joint musical performance, make a triangular configuration, reflecting the spatial orientation of the island.

The main opportunities for making music are competitive singing and dancing after shared feasts on Christmas; a hymn-singing contest with new compositions (*īmene tuki*) to mark New Year's; incidental songs throughout the month-long sports extravaganza that follows; and celebrations in dance (*ula pau*) and song (*pātautau*) by the victorious village. Wrestling chants (*tila*) mark each bout won in exhibitions on mornings of the athletic celebrations. In February, for the fishing contest (*kavekave*), villages perform fishing chants (*lalau*) and love chants (*kupu*). At wakes, people usually sing hymns. Periodically, musical contests between villages or smaller entities occur.

Since the passing of the last experts, vocal traditions have changed markedly, and their social functions—maintenance of group solidarity, display of prowess and competitive superiority, ritualized ridicule of competitors—have largely yielded to acculturated styles. The juxtaposition of new and old styles is most clearly audible during the fishermen's contest, when popular songs (*īmene lōpā* 'songs of youth') serve as *patenga* 'codalike complements': interspersed between the chanted sections, they provide light relief, plus an opportunity for onlookers to bring monetary donations and join the dancing (Salisbury 1984).

### Dance

Ancient chants contain references to accompanying movements and formations. The most common organization was in two or three ranks, but circular configurations were also prominent. In a circular dance witnessed in the mid-1800s (Gill 1876), men and women performed different actions, with elaborate headdresses and paddle-like implements.

A Tahitian style of dancing (called *upaupa*), with men and women in alternating parallel columns, developed into the modern drum-accompanied dance (*ula pau*), with traces of former styles of Pukapukan movements. Gestures (*yaka*) portray the meaning and feelings of an underlying text, the basis for the drumming. The Pukapukan *ula pau* is a suite of items: *taki,* a sequence for entrances and exits; *akatikatika,* a preparatory straightening up of the dancers' rows and columns; a routine introduced with the call *lunga, lalo* 'up, down' (figure 18); the main dance (*vāeau* 'army'); and *latailila,* a short, repeated coda. Repetition occurs on several levels, including basic rhythmic patterns, sequences, and items. A leader dances in front of the group, calling and whistling cues.

Particularly since 1972, when troupes began attending the Constitutional Celebrations, units in the Southern Cooks (such as Cook Islands National Arts Theatre) copied actions that identify Pukapukan dancing. In the 1990s, people on the island imitated videotaped performances by compatriots in Auckland, and migrants participated in composing and rehearsing dances for the annual cultural festival there.

FIGURE 18  A routine in a modern Pukapukan drum-accompanied dance, showing the leader's calls and rhythmic vocables for the drummed rhythms. After Salisbury 1983:108.

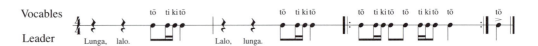

For cultural competitions in Rarotonga, Pukapukan groups compose and choreograph items in the Southern Cooks genres *ūtē* and *kaparima*. *Ula papaʻa* 'European dancing' is a common form of evening entertainment. It uses popular songs with accompaniment from guitars, ukuleles, and sometimes electric guitars. In form and sound, these songs usually resemble *īmene māpū* as sung elsewhere in the Cooks, though lyrics are occasionally in vernacular Pukapukan.

### Traditional chant

The general term for chant is *mako*. By structure and style of performance, Pukapukans distinguish two classes: *tila*, short, recited chants, associated with sports and contests; and *mako*, intoned, monophonic, chants of personal or group ownership. Several named subvarieties of *tila* once described the content or context of the songs; other known genres (*kapa, yiva, wakatapatapa* 'recital of genealogy', *talotalo* 'incantation') are obsolete.

People recite *tila* in heightened speech, with considerable fluctuation in pitch. The tempo is fast; through successive repeats, it accelerates into a climax. Textual rhythms may adjust to fit a triple meter, reinforced by clapping; they may pattern simply in duple meter, creating a syncopation. Metrical claps and textual stress coincide mainly on the penultimate mora of each textual line. In the wrestling chant in figure 19, the prevalence of a short–short–long–long pattern effectively creates an artificial long vowel on the final syllable of each line. The terseness of its text is typical:

| | |
|---|---|
| Pepelu mai Ngake. | Ngake prepares to challenge. |
| Omo ki te yinu ngavali | Rubbed with shiny oil |
| Te lau o te maile. | Are leaves of the fern. |
| Koa motu, koa teka, | Nearly breaking, out of place, |
| Toku malo nuanua. | Is my rainbow belt. |
| Uwia! Pelu! | Tripped! Prepared! |

The last line has this sense: "I've tripped my opponent, and am ready for the next."

*Mako* include fishing chants (*lalau*), boasts about skills or exploits (*tangitangi*), love-related chants (*kupu, pinga*), and laments (*tangi*). In the *kupu*, symbols drawn from nature and culture show the recipient's matrimoiety (Salisbury 1991). A *pinga* is a special chant, composed in the underworld by a deceased lover, and dreamed by the living partner. All chants are village property.

Composers continued creating *mako* into the twentieth century. Postcontact *kupu* contain copious biblical references and allusions to places and persons of the outside world. Like travelogues, three documented *tangitangi* composed by men who had ventured to the Society Islands in the 1880s and Sāmoa in 1922 show the authors' perspectives and attitudes. In the 1930s, seven men of Ngake composed fourteen new *lalau* for celebrating victories in the fishing contest. The texts depict the social and cultural milieu of that period, but an abundance of Rarotongan and

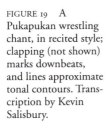

FIGURE 19 A Pukapukan wrestling chant, in recited style; clapping (not shown) marks downbeats, and lines approximate tonal contours. Transcription by Kevin Salisbury.

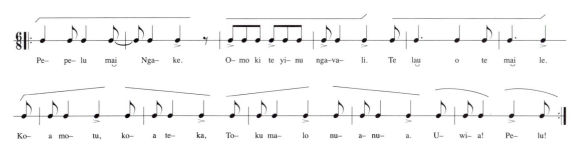

*Pātautau*—improvisatory dance-songs with origins in French Polynesia—developed a composite Pukapukan form. They contain short sections, drawing on stereotyped harmonic sequences and melodic formulas, recreated with new lyrics. A leader cues most sections and repeats.

Sāmoan words reveals the impact of other languages on Pukapukan. Since 1980, for intervillage competitions in Pukapuka and Auckland, composers have created chants in both genres.

### Chant forms

For the procedures of chanting (*tānga,* from *tā* 'chant'), Pukapukans once had a range of terms, documented in 1935 (Beaglehole and Beaglehole n.d.:106–107; Salisbury 1983:97). Linguistic analysis has revealed a hierarchy of interacting metrical and phonological principles, set in terms that differentiate pitch, tempo, meter, timbre, and the accentuation of textual rhythms.

In the intoned style, the natural textual rhythm normally falls into even groupings of syllables. Despite the syncopation of unusual verbal rhythms, a sense of duple meter prevails. Each line optimally has twelve moras in two equal colons. Some lines have eighteen moras in three colons.

For one or two lines, or for as many as forty, secondary metrical procedures may occur. An excellent example of metrical precision is the procedure known as *tānga wakatotō* 'drag out, attenuate': successive phrases contain eight moras each, and the penultimate mora is long. Two other *tānga* correspond to rhythmic organization in triple meter: *wakamotumotu* 'broken up' describes a succession of long–short patterns, and *wakatokutoku* 'sobbing' describes a syncopated short–long pattern. The intoned style employs these patterns as expressive devices, often at the beginning or end of a piece. In *tila,* they anchor the rhythmic organization.

In the intoned style, the short lower vowels /a e o/ assimilate to the quality of a following higher vowel. When certain *tānga* suspend this principle, its absence has a noticeable effect on the frequency of a predictable lower auxiliary (a minor third below the intoning note) that falls only on the high vowels /i u/ in isolation, or on those that end a sequence of high vowels.

### Acculturated music

Transitional songs (*amu*) portray the historical development of genres on Pukapuka. These are ephemeral, topical ditties, which children formerly sang for improvised dancing (Beaglehole and Beaglehole 1938:359–360). Melodic shape reflects the structure of the intoned genre with a minor third below the tonic (figure 20), but many examples feature other notes, mostly drawn from the tonic triad.

After the 1890s, *pātautau,* improvisatory dance-songs with origins in French Polynesia, developed a composite Pukapukan form, which, after games, winners sang to humor and ridicule losers. *Pātautau* still grace special celebrations. They contain short sections, drawing on stereotyped harmonic sequences and melodic formulas, recreated with new lyrics. A note intoned by a leader cues most sections and repeats. Some sections are in a stylized version of the intoned style, predominantly in unison

FIGURE 20   This Pukapukan children's song has two repeated lines, glossable as "See the birds flying this way" and "Alight on the trees there at Awanga." Transcription by Kevin Salisbury.

with a minor third below. Harmonic progression resembles that of the style of *īmene tuki*, with obligatory "perfect cadences" to conclude sections. Movement in parallel thirds or sixths is more common than responsorial phrasing between men's and women's parts. Texts come from old chants, *amu*, sung rhythms for drumming, and unison quotations of speech. Emphasis on novelty and humor makes the genre highly entertaining. An essential element is a terminal climax, featuring a pop song accompanied by drums, concluding with an accelerating *patenga* (a repeated, rhythmic couplet used as a coda), which ends abruptly.

### Hymnody

On Pukapuka, two genres of indigenous Protestant hymnody occur: *īmene tapu* and *īmene tuki,* both sung in Rarotongan. The former, including examples the missionaries printed in hymnals, are also known as *īmene reo-metua* 'old-melody hymns'. The melodic outlines of some European songs are recognizable, though the original harmony hardly recurs in the men's and women's vocal parts, which often move in parallel fourths and fifths. Stylized responsorial treatment of the text by the vocal parts characterizes later settings of earlier texts, and shows that Pukapukan styles of singing hymns developed under the influences of new pastors and Pukapukans returning from abroad. The tendency to alter certain vowel qualities, particularly at the ends of textual lines, is a notable feature.

*Īmene tuki,* the most popular style, features grunted (*tuki*) rhythmic vocalization in the men's part. The musical style is similar to that of *īmene tapu,* but is much more contrapuntal. Biblical or freely created texts occur, and the genre extends beyond religious contexts. Composers like to enhance their hymns with snatches of Pukapukan or English. For festivals at Christmas and New Year's, each village group may compose a dozen or more hymns [see MUSICAL MIGRATIONS, figure 19].

Since the 1940s, Rarotongan pastors have introduced a third style of Protestant hymnody, Sunday-school hymns (*īmene āpī-Sāpati*). These pieces, from so-called Moody-and-Sankey hymnals, provide an alternative means of singing the lyrics from the original Rarotongan hymnal. Roman Catholic liturgical repertories arrived from Sāmoa in the 1930s. The music that old people know includes imported and locally composed styles—in Latin, Rarotongan, Sāmoan, and Tahitian.

### Musical instruments

During the twentieth century, the local use of musical instruments changed. Percussion no longer accompanied traditional singing and dancing. From the southern Cooks, Pukapukans took names for percussive instruments: *pātē* 'log idiophone' (replacing *nawa*) and *pau mangō* 'sharkskin drum' (replacing *payu*). By 1960, the latter was of foreign manufacture, with an animal skin; an empty biscuit tin or kerosene tin (*tini*) doubles its part, and a bass drum (*pau*) completes the ensemble. The distinctive feature of Pukapukan drumming is an emphasis on unison drumming by *pātē,* reflecting and reinforcing an underlying text.

—KEVIN SALISBURY

## HAWAI'I

The Hawaiian archipelago includes the principal eight high volcanic islands and a chain of more than two hundred uninhabited atolls stretching more than 320 kilometers from southeast to northwest. The original settlers were Polynesian seafarers from the Marquesas Islands (as early as about A.D. 650); settlers from the Society Islands followed, beginning about 1150.

Indigenous Hawaiian society had three classes: chiefs (*ali'i*), believed to have descended from gods; commoners (*maka'āinana*), unable to trace descent from gods; and slaves and untouchables (*kauā*). At the heart of the beliefs that guided social practices was the concept of mana, sacred power, manifested in varying degrees in animate forces (including people) and inanimate objects. Rituals and prohibitions (*kapu*) reinforced social differentiation, guarding the sacred from pollution and protecting the profane from the potentially dangerous consequences of contact with sacredness.

In January 1778, two ships of a British expedition of discovery led by Captain James Cook were the first European vessels to visit Hawai'i. Within two decades, the resources of the islands were attracting American and European traders, of whom, in the wake of whaling and commerce in sandalwood, hundreds took up residence.

Missionaries of the American Board of Commissioners for Foreign Missions commenced Christian evangelization in 1820; within five years, conversion was effectively accomplished. By the mid-1800s, owners of sugar plantations were importing laborers from China and Japan; by 1900, laborers were also coming from the Philippines and Portugal.

The Hawaiian constitutional monarchy, established after King Kamehameha I (d. 1819) brought the islands under unified rule, was overthrown in 1893 by American businessmen, who formed and controlled a republic until 1898, when the United States annexed the islands. In the twentieth century, tourism was a major source of economic development, and many Hawaiians pursued assimilation as a social goal. Hawai'i attained U.S. statehood on 21 August 1959.

In the 1990 census, the state's population was about 1.1 million. Major ethnic groups included not only Hawaiians (less than 20 percent of the total), but Caucasians, Portuguese (censused separately from Caucasians), Chinese, Japanese, and Filipinos [see MUSICAL MIGRATIONS]. After the 1960s, immigration from mainland southeast Asia increased. Since the 1970s, Hawai'i has experienced a resurgence of interest in indigenous culture. For Hawaiians, performative traditions continue to serve as markers of identity.

### Traditional music

Despite missionaries' attempts at suppression and various periods of Hawaiians' neglect, indigenous musical traditions that flourished at the time of European contact survive, coexisting with Western musical styles and repertories. During the past two centuries, they have experienced multiple revivals of interest and popularity.

#### Indigenous styles

A historical understanding of Hawaiian music and dance stems from two channels: one is the knowledge of practitioners who embody the persistence of oral-aural transmission; the other is massive quantities of documentation in manuscript, print, audio, and visual media. Descriptions by explorers and adventurers provide a glimpse of musical performance before conversion to Christianity [see ENCOUNTERS WITH "THE OTHER"]. Beginning in the late 1800s, interest in Polynesian origins led to antiquarian collections of legends, lore, and poetic texts, written in manuscripts now housed mainly in the Bishop Museum Archives and the State of Hawai'i Archives; in the same period, especially between the 1860s and 1920s, Hawaiian-language newspapers published hundreds of poetic texts. Recordings housed at the Bishop Museum Archives document less-syncretized styles of performance in the 1920s and 1930s and oral histories from the 1950s and 1960s. The repertory itself flourishes in the context of commercial dissemination, via published songbooks since 1888, recordings since 1905, and televised broadcasts of hula-performing competitions since 1984.

The beginnings of scholarly inquiry are marked by monographs by Nathaniel B. Emerson (1909) and Helen H. Roberts (1926). The latter resulted from one year of fieldwork and recording (1923–1924), sponsored by the Hawaiian Legend and Folklore Commission. Elizabeth Tatar (1982) reexamined Roberts's recordings. In the mid-1970s, the Hawaiian Music Foundation began publishing *Ha'ilono Mele,* a monthly newsletter, and began sponsoring research that culminated in an encyclopedia (Kanahele 1979). Other important scholarly studies are by Adrienne L. Kaeppler (1973, 1993), Glenn Silva (1989), Amy Ku'uleialoha Stillman (1982), and Tatar (1993).

*Categories of poetry*

The term *mele* denotes a poetic text and its performed vocalization. The *mele* is the basis of all performance; without it, there can be no performance. Poetic texts are named in two ways: one is by topic; the other is by style or styles of recitation, the choice of which usually stems from the topic.

Numerous named categories of Hawaiian poetic texts can be arranged on a continuum from sacred to secular. The most general categories are as follows; each includes additional subcategories (not listed).

1. *Mele pule* are prayers dedicated to gods. The most sacred are prayers that ritual specialists (*kahuna*) performed for rituals associated with state religion. For family gods and personal supplications, households used separate prayers. Prayers specific to occupations, often within the purview of trained specialists, include prayers surrounding medicinal specialists' work, prayers for aspects of making canoes, and prayers associated with dancers' training and performance.

2. *Mele ko'ihonua* and *mele kū'auhau* are genealogical chants, typically tracing lineages from humans back to gods. The most celebrated, *Kumulipo,* traces human history back to the origin of the universe.

3. *Mele inoa* 'name songs' are chants that name and honor people. This category has several important subcategories. *Mele ma'i* are genital chants, whose function is to celebrate procreative ability. Animal-oriented chants, individually named by species (such as *manō* 'shark', *pua'a* 'pig') are usually addressed to individuals, or to animal forms of ancestral gods. *Mele kanikau,* laments and funerary dirges, are composed and performed during periods of mourning, in honor of the deceased.

4. *Mele ho'oipoipo* (also called *mele ho'oheno*) 'lovemaking songs' are dedicated to specific, though often unnamed, individuals. This poetic emphasis is predominant among *mele* composed in the twentieth century.

5. Assorted texts for informal occasions, performed and occasionally composed spontaneously. These include texts of welcome (*mele kāhea*), admiration (*mele aloha*), and criticism (*mele nema*).

*Styles of vocalization*

Hawaiians distinguish between *mele* accompanied by dance and *mele* not accompanied by dance. The former are usually called *mele hula*; the latter, *mele oli.* A musical distinction lies in the presence or absence of metered pulse, a requirement for synchronizing dancers' movements. Pulse in *mele hula* occurs in sets of even numbers of beats, with duple subdivision of beats.

Vocalizations include six named styles of vocal delivery, of which five are used in *mele oli* and the sixth in *mele hula*. These styles range on a continuum from spoken recitation with indeterminate pitch to prolonged and patterned phrasing. Each has particular poetic associations: *kepakepa*, speechlike vocalization with a crisp and rapid delivery of syllables, particularly suited for reciting long prayers and genealogies; *kāwele*, speechlike vocalization with a clearer sense of pitched contour, also suited for reciting genealogical texts and prayers; *olioli*, vocalization with sustained pitch, using one principal tone (which may occasionally receive embellishment from auxiliary tones, usually lower) and applicable to the full range of poetic types, except laments and funerary dirges; *hoʻāeāe*, vocalization with prolonged sustained pitch and elaborate patterned vibratos, appropriate for lovemaking songs; *hoʻouwēuwē*, vocalization with extremely prolonged sustained pitch and wailing, appropriate only for laments and funerary dirges; *ʻai haʻa,* vocalization for *mele hula,* using regular patterns of pitch with metered pulse.

### Vocal ornaments

On the most detailed level, particular vocal ornaments are associated with each of the vocal styles. These ornaments involve articulatory techniques related to pronunciation; many of them are associated with particular styles of vocal delivery. The most prominent ornament is vibrato (*ʻiʻi*), used extensively in *olioli, hoʻāeāe, hoʻouwēuwē,* and *ʻai haʻa.* Other ornaments include: *aeae,* a glide; *ʻalalā,* vibrato and laryngealization combined; used especially in *ʻai haʻa; haʻanoʻu,* a loud-tone attack; used in all styles but *kāwele; haʻi* or *haʻihaʻi,* a yodel, with a break in the vocal line to emphasize the shift between vocal registers; *heʻu,* laryngealization ("creaky voice"), used extensively in *hoʻāeae, hoʻouwēuwē,* and *ʻai haʻa* styles; *kōhi,* velarization, used in *olioli* and *hoʻāeāe* styles; *koʻu,* pharyngealization, used in *kepakepa, olioli,* and *ʻai haʻa; uwē,* wailing, used in *hoʻouwēuwē.*

### Musical instruments

Most indigenous musical instruments are associated with dancing. Anciently, a conch (*pū*) served for signaling, especially in battle; it continues to be used thus, at the beginning of concerts and pageants. Lovers communicated by playing flutes (*ʻohe hano-ihu*), whose repertory especially included lovemaking songs. Instruments used for dancing fulfill one of two basic functions, depending on who plays them.

For dances by standing performers, three instruments are played by musicians (*hoʻopaʻa*), who vocalize the *mele.* The function of these instruments is to provide a pulse that guides the dancers' lower-body movements. A pair of membranophones—the *pahu* (a sharkskin drum, struck with bare hands) and the *pūniu* (a fishskin coconut-shell drum, usually tied to the musician's right thigh, and struck with braided leaves or a cord)—are most often played in combination. The *ipu* is a gourd idiophone; two gourds glued together at the neck are *ipu heke.* The *pahu* and the *ipu* have a basic inventory of named rhythmic patterns. Those for the *pahu* are named after specific textual passages in the dances in which they occur; for example, the pattern *kaulilua* derives its name from the first word of the piece "*Kaulilua,*" and the pattern *e uē* derives its name from the phrase "*e uē.*" For the *ipu,* the rhythms are not textually specific, but are universally applicable. The player, grasping the gourd by its neck, alternately thumps it on the ground and slaps it on its side (figure 21).

For dances by seated performers, instruments are played by the dancers (*ʻōlapa*), who also vocalize the *mele.* These instruments include the *ʻulīʻulī,* a small, seed-filled gourd, with an attached handle and feathers; *pūʻili,* a length of split bamboo, closed

TRACK 27

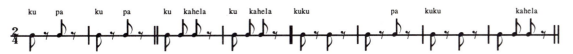

FIGURE 21 Three
named rhythmic pat-
terns for Hawaiian
gourd idiophones.
Downward stems indi-
cate thumping on the
ground or a mat;
upward stems indicate
right-hand slaps on the
side of the gourd.
Transcriptions by Amy
Ku'uleialoha Stillman.

at the end of the handle; *'ili'ili,* water-worn pebbles, one pair held in each hand; and *kālā'au,* a pair of hardwood sticks. In addition to acoustically enhancing the performance, these instruments function as an extension of the dancers' hands.

### Mele hula

Among *mele* composed for dancing, important distinctions can be drawn between two styles, *hula pahu* and *hula 'ala'apapa,* based not only on the accompanying instruments, but on the format of the poetry. *Mele hula pahu* are *mele* composed for performance with the *pahu.* These *mele* are through-composed, with no regularly recurring melodic or rhythmic patterns, though in a given *mele* identifiable rhythmic motifs may occur, with specific sequences of movements at particular points. The known repertory of *hula pahu* numbers about ten pieces, all of which have been transcribed (Tatar 1993).

*Mele hula 'ala'apapa* are *mele* composed for performance with the *ipu.* These *mele* are also through-composed, but share two overall structural attributes. First, the text is arranged into sections (*paukū*), of which some *mele* contain only one. Though *mele* may have multiple *paukū,* these sections may not be identical in length, melody, or number of gourd-marked beats; thus, despite the appearance of having stanzas, these *mele* are not, strictly speaking, strophic. Second, each *paukū* precedes a sequence of movements associated with a specific set of rhythms, as in figure 22, from a *mele* dedicated to Hi'iaka, sister of Pele, goddess of volcanoes. The *paukū* of the text, as taught by Zaneta Ho'oūlu Richards and translated by me, reads:

> No luna e ka Halekai, o ka ma'alewa,
> Nānā ka maka iā Moananuikalehua lā,
> Noho i ke kai o mali'o mai
> I kū a'e lā ka lehua i laila lā.
> > 'Ea lā, 'ea lā, 'ea.
> > I laila ho'i.

> From above at Halekai, from the mountain-ladder,
> The eyes gaze upon Moana-nui-ka-lehua,
> Sitting in the calm sea
> Where the *lehua* blossoms stood upright.
> > Tra la, tra la.
> > There, indeed.

The nonidentity of the structures of the *paukū* illustrates the primacy of the poetry in *mele hula 'ala'apapa,* showing how the melody and the rhythms accommodate poetical requirements.

### Styles introduced in the 1800s

In the 1800s, Hawaiian society underwent turbulent changes, including the rejection of the indigenous state religion, the acceptance of Christianity, the widespread embracing of Western goods, customs, and government, and the loss of national sovereignty. Relevant to the practice of music are the introduction of Christian hymnody, a major revival of *oli* and *hula* in the 1870s and 1880s, and the emergence of highly Westernized musical genres, which remain popular.

FIGURE 22
Beginning of "*No luna e ka Halekai*," a *mele hula ʻālāʻapapa*, in the version taught by Zaneta Hoʻoūlu Richards. Transcription by Amy Kuʻuleialoha Stillman.

### Sacred music: hīmeni haipule

The term *hīmeni* is the Hawaiianized form of the English word *hymn*. Because the term *hīmeni* had by 1900 come to be used for secular songs, and even for "any song not used for hulas" (Pukui and Elbert 1986), further qualification by the term *haipule* 'religious' specifies Christian hymns.

Throughout the 1800s, Calvinistic missions dominated Christian hymnody. Other missions were established by Roman Catholics in 1827, the Church of Jesus Christ of Latter-Day Saints (Mormons) in 1850, and the Church of England in 1862. These missions produced series of hymnals beginning in 1852, 1924, and 1874, respectively.

Missionaries translated Anglo-American psalms and hymns into Hawaiian (figure 23). These were strophic melodies in three of four parts, sung in note-against-note harmonies. Sources they drew upon included the *The Boston Handel and Haydn Society's Collection* (especially editions of about 1830) and *Christian Lyre* (1831). The first printed collection of Hawaiian-language texts for hymns appeared in 1823. After several editions of that and a second collection, a songbook was issued in 1834, with a primer on how to read musical notation. Throughout the 1830s and 1840s, Protestant missionaries, in contrast to other missionaries, gave music lessons, which

**58**

8.          Waimaka.

Ma - ke auwe! ua     ie - o nei,     Ka

mea hooweli - weli mai;     Nou, nae, e Iesu,

ka manao,     E   make kama - lii a pau.-

FIGURE 23    The hymn "Waimaka" as printed in an early Hawaiian hymnal (*Na Himeni Kamalii* 1842:59).

became quite popular. By the mid-1800s, musical literacy was widespread in the islands.

Around the 1860s, the repertory of psalms and hymns yielded to a new style, known as gospel hymns, and associated with the American evangelist Dwight Moody. In the 1880s, the Reverend Lorenzo Lyons translated into Hawaiian three books of gospel hymns collected by Ira D. Sankey. These hymns have refrains and simple harmonies, almost exclusively tonic, subdominant, and dominant. The most recently published Protestant hymnal in Hawaiian, *Na Himeni Haipule Hawaii* (1972), contains mostly nineteenth-century gospel hymns.

In addition to church and Sunday school, important events in Hawaiian parishes are annual conventions of parishes. Stemming from quarterly and annual examinations of Sunday-school pupils in the 1800s, the choral singing of hymns is a central feature of these gatherings.

*Secular music: hīmeni*

By the 1860s, secular songs were being composed by Hawaiian songwriters, who, as descendants of chiefs and their associates, formed educated elites. Among the most prominent were the siblings known collectively as *Nā Lani ʻEhā* 'The Four Majesties': King David Kalākaua (reigned 1874–1891), Queen Liliʻuokalani (reigned 1891–1893), Prince William Pitt Leleiohoku (1835–1877), and Princess Miriam Likelike (1851–1887).

The diction of secular *hīmeni* fused Victorian sentimentality with Hawaiian poetic conventions. The songs followed the verse-refrain alternation of gospel hymns. The compositions were performed unaccompanied by glee clubs, which frequently engaged in friendly competition. This choral tradition became institutionalized by the Kamehameha Schools, whose annual musical contest, begun in 1921, features competition in three divisions: girls, boys, and mixed classes [see MUSIC AND EDUCATION: Hawaiʻi]. Among adults, opportunities to participate in choral activities are offered by the Hawaiian Civic Clubs, whose statewide association convenes a choral competition during its annual convention. Glee clubs have been maintained by employers of large numbers of Hawaiians, including the Honolulu Police Department, the Hawaiian Electric Company, and the Hawaiian Telephone Company.

By the 1870s, songs were being published as sheet music; beginning in 1888, published songbooks appeared. Songbooks containing only lyrics followed the format used in hymnals: setting each stanza in a block of four lines, and labeling the chorus as *CHO.*, or its Hawaiian equivalent, *HUI* 'together'. Songbooks with notation contained piano-vocal arrangements, and the refrain was frequently arranged for four-part choral singing. Important collections include Henry Berger's *Mele Hawaii* (1898), Charles Hopkins' *Aloha Collection* (1899), A. R. "Sonny" Cunha's *Famous Hawaiian Songs* (1914), Charles E. King's *Book of Hawaiian Melodies* (1916–1948) and *Songs of Hawaii* (1942, 1950), and Johnny Noble's *Royal Collection of Hawaiian Songs* (1915).

*Hula kuʻi*

The reign of King David Kalākaua holds special significance for Hawaiian traditions. After decades of missionary-led censure, Hawaiian customs became revitalized when Kalākaua encouraged their revival. Master teachers (*kumu hula*) were summoned to the court at Honolulu, where they enjoyed royal patronage. Out of this atmosphere, a new style of dancing emerged, that of the *hula kuʻi* (figure 24).

The term *kuʻi* means 'to join old and new', and refers to the mix of old and new components of poetry, music, dance, and costume. Traditional conventions gained a

Throughout the 1900s, much of the development of Hawaiian music occurred in response to tourism. Indigenous styles of performance coexisted alongside Westernized styles.

FIGURE 24     *Hula* dancers and musicians, about 1883. Photo Hawai'i State Archives.

new format: texts were strophic, and each strophe consisted of a couplet. Indigenous vocal styles and ornaments were added to melodies based on tempered tones and simple harmonies. Each couplet was uniform in length, most commonly eight or sixteen beats. The format mandated the repetition of the melody for each couplet, and each couplet was commonly performed twice. An instrumental interlude, popularly called a vamp, separated the stanzas. In dances by seated performers, this interlude is called *kiʻi pā.* New sequences of movements joined preexisting, named, lower-body motifs. Locomotive lower-body motifs were emphasized over stationery ones, favored in earlier dancing. The shredded-grass skirt brought to Hawaiʻi by Gilbertese laborers came to be favored. Male dancers wore long-sleeved shirts and slacks, with a skirt over the slacks. Ankle-length Victorian gowns, especially the white gown worn at academic commencements, also became a costume for dancing.

The defining distinction of the *hula kuʻi* was accompaniment from guitars and *ʻukulele.* For dances by standing performers, *mele* composed in the new format also had the accompaniment of *ipu* or other indigenous percussive instruments. In the twentieth century, performances of those *mele* came to be called either ancient hula or *hula ʻōlapa,* referencing the division of labor between dancers (*ʻōlapa*) and musicians (*hoʻopaʻa*). The same, or other, *mele* performed with the accompaniment of stringed instruments were called *hula kuʻi*—a term that in the twentieth century was more commonly replaced by *modern hula.*

The following text is a representative *mele inoa,* the poetic type that dominated

FIGURE 25    The first stanza of the *mele inoa* "*Kalākaua*" in two versions: *a*, as a *hula ʻōlapa*, in the version taught by Zaneta Hoʻoūlu Richards; *b*, as a *hula kuʻi*. Transcriptions by Amy Kuʻuleialoha Stillman.

poetic composition in couplets during the 1870s and 1880s. This song is extant in two forms: *hula ʻōlapa* (figure 25*a*) and *hula kuʻi* (figure 25*b*).

| | |
|---|---|
| Kalākaua he inoa, | Kalākaua is a name, |
| ʻO ka pua mae ʻole i ka lā, | The never-fading flower in the sun, |
| | |
| Ke pua mai lā i ka mauna, | Blossoming forth on the mountain, |
| I ke kuahiwi o Mauna Kea, | On the height of Mauna Kea, |
| | |
| Ke ʻā lā i Kilauea, | The fieriness there at Kilauea, |
| Mālamalama o Wahinekapu, | Illuminating Wahinekapu, |
| | |
| A luna o ʻUwēkahuna, | Above ʻUwēkahuna, |
| I ka pali kapu o Kaʻau, ʻeā. | At the sacred cliff of Kaʻau, tra la. |
| | |
| Ea mai ke aliʻi kia manu, | The birdcatching chief arises, |
| Ua wehi i ka hulu o ka mamo. | Adorned with feathers of the *mamo*. |
| | |
| Ka pua nani aʻo Hawaiʻi— | The beautiful flower of Hawaiʻi— |
| ʻO Kalākaua he inoa. | Kalākaua is a name. |

In the 1920s and 1930s, about twenty orally transmitted *mele* were set to newly composed melodies, which adhered to the basic structural format of two phrases of identical length.

### Styles originating in the 1900s

Throughout the 1900s, trends in the performance of Hawaiian music often mirrored trends in popular music of the North American mainland. Much of the development of Hawaiian music occurred in response to tourism. Indigenous styles of performance coexisted alongside Westernized styles. Perpetuation of indigenous styles before the 1970s was largely supported by agencies such as the Bishop Museum, the University of Hawaiʻi, and the State Council on Hawaiian Heritage.

In the first decade of commercial recording (which began in Honolulu in 1905), violins and flutes were common. In the 1920s and 1930s, Hawaiian orchestras in hotels emulated big-band instrumentations. During World War II, performers who entertained military personnel adopted a scaled-back trio (*ʻukulele,* guitar, string bass), sufficient to accompany one or more dancers. Electrically amplified guitars and bass became common in the 1950s and 1960s, but in the 1970s, many local musicians again favored acoustic instruments.

Around 1900, a new genre, hapa haole song (from *hapa* 'half,' and *haole* 'foreigner') emerged. The term emphasizes that the lyrics are in English. These songs romanticize Hawaiʻi or some aspect of Hawaiian culture, and use Hawaiian-language

FIGURE 26 "One Two Three Four: Famous Hawaiian Song." Sheet music, 1917. Collection DeSoto Brown.

FIGURE 27 Richard and Solomon Hoʻopiʻi, renowned for singing and playing ʻukulele, received a National Heritage Fellowship from the U.S. government in 1996. Photo by Tibor Franyo. Courtesy of the Hawaiʻi State Foundation for Culture and the Arts.

words for flavor (figure 26). A thirty-two-measure $A_1A_2BA_2$ form, used extensively in American popular songs, became the standard format for hapa haole songs.

After the 1915 Panama-Pacific Exposition in San Francisco, a Hawaiian-music fad swept the mainland. During the late 1910s and throughout the 1920s, composers in New York's Tin Pan Alley turned out dozens of songs marked by pseudo-Hawaiian words—songs like "Oh How She Could Yacki Hacki Wicki Wacki Woo." In the 1920s and 1930s, a development of the Hawaiian-music craze was a boom in the publication of instructional materials for ʻukulele and guitar.

*Hawaiian guitar* denotes a particular method of playing. Its invention is credited to a schoolboy, Joseph Kekuku, who discovered a distinct sound by accident when he dropped a comb onto the strings of a guitar. This method stops the strings with a steel object, instead of fingers. In the 1930s, when guitars were electrically amplified, the instrument became capable of sustaining tones with the addition of a pedal, and became known as steel guitar. Its plaintive wailing became synonymous with the sound of Hawaiian songs.

In the 1950s, slack-key style emerged. On acoustic guitars, players altered tunings by slackening strings. In addition to playing the main melody, they performed accompanying figures. Common techniques of playing include chimes (harmonics), hammering on an already plucked string to produce a second tone, and pulling off an already plucked string.

### Published songbooks

Hawaiian music leads other Polynesian musics in quantity of output and bibliographic control (Stillman 1987a). Popular Hawaiian songs were issued as sheet music beginning in 1869. Since 1888, more than two hundred published collections of Hawaiian songs have appeared. The first issued sheet music came from mainland American publishers, but the publication of songbooks was centered in Honolulu.

The most popular Hawaiian songs have been published in songbooks compiled at various times and for various publishers by Sonny Cunha, Charles Hopkins, Charles E. King, and Johnny Noble. Most of these songs are arranged for voice and piano; many include tablature for fingering chords on a guitar or a ʻukulele. Some contain only lyrics; since 1970, the use of orthographic symbols in Hawaiian-language lyrics has aided pronunciation.

The international popularity of Hawaiian music after 1915 contributed to an explosion of publication. Composers in New York's Tin Pan Alley churned out pseudo-Hawaiian songs, whose influence was felt as far away as Australia. The ʻukulele and Hawaiian-guitar fads sparked publication of instructional books in Honolulu, New York, San Francisco, and even Cleveland. Since the 1920s, for broader appeal, Hawaiian songbooks have included increasing numbers of English-language songs, and mainland companies have come to dominate publication. Most of the published repertory is now controlled by two entities, Miller Music Corporation and United Artists.

### The Hawaiian renaissance

A resurgence of interest in Hawaiian music began in the 1970s (figure 27). New musicians emerged in unprecedented numbers. Many of them approached Hawaiian music from backgrounds in rock. Younger musicians shunned conventional sounds, especially those of steel guitar and ʻukulele, favoring a more guitar-dominated instrumentation. Students also flocked to *hula* studios. New songs issued from composers who seriously studied the Hawaiian language. Levels of linguistic competency varied, and rudimentary poetic expression coexisted with the sublime. Composition in

Hawaiian was exceeded, however, by composition in English. Songs took their material from the multiethnicity that descended from late-nineteenth-century interactions on plantations. Local themes were shared concerns, which unified residents of varying backgrounds; as land increasingly passed into foreign hands and private-property rights excluded residents, texts asserted opposition to commercial development and demanded access to natural resources.

What continues to mark this renaissance is the symbolic significance of Hawaiian music as a marker of ethnic identity and heritage. The primary venue for the performance of *hula* is competitions among *hula* schools (*hālau hula*). Among the most established are the Merrie Monarch Festival Hula Competition, begun in 1971; the King Kamehameha Hula and Chant Competition, begun in 1973; and the Queen Lili'uokalani Keiki Hula Competition, begun in 1975. The Iā 'Oe E Ka Lā Hula Competition in California, begun in 1981, provides analogous opportunities for groups from mainland Hawaiian communities unable to visit Hawai'i.

The contexts of these competitions have spawned the recognition of two added categories: *hula kahiko* 'old hula' denotes singing and dancing in an indigenous style of performance; *hula 'auana* 'stray hula' denotes singing and dancing in a Westernized style. This classification creates a division between *hula* and *mele hula* in couplets of the mid-1800s: *mele* performed with *ipu* and other indigenous instruments are classed as *hula kahiko,* and *mele* performed with guitar and *'ukulele* are classed as *hula 'auana,* though many couplet-format *mele* are performed in ancient and modern styles.

—AMY KU'ULEIALOHA STILLMAN

## "Art music"

The supremacy of vocal expression in Hawaiian culture informs the discussion of "art music" and especially "art song," Western musical concepts incorporated into Hawaiian culture. The traits of Hawaiian "art song" include music written by a supposedly professional composer; text, usually poetry, of high quality, preferably in the Hawaiian language, using accepted conventions such as hidden meaning (*kaona*) and linked assonance; instrumental accompaniment specified by the composer, rather than improvised by the performer; and songs intended for the concert stage with the goal of transmitting artistic messages through artistic interpretation.

The introduction of Western music theory and vocal methods began in 1820 with the arrival of Hiram Bingham and his company of Protestant missionaries, who taught Hawaiians the Christian hymns then popular in New England. This process culminated in the Hawaiian people's adoption of the musical language of Protestant hymnody, whose melodic, rhythmic, and harmonic style remains influential in Hawaiian music.

In 1872, Henry Berger arrived to direct the Royal Hawaiian Band [see POPULAR MUSIC: Musical Ensembles], which popularized the performance of music outside churches. He composed and arranged more than five hundred marches and songs, and "was responsible for directing the development of Hawaiian music toward the end of the transition period from the *hīmeni* . . . to the secular form of modern Hawaiian music" (Billam-Walker 1979:36). His impact inspired Queen Lili'uokalani in 1914 to call him the Father of Hawaiian Music.

The Royal Hawaiian Band continues to give weekly concerts presenting arrangements of Hawaiian songs, plus standards from the classical repertory. To render vocal selections, it engages female vocalists able to project over the ensemble. European-American music figures frequently in the programs given by the band, since 1981 led by Aaron David Mahi. Students regularly receive Western-style vocal training in the Music Department of the University of Hawai'i and other educational venues.

FIGURE 28   Queen Lili'uokalani's portrait graces the cover of the sheet music for her "Prayer and Serenade," about 1895. Bishop Museum Library.

### Hawaiian performers and composers

Hawaiian singers who have opted to develop their technique and pursue careers as performers of "art music" include Nani Alapai, Charles K. L. Davis, Ululani Robertson Jabulka, Tandy Kaohu MacKenzie, Miu Lan Naiwi, and Emma Veary, each of whom adopted a Western-training approach to the vocal arts and received acclaim for performing "art music" and Hawaiian song. Some achieved renown in the operatic repertory, for which an opera house was built near the palace.

Hawaiian composers whose music belongs to the genre of "art music" are few. One of the first was Queen Lili'uokalani. In 1869, with the publication of her composition "*Nani Nā Pua*" ('Beautiful Are the Flowers'), she initiated the movement toward combining Hawaiian poetry with Western melody and harmony (figure 28). But it was the queen's student, Charles E. King—composer, publisher, bandleader, statesman, cultural historian, producer, broadcaster—whose songs and publications gained wide recognition, reconfiguring the Hawaiian music world for much of the twentieth century.

King's musical accomplishments include a three-act operetta, *Prince of Hawaii,* first performed in Honolulu on 4 May 1925. King wrote its twenty-four songs, including "*Ke Kali Nei Au*" (which later came to be known as the Hawaiian Wedding Song) and "*Kuʻu Leialoha*." The show garnered critical praise. In 1926, after it had been revised and remounted in Honolulu, fifty members of the original cast performed it in Los Angeles and San Francisco (Kanahele 1979:305–306). King's works maintain a broad cultural appeal, in part because of the quality of the Hawaiian verse he set, and in part because of its continuing importance for Hawaiians' musical identity. His significance also derives from his being among the first Hawaiian composers to copyright and publish their own works. All his songs are set for piano and strings; the range and contour of many of their melodies are demanding, in reflection of his craft as a composer. He carried on his royal predecessors' style, but refined it into new, more sophisticated musical domains.          —KAʻALA CARMACK

## Dance

Hawaiian poetry is conveyed through vocalized rhythmic and melodic motifs and movements of the human body. Organized according to text phrases, movement motifs are based in a system of knowledge of Hawaiian structured-movement systems. Ancient Hawaiʻi had two such systems: *haʻa*, ritual movements performed on outdoor temples (*heiau*); and *hula*, formal or informal entertainment. Movements visually enhanced vocalized texts by objectifying them in *haʻa* or alluding to them in *hula*. Today, these systems have coalesced into one, *hula* (Kaeppler 1993).

### Aesthetics, composition, performance

An important Hawaiian value is indirectness (*kaona* 'hidden or layered meaning'), a concept that pervades Hawaiian life, bringing to many cultural forms an aesthetically evaluative way of thinking. Indirectness and skill (*noʻeau*) are important elements in Hawaiian music and dance. A poetic text incorporated its initial *kaona* through the composition of one or more verbal artists (*haku mele*). These artists, specialists, or performers could compose melodic-rhythmic contours. A movement artist choreographed the text, using motifs from the Hawaiian structured-movement system. The movements suggested or depicted certain words, or enhanced the text through veiled or hidden meanings, alluding to genealogical lines, chiefs, or events. Especially in relation to words and their combinations, *kaona* had a power that could harm as well as honor. From cultural knowledge, observers had to deduce the meaning of *kaona*-laden texts.

By honoring and validating social distinctions based on divine descent, performances reinforced the sociopolitical system. Audiences brought to performances aesthetic evaluations of poetical composition, musical sound and appropriateness, movement allusion, and choreographic structure. The order of the dances, the placement of individuals within the ensemble, and the clothing—all imparted information about the performers' ranks and genealogies.

Training occurred in a *hula* school (*hālau hula*), taught by a master (*kumu hula*) under the religious restrictions of Laka, patron-god of *hula*. These schools observed taboos (*kapu*) and performed religious rites, including formal graduation (*ʻūniki*). Young people were eager to attend these schools, for they gave an entrée into court life. Chiefs subsidized troupes of dancers, whose performances praised the chief and honored the gods and his ancestors. Composed for a specific occasion, a *hula* became part of the repertory belonging to the chief it praised. Subsequent artists might choreograph the text differently, alluding to different words, or to a variant meaning of a phrase, or (if the poetry was incorrectly heard or remembered) to a different meaning of a phrase. A *hula* text therefore has no single correct sequence of movements (though *haʻa* movements should not change), and part of the excitement of

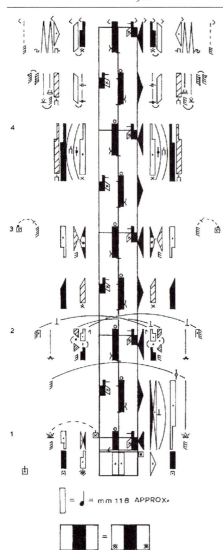

$$\Box = \; \downarrow \; = \text{mm 118 APPROX.}$$

FIGURE 29    Labanotation of the beginning of
"*Kaulilua.*" Notation by Judy Van Zile.

watching is to discover how skillfully the choreographer makes the text visible in a culturally satisfying way.

For uninformed observers, the poetry and movements do not tell an integrated story; performers orally and visually relate concepts intended for those who know the poetic and movement metaphors and understand the sociocultural context of the performance. To an uninformed spectator, a *hula* appears fragmentary, whereas to a knowledgeable beholder, its concepts are readily apparent. The resulting products, passed from generation to generation, became chronicles of history, objectified in verbal and visual forms.

Christian missionaries discouraged *ha'a* performed with *pule,* religious incantations used to call upon the gods, often associated with fertility of the land, the sea, and the people. Name songs (*mele inoa*) continued to be created in praise of chiefs. Belief in the power of words hastened the nineteenth-century demise of compositions in the Hawaiian language, as would-be composers feared that because they did not know all the hidden meanings, they might inadvertently harm the person they intended to honor. The poetic beauty and hidden metaphor became less apparent, and in the twentieth century many compositions incorporate foreign ideas translated into Hawaiian contexts. Many of the old *mele inoa,* however, are still performed.

Traditional interpretation was a kind of storytelling. The performer never became an actor or a character in a drama, but performed a story audibly and visually, telling about persons, places, and events. Performances were not dramatic in any Western sense: they had no conflict, nor did they express emotions. The introduction of characterization distinguishes later Hawaiian dances from earlier ones: performances became more pantomimic, and storytellers became like actors telling stories to audiences that did not have full command of the language.

### Structures and movements

The vocalization of *mele hula* is akin to that of *oli,* though it has less *'i'i* (see above). The rhythm, in 2/4 or 4/4 time, is more regular, permitting people to perform together as singer-instrumentalists (*ho'opa'a*) and dancers (*'ōlapa*), who might number one or more.

*Hula* are performed standing or seated. In the seated position, the body's weight is supported on the knees and lower legs, folded under the upper legs or at the sides; the knees are far enough apart that the buttocks can be placed on the ground between the feet. This position may strain the upper leg muscles, as some movements require that the body be raised and lowered and the torso make circling movements that can place the back on or near the floor. Seated performers may play percussive instruments and sing. In the standing position, the lower body conveys the rhythms or furnishes the rhythmic environment for motifs of hands and arms. Lower-body motifs have names, and include the interrelated movements of feet, legs, and hips. The feet are close together, flat on the floor, with knees bent. The amount of flexion of the knees and turnout of the ankles varies according to teachers' and performers' preferences. The back is straight, and the shoulders do not usually move, except as required by movements of the arms. The head, and especially the eyes, follow the hands. If both arms are not doing the same movement, the eyes usually follow the hand farther away from the body, usually the one alluding to the text.

The structure of a *hula* begins with a *kāhea,* a recitation of the first line of its text. A percussive instrument then sets the rhythm, and movement-accompanied poetry (through-composed or in couplets) follows. Between stanzas, a short instrumental phrase may occur, and one of the performers may recite part of the succeeding line of text. The dance concludes with an ending motif and a final *kāhea* announces the name of the honored person, place, or event. A set of dances follows

FIGURE 30    Hauʻolionalani Lewis demonstrates the entrance motif (*top*) and the lower-body-movement motif *hela* (*middle and bottom*) in the *hula* "*Kaulilua*." Photos by Adrienne L. Kaeppler, 1985.

an entrance dance (*kaʻi*), and precedes an exit dance (*hoʻi*). Lower-body motifs, with movements of the hands and arms, are choreographed—combined simultaneously and sequentially—as meaningful imagery based on a text. Through a specific choreography, a sequence of motifs has meaning as one component of a larger social activity.

### Lower-body motifs

Important lower-body movement motifs are *hela*, *kāholo*, *ʻuwehe*, *ʻami*, and *kāwele*. For *hela*, while bending the left knee and swaying the hips to the left, the performer extends the right leg forward from the hips, and with the ball or the whole sole touches the floor to the front, or slightly to the right, of the foot's beginning position. The touching foot turns out a little. The right foot moves back to step in place with a bent knee, and the performer repeats the whole motif on the opposite side. The motif may begin in a bent-knee position, or the knee may bend simultaneously with the extension of the foot for the first touch. Figures 29 and 30 show the *hula* "*Kaulilua*" using the *hela* motif.

For *kāholo*, with knees bent and hips moving with (or anticipating) the leg movements, the right foot steps side right, the left foot steps in place alongside the right, the right foot steps side right, and the left foot touches in place, but does not take the weight, leaving the left foot free to repeat the motif to the opposite side. The performer may face forward or to the diagonal of the performing space.

The essence of *ʻuwehe* is a lift of the heels, which moves the knees either forward or open to the sides. The essence of *ʻami* is a circular rotation of the hips. *Kāwele* resembles *kāholo*, except that the first side step makes a circular motion above the floor as it moves to the side.

### Motifs of the hands and arms

Movements of the upper limbs are not organized into named motifs, except for their nonspecific association with words. Some might depict a noun: bringing the finger and thumb to meet at their tips can allude to a flower; touching fingertips to their respective shoulders and dipping the wrists while extending the arms to the sides can allude to a bird; holding up two fingers can signify the number two; moving the fingers at eye level can refer to eyes; touching the cheeks can refer to cheeks; and holding the fingers at lip level can refer to lips, singing, or poetry. Other motifs of hands and arms are abstract, and do not refer directly to the words of a text. They often function as fillers between alluding movements, or cover the rest of a line of poetry after the end of the alluding movement. For each line of poetry, older dances usually have one alluding movement, and use an abstract movement to cover the rest of it.

A dividing motif often occurs at the end of each stanza. Usually an abstract motif, called the common movement or common position is used: one hand is placed at chest level with the palm down and the elbow to the side, the other arm is extended to the opposite side, and the fingers and wrists are flexed and extended. This pattern is then performed on the opposite side of the body.

The positions of the arms place the hands at the alluding level, while formations of the fingers or subtle flexions and extensions of fingers and wrists depict or give pulse. Depictions usually refer to the surface meaning of the text, sometimes masking the *kaona*: a flower depicted by fingers may refer, not to a flower, but to a person; the depiction of the prow of a canoe may refer, not to a canoe, but to a place.

### Categories of hula

The most important danced *mele* were *mele inoa*, honoring a god or a chief, and *mele hoʻipoipo*, songs of a topical or endearing nature. *Mele inoa* were composed as *'ālā'apapa,* texts composed in sections, sung with the playing of a gourd idiophone. Movements alluded to words of the text, with often only one allusion per line. In the 1800s, the style of *mele inoa* evolved into *hula ku'i,* joining the old and the new, or *'ōlapa* (depending on the music), composed in couplets that usually repeat. Movements interpret texts. Usually, couplets are performed first to the right side of the body and then to the left. *Mele ho'oipoipo* were less formal, sometimes extemporaneous, about people, places, and current events. *Mele ma'i* 'genital songs' are a subdivision of *mele inoa.* Composed in praise of a chief's sexual parts and usually performed last in a set, *mele ma'i* honor the physical means of perpetuating the royal lines, alluding to nature symbolism; today, however, the movement references may be more explicit.

*Mele hula* are also categorized according to the musical instrument with which the sung poetry is integrally related. The poetry for *hula pahu* is performed with a *pahu,* a membranophone; *hula pā ipu,* with a gourd idiophone (figure 31); *hula kālā'au,* with sticks (*kala'au*), and sometimes with a treadleboard (*papa hehi*); *hula 'ulī'ulī* are performed with a gourd rattle; *hula pū'ili,* with a slit bamboo rattle; *hula 'ili'ili,* with stone clappers (figure 32); and *hula pa'iumauma,* with open palms striking chest and thighs. Since the 1960s, additional categories have been introduced, especially for festivals (figure 33). Thus, old *hula* (*hula kahiko*) include *hula* performed with any traditional musical instruments and less melodically variable vocal contours, and *hula 'auana* include *hula* performed with introduced musical instruments and Western harmonies.

New forms of music and dance rise and fall in popularity. Waltz, disco, reggae, rap, and beyond—all coexist with older genres. Having roots in the indigenous past or fashion in the multicultural present, dances are performed in a variety of contexts that reveal Hawaiian identity and an appropriation of the modern world.

—ADRIENNE L. KAEPPLER

## AOTEAROA

Comprised primarily of two large islands, of more about 260,000 square kilometers, and with a population of about 3.5 million, Aotearoa is isolated from its neighbors by large expanses of ocean. Its plants and animals evolved into many species, but included no mammals. Distance was a factor in Māori settlement, the final major migration of Polynesian people, which occurred before A.D. 1000. To the British, Aotearoa looked like the antipodes, the farthest place on the globe. They called it New Zealand and colonized it. Endemic plants and animals, endangered by Polynesian and European predators, endure in visual art (traditional and contemporary) and twentieth-century concert music, where the distinctive songs of local birds serve as primary musical sources.

Topographical extremes—high mountains, rugged hills, an extensive plain—encouraged settlers and their descendants to concentrate in small communities, which developed unique flavors. Māori tribal dialects developed, and woodcarving, tattooing, music, and dance acquired localized traits. Patterns of settlement preserved the musical styles of some European immigrants: Scots in Dunedin, English in Canterbury, Dalmatians in Northland. The twentieth-century concentration of Pacific Islanders in Auckland and the cosmopolitan makeup of Wellington continue this diversity.

Because communities were small, musical influence fell into the hands of a few individuals. In Nelson, Michael Balling (1866–1925), a young German musician, established the School of Music. Frederick Page (1905–1983), from Christchurch, became the first New Zealander to head a university-based music department; in Wellington in the 1960s, he promoted new European music. H. C. A. Fox

FIGURE 31    Iolani Luahine, dancer, and Lokalia Montgomery, musician, perform a *hula pā ipu*. Photo by George Bacon, 1945.

(1889–1960) conducted bands, choirs, and orchestras in Hawera, a small south Taranaki town, giving it an outstanding musical tradition. Other individuals have continued the development of European traditions. In a field that espoused the English choral manner, Maxwell Fernie (b. 1910) set up a choir to perform continental-style plainsong and polyphony. Robert Oliver (b. 1936) pioneered Baroque and other performance of early music, and Philip Dadson (b. 1946) created a style of playing newly devised percussion instruments (figure 34). By basing compositions on recordings from Indonesia, China, and elsewhere, and organizing performances of Asian musics, Jack Body (b. 1944) developed connections with worldwide traditions (figure 35).

Isolation magnified overseas musical influences, popularly called the cultural cringe. The public overvalued artists abroad, including expatriate New Zealanders; nevertheless, the local musical world learned from developments overseas. In 1886–1889, Māori people eagerly followed the tours of the Fisk Jubilee Singers, to the point of pursuing them around the country. In 1910, the Sheffield Choral Society brought to choral societies and audiences the latest pieces and a new choral sound. Brass-band tours (Besses o' the Barn, 1906; Sousa, 1910) confirmed a strong tradition in Māori communities, and in military, religious (Salvation Army), and working-class areas. Pacific Islanders provided models for understanding Polynesian traditions, as in Christchurch in 1906, when local Māori copied Cook Island styles. Virtuoso pianists, including the legendary Lili Kraus (1905–1986), who received New Zealand citizenship, played to local audiences.

Local developments were also important. Te Puea Herangi (1883–1952) established the troupe Te Pou O Mangatawhiri, which, to raise funds for housing and farming around Waikato, traveled widely after 1923, inspiring in the Māori a new sense of tradition. In 1939, Fred Turnovsky (b. 1916), a businessman from Prague, developed the Wellington Chamber Music performances into the nationwide Music Federation, which organized tours of internationally famous musicians. Since 1980, pressing and distributing Flying Nun Records, Roger Shepherd has given an international profile to many local rock-and-roll bands.

FIGURE 32    Using stone clappers, dancers from the studio of Hoakalei Kamau'u perform a *hula 'ili'ili* at the East-West Center. Photo by Bill Feltz, 1977.

FIGURE 33    At the Festival of American Folklife, three generations of Zuttermeisters perform a *hula ʻauana*. In 1984, Kauʻi Zuttermeister (*center*) became the first recipient from Hawaiʻi to be awarded the National Heritage Fellowship by the U.S. government. Photo by Adrienne L. Kaeppler, 1985.

### Competitions

Competitions provide an important focus. Brass-band contests began in 1880, modeled on British practice. In many cities and towns in the first decades of the twentieth century, competitions for children and young adults included elocution, dramatic readings, piano and other instrumental performance, singing, ballet, and other kinds of dance.

As part of the competitive ethos, Māori cultural rivalry continues. During the 1990s, biennial Māori Cultural Competitions attracted thousands of performers, inspired new compositions, and revived older ones. Judging featured the highest artistic authorities in the Māori world. Adjudicative meetings, later accessible in written minutes, invoked important aesthetic values, adapting the arts to new conditions and surroundings. Each competing company performed examples of three genres (*haka, poi, waiata*) and recent or innovated ones.

### The 1900s

For the Māori community, the early years of the twentieth century were decisive. Māori recovered from depopulation and disease. Traditional arts were revived, and a

FIGURE 34    In 1988, the percussion ensemble From Scratch performs *Pacific 3.2.1 Zero* (1982), their composition protesting French nuclear tests in Oceania. *Left to right:* Philip Dadson, Wayne Laird, James McCarthy.

FIGURE 35   Jack Body (*left*), who incorporates Asian and Pacific musical styles into his compositions, discusses the Chinese *lusheng* with musician Gong Hong-Yu. Photo by John Casey, 1989.

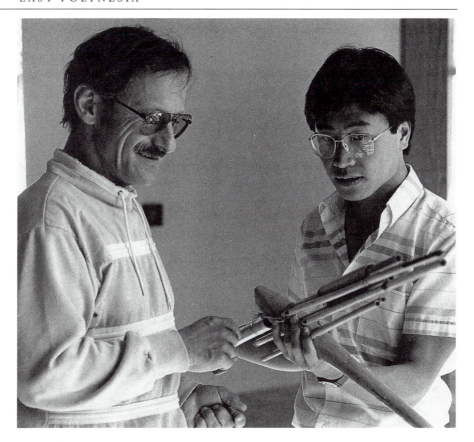

FIGURE 35   Jack Body (*left*), who incorporates Asian and Pacific musical styles into his compositions, discusses the Chinese *lusheng* with musician Gong Hong-Yu. Photo by John Casey, 1989.

new genre, *waiata-a-ringa,* with an important role in Māori resurgence, was born. An equally decisive period was the 1940s, just after the celebration of the national centenary: the arts received governmental funding; the National Orchestra came into being; a radio network developed; and the compositions of Douglas Lilburn (b. 1915), the nation's premier composer, first came to public notice.

The 1980s saw rapid change. Popular music and rock developed local forms, including Māori songs of protest, reggae, and a proliferation of styles of concert music. The government extended funding, once reserved for European concert music, to Oceanic music. Significant in the decade was the promulgation of a bicultural national path, a partnership between Māori and non-Māori, in which some composers and educators discovered new directions. Many pieces by non-Māori composers had included Māori titles, but this inclusion had usually implied little interaction between the musical systems. In the 1980s, developments in concert music, the visual arts, and dance, paying closer attention to Māori sensitivities, produced adventuresome new forms. In contrast, for more than a century, Māori composers frequently innovated, using musical materials from European traditions. Tuini Ngawai (1910–1965) used more than 160 hit-parade songs for her compositions, continuing the Māori tradition of emphasizing texts or messages. Her compositions varied from profound laments to cheeky ditties; her company, Hokowhitu A Tu, sang and danced her works throughout the country.

Some nineteenth-century popular songs—ballads, work-accompanying songs, ditties—survive but are not so widely known as English songs, Māori acculturated songs (like "*Pōkarekare Ana*" and "*Hine Hine*"), and internationally popular songs of the twentieth century. Two songs known throughout Aotearoa are "Now Is the Hour When We Must Say Goodbye" and "*Ka mate, ka mate,*" a Māori *haka.* The former farewelled shipboard passengers, including soldiers leaving for war. Since before

TRACK 53

1886, the national rugby team, the All Blacks, have performed the latter, a composition attributed to the renowned nineteenth-century warrior Te Rauparaha. People acknowledge its performance to be in keeping with tradition, but controversy about it has surfaced, as in its use in 1990 by a women's hockey team. Composers attracted by this *haka* and the rhythms of traditional dances included Alfred Hill (1870–1960) and Jenny McLeod (b. 1941).

### Musical studies

The collecting and recording of Māori music began in the mid-1800s, when several Europeans collected texts from knowledgeable performers. An eminent undertaking—still the main published collection—is *Ngā Mōteatea* (1928, 1961, 1970), begun by Sir Apirana Ngata (1874–1950). It drew on nineteenth-century collections, but sought examples from many tribal areas, including Ngata's own Ngāti Porou. Helped by Pei Te Hurinui, Ngata completed a four-volume collection of texts in English and Māori. He annotated each text with information on its tribal origin and composer, the reason or inspiration for its composition, and its class or purpose.

Early recordings of Māori texts used various technologies, including cylinders, wires, and disks. In 1946–1948, on the initiative of the mobile recording unit of the National Broadcasting Service a more thorough survey began. Staffers traveled to towns and country districts, recording schoolchildren, pipe bands, church choirs, instrumentalists, Māori elders, mayors, and other sources. They discovered little new talent, but their survey provides a definitive record of local speech, includes important recordings of Māori songs, and provides extensive documentation of local performers. Radio-sponsored recordings supplemented it later. Particularly noteworthy in collecting music has been the pioneering work of Māori broadcasters Wiremu Parker (d. 1986) and Wiremu Kerekere (b. 1923). In the 1950s, Mervyn McLean began musical research that culminated in the creation of the Archive of Māori and Pacific Music at Auckland University and a monograph on Māori music (1996).

In the 1980s, the study of concert music received impetus from the work of John Mansfield Thomson (1990, 1991), and the study of popular music, from the work of John Dix (1982). The journal of the Composers Association of New Zealand documents activities of local composers, who published many works at the Waiteata Press of the School of Music, Victoria University of Wellington. An archive established in 1974 at the Turnbull Library of the National Library of New Zealand, Wellington, encouraged the preservation of composers' works and memorabilia, and made materials available for research. In promoting local music, the New Zealand Music Centre, established in 1991, has undertaken a more commercial role.

Academic departments of music, established in universities in the late 1800s, were originally the preserve of transplanted European classical traditions. As late as 1947, Lilburn was the only New Zealand composer who held a position in a university; but by 1990, the faculties of music in each of the four main universities—Auckland, Canterbury, Otago, Victoria University of Wellington—included composers. Some faculties offered courses on music in New Zealand, and in musical surveys included Māori music. By the 1980s, educators had begun encouraging multiculturally varied musical activities and studies. In the 1990s, curricula included the teaching of Polynesian music as an examination subject at the secondary level.

### Reviving Maori aerophones

In the late twentieth century, important work in music scholarship and performance included the revival of Māori flutes (*nguru, kōauau,* and others), traditionally associated with birth, death, fertility, and healing. Revivalists communicated their work largely by performing. Under Christian missionaries' influence, the use of these instruments waned, and after the mid-1800s it died out. Mrs. Paeroa Wineera, the last surviving *kōauau* player who had learned in the traditional fashion, died in the 1960s. Māori flutes were portable, and because owners readily traded them to European explorers, the world's museums have many superbly carved specimens. Controversy about their status as nose-blown or mouth-blown instruments now excites popular interest.

In addition to flutes, the *pūtōrino* is an unusual aerophone because it probably served as flute, bugle, and megaphone. A *pūtōrino* was illustrated during Captain Cook's first voyage to the Pacific. Other instruments include bone castanets (*tōkere*); a mouth-resonated bow (*kū*); a whirring disk, into which priests sang incantations (*kōrorohū*); a swung slat (*pūrerehua*) or gourd (*poiawhiuwhiu*); a swung ball (*poi*); a tapped whale's rib (*pākuru*); and a lamellaphone (*rōria*). These instruments present many sounds, drawn from a wide variety of materials: jade, wood, whales' teeth, and birds' and humans' bones.

By copying museum specimens, makers reconstruct instruments; by experimenting with sounds, performers try to recapture old techniques of playing. Māori elders' memories of the contexts in which flutes were played, and their assent to the validity of experimental sounds, permit the revival of the traditions. Awakening local curiosity, several musicians—Mark Dashper (1996), Brian Flintoff, Richard Nunns, Hirini Melbourne—have given courses and demonstrations on formal grounds (*marae*) and in educational institutions and museums throughout the country.  —ALLAN THOMAS

## Māori music

Māori music is whatever music Māori people perform: operatic performances of Dame Kīri Te Kānawa, entertainments of the late Billy T. James, choral singing, band music, traditional recreations, and brave innovations. What links these expressions comes from Māori identity. Listeners know these performers' families and tribes. Their music comes together in shared values and histories.

In precontact times, the power of the word was direct and inviolate. Information necessary to preserve old customs passed by word of mouth. Special schools, with select pupils and intense teaching, aimed for minimal transmissive loss. Songs were an important vehicle for conveying this information. Covering all topics, and bearing symbols and images of pride and affection, they became expressions of collective identity. Every song served a social function, its relevance enhanced with poetry to evoke emotional responses.

Māori songs were performed in unison. To sing in parts would have been a bad omen, and the theoretical existence of microtones would have made such singing awkward. Melodies kept within narrow ranges, and movement was mainly stepwise, with rare leaps of a third or fourth. Though melodic patterns returned repeatedly to a drone (*oro*), additive rhythms accommodated extra words, to provide subtle variations.

European explorers thought these songs mournful and monotonous. Over the years, researchers have collected and translated hundreds of their texts, but their melodies (*rangi*) have disappeared. Their words remain as poetic expressions of their times. As a relish (*kīnaki*) to speeches, performances of surviving songs still occur in traditional settings on *marae*.

In traditional songs (*waiata tawhito*), incidents of the past and their highborn composers live again. When sung now, these songs are not just formulas of notes and words, however beautiful, but a reforming of the community of the present, a recollection of the community of the past. These songs put Māori people in touch with their identities and roots: in the singing, Māori like to think, "The vanished world

FIGURE 36    Māori aerophones: *a,* a *kōauau; b,* a *pūtōrino.* Museum of Archaeology and Anthropology, Cambridge University.

*(a)*                                    *(b)*

materializes, and visions of ancestors pass before our eyes; for a moment, times merge, and the present and past are one."

### Musical influences from abroad

When the indigenous population received the European intruders, new musical influences came from sailors and missionaries. Locked into intertribal conflict, the Māori made getting firearms a high priority. In 1840, the Treaty of Waitangi (New Zealand's founding document) recognized a balance of power between Europeans and Māori; but the situation changed rapidly, with the unwitting introduction of diseases, the unwarranted encroachment on lands, and the unbridled despoilment of nature. Eventually, the Māori accepted a stable colonial government as a tolerable price to pay for ending tribal strife and controlling lawlessness in the ports. In the 1860s, confiscation of Māori lands erupted into wars, which had the effect of segregating the two peoples.

The sailors' use of hornpipes and bosun's whistles appealed to the Māori, who loved their own flutes and held flutists in high regard. The most common Māori flute was the *kōauau,* a stumpy wooden or bone instrument with three holes bored into its side. It produced a penetrating sound and had a phallic appearance (figure 36*a*). Performers could supposedly mouth intelligible words, conveying secret messages to their lovers. Interest in making and playing the *kōauau* has revived, but the technique of mouthing words while blowing is not used. Other flutes—the *pūtōrino* (figure

36*b*), the *pōrutu,* the *nguru,* each distinct in timbre—have not enjoyed a similar revival.

The love of flutes probably influenced the formation of Māori fife-and-drum corps. In 1901, one such corps, said to be from Tūhoe, performed at a reception for the Duke of York (later King George V). Parihaka, the center of the prophet Te Whīti's nonviolent resistance to governmentally approved expropriation of land, had a famous ensemble, of about thirty players.

Many of the naval ships that called in Aotearoa had brass bands; but the introduction of brass instruments among the Māori probably came from the work of the Salvation Army. In the central parts of the north island, brass bands supported social movements. In 1925, the Rātana Church gained ascendancy there, drawing people from other religious movements. The promotion of brass bands became a focus of this church, and its association with brass-band music continues. In 1989, brass-band enthusiasts of the Rātana Church formed Te Pēne o Aotearoa, a national band, which in 1990 performed at the sesquicentennial celebrations at Waitangi.

### Christian music

Missionaries profoundly changed Māori cultural life. They learned the language, reduced it to writing, and published tracts and hymns in it. They set up schools, and taught reading and writing. By the late 1800s, Māori communities were singing hymns daily. The people found few faults with the tenets of Christianity, which shared with the old Māori religion many points of agreement, particularly on notions of an afterlife. Some persons accepted completely the Christian system of thought; others adapted it to their cultural ways. The Māori recognized the existence of spiritual forces, and they had always taken protective measures against malevolent forces. Māori representations of gods and ancestors stood in awkward attitudes. Dancers imitated these, not to decorate and entertain, but to challenge and protect. As the old system broke down, troupes began to use posturing dances (*kapa haka*) for entertainment.

One church took the singing of hymns further, to anthems and oratorios, and encouraged participation of its members in the cultural and choral competitions of the Hui Tau, an annual conference. It held the first of these conferences in 1886, and the competitions became the forerunner of similar competitions in other conferences and festivals. In 1913, at Korongatā, the Church of Jesus Christ of Latter-Day Saints (Hunga Tapu) opened Māori Agriculture College, a school for boys; its music department had a teacher of voice and instruments. In 1914, Walter Smith, a Māori musician who had lived in the United States, joined the staff. For years, by selecting the music and judging the choirs, he made important contributions to the choral competitions of the Hūi Tau. The school featured a brass band, several small combinations, a choir, and a glee club. These ensembles performed in and around Hastings, and occasionally on radio. In 1915, the band made an extended tour of the north island, visiting towns in Manawatū, Taranaki, King Country, Bay of Plenty, Auckland, and Northland. To many, the sight of Māori youths neatly uniformed and performing with discipline made a curious sight; but to Māori parents, it evidenced a worthy goal, an attainable hope. The Napier earthquake (3 February 1931) devastated the school, which abruptly closed; however, the musical influence of the school remained, as alumni formed bands and choirs. The Hui Tau competitions continued into the late 1950s, when conferences ceased and church administration devolved to local units, whose activities centered in local areas. The choral tradition of the Hui Tau passed to the annual conferences of other churches.

Several choirs attained renown. Ōhinemutu Rotorua Māori Choir, founded in the late 1920s, provided an example of singers in transition; Waiata Methodist Choir

The pathway from village hall to world stage involved recordings, promotions, television, and luck. From the late 1950s, rock stars came from abroad. Local troupes joined the stars' entourages, content for the moment to bask in reflected light.

of the 1930s contained exceptional singers, one of whom was Īnia Te Wīata, an internationally famous bass; Te Arohanui Company, a 150-voice choir, went to Hawai'i to take part in the opening of the Polynesian Cultural Center. Singing in the Mormon Tabernacle, at Salt Lake City, Te Arohanui moved the audience to tears. Jerry Ottley, conductor of the Mormon Tabernacle Choir, spent three years at school in Aotearoa, sometimes conducting the massed choir at the Hui Tau. In 1974, the choir that backed "Join Together," the winning Commonwealth Games song, went on to call themselves The New Zealand Māori Chorale, with the market in mind. They succeeded in getting several gold discs and a platinum one.

Since the 1980s, the Aotearoa Arts Festival, the biennial national competition, has had a choral section. To draw this section closer to the spirit of the old Māori competitions, some groups favored traditional songs and movements, which imparted a Māori feel instead of the echo of a bygone churchiness. In 1989, to take part in the sesquicentennial celebrations, a national Māori choir came into existence.

Throughout the twentieth century, Māori communities thrived on music. On Saturday nights, the *wharekai* (dining room of the meetinghouse) served for dancing, and people would bring instruments to support the pianist. On special occasions, the whole community would come to the hall to sing and dance the ballroom standards of the day. In the 1920s and 1930s, bands would air the latest music from Tin Pan Alley and Hawai'i. Songs that caught the community's fancy would sometimes serve with gestures to convey tribal statements at Māori conferences. Tuini Ngawai and other composers borrowed music to exploit this popularity. Her songs "*Ē Te Hokowhitu Atū*" and "*Ārohinā Mai*" exemplify the unity of song, movement, and purpose. Most important were the words, which became collective statements on the business of the conference or its contemporary philosophical drift.

### Concert parties and their legacies

By the 1880s, the thermal springs of Rotorua had become a focus of tourism. The Māori response was the concert party. Rotorua became famous for its singers. Māori entertainment and showmanship opened avenues of intercultural communication. In 1910, Maggie Papakura took a troupe to Sydney; and in 1911, it went to London for the Coronation Jubilee. The English public received them well, partly because of the exoticism of the presentation. In the 1960s, Māori performers moved into live theater and became involved in musicals, drama, and opera; only then did they understand how the stage defined the theater and why it should not be subject to traditional protocol. The concert-party concept was popular. To raise funds, other tribes soon took it up; when the need vanished, each troupe dissolved.

The work of Sir Apirana Ngata generated a wave of cultural resurgence. In Wellington, he gathered workers to do restorative work in the Dominion Museum. In 1935, a supporting group of elders formed the Ngāti Pōneke Club, an association for their families and friends. It became the center for Māori social life in the capital

FIGURE 37 On Aotea Quay to welcome back the Māori Battalion in 1946, the Ngāti Pōneke Club performs. John Pascoe Collection, Alexander Turnbull Library, National Library of New Zealand, Te Puna Mātauranga o Aotearoa, Wellington, N.Z.

(figure 37). Throughout the country, tutors and supporting groups formed clubs in affiliation with it. Their Polynesian Festival of Arts, inaugurated in 1972, aimed at showcasing Māori and Pacific Islander culture. The event attracted so much Māori interest, the Māori portion of the festival continued as the Aotearoa Festival of Arts, a nationwide competition. By the 1990s, the competition had become fierce, and contenders trained intensely. Testing cultural limits, composers stretched to combine innovative music, texts, and movements. In 1963, an artistic revelation appeared in the work of the Te Arohanui Company when they returned from a tour of the United States, where producers and choreographers had developed their program. The effect was stunning, and *choreography* became a buzzword among the clubs. Until then, performers had called movements in lines drills.

The instrument associated with concert parties was the piano. In 1901, at the reception for the Duke of York, a pianist accompanied the singers. For percussive strength, the piano remained the preferred instrument so late as 1946, when, to welcome the Māori battalion back from World War II, Ngāti Pōneke trucked a piano down to the Aotea Quay. A move to guitars gave the clubs increased mobility. In the 1950s, electric guitars became more readily available. Listeners preferred the sound to that of the piano, which they began to consider a quaint, un-Māori instrument.

In 1976, an exciting development began with the Māori and Polynesian Secondary Schools' Festival, organized by the Four Schools, mostly Māori high schools in Auckland. It grew to include forty participating institutions, with a standard of performance that challenged that of the Aotearoa Festival. The formats of both festivals were similar: *whakaeke* (entry), *waiata* (traditional song), *poi, waiata-a-ringa* (song with gestures, "action song"), *mau rākau* or *patu* (drill with weapons), *haka* (declamatory rhythmic dance), *whaikorero* (oratory), and *whakawatea* (exit). Thousands of spectators attended.

### Rock and its effects

The pathway from village hall to world stage involved recordings, promotions, television, and luck. From the late 1950s, rock stars came from abroad, and crowds flocked to airports and concert halls. For experience and exposure, local troupes joined the stars' entourages, content for the moment to bask in reflected light. Many Māori artists went on Australian and Asian tours. A highly successful group from

Aotearoa was the Māori Hi Fives, whose members often switched instruments. They prospered in England and Europe; but on a visit home, they drew only small crowds.

In the 1950s, the barometer of musical fame was the *Hit Parade*, the television show that presented the nation's favorite songs of the week. Howard Morrison, a Māori showman, exploited this medium. He first sang with the Clive Trio, a group formed by the Whatarau Sisters. Of these, Kahu Pineaha later left to sing in Auckland and Sydney, and Isabel Whatarau followed to become a showbiz personality in Sydney. Morrison then formed the Ohinemutu Quartet, which appeared in a talent show in Hamilton. After experience in local performances, the quartet hit the promotion trail as The Howard Morrison Quartet. Their recording of "The Battle of Waikato," a parody of Lonnie Donegan's "The Battle of New Orleans," gave them national fame, topping the charts for weeks. Then followed "My Old Man's an All-Black," which spoofed the controversy that arose in 1960 when the national Rugby Union sent to South Africa an all-white All-Black team. This too parodied one of Lonnie Donegan's songs, "My Old Man's a Dustman." Harry Miller, a producer of pop music, promoted *Showtime Spectacular,* a show in which the Howard Morrison Quartet took top billing and filled theaters twice a day for nineteen weeks. The quartet went on to perform in Australia and before Queen Elizabeth II (at Dunedin in 1963). In later years, Morrison often performed solo; his singing of "*Whakaaria Mai*" made that song memorable.

Other outstanding Māori artists also reached national stardom. These included Ricky May, ebullient showman, suave professional, unforgettable vocalist; Prince Tūi Tēka, guitarist, with affecting vocal technique; and Dalvanius Prime, master of musical technology. In a recording of "*Poi Ē,*" working with the Pātea Māori Club, Prime cultivated raw vocal aggressiveness, backed by the power of electronic sounds.

In the early 1990s, Māori bands enjoyed top ratings and performed throughout the country. Some indulged old and familiar styles; others shifted with newer currents. The female trio Moana and the Moahunters achieved international recognition and distribution of their recordings. Māori musicians believed one truth certain: their living music would explore, changing with the general mood, taking from here, adapting from there, always returning to the *kāupapa Māori,* a feeling that identified the people with the land, the sea, and the unifying values of a national spirit.

—TE PUOHO KATENE

## Mōteatea: Māori musical poetry

*Mōteatea* is a tradition of the Māori people. Like art and literature in oral societies worldwide, it is a multipurpose compositional and performative tradition. Neither simply music nor simply poetry, a single *mōteatea* may employ a single form (such as that of the lullaby), and it may be an important educational tool, used to impart to children important information about history and philosophy. Because it employs many forms, composed and performed for every kind of situation, the tradition is a huge presence in of Māori society. *Mōteatea* can be trivial and profound, sacred and profane, instructive and amusing:

> Songs were composed in connection with every known feeling, with every human activity. The Māori broke into song to express joy, sadness, love, hatred, contempt, ridicule, mirth, and the whole range of emotions known to man. He sang himself into a fight, and out of it. He sang to avenge an insult or a trifling slight; he sang when a relative died, and also when he lost a fish hook. He sang when he was short of food and in days of plenty. He sang his prophetic visions and his dreams. (Best n.d.:0072–19c)

For all these purposes, genealogies provided conceptual frameworks by which Māori philosophers understood the great questions of existence. Concepts relating to the origin of the universe and everything in it, including music, appear in these traditions. The philosophers conceived of the universe as being completely spirit, the ultimate reality of Māori culture. Genealogies explain the existence of spiritual forms from which the physical realm arose. One such form, the *whē,* was the primordial element, whose later applications in the physical world came to be known in English as sounds. Genealogies continue by describing the creation of the physical realm represented in the sky father (Ranginui) and the earth mother (Papatuanuku), who, having been bound together for aeons, were separated by their children. The universe as we know it then came into existence.

The next genealogically recorded period that explains the physical realm was inhabited by the children of Ranginui and Papatuanuku, creating their own domains. Thus arose what may be called, again in English, the departmental gods (*atua*)—gods of wind, sea, and so on. A creative activity of the departmental gods was the application of *whē* in their domains, giving them voice (*reo*). Hence the sea and other natural phenomena received voices.

As gods begat new generations of divine progeny, these domains became populated with all the living beings of the natural world. Tāne Mahuta, a child of Ranginui and Papatuanuku, became the progenitor of forests, and his descendants gave birth to the plants of the forests, so genealogical sections represent botanical systems. Families of birds are classified like those of plants. As in the previous time, these generations received their voices, drawn from the primordial *whē.* Into this system, humanity was created, and it too received a voice created through *whē.* As this voice evolved into words and phrases, the compositional constructions of language developed.

### Kinds of song

The collection of *mōteatea* gathered by Sir Apirana Ngata (figure 38) and edited by Dr. Pei Te Hurinui contains 393 songs, including the following types.

> *waiata tangi,* laments for the dead
>
> *waiata aroha,* love songs, songs of sorrow
>
> *waiata whaiāipo,* lovers' songs
>
> *apakura,* laments composed for varying reasons
>
> *oriori,* lullabies
>
> *waiata nā te tohunga,* seers' songs
>
> *waiata whakautu tono pākūwhā,* songs to answer marriage proposals
>
> *waiata mō te moe punarua,* songs about the "tradition of two wives"
>
> *tangi mokemoke,* soliloquies
>
> *waiata nā te tūrehu,* songs by the "fairy folk"
>
> *waiata whakautu taunu,* songs in reply to taunts and slander
>
> *waiata ki tōna whenua,* laments for land lost or abandoned
>
> *waiata whakautu whakapae,* songs composed as a reply to questions
>
> *matakite,* vision songs
>
> *pātere,* songs composed in reply to jealousies, sometimes used to accompany *poi* (see below)
>
> *tau,* intoned recitations
>
> *waiata nā te puhi mō tōna haranga,* songs by a virgin maiden about her misconduct
>
> *waiata mō ngā whakapae,* gossip songs
>
> *waiata mō te maunga-ā-rongo,* songs about making peace
>
> *waiata tawhito,* ancient songs

*waiata pouwaru,* songs by widows and widowers

*tangi mō te manu,* songs for birds

*waiata mō tōna whare,* songs for a house

*mata,* prophetic songs

*tangi mō te māra kai,* songs for gardens and plantations

*waiata whakaaraara pā,* sentinels' songs

*kaioraora,* cursing songs

*waiata mō te waipiro,* drinking songs

*waiata makamaka kai-hau-kai,* songs for presentation at a feast

*waiata kī mōkai,* songs of degradation

*waiata karakia,* ritualistic songs

*waiata wawata,* songs of daydreaming

*waiata ātahu,* songs of love-controlling charms

*waiata hiahia ki te pū,* songs about coveting guns

*waiata titotito,* provoking songs

*waiata kanga,* surfing songs

*waiata pūtōrino,* songs to accompany aerophones (*pūtōrino*)

*Mōteatea* are multifunctional. When *ātahu, kaioraora, waiata karakia,* and *waiata mō te maunga-a-rongo* are performed in series, they have ritualistic functions effecting a deep response among the parties to a proceeding.

Māori composers did not create music purely as sonic entertainment, though they did develop criteria for appraising the qualities of a performance. With dance, oratory, and other arts, *mōteatea* were cherished for reaching into the spirituality of people's lives. Māori looked for the revisitation of spirit—the juxtaposition of time, place, and people, the melancholy reminder of past events and their meaning for present circumstances.

### A lament by Te Rauparaha

In the early 1800s, Te Rauparaha, a leader of the Ngāti Toa people, lived at Kāwhia, on the western coast of Te Ika-a-Māui. In the 1820s, he led his people southward, seeking new lands. Before leaving, he composed a song that, in the Ngāti Toa version, became his lament for Kāwhia, the land long inhabited by his people. This kind of song is a ceremonial farewell. It begins: *Tērā ia ngā tai o Honipaka, / Ka wehe koe i au, ē! / He whakamaunga atu nāku / Te ao ka tākawe / Nā runga mai o Te Motu. / Ka mihi mamao au ki te iwi rā ia: / Moe noa mai, i te moenga roa* 'Those waters of Honipaka, / I leave you now, *ē! / But my spirit still clings / To that cloud floating / Above Te Motu. / I pay respect to those distant people: / Sleep on, in the great sleep' (after Ngata 1928:92). To enunciate grief on leaving, Te Rauparaha uses classical Māori associations of spirit and land. He links his spirit to the clouds floating above Te Motu, an island in Kāwhia Harbor, where people would go to present songs and stories to one another.

The migration of Ngāti Toa tells an epic story of enterprise common in Māori history. Even in the 1990s, descendants of Te Rauparaha and Ngāti Toa sing this lament, as a reminder of Kāwhia and a reaffirmation of their identity. It continues:

> Ka pāria e te tai,
> Pikitū, pikirere, piki takina mai rā.
> Te kawea au e te tere,
> Te Kawau i Muriwhenua,
> Tēnā taku manu, he manu ka onga noa,
> Rūnā ki te whare, te hau o Matariki.
> Mā te whare pōrutu,
> Mā te rahi Āti Awa e kautere mai rā,
> Whakaurupā taku aroha nā.

> The tides ebb and flow,
> Standing, rising, lamenting.
> Taken fugitive in this destiny,
> Te Kawau at Muriwhenua,
> My bird left there, a decoy,
> Held captive in that house, the winds of Matariki.
> Let the House of Mourning,
> Let great Te Āti Awa go forth,
> And I shall bury all my sorrow.

To Māori, the beauty of this text arises not just from the sounds of its words, but from knowledge of its composer. Brought together, words and knowledge multiply in meaning. As in this lament, composers use beautiful elements in the natural world—birds, clouds, spirits, tides, and so on—as symbols of their exploits and their lives. In the fatalistic phrase *te kawea au e te tere* 'taken fugitive in this destiny', Te Rauparaha hints at events that surrounded him. For his descendants, these phrases are important, for they reveal facets of the man's character, unavailable through orthodox means of discovery.

### A lament by Kahukōkā

Another famous composition from the Tainui nation is the lament by Kahukōkā for her husband, Te Maunu, and their son, Ngāhua. According to Tukumana Te Taniwha of Ngāti Whanaunga, the father and son were visiting Aotea Island to see relatives and work in their gardens. Fishermen of Ngā Puhi, a tribe from the north, canoed across the Tīkapa Moana-o-Hauraki (Hauraki Gulf), and landed at Aotea. They asked Te Maunu if he could show them where certain fish frequented. At sea, they murdered Te Maunu and Ngāhua. On learning of these deaths, Kahukōkā composed a lament that describes the dread and horror she felt. It begins: *Tū tonu ko te rae, ē, i haere ai te makau. / E kai ana au, ē, i te ika wareware. / E aurere noa, ē, i te ihu o te waka!* 'Upstanding is the headland, oh, where my loved one went. / I am consumed, oh, because of forgetfulness. / The despairing cry, oh, at the prow of the canoe!' (after Ngata 1928:170).

### Musical contexts and functions

Texts are one component of Māori music. The circumstances of performance are another. Ritual meetings, where performances of classical Māori music most often occur, involve performers' and listeners' formal interactions in prescribed ways. Historically, music reinforced, challenged, and sometimes disparaged interpersonal and intertribal relationships.

#### Music as judicial evidence

In the 1820s, Ngāti Raukawa migrated from Maungatautari, the mountain that had been their traditional homeland. Their leader, Te Whatanui, was in the same mood as Te Rauparaha on leaving Kāwhia. After Te Whatanui had settled in the south, an old friend of his, Te Heuheu, asked him to move back. He replied by saying the way of the chiefs (*rangatira*) dictates that return is impossible: the words have been said, the deeds done; to go back on one's word is not the chiefs' way (after Ngata 1990:132; my translation):

| | |
|---|---|
| Rongo kōrero au e ko Tūkino | I've heard of the word |
| Te tuku mai nei. | Sent by Tūkino. |
| E haramai ana pea | Perhaps he has come |
| Ki te tiki mai Irawaru, | To collect Irawaru, |
| Kia whakakurī au, | To turn me into a dog, |
| Kia whakapai au. | To correct me. |
| He kāewaewa, he rau harakeke | My bones wander |
| Te āhua o taku kōiwi. | Like a flax leaf. |

Some fifty years later, in a case heard by the Native Land Court, a Ngāti Raukawa delegation did indeed return to Maungatautari to reclaim the mountain. A member of the tribe that had settled there sang this song. The performance rebutted Ngāti Raukawa, who then abandoned the claim. This kind of interaction was commonplace in Māori society. Musical and poetical arts belonged to the political process of making decisions as much as making speeches did.

The scene was the Native Land Court, introduced by European settlers. Such courts settled disputes over tribal lands, hastening the process of alienation. They brought feuds to a head. The proceedings occurred on tribal lands, often in the open. At a table sat a European judge, a European assessor, and a Māori interpreter. Besides these functionaries, the court at Maungatautari would have resembled a thousand tribal meetings from ages past.

After an intense debate, which by thrust and counterthrust elicited every conceivable detail of the case, the claim hinged on the rendition of a song composed some fifty years before. The simplicity and ease with which the debate ended highlights the Māori ability to understand an opponent. For Ngāti Raukawa to contradict publicly the edicts of their sacred leader was not an option: demeaning Te Whatanui would demean themselves. His song—a sweet chant, rich in inner melodic movement—silenced them, for they knew they had heard an undeniable defense (after Ngata 1990:132; my translation):

| Tae rawa atu au | I really arrived |
|---|---|
| Ki Tīuriura, | At Tīuriura, |
| Ki runga riro rā, | There above, |
| Ki te kāinga i paea ai | To the home that received |
| Te kura a Taunīnihi. | The treasure of Taunīnihi. |

| Koia rānei, a Ngāti Raukawa, | Perhaps, Ngāti Raukawa, |
|---|---|
| Me hoki au ki Maungatautari, | I should return to Maungatautari, |
| Ki te kāinga i whakarerea nei e te ngākau. | To the homeland my heart abandoned. |
| Me hoki kōmuri au ki te whenua, | Should I return to that land, |
| Kia whakawaia mai au e te ruru? | To be resented by the owl? |
| He raru tōku ki te nohanga pahī. | I do not wish to live in constant battle. |

### Music as catalyst

In 1984, Ngāti Toa and Ngāti Raukawa helped open a meetinghouse at Kāwhia. The return to Kāwhia was an opportunity to revisit the literature created in the 160 years since Ngāti Toa had migrated. As is the custom, the opening began at dawn. Busloads of Ngāti Toa and Ngāti Raukawa arrived for a greeting on the *marae* by the Waikato-Maniapoto people. Women sounded the *karanga* (announcing the issues and groups of the day), and the Toa-Raukawa delegation walked slowly into the public space. From Ngāti Toa came a *karanga* in reply. Waikato-Maniapoto then began their welcoming dance (*haka pōwhiri*). Toa-Raukawa replied with a similar one. As the songs and dances reiterated Ngāti Toa migration and later history, they revisited events, remembered the dead, reinforced decisions, and recalled the drives in the intervening years to create unity among the tribes by setting up the King Movement, Kingitanga: *Taku waka whakairo, ē! / Taku waka whakateretere: / Ki runga i te ngaru na, ī! / Tēnā ka pakaru, ē! / Kei te manuao e pūkai ana / Ngā maramara na, ī!* 'My carved canoe, *ē!* / My nimble canoe: / There on those waves, *ī!* It will shatter, *ē!* / The pieces are heaping / Upon the man-of-war, *ī!*' (after Burns 1983:281; my translation). As a member of the Toa-Raukawa delegation, I felt the crowd's alertness to subtle tensions, poetical allusions, public decisions, and the private weight of the occasion. In those moments, the awakening dawn, cries, and songs in the silence, space and time had been transformed. Ancestors had been summoned. Their presences animated leaves, and the currents of ghost winds affected the mellow inflection of voices held in song.

### The legacy of mōteatea

*Mōteatea* traditions persist. Parts of an immeasurable literary legacy, they underpin and ornament Māori society with exquisite expressions and philosophical explanations. Māori composers are acute witnesses of human acts and the circumstances that surround them; they often provide alternative interpretations of critical events, supplementing the historical record.

Māori society is undergoing reconstruction and redevelopment. In this process, *mōteatea* perform an important function: from ancient literature and traditions, tribes preparing for the future are seeking guidance. Their endeavors attest the endurance of certain features of the human condition and the *mōteatea* that discuss them.

Since the 1970s, courses have been taught in the study of *mōteatea*. They are now being retaught in schools and homes, in formal public spaces, and elsewhere. The people of Aotearoa are beginning to see them as embodying a noble tradition of music and literature. More young Māori are learning their ancestral language. As English-speakers value Shakespeare, Māori-speakers value *mōteatea*. Young second-

Feet must be ready to move to a new position, deliver an attack, make a threat, alter the body alignment, or defend by dodge or parry. A proverb warns that "slow feet are wet feet"—wet with blood.

language speakers may not understand every point in a particular text, but they learn the text eagerly. Through *mōteatea* they find they can quickly attain more depth in their knowledge of language. As new levels within *mōteatea* reveal themselves, the text endures as an important symbol, adding to their knowledge of themselves.

The revival of *mōteatea* has paralleled a revitalization of tribal systems and institutions. Māori people are reworking and reestablishing traditional institutions, such as *whare wānanga,* traditional schools of higher learning. Literature is a large part of the curriculum, and *mōteatea* have aided the philosophical empowerment of those institutions: "With regard to making speeches in the Māori language, there is no better qualification than a knowledge of the songs. They embody expressions applicable to every circumstance, to every circumstance of the Māori" (Ngata 1961:xxxviii). Reexamining traditional theatrical institutions, many tribes are giving attention to *mōteatea* and musical instruments. Identifying theater as a vehicle for development, young Māori attend schools dedicated to drama and other arts, and represent their experiences by reworking traditional forms of making music.

Another important activity is archiving. Within tribes and governmental organizations, recording *mōteatea* is a high priority. Television and radio programs devoted to preserving tribal histories and traditions have been responsible for recording many examples. After a gap of some twenty years, publication of *mōteatea* resumed with the fourth volume of *Ngā Mōteatea.* Several tribes are planning to publish their own material on *mōteatea,* and have commissioned researchers to prepare books of tribal classics.

—Te Ahukaramū Charles Royal

## Dance

Dance has great mana within Māori cultural contexts, where it is, and has always been, a powerful message-bearing expression. The significance of any aspect of it cannot be dissected from that expressive purpose, any more than from the language of its texts, the music of its delivery, or the customs surrounding its performance. There are three main types: *haka, waiata-a-ringa,* and *poi.*

### Haka

*Haka peruperu* and *haka taparahi* are vigorous, bellicose, awe-inspiring, spirited, yet anchored war dances. Angry, aroused men—maybe a hundred, maybe a thousand—raise a storm of elemental force. To lift morale, inspire warriors before battle, and terrorize enemies, *haka taparahi* was a classic war dance, performed without weapons and requiring all the body's committed involvement. *Peruperu,* danced with weapons, was the classic battle-line *haka. Tū ngārahu* used *haka* as a divinatory exercise to determine the likely outcome of an impending battle.

Foot-leg movements (*waewae takahia*) set the pulse by repeated rhythmic plantings of feet on the ground, establishing a surefooted sense of precisely where the body's weight and balance are placed. The footfall conveys a sense of warriors holding their ground while displaying an ever-watchful alertness, focusing attention on the opponent. Feet must be ready to move swiftly to a new position, deliver an attack, warn with a threat, alter the body alignment, or defend by dodge or parry. A proverb warns that "slow feet are wet feet"—wet with blood. That proverb seems danced out in a particularly agile leap when the legs are pulled swiftly up underneath the body to avoid an enemy's sweeping weapon. By contrast, other jumps, taken from a stance of feet wide and legs bent, may land on the knee, emphasizing occupation of the land.

Textual messages are delivered in a sequence of arm gestures (*ringa*), thrust in particular directions. The hands may be clenched as fists, or, expanded, may strike the torso, chest, shoulders, hips, or thighs with forceful percussive effect. Some gestures are directed toward the body, some away from it, some downward, some upward, some at the enemy (audience). Most emphasize textual themes and moods, but a few may serve as rhythmic or patterning links, providing contrast to the interpretive gestures. Movements are uniform for the group, but considerable scope for individuality, particularly in facial expression, remains.

*Wiri,* in which arms and hands quiver in rapid vibrations or rotations, is said to bring Māori dance to life. The distinctive quivering crosses back and forth between what can be seen and what can only be felt. Connecting overt and trace movements signals that the performer's body and mind are on the same continuum. At times, warriors seem to internalize *wiri* into minuscule vibrations of the torso, neck, head, and limbs, bringing the body to a feverish standstill, preceding an explosion of rage. *Wiri, whakapī* (contorting the facial features), *pūkana* (a fixed glare, rolled or protruded eyeballs), *te arero* (a protruded tongue), belligerent snorts, and vocalizations—all combine to deliver warnings, threats, and challenges.

### Waiata-a-ringa, also known as waiata kori

These are dances developed in the early twentieth century from features of older dances, chants (especially *pātere*), and innovated movements, with texts set to melodies from borrowed popular songs. From these beginnings, they have developed into major compositions. Many incorporate obvious influences from *haka* (Shennan 1984).

*Waiata-a-ringa* are frequently performed in *marae* situations, on other formal occasions, and at informal gatherings. The particular compositions, whether classics associated with particular composers or events, or songs newly composed especially to reflect the circumstances of the occasion, are carefully selected for their significance and relevance. The texts and interpretive gestures make significant thematic contributions to the subject of the gathering.

### Haka poi

*Poi* dances involve the rhythmic tossing, hitting, and catching of a ball or several balls, traditionally made from bulrushes and attached to strings, which may be short (about 15 centimeters) or long (about 120 centimeters). Skilled performers may hold one or two short *poi,* or one or two long *poi* in each hand (figure 39). Warriors formerly used *poi* actions to maintain wrist flexibility, but *poi* have developed as a women's dance today, with new compositions emerging. Classic *poi* dances and songs are reputed to have been those of the people of the Taranaki, Rotorua, and Whanganui tribal areas, but *poi* are now performed everywhere in Aotearoa. The dancers' singing points the rhythm for the movements. The sounds of the *poi* hitting parts of the body and the rustling of the swinging skirts provide distinctive accompanimental elements.

FIGURE 39 At the Pacific Festival of Arts, Māori women, members of Ngāti Rangiwewehi, perform with *poi*. Photo by Adrienne L. Kaeppler, 1996.

### Dance within the protocol of a welcome

Formal gatherings on *marae* require a series of rituals. To announce visitors' approach, leading women make *karanga* 'calls', high-pitched keening. Men issue a *wero* 'challenge' by manipulating a weapon (figure 40), often a *taiaha* 'long weapon'. Visitors must declare the purpose of their visit, which the hosts assume to be hostile until proven friendly. Even visitors whose peaceful purpose is already known are treated with warriorlike watchfulness, as enemies would have been.

The *marae* is the domain of Tū Matauenga, the war god. Precise timing and fastidious control of this potentially volatile arena between the home and the visiting groups is rigorously exercised. The rituals of *marae* protocol guide the gradual neutralizing and reducing of this space until the visitors and home people merge as one, marked by interpersonal pressing of noses (*hongi*).

Oratory (*whaikōrero*), a highly developed art, advances the business of the gathering. The orator speaks while pacing back and forth, brandishing a weapon or stick and employing stylized lunges and gestures to emphasize his words.

Women take an important solo exhortatory role (*manungangahu*), when they may use *taiaha* or short weapons (*mere*). Different tribal areas have varying practices regarding the involvement of women on *marae*, including their rights to speak in oratory, and women may perform their own *haka* as part of those traditions.

Rituals of the assembly include *haka pōwhiri*, the welcoming dance to visitors. Female elders of the home people lead, with repeated beckoning gestures, waving branches of fresh greenery. The textual imagery suggests that the visitors form a canoe being hauled onto the *marae*.

Other group dances of distinct character and mood—*waiata-a-ringa* and *poi* dances—are likely included in formal gatherings, but on rare occasions a striking

FIGURE 40 At the Pacific Festival of Arts, Māori men, members of Ngāti Rangiwewehi, perform a *haka peruperu*. Photo by Adrienne L. Kaeppler, 1996.

contrast occurs moments after the formal ceremonies of the exchange rituals have ended. Some senior women of the home people may break into a spontaneous *kopikopi,* a snatch of improvised dancing with suggestive hip movements and pelvic thrusts that normally have no part in formally presented group dances. This stylized clowning is over quickly, but makes a memorable impact in the ambiguity of old women assuming sexual allure.

### Accounts of Māori dance

Colorful and sometimes detailed descriptions with illustrations of Māori dancing appear in journals kept by people on board the ships of Cook's, de Sainson's, and others' voyages in the late 1700s and early 1800s. Later, missionaries' and settlers' journals reveal various responses to the power of Māori dancing. Some diarists left brief but invaluable accounts; some found the dancing repugnant and called it the work of the devil.

The International Exhibition held in Christchurch in 1906–1907 marked the official transition of New Zealand from colony to dominion. The daily and weekly press accounts of the time contain detailed descriptions of the lengthy seasons of Māori dance performance, which were a prominent part of the gathering and enabled the Māori groups to see performances by people from the Cook Islands, Niue, and Fiji.

Twentieth-century scholarship has focused on traditional dance content (Armstrong 1964; Armstrong and Ngata 1960; Best 1925–1926; Kāretu 1978, 1993; Kururangi 1963, 1972; and Smithells et al. 1972) and contexts ranging from *marae* protocol (Awatere and Dewes n.d.; Sharples 1985) to specific performances (Loughnan 1902; Sutherland 1949), people (Dewes 1974; Peiwhairangi 1985), and protest (Kāretu 1991).

### Māori dance today

The texts of newly composed *haka* air long-standing issues concerning the Treaty of Waitangi, land rights, or intercultural relations, and challenge the authorities to honor their responsibilities. *Haka* continue in their time-honored tradition of confronting an opponent, of raising a question, and of "dancing out the answer."

The history of almost a millennium of indigenous occupation saw a complex network of alliances, affiliations, or enmities between tribal areas develop. These identities are forged in different tribal histories, which include distinctive dance practices—within the actual repertory and ownership of *haka* compositions, in varying customs of gender participation in dance performance, and in contrasting use of particular leg, foot, or hip movements, and style of performance.

Competitiveness between tribes has found outlets in the formally organized network of regional cultural competitions held since the 1920s. These now culminate in a national competitive festival, held regularly in different locations around the country, providing groups with considerable challenge in the performance, composition, and costume standards expected. Over time, there has been a demonstration of old and new forces at work in dance composition. Outstanding in the contemporary Māori scene is Pita Sharples, leader of the cultural group Te Roopu Manutaki, in West Auckland. He has drawn on his experiences as educator, community leader, martial-arts exponent, *haka* teacher, composer, and performer to make significant interpretations of Māori dance concepts to non-Māori.

From the 1950s, there have been attempts to incorporate Māori themes or movement style into the choreography of ballet, modern dance, or music in the theater. Some—Jenny McLeod's *Earth & Sky* (1968), Moana Nepia's *Koru* (1984), Gray Veredon's *Tell Me a Tale* (1988), Helen Fisher's *Karanga* (1994)—have made memorable impacts. Increasing numbers of Māori who have trained in theatrical dance techniques are calling on the dance experience of their cultural background and emerging as a new force in modern dance.

Prominent in this work have been Stephen Bradshaw with his company, Taiao, who, since 1990, have performed on many *marae* in rural areas; Taiaroa Royal in his renowned solo, *Te Pō* (1992), and Tanemahuta Gray in *Equus* (1995), both based on *taiaha* rituals; Charles Neho in *Dancescape* (1989), a dramatic work exploring myth; and Merenia Gray in *Interiors versus Exteriors* (1994), a modern-dance study of Māori spiritual themes.　　　　　　　　　　　　　　　　　　　　　—JENNIFER SHENNAN

### Māori dance: an indigenous view

In July 1996, Jan Bolwell, head of the Department of Performing Arts Education at Wellington College of Education, talked with the Māori educator and artist Keri Kaa. A transcript of their conversation follows.

KERI. We do *haka* to tell stories and score political points (figure 41). It's actually social comment; and for the men, the most powerful *haka* is political comment. Often they're political protests; they're vehicles for the protest. In the actual words, some quite vicious things are said. I remember my father being appointed the interpreter when the Commissioner of Lands came to the East Coast in the forties, and my father was thrilled to be the interpreter and to escort this minister. It wasn't until halfway through the ceremonies that he realized his cousins had appointed him as the translator because the whole *haka* was actually a protest against the government, and our poor father had to sit there and give this gracious translation, when in fact they called the Parliament things like: "Barking dogs are here to grind away at us in the form of taxes." They saw a whole lot of governmental decisions as financial punishments, and they called the Commissioner of Lands bluntly: "Welcome, you bloody bugger; you've come here to eat our lands."

JAN. So are you saying that the way the *language* works is more important than the *gesture* or the *form* of the dance?

KERI. A lot of the language is hard-hitting. Some of the gestures are graphic, and if you were just looking at them as gestures, they would be obscene. For instance, if you ever see an action where the fist is made, that's usually to do with the phallus. When you wave that at people, you're making a statement about the anger and the bitterness you feel. In many dances where people are making this angry kind of state-

FIGURE 41　Men of the Māori contingent to the Pacific Festival of Arts perform a *haka*. Photo by Adrienne L. Kaeppler, 1992.

ment, they frequently gesture, talking about the males to the genital area, and you know, the pelvis sort of does a rotation, and they hoist their hips up.

JAN. So are you saying that Māori dance can serve as a cathartic release?

KERI. Oh, it is! If people watching the dance are applauding the exciting movement, I have a chuckle, because if they really knew what was said, some of the dances would not be permitted to be done in public, but it's the people's way of expressing how they're feeling. Probably the most contemporary composer of *haka* who can do that and do it effectively is Bub Wehi, and he does it with words and gestures. Tīmoti Kāretu in some of his *haka* does it with the words, but you have to be a skilled linguist to appreciate what's actually happening. There are gestures where all the lines get down on the ground, and they make a fist and they pound the ground before they rise again.

And *haka* can also be celebratory, where you can have fun *haka*. We have got a hilarious one that we learned as children, all about eating fermented corn. It's still danced in our valley, and the little kids at the last tribal festival, they got up and did the *kanga kopu haka,* and of course those of us who had learned it as children stood up in the audience and did it with these little kids, and the leader was a six-year-old!

And we've got dances where one tribe belittles another tribe; and the belittling might have taken place fifty years ago, but the dance is retained, and now they're done for fun. My people, from my valley, went to see the people from Kuini Moehau's valley. (She's a Māori woman, probably the best one we've got of contemporary *haka*.) And something went wrong with the food. The people from my village came back saying that her people weren't hospitable because they gave my people little eels and what people now call hearts of palm, but they were cabbage-tree shoots. It was probably all the poor things had in their food pits. It wasn't considered a good lunch to have given to visitors, so my lot have this *haka*. Whenever they see the people from that valley, they get up and they welcome them and they say, "Welcome you people from your side of the river who eat little weenie *kūmera* [sweet potatoes], and can only afford to cook up cabbage-tree shoots." And one of the people who loves to do the *haka* is my father's last surviving brother, who's in his eighties, and whenever he spies this family from there, that's how he greets them, with this little dance.

JAN. Is there a history in those relationships between the tribes?

KERI. Oh yes, it's a wonderful way to do it, but my fear is that the knowledge about such matters is really held in only a few people's heads.

JAN. Is there a releasing of that knowledge, or is it still contained within a tribal context?

KERI. Oh, people make assumptions that they actually all know this stuff, and they don't. Not everybody knows it because only some families talk about such incidents and recreate all those dances. So you see, the *haka* for us is quite significant, because it contains a whole lot of stories. There's one, probably the most famous one, that everybody else does and most people do badly, a *haka* called "*Kura Tīwaka*." The *Kura Tīwaka* was a sacred canoe, which had all these people on board, brothers or cousins, and there was rivalry amongst them. A lot of it had to do with who was the most important person on the *waka* [canoe], and it's a *haka* which has up to thirteen changes of rhythm. It's a real masterpiece to do, and that's why it's so difficult to perform. There's this flood that comes up at sea, and huge swells, and one of them manages to get back to shore because he summons up help from the depths of the ocean. It's a famous dance, and it's a myth really. It's a myth that people still dance in town, but it also serves as a warning to tribes about what happens when you don't have unity in good working relationships within a group.

JAN. Are you saying that the dances are tribally specific?

KERI. Oh yes! "*Rūahuka,*" the one that everyone says is about the earthquake god, for instance, is really nothing to do with earthquakes. "*Rūaumoko*" was written by a woman, and so that bit is never acknowledged, because "*Rūaumoko*" is about the phallus in action. I was about thirty before I clicked at what the *haka* was really saying. The explanation is that only a woman could describe what the penis was doing, because she was the recipient of it. So, it's about the penis in motion, and it's graphically expressed in the actions. But of course for public viewing and for public consumption, there's another story attached to it, partly to make it palatable for audiences.

JAN. So a lot of *haka* were sexually explicit?

KERI. Oh yes, a lot of them were, and a lot were explicit about the activity of eating people, killing them. There's one that says, "*Homai kia whitiwhiti*," and you illustrate when you do it, you're actually disemboweling somebody—literally, "Give me your guts, and I'll tear them apart for you." And you realize there's been an incident where somebody has actually been killed in battle and accordingly disemboweled. So in a lot of the *haka,* the lyrics are ferocious. To have an appreciation of *haka,* you have to have a good understanding of the language. A lot of *haka* have been watered down to make them palatable for audiences.

JAN. Is this the influence of Christianity?

KERI. Yes, then you have got to thank missionaries for that—and because people turned away from warfare, and turned to singing together and praying together.

JAN. Well, what's your view of this? I mean, when we think about Māori dance, if we use the word *traditional* as opposed to *contemporary,* what meaning does that have for you?

KERI. I think when you're watching *haka* today, sometimes I think we're watching only the surface of it. But the real guts of it sometimes cannot be readily understood except by a learned few, and I think that's beginning to change with the *haka* schools that are developing round the country, where young men who are qualified in the *reo* [language], who are good speakers of it, are starting to ask probing questions, starting to unearth information they feel they need. Irirangi, for instance, one of the great storehouses of knowledge, would tell so much information to his classes and then stop, because he felt that some of the knowledge was probably knowledge that they wouldn't have been able to handle.

JAN. Are you saying that some of that knowledge will never be passed down?

KERI. Yes. Because he probably felt it was unsafe. Irirangi was the last person I know of who fought a duel. He was challenged to this fight, and said to this man, "Choose your weapons." I don't know what the man chose, but Irirangi chose his *patu,* his short fighting club. It was a fight to the death, but Irirangi stopped short of the killer blow, with his *patu* raised for the killer strike. He stopped when he got that far. Now he has done the same thing to his pupils: he stopped short of the killer strike. That's why it was a sad time when he died. There were things he could never discuss with anybody except men as learned as he was, so some of that knowledge has gone to his grave with him.

JAN. So where does that leave young people today?

KERI. Some of them learn the material. They learn the words, the actions, how to coordinate it; and they learn how to perform it. But I think some of them need to go a step further and start reading, and talking, and going to workshops to talk things through, because to me there's a gap in the learning. They don't understand about movements, which, when you're teaching them to new students, are physically quite dangerous, and can wreck people's ankles and feet if people's bodies aren't properly prepared.

I'll be interested to see where people take *haka* in the next century, whether it'll reshape and recreate itself. What I see the groups doing, and what I see them as signaling, is the development of a new kind of dance, a dance that's telling the stories of now. We've got dances about drugs, about AIDS, and one of the dances I find most entertaining is about space people. In the thirties and forties, people were creating dances about things they saw happening, about airplanes.

JAN. Well, look at the music they took from that age. You could call it appropriation, but they were taking from everything that was happening around them in popular culture.

KERI. Rarotonga is a wonderful example. They've got a dance for men where the men have their arms out like airplane wings. It was clear to me what that was the minute I saw it, because they would have been miming what they saw coming down from the sky. They've got a really entertaining dance about a man on a horse, and you can tell because the dancer actually raises one leg and mounts his imaginary horse, and then rides it about. And of course you and I have seen their entertaining butt-dance, so people are being presented with these new things and then creating what they have seen. And, hey, presto! you get a new dance.

JAN. But still rooted in the traditional form?

KERI. Yes. And a *haka* that diverts from that gets itself into difficulties rhythmically, because if you don't have that solid, basic beat going, the rest of the dance goes haywire. I've seen some *haka* where people have tried to fly through the air, and they've not quite managed it because they haven't come back to the basic rhythm. But I always think, well, that's great, because people are experimenting with an idea. I've seen *haka* movements used in aerobic sessions—which my father would have been frowning heavily at.

A lot of tutors need to go back to school, because there's a need for good, solid teaching. You should tell people why they're doing what they're doing. Many tutors don't even tell their performers why they stand in lines. I heard one say because it's neat and tidy! People need to have an understanding of where this has come from. We have to get up off our chuffs and do it ourselves, because we're coming from inside the dance.                                              —JAN BOLWELL, KERI KAA

## RAPA NUI

An overseas territory of Chile, Rapa Nui lies 2,000 kilometers from its nearest Polynesian neighbor, Pitcairn, and 3,200 kilometers from the coast of South America. With an area of about 160 square kilometers and a population of slightly more than two thousand, Rapa Nui is one of the most isolated spots on earth. It was devastated by civil wars in precontact times, and by introduced diseases and slaving since Easter 1722, when the Dutch explorer Roggeveen visited and named it Easter Island. The ensuing cultural disintegration included the loss of much local music and dance. Nevertheless, these arts have again become a living tradition, and are evolving styles of their own out of the remnants of the past and introductions from other Polynesian areas.

Probably numbering several thousand before the 1800s, the population of Rapa Nui fell to 111 in 1877 (Métraux 1940). Since then, the people have increased in numbers, and have recast their musical life. Landmarks of this process have been Roman Catholic evangelization, started in 1864; Chilean naval control of the island since 1917; and the influence of the American continent and tourism since the 1950s.                                              —ADRIENNE L. KAEPPLER

## Music

Rapa Nui musical history can be divided into four periods (Campbell 1971, 1988), but these are tentative, and historical certainty is impossible. Musical genres surviving from precontact times include rhythmic recitations (*kaikai*), songs to dangerous spir-

Dance in Rapa Nui is based on sung poetic texts.
But since the words of the old songs are no longer
completely understood and new songs are often
adapted from other Polynesian languages, the
movements have become more decorative and
superficially interpretative.

its (*akuaku*), funeral laments and songs to recall sad events (*riu*), and songs of praise
(*ate*) and ridicule (*'ei*). Visitors to the island documented other terms for musical genres, but their place in indigenous thinking about music is unclear. Songs bearing
these names are still composed and performed. They have rhythmic accompaniment
from percussion staffs (*ua*), concussed stones (*ma'ea*), struck stone slabs (*keho*), and a
postcontact instrument, a horse-jaw rattle (*kauaha*).

The oldest known examples of Rapa Nui music use irregular, word-based meter
with a stable pulse. Melodic ranges are narrow, and recitations are mostly monotonic.
This style characterizes songs associated with string figures. Children sing in a similar
style when they play with tops (*mako'i*), made of a local fruit.

The first wave of external influence occurred from 1864, when Roman Catholic
missionaries arrived, to 1917. Genres new in this period include songs of gratitude
(*hakakio*) and Tahitian genres or locally developed genres based on Tahitian models:
nuptial songs (*hāipoipo*) accompanied with a cane flute (*hio*), *hīmene, hulahula,* and
*'ūtē.* Meters are binary, and harmonies feature simple triads, often with a drone or
near-drone on the tonic.

From 1917 to 1954, newly introduced genres included the Chilean *cueca* and
*vals*; the *tāmūrē,* based on a Tahitian dance; and the *sausau,* said to derive from
Sāmoa. Music with dance is more important than narrative music. The Rapa Nui
adopted Spanish guitars, but used only four strings, influenced by ukuleles.

After 1954, an array of styles and genres from international sources reached the
island. Locally popular dances include the tango, the Mexican *corrido,* the fox-trot,
the twist, rock, and disco. During this period, performers adopted the button accordion (*upaupa*), and families acquired radios, phonographs, televisions, and cassette
players (Loyola 1988).

The public schools teach ancient Rapa Nui music and modern Polynesian
music. The Hito-Atan and Pakarati families most avidly preserve the tradition of
family-based musical ensembles. Rapa Nui presentations of music and dance, heavily
influenced by Tahitian genres and styles, have been seen by tourists in increasing
numbers since the 1950s, changing family-based festivities to commercial ones.

—Juan Pablo González

## Dance

Remnants of the past comprise reconstructions and recombinations of movement
motifs taken from written and pictorial sources and oral traditions known today primarily through the knowledge of one man, Kiko Pātē. Essentially, Rapa Nui has two
traditional genres: dances performed with a carved or painted paddle in abstract
anthropomorphic form, and a dance simultaneously combining two sets of movements performed by men and women. Dances with paddles are performed either in a
squatting position, in which the paddle is twirled between the palms while the distal
end rests on the floor, or in a standing position, in which the distal end is held

FIGURE 42    At the Pacific Festival of Arts, men of the Rapa Nui contingent wield paddles while a kneeling woman raises her hands to show a string figure. Photo by Adrienne L. Kaeppler, 1985.

FIGURE 43    At the Pacific Festival of Arts, Rapa Nui women wearing feather-tasseled skirts perform an improvised dance. Photo by Adrienne L. Kaeppler, 1996.

between the toes and the head of the paddle is held in the hand. In the latter, the movements consist primarily of hopping on one foot, either in place or moving in a backward circle. In the other old genre, seated men make rowing motions while standing women perform graceful arm and lower-body movements. For presentations at the Pacific Festival of Arts, a contingent from Rapa Nui combined these ideas: kneeling women demonstrated the making of string figures while standing men wielded paddles (figure 42).

The movements of these genres derive from the forebears of the historic Rapa Nui, who migrated to this island from central Polynesia; therefore, the movements combine successfully with later importations from the same area, especially Tahiti and the Cook Islands. These introductions combine side-to-side hip movements in various rhythms with graceful hand-and-arm movements typical of central Polynesian storytelling dances (*aparima*). Another dance now considered traditional is *simosimo,* said to be based on a Sāmoan song, but with hip movements borrowed from central Polynesia.

Dance in Rapa Nui is based on sung poetic texts. But since the words of the old songs are no longer completely understood and new songs are often adapted from other Polynesian languages, the movements have become more decorative and superficially interpretative (figure 43) than the more allusive enhancement of poetry and ritual movements done with religious humility that probably existed in precontact times.                                                —ADRIENNE L. KAEPPLER

# REFERENCES

Armstrong, Alan. 1964. *Maori Games and Hakas.* Wellington: A. H. and A. W. Reed.

Armstrong, Alan, and Reupena Ngata. 1960. *Maori Action Songs.* Wellington: A. H. and A. W. Reed.

Awatere, Arapeta, and Te Kapunga Dewes. N.d. *Maori Literature—Te Kawa o te Marae.* Wellington: Department of Anthropology, Victoria University of Wellington.

Beaglehole, Ernest, and Pearl Beaglehole. 1938. *Ethnology of Pukapuka.* Bulletin 150. Honolulu: Bishop Museum.

———. N.d. "Myths, Stories, and Chants from Pukapuka." Manuscript. Honolulu: Bishop Museum.

Beechey, F. W. 1831. *Narrative of a Voyage to the Pacific and Bering's Strait . . . in the Years 1825, 26, 27, 28.* London: H. Colburn and R. Bentley.

Berger, Henry. 1898. *Mele Hawaii.* Honolulu: Hawaiian News Co.

Best, Elsdon. N.d. Manuscript. Wellington: Alexander Turnbull Library, Best Papers.

———. 1925–1926. *Games and Pastimes of the Maori.* Wellington: Government Printer.

Billam-Walker, Donald. 1979. "Berger, Kapena (Captain) Henry né Heinrich Wilhelm." In *Hawaiian Music and Musicians: An Illustrated History,* ed. George S. Kanahele, 34–44. Honolulu: University Press of Hawai'i.

Buck, Peter H. (Te Rangi Hiroa). 1932. *Ethnology of Manihiki and Rakahanga.* Bulletin 99. Honolulu: Bernice P. Bishop Museum.

———. 1938. *Ethnology of Mangareva.* Bulletin 157. Honolulu: Bishop Museum.

Burns, Patricia. 1983. *Te Rauparaha, a New Perspective.* Auckland: Penguin Books.

Burrows, Edwin G. 1933. *Native Music of the Tuamotus.* Bulletin 109. Honolulu: Bishop Museum.

———. 1934a. "Music of the Tahaki Chants." In *The Legends of Maui and Tahaki,* ed. J. Frank Stimson, 78–88. Bulletin 127. Honolulu: Bishop Museum.

———. 1934b. "Polynesian Part-Singing." *Zeitschrift für Vergleichende Musikwissenschaft* 2:69–76.

Campbell, Ramón. 1971. *La herencia musical de Rapanui.* Santiago: Editorial Andrés Bello.

———. 1988. "Etnomusicología de la Isla de Pascua." *Revista Musical Chilena* 42(170):5–47.

Cunha, A. R. "Sonny." 1914. *Famous Hawaiian Songs.* Honolulu: Bergstrom Music Co.

Dashper, Mark. 1996. *He Nguru, he Koauau: A User's Guide to Maori Flutes.* Waipukurau, New Zealand: Central Hawkes Bay Print.

Dewes, Te Kapunga. 1974. *Nga Waiata Haka a Henare Waitoa.* Wellington: Department of Anthropology, Victoria University of Wellington.

Dix, John. 1982. *Stranded in Paradise: NZ*

*Rock'n'Roll 1955–1988.* Wellington: Paradise Publications.

Emerson, Nathaniel B. 1909. *Unwritten Literature of Hawaii: Sacred Songs of the Hula.* Washington, D.C.: Bureau of American Ethnology.

Emory, Kenneth P. 1976. "Tuamotuan Chants and Songs from Napuka." In *Directions in Pacific Traditional Literature,* ed. Adrienne L. Kaeppler and H. Arlo Nimmo, 173–193. Special publication 62. Honolulu: Bishop Museum Press.

Gill, William Wyatt. 1876. *Life in the Southern Isles.* London: Religious Tract Society.

Handy, E. S. Craighill. 1923. *The Native Culture in the Marquesas.* Bulletin 9. Honolulu: Bishop Museum.

———. 1930. *Marquesan Legends.* Bulletin 69. Honolulu: Bishop Museum.

Handy, E. S. Craighill, and Jane Lathrop Winne. 1925. *Music in the Marquesas Islands.* Bulletin 17. Honolulu: Bishop Museum.

Hanson, F. Allan. 1970. *Rapan Lifeways: Society and History on a Polynesian Island.* Boston: Little, Brown.

Hodée, Paul. 1983. *Tahiti 1834–1984:150 ans de vie chrétienne en Église.* Tahiti: Archevêché de Papeete.

Hopkins, C. A. 1899. *Aloha Collection of Hawaiian Songs.* Honolulu: Wall, Nichols Co.

Jonassen, John. 1991. *Cook Islands Drums.* Rarotonga, Cook Islands. Ministry of Cultural Development.

Kaeppler, Adrienne. 1973. "Music in Hawaii in the Nineteenth Century." In *Musikkulturen Asiens, Afrikas und Ozeaniens im 19. Jahrhundert,* ed. Robert Gunther. Regensburg: Gustav Bosse Verlag.

———. 1993. *Hula Pahu: Hawaiian Drum Dances.* Vol. 1, *Ha'a and Hula Pahu: Sacred Movements.* Bulletin in Anthropology 3. Honolulu: Bishop Museum.

Kanahele, George S., ed. 1979. *Hawaiian Music and Musicians: An Illustrated History.* Honolulu: University Press of Hawai'i.

Kāretu, Tāmoti S. 1978. *Nga Waiata ma nga Haka a Taua a te Maori.* Waikato, New Zealand: University of Waikato.

———. 1991. "Te Ngahuruhuru: A Decade of Protest, 1980–1990." In *Dirty Silence,* ed. Graham McGregor and Mark Williams, 159–175. Oxford: Oxford University Press.

———. 1993. *Haka.* Wellington: A. W. and A. W. Reed.

King, Charles E. 1916–1948. *Book of Hawaiian Melodies.* Honolulu: Charles E. King.

———. 1942, 1950. *Songs of Hawaii.* Honolulu: Charles E. King.

Kururangi, Mere. 1963. *Action Songs.* Wellington: Government Printer.

———. 1972. *Single Long Poi.* Wellington: Government Printer.

Loughnan, R. E. 1902. *Royalty in New Zealand.* Wellington: Government Printer.

Loyola, Margot. 1988. "Mis Vivencias en Isla de Pascua." *Revista Musical Chilena* 42(170):48–86.

McLean, Mervyn. 1996. *Maori Music.* Auckland: Auckland University Press.

Matheson, Trevor. 1987. "The Absent Majority: The Case of Rakahanga." In *Land Tenure in the Atolls,* ed. R. G. Crocombe, 169–187. Suva: Institute of Pacific Studies, University of the South Pacific.

Mesplé, Raymond. 1986. "Les Hīmene en Polynesia Française." Mémoire de Maîtrise, U.E.R. de Musicologie, University of Lyons 2.

Métraux, Alfred. 1940. *Ethnology of Easter Island.* Bulletin 160. Honolulu: Bishop Museum Press.

Moulin, Jane Freeman. 1979. *The Dance of Tahiti.* Pape'ete: Christian Gleizal/Les éditions du Pacifique.

———. 1989. "Field recordings for the Territorial Survey of Oceanic Music: Music in the Southern Marquesas." Auckland: Archive of Maori and Pacific Music, University of Auckland.

———. 1991a. *Territorial Survey of Oceanic Music: Music in the Southern Marquesas.* 5-volume catalog of field recordings. Auckland: Archive of Maori and Pacific Music, University of Auckland.

———. 1991b. "He Ko'ina: Music, Dance, and Poetry in the Marquesas Islands." Ph.D. dissertation, University of California at Santa Barbara.

———. 1994. *Music of the Southern Marquesas Islands.* Occasional Papers in Pacific Ethnomusicology, 3. Auckland: University of Auckland, Department of Anthropology.

*Na Himeni Kamalii.* 1842. Honolulu: The Missionaries.

Ngata, Apirana T. 1928. *Nga Moteatea.* Vol. 1. Wellington: Polynesian Society.

———. 1961. *Nga Moteatea.* Vol. 2. Edited by Pei Te Hurinui. Wellington: Polynesian Society.

———. 1970. *Nga Moteatea.* Vol. 3. Edited by Pei Te Hurinui. Wellington: Polynesian Society.

———. 1990. *Nga Moteatea.* Vol. 4. Wellington: Polynesian Society.

Noble, Johnny. 1915. *Royal Collection of Hawaiian Songs.* Honolulu: Johnny Noble; San Francisco: Sherman Clay.

Oliver, Douglas L. 1974. *Ancient Tahitian Society.* 3 vols. Honolulu: University of Hawai'i Press.

O'Reilly, Patrick. 1977. *Dancing Tahiti.* Société des Océanistes, dossier 22. Paris: Nouvelles éditions latines.

Peiwhairangi, Ngoi. 1985. *Tuini—Her Life and Songs.* Gisborne: Te Rau Press.

Pukui, Mary Kawena, and Samuel H. Elbert. 1986. *Hawaiian Dictionary.* Revised and enlarged. Honolulu: University of Hawai'i Press.

*Pupu Himene no Rurutu 2.* 1980. Rama R–003. Cassette.

Roberts, Helen H. 1926. *Ancient Hawaiian Music.* Bulletin 29. Honolulu: Bishop Museum.

Salisbury, Kevin. 1983. "Pukapukan People and Their Music." M.A. thesis, University of Auckland.

———. 1984. "Tradition and Change in the Music of Pukapuka." *Pacific Arts Newsletter* 19:42–55.

———. 1991. "The Oral Poetic Tradition of Pukapuka: Treasure Trove of the Ancestors." *Rongorongo Studies* 1(2).

Sharples, Peter. 1985. "Maori Dance Forms and Their Role in Contemporary Maori Society." In *Dance—The New Zealand Experience,* ed. Jean Silver. Auckland: Dance and the Child International.

Shennan, Jennifer. 1984. *The Maori Action Songs.* Wellington: New Zealand Council for Educational Research.

Silva, Glenn [Kalena]. 1989. "A Comparative Study of the Hymnody of Two Hawaiian Protestant Denominations: Hoʻomana Iā Iesū and Hoʻomana Naʻauao." Ph.D. dissertation, University of Washington.

Smithells, Philip, et al. 1972. *Games and Dances of the Maori.* Wellington: Government Printer.

Stillman, Amy K. 1987a. "Published Hawaiian Songbooks." *MLA Notes* 44:221–239.

———. 1987b. *Report on Survey of Music in Mangareva, French Polynesia.* Working Papers in Anthropology, Archaeology, Linguistics, Maori Studies, 78. Auckland: University of Auckland, Department of Anthropology.

———.1991. "*Hīmene Tahiti:* Ethnoscientific and Ethnohistorical Perspectives on Choral Singing and Protestant Hymnody in the Society Islands, French Polynesia." Ph.D. dissertation, Harvard University.

Stillman, Amy Kuʻuleialoha. 1982. "The Hula Kuʻi: A Tradition in Hawaiian Music and Dance." M.A. thesis, University of Hawaiʻi.

Stillman, Amy Kuʻuleialoha, and Monica Paheo. 1985. "E Mau Takao no Mangareva." Typescript. Territorial Survey of Oceanic Music, Mangareva.

Sutherland, I. L. G. 1949. *The Ngarimu Hui.* Wellington: The Polynesian Society.

Tatar, Elizabeth. 1982. *Nineteenth Century Hawaiian Chant.* Pacific Anthropological

Records, 33. Honolulu: Department of Anthropology, Bishop Museum.

———. 1993. *Hula Pahu: Hawaiian Drum Dances. Vol. 2: The Pahu: Sounds of Power.* Bishop Museum Bulletin in Anthropology, 3. Honolulu: Bishop Museum Press.

Thomson, John Mansfield. 1990. *Biographical Dictionary of New Zealand Composers.* Wellington: Victoria University Press.

———. 1991. *The Oxford History of New Zealand Music.* Oxford and Auckland: Oxford University Press.

Tregear, Edward. 1899. *A Dictionary of Mangareva.* Wellington, New Zealand: Government Printing Office.

Walsh, D. S., and Bruce Biggs. 1966. *Proto-Polynesian Word List 1.* Auckland: Linguistic Society of New Zealand.

# MUSIC AND DANCE

The Polynesian, perpetually threatened with sudden death, believed in living fully while he could. Music and dancing were major parts of his day-to-day life.

**SISTRUM**

Some Hawaiian dances, which depended on very delicate movements for effect, were accompanied by rustling sounds from instruments such as this.

**WHIZZER GOURDS**
Hawaii

The middle gourd was held in one hand. When the string, wound around the stick inside, was pulled rapidly with the other hand, the end gourds rotated, producing a whizzing sound. The string would rewind itself.

**DANCE SKIRT**
Samoa

The Polynesians fashioned their dance costumes from many kinds of fibers.

**MUSICAL BOW**

Although Polynesians did not have true stringed instruments, the Hawaiians developed a musical bow. The notched end was held in the mouth which acted as a resonance chamber. The player tałed as he picked the strings, giving the effect of musical speech.

**UKULELE**

The ukulele is not native to Hawaii, but was developed from a similar Portuguese instrument, introduced into Hawaii about 1879.

**DANCE WANDS**
Tuamotu Islands

Polynesian dancers did not touch each other, but most of them liked to hold valued ornaments in their hands as they danced. In the Tuamotus tapa cloth was scarce and valuable, thus suitable for covering wands carried in a dance.

# *Part 4*
# Resources and Research Tools

How do we preserve and access the tangible products of music and dance? Where do we keep them and why? Most important to Oceanic peoples are the living repositories of respected elders, who hold the systems of knowledge in memory. Becoming more and more useful today are museums and archives, which preserve musical instruments, costumes, and aural and visual records—in recordings, transcriptions, moving images, photographs, and texts. Navigating through recordings, films, videos, and printed matter leads us to the treasures of our Oceanic heritage.

Musical treasures from Polynesia on exhibit at the Smithsonian Institution, Washington, D.C.: *left wall,* a Sāmoan panpipe and a Hawaiian vessel flute; *back wall, upper left,* a Tongan flute, a Hawaiian ʻukulele, a Hawaiian musical bow (*ūkeke*), and a Hawaiian split-bamboo rattle (*pūʻili*); *back wall, lower left,* a Tuamotu feathered dance wand; *floor, left to right,* a conch trumpet, a small log idiophone from Aitutaki (Cook Islands), a Hawaiian gourd rattle (*ʻulīʻulī*), a Hawaiian large-gourd idiophone (*ipu*), two Hawaiian drums (*pahu* and *pūniu*), and a Hawaiian whizzer-gourd rattle (*ʻūlili*); *right wall,* Hawaiian dance sticks (*kālaʻau*). Behind the *ipu* and the *pahu* hangs a Sāmoan skirt. Photo by Smithsonian Institution.

# Archives and Institutional Resources

Adrienne L. Kaeppler
Helen Reeves Lawrence
Grace Koch
Don Niles
David Akin
Lawrence Foanaota
Raymond Ammann
Kirk Huffman
Barbara B. Smith

Betty Kam
Karen Peacock
Dale B. Robertson
Amy Kuʻuleialoha Stillman
J. W. Love
Suzanne Mudge
Robert Reigle
Kathryn Creely
Anthony Seeger

Pamela Wintle
Daisy Russell
Judith A. Gray
Joseph C. Hickerson
Susanne Ziegler
Rolf Husmann
Helga Thiel

**Archives and Museums in Oceania**
**Archives and Museums in North America**
**Archives and Museums in Europe**

The principal Oceanic resources that preserve information about the performing arts are people—respected individuals having knowledge and skill, often elders who serve as trustees of traditions (figure 1). The immediacy of personal authority is augmented by observers' accounts, written and aurally and visually recorded, and deposited in public and private archives and museums. Useful institutions are in Oceania itself and elsewhere around the world, mainly in the United States and Europe; however, information on some of these is difficult to access.

## ARCHIVES AND MUSEUMS IN OCEANIA

Numerous institutions in Oceania conserve collections useful for pursuing research on the performing arts, including recorded sounds, films, and videos, photographs, musical instruments, and costumes. These resources include small, local museums in Port Moresby, Honiara, Nouméa, Majuro, Suva, and elsewhere, and large museums and archives in Australia, French Polynesia, Hawaiʻi, and Aotearoa. Radio and TV stations throughout Oceania record important events, archive the tapes, and play excerpts daily. In French Polynesia, the department of oral tradition at the Musée de Tahiti et des Îles has recordings, as does Radio Télé Tahiti. OTAC (Office Territorial d'Action Culturelle) preserves recordings of Heiva competitions. In Micronesia, radio stations feature recordings of traditional music made by local and expatriate performers. In ʻUvea, RFO Wallis et Futuna has since 1979 archived its recordings of performances taped on religious feasts. And daily in Tonga, radio station A3Z airs a program featuring tapes made during important events.  —ADRIENNE L. KAEPPLER

### Australia

The federal capital (Canberra), state capitals, and some towns have museums, libraries, archives, universities, and other institutions that contain collections relating to Oceanic music and dance [see THE MUSIC AND DANCE OF AUSTRALIA: Research Institutions].

Canberra has major archives. The **Australian Institute of Aboriginal and Torres Strait Islander Studies** (AIATSIS) has the largest collection of indigenous

FIGURE I   Human archives: *a,* Faʻanimo
(1874–1974), a repository of Sāmoan musical
knowledge (photo by J. W. Love, 1973); *b,*
Kameol (1901–1972), a choreographer of
Namoluk Atoll, Chuuk, Federated States of
Micronesia (photo by Mac Marshall, 1971).

(b)

(a)

Australian music, preserved in recordings, manuscripts, films, and videos. The **National Library of Australia** houses Pacific materials, and its oral-history unit contains recordings of Australian music, with associated documentation. It has published a directory to collections held in libraries in Oceania except Hawaiʻi (Cunningham 1997). The **National Film and Sound Archive** has anthropological and commercial films and a comprehensive collection of commercial recordings from the start of the recording industry to the present. The **Pacific Manuscripts Bureau,** at the Australian National University, has microfilm copies of many documents, some of which contain information on music and dance. The bureau sponsors documentation-oriented projects throughout the Pacific Islands.

Recordings of indigenous Australian musics and some Pacific musics are held in the archives of the national public broadcaster, the **Australian Broadcasting Corporation.** Smaller broadcasters, including the **Central Australian Aboriginal Media Association** and the **Torres Strait Islander Media Association,** have recordings of contemporary indigenous music, and produce commercial releases on cassette and disk.

The **Mitchell Library** (Sydney) and the **John Oxley Library** (Brisbane) house substantial collections of indigenous Australian and Pacific materials, including manuscripts, photographs, and published works. Many state libraries hold collections relating to indigenous Australian histories; some materials, including diaries and photographs, contain information on music and dance. The major university libraries and archives hold collections relating to indigenous cultures and histories; those of the east coast have collections of Pacific Islander materials. Other academically affiliated institutions, such as the **Grainger Museum** (see below), have small collections of Oceanic musical materials.

Every territorial and state museum in Australia has a substantial collection of indigenous artifacts (including artworks) and archival material. Some house Pacific Islander materials and archives of recorded sounds. Most contain examples of musical instruments, dance costumes, masks, and other music-related artifacts. In 1996, Gregg Howard (of Griffith University, Brisbane) undertook the first thorough survey of musical instruments in Australian collections (Howard 1996; www.gu.edu.au/gwis/qcm/instdb/contents.htm). Many regional museums, cultural centers, and Aboriginal community "keeping places" hold collections containing relevant materials. The **Strehlow Research Centre** (Alice Springs) and other institutions have archival materials relating to Aboriginal music and dance. The **Australian Music Centre** (Sydney) does not normally acquire items associated with indigenous musics.

At a new site in Canberra, the federal government is constructing buildings to house the **National Museum of Australia.** AIATSIS may be relocated to this site. Also in progress is the **National Networked Facility for Research in Australian Music** (http://online.anu.edu.au/nfram), a directory of collections of music-related materials throughout Australia, with links to detailed information about Australian musical resources.      —HELEN REEVES LAWRENCE

### *AIATSIS*

The largest collection of recordings, photographs, videos, and films of Australian indigenous music and dance is that of the **Australian Institute of Aboriginal and Torres Strait Islander Studies** (AIATSIS, GPO Box 553, Canberra ACT 2601, Australia; www.aiatsis.gov.au). These materials are kept in temperature- and humidity-controlled vaults, meeting international archival standards. Access is by appointment. Conditions of deposit regulate the use of each collection.

Most collections consist of material generated by research funded by the institute, though staffers seek out copies of relevant items from other institutions and organizations. The holdings of the archives of film and sound date from 1898. Samples from the 1990s include videos and commercial tapes issued by country, rock, and reggae groups.

The charter of AIATSIS authorizes the funding of research, some of which covers music and dance. The Research Officer in Ethnomusicology gives researchers advice and assistance. Researchers are responsible for disseminating their work, which they often do via the Aboriginal Studies Press, controlled by the institute. Recordings and videos of indigenous music and dance are available on order from the press, as are books.

The Sound Archive, founded by the federal government in 1964, was the first governmentally institutionalized aural archive in Australia. It contains twenty-two thousand hours of recordings, about eight thousand of which document indigenous music. Its library houses transcriptions, musical texts, notes, dissertations, books, and articles pertaining to the recordings. The archive holds copies of the Norman B. Tindale tape collection of the South Australian Museum and tape transfers of the 1898 cylinder collection of the Cambridge Expedition to the Torres Strait.

Alice Moyle donated the widest-ranging collection of tapes of Australian traditional music. In the 1960s and 1970s in Cape York, Arnhem Land, the Gulf of Carpentaria, and the Kimberleys, she recorded more than 185 hours of musical performances and instrumental demonstrations. Her collection includes photographs and videotapes. The library holds copies of her publications. The largest collection of tapes of Aboriginal music is that of Richard Moyle, dating from 1974 to 1977. It consists of more than 350 hours of mostly ceremonial music performed by Western Desert and Arandic people of Central Australia. The Aboriginal Studies Press has published two books based on these recordings. Other notable collections of music or dance or both are those of Stephen A. Wild (Warlpiri, Central Arnhem Land), Andrée Grau (Bathurst and Melville Islands), Wolfgang Laade (Torres Strait, North Queensland), Catherine Ellis (Southeast Australia, Victoria), and Luise Hercus (Southeast Australia, Central Australia, Victoria).      —GRACE KOCH

### Grainger Museum

Established in 1938 by the pianist and composer Percy Aldridge Grainger, the Grainger Museum (University of Melbourne) contains musical and nonmusical materials, mostly acquired by Grainger. It has two separate areas: the **Grainger Collection** and the **Music Museum Collection.** Grainger wanted a small museum with intimate spaces, where he could present the personal and creative sides of music. He thought exhibits should be displayed so visitors with no musical knowledge could appreciate the connections between life and art. He did not ignore the intellectual side of music: he wanted the archived collection to become a primary resource for researchers.

The museum contains about three hundred phonograph cylinders, recordings of Māori and Cook Islanders singing, Danish music and culture, and English folk songs. In 1940, the Library of Congress dubbed this material onto acetate discs. Other materials include musical instruments, ethnographic artifacts from Oceania and Africa, music manuscripts and publications, costumes, furniture, visual artworks, photographs, correspondence, a library, and memorabilia.

A citizen of the United States from 1918, Grainger spent much of his life in New York, but he concertized around the world. He maintained a close association with Aotearoa and Australia, especially Melbourne, his birthplace. On tour in 1908–1909, he heard recordings of Rarotongan and Aotearoa Māori music made by Alfred J. Knocks, a resident of Otaki, Aotearoa. Grainger spent an evening at Knocks's house, transcribing wax-cylinder recordings of Rarotongan music. At the International Exhibition in Christchurch in 1906–1907, Knocks had recorded music performed by visitors from the Cook Islands (Reeves 1982).

Knocks also recorded Māori *tangi* and *haka.* Married to a Māori, he spoke Māori fluently, and translated many recorded texts. Grainger liked this music:

> O the Maori hakas! The grand wild rhythms of them ring bewitchingly in the memory of my ears. . . . To perform a haka must give more joy than to perform any other art I know, almost. For one not only shouts wild bold words, with the rhythmic pulse of a lot of fellow hakamen floating one along, but accompanies the chanting with desperate violent wanton abandoned movement of the whole body! Musical football. (Grainger 1909)

Years later, Grainger borrowed the cylinders and had their recordings copied onto other cylinders, now housed in the museum, with manuscripts of Grainger's (incomplete) transcriptions of them. In 1984, the recordings were dubbed onto tape (Reeves 1984). Other copies of the recordings are housed in the Archive of Maori and Pacific Music (Auckland). Tapes of the songs from the Cook Islands are in the Cook Islands National Archives (Rarotonga). When Grainger made recordings, he sounded a pitch pipe at the start of each item. Knocks did not, so finding the correct speed for playing his cylinders is problematic.          —Helen Reeves Lawrence

### Papua New Guinea

The **Music Archive of the Institute of Papua New Guinea Studies** (from 1988 to 1995 the Cultural Studies Division of the National Research Institute) holds the world's largest collection of recordings of Papua New Guinean music. In 1974, a year before national independence, the colonial government set up the Institute of Papua New Guinea Studies to record the music of the country. Beginning with staff-made recordings, the archive has expanded to include copies of recordings made by visiting researchers, plus a nearly complete collection of commercial recordings of local musics. It has copies of field recordings beginning in 1898; the originals are over-

FIGURE 2   Entrance pavilion of the National Museum and Art Gallery, Papua New Guinea. Designed by David Lasisi, it resembles the entrances of Sepik meetinghouses, where men stored sacred musical instruments and other valuable objects. Photo by Adrienne L. Kaeppler, 1977.

seas—in Berlin, Canberra, Hamburg, Helsinki, London, Paris, Vienna, Washington, and elsewhere. An early catalog formed the basis for the present one (Niles 1981). The Music Archive contains about seven thousand hours of music. An extensive collection of printed materials—articles, books, theses, unpublished papers—supplements this collection. The extent of the recorded and printed materials has made the archive the main center for researching local music (Niles 1992).

In 1988, the Institute of Papua New Guinea Studies merged with the Institute for Applied and Social Economic Research and the Education Research Unit to form the National Research Institute. In January 1996, it was reestablished separately as the Institute of Papua New Guinea Studies. The Music Department disseminates the results of research on local musics. It has published a bibliography, a series of musical texts, catalogs of commercial recordings of local musics, a translation of a monograph on musical instruments, an academic series (*Apwitihire: Studies in Papua New Guinea Musics*), and an annual series on music (*Kulele: Occasional Papers on Pacific Music & Dance*).

Other national archives are smaller or narrower in scope. The **Papua New Guinea Service of the Australian Broadcasting Commission** broadcast from 1946 until 1973, when the National Broadcasting Commission took over its functions (Mackay 1976). Radio stations have sprung up in all nineteen provinces. Each station retains recorded materials. Since the establishment of each station, teams of broadcasters have occasionally recorded local music and aired the recordings. The stations do not usually retain recordings permanently: they keep them simply for broadcast, and masters may not survive the rigors of repeated play. Though personnel have lamented the lack of archival storage for valuable recordings the NBC stations hold, many original recordings will probably perish. The **Papua New Guinea National Archives** houses the government's official documents, but no recordings. The **New Guinea Collection** at the Michael Somare Library (University of Papua New Guinea) and the **Papua New Guinea Collection** of the National Library hold scattered recordings. The **National Museum** (figure 2) holds a collection of musical instruments.
—DON NILES

## Solomon Islands

The **National Museum of the Solomon Islands** (P.O. Box 313, Honiara Guadalcanal) holds hundreds of cassettes and some reel-to-reel tapes, collected by museum-related projects and donated by outside researchers, including David Akin, Ben Burt, Christine Jourdan, Roger Keesing, Elli Köngäs-Maranda, Pierre Maranda, and Hugo Zemp. These recordings contain musical, ethnographic, and oral historical information, and are available for use within the museum. The material from Malaita is particularly rich.

The museum holds videotapes of cultural performances and events from the 1970s on. David Akin's videotapes document Kwaio drumming, panpiping in several genres (*'aukaakaba'ii, 'aukwa'ikwa'i, 'aulebi, 'ausango*), tube-stamper playing (*gilo*), singing-accompanied dancing (*mao*), *'aulebi* panpipe-accompanied dancing (*tootola*), and most extensively, *sango,* a ritual dance accompanied by eight panpipers and performed about every four years for ancestral spirits at the spirits' request, in front of the shrine where the spirits' skulls rest. In addition to ritual performances, these videos document instruction and practice in *sango* dancing and panpiping.

Of the museum's musical instruments, culturally important idiophones include sets of tube stampers, mortars and pestles, log idiophones, struck bamboo idiophones, bamboo lamellaphones, and handheld and leg-tied nut rattles. The main chordophone is a two-stringed zither with bamboo bridges; the strings are plucked with a plectrum, and the player's mouth serves as a resonator. The aerophones feature

FIGURE 3   Dancing is an activity documented by the MABO Project, as in this occasion on Santa Isabel, Solomon Islands. Photo by the MABO Project.

FIGURE 4   At a chief's installation, Baelelea men carry painted staves and stamp their rattle-clad right feet. Photo by Adrienne L. Kaeppler, 1976.

numerous side-blown and end-blown bamboo flutes, many kinds of panpipes and panpipe sets (played in ensemble), singing tops, humming toys, and a holed nut threaded with strings, which the player pulls to make the nut spin and hum. The museum's collection includes costumery and carved and decorated sticks and wands (carried by dancers) from Malaita, Vanikoro, and elsewhere. On a large TV screen in the main gallery, the museum shows videos from its collection.

The **Solomon Islands Broadcasting Corporation** (SIBC) is an independent statutory body with English and Pijin programming. SIBC maintains hundreds of recordings of Solomon Islands music, including traditional, popular, and church music, and performances by vocal groups, string bands, and rock bands. For a small charge, SIBC copies material from its collection onto cassettes brought to its offices. The station regularly broadcasts traditional music.    —DAVID AKIN

### The MABO Project

A multinational enterprise in cultural documentation, the **MABO Project** unites the musical efforts of the National Museum of the Solomon Islands, the National Archives, the Solomon Islands Broadcasting Corporation, and Osaka University. Its name is an acronym of *Museum, Archives, Broadcasting, Osaka*. Happily, in a local language, the word *mabo* means 'peace'.

The primary goal of the project is to document the music and dance of all cultures in the country (figure 3). Osaka University provides personnel and funding, including equipment, shared with the National Museum and the Broadcasting Corporation. A secondary goal is to train Solomon Islanders to use the equipment so they can record performances on their own. Research in the Solomon Islands is controlled by a governmental act requiring researchers to apply for permission more than nine months ahead of their prospective work. Projects like MABO—coordinated by the government, or involving governmental institutions—bypass this requirement and may proceed as the situation warrants. Another aspect of training is to acquaint museum personnel with standard methods of preserving tapes and films.

The project has three phases. The first, begun in 1986, involved informing provincial authorities about the project, obtaining their consent for research, and planning the order by which cultures would be documented. The original idea was to start in the southeast, in the Santa Cruz Islands, and to work northwestward, documenting cultures most rapidly losing their traditional music and dance. Since a good opportunity arose early in the Russell Islands, the project made its first recordings there, and research continued in the central and northwestern part of the country. Ryūichi Tai, from Osaka University, sometimes accompanied by the museum archivist, has undertaken research in Central, Isabel, and Western provinces.

The second phase is to conduct research in areas that have already been covered, by outside researchers or indigenous institutions. The third phase is to revisit the cultures of phase one, studying changes that have happened since the original documentation. The recordings are housed in the National Museum, the National Archives, and Osaka University. Years before the project began, the museum had been maintaining archival copies of audiotapes, videotapes, and films, including materials generated by a UNESCO workshop in 1976 (figure 4).

An event that invigorated the project was the tenth anniversary of national independence, whose celebrations occurred in July 1988. As chairman of the Cultural Arts and Entertainment Committee, Lawrence Foanaota organized performances of representative cultural groups, which traveled to Honiara to perform. The project learned which dances were current in the provinces and which individuals were organizing and presenting them. The performances were audiotaped and videotaped.

—LAWRENCE FOANAOTA

FIGURE 5    Fo'aanamae, a Kwaio man, works on one of a set of eight *'aulebi* panpipes. The set consists of four pairs of instruments, each pair having a unique size and each instrument having eleven pipes. Photo by David Akin, 1996.

### Kwaio Cultural Centre

The **Kwaio Cultural Centre,** in the East Kwaio mountains behind Sinalagu Harbor, consists of a main school and two satellite schools, taught by local teachers in the Kwaio language (Akin 1994). In 1986, cyclone Namu destroyed the center's collection of musical and other cassettes, photos, and papers. Plans to house an expanded replacement set of these in the National Museum in Honiara are under way. The material will include copies of about four hundred cassettes, including more than fifty hours of music; musical and other videos; and other materials collected by anthropologists Roger M. Keesing and David Akin. The Melanesian Resource Center at the University of California in San Diego (see below), where copies of these materials will be held, is aiding the project. Kwaio chiefs will control access to the materials in the National Museum.

The center sponsors or supervises many cultural activities. Musical classes taught at the center have included making and playing panpipes and other flutes, dancing, and playing the center's set of eight log idiophones (*baleeo'o'o*), instruments which men holding a short stick in each hand traditionally struck to convey signals and accompany dancing. The center is planning eighteen courses to be taught by local musicians and artisans. Ten of the courses will relate to music, including the making and playing of instruments, singing, and dancing. To aid this effort, the Peace Corps has agreed to place volunteers at the center.

Kwaio Arts, one of the center's main cultural projects during the 1980s, encouraged young people to study endangered traditions, including playing indigenous musical instruments and making these instruments for use and sale (figure 5). From 1979 to 1983, marketing these instruments in Honiara earned local artists more than US$30,000. Kwaio musical artifacts are still being made and sold, but the center no longer organizes their sale.

During the early 1980s, the center was funded by the Peace Corps, the Organization for International Development Cooperation (Netherlands), and Freedom from Hunger (Australia). In 1996, the center received grants from the Pacific Development and Conservation Trust (Aotearoa) and the South Pacific Cultures Fund (Australia). Designed to serve local people, the center is unprepared to host visitors, but researchers receiving the center's written permission can access the center's materials in the National Museum.                                          —DAVID AKIN

### New Caledonia

New Caledonia has three official institutions that archive books, documents, recorded music, and films on local subjects: the **Territorial Museum** (Musée Territorial de Nouvelle-Calédonie), the **Agence de Développement de la Culture Kanak** (ADCK), and the **Territorial Archives** (Archives Territorials), all in Nouméa. The archives' collections hold many books and documents on Kanak culture, but only the museum and the ADCK hold important musical recordings, videos, 16-millimeter films, and musical instruments. The museum and the ADCK cooperate closely. Each borrows and archives items belonging to the other.

A showcase with a small selection of musical instruments stands on permanent exhibit in the museum. A bamboo-tube stamper and paired bark clappers from Grande Terre, with a leaf parcel from the Loyalty islands, represent local idiophones. A small panpipe, a Kanak flute, and a coconut-palm leaf represent the aerophones. In the 1990s, more numerous Kanak musical instruments were collected by Raymond Ammann. They are designated to be on exhibit in the ADCK's Jean Marie Tjibaou Cultural Center (Centre Culturel Jean Marie Tjibaou).

The ADCK holds New Caledonia's most important films, photographs, and musical recordings, and collects ethnographically valuable postcards and photographs. The ADCK and museum's photographer, David Becker, has taken thousands of photos documenting contemporary Kanak life, including performances of music and dance. One of his projects is a photo exhibition that will occur in a hundred years. In the interim, the negatives will be stored in the archives.

The ADCK and the museum collect old films and copies of old films dealing with New Caledonia's people. In the 1980s, the ADCK (then still named Office Culturelle) began producing films, first with 16-millimeter equipment, and since 1991 with video cameras. In a workshop in 1991, young Kanak learned to produce documentary films. Each year thereafter, the ADCK has released several films on local subjects. Later films have been coproduced and broadcast by RFO. Public audiences can see them in the ADCK's media center (*médiathèque*). The ADCK's video collection includes about thirty films of Kanak dances.

The ADCK collects recordings of speech and music. It holds copies of important musical recordings made by Marie-Joseph Dubois between 1943 and 1967 on Maré. The Territorial Museum houses recordings made by Maurice Leenhardt in the 1930s and 1940s in Ajië (Houaïlou area, central Grande Terre). In the 1980s, Jean-Michel Beaudet recorded singing and dance-music, mainly on Grande Terre. In the 1990s, Raymond Ammann recorded music on Grande Terre and in the Loyalty Islands. The ADCK collects commercial recordings of *kaneka*, popular Kanak music. All recordings are accessible to the public. On school-free days, young Kanak crowd the media center to watch videos of *kaneka* concerts and listen to newly released *kaneka* cassettes. To ease the search for specific recordings and reduce storage space, the ADCK is copying its sound-archive items onto compact discs.

—RAYMOND AMMANN

## Vanuatu

The audiovisual collections of the **Vanuatu Cultural Centre** include about twenty-five hundred hours each of audiotape and videotape, twenty-five hours each of 16- and 8-millimeter film, copies of the earliest recordings and movies made in the country, three thousand black-and-white photos taken before 1960, four thousand color slides and negatives, and some black-and-white negatives taken since 1977.

In 1976, with financial assistance from UNESCO and the South Pacific Commission, Peter Crowe began the center's Oral Traditions Collection Project in Ambae and Maewo, aided for six months by Jean-Michel Charpentier from the Cultural Centre in Vila. From 1977, the project continued, subsidized since 1980 by the Australian government's South Pacific Cultures Fund. By late 1977, two local workers were documenting their own cultural areas. By 1995, forty-eight volunteers were working on the project.

The project aims to preserve, promote, and develop the country's cultural heritage. The center's paramount goal is to amass customary resources to serve the needs of future generations. On request, if holders of the traditional copyright grant permission, outsiders may use particular items for promotion, study, or display, but the collection's development is geared toward Ni-Vanuatu. For curricular use, the center's workers are producing dictionaries of their languages (under Darrell Tryon's direction), ethnographies of their cultures, and transcriptions of their myths, legends, and histories. From recordings, staffers regularly produce and broadcast programs, introduced in Bislama.

The center began videotaping in 1984. Until then, it used 8-millimeter film. Highlights of the center's collections are:

- Peter Crowe's films of rituals, graded ceremonies, and drinking kava on Ambae, 1976–1977.

- James Gwero's films of graded rituals, funerary rituals, gardening, and mat-work on West Ambae, 1977–1984.
- Kaindum Baiagk Atis's silent films of Nalawan and yam-exchange rituals in Southwest Bay, Malakula; and female tooth-evulsion rituals in South-Central Malakula, 1980–1981.
- Walter Bebe's films of land diving in South Pentecost, 1979–1982.
- Jack Keitadi's documentation of graded rituals and flute music in central Pentecost; films on Tanna, and reef fishing on Anatom, 1984–1987.
- Kirk Huffman's films on South and Southwest Malakula Nalawan and female graded rituals and South-Central Malakula (Small Nambas) funerary rituals; sand drawing, gradetaking, and sacred men's hut opening on West and North Ambrym; land diving in South Pentecost; music and ritual in custom areas of Tanna, 1977–1989.
- Vianney Atpatoun's films and videos on pottery of the West Coast of Santo; launching canoes, carving log idiophones, initiation, and gradetaking in Vao; graded rituals of the Big Nambas of Northwest Malakula; postinitiatory rituals and gradetaking of the Small Nambas of South-Central Malakula; land diving in South Pentecost; the Malakula Arts Festival; rituals on Tanna, 1980–1996.
- Alben Reuben and James Teslo's videos of Nalawan rituals of Southwest and South Malakula; initiation, marriage, graded, and funerary rituals of the Small Nambas, 1986–1995.
- Jacob Sam's videos on ritual, cultural, and historical material throughout Vanuatu, 1986–1996.
- Hardy Ligo's firewalking- and jumping-ritual video, South Santo, 1994.

Taboo material is restricted. Certain performers allow videotaping only if the center agrees not to let the public view the tapes; others restrict viewing to members of the same sex as the performers. Rights to videos of certain rituals belong to traditional sponsors or owners. The public may freely view other material.

Videotape has served practical uses in the process of cultural revival. Sponsors of a ritual may try to guarantee a performance so accurate as not to offend ancestral spirits, and video provides a means of checking performances. At least twice when ritual leaders viewed a video, they noticed unacceptable deviations—and fined, in pigs, the mistaken performers.

### Ongoing work

The center's urgent work is to film complete events, not to produce edited versions. Local viewers usually want to watch the record of a whole ritual. They can thus monitor its exchange-payment content, including how many taros, yams, kava roots, mats, and pigs were exchanged and how many pigs were killed. Vianney Atpatoun's twelve hours of video of a ritual held at Norohure on Vao in February 1986 is typical of the center's videos, as are his twenty-five hours covering the Malakula Arts Festival of 1985 and twenty-two hours covering the National Arts Festival of 1991. Jacob Sam, head of the center's National Film Unit, coordinates filming, chooses and edits sequences for Vanuatu TV (introduced in 1992), and copies material for safety and storage.

Audiovisual documentation enables viewers to appreciate singing, instrumental playing, dancing, and bodily painting. "Art" (for which Ni-Vanuatu languages have no term) is not just the material objects found in museums, or the masks and drums used in rituals: it is the living complex of ceremonial life. Tanna Island, though deemphasizing material arts, is yet, with vibrant cycles of songs and dances, one of the artistically richest islands of the country. Looking at collections in museums abroad, and trudging around the islands showing copies of early photographs and films, proved that, though much has disappeared, much has survived, and much more will reawaken. For an interlinked series of cultures, collections and audiovisual documents represent particular points on a timeline, which shifts and flows, as in the rest of the world.

Ni-Vanuatu highly value the collections of their art and culture in museums overseas. Since much of their material art is fragile, made for a single performance, they know that time, work, money, and luck have enabled the preservation of these collections, which they hope to use to stimulate cultural continuity and renewal.

—KIRK HUFFMAN

## Micronesia

Archives in Micronesia hold none of the original cylinders of the earliest recordings made in the islands. Some dubbings (in useful contemporary formats) of extant recordings made by foreigners during the colonial period and housed in foreign institutions have been repatriated. In preparation for self-rule, politicians gave higher priority to economic, educational, medical, and political development than to conservation of traditional culture as documented on materials such as magnetic tapes, whose preservation requires special storage facilities to minimize climatic effects, and whose use requires special equipment.

Three archives with important collections of recordings of Micronesian cultures, including the performing arts, are components of museums devoted primarily to local cultures (Cohen 1993). The **Belau National Museum Research Library** (P.O. Box 666, Koror, Palau 96940) keeps locally made audio and video recordings among its resources for museum functions, governmental agencies, citizens, and visitors. Its collection of traditional Palauan musics was expanded in 1994 by Osamu Yamaguti's gift of a copy of the collection of audiotapes which he recorded during ethnomusicological research in Palau in 1965–1966. The **Kosrae State Museum Archives** (P.O. Box AD, Kosrae, FSM 96944), established to document Kosraean culture, has a small but important collection of audiotapes and videotapes of recent performances of Kosraean music and dance. The **Alele Museum** (P.O. Box 629, Majuro, Marshall Islands 96960), as part of its mission to preserve the history and conserve the traditional arts and skills of the Marshallese people, records Marshallese oral history and performing arts. The archive of audio and video recordings—in Micronesia, the most extensive collection of ethnographic materials in this form—includes recordings of music and dance, appropriately documented, catalogued, and housed. They were the initial resource for the project on Marshallese music of the Territorial Survey of Oceanic Music (conducted by Mary E. Lawson Burke and museum staff in 1988), which, in turn, yielded new recordings for the collection. Some archived materials are used for the museum's regular broadcasts about Marshallese culture.

Governmental archives are primarily repositories for proceedings of official meetings, periodic reports by government administrators, and so on, but some departments have audiotapes or videotapes. The **Office of Public Information** of the Federated States of Micronesia (P.O. Box 34, Palikir, Pohnpei, FSM 96941) has an extensive collection of videotapes of official governmental functions (including inaugurations and visitations to outer islands), with footage of dances performed at, and significant to, those occasions. The **Kiribati Ministry of Education** (P.O. Box 263, Tarawa, Kiribati) has a small collection of videotapes of cultural performances.

Some local radio stations, and increasingly TV stations, have valuable material. In the late 1960s, **WSZA-Radio** in Yap (Colonia, Yap, FSM 96943) began recording performances of traditional Yapese music and dance at civic functions and events, including intervillage feasts. Its collection is catalogued. The station receives cassettes recorded by local pop-music bands eager to have their performances broadcast.

Two major research institutions maintain collections of audio and audiovisual materials. The **Micronesia Seminar Library** (formerly in Chuuk; now P.O. Box 160, Kolonia, Pohnpei, FSM 96941) supports research and the work of the Roman Catholic Church in Micronesia, especially in the diocese of the Caroline Islands. It holds rare early documents relating to missionization. The **Micronesian Area Research Center** (University of Guam, UOG Station, Mangilao, Guam 96923) has a large collection of printed materials and an extensive photo collection, and translates and publishes old materials and current research.

## Fiji

The **Fiji Museum** (P.O. Box 2023, Suva, Fiji) holds about four hundred cassettes of oral history and music, including copies of collections made by Bruce Biggs, Paul Geraghty, Chris Saumaiwai and Vula Saumaiwai, and Saimoni Vater, head of the project for recording oral histories from 1976 to 1978 (Vater 1977). The **Pacific Collection** of the library of the University of the South Pacific (P.O. Box 1168, Suva, Fiji; http://www.usp.ac.fj) holds about fifty-five thousand volumes of books, periodicals, theses, conference proceedings, and South Pacific Commision papers, including more than three hundred videos, many made by USP's Media Centre. It holds copies of tape recordings and their documentation made by David Fanshawe in the Pacific Islands beginning in 1978.     —BARBARA B. SMITH

## Hawai'i

The state of Hawai'i has major library, archival, and audiovisual resources in public collections. Important materials remain in private hands. Most collections emphasize Hawaiian history and culture, but the collections of the Bernice Pauahi Bishop Museum Library and Archives and the University of Hawai'i Library are important for the study of Oceanic music and dance.

### Bernice Pauahi Bishop Museum

Founded by Charles Reed Bishop in memory of his wife, **Bishop Museum** (1525 Bernice Street, Honolulu HI 96817; www.bishop.hawaii.org) played a major role in Oceanic scientific research from 1900 to 1930 (figure 6), when interest in indigenous cultures stimulated discovery, exploration, and documentation, and the museum stated its focus to be subjects of "Polynesian and kindred antiquities, ethnology, and natural history." Accordingly, early research and expeditions sponsored by the museum targeted Polynesian cultures and traditions.

Key resources documenting Oceanic music in the Bishop Museum Archives are an audio collection (nearly seven thousand items), a manuscript collection (about 30 cubic meters), historical photographs (one million images), and a motion-picture collection (more than a thousand titles). The archives houses the museum's records, reflecting the museum's history and involvement in Oceanic research.

Among the earliest recordings at the museum are those made by staff and associates who recorded indigenous music. Helen H. Roberts received funding from the territorial government and worked with the museum to document Hawaiian songs. In 1923–1924, she recorded *mele,* on paper and on cylinder, mostly from elderly performers. She published (1926) some of her findings. Much later, to acknowledge the Hawaiians who had contributed songs and honor the hundredth anniversary of the birth of Mary Kawena Pukui (who had translated the texts into English), the museum published *Nā Mele Welo: Songs of Our Heritage* (Bacon and Napoka 1995). In 1933, the museum sponsored the recording, in written and audio forms, of singing

FIGURE 6    In Honolulu, the Bernice Pauahi Bishop Museum, built in 1889 in Richardsonian romanesque style, houses important collections of cultural material of the Pacific Islands. Photo by Adrienne L. Kaeppler, 1996.

by J. P. K. Kuluwaimaka, who had performed for Hawaiian royalty during the late 1800s (Tatar 1980, 1982, 1993). In the 1930s, Vivienne Huapala Mader studied music and dance with respected Hawaiian teachers. In 1981, her collection—artifacts, costumes, films, recordings, manuscripts, photographs—-was presented by her son to Bishop Museum (Tatar 1984).

Outside Hawai'i, staffers continued this collecting, first in Polynesia and then farther afield. Wax cylinders and notes documented music and stories. Recordings of this period include the music and songs of Tahiti, recorded by E. S. Craighill Handy, 1921 and 1923 (Handy and Winne 1925); the Austral Islands, recorded by Robert T. Aitken, Bayard Dominick Expedition, 1922; the Austral Islands, recorded by John F. G. Stokes, 1924 and 1925; Tuamotu, recorded by Kenneth P. Emory and J. Frank Stimson, Tuamotu Expedition, 1929–1930 (Emory 1976) and Mangareva Expedition, 1934; and a Tahitian performance in Honolulu, recorded by Kenneth P. Emory, 1938 (figure 7). Stimson's recordings in the Tuamotus included important performances covering "a wide field: religious, epic, lyric and ethnologic" (Bishop Museum 1930). Other archived recordings from this period include dance-songs of the Gilbert Islands (1924), and songs of 'Uvea and Futuna (Burrows 1945). Polynesians of Kapingamarangi were recorded in 1947 by Emory and Te Rangi Hiroa (Sir Peter H. Buck).

In 1935, the museum participated in the Micronesian Expedition, for which Iwakichi Muranushi served as ethnologist. An outstanding product of this expedition is the Muranushi collection of Micronesian music, captured on about forty cylinder recordings, from which a cassette, *Call of the Morning Bird* (1985) was compiled. The audio collection has grown with later additions, including important collections by Bengt Danielsson, Raroia, 1952, and Tahiti, 1953; Jack Ward, Society Islands, 1959; R. K. Johnson, Tuamotus and Marquesas, 1960; Yosihiko Sinoto, Society Islands, 1960–1962; Adrienne L. Kaeppler, Tonga, 1964–1969; Vern Williams, Sāmoa, 1967–1972; Adrienne L. Kaeppler and Kenneth P. Emory, Tuamotu, 1976.

*Other resources within the museum*

Recordings at Bishop Museum include important interviews of Hawaiian people, recorded from 1950 through the mid-1960s. These interviews, some in Hawaiian, document traditions. Many discuss music. Most were conducted by Mary Kawena

FIGURE 7    On a boat with Honolulu's Diamond Head in the background, Kenneth P. Emory (squatting) interviews Tahitian musicians singing and playing a guitar and a small log idiophone. Photo Bishop Museum, 1938.

Pukui, who provided recordings of songs she had known as a child. More than twelve thousand Hawaiian musical texts in the archives' manuscript collection, indexed primarily by Pat Namaka Bacon, are accessible electronically.

The archives includes numerous collections of photographs relevant to research on music and dance. Another visual resource is the moving-image collection, spanning the 1920s through the 1970s and including important films on Oceanic music, especially of Hawai'i and Tahiti. The museum has early artworks and documentation of ceremonies, music, and dance recorded by artists on early Pacific voyages and expeditions during the 1700s and 1800s.

The museum supports research in Oceanic music by making documentation available. Inquiries received through mail, E-mail, phone, and fax are handled by departmental archivists. Copies of most archived items can be requested. In 1992, to ease search and access to the collections, the archives set up a cataloguing program through the Colorado Alliance of Research Libraries (uhcarl.lib@hawaii.edu). The program catalogs published materials, manuscripts, recorded interviews, and visual images, and indexes Hawaiian songs.                —BETTY KAM

### University of Hawai'i

The **Pacific Collection of the University of Hawai'i Library** (2550 The Mall, Honolulu HI 96822) houses materials relating to New Guinea, Melanesia, Micronesia, and Polynesia. Its holdings include about eighty thousand books, twelve hundred serials, thirty-three newspapers currently being published in Oceania, more than twelve thousand reels of microfilm, and four hundred videotapes. Its acquisitions comprehensively cover written material in any format or language that relates to the Pacific Islands. Holdings include a copy of the archives of the U.S. Trust Territory of Micronesia: 2,169 reels of documents on microfilm and fifty thousand photographs. A founding member of the Pacific Manuscripts Bureau, the library is a depository for publications of the South Pacific Commission.

The Pacific Collection houses copies of most published materials relating to music in the Pacific Islands: monographs, theses and dissertations, conference papers, and reprints of journal articles. Nearly all relevant periodicals published in Oceania are present in the collection. For articles on Oceanic music in U.S. and international journals, the holdings of the general collections (in 1997, 2.8 million volumes and thirty thousand serials) and the music collection in Sinclair Library provide access.

The library's periodical index for Oceania, the Hawaii and Pacific Journal Index, offers a keyword search of titles of periodical articles. The index is available on UHCARL, the library's catalog system, via the internet and the CARL network.

*Other resources within the university*

More than five hundred archived recordings of Oceanic music are housed in the library's **Wong Audiovisual Center**; most are cassettes of popular music produced in Oceania since the mid-1960s. The library tries hard to acquire videotapes from and about Oceania. Many of these resources, with films of the Pacific Festivals of Art, show dance and music.

The library's **Hawaiian Collection** has extensive holdings on all aspects of Hawaiian history and culture. These include a computerized sheet-music index covering Hawaiian-related holdings in the Bishop Museum, the Hawai'i State Library, and the university, and typewritten indexes of Hawaiian musical repertories in published songbooks and Protestant hymnals. The library's audiovisual holdings of Hawaiian music and dance are comprehensive. The library acquires copies of televised programs and live broadcasts of hula competitions (Minatodani 1994). Contents of the two largest such events—the Merrie Monarch and King Kamehameha hula competitions—have been indexed (Stillman 1996).

In the Music Department (2411 Dole Street, Honolulu HI 96822; www2.hawaii.edu/~uhmmusic), the **Hawai'i Archives of Ethnic Music and Dance** holds Oceanic material including more than 250 commercial disc recordings of Hawaiian musics and three hundred of other Pacific Islands musics; fifty commercial cassettes; 150 open-reel and cassette recordings resulting from research projects done by students and faculty, especially in Polynesia and Micronesia; dubbings of audio collections held elsewhere; fifty videotapes and films of local and overseas performances; students' research papers from 1962 and later; and programs and other printed materials.

At the School of Hawaiian, Asian & Pacific Studies (315 Moore Hall, 1890 East–West Road, Honolulu HI 96822; www2.hawaii.edu/shaps/index/html), the **Center for Pacific Islands Studies** coordinates many of the university's Pacific-related activities, including publishing and degree-granting programs, and projects cosponsored with the Pacific Islands Development Program at the East–West Center. "Moving Images of the Pacific" (www2.hawaii.edu/oceanic/film) is the center's searchable guide to more than 1,700 films and videos about the Pacific Islands, including music and dance.     —KAREN PEACOCK

### Institute for Polynesian Studies

The **Institute for Polynesian Studies** (Box 1997, Brigham Young University, Lā'ie HI 96762) has been in existence since 1959, when, to preserve the cultures of Oceania while providing employment for students, Jerry Loveland and other faculty members of Church College of Hawaii, now Brigham Young University–Hawai'i Campus, organized the Polynesian Institute. One of the institute's first functions was to transport students to Honolulu and other cities in O'ahu so they could perform there.

The keystone of the institute is an interdisciplinary journal, *Pacific Studies,* which began publishing in 1977. The journal often prints articles on the arts. Of note was an issue on the arts and politics in Oceania (December 1992), in which fifteen scholars explored relationships among politics, dance, drama, and visual arts. The institute has produced pamphlets and other publications on music and dance. Its other activities include supporting research, conferences, and visual documentation.

Since 1992, the institute has sponsored student-faculty research groups. In 1994, one of these groups produced a special issue of the journal *Social Process in Hawaii,* on Pacific Islanders in Hawai'i. In 1995, the same group produced *Pacific Islander Americans: An Annotated Bibliography in the Social Sciences,* by Blossom Fonoimoana, Karina Kahananui Green, David Hall, Dorri Nautu, Tupou Hopoate Pau'u, Paul R. Spickard, John Westerlund, and Debbie Hippolite Wright.

In 1995, the institute formed an advisory board of fellows, drawn from faculty and administrators at Brigham Young University–Hawaii Campus and the Polynesian Cultural Center. The first fellows were Robert Akoi, Jr., Logoitino Vaovai Apelu, Jeffrey Belnap, Cy M. Bridges, 'Inoke F. Funaki, Pulefanolefalasa F. Galea'i, A. LaMoyne Garside, Jon Tikivanotau Michael Jonassen, Raymond T. Mariteragi, Riley Moffat, Mele Nunia Ongoongotau, Dale B. Robertson, Paul R. Spickard, Max E. Stanton, Inoke Seru Suruturaga, William Kauaiwiulaokalani Wallace III (chair), Vernice Wineera (director of the institute), and Debbie Hippolite Wright.

### Polynesian Cultural Center

The **Polynesian Cultural Center** (55–370 Kamahameha Highway, Lā'ie HI 96762; www.polynesia.com) was created in 1962 to provide employment for students enrolled in Brigham Young University–Hawai'i Campus and preserve the cultures of Polynesia (figure 8). About six hundred students work at the center, demonstrating artistic and cultural activities. More than twenty-five thousand students have worked there.

On about 17 hectares of land, the center features representations of villages in Aotearoa, Fiji, Hawai'i, the Marquesas, Sāmoa, Tahiti, and Tonga. It has an IMAX theater, a museum, shopping areas, and two halls for performances. Shows occur several times daily. The evening show features about a hundred performers presenting Polynesian music and dances. The center provides an educational service to the state of Hawai'i: each year, about thirty-five thousand children from schools and other organizations visit to participate in special cultural activities. The center is the major financial contributor to the Institute for Polynesian Studies. —DALE B. ROBERTSON

### Aotearoa

The **Archive of Maori and Pacific Music** (Anthropology Department, University of Auckland, Private Bag 92019, Auckland 1, New Zealand; www.auckland.ac.nz/ant/archived.htm), conceived as a national resource to serve Māori and other indigenous peoples of Oceania, was established in the Department of Anthropology, University

FIGURE 8 Students from the Society Islands perform a Tahitian *'ōte'a* at the Polynesian Cultural Center. Photo by Adrienne L. Kaeppler, 1964.

of Auckland, in 1970. The planning committee included representatives from the Māori Affairs Department, the New Zealand Broadcasting Service, the Dominion Museum, Otago University, the University of Auckland, and the University of Waikato.

The archive initially aimed to encourage the collection of Māori music, develop a comprehensive collection of Oceanic musics by acquisition and exchange with other archives and institutions, catalog Māori and Pacific recorded music, sponsor and support musical research in Aotearoa and elsewhere in the Pacific, and assist Māori who wanted to use recordings to learn Māori music. The archive's initial collection consisted mainly of Māori data, including oral traditions and linguistic material from the university's Department of Anthropology, and more than a thousand items of music recorded by Mervyn McLean. Subsequent Māori resources include recordings from the Maori Purposes Fund Board and wax-cylinder recordings from the National Museum.

The archive has become a repository for collections made during musical research outside Aotearoa, in open-reel and cassette formats. Among these collections are Vida Chenoweth's recordings of the Usarufa of Papua New Guinea; Peter Crowe's recordings from Vanuatu; Mervyn McLean's, Kevin Salisbury's, and Helen Reeves Lawrence's recordings from the Cook Islands; Richard Moyle's recordings from Sāmoa, Tonga, and the Lau Islands; and Amy Stillman's recordings from the Society Islands. The archive's visual resources include photographs, films, and videotapes, in various formats. Highlights include films of the second Pacific Festival of Arts.

### Territorial Surveys

To document traditional musics, the archive entered into an association with the New Zealand National Commission for UNESCO to administer the Territorial Survey of Oceanic Music, funded by UNESCO and the Institute for Polynesian Studies at Brigham Young University, Hawai'i. The purpose of the survey was to sponsor short-term research, mainly in undocumented areas of Oceania.

Researchers for the survey are affiliated with a local academic institution or cultural center. They ideally work with a local person, who gains experience in documentary techniques. The original recordings or dubbed copies are housed at the archive; copies of the archival recordings are to be disseminated to the sponsoring institutions, and especially within Oceania to relevant museums and cultural centers, and are to be available for broadcast and academic use.

Researchers try to record representative samples of all locally extant kinds of singing and instrumental playing. On finishing fieldwork, each researcher submits a report describing the findings, and compiles a sample tape of musical genres and styles, to be available from the archive on request. At least a dozen surveys, ten of which cover Polynesian cultures, have been completed:

- Niue: Richard Moyle, with Mrs. D. Puheketama (in Auckland) and Mrs. E. F. Talagi (on Niue); September to November 1984
- Northern Cook Islands (Penrhyn and Manihiki): Richard Moyle, with Tony Tauraki; eight weeks in fall 1985
- Austral Islands (Tubua'i): Amy Stillman, with Michel Yieng Kow; August 1985
- Mangareva: Amy Stillman, with Monica Paheo; September and October 1985
- Fiji (Kadavu, Taveuni): David Goldsworthy with Mali Tugota; 1986
- Tokelau: Allan Thomas, with Kotelano Kele (on Nukunonu) and Ineleo Tuia (in Wellington); September and October 1986

- Marshall Islands: Mary E. Lawson Burke, with the Alele Museum, 1988
- Southern Cook Islands (Mauke, Mitiaro, Atiu): Jenny Little, with Nga Foster, Teiroa Makara, and No'oroa Teio; April to September 1988
- Southeast New Britain (Lote of Uvol, Mengen of Jacquinot Bay): Wolfgang Laade; August to October 1988
- Marquesas Islands: Jane Freeman Moulin, with Robert Te'ikitautua LeBronnec (on Hiva'oa and Tahuata) and Paloma Gilmore Ihopu (on Fatuiva); June to August 1989
- West Futuna: Allan Thomas, with Takaroga Kuautoga; August to September 1990
- Takuu: Richard Moyle, September to October 1994

The dissemination of researchers' reports was initially carried out by the **Department of Anthropology** (University of Auckland, Private Bag 92019, Auckland 1, New Zealand), in the series Working Papers in Anthropology, Archaeology, Linguistics, Maori Studies, which included reports for surveys on Niue (number 67), the Northern Cook Islands (70), Mangareva (78), Tokelau (79), and the Southern Cook Islands (80). In 1991, the archive launched its own series, Occasional Papers in Pacific Ethnomusicology. Reports from surveys on West Futuna, the Marquesas Islands, and Takuu have been issued as numbers 2, 3, and 5, respectively.                                          —AMY KU'ULEIALOHA STILLMAN

### Other resources

The **National Library of New Zealand, Te Puna Mātauranga o Aotearoa** (P.O. Box 1467, Wellington, New Zealand; www.natlib.govt.nz), holds the world's largest collection of printed Māori material. The **Alexander Turnbull Library** (P.O. Box 12-349, Wellington, New Zealand), opened in 1920 and a component of the National Library since 1966, houses the national documentary collection relating to Aotearoa and the Pacific (Barrowman 1995). It holds nearly three hundred thousand books, 1.65 million photos, and about twenty-five thousand disks, tapes, and cassettes. Its **Oral History Centre** promotes the recording of oral histories of Māori and Pacific Islanders throughout the country. The library's **Archive of New Zealand Music** collects printed matter, manuscripts, recordings, photos, and other items relating to classical, band, jazz, country, popular, rock, and Māori music. It holds Aotearoa composers' scores and papers, documents of the Composers' Association of New Zealand and the New Zealand Opera Company, and recordings of the Concert FM New Zealand Composer Tape Archive. A computerized system catalogs many unpublished materials. The library is publishing CDs of its archived historic musical recordings. At the University of Canterbury, the **Macmillan Brown Library** (http://library.canterbury.ac.nz/mb/mb.htm) holds manuscripts, photos, maps, cassettes, videotapes, and ninety thousand published items of Aotearoa and Pacific Island material. In Wellington, the **Museum of New Zealand, Te Papa Tongarewa** (www.tepapa.govt.nz), has sixteen thousand Māori artifacts, the largest such collection in the country. These artifacts include musical instruments and costumes.
                                                                        —J. W. LOVE

## ARCHIVES AND MUSEUMS IN NORTH AMERICA

Institutions in North America do not focus on Oceania, yet many have collections useful for the study of Oceanic music, and most large U.S. museums house musical instruments from Oceania (Kaeppler and Stillman 1985). These include the Smithsonian Institution (Washington, D.C.), the Field Museum (Chicago), the American Museum of Natural History (New York), and the Peabody museums at

Harvard and Yale universities and in Salem, Massachusetts. Of note is the Department of Musical Instruments at the Metropolitan Museum of Art (New York), housing the Crosby Brown Collection, which includes musical instruments from Oceania.

Musical treasures exist in unexpected places. The Martin and Osa Johnson Safari Museum (Chanute, Kansas) includes film footage made by the Johnsons' expeditions to Melanesia. The Vanderbilt Museum (Centerport, New York) houses film footage made by the Vanderbilt family in the 1920s. Laura Boulton's recordings are housed at Columbia University and the Library of Congress, her film footage is in the Human Studies Film Archive at the Smithsonian, and her musical instruments are in the Mathers Museum, University of Indiana (Bloomington). Materials about the films of Robert J. Flaherty are in the Special Collections, Columbia University Libraries ("Ninety-Two Boxes" 1995). The Sāmoan photographs of Frances Hubbard Flaherty and other Flaherty materials are in the Robert and Frances Flaherty Study Center in Claremont, California (Mesenholler and Nordstrom 1995). Margaret Mead's notebooks, manuscripts, and other memorabilia are in the Library of Congress, and her collection of objects is in the American Museum of Natural History.

—ADRIENNE L. KAEPPLER

## Indiana University

The **Archives of Traditional Music** (Morrison Hall 117 & 120, Indiana University, Bloomington IN 47405-2501; www.indiana.edu/~libarchm), founded at the university by George Herzog in 1948, is the largest university-based archive of ethnographic sounds in the United States. Its houses recordings of music, tales, stories, interviews, oral histories, and languages. These recordings contain more than two hundred thousand hours of sound—on cylinders, wires, open-reel tapes, cassettes (analog and DAT), discs (including CDs), and videotapes. Two temperature- and humidity-controlled storage vaults house these materials, on about 125 square meters of compact shelving.

Collections include manuscripts, transcriptions, correspondence, linguistic files, photographs, slides, and published articles and films. Many collections have come from the collectors, in exchange for high-quality copies. The archives purchases commercial recordings, and receives them through donations or exchange. The catalogued noncommercial collections are in the OCLC database (available through FirstSearch) and accessible through the Internet. The listening library is open to the public five days a week. For about two-thirds of the collection, copies are available for listening; copies of other examples are made on request. Anyone may purchase copies, except of recordings whose use depositors have restricted.

### Oceanic materials

The archives have collections from most areas of Oceania. In addition to several worldwide collections that include Oceanic materials, the archives have about sixty collections devoted exclusively to Oceania, dating from about 1900 on. Major collections that include Oceanic materials are Berlin Phonogramm-Archiv Demonstration Collections, 1900–1913, including 120 cylinders of songs, instrumental music, rites, and ceremonies from Australia, New Guinea, Micronesia, and Sāmoa; the Laura Boulton Collection, including recordings, interviews, and lectures on music and culture from New Guinea, Micronesia, and Polynesia; and the C. F. and F. M. Voegelin Archives of the Languages of the World, containing linguistic materials from most of Oceania, including Australia, New Guinea, the Solomon Islands, Vanuatu, and Polynesia.

Major Oceanic collections from Australia are those by Richard A. Waterman,

1952–1953 (fifty-three reels of Aboriginal songs and music from Arnhem Land); LaMont West, 1964–1965 (137 reels, plus 16-millimeter films of music and linguistic material from northern Queensland); Stephen A. Wild, 1969–1971 (121 reels of performances from Hooker Creek (now Lajamanu), Northern Territory; Adam Kendon, 1981–1985 (sixty-two videos of Aboriginal sign-language, copied from AIATSIS-held originals); and Adrienne L. Kaeppler, 1988 (ten videos from the fifth Festival of Pacific Arts).

From Papua New Guinea, the archives hold major collections by Steven Feld, 1976–1977 (159 reels of Samo music, Kaluli music, oral traditions, and interviews); Douglas Newton, 1967 (nineteen reels of songs, ceremonies, narratives, and instrumental music from East Sepik Province); and Edward Schieffelin, 1966–1968 and 1976 (eighteen reels, primarily of *gisalo,* ceremonial Kaluli music). A major collection from the Solomon Islands is that by Richard Feinberg, 1972–1973 and 1983–1984 (thirty-seven cassettes of music, oral traditions, and interviews from Anuta and other locations, including New Guinea, Guadalcanal, and Polynesia). A major collection from Fiji is that by Dorothy Sara Lee, 1976–1977 and 1982 (eighty-one cassettes and fourteen reels of interviews, poetry, narratives, and other spoken forms from various locations).
—Suzanne Mudge

## University of California at Los Angeles

The **Ethnomusicology Archive** (1630 Schoenberg Hall, Box 951657, Los Angeles CA 90095-1657; www.ethnomusic.ucla.edu/archive) began operating in 1961 under the direction of Ann Briegleb (now Schuursma), who served until 1984. Louise Spear has been the director since 1985. The Department of Ethnomusicology and the UCLA Library fund the archive's activities, which include acquiring and preserving commercial and field recordings and providing reference services and listening facilities. The archive is open to the public Monday through Friday. The archive does not allow copying of commercial recordings. Copies of noncommercial recordings may be purchased, provided the user obtains the collector's permission. The archive has dissertations, books, periodicals, photographs, and copies of academic articles. Most holdings are catalogued in Orion, UCLA's information system.

The archive holds theses and dissertations, seven collections of Oceanic field recordings, 119 LP disks, numerous CDs, and other materials, mostly concerning "traditional" musics. Archived syncretic recordings are notably from Hawai'i and Tahiti. The most extensive field collection is J. W. Love's 1972–1975 recordings of Sāmoan music, consisting of twenty-six reels and 350 pages of documentation. Additional Sāmoan materials include four reels recorded by Raymond Belisle in 1962 and a National Public Radio program on Sāmoan music. Hawaiian recordings include a four-part seminar on Hawaiian dance, taught by Eleanor Williamson and Hoakalei Kamau'u in 1972. The archive has original tapes or dubs of recordings by Bruce Biggs (Māori, 1954–1957), Adrian A. Gerbrands (Asmat, 1962), Raymond Kennedy (Papua New Guinea), the Rev. Louis Luzbetak (Papua New Guinea), Elizabeth May (Australia, 1965), N. R. Nuttycombe (Vanuatu, 1968), and Ray Sheridan (Papua New Guinea), and recordings of lectures by Trevor Jones and Donald Peart (both 1967).

The **Department of World Arts & Cultures** (124 Dance Building, Box 951608, Los Angeles CA 90095-1608; www.arts.ucla.edu) has extensive, fully catalogued video resources covering the Pacific Festivals of Arts in Townsville (1988), Rarotonga (1992), and Sāmoa (1996). Led by Judy Mitoma, then head of the program, student teams recorded, photographed, and videotaped performances of music and dance and other facets of the festivals, including the demonstration of crafts.
—Robert Reigle

## University of California at San Diego

The **Melanesian Archive** (Geisel Library, 0175-R, UCSD, La Jolla CA 92093-1075; http://gort.ucsd.edu/melanesia) collects, preserves, disseminates, and repatriates unpublished materials on the cultures of Melanesia, including New Guinea (Creely 1992). Housed in the Mandeville Special Collections Library, the archive has extensive holdings of anthropological fieldnotes and accompanying materials, such as audiotapes and videotapes. The archive sends libraries in Melanesia microfiched copies of its unpublished materials. UCSD has notable holdings of microform sets of archival materials from other institutions, especially Papua New Guinea patrol reports, missionary documents, and other colonial-era literature. The archive has participated in microfilm-preservation projects, including those of the Pacific Manuscripts Bureau and the Oceania Marist Province Archives.

From Papua New Guinea, the archive houses Mary Clifton Ayres's papers, including recordings of songs, documenting her work from 1979 to 1981 in the Morehead area of Western Province. Also from Western Province are Bruce Knauft's recordings of Gebusi songs, particularly from séance rituals. From the Jimi River area of the Western Highlands, Edwin Cook's papers include recordings of Manga songs. The archive's copies of Stephen Leavitt's recordings from the Bumbita Arapesh, East Sepik, include songs, log-idiophone signals, whistle-talk, and men's-cult sounds. Also from the East Sepik are Anthony Forge's extensive recordings of music of the Abelam, including singing and performing on flutes and kundus. From the Solomon Islands, the archive houses original tapes of every kind of Kwaio music, recorded by David Akin and Roger M. Keesing, and about thirty hours of Akin's Hi8 videos, many of which document Kwaio music and dance. It holds a few other recordings of indigenous music from Malaita and Guadalcanal, and recordings of string-band and guitar songs from the 1960s and 1970s. From Vanuatu, the archive has copies of musical material collected by John Layard in 1914 and 1915 in Malakula, Atchin, and Vao. This material includes manuscript notebooks (annotating songs with words and music) and photos, notes, and other data on log idiophones, dance, and music, particularly in ritual contexts. The archive holds four reel-to-reel tapes of Malakula log-idiophone music made by Raymond Clausen in 1961.

The university has the largest North American collection of monographs, journals, dissertations, and audiovisual materials about Melanesian cultures. Fully catalogued on OCLC and the MELVYL system, these materials are integrated with the general collections of the UCSD libraries. Reference consultations are provided to visitors, as is more limited reference service by E-mail, telephone, and correspondence.

Related collections of published material at UCSD include the **Kenneth E. Hill Collection of Pacific Voyages,** a preeminent collection of early European voyages of discovery and exploration, containing more than two thousand published volumes dating from the 1500s to the mid-1800s. The library of the **Scripps Institution of Oceanography** (http://scilib.ucsd.edu/sio) contains reports of nineteenth- and twentieth-century scientific expeditions to the Pacific. Descriptions of these holdings are accessible on the MELVYL system.

—Kathryn Creely, Amy Ku'uleialoha Stillman

## Smithsonian Institution

### Center for Folklife Programs & Cultural Studies

The **Archive of the Center for Folklife Programs & Cultural Studies** (955 L'Enfant Plaza Suite 2600, Smithsonian Institution MRC 914, Washington DC 20560; www.si.edu/folklife) is staffed by an archivist and an assistant archivist. Except on certain holidays and Folklife Festival periods, it is open from 9:00 A.M. to

5:00 P.M., Mondays through Fridays. Arranging for an appointment ensures needed playback equipment will be reserved.

The archives' holdings fall roughly into two parts. One part is the tapes, other recordings, correspondence, and paper and photographic files of the record companies acquired by the Smithsonian Institution as collections (Cook, Dyer-Bennet, Folkways, Paredon), and kept in print. The center maintains and publishes the files ♦⑨⁻20, 27, 28, 53 of Smithsonian Folkways Recordings. The other major holdings are the audio, film, and video recordings, photographs, and paper files of the Smithsonian Festival of American Folklife, an event held annually on the Mall since 1967. In addition to these, the archive holds individual collections on Oceania.

Among the record-company collections, only Folkways Records has many recordings related to Oceania. Every published Folkways title remains available on cassette and CD. The quality of the recordings and documentation is uneven; the recordings gain significance because of their age. The titles on Smithsonian Folkways Recordings, established in 1988, are more consistently compiled and annotated. At www.si.edu/folkways/start.htm, all thirty thousand items are available for searching—by performer, title, location, and cultural group.

Musicians from Oceania have appeared at several Festivals of American Folklife. The festival recordings of live musical performances are of variable quality, severely affected by the settings—which may make them useful for certain types of research. Of perhaps greater use to researchers are recordings of fieldwork interviews and so-called narrative stages. The fieldwork tapes are usually individual interviews; the narrative stages are usually panel discussions with the performers, often mixing performers from different cultures. The 1988 and 1989 festivals, which featured participants from Hawai'i [see MUSICAL MIGRATIONS, figure 21; EAST POLYNESIA, figure 33], are examples of such contents. In addition to festival performances of music, the narrative stages included the topics "plantation life," "instrument workshop, 'ukulele styles," "preserving, presenting, pretending," and "the sacred, the personal, and the offensive." These are rare recordings of performers talking about what they think and do, comparing their ideas with those of performers from other backgrounds. Each festival is documented with thousands of color slides, but is spottily documented on film and video.

Rights in the center's record-company sounds and texts are governed by contracts with compilers and artists. Participants at the Festival of American Folklife sign releases making their voices and images available for research and education. Commercial use must be cleared with the artists or their heirs. —ANTHONY SEEGER

### Human Studies Film Archives

The **Human Studies Film Archives** (HSFA, Natural History Building, room E307, stop 123, Smithsonian Institution, Washington DC 20560; hsfa@sivm.si.edu) collects, preserves, documents, and disseminates a broad range of ethnographic and anthropological moving-image materials. Located in the Department of Anthropology, National Museum of Natural History, the archives was established in 1981 as a successor to the National Anthropological Film Center, founded in 1975.

The HSFA collection consists of more than 1.8 million meters of motion-picture film and more than five hundred hours of videotape. These resources include edited productions, outtakes, unedited films and videos, professional travelogs, and amateur films. The HSFA emphasizes documentation by acquiring associated texts, tapes, manuscripts, photographs, and synchronous commentaries recorded by the creators.

In 1995, the HSFA published *Guide to the Collections of the Human Studies Film Archives,* commemorating the hundredth anniversary of motion pictures. The guide draws on the HSFA database, which catalogs all films and videos acquired before 1994. The database can be accessed on the internet through the Smithsonian Institution Research Information System (SIRIS), Telnet to siris.si.edu. The HSFA database is located in the Archives and Manuscripts Catalog. The guide can be browsed, searched, or downloaded via the gopher server http://nmnhgoph.si.edu and the site http://nmnhwww.si.edu/departments/anthro.html.

*Oceanic materials*

Many HSFA films and videos on Oceania house sound and silent aspects of music and dance. Highlights among these are:

- *Duke of Edinburgh Culture Festival—Cook Islands, 1978,* a research-film project produced by the National Anthropological Film Center, documenting dances on Aitutaki Atoll during an interisland festival
- *Fourth Pacific Festival of Arts, Tahiti, 1985,* and *Fifth Pacific Festival of Arts, Townsville, Australia, 1988,* video projects by Adrienne L. Kaeppler, including extensive documentation of music and dance
- *Songs from Papua New Guinea, 1982,* film shot by Christopher Roberts, documenting traditional songs from Southern Highlands, Western, and West Sepik provinces
- *Leahy Footage of Papua New Guinea, about 1930–1952,* film shot by Michael Leahy, including singsings in the area of Mount Hagen
- *Film Study of the Lifestyle of the Western Caroline Islands of Micronesia, 1976, 1981–1982,* research-film projects produced by the National Anthropological Film Center, documenting life in villages on Woleai and Ifalik, including dancing
- *Laura Boulton Film Collection: Micronesia, 1976,* documenting dances performed on Palau, Ulithi, and Yap. Other HSFA films overseen by Laura Boulton document music and dance in Papua New Guinea and Sāmoa
- *Fiji War Dance at Beqa, about 1925,* an incomplete copy of an edited film documenting three Fijian dances
- *Hawaiian Hula, 1943,* showing Patience Wiggin (Bacon) performing traditional Hawaiian dances

Reference copies of these and other films and videos can be viewed on the premises of the HSFA at no charge. (Viewing archival original or preservational materials is not allowed.) The HSFA is open from 9 A.M. to 5 P.M. Mondays through Fridays, but an appointment is required, forty-eight or more hours in advance.

—PAMELA WINTLE, DAISY RUSSELL

## Library of Congress

TRACK 2, 9, 32, 40

The **Archive of Folk Culture,** established in 1928 as the Archive of American Folk-Song within the Library of Congress (Washington DC 20540–4610; http://lcweb.loc.gov/folklife), contains ethnographic collections from around the world, including every region and state of the United States. The archive holds more than twenty-five hundred ethnographic collections of traditional music and lore, documenting communities, occupations, and ethnic groups. These collections include about fifty-thousand hours of recordings, five hundred thousand photographs, a million pages of manuscript material, videos, microfilms, and data in other formats.

Of the archive's collections of Oceanic music, the most important are:

FIGURE 9    Vida Chenoweth interviews Taaqiyáa, a contributor of Usarufa music and texts, 1967. American Folklife Center.

- *Peabody Museum–Benjamin Ives Gilman Collection:* seventy- four cylinders recorded at the 1893 World's Columbian Exposition, including thirty cylinders of performances by Fijians, Sāmoans, and 'Uveans
- *H. E. Crampton Collection:* Tahiti, 1906; forty-five cylinders
- *Helen Heffron Roberts Collection:* Hawai'i, 1923; sixty-five cylinders
- *Cornelius Crane Expedition Collection:* mostly in East Sepik Province, but partly in West Sepik and Morobe, Papua New Guinea, 1937; forty-eight cylinders
- *Fahnestock South Sea Collection:* American Sāmoa, Fiji, Marquesas Islands, New Caledonia, Society Islands, 1940–1941; disks, films, manuscripts, photos
- *Laura Boulton Collection* (1960s–1970s): Micronesia, thirty-three tapes; Papua New Guinea, seven tapes; Hawai'i, six tapes
- *Vida Chenoweth Collection:* Usarufa, Papua New Guinea, 1966–1973 (figure 9); fifty-six tapes, five cassettes; additional materials from Vanuatu and elsewhere pending

The archive is accessed through the Folklife Reading Room, open Monday through Friday, 8:30 A.M. to 5 P.M., except on federal holidays. Visitors must present a Library of Congress reader card, which requires valid photo identification. Researchers may contact the archive by phone (202-707-5510), fax (202-707-2076), or E-mail (folklife@loc.gov). Information about certain collections and topics is available via gopher://marvel.loc.gov.    —JUDITH A. GRAY, JOSEPH C. HICKERSON

## ARCHIVES AND MUSEUMS IN EUROPE

Museums in Europe have the oldest collections of musical instruments from the Pacific Islands, acquired during voyages of discovery in the 1700s. European archives have some of the oldest recordings, dating to 1898 in Berlin and 1904 in Vienna. Many photographs survive in European collections (figure 10).

### Berlin: Phonogramm-Archiv

In Berlin, the **Phonogramm-Archiv** holds important historical recordings of Oceanic music. It was founded by physiologist-psychologist Carl Stumpf in 1900. It was first housed in the Psychological Institute, University of Berlin, but later joined the collections of the Museum für Völkerkunde. During World War II, many of its recordings were taken to the Soviet Union, and later to East Germany. With the reunification of Germany, the archive is now being reorganized in the museum.

FIGURE 10    On Weno, Chuuk, standing girls dance. Photo by Elisabeth Krämer, 1909. Institute of Ethnology, University of Tübingen.

Guided by Erich M. von Hornbostel (director, 1905–1933), the archive grew to contain ten thousand wax-cylinder recordings. Its contributors were colonial administrators, scientists, and informed travelers, to whom the archive issued suggestions on what to record and how to go about doing so. On the Nazis' rise to power, Hornbostel left Germany, but the archive's activities continued, first under Marius Schneider (director, 1934–1945), then under Kurt Reinhard (1948–1968), Dieter Christensen (1968–1972), and Artur Simon (since 1972). In 1963, the name of the institution was changed to *Abteilung Musikethnologie*. During the 1960s and 1970s, comprehensive collections of Oceanic music on tape were recorded by Gerd Koch, Artur Simon, and Ekkehard Royl.

Using the archive's recordings, Hornbostel and his students transcribed and published music from around the world. Several of these students became leading researchers. These included George Herzog, who in Berlin studied Micronesian music, and Mieczyslaw Kolinski, who wrote a doctoral dissertation (1930) partly on his transcriptions of Sāmoan recordings in the archive.

### Important Collections

Among the important Oceanic collections in the archive are these, listed by their archival titles, with numbers of cylinders in parentheses:

- Myers Murray Island, 1898, Torres Strait (2)
- Pöch Britisch Neuguinea, 1904–1906 (11 original, 36 copies of cylinders in the Vienna Phonogramarchiv)
- Stephan Melanesien, 1904, Melanesia (15)
- Felix von Luschan, 1905, Australia (5)
- Dempwolff Südsee, 1906 (8), recorded by naval physician Dr. Otto Dempwolff
- Thurnwald Südsee 1906–1910, Melanesia (343)
- Krämer Südsee, 1907 (33), recorded in the Bismarck Archipelago, Yap, and Chuuk for the Hamburg Südsee-Expedition
- Deutsche Marine-Expedition, 1907–1909 (72), recorded by Emil Stephan and Otto Schlaginhaufen in Southeast New Ireland
- Hocart Britisch-Salomonen, 1908 (19), recorded in Roviana, Solomon Islands
- Neuhauss Deutsch-Neuguinea, 1908–1910 (139)
- Winthuis Papua-Neuguinea, 1908–1909 (13)
- Hamburger Südsee-Expedition, 1909 (95), recorded by Müller Wismar in Melanesia, and Ernst Sarfert and Paul Hambruch in Micronesia
- Archiv Samoa, ca. 1910 (6), of two young scholars from Savai'i, recorded in Berlin
- Beagle-Bay-Mission, Northwest Australia, 1910 (31)
- Landtman Britisch-Neuguinea (Kiwai), 1910 (46)
- Moszkowski Holländisch-Neuguinea, 1910 (20), recorded in Irian Jaya
- Solf Samoa, 1910 (6)
- Frizzi Salomonen, 1911 (72)
- Leber Samoa, 1911 (32)
- Börnstein Südsee, 1912–1914 (108), recorded in the Bismarck Archipelago
- Deutsch Neuguinea-Expedition, 1912–1913 (175), recorded along the Kaiserin Augusta River
- Thurnwald Kaiserin-Augusta-Fluss, 1912 (139)
- Leroux Neuguinea, 1926 (16)
- Wirz Neuguinea, 1927 (45)
- Zahn, Neuguinea, 1928–1932 (211)
- Nevermann Neuguinea, 1933–1934 (36), recorded in Grande Terre and the Loyalty Islands, New Caledonia
- Kasprus Nord-Neuguinea, 1934–1938 (44).
- Ernest Worms, northwest Australia, 1937 (12)
- Frobenius-Expedition to northwest Australia, 1938–1939 (70)
- Held Holländisch-Neuguinea, 1939 (18), recorded in Geelvink Bay, Irian Jaya
- Siemer Südsee, 1936 (42), recorded in Palau
- Verschueren Holländisch-Neuguinea, 1936–1937 (24), recorded in Merauke Regency, Irian Jaya
- Kunst Süd-Neuguinea (5)
- Wirz Holländisch-Süd-Neuguinea (34)

Some of these collections include written texts and collectors' remarks.

—SUSANNE ZIEGLER

## Göttingen: Institut für den Wissenschaftlichen Film

In Göttingen, Germany, the **Institut für den Wissenschaftlichen Film** (Institute for Scientific Film, IWF) is the largest handler of scientific films in Europe. It houses more than fifteen hundred ethnographic films. Mainly serving German researchers, it covers multiple academic disciplines. Its department of anthropology, subdivided into divisions of Volkskunde (European ethnology) and Völkerkunde (non-European ethnology), is one of its most productive sections. In 1956, the institute was established with financial support from federal-government sources. Since then, it has assisted scientists in carrying out visual research and documentation by producing, publishing, archiving, and distributing their films. Free of charge, it rents ethnographic films to academic institutions and their staffs.

The IWF holds about 320 films on Oceania, listed in its catalogue *Australia/ Oceania* (published in 1990, supplemented annually). Many of these films, about five to twenty minutes long, focus on material culture. The IWF holds large numbers of films on New Guinea, Kiribati, Tuvalu, and the Solomon Islands. Most of them were produced and are rented as 16-millimeter films, but are available for sale as videos, and include written accounts discussing the filmed ethnic group, the topic, and technical data of the production.

In the 1950s and 1960s, Gerd Koch carried out several expeditions to make ethnographic films in Oceania. He first worked in Tonga, on which IWF has published five of his films, including *Village Life,* a series of three films. In 1960, Koch filmed in Niutao, Ellice Islands. The publication of fifteen films resulted. He then worked in the Gilbert Islands, where he shot seventy films: forty-three on Nonouti, fifteen on Tabiteuea, and twelve on Onotoa. His last expedition, in 1967, was to the Santa Cruz Islands, where he shot seventeen films. Most of his films document material culture, fishing, the production of food, games, and dancing.

For New Guinea, some of the institute's films date back to the early 1900s, but most come from 1975–1976, when IWF participated with German researchers in Irian Jaya. The resulting films—fifty-two on the Eipo, eight on the Fa, six on the Bime—constitute an important body of visual documentation, complementing the other results of the project. IWF films have covered other New Guineans in cooperation with Swiss anthropologists from Basel: Christian Kaumann, Meinhard Schuster, Milan Stanek, and Jürg Wassmann. Made in the 1960s and 1970s, these films show everyday and ritual activities of the Aibom (twenty films), the Iatmul (twenty-nine films), the Kwoma (ten films), the Kwaiut (two films), and the Sawos (five films).

In the 1990s, IWF produced few new films on Oceania. The latest example is *Maire Nui Vaka,* a forty-three-minute video by Gundolf Krüger on the sixth Pacific Festival of Arts, held in 1992 in Rarotonga.    —ROLF HUSMANN

## Vienna: Phonogrammarchiv and other archives

In the Austrian Academy of Sciences, Vienna, the **Phonogrammarchiv** (founded in 1899) holds recordings of Oceanic music, which it makes accessible to the public. These holdings stem from Austrian researchers and others having close contact with the institution. Some of these holdings are a product of chance. Some resulted from researchers' investigative plans. All the acoustic sources, old or new, are accompanied by protocols that contain three sets of information: *personal data,* about the individual or group recorded, the language of vocal pieces, the names of instruments (indigenous and systematic), and the place and date of the recording; *technical data,* about equipment used to make the original recording and equipment by which dubs have been made; and *administrative data,* about authorship, use, restrictions (if any), and archival numbers. Annexed to these data are notes on the content of every item, including title, genre, and performance. The protocols do not contain musical transcriptions. Some include linguistic comments and cultural observations.

For the Phonogrammarchiv, Rudolf Pöch began recording in German New Guinea in 1904. He then worked in British New Guinea—at Cape Nelson in 1905 and Port Moresby in 1906. He recorded music of the Motu, an Austronesian-speaking people, but focused on non-Austronesians, especially the Koitapu and the Monumbo. He obtained songs of Arifamu, Baifa, Hula, Irewowona, Juwo, Karesau, Maisin, Maiwa, Mokuru, Okena, and Suau peoples, and made isolated recordings of Arop, Malol, Oian, Onjob, Tumleo, and Yasiyasi (a tribe at Irewowona) music.

From 1957 to 1973, Walter Graf was director of the archive; from 1963 to 1973, he held the chair of Comparative-Systematic Musicology at the Institute of Musicology, University of Vienna. His student, Gerald Florian Messner, working at the institute from 1973 to 1988, recorded music in Papua New Guinea, assisted by Philip Lamasisi Yayii, a New Irelander. Five published catalogues of the archive's holdings (Exner 1922; *Katalog der Tonbandaufnahmen* 1960, 1966, 1970, 1974) are available.

### Oceanic materials

In chronological order, the following list of the archive's holdings refers to the music of Oceania, defined broadly—the music of Oceanic peoples and that of Oceanic residents of non-Oceanic origin. The collections are identified by collectors' names:

- Rudolf Pöch: expedition to British New Guinea and German New Guinea, 1904–1906. These are the oldest original Oceanic recordings extant in Austria.
- Emil Stephan: expedition to New Britain (Baining people) and New Ireland (King people), 1904. These recordings are copies of originals in the Phonogrammarchiv Berlin.
- Wilhelm Schmidt: 1907, recorded in Vienna; songs of Pritak Mawi, a young Karesau man of East Sepik Province, with texts in Kairiru, an Austronesian language.
- Josef Winthuis: expedition to New Britain, 1908–1909. These recordings are copies of cylinders now in the Phonogramm-Archiv Berlin.
- Friedrich Zander: Māori from Christchurch, Aotearoa; recorded in the archive, 1957.
- Käthe Hye-Kerkdal: a U.S.-born woman of Hawaiian descent; recorded in the archive, 1959.
- Ray Sheridan: recordings in Papua New Guinea, 1962, 1963, 1969. The oldest recordings are of Sio men of Morobe Province. Later recordings include a dance-song (*bot*) of a man from Sosson Island, New Ireland, and a Telefol men's dance-song. Other recordings include men's performances from Rossel Island (Louisiade Archipelago) and a men's dance-song (*sorai*) of Pak Island (Admiralty Islands).
- Hanns Peter and Brigitte Peter: east Papua New Guinea, 1969. The recordings include songs of the Yuri, a non-Austronesian group of the West Sepik.
- Gerald Florian Messner: east Papua New Guinea, 1977. The recordings include music of New Ireland, the Admiralty Islands, and Eastern Highlands Province. Many of the recordings are interviews.
- Károly Gaál and Edith Gaál: expedition to New Zealand (Māori and non-Māori), 1982–1983. The Gaáls studied the lives of Austrian and Hungarian immigrants in Aotearoa, mainly in Christchurch. The recordings are mainly of Austrian mainstream popular music, with participating audiences of

Austrians and their Aotearoa relatives and friends. The Gaáls recorded Christian religious music on the North Island.

The Phonogrammarchiv houses no printed music, written contributions dealing with Oceanic music, or recordings of broadcasts on radio and television. The film *Neuguinea: In Memoriam Prof. Dr. Rudolf Pöch* (1958), using clips made in 1904–1906, is in the holdings of the **Austrian Federal Institute of Scientific Film.** It shows dancing, but has no music.

—HELGA THIEL

## REFERENCES

Akin, David. 1994. "Cultural Education at the Kwaio Cultural Centre." In *Culture, Kastom, Tradition: Developing Cultural Policy in Melanesia,* ed. Lamont Lindstrom and Geoffrey White, 161–172. Suva: Institute of Pacific Studies, University of the South Pacific.

Bacon, Pat Namaka, and Nathan Napoka, ed. 1995. *Nā Mele Welo, Songs of Our Heritage.* Honolulu: Bishop Museum.

Barrowman, Rachel. 1995. *The Turnbull: A Library and Its World.* Auckland: Auckland University Press.

Bishop Museum. 1930. *Report of the Director.* Honolulu: Bishop Museum.

Burrows, Edwin G. 1945. *Songs of Uvea and Futuna.* Bulletin 113. Honolulu: Bishop Museum.

*Call of the Morning Bird: Chants and Songs of Palau, Yap, and Ponape, Collected by Iwakichi Muranushi, 1936.* 1985. Edited by Elizabeth Tatar. Department of Anthropology, Bishop Museum. Cassette.

Cohen, Arlene, ed. 1993. *Directory of Libraries, Archives and Museums in Micronesia.* MARC working paper 59. Mangilao: Micronesian Area Research Center, University of Guam.

Creely, Kathryn. 1992. "Melanesia Studies at the University of California, San Diego." *The Contemporary Pacific* 4:210–214.

Cunningham, Adrian, comp. 1997. *Directory of Libraries and Archives in the Pacific.* Edited by Susan McDougal. Canberra: Australian Library and Information Assocation, National Library of Australia, and APSIG.

Emory, Kenneth P. 1976. "Tuamotuan Chants and Songs from Napuka." *Directions in Pacific Traditional Literature: Essays in Honor of Katharine Luomala,* ed. Adrienne L. Kaeppler and H. Arlo Nimmo, 173–193. Special publication 62. Honolulu: Bishop Museum.

Exner, Sigmund. 1922. *Katalog der Platten 1–2000 des Phonogramm-Archives der Akademie der Wissenschaften in Wien.* Vienna: Phonogramm-Archiv der Akademie der Wissenschaften.

Grainger, Percy. 1909. Letter to Karen Holten, 18 February 1909. Grainger Museum, University of Melbourne.

Handy, Edward S. Craighill, and Willowdean Chatterson Winne. 1925. *Music in the Marquesas Islands.* Bulletin 17. Honolulu: Bishop Museum.

Howard, Gregg. 1996. "An Introduction to the *National Survey of Musical Instruments in Australian Collections* and the *Directory of Australian Collections Holding Musical Instruments.*" *Australasian Music Research* 1:231–325.

Kaeppler, Adrienne L., and Amy Ku'uleialoha Stillman. 1985. *Pacific Island and Australian Aboriginal Artifacts in Public Collections in the United States of America and Canada.* Paris: UNESCO.

*Katalog der Tonbandaufnahmen B1 bis B3000 der Phonogrammarchives der Österreichischen Akademie der Wissenschaften in Wien.* 1960. Vienna: Herman Böhlaus.

*Katalog der Tonbandaufnahmen B3001 bis B7000 der Phonogrammarchives der Österreichischen Akademie der Wissenschaften in Wien.* 1966. Vienna: Herman Böhlaus.

*Katalog der Tonbandaufnahmen B7001 bis B10000 der Phonogrammarchives der Österreichischen Akademie der Wissenschaften in Wien.* 1970. Vienna: Herman Böhlaus.

*Katalog der Tonbandaufnahmen B10001 bis B13000 der Phonogrammarchives der Österreichischen Akademie der Wissenschaften in Wien.* 1974. Vienna: Herman Böhlaus.

Kolinski, Mieczyslaw. 1930. "Die Musik der Primitivstämme auf Malaka und ihre Beziehungen zur samoanischen Musik." *Anthropos* 25:585–648.

Mackay, Ian K. 1976. *Broadcasting in Papua New Guinea.* Melbourne: Melbourne University Press.

Mesenholler, Peter, and Alison Devine Nordstrom. 1995. *Picturing Paradise: Colonial Photography of Samoa, 1875–1925.* Daytona Beach: Daytona Beach Community College.

Minatodani, Dore. 1994. "Videotapes on Hula Available in the Wong Audiovisual Center, Sinclair Library." Typescript. University of Hawai'i.

*Neuguinea: In Memoriam Prof. Dr. Rudolf Pöch.* 1958. Vienna: SHB. Film.

Niles, Don. 1981. "The Music Department of the Institute of Papua New Guinea Studies." *International Association of Sound Archives Phonographic Bulletin* 29(March):33–40.

———. 1992. "Collection, Preservation, and Dissemination: The Institute of Papua New Guinea Studies as the Centre for the Study of All Papua New Guinea Music." In *Music and Dance of Aboriginal Australia and the South Pacific,* ed. Alice Marshall Moyle, 59–75. Sydney: University of Sydney.

"Ninety-Two Boxes (1970)." 1995. *Wide Angle* 17:384–401.

Reeves, Helen. 1982. "A Universalist Outlook: Percy Grainger and the Cultures of Non-Western Societies." *Studies in Music* 16:32–52.

———. 1984. "From the Phonograph Cylinder Collection in the Grainger Museum." *I.A.S.A. Australian Branch Newsletter* 17(July):14–28.

Roberts, Helen H. 1926. *Ancient Hawaiian Music.* Bulletin 29. Honolulu: Bishop Museum.

Stillman, Amy Ku'uleialoha. 1996. "Competition Hula: An Index of Mele and Hālau in the King Kamehameha Hula Competition (1982–1995) and the Merrie Monarch Hula Competition (1980–1995)." Typescript. Pacific Collection, University of Hawai'i Library.

Tatar, Elizabeth. 1980. *Nā Leo Hawai'i Kahiko (Voices of Old Hawai'i).* Bishop Museum Audio-Recording Collection ARCS-1. 2 LP disks.

———. 1982. *Nineteenth Century Hawaiian Chant.* Pacific Anthropological Records, 33. Honolulu: Department of Anthropology, Bishop Museum.

———. 1984. *Ka Pō'e Hula Hawai'i Kahiko: The Hula People of Old Hawai'i.* Honolulu: Department of Anthropology, Bishop Museum.

———. 1993. *Hula Pahu: Hawaiian Drum Dances: Volume 2, The Pahu: Sounds of Power.* Bishop Museum Bulletin in Anthropology, 3. Honolulu: Bishop Museum Press.

Vater, Saimoni, comp. 1977. *Na Veitalanoa me Baleta na i Tukutuku Maroroi* (Talking about oral tradition). Suva: Fiji Museum.

# Recordings of Oceanic Music

*Adrienne L. Kaeppler*     *Peter Russell Crowe*

*J. W. Love*     *Barbara B. Smith*

*Stephen A. Wild*     *Amy Ku'uleialoha Stillman*

*Don Niles*     *Philip Hayward*

**Australia**

**New Guinea**

**Melanesia**

**Micronesia**

**Polynesia**

**Contemporary Cross-Cultural Syntheses**

Most recordings of Oceanic music remain unpublished. These include, beginning in 1893, thousands of wax cylinders, housed mainly in archives around the world. The latest large-scale recording effort is sponsored by UNESCO, which has so far made a dozen territorial surveys [see ARCHIVES AND INSTITUTIONAL RESOURCES: Aotearoa]. Commercial releases include those made and distributed by museums (Basel, Berlin, Paris, Hawai'i), Smithsonian Folkways, the Australian Institute of Aboriginal and Torres Strait Islander Studies, and record companies in Australia and the Pacific Islands. The most prolific LP labels were Hibiscus and Viking. The latter listed more than four hundred albums. An important series derives from the Pacific Festivals of Art, especially the first festival (1972), from which Viking published ten "spectaculars"—LP disks of music by ensembles from the Solomon Islands, Kiribati, Fiji, Tonga, American Sāmoa, Niue, Tuvalu, and the Cook Islands, and a disk of musical highlights of the festival. The sixth festival resulted in the cassette *Visions of the Pacific* (1992), plus a lavishly illustrated coffee-table book and videos.

By the 1950s, radio organizations in several countries had begun recording and archiving indigenous music. In Papua New Guinea, the broadcaster Ray Sheridan (1972) made important musical recordings. In Aotearoa, Māori broadcasters Wiremu Parker and Wiremu Kerekere fostered the recording of Māori music. For radio stations in the 1950s, the South Pacific Commission (1956, 1957, 1959) published catalogs of local music. Many radio stations broadcast traditional music, simultaneously defining and promoting cultural identities. The Australian Broadcasting Corporation (formerly Commission) broadcast the weekly programs "Music Deli," featuring Australian multicultural and indigenous music, and "Away," considering indigenous affairs. The ABC weekly indigenous-oriented TV series "Blackout," which ran for years, often broadcast musical performances. The TV programs "Countdown" and "Rage," featuring Australian popular music, have always included Aboriginal popular music. Aboriginal people now run radio and television stations that serve Aboriginal audiences. In Hawai'i from 1922 on, radio programs have given local music crucial international recognition (Tatar 1979a). In Aotearoa, primarily in Auckland and Wellington, programs of independently produced music target immigrant Pacific Islanders (Mitchell 1994).

With the miniaturization of recording equipment, especially cassette recorders, outsiders who do not ordinarily focus on music—missionaries, administrators, expatriate teachers—have made useful recordings, as have anthropologists, linguists, and other specialists. Some of these recordings have been deposited in the outsiders' home institutions or local archives. Some remain in private hands.

Increasingly, audio materials are available on the internet. An example is "The Keali'i Reichel Songbook" (www.interpac.net/~nahenahe/kealii/songbook). It features a discography of Keali'i Reichel's commercial releases, lyrics of the songs, and sound files, which can be heard on line or downloaded for off-line listening.

Countless tapes, cassettes, and compact discs, produced at varying technical levels, are distributed mainly within Oceanic communities. Because distribution serves limited purposes, the appreciation of Oceanic music depends on being in the right place at the right time. Many recordings are homemade dubs, passed from friend to friend. Other recordings are issued by commercial enterprises. The Central Australian Aboriginal Media Association, established in 1980 in Alice Springs, records and distributes, mostly to Aboriginal markets, cassettes of music created and played by central and northern Australian Aboriginal bands. In Hawai'i, instructors in *hula* studios used recordings issued by 49th State Records (Hopkins 1979). In Vanuatu in the 1980s, expatriates ran studios that produced commercial cassettes of stringband music. The Black Brothers, a band whose members had immigrated from Irian Jaya, operated one such studio. An immigrant from France operated the other.

Specialized audiographies have been published: for Australia, by Alice M. Moyle (1966) and Linda Barwick and Allan Marett (1996); for Papua New Guinea, by Don Niles (1984, 1985, 1987a, 1987b, 1988, 1991, 1992, 1993) and Niles and Clement Gima (1993a, 1993b, 1994); for Hawai'i by Amy Ku'uleialoha Stillman [see ARCHIVES AND INSTITUTIONAL RESOURCES] and Elizabeth Tatar (1979b). For particular regions and styles, critical analyses of Oceanic recordings have appeared in works by Raymond Ammann (1997), Peter Crowe (1995), A. P. Elkin and Trevor A. Jones (1953–1956), Philip Hayward (1996), Alice M. Moyle (1968–1969), and Michael Webb (1993).

—ADRIENNE L. KAEPPLER, J. W. LOVE

## Multicultural recordings

*Australia & New Guinea.* N.d. Recordings by A. P. Elkin, the Australian Broadcasting Commission, and André P. Dupeyrat. Notes by A. P. Elkin and André P Dupeyrat. Columbia World Library of Folk and Primitive Music, compiled and edited by Alan Lomax. Columbia SL-208. LP disk.

*The Gilbert and Ellice Islands Festival Company.* N.d. Hibiscus HLS 49. LP disk.

*Gilbert and Ellice Islands Songs.* N.d. Music from Kiribati and Tuvalu. Viking VE 218. EP disk.

*Gilbert and Ellice Spectacular: Gilbert & Ellice Dance Group.* 1973. Viking VP 365. LP disk.

*Island Music of the South Pacific.* 1981. Recordings and notes by David Fanshawe. Explorer Series. Nonesuch Records H-72088.

*Music of Micronesia: Songs from the Gilbert and Ellice Islands.* N.d. Viking VP 205. LP disk.

*Music of the Orient in Hawaii: Japan / China / Korea/Philippines.* 1963. Recorded by Jacob Feuerring. Folkways FW 8745. LP disk.

*Musical Mariner: Pacific Journey.* 1989. Music of the Highlands Region and Sepik Province of Papua New Guinea, Wagi Brothers Bamboo Band, Solomon Islands, Tahiti, and Rapa Nui. Recordings by David Fanshawe. Compact disc.

*Musics of Hawai'i: "It All Comes from the Heart": An Anthology of Musical Traditions in Hawai'i.* 1994. Folk Arts Program, State Foundation on Culture and Arts. Booklet and five cassettes.

*Puerto Rican Music in Hawai'i: Kachi-Kachi.* 1989. Recordings and notes by Ted Solís. Smithsonian Folkways 40014. Compact disc.

*Puerto Rico in Polynesia: Jíbaro Traditional Music on Hawaiian Plantations.* 1994. Original Music OMDC 020. Compact disc.

Tsounis, Demeter. 1990. *Shoulder to Shoulder.* Greek music in Australia. Adelaide: Multicultural Artworkers Committee of South Australia. Cassette.

*Visions of the Pacific.* 1992. Music at the sixth Pacific Festival of Arts: Papua New Guinea, Guam, Rotuma, Tonga, Tokelau, French Polynesia (Tahiti), Cook Islands, Hawai'i, Aotearoa. Recorded by Te Reo O Aotearoa (Maori and Pacific Islands Programme Unit, Radio New Zealand). Distributed by Ministry of Cultural Development, Rarotonga, Cook Islands. Cassette.

**AUSTRALIA**

Recordings of Australian Aboriginal and Torres Strait Islander music date back to 1899, when the singing of Mrs. Fanny Cockrane Smith, a Tasmanian Aboriginal woman, was recorded on wax cylinders in the rooms of the Royal Society of Tasmania. Recording on cylinders continued until World War II. It produced collections by W. B. Spencer and F. J. Gillen in central Australia (1901); Spencer in northern Australia (1912); A. R. Radcliffe-Brown in northern Western Australia (1912); E. H. Davies in South Australia (1926–1929); H. Basedow in central Australia (1926); W. L. Warner in Milingimbi, Northern Territory (1926–1929); C. W. M. Hart on Bathurst and Melville Islands, Northern Territory (1928–1930); N. B. Tindale in central and southern Australia (1930–1937), western New South Wales (1938), and south-coastal New South Wales (1939); A. P. Elkin in central coast New South Wales (1930); Ursula McConnel in Cape York, Queensland (1934–1937); and R. M. and C. H. Berndt in South Australia (1943).

After 1945 occurred a brief wire-recording period, led by C. P. Mountford and C. Simpson during the American-Australian Expedition to Arnhem Land, Northern Territory (1948). Wire recording continued until 1955, but was largely replaced by tape recording from 1949. Cylinders recorded only for minutes, but tape recordings could continue for hours. The first major taped collection, sixteen hours of recordings made by Elkin in 1949, 1952, and 1953, is an important sample of Arnhem Land music. A selection of these recordings was published on three LP disks as *Arnhem Land: Australian Aboriginal Songs and Dances.*

Other large taped collections soon followed: by T. G. H. Strehlow in central Australia (1949–1950, 1953–1955, 1960), R. A. Waterman in northeast Arnhem Land (1952–1953), Jeremy Beckett in the Torres Strait Islands (1958–1961), and LaMont West Jr. in Cape York and northern Northern Territory (1961–1962). The early 1960s saw an exponential growth of recordings of Australian Aborigines, particularly those produced by Catherine J. Ellis, Alice M. Moyle, Richard M. Moyle, and Stephen A. Wild. Most recordings since 1960, sponsored by the Australian Institute of Aboriginal and Torres Strait Islander Studies, are deposited in the Institute's archive, which holds copies of older recordings.

**Commercial recordings**

The most notable commercial recordings of Australian music are albums recorded and edited by Alice M. Moyle between 1964 and 1981. Many recordings have been published by the Australian Institute of Aboriginal Studies (now Aboriginal Studies Press). Ethnic Folkways published several albums, including *Songs of Aboriginal Australia and Torres Strait.* That company's new label, Smithsonian Folkways, has continued the tradition with *Bunggridj-Bunggridj: Wangga Songs from Northern Australia by Alan Maralung* (1993). Aboriginal Studies Press, publishing jointly with the National Library of Australia, has ventured into historical recordings of Aboriginal music with *The Songs of Dougie Young* (1994). A country singer-composer, Young was first studied by Jeremy Beckett in the 1950s.

Studio recordings of indigenous popular music are being issued on commercial labels in increasing numbers. The Central Australian Aboriginal Media Association (CAAMA) has issued albums by Blekbala Mujik, Coloured Stone, Hermannsburg Ladies Choir, Sunrize Band, and others. Its 1995 catalogue listed more than fifty music albums (CDs and cassettes). Aboriginal bands, including Tiddas and Yothu Yindi (www.yothuyindi.com), and soloists, including Archie Roach, have had albums issued by mainstream labels.

—STEPHEN A. WILD

## Traditional Aboriginal Music

*Aboriginal Sound Instruments*. 1981. Recordings by Alice M. Moyle. Australian Institute of Aboriginal Studies AIAS 14. Cassette, LP disk.

*Arnhem Land: Authentic Australian Aboriginal Songs and Dances*. N.d. Recordings by A. P. Elkin. His Master's Voice/E.M.I. Australia. OALP 7504–7505. 3 LP disks.

*Australia: Songs of the Aborigines*. 1965? Recordings and notes by Wolfgang Laade. Lyrichord LYRCD 7331. Compact disc.

*Bunggridj-Bunggridj: Wangga Songs from Northern Australia by Alan Maralung*. 1993. Recordings and notes by Allan J. Marett and Linda Barwick. International Institute for Traditional Music: Traditional Music of the World, 4. Smithsonian Folkways CD 40430. Compact disc.

Dargin, Alan. N.d. *Bloodwood: The Art of the Didjeridu*. Compact disc.

*Didgeridoos: Sounds of the Aborigines*. N.d. Produced by Murdo McRae and Harry Wilson. Nesak International 19812–2. Compact disc.

*Djambidj: An Aboriginal Song Series from Northern Australia*. 1982. Australian Institute of Aboriginal Studies AIAS 16. Cassette.

*Goyulan the Morning Star: An Aboriginal Clan Song Series from North Central Arnhem Land*. 1988. Recordings and notes by Margaret Clunies Ross and Johnnie Mundrugmundrug. Australian Institute of Aboriginal Studies AIAS 18. Cassette.

*Modern Music of Torres Strait*. 1981. Recordings by Jeremy Beckett. Australian Institute of Aboriginal Studies AIAS 15. LP disk.

*Songs of Aboriginal Australia*. 1987. Recordings by Paddy Naughton. Australian Institute of Aboriginal Studies AIAS 17. Cassette.

*Songs of Aboriginal Australia and Torres Strait*. 1964. Recordings by Geoffrey N. O'Grady and Alix O'Grady. Musicological notes by Alice M. Moyle. Edited by George List. Ethnic Folkways FE 4102. LP disk.

*Songs from the Kimberleys*. 1977 [1968]. Recordings and notes by Alice M. Moyle. Australian Institute of Aboriginal Studies AIAS 13. Cassette.

*Songs from the Northern Territory*. 1964. Recordings and notes by Alice M. Moyle. Monograph Series, 3. Institute of Aboriginal Studies M-001–5. 5 LP disks.

*Songs from North Queensland*. 1977 [1966]. Recordings and notes by Alice M. Moyle. Australian Institute of Aboriginal Studies AIAS 12. LP disk.

*Songs from Yarrabah*. 1970. Recordings and notes by Alice M. Moyle. Australian Institute of Aboriginal Studies AIAS 7. Cassette.

*Traditional Music of the Torres Strait*. 1981 [1972]. Recordings by Jeremy Beckett and Trevor Jones. Australian Institute of Aboriginal Studies AIAS 11. LP disk, cassette.

*Tribal Music of Australia*. 1953. Recordings and Notes by A. P. Elkin. Ethnic Folkways FE 4439. LP disk.

Walley, Richard. N.d. *Bilya*. SMACD-06. Compact disc.

———. N.d. *Boolong*. Reissue of thirteen remastered tracks from most of Walley's earlier CDs. SMACD-18. Compact disc.

Wandjuk Marika. 1977. *Wandjuk Marika in Port Moresby: Didjeridu Solo*. Notes by Jennifer Issacs. Larrikin Records LRE 014. EP disk.

## Pop Aboriginal Music

*AIDS! How Could I Know*. 1989. CAAMA Music 203. Cassette.

Anu, Christine. 1995. *Stylin Up*. Mushroom Records D 24325. Compact disc.

Areyonga Desert Tigers. 1988. *Light On*. Imparja Recordings 21. Cassette.

Blekbala Mujik. 1995. *Blekbala Mujik*. CAAMA Music 245. Compact disc.

Casso and the Axons. 1987. *Australia for Sale*. Mantree Industries. Cassette.

Coloured Stone. 1987. *Black Rock from the Red Centre*. Rounder Records 5022. LP disk.

———. 1989. *Crazy Mind*. CAAMA M207. Cassette.

Desert Oaks Band. 1989. *Titjikala*. CAAMA Music. Cassette.

Geia, Joe. 1988. *Yil Lull*. Gammin Records D3129. LP disk.

*Hermannsburg Ladies Choir*. N.d. CAAMA M115. Cassette.

*In Aboriginal*. 1994. CAAMA Music 241. Compact disc.

No Fixed Address and Us Mob. 1981. *Wrong Side of the Road*. Black Australia Records PRC 196. Cassette.

Roach, Archie. 1990. *Charcoal Lane*. Mushroom 30386. Cassette.

Shillingsworth, Les, et al. 1988. *Justice Will Be Done*. Privately published. Cassette.

*Stompem Ground: Highlights from the 1992 Kimberley Aboriginal Arts and Cultural Festival*. 1993. Australian Broadcasting Corporation 518 0202. Cassette, compact disc.

*Sunrize Band*. N.d. *Sunset to Rise*. CAAMA M069. Cassette.

*Tiddas: Sing About Life*. 1993. Id Phonogram 518 3482. Cassette, compact disc.

*UPK: Uwankara Palyanka Kanyinijaku* (A strategy for well-being). 1989. CAAMA Music 208. Cassette.

Warumpi Band. 1987. *Go Bush!* Festival Records C38707. Cassette.

Yothu Yindi. 1989. *Homeland Movement*. Mushroom Records. Cassette, compact disc.

———. 1991. *Tribal Voice.* Mushroom 30602. Cassette, compact disc.

———. 1993. *Freedom.* Hollywood Records HR–61451-2. Compact disc.

———. 1995. "Jailbreak." In *Fuse/Box: The*

*Alternative Tribute.* BMG 74321 286814. Compact disc.

Young, Dougie. 1994. *The Songs of Dougie Young.* National Library of Australia, Aboriginal Studies Press 19. Cassette, compact disc.

## NEW GUINEA

The first commercial release of recordings made in New Guinea occurred in 1949, with the sale of disc versions of wire recordings made by the Australian journalist Colin Simpson and his technician, John Cunningham (Australian Broadcasting Commission 1949). A record edited by Ray Sheridan (1958) provided the first overview of the music of Papua New Guinea. In 1947–1949, his years in the country as an army officer, he interested himself in music, as his manuscripts, collection of drawings of instruments, and photographs prove. These materials are in the Papua New Guinea Collection of the National Library.

Several commercial recordings by missionaries, including André Dupeyrat, and anthropologists, including A. P. Elkin, appeared in the 1950s. In the next decade, indigenous music appeared in several anthologies, and Ethnic Folkways issued similar recordings.

Besides examples in large collections, commercial studios ignored locally produced popular music until 1968, when Viking, in Aotearoa, began issuing disks concentrating on contemporary music, though photographs on some albums imply that the recordings treat traditional music. Many of these releases duplicated recordings supplied by the Australian Broadcasting Commission in Port Moresby. Viking made about forty releases of this music. In 1974, the ABC supplied recordings to CBS. Gospel Recordings, in the United States, has issued hundreds of recordings of readings of biblical texts in local languages. In 1973, the Papua New Guinea government set up the National Broadcasting Commission, which provided material for further releases with RCA and EMI. The ordinance that established NBC empowered the agency to produce and manufacture recordings.

A few years after independence, a shift in commercial-recording producers' nationality occurred. Viking continued producing records until 1977, but local companies soon dominated. In 1975, the Institute of Papua New Guinea Studies released its first recordings, initially on discs through Ocora, in France, then on its own label, and later still on Larrikin Records, in Australia. In 1976, Kristen Kaset began a series of religious recordings. In 1977, the NBC began releasing recordings on cassettes, locally a more convenient format than LP disks.

Most NBC releases featured popular music, as did those of other entities except the Institute of Papua New Guinea Studies, which has issued sixteen discs and cassettes of mostly traditional music. Among the most productive cassette-releasing companies in New Guinea, listed with years of operation and approximate number of cassettes released to the end of 1992, are Kristen Kaset (since 1976, ninety-four cassettes), National Broadcasting Commission (since 1977, 362), Paradise Recording Company (1978, ten), Chin H. Meen (since 1980, 783), Soundstream (1980–1985, fifty-one), Vista (since 1981, 210), Communication Institute (since 1981, forty-seven), Lowkal (1981–1982, twenty-eight), Cassette Ministry (1981–1984?, fifty-seven), Pacific Gold Studio (since 1983, 611), Kuanua (1983–1985?, seventy-one), and Tumbuna Traks (since 1988, thirty-three) (figure 1). Since independence, local companies have issued nearly three thousand releases. In 1991, Chin H. Meen began issuing videos of excerpts from "Mekim Musik" and "Fizz," programs on EMTV, a television station based in Papua New Guinea.

Schools and churches have sporadically released cassettes. Highly important has

FIGURE 1 Chris Seeto, producer of commercial music, works at Tumbuna Traks, the studio in his home in Madang. Photo by Don Niles, 1989.

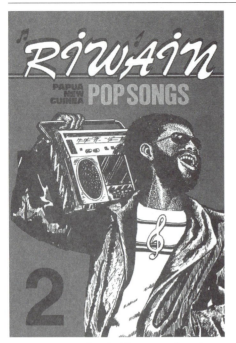

FIGURE 2 As in this double cassette, featuring fifty songs by nearly fifty bands, the Institute of Papua New Guinea Studies issues recordings of popular music.

been the compilation and release of the *Papua New Guinea Music Collection* (1987). Containing more than three hundred musical examples, it surveys the work done in Papua New Guinea. By providing students with examples of traditional music, it has influenced the national curriculum in music. The Institute of Papua New Guinea Studies has released cassettes of popular music (figure 2).

Foreign companies have sporadically issued recordings of Papua New Guinea musics, many the results of endeavors by William Mitchell (Folkways), Ragnar Johnson (!Quartz), Wolfgang Laade (Folkways, Jecklin), and the series begun in 1981 on Bärenreiter by Steven Feld, Brigitta Hauser-Schäublin, Jacqueline Pugh-Kitingan, and Gordon Spearritt. Catering to overseas audiences, these companies focused on traditional music. The first compact disc devoted to New Guinean music—Steven Feld's *Voices of the Rainforest* (1991)—brought international attention to musical and environmental issues. The first locally produced CDs of New Guinean bands were issued in 1994.

Since 1984, the National Research Institute has published annual listings of commercial recordings of Papua New Guinea musics (Niles 1984, 1985, 1987a, 1987b, 1988, 1991, 1993; Niles and Gima 1993a, 1993b, 1994). Each entry lists company, number, title, date of release, group(s), catalog-number in the Music Archive of the institute, and contents.    —DON NILES

## Collections

*Australia and New Guinea.* 1954. Recordings by A. P. Elkin and A. P. Dupeyrat. Edited by A. P. Elkin. Columbia World Library of Folk and Primitive Music, 5. Columbia Masterworks KL-208. LP disk.

*Indonesia.* 1954. Recordings by André Dupeyrat and J. Hobbel. Edited by Jaap Kunst. Columbia World Library of Folk and Primitive Music, 7. Columbia Masterworks KL-210. LP disk.

*Music of the Anga.* 1983. Recordings by Bergh Amos, Ilaita Gigimat, Lisa Lawson, and Don Niles. Institute of Papua New Guinea Studies IPNGS 006. Cassette.

*Music of New Guinea: The Australian Trust Territory: An Introduction.* 1958. Recordings by Ray Sheridan and W. E. Smythe. Edited by Ray Sheridan. Wattle Recordings D2. LP disk.

*New Guinea and Papuan Native Music.* 1949. Recordings by Colin Simpson and John Cunningham. Australian Broadcasting System NAT 14. Seven 78-RPM disks.

*Ol Singsing Bilong Ples.* 1990. Recordings by Michael Webb and Don Niles. Boroko: Institute of Papua New Guinea Studies IPNGS 010. Book with two cassettes.

*Papua New Guinea Music Collection.* 1987. Edited by Don Niles and Michael Webb. Institute of Papua New Guinea Studies IPNGS 008. Book with eleven cassettes.

*Primitive Sounds: An Authentic Sound Picture of New Guinea.* 1971. Recordings by James L. Anderson. Hibiscus Records HLS 31. LP disk.

*This Is New Guinea: A Recorded Sound Picture.* N.d. Recordings by James L. Anderson. Hibiscus Records HLS 19. LP disk.

## Popular music

Amazil Local. 1981. *Amazil Local.* Walter Bay Trading Company. Vista NGK 6028. Cassette.

*The Best of PNG Pidgin Rock.* 1991. Institute of Papua New Guinea Studies IPNGS 220.

Delapou Band, The Rainbows, and The Kopy Kats. 1968. *New Guinea Music Today.* Viking VP 266. LP disk.

Hollie Maea Band. N.d. *Mangi Moresby.* CHM Supersound 702. LP disk.

*The New Guinea Scene.* 1969. Recordings by the Australian Broadcasting Commission. Viking Records VP 318. LP disk.

*Papua/New Guinea Independence Celebrations: Song Contest Finalists.* 1975. Viking VPS 392. LP disk.

*Riwain! Papua New Guinea Pop Songs.* 1986. Compiled by Michael Webb and Don Niles. Institute of Papua New Guinea Studies IPNGS 007. Book with two cassettes.

## Papuan Region

*The Coast of the Western Province, Papua New Guinea.* 1993. Recordings and notes by Wolfgang Laade. Music of Man Archive. Jecklin-Disco JD 655-2. Compact disc.

*The Coast of the Western Province, Papua New Guinea.* 1993. Recordings and notes by Wolfgang Laade. Music of Man Archive. Jecklin-Disco JD 655-2. Compact disc.

*Kamu Mariria: Music of the Maopa and Aloma.* 1981. Recordings by Les McLaren and Ilaita Gigimat. Compiled by Don Niles. Institute of Papua New Guinea Studies IPNGS 003. Cassette.

*Music from the D'Entrecasteaux Islands.* 1983. Recordings by Lisa Lawson, Hape Haihavu, Charles Asshy, and Pio Renssy. Produced in collaboration with the National Arts School. Institute of Papua New Guinea Studies IPNGS 005.

*Music from South New Guinea.* 1971. Recordings and notes by Wolfgang Laade. Folkways AHM 4216. LP disk.

*Traditional Music of the Gizra and Bine People: Papua New Guinea, Western Province.* 1978. Recordings and notes by Frédéric Duvelle, assisted by Billai Laba. Larrikin Records LRF 031. LP disk.

## Highland Region

*Chimbu Music: Kukane Traditions.* 1975. Recordings and notes by Frédéric Duvelle, assisted by Paul Kuange. Papua New Guinea, 1. Institute of Papua New Guinea Studies. LP disk.

*Enga Traditional Music.* 1974. Recordings by Frédéric Duvelle. Notes by Kundopen Talyaga. Institute of Papua New Guinea Studies. LP disk.

*The Huli of Papua Niugini.* 1986. Recordings by Jacqueline Pugh-Kitingan. Bärenreiter-Musicaphon BM 30 SL 2703. LP disk.

*The Kaluli of Papua Niugini: Weeping and Song.* 1985. Recordings by Steven Feld. Bärenreiter-Musicaphon BM 30 SL 2702. LP disk.

*Music of the Kaluli.* 1981. Recordings by Steven Feld. Institute of Papua New Guinea Studies IPNGS 001. LP disk.

*Voices of the Rainforest: Bosavi, Papua New Guinea.* 1991. Recordings and notes by Steven Feld. Rykodisc RCD 10173. Compact disc.

## Mamose Region

*The Iatmul of Papua Niugini.* 1980. Recordings by Robert MacLennan and Gordon Spearritt. Notes by Meinhard Schuster and Gordon Spearritt. Bärenreiter-Musicaphon BM 30 SL 2701. LP disk.

*Kovai and Adzera Music.* 1981. Recordings by Bergh Amos, Thomas Lulungan, Don Niles, and Jesse Pongap. Adzera translations by Soni Timo Maraba. Institute of Papua New Guinea Studies IPNGS 002. Cassette.

*Papua Niugini: The Middle Sepik.* 1980. Recordings by Robert MacLennan, Fred Gerrits, and Gordon Spearritt. Notes by Meinhard Schuster and Gordon Spearritt. Bärenreiter-Musicaphon BM 30 SL 2700. LP disk.

*Rhythms and Music of Oceanic Islands, Following N. N. Miklouho-Maclay.* 1978. Recordings by Boris N. Putilov. Leningrad: Melodiya M80–39597–39602. Three LP disks.

*Sacred Flute Music from New Guinea: Madang.* 1977. Recordings by Ragnar Johnson and Jessica Mayer. Quartz Publications: !Quartz 001. LP disk.

*Windim Mambu: Sacred Flute Music from New Guinea: Madang.* 1978. Recordings by Ragnar Johnson and Jessica Mayer. Quartz Publications: !Quartz 002. LP disk.

## Irian Jaya

*Musik aus dem Bergland West-Neuguineas (Irian Jaya): Eine Klangdokumentation untergehender Musikkulturen der Eipo und ihrer Nachbarn/Music from the Mountainous Region of Western New Guinea (Irian Jaya): A Documentation in Sound of the Vanishing Musical Cultures of the Eipo and Their Neighbors.* 1993. Recordings and notes by Artur Simon. Museum Collection Berlin CD 20, vols. 1 and 2. Six compact discs.

*Music of Biak, Irian Jaya.* 1996. Recordings by Philip Yampolsky. Notes by Danilyn Rutherford and Philip Yampolsky. Produced in collaboration with the Indonesian Society for the Performing Arts. Music of Indonesia, 10. Smithsonian Folkways CD 40426. Compact disc.

## MELANESIA

Recordings of Melanesian music began in the Island Region of Papua New Guinea in the first decade of the twentieth century, with wax-cylinder collections made by Emil Stephan in New Britain and New Ireland in 1904, Richard Thurnwald in 1907, and Josef Winthuis in New Britain in 1908. In each decade thereafter, the region has been represented with important recordings [see THE MUSIC AND DANCE OF NEW GUINEA; RECORDINGS: Papua New Guinea].

In the Solomon Islands in 1908, A. M. Hocart made nineteen wax-cylinder recordings, now archived in Berlin. There too, about 1910, W. H. R. Rivers made six cylinders, now in the British Institute of Recorded Sound, London. About 1946, the linguist George B. Milner made local recordings, published on an obscure label, "The British Homophonic Company," in a series of ten-inch shellac 78-RPM disks, including, from Vella Lavella, a remarkable lament—to which the gods reply by thunder, clearly audible in the recording.

The first musical recordings in New Caledonia were made by Paul Montague in 1913. These recordings and Montague's writings remain unpublished. The recordings are housed in the British Library, London. Other early New Caledonian recordings were made by Marie-Joseph Dubois on Maré Island (Nengone language) and Maurice Leenhardt in the Houaïlou area (Ajië language). Copies of both collections are in the archive of the Agence de Développement de la Culture Kanak (ADCK). Other New Caledonian materials are thirty-six recordings made by Hans Nevermann on Grande Terre and the Loyalty Islands in 1933–1934, archived in Berlin, and iso-lated recordings made in 1940 by Bruce and Sheridan Fahnestock, archived in the Library of Congress, Washington, D.C. Recordings of Kanak singing were made in France by the Institut de Phonétique (Paris), which in 1931 recorded the singing of a group that went to Paris to participate in the Colonial Exposition and in 1945 recorded the singing of Kanak soldiers stationed in France after the war ended. These recordings remain unpublished. They are housed in the Phonothèque National. In 1990, Jean-Michel Beaudet and Raymond Ammann produced important collections. The ADCK and more particular institutions, especially the Centre Culturel Yéiwéné Yéiwéné, have released recordings for local consumption.

In 1914–1915, John Layard, using an Edison type-2 "standard" wax-cylinder phonograph, made the first musical recordings in Vanuatu. Twenty-six tracks were copied onto sixteen-inch 33-RPM acetate disks, of which copies are in the Musée de l'Homme, Paris. These tracks include two-part songs and conch-shell calls for announcing stages of pig-killing rites—all now rare or extinct. In and after 1959, Michael Allen used a Butoba spring-wound tape recorder on Ambae, with good results.

Since the 1950s, when transistor-wired, battery-powered machines became avail-able, many researchers and tourists have recorded Melanesian music. Some of these recordings remain in private hands. "Professional-quality" recordings have been made since the 1960s. In the Island Region of Papua New Guinea, Charles and Frédéric Duvelle's collections include Manus and the Tolai. With a Nagra in 1989, Wolfgang Laade made a substantial collection in southeast New Britain. Music of the Solomon Islands is available on Hugo Zemp's publications on vinyl, of which some have been reissued and augmented on compact discs. Two compact discs (Chants Kanaks 1990; Nouvelle-Calédonie 1997) survey music of New Caledonia. One compact disc (Crowe 1994) samples music of Vanuatu. In all regions, locally made and distributed cassettes have appeared.

—PETER RUSSELL CROWE

### Multicultural recordings

*Manus; Bougainville.* 1975. Recordings by Charles Duvelle and Frédéric Duvelle. Notes by Kakah Kais and Leo Hannett. Ocora OCR 86. LP disk.

### Island Region of Papua New Guinea

*Music and Sounds of Melanesia.* 1962. Music of the Duke of York Islands. Recordings and notes by Sandra LeBrun Holmes. HMV OELP 9189. LP disk.

*Tolai Traditional Music from the Gazelle Peninsula.* 1977. Recordings and notes by Frédéric Duvelle, assisted by Jacob Simet and Apisai Enos. Larrikin Records LRF 013. LP disk.

ToUna, Blasius. 1978. *Guitar Songs of Papua New Guinea.* Recordings and notes by Frédéric Duvelle. Larrikin Records LRF 030. LP disk.

*Tribal Heart.* 1994. Music popular of Rabaul. Larrikin Entertainment AIM 1042. Compact disc.

## Solomon Islands

*Fataleka and Baegu Music: Malaita: Solomon Islands.* 1990 [1973]. Recordings and notes by Hugo Zemp. Augmented reissue. Auvidis-Unesco D 8027. Compact disc.

*Îles Salomon: Ensembles de flûtes de pan 'Are'are.* 1994. Recordings and notes by Hugo Zemp. Le Chant du Monde LDX 274 961–62. 2 compact discs.

Meja, Nelson, and His Bamboo Band, with Solomon Dakei. N.d. *Bamboo Beat.* Notes by Ron Calvert. Viking VE 163. EP disk.

*Melanesian Music, 'Are'are, Vol. 3.* 1973. Recordings and notes by Hugo Zemp. Collection Musée de l'Homme. Vogue LDM 30106. LP disk.

*Musique de Guadalcanal: Solomon Islands.* 1994. Recordings and notes by Hugo Zemp. Ocora Radio France C 5580049. Compact disc.

*Polyphonies of the Solomon Islands (Guadalcanal and Savo).* 1990. Recordings and notes by Hugo Zemp. Augmented reissue. Collection Centre National de la Recherche Scientifique and Musée de l'Homme. Le Chant du Monde LDX 274663. Compact disc.

*St. Joseph's Temaru: Pan Pipers.* 1986. Produced by St. Joseph's Temaru. Cassette.

*Solomon Islands: 'Are'are Intimate and Ritual Music.* 1995. Recordings and notes by Hugo Zemp. Collection Centre National de la Recherche Scientifique and Musée de l'Homme. Le Chant du Monde CNR 274 963. Compact disc.

*The Solomon Islands: The Sounds of Bamboo: Instrumental Music and Song of the 'Are'are People of Malaita.* N.d. Recordings by the MABO Project. Music of the Earth MCM 3007. Compact disc.

## New Caledonia

Bwanjep. 1993. *Vie.* Popular music by a band from northern Grande Terre. Nouméa: Studio Mangrove. Cassette, compact disc.

*Cada et ayoii: chants de Hienghène.* 1992. Recordings by Jean-Michel Beaudet. Nouméa: Agence de Développement de la Culture Kanak. Cassette.

*Chants kanaks: cérémonies et berceuses.* 1990. Recordings by Jean-Michel Beaudet and Lionel Weiri. Notes by Jean-Michel Beaudet and Kaloonbat Tein. Collection Centre National de la Recherche Scientifique and Musée de l'Homme. Le Chant du Monde LDX 274909. Compact disc.

*Chants et musiques Drehu.* 1994. Recordings and notes by Raymond Ammann. Collection Musiques Kanak, 2. Nouméa and Maré: Centre Culturel Yéiwéné Yéiwéné and Agence de Développement de la Culture Kanak. Cassette. Cassette.

*Chants et musiques Iaaï.* 1994. Recordings and notes by Raymond Ammann. Collection Musiques Kanak, 1. Nouméa and Maré: Centre Culturel Yéiwéné Yéiwéné and Agence de Développement de la Culture Kanak. Cassette.

*Chants et musiques Nengone.* 1994. Recordings and notes by Raymond Ammann. Collection Musiques Kanak, 3. Nouméa and Maré: Centre Culturel Yéiwéné Yéiwéné and Agence de Développement de la Culture Kanak. Cassette.

Gurejele. 1993. *Wabeb bulu.* Popular music by a band from Maré Island. Nouméa: Studio Mangrove. Cassette, compact disc.

*Kanaké: Musiques canaques de Nouvelle-Calédonie: Festival Melanesia 2000.* 1984 [1975]. Nouméa. LP disk, cassette.

*Kanak Modern Music.* 1987? Recordings by Warawi Wayenece, with the participation of l'Association Boenando. Amakal Productions. Cassette.

Mexem. 1995. *Kadely.* Popular music by a band from Lifou Island. Nouméa: Studio Mangrove. Cassette, compact disc.

*Nouvelle-Calédonie: danses et musiques kanak/New Caledonia: Kanak Dance and Music.* 1997. Recordings by Raymond Ammann. Geneva: Musée d'Ethnographie, AIMP XLVIII. VDE CD-923. Compact disc.

*Pilou-Pilou: Songs and Dances of New Caledonia: Authetic Folk Music from New Caledonia, The Isle of Pines and Loyalty Islands.* 1969. Viking Records VP 278. LP disk.

Shabatan. 1995. *Waica ri kae deng.* Popular music by a band from Maré Island. Nouméa: Studio Mangrove. Cassette, compact disc.

Vamaley. 1993. *Echos du passé.* Popular music by a band from northern Grande Terre. Nouméa: Studio Mangrove. Cassette, compact disc.

## Vanuatu

Black Brothers. N.d. *Best of the Black Brothers.* Vila: Sound Centre AGP 15. Cassette.

Black Revolution. 1986. *Everyday.* Studio Vanuwespa SAEP 8611. Cassette.

Magawiarua. 1992. *Magawiarua.* Vanuatu Productions V-PRO 92-11. Cassette.

Nahabau. N.d. *Radio Vanuatu and The Sound Centre.* Alain Gault Productions. TC AGP 17. Cassette.

*New Hebrides Music Today.* 1969. Recordings by Radio Nouméa. Viking VP 284. LP disk.

Noisy Boys. 1982. *Fes Tua.* Alain Gault Productions. TC AGP 10. Cassette.

———. 1986. *1986 Tanna Inta Distrik Gems.* Vanuata [sic] Production (Société de Promotion de Musique Mélanésienne) VP 24. Cassette.

*Les Nouvelles-Hébrides.* N.d. Recordings by Maurice Bitter. Musique Folklorique du Monde. Musidisc 30 CV 1273. LP disk.

*Songs and Dances of the New Hebrides.* 1969. Recordings by Radio Nouméa. Viking VP 280. LP disk.

*Traditional Music of Vanuatu (New Hebrides) from the Cultural Centre Archives.* 1977. Recordings by Joseph Boe, James Gwere, and Kirk Huffman. Cultural Centre. Cassette.

*Vanuatu: Custom Music/Singsing-Danis Kastom.* 1994. Recordings and notes by Peter Crowe and other participants in the New Hebrides Oral Traditions Project. Geneva: Musée d'Ethnographie, AIMP XLVIII. VDE 796. Compact disc.

Western Boys. 1992? *Again.* Vila: Sum Productions SP 160. Cassette.

## MICRONESIA

The first recordings of Micronesian music were made on Yap in 1903 by William Henry Furness (1910). Also on Yap, in 1907, a German researcher made the first of the recordings that, as transcribed by George Herzog (1932, 1936), became the base line for studies of music of the Caroline Islands. One hundred wax-cylinder recordings were made in the Caroline Islands by the Hamburg Südsee-Expedition of 1908–1910. In the Ellice Islands in 1924, Kenneth P. Emory recorded Gilbertese residents. In the Carolines and Marshalls in 1934, Hisao Tanabe made wax-plate recordings from which a selection, *The Music of Micronesia,* was issued on vinyl around 1978. In the Carolines in 1936, Iwakichi Muranushi made wax-cylinder recordings, from which Elizabeth Tatar's selection, *Call of the Morning Bird,* appeared on cassette in 1985.

Soon after the war, U.S. government agencies sent anthropologists, educators, and others to Guam and the Trust Territory of the Pacific. Among these researchers, Edwin G. Burrows in Ifaluk, Paul Garvin in Ponape, William A. Lessa in Ulithi, and Ernest McClain in Guam recorded on wire or tape. Some of their recordings are in U.S. institutions; no commercial releases have been made from them. In 1963, Barbara B. Smith, surveying indigenous music and dance at the request of Micronesian students at the University of Hawai'i, recorded performances in the Carolines and Marshalls. In the Gilbert Islands, H. G. A. Hughes from Wales recorded traditional music, hymns, and legends in the early 1950s, and Gerd Koch recorded for the Museum für Völkerkunde (Berlin) in 1963–1964.

Important collections, of which some dubbings are housed in Micronesian institutions, have been made by graduate students: in the 1960s, Osamu Yamaguchi (now Yamaguti) in Palau; in the 1970s, Kim Bailey in Ponape and Virginia Marion in the Gilberts; in the 1980s, Junko Iwata (now Konishi) in Yap and Mary Elizabeth Lawson (now Burke) in Kiribati; in the 1990s, Deirdre Marshall (now Marshall-Dean) in Yap and Mark Puryear in several islands. Increasingly since the 1980s, indigenous scholars are researching the musical heritage of their families, villages, and islands.

Since the 1960s, a few radio stations have recorded their islands' musics for broadcast and have accumulated important collections. Most early recorded performances occurred in administrative centers. In 1979, for use in indigenous-language radio programs, the Folk Arts Program of the National Endowment for the Arts funded a project in which Kim Bailey trained Trukese and Ponapeans, who then visited outlying parts of their districts to record musical performances. The tapes made in Truk were deposited in the Micronesian Area Research Center (Guam).

In 1976, an independent researcher, Laura Boulton, documented dances and music performed on Palau, Ulithi, and Yap. For the Territorial survey of Oceanic Musics in 1988, Mary E. Lawson Burke, working with the Alele Museum (Majuro), surveyed Marshallese music. No collection of musical recordings for academic documentation or study has been made in Nauru, though for personal enjoyment many Nauruans—a large number of whom own fine recording equipment—record performances of Nauruan music.

Few vinyl records of Micronesian musics have been issued. The first, *Enchanted Evening in Micronesia,* was a 7-inch disk of music performed by students in the Micronesian Club of Honolulu. Of major labels, Viking issed three LP disks (one of music of the Marshalls and two of the Gilberts, with the Ellice Islands). LPs resulting from local initiatives include one of musics of six Micronesian cultures for sale in Saipan, one of the Danpei Youth Choir of Ponape, a two-disk set of songs and legends of Guam (arranged and produced for the Guam Economic Development Authority by a prominent Hawaiian musician), and disks of Guam's popular singer-entertainers. With few exceptions, outsiders have purchased more of these recordings than have Micronesians.

Small, inexpensive cassette recorders dramatically changed the content of, and market for, recordings of indigenous musics, especially popular musics. Some cassettes were made primarily for tourists in Guam and Saipan, and a cassette of traditional Chamorro music (*Musikan Guahan*) was inspired by a cultural renaissance, but most commercial cassettes there and on other islands feature popular songs with lyrics in English or indigenous languages, composed and performed by young Micronesians to convey local or personal concerns to their own people—those living on their island and those relocated elsewhere. Expatriate Micronesians have made commercial cassettes that have become popular overseas and in home islands. In the 1990s in Palau, Guam, and Saipan, the number of commercially released cassettes grew tremendously, and compact discs began to appear.   —BARBARA B. SMITH

## Multicultural recordings

*Enchanted Evening in Micronesia: Songs and Dances from Marshalls, Ponape, Truk, Yap and Palau.* 1960. Performed by The Micronesian Club of Honolulu at the University of Hawai'i. Seven-inch LP disk.

*Guam, Northern Marianas, Federated States of Micronesia, Marshall Islands.* 1994. Recordings and notes by Hikaru Koide. JVC World Sounds Special, Music of Micronesia. JVC VICG-5277. Compact disc.

*Micronesia: A Musical Glimpse.* N.d. Six island cultures spanning Palau in the west to the Gilberts in the east. Trutone Records for J. C.

Tenorio Enterprises, Saipan, Northern Marianas. LP disk.

*The Music of Micronesia, the Kao-Shan Tribes of Taiwan, and Sakhalin.* 1978? Side A: recordings by Hisao Tanabe in Palau, Truk, Ponape, and the Marshall Islands. Side B: Taiwan and Sakhalin. Toshiba TW- 80011. LP disk.

*Spirit of Micronesia: Traditional Music Recorded between 1978–1984: Chants, Hymns, Dances from Kiribati, Marshall Islands, Kosrae, Pohnpei, Chuuk, Yap & Palau.* 1995. Recordings by David Fanshawe. Saydisc Records SDL-414. Compact disc.

## West Micronesia

*Call of the Morning Bird: Chants and Songs of Palau, Yap, and Ponape, Collected by Iwakichi Muranushi, 1936.* 1985. Edited by Elizabeth Tatar. Honolulu: Bishop Museum, ARCS 2. Cassette.

Waab-Palau Trio (Rodol Ruethin, Kasiano Kelulau, Josino Joseph). [Palau and Yap.] 1983? *Kasinoma.* MRM Productions MRMC-1001. Cassette.

### *Palau*

Bekebekmad, Johnny "B." N.d. *"Johnny B."* Gem Records CS-1113. Cassette.

Eriich, Halley. N.d. *Ngerbuus.* ET Records. Cassette.

———. N.d. *Manterang.* ET Records. Cassette.

———. N.d. *Ai Sa Nangyo.* ET Records. Cassette.

Kanai, Virian. 1995. *Bertau.* BKE 10995. Cassette.

### Yap
Wallow, led by Jesse Maw. 1995. *Wallow.*
Recorded at the radio station. Cassette.

### Pohnpei
*The Danpei Youth Choir of Ponape, Micronesia: On Tour.* [1980.] Produced by the Rev. Elden Buck, tour director. Triad Recording Studio. LP disk.

## Mariana Islands

### Guam
Bias, Jesse. 1985. *Guam on My Mind.* Alifan Productions 85-12-001. LP disk and cassette.

———. N.d. *Language of Love.* LP disk and cassette.

———. N.d. *We Are One.* LP disk and cassette.

*Biggest Chamorro Stars: Greatest Chamorro Hits, Vol. 2.* 1994. Naou Records International VA-CS. Cassette.

Guerrero. 1987. *Chamorro Songs [Guam/Saipan]: Palao'an Matulaika Hao.* Produced by Tony R. Guerrero. Cassette.

*Makpo.* 1990. Songs composed or arranged by Maria Santos Yatar. Cassette.

*The Music and Legends of Guam.* 1978. Produced and directed by Jack de Mello for the Guam

Economic Development Authority. Notes by Jack de Mello. 2 LP disks, 2 cassettes.

*Musikan Guahan.* 1992. Edited by Judy Flores. Agaña: Guam Council on the Arts & Humanities. Cassette.

Sablan, Johnny. 1960s. *Dalai Nene.* Hafa Adai Records HAC 3300. Cassette.

———. N.d. *Chamorro Country-Western.* Hafa Adai Records HAC 3313. Cassette.

———. N.d. *Feliz Navidad!* Hafa Adai Records HAC 3315. Cassette.

———. 1982. *Shame 'n Scandal.* Hafa Adai Records HAC 3325. Cassette.

### Northern Mariana Islands
AFETNAS II. 1984. *Maila Ta Na' Mames Este Na Momiento.* Saipan: Tenda Store Production. TS4802. Cassette.

Cabrero, Joe. N.d. *Fiesta.* Saipan: A & E Productions. Cassette.

The Commonwealth. N.d. *Marianas Despedida.* CM1980-01. Cassette.

De la Cruz, Eddie. 1991. *Edwardo.* Guam: Doe Productions. Cassette.

De la Cruz, Frank. N.d. *Tinian.* Guam: Ke Productions. Cassette.

Diaz, Joseph M. N.d. *Fan Respeta Gi Manaina Mu.* Saipan: Tenda Store Production TS4812. Cassette.

Dinana i famililian "Camacho." 1989. *Dinana i famililian "Camacho."* Saipan: S. D. Camacho Quality Productions. Cassette.

Indelecio, Cindy. N.d. *Un Tunoco Va.* Tinian: Guam Sirena Production. Cassette.

Kunados Tinian II. 1984. *Lao Hu-ouive Hao.* Tinian: Kunados Tinian Productions Enterprises. Cassette.

Muna, Jesse. 1990. *Fiestan Luta.* Rota: LJ's Production. Cassette.

Pangelinan, Frank M. N.d. *Chikko Va.* Saipan: no producer. Cassette.

———. N.d. *Memorias Marianas.* Saipan: Tenda Store Production TS6809. Cassette.

Sablan, Alesandro. 1993? *Jose Maria.* Saipan: Chamorro Hit Radio FM. Cassette.

Tropicsette. N.d. *Nobia.* Saipan: Tropicsette. Cassette.

## East Micronesia

### Marshall Islands
Bwil 'm Molo. 1994. *Ebwil!* Majuro: privately produced. Cassette.

Jabe in Nebar. N.d. *Jej family eo an Iroij.* V7AB Recording Studio. Cassette.

Kakinono. 1996. *Kakinono kein kaiuon.* Chaninway KK-1. Cassette.

Likajer. 1995. *Inedral.* Manufactured in Fremont, Calif. Cassette.

Skate-Em-Lā. 1985. *Mour Ilo Aelōñ Kein.* Recorded in Majuro by Bill Graham in association with Marshall Islands Yacht Club. Remastered in Honolulu by Academics Hawaii. Cassette.

*Songs from Micronesia.* N.d. Reissue of an untitled LP disk produced and recorded by Lee Webb in the Marshall Islands. Viking VP 265. LP disk.

### *Kiribati*

Foon, Peter. 1986. *Bata Peter: Bibitakin te Moanoua.* Suva: Foon's Home Studio CPR 10. Cassette.

Nenem, Isaia. 1986. *Te Roro N Rikirake.* Suva: Foon's Home Studio CPR 17. Cassette

## POLYNESIA

Commercial recordings of Polynesian music address two goals: ethnographic recordings focus on preserving and informatively presenting traditional or older styles of music, and popular-music releases aim to please broad audiences. Ethnographic recordings usually sample collections made by academic researchers working with nonprofessional performers. Written commentaries introduce cultural contexts and specific pieces. Ethnographic recordings of Polynesian musics are listed in the catalogs of companies that specialize in documenting musics of the world, including Folkways Records (now Smithsonian Folkways, Washington, D.C.); Le Chant du Monde (Paris), of recordings produced by the Centre National de la Recherche Scientifique, Musée de l'Homme; Hibiscus Records (Aotearoa), important for recordings from the 1976 South Pacific Festival of the Arts; Playa Sound (Paris); and most recently, Pan Records (Netherlands). The Bishop Museum has released a recording of archival Hawaiian material (*Nā Leo Hawaiʻi Kahiko* 1981). Commercial recordings of popular Polynesian musics date from the early 1900s. Only in Aotearoa and Hawaiʻi is the history of recordings well documented.

Throughout Polynesia, a cottage industry produces musical materials—homemade products, sold in markets and fairs and heard on radio. The music presented on cassettes and compact discs varies from traditional to modern—a distinction advertised in the designs of the packaging (figure 3).     —AMY KUʻULEIALOHA STILLMAN

### West Polynesia

Most nations of West Polynesia do not have a commercial-recording industry. Except for Fiji, recording is done by local radio stations and home studios, or at live performances. Numerous cassettes are available from these sources, sold in local shops and sent to relatives overseas. CDs are usually made by outsiders and bought primarily by outsiders and tourists. The numerous LPs made by commercial companies are no longer available, and have not yet been remastered or rereleased.

### *Fiji*

Fiji has a flourishing commercial-recording industry, dominated by two companies: South Pacific Recordings, dating from 1970, and Procera, dating from 1972. Both

FIGURE 3  Traditional and modern styles of music advertised visually: *a,* the cover of the Hawaiian Style Band's *Rhythm of the Ocean* features a drawing of a *pahu*; *b,* the cover of The Peter Moon Band's *Iron Mango* is an abstract modern painting.

(*a*)          (*b*)

companies issue recordings of Fijian and Fiji-Indian performers. SPR maintains an active catalog of more than seven hundred Fijian and more than 350 Fiji-Indian releases. Procera has issued more than fifteen hundred recordings, and currently issues more than sixty new releases a year. Recordings of Fijian performers include traditional *meke,* string-band, and popular styles, and Christian musics in traditional Fijian and modern gospel styles. Recordings of Fiji-Indian performers include traditional genres from India, especially Bihar (where ancestors of most Fiji-Indians came from), other secular and devotional musics, and popular musics. Since the mid-1990s, SPR has recorded popular musics of Rotumans and Banabans resident in Suva. Local people buy mostly cassettes. Some traditional Fijian and current popular favorites are issued on compact discs, mainly for tourists. Both companies produce and market music videos.                                          —BARBARA B. SMITH

## East Polynesia

In East Polynesia, the production and distribution of recorded popular songs attest to a flourishing musical scene. Outside the region, the extent of this activity is little known. Libraries and aural archives, many of which concentrate on ethnographic recordings, have not systematically collected these items. Enterprising record companies are remastering their stocks, acquiring inactive catalogs, and reissuing on compact discs earlier recordings and newly compiled anthologies. So-called vintage Hawaiian music from before the 1940s has been rereleased by Arhoolie, Harlequin, and Rounder. Hula Records (Honolulu) has been prominent in rereleasing on CDs its earlier products. In 1994, Hana Ola Records (California) began anthologizing Hawaiian music from 49th State Records and Bell. Tahitian music from Criterion Records is being rereleased and distributed internationally on the Manuiti label.

### Tahiti

Recordings of Tahitian popular music have occasionally appeared outside French Polynesia. For use by dance troupes paid to entertain tourists, Hawaiian record companies have sold recordings of ʻōtéʻa and ʻaparima. In the 1960s on the Tiare Tahiti label, Criterion Records (Los Angeles) set up international distribution of Tahitian popular music recorded in Tahiti. Major Tahitian dance troupes—Heiva, Ia Ora Tahiti, Royal Tahitian Ballet, Te Maeva—have issued recordings in ethnographic series. Since 1993, Triloka and Shanachie Records have issued recordings of Tahitian-style choral singing (*hīmene*) that have enjoyed international popularity (figure 4). In Tahiti in the 1980s and 1990s, Gabilou, Irma Prince, Esther Tefana, Andy Tupaia, and other entertainers have released Tahitian popular music on labels including Here, Océane, Puhi Hau, Rama, and Studio Alphonse.

### Hawaiʻi

The first U.S. record company to produce recordings of Hawaiian musicians in Honolulu was Victor, in 1905. Columbia joined the competition in 1910. Other mainland companies active in Hawaiian music included Brunswick, Capitol, and Decca. In 1930, Hawaiian Transcription Productions became the first locally owned recording company. Bell was founded in 1944. These companies were eclipsed in 1948 by 49th State Records. Other local record companies were Hula, Lehua, Mahalo, Poki, Tradewinds, and Waikiki. During the cultural resurgence of the 1970s, these companies were joined by more local labels, including Kahanu, Kanikapila, Mountain Apple, and Pumehana. Musicians in the 1980s and 1990s preferred independent production companies, which let them exercise greater control over their artistic and financial affairs.

The Hawaiian recording industry recognizes excellence annually with an award ceremony, Nā Hōkū Hanohano (Stars of Distinction), organized since 1978 by the

FIGURE 4   On the Triloka label, the Tahitian Choir sings songs from Rapa, the southernmost of the inhabited Austral Islands.

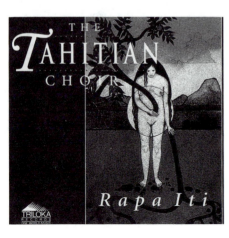

Hawai'i Academy of Recording Arts. Modeled on the Grammy awards, the categories favor Hawaiian musical styles, but categories like Best Contemporary Album accommodate musicians who specialize in other styles.

### Aotearoa

In Aotearoa, where commercial recordings date from 1948, four companies—Hibiscus, Kiwi, Seven Seas, Viking—have associated themselves with Māori and other Polynesian musics (Mitchell 1994). Since the 1960s, the Ode label has included recordings of Cook Islander, Māori, Sāmoan, and Tongan popular musics. Since the 1980s, Māori popular-music artists have been adapting styles associated with rap and reggae. Artists performing Māori-language material have not enjoyed widespread access to multinational recording companies (including BMG, EMI, Polygram, and Sony-CBS), which dominate the country's popular-music industry. Prominent independent labels include Flying Nun (founded in 1981), Jayrem (1982), Pagan (1985), Southside (1990), and Tangata (1991).          —AMY KU'ULEIALOHA STILLMAN

## Multicultural recordings

*Pacific Rhythm, Vol. 1: The First Compilation of the Pacific Islands Top Dance Hits.* 1997. Music of Fiji, Tonga, Sāmoa, Rarotonga. Produced by Kennedy Tau. Evander Kennedy Music EKM 001. Cassette.

*Polynesian Panorama: 20 Authentic Songs and Chants of the Southern Polynesian Islands Performed by Native Islanders Representing the* Polynesian Institute at Laie, Oahu, Hawaii. N.d. Music from Fiji, Tonga, Sāmoa, Tokelau, Cook Islands, Aotearoa. Recordings by Jacob Feuerring. Produced by Bob Bertram. Polynesian PM 700. LP disk.

*Songs and Dances of the Cook Islands.* N.d. Music from Tokelau and the Cook Islands. Viking Records VP 135.

## West Polynesia

*Music of Marginal Polynesia: Fiji, Wallis and Futuna, Tuvalu.* 1994, recorded in 1977–1985. JVC World Sounds Special, Music of Polynesia, 5. VICG-5276-2. Compact disc.

*Samoa, Tonga.* 1988, recorded in 1977–1985. JVC World Sounds Special, Music of Polynesia, 4. VICG-5274. Compact disc.

### Fiji

Chet, Titau, and the Chequers Gold Band. 1996. *Titau Chet & the Chequers Gold Band.* Banaban music. South Pacific Recordings SPR 733. Cassette.

Drola Entertainment Group of Na Cula Village, Yasawa. 1997. *Traditional Fijian Songs and Mekes.* Procera DRO 2059.

*Fiji Calls.* N.d. Viking Records VP 47. LP disk.

*Fiji on Parade: The Band of the Fiji Police Force.* N.d. Viking VP 351. LP disk.

Garden Island Resort Band. 1997. *Garden Island Resort Band: Taveuni—Fiji.* South Pacific Recordings. Compact disc.

*High Lights Music Man.* 1991. Reggae by Epeli Kurualeba. South Pacific Recordings SPR 450. Cassette

Kumar, Ashok. 1997. *Bakhti Kirtan, Vol. 3.* Fiji-Indian music. South Pacific Recordings SPR 316H. Cassette.

Matasiga Choral Group. 1995. *Jisu Jisu.* Procera MCG 2118. Cassette.

Nawaka Entertainment Group. 1991. *Bula Fiji Bula.* South Pacific Recordings. Compact disc.

Rawasese Entertainment Group. 1991. *Mana Island.* South Pacific Recordings. Compact disc.

Serevi, Seru. 1993. *Vude Mai!* South Pacific Recordings. Compact disc.

———. 1997. *The Best of Seru Serevi.* Procera. Compact disc.

Wai Koula ni Gauna Vou Kei Tavua. 1996. *Ocei-e-Bolei Au.* South Pacific Recordings SPR 732. Cassette.

Wilson, Eddie. 1996. *Eddie Wilson's Tarana.* Fiji-Indian popular music. South Pacific Recordings SPR 284H. Cassette.

### Tonga

Bill Sevesi and the Royal Tongans. 1965. *Tunes from Tonga.* Viking VE 103. EP disk.

*Ifi Palasa: Tongan Brass.* 1994. Recordings by Ad Linkels and Lucia Linkels. Notes by Ad Linkels. Anthology of Pacific Music, 4. PAN Records 2044. Compact disc.

Kaho, Tuʻimala. 1988. *Songs of Love.* Warrior Records Pacific Division WARC 2011. Cassette.

*Music from Tonga: The Friendly Islands.* 1976. Recordings by Lavinia ʻA. Finau. Tangent Records TGM 122. LP disk.

*Music of Tonga.* N.d. Recordings by Tonga Broadcasting Commission. Notes by R. MacDonald. Viking Records VP 108. LP disk.

*The Music of Tonga.* 1972. Recordings and notes by Luis Marden. National Geographic Society 3516. LP disk.

Nukuʻalofa Wanderers. 1972? *The Friendly Islands: Music from Tonga.* Viking Records VP 263. LP disk.

Tauhola, Fola ʻOfa, and Siale Hae Vala [groups].

1973. *Tonga Spectacular.* Viking Records VP 353. LP disk.

*Tongan Coronation 1967.* 1967. Viking VE 237. EP disk.

Tongan Festival Contingent, led by The Honourable Veʻehala. 1972. *Music of Tonga.* Recordings by John Ruffell. Hibiscus Records HLS-39, 40. Two LP disks.

*Traditional Music of Tonga: An Authentic Sound Picture.* 1975. Recordings and notes by Richard M. Moyle. Hibiscus Records HLS-65. LP disk.

Tui Mala Group, Queen Salote College Choir, and Tongan Entertainers. N.d. Recordings by Tonga Radio and James Siers. Notes by James Siers. Hibiscus Records HLS-4. LP disk.

### Sāmoa

Choir of the American Samoa Arts Council. 1972. *American Samoa Spectacular.* Viking Records VP 360. LP disk.

*Faʻa-Samoa: The Samoan Way . . . between Conch Shell and Disco.* 1995. Recordings by Ad Linkels and Lucia Linkels. Anthology of Pacific Music, 6. Pan Records. Pan 2066CD. Compact disc.

*Popular Songs of Samoa.* 1996. The Five Stars Collection, 3. Hibiscus Records CD HLS160. Compact disc.

*RSA Band Vol. 4—Apia W. Samoa.* 1996. RSA. Cassette.

*The Music of Samoa: An Authentic Sound Picture.* 1973. Recordings and notes by Richard M. Moyle. Hibiscus HLS-55. LP disk.

*Samoan Songs: A Historical Collection.* N.d. Musicaphon BM 2705. LP disk.

*Songs and Dances of Samoa.* N.d. Viking Records VP 134. LP disk.

Western Samoa Teachers Training College. 1972. *Samoan Song and Rhythm.* Hibiscus Records TC HLS-24. Cassette.

### ʻUvea and Futuna

*Chants et Danses des Îles Wallis.* 1972? [1963?] Recordings by Maurice Bitter. Disque BAM LD 5749. LP disk.

*"Dance to the Wallis Island Beat."* 1969? Recorded by Radio Nouméa. Viking VP 304. LP disk.

*Songs and Dances of Wallis Island.* 1969? Viking Records VP 293. LP disk.

### Niue

*Festival Company of Niue.* 1972. Recorded at the South Pacific Festival of Arts. Hibiscus HE-10. EP disk.

*Niue Island Magic: South Seas Souvenir.* 1973. Viking Records VP 347. LP disk.

*Niue Island Spectacular: Souvenir Record of the South Pacific Arts Festival.* 1973. Viking Records VP 354. LP disk.

### Rotuma

Island Drifters. 1996. *Katoʻaga Helava Fau 150 Ne Rotu Katoliko ʻE Rotuma.* South Pacific Recordings 740. Cassette.

### Tuvalu

*An Evening in the Ellice Islands.* N.d. Salem Record Company XP 5033. LP disk.

*Tuvalu: A Polynesian Atoll Society.* 1994. Recordings and notes by Ad Linkels. PAN 2055CD. Compact disc.

## Polynesian Outliers

Fatuana Matua. 1987? *Mi Laikem Yu . . . Long Fasin Blong Yu.* Music of West Futuna. Vanuata [sic] Productions VP 45. Cassette.

*Ouvea: Chants, Danses et Documents.* 1972? Music of West ʻUvea. Recordings by Maurice Bitter. Disque BAM LD 5754. LP disk.

*Polynesian Dances of Bellona (Mungiki): Solomon Islands.* 1978. Recordings by Jane Mink Rossen and Hugo Zemp. Notes by Jane Mink Rossen. Folkways FE 4274. LP disk.

*Polynesian Songs and Games from Bellona (Mungiki): Solomon Islands.* 1976. Recordings and notes by Jane Mink Rossen. Folkways FE 4273. LP disk.

*Polynesian Traditional Music of Ontong Java (Solomon Islands).* 1971. Music of Luangiua.

Recordings and notes by Hugo Zemp. Collection Musée de l'Homme. Vogue LD 785 and LDM 30.109. Two LP disks.

*Tikopia Songs: Poetic and Musical Art of a Polynesian People of the Solomon Islands.* 1991. Recordings and notes by Raymond Firth, with Mervyn McLean. Cassette.

## East Polynesia

*Easter Island, Marquesas Islands.* 1994, recorded in 1977–1985. JVC World Sounds Special, Music of Polynesia, 3. VICG-5273. Compact disc.

*The Gauguin Years: Songs and Dances of Tahiti.* Music of the Marquesas, Society Islands, Tuamotus. 1966?, recorded in 1965. Recordings by Francis Mazière. Notes by Jane Sarnoff. Explorer Series. Nonesuch H-72017. LP disk.

*Îles Marquises et Tuamotu: Chants et Musique.* 1976. Recordings by Henri Lavondes. Orstom SETO 755. LP disk.

*1980—Année du Patrimoine: Îles Marquises— Tahiti.* 1980. Manuiti 3038. LP disk.

*Tahiti, Dream Island.* N.d. Tracks 1–9 are Tahitian; 10–23, Marquesan. Productions Musicales Polynésiennes. Manuiti/Playa Sound PS 65007. Compact disc.

*Tahiti, Society Islands.* 1988. JVC World Sounds Special, Music of Polynesia, 1. VICG-5271. Compact disc.

*Tuamotu, Austral Islands.* 1994, recorded in 1977–1990. JVC World Sounds Special, Music of Polynesia, 2. VICG-5272. Compact disc.

### *Society Islands*

Le Ballet Polynésien Heiva. N.d. *O Tahiti.* Directed by Madeleine Moua. Chant du Monde LDX 74342. LP disk.

*Chants & Rythmes du Pacifique Sud: South Pacific Songs and Rhythms.* 1968. Productions Musicales Polynésiennes. Manuiti/Playa Sound PS 65018. Compact disc.

Coco et son groupe folklorique Temaeva. N.d. *Tiurai: Tahiti Festival.* Manuiti 3 203. LP disk.

*Drums of Bora Bora and Songs of Tahiti.* 1993. Tracks 1–17 recorded by Gaston Guilbert in 1956; tracks 18–32 produced by Yves Roche for Criterion Records in 1993. Crescendo Records GNPD 2214. Compact disc.

*Escale à Tahiti: A Journey to Tahiti.* 1994. Productions Musicales Polynésiennes. Manuiti/ Playa Sound PS 66501. Compact disc.

*Heiva à Tahiti, 1: Himene, ute, toere: Les plus beaus moments du Heiva.* N.d. Recorded at Vai'ete by Francis Teai. Produced by OTAC—Te Fare Tauhiti Nui. JMC Production Rama R016. Cassette.

Hiriata et son Choeur, Salamon et ses Batteurs, and Maono et le Groupe de Patutoa. N.d. *Eddie Lund Presents . . . Aparima et Otea.* Tahiti Records EL 1017. LP disk.

Joël et son Groupe Folklorique Maeva Tahiti. 1976. *Pirogues Tahitiennes: Ballet—Aparima.* Editions Manuiti 1712. EP disk.

Lund, Eddie, and His Tahitians and Mila. N.d. *Eddie Lund Presents . . . To the South Seas with the Tahiti Yacht Race.* Tahiti Records EL-1003. LP disk.

Manuia and Maeva. 1965? *Otuitui Tahiti: Et d'autres grands succes de Tahiti.* Produced by Michael H. Goldsen. Reo Tahiti Records/ Criterion Records RTS 520. LP disk.

Moua, Madeleine, and Les Ballets Heiva. N.d. *À Vous Tahiti.* Philips 844.915. LP disk.

L'Orchestré [sic] Hotel Tahiti, Paulina et Salamon, and Les Mama Ruau Ma. N.d. *Eddie Lund Presents . . . Tahiti—Mon Amour.* Tahiti Records EL 1016. LP disk.

*Pahu Tahiti! Authentic Drums of the South Seas.* N.d. Recordings by Gaston Guilbert. Criterion Records SRT-560. LP disk.

*Paparai: Himene Tarava, Ute, Tuki.* 1991. Océane Production OCN CD11. Compact disc.

*Percussions Polynésiennes: South Pacific Drums.* 1990, recorded from 1965 to 1990. Productions Musicales Polynésiennes. Manuiti/Playa Sound PS 65066. Compact disc.

Royal Folkloric Troupe of Tahiti. 1992, recorded in 1966, 1970, and 1972. *Coco's Temaeva.* Manuiti Productions Musicales Polynésiennes S 65808. Compact disc.

Royal Folkloric Troupe of Tahiti. 1994, recorded in 1966, 1970, 1972, and 1987. *Coco's Temaeva.* Vol. 2. Manuiti Productions Musicales Polynésiennes S 65815. Compact disc.

Royal Tahitian Dance Company. 1974. *Royal Tahitian Dance Company.* 1974. Monitor Records MCD 71758. Compact disc.

*Tahiti, Belle Époque: All Time Tahitian Favorites.* 1991, recorded from 1940 to 1967. Productions Musicales Polynésiennes S 65807. Compact disc.

*Tahiti, Belle Époque 3: Original Barefoot Boys from the 60's: Ensemble original du Bar Lea.* 1992, recorded in 1967 and 1968. Productions Musicales Polynésiennes S 65811. Compact disc.

*Tahiti, Belle Époque 4: Songs of the Atolls & the Islands.* 1994. Recordings by Gaston Guilbert in

1955–1959 and 1966. Productions Musicales Polynésiennes/Playa Sound PS 65816. Compact disc.

*Tahiti Fête! Authentique Folklorique.* 1997? Criterion Records SST-1800. LP disk.

*Tahiti: Islands of Paradise: Authentic Tahitian Music Recorded by Gaston Guilbert in Papeete during the Filming of "Mutiny on the Bounty."* 1956? MGM E 4082. LP disk.

### Austral Islands

*Pupu Himene no Rurutu 1.* 1980? Recorded by Studio Hei Tiare. Rama R–002. Cassette.

*Pupu Himene no Rurutu 2.* 1980? Recorded by Studio Hei Tiare. Rama R–003. Cassette.

*The Rurutu Choir: Polynesian Odyssey.* 1996. Recordings by Pascal Nabet-Meyer. Shenachie Entertainment SH-64065. Compact disc.

*The Tahitian Choir: Rapa Iti.* 1992. Recordings by Pascal Nabet-Meyer. Triloka Records 7192-2. Compact disc.

### Tuamotu Islands

Lund, Eddie, and his Tahitians. N.d. *Paumotu Drums, Songs and Chants.* Viking Records VP 56.

Mariterangi. N.d. *Ua Reka.* Music arranged by Eddie Lund. Tahiti Records EL 108. LP disk.

### Marquesas Islands

Kanahau Trio. 1990s. *Haavei i Ua Huka.* Recordings by Here Recording. Océane Production STT 40, vol. 2. Compact disc.

Rataro. 1990s. *Kaoha, les Marquises.* Recordings by Here Recording. Océane Production A063. Cassette.

———. 1994. *Marquises Terre Sauvage.* Océane Production OCN CD38. Compact disc.

Salomon et son Groupe avec Kapuhia. N.d. *Polynesian Primitive.* Tahiti Records EL 1035. LP disk.

*Te Eo Hiva Oa.* 1990s. Recorded at Studio JMC

### Cook Islands

*Cook Islands Musical Spectacular, Silver Anniversary 1965–1990.* 1990. Recorded by Capricorn Studios. Produced by the Ministry of Cultural Development and Capricorn Studios. Capricorn CPR 206. Cassette.

*Imene Tuki: Cook Islands Traditional Singing.* 1990. Recorded by Capricorn Studios. Produced by the Ministry of Cultural Development and Capricorn Studios. Capricorn CPR 207. Cassette.

### Hawai'i

*Aloha Hula Hawaiian Style.* 1995. Remastered recordings. Vintage Hawaiian Treasures, 9. HanaOla HOCD 26000. Compact disc.

Apaka, Alfred. N.d. *The Golden Voice of the Island.* Hula Records C-HS408. LP disk.

———. 1984. *Hawaiian Paradise.* Capitol Records 541–56636. LP disk.

*Tahiti Variétés.* 1986. Océane Production OCN CD01. Compact disc.

Temaeva and Coco Hotahota. N.d. *Te Vahine Maohi.* Tupuna Production/Editions JMC Rama R012. Cassette.

Les Voix des Atolls and Le Zizou Bar Trio. N.d. *Ta'u Tahiti (Mon Tahiti).* Recordings by Gaston Guilbert. Criterion Records STT-2000. LP disk.

*The Tahitian Choir Vol. II.* 1994. Recordings by Pascal Nabet-Meyer. Shanachie Entertainment SH-64055. Compact disc.

*Tamarii Manureva no Rurutu.* 1980s. Océane Production C-008. Cassette.

*The Tubuai Choir.* 1993. Recordings by Pascal Nabet-Meyer. Shenachie Entertainment SH-64049. Compact disc.

*Paumotu: Teaitu Mariterangi.* N.d. Produced by Michael H. Goldsen. Criterion Records RT-419. EP disk.

Production. Te Eo, 1. Océane Production. Cassette.

*Te Hakamanu: La Danse de l'Oiseau.* 1990. Légende Marquisienne avec musique et chants du Festival des Arts des Îles Marquises. Haere Po no Tahiti. Rama 013. Cassette.

*Te Ka'ioi.* 1991. Recorded at Studio de l'I.C.A. Océane Production CO13. Cassette.

*Îles Marquises et Tuamotu: Chants et Musique.* 1981. Recordings by Henri Lavondès. Collection Traditional Orale. ORSTOM-SELAF. Cassette.

*Tapuahua Boys.* 1990. Recorded by the T & A Onu Studio. T & A Onu Studio TO25. Cassette.

*Tumutevarovaro Live—Rarotonga, Cook Islands.* 1990. Recorded by Capricorn Studios. Capricorn CPR 202. Cassette.

Beamer, Keola. 1995. *Moe'uhane Kīkā: "Tales from the Dream Guitar."* Dancing Cat Records 08022–38023. Compact disc, cassette.

Bruddah Waltah & Island Afternoon. 1990. *Hawaiian Reggae.* Platinum Pacific Records PPR 1005CD. Compact disc.

Cazimero, Brothers. 1977. *The Brothers Cazimero in Concert*. Produced by Jack DeMello. Music of Polynesia 32672. Cassette.

———. 1987. *The Best of the Brothers Cazimero*. Mountain Apple MACD-2011. Compact disc.

———. 1997. *Twenty Years of Hōkū Award-Winning Songs*. Mountain Apple MACD-2042. Compact disc.

*Chuck Machado's Luau Inc.: Recorded Live on the Beach at Waikiki*. N.d. Recording by Sounds of Hawaii. CPM-9318. LP disk.

Denny, Martin. 1996. *Exotica: The Sounds of Martin Denny*. Scampi SCP 9712. Compact disc.

Edwards, Webley. 1997 [1975]. *Hawaii Calls: Hawaii's Greatest Hits*. Hawaii Calls, Inc. HCS 921A, 922A. Two compact discs.

*The Extraordinary Kui Lee*. 1997. Remastered recordings. Hawaiian Legends, 2. HanaOla HOCD 28000. Compact disc.

*Felix Mendelssohn & His Hawaiian Serenaders*. 1997. Remastered recordings. Music of Hawaii, 5. Harlequin HQ CD 93. Compact disc.

*Folk and National Music Recordings, Volume 1: Foreign Countries*. 1958. Recordings by the British Broadcasting Commission. Recorded Programmes Permanent Library, 239–243, record 23176. LP disk.

*Hapa Haole Hawaiian Hula Classics*. 1993. Remastered recordings. Vintage Hawaiian Treasures, 1. HanaOla HOCD 17000. Compact disc.

*Hawaiian Chants, Hula and Love-Dance Songs*. 1989 [1972]. Vocals by Kaulaheaonamoku Hiona. Recorded by Jacob Feuerring. Reissued with revised notes by Elizabeth Tatar. Smithsonian Folkways 4271. LP disk.

*Hawaiian Chant, Hula and Music*. 1989 [1962]. Vocals by Kaulaheaonamoku Hiona. Recorded by Jacob Feuerring. Reissued with revised notes by Elizabeth Tatar. Smithsonian Folkways 8750. LP disk.

*Hawaiian Drum Dance Chants: Sounds of Power in Time*. 1989. Notes by Elizabeth Tatar. Smithsonian Folkways SF-40015. Cassette, compact disc.

The Hawaiian Festival Contingent. 1976. *Festival Music from Hawaii*. Hibiscus Records HLS-71. LP disk.

*Hawaiian Masters Collection, Vol. 1*. 1991. Remastered recordings. Tantalus Records TRCD 1002. Compact disc.

*Hawaiian Masters Collection, Vol. 2*. 1993. Remastered recordings. Tantalus Records TRCD 1003. Compact disc.

*Hawaiian Slack Key Guitar Masters: Instrumental Collection*. 1995. Dancing Cat Records 08022-38032-2. Compact disc.

*Hawaiian Song Bird Lena Machado*. 1997. Remastered recordings. Hawaiian Legends, 3. HanaOla HOCD 29000. Compact disc.

Hawaiian Style Band. 1994. *Rhythm of the Ocean*. Top Flight Records 2936. Compact disc.

*The History of Slack Key Guitar*. 1995. Remastered recordings. Vintage Hawaiian Treasures, 7. HanaOla HOCD 24000. Compact disc.

Ho'opi'i Brothers. 1975. *No Ka Oi*. Poki Records SP 9006. Cassette.

———. 1996. *Ho'opi'i Brothers: Ho'omau—To Perpetuate*. Produced by Jay W. Junker and Diane Sunada Koshi for Honu Productions. Notes by Jay W. Junker. Mountain Apple. Compact disc.

*Hula Hawaiian Style*. 1994. Remastered recordings. Vintage Hawaiian Treasures, 2. HanaOla HOCD 18000. Compact disc.

Kahumoku, George Jr. 1997. *Drenched by Music*. Produced by George Winston and George Kahumoku Jr. Dancing Cat Records 08022-38038-2. Compact disc.

*The Kalima Brothers and the Richard Kauhi Quartette*. 1996. Remastered recordings. Hawaiian Legends, 1. HanaOla HOCD 27000. Compact disc.

Kamakawiwo'ole, Israel. 1993. *Facing Future*. Bigboy Record Company BBCD 5901. Compact disc.

Kanaka'ole, Aunty Edith. 1978. *Ha'aku'i Pele i Hawai'i!* Produced by Don McDiarmid Jr. Notes by Kalani Meinecke. Hula Records HS-560. LP disk.

———. 1979. *Hi'ipoi i ka 'Āina Aloha: Cherish the Beloved Land*. Hula Records HS-568. LP disk.

Kāne, Raymond. 1988. *Music Recorded for the Robert Mugge Film HAWAIIAN RAINBOW*. Produced by Robert Mugge. Rounder Records 6020. LP disk.

———. 1994. *Punahele*. Dancing Cat Records 08022-38001-2. Compact disc.

Kapena. 1992. *The Kapena Collection*. Remastered recordings. KDE Records KDE-1059CD. Compact disc.

*KCCN's 25th Anniversary Collection: 25 of Hawaii's Most Beloved Songs*. 1991, recorded between 1957 and 1990. Two cassettes.

*Kodak Hula Show*. N.d. Produced by Tommy Kearns. Waikiki Records WC-302. Cassette.

Kotani, Ozzie. 1995. *Kani Hō'alu (The Sound of Slack Key)*. Dancing Cat Records 08022-38013. Compact disc.

Ku, Tony, accompanied by Tomomi Sugiura. 1979. *Original Hawaiian Steel Guitar*. Notes by Isami Uchizaki. Folkways FW 8714. LP disk.

Maiki Aiu Lake and The Kahauanu Lake Trio and Singers. 1992. *Maiki: Chants and Mele of Hawaii*. Hula Records CHDS-588. Compact disc.

*Mehe Hula Hawaiian Style*. 1994. Remastered recordings. Vintage Hawaiian Treasures, 4. HanaOla HOCD 20000. Compact disc.

*Mele-Hula*. N.d. Produced by H. Skippy Hamamoto. Collectors Series, 1–2. Noelani Records NRS 102–103. Two LP disks.

*The Music of Hawaii*. 1974. Recordings by Marc J. Aubort. Notes by Mary McPeak and Robert E. Pullman. National Geographic Society 706. LP disk.

*Musics of Hawai'i: "It All Comes from the Heart."* 1994. Folk Arts Program, State Foundation on Culture and Arts. Five cassettes.

*Na Mele Ho'oheno: A Musical Tradition.* 1997. Retrospective of 75 years of the choral-singing contest. Kamehameha Schools/Bernice Pauahi Bishop Estate. Two compact discs.

Nahenahe Singers. 196? *Hawaii's Folk Singers.* Tradewinds-Records TS-115. LP disk.

*Nā Leo Hawai'i Kahiko: Voices of Old Hawai'i.* 1981. Notes by Elizabeth Tatar. Audio-Recording Collection Series, 1. Bishop Museum ARCS-1. Two LP disks.

*Na Mele Paniolo: Songs of Hawaiian Cowboys.* 1992 [1987]. Notes revised by Ricardo D. Trimillos, with an introduction by Lynn Martin. Folk Arts Program, State Foundation on Culture and the Arts. Two cassettes.

Naope, George. 1985. *The Other Side of Hawaii's Golden Treasure: Na Mele o Kawa Kahiko (Chants of Hawaii).* 1985. MDL-6430. Compact disc.

*Nature's Mystic Moods: The Sounds of Hawaii.* 1975. Recorded by Brad Miller. Bainbridge Entertainment BT6240. LP disk.

*Night Club Hula Hawaiian Style.* 1995. Remastered recordings. Vintage Hawaiian Treasures, 6. HanaOla HOCD 23000. Compact disc.

*On the Beach at Waikiki (1914–1952).* 1995. Remastered recordings. Music of Hawaii, 3. Harlequin HQ CD 57. Compact disc.

*On a Coconut Island.* 1994. Remastered recordings. Music of Hawaii, 2. Harlequin HQ CD 46. Compact disc.

Pahinui, Gabby. 1972. *Gabby.* Panini Records PS-1002. LP disk.

Peter Moon Band, with David Choy, Martin Pahinui, and Palani Vaughan. 1994. *Iron Mango.* Kanikapila Records KCD-1014. Compact disc.

Reichel, Keali'i. 1994. *Kawipunahele.* Punahele Records PP001. Compact disc.

———. 1997. *Lei Hali'a.* Punahele Records. Compact disc.

*Rhythm of the Islands, 1913–1952.* Remastered recordings. Music of Hawaii, 4. Harlequin HQ CD 92. Compact disc.

*The Royal Hawaiian Band: Live at Carnegie Hall.* N.d., recorded in 1988. FRB CD 002–003. Two compact discs.

*Santa's Gone Hawaiian.* 1995. Remastered recordings. Vintage Hawaiian Treasures, 8. HanaOla HOCD 25000. Compact disc.

*Show Biz Hula Hawaiian Style.* 1995. Remastered recordings. Vintage Hawaiian Treasures, 5. HanaOla HOCD 22000. Compact disc.

*Sons of Hawaii: The Folk Music of Hawaii in Book and Record.* 1971. Produced by Steve Siegfried, Witt Shingle, and Lawrence Brown. Notes by Carl Lindquist. Island Heritage KN 1001. LP disk.

Ta'ua, Keli'i. 1977a. *Kamehameha Chants.* Pumehana Records PS-4918. Compact disc.

Ta'ua, Keli'i. 1977b. *The Pele Legends.* Pumehana Records PS-4903. Compact disc.

*Tickling the Strings, 1929–1952.* 1993. Remastered recordings. Music of Hawaii, 1. Harlequin HQ CD 28. Compact disc.

Topolinski, Kaha'i. 1986. *Nou E, Kawena: For You, Kawena.* Pumehana Records PS-4926. LP disk.

*Traditional Music from Hawai'i: Music from the Motion Picture Soundtrack TROUBLED PARADISE.* 1992. Flying Fish Records FF70607. Compact disc.

*We Are Hawaii.* N.d. Hula Records P 21. Two LP disks.

Wong, Kaupena, and Pele Pukui. 1974. *Mele Inoa: Authentic Hawaiian Chants.* Poki Records SP 9003. LP disk.

### Aotearoa

*Authentic Maori Chants.* N.d. Recordings prepared by the Maori Purposes Fund Board. Kiwi EC 8–10. Three EP disks.

*Maori Songs of New Zealand: Haka, Tangi, Oriori, Waiata, Maemae, Karakia, Apakura.* 1952. Recordings by the New Zealand Broadcasting Service. Ethnic Folkways P433. LP disk.

Polynesian Studies Group. N.d. *The Magic of Maori Song.* Salem XP 5025. LP disk.

Putiki Maori Club. N.d. *Maori Action Songs.* M3D-1. EP disk.

Te Wiata, Inia. N.d. *The Maori Flute: The Hinemoa Legend in Song and Story.* Kiwi EA-120. EP disk.

Turakina Maori Girls' College Choir, Marton, New Zealand. N.d. *The Maori Girls of Turakina.* Viking VP 255. LP disk.

### Rapa Nui

*The Easter Island.* 1976. Recordings by Claude Jannel. Edited by Ariane Segal. Peters International FARN 91040. LP disk.

*Isla de Pascua.* 1965. Recordings by Jorge di Lauro. Odeon Chilena/EMI LDC-36547/36548. Two LP disks.

*Ka Oho Mai.* N.d. Contemporary music by Sergio Teao and friends. Private issue. Cassette.

*Música de Isla de Pascua.* 1991. Recopilación Ramón Campbell. Collección Música Chilena, Serie 1, Música Vernácula. Sección de Musicología, Facultad de Artes, Universidad de Chile. Cassette.

*Musiques de l'Île de Pâques (Rapa-Noui).* 1976. Recordings by Christos Clair-Vasiliadis. Société Française de Productions Phonographiques AMP 7 2908. LP disk.

*Rapa Nui: Music and Natural Sounds.* 1995.

Recordings and notes by Jörg Hertel. Noiseworks 130. Compact disc.

Tepano, Tomás Tepano. 1996. *Rapa Nui.* Arion ARN 64345. Compact disc.

## CONTEMPORARY CROSS-CULTURAL SYNTHESES

In the spread of the international, syncretic practice known as worldbeat, Oceania has been less subject to projects of the North American and European music industry than have Africa, South America, or, to a lesser extent, Asia. An early cross-cultural engagement in Oceania was the collaboration between Hawaiian slack-key guitarist Gabby Pahinui and North American blues guitarist Ry Cooder. Pahinui performed on Cooder's album *Chicken Skin Music* (1976), and Cooder played on Pahinui's album *Volume One* (1977). These performers' involvement on each other's recordings was essentially that of guest players, conforming to their hosts' musical styles.

In the production of cross-cultural musical innovations, the most notable project in Oceania has been that undertaken by the Melbourne-based experimental rock band Not Drowning, Waving (NDW) and musicians from Papua New Guinea, particularly vocalist George Telek, beginning in 1986. The first product of this liaison was released in 1990 under the title *Tabaran.* This album included recordings of compositions by NDW and Telek and versions of traditional New Guinean material. It was notable for arranging and recording these items in a rich, complex mix and with subtle dynamics, which derived from the work of Brian Eno and Obscure Records artists, including John Hassell, in the late 1970s and early 1980s (Hayward 1996). In 1996, after NDW broke up, the band's vocalist and keyboardist, David Bridie, produced an album (*Telek* 1997) that featured Australian and Papua New Guinean musicians and explored multiple musical approaches. Critics in Australia and Papua New Guinea praised *Tabaran* and *Telek* as models of successful and mutually respectful musical syntheses.

In 1994, after working with NDW, Ben Hakalits and fellow Papua New Guinean musician Buruku Tau joined Australian Aboriginal band Yothu Yindi, whose subsequent album, *Birrkuta: Wild Honey* (1996) featured traditional Papua New Guinean instrumentation and can be considered a cross-cultural recording. Other musicians have combined Polynesian, Melanesian, and Aboriginal musical instrumentations, drawing on musical styles and performers from outside their culture. A notable example is the incorporation of the didjeridu in the lineup of the Tahitian band Manahune (1995).

An impediment to further cross-cultural musical collaborations in Oceania is the cost of interinsular travel for most musicians, who receive little compensation for their activities and are signed to low-profit or low-overhead companies, which hesitate to engage in speculative projects. In Australia and Aotearoa, another impediment is the conservatism of the music industries, which remain reluctant to explore the market for locally originated worldbeat projects. —PHILIP HAYWARD

### Recordings

Anthill, John. 1977. *Corroboree: Symphonic Ballet.* Sydney Symphony Orchestra, conducted by John Lanchbery. EMI Records Australia OASD 7603. LP disk.

Atherton, Michael. N.d. *Windshift.* Compact disc.

*Australia: Reconciliation: Two Stories in One.* N.d. Compact disc.

Cooder, Ry, with Gabby Pahinui. 1975. *Chicken Skin Music.* Reprise Records K54083. LP disk.

The Gabby Pahinui Hawaiian Band, with Ry Cooder. 1977, recorded in 1974–1975. *Volume One.* Warner Brothers BS 3023. LP disk.

Laurens, Guy. 1995? *Fenua.* Tahitian techno. Océane Production OCN CD58. Compact disc.

Manahune. 1995, recorded in 1992. *The Nurturing Hand.* Tahitian worldbeat. Recorded at Studio Hei Tiare. Hula Records International CDHS-1001. Compact disc.

Not Drowning, Waving, and the Musicians of

Rabaul, PNG (featuring Telek). 1990. *Tabaran.* WEA 903172999. Two compact discs.

*Polynesian Music Festival '93.* 1994. Music from Fiji, Tonga, Sāmoa, Tuvalu, Tahiti, Cook Islands, Hawai'i, Aotearoa, Rapa Nui. Produced by Nigel Stone. Raging Goose Productions PMFT 001. Cassette, compact disc.

Rasta Nui. 1995. *Tahiti Reggae Beat.* Tahitian reggae. Recorded at Studio Hei Tiare. Produced by Tupuna Production. Hula Records CD HS-1002. Compact disc.

Royal Band. 1995. *Royal Band Live: En direct du Royal Papeete.* Océane Production OCN CD 55. Compact disc.

Telek, George. 1997. *Telek.* Origin OR 030. Compact disc.

Yothu Yindi. 1996. *Birrkuta: Wild Honey.* Mushroom Records. Compact disc.

## REFERENCES

Ammann, Raymond. 1997. *Kanak Dance and Music: Ceremonial and Intimate Performance of the Melanesians of New Caledonia, Historical and Actual.* London: Kegan Paul.

Barwick, Linda, and Allan Marett. 1996. "Selected Audiography of Traditional Music of Aboriginal Australia." *Yearbook of Traditional Music* 28:174–188.

Crowe, Peter. 1995. "Melanesian Music on Compact Disc: Some Significant Issues." *Pacific Studies* 18(3):147–159.

Elkin, A. P., and Trevor A. Jones. 1953–1956. *Arnhem Land Music (North Australia).* Oceania monograph 9. Sydney: The University of Sydney.

Furness, William Henry. 1910. *The Island of Stone Money: Uap of the Carolines.* Philadelphia: J. B. Lippincott.

Hayward, Philip. 1996. *Music at the Borders: Not Drowning, Waving and Their Engagement with Papua New Guinean Culture (1986–96).* Sydney: John Libbey.

Herzog, George. 1932. "Die Musik auf Truk." In *Truk,* part 2, by Augustin Krämer. Ergebnisse der Südsee Expedition 1908–1910, II.B.5. Edited by Georg Thilenius. Hamburg: Friedrichsen de Gruyter.

———. 1936. "Die Musik der Carolinen-Inseln." In *Westkarolinen,* by Anneliese Eilers. Ergebnisse der Südsee Expedition 1908–1910, II.B.9. Edited by Georg Thilenius. Hamburg: Friedrichsen de Gruyter.

Hopkins, Jerry. 1979. "Record Industry in Hawai'i." In *Hawaiian Music and Musicians: An Illustrated History,* ed. George S. Kanahele, 325–334. Honolulu: University Press of Hawai'i.

Mitchell, Tony. 1994. "Flying in the Face of Fashion: Independent Music in New Zealand." In *North Meets South: Popular Music in Aotearoa/New Zealand,* ed. Philip Hayward, Tony Mitchell, and Roy Shuker, 28–72. Sydney: Perfect Beat Publications.

Moyle, Alice M. 1966. *A Handlist of Field Collections of Recorded Music in Australia and Torres Strait.* Canberra: Australian Institute of Aboriginal Studies. Occasional Papers in Aboriginal Studies, 6. Ethnomusicology Series, 1.

———. 1968–1969. "Aboriginal Music on Cape York." *Musicology* 3:1–20.

Niles, Don. 1984. *Commercial Recordings of Papua New Guinea Music: 1949–1983.* Boroko: Institute of Papua New Guinea Studies.

———. 1985. *Commercial Recordings of Papua New Guinea Music: 1984 Supplement.* Boroko: Institute of Papua New Guinea Studies.

———. 1987a. *Commercial Recordings of Papua New Guinea Music: 1985 Supplement.* Boroko: Institute of Papua New Guinea Studies.

———. 1987b. *Commercial Recordings of Papua New Guinea Music: 1986 Supplement.* Boroko: Institute of Papua New Guinea Studies.

———. 1988. *Commercial Recordings of Papua New Guinea Music: 1987 Supplement.* Boroko: Institute of Papua New Guinea Studies.

———. 1991. *Commercial Recordings of Papua New Guinea Music: 1988 Supplement.* Boroko: National Research Institute.

———. 1992. "The Chinese and Music in Papua New Guinea." *Association for Chinese Music Research Newsletter* 5(2):31–35.

———. 1993. *Commercial Recordings of Papua New Guinea Music: 1989 Supplement.* Boroko: National Research Institute.

Niles, Don, and Clement Gima. 1993a. *Commercial Recordings of Papua New Guinea Music: 1990 Supplement.* Boroko: National Research Institute.

———. 1993b. *Commercial Recordings of Papua New Guinea Music: 1991 Supplement.* Boroko: National Research Institute.

———. 1994. *Commercial Recordings of Papua New Guinea Music: 1992 Supplement.* Boroko: National Research Institute.

Sheridan, Ray. 1972. "Music (2)." In *Encyclopaedia of Papua New Guinea,* ed. Peter Ryan, 817–821. Melbourne: Melbourne University Press.

South Pacific Commission. 1956. *Clearing House Service for Broadcast Recordings.* Technical paper 93. Noumea: South Pacific Commission.

———. 1957. *Clearing House Service for Pacific Broadcast Recordings.* Technical paper 93, supplement 1. Noumea: South Pacific Commission.

———. 1959. *Pacific Islands Broadcast Recordings Service.* Technical paper 93, supplement 2. Noumea: South Pacific Commission.

Tatar, Elizabeth. 1979a. "Radio and Hawaiian Music." In *Hawaiian Music and Musicians: An Illustrated History,* ed. George S. Kanahele, 320–325. Honolulu: University Press of Hawai'i.

———. 1979b. "Selected Discography." In *Hawaiian Music and Musicians: An Illustrated History,* ed. George S. Kanahele, 419–482. Honolulu: University Press of Hawai'i.

Webb, Michael. 1993. *Lokal Musik: Lingua Franca Song and Identity in Papua New Guinea.* Apwitihire, 3. Boroko: National Research Institute.

# Films and Videos of Oceanic Performing Arts

*J. W. Love*

**Pacific Festivals of Art**
**Multicultural Films and Videos**
**Australia**
**New Guinea**
**Melanesia**
**Micronesia**
**Polynesia**

More fully than other media, films convey the presence of music and dance. But like texts, transcriptions, and other edited realities, films play with illusion. Their appeal is partial. Filling two spatial dimensions and breaking the flow of time, they capture only pieces of the world they depict. Giving structure to those pieces, they make a world of their own—an illusion that any depicted performers and savvy viewers, facing its immanent unreality, readily see through. Because films frame their subject, they temper what they picture. To tell their truth, they always lie. Hence, how the maker shapes the show is the crux of cinematic analysis (Heider 1976; Loizos 1993). Implications extend to questions of politics and power. Who controls filmed representations of life in Oceania has emerged as an issue in current discourse on *kastom,* tradition, identity, and cultural construction (Hanson 1989; Linnekin 1992).

Films record encounters between the people behind the camera and the people in front of it [see ENCOUNTERS WITH "THE OTHER": Filmmakers]. Viewing compounds the transaction. Analysis, assuming neutral perspectives at safe removes, explores what celluloid or digital images tell about these encounters. It may focus on images seen in stills (Blanton 1995; Poignant 1996) or in motion (Barclay 1988; Blythe 1988; Rollwagen 1988). In the late twentieth century, Aboriginal Australians and Pacific Islanders increasingly understand the intercultural dynamics of film-related encounters. Improving technology and increasing prosperity enable them to go behind the lens to produce films for their own purposes [see MUSIC AND POLITICS: Hawaiian Documentary Videos as Political Tools]. These purposes fundamentally differ from those of most academic filmmakers, typically outsiders, drawn to view "the other" from bases in Australia, Europe, Japan, and North America.

Films of Oceanic music and dance range from the common fare of Hollywood entertainment, as in Elvis Presley's *Blue Hawaii,* to the unique artistry of Robert J. Flaherty (Calder-Marshall 1963). Some filmmakers explore critical issues and cultural processes. Along these lines, Chris Owens has studied expressive behavior in Papua New Guinea (Volkman 1986) and Hugo Zemp has studied indigenous musical instruments and theory in the Solomon Islands (*'Are'are Music* and *Shaping Bamboo,* Solomon Islands). Some films show performances of music and dance at major gatherings. Such items include *Lockhart Dance Festival* (Australia: Queensland) and *Songs of the Rainbow* (New Guinea: Highland Region). Some films show how music informs events, including official visits by a British governor (*Governor General's Tour,* New Guinea), prince (*Scenes at the Rotorua Hui,* Polynesia: East Polynesia: Aotearoa), and queen (*Turou Aere Mai,* Polynesia: East Polynesia: Cook Islands). Some films show how music and dance reveal or structure social contexts and concerns. Some films—including those made by Alice M. Moyle and E. C. Snell in Northern Australia for the Groote Eylandt Field Project, affiliates of the Agence de Développement de la Culture Kanak in New Caledonia, and Gerd Koch in Kiribati—document specific genres.

Throughout Oceania, festivals attract photographers and filmmakers expecting easily to sample multiple performing groups and cultures. Some festivals have spawned ongoing series of videos, of which those on Hawaiian festivals—including videos produced by the Alpha Media Corporation, KITV4 TAK Communications, and the State Council on Hawaiian Heritage—cover the King Kamehameha Traditional Chant and Hula Competition, the Merrie Monarch Festival, and the Queen Lili'uokalani Keiki Hula Festival.

The rise of MTV and the spread of rock videos have inspired Oceanic musicians (Hayward 1995). In Hawai'i, Peter Moon and the Brothers Cazimero made music videos in the early 1980s. Henry Kapono's video *Sovereignty,* celebrating a Hawaiian prosovereignty event, and Keali'i Reichel's video *Kukahi 1996,* documenting a major concert, have received uncommon public interest. Gaining in circulation are instructional videos, including Keola Beamer's *The Art of Hawaiian Slack Key Guitar* and Raymond Kāne's *Ki Hō'alu: Play & Learn.*

Detailed catalogs of published films and videos showing Oceanic music and dance are those of the Institut für den Wissenschaftlichen Film (*Filmkatalog: Ethnologie: Australien/Ozeanian*) and the Center for Pacific Islands Studies (Aoki 1994, updated at www2.hawaii.edu/oceanic/film). Surveys of related issues include those by Douglas (1981), Heider and Hermer (1995), Pike and Cooper (1980), Reyes (1995), and Schmitt (1988). A list of Hawaiian music in Hollywood films is available at www.concentric.net/~hookupu/htdocs/movhaw.html.

To enhance the illusion of authenticity, Oceanic travelogs and other films present clips of music and dance. The list below selects films primarily devoted to these topics. It sorts published films as items stemming from the Pacific Festivals of Arts, items showing more than one major culture, and items particular to individual cultures. The order of headings and subheadings follows that of Part 3 of the volume. Featured cultures, places, performers, and topics appear in brackets.    —J. W. LOVE

## REFERENCES

Aoki, Diane, ed. 1994. *Moving Images of the Pacific Islands: A Catalogue of Films and Videos.* Occasional Paper 38. Honolulu: Center for Pacific Islands Studies, School of Hawaiian, Asian, and Pacific Studies, University of Hawai'i at Mānoa.

Barclay, Barry. 1988. "The Control of One's Own Image." *Centerviews* 6(5):1, 4.

Blanton, Casey, ed. 1995. *Picturing Paradise: Colonial Photography of Samoa, 1875 to 1925.* Daytona Beach: Southeast Museum of Photography, Daytona Beach Community College; in collaboration with the Rautenstrauch-Joest-Museum of Ethnology, Cologne, Germany.

Blythe, Martin. 1988. "From Maoriland to Aotearoa: Images of the Maori in New Zealand Film and Television." Ph.D. dissertation, University of California at Los Angeles.

Calder-Marshall, Arthur. 1963. *The Innocent Eye: The Life of Robert J. Flaherty.* London: W. H. Allen.

Douglas, Norman. 1981. "Films for Pacific Studies: A Select List." *Pacific History Association Newsletter 4,* May.

*Filmkatalog: Ethnologie: Australien/Ozeanian.* 1990. Göttingen: Institut für den Wissenschaftlichen Film.

Hanson, Allan. 1989. "The Making of the Maori: Culture Invention and Its Logic." *American Anthropologist* 91(4):890–902.

Hayward, Philip. 1995. "A New Tradition: Titus Tilly and the Development of Music Video in Papua New Guinea." *Perfect Beat* 2(2):1–19.

Heider, Karl G. 1976. *Ethnographic Film.* Austin: University of Texas Press.

Heider, Karl G., and Carol Hermer. 1995. *Films for Anthropological Teaching.* 8th edition. Special publication 29. Arlington, Va.: American Anthropological Association.

Linnekin, Jocelyn. 1992. "On the Theory and Politics of Cultural Construction in the Pacific." In *The Politics of Tradition in the Pacific,* ed. Margaret Jolly and Nicholas Thomas, 249–263. *Oceania* 62(4).

Loizos, Peter. 1993. *Innovations in Ethnographic Film: From Innocence to Self-Consciousness, 1955–85.* Chicago: University of Chicago Press.

Pike, Andrew, and Ross Cooper. 1980. *Australian Film 1900–1977.* Melbourne: Oxford University Press.

Poignant, Roslyn, with Axel Poignant. 1996. *Encounter at Nagalarramba.* Canberra: National Library of Australia.

Reyes, Luis I. 1995. *Made in Paradise: Hollywood's Films of Hawai'i and the South Seas.* Honolulu: Mutual Publishing.

Rollwagen, Jack R., ed. 1988. *Anthropological Filmmaking.* Chur, Switzerland: Harwood Academic Publishers.

Schmitt, Robert C. 1988. *Hawaii in the Movies 1898–1959.* Honolulu: Hawaiian Historical Society.

Volkman, Toby Alice. 1986. *Expressive Culture in Papua New Guinea: A Guide to Three Films Produced by Chris Owen.* Watertown, Mass.: Documentary Educational Resources.

## PACIFIC FESTIVALS OF ART

### First festival: Suva, Fiji; 1972

*South Pacific Arts and Crafts.* [Melanesia, Micronesia, Polynesia.] 1972. Pacific Educational Network. 30 min. Video.

*South Pacific Festival.* 1972. Produced by Allen Keen for the government of Fiji. 53 min. Film.

### Third festival: Papua New Guinea; 1980

*Wantok.* [New Guinea, Melanesia, Micronesia, Polynesia.] 1980. Commentary in English. Produced and directed by Ellen Umlauf. West Germany: Mana Film. 60 min. Video.

### Fourth festival: Tahiti, French Polynesia; 1985

*A Koe No Na Pua: Hawai'i's Delegations to the Pacific Arts Festivals.* [Performers discuss their plans and experiences.] 1985. Produced by Alu Like Library. 30 min. Film video.

*Contemporary Music of the Arts Festival.* 1985. L'Institut de la Communication Audiovisuelle de Polynésie Française. 57 min. Video.

*Mélanésie.* [Part 1, Solomon Islands and New Guinea; part 2, Australia, New Caledonia, Fiji.] 1985. L'Institut de la Communication Audiovisuelle de Polynésie Française. Video.

*Micronésie.* [Part 1, Guam, Federated States, and Tuvalu; part 2, Nauru and Northern Marianas.] 1985. Produced by L'Institut de la Communication Audiovisuelle de Polynésie Française. 2 parts, 55 min. each. Video.

*Official Film of the Fourth Arts Festival of the Pacific.* [Summarizes each delegation's show.] 1985. L'Institut de la Communication Audio visuelle de Polynésie Française. 52 min. Video.

*Polynésie.* [Part 1, French Polynesia and Cook Islands; part 2, Hawai'i, Aotearoa, and Rapa Nui; part 3, American Sāmoa and Tokelau.] 1985. Produced by L'Institut de la Communication Audiovisuelle de Polynésie Française. 3 parts, totaling 220 min. Video.

*The Tradition Bearers: IV Festival of Pacific Arts.* 1985. Produced and directed by Summer Banner. Pape'ete, Tahiti. 28 min. Video.

### Fifth festival: Townsville, Queensland; 1988

*Dance Highlights from the 5th Festival of Pacific Arts, 1988.* 1989. Produced by Coral Sea Imagery. 30 min. Video.

*Dancing in the Moonlight.* [Participants from various cultures perform and discuss political issues.] 1988. Produced by Yarra Bank Films & Islander Media Association. Video.

*Fifth Festival of the Pacific Arts.* 1989. Produced by the UCLA World Arts and Culture Program. 68 min. Video.

*5th Festival of the Pacific Arts: The Melanesians.* [Participants from Melanesia and New Guinea.] 1989. Produced by Nā Maka o Ka 'Āina. 60 min. Video.

*5th Festival of the Pacific Arts: The Polynesians.* [Participants from Polynesia.] 1989. Produced by Nā Maka o Ka 'Āina. 60 min. Video.

*Nā Mamo O Hawai'i.* [Hawaiian delegation.] 1988. Produced by Nā Maka o Ka 'Āina. 60 min. Video.

*New Caledonia.* [New Caledonian contingent.] 1988. Produced and distributed by Coral Sea Imagery. 65 min. Video.

*Papua New Guinea Delegation.* [Oro and West Sepik provinces, Trobriand Islands, Manus, West New Britain, Gogodala, Mekeo, Pari, Sia; Raun Raun Theatre and Dua Dua Dance Group.] 1988. Queensland: Coral Sea Imagery. 30 min. Video.

*Tahiti at the Festival.* 1988. Produced by Nā Maka o Ka 'Āina. 60 min. Video.

### Sixth festival: Rarotonga, Cook Islands; 1992

*Maire Nui Vaka.* 1992. Directed by Gundolf Krüger. Institut für den Wissenschaftlichen Film. 43 min. Video.

*Tanz der Cook-Inseln.* [Cook Islands National Arts Theatre.] 1994. Directed by Andrea Weisser. Cologne: Deutsche Sporthochschule. 45 min. Video.

*Visions of the Pacific.* [Australia, Papua New Guinea, New Caledonia, Guam, Samoa, Niue, Tahiti, Cook Islands, Hawai'i, Aotearoa.] 1992? Produced by Kenzo for the Ministry of Cultural Development, Cook Islands. 60 min. Video.

### Seventh Festival: Apia, Sāmoa; 1996

*Opening Ceremony.* 1996. Produced by Televise Samoa. Video.

*Performing Arts.* 1996. Produced by Televise Samoa. Video.

## MULTICULTURAL FILMS AND VIDEOS

*Aus den Hamburgische museum fur Völkerkunde: Völkerkunde Filmdokumente aus der Sudsee aus den Jahren 1908–1910.* [Dances from the Mortlock Islands, Chuuk, and the Bismark Archipelago.] N.d. Edited by Hans Tischner. Hamburg: Museum für Völkerkunde. Film.

*Dancing in One World.* ['Uveans, Hawaiians, and others.] 1993. Directed by Stephanie Bakal and Mark Obenhaus. New York: RM Arts, BBC-TV, and Thirteen/WNET. 57 min. Film.

*JVC Video Anthology of Music and Dance.* Vol. 29. [Australia: Djinang, of Arnhem Land; New Guinea: Iatmul, Sawos, Eipo; Melanesia: New Caledonia (Tiga, Ouvea, and eastern Grande Terre); Micronesia: Federated States (Pohnpei), Northern Marianas (Saipan); Polynesian outlier:

Bellona. The New Caledonian, Micronesian, and Bellonese performances were shot at the fifth Festival of Pacific Arts.] 1990. Edited by Tomoaki Fujii, in collaboration with the National Museum of Ethnology, Osaka. Produced by Nakagawa Kunihiko and Yuji Ichihashi. Distributed by Rounder Records, Cambridge, Mass. 92 min. Video.

*Pacific Passages.* 1997. Produced and directed by Caroline Yacoe, Wendy Arbeit, and G. B. Hajim. Pacific Pathways. 30 min. Video.

*South Pacific.* [Rogers and Hammerstein musical, starring Rossano Brazzi and Mitzi Gaynor; island scenes filmed on Kaua'i, Hawai'i.] 1957. CBS/Fox. 150 min. Film, video.

## AUSTRALIA

Aboriginal people consider that the starred films, because they show secret rites, may not be screened publicly in Australia. The Australian Institute of Aboriginal and Torres Strait Islander Studies prefers that the starred films not be screened anywhere.

### Multicultural films and videos

*The Coolbaroo Club.* [An Aboriginal dance club in Perth, popular from 1946 to the 1960s.] 1996. Directed by Robert Scholes. Research funded by the Australian Institute of Aboriginal and Torres Strait Islander Studies. Ronin Films and Coolbaroo Club Productions. 55 min. Film, video.

*Harold.* [Documentary portrait of Aboriginal singer Harold Blair, Australia's last great concert-hall tenor of the 1940s and 1950s.] 1994. Directed by Steve Thomas. 56 min. Film.

*MIMI: Aboriginal Islander Dance Theatre.* [Interviews with and demonstrations by the troupe's principal dancers.] 1980s? Kim Lewis Marketing. 58 min. Video.

*Sunny and the Dark Horse.* [Biography of an Aboriginal station manager; music by Harry and Wilga Williams and the Country Outcasts.] N.d. Directed by David MacDougall and Judith MacDougall. Canberra: Ronin Films. 86 min. Film, video.

*The Wrong Side of the Road.* [Two days in the lives of Aboriginal bands No Fixed Address and Us Mob.] 1981. Directed by Ned Lander. Produced by Ned Lander and Graeme Isaac. Australian Film Institute, with assistance from the Department of Aboriginal Affairs. 80 min. Film.

### Northern Australia

*Aboriginal Dances.* [Anindilyaugwa, Groote Eylandt, Arnhem Land.] 1969. Directed by Alice M. Moyle and E. C. Snell. Groote Eylandt Field Project, 8.3. Australian Institute of Aboriginal Studies. 30 min. Film.

*Djalambu—Ceremonial Disposal of Human Remains in a Hollow Log Coffin.* [Arnhem Land.] 1963. Directed by C. Holmes. Australian Institute of Aboriginal Studies. 47 min. Film.

*The Djunguan of Yirrkala.* [Yolngu, Arnhem Land.] 1966. Directed by Roger Sandall. Australian Institute of Aboriginal Studies. 56 min. Film.

*Eight Aboriginal Songs with Didjeridu Accompaniment.* [Anindilyaugwa, Groote Eylandt, Arnhem Land.] 1969. Directed by Alice M. Moyle and E. C. Snell. Groote Eylandt Field Project, 8.6. Australian Institute of Aboriginal Studies. 20 min. Film.

*Five Brolga Dances.* [Anindilyaugwa, Groote Eylandt, Arnhem Land.] 1969. Directed by Alice M. Moyle and E. C. Snell. Groote Eylandt Field Project, 8.4. Australian Institute of Aboriginal Studies. 15 min. Film.

*Good-Bye Old Man.* [Tiwi mortuary rites, Melville Island.] 1977. Directed by David MacDougall. Australian Institute of Aboriginal Studies. 70 min. Film.

*Gunabibi: An Aboriginal Fertility Cult.* [Arnhem Land.] 1966. Directed by Roger Sandall and Nicolas Peterson. Australian Institute of Aboriginal Studies. 54 min. Film.

*Madarrpa Funeral at Gurka'wuy.* [Yolngu, Arnhem Land.] 1979. Directed by Ian Dunlop. Sydney: Film Australia. 88 min. Film.

*Mourning for Mangatopi.* [Tiwi mortuary rites, Melville Island.] 1975. Directed by Roger Sandall. Australian Institute of Aboriginal Studies. 56 min. Film.

*Primitive People: Australian Aborigines.* [The Mewite people, Arnhem Land; includes mortuary rites.] 1950. University of California Extension Media Center. 33 min. Film, video.

*Waiting for Harry.* [Anbarra, north-central Arnhem Land.] 1980. Directed by Kim McKenzie. Australian Institute of Aboriginal Studies. 57 min. Film.

## Gulf of Carpentaria

*Dance on Your Land.* [Fifty Yanyuwa (of Mornington Island) and Borroboola perform in fourteen Aboriginal communities; songs sung in Garawa and Lardil.] 1991. Produced by SBS TV, Sydney, with the Woomera Aboriginal Corporation. 28 min. Film, video.

*Ka-Wayawayama—The Aeroplane Dance.*

[Yanyuwa.] 1994. Directed and produced by Trevor Graham. Film Australia 01269756. 56 min. Film.

*Lurugu.* [Lardil, Mornington Island.] 1974. Directed by Curtis Levy. Australian Institute of Aboriginal Studies. 59 min. Film.

## Queensland

*Dances at Aurukun.* [Cape York.] 1962. Directed by Ian Dunlop. Australian Institute of Aboriginal Studies. 31 min. Film.

*Five Aboriginal Dances from Cape York.* 1966. Directed by Ian Dunlop. Sydney: Australian Commonwealth Film Unit. 8 min. Film.

*The House Opening.* [Aurukun (place), Cape

York.] 1980. Directed by Judith MacDougall. Australian Institute of Aboriginal Studies. 45 min. Film.

*Lockhart Dance Festival.* [Cape York.] 1974. Directed by Curtis Levy. Australian Institute of Aboriginal Studies. 30 min. Film.

## Western Australia

*Bran Nue Dae.* [The life of Jimmy Chi, with the Broome band Kuckles.] 1991. Produced by Tom Zubrycki, with Bran Nue Dae Corporation. Ronin Films. 55 min. Film, video.

*Milli Milli.* [Kimberleys.] 1993. Directed by Wayne Barker. Ronin Films. 53 min. Film, video.

## Central Australia

*The Mulga Seed Ceremony.* 1966. Directed by Roger Sandall. Australian Institute of Aboriginal Studies. 25 min. Film.

*The Native Cat Ceremonies of Watarka, Loritja Tribe.* [Central Australian totemic rites.] 1950. Directed by T. G. H. Strehlow. Adelaide: Adelaide University. 21 min. Film.

*Peppimenarti.* [Aboriginal ranching; features sacred rites.] 1980s? Produced by Film Australia. 50 min. Video.

*A Walbiri Fire Ceremony: Ngatjakula.* [Walpiri.]

1977. Directed by Roger Sandall. Australian Institute of Aboriginal Studies. 21 min. Film.

*Walbiri Ritual at Gunadjari.* [Walpiri.] 1967. Directed by Roger Sandall and Nicolas Peterson. Australian Institute of Aboriginal Studies. 29 min. Film.

*Walbiri Ritual at Ngama.* [Walpiri.] 1966. Directed by Roger Sandall and Nicolas Peterson. Australian Institute of Aboriginal Studies. 26 min. Film.

## Southeastern Australia

*Eelarmarni.* 1988. Produced by Lorraine Mafi-Williams. Sydney: Australia Film Institute. Film, video.

### Torres Strait Islands

*Islanders.* [Instruments and dances.] N.d. Distributed by Film Australia. 22 min. Video.

*Wame: Traditional String Figures from Saibai Island, Torres Strait.* [Includes singing.] 1965.

Directed by Wolfgang Laade and Roger Sandall. Australian Institute of Aboriginal Studies. 26 min. Film.

## NEW GUINEA

### General and multicultural films and videos

*Dances of New Guinea.* 1965. Produced by the Australian Broadcasting Corporation. 7 min. Film.

*Festival of the Pig.* 1950. Produced by Peerless Films. 11 min. Film.

*Governor General's Tour of Papua New Guinea.* 1964. Produced by the Commonwealth Film Unit for the Australian Department of External Affairs. 25 min. Film.

*Neu-Guinea 1904–1906: In Memoriam Prof. Dr. Rudolf Pöch.* 1958. Edited by P. Spinder. Includes clips filmed by Rudolf Pöch in 1904–1906. Vienna: Austrian Federal Institute of Scientific Film. 16 min. Film.

*Port Moresby: Coronation Celebrations.* [Marking the crowning of Queen Elizabeth II.] 1953. Produced by Pacifilm. 15 min. Film.

*Songs of a Distant Jungle.* [A visitor's musical experiences in Western Province and the Trobriand Islands, Milne Bay Province.] 1985. Distributed by the University of California Extension Media Center. 20 min. Video.

*Songs from Papua New Guinea.* [Bultem and Tifalmin, West Sepik; Kopiri, Southern Highlands.] 1986. University of California Extension Media Center. 21 min. Video.

*When Headhunters Reigned.* 1954. Produced by W. A. Deutscher. 42 min. Film.

*Yesterday, Today and Tomorrow: The Women of Papua New Guinea.* [Examines the place of custom in modern society; includes Mendi women's self-mutilation and girls' courtship rituals.] 1987. Produced by Center Productions. Distributed by Barr Films. 27 min. Video.

*Yumi Yet.* [Celebrations of Papua New Guinean political independence, 1975.] 1977. Film Australia and Ronin Films. 54 min. Film, video.

### Papuan Region

*Bespannen von Trommeln.* [Me'udana, Milne Bay Province.] 1963. Directed by E. Schlesier. Institut für den Wissenschaftlichen Film. 8 min. Film.

*Gogodala: A Cultural Revival?* [Gogodala, Western Province.] 1977. Directed by Chris Owen. Institute of Papua New Guinea Studies. 90 min. Film.

*Kama Wosi: Music in the Trobriand Islands.* [Milne Bay Province.] 1979. Directed by Les McLaren. Focal Communications. 49 min. Film, video.

*Mailu Story.* [Mailu, Central Province.] 1962. Produced by the Commonwealth Film Unit. 25 min. Film.

*Man without Pigs.* [Binandere, Oro Province: Professor John Waiko returns home to Tabara Village.] Directed by Chris Owen. 90 min.; short version, 50 min. Film.

*Sagari-Tänze.* [Me'udana, Milne Bay Province.] 1963. Directed by Erhard Schlesier. Institut für den Wissenschaftlichen Film. 10 min. Film.

*The Spirit World of Tidikawa.* [Nomad, Western Province.] 1974. Produced by Jef Doring and Su Doring. Distributed by Documentary Educational Resources. 50 min. Film.

*Tidikawa and Friends.* [Nomad, Western Province.] 1973. Produced by Jef Doring and Su Doring. Distributed by Focal Communications. 84 min. Film.

*Trobriand Cricket: An Ingenious Response to Colonialism.* [Milne Bay Province.] 1973. Directed by Jerry W. Leach and Gary Kildea. Produced by the Office of Information, Government of Papua New Guinea. Distributed by the University of California Extension Media Center, California. 54 min. Film.

*The Trobriand Islanders.* [Milne Bay Province.] 1951. Directed by H. A. Powell. London: Anthropology Department, Royal Anthropological Institute, University College. Film.

### Highland Region

*Bark Belt.* [Southern Highlands: manufacture of and dance with a bark belt.] 1987. Produced by the Institute of Papua New Guinea Studies. 35 min. Video.

*Bugla Yunggu.* [Chimbu, Chimbu Province.] 1973. Directed by Gary Kildea. Distributed by the Office of Information. 44 min. Film.

*Gisaro: The Sorrow and the Burning.* [Kaluli, Southern Highlands.] 1986? Produced by Yasuko Ichioka. Distributed by Nippon A-V Productions. 43 min. Video.

*Guardians of the Flutes.* [Sambia, Eastern Highlands.] 1994. Produced by Raul Reddish. New York: Filmmakers Library. 55 min. Video.

*Maring in Motion.* [Maring, Western Highlands.] 1968. Directed by Allison Jablonko. College Park: Pennsylvania State University. Film.

*Moka Festival.* [Melpa, Western Highlands.] 1951. Produced by Peerless Films. 10 min. Film.

*Ongka's Big Moka.* [Melpa, Western Highlands.] 1976. Granada Productions. 52 min. Film.

*Sinmia; Haus Bilas Bilong Manmeri Bilong Baruya.* [Baruya, Eastern Highlands.] 1985. Directed by Kumain. Distributed by Skul Bilong Wokim Piksa. 40 min. Film.

*Songs of the Rainbow.* [Singsing at Mount Hagen, Western Highlands.] N.d. Directed by Albert Falzon. Produced by Beyond, Australia. Festivals of the World series. 27 min. Video.

*Tidikawa and Friends.* [Bedamini; includes initiatory and mortuary rites.] 1972. Vision Quest. 82 min. Film.

*Tighten the Drums: Self-Decoration Among the Enga.* [Enga, Enga Province.] 1983. Directed by Chris Owen. Institute of Papua New Guinea Studies. 58 min. Film.

*Towards Baruya Manhood Series.* [Baruya, an Angan people of the Eastern Highlands.] 1972. Directed by Ian Dunlop and Maurice Godelier. 465 min. in 9 parts. Film.

*Turnim Hed: Courtship and Music in Papua New Guinea.* [Chimbu Province.] 1992. Produced by James Bates and Phil Agland. Princeton, New Jersey: Films for the Humanities and Sciences. 52 min. Film.

*Usarufas: Music from the Eastern Highlands.* [Usarufa, Eastern Highlands.] 1985. Produced by John Caldwell and Vida Chenoweth. 22 min. Video.

*Werberitual (Amb Kanant).* [Melpa, Western Highlands.] 1972. Directed by Irenäus Eibl-Eibesfeldt. Institut für den Wissenschaftlichen Film. 28 min. Film.

*Werbetanz ("Amb Kenan"/"Tanim Het").* [Melpa, Western Highlands.] 1972. Directed by Irenäus Eibl-Eibesfeldt. Institut für den Wissenschaftlichen Film. 16 min. Film.

## Mamose Region

*Auftritt der "Mai"-Masken in Korogo.* [Iatmul, East Sepik.] 1984. Directed by Hermann Schlenker and Milan Stanek. Institut für den Wissenschaftlichen Film. 7 min. Film.

*Aus dem Leben der Kate auf Deutsch-Neuguinea: Aufnahmen aus dem Jahre 1909.* [Kate, Morobe.] Directed by Richard Neuhauss. 1939. Filmed in 1909. Institut für den Wissenschaftlichen Film. 10 min. Film.

*Bespannen und Herrichten einer Handtrommel.* [Iatmul, East Sepik.] 1984. Directed by Hermann Schlenker and Milan Stanek. Institut für den Wissenschaftlichen Film. 6 min. Film.

*Cannibal Tours.* [Mostly East Sepik.] 1987. Directed by Dennis O'Rourke. Direct Cinema, Los Angeles. 77 min. Film.

*Fadenspiele "Ninikula."* [Kaile'una, Trobriand Islands.] 1987. Directed by Irenäus Eibl-Eibesfeldt. Institut für den Wissenschaftlichen Film. 21 min. Film.

*Fertigstellung eines Lieder-Memorierstabes, Gesänge und Schlitztrommelschlagen bei einer Kanuweihe in Yindabu.* [Iatmul, East Sepik.] 1988. Directed by Hermann Schlenker and Milan Stanek. Institut für den Wissenschaftlichen Film. 22 min. Film.

*Fest zur Kanueinweihung in Kanganamun, Auftritt von Waldgeistern und Ahnfrauen.* [Iatmul, East Sepik.] 1984. Directed by Hermann Schlenkjer and Milan Stanek. Institut für den Wissenschaftlichen Film. 21 min. Film.

*Flötenorchester auf einem sakralen Felsen (7 Bambusflöten, 2 Schlagstöcke.* [Aibom, East Sepik.] 1984. Directed by Hermann Schlenker. Edited by D. Kleindienst-Andrée. Institut für den Wissenschaftlichen Film. 18 min. Film.

*Flötenorchester in Männerhaus.* [Aibom, East Sepik.] 1984. Directed by Hermann Schlenker. Edited by D. Kleindienst-Andrée and M.

Schuster. Institut für den Wissenschaftlichen Film. 16 min. Film.

*Herstellen und Spielen der einsaitigen Stielzither "Tagarangau."* [Iatmul, East Sepik.] 1984. Directed by Hermann Schlenker and Milan Stanek. Institut für den Wissenschaftlichen Film. 11 min. Film.

*Herstellen und Spielen der einsaitigen Stielzither "Woragutngau."* [Iatmul, East Sepik.] 1984. Directed by Hermann Schlenker. Edited by D. Kleindienst-Andrée and Milan Stanek. Institut für den Wissenschaftlichen Film. 6 min. Film.

*Initiationsfest.* [Pasum, Morobe Province.] 1958. Directed by Carl A. Schmitz. Institut für den Wissenschaftlichen Film. 16 min. Film.

*Kandem erzählt von Schlitztrommel und Kopfjagdtrompete: Spiel auf beiden Instrumenten.* [Iatmul, East Sepik.] 1984. Directed by Hermann Schlenker and Milan Stanek. Institut für den Wissenschaftlichen Film. 13 min. Film.

*Kopfjägertanz in Chambri aufgeführt vor Touristen.* [Aibom, East Sepik.] 1984. Directed by Hermann Schlenker. Edited by D. Kleindienst-Andrée and Milan Stanek. Institut für den Wissenschaftlichen Film. 11 min. Film.

*Männerinitiation in Japanaut: "Tod der Novizen."* [Iatmul, East Sepik.] 1984. Directed by Hermann Schlenker. Edited by D. Kleindienst-Andrée and Jürg Wassmann. Institut für den Wissenschaftlichen Film. 51 min. Film.

*Männerinitiation in Japanaut: "Novizen in der Urzeit."* [Iatmul, East Sepik.] 1984. Directed by Hermann Schlenker. Edited by D. Kleindienst-Andrée and Jürg Wassmann. Institut für den Wissenschaftlichen Film. 90 min. Film.

*Männerinitiation in Takgei.* [Iatmul, East Sepik.] 1984. Directed by Hermann Schlenker. Edited by D. Kleindienst-Andrée, Jürg Wassmann, and J.

Schmid-Kocher. Institut für den Wissenschaftlichen Film. 51 min. Film.

*Männerinitiation in Tamanumbu.* [Iatmul, East Sepik.] 1984. Directed by Hermann Schlenker. Edited by D. Kleindienst-Andrée, Jürg Wassmann, and J. Schmid-Kocher. Institut für den Wissenschaftlichen Film. 18 min. Film.

*Maultrommelspielen beim abendlichen Zusammensein.* [Iatmul, East Sepik.] 1984. Directed by Hermann Schlenker. Edited by D. Kleindienst-Andrée and Milan Stanek. Institut für den Wissenschaftlichen Film. 9 min. Film.

*Mythologischer Gesang über die Vorfahren der Klane Mbowi-Semal.* [Aibom, East Sepik.] 1984. Directed by Hermann Schlenker and Milan Stanek. Institut für den Wissenschaftlichen Film. 11 min. Film.

*Namekas: Music in Lake Chambri.* [Pondo, East Sepik.] 1979. Directed by Les McLaren. Canberra: Ronin Films. 53 min. Film, video.

*The Red Bowmen.* [Umeda, West Sepik: the *ida* ritual.] 1976. Directed by Chris Owen. Institute

of Papua New Guinea Studies. 130 min.; short version, 58 min. Film.

*Riten bei Knabeninitiation.* [Kambrambo, East Sepik.] 1963. Filmed in 1930. Directed by Felix Speiser and C. A. Schmitz. Institut für den Wissenschaftlichen Film. 6 min. Film.

*Le Sang du Sagou.* [Yafar, West Sepik.] 1985? Produced by Bernard Juillerat, Centre Nationale de Recherche Scientifique. 60 min. Film.

*Singsing Tumbuan (Mask Dance).* [Birap Village, Madang.] 1992. Asples Productions. 48 min. Video with 64-page booklet.

*Tanzfest mit der Flöte "Yawanganamak" in Palimbei.* [Iatmul, East Sepik.] 1984. Directed by Hermann Schlenker and Milan Stanek. Institut für den Wissenschaftlichen Film. 38 min. Film.

*Totenfest in Gaikorobi: Anrufung und Tanz der Ahnen, Gesänge und Flötenspiel.* [Sawos, East Sepik.] 1979. Directed by Hermann Schlenker and Markus Schindlbeck. Institut für den Wissenschaftlichen Film. 18 min. Film.

### Irian Jaya

*Asmat.* [Study of a six-week funerary ritual.] 1990. Produced by Dea Sudarman. 52 min. Film.

*Dead Birds.* [Dani.] 1963. Directed by Robert Gardner. Cambridge: Harvard University. 83 min. Film, video.

*Herstellen einer Maultrommel.* [Eipo.] 1976. Directed by F. Simon. Institut für den Wissenschaftlichen Film. 12 min. Film.

*Herstellen einer Sanduhrtrommel.* [Asmat.] 1961. Directed by Adrian A. Gerbrands. Institut für den Wissenschaftlichen Film. 16 min. Film.

*Ornamentieren eines Blashorns aus Bambus.*

[Asmat.] 1961. Directed by Adrian A. Gerbrands. Institut für den Wissenschaftlichen Film. 5 min. Film.

*Singen bei der Arbeit.* [Eipo.] 1976. Volker Heeschen. Eipo people. Institut für den Wissenschaftlichen Film. 9 min. Film.

*Spielen einer Maultrommel.* [Eipo.] 1976. Directed by F. Simon. Institut für den Wissenschaftlichen Film. 8 min. Film.

*Wow.* [Asmat.] 1975. Directed by William Leimbach, Jean-Pierre Dutilleux, and Peter Van Arsdale. London: Survival Films. Film.

## MELANESIA

### Island Region of Papua New Guinea

*Cultural Performances at the 1989 West New Britain Provincial Show.* 1989. Produced by Asples Productions. 60 min. Video.

*The Drum and the Mask: Time of the Tubuan.* 1996. Produced by Caroline Yacoe. Pacific Pathways. 30 min. Video.

*Malangan Labadama: A Tribute to Buk-Buk.* [Mandak mortuary rites, New Ireland.] 1982. Directed by Chris Owen. Institute of Papua New Guinea Studies. 58 min. Film.

*Nausang Masks: Performance.* [Kilenge, West New Britain.] 1973. Directed by Adrian A. Gerbrands. Institut für den Wissenschaftlichen Film. 35 min. Film.

*The Sharkcallers of Kontu.* [Kontu, New Ireland.] 1982. Directed by Dennis O'Rourke. 54 min. Film, video.

*Sia Chorus.* [Kilenge, West New Britain.] 1971. Directed by Adrian A. Gerbrands. Institut für den Wissenschaftlichen Film. 21 min. Film.

*Tui; Wokim Garamut.* [Arawa, North Solomons.] 1983. Produced by Divisin Bilong Infomesin. 60 min. Video.

*Vukumo Mask: Construction and Performance.* [Kilenge, West New Britain.] 1971. Directed by Adrian A. Gerbrands. Institut für den Wissenschaftlichen Film. 17 min. Film.

### Solomon Islands

*Anlegen des Tanzschmuckes und Tänze.* [Ndende, Santa Cruz Islands, Temotu Province.] 1971. Directed by Gerd Koch. Institut für den Wissenschaftlichen Film. 35 min. Film.

*'Are'are Maasina.* ['Are'are, Malaita Province.] 1971. Produced by Daniel de Coppet and Christa de Coppet. Sound by Hugo Zemp. Axe Films. 33 min. Film.

*'Are'are Music* and *Shaping Bamboo*. ['Are'are, Malaita Province.] 1993. Produced by Hugo Zemp. Audiovisual Series, 1. Society for Ethnomusicology. Video.

*Iu Mi Nao: Solomon Islands Regains Independence*. [Various groups.] 1979. Directed by Graham Chase and Martin Cohen. Film Australia. 50 min. Film, video.

*Kwaio Artists*. [Kwaio, Malaita Province: manufac-ture of musical instruments and costumes.] 1985. University of Hawai'i. 360 min. Video.

*Totora and Siwa*. [Feasts of Malaita Province: *toto-ra* for courting, *siwa* for a murdered person.] 1980. Solomon Islands Culture series. Film Australia. 10 min. Film.

*Wogasia*. [Santa Catalina Island, Makira Province: garden-blessing rite.] 1980. Solomon Islands Culture series. Film Australia. 53 min. Film.

## New Caledonia

*Ae-ae se chante la nuit*. [Arhâ area of Grande Terre.] 1994. Produced by Brigitte Travant. Nouméa: Agence de Développement de la Culture Kanak. Film.

*Chants kanak: ayoii et cada*. [Rehearsals and the making of costumes and percussion instruments as performers from Hienghène prepare for a con-cert in Nouméa.] 1995. Produced by Gilles Dagneau. Nouméa: Agence de Développement de la Culture Kanak and RFO. 58 min. Film.

*Danser avec les lutins*. [Paicî area of Grande Terre explain their dance]. 1992. Produced by Auguste Cidopua. Nouméa: Agence de Développement de la Culture Kanak. 15 min. Film.

*Danse de Ti.Ga.* [Performances by Ti.Ga., a troupe from Tioumidou and Galilé villages, cen-tral Grand Terre.] 1994. Produced by Raymond Ammann. Nouméa: Agence de Développement de la Culture Kanak. 18 min. Film.

*La Danse tchap*. 1994. Produced by Brigitte Whaap and André Ravel. Nouméa: Agence de Développement de la Culture Kanak and Centre Culturel Provincial Yéiwéné Yéiwéné. 10 min. Film.

*La Danse bua*. 1994. Produced by Brigitte Whaap and André Ravel. Nouméa: Agence de Développement de la Culture Kanak and Centre Culturel Provincial Yéiwéné Yéiwéné. 10 min. Film.

*La Danse drengeju cileje trohemi*. 1994. Produced by Brigitte Whaap and André Ravel. Nouméa: Agence de Développement de la Culture Kanak and Centre Culturel Provincial Yéiwéné Yéiwéné. 15 min. Film.

*La Danse de Wetr*. [Structure and content of a dance of Lifu, created in 1992.] 1993. Produced by Marc-Arnaud Boussat and Raymond Ammann. Nouméa: Agence de Développement de la Culture Kanak. 26 min. Film.

*Le Cricket en Nouvelle-Calédonie*. 1990. Produced by Michel Bironneau. Nouméa: Centre Territorial de Recherche Pédagogique. 12 min. Film.

*Les Danses drui et trutru abo*. 1994. Produced by Brigitte Whaap and André Ravel. Nouméa: Agence de Développement de la Culture Kanak and Centre Culturel Provincial Yéiwéné Yéiwéné. 11 min. Film.

*Jêmââ*. [The Kaneka band Jêmââ, from Poindimié, central Grande Terre, Paicî area.] 1992. Produced by Jean-François Lalié. Nouméa: Agence de Développement de la Culture Kanak. 19 min. Film.

*Kanak et fier de l'être*. N.d. Produced by Office Cultural Scientifique et Technique Kanak. 55 min. Video.

*La Légende de Mwaxrenu*. [Drubéa and Noumèè areas of Grande Terre.] 1992. Produced by Élie Peu. Nouméa: Agence de Développement de la Culture Kanak. 16 min. Film.

*Levée de deuil à Tiaoué*. [Fwâi and Nemi areas of Grande Terre.] 1995. Produced by Gilles Dagneau. Nouméa: Agence de Développement de la Culture Kanak and RFO. 20 min. Film.

*Mélanésia 2000*. [Festival performances.] 1975. Produced by Georges Ravat and Guy Chanel. Chanel Production. 17 min. Film.

*Mwakheny*. [Fwâi and Nemi areas of Grande terre.] 1992. Produced by Brigitte Whaap. Nouméa: Agence de Développement de la Culture Kanak. 17 min. Film.

*Nouvelle-Calédonie, Terre Missionaire*. 1931. Produced by Alphonse Rouel. Society of Mary. 37 min. Film.

*Remember New Caledonia*. [Films made by U.S. soldiers in 1942–1945, including excerpts of Kanak dancing.] 1996. Produced by Gilles Dagneau. Nouméa: R.F.O. Film.

## Vanuatu

*Blong Save Hu Nao Yumi*. [Activities of the Arts Festival held by the people of Malakula in 1986.] 1986. Produced by Film Australia. 52 min. Video.

*Taem Bifo—Taem Nao*. [First National Arts Festival (Vila, 1979): crafts, singing, dancing.] 1980. Film Australia. 27 min. Film.

*Vanuatu*. [Celebrations of political indepen-dence.] 1983. Radharc Films. 26 min. Film.

*Vanuatu: Struggle for Freedom*. [Celebrations of political independence.] 1981. Film Australia. 75 min. Film.

## MICRONESIA

*Celebrating the Arts of Micronesia.* [Palau, Chuuk, Pohnpei, Marshalls; performances at the Micronesian Cultural Fair, University of Hawai'i.] 1986. Produced by Carl Hefner. 30 min. Video.

*Micronesia.* [Carolines, Marshalls.] 1954. Produced by Oceania Films. 10 min. Film.

### West Micronesia

#### Palau

*Beldeklel a Ngloik: The Process.* 1993. Directed by Lynn Kremer Babcock. Worcester, Mass.: Lynn Kremer Babcock, Holy Cross College. 62 min. (Palauan-language version), 47 min. (English version). Film.

#### Federated States

*Kamadipw.* [Dances by performers from the Net Cultural Center, Pohnpei, and synchronized pounding of kava by twenty-four pounders.] 1983. Produced by Steve Arvisu and Joseph R. Camacho. 60 min. Film.

*Kosrae Singing Group: Christmas.* [Kosraean performances in Uliga Church, Majuro, Marshall Islands.] 1987. Alele Museum, Majuro. 198 min. Video.

*Lamotrek: Heritage of an Island.* [Lamotrek Atoll, Yap: studies *rong* 'special skill and knowledge'; songs translated in subtitles.] 1988. Directed by Eric Metzger. Triton Films. 27 min. Video.

*Mwan Mwich.* [Moen, Chuuk.] 1979. Produced by Triton Films. Micronesian Transitions series. 30 min. Video.

*The Navigators: Pathfinders of the Pacific.* [Satawal, Chuuk.] 1983. Directed by Sanford Low. Produced by the Public Broadcasting System. Distributed by Documentary Educational Resources. 59 min. Film, video.

*Satawalese Canoe Departure from Saipan, Spring 1988, and Traditional Dances.* [Festivities for a canoe's departure for home in Satawal; includes dancing by the crew and Carolinean residents of Saipan.] 1988. Produced by M. L. Kenney. 90 min. Video.

*Spirits of the Voyage.* [Studies *pwo*, a navigator's rite of passage.] 1996. Directed by Eric Metzger. Triton Films. 88 min. Video.

#### Mariana Islands (Guam and the Northern Marianas)

*Belembaotuyan.* [Chamorro.] 1980. Directed by Lee Soliwada. Agaña: Guam Council on the Arts & Humanities Agency. 30 min. Video.

*Chamorro Music.* [*Kantan chamorrita* and *belembaotuyan.*] 1990. Produced by Kathy Coulehan for KGTF-TV. Portraits of Guam, 8. 30 min. Video.

*Guam's History in Songs.* 1993. Script by Carmen L. Santos and Anthony P. Sanchez. Produced by Carmen L. Santos. Underwritten by the Guam Quincentennial Commission. Shooting Star Production. 30 min. Video.

### East Micronesia

#### Marshall Islands

*Alele Festival.* 1986. Alele Museum, Majuro. Video.

*Alele Festival.* 1994. Alele Museum, Majuro. Video.

*Interview with Cultural Expert, Laimaaj Barmoj.* [About the *jebwa* (dance) and Marshallese navigational singing.] 1988. Alele Museum, Majuro. Video.

#### Kiribati

*"Batere"-Tanz.* [Nonouti.] 1967. Directed by Gerd Koch. Institut für den Wissenschaftlichen Film. 3 min. Film.

*"Bino"-Tanz.* [Tabiteuea.] 1965. Directed by Gerd Koch. Institut für den Wissenschaftlichen Film. 3 min. Film.

*"Ruoia"-Tanz "Kamei."* [Nonouti.] 1967. Directed by Gerd Koch. Institut für den Wissenschaftlichen Film. 3 min. Film.

*"Ruoia"-Tanz "Kawawa."* [Tabiteuea.] 1967. Directed by Gerd Koch. Institut für den Wissenschaftlichen Film. 3 min. Film.

*"Ruoia"-Tänze.* [Tabiteuea.] 1965. Directed by Gerd Koch. Institut für den Wissenschaftlichen Film. 4 min. Film.

*"Tirere"-Tanz "Ngeaba."* [Nonouti.] 1967. Directed by Gerd Koch. Institut für den Wissenschaftlichen Film. 3 min. Film.

## POLYNESIA

### General items

*Islands of Light: South Pacific Dance.* [Sāmoa, Cook Islands, Aotearoa.] 1980s? Produced by Huia Films.

*JVC Video Anthology of Music and Dance.* Vol. 30. [Fiji, Tonga, Western Sāmoa, Tokelau, Tuvalu, Tahiti, Marquesas, Cook Islands, Aotearoa. The performances from Fiji and Aotearoa were shot in Japan; the other performances were shot at the fifth Festival of Pacific Arts.] 1990. Edited by Tomoaki Fujii, in collaboration with the National Museum of Ethnology, Osaka. Directed by Nakagawa Kunihiko and Yuji Ichihashi. Distributed by Rounder Records, Cambridge, Mass. 92 min. Video.

*Song of the South Seas.* [Cross-cultural musical experiences: Tonga and Aotearoa.] 1992. Distributed by the New Zealand National Film Unit. 25 min. Film.

*Story Telling.* [Tonga, Sāmoa, Hawai'i.] 1990. Directed by Jeff Gere. Honolulu: KHET Television. 30 min. Video.

### West Polynesia

#### Fiji

*Fijian Things.* [Children's games and dances.] 1972. 13 min. Film.

*South Pacific Island Children.* [Viti Levu.] 1951. Produced by Educational Films. 11 min. Film.

#### Tonga

*The Honourable Out-of-Step.* [Music and dance at the Centennial celebration of the Tongan Constitution, November 1975.] 1976. British Broadcasting Corporation. 50 min. Film.

*Kawa-Gesellschaft und Tänze.* 1954. Directed by Gerd Koch. Dorfleben im Tonga-Archipel, 3. Institut für den Wissenschaftlichen Film. 13 min. Film.

*Laumatanga, Pride of Locality in Tongan Poetry.* 1986. Distributed by the University of Hawai'i. 30 min. Video.

*From Mortal to Ancestor: The Funeral in Tonga.* 1994. Produced by Wendy Arbeit. Palm Frond Productions. Video.

*Tonga Royal.* 1977. Produced by the Journal Library. 20 min. Film.

*Village Life in Tonga.* [Hoi Village; natural sounds and music.] Produced by Tony Ganz for Harvard University. 20 min. Film.

#### Sāmoa

*Fa'a Samoa: The Samoan Way.* N.d. Directed by Lowell D. Holmes. 17 min. DFA. Film.

*Moana: A Romance of the Golden Age.* 1926. Directed by Robert Flaherty. Produced by Paramount. Distributed by Museum of Modern Art. 66 min. Silent film.

*Moana of the South Seas.* 1980. Directed by Robert Flaherty. Sound added by Monica Flaherty Frassetto. Brattleboro, Vt.: Monica Flaherty Frassetto. 83 min. Film.

*Samoa.* 1948? Directed by F. W. Murnau and Robert Flaherty. 16 min. Film.

#### Tokelau

*Tokelau Tafaoga: Games.* 1995. Directed by Allan Thomas. Asia Pacific Archive, School of Music, Victoria University of Wellington. Video.

#### Tuvalu

*Fakanau-Tänze.* 1961. Directed by Gerd Koch. Institut für den Wissenschaftlichen Film. 6 min. Film.

*Fatele-Tänze.* 1961. Directed by Gerd Koch. Institut für den Wissenschaftlichen Film. 9 min. Film.

*Siva-Tanz.* 1961. Directed by Gerd Koch. Institut für den Wissenschaftlichen Film. 3 min. Film.

*Viiki-Tanz.* 1961. Directed by Gerd Koch. Institut für den Wissenschaftlichen Film. 3 min. Film.

### East Polynesia

#### French Polynesia

*Aroha Mai.* [Show staged by Coco Hotahota, with commentary in French by Coco.] 1986. Produced by L'Institut de la Communication Audiovisuelle de Polynésie Française. 49 min. Video.

*Heiva i Tahiti: Tahiti July Festival.* 1993. Produced by L'Institut de la Communication Audiovisuelle de Polynésie Française. 90 min. Video.

*Heiva i Tahiti: Tahiti July Festival.* 1994. Institut de la Communication Audiovisuelle de Polynésie Française. 59 min. Video.

*Island Dreaming: The Heiva i Tahiti Fête.* 198? Directed by Albert Falzon. 26 min. Video.

*Place of Power in French Polynesia.* [A Tahitian dancer's view of the cultural renaissance.] 1983. Produced by Film Australia. 30 min. Video.

*Religious Songs.* [At the Heiva, choirs of Adventist, Mormon, and Sanito churches perform.] 1986. L'Institut de la Communication Audiovisuelle de Polynésie Française. 26 min. Video.

*Sacred Ceremony of Umu-Ti.* [Sacred singing, ritualizing, dancing, firewalking; filmed on Magnetic Island.] 1988. Soundtrack recorded by David Fanshawe. Coral Sea Imagery. 27 min. Video.

### Cook Islands

*Moana Roa.* [Singing, dancing, fishing, basketry.] N.d. Distributed by Indiana University Audio Visual Center. 32 min. Film.

*Sex and Social Dance.* 1993. Directed by Stephanie Bakal and Mark Obenhaus. New York:

### Hawai'i

*Act of War: The Overthrow of the Hawaiian Nation.* 1993. Directed by Puhipau and Joan Lander. Produced by Nā Maka o ka 'Āina, with singing by activist Didi Lee Kwai. Video.

*Aloha 'Āina Concert.* [Speeches and music at Andrews Amphitheatre, University of Hawai'i.] 1988. Produced by Nā Maka o Ka 'Āina. 120 min. Video.

*And Then There Were None.* 1995. Directed by Elizabeth Kapu'uwailani Lindsey. Honolulu: Pacific Islanders in Communication. 21 min. Video.

*The 'Āina Remains.* 1983. Narrated by Auntie Ma'iki Aiu Lake. Produced by Clarence Ching and Jeannette Paulson. Video.

Beamer, Keola. [Instructional video.] N.d. *The Art of Hawaiian Slack Key Guitar.* Homespun Tapes VD-KEO-GT01. Video.

*Blue Hawaii.* [Elvis Presley sings fourteen songs.] 1961. Paramount. 100 min. Video.

*Danny Kaleikini.* [Includes performances on nose-blown flute and 'ukulele.] 1985. Media Resources International. 45 min. Video.

*Don Ho: In Love with Hawaii.* [Music and commentary.] 1984. Media Resources International. 30 min. Video.

*First Two Aloha Week Celebrations.* [Crafts, hula, parades.] 1948. Bishop Museum. 15 min. Video.

*Fourteenth Annual King Kamehameha Hula Competition.* 1987. Media Resources International. 90 min. Video.

*Gift Giving Ritual of Old Hawaii.* [Recreated pageant staged at Pu'ukoholā heiau.] 1973. Cine Pic Hawaii 10 min. Film.

*Hawaiian Rainbow.* [Ricardo Trimillos and George S. Kanahele narrate the history of Hawaiian music; slack-key guitarist Raymond

*The Tahitian Choir: Rapa Iti.* 1995. Produced by Pascal Nabet-Meyer. Shanachie SH 105. 60 min. Video.

*Tahitian Scenes and Dancing.* 1937. Bishop Museum. 15 min. Silent film.

*Tahiti Fête of San Jose: A Polynesian Dance Extravaganza.* 1992. Produced by the Polynesian Cultural Association. Playback Memories, San Jose, California. 4 parts, about 135 min. each. Video.

*Tarava.* N.d. Filmed by Harris Aunoa. Text by Henri Hiro. OTAC. 60 min. Film.

*Te Moana Nui.* [Performances at the OTAC Grand Theater.] N.d. Institut de la Communication Audiovisuelle de Polynésie Française. 58 min. Video.

RM Arts, BBC-TV, and Thirteen/ WNET. 57 min. Film.

*Turou Aere Mai.* [Presentations welcoming Queen Elizabeth II.] 1974. New Zealand National Film Unit. 9 min. Film.

Kane, singers Auntie Genoa Keawe, the Ho'opi'i brothers, Jerry Santos, and others.] 1988. Mug-Shot. 85 min. Video.

*The Hawaiian Way: The Art and Tradition of Slack Key Music.* 1993. Directed by Eddie Kamae. Produced by Myrna J. Kamae and Rodney A. Ohtani. Honolulu: Hawaii Sons. 68 min. Video.

*Hawai'i Ponoi.* [Hana Music Festival: 'Iolani Luahine, Auntie Genoa Keawe, the Sons of Hawai'i, Palani Vaughan, and others.] 1970. Bishop Museum. 60 min. Video.

*Ho'āla: Awakening.* 1992. Produced by Heather Haunani Giugni and Juniroa Productions. Video.

*Ho'okupu Mele: Hawaiian Song Offerings.* [Kawai Cockett and others.] 1987. Alu Like Library. 30 min. Video.

*Ho'olaule'a: The Traditional Dances of Hawaii.* ['Iolani Luahine performs hula.] 1965. Honolulu Academy of Arts. 33 min. Film.

*Hula Dancers, Surf Riding at Waikiki, Native Life.* [Dancing, surfing, crafts.] Bishop Museum. 15 min. Silent film.

*Hula Dancing Steps.* [Pat Bacon demonstrates.] Bishop Museum. 15 min. Video.

*Hula: The First 30 Years: Merrie Monarch Festival: A Collection of Memorable Performances.* 1994. Produced and directed by Roland Yamamoto. KITV4, TAK Communications. Video.

*Hula Ho'olaulea: Traditional Dances of Hawaii.* 1960. Directed by F. Haar. Honolulu Academy of Arts. 22 min. Film.

*Hula Hou: A Program on Hula Auwana.* [Choreographers discuss modern hula.] 1985. Alu Like Library. 31 min. Video.

*Hula Pa'aloha: The Beamers.* [Members of the Beamer family perform.] 1930–1935. Bishop Museum. 20 min. Silent film.

Kāne, Raymond. [Instructional video.] N.d. *Ki Hoʻalu: Play & Learn.* Video, with lyrics and tablature for twelve songs.

*Ka Poʻe Hula Hawaii Kahiko.* 1984, filmed 1930–1935. Directed by Vivienne Huapala Mader. Edited by Elizabeth Tatar. Bishop Museum. 16 min. Film.

*Kī Hōʻalu: That's Slack Key Guitar.* 1994. Directed by Susan Friedman. Half Moon Bay: Studio on the Mountain. 58 min. Video.

*Kukahi 1996.* 1996. Performances by Kealiʻi Reichel and others on 16 March 1996 at the Waikīkī Shell. M005-US. Video.

*Kuoha Mele Aloha: Inspiring Songs of Love.* [Frank Kawaikapua Hewett and women of Kuhai Hālau Kawaikapua Pā ʻOlapa Kahiko.] 1987. Alu Like Library. 26 min. Video.

*Kuʻu Home: Hawaiian Songs of Home.* 1991. KGMB Television (Hawaiʻi), channel 9. Video.

*Kumu Hula: Keepers of a Culture.* N.d. RHAP-80363. Video.

*Lia.* 1988. Directed by Eddie Kamae. Honolulu: Hawaii Sons. 60 min. Video.

*Malie: The Peter Moon Band.* [Interviews; songs from the album *Malie.*] 1981. Media Resources International. 20 min. Video.

*Merrie Monarch Hula Festival: Auwana.* [Modern-style performances at the twenty-second festival.] 1985. Media Resources International. 240 min. Video.

*Merrie Monarch Hula Festival: Highlights.* [Performances at the twenty- second festival.] 1985. Media Resources International. 60 min. Video.

*Merrie Monarch Hula Festival: Kahiko.* [Ancient-style performances at the twenty-second festival.] 1985. Media Resources International. 240 min. Video.

*Merrie Monarch Hula Festival: Miss Aloha Hula.* [Female soloists' performances at the twenty-second festival.] 1985. Media Resources International. 240 min. Video.

*Molokai Ka Hula Piko.* [John Kaimikaua's version of the origin of ancient Hawaiian dance.] 1985. Alu Like Library. 28 min. Video.

*1987 Merrie Monarch Festival Auwana.* [Modern-style performances at the twenty-fourth festival.]

1987. Media Resources International. 3 parts, 120 min. each. Video.

*1987 Merrie Monarch Festival Highlights.* [Performances at the twenty- fourth festival.] 1987. Media Resources International. 120 min. Video.

*Pacific Sound Waves.* [Music of political protest and power.] 1987. Produced by Nā Maka o Ka ʻĀina. 60 min. Video.

*Paniolo o Hawaiʻi: Cowboys of the Far West.* 1997. Produced and directed by Edgy Lee. Written by Paul Berry and Edgy Lee. Film.

*Papakōlea: A Story of Hawaiian Land.* 1993. Directed by Edgy Lee and Haskell Wexler. 57 min. Video.

*Paradise, Hawaiian Style.* [Elvis Presley's second Hawaiian film.] 1966. Distributed by CBS/Fox. 91 min. Video.

*Puamana.* [Life and Music of Auntie Irmgard Farden Aluli.] 1990. Directed by Les Blank. Sound by Chris Simon. Produced by Meleanna Aluli Meyer. 37 min. Video.

*The Slack Key Secrets of Ray Kane.* 1995. Lonetree Productions. 110 min. Video.

*Sovereignty: A Celebration of Life.* [Performances by Roland Cazimero, Hula Hālau Olana, Israel Kamakawiwoʻole, and Cyril Pahinui.] 1993. Produced by Henry Kapono. Honolulu: KHON-TV. 60 min. Video.

*The Story of the Struggle of the Native Hawaiian People for Self-Determination.* 1988. Directed by Puhipau and Joan Lander. Produced by Nā Maka o ka ʻĀina. 22 min. Honolulu. Video.

*A Tour of the Hawaiian Islands.* [Views of Kauaʻi, Oʻahu, and the Kodak Hula Show.] 1939–1940. Bishop Museum. 25 min. Silent video.

*Tropical Storm: The Peter Moon Band.* [Interviews; songs from the album *Tropical Storm.*] 1983. Media Resources International. 30 min. Video.

*Ula Nōweo.* [Instruction for the *hula* "*Ula Nōweo.*"] 1966. Directed by Dorothy Kahananui Gillette and Barbara B. Smith. Performed by Eleanor Leilehua Hiram. Committee for the Preservation and Study of Hawaiian Language, Art, and Culture, University of Hawaiʻi. 30 min. Film, with booklet and 7-inch 45-RPM disk.

## Aotearoa

*Heritage of Maori Song.* [Twenty-three songs performed by various ensembles.] N.d. Distributed by Myriah's Polynesian Bazaar. 56 min. Video.

*Hirini Melbourne.* [Life and music of Māori composer Hirini Melbourne, of Ngāti Tuhoe.] 1994. Produced by Television New Zealand. 39 min. Video.

*Kapa Haka: The People Dance.* 1996. Directed by Allison Carter. Produced by Derek Kotuku Wooster. Distributed by Television New Zealand. 46 min. Video.

*The Maori: Featuring Ngati-Rangiwewehi of*

*Rotorua.* N.d. New Zealand Video Tours. 20 min. Video.

*Mawai Fillers.* [Mawai Hakona Maori Group sings and dances myths and legends.] 1978. New Zealand National Film Unit. 21 min. Film.

*The Power of Music.* [The all-Māori band Herbs promotes its new album in a rural town.] 1988. Directed by John Day and Lee Tamahori. Distributed by Matte Box Films. 24 min. Video.

*Scenes of Maori Life on the East Coast: He Pito Whakaatu i te Noho a te Maori i te Tairawhiti.* [Ngāti Porou's crafts and customs, including singing.] 1923. Directed by Johannes Andersen, Elsdon Best, and James McDonald, with Te Rangi Hiroa. New Zealand Film Archive. 26 min. Film.

*Scenes of Maori Life on the Whanganui River: He Pito Whakaatu i te Noho a te Maori i te Awa o Whanganui.* [Whanganui River people's crafts and customs, including string games and divinatory rites.] 1921. Directed by Johannes Andersen, Elsdon Best, and James McDonald, with Te Rangi Hiroa. New Zealand Film Archive. 48 min. Film.

*Scenes at the Rotorua Hui: He Pito Whakaatu i te Hui i Rotorua.* [Performances welcoming the Prince of Wales to the Rotorua Racecourse: singing, dancing, playing flutes and games.] 1920. Produced by James McDonald. 24 min. Film.

*Songs of the Maori.* [Maori Mormon Choir.] 1963. Produced by the New Zealand National Film Unit. 19 min. Film.

*Tangi and Funeral of Te Rauparaha's Niece, Heeni Te Rei, Otaki, New Zealand.* [Māori mortuary rites.] 1921. Produced by New Zealand Moving Picture Company and Maoriland Films. New Zealand Film Archives. 10 min. Silent film.

*Te Amokura a te Aronui-A-Rua.* N.d. New Zealand Maori Arts & Crafts Institute. New Zeland Video Tours. 30 min. Video.

*Te Maori: A Celebration of the People and Their Art.* [Exhibit of Māori culture, including singing and orating.] 1985. New Zealand National Film Unit. 58 min. Film.

*Waituhi: The Making of a Maori Opera.* [Tracks the production of *Waituhi* through rehearsals to the premiere at the State Opera House, Wellington.] 1985. New Zealand National Film Unit. 59 min. Film.

### *Rapa Nui*

*Easter Island.* 1934. Produced by the Franco-Belgian Expedition to Easter Island, sponsored by the Trocadéro Museum (Paris) and the Musée Royale (Brussels). Museum of Modern Art. 25 min. Film.

# Books for Further Reading

## GENERAL WORKS

*The Arts and Politics.* 1992. *Pacific Studies* 15(4). Special issue. Edited by Karen L. Nero.

Bellwood, Peter, et al., eds. 1995. *The Austronesians: Historical and Comparative Perspectives.* Canberra: Australian National University.

Beloff, Jim. 1997. *The Ukulele: A Visual History.* San Francisco: Miller Freeman Books.

Chenoweth, Vida. 1972. *Melodic Perception and Analysis: A Manual on Ethnic Melody.* Ukarumpa, Papua New Guinea: Summer Institute of Linguistics.

Finnegan, Ruth, and Margaret Orbell, eds. 1995. *South Pacific Oral Traditions.* Bloomington: Indiana University Press.

Fischer, Hans. 1986. *Sound-Producing Instruments in Oceania.* Edited by Don Niles. Translated by Philip W. Holzknecht. Boroko: Institute of Papua New Guinea Studies.

Goodenough, Ward H., ed. 1996. *Prehistoric Settlement of the Pacific.* Philadelphia: American Philosophical Society.

Götzfridt, Nicholas J. 1995. *Indigenous Literature of Oceania: A Survey of Criticism and Interpretation.* Westport, Conn., and London: Greenwood Press.

Hiroa, Te Rangi [Peter H. Buck]. 1953. *Explorers of the Pacific: European and American Discoveries in Polynesia.* Special Publication 43. Honolulu: Bishop Museum.

Irwin, Geoffrey. 1992. *The Prehistoric Exploration and Colonisation of the Pacific.* Oakleigh, Victoria, Australia: Cambridge University Press.

Johnson, L. W. 1983. *Colonial Sunset: Australia and Papua New Guinea 1970–1974.* St. Lucia: University of Queensland Press.

Kaeppler, Adrienne L., and H. Arlo Nimmo, eds. 1976. *Directions in Pacific Traditional Literature: Essays in Honor of Katharine Luomala.* Special Publication 62. Honolulu: Bishop Museum Press.

Linnekin, Jocelyn, and Lin Poyer. 1990. *Cultural Identity and Ethnicity in the Pacific.* Honolulu: University of Hawai'i Press.

McLean, Mervyn. 1995. *An Annotated Bibliography of Oceanic Music and Dance.* Revised and enlarged second edition. Detroit Studies in Music Bibliography, 74. Detroit: Harmonie Park Press.

Moyle, Alice Marshall, ed. 1992. *Music and Dance of Aboriginal Australia and the South Pacific: The Effects of Documentation on the Living Tradition.* Papers and discussions of the Colloquium of the International Council for Traditional Music, held in Townsville, Queensland, in 1988. Oceania monograph 41. Sydney: University of Sydney.

Siikala, Jukka, ed. 1990. *Culture and History in the Pacific.* Helsinki: Finnish Anthropological Society.

Smith, Bernard. 1992. *Imagining the Pacific: In the Wake of the Cook Voyages.* New Haven: Yale University Press.

Wendt, Albert, ed. 1995. *Nuanua: Pacific Writing in English since 1980.* Honolulu: University of Hawai'i Press.

## AUSTRALIA

Barwick, Linda, Allan Marett, and Guy Tunstill, eds. 1995. *The Essence of Singing and the Substance of Song: Recent Responses to the Aboriginal Performing Arts and Other Essays in Honour of Catherine Ellis.* Oceania monograph 46. Sydney: University of Sydney.

Berndt, R. M., and E. S. Phillips, eds. 1973. *The Australian Aboriginal Heritage: An Introduction Through the Arts.* Sydney: Australian Society for Education through the Arts and Ure Smith.

Borsboom, Adrianus P. 1978. *Maradjiri: A Modern Ritual Complex in Arnhem Land, North Australia.* Nijmegen: Katholieke Universiteit.

Breen, Marcus, ed. 1989. *Our Place Our Music: Aboriginal Music.* Australian Popular Music in Perspective, 2. Canberra: Aboriginal Studies Press.

Chatwin, Bruce. 1987. *The Songlines.* Harmsworth, England: Penguin.

Clunies Ross, Margaret, and Stephen A. Wild. 1982. *Djambidj: An Aboriginal Song Series from Northern Australia.* Canberra: Australian Institute of Aboriginal Studies.

Covell, Roger. 1967. *Australia's Music: Themes of a New Society.* Melbourne: Sun Books.

Dixon, Robert M. W., and Grace Koch. 1996. *Dyirbal Song Poetry: The Oral Liberature of an Australian Rainforest People.* St. Lucia: University of Queensland Press.

Elkin, A. P., and Trevor A. Jones. 1953–1957. *Arnhem Land Music (North Australia).* Oceania monograph 9. Sydney: University of Sydney.

Ellis, Catherine J. 1985. *Aboriginal Music: Education for Living.* St. Lucia: University of Queensland Press.

Grieve, Ray. 1995. *A Band in a Waistcoat Pocket: The Story of the Harmonica in Australia.* Sydney: Currency.

Hayward, Philip, ed. 1992. *From Pop to Punk to Postmodernism: Popular Music and Australian Culture from the 1960s to the 1990s.* North Sydney: Allen & Unwin.

Johnson, Bruce. 1987. *The Oxford Companion to Australian Jazz.* Melbourne: Oxford University Press.

Mitchell, Ewen. 1996. *Contemporary Aboriginal Music.* Port Melbourne: Ausmusic.

Moyle, Alice M. 1974 [1967]. *Songs from the Northern Territory.* Canberra: Australian Institute of Aboriginal Studies.

———. 1978. *Aboriginal Sound Instruments.* Australian Institute of Aboriginal Studies AIAS 14. LP disk.

Moyle, Richard M. 1979. *Songs of the Pintupi: Musical Life in a Central Australian Society.* Canberra: Australian Institute of Aboriginal Studies.

Narogin, Mudrooroo. 1990. *Writing from the Fringe: A Study of Modern Aboriginal Literature.* Melbourne: Hyland House.

Neuenfeldt, Karl William. 1996. *The Didjeridu: From Arnhem Land to Internet.* Sydney: Perfect Beat and John Libbey Publications.

Smith, Jazzer, ed. 1984. *The Book of Australian Country Music.* Sydney: BET Publishing Group.

Sutton, Peter, ed. 1989. *Dreamings: The Art of Aboriginal Australia.* Ringwood, Australia, and London: Viking Penguin.

Turner, Ian. 1969. *Cinderella Dressed in Yella: Australian Children's Play-Rhymes.* Melbourne: Heinemann Educational.

von Brandenstein, C. G., and A. P. Thomas. 1975. *Taruru: Aboriginal Song Poetry from the Pilbara.* Honolulu: University Press of Hawai'i.

Walsh, Michael, and Colin Yallop, eds. 1993. *Language and Culture in Aboriginal Australia.* Canberra: Aboriginal Studies Press.

Wild, Stephen A., ed. 1986. *Rom: An Aboriginal Ritual of Diplomacy.* Canberra: Australian Institute of Aboriginal Studies.

## NEW GUINEA

Brennan, Paul W. 1977. *Let Sleeping Snakes Lie: Central Enga Religious Belief and Ritual.* Adelaide: Australian Association for the Study of Religions.

Chenoweth, Vida, ed. 1976. *Musical Instruments of Papua New Guinea.* Ukarumpa: Summer Institute of Linguistics.

———. 1979. *The Usarufas and Their Music.* Publication 5. Dallas: Summer Institute of Linguistics Museum of Anthropology.

———. 1980. *Music for the Eastern Highlands.* Ukarumpa: Summer Institute of Linguistics.

Crawford, Anthony L. 1981. *Aida: Life and Ceremony of the Gogodala.* Bathurst: National Cultural Council and Robert Brown & Associates.

Feld, Steven. 1990. *Sound and Sentiment: Birds, Weeping, Poetics, and Song in Kaluli Expression.* 2nd ed. Philadelphia: University of Pennsylvania Press.

Gell, Antony Francis. 1975. *Metamorphosis of the Cassowaries: Umeda Society, Language and Ritual.* London: Athlone Press.

Goodale, Jane C. 1995. *To Sing with Pigs Is Human: The Concept of Person in Papua New Guinea.* 1995. Seattle: University of Washington Press.

Harrison, Simon. 1982. *Laments for Foiled Marriages: Love-Songs from a Sepik River Village.* Boroko: Institute of Papua New Guinea Studies.

Herdt, Gilbert H. 1981. *Guardians of the Flutes: Idioms of Masculinity.* New York: McGraw-Hill.

Kasaipwalova, John, and Ulli Beier, eds. 1978. *Yaulabuta: The Passion of Chief Kailaga: An Historical Poem from the Trobriand Islands.* Port Moresby: Institute of Papua New Guinea Studies.

Kunst, Jaap. 1967. *Music in New Guinea: Three Studies.* Translated by Jeune Scott-Kemball. Verhandelingen van het Koninklijk Instituut voor

Taal-, Land- en Volkenkunde, 53. The Hague: Martinus Nijhoff.

Lohia, Simon, and Raka Vele. 1977. *Central Guitar Songs.* Boroko: Institute of Papua New Guinea Studies.

McLean, Mervyn. 1994. *Diffusion of Musical Instruments and Their Relation to Language Migrations in New Guinea.* Kulele: Occasional Papers on Pacific Music and Dance, 1. Boroko: Cultural Studies Division, National Research Institute.

Paia, Robert, and Andrew Strathern. 1977. *Beneath the Andaiya Tree: Wiru Songs.* Boroko: Institute of Papua New Guinea Studies.

Schieffelin, Edward L. 1976. *The Sorrow of the Lonely and the Burning of the Dancers.* New York: St. Martin's Press.

Strathern, Andrea, ed. 1974. *Melpa Amb Kenan.* Port Moresby: Institute of Papua New Guinea Studies.

Talyaga, Kundapen. 1975. *Modern Enga Songs.* Boroko: Institute of Papua New Guinea Studies.

Van Arsdale, Kathleen O. 1981. *Music and Culture of the Bismam Asmat of New Guinea: A Preliminary Investigation.* Hastings, Neb.: Crosier Press.

Waiko, John D. D. 1993. *A Short History of Papua New Guinea.* Melbourne: Oxford University Press.

Wassmann, Jürg. 1991. *The Song to the Flying Fox: The Public and Esoteric Knowledge of the Important Men of Kandingei about Totemic Songs, Names and Knotted Cords (Middle Sepik, Papua New Guinea).* Translated by Dennis Q. Stephenson. Apwitihire, 2. Boroko: National Research Institute.

Webb, Michael. 1993. *Lokal Music: Lingua Franca Song and Identity in Papua New Guinea.* Apwitihire, 3. Boroko: National Research Institute.

Webb, Michael, and Don Niles. 1986. *Riwain: Papua New Guinea Pop Songs.* Goroka and Boroko: Goroka Teachers College and Institute of Papua New Guinea Studies.

———. 1990. *Ol Singsing Bilong Ples.* Boroko: Institute of Papua New Guinea Studies. IPNGS 010. Book with two cassettes.

Weiner, James F. 1991. *The Empty Place: Poetry, Space and Being among the Foi of Papua New Guinea.* Bloomington: Indiana University Press.

Williams, Francis Edgar. 1940. *Drama of Orokolo: The Social and Ceremonial Life of the Elema.* Oxford: Clarendon Press.

Yamada, Yoichi. 1997. *Songs of Spirits: An Ethnography of Sounds in a Papua New Guinea Society.* Apwitihire, 5. Boroko: Institute of Papua New Guinea Studies.

Zahn, Heinrich. 1996. *Mission and Music: Jabêm Traditional Music and the Development of Lutheran Hymnody.* Edited by Don Niles. Translated by Philip W. Holzknecht. Apwitihire, 4. Boroko: Institute of Papua New Guinea Studies.

## MELANESIA

Ammann, Raymond. 1994. *Les Danses Kanak: Une Introduction.* Nouméa: Agence de Développement de la Culture Kanak.

———. 1997. *Kanak Dance and Music: Ceremonial and Intimate Performance of the Melanesians of New Caledonia, Historical and Actual.* Nouméa: Agence de Développement de la Culture Kanak. Book with compact disc.

Bonnemaison, Joël, Kirk Huffman, Christian Kaufmann, and Darrell Tryon, ed. 1997. *Arts of Vanuatu.* Bathurst, Australia: Crawford House Publishing.

Chenoweth, Vida. 1984. *A Music Primer for the North Solomons Province.* Ukarumpa: Summer Institute of Linguistics.

Hesse, Karl, with Theo Aerts. 1982. *Baining Life and Lore.* Boroko: Institute of Papua New Guinea Studies.

Layard, John. 1942. *Stone Men of Malekula: Vao.* London: Chatto & Windus.

Lindstrom, Lamont, and Geoffrey White. 1995. *Culture, Kastom, Tradition: Developing Cultural Policy in Melanesia.* Suva: Institute of Pacific Studies, University of the South Pacific.

Stella, Regis. 1990. *Forms and Styles of Traditional Banoni Music.* Apwitihire, 1. Boroko: National Research Institute.

Suri, Ellison. 1980. *Ten Traditional Dances from the Solomon Islands.* Honiara: Solomon Islands Centre, University of the South Pacific.

Tjibaou, Jean-Marie. N.d. *Kanaké: The Melanesian Way.* Translated by Christopher Plant. Pape'ete: Éditions du Pacifique.

Zemp, Hugo. 1995. *Écoute le bambou qui pleure: récits de quatre musiciens mélanésiens.* Collection "L'aube des peuples." Paris: Éditions Gallimard.

Zemp, Hugo, and Daniel de Coppet. 1978. *'Aré'aré: un peuple mélanésien et sa musique.* Paris: Éditions du Seuil.

## MICRONESIA

Browning, Mary. 1970. *Micronesian Heritage.* Dance Perspectives, 43. New York: Dance Perspectives Foundation.

Burrows, Edwin G. 1963. *Flower in My Ear.* Seattle: University of Washington Press.

Fischer, John L. 1970 [1957, 1966]. *The Eastern Carolines.* Revised edition. New Haven, Conn.: Human Relations Area Files Press.

Grimble, Arthur Francis. 1989. *Tungaru Traditions: Writings on the Atoll Culture of the*

*Gilbert Islands.* Edited by H. E. Maude. Pacific Islands Monograph Series, 7. Honolulu: University of Hawai'i Press.

Hijikata, Hisakatsu. 1996. *Myths and Legends of Palau.* Edited by Hisashi Endo. Collective Works of Hijikata Hisakatsu. Tokyo: Sasakawa Peace Foundation.

Maude, Honor. 1971. *The String Figures of Nauru Island.* Adelaide: Libraries Board of South Australia.

Tanabe, Hisao. 1968. *Nanyō, Taiwan, Okanawa Ongaku Kikō* (A musical journey to the South Seas, Taiwan, and Okinawa). Edited by Toyo Ongaku Gakkai. Tokyo: Ongaku no Tomosha.

## POLYNESIA

Andersen, Johannes C. 1933. *Maori Music with Its Polynesian Background.* Polynesian Society Memoir 10. New Plymouth, New Zealand: Thomas Avery & Sons.

Barrère, Dorothy B., Mary Kawena Pukui, and Marion Kelly. 1980. *Hula: Historical Perspectives.* Pacific Anthropological records, 30. Honolulu: Bishop Museum.

Burrows, Edwin. 1933. *Native Music of the Tuamotus.* Bulletin 109. Honolulu: Bishop Museum.

———. 1945. *Songs of Uvea and Futuna.* Bulletin 183. Honolulu: Bishop Museum.

Christensen, Dieter, and Gerd Koch. 1964. *Die Musik der Ellice-Inseln.* Veröffentlichungen des Museums, Neue Folge 5, Abteilung Südsee 2. Book with 45-RPM record. Berlin: Museum für Völkerkunde.

Davey, Tim, and Horst Puschmann. 1996. *Kiwi Rock: A Reference Book.* Dunedin: Kiwi Rock Publications.

Dix, John. 1982. *Stranded in Paradise: NZ Rock 'n' Roll 1955–1988.* Wellington: Paradise Publications.

Elbert, Samuel H., and Noelani Mahoe. 1970. *Nā Mele o Hawai'i Nei: 101 Hawaiian Songs.* Honolulu: University of Hawai'i Press.

Elbert, Samuel H., and Torben Monberg. 1965. *From the Two Canoes: Oral Traditions of Rennell and Bellona Islands.* Copenhagen: Danish National Museum.

Firth, Raymond, with Mervyn McLean. 1991. *Tikopia Songs: Poetic and Musical Art of a Polynesian People of the Solomon Islands.* Cambridge Studies in Oral and Traditional Culture, 20. Cambridge: Cambridge University Press.

Handy, E. S. Craighill, and Jane Lathrop Winne. 1925. *Music in the Marquesas Islands.* Bulletin 17. Honolulu: Bishop Museum.

Harding, Mike. 1992. *When the Pakeha Sings of Home: A Source Guide to the Folk and Popular Songs of New Zealand.* Auckland: Godwit.

Hayward, Philip, Tony Mitchell, and Roy Shuker, ed. 1994. *North Meets South: Popular Music in Aotearoa/New Zealand.* Umina, Australia: Perfect Beat Publications.

Hereniko, Vilsoni. 1995. *Woven Gods: Female Clowns and Power in Rotuma.* Honolulu: University of Hawai'i Press.

Highland, Genevieve A., Roland W. Force, Alan Howard, Marion Kelly, and Yosihiko H. Sinoto, eds. 1967. *Polynesian Culture History: Essays in Honor of Kenneth P. Emory.* Special Publication 56. Honolulu: Bishop Museum Press.

Jonassen, John. 1991. *Cook Islands Drums.* Rarotonga: Ministry of Cultural Development, Cook Islands.

Jones, Pei Te Hurinui. 1995. *Nga Iwi O Tainui: Traditional History of the Tainui People.* Translated by Bruce Biggs. Auckland: Auckland University Press.

Kaeppler, Adrienne L. 1993a. *Hula Pahu: Hawaiian Drum Dances: Volume 1: Hā a and Hula Pahu: Sacred Movements.* Bishop Museum Bulletin in Anthropology 3. Honolulu: Bishop Museum Press.

———. 1993b. *Poetry in Motion: Studies of Tongan Dance.* Nuku'alofa: Vava'u Press, in association with the East–West Center's Pacific Islands Development Program.

Kaho, Tu'imala. 1988. *Songs of Love by Tu'imala Kaho of the Kingdom of Tonga.* Nuku'alofa, Tonga: Vava'u Press.

Kanahele, George S. ed. 1979. *Hawaiian Music and Musicians: An Illustrated History.* Honolulu: University of Hawai'i Press.

Kirtley, Bacil F. 1971. *A Motif-Index of Traditional Polynesian Narratives.* Honolulu: University of Hawai'i Press.

Love, Jacob Wainwright. 1991. *Sāmoan Variations: Essays on the Nature of Traditional Oral Arts.* Harvard Dissertations in Folklore and Oral Tradition. Edited by Albert B. Lord. New York and London: Garland Publishing.

McLean, Mervyn. 1991. *The Structure of Tikopia Music.* Occasional Papers in Pacific Ethnomusicology, 1. Auckland: Archive of Maori and Pacific Music.

———, ed. 1995. *Catalogue of Maori Purposes Fund Board Recordings Recorded by W. T. Ngata 1953–58.* 2nd ed. Auckland: Archive of Maori and Pacific Music, Anthropology Department, University of Auckland.

———. 1996. *Maori Music.* Auckland: Auckland University Press.

McLean, Mervyn, and Margaret Orbell. 1979. *Traditional Songs of the Maori.* Auckland: Auckland University Press.

Mayer, Raymond. 1976. *Les Transformations de la Tradition Narrative à l'Île Wallis (Uvea).* Publications de la Société des Océanistes, 38. Paris: Musée de l'Homme.

Moulin, Jane Freeman. 1979. *The Dance of Tahiti.* Pape'ete: Christian Gleizal/Les éditions du Pacifique.

———. 1994. *Music of the Southern Marquesas Islands.* Occasional Papers in Pacific Ethnomusicology, 3. Auckland: Department of Anthropology, University of Auckland.

Moyle, Richard M. 1985. *Report on Survey of Traditional Music of Northern Cook Islands.* Working Papers in Anthropology, Archaeology, Linguistics, Maori Studies, 70. Auckland: Department of Anthropology, University of Auckland.

———. 1987. *Tongan Music.* Auckland: Auckland University Press.

———. 1988. *Traditional Samoan Music.* Auckland: Auckland University Press.

———. 1995. *Music of Takuu (Mortlock Is.), Papua New Guinea.* Occasional Papers in Pacific Ethnomusicology, 5. Auckland: Archive of Maori and Pacific Music, Department of Anthropology, University of Auckland.

Quain, Buell Halvor 1942. *The Flight of the Chiefs: Epic Poetry of Fiji.* New York: J. J. Augustin.

Roberts, Helen H. 1926. *Ancient Hawaiian Music.* Bulletin 29. Honolulu: Bishop Museum.

Rossen, Jane Mink. 1987. *Songs of Bellona Island.* 2 vols. Language and Culture of Rennell and Bellona Islands, 6. Copenhagen: Forlaget Kragen.

Stillman, Amy Kuʻuleialoha. 1987. *Report on Survey of Music in Mangareva, French Polynesia.*

Working Papers in Anthropology, Archaeology, Linguistics, Maori Studies, 78. Auckland: University of Auckland, Department of Anthropology.

Tatar, Elizabeth. 1982. *Nineteenth Century Hawaiian Chant.* Pacific Anthropological Records, 33. Honolulu: Department of Anthropology, Bernice P. Bishop Museum.

———. 1987. *Strains of Change: The Impact of Tourism on Hawaiian Music.* Special Publication 78. Honolulu: Bishop Museum Press.

———. 1993. *Hula Pahu: Hawaiian Drum Dances: Volume II: The Pahu: Sounds of Power.* Bulletin in Anthropology, 4. Honolulu: Bishop Museum.

Thomas, Allan. 1996. *New Song and Dance from the Central Pacific: Creating and Performing the Fatele of Tokelau in the Islands and in New Zealand.* Dance and Music, 9. Stuyvesant, N.Y.: Pendragon Press.

Thomas, Allan, and Takaroga Kuautoga. 1992. *Hgoro Futuna: Report of a Survey of the Music of West Futuna, Vanuatu.* Occasional Papers in Pacific Ethnomusicology, 2. Auckland: Department of Anthropology, University of Auckland.

# Glossary

Page numbers in *italics* indicate pages on which illustrations appear.

**aerophone** A musical instrument whose principal sound is the vibration of air enclosed within it or immediately surrounding it (22, 371, 392, 402)

**AIATSIS** Australian Institute of Aboriginal and Torres Strait Islander Studies (415, 440, 960)

*aloha* A prime Hawaiian cultural value, often conveyed in greeting, farewell, and lyrics, emphasizing sharing, cooperation, respect for self and others, responsibility, and industriousness (167, 273–74)

*"Aloha 'Oe"* Hawaiian song that in 1878 Princess (later Queen) Lili'uokalani textually composed and musically adapted from part of Charles Crozat Converse's hymn "The Rock Beside the Sea" (43, 45, 159, 353)

**Aotearoa** [Māori, 'Long White Cloud'] Indigenous name of the South Pacific islands that Europeans colonized and named New Zealand (111)

*'arioi* Eighteenth-century professional traveling entertainers of the Society Islands (229, 769, 875)

**armshell** A shell cut into a ring, often decorated with suspended small shells and worn on the upper arm (492)

**art** Any cultural process or product that uses words, sounds, movements, materials, scents, or spaces to formalize the nonformal, much as poetry intensifies the formalization of language (785, 923)

*bai* Spectacular Palauan structure, profusely decorated with carved and painted interior beams and gables illustrating events and symbolizing wealth (722–24, *725, 743*)

**bamboo band** A band of guitars and tuned lengths of bamboo, whose open ends players strike with a rubber thong or thongs in patterns evoking a boogie-woogie bass (90, 155–56, 657)

*bātere* Kiribati short song with interpretive movements, adapted from the Tokelauan *fātele* (761–62, 764)

*bêche de mer* (also *trepang*) Large sea cucumbers, boiled, dried, and used mostly by Chinese for making soup (84)

**Belau** An alternate spelling of *Palau* (722, 967)

*belembaotuyan* [from *berimbau,* a Brazilian chordophone, possibly derived from an Angolan gourd-resonated musical bow] An introduced musical bow of the Mariana Islands that has become an icon of Chamorro cultural identity (387, 745–46)

**Benesh notation** (also *Benesh Movement Notation*) The system of notation on five-line staffs running left to right developed between 1947 and 1955 by Rudolf Benesh (1916–1975) and Joan Benesh (b. 1920) to transcribe human movements; compare *Labanotation* (316–17, *461, 466*)

**betel** The kernel of the seed of the areca palm, chewed with the leaves, stems, or catkins of betel pepper, slaked lime, and flavorings (177, 179, 602, 608, 636, 638)

**big-band music** Popular orchestral music of the 1930s and 1940s, often played for dancing (25, 921)

**bird of paradise** Any of numerous brilliantly colored birds of family Paradiseidae native to New Guinea and important for their plumage, often used in costumes (55, *179,* 349–50, 484–85, 496, 523, 529, *599*)

**Bislama** [English *beach-la-mar,* from French *bêche de mer*] The common pidgin of Vanuatu (214, 259, 690, 709, 861)

**Bismarck Mountains** Papua New Guinean mountain chain defining the border of Madang and the Highlands provinces, south of the Ramu River (484, 514)

**Bongu** Papua New Guinean village near the western end of the Rai Coast (23, 561)

**Bon Odori** A dance performed to celebrate O-Bon (317, 739)

**boogie-woogie** A style of playing blues on the piano, characterized by a fast, steady rhythmic bass, often outlining triads (25, 90, 139, 387)

**brass band** Band basically consisting of brass instruments, but sometimes joined by other aerophones and percussion (66, 80, 126–34, *128, 129, 131, 132,* 261, 382, 383, 719, 743, 755, 771, 793, *808,* 817, 901, 906, 929, 930, 935)

**brolga** An Australian crane that performs elaborate movements, possibly as part of a courtship display, often the subject of singing and dancing by Aboriginal Australians (421)

**butcher-bird** Any of several Australian and New Guinean shrikes of genus *Cracticus,* so called because they impale their prey (including small birds) on spikes or thorns, or wedge it in the forks of trees (564)

**button accordion** A musical instrument having two hexagonal headboards connected by a folding bellows and eliciting sounds from free-beating metal tongues set into vibration by the actions of buttons; compare *piano accordion* (99, 103, 141, 159, 745, 905, 907, 909, 952)

**cassowary** Any of several large birds of genus *Casuarius,* closely related to the emu and symbolically important in many highland New Guinean cultures (384, 484, 499, 525, 547, 553, 618)

*céilí* An evening gathering, in Australia usually held monthly by people of Irish ancestry and often involving social dances (including the waltz), solo or group displays, and vocal solos (78)

**cent** One one-hundredth of an equal-tempered semitone, a unit of measurement introduced by Alexander J. Ellis (1814–1890) (399–400)

*chalangalang* (also *changalang*) Hawaiian manner of strumming *'ukulele* and guitar, sometimes called twangy (127–28)

**Chamorro** (also *Chamoru*) The indigenous people and language of the Mariana Islands (26, 116, 158, 717, 719–20, 743, 995)

**chant** Recitational singing, often on one or two tones, with rhythms deriving from those of the words (36, 321, 890–94)

**chordophone** A musical instrument whose principal sound is the vibration of one or more stretched strings (371, 385–91)

**Chuuk** The main island complex, and a state, of the Federated States of Micronesia (91, 159, 160, 178, 181, 324, 328, 712, 716, 719, 726, 728, 733–38, 758, 968, 981)

**clansong** a song owned by a clan (546); in Aboriginal Australia, a song created by totemic ancestral spirits and performed publicly to celebrate the spirits' activities (243, 301–302, 355–56, 394–95, 418–22)

**clapsticks** In Aboriginal Australia, a concussed pair of sticks or boomerangs (60, 61, 243, *433; see also* General Index)

**conch band** A musical ensemble formed of conch trumpets, with one performer and one note per instrument, invented around 1925 in Morobe, New Guinea, by the Lutheran missionary Heinrich Zahn (1880–1944) (89, 128–29, 195–96, *197*, 288, 393, 794)

**conch trumpet** Trumpet made from the empty shell of a conch of genera *Cassis, Fusus, Strombus,* or *Triton*; possibly the most widespread indigenous instrument of Oceania (393, 476; *see also* General Index)

**concussive idiophone** An idiophone made to sound by the action of one part against another, as with clapsticks, paired stones, and castanets; compare *percussive idiophone* (373)

**copra** Dried coconut meat, exported from many Pacific islands for processing into palm oil (237, 755, 795, 904)

**coordinate monophony** The simultaneous performance of two or more melodies, unrelated or related only through a common tone, as in Angan choral singing (497), or meter, as in Yupno *njaguo konggap* (304) and among the Isirawa (583)

**coordinate polyphony** The simultaneous performance of two or more independent phrases, as in the Bellonese *suahongi* and the Tongan *me'etu'upaki* (308–309)

**cordyline** Relating to ti plants (339, 518, 629)

**corrido** Mexican balladic musical genre, derived from the Spanish *romance,* with texts usually concerning local, historical, or legendary events, set in stanzas of eight-syllable lines (952)

**corroboree** An Aboriginal Australian nocturnal festivity with singing and dancing (60, 408, *410,* 426, 430, 440–41, 461)

**Creative Nation** The Australian federal policy implemented in 1994 to further "cultural industry," tourism, and artistic technology, and to assist emerging artists (253, 407)

**creole** A language deriving from two or more languages and serving as its speakers' native language; compare *pidgin* (102, 140)

**cuatro** [Spanish 'four'] A Puerto Rican creole lead guitar with five steel-stringed double courses, originally four gut single strings (99, 102–103)

**cueca** A Chilean dance in alternating 3/4 and 6/8 meter, usually with text set in quatrains of eight-syllable lines and melody sung in parallel thirds on tonic and dominant triads accompanied by handclaps and guitars (82–83, 952)

**dance** A specially marked or elaborated and culturally specific system of movement resulting from creative processes that manipulate human bodies in time and space to formalize and intensify movement, much as poetry intensifies and formalizes language (311, 312)

**danza** [Spanish 'dance'] A couple dance, usually without sung text, in duple meter and

sectional form, often involving an initial promenade (*paseo*) (101–102)

**decibel** [abbreviated *dB*] A logarithmic unit for expressing relative power levels. The sound-pressure level of 0 dB is ordinarily referred to as a pressure level of 20 micropascals, the approximate threshold of human hearing. The average threshold of pain is about 130 dB (381)

**décima** [Spanish 'tenth'] A Spanish poetic form having ten eight-syllable lines rhyming *abba:accddc,* the colon denoting a pause; also called *décima espinela* (101)

**didjeridu** A wooden trumpet, about 1 to 1.5 meters long, played mainly by Aborigines of northern Australia (61, 243, 293–94, 393–98, *394, 420, 427; see also* General Index)

**difference tone** A sound of frequency $f_1$–$f_2$ or $f_2$–$f_1$, generated when pure sounds of frequency $f_1$ and $f_2$ are fed simultaneously into a nonlinear system (396)

**djalkmi** A clansong style of Central Arnhem Land (421–22)

**djatpangarri (also *djedbangari,* often in writing called fun songs)** Didjeridu-accompanied songs with formulaic, mainly "nonsense" texts, sung by young unmarried men, especially in northeastern Arnhem Land (394, 420–21, 445)

**Dreaming** The realm of Aboriginal Australians' ancestral and totemic spirits, accessible in dreams (185, 187–88, 241, 345, 355, 417, 419, 422, 425–26, 431, 434, 436, 439, 443, 450–51, 453, 456, 460, 464–67)

**drone** A sustained musical tone or pattern of tones, against which one part or several parts may move (14, 294, 395–98; *see also* General Index)

**dukduk** In New Britain and the Duke of York Islands, male (in Nissan, female) masks with heavy pandanus-leaf skirts, worn by men who perform gyrating movements before seated drummers; complementary to *tubuan (tumbuan)* (596, 632, *634*)

**dulcimer (often *hammer dulcimer*)** A trapezoidally shaped chordophone played with light, handheld hammers (73)

**electric band** Common Oceanic name for an electrically amplified musical ensemble (90, 137–40, 153, 246, 485–86)

**Ellice Islands** The former name of Tuvalu (5, 758, 828)

**emic** [from *phonemic*] Of sounds, perceivable as distinctive according to the subjective sense they make to participants in the cultures that generate or value them; compare *etic* (283, 289, 313, 317, 322, 501, 697, 778)

**etic** [from *phonetic*] Of sounds, perceivable as present and actual acoustic events according to an assumed objective measurement or description; compare *emic* (283, 289, 313, 322, 501, 778)

**exogamy** Marriage outside one's own group, especially as required by custom or law (419, 457, 460, 506, 516, 592, 602)

**fa'ataupati** Sāmoan dance with slapping, usually done by men (104, 805, *806*)

**falsetto** A timbre, usually with high pitch, resulting from forced limitations of the larynx (27, 297, 490, 538; *see also* General Index)

**fātele** Tokelauan short song with interpretive movements, adapted in Kiribati as the *bātere* (113, 278, 354, 379–80, 762, 825–31)

**Finisterre Range** Papua New Guinean mountains running inland of the Rai Coast, between the coast and the border with Morobe (303, 545, 561)

**formant** Any of several frequency bands comprising groups of prominent overtones of a complex tone, in the human voice determining the phonetic identity of vowels (297, 396)

**formula, melodic** A tone or series of tones (some variously optional or alternative), whose rhythmic realization depends mostly on the words that give it breath (256, 300–301, *561,* 603, *648,* 723, 728, 799, *800, 912*)

**Fourier analysis** A mathematical procedure, automated in signal-analysis equipment, that decomposes a complex waveform into sine waves (fundamental and overtones) of well-defined frequencies (381)

**frequency** The number of repetitions of a periodic process in a unit of time; in the analysis of sound usually measured in hertz (286, 291, 292–94, 373, 385–86, 392, 395–96, 570)

**frigate bird** Any of several rapacious seabirds of family Fregatidae; a dance or mimetically performed motif or set of motifs of Kiribati, Nauru, and other islands; compare *tropic bird* (231, 262, 336, 663, 664, 686, 754, 757, 885)

**FSM** The Federated States of Micronesia, comprised of Chuuk, Kosrae, Pohnpei, and Yap (726)

**fundamental** The component of a musical sound having the lowest frequency and upon which a series of overtones may be based (293–94, 373, 395, 412–13, 542, 556, 669)

**garamut** Any hollowed log idiophone of Papua New Guinea (22, 23, 245, 375–77, 475–76; *see also* General Index)

**gender** The social construction of male and female sexuality, involving expectations about behavior and attributions of intent (241–49)

**Gilbert Islands** An archipelago formerly part of the Gilbert and Ellice Islands Colony and now part of the Republic of Kiribati (758)

**glottal stop** During vocalization, the interruption of the breath by closure of the glottis (the space between the vocal cords); also, a typographical sign for this action (503, 575, 697)

**glottochronology (also *lexicostatistics*)** A method of measuring the history of related languages by quantifying the degree to which they share cognate words (321)

**Great War** The European military conflict of 1914–1918, retrospectively called World War I (115)

**Gregorian chant** The ancient, rhythmically free, liturgical, unison singing of the Roman Catholic Church (88, 199, 889)

**Guam** The southern and largest of the Mariana Islands, governmentally separate from the Northern Marianas (744–46)

*guaracha* Medium-fast strophic song-dance of Cuban origin, in duple meter and stanza-refrain form (101–102)

*güiro* [Spanish 'bottle gourd'] Gourd (sometimes in Hawai'i, metal) scraper, of Amerindian origin, providing usually stressed downbeats and rhythms varied according to the dance accompanied (99, 102)

**gutbucket** Chordophone consisting of a string stretched across a board inserted into a washtub or large empty can (27, 157)

*hālau* Hawaiian school of *hula*, requiring long apprenticeship and the study of customs (117, 923, 925)

**hapa haole** [Hawaiian, from *hapa* 'half' (from English *half*) and *haole* 'foreign'] Of part-European ancestry or origin, especially Hawaiian-European (921–22)

**harmonic** An overtone whose vibrational frequency is an exact integer multiple of that of the fundamental; the component with frequency *n* times that of the fundamental is the *n*th harmonic (294, 296–97, 389, 392, 395–96, 511, 546, 922)

**Heiva** The principal festival of French Polynesia, held in Tahiti each July (56–57, 65–66, 867–68, 873, 880)

*heliaki* In Tongan verbal expression, indirectness or veiled meaning (336, 365, 367–68, 783, 785, 789, 793, 794)

**Helmholtz resonator** [after Hermann von Helmholtz (1821–1894)] Any sound-making object partly enclosing an air-filled cavity, whose pitch is set by the size(s), not the position(s), of the opening(s), as with hollowed log idiophones and vessel flutes (374, 393)

**hermaphrodite pig (also *intersex pig*)** A pig with male and female genitalia, highly valued in Vanuatu for use in grade-taking rituals (198)

**hertz** [abbreviated Hz] The number of oscillations per second produced by a vibrating body or a sound wave (286, 291–94, 395–96)

*hīmene* (Society Islands, Manihiki), *hīmeni* (Hawai'i), *īmene* (Pukapuka), *'īmene*

**(southern Cook Islands)** [from French *hymne* or English *hymn*] East Polynesian choral singing, originally combining indigenous musical textures with European harmonies and now perceived as an original cultural expression (37, 85, 112, 166, 187, 209, 308, 869–73, 894, 898, 905, 913, 918–19)

*hiri* A trading network of the Motu people of southern New Guinea (489, 492–93)

**Hiri Motu (also *Police Motu*)** A pidgin commonly spoken in Papua New Guinea, especially in the Papuan Region (90, 179, 474, 488, 492, 494–95, 506)

*hiva kakala* Tongan popular song (104, 117, 130–31, 313, 365, 366–67, 783, 787, 793)

**hocket** Texture in which two or more voices rapidly alternate melodic notes or groups of notes, one part resting while the other sounds (64, 65, 556, 565)

*hula 'auana* [Hawaiian, 'modern *hula*'] *Hula* style incorporating newer movements, with harmonized sung text accompanied by plucked chordophones of Western origin (66–67, 923, 926)

*hula kahiko* [Hawaiian, 'ancient *hula*'] *Hula* style incorporating older movements, with monophonically recited text accompanied by indigenous instruments (66–67, 391, 923, 928)

**idiophone** A musical instrument whose principal sound is the vibration of its primary material (22, 371, 373–82)

**Ifaluk** A former spelling of Ifalik, an atoll in Yap State (994)

**I-Kiribati** The people of Kiribati (758)

**inharmonicity** The quality arising when the overtones in a complex musical sound are not harmonics of the fundamental, as with instruments excited percussively, such as bells and gongs (395)

**inner tempo** The number of rhythmic impulses per minute, regardless of their periodicity or regularity of occurrence, the distribution of accents, and the presence of a meter (290–91)

**Jamoan** Jamaican-Sāmoan reggae, cultivated by the I Don't Know Band, a Saipan-based musical ensemble (160)

**Jawaiian** A Hawaiian adaptation of reggae, most popular in the 1980s (164, 166–67)

**jitterbug** A jazz variation of the two-step, in which mixed couples vigorously swing and twirl in quick, often jerky, movements (25, 26)

**John Frum movement** A religious-political movement ("cargo cult") that originated in Tanna in the 1940s (32, 214–15)

**jolting** The log-idiophone-playing technique by which the player hits the instrument with the end of a thick stick or a bundle of sticks; compare *striking* (374, 375, 476, 547, 552, 601, 615, 639, 651)

*kachi-kachi* Japanese-Hawaiian plantation term for the scratching of a *güiro*; in Hawai'i, a generic term for Puerto Rican dance-music (102)

*kailao* 'Uvean and Tongan men's dance performed with clubs (379, 792–93, 809, 812–13, 816)

**Kamehameha Day** Hawaiian state holiday honoring King Kamehameha I (1758?–1819), the monarch who first united the islands (67, 95)

**Kanak** Name the indigenous people of New Caledonia call themselves (213–14, 671)

**Kanaky** Name the indigenous people of New Caledonia call their country (213–14)

*kaneka* The contemporary indigenous music of Kanaky (213–14)

*kantan chamorrita* Chamorro songs distinguished by metaphors and other allusive verbal devices (158)

*kaona* [Hawaiian] Veiled or layered verbal meaning (222, 299, 336, 923, 925, 927)

*kastom* [pidgin, from English *custom*] Indigenous attitudes, beliefs, concepts, and behavior, especially in New Guinea and Melanesia (212)

**kava** The plant *Piper methysticum* or an infusion of its pulverized or formerly masticated roots or stems, serving as a beverage often consumed with formalities encoding important elements of social structure (104, 161, 172–77, 202, 216–17, 348, 363, 689, 694, 702, 703, 717, 739, 740, 741, 774, 781, 793, 802, 803, 809, 815–16, 897)

**kina** [Tok Pisin] A large mother-of-pearl, traditionally used for trade in the Papua New Guinea highlands; since 1975, the basic unit of Papua New Guinea currency, divided into 100 toea (534, 536)

**kineme** The minimal unit of movement recognized as contrastive by people of a given dance tradition (313)

**Kodak Hula Show** A Hawaiian music-and-dance show, founded in 1937 by Louise Akeo and the Royal Hawaiian Girls' Glee Club and still presented once or more often a week outdoors at Waikīkī (56, 67, 105)

*konggap* [Yupno, 'ghost voice'] Any short tune uniquely identified with an individual Yupno, of Madang Province, Papua New Guinea (303–304, 545)

**Kosrae** An island and state of the Federated States of Micronesia (726, 740–43)

*koto* Japanese zither having thirteen silk strings set on movable bridges and played with ivory picks (97)

*kula* An extensive trading network of southeast New Guinea (53, 490, 492, 498–99)

*Kumulipo* The long, versified genealogical narrative honoring Lono-i-ka-Makahiki, an ancestor of King Kalākaua of Hawai'i (915)

*kundiman* Lowland Filipino song, composed in an art-song style with piano accompaniment (100)

**kundu** A Papua New Guinean hourglass-shaped drum, held with one hand and struck with the other, mostly by men (28, *242*, 245, 382–84, 476; *See also* General Index)

**Kundu** A network service of the National Broadcasting Commission of Papua New Guinea (91)

*kupuna* (pl. *kūpuna*) Hawaiian-speaking elder, revered by Hawaiians as a living repository of indigenous culture (222, 273, 275)

*kutu* An Okinawan zither (98)

**Labanotation** (also *Kinetography Laban*) The system of notation running from bottom to top developed in the 1920s by Rudolf von Laban (1879–1958) to transcribe human movements; compare *Benesh notation* (316–17, *454*, *466*, *793*, *926*)

*lagatoi* Trading vessels of the Motu people of New Guinea (492–93)

*lakalaka* Formal Tongan dance developed from the *me'elaufola* in the 1800s; generic term for dance in the Banks Islands, Vanuatu (117, 224, 241, *242*, 308–309, 351–52, 365, 367–68, 698, 783, 789, 809, 812–13)

**lamellaphone** A musical instrument whose sound is the vibration of a tonguelike projection (286, 374, 476)

**Lapita cultural complex** An archaeologically documented tradition of earthenware ceramics from the Bismarck Archipelago, the coast of New Guinea, Melanesia, and West Polynesia (2–4, 598, 689, 771, 809)

**lexicostatistics** (also *glottochronology*) A method of measuring the history of related languages by quantifying the degree to which they share cognate words (321, 688)

**lion dance** Movements made by a lionlike effigy worked from inside, usually by members of martial-arts organizations; an important marker of Chinese identity on celebratory occasions (71, 96, 106, 109)

**live band** [Tok Pisin *laiv ben*] New Guinean name for an electrically amplified musical ensemble (90, 137–40, 153, 246, 485–86)

**LMS** London Missionary Society (See below)

**log idiophone** A hollowed log, branch, or other piece of timber, played by being struck or jolted, often in ensemble (14, 374–77; *see also* General Index)

**London Missionary Society** British interdenominational Christian organization that began sending missionaries to Oceania in 1797 (84–85, 88, 193–95, 204, 206, 208–209, 412, 429, 493, 506, 682, 720, 763, 795, 816, 823, 828, 831, 905)

**longtom** Any of various elongate Australian marine and estuarine fishes of family Belonidae (421)

**lotusbird** The northern and eastern Australian jacana, a bird of genus *Jacana*, able to run on floating vegetation (421)

**lute** A chordophone having a usually pear-shaped body, a fretted fingerboard, and a head with tuning pegs, often angled backward from the neck (73, 98)

**macron** Long mark, written above a vowel to show that in pronunciation the vowel takes more time than typical unmarked vowels (285)

*makahiki* Three-month precontact Hawaiian festival in which competitive games and sports were played under the eye of Lono, god of peace and agriculture (66)

*malae* (Sāmoan), *mala'e* (Tongan), *marä'e* (Rotuman), *marae* (East Polynesian) Formal communal grounds, in East Polynesia serving as a sacred space usually marked with imposing stone or wooden structures (57, 236, 237, 277, 787, 809, 812, 818, 846, 861, 863, 933, 943, 945–46, 947)

*malaga* A ceremonial Sāmoan visit, often marked by formalities including orations and kava and celebrated with singing and dancing (53, 802)

*malanggan* Dramatic commemorative rites of northern New Ireland, involving masked performers who often voice their messages through the sounds of musical instruments (350, 600–601, 628–29)

**mana** [from Polynesian] Supernatural power and authority (175, 200, 207, 209, 325, 349, 781, 835, 914, 944)

**Māori** Term used by Polynesians of Aotearoa and the Cook Islands to refer to themselves (896, 928, 930–51)

**Marley, Robert Nesta "Bob" (1945–1981)** Jamaican reggae musician who toured parts of Oceania in 1979 (145, 166, 168, 213)

**Mass** The liturgy of Holy Communion, the essential rite of the Roman Catholic and other apostolic churches (199–200, 204, 206)

**matrilineal** Tracing descent through the female line; compare *patrilineal* (115, 457, 662, 688, 715, 722, 738)

*mā'ulu'ulu* Sāmoan and Tongan sung speech with choreographic movements (104, 278, 789–90, 803, 814, 823, 827)

**mazurka** A Polish dance in moderate triple meter (101, 141)

*me'elaufola* Tongan dance observed during Cook's third voyage; prototype of the *lakalaka* (12, 241, 789)

*me'etu'upaki* Tongan dance in which standing men manipulate paddles (13, 309, 316, 790–91)

**megapode** A bird that lays its eggs in mounds of debris, where heat from composting vegetable matter incubates the eggs (384, 476)

**mel** The unit of measurement of pitch: if a sound of frequency 1000 Hz is arbitrarily taken to have a pitch of 1000 mels, people trying to set a pitch half as high (500 mels) choose a sound of about 400 Hz, and peo-

ple trying to set a pitch twice as high (2000 mels) choose a pitch of about 3000 Hz (290)

*mele* A Hawaiian poetic text and its vocalization: *mele hula*, singing with dancing; *mele oli*, singing without dancing (276, 299–300, 915)

**membranophone** Any musical instrument whose principal sound is the vibration of a stretched skin (22, 371, 381–85)

**menarche** An individual's first menstrual period (613)

**metaphor** Figure of speech by which a stated denotation, sometimes called a vehicle, delivers an unstated message, sometimes called a tenor (215–19, 330, 336–43, 359, 361, 363, 479, 514, 517–18, 550, 566, 583, 645, 673, 768, 783, 785, 787, 836, 862)

**meter** The underlying pattern of strong and weak stresses per musical measure; compare *rhythm* and *tempo* (289–90, 324)

**MIDI** Musical Instrument Digital Interface, a hardware and software specification that permits the exchange of information among musical instruments or electronic devices such as computers, lighting controllers, mixers, and sequencers (144)

*minyo* Japanese genre of rural song (97)

**modern dance** Styles and techniques of theatrical dancing that developed during the early twentieth century as an alternative to the strict disciplines of classical ballet (107, 109, 416–17)

**moiety** One of two basic complementary subdivisions of a group of people (198, 340, 381, 419, 427, 431, 457, 489, 498, 506, 553, 557, 624, 695, 702)

**mora** In a given language, the duration of a typical short syllable (324–25, 695, 803, 912)

**morphokine** The smallest unit that has meaning as movement in the structure of a movement system (313)

**motif** In dance analysis, a culturally grammatical sequence of movement combining kinemes and morphokines in a characteristic way and verbalized and recognized by people indigenous to the culture (12, 313, 793, 927, 952–53)

**Mwai (Mai)** Iatmul men's ceremony involving masks (555–56)

*mwai* (*mai*) Iatmul paired, end-blown, bamboo voice modifiers used during the Mwai (555–56)

*nahenahe* A prime Hawaiian cultural value, emphasizing gentleness, calmness, and laid-back ease, often used to differentiate Hawaiian musical styles from others (166, 167, 390)

**NAISDA** National Aboriginal Islander Skills Development Association (228–29, *254*, 442–43)

**neo-Melanesian** Any local pidgin spoken in Melanesia (198)

**New Hebrides** Former name of Vanuatu (688)

**newsong verse** [for Yolngu *yuṯa manikay* 'new song'] A newly composed song of north-eastern Arnhem Land (355–56)

*ngarkana* A clansong style of Central Arnhem Land (421)

**Ni-Vanuatu** The people of Vanuatu (84, 198, 691)

**Noisy Boys** A Vanuatu band (32–33, 709)

**nonlinearity** A situation in which increasing the input energy (or force) increases the loudness of the output and changes its timbre, as with sustained-tone instruments, whose sound-generating mechanism makes the overtones exact harmonics, and with electronic sound systems, whose nonlinearity produces harmonic distortion (396)

**no-no language** Any of several southeast Australian Aboriginal languages whose names consist of the repeated local word for *no* (439, 441)

**normal score** A melody found by quantitative inference from transcriptions of sampled performances (292, 294–96)

**note** A tone occurring as part of a musical piece; a transcriptive sign of such a tone or any other musically significant sound (291)

**no-with language** Any of several southeast Australian Aboriginal languages whose names consist of local words for *no* and *with* (439, 441)

**O-Bon** Japanese Buddhist commemoration of deceased friends and relatives (95, 97, 106)

**octave** A musical interval encompassing eight diatonic degrees; the interval between a referential sound and a sound of twice or half its frequency; people trying to set tones an octave apart typically stretch this interval by about 1 percent (292–94, 434)

**OTAC** Office Territorial d'Action Culturelle, based in Papeʻete, Tahiti (958)

**Ouvéa** French name of the island sometimes called West ʻUvea (671, 682)

**overtone** Any of the high, quiet sounds produced with a fundamental and joining with that fundamental in comprising a tone (373, 381, 386, 395–96, 412–13)

**Pacific Festival of Arts** A quadrennial international festival featuring cultural displays from the nations of Oceania, first held in 1972 (53, *54*, 57–59; *see also* General Index)

*pahu* East Polynesian hand-struck footed drum having a shark- or ray-skin head and a body usually carved from coconut or breadfruit wood, ranging from 22 to 114 centimeters high (286, 382, 384–85, 865, 869, 895, 916; *see also* General Index)

**panpipe** A set of differently pitched tubular flutes, usually bound in a bundle or row (23, 393, 398–401; *see also* General Index)

**partial** [for *upper partial tone*] An overtone (399–400, 542, 556)

**patrilineal** Tracing descent through the male line; compare *matrilineal* (419, 455–56, 457, 460, 516, 553, 557, 602, 776)

**percussive idiophone** An idiophone made to sound by the action of a beater, as with log idiophones, wooden plaques, and xylophones; compare *concussive idiophone* (373)

*peroveta anedia* **'prophet song'** Twentieth-century New Guinean musical genre whose melodic, rhythmic, harmonic, and textural style, and originally language, were brought by Polynesian LMS missionaries (88, 90, 494)

**phoneme** The minimal unit of distinctive linguistic sound (322, 326–28)

**piano accordion** A musical instrument having two rectangular headboards connected by a folding bellows and eliciting sounds from free-beating metal tongues set into vibration by the actions of keys on a pianolike keyboard on the right side and buttons on the left; compare *button accordion* (81)

**pidgin** A simplified speech serving for communication among peoples having different native languages; compare *creole* (58, 214, 387, 441, 488, 690, 844)

**Pijin** A pidgin commonly spoken in the Solomon Islands (158)

*pilu* [taken into French as *pilou*] Presentational Kanak dancing, often by numerous ensembles (213)

**pipe band** A musical ensemble formed of bagpipes and usually a battery of side and bass drums (89, 95, 115, 135–36, *136*; *see also* General Index)

**pitch** The perceived height or "location" of sound, measurable in mels; compare *frequency, note,* and *tone* (291–96)

*plena* Fast song-dance genre, of African–Puerto Rican origin, in duple meter and sometimes improvised stanza-refrain form (102)

**Pohnpei** The main island, and a state, of the Federated States of Micronesia (726, 739–40)

**polykinetic** Having multiple movements, as a dance in which individuals or groups perform movements that differ from those of other individuals or groups, or in which movements of some of an individual's body parts differ from those of the same individual's other body parts as they move together (784–85, 798–99)

**Ponape** The entity now known as Pohnpei (726)

**power band** [Tok Pisin *pawa ben*] New Guinean name for an electrically amplified musical ensemble (90, 137–40, 153, 246, 485–86)

**Prince Alexander Mountains** Papua New Guinean mountains in East Sepik, an extension of the Torricelli Range (548, 549)

**Proto-Polynesian** A hypothesized language ancestral to the Polynesian languages (320)

*qeej* **(Lao** *khaen***)** A Hmong multiple free-reed pipe (75–76)

**Rai Coast** The Papua New Guinean coast of Madang Province, extending from the town of Madang eastward to the Morobe border (297, 476, 546, 547, 561–66)

**recitative** A style of singing in imitation of the rhythmic and sometimes tonal inflections of ordinary speech (769, 830, 884)

**RFO** Radiodiffusion Télévision Française pour Outre-Mer, the French overseas TV broadcasting system (958)

**rhythm** A pattern of strong and weak elements in a flow of sound, musically often recurring or grouping at several levels of organization; compare *meter* and *tempo* (290)

**Rom** A ceremony performed by Aboriginal Australians of Arnhem Land as a mark of friendship, with singing and dancing (47, 227–28, *346*, 419, *420*, 467)

*rondalla* Filipino string band, consisting of mandolinlike melodic instruments (*bandurria* and *laud*), guitars, and a bass (100)

**Saidor** Papua New Guinean town on the Rai Coast, immediately east of Serieng (547–48, 562)

**Saipan** The capital island of the Commonwealth of the Northern Mariana Islands (91, 160, 712, 743, 746)

*sakau* [Pohnpeian] Kava (175, 717, 719, 740, 741)

**samba** A Brazilian dance having syncopated rhythms in 2/4 meter (83, 84, 213, 407)

**saratoga** An Australian freshwater fish of genus *Scleropages* (421)

**Saruwaged Range** Papua New Guinean mountains in Morobe, between the Markham River and the border with Madang (545)

*sawagoro* A Vanuatu genre of popular song (198, 361)

*seis* [Spanish 'six'] Medium-fast duple strophic song-dance, set to the poetic form of a *décima* (101–102)

**Serieng** Papua New Guinean village in the center of the Rai Coast, immediately west of Saidor (564–65)

*shakuhachi* Japanese end-blown bamboo flute with five holes for fingering (97, 444)

*shamisen* Japanese box-shaped three-stringed long-necked fretless lute, played with a plectrum (97)

*shigin* Japanese recited poetry (97)

*sia* A nocturnal mimetic dance that originated in the Siasi Islands and spread to become a cultural icon of the Mamose Region of Papua New Guinea (336, 545–46, 572–74, 610–11, 616, 619)

**singsing** In Papua New Guinea, the performance of a song or songs, especially in public, with dancing by decorated performers (56, 62, 147–48, 245, 477, 496–97, 502–503, 526, 529–30, 533–34, 545–46, 549, 560–61)

**sit-down dance** Torres Strait Islanders' adaptation of Sāmoan singing and dancing (85)

**slack-key tuning** [Hawaiian *kī hōʻalu*] A Hawaiian-developed method of playing acoustic guitar by which the player loosens the strings to alter the tuning (160, 388–89, 922)

**sonagram** Graphic printout of an electronically analyzed segment of sound (136, 160, 381, 399–400)

**songline** Term popularized by Bruce Chatwin to denote the geographical path evoked or taken by a series of related Aboriginal Australian ceremonial songs (292–93, 345, 411, 707)

**sonics** The study of the pure sound of utterances (325)

*son montuno* Slow-medium song-dance of Cuban origin, in duple meter and stanza-refrain form, followed by an African-influenced improvised responsorial section (101)

**Southern Cross** A constellation visible in the southern hemisphere, often seen as a Christian symbol (45, 55, *219*)

**stanza** A division of a poem, consisting of verses sometimes arranged in a recurring pattern, as of meter, rhyme, or syntax (101–102, 205, 306, 704, 778, 791, 821, 825, 850, 854, 882, 887, 888, 952)

**steel guitar** [Hawaiian *kikā kila*] Hawaiian-developed style of playing the guitar by sliding a steel bar along the strings to make microtonal slides, harmonics, and timbral variations (127, 142, 389–90, 922)

**striking** The log-idiophone-playing technique by which the player hits the instrument with the side of a stick or two short sticks, one in each hand; compare *jolting* (374, 375, 476, 601)

**string band** [Tok Pisin *stringben*] A musical ensemble formed mainly of chordophones, usually guitars, sometimes incorporating ukuleles and rarely banjos (27, 90, 95, 100, 136–40, 485; *see also* General Index)

**string figure** A loop of string manipulated into a pattern or patterns perceived as meaningful and often accompanied by or interpreting a sung text (253, 263, 267, *268*, 656, 661, 758, 952)

**strophic** Designation for a poem consisting of two or more lines whose rhythmic pattern repeats as a unit, or a song in which each stanza of the lyrics is sung to the same music (301, 330–35)

**sum and difference frequencies** Frequencies of $f_1+f_2$ (the sum frequency) and $f_1-f_2$ (the difference frequency), generated when pure pitches of frequency $f_1$ and $f_2$ are fed into a nonlinear system; the most prominent

members of a set of nonlinearly generated pitches of frequency $nf_1 \pm mf_2$, where $n$ and $m$ are integers (396)

**susap** [Tok Pisin, from English *Jew's harp*] A mainly Papua New Guinean lamellaphone, usually played for private entertainment by males (178, 476, 503; *see also* General Index)

**swing** A musical genre developed in North America in the 1920s and popularized in the 1930s to accompany jazz dancing in moderate tempo with smooth syncopation (25, 100, 144, 266, 387, 390)

**swung slat** A simple, but often sacred, aerophone consisting of a thin, lens- or rhomboid-shaped wooden slat attached to a string and made to hum by being whirled through the air (23, 168, 245, 252, 392; *see also* General Index)

**syncretism** The combination of two or more different cultural systems of belief or practice (187, 193, 361)

*tabu* (also **taboo**, *tapu*, *kapu*) Interdictions and protocols serving to protect mana and keep the sacred separate from the secular (15–16, 22–23, 200–201, 202, 207–209, 230, 245, 349, 402, 467, 492, 563, 583, 609, 652, 705, 708, 781, 787–88, 835, 914, 925)

*taibobo* (also *taibubu*) The so-called Kiwai dance, a genre of singing and dancing adapted from Rotuman genres and performed by Torres Strait Islanders and coastal peoples of Western Province, Papua New Guinea (85, *490*, 507)

*taiko* A Japanese large barrel-shaped two-headed drum, whose skins are usually tacked (97)

*taiko* **drumming** A contemporary presentational ensemble, based on Japanese drumming genres and sometimes including flutes, gongs, or stringed instruments (97)

**tambaran** [Tok Pisin] In Papua New Guinea, a spirit or its representation, in sight (as by carved wood) or sound (as by a flute) (245, 477, 546, 547–48, 552, 561–62)

*tāmūrē* Popular term for *ʻori tahiti*, Tahitian couple dancing, associated in Tahiti with joy and pleasure (211, 874, 952)

**tapa** Cloth made from pounded bark, usually of the paper mulberry (21, 57)

*taralala* [rightly *tarālalā*, probably from English *tra-la-la*] Fijian mixed couples' dance in duple meter and lively tempo, with cheerful text and music deriving from European popular styles of the 1800s (149, 157, 162, 779–80, 782)

*taualuga* Finale of a Sāmoan performance of singing and dancing, featuring a distinguished woman (*tāupou*) and attendants (*ʻaiuli*) (104, 231, 349, 798, 802)

*tauʻolunga* A Tongan dance performed by women (117, 231, 787, 793)

**tempo** The perceived speed of a musical per-

formance; compare *meter* and *rhythm* (290–91)

**ti** Any of several Oceanic shrubs of genus *Cordyline*, of the lily family (66, 67, 177, 313, 821)

*tigul* (Nissan), *tsigul* (Banoni, Buka) Nocturnal session of dancing, drumming, and singing; the genres performed at such sessions (633–36, 644–45)

**tiki** Polynesian stone or wooden image of a supernatural power (55)

**timbre** The perceived quality of a sound, defined by the presence and intensities of overtones (296–300)

**Tin Pan Alley** A musical style that originated in New York in the 1890s and became popular from about 1912; a neighborhood or area where large numbers of musical composers and publishers work (25)

**toddy** Fermented coconut-palm sap (178, 179, 181, 754, 758, 845)

**Tok Pisin** [English *talk pidgin*] A pidgin commonly spoken in Papua New Guinea (90, 151–52, 153, 179, 195, 257, 474, 488, 568)

**tonal center** In any melody, the tone that serves as a typical structural goal or point of repose (292, 296, 302–303)

**tone** A pitch of definite frequency; a pitch or range of pitches treated within a musical system as a sonic identity, analyzable as a scalar unit; compare *frequency, note,* and *pitch* (291)

**Torricelli Mountains** Papua New Guinean coastal mountains at the border of East and West Sepik, an extension of the Prince Alexander Range (545, 548)

**totem** An object, as a plant or an animal, or a depiction of an object serving as the sign of a family or a clan (340–42, 411, 419, 421, 430, 445, 460–61, 463, 474, 482–83, 489, 550, 556, 557, 662, 685–686, 729)

**traceform** The shape of the pathways traced by an individual's limbs as they move through space (314)

**tradition** The continual (re)creation of culture by the manipulation of symbolic elements and the reordering and refocusing of inherited cultural constructs to reflect present-day needs and desires (146, 212, 361, 950)

**trepang** (also *bêche de mer*) Large sea cucumbers, boiled, dried, and used mostly by Chinese for making soup (84)

**triad** Any chord of three tones, usually a root and its third and fifth, forming the harmonic basis of tonal music (14, 257, 308, 576, 794, 822, 912)

**tritone** The tonal interval of an augmented fourth or diminished fifth (530)

**trochus shell** Conical shell produced by a mollusk of genus *Trochus* (655, 657)

**tropic bird** Any of several web-footed birds of genus *Phaethon*, often seen far from land; in some cultures, a dance so named; compare *frigate bird* (349, 882)

**Truk** The entity now known as Chuuk (726)

*tubuan* (**also** *tumbuan*) Southern New Ireland commemorative rites involving masked dancers: in New Britain and the Duke of York Islands, female (in Nissan, male) masks with heavy pandanus-leaf skirts, worn by men who perform gyrating movements before seated drummers; complementary to *dukduk* (600–601, 609–10, 619, 621, 625, 632, *634*)

**tuning** [Tok Pisin *ki* 'key'] An array of tones to which the strings of a chordophone are set (90, 160, 286, 387)

*'ukulele* Hawaiian name given during the 1880s to the *braguinha,* a small four-stringed Portuguese musical instrument of the guitar family (27, 95, 390–91, *807, 922*; *see also* General Index)

**unison** The conception or performance of musical parts on the same tone or, in loose speech and writing, at the octave; the consonant simultaneous sounding of multiple instruments, as of kundus beaten together in precise rhythm (301, 376, 434, 491, 933)

**USO** United Service Organization, a morale-building entity serving the U.S. military (26, 28, 67, 149, 160)

**verse** A line of text (205, 247, 306, 324)

**vibrato** The tremulous quality given to a musical tone by rapid variations in its pitch or intensity (205, 503, 779, 808, 916)

**vocable** A spoken or sung wordlike sound having no lexical meaning (320, 482, 489, 513, 530, 564, 568, 592, 603, 652–53, 657, 664, 704, *892, 905, 910*)

**waltz** A ballroom dance in moderate triple time (78, 99, 101, 102, 147, 213, 744, 750, 874, 905, 928)

*wangga* Aboriginal northwestern Australian songs, usually received from spirits in dreams (243, *244*, 317, 355, 394; 423–27, 431–32, 453–55)

**Western Sāmoa** Until July 1997, the administrative and national name of the western and most populous part of Sāmoa, mainly Savai'i and 'Upolu islands (213, 795)

**Wilhelm, Mount** Papua New Guinean mountain at the intersection of Chimbu, Madang, and Western Highlands (511)

*wowipits* [Asmat] Any man skilled at carving wood (190)

**Yap** The main island complex, and a state, of the Federated States of Micronesia (726, 729–33)

*yaqona* [Fijian] Kava (161, 176, 774)

**yodel** The rapid alternation of falsetto and full-voice singing (49–50, 151, 297, 298–300, 467, 478, 538, 540–41, 543, 665, 706, 709, 916)

# Notes on the Audio Examples

1. Fijian club dance (*meke i wau*) (1:00). Sung by two female soloists (*laga, tagica*) and a chorus (*druku*), with additional sounds from a small log idiophone (*lali ni meke,* held against one person's chest and struck by another), choral clapping with cupped hands (*cobo*), and rattles tied to the dancers' ankles. Performed at a church fundraiser in Suva, Viti Levu, Fiji.
   Recorded by Adrienne L. Kaeppler, 7 December 1984.

2. Tannese conch-shell trio (0:23). The musicians play a pattern that warns women to look away during men's circumcision-related rituals and activities. Performed by three men of Lamakaun Village, Tanna, Vanuatu.
   Recorded by Vida Chenoweth, 5 June 1994. American Folklife Center, AFC 1995/038, cassette C94/799, item 2.

3. Pohnpei kava-pounding rhythms (*sukusuk*) (1:30). Four men sit beside each of eight large kava stones (*peitehl*) brought from the mountaintop before 1800. Each man uses a fist-sized stone (*soahl*) to pound kava roots in prescribed rhythms. [*a*] First, all pound together on the edge of the stones; after a short pause, two men at each kava stone begin pounding on downbeats (*tempel*) while the other two pound less vigorously on offbeats (*wokpekid*). [*b*] As the roots become well mashed, the sound becomes more brilliant. [*c*] The tempo increases, and the process ends with a decrescendo and a sudden loud flourish. Though not conceptualized as music, kava-pounding rhythms are locally classified as *keseng* with such nonvocal sounds as those of harmonicas. Performed by thirty-two men of Madolenihmw (then Metalanim) Municipality, Pohnpei.
   Recorded by Barbara B. Smith in Madolenihmw, December 1963.

4. Manihiki polyphonic hymn (*hīmene tuki tapu*) (2:15). Performed by members of the Cook Islands Christian Church, Tūkao Ekalesia.
   Recorded by Helen Reeves Lawrence in Tūkao, Manihiki, Cook Islands, 29 November 1987.

5. "*Ieōvae, le Atua, le e afio i lugā,*" Sāmoan Protestant hymn (*pese lotu*) (1:30). Sung by the congregation of the Congregational Christian Church in Vaotupua, Falealupo, Savai'i, Sāmoa, accompanied on pedal organ by Togia Kalepo.
   Recorded by J. W. Love, 29 July 1973.

6. Sāmoan performance of the Gloria, an ordinary text of the Mass (1:00). Sung in Sāmoan, with the ringing of a low-pitched bell in the tower outside the church and high-pitched bells in the sanctuary. Performed during the Vigil and Mass of Easter by the congregation of the Roman Catholic church of Falealupo, Savai'i, Sāmoa.
   Recorded by J. W. Love, 1 April 1972.

7. Rapa Nui string-figure song (*pātaʻutaʻu*) (0:25). Performed by Kiko Pātē while manipulating a string figure (*kaikai*).
   Recorded by J. W. Love in Hangaroa, Rapa Nui, 29 August 1980.

8. *"Pale (h)ipm"* ('This is a shell'), Baluan lullaby (0:28). Performed twice by a man and two women of Parioi Village, Baluan, Manus Province, Papua New Guinea.
   Recorded by Gerald Florian Messner, 28 December 1980.

9. Sāmoan responsorial dance-song (*mā'ulu'ulu*) (1:05). Performed by eight men and ten women, mostly of Sāmoa, accompanied by clapping and a small struck log idiophone (*pātē*).
   Recorded by Benjamin Ives Gilman in the Sāmoan Exhibit on the Midway Plaisance at the World's Columbian Exposition, Chicago, 23 September 1893—the earliest date from which a recorded performance of Oceanic music survives. Although the original recording captured only a narrow range of frequencies and added extraneous noise, it shows the basic texture and the repeated alternation of phrases. American Folklife Center, AFS 14,741:A16 (cylinder 4323). Peabody Museum of Archaeology and Ethnology, Harvard University.

10. *"E yo yara waya,"* Chimbu courtship song (*kaungo*) (0:54). Sung in the second style (*giglang dingwa*), mostly in high falsetto, by three men of Bongugl Village, Chimbu Province, Papua New Guinea.
    Recorded by Frédéric Duvelle, 1974. Institute of Papua New Guinea Studies, IPNGS 79-006, It. 19.

11. Huli ceremonial music (1:00). With feet together, men in two facing rows jump sideways in time to the beat of their kundus as they sing in two parts, a repeated shout and a sustained tone. Beside these rows, paired women may dance, holding a stick between them and jumping clockwise in a circle. Performed by people of Hedemali clan, Southern Highlands Province, Papua New Guinea.
    Recorded by Charles Duvelle, 1974. Institute of Papua New Guinea Studies, IPNGS 79-001, It. 20.

12. Anutan lament for a father (*puatanga o te pa*) (1:10). Performed with sobbing at the funeral of Pu Teputuu by the people of Anuta.
    Recorded by Richard Feinberg in December 1972.

13. Tongan coordinate polyphony (1:45). Demonstration of how three independent phrases combine to form the complex texture of a *me'etu'upaki*. [*a*] On the words *"'Oie, 'oie, ka ma'u, ka ma'u, e kau savoli mo tui laulua."* [*b*] On the words *"He kau sa tū ulie! he ie aue!"* [*c*] On the words *"'Ioē! ō nai value, ō nai value! E fotu mai faliki toalua. Ē 'iē kasē! 'iē kasē!"* [*d*] All three phrases together.
    Performed by Vaisima Hopoate and others in Lapaha Village, Tonga.
    Recorded by Adrienne L. Kaeppler, 1967.

14. Tongan formal dance-song (*lakalaka*) (1:30). The introduction (*fakatapu*), sung in the classical style and illustrating rhythmic clapping. Later, one of the climaxes of the performance illustrates audience appreciation, with laughter and calls of *"Malie!"* Composed by Malukava, this *lakalaka* is emblematic of Tatakamotonga Village, Tongatapu, Tonga. Performed by the people of Tatakamotonga at the centennial celebration of Roman Catholic education in Tonga, Lapaha, Tongatapu.
    Recorded by Adrienne L. Kaeppler, 16 December 1986.

15. Santa Cruz three-line strophic song (0:45). Sung and danced by about 150 people of Temotu-Neo, Te Motu Province, Solomon Islands. Rattles tied to each knee accent the beats.
    Recorded by William Davenport at Neo Village, Temotu-Neo, 10 October 1974.

16. *"Anawa, anawa,"* Kiribati women's hip-shaking dance (*kabuti*) (1:35). Performed by people of Tekuanga Village, Marakei Island, Kiribati.
    Recorded by Mary E. Lawson Burke, 12 March 1985.

17. Sāmoan men's body-percussion dance (*fa'ataupati*) (0:30). Slaps, claps, tramps, and shouts performed by eight men on the staff of Aggie's, Apia, 'Upolu, Sāmoa.
    Recorded by J. W. Love in the guest hall at the hotel, 8 October 1971.

18. Sounds of a Huli two-stringed musical bow (*gāwā*) (0:44). Performed by a man of Walete, Southern

Highlands Province, Papua New Guinea.
Recorded by Bronwyn Peters and Jacqueline Pugh-Kitingan at Walete, 26 December 1974. Institute of Papua New Guinea Studies, IPNGS x82-161, It. 19-20.

19. Sounds of a Tongan nose-blown flute (0:45). This instrument is now in the collection of Bernice Pauahi Bishop Museum, Honolulu. Performed by Ve'ehala.
Recorded in Honolulu, Hawai'i, by Adrienne L. Kaeppler, 1970s.

20. Sounds of a susap (1:20). Performed by Amadu at Buji, Western Province, Papua New Guinea.
Recorded by Wolfgang Laade, 1964. Asch Mankind Series AHM 4216. Smithsonian Folkways cassette 04216, track 19 (B12).

21. Manihiki choreographed dance (*hupahupa*) (3:55). The main section (*taki*) composed by Mehau Karaponga about 1978. Performed, with intermittent shouts, by Nehemia Tauira (leader), Kimi Tauira, Tangi Toka, Tepania Junior, Grand Charlie, and Takaia Tamata (all on *kōriro*); Tahinu Aporo (*tini*); Kaikohe Kauraka and Ro John (single-headed *pahu*); and Munokoa Tepania (double-headed *pahu*). The first instrument sounded is the *tini*.
Recorded by Helen Reeves Lawrence in Tauhunu, Manihiki, Cook Islands, 26 June 1986.

22. "*Di Vozi*" ('A Gasping Man Climbs the Hill'), piece for two large friction blocks (0:19). Performed by two men of Madina Village, Nalik area, New Ireland Province, Papua New Guinea.
Recorded by Gerald Florian Messner, 29 July 1979.

23. Piece for small friction block (0:20). The name of the piece is secret. Performed by a man of Paruai Village, Kara area, northern New Ireland Province, Papua New Guinea.
Recorded by Gerald Florian Messner, 15 March 1977.

24. Sounds of a small swung slat (0:23). Performed by a man of Madina Village, Kara area, northern New Ireland Province.
Recorded by Gerald Florian Messner, 26 July 1979.

25. Sounds of four ribbon reeds and six human moaners (0:21). Most moans occur just at the end. Performed by ten people of Madina Village, Kara area, northern New Ireland Province, Papua New Guinea.
Recorded by Gerald Florian Messner, 28 July 1979.

26. Sounds of large and small friction blocks, a swung slat, ribbon reeds, and human moaners (0:40). Performed by men of Madina Village, Nalik area, northern New Ireland Province, Papua New Guinea.
Recorded by Gerald Florian Messner, 30 July 1977.

27. "*Kaulilua i ke anu Wai'ale'ale*," Hawaiian dance-song (*hula pahu*) (1:58). Performed by Noenoelani Zuttermeister Lewis, accompanying herself on a *pahu* and a *kilu*.
Recorded by Cine-pic Hawaii in Honolulu, 4 March 1989. *Hawaiian Drum Dance Chants*, Smithsonian Folkways CD 40015, track 4.

28. "Green Frog," Arnhem Land *wangga* song (2:05). Sung, with clapsticks, by Alan Maralung; didjeridu played by Peter Manaberu.
Recorded by Allan Marett in Barunga, Northern Territory, Australia, 14 November 1988. *Wangga Songs by Alan Maralung*, Smithsonian Folkways CD 40430, track 4.

29. "*Sauke*" (the name of a bird), Baluan commemorative song (*kolorai*) (4:27). [a] Before the singing,

men play a *kileŋ kolorai* on struck garamuts. [*b*] The lead (*yaret*) exclaims *oi!* and continues; the second (*isiol*) varies this phrase and sings the tonal center as a drone; the men then repeat the song. [*c*] After the singing, men whoop and play a *kileŋ kolorai* on struck garamuts. Performed by Konda'i Lipamu (lead singer), Pokut Narumbuai (second singer), and other men of Parioi Village, Baluan Island, Manus Province, Papua New Guinea.
Recorded by Gerald Florian Messner, 10 May 1977.

30. Music at a Waina *ida* (1:50). The ritual promotes the fertility of sago and other crops. Performed by male singers and players of five differently pitched wooden trumpets (*fuf*), with sounds made by painted and masked male dancers, who, against their pig-bone belts (*oktek*), click the elongated gourds (*pedasuh*) into which they have inserted their penises. Performed by people of Punda Village, West Sepik Province, Papua New Guinea.
Recorded by Don Niles and Thomas Waeki, 1986. Institute of Papua New Guinea Studies, IPNGS 86-162, *3B.

31. Wiru poetic recitation (1:10). While one man recites the words, another man sounds them via a two-stringed musical bow (*wapiela*), which he holds perpendicular to the ground with one end in his mouth, plucking the strings with a wooden plectrum. Performed by men of Andua Village, Southern Highlands Province, Papua New Guinea.
Recorded by Don Niles, 1983. Institute of Papua New Guinea Studies, IPNGS 83-047, It. 22.

32. Usarufa blood-song (*naa-ímá*) (2:45). One man shouts *tinutinu,* the sign that an arrow has struck a man; other men shout *wōwō* and *wōpī* (*pī* is the sound of spurting blood) and vaunt their bows; others shout the names of lethal arrows and laugh, anticipating victory. Performed by men of Kaagu Village, Eastern Highlands Province, Papua New Guinea.
Recorded by Vida Chenoweth in October 1968. American Folklife Center, R68/102, track 9.

33. "*Sakiraring,*" Rai Coast sacred music (*kaapu kak sari*) (2:05). Introductory excerpt from a multisectional texted song. Performed on two voice-modifying gourds (*kaapu naing*) and two long voice-modifying bamboos (*kaapu simang*) by men of Serieng Village, Madang Province, Papua New Guinea.
Recorded by Robert Reigle, 6 September 1997.

34. Asmat "ghost-celebrating song" (1:20). Performed by about ten men, accompanied by hourglass-shaped iguana-skinned drums (*tifa*).
Recorded by J. W. Love and Adrienne L. Kaeppler in the Baird Auditorium, Museum of Natural History, Smithsonian Institution, Washington, D.C., 13 June 1991.

35. Dani singing in coordinate monophony (1:20). Performed by about ten men.
Recorded by J. W. Love and Adrienne L. Kaeppler in the Baird Auditorium, Museum of Natural History, Smithsonian Institution, Washington, D.C., 13 June 1991.

36. "*Ri daula,*" Tigak shark-catching song (0:58). Performed in a canoe, accompanied by a rattle shaken in the water, by a man of Ngavalus Village, northern New Ireland Province, Papua New Guinea. The rattle (*roroq*) consists of halved coconut shells, threaded through central holes onto a doubled, circular cane frame.
Recorded by Filip Lamasisi Yayii, 1982. Institute of Papua New Guinea Studies, IPNGS 83-005, It. 24.

37. Baluan bridewealth-paying song (*w(e)ii*) (1:50). Performed by two women of Parioi Village, Baluan Island, Manus Province, Papua New Guinea.
Recorded by Gerald Florian Messner, 21 April 1977.

38. Nasioi celebratory dance-music (*singsing kaur*) (1:45). Men and women sing vocables, accompanied

by the *kobi* ensemble: double-row panpipes, each row having four pipes, the proximal row blown and the distal row sounding sympathetically; end-blown bamboo trumpets (*kavaronta*), four tubes tied in row and tuned to the pitches of the panpipes; and end-blown wooden trumpets (*kororon*) having a cylindrical or conical body topped by a holed half-coconut shell. Players of wooden trumpets dance in a clockwise circle while the singers and other instrumentalists circle them counterclockwise. Performed by people of Mongontoro Village, Bougainville, North Solomons Province, Papua New Guinea.
Recorded by Charles Duvelle, 1974. Institute of Papua New Guinea Studies, IPNGS 79-004, It. 1.

39. Nissan music for masked dancers (1:20). Sung, to the beat of kundus, by men of Nissan, North Solomons Province, Papua New Guinea.
Recorded by Steven R. Nachman, 1971.

40. New Caledonian festal dance-song (*cada*) (1:30). Sung mainly in two-part polyphony, accompanied by stamped bamboo tubes and concussed bark clappers. Performed by two male soloists and other men of the Hienghène area, Grande Terre.
Recorded by the brothers Bruce and Sheridan Fahnestock, 12 September 1940. American Folklife Center, AFS 25,848, disc 41, side A, song 1.

41. "*Jourur tak armej,*" Marshallese staff-dance music (*jebwa*) (1:45). Performed by men of Ujae Island, comprising the troupe about to go to the Pacific Festival of Arts to display Marshallese cultural identity.
Recorded by Mary E. Lawson Burke at Marshall Islands High School, Majuro Island, Marshall Islands, 8 August 1988.

42. "*Nunnwey,*" Yapese sitting men's dance (*parubut', par u buut, par-nga-but*) (1:07). Composed before 1900 on a Carolinean atoll in anticipation of a voyage westward to Ulithi, and subsequently given to a Yapese chief in a ceremonial exchange (*sawei*). Performed in celebration of United Nations Day, with gestures and claps, by about thirty men of Kanifaay Municipality.
Recorded by Barbara B. Smith in Colonia, then the district center of Yap, in October 1963.

43. "*Turim im bök jän ikjet bök na iaejet,*" Marshallese erotic song (*alin mweina*) (2:05). Composed by Alwoj Luke and Ajnij Helbi. Performed by the women Wina Lakjohn (soprano) and Nermey Elbon (alto) and the man Donsay Helmos (tenor and guitar).
Recorded by Mary E. Lawson Burke in Wotje Village, Wotje Island, Marshall Islands, 25 June 1988.

44. "*Küttak dailli kwon bar küttak lo,*" Marshallese song for sailing (*alin jerakrök*) (1:30). The singer intermittently speaks inspirational recitations (*roro*). Performed by Arento Lobo, a 70-year-old man of Ailinglaplap Island, who had learned the song from his grandfather.
Recorded by Mary E. Lawson Burke on Majuro Island, Marshall Islands, 30 July 1988.

45. "*E tataekinaki aron abara ae Onotoa,*" Kiribati song for the *bino* (1:30). Danced by seated performers after a nonmetrical section. Sung, with clapping, by men and women of Tanimaiaki Village, Abaiang Island, Kiribati.
Recorded by Mary E. Lawson Burke in the main *maneaba* of Tanimaiaki, 24 January 1985.

46. "*Te kaurea ma atuna,*" Kiribati secular choral song (*kuaea*) (1:32). Accompanied by guitar and ukulele in a contemporary East Polynesian style. Performed by people of Bikati Islet, Butaritari Island, Kiribati.
Recorded by Mary E. Lawson Burke at Tereitannano *maneaba*, Bikati, 3 November 1985.

47. "*Kauririko ma barebareiko,*" Kiribati contemporary dance-song (1:05). Danced as a *kaimatoa* by

standing men and women accompanied by seated singers and a struck percussion box. Performed by the Rotorua Dance Troupe at the Otintai Hotel, Bikenibeu Village, Tarawa, Kiribati.
Recorded by Mary E. Lawson Burke on a patio outside the hotel, 11 June 1981.

48. Sāmoan homemade ukulele (0:40). Designed to have four strings, the instrument has only three. Chordal patterns performed by Ropati Onofia. [*a*] Strummed (*salu*). [*b*] Picked (*piki*).
Recorded by J. W. Love in Falealupo, Savai'i, Sāmoa, 17 and 29 May 1972, respectively.

49. Sāmoan store-bought ukulele (0:35). Chordal patterns performed by Lemi A'e'au.
Recorded by J. W. Love in Falealupo, Savai'i, Sāmoa, 18 March 1972.

50. "*E a te talatala ni matala mai haahine*" ('As to the tale the women told'), Sikaiana danceless song (*olioli*) (1:00). Performed by Reuben Tenai and several men and women of Loto Village, Sikaiana.
Recorded by William Donner, 1981.

51. "'*Otamu*" (now known to some as "*Ueue*") and "*Tākoto*," Tahitian rhythmic patterns (0:47). Performed, for accompanying an '*ōte'a*, by five percussionists (three *tō'ere*, one *fa'atete*, one *pahu*) of the troupe Tahiti Nui, directed by Muna Nui.
Recorded by Jane Freeman Moulin in Puna'auia, Tahiti, 11 December 1976.

52. Marquesan pig dance (*maha'u*) (0:36). Performed, with clapping, by about twenty-five men of the dance troupe of Taioha'e, Nukuhiva, directed by Lucien Ro'o Kimitete.
Recorded by Jane Freeman Moulin in Taioha'e, Marquesas Islands, 22 June 1989.

53. Māori bellicose dance-song (*haka*) (1:30). Composed by Te Rauparaha (1768–1849).
Recorded by the New Zealand Broadcasting Service in cooperation with the Maori Affairs Department, 1952? Smithsonian Folkways LP 433, track 45.

54. Rapa Nui popular song (1:40). Sung, to accompaniment by guitars and percussion, by people of Rapa Nui.
Recorded by Adrienne L. Kaeppler in Hangaroa, Rapa Nui, 18 September 1984.

# Index